Frommer's®

KT-217-807

Europe by Rail

1st Edition

Here's what the critics say about Frommer's:

"Amazingly easy to use. Very portable, very complete."

—*Booklist*

"Detailed, accurate, and easy-to-read information for all price ranges."
—*Glamour Magazine*

"Hotel information is close to encyclopedic."

—*Des Moines Sunday Register*

"Frommer's Guides have a way of giving you a real feel for a place."
—*Knight Ridder Newspapers*

WILEY

Wiley Publishing, Inc.

Published by:

Wiley Publishing, Inc.

111 River St.
Hoboken, NJ 07030-5774

Copyright © 2004 Wiley Publishing, Inc., Hoboken, New Jersey. All rights reserved. No part of this publication may be reproduced, stored in a retrieval system or transmitted in any form or by any means, electronic, mechanical, photocopying, recording, scanning or otherwise, except as permitted under Sections 107 or 108 of the 1976 United States Copyright Act, without either the prior written permission of the Publisher, or authorization through payment of the appropriate per-copy fee to the Copyright Clearance Center, 222 Rosewood Drive, Danvers, MA 01923, 978/750-8400, fax 978/646-8600. Requests to the Publisher for permission should be addressed to the Legal Department, Wiley Publishing, Inc., 10475 Crosspoint Blvd., Indianapolis, IN 46256, 317/572-3447, fax 317/572-4447, E-Mail: permcoordinator@wiley.com.

Wiley and the Wiley Publishing logo are trademarks or registered trademarks of John Wiley & Sons, Inc. and/or its affiliates. Frommer's is a trademark or registered trademark of Arthur Frommer. Used under license. All other trademarks are the property of their respective owners. Wiley Publishing, Inc. is not associated with any product or vendor mentioned in this book.

ISBN 0-7645-4110-2

Editor: Naomi P. Kraus
Production Editor: Heather Wilcox
Cartographer: Roberta Stockwell
Photo Editor: Richard Fox
Production by Wiley Indianapolis Composition Services

Front cover photo: Switzerland: Crystal Panoramic Express
Back cover photo: Switzerland: Rhaetian Railways' Bernina Express, as it passes over a viaduct on its way to St. Moritz

For information on our other products and services or to obtain technical support, please contact our Customer Care Department within the U.S. at 800/762-2974, outside the U.S. at 317/572-3993 or fax 317/572-4002.

Wiley also publishes its books in a variety of electronic formats. Some content that appears in print may not be available in electronic formats.

Manufactured in the United States of America

5   4

Contents

List of Maps

Bonus Coverage!

This book covers rail travel in western Europe, as well as Hungary and the Czech Republic. If you're interested in riding the less-traveled rails of eastern Europe and the Balkans, check out our special coverage of that region's rail options and highlights at **Frommers. com** (www.frommers.com).

About the Authors

Darwin Porter, a native of North Carolina, was assigned to write the very first edition of a Frommer's guide devoted solely to one European country. Since then, he has written many bestselling Frommer's guides to all the major European destinations. In 1982, he was joined in his research efforts by **Danforth Prince,** formerly of the Paris bureau of the *New York Times,* who has traveled and written extensively about Europe.

Suzanne Rowan Kelleher is a freelance travel writer and the former Europe Editor of *Travel Holiday* magazine. She has traveled extensively in Ireland, is married to an Irishman, and currently lives in County Dublin. She is the author of *Frommer's Ireland* and a co-author of *Frommer's Europe from $70 a Day.*

Native New Yorker **Joseph S. Lieber** lived in Hungary for several years in the early 1990s. He presently practices law in Boston and is the co-author of *Frommer's Budapest & the Best of Hungary.* **Christina Shea** served as a Peace Corps volunteer in Hungary and subsequently directed Peace Corps language-training programs in Lithuania and Kyrghyzstan. She's the author of the novel *Moira's Crossing* (St. Martin's) and a co-author of *Frommer's Budapest & the Best of Hungary.*

George McDonald has lived and worked in both Amsterdam and Brussels as deputy editor of the KLM in-flight magazine and as editor-in-chief of the Sabena in-flight magazine. Now a freelance journalist and travel writer based in Germany, he is the author of *Frommer's Amsterdam* and *Frommer's Belgium, Holland & Luxembourg,* and a co-author of *Frommer's Europe from $70 a Day.*

Hana Mastrini is a native of the western Czech spa town of Karlovy Vary who became a veteran of the "Velvet Revolution" as a student in Prague in 1989. She began contributing to Frommer's guides while helping her husband, John, better understand his new home in the Czech Republic.

Donald Olson is a novelist, playwright and travel writer. His play, *Beardsley,* was produced in London. He is the author of *England For Dummies,* which won the Lowell Thomas Travel Writing Award for Best Guidebook in 2002. He is also a co-author of *Frommer's Europe from $70 a Day.* He has contributed travel stories to the *New York Times,* National Geographic Books, and many other national publications.

New-York based **Sascha Segan** is a freelance journalist who has lived on three continents and spent quite a lot of time riding the rails of Europe. He has worked for *Expedia Travels* magazine, ABCNEWS.com, and *The Guardian* in the U.K. He is currently a columnist at Frommers.com and is the author of *Frommer's Fly Safe, Fly Smart.*

Born in Chicago, **Theodora Tongas** traveled around her parents' native Greece many times as a child. After earning a master's degree in journalism from Northwestern University's Medill School of Journalism, she went to work as a reporter for the Associated Press in Athens, and has lived there ever since. With Athens as her base, she has toured the entire mainland—and many islands—by plane, train, and automobile.

An Invitation to the Reader

In researching this book, we discovered many wonderful places—hotels, restaurants, shops, and more. We're sure you'll find others. Please tell us about them, so we can share the information with your fellow travelers in upcoming editions. If you were disappointed with a recommendation, we'd love to know that, too. Please write to:

Frommer's Europe by Rail, 1st Edition
Wiley Publishing, Inc. • 111 River St. • Hoboken, NJ 07030-5774

Acknowledgments

Many people worked behind the scenes and lent us a helping hand to make keep this book on track. I'd like to give special thanks **Cece Drummond, Nico Zenner, Michele Topper,** and **Anthony Cefaloni** at Rail Europe for all of their invaluable assistance. **Sascha Segan** is a veritable fountain of rail information whose expertise made planning the book a great deal easier. You can't ask for a better cartographer than **Roberta Stockwell,** the woman behind all the maps in this book. Thanks also to **Nick Trotter** for the great illustration. Major thanks to **Heather Wilcox** and **Christina Van Camp** in Indianapolis for their unbelievable patience and much-needed advice. Thanks also to **Kelly Regan, Brice Gosnell, Mike Spring, Alexis Lipsitz, John Vorwald, Kathleen Warnock,** and **Amy Lyons** at Frommer's whose timely assistance was crucial to the success of this book, even if they didn't realize it. And thanks to my family for making sure I stayed sane while juggling rail maps, timetables, and train itineraries for 6 months.

—Naomi P. Kraus

An Additional Note

Please be advised that travel information is subject to change at any time—and this is especially true of prices. We therefore suggest that you write or call ahead for confirmation when making your travel plans. The authors, editors, and publisher cannot be held responsible for the experiences of readers while traveling. Your safety is important to us, however, so we encourage you to stay alert and be aware of your surroundings. Keep a close eye on cameras, purses, and wallets, all favorite targets of thieves and pickpockets.

Other Great Guides for Your Trip:

Frommer's Europe
Frommer's Europe from $70 a Day
Frommer's Gay & Lesbian Europe
Europe For Dummies
Hanging Out in Europe

Frommer's Star Ratings, Icons & Abbreviations

Every hotel, restaurant, and attraction listing in this guide has been ranked for quality, value, service, amenities, and special features using a **star-rating system.** In country, state, and regional guides, we also rate towns and regions to help you narrow down your choices and budget your time accordingly. Hotels and restaurants are rated on a scale of zero (recommended) to three stars (exceptional). Attractions, shopping, nightlife, towns, and regions are rated according to the following scale: zero stars (recommended), one star (highly recommended), two stars (very highly recommended), and three stars (must-see).

In addition to the star-rating system, we also use **five feature icons** that point you to the great deals, in-the-know advice, and unique experiences that separate travelers from tourists. Throughout the book, look for:

Finds	Special finds—those places only insiders know about
Moments	Special moments—those experiences that memories are made of
Warning	Warning—traveler's advisories are usually in effect
Tips	Insider tips—great ways to save time and money
Value	Great values—where to get the best deals

The following **abbreviations** are used for credit cards:

AE	American Express	DISC	Discover	V	Visa
DC	Diners Club	MC	MasterCard		

Frommers.com

Now that you have the guidebook to a great trip, visit our website at **www.frommers.com** for travel information on more than 3,000 destinations. With features updated regularly, we give you instant access to the most current trip-planning information available. At Frommers.com, you'll also find the best prices on airfares, accommodations, and car rentals—and you can even book travel online through our travel booking partners. At Frommers.com, you'll also find the following:

- Online updates to our most popular guidebooks
- Vacation sweepstakes and contest giveaways
- Newsletter highlighting the hottest travel trends
- Online travel message boards with featured travel discussions

Touring Europe by Rail

Rich, ancient, and incredibly diverse, the nations of Europe offer a vast array of sights, climates, cultures, and cuisines. The ten trips outlined below show the full reach of the European rail system; feel free to mix and match parts of them to create your ideal vacation.

Where possible, we've used overnight trains on these trips, as they save you the cost of a hotel night, maximize your sightseeing time, and are a rail experience in and of themselves. Remember that overnight trains, as well as the Eurostar Chunnel train, French TGV trains, and most high-speed trains, require extra reservation fees over the price of your railpass. (See p. 35 for more on overnight trains.)

We've recommended railpasses for those itineraries below that would make good use of them; where point-to-point tickets are cheaper, we've noted that as well. (For an overview of when to buy a pass and when to go point-to-point, see p. 42.)

Exact train times and prices are subject to change—the details in these pages were accurate as of December 2003, but you should double-check all train schedules when plotting out your journey. For more on navigating rail schedules, see p. 30.

1 1-Week Itineraries

The average North American vacation is a mere 7 days long (we know, too short!). To help you make the best of your time in Europe, we've put together five 1-week rail itineraries that will give you a taste of some of the best Europe has to offer. Whether you're a royalty fanatic who can't get enough of the continent's magnificent palaces or a nature buff who'd rather tackle the magnificent scenery of Scandinavia, you'll find an itinerary below that will suit your needs. And if you happen to have more than a week to spend (lucky you!), you can mix and match these itineraries or check out the 2-week itineraries we offer in the next section.

ITINERARY 1   EUROPE'S BEST CASTLES & PALACES

Duration:	8 days, 7 nights
Best time of year:	Spring or fall
Recommended passes:	Second-class Eurostar ticket, plus 3-country 6-day Eurail Selectpass
Arrive in:	London
Depart from:	Munich

Europe is practically overflowing with medieval castles and ornate palaces. And many of these world-famous residences (and former residences) are open to exploration by those of us whose blood isn't Royal Blue. Touring all these bastions of nobility could take years, but we've put together an itinerary that will introduce you to a few of the most noteworthy castles and palaces on the Continent and in London.

Day 1

Arrive in London. After checking into your hotel, take a tour of **Buckingham Palace** in the morning, if it's open (only in summer); otherwise, take in the adjacent **Royal Mews** and the magnificent **Queen's Gallery,** both of which are open year-round and feature lots of fabulous royal treasures. Spend the afternoon exploring the **Tower of London,** an imposing castle complex built by William the Conqueror and home to Britain's fabulous crown jewels. If you have time, indulge in a traditional afternoon tea, or try a night out at the theater. See "London" in chapter 10 for more sightseeing options in this historic city.

Day 2

Fortify yourself with a good English breakfast before taking the Eurostar train on a 2½-hour jaunt to Paris, a journey that's discounted with your Eurail Selectpass. If you've got time once you've settled into your hotel, visit the **Louvre,** which would be the largest palace in the world, if it were still a palace and not one of the world's greatest art museums. Pay homage to the *Mona Lisa,* the *Venus De Milo,* and 300,000 or so of their fellow artworks. It's a royal treat, palace or not. See "Paris" in chapter 8 for other things to do in the city.

Day 3

Get an early morning start and take the RER C-line commuter train (the train is covered by your railpass) out to **Versailles** (p. 272) and spend a half day touring Louis XIV's masterpiece, a structure so magnificent, that building it practically bankrupted the state treasury. Return to Paris in the afternoon for a stroll or some other sightseeing before taking an evening TGV high-speed train for the 1-hour ride to

Tours, in the Loire valley. Check into your hotel (see "Tours" in chapter 8 for accommodations options) and rest up.

Day 4

If ever there were a spot for castle lovers, it's the **Loire valley.** Unfortunately, it's not the most train-friendly spot in France, so the best way to see the region's famous castles is to get up early and take a full-day bus tour of the Loire chateaux. Tours leave at 9 am daily from the city's tourist office and, alas, Tours tours aren't covered by railpasses. Should you wish to explore on your own, a few chateaux are reachable from Tours by rail. Try the Gothic and Renaissance **Château of Amboise** or the historic **Château de Blois.** Stay in Tours a second night. See "Tours" in chapter 8 for more chateaux excursions out of Tours.

Day 5

More chateaux! Take a 25-minute train ride to **Chenonceaux** (p. 285), noted for its startling river-spanning castle. Return to Tours for a final dinner, then take the 7:34pm TGV back to Gare Montparnasse in Paris, arriving at 8:45pm, to connect to the 10:58pm overnight train from Paris Est station to **Munich,** which arrives at 8:54am. (*Note:* You'll have to get from Montparnasse to Paris Est station by Metro or taxi, but you've got plenty of time to make the connection.)

Day 6

From the Munich Hauptbahnhof, take the first available train to **Füssen;** you should arrive there around lunchtime. Take one of the hourly buses to **Hohenschwangau** (p. 377) and tour that castle (the line there should eat up most of your afternoon) and then return to Füssen for the evening. See chapter 9 for more on Munich and the Romantic Road.

Itinerary 1: Europe's Best Castles & Palaces

Day 7

In the morning, take a bus to **Neuschwanstein** (p. 377), Mad King Ludwig's fairy-tale folly. (This was the model for Walt Disney's Cinderella Castle and the real thing is a heck of a lot better!). After lunch, take the bus back to Füssen for the 2-hour train ride to Munich, where you can tour the downtown **Residenz Palace** after checking into your hotel.

Day 8

If you have an afternoon flight, you might be able to get to **Schloss Nymphenburg** (p. 349), on the edge of Munich, in the morning. Otherwise your castle hopping will come to an end as you fly home from Munich.

ITINERARY 2   SMALL CITIES OF THE BENELUX

Duration:	8 days, 7 nights
Best time of year:	Summer
Ideal passes:	Point-to-point tickets
Arrive in:	Amsterdam Schiphol
Depart from:	See below

Relaxing, romantic small cities can be an antidote to the typical European big-city bustle. Tack part of this itinerary onto a Paris or Amsterdam trip for a change of pace, or do the whole thing for a truly intimate week. All the Dutch and Belgian destinations in this itinerary are within a few hours of Amsterdam or Brussels, and you won't have to worry about catching a train at a specific time within Holland or Belgium because all trains run on at least an hourly basis.

Day 1

Arrive at Amsterdam Schiphol airport, and take a train from the station beneath the airport terminal directly to The Hague, just 50 minutes away. Check into your hotel for a 3-night stay. Once you're settled in, head for **Madurodam,** a fascinating scale-model replica of dozens of Dutch landmarks and attractions. After you've had your fill of miniatures, and if you still have time, take Tram 1 all the way up to the beach resort of **Scheveningen** to see how the Dutch spend sunny days. See "The Hague" in chapter 15 for more information.

Day 2

Take Local Tram 1—not the train—from The Hague to **Delft** and spend the day in that charming city, strolling its atmospheric canals, touring its two churches, and visiting its renowned **Prinsenhof Museum** (p. 660). Head back in the evening to The Hague and relax.

Day 3

In the morning, grab a train to **Haarlem,** a compact town, just 35 minutes away, that's ideal for strolling. Start first at its impressive **Grote Markt (market square)** and catch a recital on the 98-foot-tall organ inside the **Church of St. Bavo.** Finally, take in the city's finest attraction, the **Frans Hals Museum,** which sports both great art and a charming 17th-century setting. For more information, see "An Excursion to Haarlem" in chapter 15. In the afternoon, head back to The Hague and tour the **Mauritshuis,** whose must-see art collection includes the quintessential Benelux city land-scape—Vermeer's *View of Delft.*

Day 4

It's time to leave The Hague behind. Take a morning train to Antwerp's Centraal Station, store your luggage there, and then lose yourself on the streets of Antwerp, a hidden gem that's the capital of Europe's diamond trade. Don't miss the largest church in the Benelux, the **Cathedral of Our Lady,** situated right off the city's medieval and picturesque **Grote Markt.** For a touch of culture, visit the impressive **Rubens House,** where artist Peter Paul Rubens once lived and worked. For more on Antwerp, see "An Excursion to Antwerp" in chapter 4. In the evening, head back to the rail station and catch a 2-hour train to the city of Liège in the heart of Belgium's Wallonia province. Check into your hotel and give yourself a well-earned rest.

Day 5

Spend you day exploring the "Passion-ate City" of Liège. Don't miss this the **Museum of Walloon Life** (p. 148), especially its fabulous puppet collec-tion. The Romanesque **Church of St. Bartholomew** has a 12th-century bap-tismal font that's regarded as one of the greatest treasures in Belgium. For more options, see "Liège" in chapter 4.

Day 6

Eat an early breakfast before catching a train to your final base in the Benelux—the World Heritage city of **Bruges.** The trip will take about 2 hours and 10 min-utes. Once you've settled into your hotel, wind your way through the medieval streets of Bruges, making sure to visit the city's famous **Belfry and Market Halls,** the **Begijnhof,** and the **Church of Our Lady** with its sculpture by Michelangelo. See "Bruges" in chap-ter 4 for more on the city.

Itinerary 2: Small Cities of the Benelux

Day 7

If you can draw yourself away from Bruges for the day, get on a train for the 20-minute ride to **Ghent,** another breathtaking medieval city. Make sure to see its **Cathedral,** the **Belfry** and the grim **Castle of the Counts,** and then stroll along Graslei. Return to Bruges before dinner and spend the rest of the evening soaking up the city's medieval atmosphere. For more on Ghent, see "An Excursion to Ghent" in chapter 4.

Day 8

Bruges is close to several international airports: Brussels is about 1½ hours away, Amsterdam Schiphol is a little over 3 hours, and Charles de Gaulle in Paris is only 2¾ hours. Fly home from whichever airport works best for you.

ITINERARY 3   **RIDING THE SCENIC ROUTE**

Duration:	8 days, 7 nights
Best time of year:	Spring
Ideal passes:	Second-class point-to-point tickets (cheapest) *or* First-class 5-day Switzerland 'n Austria Pass, plus a ticket from Milan to Swiss border of Chiasso
Arrive in:	Milan
Depart from:	Vienna

There's some intense rail riding on this weeklong trip, but you'll be rewarded with a number of the world's most thrilling and dramatic rail journeys as you travel across the Alps. Two noteworthy trains you'll be riding are the magnificent Centovalli Railway traversing Italy and Switzerland, and the only railway deemed worthy of UNESCO's World Heritage Site designation, the Semmering Pass Railway in Austria.

Before leaving home: Call to make reservations to see Leonardo's *Last Supper* in Milan.

Day 1

Arrive in Milan in the morning. After checking into your hotel, see the **Duomo,** and then head for the *Last Supper* if you nabbed a reservation. Spend the afternoon in the **Brera Picture Gallery** and checking out the shops and antiques stores on the side streets off of **Via Brera,** which are open until 7:30pm on most evenings. See "Milan" in chapter 14 for more information on the city.

Day 2

Today you head off on one of the best railroad journeys in Europe: a ride on the **Centovalli Railway.** Grab the 9:25am InterCity train to Bellinzona, arriving at 11:23am. Connect there to a 12:07pm train to Locarno, arriving at 12:30pm, and then get on the Centovalli Railway to Domodossola, one of the lesser-known scenic treasures of the Alps. The hourly frequency of the Centovalli line means you can get off at any of the charming villages it serves (we recommend Verdasio or Intragna for their cable cars) and get back on again. There are local and express Centovalli trains, so take a local (leaving at 1:09pm) if you want to stop and an express (leaving at 12:55pm) if you want to shoot straight through. If you take the local, make sure to get back on the train to arrive in Domodossola no later than 7pm, so you can catch the 7:25pm Cisalpino to Brig, and from there, connect to **Bern.** If you take the express train straight through, you'll arrive in Domodossola at 2:40pm; from there, hop the 2:52pm train to

Brig and change there to the 3:22pm to Bern, where you'll arrive just after 5pm and can check into your hotel for a well-earned rest.

This all sounds very complicated, but the views offered by the Centovalli trains are exceptional, and these are common and frequent connections. The conductors on any of the trains we mention above will tell you where to go if you ask. And if you miss a train, there will usually be another one along in an hour or so.

Day 3

Bern is lovely, but the best railway scenery is in nearby Interlaken. In the morning, make the 1-hour journey to the Interlaken Ost train station and you'll get a view of the mountains in the distance, the 13,000-foot peaks of the **Jungfrau** (p. 861). An intricate network of railways climbs these mountains, and you can ride one or two of them today out of the Interlaken station; a Eurailpass doesn't cover these trains, but passholders do get a 25% discount. Rail Europe also sells Jungfrau tickets. Once you've had your fill of the magnificent scenery, head back to Bern and have dinner in one of the city's wine taverns. See "Bern" in chapter 20 for more nightlife options.

Day 4

Say goodbye to Bern, grab your luggage and head back to Interlaken Ost. The famous **Golden Pass Line** (p. 859) heads through the mountains outside of Interlaken along an incredibly scenic route to Luzern (Lucerne). Take the 10:30am **Golden Pass Panoramic** train from Interlaken Ost

Itinerary 3: Riding the Scenic Route

to Luzern (you'll arrive at 12:24pm), connecting there to Zurich.

Five trains a day from Zurich depart for the 3¾-hour trip to Innsbruck, Austria, and you could get into Innsbruck as early as 5:18pm. Check into your hotel and eat dinner. If you have some energy left, take a tram to the **Hungerburg cable railway** (p. 112), which takes you up a mountain overlooking the city and offers especially beautiful nighttime views of Innsbruck.

Day 5

Spend the morning strolling the beautifully preserved **Altstadt** (Old Town) in **Innsbruck.** After an early lunch, catch the 1:30pm train to **Salzburg,** a 2-hour ride through spectacular Alpine scenery. Take some time to stroll through this picturesque city and check out the **Residenz State Rooms,** where Mozart once played for royal guests. See "Innsbruck" and "Salzburg" in chapter 3 for more on these Austrian cities.

Day 6

Take the 11:18am train from Salzburg to Leoben. Arriving at 2:32pm, you'll make a quick connection to the 2:48pm train to Vienna aboard the 150-year-old **Semmering Pass Railway**—the only rail line on UNESCO's list of World Heritage sites. Arrive in Vienna at 5:02pm, check into your hotel and have dinner. Have a piece of the city's famous dessert, the *Sachertorte*—you've earned it.

Day 7

Start your day off at **St. Stephen's Cathedral** in the heart of Vienna. Climb its south tower for a panoramic view of the city, and then stroll down Kärntnerstrasse, the main shopping street. Stop off at one of the city's grand cafes at 11am for coffee. In the afternoon, visit the **Schönbrunn Palace,** summer seat of the Hapsburg Dynasty. Have dinner in a Viennese wine tavern and, if you can, attend a concert or theater performance. If you're an opera fan, the **Vienna State Opera** is one of the best in the world.

Day 8

If there's time in the morning, try and cram in a visit to the city's **Hofburg Palace Complex** before flying home out of Vienna.

ITINERARY 4   EASTERN EUROPE

Duration:	8 days, 7 nights
Best time of year:	Summer
Ideal passes:	Point-to-point tickets are cheapest, but First-class European East Pass is only $70 more and offers a lot more flexibility and convenience
Arrive in:	Prague
Depart from:	Budapest

Liberated and bustling, but also ancient, eastern Europe is blooming as a rail destination. And, compared to western Europe, it's cheap, too. This weeklong jaunt takes you to three very different capitals on both sides of the former Iron Curtain: hip Prague, historic Budapest, and cultured Vienna.

Day 1

Arrive in **Prague** in the morning. After checking into your hotel, walk the city's famous Royal Route, touring **Prague Castle** before walking across the Charles Bridge into **Old Town.** From there, head for **Wenceslas Square,** site of the demonstrations that led to the Velvet Revolution in 1989. See "Prague" chapter 5 for more on the city.

Day 2

Prague's greatest strengths are its architecture and atmosphere; both are best experienced by strolling and wandering the city's streets. So spend your day exploring Prague's **Old Town** and **Jewish Quarter** in more depth. In the **Jewish Quarter (Josefov),** be sure to visit the **Old Jewish Cemetery.**

Day 3

Take a morning train to beautiful, medieval **Český Krumlov,** changing trains in Česke Budějovice. If you can

stomach it, there's a 7:17am from Prague, which will get you into Krumlov around 11:30am; otherwise, take the 9:17am and get in around 1:20pm. Spend the day exploring this World Heritage Site (be sure to see the city's famous castle) and stay overnight. For more information, see "Český Krumlov" in chapter 5.

Day 4

Get up early this morning because you'll need to hop an 8:19am train from Krumlov back to **České Budějovice.** You'll have about 2½ hours to explore this former fortress town and original home of Budweiser beer. See "České Budějovice," in chapter 5 for sightseeing options in the town. Make sure you're back in the station in time to catch the 11:54am train to Linz. You'll connect there to a train to Vienna and should arrive in the Austrian capital at about 4:30pm. Check into your hotel, have dinner (don't skip dessert in this city renowned for its pastries!), and

Itinerary 4: Eastern Europe

perhaps take in a concert. For more on Vienna, check out "Vienna" in chapter 3.

Day 5
See Day 7 of the "Riding the Scenic Route" itinerary on p. 8.

Day 6
Take the 8:45am train out of Vienna to Budapest. After arriving at 11:43am, check into your hotel and eat lunch. Spend your afternoon exploring the **Inner City** and **Central Pest.** Walk down **Vaci útca,** the city's trendiest shopping street. Then stroll along the Danube to the neo-Gothic **Parliament** building. Have a hearty Hungarian dinner and, if you're an opera fan, join the rest of Budapest at the **Hungarian State Opera.** See "Budapest" in chapter 12 for more information on the city.

Day 7
Today, focus on Budapest's Castle District. Be sure to see the 13th-century **Matthias Church and the Budapest History Museum.** On your way back into Pest, stop for coffee and a slice of *dobos torta* (layer cake) at **Gerbeaud's,** one of the city's classic coffeehouses. Then drop in at **St. Stephen's Church,** the country's largest before heading over to the striking Moorish and Byzantine **Dohány Synagogue,** the largest in Europe. After dinner, take in one the city's many musical concerts.

Day 8
Fly home from Budapest.

ITINERARY 5

EXPLORING THE SCANDINAVIAN TRIANGLE

Duration:	8 days, 7 nights
Best time of year:	Summer
Ideal passes:	Point-to-point tickets (cheapest) or Scanrail Pass
Arrive in:	Copenhagen
Depart from:	Stockholm

Summer in Scandinavia brings days that stretch forever. Take advantage of all those sunny hours to explore three of the region's key cities: Copenhagen, Stockholm, and Oslo.

Day 1

Arrive in Copenhagen in the morning and check into your hotel. Take a couple of hours to stroll the old city's cobblestone streets and its many canals. Spend the late afternoon at **Christiansborg Palace.** Early in the evening, sample the rides and entertainment at the city's famous **Tivoli.** See "Copenhagen" in chapter 6 for more sightseeing options.

Day 2

In the morning, visit **Amalienborg Palace,** see the changing of the guard there, and then walk to the statue of the **Little Mermaid.** In the afternoon, see the art treasures of the **Ny Carlsberg Glyptotek,** and in the evening, drop in on one of the city's many jazz clubs.

Day 3

Spend your morning perusing works by the Old Masters at **The Royal Museum of Fine Arts,** then have an early lunch and leave Copenhagen on the 1:36pm X2000 express train to Gothenburg, and switch there to the 5:35pm train to Oslo. Eat dinner on the train because you won't arrive in Oslo until 9:45pm. Check into your hotel and get some rest.

Day 4

After breakfast, stroll past **Akershus Castle** before catching the bus to the Bygdøy peninsula for the city's renowned ship museums. In the afternoon, if you have time, take in the **Edvard Munch Museum** or head to the **Tryvannstårnet** tower for a panoramic view of Oslo. See "Oslo" in chapter 16 for more information.

Day 5

Get up early and pay quick respects to the world-famous Munch painting, *The Scream,* at the **Nasjonalgalleriet.** Then hop the 11:27am X2000 train to Stockholm, which will put you in the Swedish capital at 4:15pm. After checking into your hotel, take a walk around Stockholm's **Gamla Stan (Old Town)** and have dinner at one of its restaurants. See "Stockholm" in chapter 19 for information on the city.

Day 6

Get an early start and take a ferry to Djurgården to visit the *Vasa* ship museum and the **Skansen** folk museum. In the afternoon, head to the **Royal Palace & Museums** and check out the Swedish crown jewels, among other royal treasures. Have dinner in Old Town and, if you can, take in a performance in the exceptional **Drottningholm Court Theater.**

Day 7

Take a morning train to **Uppsala**— trains leave every half hour and take 40 minutes—and spend some of the

Itinerary 5: Exploring the Scandinavian Triangle

morning walking around the university and visiting its famous Gothic cathedral. After lunch, take the local bus to historic **Gamla Uppsala** and explore the archaeological remains there. For more sightseeing options, see "Uppsala" in chapter 19. Return to Stockholm by train before dinnertime.

For dinner, try the smorgasbord-style buffet at the **Grand Veranda.**

Day 8
If you're flight doesn't leave until the afternoon, spend the morning in the **National Museum of Art.** Catch the 20-minute Arlanda Express train to the airport and fly home.

2 2-Week Itineraries

Though you can do a 1-week rail vacation in Europe if you limit your travels to a small region, if you want to cut a wider swath, you'll need at least 2 weeks to see things without feeling rushed. In this section we offer a couple of specialized itineraries for architecture buffs and food-lovers, as well as a few "grand tour" suggestions for travelers who want to sample Europe's various regions and cities at a reasonable pace.

ITINERARY 6   EUROPE'S BEST ART & ARCHITECTURE

Duration:	15 days, 14 nights
Best time of year:	Spring
Ideal passes:	First-class 6-day 4-country Eurail Selectpass, plus ticket from Brussels to Bruges
Arrive in:	Brussels
Depart from:	Venice

This trip lets you bury yourself among the masterpieces of European art—it's a museum buff's dream. You'll hit four of the world's greatest museums—the Louvre, the Prado, the Vatican and the Uffizi—as well as three open-air museums filled with great architecture in Bruges, Barcelona, and Venice.

Day 1
Arrive at Brussels National Airport, then take the train into Brussels Nord station and immediately connect to a train to **Bruges;** the entire train trip should take about 1½ hours. In Bruges, tour the medieval streets and enjoy the city's unique architecture. See "Bruges" in chapter 4 for more on the city.

Day 2
There is one direct morning train from Bruges to Paris, but it departs at 6:36am, so unless you're a really chipper morning person, forget it and take one of the hourly trains that leave Bruges for Brussels, and then catch a Thalys trains to Paris. If you time it right, the entire trip shouldn't take more than 3 hours. Once you're settled in **Paris,** start off at the **Arc de Triomphe,** then stroll down the Champs-Elysees to the **Egyptian obelisk** at the Place de la Concorde. Next up is the **Eiffel Tower.** Around sunset, head for **Notre Dame Cathedral** to top off your Paris monuments tour. See "Paris" in chapter 8 for more on the City of Light.

Day 3
If you're a fan of great art, then we don't have to tell you that the **Louvre** warrants an entire day. But if you need a change of pace in the afternoon, the **Centre Pompidou** will yank you into the 20th Century.

Day 4
So many riches: The **Musée National Auguste Rodin?** The **Musée Picasso?** How about the **Musée d'Orsay?** Choose two, and enjoy one in the morning and one in the afternoon. After an early dinner, head to Paris' Austerlitz station for the 7:43pm overnight train to Madrid, arriving at 8:58am. This train, the *Francisco de Goya,* is one of Spain's Elipsos train hotels and one of Europe's most luxurious rides (p. 38).

Day 5
Check into your hotel, then start your day in Madrid at the **Royal Palace** and work your way east to the **Monasterio de las Descalzas Reales.** Spend the night as locals do by Tasca hopping. See "Madrid" in chapter 18 for more on information.

Day 6
How does the **Prado** compare to the Louvre? Today's your day to find out. If there's time, head over to the **Museo Nacional Centro de Arte Reina Sofia,** home of Picasso's famous *Guernica.* If you aren't too exhausted, take in a Flamenco show after dinner.

Day 7
Take the 9am Talgo high-speed train from Chamartin station to **Barcelona,**

Itinerary 6: Europe's Best Art & Architecture

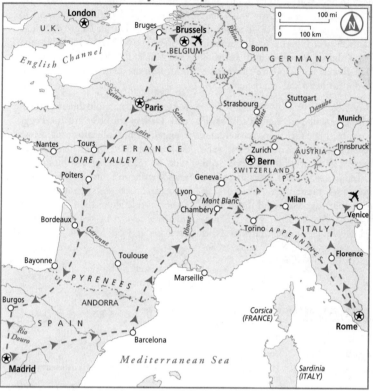

arriving at 4:03pm. Spend the afternoon and evening strolling the **Barri Gòtic,** the city's Gothic quarter, or the famous promenade of **La Rambla.** For more sightseeing options, see "Barcelona" in chapter 18.

Day 8

Start your morning with a tour of **La Sagrada Família;** then head either to **Parc Güell** for more Modernist masterpieces, or take in the **Fundació Joan Miró** or **Museu Picasso** museums. (This is a good time to take a break from museums, and lounge on a bench in Parc Güell staring at the sky.)

Take the 8:38pm Talgo night train to Milan, where you'll transfer to the 10am Eurostar Italia train bound for Rome, arriving at 2:30pm on Day 9.

Day 9

Check into your hotel in **Rome** and spend the afternoon and evening touring the ruins of Ancient Rome, starting at the **Capitoline Hill** and walking along the **Via dei Fori Imperiali** to the ruins of the **Colosseum.** See "Rome" in chapter 14 for more sightseeing options in the city.

Day 10

Spend the entire day perusing the contents of the **Vatican Museums.** Seeing the **Sistine Chapel** is a given, but don't miss the **Pinacoteca** (picture gallery), which is loaded with masterpieces.

Day 11

Say goodbye to Rome and take a morning train—trains run twice an hour—for the 95-minute journey to

Florence. Florence is fortunately compact, so once you've checked into your hotel, you can spend your day strolling the axis from the **Basilica di Santa Maria Novella** to **Il Duomo,** the **Palazzo Vecchio,** and **Giotto's Bell Tower.** See "Florence" in chapter 14 for further details on the city.

Day 12

Check out of your hotel early, stash your bags at the train station and spend your entire day, if possible, submerged in the art of the **Galleria degli Uffizi.** Tear yourself away from the museum's masterpieces in order to grab your bags and board the 6:30pm train to Venice, arriving at 9:27pm. (Have dinner in the Eurostar Italia train's dining car.) See "Venice" chapter 14 for more details.

Day 13

Venice *is* art. Explore the **Piazza San Marco** in the morning—be sure to stop in at the **Ducale Palace & Bridge of Sighs** and **St. Mark's Basilica**—and then wander the city's many canals and bridges in the afternoon.

Day 14

Museum buffs should hit the **Academy Gallery** for older art, the **Peggy Guggenheim Collection** for newer works, and **Ca' d'Oro,** where a multitude of masterpieces are hung in a grand setting in a former palace. If you prefer architecture to museums, take a *vaporetto* ride along the Grand Canal and visit several of Venice's beautiful churches and guild houses.

Day 15

Bid farewell to Europe and fly home out of Venice.

ITINERARY 7	EUROPE FOR FOOD LOVERS

Duration:	15 days, 14 nights
Best time of year:	Spring or Fall
Ideal passes:	First-class 3-country Eurail Selectpass (5, 6, or 8 days depending on the side trips you take), plus Eurostar ticket
Arrive in:	London
Depart from:	Barcelona

This 2-week trip features a walk through some of the best and most recognized regional cuisine and dining experiences in Europe. We start you off in London, where you can take afternoon tea or dine on classic pub grub, then head off to indulge in the renowned food mecca of Paris plus the celebrated cuisines of Tuscany and Spain with a side trip to Provence as a bonus. Loosen your belt as you eat your way through Europe.

Before you leave: If you don't want to be left out in the cold, it is crucial to make dinner reservations by phone in advance before you leave home.

Day 1

Arrive in the morning in **London.** The city is actually a center of global cuisine where you can eat a different country's food every day for weeks—it's an often-underrated foodie capital that's about a lot more than fish and chips (though you should have those too!). Spend the day visiting the sites of Westminster: **Westminster Abbey, 10 Downing Street, Big Ben,** and the **Houses of Parliament.** For dinner, sample the cuisine of one of Britain's best chefs, Marco Pierre White, at **Mirabelle.** Top off the evening with a pint at a pub near your hotel. See "London" chapter 10 for more on dining and sightseeing in the city.

Itinerary 7: Europe for Food Lovers

Day 2

Today's a royal day in London. Spend a long morning at the **Tower of London,** have lunch, and then head off to **Kensington Palace.** Grab a pre-theater dinner at Michelin-starred chef Nico Ladenis's **Incognico,** then head off to the West End and see a show.

Day 3

In the morning, visit the **British Museum.** Shop a bit in Covent Garden and stop in at one of Soho's many patisseries for a traditional afternoon tea. Then, head off to South Kensington for a stroll and perhaps pop in at the **Victoria & Albert Museum.** For your final night in London, dine at the ultra-British but thoroughly modern cuisine at **Rules Restaurant.**

Day 4

After a good English breakfast, take a morning Eurostar train for the 2½-hour ride to Paris. Your Eurail Select-pass gives you a discount on this speedy train. (See p. 386 for more on Eurostar.) Spend the afternoon at the **Louvre** and have dinner in a traditional French brasserie. See "Paris" in chapter 8 for dining options in the city.

Day 5

Get acquainted with monumental Paris. Begin at the **Arc de Triomphe** and stroll down the Champs-Elysees to the **Egyptian obelisk;** then either stand in line for the Eiffel Tower or explore the **Ile St-Louis** and the **Quartier Latin.** Take a break at a Left Bank cafe for coffee and pastries, and around sunset, head for **Notre-Dame**

Cathedral to top off your Paris monuments tour. Have dinner in a Left Bank bistro.

Day 6

Explore a Parisian food market this morning to see where chefs get their inspiration. Then visit **Fauchon,** the ultimate gourmet food store, for the ingredients of a picnic lunch. Spend the rest of the day exploring the sights of the **Ile de la Cité** and **Le Marais** before seeing what all that three-star Michelin stuff is about at **L'Ambroisie** (just be prepared to empty your wallet). Get some rest—you'll have an early start and a very long day tomorrow.

Day 7

Depart Paris on the 9:34am TGV train to **Avignon,** in Provence (arriving at 12:15pm). This former capital of Christendom offers excellent dining and the magnificent **Palais des Papes** (Palace of the Popes) for touring. Have an early dinner because you'll need to hop the TGV back to Paris at 9pm to arrive at 11:40pm. Fall into bed and get a well-deserved night's sleep. See "Avignon" in chapter 8 for dining options in the city.

Day 8

Sleep in a little, have a leisurely breakfast and then spend the day at the **Musée d'Orsay** and **Centre Pompidou.** In the afternoon, take tea (or hot chocolate—it's exceptional) at **Angelina,** a legendary *salon de thé.* You can bring along Parisian takeout or have dinner on the 7:09pm overnight train to Florence, your base for Tuscany. You'll arrive at 7:45am on Day 9.

Day 9

Work up your appetite today by strolling **Florence** from the **Basilica di Santa Maria Novella** to the Duomo, the **Palazzo Vecchio,** and finally **Santa Croce.** Have lunch at a simple Italian restaurant such as **Buca dell'Orafo** or **Da Ganino.** For dinner, eat at the legendary Tuscan restaurant

Paoli. See "Florence" in chapter 14 for more on dining in the city.

Day 10

It's excursion time: Catch the 9:25am train to the Tuscan city of Pisa. You'll arrive at 10:27am and should immediately set out for the famous **Leaning Tower.** For lunch, sample excellent Pisan cuisine at **Antica Trattoria Da Bruno,** near the tower. Then tour the **Duomo** and the **Baptistery** before returning to Florence on the 4:28pm train (arriving 5:30pm). Sample some more delectable Tuscan cuisine at dinner, then have dessert and coffee at one of the city's many sidewalk cafes and people-watch.

Day 11

Spend the morning at the **Boboli Gardens** and the **Palazzo Pitti.** Take a long lunch at **Cantinetta Antinori,** sampling the wines. After a siesta, do some shopping and have a final Tuscan dinner at **Trattoria Garga.**

Day 12

Get up early and spend the day in the **Galleria degli Uffizi,** one of the world's greatest art museums. Take the 4:13pm express train from Florence to Milan, where you'll have a 1-hour layover before connecting to the 8pm overnight train to Barcelona. Have dinner on the train or grab something in Milan's station before you depart. You'll arrive in Barcelona at 9:31am.

Day 13

Barcelona has an embarrassment of riches, both culinary and architectural. Check into your hotel and then start your day off at **La Sagrada Familia** cathedral, the city's famous cathedral, and wander the city's Gothic Quarter. Take lunch at **Garduña,** located in the back of Catalonia's best food market, before visiting the **Museu Picasso.** Retire to your hotel room for a siesta, then eat a late dinner and spend the night downing bubbly at Barcelona's numerous *cava* (champagne) bars. See

"Barcelona" in chapter 18 for more on dining in the city.

Day 14

Start your day off by visiting the **Parc Güell** and the **Fundació Joan Miró.** Spend a relaxing afternoon sipping cava and munching tapas at **El Xampanyet,** and eat a late dinner at one of Barcelona's excellent Catalonian restaurants—**Jean Luc Figueras** is a good choice.

Day 15

Say *adios* to Europe and fly home from Barcelona.

ITINERARY 8   WARM-WEATHER EUROPE

Duration:	15 days, 14 nights
Best time of year:	Summer
Ideal passes:	First-class 8-day 4-country Eurail Selectpass
Arrive in:	Athens
Depart from:	Barcelona

There's a mellow Europe where 3-hour lunches and lounging on the beach is the norm. It's also an ancient and beautiful place, settled thousands of years ago by Greece and Rome. This 2-week trip brings you along that ancient coastline and lets you sun yourself on the beaches of four countries. Bring your bathing suit and plenty of sunblock!

Day 1

Arrive in Athens. After checking into your hotel, start at the **Acropolis,** strolling downhill to the ancient Agora. Have lunch in the nearby Monastiraki or Plaka districts, then take a taxi to the **National Archaeological Museum** (it reopens after a 2-year renovation in 2004) to see the Mycenaean gold, Cycladic idols, and classical bronze statues. Head back to your hotel for a siesta, before returning to the Plaka for dinner. If you're in town during the city's famous Athens Festival, try to see a play at the Acropolis's **Odeon of Herodes Atticus.** For more on Athens, see "Athens" in chapter 11.

Day 2

Rise with the sun this morning (it'll be worth it) and catch the 8:29am train to the seaside village of **Diakofto.** After arriving at 11:36am, hurry and make the 11:48am connection to the **rack-and-pinion railroad** (p. 457) that runs the 1-hour mountain route between Diakofto and Kalavryta. This hidden gem is one of the most scenic in all of Europe. Eat lunch and spend some time exploring the charming town of **Kalavryta,** but be sure to get back to the train station in time to catch the 5pm train back to Diakofto, where you'll need to grab the 6:19pm Inter-City train back to Athens. Have a late dinner and get some well-earned sleep.

Day 3

Start your morning off in Athens at the **Benaki Museum,** where all of Greek history is housed under one roof. Afterwards, get some lunch and do a little shopping in the Plaka. Be sure to get to the train station in time to catch the 4:06pm train to Nafplion. You'll arrive in the scenic town at 7:04pm. Take a taxi to your hotel, then grab dinner at a local taverna and call it a day.

Day 4

Spend your day in **Nafplion,** wandering the beautiful town's streets and enjoying the scenery and the beach. Walk up to the **Acronafplia,** and take a taxi to the top of the **Palamidi** before walking down. Cap your day by having coffee at one of the city's many waterfront cafes while watching the sunset.

Day 5

It's time to cross the Adriatic. Take the 11:27am train from Nafplion to Corinth, and switch to the 1:25pm train to Patras, arriving at 3:29pm. At 6pm, get on the overnight ferry to Bari, Italy, arriving at 8:30am. (For more on this ferry, see p. 575.)

Day 6

Spend the morning in Bari, then a 1:43pm express train for the 4½-hour journey to Rome. Check into your hotel, and then have dinner near the **Pantheon** and visit the **Trevi Fountain.** See "Rome" in chapter 14 for more sightseeing options in the city.

Day 7

Explore ancient Rome today starting at the **Capitoline Hill** and walking along the Via dei Fori Imperiali to the ruins of the **Colosseum.** Nearby you'll find the ruins of the **Roman Forum** and the **Palatine Hill.** Have dinner near the **Piazza Navona,** then explore that famous square and see **Bernini's Fountain.** For more information, see "Rome" in chapter 14.

Day 8

Spend today exploring the treasures of the Vatican. Take in **St. Peter's Basilica** in the morning and the **Vatican Museums** in the afternoon. Have dinner in Trastevere.

Day 9

Take a day trip to the ancient city of **Pompei,** just 2½ hours from Rome by train. Trains run via Naples and if you leave Rome at 8:45am and return from Pompeii at 4:40pm, you'll have time for dinner in Naples before returning to Rome.

Day 10

During the morning, shop and stroll around the **Spanish Steps.** In the afternoon, take in another museum,

such as the **Galleria Borghese,** or enjoy people-watching on the Piazza della Rotonda near the Pantheon. Take the 11:27pm overnight train to Ventimiglia, a border town in Italy where you'll change for the 8:44am TGV high-speed train to Cannes, arriving at 10:03am.

Day 11

You're only on the **Riviera** for the day. Stash your luggage in lockers at the station and spend the day ogling beachgoers (as Cannes' rocky beach isn't very comfortable), window-shopping on **La Croisette,** and pretending to be rich and famous. (See chapter 8 for more on the Riviera.) Then get on the 10:58pm overnight train to Portbou, a border town in Spain where you'll arrive at 6:14am; wait a bit, then hop the 7:35am train to Barcelona.

Day 12

You'll arrive in **Barcelona** at 9:42am. After checking into your hotel, visit Gaudí's **La Sagrada Familia** cathedral. In the evening, stroll the **Barri Gòtic,** the city's Gothic quarter, or the famous **La Rambla** promenade. For more sightseeing options, see "Barcelona" in chapter 18.

Day 13

Start your morning off with a tour of the **Museu Picasso,** and then spend the afternoon among the surreal architecture of beautiful **Parc Güell.**

Day 14

Head to the **Fundació Joan Miró** museum in the morning, and then ride the funicular up Tibidabo Mountain to the **Mirador Torre de Collserola;** the tower offers spectacular vistas of the coast and city. In the afternoon, stroll the city's Gothic quarter and check out **Catedral de Barcelona.** Spend a fun evening sampling the bubbly at Barcelona's many *cava* (champagne) bars.

Day 15

Fly home from Barcelona.

Itinerary 8: Warm-Weather Europe

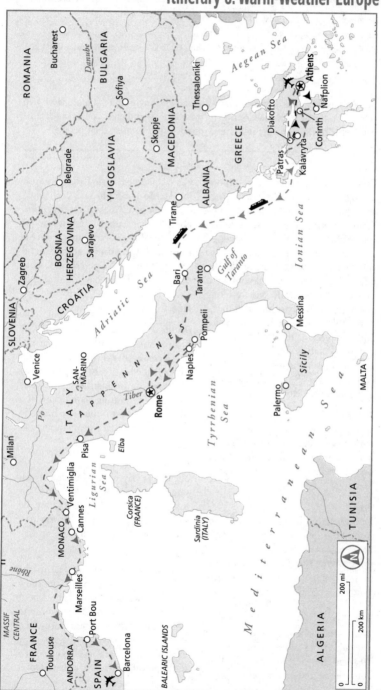

ITINERARY 9   GREAT CITIES OF EUROPE

Duration:	15 days, 14 nights
Best time of year:	Spring or Fall
Ideal passes:	First-class 5-day, 4-country Eurail Selectpass, plus Eurostar ticket
Arrive in:	Rome
Depart from:	Berlin

Europe has been the center of many a globe-girdling empire. This 2-week trip gets you to the heart of the Continent's great cities—and gives you as much time as possible to explore their sights and sounds—and to meet their people.

Day 1

Land at Rome's Fiumicino airport, starting your European rail journey with the train shuttle to the Roma Termini Station (don't waste a day on your railpass for this ride, though— the ticket is very cheap). Check into your hotel before starting your exploration of ancient Rome, beginning at the **Capitoline Hill** and walking along the Via dei Fori Imperiali to the ruins of the **Colosseum.** Nearby you'll find the ruins of the **Roman Forum** and the **Palatine Hill.** Have dinner near the **Pantheon** and visit the **Trevi Fountain.** See "Rome" in chapter 14 for more on the city.

Day 2

Spend today exploring the treasures of the Vatican. Take in **St. Peter's Basilica** in the morning and the **Vatican Museums** in the afternoon. Have dinner in Trastevere.

Day 3

During the morning, shop and stroll around the **Spanish Steps.** In the afternoon, take in another museum, such as the **Galleria Borghese,** or enjoy people-watching on the Piazza della Rotonda near the Pantheon. Around 5pm, head to Stazione Termini for your first major rail trip: The **Artesia France-Italy Night train** departing at 7:07pm from Rome, arriving at 10:13am the next morning in Paris. For more on the Artesia, see p. 554.

Day 4

Get acquainted with Paris. Begin at the **Arc de Triomphe** and stroll down the Champs-Elysees to the **Egyptian obelisk;** then either stand in line for the **Eiffel Tower** or explore the **Ile St-Louis** and the **Latin Quarter.** Around sunset, head for **Notre-Dame Cathedral** to top off your day. Eat dinner in a Left Bank cafe. See "Paris" in chapter 8 for more information.

Day 5

Start your day off exploring the **St–Germain–des–Prés** area. Move on to the Ile de la Cité, before heading to the **Place de la Bastille.** Finish your day off by touring fashionable **Le Marais.** Then eat dinner at a brasserie and spend the night people-watching at a sidewalk cafe.

Day 6

Spend the day at the **Louvre;** if you want a change of scenery, tack on a visit to the magnificent **Musée d'Orsay.** Be sure to indulge in some Parisian pastries before the day is through.

Day 7

Grab a croissant on the way to the Gare de Lyon and take a morning Eurostar train to London. The 3-hour journey rockets across France at up to 186 mph. It may appear costly, but the $75 passholder fare is no more expensive than the combined fare for a high-speed ferry from Calais to Dover

Itinerary 9: Great Cities of Europe

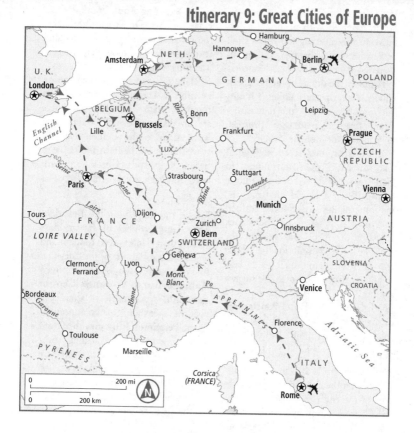

and a local train from Dover to London. (See p. 386 for more on Eurostar.)

You'll arrive in **London** around lunchtime. Leave your bags at your hotel and grab lunch at a nearby pub. Spend the afternoon touring the sights of Westminster: **Westminster Abbey, 10 Downing Street, Big Ben,** and the **Houses of Parliament.** Have dinner in Covent Garden. See "London" in chapter 10 for more on the British capital.

Day 8

If you couldn't get into Westminster Abbey on Day 7, try again. Otherwise, spend the morning at the **British Museum,** and after lunch head over to the **Tower of London.** If you have time, take a ride on the **British Airways London Eye,** just across the river. After a quick dinner, head over to the West End and catch a show.

Day 9

If one of your days in London is a weekend, spend some time at one or two of the major markets, such as Camden or Portobello Road. If you're here mid-week, wave hello to the pigeons in **Trafalgar Square** and tour the **National Gallery,** one of Europe's finest art museums (and it's free!). Grab some lunch, shop a bit at Covent Gardens, and end your day at the **Victoria & Albert Museum**—home to the world's greatest collection of decorative arts (don't miss the British Galleries).

Day 10

Fortify yourself with a good English breakfast this morning and take a stroll near your hotel before heading to Waterloo station for the 12:27 Eurostar to **Brussels,** the capital of the European Union. The trip takes under 3 hours, but you'll arrive after 4pm thanks to a 1-hour time difference. See "Brussels" in chapter 4 for more on the city.

In Brussels, stash your luggage at Gare du Midi, then hop a train to Gare Central and head to the medieval **Grand-Place,** a World Heritage site, for some of the city's famous seafood and mussels. After dinner, head back to Gare du Midi and get on the 8:37pm InterCity train for the 3-hour trip to Amsterdam. You'll get in late, so take a cab to your hotel. We suggest staying near Centraal Station at a hotel such as the **Hotel Amsterdam** or the **Amstel Botel.** See "Amsterdam" in chapter 15 for more hotel options.

Day 11

You've only got 2 days in Amsterdam, so focus on the city center. Explore the core of the city either by foot or on a canal boat, stopping at the **Dam Square,** the picturesque **Flower Market** at **Muntplein,** the immense market at **Waterlooplein,** and the lively **Leidseplein.** After a late lunch, stop at the renowned **Rijksmuseum** to see its current "greatest hits" exhibition of Dutch art. For dinner, sample one of the city's **Indonesian *rijsttafel* buffets.** After dinner, if you dare, take an evening walk through the Red Light District on the way back to your hotel—it only gets livelier as it gets later.

Day 12

Check out of your hotel, store your luggage, and head to the western part of the city this morning, past the Dutch Renaissance-style **Westerkerk,** to the haunting **Anne Frank House.** Have lunch at **De Prins,** right across the canal. Unwind with a coffee and "brown-cafe" style food while people-watching along the canal.

Make sure to be at Centraal Station in time to catch the zippy 3:13pm InterCity train to Berlin (alas, there are no decent overnight trains from Amsterdam to the German capital). Have dinner on the train and arrive in Berlin at 9:11pm. Check into your hotel and get a good night's sleep.

Day 13

In the morning, visit the **Branden-burg Gate,** symbol of Berlin, then walk down Unter den Linden and enjoy breakfast at one of the cafes that line the street. Head to the store-lined **Kufurstendamm** to witness German capitalism in action. In the afternoon, visit the Greek and Roman antiquities in the **Pergamon Museum,** then head south to explore the charming 16th-century **Nikolai Quarter.** If they are playing when you are in town, the **Berlin Philharmonic Orchestra** is one of the best in the world. For more on the city, see "Berlin" in chapter 9.

Day 14

Visit the masterpieces at the **Gemälde-galerie,** then tour **Charlottenburg Palace** and its museums. Spend any leftover time strolling through Berlin, perhaps stopping at the Cold War's **Checkpoint Charlie.** Or take a day trip to beautiful **Potsdam,** just 23 minutes away by train (29 trains depart throughout the day), and explore the **Sans Souci Palace** and its surrounding parkland. After dinner, do as Berliners do and have a drink at a *Kneipe,* the local version of a British pub.

Day 15

Fly back to your home from Berlin.

ITINERARY 10   THE GRAND TOUR

Duration:	15 days, 14 nights
Best time of year:	Any time
Ideal passes:	First-class 15-day Eurailpass
Arrive in:	Lisbon
Depart from:	Berlin

The European Union may have a single currency (well, minus a few pesky hold-outs here and there), but it's got more than a dozen unique cultures. A dozen in 15 days is a bit too much of a challenge for us, but this long-distance journey lets you experience six distinctly different flavors of Europe without having to change your money once—the most diversity and least hassle you can get in 2 weeks. Note that the five rail legs used in this itinerary are night trains, so you'll save on hotel rooms, but will have to budget for sleeper supplements.

Day 1
Time your flight to arrive in Lisbon as early as possible. Start your day with a stroll through the **Alfama,** the most atmospheric quarter of Lisbon. Visit the city's 12th-century cathedral and take in a view of the city and the river Tagus from the **Miradouro de Santa Luzia.** Climb up to the **Castelo de São Jorge** and take in another breathtaking view from the castle's observation platform. Consider a nap before spending a late night at a **fado club** in the Alfama. See "Lisbon" in chapter 17 for more information on the Portuguese capital.

Day 2
Head to the suburb of Belém to see the **Mosteiro dos Jerónimos (Jerónimos Monastery),** the **Torre de Belém,** and the **Museu Nacional dos Coches (National Coach Museum).** After lunch, see the artworks at the **Museu de Fundação Calouste Gulbenkian,** or shop at the open-air **Feira da Ladra.** Take the overnight *Lusitania* hotel train to Madrid (p. 38).

Day 3
Drop your luggage at your hotel, then start your day in Madrid at the **Royal Palace** and work your way east to the **Monasterio las Descalzas Reales.** After checking into your hotel, snack your way around the many tapas bars in the Plaza Mayor area. See "Madrid" in chapter 18 for more on the city.

Day 4
Check out the masterpieces at the **Museo Lazaro Galdiano** in the morning and shop the El Rastro flea market in the afternoon. Or take a day trip to explore the Moorish architectural riches of **Cordoba**—hourly AVE express trains leave from Madrid's Atocha station for the 2½-hour journey. See "Cordoba" in chapter 18 for more on this Moorish city.

Day 5
Spend your day at the **Prado,** and take the overnight train to Paris. This train, one of the *Elipsos* series, is one of Europe's most luxurious regular trips; even the most basic accommodation is a four-berth sleeper, not a six-berth couchette room like those on many other trains (p. 38).

Day 6
See Day 4 of the " Great Cities of Europe" itinerary (p. 20).

Day 7
See Day 5 of the "Great Cities of Europe" itinerary (p. 20).

Day 8
Spend the day immersed in art at the **Louvre** and the **Musée d'Orsay.** Grab

Itinerary 10: The Grand Tour

some gourmet French takeout at **Fau-chon** for dinner and take the overnight train to Florence, departing Paris at 7:07pm and arriving at 7:45am.

Day 9

Florence is all about art. Spend your day strolling the city from the **Basilica di Santa Maria Novella** to the **Duomo,** the **Palazzo Vecchio,** and finally **Santa Croce.** Florence is all about food, too, so load up on Tuscan cuisine at dinner. See "Florence" in chapter 14 for dining options in the city.

Day 10

Allot the entire day for the **Galleria degli Uffizi,** one of the world's greatest art museums. If you need a change of scenery, stroll the **Boboli Gardens**

and take in the art at the **Palazzo Pitti.** Take the 10:09pm overnight train to Vienna, arriving at 8:47am. If you can, get up around 6:45am to watch the train go over the 150-year-old Semmering Pass Railway, the only rail line on UNESCO's list of World Heritage Sites.

Day 11

See Day 7 of the "Riding the Scenic Route" itinerary (p. 8).

Day 12

Explore other major Vienna attractions, such as the **Hofburg Palace Complex** and the **Kunsthistorisches Museum.** Get to the train station in time to take the 9:28pm overnight train to Berlin (arriving at 7:52am).

Day 13

You'll get to **Berlin** by breakfast time, so head for **Unter den Linden** and enjoy breakfast at one of the cafes that line the street. Head to the store-lined **Kufurstendamm** to shop until you feel like eating lunch. In the afternoon, visit the Greek and Roman antiquities in the **Pergamon Museum,** then head south to explore the charming 16th-century **Nikolai Quarter.** If they are playing when you are in town, the **Berlin Philharmonic Orchestra** is one of the best in the world. For more on the city, see "Berlin" in chapter 9.

Day 14

Visit the masterpieces at the **Gemälde-galerie,** then tour **Charlottenburg Palace** and its museums. Spend any leftover time strolling through Berlin, perhaps stopping at the Cold War's **Checkpoint Charlie.** Top off your trip with a drink at one of Berlin's vaunted wine cellars.

Day 15

Fly home from Berlin.

2

Planning Your European Rail Trip

Rails are the veins of Europe. When you travel on the continent's speedy, affordable, and surprisingly complete rail system, you'll get to cross terrain where no cars go, make friends you would never otherwise have met, and travel without the worries of traffic, parking, and airport security.

Speedy trains zip across Northern Europe at up to 186 mph; slower trains stop in the depths of Swiss mountain valleys and meander past quaint Dutch villages. And somehow, trains make people open up in ways they never would if they were traveling by air, bus, or car. In one car of a French night train, we once met a college student from Nashville, an artist from Florence, and five members of an Ethiopian soccer team. Riding a high-speed train along the backbone of Italy, we were charmed by a young man heading to his exams for the *carabinieri* who led us, patiently, through the chaos of Rome's Termini Station.

Thousands of students first see Europe from the inexpensive perch of a six-berth couchette, but more mature travelers who seek luxury are sure to find it in Europe's top-class trains, where cabins include private showers and waiters bring restaurant-quality meals straight to your room, as the Pyrenees or the Mediterranean coast slide by your window.

Those who haven't traveled on European trains in a while will be startled by the range of ticket classes and the bewildering number of trains. But traveling by train doesn't have to be confusing: Take a deep breath, leave yourself some time at the station, and enjoy traveling the way Europeans do.

Modern trains are romantic, comfortable and an easy way to get around, and they even get you to where you're going on time. What more can you ask?

1 Visitor Information

Your first step in planning your Europe trip should be to decide which countries or regions you'd like to visit. Browse chapters 3 through 20 of this book to get an idea of the highlights of each major European country. Should you want more detailed information to help you make your selections, contact the **European tourist offices** in your own country; for a complete list, see below:

AUSTRIAN NATIONAL TOURIST OFFICE

www.anto.com or www.Austria-tourism.com

IN THE U.S. P.O. Box 1142, 500 Fifth Ave., New York, NY 10110 (© **212/944-6880;** fax 212/730-4568).

IN CANADA 2 Bloor St. W., Suite 3330, Toronto, ON M4W 1A8 (© **416/967-3381;** fax 416/967-4101).

BELGIAN TOURIST OFFICE

www.visitbelgium.com

IN THE U.S.   780 Third Ave., New York, NY 10017 (✆ **212/758-8130;** fax 212/355-7675).

IN CANADA   P.O. Box 760 NDG, Montreal, PQ H4A 382 (✆ **514/457-2888;** fax 514/489-8965).

BRITISH TOURIST AUTHORITY
www.visitbritain.com or www.travelbritain.org

IN THE U.S.   551 Fifth Ave., Suite 701, New York, NY 10176-0799 (✆ **800/462-2748** or 212/986-2266; fax 212/986-1188).

IN CANADA   5915 Airport Rd., Mississaugua, ON L4V 1TI (✆ **888/ VISITUK;** fax 905/405-1835).

CZECH TOURIST AUTHORITY
www.czechcenter.com or www.czech.cz

IN THE U.S.   1109 Madison Ave., New York, NY 10028 (✆ **212/288-0830;** fax 212/288-0971).

IN CANADA   c/o Czech Airlines, 401 Bay St. Suite 1510, Toronto, ON M5H 2Y4 (✆ **416/363-9928;** fax 416/363-0239; ctacanada@iprimus. ca).

FRENCH GOVERNMENT TOURIST OFFICE
www.franceguide.com

IN THE U.S.   444 Madison Ave., 16th Floor, New York, NY 10022 (✆ **212/838-7800;** fax 212/838-7855). To request information at any of these offices, call the **France on Call hot line** at ✆ **900/990-0040** (50¢ per min.).

IN CANADA   Maison de la France/French Government Tourist Office, 1981 av. McGill College, Suite 490, Montreal, PQ H3A 2W9 (✆ **514/876-9881;** fax 514/845-4868); 30 St. Patrick St., Suite 700, Toronto, ON M5T 3A3 (✆ **416/ 491-7622;** fax 416/979-7587).

GERMAN NATIONAL TOURIST OFFICE
www.visits-to-germany.com

IN THE U.S.   122 E. 42nd St., 52nd Floor, New York, NY 10168-0072 (✆ **800/637-1171** or 212/ 661-7200; fax 212/661-7174).

IN CANADA   P.O. Box 65162, Toronto, ON M4K 3Z2 (✆ **877/ 315-6237;** fax 416/968-1986).

GREEK NATIONAL TOURIST ORGANIZATION
www.gnto.gr

IN THE U.S.   645 Fifth Ave., Suite 903, New York, NY 10022 (✆ **212/ 421-5777;** fax 212/826-6490).

IN CANADA   91 Scollard St., Toronto, ON 1G4 3K8 (✆ **416/968-2220;** fax 416/968-6533).

HUNGARIAN NATIONAL TOURIST OFFICE
www.hungarytourism.hu or www.gotohungary.com

IN THE U.S. & CANADA   150 E. 58th St., 33rd Floor, New York, NY 10155 (✆ **212/355-0240;** fax 212/ 207-4103).

IRISH TOURIST BOARD
www.ireland.travel.ie or www.irelandvacations.com

IN THE U.S.   345 Park Ave., New York, NY 10154 (✆ **800/223-6470** or 212/418-0800; fax 212/371-9052).

ITALIAN GOVERNMENT TOURIST BOARD
www.enit.it or www.italiantourism.com

IN THE U.S.   630 Fifth Ave., Suite 1565, New York, NY 10111 (✆ **212/ 245-4822;** fax 212/586-9249).

IN CANADA   175 Bloor St. E., South Tower, Suite 907, Toronto, ON M4W 3R8 (✆ **416/925-4882;** fax 416/925-4799).

NETHERLANDS BOARD OF TOURISM
www.holland.com

IN THE U.S.   355 Lexington Ave., 19th Floor, New York, NY 10017 (✆ **888/464-6552** or 212/557-3500; fax 212/370-9507).

PORTUGUESE NATIONAL TOURIST OFFICE

www.portugal.org or www.portugalinsite.pt

IN THE U.S.   590 Fifth Ave., 4th Floor, New York, NY 10036 (© **212/354-4403;** fax 212/764-6137).

IN CANADA   60 Bloor St. W., Suite 1005, Toronto, ON M4W 3B8 (© **416/921-7376;** fax 416/921-1353).

SCANDINAVIAN TOURIST BOARDS (DENMARK, FINLAND, NORWAY & SWEDEN)

www.goscandinavia.com, www.visitdenmark.com, www.gofinland.org, www.visitnorway.com, or www.visit-sweden.com

IN THE U.S. & CANADA

P.O. Box 4649, Grand Central Station, New York, NY 10163-4649 (© **212/885-9700;** fax 212/885-9710).

SWITZERLAND TOURISM

www.switzerlandtourism.com

IN THE U.S.   608 Fifth Ave., New York, NY 10020 (© **800/794-7795,** 877/794-8037, or 212/757-5944; fax 212/262-6116).

TOURIST OFFICE OF SPAIN

www.okspain.org

IN THE U.S.   666 Fifth Ave., 35th Floor, New York, NY 10103 (© **212/265-8822;** fax 212/265-8864).

IN CANADA   2 Bloor St. W., 34th Floor, Toronto, ON M5S 1M9 (© **416/961-3131;** fax 416/961-1992).

2 When to Go

Europe is a continent for all seasons, offering everything from a bikini beach party on the Riviera in summer to the finest skiing in the world in the Alps in winter.

Europe has a continental climate with distinct seasons, but there are great variations in temperature from one part to another. Northern Norway is plunged into Arctic darkness in winter, but in sunny Southern Italy the climate is usually temperate—though snow can fall even on the Greek Islands in winter, and winter nights are cold anywhere. Europe is north of most of the United States, but along the Mediterranean they see weather patterns more along the lines of the U.S. southern states. In general, however, seasonal changes are less extreme than in most of the United States.

The **high season** lasts from mid-May to mid-September, with the most tourists hitting the Continent from mid-June to August. In general, this is the most expensive time to travel, except in Austria and Switzerland, where prices are actually higher in winter during the ski season. And because Scandinavian hotels depend on business clients instead of tourists, lower prices can often be found in the fleeting summer, when business travelers are scarce and a smaller number of tourists take over.

You'll find smaller crowds, relatively fair weather, and often lower prices at hotels in the **shoulder seasons,** from Easter to mid-May and mid-September to mid-October. **Off season** (except at ski resorts) is from November to Easter, with the exception of December 25 to January 6. Much of Europe, Italy especially, takes August off, and from August 15 to August 30 is vacation time for many locals, so expect the cities to be devoid of natives but the beaches packed.

WEATHER

BRITAIN & IRELAND   Everyone knows it rains a lot in Britain and Ireland. Winters are rainier than summers; August and from September to mid-October

> ## ⟨Tips⟩ What Time Is It, Anyway?
>
> Based on U.S. **Eastern Standard Time (EST),** Britain and Ireland are 5 hours ahead of New York City; Greece is 7 hours ahead of New York. The rest of the countries in this book are 6 hours ahead of New York. For instance, when it's noon in New York, it's 5pm in London and Lisbon; 6pm in Paris, Copenhagen, and Amsterdam; and 7pm in Athens. The European countries now observe daylight savings time, but the time change doesn't usually occur on the same day or during the same month as in the United States, so be advised that the time difference can vary by as much as 2 hours during those few weeks when some countries have switched to or from daylight savings time ahead of North America.
>
> If you plan to travel to Ireland or continental Europe from Britain, keep in mind that the time will be the same in Ireland, 2 hours later in Greece, and 1 hour later in the other countries in this guide.
>
> And *one last warning:* Departure and arrival times on train schedules are almost always given in 24-hour military time. So a train leaving at 1:23pm, would be listed as leaving at 13:23.

are the sunniest months. Summer daytime temperatures average from the low 60s Fahrenheit (10s Celsius) to the mid-60s (20s Celsius), dropping to the 40s (5s Celsius) on winter nights. Ireland, whose shores are bathed by the Gulf Stream, has a milder climate and the most changeable weather—a dark rainy morning can quickly turn into a sunny afternoon, and vice versa. The Scottish Lowlands have a climate similar to England's, but the Highlands are much colder, with storms and snow in winter.

CENTRAL EUROPE   In Vienna and along the Danube Valley the climate is moderate. Summer daytime temperatures average in the low 70s Fahrenheit (20s Celsius), falling at night to the low 50s (10s Celsius). Winter temperatures are in the 30s Fahrenheit (below 0 Celsius) and 40s (10s Celsius) during the day. In Budapest, temperatures can reach 80°F (25°C) in August and dip to 30°F (0°C) in January. Winter is damp and chilly, spring is mild, and May and June are usually wet. The best weather is in the late summer through October. In Prague and Bohemia, summer months have an average temperature of 65°F (18°C) but are the rainiest, while January and February are usually sunny and clear, with temperatures around freezing.

FRANCE & GERMANY   The weather in Paris is approximately the same as in the U.S. mid-Atlantic states, but like most of Europe, there's less extreme variation. In summer, the temperature rarely goes above the mid-70s Fahrenheit (mid-20s Celsius), though heat waves (such as the one that struck all of Europe in 2003) can occur. Summers are fair and can be hot along the Riviera. Winters tend to be mild, in the 40s Fahrenheit (10s Celsius), though it's warmer along the Riviera. Germany's climate ranges from the moderate summers and chilly, damp winters in the north to the mild summers and very cold, sunny winters of the alpine south.

NORTHERN EUROPE   In the Netherlands, the weather is never extreme at any time of year. Summer temperatures average around 67°F (20°C) and the winter average is about 40°F (5°C). The climate is rainy, with the driest months from February to May. From Mid-April to mid-May, the tulip fields burst into color. The climate of northern Germany is very similar. Belgium's climate is moderate, varying from 73°F (23°C) in July and August to 40°F (5°C) in December and January. It does rain a lot, but the weather is at its finest in July and August.

SCANDINAVIA   Summer temperatures above the Arctic Circle average around the mid-50s Fahrenheit (mid-10s Celsius), dropping to around 14°F (–10°C) during the dark winters. In the south, summer temperatures average around 70°F (22°C), dropping to the 20s Fahrenheit (below 0 Celsius) in winter. Fjords and even the ocean are often warm enough for summer swimming, but rain is frequent. The sun shines 24 hours in midsummer above the Arctic Circle, where winter brings semi-permanent twilight. Denmark's climate is relatively mild by comparison. It has moderate summer temperatures and winters that can be damp and foggy, with temperatures just above the mid-30s Fahrenheit (0 Celsius).

SOUTHERN EUROPE   Summers are hot in Italy, Spain, and Greece, with temperatures around the high 80s Fahrenheit (30s Celsius) or even higher in some parts of Spain. Along the Italian Riviera, summer and winter temperatures are mild, and except in the Alpine regions, Italian winter temperatures rarely drop below freezing. The area around Madrid is dry and arid, and summers in Spain are coolest along the Atlantic coast, with mild temperatures year-round on the Costa del Sol. Seaside Portugal is very rainy but has temperatures of 50°F to 75°F (10°C–25°C) year-round. In Greece, there's sunshine all year, and winters are usually mild, with temperatures around 50°F to 54°F (10°C–12°C). Hot summer temperatures are often helped by cool breezes. The best seasons to visit Greece are from mid-April to June and mid-September to late October, when the wildflowers bloom and the tourists go home.

SWITZERLAND & THE ALPS   The alpine climate is shared by Bavaria in southern Germany and the Austrian Tyrol and Italian Dolomites—winters are cold and bright, and spring comes late, with snow flurries well into April. Summers are mild and sunny, though the Alpine regions can experience dramatic changes in weather any time of year.

3 Finding Your Rail Route

Thousands of trains run across Europe every day, and on many routes you can just show up at the station and be assured a train will be leaving pretty soon. But there are many reasons to plan your trip in advance: Some trains require advance reservations, and some only run a few times a day, and several lines have both fast and slow trains.

The **Rail Europe** website (**www.raileurope.com**) has train schedules for routes between major European destinations, but not all smaller towns and cities are included on their site, and if you want to check intermediate stops on a given train, you'll have to look elsewhere. The site also offers prices for point-to-point tickets (a major plus when budgeting for a trip), seat reservations, passes when purchased in North America (some passes can only be purchased on this side of the Atlantic), and a list of accommodations on night trains.

A better site for timetables—and our personal favorite—is produced by German railway **Die Bahn** at **www.bahn.de** (click the "Int. Guests" tab at the top of the Web page). The DB site covers all major rail lines in all Eurail countries. It also features many bus and ferry services, and will tell you which trains will require reservations. Within Germany, it gives train prices and even tells you what tracks you can expect your trains to appear on.

But even the DB site is missing some small stations and lines, and it can be hard to find the correct station for some smaller cities when the station name doesn't match the location name (we had a heck of a time getting the correct routing for Szigliget in Hungary). Note also that the website uses European and not American spellings, so you won't be looking for Florence and Naples, you'll be looking for Firenze and Napoli.

If the DB site doesn't meet your needs, you'll need to go to the national rail site for the destination you're interested in. Choose your desired country from the "National Railway Websites & Phone Numbers" chart below, or from a more comprehensive list at **http://mercurio.iet.unipi.it/misc/timetabl.html**. Many of the national rail sites will display prices for domestic itineraries only; if you are traveling through several countries, you'll need to call the national rail company or you can check Rail Europe's website. **Warning:** Keep in mind that some European national rail sites don't have English versions, so if you don't speak the local language, navigating these sites will be extremely difficult.

National Railway Websites & Phone Numbers

Country	Website	Phone Number (International)
All countries	www.raileurope.com	1/877-272-RAIL (E)*
Austria	www.oebb.at	43/1 930 000
Belgium	www.b-rail.be	32/2 528 2828
Czech Republic	www.cdrail.cz	420/2 2422 5849 (E)
Denmark	www.dsb.dk	45/70 13 14 16
Finland	www.vr.fi	358/307 20 902
France	www.sncf.com	33/1 53 90 10 10
Germany	www.bahn.de	44/870 243 53 63 (E)
Greece	www.ose.gr	30/210 529 7777
Hungary	www.mav.hu	36/1 461 5500
Ireland	www.irishrail.ie	353/1 836 6222 (E)
Italy	www.trenitalia.it	39/89 20 21
Luxembourg	www.cfl.lu	352/49 90 49 90
Netherlands	www.ns.nl	31/900 92 96
Norway	www.nsb.no	47/815 00 888 x 4 (E)
Portugal	www.cp.pt	351/213 215 700
Spain	www.renfe.es	34/93 490 11 22
Sweden	www.sj.se	46/771 75 75 75 (E)
Switzerland	www.sbb.ch	41/512 20 11 11
United Kingdom	www.nationalrail.co.uk	44/845 7 48 49 50 (E)

Note: *All phone numbers above (except for Italy, which has only a local number) are shown as you would dial them from North America (dial the international access code of* **011,** *then the number as listed above).*

* *Phone numbers marked with an "E" respond immediately in English. For other countries, you'll have to wait through a taped message in the local language. Hang on—the operators usually speak, or can find someone who speaks, English.*

> ## *Tips* Staying on Track
>
> Americans used to Amtrak, which gets you to your destination sort of whenever, will be amazed by the timeliness of European trains. By and large, trains on the Continent run on time to the minute. There are exceptions, though:
>
> Local trains in **Greece, southern Italy,** and **southern Spain** may follow timetables that are "a bit lax," according to Rail Europe, so plan extra time in those regions.
>
> The **British** railway system has been plagued by delays in recent years, with as many as one in five trains in some parts of the country running late, so have some patience there. (Eurostar generally isn't affected by these problems.)
>
> **France** and **Italy** are prone to seasonal strikes and labor actions that may impact train travel, often in the fall and around Christmas. Unfortunately, these can't be planned for, so take solace in the fact that everyone else will be as stuck as you are.

Off-line, the ultimate bible for European rail schedules is the **Thomas Cook European Timetable.** At 550 pages, it's chunky, but it covers every major railway line on the continent, as well as many bus and ferry services. It's updated monthly, so buy it as close to your travel date as possible, allowing 2 weeks for delivery. The Timetable is available online from Thomas Cook Publishing (www.thomascookpublishing.com) for £9.45 plus £5 shipping (approximately $24 total) to the U.S. To order by phone (it'll cost you about 10% more), call ⓒ **44/1733 416 477.** It's also sold by Rail Europe (ⓒ **877/272-RAIL**) for $28.95 plus a $15 2-day delivery charge.

4 Choosing the Train That's Right for You

If you have a limited time in Europe, then speed will be an issue for you when traveling by train, and there are plenty of high-speed options that will zip you around Europe. But it can be hard to look out at some of the country's grandest scenery when you're flying by at 250 mph (400kmph), so perhaps you'd rather take a slower train every now and then. (Those people who suffer from motion sickness may find that looking out a window as a high-speed train is zipping along can be disquieting, so they might want to stick to slower, local trains.)

Depending on your budget, you may want to travel only in first class, or you may want to spend your money on other things and won't want to shell out the extra money to get out of second class. And if you opt to travel after dark, a plethora of sleeping options await you on Europe's vast array of night trains. In this section, we outline all of the major train and accommodations options you'll encounter when traveling through Europe by rail. Read through the descriptions and then choose the train that will best suit your needs.

HIGH-SPEED TRAINS

Note: See the tear-out map at the back of this book for a look at all of the major high-speed routes in Europe.

Europe's high-speed trains are true marvels, zipping you across the country-side at speeds up to 186 miles per hour (and in some cases, a whole lot more). Some of them, like the Pendolino and Cisalpino trains, even "tilt" so they can glide through curves without having to slow down (don't worry, you'll hardly feel a thing.) In many cases, taking high-speed trains is faster than flying!

France, Italy, Germany, Spain, and Sweden offer the most developed high-speed networks, but most European countries have some form of high-speed service. These trains are worth seeking out: TGV, Eurostar, and Thalys trains, especially, can turn a full day's journey into a 3-hour trip.

You'll pay extra for the privilege of riding on one of these rail rockets, but shelling out the extra cash is worth it when you consider the time you'll save. A nonstop express ticket from Munich to Berlin, for instance, is 83.60€ ($96.15) if bought in Germany, with the ride taking 6½ hours. You can pay as little as 66.60€ ($76.60) for a regular ticket, but you'll be forced to change trains four times en route and the trip will take 10 hours!

High-speed trains are also generally more comfortable and safer than regional and local trains, as they attract a more upscale crowd than cheaper trains do. First-class accommodations on these trains are truly posh; you might get a news-paper, free drinks, an in-seat video screen, on-board music channels, and a meal with wine. If you want to sit in a nonsmoking section on a train, you're also far more likely to find space in first class than you are in second. So if you're pur-chasing a railpass and you want legroom and luxury, go for first class.

For passholders, some high-speed trains will require extra fees, such as a seat reservation fee, but you'll still get a huge discount over what non-passholders pay. (For passholder fares below, we're assuming you've got a pass that covers all the countries the train travels through. For more on reservation fees, see p. 42.) In the "High-Speed Trains in Europe" chart below, we detail the high-speed trains in all of the Eurailpass-covered countries. We list second class, one-way adult fares on the chart because those are what most leisure travelers with point-to-point tickets buy; for first-class fares, add 50%. Most trains also have dis-counted children's, youth, and senior fares.

EXPRESS, REGIONAL & LOCAL TRAINS

Typically, there are four levels of trains below the posh, high-speed services, though some countries may have less or more (Germany has seven.) As all of these trains typically cost the same—and all are included in a railpass. You should just take whichever is the fastest train that stops at your destination.

EuroCity (EC) trains are express trains, typically crossing borders. EC trains sometimes require reservations, so make sure to ask when booking your ticket.

InterCity (IC) trains are express trains, stopping at major cities. Some require reservations, so make sure to check.

High-Speed vs. Regular Trains

Route	Fastest Regular Train	High-speed Train	Time Saved
Paris–Avignon	8 hr. 5 min.	2 hr. 40 min.	5 hr. 25 min.
Copenhagen–Stockholm	8 hr. 57 min.	4 hr. 52 min.	4 hr. 5 min.
Rome–Florence	3 hr. 22 min.	1 hr. 35 min.	1 hr. 47 min.
Munich–Berlin	7 hr. 28 min.	6 hr. 33 min.	55 min.
London–Paris	9 hr. 20 min.	2 hr. 35 min.	6 hr. 34 min.

High-Speed Trains in Europe

Nation & Train Name	Route	Time	One-Way Fare (2nd Class)	Pass Fare/Res. Fee (1st Class)	Reservations
Belgium					
Thalys	Brussels–Paris	1 hr. 25 min.	$43–$188	$18	Yes
Denmark					
X2000	Copenhagen–Stockholm	5 hr. 18 min.	$171	$11	Yes
England					
Eurostar	London–Paris	2 hr. 35 min.	$90	$75*	Yes
	London–Brussels	2 hr. 15 min.	$90	$75*	Yes
Finland					
Pendolino	All major cities	Varies	Varies	$11	Yes
France					
Artesia	Paris/Lyon–Milan	6 hr. 50 min.	$123	$11	Yes
TGV	Paris to many major cities	Varies	Varies	$11	Optional
Germany					
ICE	All major cities	Varies	Varies	Free	Optional
Italy					
Cisalpino	Florence–Zurich	6 hr. 52 min.	$83	$15	Optional
	Milan–Stuttgart	6 hr. 48 min.	$94	$15	Optional
	Milan–Basel	4 hr. 30 min.	$73	$15	Optional
	Venice–Geneva	6 hr. 48 min.	$84	$15	Optional
Eurostar Italia	All major cities	Varies	Varies	$20	Yes
Netherlands					
Thalys**	Brussels–Amsterdam	2 hr. 39 min.	$28–$72	$18	Yes
Norway					
Signatur	All major cities	Varies	Varies	$40 ($11 2nd class)	Yes
Portugal					
Alfa	Lisbon–Porto	3 hr.	$29	$11	
Spain*					
AVE	Madrid–Cordoba	1 hr. 45 min.	$53–$59		
	Madrid–Seville	2 hr. 30 min.	$72–80	$29	Yes
Talgo	Barcelona–Montpellier	7 hr. 30 min.	$58	$11	Yes
	Cartagena–Montpellier	4 hr. 30 min.	$102	$11	Yes
Talgo 200	Madrid–Malaga	4 hr. 10 min.	$59–$67	$29	Yes
Alaris	Madrid–Valencia	3 hr. 50 min.	Varies	Varies	Yes
Altaria	Madrid–Alicante	3 hr. 45 min.	Varies	Varies	Yes
Euromed	Barcelona–Alicante	4 hr. 30 min.	Varies	Varies	Yes
Arco	Barcelona–Valencia	Varies	Varies	Yes	
Sweden					
X2000	All major cities	Varies	Varies	$11	Yes
Switzerland	Served by Cisalpino trains from Italy, TGV trains from France, and ICE trains from Germany				

* Second-class passholder fare for Eurostar; holders of all passes can use this fare. First class is $135.

** Thalys trains from Belgium continue into the Netherlands at regular speed. We strongly recommend against spending extra to ride Thalys on this route as the trip takes just as long as it would on a normal express train.

*** Spain doesn't have more high-speed trains than France or Germany, they just give the trains a slew of different names.

Regional or **Local** trains have different names in every country. In Belgium they're "L" trains, in the Netherlands they're "stoptreins," and in Germany they're "Regional Bahn." Whatever they're called, these are the slow trains that stop at every tiny station, and you should avoid them whenever possible. (In Germany, there are also three classes of middling express trains called—from fastest to slowest—InterRegio, InterRegioExpress, and Regional Express. These are essentially different grades of regional trains.)

Suburban trains connect major cities and nearby destinations, and usually leave from a different train station than long-distance trains. Except for the Paris RER Lines B and C to the airports, these trains are not covered by a railpass, nor are **local city transport systems** such as trams and subways. One exception is Switzerland when you travel on a Swiss Pass.

FIRST VERSUS SECOND CLASS

Most European trains have two classes of seats: first and second class.

On **local, regional,** and **express trains,** there's not as much difference between the classes as there is on the high-speed trains. First-class cars usually have either three seats per row (a seat on one side of the aisle, two seats on the other) or six seats per compartment; second-class cars have four seats per row (two on each side of the aisle) or eight per compartment. First class has more legroom, and the upholstery may be plusher or better kept.

Note that second class tends to fill up a lot faster than first class, so if you're traveling second class on a major route where reservations are not required, you'll likely need to show up a lot sooner at the train station in order to guarantee yourself a seat.

The major difference between first and second class on most trains is the clientele; the folks in the first-class compartment will be older and more sedate, with a lot of business travelers. Most families and young backpackers will be in second class. Both classes, of course, get to their destinations at the same time.

On **high-speed trains** there's more of a difference. First class on high-speed trains often includes airline-style amenities (see "Fabulous in First," below, for some examples of these amenities) and very spacious seating. In the individual country chapters in this book, we point out where the difference between second class and first class isn't enough to justify paying the higher fee. And we also point out instances where going first-class (in Greece, for example) is almost a must if you want to have anything approaching a comfortable ride.

If you feel like switching classes, first-class pass and ticket holders can sit in second class any time they like. Second-class ticket holders can upgrade on board the train by paying the price difference, usually 50% of the price of a second-class point-to-point ticket, if a seat is available.

NIGHT TRAINS

Most major European cities that are at least 7 hours apart by rail are connected by night trains. Not only do night trains save you the price of a hotel, they give you more time to sightsee. And some night trains even have some hotel-type amenities, such as private bathrooms with showers. We recommend taking night trains whenever possible.

The average European night train will have sleeper cars, which sleep between one and four people; couchettes, which are affordable compartments for three to six people with less-comfortable, but still perfectly serviceable bunk beds; and sometimes airline-style coach seats as well. True cheapskates can sleep in coach

First-class compartment, Euromed train. *(photo: Courtesy of Rail Europe)*

First Class

The photo features the standard first-class configuration on most modern European trains; older trains (such as the Corail trains in France) have compartment seating, but these are gradually being phased out.

seats on trains that offer this option, but because a berth in a 6-bunk couchette may cost passholders as little as $28 on most trains, there's no need to give yourself a neck cramp. Keep in mind that some trains require that you have a first-class pass to sleep in certain types of cabins. Except in France, however, there are no first-class couchettes—you can go second-class only. *Note:* Couchettes, except in a few countries (see below), are not segregated by sex.

Sleepers offer a somewhat more posh travel experience than other train sleeping arrangements: You have a steward at your beck and call who will deliver snacks, drinks, and a complimentary breakfast to your room. Most sleeper cabins also have sinks (and some have bathrooms with showers), while most couchette cabins don't.

Whether you're traveling in a couchette or sleeper, the compartment you sleep in will start out with benches or sofas during the evening. At some point after dark, an attendant will come by to snap down the bunks and make them up as beds (or give you the necessary equipment for you to make your own), with

Fabulous in First

Country	Train	First Class Bonus
Belgium/France/Netherlands	Thalys	Meals, alcoholic drinks, newspaper
England/Belgium/France	Eurostar	Meals, alcoholic drinks, newspaper
France	TGV Med	Meals served at seat (additional cost)
Germany	ICE	Newspapers, phones
Italy	Eurostar Italia	Drink and snack
Italy/Switzerland/Germany	Cisalpino	In-seat music system
Norway	Signatur	Meals, phones, in-seat music
Spain	AVE	Meals included
Sweden	X2000	Free coffee/tea, in-seat music, newspapers

Second-class compartment, Euromed train. *(photo: Courtesy of Rail Europe)*

Second Class

The photo features the standard second-class configuration on most modern European trains. Second-class seats on high-speed trains are usually far more comfortable than those on local and regional trains.

sheets included. Some attendants may also take your passport, if you're traveling across a border with passport control so you aren't disturbed at night.

After the bunks are down, everyone's expected to at least be quiet. In couchettes, nobody undresses; just stash away your shoes, curl up under the covers and let the rocking of the train lull you to sleep. (And make sure to keep your valuables firmly attached to you or you may wake up without them!)

The attendant will wake you up in time for your stop, but if you want to have control over your morning, you can bring your own alarm clock. Forget sleeping in: When morning comes around, the attendant will return to the car to turn the bunks back into seats.

If you're a woman creeped out by the idea of sleeping near strangers of the opposite sex, French and Austrian couchettes offer the option of women-only

---

(Tips Tasty Train Rides

If you don't have time to eat before you get on the train, don't worry: Long-distance trains in Europe have dining cars, and even the dinkiest Dutch *stop-trein* will send an attendant past your seat with snacks on a rolling cart. The muffins are usually edible, if extremely unhealthy. Note that though food is available, it's often very expensive for the amount received.

Premium-class tickets on many high-speed and night trains (for instance, on AVE, Eurostar, and Thalys) include meals, and if you're in a first-class sleeper on one of the premier night trains, they'll even serve you breakfast in your cabin. Ask about food arrangements when making your reservation.

Trenhotel restaurant car. *(photo: Courtesy of Rail Europe)*

Restaurant Cars

Though most long-distance trains feature some type of dining option, premiere trains, such as Spain's luxurious Trainhotel Elipsos, feature top-quality restaurant cars.

cars. (Sorry, guys, you don't get any couchette cars to yourselves.) Otherwise, your only option is to get a bed in a sleeper: Sleepers are segregated by sex unless you're booking the whole sleeper at once.

All sleeping compartments are supposed to have locks, but with the number of strangers coming in and out of a couchette, you shouldn't count on the lock to protect your valuables. Lock your bags and chain them to seats or bunks if possible.

Parents concerned about their children's' safety in bunk beds can request "safety nets" on French sleepers at no charge; this webbing prevents the kids from rolling out of bed. Still, if you want complete control over your environment, get a sleeper rather than a couchette seat.

HOTEL TRAINS

The elite of European night trains are the "hotel trains." They're spotless and comfortable, with amazing top-class cabins and full restaurants, but they're a huge headache for budget travelers because they lack couchettes. They include:

- **Trainhotel Elipsos.** The bane of the budget traveler, but absolutely perfect for someone looking for a high-end rail travel experience, this super-classy overnight service runs between Madrid and Paris, between Barcelona and Paris, between Barcelona and Milan, and between Zurich and Milan. The train has a full restaurant on board and individually air-conditioned sleepers. Opt for the top "Gran Class" and you'll get all meals and a private bathroom with shower. There are no couchettes. The minimum passholder fare is $79 to stay in a second-class four-bed sleeper, and it climbs all the way up to $218 for a single Gran Class cabin. Double cabins for passholders are $120. Find out more at **www.elipsos.com** or at **www.raileurope.com**.
- **Lusitania Trenhotel.** This train runs from Lisbon to Madrid. Four-berth sleepers (the minimum on this train) cost only $32 for passholders. Singles

Snack Bar on Spanish high-speed train. *(photo: Courtesy of Rail Europe)*

Snack Bars

Most new or upgraded high-speed and international trains have a fast-food snack bar where passengers can get a quick bite.

in Gran and regular class are $149 and $104 for passholders; double berths are $89 and $56 per person.

- **CityNightLine.** These trains run various routes through Germany, Switzerland, and Austria. They offer deluxe single ($234 off-peak) and double sleeper cabins with private bathrooms and showers, as well as economy four-bed cabins with shared bathrooms ($67 off-peak). All cabins have electronic locks, and are air-conditioned and nonsmoking. Astonishingly, there are no reduced rates for passholders. To find out more, check out **www.citynight line.ch**.

TYPES OF ACCOMMODATIONS

If the last time you rode on a European night train was as a college student, crammed into a six-berth couchette compartment, you'll be pleasantly surprised by the range of accommodations on modern night trains. At their best, they bring back the classic age of train travel, with a uniformed attendant serving you an aperitif as you board, air-conditioning, private showers, and phones in every room. Of course, a top-class bed will cost you; a full-fare ticket for a single, private, top-class compartment from Madrid to Paris runs $443.

Tips **Cleaning Up**

If you can't stand the idea of an overnight ride without bathing, these trains provide showers:

Private Showers
- Artesia de Nuit trains between Paris and Rome, Milan, or Venice in "Excelsior" class
- Elipsos trains from Madrid–Paris, Barcelona–Paris, Barcelona–Zurich, or Barcelona–Milan in "Gran" class
- Lusitania Trenhotel from Madrid to Lisbon in "Gran" class
- CityNightLine trains throughout Germany, Switzerland, Austria, and the Netherlands in "Deluxe" class
- Sweden's Northern Arrow from Gothenburg to Stockholm and Östersund in "Exclusive" class
- Some sleeping compartments on the Berlin Night Express from Berlin-Stockholm

Corridor Showers
- Elipsos trains in "Club" class
- 2-berth and 3-berth sleepers on Sweden's Northern Arrow
- Single and double sleepers on German "NachtZug" trains within Germany and to Brussels, Paris, Milan, Florence, and Copenhagen

Not every train has every one of these accommodations, but the range of accommodations on night trains usually includes the ones listed below.

Coach Seats are the cheapest way to travel overnight. These are airline-style seats, with toilets and sinks at one end of the car. Reservations will usually cost you around $11. We recommend you add another $17 to upgrade to a couchette.

Couchettes (aka **T6**) are the sleeping cars of the masses, and they're where you'll find most budget travelers. Second-class couchette accommodations start at $28 for passholders on most European trains. The compartment has two long, benchlike seats during the day, with three people sitting on each side and two top bunks up near the ceiling; at night, the back of each bench snaps up to become a middle bunk. Couchette cars usually have toilets and sinks at one end, but no showers.

First-class Couchettes are offered on some French trains. They seat and sleep four (two on each side) and usually cater to an older, more business-oriented clientele than second-class couchettes.

Four-berth sleepers (aka **T4**) have two beds on each side. These are most often seen on high-class night trains such as the Elipsos hotel trains, which don't offer couchettes. On those trains, these are the cheapest beds.

Triple sleepers (aka **T3**) have three beds that fold down from one side of the compartment, with a table and a sink on the other side.

Double sleepers (aka **T2**) offer two bunk beds, a table, and a sink.

"Matrimonial" sleepers are only available on the Artesia trains between Paris and Italy in "Excelsior" class. They're the only sleepers in Europe offering a double bed. During the daytime, the compartment has a sofa and a small table.

Train Sleeping Accommodations

Regular sleeper, Spanish night train

REGULAR SLEEPERS
- One to four beds per cabin
- Secure compartments with reserved bathrooms
- Available in either first- or second-class (on some trains)
- Air conditioning in most cabins
- Sink, mirror, and luggage storage space
- Mineral water
- Breakfast often included in the rate

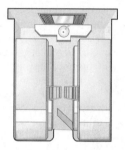

Deluxe sleeper, Trenhotel Elipsos

DELUXE SLEEPERS
- One to three beds per cabin
- Secure compartments with private attendant
- Private bathroom with shower and toiletries
- Sitting area (only on some trains)
- Electronic door locks, luggage storage areas, panoramic windows, individual climate controls
- Mineral water
- Breakfast always included in rate

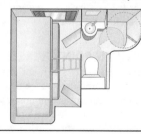

Single sleepers (aka **T1**) give you the most personal space you'll have on a train: a compartment all to yourself, complete with sink and locking door.

Top-class or **Deluxe sleepers** are available on hotel trains such as the Artesia, Elipsos, and CityNightLine series. Many of these have private showers, and you're sure to get very attentive service.

5 The Price of Rail Travel

RESERVATIONS & SUPPLEMENTS

A railpass means you've paid up front and can just hop on a train, right?

Alas, no. Most high-speed trains (including some EuroCity and InterCity), scenic trains, and all sleepers require reservations—and reservation fees will cost you over and above the price of your railpass. Some fast trains have "Passholder Fares," which are essentially fancy, pumped-up reservation fees.

Some exceptions: Reservations aren't necessary on German high-speed trains (although they're helpful, as they guarantee you a seat). They're also unnecessary on British trains (except on some trains to Scotland) or Swiss trains (except certain scenic trains).

We say, don't nickel and dime yourself to avoid reservation fees. The difference in speed between regular and high-speed trains is so striking, that for your extra $15 or so you'll usually get several hours more to spend at your destination.

You can make your reservation as little as a few hours in advance at European train stations, and you probably won't have to worry, but trains do sell out, especially overnight and peak vacation trains. You'll also save money by making reservations in Europe: While the reservation fee on most trains is $11 if booked from the U.S., it's 3€ to 6€ ($3.45–$6.90) if you're booking in Europe.

There are, of course, exceptions: If you're traveling on international night trains during the summer, we advise you to reserve well in advance through **Rail Europe** (© **877/272-RAIL** in the U.S., **800/361-RAIL** in Canada; www.rail europe.com). The same rule applies if you will be traveling during a holiday period. We let you know in the individual country chapters when a reservation should be made before you leave home. You can make reservations up to 270 days in advance for Eurostar, up to 90 days in advance for Thalys, Elipsos, and international TGV trains, and up to 60 days in advance for most other trains. Reservations in Bulgaria, Greece, Portugal, and Romania can't be made from North America.

Note: If you did reserve a seat, there is one quirk you might want to watch out for—some countries (Greece, for example) don't mark seats as reserved and confusion occasionally reigns when people occupy seats they didn't know were reserved. If you show up at your reserved seat and someone's sitting in it, politely but firmly inform him or her you have a reservation and ask him or her to vacate. Don't let them talk you out of your own seat (and some people will try to do just that).

PASSES VERSUS POINT-TO-POINT TICKETS

Ah, the great debate: to buy a pass or to buy point-to-point tickets?

That depends on what kind of traveler you are. If you're an extreme penny-pincher who's just staying in a few cities, planning out your trip in advance, and traveling second class, you may find that point-to-point tickets are cheaper. But if convenience, style, or speed attracts you, you'll find big discounts and spend a lot less time waiting in line to buy tickets if you go with railpasses.

PASS PLUSES

- **Passes allow for spontaneity.** Some itineraries will be cheaper if you buy point-to-point tickets rather than a pass. But what a pass gives you is the flexibility to dodge ticket lines, to walk right by vending machines, and often to ignore schedules, simply showing up at the station to hop onto the next train to anywhere.

Country	Train	Res. Fee/Pass Fare in U.S.	Res. Fee/Pass Fare
England–France/Belgium	Eurostar	$75	N/A
France	TGV	$11	3€
France–Belgium/Netherlands	Thalys	$13	10€
France–Italy	Artesia de nuit	from $29	
France–Italy	Artesia (day)	$11	4€
Germany–Sweden	Berlin Night Express	N/A	55€ (couchette)
Italy	Eurostar Italia	$16	10€–15€
Italy–Switzerland	Cisalpino	$12	18€
Most countries	Night trains	$29 (couchette)	20€
Most countries	High-speed trains	$11	6€
Spain	AVE	$12	10€ (with pass only)
Spain	Talgo 200	$13	10€ (with pass only)
Spain–France/Italy	Elipsos night trains	$79	
Spain–Portugal	Lusitania	$11 (seat) $34 (T4)	
Switzerland	Glacier Express	$18	6€
Switzerland	William Tell Express	$42	27€
Switzerland	Bernina Express	$12 ($28 for bus train)	4€
Switzerland	Golden Pass Line	$18	
Switzerland	Chocolate Train	$22	

Reservation Fees

* Unless otherwise noted, all reservation fees above were calculated for second-class seats and lowest-price accommodations.

If you're a peripatetic traveler who wants to see every new day in a different city, or a spontaneous traveler who wants your whims of the moment to be able to dictate your travel plans, railpasses are for you. Admittedly, you've still got to make reservations for high-speed or overnight trains, but, if you choose to avoid the reservation counter entirely, it'll just make your trip more spontaneous, as slower trains stop in fascinating small towns you'd zip by otherwise.

• **Passes offer big discounts over high-class tickets.** If you think you'd enjoy the comfort of first class, with spacious, high-quality seats and quiet cars, go with passes every time. If you're taking any long-distance journeys, you'll find a first-class railpass swiftly becomes a bargain when compared to the standard first-class rail fares or high-quality sleeper prices.

For example, take a triangle run from Paris to Rome to Venice and back to Paris, using a day train in Italy and sleepers on the night legs. If you ride first class and take an "Excelsior" class double sleeper, you'll end up paying $608 for your point-to-point tickets, but only $509 if you use a 4-day France 'n Italy Pass and pay the various supplements involved.

Similarly, a single first-class TGV round-trip between Paris and Avignon costs $131. For only $26 more, you could get 4 days of unlimited, first-class travel throughout the whole nation of France. Clearly, the pass is the way to go if you're going first-class over long distances.

Tips Protecting Your Pass

Rail passes are expensive and may be lost or stolen. Get peace of mind through Rail Europe's Rail Protection Plan, which reimburses you for your pass's remaining value if the pass disappears and has been replaced by locally bought tickets or passes. We strongly recommend buying the Rail Protection Plan for Eurailpasses and Selectpasses ($14) and for single-country and regional passes ($10). Rail Europe also sells a Rail Protection Plan for individual tickets, for $10 per ticket, and for multiperson Saverpasses starting at $17. While that's a great idea for a $180 round-trip TGV ticket, you can probably do without it for a $21 hop from Amsterdam to Delft. *Note:* The Rail Protection Plan doesn't cover sleepers or reservations, so keep a very close eye on that $482 Gran Class sleeper ticket from Madrid to Paris.

- **Speedy trains mean big savings for passholders.** Generally, if you're traveling several long-distance legs on high-speed trains, especially within France or Germany, a single-country pass will pay off big-time.

  For instance, if you're traveling the triangle route of Berlin-Munich-Frankfurt-Berlin in Germany, that'll cost you $247 for point-to-point tickets in second class. But a 4-day (non-consecutive), second-class German Rail Pass for the same trip will only run $180—and you'll have an extra rail day left on the pass.

  If you're basing yourself in Paris and zipping off to Avignon (for Provence) and Dijon (for the castles), you'll have hit yourself for over $300 in point-to-point TGV tickets. A second-class France Railpass is a mere $218—a big-time bargain.

- **If you're staying in one or two countries and taking long trips, passes are winners.** The France 'n Italy pass is a great deal because it reduces the huge fare on overnight trains between those two countries to a cool $28 (if you're sleeping in a couchette). Even if you're just going from Paris to Rome, and Florence and back, you end up saving $55 by getting a France 'n Italy pass over buying point-to-point tickets.

  Two new passes in 2004—the France 'n Switzerland Pass and Switzerland 'n Austria Pass—are equally good deals.

  The France 'n Spain pass is less helpful because overnight trains between France and Spain don't have couchettes, but it still pays off if you're taking a high-class sleeper. And if you're planning to take long sleeper trips between two countries where couchettes are available, often getting two single-country passes is less expensive than paying the standard couchette fare.

POINT-TO-POINT ADVANTAGES

- **If you're not traveling far, don't bother with a pass.** It's almost impossible to make the Benelux Tourrail Pass pay off because trips in Belgium and the Netherlands are so short and cheap. Even if you cram Amsterdam, Haarlem, Leiden, Delft, the Hague, Antwerp, Bruges, Ghent, and Brussels into your trip, you'll only have spent around $115 on point-to-point tickets—well short of the $163 you'd pay for a Benelux Tourrail Pass.

  In Italy, a 4-day Trenitalia Pass will cost you $191 (plus reservation fees if you're taking Eurostar Italia trains). But if you're just riding from Rome to Florence to Venice to Pisa and back to Rome—with no journey longer than

No Passes Please, We're Basque

Some trains in Europe won't accept *any* railpass. You'll have to buy point-to-point tickets for these trains in Europe whether or not you have a pass:

- Regional trains in Spain not run by RENFE (along the northern coast, in the Basque country, around Valencia, and FGC-run trains around Barcelona) don't take passes. You'll have to pay cash for these tickets, and you can't buy the tickets from Rail Europe.
- The Metropolitan, a super-high-speed express between Cologne and Hamburg, in Germany isn't covered by railpasses and Rail Europe will not book tickets on this train. The good news: Regular EC and IC trains also ply this route, and they *are* covered.
- The Desentis-Brig-Zermatt portion of the Glacier Express, in Switzerland is going to cost you extra. While the rest of the train is covered by a Eurailpass (with a reservation fee; see the "Reservation Fees" chart above), you have to shell out $95 (1st class) or $56 (2nd class) for this part of the run. Swiss Passes are accepted on the entire Glacier Express run. Rail Europe will help you book this ticket.
- Scenic private railways in Switzerland and Austria don't take Eurailpasses. A number of scenic railways (the famous Jungfrau trains in Switzerland, for example) aren't covered by your railpass, though it will get you a discount. Rail Europe will help you book the tickets on these railways.

4 hours—you'll pay only $145 (plus reservation fees) for the point-to-point tickets. You're not covering enough ground, and not in a costly enough country, to warrant the pass.

- **A quick trip across a border is best done point-to-point.** If you're just slipping from Germany into Austria, or from the Benelux into Germany, a three-country Eurail Selectpass is overkill. Get a single-country pass for the country you're spending more time in, and supplement it with a point-to-point ticket or two. But if you're spending a considerable amount of time in two countries, look into getting two one-country passes (or a combo pass such as the France 'n Italy Pass).

Don't Forget the Service Charges!

Be advised that Rail Europe charges two additional fees when you buy tickets or passes in the U.S. They charge a $7 extra fee for every reservation on a high-speed train, and a $15 shipping and handling fee for each order. (You only have to pay one $15 fee, even if you're ordering a dozen tickets.) While these fees shouldn't affect your purchase of a railpass or a slew of tickets from Rail Europe, you'll need to account for them in any rail budget that you put together.

Tip: Though this isn't always feasible, if you're traveling to Europe with a group of friends or family members, you'll save a bundle on shipping fees if one person for the group buys the passes for all members.

Pricing the Difference: Fast vs. Slow Trains

Route	Rail Europe price	European price
Fast or Long-Distance Trains		
Munich–Berlin	$99	$97.80
Paris–Avignon	$102	$133
Madrid–Seville	$72	$74.90
Rome–Venice	$59	$52.55
Milan–Zurich	$62	$62.30
Slow or Short-Distance Trains		
Amsterdam–Haarlem	$10	$3.60
Bruges–Ghent	$15	$5.60
Barcelona–Girona	N/A	$5.85
Copenhagen–Malmo	$16	$9
Cologne–Aachen	$20	$12.50

- **Eastern Europe is really cheap.** Point-to-point tickets in eastern Europe are so inexpensive that railpasses become difficult to justify unless you're continually hopping on and off trains. For the eastern European itinerary (p. 8) we recommend in chapter 1, which is pretty much the most you can do in a week and still stay sane, point-to-point tickets cost a mere $119, but the European East Pass would cost $158.

Home or Away?

If you're buying point-to-point tickets, you've got to decide whether to get them while you're in North America or when you arrive in Europe. Fortunately, there's a pretty simple rule. Buy tickets for overnight journeys or tickets for high-speed trains in North America. For shorter trips, you'll generally find much cheaper prices in Europe.

Take a look at the chart above. The first five routes are all on high-speed trains, where reservations are suggested (in Germany) or required (in France.) In all of those cases, the North American prices come close to, match, or beat the European ticket prices (though you have to factor in shipping and handling charges as well).

For night trains, another factor comes into play: convenience. Night trains on popular routes sell out, especially during the peak summer months, so you'll want to buy them well in advance. If you buy your ticket before you leave home, you'll deal with a polite, native-English-speaking agent who can walk you through the complicated accommodation arrangements.

But if you're taking short trips—for instance, on practically any train in Belgium or the Netherlands, from Denmark to Sweden, or on local trains in Spain and Italy—buying tickets when you're in Europe really makes sense. For one thing, you can generally buy unreserved tickets at vending machines, zipping past lines. (Make sure to have enough change, though, as some vending machines don't take bills.) For another, short-haul tickets are much cheaper over there than they are in North America.

FARE DISCOUNTS

There's one other advantage to buying tickets in Europe: You can get discounts that aren't offered when you're buying your tickets in North America. Often,

Is the U.K. Okay?

The one glaring omission from the Eurailpass system is Great Britain. Eurail-passes and Eurail Selectpasses are not valid in England, Scotland, or Wales. But there are still several railpass options for travelers going to Britain. **BritRail** passes cover the mainland U.K.; the **Days Out From London Pass, Freedom of Scotland Pass,** and **BritRail England Pass** focus on specific parts of the kingdom. The **BritRail Pass + Ireland** lets you roam freely through-out the U.K. and Ireland, and includes a round-trip voyage by ferry.

Finally, if you only intend to visit London from France, look at getting a Eurostar ticket.

---

these discounts require buying tickets in advance, but you can usually buy them over the phone, with a credit card, by calling the relevant national rail system's phone number (see the "National Railway Websites & Phone Numbers" chart on p. 31). That said, you may have to negotiate these purchases in a foreign language, prices will be in foreign currency, and you will need to pick up your tick-ets at the appropriate station.

In **France,** the "Decouverte à Deux" fare gives parties of two to nine people a 25% discount on tickets for TGV trains (except overnight trains) and couchettes on non-TGV trains. The "Decouverte de Sejour" fare offers a 25% discount if you're making a round-trip of more than 124 miles (200km) and staying over a Saturday night. And the "Decouverte J8/J30" fares offer even greater discounts for those who book at least 8 to 30 days in advance.

German trains offer two big discounts. The "Plan & Spar" fare gives you 25% off a round-trip ticket that involves a Saturday-night stay, if you buy 7 days in advance. The "Plan & Spar Plus" fare bumps the discount up to 40% if you buy 14 days in advance. Both special fares require that you make reservations on your trains, and both apply to some extent to international services between Germany, Belgium, and Denmark.

In **Sweden,** you'll fork up less if you ask for the "förköpsbiljett" fare, which requires a 7-day advance purchase.

Great Britain has a complex system of discounts. **Saver** fares are available for off-peak trains, **Super Advance** fares must be bought a day in advance, and **Apex** and **Bargain Return** fares must be bought a week in advance. Apex fares become available 8 weeks in advance and can sell out, so buy them as far ahead as possible.

Most European nations have extremely reduced **children's fares.** In Italy, for example, one child under 12 rides free when accompanied by two paying adults. Children under 12 pay 1€ ($1.15) on many Belgian trains, and kids under 15 travel for free if accompanied by an adult in Germany. If you will be traveling with kids on your rail trip, ask ahead of time if you can get any kind of discount for them.

For more country-specific fare discounts, see the individual country chapters.

6 The Train Passes

So you've decided you're going to buy a railpass. Rail Europe offers dozens of passes, and the choices can be overwhelming. Fortunately, all you need to do to get the right pass is answer four questions:

1. **How much ground do you want to cover?**
   If you're going to confine your travels to one country, look for a **single-country pass** (or point-to-point tickets; see "Passes vs. Point-to-Point Tickets," above). If you plan on visiting up to five countries, look at buying a **regional pass.** For six or more countries, an **all-Europe pass** is probably the way to go.

2. **Will you be continually on the move, or want to linger in some places for a few days?**
   If you plan on being continually on the move, get a **consecutive-day pass.** The clock on these passes starts the day you first use it and expires after a requisite number of days. If you'll be staying in cities for several days at a time, get a **non-consecutive pass.** This type of pass covers travel for a certain number of non-consecutive days in a given time period—5 days in a 30-day period, for example. The clock on the 30 days starts running the day you first use the pass.

Once you've determined the best kind of railpass for your trip, answering two more questions will help you get the best price:

3. **How old are you?**
   If you are under 26, **youth passes** and **children's rates** are available. If you are at least 60, discounted **senior passes** are the way to go.

4. **How many people are you traveling with?**
   The more the merrier when you're traveling by train. If at least two people are traveling together, **group passes** cost less than buying several single passes. Groups of 10 traveling together can get special discounts—call the Eurogroups Department at Rail Europe at © **800/462-2577.**

We divide all the available pass options into six categories in the sections below so you can find the one that's best for you, and then describe youth, senior, and group savings options.

SINGLE-COUNTRY, CONSECUTIVE-DAY PASSES

These three passes are for whirlwind journeys either through the U.K. or Switzerland. As with all single-country passes, they're not always cheaper than point-to-point tickets, especially for brief trips.

BritRail Consecutive Pass: This pass offers 4, 8, 15, 22 days, or 1 month of consecutive travel in the U.K. (except Northern Ireland). **First-class prices:** 4 days $279, 8 days $405, 15 days $599, 22 days $765, 1 month $909. **Second-class prices:** 4 days $189, 8 days $269, 15 days $399, 22 days $509, 1 month $605.

BritRail England Pass: Covers 4, 8 days, or 1 month of consecutive travel within England. **First-class prices:** 4 days $225, 8 days $325, 1 month $725. **Second-class prices:** 4 days $149, 8 days $215, 1 month $485.

Swiss Pass: Covers 4, 8, 15, 22 days or 1 month of consecutive travel in Switzerland, including travel on postal buses, lake steamers, and public city transportation. **First class prices:** 4 days $260, 8 days $360, 15 days $440, 22 days $500, 1 month $560. **Second class prices:** 4 days $170, 8 days $240, 15 days $290, 22 days $335, 1 month $375.

The Swiss Pass also offers several discounts: 25% discount on most mountain railways and cable cars. 10% discount on ski rentals. Reduced rates on many hotels and tours. 25% discount on entrance fees to Lausanne Olympic Museum, Lucerne Transport Museum, and Open-air museum Brienz/Ballenberg. 15% discount on entrance fee to Swiss Miniature Lugano-Melide. 5% discount at Gübelin stores on watches and jewelry.

SINGLE-COUNTRY, NON-CONSECUTIVE PASSES

If you're planning to explore one country for a week or 2, this is the kind of pass to get. Watch out when buying these passes: In many cases, especially with short pass durations or in very small countries (such as the Netherlands), point-to-point tickets will be cheaper.

One-country passes can also be used as add-ons to regional passes, or stacked on top of each other for a two-country trip. If you're going to France and Germany, for instance, the combined price of two one-country passes can often be cheaper than point-to-point tickets.

If you're interested in Greece, see "Rail-Drive & Rail-Fly Passes" below.

Austrian Railpass: Covers 3 to 8 days of travel within a 15-day period. **Price for 3 days:** $160 first class, $109 second class. **Additional days:** $20 first class, $15 second class.

Discounts: Special prices on steamers of Donauschiffahrt Wurm and Kock operating between Passau and Linz and on DDSG steamers operating between Melk, Krems, and Vienna.

BritRail England Flexipass: Covers 4, 8, or 15 days of travel in a 2-month period. **Price for 4 days:** $279 first class, $189 second class. **Price for 8 days:** $409 first class, $275 second class. **Price for 15 days:** $619 first class, $415 second class.

BritRail Flexipass: Covers 4, 8, or 15 days of travel within a 2-month period in the U.K., except Northern Ireland. **Price for 4 days:** $349 first class, $239 second class. **Price for 8 days:** $515 first class, $345 second class. **Price for 15 days:** $773 first class, $519 second class.

Czech Flexipass: Covers 3 to 8 days travel within a 15-day period. **Price for 3 days:** $68 first class, $48 second class. **Additional days:** $9 first class, $6 second class.

Finrail Pass: Covers 3, 5, or 10 days of travel within a 1-month period in Finland. **First class:** 3 days $214, 5 days $286, 10 days $387. **Second class:** 3 days $143, 5 days $191, 10 days $259. Add-on day trips to Tallinn, Estonia available for $79 to $129 depending on pass. Add-on trips to St. Petersburg available for $145 to $225 depending on class of travel.

France Railpass: Covers 4 to 10 days of travel within a 1-month period. **Price for 4 days:** $252 first class, $218 second class. **Additional days:** $32 first class, $28 second class.

Discounts: 50% reduction on Seine River cruises with Bateaux Parisiens. 50% reduction on the private scenic rail line from Nice to Digne, "Chemin de Fer de Provence." 50% reduction on passenger fares on Sea France ferries operating between Calais and Dover. 30% reduction on SNCM ferry routes between Corsica and Mainland France. 50% reduction on the railway network in Corsica. 20% discount on the discovery pass for guided tours and museums in Dijon. 50% reduction on the Paristoric tourist attraction (film on the history of Paris). Reductions at the famous Grevin Waxwork Museums in Paris, Lourdes, Tours, Salon de Provence, or St Jean de Luz; and on the entrance price to the Railway Museum in Mulhouse.

Freedom of Scotland Pass: Covers 4 days out of 8 or 8 days out of 15. **Price for 4 days:** $145. **Price for 8 days:** $189.

Discounts and bonuses: Includes Caledonian MacBrayne and Stratclyde ferries. Discounts on some P&O ferries.

German Rail Pass: Covers 4 to 10 days travel within a 1-month period. **Price for 4 days:** $260 first class, $180 second class. **Additional days:** $34 first class, $24 second class.

Discounts and bonuses: Includes KD German Rhine Line ferries. 50% off BSB steamers on Lake of Constance. Discount on Romantic Road and Castle Road buses.

Holland Rail Pass: Covers 3 or 5 days of travel within 1 month. **Price for 3 days:** $120 first class, $80 second class. **Price for 5 days:** $171 first class, $122 second class.

Hungarian Flexipass: Covers 5 days of travel within a 15-day period, or 10 days within a month. First class only. **Price for 5 days:** $76. **Price for 10 days:** $95.

Norway Rail Pass: Covers 3 to 8 days within 1 month. Second class only. **Price for 3 days:** $209. **Additional days:** $35.

Discounts: 30% discount on Flam Line. 50% discount on HSD ferry Bergen-Haugesund-Stavanger.

Portuguese Railpass: Covers 4 days of travel within a 15-day period. First class only: $105.

Spain Flexipass: Covers 3 to 10 days of travel within a 2-month period. **Price for 3 days:** $225 first class, $175 second class. **Additional days:** $35 first class, $30 second class. Does not apply on FEVE, FCG, FGV, and EUSOKTREN private railways.

Swiss Flexipass: Covers 3, 4, 5, 6, or 8 days within 1 month. **Price for 3 days:** $250 first class, $166 second class. **Additional days:** $48 first class, $30 second class *except* 8-day pass is discounted to $450 first class, $300 second class.

For bonuses, see "Swiss Pass" above.

Trenitalia Pass for Italy: Covers 4 to 10 days of travel within 2 months. **Price for 4 days:** $239 first class, $191 second class. **Additional days:** $24 first class, $19 second class.

Discounts and bonuses: Includes ferries to Sicily; doesn't include international Artesia, France-Italy Night, and Elipsos trains, but offers passholder fare on those trains.

REGIONAL, CONSECUTIVE-DAY PASSES

There are no regional, consecutive-day passes available for travel in Europe. If you're going to be zipping through a chunk of Europe and getting on trains nearly every day, the classic Eurailpass (p. 52) may still make sense for you.

Tips And Norway Connects to Denmark . . .

The Eurail Selectpass applies to "adjoining"' countries. Most of these are obvious—countries that share a border, such as France and Germany, are adjoining. But there are a few tricks. Ireland and France are considered adjoining, due to ferry connections, as are Greece and Italy; Norway and Denmark; and Germany, Sweden, and Finland. Norway and Finland share a border, but they're *not* considered adjoining as no rail or ferry line crosses that border.

Selectpass Pricing

Pricing on the Eurail Selectpass is complicated and is based on the number of travel days you want and the number of countries you plan to visit. Further confusing things, there are cheaper prices for couples, groups, and people under 26. At press time, these were the Selectpass prices for a person over 26, traveling in first class:

Eurail Selectpass Pricing Chart

	3 Countries	4 Countries	5 Countries
5 days	$356	$398	$438
6 days	$394	$436	$476
8 days	$470	$512	$552
10 days	$542	$584	$624
15 days	No pass	No pass	$794

REGIONAL, NON-CONSECUTIVE PASSES

Most travelers on 1-week or 2-week trips are going to go for this kind of pass, which lets you take a few, defined trips covering a specific chunk of Europe.

The king of the regional passes is the do-it-yourself **Eurail Selectpass.** Selectpasses allow you to cover 3 to 5 adjoining countries with 5, 6, 8, 10, or 15 days of travel within a 2-month period. (The Benelux region—Belgium, the Netherlands, and Luxembourg—counts as one country.) The ultimate do-it-yourself pass, it will satisfy most desires for trips up to a month long. See the "Selectpass Pricing" box above to figure out which version of the pass will work best for your trip.

There are various other, pre-defined regional passes as well, and they're all cheaper than the Eurail Selectpass. Some of these passes also come with bonus features and discounts, so if you'll only be traveling in specific regions, these will likely offer you more value for your money. Regional pass options in Europe include:

Balkan Flexipass: Covers 5, 10, or 15 days of travel within a 1-month period in Yugoslavia, Bulgaria, Macedonia, Romania, Greece, and Turkey. First class only. **5 days:** $189. **10 days:** $330. **15 days:** $397.

Discounts: Special prices on the ferry crossings between Italy and Greece operated by Superfast Ferries/Blue Star Ferries (routes Ancona-Patras and Bari-Patras). 25% discount on a 1-day cruise from Athens to the Greek islands Egina, Hydra, and Poros. Reduction of 30% on Attica Enterprises/Blue Star Ferries ferries.

Benelux Tourrail Pass: Covers 5 days of travel within a 1-month period in Belgium, the Netherlands, and Luxembourg. **First class:** $228. **Second class:** $163.

BritRail Pass + Ireland: Covers 5 or 10 days of travel in a 1-month period in Great Britain and Ireland; includes Stena Line ferry crossings. **5 days:** $515 first class, $369 second class. **10 days:** $849 first class, $595 second class.

European East Pass: Covers 5 to 10 days of travel within a 1-month period in Austria, the Czech Republic, Hungary, Poland, and Slovakia. **Price for 5 days:** $225 first class, $158 second class. **Additional days:** $25 first class, $18 second class.

Discounts: Special prices on steamers of Donauschiffahrt Wurm and Kock operating between Passau and Linz. 20% discount on DDSG steamers operating between Melk, Krems, and Vienna. Reduced price on Schneeberg rack railways. 20% discount on steamers operating on the Lake Wolfgangsee.

France 'n Italy Pass: Covers 4 to 10 days of travel within a 2-month period. **Price for 4 days:** $299 first class, $259 second class. **Additional days:** $30 first class, $27 second class.

Discounts: 50% reduction on Seine River cruises with Bateaux Parisiens. 50% reduction on the private scenic rail line from Nice to Digne, "Chemin de Fer de Provence." 50% reduction on passenger fares on Sea France ferries operating between Calais and Dover. 30% reduction on SNCM ferry routes between Corsica and Mainland France. 50% reduction on the railway network in Corsica. 20% discount on the discovery pass for guided tours and museums in Dijon. 50% reduction on the Paristoric tourist attraction (film on the history of Paris). Reductions at the famous Grevin Waxwork Museums in Paris, Lourdes, Tours, Salon de Provence, or St Jean de Luz, and on the entrance price to the Railway Museum in Mulhouse.

France 'n Spain Pass: Covers 4 to 10 days of travel within a 2-month period. **Price for 4 days:** $299 first class, $259 second class. **Additional days:** $35 first class, $29 second class.

France 'n Switzerland Pass: Covers 4 to 10 days of first-class travel within a 2-month period. **Price for 4 days:** $299. **Additional days:** $36.

Iberic Railpass: 3 to 10 days travel within a 2-month period in Spain and Portugal. First class only. **Price for 3 days:** $249. **Additional days:** $35 each.

Scanrail Pass: Covers 5 or 10 days of travel within a 2-month period or 21 consecutive days in Denmark, Sweden, Norway, and Finland. Second class only. **5 days:** $291. **10 days:** $390. **21 days:** $453.

Discounts: Discounted travel on selected ferries, boats, and buses. Most ferries offer 50% discount. Discount on Railway museums in Denmark (25%), Sweden (50%), Norway, and Finland (free). 25% discount on the Inlandsbane card (valid for 4 days of unlimited travel on the Inlandsbanan). 30% discount on the Flam Railway in Norway (Myrdal-Flam). 50% discount on the private railway lines: Frederikshavn-Skagen (Skagensbanan, Denmark) and Hjorring-Hirtshals (Hjorring Privatbaner, Denmark).

Switzerland 'n Austria Pass: Covers 4 to 10 days of first-class travel within a 2-month period. **Price for 4 days:** $300. **Additional days:** $36.

ALL-EUROPE, CONSECUTIVE-DAY PASSES

The classic **Eurailpass** is your best choice if you want the ultimate in flexibility, or you're covering very long distances. It covers 15 days, 21 days, or 1, 2, or 3 months of first-class travel and includes most of the bonuses listed in the single-country passes above. The pass is priced as follows: 15 days costs $588; 21 days $762; 1 month $946; 2 months $1,338; and 3 months $1,654. With the 15-day pass, you've got to take some very long trips or be on the train constantly for you to get your money's worth, but as the pass durations get longer, the Eurailpass compares better and better to point-to-point tickets.

ALL-EUROPE, NON-CONSECUTIVE PASSES

The king of the non-consecutive passes is the **Eurailpass Flexi,** which covers 10 or 15 days of first-class travel within a 2-month period. The past costs $694 for

> **Value Point-to-Point-to-Point**
>
> Unreserved, point-to-point tickets in Europe let you get off and back on again at any number of stops, as long as you start and end your trip on the same day. So you don't need to book two tickets or use a pass if you want to visit Orléans on the way from Paris to Tours. If you're using high-speed trains such as Eurostar, TGV, or Thalys, however, you'll need separate reservations for each segment of the journey.

10 days and $914 for 15 days and includes most of the bonuses listed under the single-country passes outline above. Plot your trip out before comparing the prices for the Eurailpass and the Eurailpass Flexi. For many trips, you'll find the original Eurailpass is a better deal. The Flexi is good, however, if you're visiting eight cities over the course of 2 months without taking many side trips.

ADD-ON PASSES
These passes function mostly as add-ons, allowing you to dip into an extra country your pass doesn't cover.

> **Prague Excursion Pass:** Adds a trip to Prague (for up to 1 week) from the Czech border. $55 first class, $40 second class.

> **Swiss Card:** Adds a trip to one Swiss destination (for up to 1 month) from the Swiss border, plus a 50% discount on tickets purchased in Switzerland. $158 first class, $116 second class.

RAIL-DRIVE & RAIL-FLY PASSES
Not all of Europe is accessible by train—many charming small towns and rural areas are best visited by car, and you've got to take a boat or a plane to get to the Greek Islands. So Rail Europe offers a range of passes combining car rentals or plane tickets with railpasses. Remember to factor in gas, though, which can often cost over $4 per gallon, so be sure to use the car for local exploration and save the train for the long hauls.

The price of rail 'n drive passes is based on the class of car you drive, and the available cars vary from country to country, so check out **www.raileurope.com** for the full details. Generally, you'll pay a big premium for an automatic transmission.

Car rentals in Europe are generally much more expensive than in North America, and although these passes are discounted, U.S. and Canadian travelers may get hit by sticker shock. For instance, an add-on car day for a tiny economy car with the EurailDrive Pass is $49; for a car with automatic transmission, you'll pay $95 a day. Single-country passes are cheaper; in France, an economy car day is $37 and a full-size is $71. But before you decide you absolutely need a car, make sure you can't get where you need to go by train or bus.

These passes are all for non-consecutive days (prices are per person, based on two people traveling together). **Rail 'n Drive** passes include:

> **EurailDrive Pass:** Covers 4 to 10 days of train travel, and at least 2 days car rental within 2 months in Austria, Belgium, Denmark, Finland, France, Germany, Greece, Holland, Hungary, Italy, Luxembourg, Norway, Portugal, Republic of Ireland, Spain, Sweden, and Switzerland. Cars are rented from Hertz or Avis; manual and automatic-transmission cars are available, but beware that the largest cars available are "intermediate," seating five. **Price:** $415 and up.

Eurail Selectpass Drive: Covers 3 to 7 days of train travel, and at least 2 days car rental within 2 months in 3, 4, or 5 adjoining European countries. Rent from Hertz or Avis; manual and automatic-transmission cars are available, but beware that the largest cars available are "intermediate," seating five. **Price:** $295 and up.

BritRail Pass 'n Drive: Covers 3 days of train travel, and 2 to 7 days of car travel within 2 months in the U.K. (except Northern Ireland). Manual and automatic-transmission cars are available; the largest car seats five. **Price:** $259 and up.

France Rail 'n Drive: Covers 4 to 10 days of train travel, and at least 2 days car travel within 2 months in France. The largest car is a minivan. **Price:** $205 and up.

German Rail 'n Drive: Covers 2 to 5 days train travel, and at least 2 days car travel within 1 month in Germany. Manual and automatic-transmission cars are available; largest car seats five. **Price:** $159 and up.

Italy Rail 'n Drive: Covers 4 days of train travel, and 2 or more days of car travel within 2 months in Italy. Manual and automatic-transmission cars are available; the largest car seats five. **Price:** $245 and up.

Scanrail 'n Drive: Covers 5 days of train travel, and at least 2 days car rental within 2 months in Denmark, Norway, and Sweden. Only manual transmission cars are available; the largest car seats five. **Price:** $339 and up.

Spain Rail 'n Drive: Covers 3 to 5 days of train travel, and at least 2 days car rental within 2 months in Spain. Manual and automatic-transmission cars are available; the largest car seats five. **Price:** $249 and up.

There's one Rail 'n Fly pass that helps travelers get to the Greek islands. The **Greek Flexipass Rail 'n Fly** offers 3 days of first-class train travel within 1 month, plus two domestic flight coupons on Olympic Airways; you've got to reserve the flights in advance. It costs $251 for adults.

DISCOUNTS
YOUTH & SENIOR DISCOUNTS
Many railpasses offer discounted versions for travelers under 26 and over 60.

All **youth passes** except the Balkan, Swiss, Greek, and French versions are for second-class travel only, but they offer big savings. There are youth versions of the Eurailpass, Eurail Selectpass, Eurailpass Flexi, BritRail Classic, BritRail Flexipass, BritRail England Pass, Balkan Flexipass, Benelux Tourrail, France Pass, France 'n Italy, France 'n Spain, France 'n Switzerland, Switzerland 'n Austria, Holland, German, Greek, Italy, Norway, Prague Excursion, Scanrail, and Swiss passes.

Senior passes, for travelers over 60, are just like the standard versions—but cheaper. Senior passes include the Balkan Flexipass, BritRail Classic, BritRail Flexipass, BritRail England Pass, France Pass, Norway Pass, and Scanrail Pass.

Children between 4 and 11 also get discounted rates on most passes, usually 40–50% off the adult rate. Adults with a Swiss Pass, Swiss Flexipass, or Swiss Card can also get the Swiss Family Card for free; the card will let you tote along any number of your own children under age 16 for free.

COUPLE, GROUP & FAMILY DISCOUNTS
If you're traveling with a small group, more discounts are available. "Saver" passes offer discounts to two or more people. Generally, if you're under 26, the youth discount is better than the saver discount, so go with a youth pass instead.

Tips   Validating Your Pass

You must validate your railpass before you step on your first train. Just head to a ticket office at any European train station and ask the ticket agent to validate your pass. The agent will write in the first and last days you can use your pass, and you're on your way. *Train conductors cannot validate your pass, so don't board a train until your pass has been validated.*

Single-country passes don't have to be validated in the country they're being used for. For instance, if you've got a France Pass and you're heading to the Riviera from Barcelona, you can get your pass validated in Spain, buy a ticket from Barcelona to the border, and use your pass for the rest of the journey.

If you're using a Eurailpass Saver or another kind of pass that affects more than one person, all the relevant people must be present when the pass is validated—but not necessarily every time it's used.

If you're using a nonconsecutive-day pass such as a Eurail Selectpass, there's one more thing you have to do after validation. Each day you plan to use the pass, write the day and month in ink in one of the boxes below "Last Day." If you're taking an overnight train that leaves after 7pm, write in the next day's date. (You get the evening part of the train free!) All trips must be completed in the days marked on your pass. And be sure to write in the date before you get on the train or you might get fined when the conductor comes round.

Note: Dates should be entered European style—date first, then month. So May 10 would be written 10–5 and not 5/10.

Saver passes or group discounts include All Rail 'n Drive passes and the Eurailpass, Eurailpass Flexi, Eurail Selectpass, France Saverpass, German Rail Twin Pass, Trenitalia Pass Saver, Iberic Saverpass, Swiss Saverpass, Swiss Saver Flexipass, BritRail Party Pass, BritRail Flexi Party Pass, and BritRail England Party Pass.

Note: The British Saver passes require three or more people to travel together; otherwise the minimum is two people.

7 The Rail Experience

AT THE TRAIN STATION

If you're traveling Europe by rail, you'll spend a lot of time in train stations. That's not a bad thing. Many European train stations are masterpieces of architecture—glorious palaces of glass and light that will make you feel thrilled to travel. Even more prosaic stations in Europe are generally clean, safe, and well kept, though you should keep an eye on your bags (like in any public place).

Many European cities have more than one train station: Paris has six, London has nine, and Brussels has four. Make sure you know which station your train leaves from, as they can be miles apart and stations aren't necessarily connected to each other by efficient means. If you have to transfer between stations in a major city, check the appropriate country chapter in this book to see how long it takes to switch stations.

In some cases, the station most trains come into isn't the most convenient one for downtown tourist attractions. See if you can hop a short-distance train to get to the more central station. In Antwerp, for instance, international trains stop at Antwerp Berchem station, in the southern suburbs. But you can change at Berchem to get to Antwerp Centraal, which puts you in the heart of the action.

If you're just in town for a few hours, most train stations offer lockers for no more than $5 per day—but the lockers only take coins, so make sure you've got plenty of change on you. Train station lockers can fit even sizeable suitcases. Some stations that lack lockers have luggage checkrooms where you can leave your bags. If a station has porters, they'll be uniformed. Never hand your bag over to a guy on the platform who isn't wearing a clearly identifiable uniform.

Feeling peckish? Most train stations will have fast food restaurants (or at least a vending machine or two). Larger stations have sit-down restaurants and pubs. If you need cash, stations generally have ATMs (automated teller machines) and currency-exchange windows. The ATMs will offer a better rate; if you need to use an exchange window, local banks generally have a better rate than train stations do.

When nature calls, check your pockets. While European train stations have bathrooms, they almost all cost money to use. (Usually, the price is around 50¢.) Paid toilets mean clean, safe, and well-attended toilets; the pay turnstile will often be handled by a live attendant, who makes sure things are kept neat and tidy. Larger stations offer showers, also for pay.

As you go to buy your ticket, remember that many stations have separate domestic and international reservations counters. Even though some European countries are tiny, "International" still means just that—a ticket from the Netherlands to Belgium must be booked at the international counter.

To help you find the right train, stations offer printed schedules and departure boards. Printed schedules are usually posted up on gigantic boards, both on the tracks and in the main hall of the station. Departure schedules are usually on a yellow background; arrival schedules are on a white background. On the schedules, train times are shown according to a 24-hour clock, with fast trains in red and slower trains in black. Larger stations have computerized departure boards.

Buses and taxis are usually available outside stations. Taxi touts working inside stations may be scam artists. Walk past them to the official taxi rank instead.

GETTING ON BOARD

Be on the platform a few minutes before your train is due to arrive. European trains wait for no one, and stops can be as short as a minute.

When your train shows up, don't just jump into the first door you see (unless you're in a real hurry). While you're safe with short-distance trains, many long-distance trains tend to split and rejoin, with different cars going to different destinations. Ask a conductor on the platform which cars are going your way. If you're in a hurry, get on board and ask the conductor once the train leaves which car you need to be in—you'll be able to move between cars using the connecting doors.

You'll also need to pay attention to whether you're in a first-class or second-class car: Classes are marked by a big "1'" or "2'" on the side of the carriage. There may also be a yellow stripe on the car for first class, and a green stripe for second class. And if you are sensitive to smoke, be sure you get yourself into a nonsmoking car or section (just be advised that nonsmoking signs tend to be ignored a lot more in Europe than they are in North America).

If you have a reservation, you'll need to match up your car number and seat number. Car numbers are listed right by the outside car doors and boards on the

> **Tips** **Special Needs**
>
> Many, but not all trains and stations in Europe have accessible toilets, ramps, and elevators for mobility-impaired passengers. If you think you'll need help, or want to scope out the situation in advance, ask Rail Europe or your travel agent when you make your train reservation. Station staff are willing to help travelers with mobility issues to the best of their abilities, but help must be reserved in advance.

tracks will indicate where you should stand on the platform for your particular car. Seat numbers are usually over the seats, inside the train. Once more, if you're in a hurry, jump onto the train and sort things out after the train gets moving.

Most train cars have a space for luggage near the entrance and baggage racks above the seats. If you have more baggage than you can handle, check it; we don't recommend letting your bags out of your sight. Theft is common enough that you'll need to be vigilant. Anyway, if you're traveling by rail in Europe, you'll be walking up and down a lot of stairs and along a lot of long platforms. Packing as light as possible is a good idea.

8 When a Train Just Won't Do

Trains are the best way to see Europe, but there are going to be times when you might find that alternative forms of transportation will get you someplace faster, or, in some of the more remote locations, when a train isn't even an option. Sometimes, a quick trip by air, a short bus leg, a ferry ride, or a rental car can save you a long, roundabout trip by train.

WHEN TO FLY

Trains are usually the cheapest and most efficient way to get from Point A to Point B in Europe. But scheduling a flight can help you cover a great distance very quickly (for instance, from London to Italy, or from Dublin to pretty much anywhere else) if you're short on time. So if you want to travel a number of countries that aren't all that close together and have a limited amount of time in Europe, a quick flight used in conjunction with your railpass may make sense.

The lowest one-way fares in Europe are available from **low-fare airlines** that offer no meal service, no intercontinental connections, and often fly from satellite airports well outside their target cities. It's not uncommon to get a flight halfway across Europe for as little as $40 to $70, including taxes and fees.

The two biggest low-fare players in Europe are **Ryanair** (© **353/1249 7851,** with toll-free numbers in many European countries; www.ryanair.com) and **easyJet** (© **44/870 600 0000;** www.easyjet.com). Both are profitable, solid carriers. Ryanair has major bases in Dublin, London, and Frankfurt; easyJet offers the most flights out of London and Amsterdam, but both airlines cover dozens of European destinations.

A wild array of smaller budget carriers blankets Europe as well, with nearly every country having its budget-flight solution. To find out where these carriers fly and get links to their websites, where you can get fare information and book flights, go to **www.flybudget.com**, an independent and regularly updated guide to low-fare airlines.

Because discount prices are always changing on air routes within Europe, it's best to check in with **Air Travel Advisory Bureau** in London (© **44/207 306**

3000; www.atab.co.uk). This bureau offers a free service directory to the public for suppliers of discount airfares from all major U.K. airports.

Warning: When pricing and timing planes against trains, factor in the price of getting to the airport and the time you'll need to spend in the airport before getting anywhere. For example, even though it isn't fully covered by the Eurail-pass, Eurostar is actually a far more economical choice than flying from London to Paris once you've factored in the time and cost of getting to the airport.

WHEN TO TAKE A BUS

Local buses pick up where the rail network leaves off, and they can be lifesavers. Taking a train from Portugal's Algarve to Spain's Costa Del Sol is a 12-hour agony by train; by bus, the ride is an hour and a half. Many small towns in Ireland, archaeological sites in Greece, and small villages in eastern Europe are also only reachable by bus.

The most useful bus services for rail travelers are small, local outfits that will be discussed in each of the following country chapters. The major international bus company **Eurolines** (℡ **44/870 514 3219;** www.eurolines.com) will hook you up with routes in Ireland and some eastern European countries, but not the Algarve route or anything in Greece. If you're truly adventurous, the website **www.busstation.net** offers hundreds of links to local bus companies. (Many of the bus companies' websites are in the local languages, and you usually can't buy tickets online in advance.)

WHEN TO TAKE A FERRY

Many ferries are covered by the Eurailpass, including international routes from Italy to Greece, from Germany to Sweden, from Denmark to Norway, and from Germany and Sweden to Finland. The Eurailpass also offers discounted fares on several other routes, including ferries from Ireland to France. On many routes—especially the Scandinavian and Adriatic ones—the modern, comfortable ferry-boats are great ways to cross borders while you sleep.

European ferries are generally even more plush than European trains. They may have onboard swimming pools, movie theaters, sit-down restaurants, or even casinos. On the Adriatic ferries, accommodations range from chaises on the deck to luxurious, hotel-room-like private cabins equipped with showers, refrigerators, and TVs, with views of the water. In colder waters, nobody's forced to sleep on the deck—accommodations start with reclining, airline-style seats or four-berth cabins and work their way up to two-berth cabins with a view.

Note however, that your railpass usually covers only the lowest possible fare. Depending on the route, that may give you an unreserved seat, a bed in a four-berth cabin or a little space on the deck overnight. If you want better accommodations, you'll have to pay more. You'll also likely have to pay port fees (ranging from 6€/$6.90 to 20€/$23) and/or high-season supplements, even if you have a railpass. These fees are usually payable at the port when you're about to board the ferry, so have some cash on you.

Keep an eye on schedules, too. Ferry schedules vary from season to season, and some ferries don't run every day. For example, the Ireland-France ferries don't run in February, and the ferry from Rostock (Germany) to Tallinn (Estonia) only runs from June through early September. You can get schedules from the individual ferry firms' websites (see "Major European Ferry Lines," below for the major ferry company websites).

If possible, reserve your ferry in advance. Ferries do sell out, just like overnight trains. Many ferry companies allow you to book seats and cabins online; though you usually can't book online if you're holding a railpass, you can make a reservation by calling the ferry company direct.

Complicating the issue, a growing number of ferry companies now offer airline-style pricing. Irish Ferries, for instance, has seven price levels, varying by individual sailing. If you're intending to take a ferry, you can save lots of money by planning ahead and getting on one of the cheap sailings—dropping the high-season fare from Ireland to France from 120€ to 90€ ($138–$104).

Two of these ferry routes are so well trodden by low-fare airlines and other options, they're not worth taking unless you're unwilling to plan ahead. The ferries between Ireland and France are 19-hour trips, and they don't even leave daily. But if you plan ahead and book a flight on low-fare Ryanair a few weeks in advance, you can shrink that trip to an hour and a half for 45€ ($51.75).

The Calais-Dover ferry, meanwhile, is a lousy way to get from Paris to London—it makes the total trip in 7 hours, and you've got to buy a Dover-London train ticket on the U.K. end. You might as well take Eurostar (which has a $75 passholder fare) or fly Ryanair.

Aside from the major international ferry routes, your railpass also gives you discounts on a wide range of sightseeing boats. None of these smaller boats are the most efficient way to get from point A to point B, but many are scenic. Discounts on these scenic options include:

Austria: 25% off DDSG Blue Danube Schiffahrt (© **43/1 588 800,** ext. 1; www.ddsg-blue-danube.at) boats between Melk and Krems, between Vienna and Burnstein (on Sun), and sightseeing trips in Vienna. Special price on Wurm and Köck steamers (© **43/732 783 607;** www.donau schiffahrt.de) between Linz and Passau. 50% off BSB, SBS, and ÖBB boats on Lake Constance from May to October.

Germany: Free passage on KD German Rhine Line (© **49/221 2088 318;** www.k-d.com) between Koblenz and Cochem and Köln and Mainz (with some exceptions). 50% off BSB, SBS, and ÖBB boats on Lake Constance from May to October. 50% off URh (© **41/52 634 0888;** www.urh.ch) boats from Constance to Schaffhausen (Switz.). Special price on Wurm and Köck steamers (© **43/732 783 607;** www.donauschiffahrt.de) between Linz and Passau.

Greece: 25% off 1-day cruises from Athens to Aegina, Poros, and Hydra with Ionian Travel (© **30/610 523 9609**).

Switzerland: Free passage on boats operated by BSG (© **41/32 329 88 11;** www.bielersee.ch) from Biel to Solothurn. 50% off BSB, SBS, and ÖBB boats on Lake Constance from May to October. 50% off URh (© **41/52 634 0888;** www.urh.ch) boats from Constance to Schaffhausen (Switz.). Free passage on various steamers on lakes Biel, Brienz, Genève, Luzern, Murten, Neuchâtel, Thun, and Zürich.

WHEN TO DRIVE

Train and bus services honeycomb much of Europe, but there are still rural areas where you might want to drive—especially in such countries as Ireland, Portugal, and Greece, where the rail networks aren't as comprehensive as in the rest of Europe. Use a car to explore these small towns and wilderness areas only—do not drive within major cities! Traffic and parking in major European cities can be nightmarish.

Though we mostly stick to the rails in this book, there are a few spots in Europe that we point out are better explored by car (the Ring of Kerry in

Major European Ferry Lines

Countries	Route	Ferry Line	Website	Phone Number
Denmark–Norway	Hirtshals-Oslo Frederikshavn- Larvik Hirtshals- Kristiansand	Color Line	www.colorline.com	47/810 00 811
France–Corsica	All routes	SNCM FerryFrance	www.sncm.fr/us	33/8 91 701 801
France–England	Calais–Dover	SeaFrance	www.seafrance.com	44/8705 711 711
Germany– Denmark	Puttgarden- Rødby Faerge	Scandlines	www.english. scandlines.dk	45/33 15 15 15
Germany–Estonia	Rostock–Tallinn	Finnjet	www.silja.com/english	800/533-3755, ext. 113
Germany–Finland	Rostock–Hanko	Superfast Ferries	www.superfast.com	30/210 8919130
Germany–Finland	Rostock-Helsinki	Finnjet	www.silja.com/english	800/533-3755, ext. 113
Germany–Sweden	Sassnitz–Trelleborg	Scandlines	www.english.scandlines.dk	45/33 15 15 15
Germany–Sweden	Travemünde- Trelleborg Rostock–Trelleborg	TT Line	www.ttline.com	49/40 36 01 442
Greece–Italy	Patras or Igoumenitsa to Corfu or Brindisi	HML	hml.gr/HML.htm	30/210 422 5341
Greece–Italy	Patras or Igoumenitsa to Corfu or Brindisi	Blue Star	www.bluestar ferries.com	30/210 414 1314
Greece–Italy	Patras–Bari Patras–Ancona Igoumenitsa–Bari	Superfast Ferries	www.superfast.com	30/210 969 1190
Ireland–France	Rosslare–Cherbourg Rosslare–Roscoff	Irish Ferries	www.irishferries.com	353/1 638 3333
Italy–Sicily	Villa S. Giovanni– Messina	Trenitalia	www.trenitalia.com	39/89 20 21
Netherlands– England	Hoek van Holland– Harwich	Stena Line	www.stenaline.com	44/8705 70 70 70
Norway	Stavanger–Bergen	Flaggruten ANS	www.flaggruten.nohsd/ flaggrutenEng.nsf	47/55 23 87 00
Spain	Barcelona– Balearic Is. Valencia-Balearic Is.	Trasmediterranea	www.trasmediterranea. es/homei.htm	34/902 45 46 45

| Major European Ferry Lines | | | | |
Countries	Route	Ferry Line	Website	Phone Number
Spain–Morocco	Algeciras–Tanger	Trasmediterranea	www.trasmediterranea.es/homei.htm	34/902 45 46 45
Sweden–Denmark	Helsingborg–Helsingør	Scandlines	www.english.scandlines.dk	45/33 15 15 15
Sweden–Denmark	Göteborg–Frederikshavn	Stena Line	www.stenaline.com	46/31 704 00 00
Sweden–Finland	Stockholm–Helsinki Stockholm–Turku	Silja Line	www.silja.com/english/	1/800 533 3755, ext. 113

Ireland, for example). This is when the Rail 'n Drive passes we detail on p. 53 may come in handy.

Warning: Those Rail 'n Drive passes don't include any of the following: gas, the collision damage waiver (CDW), personal accident insurance (PAI), other insurance options, fees for an additional and/or young driver, airport surcharges, registration tax, or car group upgrades made locally. Note that the minimum age for rentals on a Rail 'n Drive pass ranges from 23 to 25 depending on the country you're visiting. Also note that in some countries, or for a few car groups, a service charge is due on one-way rentals. And keep in mind that, unlike North America, most rental cars in Europe have manual transmission and that automatic will cost you more.

When reserving your car, be sure to ask what these extras cost, because at the end of your rental, they can make a big difference in your bottom line. Gasoline is very expensive in Europe. The CDW and other insurance might be covered by your credit card if you use the card to pay for the rental; check with the card issuer to be sure.

If your credit card doesn't cover the CDW (and it probably won't in Ireland), **Travel Guard International,** 1145 Clark St., Stevens Point, WI 54481 (✆ **800/826-4919** or 715/345-0505; www.travelguard.com), offers it for $7 per day. Avis and Hertz, among other companies, require that you purchase a theft-protection policy in Italy. Theft is covered with the Italy Rail 'n Drive from Rail Europe.

Should you wish to rent a car on your own for a day trip, the main car-rental companies are **Avis** (✆ **800/331-1212;** www.avis.com), **Budget** (✆ **800/472-3325;** https://rent.drivebudget.com/Home.jsp), **SIXT** (known as Dollar in the U.S.; ✆ **800/800-6000;** www.e-sixt.com), **Hertz** (✆ **800/654-3131;** www.hertz.com), **DER** (✆ **800/782-2424;** www.der.com), and **National** (✆ **800/227-7368;** www.nationalcar.com).

U.S.-based companies specializing in European rentals are **Auto Europe** (✆ **800/223-5555;** www.autoeurope.com), **Europe by Car** (✆ **800/223-1516,** or 212/581-3040 in New York; www.europebycar.com), and **Kemwel Holiday Auto** (✆ **800/678-0678;** www.kemwel.com). Europe by Car, Kemwel, and **Renault Eurodrive** (✆ **800/221-1052;** www.renaultusa.com) also offer a low-cost alternative to renting for longer than 15 days: **short-term leases** in which

Ferry Routes & Railpass Discounts

Country	Route	Length	Overnight
Ireland–France	Rosslare–Cherbourg	17 hr.	Yes
	Rosslare–Roscoff	15 hr.	
Germany–Finland	Rostock–Hanko	21 hr.	Yes
Germany–Finland	Rostock–Helsinki	23 hr.–35 hr.	Yes
Germany–Denmark	Puttgarden–Rødby Faerge	1 hr. 15 min	No
Germany–Sweden	Sassnitz–Trelleborg	3 hr. 45 min.–4 hr.	No
Germany–Sweden	Travemünde–Trelleborg	7 hr.–9 hr. 30 min.	Some
	Rostock–Trelleborg	5 hr. 55 min–7 hr.	Some
Germany–Estonia	Rostock–Tallinn	20 hr. 55 min.–24 hr. 15 min.	Yes
Greece–Italy	Patras or Igoumenitsa to Corfu or Brindisi	16 hr. 30 min.–20 hr. 30 min. (Patras–Brindisi)	Yes
Greece–Italy	Patras or Igoumenitsa to Corfu or Brindisi	Various	Yes
Greece–Italy	Patras–Bari	15 hr. 30 min.	Yes
	Patras–Ancona	19 hr.	
	Igoumenitsa–Bari	9 hr. 30 min.	
Denmark–Norway	Hirtshals–Oslo	8 hr.–12 hr. 30min.	From Oslo-Hirts.
	Frederikshavn–Larvik	6 hr. 15–10 hr. 30 min.	No
	Hirtshals–Kristiansand	2 hr. 30 min.–6 hr. 45 min.	
Netherlands–England	Hoek van Holland–Harwich	3 hr. 50 min.–9 hr. 30 min.	Some
Norway	Stavanger–Bergen	3 hr. 55 min.–4 hr. 25 min.	No
Spain	Barcelona–Balearic Is.	2 hr. 30 min.–15 hr.	Some
	Valencia–Balearic Is.	3 hr. 45 min.–14 hr. 30 min.	Some
Spain–Morocco	Algeciras–Tanger	2 hr.–2 hr. 30 min.	No
Sweden–Finland	Stockholm–Helsinki	8 hr.–11 hr.	Yes
	Stockholm–Turku	15 hr. 30 min.–17 hr. 30 min.	Some
Sweden–Denmark	Helsingborg–Helsingør	20 min	No
	Göteborg–Frederikshavn	2 hr.–3 hr. 15 min.	No
France–England	Calais–Dover	1 hr. 10 min.–1 hr. 30 min.	No
France–Corsica	All routes	Various overnight	Yes
Italy–Sicily	Villa S. Giovanni–Messina	35 min.	No

* Not including port taxes
‡ If this box reads '1', your pass only has to cover one of the two countries involved.
If it reads '2', your pass must cover both countries.

you technically buy a fresh-from-the-factory car and then sell it back when you return it. All insurance is included, from liability and theft to personal injury and CDW, with no deductible. And unlike at many rental agencies, who won't rent to anyone under 25, the minimum age for a lease is 18.

Frequency	Passholder Discount*	Non-passholder Fare	Pass Coverage‡	Pass Includes
Not daily (see site)	50%	50€–120€	1	Discount
Mon–Sat	Free	70€–143€	2	3/4 bed inside cabin
3 times per week	Special rate (108€–140€)	120–156€	2	Special rate
Every 30 min.	Free	3€	2	Seat
Up to 5 per day	Free	10€–15€	2	Seat
Up to 5 per day	50%	18€–24€	1	Discount
Up to 5 per day	50%	18€–24€	2	Discount
3 per week	Special rate	(60€–78€)	2	Special rate
Up to 5 per week	Free (20€ Jul–Aug)	24€–35€	2	Deck passage
Daily	Free (20€ Jul–Aug)	30€–48€	2	Deck passage
Daily	Free (20€ in Jul/Aug)	46€–57€ 58–80€ 46–57€	2	Deck passage
5–7 per week	30%	24€–56€	1	Discount on seat for day boats
Up to 3 per day				Discount
Up to 4 per day				Discount
3 per day	30%	40€	1	Discount
Up to 4 per day	50%	NOK 590	1	Discount
Up to 2 per day Up to 3 per day	20%	35.70€–55.70€	1	Discount
Up to 16 per day	20%	23.30€–29.90€	1	Discount
Daily	Free	36€–64€	2	4-p cabin
Daily		15€–37€		4-p cabin
Every 20 min.	Free	SEK 22	2	Seat
Up to 8 per day	30%	SEK 120–SEK 215	1	Discount
Up to 22 per day	50%	17€	1	Seat
Varies	30%	(many routes)	1	Discount
Up to 33 per day	Free	N/A	1	Seat

The **AAA** (www.aaa.com) supplies good maps to its members. **Michelin maps** (© **800/423-0485** or 864/458-5619; www.michelin.com) are made for European visitors. The maps rate cities as "uninteresting" (as a tourist destination), "interesting," "worth a detour," or "worth an entire journey." They also

The Rules of the Road: Driving in Europe

- First off, know that European drivers tend to be more aggressive than their American counterparts.
- Drive on the right except in Great Britain and Ireland, where you drive on the left. And *do not drive* in the left lane on a four-lane highway; it is truly only for passing.
- If someone comes up from behind and flashes his lights at you, it's a signal for you to slow down and drive more on the shoulder so he can pass you more easily (two-lane roads here routinely become three cars wide).
- Remember that there is no right turn on red anywhere in Europe.
- Except for the German autobahn, most highways do indeed have speed limits of around 100kmph to 135kmph (60 mph–80 mph).
- Remember that everything's measured in **kilometers** here (mileage and speed limits). For a rough conversion, 1 kilometer = 0.6 miles.
- Be aware that although gas may look reasonably priced, the price is per liter, and 3.8 liters = 1 gallon—so multiply by four to estimate the equivalent per-gallon price. (Gas prices in the U.S. don't look so bad now, do they?)
- Never leave anything of value in the car overnight, and don't leave anything visible any time you leave the car (this goes double in Italy, triple in Naples).

highlight particularly scenic stretches of road in green, and have symbols pointing out scenic overlooks, ruins, and other sights along the way.

9 Getting to Europe

FLYING FROM NORTH AMERICA

There's no train from North America to Europe (that pesky ocean gets in the way), so you'll have to fly. Most major airlines fly to Europe, but fares can vary wildly depending on the time of year and who's having a sale at any given moment.

Railpass travelers have unusual flexibility in choosing their destination; if you're going to be covering five or six countries, you can choose the cheapest one to fly into. Generally, flying into a capital city (such as Paris) is cheaper than flying to a provincial city (such as Marseille), but there are exceptions: For Germany, you'll often find better fares into **Frankfurt** than into Munich or Berlin, and fares to Milan and Rome are often equal.

London is the cheapest European destination to fly to from North America, followed by **Paris** and **Amsterdam. Frankfurt** and **Brussels** are also competitive hubs. If you're heading for eastern Europe, **Prague** may be cheaper than Vienna or Budapest.

The time of week and time of year you fly is critical. Midweek flights are almost always cheaper than weekend flights. **Low season** stretches from November to March, except December 14 to 25, and fares of $400 or less from the East Coast of the U.S. to various European destinations are the norm. **Shoulder season** is from April to May, mid-September to October, and December 14 to 25.

In **high season,** from June to early September, expect to pay $600 to $1,200 for a round-trip ticket to Europe.

Note: The cheapest way to fly to Europe is usually to fly into and out of the same city—flying into one city and out of another can sometimes add several hundred dollars to your airfare. The best way to travel by rail, however, is usually to start off in one city and end your journey in another, and unless you're covering a small region, backtracking to your starting point could cost you valuable travel time. We suggest you add up the costs and time of doing your rail trip as both a one-way or round-trip journey and then decide which option works best for your schedule and budget.

Check the "Essentials" section in chapters 3 through 20 for a list of the major airlines that service each European country's major cities out of North America.

FINDING THE LOWEST FARES ONLINE

Shopping online provides an easy way of finding low fares. The "big three" online travel agencies, **Expedia.com, Travelocity.com,** and **Orbitz.com,** sell most of the air tickets bought on the Internet. (Canadian travelers should try expedia.ca and Travelocity.ca.) Each has different business deals with the airlines and may offer different fares on the same flights, so it's wise to shop around. Expedia and Travelocity will also send you **e-mail notification** when a cheap fare becomes available to your favorite destination. Of the smaller travel agency websites, **SideStep** (www.sidestep.com) has gotten the best reviews from Frommer's authors. It's a browser add-on that purports to "search 140 sites at once," but in reality only beats competitors' fares as often as other sites do.

Also remember to check **airline websites,** especially those for low-fare carriers such as easyJet or Ryanair, whose fares are often misreported or simply missing from travel agency websites. Even with major airlines, you can often shave a few bucks from a fare by booking directly through the airline and avoiding a travel agency's transaction fee. But you'll get these discounts only by **booking online:** Most airlines now offer online-only fares that even their phone agents know nothing about.

If you're willing to give up some control over your flight details, use an **opaque fare service** like **Priceline** (www.priceline.com; www.priceline.co.uk for Europeans) or **Hotwire** (www.hotwire.com). Both offer rock-bottom prices in exchange for travel on a "mystery airline" at a mysterious time of day, often with a mysterious change of planes en route. The mystery airlines are all major, well-known carriers—and the possibility of being sent from Philadelphia to Paris via Chicago is remote; the airlines' routing computers have gotten a lot better than they used to be. But your chances of getting a 6am or 11pm flight are pretty high. Hotwire tells you flight prices before you buy; Priceline usually has better deals than Hotwire, but you have to play their "name our price" game. If you're new at this, the helpful folks at **BiddingForTravel** (www.biddingfortravel.com) do a good job of demystifying Priceline's prices. Priceline and Hotwire are great for flights between the U.S. and Europe.

PACKAGE TOURS & TRAVEL AGENTS

Packages aren't guided tours—rather, they're a way to save by buying your airfare, railpass, and accommodations from the same agent. Especially during high season, you can often get a better deal this way than if you booked all the pieces independently. You lose some freedom, though, and the hotels chosen by packagers are usually personality-free, international-style boxes. Getting a travel agent to construct a custom package may cost a bit more, but it can take a lot of stress out of the planning process and you'll get exactly the trip you want.

Rail Europe's packager subsidiary, **euro-vacations** (℃ 877/471-3876; www. euro-vacations.com) offers a slew of two- and three-city packages that include air and rail travel. They'll also help you construct complex, custom rail itineraries, and can book air tickets, hotel nights, and car rentals.

The **Society of International Railway Travelers** (℃ 800/IRT-4881; www. irtsociety.com) knows so much about rail that they publish a newsletter entirely about great train journeys. They offer organized rail tours and are also willing to function as a travel agent to design your ideal air/hotel/rail combination.

10 Money Matters

In 2002, 12 European countries merged their national currencies into the *euro*, and that's great news for rail travelers. As long as you stay in Austria, Belgium, Finland, France, Germany, Greece, Ireland, Italy, Luxembourg, the Netherlands, Portugal, and Spain, you won't need to change your money once.

One euro is broken into 100 cents. There are coins of 1, 2, 5, 10, 20, and 50 cents, and one and two euros; bills are 5, 10, 20, 50, 100, 200, and 500 euros. (500 euro bills, a common counterfeiters' target, aren't accepted at many shops.) Bills look the same in every euro country, but each country is allowed to design one side of its euro coins. They're like the "50 states" U.S. quarters—interchangeable, but collectable (it's a great game for kids to try to find all 96 varieties).

At press time, the U.S. dollar was in a free fall against the euro: 1€ equaled $1.15, up from 94¢ a year before. The exchange rate directly affects the planning of your rail journey—when the euro is low, it becomes much cheaper to buy some point-to-point tickets in Europe than to buy them at home. Check the latest currency rates in your local newspaper's business pages or by going to **www.oanda.com** before traveling.

OTHER FOREIGN CURRENCY

Seven countries in this book don't use the euro. The United Kingdom, Denmark, and Sweden are members of the European Union that have "opted out" of the euro. The Czech Republic, Hungary, Norway, and Switzerland are not members of the European Union (EU). (Note that some hotels and businesses in Budapest post their prices in U.S. dollars or euros; this is a hedge against forint inflation, and all Hungarian businesses accept forints as well as other currencies.) The box below shows how the seven "outsider" currencies break down and their rates against the U.S. dollar at press time.

Non-Euro Countries

Czech Republic	Koruna (Kč)	100 haléru	$1 = 26 Kč
Denmark	Krone (DKK)	100 øre	$1 = 6.67 DKK
Hungary	Forint (Ft)	no smaller unit	$1 = 220 Ft
Norway	Kroner (NOK)	100 øre	$1 = 7.4 NOK
Sweden	Krona (SEK)	100 oüre	$1 = 8 SEK
Switzerland	Franc (CHF)	100 centimes	$1 = CHF 1.5
United Kingdom	Pound (£)	100 pence	£1 = $1.65

GETTING CASH

It's a good idea to exchange at least some money—just enough to cover airport incidentals and transportation to your hotel—before you leave home, so you can avoid lines at airport ATMs. You can exchange money at your local American Express or Thomas Cook office or your bank. If you're far away from a bank with currency-exchange services, American Express offers travelers checks and foreign currency, though with a $15 order fee and additional shipping costs, at www.americanexpress.com or © **800/807-6233.**

The easiest and best way to get cash away from home is from an ATM. The **Cirrus** (© **800/424-7787;** www.mastercard.com) and **PLUS** (© **800/843-7587;** www.visa.com) networks span the globe; look at the back of your bank card to see which network you're on, then call or check online for ATM locations at your destination. Be sure you know your personal identification number (PIN) before you leave home and be sure to find out your daily withdrawal limit before you depart. Also keep in mind that many banks impose a fee every time a card is used at a different bank's ATM, and that fee can be higher for international transactions (up to $5 or more) than for domestic ones (where they're rarely more than $1.50). On top of this, the bank from which you withdraw cash may charge its own fee.

You can also get cash advances on your credit card at an ATM. Keep in mind that credit card companies try to protect themselves from theft by limiting the funds someone can withdraw outside their home country, so call your credit card company before you leave home.

CREDIT CARDS

Credit cards are a safe way to carry money; they provide a convenient record of all your expenses, and they generally offer good exchange rates. You can also withdraw cash advances from your credit cards at banks or ATMs, provided you know your PIN. If you've forgotten yours, or didn't even know you had one, call the number on the back of your credit card and ask the bank to send it to you. It usually takes 5 to 7 business days, though some banks will provide the number over the phone if you tell them your mother's maiden name or some other personal information. Your credit card company will likely charge a commission (1% or 2%) on every foreign purchase you make, but don't sweat this small stuff; for most purchases, you'll still get the best deal with credit cards when you factor in things like ATM fees and higher traveler's check exchange rates.

Within Europe, Visa and MasterCard are almost universally accepted (though some smaller establishments or places in rural areas will still only take cash). American Express is useful, if somewhat less omnipresent than the Big Two; leave your Discover Card at home.

VALUE-ADDED TAX (VAT)

All European countries charge a **value-added tax (VAT)** of 15% to 34% on goods and services—it's like a sales tax that's already included in the price. Rates vary from country to country (as does the name—it's called the IVA in Italy and Spain, the TVA in France, MOMS in Sweden, and so on), though the goal in EU countries is to arrive at a uniform rate of about 15%. Citizens of non-EU countries can, as they leave the country, usually get back most of the tax on purchases (not services) if they spend above a designated amount (usually $80–$200) in a single store (and, in some cases, if they don't use the items while in the country in which they were purchased). *Note:* The Czech Republic does not offer VAT refunds to foreign visitors.

> **Tips Dear Visa: I'm Off to Paris!**
>
> Some credit card companies recommend that you notify them of any impending trip abroad so that they don't become suspicious when the card is used numerous times in a foreign destination and your charges are blocked. Even if you don't call your credit card company in advance, you can always the card's toll-free emergency number if a charge is refused—a good reason to carry the phone number with you. But perhaps the most important lesson here is to carry more than one card with you on your trip; a card might not work for any number of reasons, so having a backup is the smart way to go.

Regulations vary from country to country, so inquire at the tourist office when you arrive to find out the procedure; ask what percentage of the tax is refunded, and if the refund is given to you at the airport or mailed to you later. Look for a TAX FREE SHOPPING FOR TOURISTS sign posted in participating stores. Ask the storekeeper for the necessary forms, and, if possible, keep the purchases in their original packages. Save all your receipts and VAT forms from each EU country to process all of them at the **"Tax Refund"** desk in the airport of the last country you visit before flying home (allow an extra 30 min. or so at the airport to process forms).

To avoid VAT refund hassles, ask for a Global Refund form ("Shopping Checque") at a store where you make a purchase. When leaving an EU country, have it stamped by Customs, after which you take it to the Global Refund counter at more than 700 airports and border crossings in Europe. Your money is refunded on the spot. For information, contact **Global Refund** (© **800/566-9828;** www.globalrefund.com).

11 Tips on Accommodations

Traditional European hotels tend to be simpler than American ones and emphasize cleanliness and friendliness over amenities. For example, even in the cheapest American chain motel, free cable is as standard as indoor plumbing. In Europe, however, few hotels below the moderate level even have in-room TVs.

Unless otherwise noted, all hotel rooms in this book have **private bathrooms.** However, the standard European hotel bathroom might not look like what you're used to. For example, the European concept of a shower is to stick a nozzle in the bathroom wall and a drain in the floor. Shower curtains are optional. In some cramped private bathrooms, you'll have to relocate the toilet paper outside the bathroom before turning on the shower and drenching the whole room. Another interesting fixture is the "half tub," in which there's only room to sit, rather than lie down. The half tub usually sports a shower nozzle that has nowhere to hang—so your knees get very clean and the floor gets very wet. Hot water may be available only once a day and not on demand—this is especially true with shared bathrooms. Heating water is costly, and many smaller hotels do it only once daily, in the morning.

A few other differences to note:

- **Think small.** European hotel rooms are generally smaller than hotel rooms in North America. Many have been squeezed into historic and older buildings.

As a result, these hotels offer an atmosphere that more modern hotels lack, but they also occasionally end up with some odd room configurations.

- **Double up.** Or not. When we use the term "double" in referring to hotel rates inside this book, we mean a room for two people. But you need to be careful when booking a hotel room in Europe because, in many instances, if you ask for a double, what you'll get is a room with one double bed (and beds are smaller in Europe, too!). A twin room, on the other hand, has two beds. King beds are very, very rare.
- **Cooling off.** Air-conditioning is far from a common amenity in most European hotels, and the hotels that do have it tend to fall into the top price categories. So if you must have air-conditioning (and after Europe's nightmarish summer of 2003, plenty of people will be looking for it), be prepared to pay for it.

GETTING THE BEST ROOM AT THE BEST RATE

The **rack rate** is the maximum rate that a hotel charges for a room. Hardly anybody pays this price, however. To lower the cost of your room:

- **Ask about special rates or other discounts.** Always ask whether a room less expensive than the first one quoted is available, or whether any special rates apply to you. You may qualify for corporate, student, senior, or other discounts. Find out the hotel policy on children—do kids stay free in the room or is there a special rate? Do you get a discount if you book a minimum number of days?
- **Dial direct.** When booking a room in a chain hotel, you'll often get a better deal by calling the individual hotel's reservation desk than at the chain's main number.
- **Book online.** Many hotels offer Internet-only discounts, or supply rooms to Priceline, Hotels.com, Lodging.com, or Expedia at rates much lower than the ones you can get through the hotel itself.
- **Shop around!** A little-known gem, **Travelaxe (www.travelaxe.com)** offers a free, downloadable price comparison program that will make your hotel search infinitely easier. The program searches a host of discount travel websites for the best prices for your city (and it covers most major European cities) and your travel dates. Click on the price you like and the program will send you straight to the website offering it. And, unlike most websites, Travelaxe prices almost always include hotel tax, so you actually see the total price of the room.
- **Remember the law of supply and demand.** Many hotels have high-season and low-season prices, and booking the day after "high season" ends can mean big discounts. For example, Paris hotel rates usually drop in August as natives leave town en masse for their summer vacations, and if you hit the Netherlands right after the major tulip bloom season, you'll still see plenty of colorful flora but will pay a whole lot less for your hotel room.
- **Avoid excess charges and hidden costs.** When you book a room, ask whether the hotel charges for air-conditioning (some do in the Mediterranean countries). Use your own cellphone, pay phones, or prepaid phone cards instead of dialing direct from hotel phones, which usually have exorbitant rates. And don't be tempted by the room's minibar offerings: Most hotels charge through the nose for water, soda, and snacks. Finally, ask about local taxes and service charges, which can increase the cost of a room by 15% or more.

Tips   A Traveler's Tip

If you call a hotel from home to reserve a room, *always follow up with a confirmation fax.* Not only is it what most hotels prefer, but it is also printed proof you've booked a room. Keep the language simple—state your name, number of people, what kind of room (like "double with bathroom and one bed" or "twin with bathroom and two beds"), how many nights you'd like to stay, and the starting date for the first night. Remember that Europeans abbreviate dates day/month/year, not month/day/year.

HOTEL BOOKING SERVICES

When you arrive in town, you'll find that a desk in the train station or at the tourist office (or both) acts as a central hotel reservations service for the city. Tell them your price range, where you'd like to be in the city, and sometimes even the style of hotel, and they'll use a computer database to find you a room in town.

The advantages of booking services are that they do all the room-finding work for you—for a nominal fee—and always speak English, while individual hoteliers may not. When every hotel in town seems to be booked up (during a convention or festival or just in high season), they can often find space for you at inns not listed in guidebooks or other main sources. On the downside, hotels in many countries often charge higher rates to people booking through such a service. Our recommendation: Unless you're the happy-go-lucky type, plan an itinerary and make your hotel reservations in advance.

RAILPASS HOTEL BONUSES

If you've got a European railpass, you can get discounted rates at many European hotels. Be aware, though, that the discount almost always applies to the hotel's sky-high rack rates and the final price may still be higher than what you'd get through an online reservation service such as hotels.com or Priceline.

Eurailpass, Eurailpass Flexi, and Eurail Selectpass: Discounts of 30% off of maximum double room rate on Fridays through Sundays in many major European cities. You must book via Hilton's worldwide toll-free number at ☎ 00800/444 58667 (☎ 800/774-1500 from the U.S. and Canada), quote the discount code "RM," and show your pass at check-in.

Swiss Pass: Reduced rates on Best Western Swiss hotels, Sunstar hotels, Swiss and Top International hotels, and more (a complete list of reduced hotel rates is included on the Swiss map you will receive with your pass). Ask the hotel for the railpass discount.

Scanrail Pass: Discounts on Best Western, Sokos Hotels, Choice Hotels, and VIP Backpackers Resorts. Ask the hotel for the railpass discount.

Austria

Rivaled only by Switzerland, Austria is one of the greatest destinations for rail travelers in the world, a land acclaimed for its scenic grandeur and soaring Alpine peaks. Much of the country's spectacular scenery can be seen outside your train window as you ride the rails in this once-great empire that was a major world power during the 18th and 19th centuries. You'll pass unspoiled mountain villages, epic monuments, grandiose ochre-colored baroque buildings, onion-domed churches, and miles and miles of rugged scenery in a country that is 75% mountainous.

Though just smaller than the state of Maine, Austria's geography is among the most varied in Europe. Castles and dense forests disappear as ancient glacial lakes come into view, lapping up against old spas that are bordered by acres of vineyards. But nothing can compete with the Alps, with some of the most panoramic and dramatic mountain peaks in the world—most of which you'll be able to see and reach easily through the country's extensive rail system, which stretches for nearly 3,600 miles (5,800km) of tracks.

Since ancient times, Austria has stood at the crossroads of Europe, and that is even truer today for the rail traveler. To the north, Austria is bordered by Germany and the Czech Republic, Slovakia and Hungary to the east, Slovenia and Italy to the south, and Switzerland and Liechtenstein to the west. As such, Austria is smack in the middle of most of Europe's rail networks and is easily connected to almost anywhere you're going except Britain and Scandinavia.

And you won't have much trouble getting around once you board your train. Austria's rail system is among the most intricate, efficient, and sophisticated in the world; and a passenger will find that getting around, even in the mountains, is easy and fast because of amazing engineering advances in rail technology, including aerial cableways.

Another plus: Austrians are taught English beginning in grade school, so language is hardly a barrier. And there is one final allure: Austria is a bi-seasonal country, attracting sightseers in summer to its Alpine villages and lakeside promenades, and a more sports-oriented crowd in winter. The skiing here is equaled in the world only by neighboring Switzerland.

HIGHLIGHTS OF AUSTRIA

For the rail passenger—or even the air passenger flying into Austria to begin a train journey—there are three major gateways to the country: Vienna, Salzburg, and Innsbruck. All three of these cities are easily reached by rail in some form or another, and, most important for the rail traveler, none of the major routes between these cities usually suffers any snow delays or closures during the popular winter ski season.

Although the capital of Austria, **Vienna** is not a central rail city, as it lies in one of the easternmost provinces of the nation. Unlike the country's two other major cities, it is not on the main north/south rail lines of Europe, though if you're flying into Austria or arriving by rail from eastern Europe, this will assuredly be your first stop in the country and is, therefore, where we start you off in this chapter.

If your rail trip will include an overview of Europe (western, central, and eastern) as a whole, then designate Vienna your crossroads: A dividing point between the continent's western and eastern frontiers, it makes a grand stopover of at least 3 days, especially if you're traveling by rail farther east to such cities as Budapest or Prague.

Vienna is actually a destination unto itself, and a worthy one as it's filled with scenic grandeur that rivals or even surpasses most of the other capitals of Europe. The Hapsburgs left grandiose monuments behind in Vienna after their centuries of imperial rule, and the city offers some of Europe's greatest museums and palaces.

The second city of Austria, **Salzburg,** is easily reached by rail from such cities as Vienna, Innsbruck, Munich, Zurich, or Milan. As a rail destination, it is particularly convenient for passengers who also want to see Munich and parts of Italy on the same journey.

Allow at least 2 days for a hurried visit to this city of Mozart and the von Trapps, made famous in the fabled 1965 musical, *The Sound of Music.* Rich with the splendors of the baroque age, Salzburg is one of Europe's premier architectural gems, and the setting for one of the continent's most prestigious music festivals.

Moments Festivals & Special Events

Given Austria's major contributions to the field, it's no wonder that many of the country's special events revolve around music. Vienna's musicians devote an entire week to the works of Wolfgang Amadeus Mozart during **Vienna Mozart Week.** The Neues Wiener Barockensemble sets the tone with orchestral works by the musical genius, followed by performances by the Vienna Philharmonic. Mozart Week culminates in a performance of the Coronation Mass and church sonatas during Sunday mass at the Church of the Augustinian Friars. Organizers of the festival also conduct guided walks following in "Mozart's Footsteps in Vienna." For bookings, contact Wiener Mozartwoche, Postfach 55, A-1181 Vienna (℃ **01/408-7586**). Festival dates change every year but usually begins in the second week of April.

The traditional highlight of Vienna's concert calendar, the **International Music Festival** features top-class international orchestras, distinguished conductors, and classical greats—a virtual "Who's Who" of the international world of music. The venue and also the booking address is Wiener Musikverein, Lothringer-Strasse 20, A-1030 Vienna (℃ **01/242-002**). Early May through the first 3 weeks of June.

Since the 1920s, the **Salzburg Festival** has been one of the premier cultural events of Europe, sparkling with opera, chamber music, plays, concerts, appearances by world-class artists, and many other cultural presentations. Always count on stagings of Mozart operas. Performances are staged at various venues throughout the city. For tickets, write several months in advance to the Salzburg Festival, Postfach 140, A-5010 Salzburg (℃ **0662/8045**). July 24 to August 31, 2004.

Austria

Most rail passengers entering Austria arrive from the west for a stopover in **Innsbruck,** the capital of the Tyrolean country. It is actually the third most important city to visit in Austria after Vienna and Salzburg, but if you're traveling by rail, it's the most central of the major Austrian cities. Another plus: It's a two-season city, being both a summer resort and a winter ski center, and is full of Alpine flavor.

Innsbruck is a stopover on the major rail link between Zurich and Vienna, and so makes an ideal introduction to Austria, especially if you want to concentrate on the Alpine grandeur of this small nation. Most rail visitors usually settle for a 2-night visit to Innsbruck before heading off to other countries, with the promise of a return on another occasion.

1 Essentials

GETTING THERE

From the United States, you can fly directly to Vienna on **Austrian Airlines** (✆ **800/843-0002** in the U.S. and Canada; www.austrianair.com), the national carrier of Austria. There's nonstop service from both New York and Washington, D.C. to Vienna.

British Airways (✆ **800/AIRWAYS** in the U.S. and Canada; www.british airways.com) provides excellent service to Vienna through London. Flights on

Lufthansa (𝒸 800/645-3880 in the U.S. and Canada; www.lufthansa-usa. com), the German national carrier, depart from North America frequently for Frankfurt and Düsseldorf, with connections to Vienna. **American Airlines** (𝒸 800/433-7300 in the U.S. and Canada; www. aa.com) funnels Vienna-bound passengers through gateways in Zurich or London.

AUSTRIA BY RAIL

Rail travel is superb in Austria, with fast, clean trains taking you through scenic regions. Trains will carry you nearly every place in the country, except for remote hamlets tucked away in almost-inaccessible mountain districts. Many other services tie in with railroad travel, among them car or bicycle rental at many stations, bus transportation links, and package tours, including boat trips and cable-car rides.

InterCity Express (ICE) trains connect Vienna with all major cities in the country, including Salzburg, Innsbruck, Klagenfurt, Graz, and Linz. **EuroCity (EC)** trains also connect cities within Austria as well as with several international trains. A few **EuroNight (EN)** international trains pass through the country as well. Avoid the slower RegionalExpress and RegionalBahn trains unless you have no other alternative as the other rail options in the country are faster and have more amenities.

One of the great train rides of Europe is the 8-hour journey from Venice northeast to Vienna, going through the still-emerging country of Slovenia, with a stopover at that country's capital, Ljubljana. This is a stunning route set against an Alpine backdrop, taking in vistas at every turn, including mountain lakes, vast woodlands, and towering peaks. On this trip, arrangements can be made for you to get off in Ljubljana to explore its attractions, such as its **hilltop fortress** dominating the town. Another great rail trip, also taking 8 hours, is the Vienna-to-Warsaw (or vice versa) journey, which runs through the foothills of the Carpathians, with their fertile vineyards, and trails along the banks of the River Váh before disappearing into the densely wooded mountain ranges in northern Slovakia. The rural villages of Mittel Europa pass in review. A major stopover along this route is the university city of Krakow in Poland.

And one final noteworthy route, combining two Alpine nations, is the 9-hour Zurich-to-Vienna run, which passes through panoramic valleys and takes in magnificent Alpine vistas, especially around the Arlberg Pass. This trip passes some of the most beautiful and unspoiled villages in Europe before stopping at Innsbruck and Salzburg, as the train heads east toward Vienna. If Innsbruck and Salzburg are the only two cities in Austria on your itinerary, you can change directions at Innsbruck because that Tyrolean city lies on the main rail route between Munich in the north and Venice in the southeast.

For information on short-distance, round-trip tickets, cross-country passes, and passes for all lines in the individual provinces, as well as piggyback transportation

---

Tips Austrian Spelling

Note that because of government regulations forbidding the use of the spelling "ss," Austrians use the symbol "ß" as a substitute. So Schloss in Austria is actually spelled Schloß. We've heard reports that the regulations are gradually being relaxed, but for now, when you are trying to find a street that ends in "strasse," look for "straße."

for a car through the Tauern Tunnel, check with the **Austrian Federal Railways,** c/o the Austrian National Tourist Office, P.O. Box 1142, New York, NY 10108-1142 (② **212/944-6880;** www.austria.info/us).

PASSES

For information on the **Eurailpass, Eurailpass Flexi,** the **Austrian Railpass,** and the new **Switzerland 'n Austria Pass,** see chapter 2. All passes must be purchased in North America prior to your departure. To buy a pass, contact **Rail Europe** (② **877/272-RAIL** in the U.S., **800/361-RAIL** in Canada; www.raileurope.com) or your travel agent.

Note: Children under 6 travel free in Austria, and kids ages 6 to 12 are offered a 50% discount.

SENIOR DISCOUNTS   In Austria, women 60 years of age and over and men age 65 and over, regardless of nationality, can travel on half-fare passes valid on the Austrian Federal Railways and on the bus systems of the Federal Railways and the Postal Service. The reduction is not applicable on municipal transit lines such as subways, streetcars, or buses, even in towns where the Postal Service operates the local bus service.

To purchase a half-fare ticket, a Railway Senior Citizen's Identification must be obtained in advance. This is issued at all railroad stations, at certain major post offices, and at the central railroad stations (Hauptbahnhof) in Frankfurt and Munich, Germany. In Zurich, the Senior Citizen discount pass is available at both the railway station and at the Zurich airport and the main railway station, Hauptbahnhof, in the center of the city. This makes it possible to take a train into Austria without having to break your trip at the border.

The price of the identification is 25€ ($28.75), and it's valid from January 1 to December 31. A passport photo is required, and you must present your passport to prove your age. With this Senior Citizen's Identification—not available

---

Moments **Riding Historic Rails**

One of the most breathtaking and dramatic train rides in Alpine Europe is the **Semmering Pass Railway** ★★★, one of the world's greatest feats of railway engineering. This UNESCO-protected site (the only rail line on UNESCO's Heritage list) dates back to 1842 and still pays tribute to the engineers of Imperial Austria.

Through limestone cliffs with craggy rocks and across wide valleys, the rail lines take you across 16 viaducts, through 15 tunnels, and across 129 bridges, a distance of 25 miles (41km). The railway, for the most part, is wholly preserved in its original state.

The Semmering rail links Vienna with the city of Graz, 124 miles (200km) southwest of Vienna. Nine trains per day make this run, with stopovers at Semmering. Trains from Vienna run daily from 5:30am to 9:23pm, and cost 24.70€ ($28.40) one-way for the trip. For more information, call ② **01/1717** in Vienna. The trip is covered by most railpasses.

The Semmering Pass itself is 56 miles (90km) southeast of Vienna and marks the boundary between the provinces of Styria and Lower Austria. At the peak of the pass, constructed on terraces between 3,231 feet and 3,973 feet, is a winter sports center and mountain spa.

in the United States—you can buy tickets for your half-fare travel in Austria. The reduction is also granted for express trains, first-class tickets, and for checked luggage. If a **TEE** (Trans European Express) train is used, any supplement must be paid in full.

This ID for seniors, called a *Seniorenausweis,* is sold at railroad stations in Austria as well as at major post offices.

FOREIGN TRAIN TERMS

Although German speaking, the people of Austria, including those who run the rails, are among the most well educated on earth. To millions, English is a second language, so getting around and riding the rails of Austria for English speakers should not be difficult.

It's helpful to know that Austria's federal railroad is called **Österreichische Bundesbahn (ÖBB),** and that it prints the annual *Fahrplane Kursbuch Bahn-Inland,* listing all rail, ferry schedules, and cable-car timetables in Austria. This massive timetable is sold at most train stations. It might also be helpful to know that yellow signs announce departure times, called *Ausfahrt,* and that white signs announce arrivals, known as *Ankunft.*

PRACTICAL TRAIN INFORMATION

Vienna has rail links to all the major cities of Europe. Rail travel within Austria itself is superb, with fast, clean trains taking you just about anywhere in the country and going through some incredibly scenic regions.

Any train depot in Austria will sell you an individual ticket. Sometimes these are sold at automated machines or even *Tabak* (tobacco) stands. You can often hop aboard a train and purchase a ticket from a conductor, although you're assessed a small surcharge for this service. Nearly all major stations accept credit cards such as American Express, Visa, and MasterCard. Riding without a ticket—called *Schwarzenfahren* in German—can result in a big fine.

For more on Austria's railways, Check out the ÖBB's website at **www.oebb.at**.

RESERVATIONS   Although not always required, it is still advisable to make a reservation for travel on an Austrian rail line. A seat reservation is not guaranteed even with a railpass, and it's worth the 11€ ($12.75) extra investment for the greater security in travel. During holiday seasons or busy times, such as the peak winter ski season in Innsbruck, reservations are imperative. Your rail pass will cover most high-speed trains such as EuroCity or InterCity, but some international trains will require you to pay a supplement of about 11€ ($12.75). ICE trains require this supplement, as does the **Romulus** train that goes from Vienna via Klagenfurt to Venice, Florence, and Rome.

For overnight travel, we'd recommend getting a *couchette* (a fold-down bunk bed; see chapter 2, for more details), priced at about $28. These are usually clean and comfortable on Austrian trains. Reservations can be made through travel agents or in person at any rail station in Austria. Most seat reservations only require a few hours notice. However, for a couchette reservation, a few days' notice is advised, especially during high season. *Note:* Because the price of couchette and seat reservations is the same in the U.S. as it is in Austria, if you have a firm travel itinerary, we recommend getting your train reservations from Rail Europe (see above) before you leave North America.

SERVICE & AMENITIES   Austria is a relatively small country, and you can get where you're going in most cases without any long overnight hauls. Therefore, sleeping arrangements, other than a couchette, are rarely a factor, though

Trains & Travel Times in Austria

From	To	Type of Train	# of Trains	Frequency	Travel Time
Vienna	Salzburg	EuroCity	5	Daily	2 hr. 57 min.
Vienna	Salzburg	InterCity	7	Daily	3 hr. 26 min.
Vienna	Salzburg	ICE	1	Sun–Fri	2 hr. 45 min.
Vienna	Innsbruck	EuroCity	1	Mon–Sat	5 hr. 10 min.
Vienna	Innsbruck	EuroCity	6	Daily	5 hr.
Vienna	Innsbruck	ICE	1	Sun–Fri	4 hr. 48 min.
Vienna	Innsbruck	EuroNight	1	Daily	6 hr. 23 min.

if you want to go in high style, you can get sleeper cars on the EuroNight trains that cross the country or pass through it. All InterCity and EuroCity trains have dining cars. And all, except very local services such as trains going to the suburbs of Vienna, feature minibars—which, on European trains is a trolley-style snack bar (also serving liquor) that's rolled on wheels through the train carriages.

The bad news is that drinking and dining on Austrian railways is prohibitively expensive for travelers on strict budgets, who are better advised to bring along some food and drink and have an on-train picnic while taking in all that panoramic Austrian scenery. Most stations have well-stocked kiosks that are only slightly more expensive than regular supermarkets. In Vienna, food or drink is no problem, as the two big stations have delicatessens that keep long hours, even on Sundays.

FAST FACTS: Austria

Area Codes The country code for Austria is **43**. The area code for Vienna is **01**; for Salzburg, **0662**; and for Innsbruck, **0512**.

Business Hours Banking hours vary according to the region. The exchange counters at airports and railroad stations are generally open from the first to the last plane or train, usually 8am to 8pm daily. Many stores are open 8am to 6pm Monday to Friday and 8am to noon Saturday, closing for 2 hours during the middle of each day. Most businesses and shops are closed on Sunday.

Climate In Austria, the temperature varies greatly depending on your location. The national average ranges from a low of 9°F (–13°C) in January to a high of 68°F (20°C) in July. However, in Vienna the January average is 32°F (0°C), for July 66°F (19°C). Snow falls in the mountainous sectors by mid-November, but it rarely affects the major rail routes. The winter air is usually crisp and clear, with many sunny days. The winter snow cover lasts from late December through March in the valleys, from November through May at about 6,000 feet, and year-round at above 8,500 feet. The ideal times for visiting Vienna are spring and fall, when you'll find mild, sunny days. "Summer" generally means from Easter until about mid-October. By the end of July, alpine wildflowers are in full bloom.

Documents Required Americans and Canadians need only a valid passport for travel to Austria.

Electricity Austria operates on 220 volts AC (50 cycles). That means that U.S.-made appliances that don't come with a 110/220 switch will need a transformer (sometimes called a converter) and an adaptor plug. Many Austrian hotels stock adapter plugs but not power transformers.

Embassies & Consulates The main building of the Embassy of the **United States** is at Boltzmanngasse 16, A-1090 Vienna (℗ **01/31339**). However, the consulate is at Gartenbaupromenade 2–4, A-1010 Vienna (℗ **01/31339**), and it handles lost passports, tourist emergencies, and other matters. Both the embassy and consulate are open Monday to Friday 8:30am to noon and 1 to 4pm.

The Embassy of **Canada,** Laurenzerberg 2 (℗ **01/531-380**), is open Monday to Friday 8:30am to 12:30pm and 1:30 to 3:30pm.

Health & Safety You'll encounter few health issues while traveling in Austria. The tap water is generally safe to drink, the milk is pasteurized, and health services are good. Occasionally, the change in diet and water may cause some minor gastric disturbances, so you may want to talk to your doctor. As for safety, no particular caution is needed, other than what a discreet person would maintain anywhere. Compared to the rest of the world, Austria is a very safe country in which to travel.

Holidays Bank holidays in Austria are as follows: January 1, January 6 (Epiphany), Easter Monday, May 1, Ascension Day, Whitmonday, Corpus Christi Day, August 15, October 26 (Nationalfeiertag), November 1, December 8, and December 25 and 26.

Legal Aid If arrested or charged with a crime, you can obtain a list of private lawyers from the U.S. Embassy, to represent you.

Mail **Post offices** *(Das Postamt)* in Austria are usually located in the heart of the town, village, or urban district they service. If you're unsure of your address in any particular town, correspondence can be addressed c/o the local post office by labeling it either POST RESTANTE or POSTLAGERND. If you do this, it's important to clearly designate the addressee, the name of the town, and its postal code. To claim any correspondence, the addressee must present his or her passport.

The postal system in Austria is, for the most part, efficient and speedy. You can buy stamps at a post office or from the hundreds of news and tobacco kiosks, designated locally as Tabak-Trafik. Mailboxes are painted yellow, and older ones are emblazoned with the double-headed eagle of the Austrian Republic. Newer ones usually have the golden trumpet of the Austrian Postal Service. A blue stripe on a mailbox indicates that mail will be picked up there on a Saturday. Both postcards and airmail letters weighing less than 20 grams cost 1.10€ ($1.25) for delivery to North America.

Police & Emergencies Dial ℗ **133** anywhere in Austria to summon the police. Emergency phone numbers throughout the country (no area code needed) are as follows: ℗ **133** for the police, **144** for accident service, and **122** to report a fire.

Telephone Do not dial abroad directly from your hotel room unless it's an emergency. Place phone calls at the post office or some other location. Austrian hotels routinely add 40% surcharges, and some will add as much as 200% to your call. If you do place a call from your room, for help dialing, contact your hotel's operator; or dial © **09** for placement of long-distance calls within Austria or for information about using a telephone company credit card; dial © **1611** for directory assistance; and dial © **08** for help in dialing international long distance.

Coin-operated phones can be found all over Austria. Despite the increasing automation of many aspects of local life, most public phones are still operated by coins instead of by credit card. Using one of them will require picking up the receiver, inserting a minimum of .10€ (10¢), waiting for the dial tone, and dialing the number. Know in advance that .10€ (10¢) will allow no more than about 2 minutes of talk time even to a number you're calling within Vienna, and when your talk time is finished, a recorded telephone announcement, in German, will instruct you to put in more coins. To avoid this unwelcome interruption to their calls, most Austrians insert up to .40€ (45¢) at the beginning of their call. In theory, at least, the phone will return whatever unused coins remain at the end of your call.

Avoid carrying lots of coins by buying a **Wertkarte** at Tabak-Trafik kiosks or at post offices. Each card is electronically coded to provide 3€ ($3.50), 7€ ($8), 14€ ($16), or 35€ ($40.25) worth of phone calls. Buyers receive a slight discount because cards are priced slightly lower than their face value.

Tipping A service charge of 10% to 15% is included on hotel and restaurant bills, but it's a good policy to leave something extra for waiters and 2€ ($2.30) per day for your hotel maid.

Railroad station, airport, and hotel porters get 1.50€ ($1.75) per piece of luggage, plus a .75€ (85¢) tip. Your hairdresser should be tipped 10% of the bill, and the shampoo person will be thankful for a 1.50€ ($1.75) gratuity. Toilet attendants are usually given .50€ (60¢) and hatcheck attendants expect .50€ to 1.50€ (60¢–$1.75), depending on the place.

2 Vienna ★★★

From the time the Romans selected the site of a Celtic settlement for location of one of its most important Central European forts, *Vindobona,* the city that grew up in the Vienna Basin of the Danube has played a vital role in European history. Austria developed around the city into a mighty empire, but the Viennese character formed during the long history of the country can only be said to be a rich amalgam of the blending of cultures that have made Vienna what it still is today: a cosmopolitan city whose people devote themselves to enjoyment of the good life.

Music, art, literature, theater, architecture, education, food, and drink (perhaps wine from the slopes where the Romans had vineyards in the 1st c. A.D.)—all contribute to the warm congenial atmosphere, the *gemütlichkeit,* of Vienna.

For the rail traveler exploring Austria, Vienna should and likely will be your introduction to the country. Most flights into Austria from North America land here, and the city is the center hub for the Austrian rail system.

Vienna

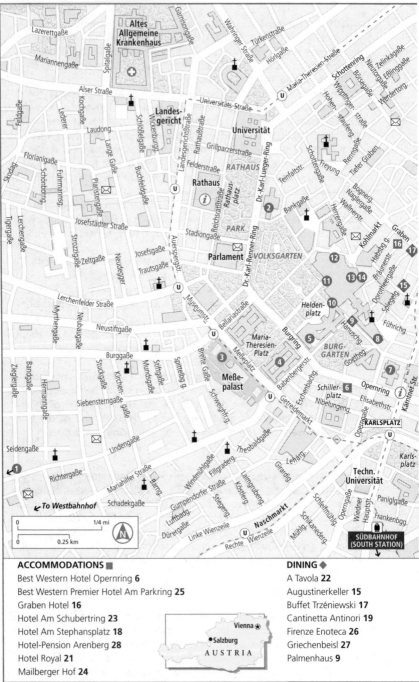

ACCOMMODATIONS ■

Best Western Hotel Opernring **6**
Best Western Premier Hotel Am Parkring **25**
Graben Hotel **16**
Hotel Am Schubertring **23**
Hotel Am Stephansplatz **18**
Hotel-Pension Arenberg **28**
Hotel Royal **21**
Mailberger Hof **24**

DINING ◆

A Tavola **22**
Augustinerkeller **15**
Buffet Trzéniewski **17**
Cantinetta Antinori **19**
Firenze Enoteca **26**
Griechenbeisl **27**
Palmenhaus **9**

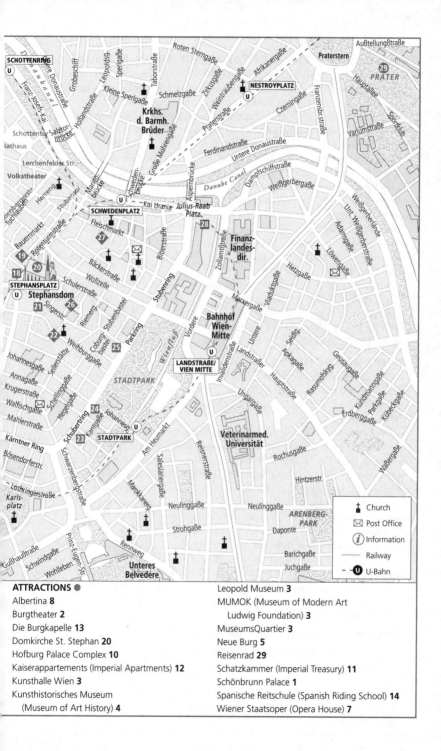

ATTRACTIONS ●

Albertina **8**
Burgtheater **2**
Die Burgkapelle **13**
Domkirche St. Stephan **20**
Hofburg Palace Complex **10**
Kaiserappartements (Imperial Apartments) **12**
Kunsthalle Wien **3**
Kunsthistorisches Museum
  (Museum of Art History) **4**

Leopold Museum **3**
MUMOK (Museum of Modern Art
  Ludwig Foundation) **3**
MuseumsQuartier **3**
Neue Burg **5**
Reisenrad **29**
Schatzkammer (Imperial Treasury) **11**
Schönbrunn Palace **1**
Spanische Reitschule (Spanish Riding School) **14**
Wiener Staatsoper (Opera House) **7**

STATION INFORMATION
GETTING FROM THE AIRPORT TO THE TRAIN STATION
Vienna International Airport (© 01/70070; http://English.viennaairport.
com) is 12 miles (19km) southeast of the city center. For a list of air carriers flying into Vienna, see "Getting There," earlier in this chapter.

A branch office of the **Vienna Tourist Information Office** in the arrival hall
of the airport is open daily: October to May 9am to 10pm and June to September 8:30am to 9pm. The office makes hotel reservations for free.

There's regular bus service between the airport and the **City Air Terminal,**
adjacent to the Vienna Hilton and directly across from the local **Wien
Mitte/Landstrasse** rail station, where you can easily connect with subway and
tramlines. Buses run every 20 minutes 6:30am to 11:30pm, and hourly at other
times. The trip takes about 25 minutes and costs 5.80€ ($6.75) per person.
Tickets are sold on the bus and must be purchased with euros. There's also bus
service between the airport and the city's two main railroad stations, the Westbahnhof and the Südbahnhof, leaving every 30 minutes to an hour. Fares are
also 5.80€ ($6.75).

Local train service, *Schnellbahn,* is available between the airport and the Wien
Nord and Wien Mitte rail stations, but it's actually slower than taking the bus
unless you're traveling during rush hours. Trains run hourly 4:30am to 9:30pm
and leave from the basement of the airport. Trip time is 40 to 45 minutes, and
the fare is 3€ ($3.50).

INSIDE THE STATIONS
Vienna has two main rail stations, which offer frequent connections to all Austrian cities and towns and from all major European cities. For train and station
information, call © **05/1717** or check on the Web at **www.metropla.net/eu/
vie/wien.htm**.

The **Westbahnhof (West Station),** Mariahilferstrasse 132, serves trains arriving from western Austria, France, Germany, Switzerland, and some eastern
European countries. It has frequent links to major Austrian cities such as
Salzburg, Innsbruck, and Linz, with longer connections to such cities as Hamburg, Amsterdam, Munich, Zurich, and Paris. Trains arrive on the second level
of the two-level station. The concourse for baggage pickup is at street level, and
there is a baggage storage office here that charges 5€ ($5.75) for 24 hours.

For reservations, rail information, and pass validation, head for an office
marked **Reisebüro am Bahnhof** on the main level. There is also a money
exchange office, *Exchange–Wechselstube,* lying to the left of the escalators on the
main level that is open daily from 7am to 10pm. Westbahnhof connects with
local trains, the U3 and U6 underground lines, and several tram and bus routes.

⌐Warning Can't Get There from Here

Most of Vienna's train stations do not have interconnecting rail service, so
you must take public transportation or a taxi to get between them. If you
opt for public transportation, it can take up to an hour (or more if you
take the wrong tram) to get from Westbahnhof to Südbahnhof. As a
result, be sure to leave plenty of time to catch a train if your journey will
require switching stations.

Südbahnhof (South Station), Wiedner Gürtel, has train service to southern and eastern Austria, and is also linked to local rail service, and tram and bus routes. At this tri-level terminal, the train platforms are located on the middle and top levels. Here trains depart for such destinations as Graz or Villach in southern Austria, as well as Rome, Venice, Krakow, Prague, Budapest, and other cities. Its currency exchange office (Exchange–Wechselstube) is on the lowest level of the station, immediately to the right of the main stairwell, and is open daily from 6:30am to 10pm.

Both of these stations house useful travel offices (**Österreichisches Verkehrsbüro**) that provide tourist information and arrange hotel reservations for free. Both information offices are open daily from 7:30am to 8:40pm. In the Westbahnhof the office is in the upper hall, and at the Südbahnhof it's in the lower hall.

INFORMATION ELSEWHERE IN THE CITY

Once you've arrived safely in Vienna, head for either of two information points that make it their business to have up-to-the-minute data about what to see and do in Vienna. The more centrally located of the two is the **Wien Tourist-Information** office at Albertinaplatz (✆ **01/211-140;** tram: 1 or 2). In the heart of the Inner City (directly behind the Opera, on the corner of Philharmoniker Strasse), it's open daily from 9am to 7pm. The staff will make hotel reservations for 3€ ($3.50). Larger and more administrative but also willing to handle questions from the public is the headquarters of the **Vienna Tourist Board,** at Obere Augartenstrasse (✆ **01/24555;** tram: 31). This office makes hotel reservations for free.

Both branches stock free copies of a tourist magazine, *Wien Monatsprogramm,* which lists what's going on in Vienna's concert halls, theaters, and opera houses. Also worthwhile here is *Vienna A to Z,* a general, pocket–size guide with descriptions and locations for a slew of attractions. This booklet is also free, but don't rely on its cluttered map to get around town.

GETTING AROUND

Whether you want to visit the Inner City's historic buildings or the outlying Vienna Woods, Vienna Transport *(Wiener Verkehrsbetriebe)* can take you there. This vast transit network—U-Bahn (subway), streetcar, or bus—is safe, clean, and easy to use. If you plan on taking full advantage of it, pay the 1€ ($1.15) for a map that outlines the U-Bahn, buses, streetcars, and local trains (Schnellbahn or S–Bahn). It's sold at the **Vienna Public Transport Information Center** *(Informationdienst der Wiener Verkehrsbetriebe),* which has five locations: **Opernpassage** (an underground passageway adjacent to the Staatsoper House); **Karlsplatz; Stephansplatz,** near Vienna's cathedral; the **Westbahnhof** (and probably the most useful for rail travelers); and **Praterstern.** For information about any of these outlets, call ✆ **01/790-9105.**

Vienna maintains a uniform fare that applies to all forms of public transport. A ticket for the bus, subway, or tram will cost 1.50€ ($1.75) if you buy it in advance at a *Tabak-Trafik* (a store or kiosk selling tobacco products and newspapers) or 2€ ($2.30) if you buy it on board. Smart Viennese buy their tickets in advance, usually in blocks of at least five at a time, from any of the city's thousands of Tabak-Trafik or at any of the public transport centers noted above. No matter what vehicle you decide to ride within Vienna, remember that once a ticket has been stamped (validated) by either a machine or a railway attendant, it's valid for one trip in one direction, anywhere in the city, including transfers.

(*Value*   **City Transportation on the Cheap**
_____

The **Vienna Card** is the best ticket to use when traveling by public transportation within the city limits. It's extremely flexible and functional for visitors because it allows unlimited travel, plus various discounts at city museums, restaurants, and shops. You can purchase a Vienna Card valid for 72 hours for 16.90€ ($19.50) at tourist information offices, public transport centers, and some hotels, or order one over the phone with a credit card (✆ **01/7984-4000128**).

You can also buy tickets that will save you money if you plan to ride a lot on the city's transport system. A ticket valid for unlimited rides during any 24-hour period costs 5€ ($5.75); an equivalent ticket valid for any 72-hour period goes for 12€ ($13.75). There's also a green ticket, priced at 24€ ($27.50), that contains eight individual partitions. Each of these, when stamped, is good for 1 day of unlimited travel. An individual can opt to reserve all eight of the partitions for his or her own use, thereby gaining 8 days of cost-effective travel on the city's transport system. Or the partitions can be subdivided among a group of several riders, allowing—for example—two persons 4 days each of unlimited rides, or three persons 2 days each of unlimited rides.

These tickets are available at Tabak-Trafiks, vending machines in underground stations, the airport's arrival hall (next to baggage claim), the DDSG landing pier *(Reichsbrücke),* and the travel agencies *(Österreichisches Verkehrsbüro)* located in the two main train stations.

U-BAHN (SUBWAY)   Most of the top attractions in the Inner City can be seen by foot, tram, or bus, but the U-Bahn is your best bet to get across town quickly or to reach the suburbs. It consists of five lines labeled as U1, U2, U3, U4, and U6 (there is no U5). Karlsplatz, in the heart of the Inner City, is the most important underground station for visitors as the U4, U2, and U1 all converge here. The U2 traces part of the Ring, the U4 goes to Schönbrunn, and the U1 stops in Stephansplatz. The U3 also stops in Stephansplatz and connects with the Westbahnhof. The underground runs daily 6am to midnight.

TRAM (STREET CAR)   Riding the city's red-and-white trams *(Strassenbahn* or *S-Bahn)* is not only a practical way to get around, it's a great way to see the city. Tram stops are well marked and lines are labeled as numbers or letters. Lines 1 and 2 will bring you to all the major sights on the Ringstrasse. Line D skirts the outer Ring and goes to the Südbahnhof, whereas line 18 goes between the Westbahnhof and the Südbahnhof (see "Can't Get There from Here," above for more on traveling between train stations).

BY BUS   Buses *(Autobus)* traverse Vienna in all directions and operate Monday to Saturday 6am to 10pm and Sunday 6am to 10pm. Buses 1A, 2A, and 3A will get you around the Inner City. Convenient night buses are available on weekends and holidays starting at 12:15am. They go from Schwedensplatz to the outer suburbs (including Grinzing). Normal tickets are not valid on these late "N" buses. Instead you pay a special fare of 1.50€ ($1.75) on board.

Vienna Public Transport

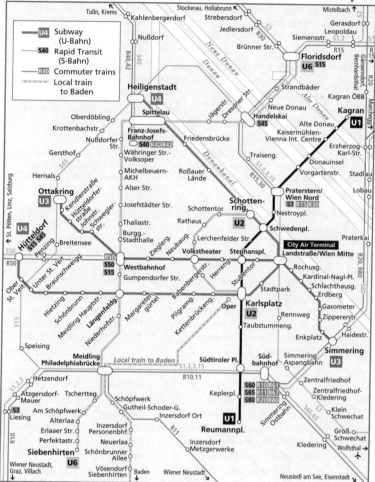

BY TAXI Taxis are easy to find within the city center, but be warned that fares can quickly add up. The basic fare is 2€ ($2.25), plus 1.20€ ($1.35) per kilometer. For night rides after 11pm, and for trips on Sundays and holidays, there is a surcharge of 1€ ($1.15). There is an additional charge of 2€ ($2.25) if ordered by phone. The fare for trips outside the Vienna area (for instance, to the airport) should be agreed upon with the driver in advance, and a 10% tip is the norm. Taxi stands are marked by signs, or you can call © **01/31300,** 60160, 81400, 91011, or 40100.

WHERE TO STAY

Best Western Hotel Opernring   Just across from the State Opera, this chain hotel puts you right in at the core of cultural Vienna. Rated 4 stars by the government, the hotel offers completely refurbished and individually designed bedrooms, which range from midsize to quite spacious. Each is tastefully and comfortably furnished; double-glazed windows keep the street noise at bay.

Opernring 11, A-1010 Vienna. ✆ **800/528-1234** in the U.S., or 01/587-55-18. Fax 01/587-55-18-29. www.
bestwestern.com. 35 units. 119€–155€ ($137–$177) double; 280€ ($322) suite. Rates include breakfast.
AE, DC, MC, V. U-Bahn: Karlsplatz. **Amenities:** Breakfast room; laundry; nonsmoking rooms. *In room:* Hair
dryer.

Best Western Premier Hotel Am Parking   A first-class hotel in the center
of Vienna, this hotel occupies three floors of a 13-story office building near
Stadtpark. An elevator sweeps you up to the well-designed and fairly large bedrooms, some with a private terrace. Windows open onto private views of
Vienna's cityscape. You'll be accommodated here in relative comfort, but don't
expect old Viennese nostalgia: Everything is too streamlined modern for that.

Parkring 12, A-1015 Vienna. ✆ **800/582-1234** in the U.S., or 01/514800. Fax 01/514-8040. www.best
western.com. 64 units. 129€–215€ ($148–$247) double. Rates include breakfast. AE, DC, MC, V. U-Bahn:
Stadtpark or Stubentor. Tram: 1 or 2. **Amenities:** Restaurant; bar; laundry; nonsmoking rooms. *In room:* Hair
dryer.

Graben Hotel   Established in 1918 at the collapse of the Austrian empire, this
hotel is great for shoppers, as it lies near some of the most famous shopping
streets of Vienna, including Kärntnerstrasse. Franz Kafka used to frequent this
hotel in the days when he was called a bohemian. The mostly Art Nouveau bedrooms are a bit small but individually designed with high ceilings. The minimalist style is a little spartan, but this is a longtime favorite of devotees who like
the atmosphere of the old city, having their coffee at the fabled Café Hawelka
across the street, where the Kafka of today might be seen hanging out.

Dorotheergasse 3, A-1010 Vienna. ✆ **01/512-15-31-0.** Fax 01/512-15-31-20. 41 units. 140€–170€
($161–$196) double. Rates include buffet breakfast. AE, DC, MC, V. U-Bahn: Karlsplatz. **Amenities:** Restaurant; nonsmoking rooms. *In room:* Hair dryer.

Hotel Am Schubertring ✮   This privately run hotel stands in the heart of
the city on the famous "ring around Vienna," the Ringstrasse, next to the opera.
The hotel has more Austrian style and tradition than many of its nearby competitors. Many of the top-floor rooms open onto panoramic views of the city.
Most of the midsize bedrooms are designed in Art Nouveau or Belle Epoque
style. The standard of comfort is high and, though you have original art and
antique mirrors, you also get all the latest modern amenities.

Schubertring 11, A-1010 Vienna. ✆ **01/717-020.** Fax 01/713-99-66. www.schubertring.at. 39 units.
128€–218€ ($147–$251) double. AE, DC, MC, V. U-Bahn: Karlsplatz. **Amenities:** Restaurant; bar; laundry.
In room: Hair dryer.

Hotel Am Stephansplatz   Next to the grandest cathedral in Austria, this
central hotel on Stephansplatz should have more Viennese atmosphere than it
does, but few can fault its exceptional location. The renovated lobby is awash
with burled woods, crystal, granite, and marble. Many of the midsize bedrooms
offer reproductions of antiques though some rooms are rather basic, with strictly
functional pieces and shower-only bathrooms. If you're a light sleeper, check in
elsewhere, as Stephansplatz is a virtual summer festival during the city's precious
few weeks of fair weather.

Stephansplatz 9, A-1010 Vienna. ✆ 01/534-05-0. Fax 01/534-05-711. 57 units. www.hotelamstephansplatz.
at. 145€–230€ ($167–$265) double. Rates include breakfast. AE, DC, MC, V. U-Bahn: Stephansplatz. **Amenities:** Restaurant; laundry. *In room:* Hair dryer.

Hotel Kaiserin Elisabeth ✮   For those nostalgic for old Vienna, this hotel is
a good choice, having hosted such musical greats as Liszt, Wagner, and Mozart

over the years. Named for the wife of Emperor Franz Joseph, the hotel lies in the vicinity of the cathedral, just five subway stops from the Westbahnhof. It has many trappings of the 19th century but the bedrooms are modernized. Oriental carpeting, skylights, marble columns, and natural wood are used in abundance.

Weihburggasse 3, A-1010 Vienna. 🕾 **01/515260.** Fax 01/515267. www.kaiserinelisabeth.at. 63 units. 200€ ($230) double; 220€ ($253) suite. Rates include buffet breakfast. AE, DC, MC, V. U-Bahn: Stephansplatz. **Amenities:** Restaurant; bar; laundry; nonsmoking rooms. *In room:* Hair dryer.

Hotel–Pension Arenberg ⭐   This small luxury hotel, under the Best Western banner, occupies the second and third stories of a 6-floor apartment house dating back to the late 1890s. A few minutes from Stadtpark (one of the city's loveliest parks) and close to the local Wien Mitte rail station, the well-run hotel offers midsize bedrooms with soundproof windows. There is certain Old World charm here evoked by the traditional furnishings and Viennese styling, both in the architecture and the decor.

Stubenring 2, A-1010 Vienna. 🕾 **800/528-1234** in the U.S., or 01/512-5291. Fax 01/513-9356. www.best western.com. 22 units. 120€–159€ ($138–$183) double; 168€–194€ ($193–$223) triple suite. Rates include breakfast. AE, DC, MC, V. U-Bahn: Schwedenplatz. **Amenities:** Restaurant; laundry; nonsmoking rooms; rooms for those with limited mobility. *In room:* Hair dryer.

Hotel Royal ⭐⭐   Less than a block from St. Stephan's, this property is unusual in that it shelters two of the city's best Italian restaurants: Firenze Enoteca (see p. 95) and Settimo Cielo. In the lobby is the original piano on which Wagner composed *Die Meistersinger von Nürnberg.* Most of the midsize to spacious bedrooms are furnished in an Art Nouveau style and are completely up-to-date, and furnishings are often a combination of antiques and reproductions. Corner rooms, with their large foyers, are the most desirable.

Singerstrasse 3, A-1010 Vienna. 🕾 **01/515680.** Fax 01/513-9696. 81 units. 130€–170€ ($150–$196) double; 175€–210€ ($201–$242) triple suite. Rates include breakfast. AE, DC, MC, V. U-Bahn: Stephansplatz. **Amenities:** Restaurant; bar; laundry; nonsmoking rooms. *In room:* Hair dryer.

Mailberger Hof ⭐ *(Finds)*   The origins of this property date from the 1300s, when it was a mansion of the knights of Malta. Later in the 17th century, it was converted into a small baroque palace before being completely recast in 1976 as a modern hotel. Classified today as a historical monument, it's located off Vienna's main thoroughfare, Kärntnerstrasse, in the heart of the city. Many old-fashioned touches remain, such as wooden doors and vaulted ceilings, even a cobblestone courtyard. The atmosphere is intimate and cozy, the hotel featuring midsize bedrooms that have been comfortably modernized with a bit of style, though most of the latter is reserved for the public lounges.

Annagasse 7, A-1010 Vienna. 🕾 **01/512-0641.** Fax 01/512-0641-10. 40 units. 195€–205€ ($224–$236) double. AE, DC, MC, V. U-Bahn: Karlsplatz. **Amenities:** Restaurant; bar; laundry; nonsmoking rooms; rooms for those with limited mobility. *In room:* Hair dryer.

TOP ATTRACTIONS & SPECIAL MOMENTS

After deliverance from the dreaded plague and the equally dreaded Turks, Vienna entered into a period of great power and prosperity that reached the zenith of empire under the long reign of Maria Theresa from 1740 to 1780. Many of the sights we describe below can be traced directly to that great empress of the Age of Enlightenment, who welcomed Mozart to her court at Schön-brunn when he was only 6 years old—a child prodigy indeed.

HOFBURG PALACE COMPLEX 𝒜𝒜𝒜

The winter palace of the Hapsburgs, known for its vast, impressive courtyards, lies in the heart of Vienna. To reach it (you can hardly miss it), head up the Kohlmarkt into Michaelerplatz, which is decorated with two enormous fountains embellished with statuary. You can also take the U-Bahn to Herrengasse or Stephansplatz, or else trams 1, 2, D, or J to Burgring. This complex of imperial edifices, the first of which was constructed in 1279, grew and grew as the empire did, so that today the Hofburg Palace is virtually a city within a city. The earliest parts were built around a courtyard, the **Swiss Court,** named for the Swiss mercenaries who used to perform guard duty here. This most ancient part of the palace is at least 700 years old.

Albertina 𝒜   The **Albertina Collection,** is another Hofburg museum, this one showing the development of graphic arts since the 14th century. Housing one of the world's greatest graphic collections, the museum's most outstanding treasure is its Dürer collection, although what you will usually see are copies, the originals being shown only on special occasions. See, in particular, Dürer's *Praying Hands,* which has been reproduced throughout the world. The some 20,000 drawings and more than 250,000 original etchings and prints include work by such artists as Poussin, Fragonard, Rubens, Rembrandt, Michelangelo, and Leonardo da Vinci. There are many changing exhibitions of both old and modern drawings and prints.

Albertinaplatz (entrance at Augustinerstrasse 1). ℂ 01/53483. www.albertina.at. Admission 7.50€ ($8.65) adults, 5.50€ ($6.35) students, free for children under 6. Thurs–Tues 10am–6pm; Wed 10am–9pm. U-Bahn: Stephansplatz.

Die Burgkapelle (Home of the Vienna Boys' Choir)   Construction of **Die Burgkapelle (Palace Chapel)** in the Gothic style started in 1447 during the reign of Emperor Frederick III, but it was subsequently massively renovated. From 1449 it was the private chapel of the royal family. Today the Burgkapelle is the scene of the **Hofmusikkapelle** 𝒜𝒜𝒜, an ensemble consisting of the Vienna Boys' Choir and members of the Vienna State Opera chorus and orchestra, performing works by classical and modern composers. Written applications for reserved seats should be sent at least 8 weeks in advance. Use a credit card; do not send cash or checks. For reservations, write to **Verwaltung der Hofmusikkapelle,** Hofburg, A-1010 Vienna. If you failed to reserve in advance, you may be lucky enough to secure tickets from a block sold at the Burgkapelle box office every Friday from 11am to 1pm or 3 to 5pm, plus Sunday 8:15 to 8:45am. The line starts forming at least half an hour before that. If you're willing to settle for standing room, it's free.

Hofburg (entrance on Schweizerhof). ℂ 01/533-9927. Mass: Seats and concerts 5€–29€ ($5.75–$33.35); standing room free. Masses (performances) held only Jan–June and mid-Sept through Dec, Sun and holidays at 9:15am. Concerts May–June and Sept–Oct Fri at 4pm. Tram: 1, 2, D, or J to Burgring.

Kaiserappartements (Imperial Apartments) 𝒜𝒜   The Hofburg complex also includes the **Reichskanzleitrakt,** or Imperial Chancellery, where the emperors and their wives and children lived on the first floor. To reach the **Kaiserappartements (Imperial Apartments),** you enter via the rotunda of the Michaelerplatz. The apartments are richly decorated with tapestries, many from Aubusson. The court tableware and silver are magnificent, revealing the pomp and splendor of a bygone era. These Imperial Apartments seem to be more closely associated with Franz Joseph than with any other emperor because of his long reign. His wife, Elizabeth of Bavaria, lived here too when she wasn't traveling,

⟨Moments⟩ The World's Most Famous Ferris Wheel

Since 1766, when Emperor Joseph II opened the Prater to the public, this extensive tract of woods and meadowland lying between the Danube River and the Danube Canal has been Vienna's favorite recreation area. Joseph, son and co–ruler of Maria Theresa, a liberal reformer and humanist, didn't always come up with changes everybody liked, but when he declared that "everybody shall be allowed to walk, ride, and drive in the Prater at their pleasure," he came up with a winner. Before that, the area had been used mostly as a hunting preserve and riding ground for the aristocracy.

The best-known attraction in the huge park is at the end nearest the entrance from the Ring. The **Riesenrad,** a giant Ferris wheel and one of the landmarks of Vienna, was constructed in 1897, and is 220 feet at its highest point. If you saw the film classic, *The Third Man,* you may recall this Ferris wheel in the scene where it appeared that Orson Welles was going to murder Joseph Cotton.

Just beside the Riesenrad is the terminus of a Lilliputian railroad, the 2.6-mile (4km) narrow-gauge line that operates in summer using vintage steam locomotives. The amusement park, right behind the Ferris wheel, has all the typical entertainment facilities: roller coasters, merry-go-rounds, tunnels of love, games arcades, etc.

The season lasts March or April to October, but the Ferris wheel operates year-round. Some of the park's more than 150 booths and restaurants stay open in winter, including the pony merry-go-round and the gambling venues. The place is usually jammed on Sunday afternoons in summer. Admission to the park (ⓒ **01/728-0516;** U-Bahn: Praterstern/3 stops from the local Wien Mitte station) is free, but you'll pay for games and rides. The Ferris wheel costs 7.50€ ($8.65) for adults, 3€ ($3.45) for children ages 3 to 14, and free for children under 3. The park is open January to February and November to December daily 10am to 8pm; March to April and October 10am to 10pm; May to September daily 9am to midnight.

which actually was most of the time until her fatal stabbing by an assassin in Switzerland. You'll see the "iron bed" of Franz Joseph, who claimed he slept like his own soldiers.

The **Leopoldinischer Trakt,** or Leopold's apartments, date from the 17th century. You can't visit the quarters once occupied by Maria Theresa as they are now used by the president of Austria.

Michaeler Platz 1 (inside the Ring, about a 7-min. walk from Stephansplatz; entrance via the Kasertor in the Inneren Burghof). ⓒ 01/533-7570. Admission 7.50€ ($8.65) adults, 5.90€ ($6.80) students under 25, 3.90€ ($4.50) children 6–15, free for children 5 and under. Daily 9am–5:30pm. U-Bahn: U-1 or U-3 to Stephansplatz. Tram: 1, 2, 3, or J to Burgring.

Neue Burg   Neue Burg, called the New Château, was the most recent addition to the Hofburg complex. Construction was started in 1881 and continued until work was halted in 1913. The palace was the residence of Archduke Franz

Ferdinand, the nephew and heir apparent of Franz Joseph, whose assassination at Sarajevo set off the chain of events that led to World War I.

The Neue Burg's collection of arms and armor is second only to that of the Metropolitan Museum in New York. It is in the **Hofjagdlung Rüstlammer** on the second floor of the New Château. On display are crossbows, swords, helmets, and pistols, plus armor, mostly the property of the emperors and princes of the House of Hapsburg. Some of the exhibits, such as scimitars, were captured from the Turks as they fled the scene of their losing sieges of Vienna. Of bizarre interest is the armor worn by the little Hapsburg princes, who had to learn the martial arts at a very early age. Another section, called **Musikinstrumentensammlung,** is devoted to old musical instruments, mainly from the 17th and 18th centuries, but with some from the 16th. Some of the instruments displayed here, especially pianos and harpsichords, were played by Brahms, Liszt, Mahler, and Beethoven.

In the **Ephesos–Museum (Museum of Ephesian Sculpture),** you'll see numerous finds from Ephesus in Turkey and the Greek island of Samothrace. It is in the Neue Hofburg, an annex of the Collection of Greek and Roman Antiquities of the Kunsthhistoriches Museum. Here the prize exhibit is the **Parthian monument** 🌟🌟, the most important relief frieze from Roman times ever found in Asia Minor. It was erected on the occasion of the victorious conclusion of the Parthian wars (A.D. 161–65) to commemorate Emperor Lucius Verus, commander of the Roman forces.

Neue Burg I, Heldenplatz (entrance behind the Prince Eugene monument). © 01/525-24-484. Admission to Hofjagd and Rüstkammer, Musikinstrumentensammlung, and Ephesos–Museum, 7.50€ ($8.65) adults, 5.50€ ($6.35) children, children under 6 free. Open Wed–Mon 10am–6pm. U-Bahn: Museumsquatier.

Schatzkammer (Imperial Treasury) 🌟🌟🌟   The Imperial Treasury, reached
by a staircase from the Swiss Court, is the greatest treasury in the world. It is divided into two sections: the Imperial Profane and the Sacerdotal Treasuries. One part displays the crown jewels and an assortment of imperial riches, and the other, of course, contains ecclesiastical treasures.

The most outstanding exhibit in the Schatzkammer is the **imperial crown** 🌟🌟🌟, which dates from 962. It is so big that even though padded, it was likely to slip down over the ears of a Hapsburg at a coronation. Studded with emeralds, sapphires, diamonds, and rubies, this 1,000-year-old symbol of sovereignty is a priceless treasure. Also on display is the imperial crown worn by the Hapsburg rulers from 1804 to the end of the empire. You will see the saber of Charlemagne and the holy lance from the 9th century. The latter, a sacred emblem of imperial authority, was thought in medieval times to be the weapon that pierced the side of Christ on the cross. The Agate Bowl was once believed to be the Holy Grail.

Among other great Schatzkammer prizes is the **Burgundian Treasure** 🌟🌟🌟 seized in the 15th century, rich in vestments, oil paintings, gems, and robes. This loot is highlighted by artifacts connected with the Order of the Golden Fleece, that romantic medieval order of chivalry. You will also see the coronation robes of the imperial family, some of which date from the 12th century. The cradle of the "King of Rome," son of Napoleon and his Austrian second wife, Marie-Louise, is in the Empire style in silver, pearl, and gilt.

Hofburg, Schweizerhof. © 01/533-7931. Admission 7.50€ ($8.65) adults, 5.50€ ($6.35) children, seniors, and students, children 5 and under free. Wed–Mon 10am–6pm.

Spanische Reitschule (Spanish Riding School) 🌟 (*Moments*   A bittersweet
nostalgia seems to permeate the Spanische Hofreitschule, a reminder of the fact

that horses were an important part of both imperial and everyday life for many centuries, with their care and training a matter of pride and honor. The school is in the white, crystal-chandeliered ballroom in an 18th-century building of the Hofburg complex, designed by J. E. Fischer von Erlach. You can marvel at the skill and beauty of the sleek Lappizaner stallions as their adept trainers put them through their paces in a show that is the same now as it was 4 centuries ago. These are the world's most famous and most classically styled equine performers. Many North Americans have seen them in the States, but to watch the Lippizaners move to the music of Johann Strauss or a Chopin polonaise in their "airs above the ground" dressage in this, their home setting in Vienna, is a pleasure you should not miss.

Michaelerplatz 1, Hofburg. ℂ **01/533-9032.** Regular performances 33€–145€ ($37.95–$167) seats, 25€ ($28.75) standing room. Classical art of riding with music 21.60€ ($24.85) adults, free for children 3–6 with an adult; children under age 3 not admitted. Training session 11.60€ ($13.35) adults, 5€ ($5.75) children. Regular shows Mar–June and Sept to mid-Dec, most Suns at 11am and some Fri at 6pm. Classical dressage with music performances Feb–June and Sept–Dec, most Sat at 11am. Training sessions Mar–June, first 2 weeks in Sept, and mid-Oct to mid-Dec Tues–Sat 10am–noon. U-Bahn: Stephansplatz.

MUSEUMSQUARTIER ☆☆☆

If you combined New York's Guggenheim Museum with that city's New York Museum of Modern Art, and then tossed in the Brooklyn Academy of Music, and added a mishmash that included everything from a children's museum to a center for architecture and design, you'd get somewhat of an idea of what the new MuseumsQuartier of Vienna is like. Of course, don't forget theaters, video workshops, art galleries, an architecture museum, and even an ecology center. Because you probably don't have a week to explore all attractions, we've highlighted only the most important for the hurried rail passenger with precious little time in Vienna. To reach any of these museums, take the U-Bahn to MuseumsQuartier (just four subway stops from the Westbahnhof and two from the center of town).

Kunsthalle Wien ☆   Cutting-edge contemporary and classic modern art is showcased here. You'll find works by everyone from Picasso and Juan Miró to Jackson Pollock and Paul Klee, from Wassily Kandinsky to Andy Warhol and, surprise, Yoko Ono. From expressionism to cubism to abstraction, exhibits reveal the major movements in contemporary art since the mid–20th century. There are five floors that can be explored in 1 to 2 hours, depending on what interests you.

Museumsplatz 1. ℂ **01/521-89-0.** Admission 6.50€ ($7.50) adults, 5€ ($5.75) seniors/students/children. Daily 10am–7pm (Thurs 'til 10pm).

Leopold Museum ☆☆   This extensive collection of Austrian art includes the world's largest treasure trove of the works of Egon Schiele (1890–1918), who was once forgotten in art history but now takes his place alongside van Gogh and Modigliani in the ranks of great doomed artists. Dying before he was 28, his collection of art at the Leopold includes more than 2,500 drawings and watercolors and 330 oil canvases. Other Austrian modernist masterpieces include paintings by Oskar Kokoschka, the great Gustav Klimt, Anton Romaki, and Richard Gerstl. Major statements in Arts and Crafts from the late 19th and 20th centuries feature works by Josef Hoffmann, Kolo Moser, and Franz Hagenauer.

Museumsplatz 1. ℂ **01/525-70.** Admission 9€ ($10.35) adults, 6€ ($6.90) students/children over 7. Mon and Wed–Sun 10am–7pm; Fri 10am–3pm. Closed Tues.

MUMOK (Museum of Modern Art Ludwig Foundation) ★★ This 5-level gallery presents one of the most outstanding collections of contemporary art in central Europe. It is comprised mainly of American Pop Art mixed with works from concurrent continental movements such as the Hyperrealism of the '60s and '70s.

Museumsplatz 1. ℂ **01/525-00.** Admission 8€ ($9.20) adults, 2€ ($2.30) children. Tues–Sun 10am–6pm; Thurs 10am–9pm.

OTHER LEADING ATTRACTIONS
Domkirche St. Stephan (St. Stephan's Cathedral) ★★★ In the very heart of the city, at Stephansplatz, a bustling intersection where legend has it that if you wait long enough you'll see anybody you're looking for in the city. St. Stephan's Cathedral was founded in the 12th century in what even in the Middle Ages was the town's center.

Stephansdom (the German name for this church) was virtually destroyed in a 1258 fire that swept Vienna, and toward the dawn of the 14th century the Romanesque basilica gave way to a Gothic building. The cathedral suffered terribly in the Turkish siege of 1683 and then again in 1945, when it was bombed towards the end of World War II by the Germans. The wooden roof of St. Stephan's was heavily damaged and has since been replaced with a steel structure. The steeple, rising to some 450 feet, has come to symbolize the very spirit of Vienna. Reopened in 1948 after restoration from war damage, today the cathedral is one of the greatest Gothic structures in Europe, rich in woodcarvings, altars, sculptures, and paintings.

The 352-foot-long cathedral is inextricably linked with Viennese and Austrian history. It was here that mourners attended Mozart's "pauper's funeral" in 1791, and it was on the cathedral door that Napoleon posted his farewell edict in 1805.

The pulpit of St. Stephan's was carved from stone by Anton Pilgrim, his enduring masterpiece. But the chief treasure of the cathedral is the carved wooden **Wiener Neustadt altarpiece** ★★ dating from 1447, richly painted and gilded, found in the Virgin's Choir. See also the curious **tomb of Emperor Frederick III** ★★ in the Apostles' Choir. Made of a pinkish Salzburg marble in the 17th century, the tomb is carved with hideous little hobgoblins trying to enter and wake the emperor from his eternal sleep. The entrance to the catacombs is on the north side of the cathedral next to the Capistran pulpit.

You can climb the 343-step south tower of St. Stephan's, which dominates the Viennese skyline and from which you have a view of the Vienna Woods. Called *Alter Steffl* (Old Steve), the tower with its needlelike spire was built between 1350 and 1433. From it, watchkeepers of earlier days kept vigil over the city. The north tower *(Nordturm)* was never finished to match the south one, but was crowned in the Renaissance style in 1579. You can reach it by elevator.

Stephansplatz 1. ℂ **01/515-52563.** Free admission Cathedral; tour of catacombs 3€ ($3.45) adults, 1€ ($1.15) children under 15. Guided tour of cathedral 3€ ($3.45) adults, 1€ ($1.15) children under 15. North Tower 4€ ($4.60) adults, 1€ ($1.15) children under 15; South Tower 4€ ($4.60) adults, 1€ ($1.15) students, 1€ ($1.15) children under 15. Evening tours, including tour of the roof, 10€ ($11.50) adults, 3.50€ ($4.05) children under 15. Cathedral, daily 6am–10pm except times of service. Tour of catacombs, Mon–Sat at 10, 11, and 11:30am, 1:30, 2, 2:30, 3:30, 4, and 4:30pm; Sun at 2, 2:30, 3, 3:30, 4, and 4:30pm. Guided tour of cathedral, Mon–Sat at 10:30am and 3pm; Sun at 3pm. Special evening tour Sat 7pm (June–Sept). North Tower, Oct–Mar daily 8:30am–5pm; Apr–Sept daily 9am–6pm. South Tower, daily 9am–5:30pm. Bus: 1A, 2A, or 3A. U-Bahn: Stephansplatz.

Kunsthistorisches Museum ★★★ The **Museum of Fine Arts** is housed in a huge building that contains many of the fabulous art collections gathered by the Hapsburgs when they added new territories to their empire. Acquisitions highlight the art of ancient Egypt and Greece. The museum is also rich in works of Dutch, German, Flemish, French, and Italian masters.

Among notable works from the German, Dutch, and Flemish schools are Roger van der Weyden's crucifixion triptych, a Memling altarpiece, and Jan van Eyck's portrait of Cardinal Albergati. But it is the works of Pieter Brueghel the Elder for which the museum is renowned. This 16th-century Flemish master did many lively studies of peasant life, and his pictures today are almost a storybook of life in his time. See especially his *Children's Games* and *Hunters in the Snow,* one of his most celebrated works.

Many visitors go to the gallery that displays the work of Van Dyck, especially to see his *Venus in the Forge of Vulcan.* Rubens, naturally, involves a big, lavish display and brings a robust Flemish enthusiasm to the museum's galleries in both religious and allegorical works. Be sure to see his *Self-Portrait* and *Woman with a Cape.* Great pride is, of course, taken in the Rembrandt collection, which includes two remarkable portraits of his mother and one of his son, Titus. Holbein the Younger, who lived in England and was famous for his royal portraits, is represented by *Jane Seymour,* third wife of Henry VIII and mother of Edward VI.

Moments Waltzing Through the Vienna Woods

The famous *Wienerwald* (the name of the Vienna Woods in German) weren't simply dreamed up by Johann Strauss Jr. as the subject of musical tales in waltz time. The Wienerwald is a land of gentle paths and trees several thousand acres in size in a delightful hilly landscape. If you stroll through this area, a weekend playground for the Viennese, you'll be following in the footsteps of Strauss and Schubert. Beethoven, when his hearing was failing, claimed that the chirping birds, trees, and leafy vineyards of the Wienerwald made it easier for him to compose.

You don't need a car to visit the woods relatively easily on your own. Board trolley car no. 1 near the State Opera, going to Schottenring. Here you must switch to tram no. 38 (the same ticket is valid) going out to Grinzing, the village that is the site of the famous *heurigen,* or wine taverns. At Grinzing, take bus no. 38A, which goes through the Wienerwald to Kahlenberg (see below). The whole trip takes about 1½ hours each way. You might rent a bicycle in Kahlenberg to make your own exploration of the woods.

When you go to the Vienna Woods by public transportation, after you reach Grinzing (if you can resist the heurigen), you board a bus up the hill to **Kahlenberg** on the northeasternmost spur of the Alps (1,585 ft.). If the weather is fair and clear, you can see all the way to Hungary from here. At the top of the hill is the small Church of St. Joseph, where King John Sobieski of Poland stopped to pray before leading his troops to the defense of Vienna against the Turks. For one of the best of all views overlooking Vienna, go to the right of the Kahlenberg restaurant. From the terrace here, you'll have a panoramic sweep, including the spires of St. Stephen's.

Moments   Boating on the "Blue" Danube

Its waters aren't as idyllic as the Strauss waltz would lead you to believe, and its color is usually muddy brown rather than blue. But despite these drawbacks, many visitors to Austria view a day cruise along the Danube as a highlight of their trip. Until the advent of railroads and highways, the Danube played a vital role in Austria's history, helping to build the complex mercantile society that eventually became the Hapsburg Empire.

The best cruises are operated by the **DDSG Blue Danube Steamship Co.**, Fredrickstrasse 7, A-1010 Vienna (② **01/588800**). The most appealing cruise focuses on the Wachau region east of Vienna, and runs April to October between Vienna and Dürnstein. The cruise departs every Sunday at 8:30am from the company's piers at Handelskai 265, 1020 Vienna (U-Bahn: Vorgartenstrasse), arriving in Dürnstein 6 hours later. The cost each way is 16.50€ ($19) adults, half-price for children 10 to 15. Eurail Pass holders get a 50% discount; Austrian Railpass holders get 20% off.

Maria–Theresien–Platz, Burgring 5. ② **01/525-24-405.** Admission 9€ ($10.35) adults, 6.50€ ($7.50) students and seniors, free for children under 6. Daily 10am–6pm. Thurs until 9pm. U-Bahn: Mariahilferstrasse. Tram: 1, 2, D, or J.

Schönbrunn Palace ✹✹✹   A Hapsburg palace of 1,441 rooms, Schönbrunn was designed by those masters of the baroque, the von Erlachs and is an absolute must-see for the Vienna visitor. It was built between 1696 and 1712 and commissioned by Emperor Leopold I, who ordered the architects to design a palace whose grandeur would surpass that of Versailles. Austria's treasury, however, could not support that ambitious undertaking, so the original plans were never carried out.

When Maria Theresa became empress, she had the original plans changed greatly, and Schönbrunn looks today much as she conceived it, with delicate, feminine rococo touches designed for her by Austrian Nikolaus Pacassi. It was the imperial summer palace during Maria Theresa's 40-year reign, from 1740 to 1780. Schönbrunn was the scene of great ceremonial balls and lavish banquets. At the age of 6, Mozart performed in the Hall of Mirrors before Maria Theresa and her court, and the empress held secret meetings with her chancellor, Prince Kaunitz, in the round Chinese Room.

The **State Apartments** ✹✹✹ are the most stunning display within Schönbrunn Palace. Much of the interior ornamentation is in 23½-karat gold, and many porcelain tile stoves are in evidence. Of the 40 rooms that you can visit, particularly fascinating is "The Room of Millions," decorated with Indian and Persian miniatures and the grandest rococo salon in the world.

In complete contrast to the grim, forbidding-looking Hofburg, Schönbrunn Palace, done in "Maria Theresa ochre," has **formal gardens** ✹, laid out in 1705, embellished by the Gloriette, a marble summerhouse topped by a stone canopy on which the imperial eagle is mounted. The park can be visited daily April to October from 6am to sunset and daily November to March 6:30am to sunset.

Schönbrunner Schlossstrasse. ② **01/81113.** www.schoenbrunn.at. "Imperial Tour" (22 state rooms with audio guide) 8€ ($9.20) adults, 4.30€ ($4.95) children 6–15, free for children under 5. "Grand Tour" (40 state rooms with audio guide) 10.50€ ($12.10) adults, 5.40€ ($6.20) children 6–15, free for children under 5. Apartments, Apr–Oct daily 8:30am–5pm; Nov–Mar daily 9am–4:30pm. U-Bahn: Schönbrunn.

WHERE TO DINE

A Tavola *Finds* *Value* ITALIAN/TUSCAN   A steady stream of frugal clients flocks to this winning choice, which occupies a site where food of some sort has been served since the 1300s. Today it's a mostly Tuscan cuisine of well-prepared specialties that lures hungry diners to this venue, where they most often begin with the tempting seafood *antipasti*. The food isn't fancy, but it's well prepared and based on fresh ingredients, with their homemade pastas and gnocchi, including one with four kinds of cheese, winning favorable reviews.

Weihburggasse 3–5. © **01/512-7955.** Reservations required. Main courses 8€–15€ ($9.20–$17.25). AE, DC, MC, V. Mon–Sat 12–3pm and 6–11pm. U-Bahn: Stephansplatz.

Augustinerkeller AUSTRIAN   One of Vienna's famous cellar restaurants, this favorite has been serving good food, wine, and beer since 1857 in one of the basements of the magnificent Hofburg palaces. Under vaulted brick ceilings, you and a host of locals can listen to *Schrammel* or folkloric music late into the night while feasting on authentic regional cuisine. Roaming accordion players will amuse you as you taste vintage wines from eastern Austria and eat some of the best schnitzels or *tafelspitz* (a famous Austria boiled beef dinner) in the area.

Augustinerstrasse 1. © **01/533-1026.** Main courses 8€–18€ ($9.20–$20.70). AE, DC, MC, V. Daily 11am–midnight. U-Bahn: Karlsplatz.

Buffet Trzésniewski *Finds* SANDWICHES   This is a virtual Viennese institution that has drawn everybody from Franz Kafka to members of European royalty over the years. To experience something authentically Viennese, get in the long line of in-the-know locals who patronize this popular establishment every day at lunch to partake of its delicious finger sandwiches, which come in nearly 20 different combinations. It's a most satisfying choice unless you are ravenously hungry or want a leisurely meal.

Dorotheergasse 1. © **01/512-3291.** Reservations not accepted. Sandwiches .80€ (90¢). No credit cards. Mon–Fri 9:30am–7:30pm; Sat 9am–5pm. U-Bahn: Stephansplatz.

Cantinetta Antinori *Finds* TUSCAN   One of a trio of restaurants in Italy and Austria run by the famous Tuscan winemakers, the Antinori family, this is a Viennese showcase for Tuscan food and wines. Near Domkirche St. Stephan and the central Stephansplatz, the high-ceiling restaurant with a "greenhouse" winter garden offers fine dining at affordable prices. The restaurant has the city's best antipasti table along with homemade pastas and flavor-filled meat, fish, and poultry dishes. A huge selection of wines is available by the glass.

3–5 Jasomirgottstrasse. © **01/533-7722.** Reservations required. Main courses 20€–25€ ($23–$28.75). AE, DC, MC, V. Daily 11:30am–11pm. U-Bahn: Stephansplatz. Closed Aug 1–10.

Firenze Enoteca *Finds Finds* TUSCAN/ITALIAN   One of Vienna's best Italian restaurants is located near St. Stephan's cathedral, inside the Hotel Royal (p. 87). It attracts discerning diners who want to escape from too many plate-size Wiener schnitzels and potato salad. With frescoes by Benozzo Gozzoli, the restaurant evokes the Renaissance style, but this is but a mere backdrop for its finely honed and mainly Tuscan cuisine. Expect an array of contrasting textures, highly evolved sauces, and succulent pastas.

Singerstrasse 3. © **01/513-4374.** Reservations recommended. Main courses 8€–26€ ($9.20–$29.90). AE, DC, MC, V. Daily noon–3pm and 6–midnight. U-Bahn: Stephansplatz.

Griechenbeisl AUSTRIAN   One of the oldest restaurants in Austria dates from 1450 and, amazingly, is still one of Vienna's best choices for authentic Austrian cuisine, which is served by waiters in the famous forest green vests of Styria. Against timeworn paneling and under vaulted ceilings and old-fashioned wrought-iron chandeliers, you are served age-old recipes, the same food once offered to Mark Twain, Mozart, and Beethoven. The cuisine would have been familiar to Emperor Franz Josef, especially the Hungarian goulash, the venison steak, or the deer stew.

Fleischmarkt 11. ℰ 01/533-1941. Reservations required. Main courses 13€–27€ ($14.95–$31.05); fixed-price menu 23€–40€ ($26.45–$46). AE, DC, MC, V. Daily 11am–1am (last orders at 11:30pm). Tram: N, 1, 2, or 21.

Palmenhaus ✦ AUSTRIAN   Under the most beautiful Art Nouveau glass canopy in Vienna, this citadel of fine cuisine opens onto the formal terraces of the Burggarten, constructed in 1901 by the former architect of the Hapsburg court, Friedrich Ohmann. Finally restored in 1998, long after the Allied bombings of 1945, Palmenhaus offers a sophisticated and seasonally adjusted menu of modern dishes, including a pan-fried breast of duck cooked pink with a spicy cabbage salad and a Morello cherry confit.

In the Burggarten. ℰ 01/533-1033. Reservations recommended for dinner. Main courses 12€–22€ ($13.80–$25.30), pastries 5.50€–7.20€ ($6.35–$8.30). AE, DC, MC. V. Daily 10am–2am. U-Bahn: Opera.

SHOPPING

The state-owned **Dorotheum,** Dorotheergasse 17 (ℰ **01/5156-0449;** U-Bahn: Stephansplatz), is Europe's oldest auction house, founded by Emperor Joseph I in 1707 as an auction house where impoverished aristocrats could fairly (and anonymously) get good value for their heirlooms. If you're interested in what's being auctioned off, pay a small fee to a *Sensal,* one of the licensed bidders, and he or she will bid in your name. The objects for sale cover a wide spectrum, including exquisite furniture and carpets, delicate *objets d'art,* valuable paintings, and decorative jewelry. If flea markets are more your style, then visit the **Flohmarkt,** Linke Wienzeille, near the Naschmarkt (no phone; U-Bahn: Kettenbrückengasse). You can find a little of everything at this flea market, held every Saturday 6am to 6pm except on public holidays. The Viennese have perfected the skill of haggling, and the Flohmarkt is one of their favorite arenas for this ritual battle of wills and wallets. It takes a trained eye to spot the treasures that are scattered among the junk.

Ö. W. (Österreichische Werkstatten), Kärntnerstrasse 6 (ℰ **01/512-2418;** U-Bahn: Stephansplatz), a three-floor, well-run store sells hundreds of handmade art objects from Austria. Leading artists and craftspeople throughout the country organized this cooperative to showcase their wares, and it's only half a minute's walk from St. Stephan's. There's an especially good selection of pewter, along with modern jewelry, glassware, brass, baskets, ceramics, and serving spoons fashioned from deer horn and bone.

Established in 1702, **Albin Denk,** Graben 13 (ℰ **01/512-4439;** U-Bahn: Stephansplatz), is the oldest continuously operating porcelain store in Vienna. The shop looks much the same as it did when Empress Elizabeth was a client. The decor of the three low-ceilinged rooms is beautiful, as are the thousands of objects from Meissen, Dresden, and other regions. If during your exploration of Vienna you should happen to admire a crystal chandelier, there's a good chance that it was made by **J. & L. Lobmeyr,** Kärntnerstrasse 26 (ℰ **01/512-0508;** U-Bahn: Stephansplatz). In the early 19th century Lobmeyr was named as a purveyor to the imperial court of Austria, and it has maintained an elevated position ever since. In addition to chandeliers of all shapes and sizes, the store also sells hand-painted Hungarian porcelain, along with complete breakfast and dinner services.

Rising five floors above the pedestrian traffic of inner Vienna's most appealing shopping street, is the well-stocked **Steffl Kaufhaus,** Kärntnerstrasse 19 (© **01/514-310;** U-Bahn: Stephansplatz), the city's most prominent department store.

Niederösterreichisches Heimatwerk, Wippaingerstrasse 23 (© **01/533-18990;** U-Bahn: Schottentor), is one of the best-stocked clothing stores in Vienna for traditional Austrian garments. Inventory covers three full floors and includes garments inspired by the folkloric traditions of Styria, the Tyrol, Carinthia, and every other Austrian province in between. If you're looking for a *loden* coat (traditional coat made of water-repellant wool); a *dirndl* (traditional folk dress); an Alpine hat (with or without a pheasant feather); an incredibly durable pair of *lederhosen* (leather shorts) for those climbs in the foothills of the Alps; handcrafted gift items, including pewter, breadboards and breadbaskets; crystal; or tableware, this is the place.

NIGHTLIFE

Music is at the heart of cultural life in Vienna. You can find places to enjoy everything from chamber music and waltzes to pop, rock, and jazz. There are small discos and large concert halls, as well as musical theaters.

Reservations and information for the four state theaters—the **Staatsoper (State Opera), Volksoper, Burgtheater (National Theater),** and the **Akademietheater**—can be obtained by contacting **Österreichische Bundestheater (Austrian Federal Theatres),** the office that coordinates reservations and information for all four theaters (© **01/5144-42959;** www.bundestheater. at). Call Monday to Friday 8am to 5pm. *Note:* The number is often busy; it's easier to get information and order tickets online. The major season is September to June, with more limited presentations in summer. Many tickets are issued to subscribers before the box office opens, and for all four theaters, box-office sales don't begin until 1 month before each performance at the **Bundestheaterkasse,** Goethegasse 1 (© **01/51-44-40**), open Monday to Friday 8am to 6pm, on Saturday from 9am to 2pm, and Sunday and holidays from 9am to noon. Credit- and charge-card sales can be arranged by telephone within 6 days of a performance by calling © **01/513-1513** Monday to Friday 10am to 6pm, and Saturday and Sunday 10am to noon. You can also order tickets for all state theater performances, including the opera, by mail by writing to the Österreichischer Bundestheaterverband, Goethegasse 1, A-1010 Vienna, from points outside Vienna. Orders must be received at least 3 weeks in advance of the performance to be booked. For more information about tickets, go online to **www. bundestheater.at.**

The **Wiener Staatsoper (Vienna State Opera),** Opernring 2 (© **01/5144-42250;** www.wiener-staatsoper.at), is one of the three most important opera houses in the world. In 1945, at the end of World War II, despite other pressing needs such as public housing shortages, Vienna started restoration work on the theater, finishing it in time to celebrate the country's independence from occupation forces in 1955. With the Vienna Philharmonic in the pit, some of the leading opera stars of the world perform here. Daily performances are given September to June and ticket prices range from 10€ to 178€ ($11.50–$205). Tours are given almost daily year-round, often 2 to 5 times a day with times posted on a board outside the theater's entrance. Tour prices are 4.50€ ($5.25) per person.

Among nightclubs and cabarets, **First Floor,** Seitenstettengasse 5 (© **01/533-7866;** U-Bahn: Schwedenplatz), a hip and worldly nightclub, is one floor above street level in an antique building in the city's historic old Jewish district. There's a long and very active bar area along with a vast, artfully illuminated aquarium so you can see the fish swimming around. There's live music—usually only a piano and bass—on Monday night. Hours are Monday to Saturday 8pm to 4am, Sunday 7pm to 3am. There's no cover charge. Although the origins of **U-4,** Schönbrunner Strasse 222 (© **01/815-8307;** U-4 to Pilgramgasse), go back to the 1920s, it continues to revitalize itself with every new generation of nightclubbers and is cited as one of the trendiest and most cutting-edge clubs in Vienna. Depending on that month's schedule, you're likely to experience such themes as Italian night; '60s, '70s, '80s, and '90s night; pop and rock music; and—every Thursday—gay night. Admission varies from nothing to 8€ ($9.20), depending on the venue. It's open nightly 10pm to around 5am, depending on business.

Café Leopold, in the Leopold Museum, Museumsplatz 1 (© **01/523-67-32;** U-Bahn: Volkstheater or Babenbergstrasse/MuseumsQuartier), proves that the city's homage to Viennese Expressionism (the Leopold Museum) can rock and roll with the sounds of dancing feet and high-energy music 3 nights a week, when the museum's restaurant fills up with drinkers, wits, gossips, dancers, and people of all ilk on the make. There's a revolving cycle of DJs, each vying for local fame and approval, and a wide selection of party-colored cocktails. The cafe and restaurant section opens daily from 10am to 2am; the disco operates only Thursday to Saturday from 9:30pm till between 2 and 3am, depending on business. There's no cover charge. **Jazzland,** Franz-Josefs-Kai 29 (© **01/533-2575;** U-Bahn: Schwedenplatz), is the most famous jazz pub in Austria, noted for the quality of its U.S. and central European–based performers. It's in a deep, 200-year-old cellar. It's open Monday to Saturday 7pm to 1am with music beginning at 9pm. Cover charge is 11€ to 20€ ($12.75–$23).

Barfly's Club, in the Hotel Fürst Metternich, Esterházygasse 33 (© **01/586-0825;** U-Bahn: Kirchengasse. Tram: 5), is the most urbane and sophisticated cocktail bar in town, frequented by journalists, actors, and politicians. The menu lists about 370 cocktails, which include every kind of mixed drink imaginable, priced at 7€ to 11€ ($8–$12.75). It's open daily 6pm to between 2 and 4am, depending on the night of the week. The ancient bricks and scarred wooden tables of **Esterházykeller,** Haarhof 1 (© **01/533-3482;** U-Bahn: Stephansplatz), famous since 1683, are permeated with the aroma of endless pints of spilled beer. An outing to this raucous spot isn't recommended for everyone, but if you decide to chance it, choose the left-hand entrance (facing from the street), grip the railing firmly, and begin your descent. The place is open Monday to Friday 11am to 11pm and Saturday and Sunday 4 to 11pm. **Loos American Bar,** Kärntnerdurchgang 10 (© **01/512-3283;** U-Bahn: Stephansplatz), is one of the most unusual and interesting bars in the center of Vienna. Once a private men's club designed by the noteworthy architect Adolf Loos in 1908, it now welcomes a crowd that tends to be bilingual and very hip, singles, and clients from Vienna's arts and media scene. No food is served, but drink specialties include six kinds of martinis, plus five kinds of Manhattans. It's open Sunday to Wednesday noon to 4am, Thursday to Saturday till 5am

Wine taverns (heurigen) on the outskirts of Vienna have long been celebrated in operetta, film, and song. **Grinzing** is the most visited district, and lies at the edge of the Vienna Woods, a short distance northwest of the center. Much of Grinzing has remained unchanged over the years, looking the same as it did in the days when Beethoven lived nearby. It's a district of crooked old streets and houses, their thick walls built around inner courtyards where grape arbors shelter Viennese wine drinkers on a summer night. The sound of zithers and accordions lasts long into the night. Most Heurigen are reached in 30 to 40 minutes. Take tram 1 from to Schottentor, and change there for tram 38 to Grinzing.

We'll start you off with some of our favorites. **Alter Klosterkeller im Passauerhof,** Cobenzigasse 9, Grinzing (© **01/320-6345**), one of Vienna's well-known wine taverns, maintains an old-fashioned ambience little changed since the turn of the 20th century. Some of its foundations date from the 12th century. Specialties include such familiar fare as tafelspitz, an array of roasts, and plenty of strudel. You can order wine by the glass or bottle. Main courses range from 15€ to 25€ ($17.25–$28.75). Drinks begin at 2.50€ ($3). Open daily from 6pm to midnight. Live music is played from 6 to 11pm. Closed in January and February.

Altes Presshaus, Cobenzlgasse 15, Grinzing (© **01/320-0203**), is the oldest heurigen in Grinzing and has been open since 1527. Ask to see their authentic cellar. The wood paneling and antique furniture give the interior character and the garden terrace blossoms throughout the summer. Meals cost 10€ to 17€ ($11.50–$19.50); drinks begin at 3€ ($3.50). It's open daily from 4pm to midnight and is closed January and February.

3 Salzburg ★★★

For passengers doing a rail tour of the Continent, Salzburg stands at the crossroads of Europe. The birthplace of Mozart makes a grand stopover on the lines running between Munich and Italy, and also lies on the main rail route linking Switzerland in the west with Vienna (and ultimately, Budapest) in the east. Because Vienna is not in the center of the country, as are some capitals, but is rather remotely located in eastern Austria, Salzburg is actually an easier gateway into the country and a more convenient transportation hub if you're arriving by rail.

On the most rushed of itineraries, Salzburg (at least its highlights) can be viewed in a day though it's better to devote at least 2 days to exploring this baroque city, world-renowned for its 17th- and 18th-century architecture. The best months to visit—unless you're planning a winter ski trip to Land Salzburg, one of Europe's greatest winter playgrounds—is from May to September to avoid the coldest weather. On the downside, all this "Sound of Music" atmosphere and great beauty carries a high price tag, as Salzburg is one of the most expensive cities in central Europe.

GETTING THERE

For some visitors, Salzburg—not Vienna—is their aerial gateway to Austria. Once in Salzburg, it's possible to begin a rail journey not only to the cities of Vienna and Innsbruck, but to all the remote corners of this little Alpine nation.

Salzburg Airport–W.A. Mozart, Innsbrucker Bundesstrasse 95 (© **0662/ 8580;** www.salzburg-airport.com), is 2 miles (3km) southwest of the city center. It has regularly scheduled air service to all Austrian airports, as well as to Frankfurt, Amsterdam, Brussels, Berlin, Dresden, Düsseldorf, Hamburg, London, Paris, and Zurich. Major airlines serving the Salzburg airport are Austrian Airlines (© **0662/85-45-11**), Air France (© **01/50-2222-403**), Lufthansa (© **081010/258-080**), and Tyrolean (© **0662/85-45-33**).

STATION INFORMATION
GETTING FROM THE AIRPORT TO THE TRAIN STATION
There is no direct rail service from the airport into the city center. Bus 77 runs between the airport and Salzburg's main rail station. Departures are frequent, and the 20-minute trip costs 2.80€ ($3.25) one-way. By taxi it's only about 15 minutes, but you'll pay at least 10€ to 15€ ($11.50–$17.25).

INSIDE THE STATION
Salzburg's main rail station, **Salzburg Hauptbahnhof,** Südtirolerplatz (© 05/1717), is connected to all of the major rail lines of Europe, with frequent arrivals not only from all the main cities of Austria, but also from a host of European cities, especially Munich (see "Munich," in chapter 9). Between 6:10am and 11:40pm, trains arrive every 30 minutes from Vienna (trip time: 2½–3½ hr.); a one-way fare costs 32€ ($36.75). There are eight daily trains that come in from Innsbruck (2 hr.); a one-way fare costs 25€ ($28.75). Trains also arrive every 30 minutes from Munich (2½ hr.); a one-way ticket costs 22€ ($25.30).

The rail station has a currency exchange office and luggage-storage lockers. There's a tourist information office on Platform 2A of the Hauptbahnhof (© 0662/88987-340) that's open daily 8:30am to 8pm.

From the train station, buses depart to various parts of the city, including the **Altstadt (Old Town).** Or you can walk from the rail station to the Old Town in about 20 minutes.

INFORMATION ELSEWHERE IN THE CITY
The **Salzburg Information Office,** Mozartplatz 5 (© 0662/88987-330; www.salzburginfo.at; bus: 5, 6, or 51 out of the Hauptbahnhof), is open in summer daily 9am to 7pm and in the off-season Monday to Saturday 9am to 6pm. In addition to dispensing information, the office can book tour guides for you or make hotel reservations for a deposit of 10% of your total hotel bill (which will be credited), plus a 2.20€ ($2.50) booking fee.

GETTING AROUND
The city buses and trams provide quick, comfortable service through the city center from the Nonntal parking lot to Sigmundsplatz, the city-center parking

---

⌒Value A Discount Pass
The **Salzburg Card** is an excellent value that not only lets you use unlimited public transportation, but also acts as an admission ticket to the city's most important cultural sights. With the card you can visit Mozart's birthplace, the Hohensalzburg fortress, the Residenz gallery, the world-famous water fountain gardens at Hellbrunn, the Baroque Museum in the Mirabell garden, and the gala rooms in the Archbishop's Residence. The card is also good for sights outside of town, including the Hellbrunn Zoo, the open-air museum in Grossingmain, the salt mines of the Dürnberg, and the gondola trip at Untersberg. The card comes with a brochure with maps and sightseeing hints.

Cards are valid for 24, 48, and 72 hours and cost 20€ ($23), 28€ ($32.25), and 34€ ($39), respectively. Children up to 15 years of age receive a 50% discount. You can buy the pass at Salzburg tourist offices, hotels, tobacconists, and municipal offices.

Salzburg

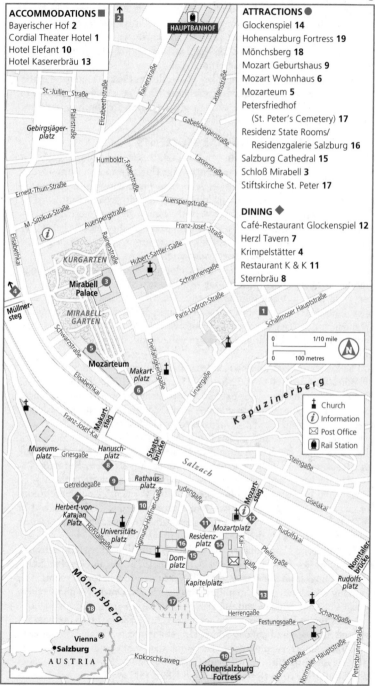

ACCOMMODATIONS ■
Bayerischer Hof **2**
Cordial Theater Hotel **1**
Hotel Elefant **10**
Hotel Kasererbräu **13**

ATTRACTIONS ●
Glockenspiel **14**
Hohensalzburg Fortress **19**
Mönchsberg **18**
Mozart Geburtshaus **9**
Mozart Wohnhaus **6**
Mozarteum **5**
Petersfriedhof
  (St. Peter's Cemetery) **17**
Residenz State Rooms/
  Residenzgalerie Salzburg **16**
Salzburg Cathedral **15**
Schloß Mirabell **3**
Stiftskirche St. Peter **17**

DINING ◆
Café-Restaurant Glockenspiel **12**
Herzl Tavern **7**
Krimpelstätter **4**
Restaurant K & K **11**
Sternbräu **8**

HAUPTBAHNHOF

St.-Julien_Straße
Plainstraße
Rainerstraße
Elizabethstraße
Lasterstraße
Gabelsbergerstraße
Gebirgsjäger-platz
Humboldt-Faberstraße
Lasserstraße
Ernest-Thun-Straße
M-Sittikus-Straße
Auerspergstraße
Auerspergstraße
Franz-Josef-Straße
Elisabethkai
KURGARTEN
Rainerstraße
Hubert-Sattler-Gaße
Schrannengaße
Mirabell Palace
MIRABELL-GARTEN
Pars-Lodron-Straße
Schallmoser Hauptstraße
Müllner-steg
Schwarzstraße
Dreifaltigkeitsgaße
Mozärteum
Makart-platz
Elisabethkai
Franz-Josef-Kai
Makart-steg
Staats-brücke
Linzergaße
Kapuzinerberg
0   1/10 mile
0   100 metres
N
Museums-platz
Griesgaße
Hanusch-platz
Salzach
Steingaße
Getreidegaße
Rathaus-platz
Judengaße
Mozart-steg
Giselakai
Herbert-von-Karajan Platz
Hofstallgaße
Sigmund-Haffner-Gaße
Universitäts-platz
Mozartplatz
Rudolfskai
Residenz-platz
Dom-platz
Kapitelplatz
Kai-Gaße
Pfeifergaße
Nonntaler-brücke
Rudolfs-platz
Mönchsberg
Herrengaße
Festungsgaße
Schanzlgaße
Nonnberggaße
Nonntaler Hauptstraße
Petersbrunnstraße
Kokoschkaweg
Hohensalzburg Fortress

† Church
ⓘ Information
✉ Post Office
🚉 Rail Station

Vienna ✱
● Salzburg
AUSTRIA

lot (the terminal and arrival points for many trams are at city lots). These buses and trams quickly shuttle passengers from the train station to all the major attractions within the city center, and also fan out to major sights in the environs. The one-ride fare is 1.70€ ($2) adults, .90€ ($1) children 6 to 15; those 5 and under travel free. Buses stop running at 11pm.

You'll find taxi stands scattered at key points all over the city center and in the suburbs. The **Salzburg Funktaxi-Vereinigung** (radio taxis) office is at Rainerstrasse 2 (© **0662/8111** to order a taxi in advance). Taxis are not cheap and fares start at 2.90€ ($3.35).

TOP ATTRACTIONS & SPECIAL MOMENTS

Most visitors head for the **Alstadt,** which lies on the left bank of the Salzach, the part stretching from the river to the Mönchsberg. This is a section of narrow streets (many from the Middle Ages) and slender houses, which stands in complete contrast with the town of magnificent buildings and large, airy squares constructed by the prince-archbishops, which lies between the Neutor and the Neugebäude.

The newer part of town is on the right bank of the Salzach, below the **Kapuzinerberg,** which is the right-bank counterpart of The Mönchsberg. This peak rises 2,090 feet, and is a lovely woodland.

The Mönchsberg itself, to the west of Hohensalzburg, is a mountain ridge slightly less than 2 miles (3.2km) long that rises over the Old Town.

A good place to begin touring the city is at **Mozartplatz,** with its outdoor cafes. From here, you can walk to the even larger **Residenzplatz,** where torchlight dancing is staged every year, along with outdoor performances, at the Salzburg Festival. While at Residenzplatz, you can visit one of the major attractions of Salzburg:

The Residenz State Rooms/Residenzgalerie Salzburg ✯✯, Residenzplatz 1 (© **0662/80-42-26-90** or 0662/84-04-51), an opulent palace, just north of the Domplatz, was the seat of the Salzburg prince-archbishops after they no longer felt the need of the protection afforded in the gloomy Hohensalzburg Fortress west of Mönchberg. The Residenz dates from 1120, but work on the series of palaces of the ruling church princes began in the late 1500s and continued until about 1782. The lavish rebuilding was originally ordered by Archbishop Wolfgang (usually called "Wolf") Dietrich. The17th-century **Residenz Fountain** ✯✯ is one of the largest and most impressive baroque fountains north of the Alps.

The child prodigy Mozart often played in the Residenz's Conference Room for guests. In 1867, Emperor Franz Joseph received Napoleon III here, and in 1871, Kaiser Wilhelm I was also a state guest at the Residenz. More than a dozen state rooms, each richly decorated, are open to the public.

On the second floor of the palace you can visit the **Residenzgalerie Salzburg** (© **0662/84-04-51**), an art gallery founded in 1923 that now displays European paintings from the 16th to the 19th centuries in 15 historical rooms. The paintings on exhibition are from the following schools: Dutch, Flemish, French, Italian, Austrian baroque, and Austrian 19th century.

Admission to the Residenz state rooms is 7.30€ ($8.50) adults, 4€ ($4.50) students 16 to 18 and seniors, 2.50€ ($3) children 6 to 15, and free for children 5 and under. A combined ticket to the state rooms and gallery is 7.25€ ($8.25). Admission to the Residenz Gallery is 4.70€ ($5.40) adults, 3.60€ ($4.25) students 16 to 18 and seniors, and 1.80€ ($2) for children 6 to 16. The palace is open January to April and November Monday to Friday 10am–5pm; May to October and December daily 10am to 4:30pm. Bus: 5 or 6.

Across from the Residenz stands the celebrated **Glockenspiel** 𝔄, Mozartplatz 1 (© **0662/80-42-27-84**), with its 35 bells. You can hear this 18th-century carillon at 7am, 11am, and 6pm daily. The idyllic way to hear the chimes is from one of the cafes lining the fringe of the Mozartplatz, while enjoying your favorite coffee or drink.

At the south side of the Residenzplatz, where it flows into the **Domplatz** (here you'll see a 1771 statue of the Virgin), stands **Salzburg Cathedral** *(Dom)* 𝔄, south side of Residenzplatz (© **0662/84-41-89**), world-renowned for its 4,000-pipe organ. When a previous edifice was destroyed by fire in 1598, Prince-Archbishop Wolf Dietrich followed up the start of work on the Residenz by commissioning construction of a new cathedral. His overthrow prevented the finishing of the project. His successor, Archbishop Markus Sittikus Count Hohenems, commissioned the Italian architect Santino Solari to build the present cathedral, which was consecrated in 1628 by Archbishop Paris Count Lodron.

Hailed as the "most perfect" Renaissance building in the Germanic countries, the cathedral has a marble façade and twin symmetrical towers. The mighty bronze doors were created in 1959 with the themes of Faith, Hope, and Love. The interior is in rich baroque style with elaborate frescoes, the most important of which, along with the altarpieces, were designed by Mascagni of Florence.

The treasures of the cathedral and a parade of the "arts and wonders" the archbishops collected in the 17th century are displayed in the **Dom Museum** (© **0662/84-41-89**), entered through the cathedral. You can also visit the **cathedral excavations,** which are accessible around the corner (to the left of the entrance to the Dom). Once here, you're treated to an exhibition of the ruins of the original foundation dating from ancient times.

Admission is free to the cathedral. Admission to the excavations is 2€ ($2.25) adults, .80€ (90¢) children 6 to 15, and free for children 5 and under. Admission to the museum is 5€ ($5.75) adults, 1.50€ ($1.75) children. Hours for the Cathedral are daily 8am–7pm (to 6pm in winter). Hours for the excavations are Easter to mid-October, Wednesday to Sunday 9am to 5pm (closed mid-Oct to Easter). Hours for the museum are Wednesday to Sunday 10am-5pm, Sunday 1 to 6pm. Closed November to April. Bus: 1, 3, or 5.

Stiftskirche St. Peter 𝔄𝔄, St.-Peter-Bezirk (© **0662/84-45-78**), is the church of St. Peter's Abbey and Benedictine Monastery, founded in 696 by St. Rupert, whose tomb is here. The church, once a Romanesque basilica with three aisles, was completely overhauled in the 17th and 18th centuries in an elegant baroque style. The west door dates from 1240. The church is richly adorned with art treasures, especially altar paintings by Kremser Schmidt. The Salzburg Madonna in the left chancel is from the early 15th century. The church is free to visit and is open daily from 9am to 6pm. Bus: 5, 6, or 55.

St. Peter's Cemetery 𝔄𝔄 *(Petersfriedhof,* in German), St-Peter-Bezirk (© **0662/84-45-78-0**), is located at the stone wall that merges into the rock called Mönchsberg. Many of the aristocratic families of Salzburg are buried here as well as many other noted persons, including Nannerl Mozart, sister of the composer. Four years older than her better-known brother, Nannerl was also an exceptionally gifted musician. You can see the Romanesque Chapel of the Holy Cross and St. Margaret's Chapel, dating from the 15th century. It's also possible to take a tour through the early Christian catacombs in the rock above the church cemetery. Admission to the cemetery is free; the catacombs cost 1€ ($1.15) adults, .60€ (70¢) children. The cemetery is open May to September daily 10:30am to 5pm; October to April daily 10:30am to 3:30pm. Bus: 1.

Moments **The Hills Are Alive . . .**

The original **"Sound of Music Tour"** offered by **Salzburg Panorama Tours,** Mirabellplatz (© **0662/88-32-11-0;** www.panoramatours.at), combines a Salzburg city tour with an excursion to the lake district and other places where the 1965 film with Julie Andrews was shot. An English-speaking guide shows you not only the highlights from the film, but also historical and architectural landmarks in Salzburg and parts of the Salzkammergut countryside. The 4-hour tour, offered daily, can be booked at the **bus terminal** at Mirabellplatz/St. Andrä Kirche (© **0662/87-40-29)**, a short walk from the main train station. The cost is 33€ ($38) for adults and 17€ ($20) for children ages 4 to 12.

Hohensalzburg Fortress 🏰🏰, Mönchsberg 34 (© **0662/84-24-30-11)**, stronghold of the ruling prince-archbishops before they moved "downtown" to the Residenz, towers 400 feet above the Salzach River on a rocky Dolomite ledge. The massive fortress crowns Festungsberg and literally dominates Salzburg. Work on Hohensalzburg began in 1077 and was not finished until 1681, during which time many builders of widely different tastes and purposes had a hand in the construction. This, the largest completely preserved castle left in central Europe, has bastions for the cannons needed in the strife-torn Middle Ages, when the scent of sanctity was often mixed with the odor of gunpowder. Functions of defense and state were combined in this fortress for 6 centuries.

The elegant state apartments once lived in by the prince-archbishops and their courts are on display. Coffered ceilings and the intricately constructed ironwork are of interest. See, in particular, an early-16th-century porcelain stove in the Golden Room.

Guided tours are available; a combined ticket of admission and tour costs 6€ ($7) for adults and 3.50€ ($4) for children. To get here, you can hike up one of the paths or lanes leading to the fortress, or you can walk from Kapitelplatz by way of Festungsgasse or from the Mönchsberg via the Schartentor. You can also take the funicular from Festungsgasse (© **0662/84-26-82)** at the station behind the cathedral. You can purchase a ticket in advance to the museum inclusive of the funicular ride for 5.50€ ($6.25) adults and 3€ ($3.50) children; or a ticket inclusive of admission, funicular ride, and guided tour, priced at 8€ ($9.25) adults, 4€ ($4.50) children.

On the grounds of Hohensalzburg, the **Burgmuseum** is distinguished mainly by its collection of medieval art. Plans and prints tracing the growth of Salzburg are on exhibit, as well as instruments of torture and many Gothic artifacts. The Salzburger Stier, or Salzburg Bull, an open-air barrel organ built in 1502, plays melodies by Mozart and his friend Haydn in daily concerts following the Glockenspiel chimes. The **Rainer Museum** has displays of arms and armor. The beautiful late Gothic **St. George's Chapel,** dating from 1501, is graced with marble reliefs of the apostles.

Admission to the fortress and museums is 3.60€ ($4.25) adults, 2€ ($2.25) children 6 to 19, free for children 5 and under. A family ticket costs 16€ ($18.50). It's open October to March daily 9:30am to 5pm; April to September daily 9am to 6pm.

West of Hohensalzburg Fortress is **Mönchsberg.** This heavily forested ridge extending for some 1½ miles (2.4 km) above the old town has fortifications dating from the 15th century. Several **panoramic vistas** ✴✴✴ can be seen from it, and a lovely view of Salzburg is possible from Mönchsberg Terrace. Express elevators leave from Gstättengasse 13 (ⓒ **0662/448-06-285**) daily from 9am to 11pm. Round-trip fare costs 2.40€ ($2.75) for adults and 1.25€ ($1.45) for children 6 to 15. Free 5 and under.

Of course, one of the reasons many music fans visit Salzburg is not only to hear the composer's splendid music but also to visit sights associated with his short and turbulent life, including **Mozart's Geburtshaus** ✴ (his birthplace), Getreidegasse 9 (ⓒ **0662/84-43-13**), a typical old burgher's house. Leopold Mozart lived on the third floor of this structure from 1747 to 1773, and it was here that Wolfgang Amadeus was born on January 27, 1756, a date all Salzburgers know. The apartment contains a number of mementos. The child prodigy Mozart, who began composing at the age of 4, wrote his early works here, and you can see the small violin on which he played and his childhood spinet. Admission is 5.50€ ($6.25) adults, 4.50€ ($5.25) students, and 1.50€ ($1.75) children. It's open daily 9am to 5pm (July–Aug 9am–7pm).

It's also possible to visit **Mozart Wohnhaus** ✴, Marktplatz 8 (ⓒ **0662/ 874-22-740**), with its multimedia exhibits. This residence of the Mozart family from 1773 to 1787 was bombed in World War II, rebuilt, and re-opened in 1996. All that remains of the original are the entrance and the **Tanzmeistersaal (dance master's hall).** Admission is 5.50€ ($6.35) adults, 4.50€ ($5.20) students, 1.50€ ($1.75) children. The museum is open June to September daily 9am to 5pm; October to May daily 10am to 5pm.

Schloss Mirabell (Mirabell Palace) ✴, Rainerstrasse (ⓒ **0662/80-72-0**), was built originally as a luxurious private residence called Altenau. Prince-Archbishop Wolfgang Dietrich had it constructed in 1606 for his mistress and the mother of his children, Salome Alt. Not much remains of the original grand structure. Lukas von Hildebrandt rebuilt the *schloss* in the first quarter of the 18th century, and it was modified after a great fire in 1818. The official residence of the mayor of Salzburg is now in the palace, which looks like a smaller

⟅Moments   A Baroque Fantasy Garden

You can live out a baroque fantasy by wandering through the **Mirabell Gardens** ✴ on the city's right bank. Fischer von Erlach laid out what are among the finest baroque gardens in Austria, evocative of a bygone era. Today, these grounds are a public park studded with reflecting pools and enough classical statuary to please a Renaissance pope. These marble statues make Mirabell Gardens virtually an open-air museum.

As you wander in the gardens at your leisure, be sure to visit the **bastion,** with fantastic marble baroque dwarfs and other figures, by the Pegasus Fountain in the lavish garden west of Schloss Mirabell. From the gardens you'll have an excellent view of Hohensalzburg Fortress. There's also a natural theater. The gardens are open daily from 7am to 8pm; in summer, free band concerts are held Wednesday at 8:30pm and Sunday at 10:30am.

edition of the Tuileries in Paris. The ceremonial marble "angel staircase" with sculptured cherubs, carved by Raphael Donner in 1726, leads to the *Marmorsaal,* a marble and gold hall used for concerts and weddings. Candlelit chamber music concerts are staged here. Admission is free but it is not open for general visits. The Staircase hours are daily from 8am to 6pm.

WHERE TO STAY & DINE

A short distance from the medieval core of town, **Cordial Theater Hotel,** Schallmooser Hauptstrasse 13 (✆ **0662/8816-810**), is one of the city's best moderately priced hotels. Located in a renovated 19th-century building, the 58-room hotel is stylish and comfortable; its well-furnished bedrooms, each named for a famous composer or writer, are spread across three floors. Many singers and musicians, especially at the time of the Salzburg Festival, make this hotel their address. Room rates run 95€ to 180€ ($109–$207) double and include breakfast. Bus: 29.

The 31-room **Hotel Elefant,** Sigmund-Haffner-Gasse 4 (✆ **0662/84-33-97**), is located on a tranquil alley off bustling Getreidegasse, and is housed in one of the city's most ancient structures, dating back some 7 centuries. Bedrooms rest under high ceilings and are traditionally and comfortably furnished. Even if you don't stay here, you might want to patronize one of the Elefant's two popular restaurants, one of which is in a converted wine cellar dating from the 17th century. Room rates run 152€ to 168€ ($175–$193) double and include a buffet breakfast. Bus: 1, 2, 5, 6, or 51.

Lying a few blocks from the Dom (cathedral), **Hotel Kasererbräu,** Kaigasse 33 (✆ **0662/84-24-450;** www.kasererbraeu.at), is a government-rated four-star hotel constructed on Roman walls in the center of the city. It has more style than many of its competitors in that its rooms feature baroque and Biedermeier furnishings, often resting on Asian carpeting. Double rooms are generally spacious and comfortably furnished. Some units are large enough to be classified as apartments, suitable for 2 to 4 persons. Double rates are 109€ to 202€ ($125–$232) and include breakfast. Apartments cost 210€ to 298€ ($242–$343) depending on the number of occupants. Bus: 55.

Bayerischer Hof, Kaiserschüzenstrasse 1 (✆ **0662/46-97-00;** www.bayerischer.com), is a worthy choice and convenient choice for rail travelers as it lies only 2 blocks from the Hauptbahnhof. The 34-room hotel is tastefully decorated in a traditional style, and its midsize bedrooms are most comfortable. This longtime favorite is mainly known for its three dining rooms, which feature old-fashioned and exceedingly good Austrian cooking. Room rates cost 85€ to 195€ ($98–$224) double and include breakfast.

A dining favorite, the **Herzl Tavern** 🍴🍴, Karajanplatz 7 (✆ **0662/808-48-89**), stands next door to the city's most glamorous hotel, Goldener Hirsch, and is entered on Karajanplatz in the center of the city. It's especially popular during the Salzburg Festival, drawing some of the leading performers with its finely tuned take on Austrian and Viennese specialties. Come here for old-fashioned favorites such as roast pork with dumplings and game stew in autumn. Main courses run 10.20€ to 20€ ($11.75–$23). Bus: 10, 29.

Restaurant K & K, Waagplatz 2 (✆ **0662/84-21-56**), near the Salzburg Cathedral, offers four floors of atmospheric and intimate dining decorated with marble, candlelight, and various antiques. The menu features a series of well-prepared Austrian and international dishes, ranging from traditional to modern. Service is formal and polite. The wine list is impressive, or you can

Moments **Cafe Society**

Its location on one of Salzburg's most colorful squares has made **Café-Restaurant Glockenspiel** 🎻, Mozartplatz 2 (📞 **0662/84-14-03-0**; bus: 55), the most popular in the city. The 100 tables with armchairs in front of the cafe are perfect for people-watching. If the day is warm enough, you might want to spend an afternoon here, particularly when there's live chamber music. The cafe's interior is dominated by a sweet tooth's dream—a glass case filled with every highly caloric delight west of Vienna. The rooms on either side of the display contain big, arched windows overlooking the statue in the square. The tastefully decorated restaurant upstairs has a big balcony overlooking Salzburg, and serves regional specialties. Many people, however, come just for the drinks and pastries. Try the Maria Theresia, which contains orange liqueur. In summer, it's open daily 9am to midnight (food served to 11pm); the rest of the year, daily 9am to 8pm (food served to 6pm). Closed the second and third weeks of November and January.

retreat to the cellar for a beer. Main courses cost 10€ to 21€ ($11.50–$24.25). Bus: 5, 6, or 51.

With a history dating back to 1548, **Krimpelstätter,** Müllner Hauptstrasse 31 (📞 **0662/43-22-74**), is awash with stone columns, heavy timbers, and vaulted ceilings, blossoming outside into a flower-filled beer garden in summer. Head to the *gastizimmer* section for beer or wine drinking, or else, if you want more formal service, opt for three intimate dining rooms upstairs. Some of the best specialties of the Land Salzburg region are served here; expect wild game in autumn or such longtime local favorites as cream of goose soup and beef stew with buttery noodles. Main courses cost 6.60€ to 14.50€ ($7.75–$16.75).

The Austro-Hungarian army used to eat at **Sternbräu,** Griessegasse 23 (📞 **0662/84-21-40**), located in the Old Town with plenty of space for every hungry diner or beer drinker. A hearty, Austrian cuisine is served nightly in a series of eight rooms, which overflow into a beer garden in summer that's shaded by chestnut trees. The food is more hearty and filling than refined, but that—and the brew served here—is why the place is so popular. Look for some good-tasting daily specials. Main courses cost 6.50€ to 16€ ($7.50–$18.50); fixed-price menus 12€ to 16€ ($13.75–$18.50).

SHOPPING

Good buys in Salzburg include souvenirs of land Salzburg, dirndls, lederhosen, petit point, and all types of sports gear. **Getreidegasse** is a main shopping thoroughfare, but you'll also find some intriguing little shops on the **Residenzplatz.** Most stores in Salzburg open at 9am and stay open until 6pm. Note that a number of them, especially the smaller places, take a 1- or 2-hour break for lunch. Stores also close down on Saturday afternoon and all day on Sunday.

Owned by the same family for four generations, **Jahn-Markl,** Residenzplatz 3 (📞 **0662/84-26-10**), is a small and elegant store with a forest-green facade trimmed with brass and wrought-iron detailing. Located in the center of the Old Town, it carries lederhosen for all sizes, leather skirts, and a full line of traditional Austrian coats and blazers.

Salzburger Heimatwerk, Am Residenzplatz 9 (© **0662/84-41-10**), is one of the best places in town to buy Austrian handcrafts. It's a dignified stone building in the least crowded section of the Residenzplatz, with a discreet (and hard to see) sign announcing its location. Items for sale include Austrian silver and garnet jewelry, painted boxes, candles, woodcarvings, copper and brass ceramics, tablecloths, and patterns for cross-stitched samplers in Alpine designs.

Wiener Porzellanmanufaktur Augarten Gesellschaft, Alter Markt 11 (© **0662/84-07-14**), is the premier shop in Salzburg for Austrian porcelain, specializing in Augarten ware. Its most famous item, which it still turns out, is a black-and-white coffee set created by architect/designer Josef Hoffmann.

NIGHTLIFE

It's said that there's a musical event—often a Mozart concert—staged virtually every night in Salzburg. To find out what's playing, visit the **Salzburg Tourist Office,** Mozartplatz 5 (© **0662/88987-330**), where you can get a free copy of *Offizieller Wochenspiegel,* a monthly pamphlet listing all major and many minor local cultural events. The annual Mozart Week is in January.

All the premier ballet, opera, and musical concerts are performed at **Festspielhaus,** Hofstallgasse 1 (© **0662/8045**), a world-famous citadel of Salzburg culture. *Grosses Haus* (Big House), the larger venue, seats 2,170. *Kleines Haus* (Small House) seats 1,323, which isn't that small. Instead of going directly to the Festspielhaus, you can purchase tickets in advance at the box office at Waagplatz 1A (© **0662/84-53-46**), close to the tourist office, Monday to Friday 8am to 6pm. Most performances begin at 7:30pm, although there are matinees from time to time at 11am and 3pm. Tickets cost 15€ to 350€ ($17.25–$403) (the higher price is for the best seats at the Salzburg Festival); average but good seats run 35€ to 80€ ($40.25–$92). Bus: 1, 5, or 6.

Festung Hohensalzburg, Mönchsberg 34 (© **0662/84-24-30-11**), stages concerts within the Hohensalzburg Fortress. Here, in historic and dramatic settings, you're likely to hear heavy doses of Mozart and, to a lesser degree, works by Schubert, Brahms, and Beethoven. Mid-May to mid-October, performances are likely to be held at 8 or 8:30pm every night of the week. The rest of the year, they're presented most (but not all) nights, with occasional weeklong breaks, usually at 7:30pm. The box office for the events is at Adlgasser Weg 22 (© **0662/82-58-58**). To reach the fortress, take the funicular from Festungsgasse. Tickets range in price from 29€ to 36€ ($33.25–$41.50).

Mozarteum, Schwarzstrasse 26 and Mirabellplatz 1 (© **066/87-31-54**), on the right bank of the Salzach River, near Mirabell Gardens, is Salzburg's major music and concert hall. All the big orchestra concerts, as well as organ recitals and chamber-music evenings, are presented here. In the old building at Schwarzstrasse, there are two concert halls, *Grosser Saal* and the *Wiener Saal.* In the newer building on Mirabellplatz, concert halls include the Grosses Studio, the Leopold-Mozart Saal, and the Paumgartner Studio. It's also a music school, and you can ask about free events staged by the students. The box office is open Monday to Thursday 9am to 2pm and Friday 9am to 4pm. Performances are at 11am or 7:30pm. Tickets cost 8€ to 185€ ($9.25–$213); the best seats run 90€ to 185€ ($104–$213). Bus: 1, 5, 6, or 51.

Despite the availability of ticket outlets in any of the below-mentioned theaters, many visitors head for the larger umbrella ticket agency that is affiliated with the city of Salzburg. Located adjacent to Salzburg's main tourist office, at Mozartplatz 5, it's called the **Salzburger Ticket Office** (© **0662/84-03-10**). Open Monday to Saturday 9am to 6pm (to 7pm in midsummer) and Sunday

9am to noon, it's the single best source for cultural information and ticket sales in town, usually with tickets to virtually every musical event in the city on sale—except, of course, to those events that are sold out long in advance.

Of course, the big event in town is the **Salzburg Festival** (see p. 72). Festival tickets are in great demand, and should be secured as early as possible. In general, drama tickets cost 25€ to 180€ ($28.75–$207), with opera tickets going from 45€ ($51.75) and ranging upward to 350€ ($403). For festival details, contact the Salzburg Festival Box office, Hofstallgasse 1, A-5020 Salzburg (© **0662/ 8045-579;** www.salzburgfestival.at).

Outside the cultural venues, the most entertaining evenings in Salzburg are at the **Augustiner Bräustübl,** Augustinergasse 4 (© **0662/43-12-46**), the city's most famous beer garden, taking its name from the old Augustinian monastery founded here. Its beer garden is the most popular place to be in Salzburg in summer, with guests retreating inside into several rooms in winter. This place has been known to house 2,200 drinkers and revelers on its busiest nights. A full liter begins at 5.40€ ($6.25), and you can enjoy it Monday to Friday 3 to 11pm and Saturday and Sunday 2:30 to 11pm.

Another place where the suds flow is **Salzburger Altstadtkeller,** Rudolfskai 27 (© **0662/84-96-88**). The setting is a medieval cellar set beneath the Altstadt Radisson Hotel, immediately adjacent to the banks of the river. Don't come here expecting fine dining: What you'll get is a short list of Austrian-style platters (Wiener schnitzel, tafelspitz, and so on), and a reverberating roster of musical acts that include swing, Latino, jazz, and blues. Every Thursday, the acts get more nostalgic and folkloric, as the stage is turned over to bands specializing in Austrian or Bavarian "evergreen" or folkloric music. Music plays from between 9:15pm and 1am, with guests then lingering over their drinks for at least another hour. There's no cover charge, but a half-liter of beer costs 3.10€ ($3.50). Main courses range from 3€ to 11€ ($3.50–$12.75), and service is Tuesday to Saturday 7pm to 2:30am.

4 Innsbruck ★★

Rivaling Vienna and Salzburg for the title of Austria's most beautiful city, Innsbruck (which means "bridge over the Inn," the Inn being the river that flows through the city) is the capital of Tyrol, one of the world's greatest Alpine playgrounds. The city is the major rail transportation hub for western Austria and a bustling arrival point in both winter and summer. In fair weather, visitors arrive at Innsbruck's rail station to hike through and explore the Alps; in winter (which many innkeepers consider high season), thousands upon thousands flock here to get to the winter ski resorts of the Tyrol, for Innsbruck is the rail gateway to such resorts as Seefeld, Zell am Ziller, and Kitzbühel. It's also a convenient stopover for those doing a grand rail tour of Europe, as trains from Innsbruck reach the German border to the north in 45 minutes or arrive at the Italian frontier to the south in only 30 minutes.

For the rail traveler, Innsbruck is a convenient overnight stopover because much of the city, whose beautiful historic areas are loaded with Gothic, Renaissance, and baroque buildings, can be seen in a day, though 2 would be better. And though it's not cheap, it's less expensive than Salzburg.

STATION INFORMATION
GETTING FROM THE AIRPORT TO THE TRAIN STATION
Less important than Vienna and Salzburg, Innsbruck is a gateway for many air passengers who prefer to begin their rail journey of Austria in the Tyrolean Alps.

Innsbruck's airport, **Flughafen Innsbruck-Kranebitten,** Fürstenweg 180 (© **0512/22525;** www.Innsbruck-airport.com), is 2 miles (3km) west of the city. Though there is no direct service from North America, there is regularly scheduled air service from Amsterdam, Frankfurt, London, Paris, and Zurich. **Tyrolean Airlines** (© **0512/2222**) serves the airport exclusively, although some foreign carriers will charter flights. The best gateways from North America are Frankfurt and Zurich.

There is no direct rail service from the airport into town. From the airport, bus F leads to the train station, which is in the exact center of town. Tickets cost 1.50€ ($1.75). A taxi ride takes about 10 minutes and costs 8€ ($9.25) and up, depending on traffic.

STATION INFORMATION

Innsbruck is connected to all the major cities of Europe by international railway links. At least 5 trains arrive daily from Munich (trip time: 3 hr.) and 8 daily trains from Salzburg (1 hr.). Travel time here from Vienna, ranges from 5 hours to about 6 hours, depends on which train you take.

Most trains arrive at the main railway station, the **Hauptbahnhof,** Südtiroler Platz. Call © **05/1717** for rail information.

There is a **Train Information Office** at the station open daily from 7am to 9:30pm, but it makes seat reservations only from 8am to 7:30pm. There is also a small tourist information kiosk inside the station, but because the station is in the center of town, it's best to use the main tourist information center we discuss below. It's larger than the one in the station, is better equipped, and will make hotel reservations for you.

Next to the information office is a baggage store area, which charges 2€ ($2.25) for 24 hours.

INFORMATION ELSEWHERE IN THE CITY

Innsbruck-Information, Burggraben 3 (© **0512/56-20-00** or 0512/53-56-30), is open Monday to Friday 8am to 6pm. Here you can stock up on printed information about Innsbruck (and other parts of Tyrol) and ask questions about virtually any feature of the town. Staff members can also arrange city tours, sell tickets to concerts and cultural events, and will make hotel reservations for free if you notify them at least a day in advance. Same-day hotel reservations carry a surcharge of 4€ ($4.50).

GETTING AROUND

A network of 3 **tram** and 25 **bus lines** covers all of Innsbruck and its close environs, and both systems use the same tickets. Single tickets in the central area cost 1.60€ ($1.75), and a booklet of four tickets goes for 5€ ($5.75). The tram is called either *Strassenbahn* or *Trambahn.* On the left bank of the Inn, the main tram and bus arteries are Museumstrasse and Mariahilfstrasse. On the right bank, trams and buses aren't routed into the pedestrian zone, but to their main stop in Marktgraben.

For information about various routes, call the **Innsbrucker Verkehrsbetriebe** (© **0512/530-7102**). Most tickets can be purchased at the Innsbruck tourist office, tobacco shops, and automated vending machines. *Tageskarte* (day passes) cost 3.20€ ($3.75) and are only available from the tourist information office, tobacco shops, and cafes.

Postal Buses heading for all parts of the Tyrol leave from the Central Bus Station *(Autobushof),* adjacent to the Hauptbahnhof on Sterzinger Strasse. The

Innsbruck

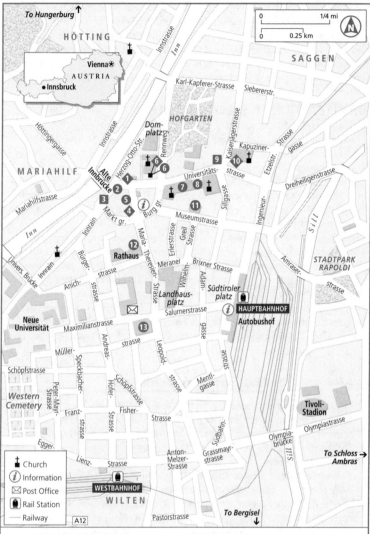

| Church |
| Information |
| Post Office |
| Rail Station |
| Railway |

ACCOMMODATIONS ■
Hotel Grauer Bär **9**
Hotel Innsbruck **3**

DINING ◆
Cáfe Sacher **6**
Hirschen-Stuben **4**
Restaurant Goldener Adler **1**
Restaurant Schwarzer Adler **10**

ATTRACTIONS ●
Annasäule (St. Anna's Column) **12**
Goldenes Dachl **2**
Herzog-Friedrich-Strasse **5**
Hofburg **6**
Hofkirche **7**
Tiroler Landesmuseum Ferdinandeum **11**
Tiroler Volkskunst-Museum
  (Tyrol Museum of Popular Art) **8**
Triumphpforte **13**

station is open Monday to Friday 7:30am to 6pm and Saturday 7am to 1pm. For information about bus schedules, call ℭ **0512/58-51-55.**

Taxi stands are scattered at strategic points throughout the city, or you can call a radio car (ℭ **0512/5311**). For a nostalgic ride, you can hire a horse-drawn carriage *(Fiaker)* from a spot adjacent to the **Tiroler Landestheater,** Rennweg. Clip-clopping along the cobblestone pavement costs around 25€ ($28.75) for 30 minutes.

TOP ATTRACTIONS & SPECIAL MOMENTS

Allow at least 4 hours to walk through and explore the Altstadt or Old Town of Innsbruck, heading up the main street, **Maria-Theresien-Strasse** 🞯, which runs north to south and is the main street of this Tyrolean city. It's about a ¼-mile (.4km) stroll from the Hauptbahnhof. People-watching is a major pastime along this street, especially when locals wear the characteristic Tyrolean dress, perhaps with a feather in their cap or hat. The shop-flanked thoroughfare is lined with many 17th- and 18th-century houses that characterize the architecture of the region.

Standing at the southern end of this broad boulevard is the **Triumphpforte** or Triumphal Arch, modeled after a similar one that stands in Rome. Dating from 1765, it was ordered constructed by Maria Theresa. The empress wanted to honor the marriage of her son, the future Emperor Leopold II, to a Spanish princess, and also wanted a monument to honor her late husband, Franz I.

If you head north from the arch, still staying on Maria-Theresien-Strasse, you'll reach **Annasäule** or St. Ann's Column commemorating the date of July 26, 1703, the birth of St. Anne—when Bavarian invaders retreated during

---

⟮*Moments*⟯ The Most Beautiful Spot in Tyrol

The **Hungerburg** 🞯🞯 mountain plateau at 2,860 feet is the most beautiful spot in Tyrol, affording the best view of Innsbruck, especially on summer nights when much of the city, including fountains and historic buildings, is brightly lit. Some of the most scenic hotels in the Innsbruck area are here.

You can take the **cable railway (Hungerburgbahn),** which departs daily about four times an hour 8am to 6pm, then about every 30 minutes until 10:30pm; one also departs at 11pm Friday and Saturday night. The departure point lies about half a mile (.8km) east of the center of Innsbruck, at the corner of Rennweg and Kettenbrücke. (It's accessible from Innsbruck's center via tram 1 or bus C.) Round-trip fares are 4.20€ ($4.75) for adults and 2.10€ ($2.50) for children. For schedules and information, call ℭ **0512/58-61-58.**

Once you reach the plateau, you can progress even farther into the Alpine wilds via the **Nordkette cable railway (Nordkettenbahn)** (ℭ **0512/29-33-44**). It will take you up to the Seegrube and the Hafelekar (7,655 ft.) for a sweeping view of Alpine peaks and glaciers. This is the starting point of high mountain walks and climbing expeditions. The cable railway runs daily (except Apr and Nov when it's closed) every hour 8am to 6pm. A round-trip ticket from Innsbruck to Hafelekar costs 21.30€ ($24.50) for adults and 10.70€ ($12.25) children.

Note: None of the railways above are covered by railpasses.

the War of the Spanish Succession in that same year. The column stands in front of the Rathaus or Town Hall dating from the 19th century. On top of this Corinthian Column stands a statue of the Virgin Mary on a crescent moon, with satellite statues of Saints Cassianus, Virgilius, Anna, and George at the base.

Close to Annasäule, the street narrows and turns into **Herzog-Friedrich-Strasse** ✸, which cuts right into the **Altstadt** ✸✸✸, the historic medieval quarter of Innsbruck. This arcaded Gothic quarter is full of rich architectural details, including bulbous belfries and intricately designed wrought-iron signs often painted gold.

At the end of Herzog-Friedrich-Strasse stands the symbol of Innsbruck, the **Goldenes Dachl** ✸✸✸, or Little Golden Roof. It's a three-story balcony on a house in the Old Town, the late Gothic oriels capped with 2,657 gold-plated tiles. It was constructed at the dawn of the 16th century for Emperor Maximilian I to serve as a royal box where he could sit and enjoy tournaments in the square below. It was built in honor of Maximilian's second marriage, to Bianca Maria Sforza of Milan, but the emperor, unwilling to alienate allies gained by his first marriage to Maria of Burgundy (she died), had himself painted on his balcony between the two women. He is, however, looking at the new wife, Bianca.

Farther north stands the **Hofburg** ✸, Rennweg 1 (✆ **0512/58-71-86**), the 15th-century imperial palace of Emperor Maximilian I, rebuilt in rococo style in the 18th century on orders of Maria Theresa. Later it was to hold sad memories for the empress, as it was here that her husband died in 1765. The palace, the exterior of which is colored Maria Theresa ochre (a yellow that the empress favored) and flanked by a set of domed towers, is a fine example of baroque secular architecture. The structure has four wings and a two-story *Riesensaal* (Giant's Hall), painted in white and gold and filled with portraits of the Hapsburgs. The rooms recall the power and heyday of that ruling family. You can wander at will through the rooms, but if you want to participate in a guided tour, the staff conducts two a day, at 11am and 2pm, in a multilingual format that includes English. Each tour lasts 30 to 45 minutes and costs 2.18€ ($2.50). Admission is 5.45€ ($6.25) for adults, 3.65€ ($4.25) students, 1.10€ ($1.25) children under 12. Open daily 9am to 4:30pm. Tram: 1 or 3.

The Gothic-style **Hofkirche,** Universitätsstrasse 2 (✆ **0512/58-43-02**), was built in 1553 by Ferdinand I. Its most important treasure is the cenotaph of Maximilian I, an elegant marble sarcophagus glorifying the Roman Empire. The tomb, a great feat of the German Renaissance style of sculpture, has 28 bronze 16th-century statues of Maximilian's real and legendary ancestors and relatives surrounding the kneeling emperor on the cenotaph, with 24 marble reliefs on the sides depicting scenes from his life. Three of the statues are based on designs by Dürer. Tyrol's national hero, Andrea Hofer, is also entombed here. The Hofkirche has a lovely Renaissance porch, plus a nave and a trio of aisles in the Gothic style.

The Tiroler Volkskunst–Museum (see below) is reached through the same entrance way.

The **Hofgarten,** a public park containing lakes and many shade trees, including weeping willows, lies north of Rennweg, across the street from the church. Concerts are often presented at the Kunstpavillon in the garden in summer. You can purchase a combined ticket to the church and the Tiroler Volkskunst–Museum for 6.50€ ($7.50). Admission to Hofkirche is 5€ ($5.75) for adults, 1.50€ ($1.75) students or children, free for children 5 and under. Hours are Monday to Saturday 9am to 5pm. Tram: 1 or 3.

Moments **The Count of Tyrol's Renaissance Palace**

Schloss Ambras 🕯🕯, Schloss Strasse 20 (✆ **0512/348-446**), is a Renaissance palace, 2 miles (3km) southeast of the heart of Innsbruck on the edge of the Mittelgebirgsterrace. It was built by Archduke Ferdinand II of Austria, count of Tyrol, in the 16th century. It's divided into a **lower** and an **upper castle** set in the remains of a medieval fortress. This was Ferdinand's favorite residence and the center of his court's cultural life. The lower castle was planned and constructed by the archduke as a museum for his various collections, including arms and armor, art, and books, all of which can be seen today. The **Spanish Hall,** one of the first German Renaissance halls, was built to house the portraits of the counts of Tyrol.

The upper castle has a small but fine collection of medieval sculpture, black-and-white frescoes on the wall of the inner courtyard, and a portrait gallery hung with dynastic paintings from the 14th to the 18th century. In some of the living rooms you can see 16th-century frescoes, late-16th-century wooden ceilings, and 17th-century furniture. Admission is 7.50€ ($8.65) adults, 4.50€ ($5.20) students and children. A guided tour costs an extra 2€ ($2.30). The castle's hours are April to October, daily 10am to 5pm. December to March, it's open daily 2 to 5pm. It's closed in November.

To reach the castle, take tram 3 or 6 from Innsbruck's Hauptbahnhof. The castle also maintains its own shuttle bus, a white-sided vehicle with the words SCHLOSS AMBRAS written on its sides, which departs from a point adjacent to the Landhaus on the Maria-Theresien-Strasse every hour during the palace's open hours. Service runs less frequently December to April. Round-trip fares cost 5.50€ ($6.35) adults and 3€ ($3.45) children.

Tiroler Volkskunst–Museum (Tyrol Museum of Popular Art) 🕯🕯, Universitätsstrasse 2 (✆ **0521/58-43-02**), is in the Neues Stift, or New Abbey, adjoining the Hofkirche on its eastern side. The abbey dates from the 16th and 18th centuries. The museum contains one of the largest and most impressive collections extant of the artifacts of life in Tyrol, ranging from handcrafts to religious and profane popular art, furniture, and national costumes. The three floors house a collection of Tyrolean mangers, or Christmas cribs, some from the 18th century. The *stuben* (the finest rooms) are on the upper floors. Displays include a range of styles from Gothic to Renaissance to baroque, as well as a collection of models of typical Tyrolean houses. Admission is 5€ ($5.75) for adults, 1.50€ ($1.75) children and students. Hours are Monday to Saturday 9am to 5:30pm, Sunday 9am to noon. Tram: 1 or 3.

Tiroler Landesmuseum Ferdinandeum (Ferdinandeum Tyrol Museum) 🕯, Museumstrasse 15 (✆ **0512/59-489**), has a celebrated gallery of Flemish and Dutch masters. This museum also traces the development of popular art in the Tyrolean country, with highlights from the Gothic period. You'll also see the original bas-reliefs used in designing the Goldenes Dachl. Admission is 8€ ($9.25) for adults, 4€ ($4.50) students and children. Hours are May to

September daily 10am to 5pm, October to April Tuesday to Saturday 10am to noon and 2 to 5pm, and Sunday 10am to 1pm. Tram: 1 or 3.

WHERE TO STAY & DINE

In the heart of Innsbruck, close to the major attractions, the 189-room **Hotel Grauer Bär**, Universitätsstrasse 7 (© **0512/59240;** www.innsbruck-hotels.at), is a government-rated 4-star hotel and a long-established favorite. Even many Tyroleans stay here on visits to Innsbruck, as they are drawn to the "Gray Bear's" midsize bedrooms, which are immaculately kept and comfortably furnished. One of the town's best restaurants is installed in a "Stube" (beer cellar) here, and other facilities include a fitness center. Room rates run 118€ to 155€ ($136–$178) double and include breakfast.

Hotel Innsbruck, Innrain 3 (© **0512/59-868;** www.hotelinnsbruck.com), is a modern 114-room property, whose windows open onto the Inn River. Constructed on the foundations of an ancient town hall, the bedrooms come in a range of sizes, the preferred units being the "dormer chambers" on the upper floor, each opening onto vistas of the Old Town. The atmospheric hotel is one of the best equipped in the area, offering a typically Tyrolean restaurant with good food and such extras as nonsmoking rooms and accommodations for those with limited mobility. Rates run 110€ to 185€ ($127–$213) double and include buffet breakfast.

Most short-term visitors prefer to dine at traditional Alpine, Tyrolean restaurants such as the **Restaurant Goldener Adler**, Herzog-Friedrich-Strasse 6 (© **0512/57-11-11**). Beautifully decorated, the restaurant is of equal appeal to visitors and locals alike, who are attracted to its robust, hearty mountain cuisine. Come here if you like all those good things your doctor warned you about, such as herb-enriched spinach dumplings in cream sauce served with *Zopfbraten,* an age-old specialty featuring strips of veal steak. Main courses run 7.80€ to 20.70€ ($9–$23.75), and set menus cost 13€ to 19€ ($15–$21.75).

Even better is the food at **Restaurant Schwarzer Adler**, in the Hotel Schwarzer Adler on Kaiserjägerstrasse 2 (© **0512/587-109**), which is installed in one of the town's most atmospheric and historic hotels, a building where Kaiser Maximilian in the 18th century housed his favorite mistress. Guests dine in artifact-decorated rooms on award-winning Austrian and Tyrolean dishes that range from grilled filets of wild boar to strips of braised gooseliver sprinkled with apple liqueur. Main courses cost 17€ to 23€ ($19.55–$26.45).

Hirschen–Stuben, Kiebachgasse 5 (© **0512/58-29-79**), serves food every bit as good as the Schwarzer Adler (see above), and also offers a historic setting beneath vaulted ceilings in a 17th-century building. Although it lacks a summer garden so beloved by Tyroleans, this is a good choice in other seasons because of its warm, cozy atmosphere and traditional country cooking, which also borrows heavily from the recipes of Italy to the south. Main courses run 8.80€ to 18.50€ ($10.10–$21.30).

The Innsbruck branch of **Café Sacher,** Rennweg 1 (© **0512/565626**), has a Bordeaux-red decor that closely emulates the rich cafe life of the original in Vienna. This is one of the few places you can get your hands on the genuine version of the chain's famous dessert, the *Sachertorte.* Rip-offs and unauthorized copies of the dish have cost contestants millions in litigation over the years, and the holders of the original 19th-century recipes (the owners of the Hotel Sacher in Vienna) have clung ferociously to their property. You can order coffee, priced at around 2.60€ ($3), and the famous pastry, at 4.50€ ($5.25) per slice.

SHOPPING

On their home turf, you can purchase such Tyrolean specialties as lederhosen, dirndls, leather clothing, woodcarvings, loden cloth, and all sorts of skiing and mountain-climbing equipment. Stroll around such shopping streets as the **Maria-Theresien-Strasse,** the **Herzog-Friedrich-Strasse,** and the **Museum-strasse,** ducking in and making discoveries of your own.

Here are a few recommendations if you're seeking something special:

Tiroler Heimatwerk, Meraner Strasse 2 (© **0512/58-23-20**), is one of the best stores in Innsbruck for such handcrafted Tyrolean items as sculpture, pewter, textiles, woolen goods, hand-knitted sweaters, lace, and bolts of silk for do-it-yourselfers. You can purchase regionally inspired fabrics and dress patterns, which you can whip into a dirndl (or whatever) as soon as you get home. Also for sale are carved chests, mirror frames, and furniture.

Zinnreproduktionen U, Kiebachgasse 8 (© **0512/58-92-24**), uses old molds discovered in abandoned Tyrolean factories. This imaginative company produces the finest reproductions of century-old pewter in the region. Owner Rudolf Boschi attends auctions throughout Europe and after discovering rare pewter objects, he reproduces them in excellent quality at reasonable prices. Look for a copy of the 18th-century pewter barometer emblazoned with representations of the sun and the four winds or hand-painted ceramic mugs whose pewter lids keep suds from flowing over the top. Each of the items for sale is cast or molded in a nearby foundry south of Innsbruck.

Lodenbaur, Brixner Strasse 4 (© **0512/58-09-11**), is the closest thing you'll find to a department store in Innsbruck devoted to regional Tyrolean dress. Most of the goods are made in Austria, including a full array of lederhosen, coats, dresses, dirndls, and accessories for men, women, and children. Be sure to check out the basement as well.

NIGHTLIFE

For something authentically Tyrolean, visit **Goethe Stube,** in the Restaurant Goldener Adler, Herzog-Friedrich-Strasse 6 (© **0512/57-11-11**), to hear melodies of the Tyrol, including zither playing. There's a one-drink minimum with a large beer going for 3.20€ ($3.75). Open daily 6 to 11pm. More Tyrolean folk entertainment is presented in shows by **Tiroler Alpenbuhne/ Geschwister Gundolf** (© **0512/26-32-63**). As you eat dinner a brass band entertains, as well as Alpine performers who perform on the zither, singing saw, the alphorn, and the folk harp. Shows are presented daily at 8:40pm at the Gasthaus Sandwirt, Reichenauerstrasse 151, and the Meese-Saal, Etzel–Strasse 35, from May to October, with tickets costing 20€ ($23). Tickets can be purchased on site at either venue.

One of the best bars is **Jimmy's,** Wilhelm-Greil-Strasse 17 (© **0512/56-50-00**), which draws a convivial crowd in their 20s and 30s daily from 11am to 2am. For a touch of Ireland, head for **Limerick Bill's,** Maria-Theresia-Strasse 9 (© **0512/582-01-11**), on the main street. Irishmen and Celtic wannabes are attracted to this fun-loving place, especially on Saturday when dancing is a feature from December to March. Sometimes live music is also offered. Hours are 8pm to midnight.

Belgium

The home of continental Europe's first railway, built way back in 1835, Belgium has one of the most extensive—nearly 2,500 miles (3,400km) of track—and reliable train networks in Europe. About the same size as Maryland and with 10 million inhabitants, Belgium is a small country, but it's not so small that if you blink you'll have missed it—it does take almost 4 hours to cross the entire country, after all. But it's compact enough that a couple of hours of riding the rails will get you from the capital, Brussels, to just about any corner of the realm you care to mention. Yet the variety of culture, language, history, and cuisine crammed into this small space would do credit to a country many times its size, making this the ideal destination for the rail traveler on a tight time budget.

Belgium's diversity is a product of its location at Europe's cultural crossroads. The boundary between the continent's Germanic north and Latin south cuts clear across the country's middle, leaving Belgium divided into two major ethnic regions, Dutch-speaking Flanders and French-speaking Wallonia. (No matter where you end up on your journey, however, you'll likely find someone who speaks English.)

The country is also at the crossroads of some of Europe's major rail networks and serves as a major hub for international rail travel. The famous Eurostar high-speed train linking Great Britain (see chapter 10) to the Continent runs from London to Brussels in only 2½ hours. The high-speed Thalys links several cities in Belgium to Paris, and Amsterdam, and Cologne, and the TGV trains arrive in Brussels from France. And Belgium is linked to most European capitals through regular EuroCity services. If you're planning a grand jaunt across the continent, Belgium makes an easy and convenient transfer point—don't miss it.

HIGHLIGHTS OF BELGIUM

Because **Brussels** has Belgium's only real international airport and is the hub of the country's rail net, it's likely that you'll visit this city first. That's not a bad proposition. Brussels is by no means the Continent's most exciting city, but the "capital of Europe" has its share of history and world-class attractions, and much to savor when it comes to dining and drinking. If you can set aside a few days for Belgium on your rail trip, devoting one of them to Brussels will be time well spent, though ideally you need 2 or 3 days to really get a grip on the place.

If you want to head straight for one of the historic Flemish cities of art and culture, then you can do no better than **Bruges.** Art, history, and Gothic architecture are what this marvel of a city is all about. It's less than an hour from Brussels by train and is small enough to be doable in a day, if all you want is to soak up the atmosphere and visit a few of its highlights.

Ghent and **Antwerp** are even closer to Brussels than Bruges. Though these two handsome Flemish cities can't boast as much sheer old-fashioned charm as Bruges, they have enough to get by on and far less of a tourist-swamped, museum-exhibit setting.

Belgium

To compete with the Flemish art cities and the Flanders region's possession of the country's seacoast, the Wallonia region offers fresh air and the scenic grandeur of the Ardennes and the Meuse River valley. Sadly, the Ardennes has few rail lines, and travel by bus is slow. You really need your own transportation and the time to take advantage of it. For a taste of francophone Belgium, however, a day trip to one of the Meuse River cities of **Liège** or **Namur** is an acceptable substitute and is easily done by train from Brussels.

And as a final option, a fairly easy side trip from the Belgian Ardennes is **Luxembourg.** The Grand Duchy may be a pocket-size nation, but size isn't everything. Its capital, Luxembourg City, is one of the small, hidden gems of Europe—off the beaten track but worth a visit in its own right.

1 Essentials

GETTING THERE

Brussels National Airport at Zaventem, 9 miles (14.5km) northeast of the city center, is the principal airport in Belgium and handles virtually all of the country's international flights. From here there is direct rail service to Brussels and many other points in Belgium.

Carriers with flights to Brussels from North America include **Air Canada** (© 888/247-2262; www.aircanada.ca), **American Airlines** (© 800/433-7300;

Moments Festivals & Special Events

If you're in Bruges on Ascension Day (5th Thurs after Easter), don't miss the **Procession of the Holy Blood.** A relic of the blood of Christ is carried through the streets, while costumed characters act out biblical scenes. Contact **Toerisme Brugge** (© **050/44-86-86**).

A major event in Brussels is **Ommegang,** which takes place in the Grand-Place on the first Tuesday and Thursday in July. It's a historic pageant that represents the entry into Brussels of Emperor Charles V in 1549. For more information, contact **Tourist Information Brussels** (© **02/513-89-40**).

Finally, a striking spectacle that should not be missed if you're in town is the **Carpet of Flowers,** in the Grand-Place, Brussels. During this event—held in mid-August in even-numbered years—the historic square is carpeted with two-thirds of a million begonias that are arranged in a kind of tapestry. Contact **Tourist Information Brussels** (© **02/513-89-40**).

---

www.aa.com), **Continental Airlines** (© **800/525-0280;** www.continental. com), **Delta Airlines** (© **800/221-1212;** www.delta.com), and **United Airlines** (© **800/538-2929;** www.united.com).

BELGIUM BY RAIL

All major tourist destinations in Belgium can be reached easily in a day trip by train from Brussels on the excellent rail net of the **Société Nationale des Chemins de Fer Belges/SNCB,** also known as NMBS in Dutch (Belgian Railways; © **02/528-28-28;** www.sncb.be). Antwerp is just 29 minutes away; Ghent, 32 minutes; Namur, 40 minutes; Bruges, 55 minutes; and Liège, 60 minutes. Main train stations, and some minor ones, also have bikes for rent.

TICKETS & PASSES

The following tickets and passes are valid only in Belgium or the Benelux countries. The first four of these options can only be purchased in train stations in Belgium. The Benelux Tourrail Pass must be purchased in North America and can be obtained from **Rail Europe** (© **877/272-RAIL** in the U.S., **800/361-RAIL** in Canada; www.raileurope.com) or through your travel agent. For details on purchasing multi-country options, such as the Eurailpass, see chapter 2.

Minitrips Discounted 1-day excursion tickets to major sightseeing destinations are available. For example, a 1-day minitrip to Bruges from Brussels, including second-class round-trip rail fare, a sightseeing tour, and admission to two museums costs 31€ ($35.75) per adult.

Weekend Return Valid from after 7pm on Friday to the last train on Sunday evening, this ticket affords a discount of 40% over the regular price. If you travel with two to six people, the discount per ticket for all travelers is 60%.

Rail Pass Valid for 10 single journeys anywhere on the Belgian railway network, except for stations at international borders, for 60€ ($69) in second class, and 93€ ($107) in first class.

Tourrail Pass   Valid for unlimited travel anywhere on the network, except for stations at international borders, on any 5 days in a 1-month period, for 68€ ($78.25) in second class, and 104€ ($120) in first class.

Benelux Tourrail Pass   The pass allows 5 days of unlimited travel in 1 month in Holland, Belgium, and Luxembourg, for 142€ ($163) in second class and 198€ ($228) in first class. Two adults traveling together benefit from a 50% companion discount. For passengers ages 4 to 25 traveling in second class, the pass is 94.85€ $109. Children under 4 travel free.

FOREIGN TRAIN TERMS

A train is a train in French and a *trein* in Dutch and there are three kinds of trains in Belgium. These are the fast **InterCity (IC)** trains; the somewhat slower **Inter-Regional (IR)** trains; and the tortoises of the network, **Local (L)** trains that stop at every station on the way. These are in addition to high-speed Thalys trains from France, the Netherlands, and Germany; high-speed TGV trains from France; and high-speed Eurostar trains from Britain.

Class is *Classe* in French and *Klas* in Dutch. Second class is *Deuxième Classe/Tweede Klas,* and first class is *Premier Classe/Eerste Klas.* A station is a *gare/station.* In big cities like Brussels and Antwerp, which have more than one station, the main station is called *Gare Centrale/Centraal Station* (Central Station). Platform is *quai/spoor* (in Dutch it rhymes with "boar").

PRACTICAL TRAIN INFORMATION

Belgian trains are invariably crowded, so should you be planning to make a trip by InterCity train, you should try to reserve a seat; otherwise, you may need to stand. On the other hand, distances between stations are short, and a bunch of people is sure to get out at whatever the next one is; so, you could just wait and grab a seat when it becomes vacant.

Because of the small size of the country, no Belgian trains have restaurant cars (some international trains do), but on most InterCity trains an attendant pushes around a small cart, from which coffee, tea, mineral water, sandwiches, potato chips, and other snacky items are dispensed. These are more expensive than the same things bought from a supermarket, so if you are on a tight budget, buy them before boarding the train.

Similarly, a lack of long-distance lines means there are no sleeper cars on trains within Belgium.

All trains, even the smallest, have a first-class section or cars. The cars themselves are open-plan—no closed compartments. Because smoking and non-smoking sections are usually found within the same car, anyone who likes to breathe air free of secondhand smoke is out of luck; you can minimize the discomfort by sitting as far as possible from the dividing line.

Train Frequency & Travel Times in Belgium*

	Ghent	Antwerp	Bruges	Ostend	Liège	Namur
Time	32 min.	48 min.	1 hr.	72 min.	70 min.	57 min.
Train frequency**	4	2	4	2	4	3

* *Travel times are calculated using Brussels as the departure point.*
** *Frequency is average number of trains out of Brussels per hour during daytime.*

FAST FACTS: Belgium

Area Codes When making phone calls within Belgium (and this includes if you're calling another number within the same area code), you always need to dial the area codes in this book. The area code for Brussels is **02**. Other area codes are Bruges **050**, Ghent **09**, Antwerp **03**, Liège **04**. Luxembourg has no area codes. When calling a local number from anywhere within the Grand Duchy, you need only dial the local number.

Business Hours Banks are generally open Monday to Friday from 9am to 1pm and 2 to 4:30 or 5pm, and some branches are also open on Saturday morning. Shops generally are open Monday to Saturday from 10am to 6pm, though some also are open on Sunday. Most department stores stay open on Friday to 8 or 9pm.

Climate Belgium's climate is moderate, with few extremes in temperature either in summer or winter. It rains a lot. You're well advised to pack a fold-up umbrella at any time of year. Likewise, carry a raincoat (with a wool liner for winter). Temperatures are lowest in December and January, when they average 42°F (6°C), and highest in July and August, when they average 73°F (23°C). Pack a sweater or two (even in July) and be prepared to layer your clothing at any time of year. Don't worry: You're allowed to leave some space for T-shirts, skimpy tops, and sneakers.

Documents Required For stays of up to 3 months, citizens of the U.S. and Canada need only to have a valid passport. For stays longer than 3 months, a visa is required.

Electricity Belgium runs on 220 volts electricity (North America uses 110 volts). So, for any small appliance up to 1,500 watts, you need to take a small voltage transformer (available in drug and appliance stores and by mail order) that plugs into the round-holed European electrical outlet and converts the Belgian voltage from 220 volts down to 110 volts. Don't try to plug an American appliance directly into a European outlet without a transformer.

Embassies These are all in Brussels. **U.S.:** bd. du Régent 25–27 ((*C*) **02/508-21-11;** www.usembassy.be; Métro: Arts-Loi). **Canada:** av. de Tervuren 2 ((*C*) **02/741-06-11;** Métro: Merode).

Holidays January 1 (New Year's Day), Easter Sunday and Monday, May 1 (Labor Day), Ascension Day, Pentecost Sunday and Monday, July 21 (Independence Day), August 15 (Assumption Day), November 1 (All Saints' Day), November 11 (World War I Armistice Day), and December 25 (Christmas). In Flanders only, July 11 is Flemish Community Day, the anniversary of the Battle of the Golden Spurs in 1302. In Wallonia only, September 27 is French Community Day, recalling liberation from Dutch rule in 1830.

Health & Safety For day or night emergency medical service, call (*C*) **02/479-18-18** or (*C*) **02/648-80-00;** for emergency dental service, call (*C*) **02/426-10-26** or (*C*) **02/428-58-58;** for police assistance, call (*C*) **101;** Each pharmacy in Belgium has a list of late-night and weekend pharmacies posted on its door.

Mail Postage for a postcard or letter to the U.S., Canada, Australia, New Zealand, and South Africa is .85€ ($1); to the U.K. and Ireland .45€ (50¢).

Police & Emergencies For emergency police assistance, call ℂ **101**. In case of accidents, call ℂ **100**. In case of fire, ℂ **100**.

Taxes On top of a 16% service charge, there's a value-added tax (TVA) of 6% on hotel bills and 21.5% on restaurant bills. The higher rate is charged on purchased goods, too. If you spend over 125€ ($144) in some stores, and you are not a resident of the European Union, you can recover it from some stores by having the official receipt stamped by Belgian Customs on departure and returning the stamped receipt to the shop. Your refund should arrive by check or be credited to your credit card within a few weeks. Not all stores participate in this scheme so it pays to ask first, particularly for major purchases.

Telephone **To call Belgium:** If you're calling from the United States, dial the international access code (011), followed by the country code for Belgium (32), then the area code (2 for Brussels) and the number. So the whole number you'd dial would be **011-32-2-000-0000**.

To make international calls: To make international calls from Belgium, first dial 00 and then the country code (U.S. or Canada 1,). Next you dial the area code and number. For example, if you wanted to call the British Embassy in Washington, D.C., you would dial **00-1-202-588-7800**.

For information inside Belgium, call ℂ **1207** or ℂ **1307**; for international information, call ℂ **1405**. Numbers beginning with 0800 within Belgium are toll-free.

You can use pay phones with a Belgacom *telecarte* (phone card), which is 5€ ($5.75), 12.50€ ($14.40), and 25€ ($28.75) from post offices, train ticket counters, tourist information offices, some tobacconists, and newsstands. Some pay phones take credit cards. A few pay phones take coins, of .05€ (5¢), .10€ (10¢), .20€ (25¢), .50€ (60¢), and 1€ ($1.15).

To charge a call to your calling card, dial **AT&T** (ℂ **0800/100-10**); **MCI** (ℂ **0800/100-12**); **Sprint** (ℂ **0800/100-14**); **Canada Direct** (ℂ **0800/100-19**); **British Telecom** (ℂ **0800/100-24**).

Tipping The prices on most restaurant menus already include a service charge of 16%, so it's unnecessary to tip. If service is good, however, it's usual to show appreciation with a tip. It's enough to round up the bill to the nearest convenient amount, if you wish, rather than leave a full-fledged tip. Otherwise, 10% is adequate, and more than most Belgians would leave. Service is included in your hotel bill as well. Taxis include the tip in the meter reading. You can round up the fare if you like, but need not add a tip unless you have received an extra service like help with luggage. For other services: Leave 20% of the bill for hairdressers (leave it with the cashier when you pay) and 1€ to 2€ ($1.15–$2.30) per piece of luggage for porters.

2 Brussels

A city with a notable history, Brussels is carving out a bright future for itself and is unquestionably the place to start your rail journey through Belgium. The "capital of Europe" has begun to act like Europe's Washington, D.C., a focus of economic and political power, where decisions are made that affect the lives of people around the world. Headquarters of the European Union (EU), Brussels both symbolizes the Continent's vision of unity and is a bastion of officialdom, a breeding ground for the regulations that govern and often exasperate the rest of Europe.

Bruxellois have ambivalent feelings about their city's transformation into a power center. At first, the waves of Eurocrats brought a new cosmopolitan air to a somewhat provincial city, but as old neighborhoods were leveled to make way for office towers, people wondered whether Brussels was losing its soul. After all, this city doesn't only mean politics and business—it helped inspire surrealism and Art Nouveau, worships comic strips, prides itself on handmade lace and chocolate, and serves each one of its craft beers in its own unique glass.

Fortunately, not all of Brussels's individuality has been lost in this transition, and though the urban landscape has suffered from wanton "development," the city's spirit survives in traditional cafes, bars, bistros, and restaurants. Whether elegantly Art Nouveau or eccentrically festooned with posters, curios, and knickknacks, such centuries-old establishments provide a warm, convivial ambience that is peculiarly Belgian.

STATION INFORMATION
GETTING FROM THE AIRPORT TO THE TRAIN STATION

There's **train** service to Brussels's Gare du Nord (where you can connect to the city's other stations), from Brussels National Airport between 5:43am and 11:14pm, for a one-way fare of 2.50€ ($3). The trip is free if you hold a validated train pass. Most airport trains have wide corridors and extra space for baggage and are the best and easiest way into town. The journey takes 20 minutes.

You'll also find **taxi** stands in front of the airplane terminal building if you prefer to head into town that way. All taxis from the airport are metered. Expect to pay around 35€ ($40.25) to get to the city center.

INSIDE THE STATION

Brussels has three major train stations. High-speed Eurostar trains from London; Thalys from Paris, Amsterdam, and Cologne; and TGV from France (not Paris) arrive at **Gare du Midi,** rue de France, south of the city center. Other international trains arrive at Gare du Midi; **Gare Centrale,** Carrefour de l'Europe, downtown, a few blocks from the Grand-Place; and **Gare du Nord,** rue du Progrès, north of the city center.

All of the stations offer currency exchange, luggage storage, and boards with train information. Note that Gare Centrale does not have an actual train information desk, and you cannot make train reservations or validate a railpass here, though it is the rail station closest to many of the attractions in the city. Gare du Midi has several snack kiosks and a few shops on its concourse.

Gare Centrale and Gare Midi have room reservations desks that do not accept phone bookings. Otherwise, tourist information and room reservations are not available in any of Brussels's train stations.

For information in English, for both domestic and international trains (including Thalys, Eurostar, and the TGV), call ✆ **02/528-28-28** or go to **www.sncb.be**.

INFORMATION ELSEWHERE IN THE CITY

In the city center, a short walk down a hill from Gare Centrale, **Brussels International Tourism (B.I.T.)** is on the ground floor of the Hôtel de Ville (Town

Brussels

Railway ──
Post Office ✉
Information ⓘ

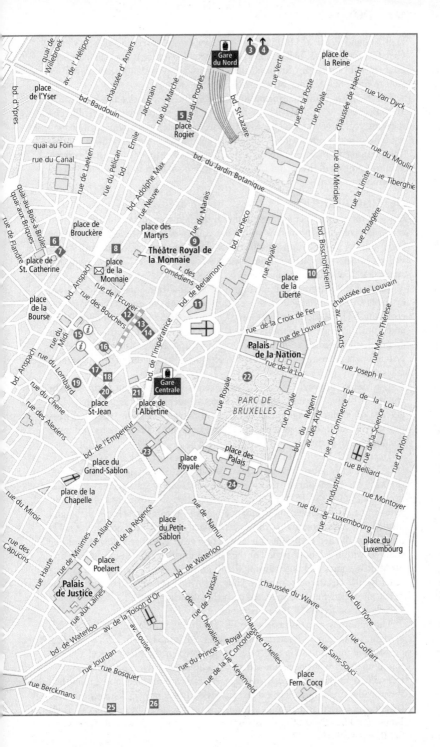

Hall), Grand-Place (℗ **02/513-89-40;** www.brusselsinternational.be; Métro: Gare Centrale). B.I.T. makes hotel reservations. The office is open June to September, daily from 9am to 6pm; October to May, Monday to Saturday from 9am to 6pm, and Sunday from 10am to 2pm.

The **Belgian Tourist Information Center,** rue du Marche-aux-Herbes 63, 1000 Bruxelles (℗ **02/504-03-90;** French-speaking region www.opt.be, Dutch-speaking region www.toervl.be; Métro: Gare Centrale), covers the entire country. The office is open June to September, Monday to Saturday from 9am to 7pm, Sunday from 9am to 6pm; October to March, Monday to Saturday from 9am to 6pm; April, May, and October Sunday from 9am to 6pm, and to 5pm November to March.

GETTING AROUND

Once in town, your feet are almost always the best way to get around, and the center is small enough to allow you to use your own leg power. Be sure to wear good walking shoes, as those charming cobblestones on the sidewalks and streets will get under your soles and onto your nerves after a while. When crossing the street, watch out for trams and bikes.

Maps of the integrated public transit network—Métro, tram, and bus—are available free from the tourist office; from offices of the public transportation company, **STIB,** Galérie de la Toison d'Or 15 (℗ **02/515-20-00;** www.stib.be); and from the Porte de Namur, Rogier, and Gare du Midi Métro stations. In addition, all stations and most tram and bus stops have transit maps. The full system operates from 6am to midnight, after which a limited night-bus service takes over.

The **Métro** (subway) net covers the city center and reaches out to the suburbs and to the Bruparck recreation zone. Stations are identified by signs with a white letter M on a blue background. An extensive network of **tram** (streetcar) lines provides the ideal way to get around the city. Trams are generally faster and more comfortable than **buses.**

Tickets are 1.40€ ($1.60) for a single journey (known as a *direct*) and 6.20€ ($7.15) for a five-journey ticket, both of which you can buy from the driver; 9€ ($10.25) for a ten-journey ticket available from Métro stations and train stations; and 3.60€ ($4.15) for a 1-day ticket valid on all urban services. You validate your ticket by inserting it into the orange electronic machines that stand inside buses and trams and at the access to Métro platforms. Though the ticket must be revalidated each time you enter a new vehicle, you are allowed multiple transfers within a 1-hour period of the initial validation, so you can hop on and off Métros, trams, and buses during that time and only one journey will be canceled by the electronic scanner. If more than one person is traveling on one ticket, the ticket must be validated each time for each traveler. Children under 12 ride free on the STIB transit network.

The minimum rate for **taxis** is 2.50€ ($3) during the day and 4.50€ ($5.20) at night. Charges per kilometer vary from 1€ to 2€ ($1.15–$2.25), depending on location and time. Tip and taxes are included in the meter price. You can round up the fare but need not add an extra tip unless there has been extra service, such as helping with heavy luggage. All taxis are metered. You cannot hail them in the street, but there are taxi stands on many principal streets, particularly in the center, and at train stations. To request a cab by phone, call **Taxis Bleus** (℗ **02/268-00-00**), **Taxis Oranges** (℗ **02/349-43-43**), or **Taxis Verts** (℗ **02/349-49-49**).

WHERE TO STAY

Comfort Art Hotel Siru ✨✨   What sets the Siru, opposite Gare du Nord, apart is that the owner of this art-gallery-cum-hotel in a redeveloped business district persuaded 130 Belgian artists to "decorate" each of the coolly modern, well-equipped rooms and the corridors with a work on travel. Given the unpredictable nature of reactions to modern art, some clients apparently reserve the same room time after time; others ask for a room change in the middle of the night.

Place Rogier 1, 1210 Bruxelles. ✆ **800/228-3323** in the U.S. and Canada, or 02/203-35-80. Fax 02/203-33-03. www.comforthotelsiru.com. 101 units. 90€–180€ ($104–$207) double. Rates include buffet breakfast. AE, DC, MC, V. Métro: Rogier. **Amenities:** Restaurant; laundry; nonsmoking rooms. *In room:* Hair dryer.

De Boeck's   In a well-maintained 19th-century town house off of chaussée de Charleroi and a short walk from Place Stephanie, this graceful hotel has unusually spacious and quiet rooms. They don't quite measure up to the Victorian elegance of the public spaces but are adequately furnished, with comfortable modern beds, soft carpeting, and floral-pattern curtains. Some rooms, ideal for families and small groups, can be used as quads or even quints.

Rue Veydt 40, 1050 Bruxelles. ✆ **02/537-40-33.** Fax 02/534-40-37. hotel.deboeck@euronet.be. 36 units. 70€–75€ ($81–$86) double. Rates include buffet breakfast. AE, DC, MC, V. Métro: Louise.

Le Dixseptième ✨✨   This graceful, 17th-century house was once the official residence of the Spanish ambassador and stands close to the Grand-Place (2 blocks from Gare Centrale) in a neighborhood of restored dwellings. Rooms have wood paneling and marble chimneys and are as big as suites in many hotels; some have balconies. All are in 18th-century style and are named after Belgian painters from Brueghel to Magritte. Two beautiful lounges are decorated with carved wooden medallions and 18th-century paintings.

Rue de la Madeleine 25, 1000 Bruxelles. ✆ **02/502-57-44.** Fax 02/502-64-24. www.ledixseptieme.be. 24 units. 180€–360€ ($207–$414) double. Rates include buffet breakfast. AE, DC, MC, V. Métro: Gare Centrale. **Amenities:** Lounge; laundry. *In room:* Hair dryer.

Les Bluets ✨✨   If you're searching for classic European charm or are a fan of American B&Bs, you'll enjoy it here. In a town house from 1864 that's close to av. Louise and just a couple of blocks from a Métro station, the effect is more that of a comfortable country residence than a hotel. You feel as though you're staying with friends when you breakfast in the antiques-filled dining room or in the sunroom. Several rooms have 14-foot ceilings and ornate moldings, and all have antiques and knickknacks. There's no elevator.

Rue Berckmans 124, 1060 Bruxelles. ✆ **02/534-39-83.** Fax 02/543-09-70. www.belge.net/bluets. 10 units. 52€–81€ ($58.75–$93.25) double. Rates include continental breakfast. MC, V. Métro: Hôtel des Monnaies. **Amenities:** Nonsmoking rooms. *In room:* No hair dryer.

Métropole ✨✨   An ornate, marble-and-gilt interior distinguishes this late-19th-century landmark from 1895 (Brussels's sole surviving 19th-c. hotel), just a few blocks away from the Grand-Place. Soaring ceilings, potted palms, and lavishly decorated public spaces on the ground floor add to the *belle époque* allure. The spacious rooms, some in Art Deco style, have a mix of classic and elegant modern furnishings. Both the French restaurant L'Alban Chambon and the Café Métropole are worth a visit in their own right.

Place de Brouckère 31 (close to Centre Monnaie), 1000 Bruxelles. ✆ **02/217-23-00.** Fax 02/218-02-20. www.metropolehotel.be. 305 units. 325€–425€ double ($374–$489); from 450€–750€ suite ($518–$863). Rates include buffet or continental breakfast. AE, DC, MC, V. Métro: De Brouckère. **Amenities:** Restaurant; lounge; cafe; sidewalk cafe; laundry. *In room:* Hair dryer.

Mozart Go a flight up from the busy, cheap-eats street level a block away from the Grand-Place, and guess which famous composer's music wafts through the lobby? Salmon-colored walls, plants, and old paintings create a warm, intimate ambience that's carried into the rooms. Although furnishings are blandly modern, colorful fabrics and exposed beams lend each room a rustic originality. Several are duplexes with a sitting room underneath the loft bedroom. Top rooms have a great view.

Rue du Marché-aux-Fromages 23, 1000 Bruxelles. ✆ **02/502-66-61.** Fax 02/502-77-58. www.hotel-mozart.be. 47 units. 90€ ($104) double. AE, DC, MC, V. Métro: Gare Centrale. **Amenities:** Lounge. *In room:* No hair dryer.

Sabina This small hostelry off of place des Barricades is like a private residence, presided over by hospitable owners. A grandfather clock in the reception area and polished wood along the restaurant walls give it a warm, homey atmosphere. Rooms vary in size, but all are comfortable and simply yet tastefully done in modern style with twin beds. Three rooms have kitchenettes.

Rue du Nord 78, 1000 Bruxelles. ✆ **02/218-26-37.** Fax 02/219-32-39. www.hotelsabina.be. 24 units. 63€–73€ ($72.50–$84) double. Rates include buffet breakfast. AE, DC, MC, V. Métro: Madou. *In room:* Hair dryer.

Welcome ★★★ The smallest hotel in the center, the Welcome is a little gem of a place that lives up to its name in full. You can think of this as a country *auberge* (inn) in the heart of town, on the old Fish Market. Rooms are styled on individual themes—Savannah, Provence, Japan, Thailand, India, Tibet, Bali, and Laura Ashley—and furnished and decorated from both local designer and antiques stores with what can best be described as tender loving care.

Rue du Peuplier 1, 1000 Bruxelles. ✆ **02/219-95-46.** Fax 02/217-18-87. www.hotelwelcome.com. 8 units. 70€–120€ ($80.50–$138) double; 150€ ($173) suite. DC, MC, V. Métro: Ste-Catherine. **Amenities:** Restaurant; lounge. *In room:* Hair dryer.

TOP ATTRACTIONS & SPECIAL MOMENTS

Atomium ★ There's nothing quite like this cluster of giant spheres representing the atomic structure of an iron molecule enlarged 165 billion times, built for the 1958 World's Fair. The view from the viewing deck is marvelous, and you can wander around inside the spheres, which often house special exhibitions.

Bd. du Centenaire, Heysel. ✆ **02/475-47-77.** Admission 6€ ($7) adults, 3€ ($3.50) seniors/students/ children 12 and under, children under 4 ft. free. Apr–Aug daily 9am–8pm; Sept–Mar daily 10am–6pm (Panorama to 9:30pm). Métro: Heysel.

Cathédrale de St-Michel ★ Begun in 1226, this magnificent Gothic church. off of bd. de l'Impératrice 2 blocks west of Gare Centrale, was officially consecrated as a cathedral only in 1961. The 16th-century Emperor Charles V donated its superb stained-glass windows. Aside from these, the spare interior decoration focuses attention on its soaring columns and arches, and the bright exterior stonework makes a fine sight.

Parvis Ste-Gudule. ✆ **02/217-83-45.** Admission Cathedral free; crypt 1€ ($1.15). Apr–Sept daily 7am–7pm; Oct–Mar daily 7am–6pm. Métro: Gare Centrale.

Centre Belge de la Bande Dessinée (Belgian Center for Comic-Strip Art) ★★ Called the CéBéBéDé for short, the center, off of bd. de Berlaimont, is dedicated to comic strips and takes a lofty view of "the Ninth Art." As icing on the cake, it's housed in a restored Art Nouveau department store from 1903, the Magasins Waucquez, designed by Victor Horta. A model of the red-and-white

---

Moments **Les Marolles**

The iconoclastic working-class Marolles district, lying beneath the long shadow of the Palace of Justice, is a special place where the old Brussels dialect called *Brusseleir* can still be heard. It's a generally poor community, under constant threat of encroachment and gentrification from neighboring, far wealthier areas—a process the Marolliens seem to want nothing to do with. Locals remain resolutely unimpressed by the burgeoning "Capital of Europe."

Most people get their Marolles initiation by visiting the daily flea market in place du Jeu de Balle, which opens at 7am and closes at 2pm (take the Métro to Porte de Hal and then walk several blocks up rue Blaes). Here the weird and wonderful is commonplace. It makes a refreshing change to explore this other Brussels, a simple neighborhood of homes, welcoming cafes, and great, inexpensive restaurants. Simply wander around for an hour or 2.

---

checkered rocket in which Tintin and Snowy flew to the Moon, long before Armstrong and Aldrin did it in mere fact, takes pride of place at the top of the elegant staircase. Beyond, is a comic strip wonderland. All the big names appear in a library of 30,000 books and in permanent and special exhibitions, including Tintin, Asterix, Thorgal, Lucky Luke, the Smurfs, Peanuts, Andy Capp, Suske and Wiske—yes, even Superman, Batman, and the Green Lantern—along with many lesser heroes.

Rue des Sables 20. ⓒ 02/219-19-80. Admission 6.25€ ($7.20) adults, 5€ ($5.75) students/seniors, 2.50€ ($3) children under 12. Tues–Sun 10am–6pm. Métro: Gare Centrale.

Hôtel de Ville (Town Hall) ✦✦ The facade of the dazzling Town Hall, from 1402, shows off Gothic intricacy at its best, complete with dozens of arched windows and sculptures—some of these, like the drunken monks, a sleeping Moor and his harem, and St. Michael slaying a female devil, displaying a medieval sense of humor. A 215-foot-tower sprouts from the middle, yet it's not placed exactly in the center. A colorful but untrue legend has it that when the architect realized his "error," he jumped off the summit of the tower. The building is still the seat of the civic government, and its wedding room is a popular place to tie the knot. In the spectacular Gothic Hall, open for visits when the city's aldermen are not in session, you can see baroque decoration. In other chambers are 16th- to 18th-century tapestries. One of these depicts the Spanish duke of Alba, whose cruel features reflect the brutal oppression he imposed on the Low Countries; others show scenes from the life of Clovis, the king of the Franks.

Grand-Place. ⓒ 02/279-43-55. Admission (for guided tours in English) 3€ ($3.50) adults, 2.50€ ($3) children 6–15, children under 6 free. Apr–Sept Tues–Wed 3:15pm, Sun 12:15pm; Oct–Mar Tues–Wed 3:15pm. Métro: Gare Centrale.

Mini-Europe ✦ Stroll among highlights from member states of the European Union, all meticulously detailed at a scale of 1:25. There's London's Big Ben, Berlin's Brandenburg Gate, the Leaning Tower of Pisa, the Bull Ring in Seville (complete with simulated sounds of fans yelling *Olé!*), and Montmartre in Paris, as well as more modern emblems of continental achievement such as the Channel Tunnel and the Ariane rocket. Mt. Vesuvius erupts, gondolas float around the canals of Venice, and a Finnish girl dives into the icy waters of a northern lake.

Bruparck, Heysel. ℂ **02/478-05-50.** Admission 10.50€ ($12) adults, 8€ ($9.25) children 12 and under, children under 4 ft. free. Apr–June and Sept 9:30am–6pm; first 2 weeks of July and last 2 weeks of Aug 9:30am–8pm; mid-July to mid-Aug 9:30am–midnight; Oct–Jan 10am–6pm. Closed Feb–Mar. Métro: Heysel.

Musée de la Ville de Bruxelles (Museum of the City of Brussels) ★   In the neo-Gothic King's House (which, despite its name, has never housed a king), this museum documents the history of Brussels. Among the most fascinating displays are old paintings and modern scale-reconstructions of the historic center, including some that depict activity along the now-vanished Senne River. There also are exhibits on traditional arts and crafts, such as tapestry and lace. The pride of the museum, however, is the more than 500 costumes—including an Elvis outfit—donated to outfit Brussels's famous *Manneken-Pis* statue, each equipped with a strategically positioned orifice so that the little sculpture's normal function is not impaired.

Grand-Place 1. ℂ **02/279-43-50.** Admission 3€ ($3.50) adults, 2.50€ ($3) children 6–15, children under 6 free. Tues–Fri 10am–5pm; Sat–Sun noon–5pm. Métro: Bourse.

Musées Royaux des Beaux-Arts ★★★   In a vast museum of several buildings at place Royale, this complex combines the **Musée d'Art Ancien** and the **Musée d'Art Moderne** under one roof (connected by a passage). The collection shows off works, most of them Belgian, from the 14th to the 20th century, including Hans Memling's portraits from the late 15th century, which are marked by sharp lifelike details; works by Hieronymus Bosch; and Lucas Cranach's *Adam and Eve.* You should particularly seek out the rooms featuring Pieter Brueghel, including his *Adoration of the Magi* and *Fall of Icarus.* Don't miss his unusual *Fall of the Rebel Angels,* with grotesque faces and beasts. But don't fear—many of Brueghel's paintings, like those depicting Flemish village life, are of a less fiery nature. Later artists represented include Rubens, Van Dyck, Frans Hals, and Rembrandt.

Moments **Special Brussels Experiences**

- **Watching the Son-et-Lumière on Summer Evenings in the Grand-Place.** This sound-and-light show in which a series of colored lamps on the Hôtel de Ville (Town Hall) are switched on and off in sequence to a piece of appropriately grand music is admittedly kind of kitsch. But who cares? It's also magical.

- **Shooting *Manneken-Pis.*** We mean with a camera, of course. Nobody can resist this statue of a gleefully tinkling little boy. Should you be any different?

- **Snapping Up a Bargain at the Flea Market.** Each day, from 7am to 2pm, the Marché-aux-Puces in place du Jeu de Balle offers everything from the weird to the wonderful at rock-bottom prices.

- **Pigging Out on Belgian Chocolates.** Those devilish little creations—handmade Belgian pralines—are so addictive they should be sold with a government health warning attached. Try the Wittamer chocolatier in place du Grand-Sablon, and eat your fill.

Moments A Neat Little Park

Once a hunting preserve of the dukes of Brabant, the **Parc de Bruxelles (Brussels Park)**, rue Royale (Métro: Parc), between Parliament and the Royal Palace, was laid out in the 18th century as a landscaped garden. In 1830, Belgian patriots fought Dutch regular troops here during the War of Independence. Later it was a fashionable place to stroll and to meet friends. Although not very big, the park manages to contain everything from carefully trimmed borders to rough patches of trees and bushes, and has fine views along its main paths, which together with the fountain form the outline of Masonic symbols.

Next door, in a circular building connected to the main entrance, the modern art section has an emphasis on underground works—if only because the museum's eight floors are all below ground level. The overwhelming collection includes works by van Gogh, Matisse, Dalí, Tanguy, Ernst, Chagall, Miró, and local boys Magritte, Delvaux, De Braekeleer, and Permeke.

Rue de la Régence 3. ✆ **02/508-32-11.** Admission 3.75€ ($4.25) adults, 2.50€ ($3) students/seniors/ people with disabilities, 1.25€ ($1.40) children 13–18, children under 13 free. Museum of Historical Art Tues–Sun 10am–noon and 1–5pm; Museum of Modern Art Tues–Sun 10am–1pm and 2–5pm. Métro: Parc.

Palais Royal (Royal Palace)   The palace, which overlooks the Parc de Bruxelles, was begun in 1820 and had a grandiose Louis XVI–style face-lift in 1904. The older wings date from the 18th century and are flanked by two pavilions, one of which sheltered numerous notables during the 1800s. Today, the palace is used for state receptions. It also contains the offices of King Albert II, though he and Queen Paola do not live here.

Place des Palais. ✆ **02/551-20-20.** Free admission. July 22 to late Sept Tues–Sun 10:30am–4:30pm. Métro: Parc.

THE GRAND-PLACE

Ornamental gables, medieval banners, gilded facades, sunlight flashing off gold-filigreed rooftop sculptures, a general impression of harmony and timelessness—there's a lot to take in all at once when you first enter the **Grand-Place** ✸✸✸ (Métro: Gare Centrale or Bourse), a World Heritage site. Its present composition dates mostly from the late 1690s, but the Town Hall dates from the early 1400s. Don't miss the cafes lodged within the opulent wooden interiors of old guild houses; their upper-floor windows overlooking the Grand-Place give some of the best views in Europe.

The famous *Manneken-Pis* statue ✸✸, on the corner of rue du Chêne and rue de l'Etuve, 2 blocks from the Grand-Place, is Brussels's favorite little boy, gleefully doing what a little boy's gotta do. It's known that the boy's effigy has graced the city since at least the time of Philip the Good, who became Count of Flanders in 1419. Among the speculations about his origins are that he was the son of a Brussels nobleman who got lost and was found while answering nature's call, and also that he was a patriotic Belgian kid who sprinkled a hated Spanish sentry passing beneath his window. Perhaps the best theory is that he saved the Town Hall from a sputtering bomb by extinguishing it—like Gulliver—with the first thing handy.

WHERE TO DINE

Chez Léon BELGIAN/MUSSELS   Think of it as "the mussels from Brussels," as this big, basic restaurant right of the Grand-Place is the city's most famous purveyor of that marine delicacy. Léon has been flexing its muscles since 1893 and now has clones all over Belgium). The mollusks in question are served in a variety of styles. If you don't like mussels, there are plenty of other fishy delights—like eels in green sauce, cod, and bouillabaisse.

Rue des Bouchers 14–24 (off Grand-Place). © **02/511-14-15**. Main courses 7.25€–24€ ($8.25–$27.50). AE, DC, MC, V. Daily Sun–Thurs noon–11pm; Fri–Sat noon–11:30pm. Métro: De Brouckère.

De l'Ogenblik ★★ FRENCH/BELGIAN   In the elegant surroundings of the Galeries Royales St-Hubert, this restaurant supplies good taste in a Parisian bistro-style setting. It often gets busy, but the ambience in the split-level, wood-and-brass-outfitted dining room, with a sand-strewn floor, is convivial, though a little too tightly packed when it's full. Look for garlicky meat and seafood dishes, and expect to pay a smidgeon more for atmosphere than might be strictly justified by results on the plate.

Galerie des Princes 1. © **02/511-61-51**. Main courses 22€–28€ ($25.25–$32.25); *plat du jour* 11€ ($12.65). AE, DC, MC, V. Mon–Thurs noon–2:30pm and 7pm–midnight; Fri–Sat noon–2:30pm and 7pm–to 12:30am. Métro: Gare Centrale.

In 't Spinnekopke ★★ *Finds* TRADITIONAL BELGIAN   "In the Spider's Web" occupies a 1762 stagecoach inn in the Place du Jardin aux Fleurs, just far enough off the beaten track downtown to be frequented mainly by "those in the know." You dine in a tilting, tiled-floor building, at plain tables. This is one of Brussels's most traditional cafe/restaurants—so much so, in fact, that the menu lists its hardy standbys of regional Belgian cuisine in the old Bruxellois dialect.

Place du Jardin-aux-Fleurs 1. © **02/511-86-95**. Main courses 10.50€–19.50€ ($12–$22.25); *plat du jour* 8.15€ ($9.25). AE, DC, MC, V. Mon–Fri noon–3pm and 6–11pm; Sat 6pm–midnight (bar Mon–Fri 11am–midnight; Sat 6pm–midnight). Métro: Bourse.

La Manufacture ★★ FRENCH/INTERNATIONAL   Even in its former incarnation, this place was concerned with style—it used to be the factory of chic Belgian leather goods maker Delvaux. Fully refurbished, with hardwood floors, leather banquettes, polished wood, and stone tables, all set amid iron pillars and exposed air ducts, it produces trendy world cuisine on a French foundation. On sunny days in summer, you can dine outdoors on a terrace shaded by giant bamboo plants. It's something of a hike from the Bourse Métro station, but well worth the journey.

Rue Notre-Dame du Sommeil 12–20. © **02/502-25-25**. Main courses 12€–22€ ($13.75–$25.25); *menu du jour* (lunch only) 13€ ($15); fixed-price menus 30€–65€ ($34.50–$74.75). AE, DC, MC, V. Mon–Fri noon–2pm and 7–11pm; Sat 7pm–midnight. Métro: Bourse.

La Truite d'Argent ★★ SEAFOOD/CLASSIC FRENCH   Understated elegance complements fine cuisine at this restaurant on the ground floor of a *maison de maître* (town house) dating from 1896. A stucco ceiling, arches, original oak paneling, chandeliers, mirrors, and old paintings, grace a dining room that has just 25 places. The menu includes a few meat choices. The presentation is professional yet relaxed. In fine weather, you can dine outdoors on a sidewalk terrace on the old Fish Market square.

Quai aux Bois-à-Brûler 23. © **02/219-95-46**. Main courses 18€–27€ ($20.75–$31); fixed-price menu 31.25€ ($36). DC, MC, V. Mon–Fri noon–2:30pm and 7–11:30pm. Métro: Ste-Catherine.

L'Auberge des Chapeliers ★★ *Value* TRADITIONAL BELGIAN   In a 17th-century building off of the Grand-Place that was once the headquarters of the hatmakers' guild, the Auberge preserves its historic charm. Behind a beautiful brick facade, the first two floors are graced with timber beams and paneling and connected by a narrow wooden staircase. The food is typical hearty Belgian fare, with an accent on mussels in season and dishes cooked in beer.

Rue des Chapeliers 1–3. © 02/513-73-38. Reservations recommended on weekends. Main courses 8.50€–17.50€ ($9.75–$20.25); set-price menus 15€–21€ ($17.25–$24.25). AE, DC, MC, V. Mon–Thurs noon–2pm and 6–11pm; Fri noon–2pm and 6pm–midnight; Sat noon–3pm and 6pm–midnight; Sun noon–3pm and 6–11pm. Métro: Gare Centrale.

Le Scheltema ★ BELGIAN   This is one of those solid restaurants in the Ilôt Sacré district off of rue des Bouchers that keep going day in, day out, year after year, serving up much the same fare but never forgetting that quality counts. Good service and fine atmosphere complement the seafood specialties at this brasserie-style restaurant, which in some ways is similar to others in the district but always goes the extra mile in terms of class and taste.

Rue des Dominicains 7. © 02/512-20-84. Main courses 16€–24€ ($18.50–$27.50). AE, DC, MC, V. Mon–Thurs noon–3pm and 6–11:30pm; Fri–Sat noon–3pm and 6pm–12:30am. Métro: Gare Centrale.

't Kelderke ★★ TRADITIONAL BELGIAN   Despite being on the Grand-Place—the square that is the focus of tourism in Brussels—this is far from being a tourist trap. As many Bruxellois as tourists throng the long wooden tables in a 17th-century, brick-arched cellar, and all are welcomed with time-honored respect. Memorable traditional Belgian fare, with little in the way of frills, is served up from an open kitchen. This is a great place to try local specialties.

Grand-Place 15. © 02/513-73-44. Main courses 9.50€–18.50€ ($11–$21.25); *plat du jour* 7.50€ ($8.75). AE, DC, MC, V. Daily noon–2am. Métro: Gare Centrale.

SHOPPING

One of Europe's oldest shopping malls, the **Galeries Royales St-Hubert** (Métro: Gare Centrale) is a light and airy arcade hosting boutiques, cafe terraces, and street musicians playing classical music. Built in Italian neo-Renaissance style and opened in 1847, architect Pierre Cluysenaer's gallery offers shopping with a touch of class and is well worth strolling through even if you have no intention of even looking in a shop window. The Galeries Royales St-Hubert is near the Grand-Place, between rue du Marché-aux-Herbes and rue de l'Ecuyer, and split by rue de Bouchers.

Among the finest—and most addictive—of Belgian specialties are the country's handmade chocolates. Two good places to buy these are **Neuhaus,** Galerie de la Reine 25 (© 02/502-59-14; Métro: Gare Centrale); and **Wittamer,** Place du Grand-Sablon 12 (© 02/512-37-42; Tram: 92, 93). And while you're in sweet-tooth mode, for spicy *speculoos* cookies (made with cinnamon, ginger, and almond) and *pain à grecque,* a thin, spicy biscuit, check out **Dandoy,** rue au Beurre 31 (© 02/511-81-76; Métro: Bourse).

Lace isn't far behind as a Brussels shopping highlight. Two fine, centrally located stores that retail top-quality handmade Belgian lace, are **Maison Antoine,** Grand-Place 26 (© 02/512-14-59; Métro: Gare Centrale), and **Manufacture Belge de Dentelle,** Galerie de la Reine 6–8 (© 02/511-44-77; Métro: Gare Centrale).

MARKETS

At the **Flea Market** on place du Jeu-de-Balle (Métro: Louise), a large square in the Marolles district, you can find some exceptional decorative items, many recycled from the homes of the "recently deceased," as well as unusual postcards, clothing, and household goods. The market is held daily from 7am to 2pm.

Every weekend, the place du Grand-Sablon hosts a fine **Antiques Market** (Tram: 92, 93, 94). The salesmanship is low-key, the interest pure, the prices not unreasonable (don't expect bargains though), and the quality of the merchandise—which includes silverware, pottery, paintings, and jewelry—is high. The market is open Saturday from 9am to 6pm and Sunday from 9am to 2pm.

Near the Grand-Place, at the top end of rue du Marché-aux-Herbes, in a square loosely called the Agora, there's a weekend **Crafts Market** (Métro: Gare Centrale), with lots of fine specialized jewelry and other items, mostly inexpensive.

NIGHTLIFE

The superb and historic **Théâtre Royal de la Monnaie** ★★, place de la Monnaie (© **02/229-12-11;** Métro: De Brouckere), founded in the 17th century, is home to the Opéra National and l'Orchestre Symphonique de la Monnaie. Ballet performances are also presented here. The present resident ballet company is local choreographer Anne Theresa de Keersmaeker's Group Rosas. The **Palais des Beaux-Arts,** rue Royale 10 (© **02/507-82-00;** Métro: Parc), is the home of Belgium's National Orchestra.

Théâtre Toone VII, in an upstairs room in a bistro of the same name, is the latest in the Toone line of puppet theaters, which dates back to the early 1800s—the title being passed from one puppet master to the next—and it may be the most popular theater in Brussels. At Toone, Puppet Master José Géal presents his adaptation of such classic tales as *The Three Musketeers, Faust,* and *Hamlet* in the Brussels dialect, but also in English, French, Dutch, and German. Impasse Schuddeveld 6, Petite rue des Bouchers 21 (© **02/513-54-86;** Métro: Gare Centrale). Ticket prices and performance times vary.

⌒Moments Puppet Shows

A special word is in order about a special sort of theater—that of the wooden marionettes that have entertained Belgians for centuries. In times past, puppet theaters numbered in the hundreds nationwide (Brussels alone had 15), and the plays were much like our modern-day soap operas. The story lines went on and on, sometimes for generations, and working-class audiences returned night after night to keep up with the *Dallas* of the times. Performances were based on folklore, legends, or political satire.

Specific marionette characters came to personify their home cities: a cheeky ragamuffin named Woltje (Little Walloon) was from Brussels; Antwerp had the cross-eyed, earthy ne'er-do-well Schele; Pierke, from Ghent, was modeled on the traditional Italian clown; and Liège's Tchantchès stood only 16 inches high and always appeared with patched trousers, a tasseled floppy hat, and his constant companion, the sharp-tongued Nanesse (Agnes).

Jazz is a popular but ever-changing scene. **Phil's Jazz Kitchen Café,** rue Haute 189 (*©* **02/513-95-88**), a relaxed bar with good atmosphere, has jazz or other music most nights of the week, and a jam session on Wednesday. **L'Archiduc,** rue Antoine Dansaert 6 (*©* **02/512-06-52**), puts on jazz concerts on Saturday and Sunday. The **Marcus Mingus Jazz Spot,** impasse de la Fidélité 10–11 (*©* **02/502-02-97**), lights up jazz, Brazilian, Latin, blues, and funk, Tuesday to Sunday at 10pm.

BARS & CAFES   Unique, to say the least, is a Brussels favorite, **A la Mort Subite,** rue Montagne-aux-Herbes-Potagères 7 (*©* **02/513-13-18**), a bistro of rather special character whose name translates to "Sudden Death," which is also the name of one of the beers you can buy here. The decor consists of stained-glass motifs, old photographs, paintings, and prints on the walls, and plain wooden chairs and tables on the floor.

Au Bon Vieux Temps, rue du Marché-aux-Herbes 12 (*©* **02/217-26-26**), hidden away at the end of a narrow alleyway, is a gloomily atmospheric old tavern that seems to hearken back to a bygone era. You should try the appropriately named *Duvel* (Devil) beer here. **A l'Image de Notre-Dame,** impasse rue du Marché-aux-Herbes 6 (*©* **02/219-42-49**), is a good, quiet place to drink and read or reflect if you're alone, or to converse with a companion without having to compete with a blaring jukebox.

A legendary 1904 Art Nouveau tavern, enlivened with a dash of Art Deco and rococo, **Le Falstaff,** rue Henri Maus 17–25 (*©* **02/511-87-89**), has shed its former, famously vain waitstaff and slipped a few notches on the hip scale as a result. If such considerations don't worry you, there's still the same stunning decor, stained-glass scenes in the style of Pieter Brueghel the Elder depicting Shakespeare's Falstaff tales, and reasonably priced brasserie food.

Rick's, av. Louise 344 (*©* **02/640-03-05**), brings a touch of Humphrey Bogart and Ernest Hemingway, accompanied by American and Mexican food, to the stylish avenue Louise.

AN EXCURSION TO GHENT ★★

In the tourism department, Ghent (Gent) is often considered a poor relation of Bruges (p. 140). Its historical monuments and townscapes are not quite as pretty as those in its sister city, and, therefore, only to be viewed if there is time after visiting Bruges. There is some truth in this—but not too much. An important port and industrial center, Ghent compensates for its less precious appearance with a vigorous social and cultural scene.

ESSENTIALS

GETTING THERE   Ghent is just a 32-minute train ride from Brussels (trains leave from all three of Brussels's major stations, so go to whichever is closest to your hotel), and there are around four trains an hour from the capital. The main train station, **Gent Sint-Pieters Station** (*©* **09/222-44-44**), is on Koningin Maria-Hendrikaplein, 1½ miles (2km) south of the city center and connected by frequent tram to the center.

VISITOR INFORMATION   The **Ghent Tourist Office (Dienst Toerisme),** Predikherenlei 2, 9000 Gent (*©* **09/225-36-41;** www.gent.be), is open Monday to Friday from 8:30am to noon and 1 to 4:30pm. More convenient for personal visits is the **Infokantoor (Inquiry Desk)** in the cellar of the Belfry, Botermarkt 17A, 9000 Gent (*©* **09/266-52-32;** fax 09/224-15-55); open April to October daily from 9:30am to 6:30pm, and November to March daily from 9:30am to 4:30pm.

⌒Moments   A Stroll Through History

Graslei 🅐🅐, a beautiful canalside street, is home to a solid row of towering, gabled guild houses built between the 1200s and 1600s, when the
neighboring waterway formed the city's harbor. To fully appreciate their
majesty, walk across the bridge over the Leie to **Korenlei** on the opposite
bank and view them as a whole, then return to stroll past each.

TOP ATTRACTIONS & SPECIAL MOMENTS

Even if you see nothing else in Ghent, you shouldn't miss **Sint-Baafskathedraal
(St. Bavo's Cathedral)** 🅐🅐🅐, Sint-Baafsplein. (© **09/225-16-26**). Don't be
put off by the exterior's uncertain mix of Romanesque, Gothic, and baroque.
The interior is filled with priceless paintings, sculptures, screens, memorials, and
carved tombs. About midway along the vaulted nave is a remarkable pulpit in
white marble entwined with oak, reminiscent of Bernini. St. Bavo's showpiece is
the 24-panel altarpiece *The Adoration of the Mystic Lamb,* completed by Jan van
Eyck in 1432. The cathedral is open April to October, daily from 8:30am to
6pm; November to March, daily from 8:30am to 5pm. Admission to the Cathedral is free; to the *Mystic Lamb* chapel 2.50€ ($3) for adults, 1.25€ ($1.40) for
children ages 6 to 12, and free for children under 6.

Just across the square from the cathedral, the richly ornate Gothic **Belfort en
Lakenhalle (Belfry and Cloth Hall)** 🅐🅐, Sint-Baafsplein (© **09/223-99-22**),
together form a glorious medieval ensemble. The Cloth Hall from 1425 to 1445
is where cloth was stored and traded and was the gathering place of wool and
cloth merchants. A World Heritage site, the Belfry, from 1314 to 1338, is 295
feet high and has a gilded copper dragon at its summit. It holds the great bells
that have rung out Ghent's civic pride down through the centuries. Take the elevator up to the Belfry's upper gallery, at a height of 215 feet, to see the bells and
a fantastic panoramic view of the city. The attraction is open mid-March to mid-
November, daily from 10am to 1pm and 2 to 6pm. Admission is 3€ ($3.50) for
adults, 1.75€ ($2) for seniors and students, and .90€ ($1.05) for children
under 12. Free guided tours are available Easter and May to September, Tuesday
to Sunday at 2:10, 3:10, and 4:10pm.

"Grim" is the word that springs to mind when you first see the **Gravensteen
(Castle of the Counts)** 🅐, Sint-Veereplein (© **09/269-37-30**). The fortress,
built by Philip of Alsace in 1180, crouches like a gray stone lion over the city. If
the castle's 6-foot-thick walls, battlements, and turrets failed to intimidate attackers, the count could always turn to a well-equipped torture chamber inside. On
a happier note, if you climb to the ramparts of the high building in the center,
the donjon, your reward is a great view of Ghent's rooftops and towers. The castle is open April to September, daily from 9am to 6pm; October to March, daily
from 9am to 5pm. Admission is 6.20€ ($7.25) for adults; 2.50€ ($3) for seniors, students, and visitors ages 12 to 26; and free for children under 12.

WHERE TO DINE

In a town where the Middle Ages are *big,* the **Brasserie Pakhuis** 🅐🅐, Schu-
urkenstraat 4 (© **09/223-55-55**), located off of Veldstraat, is almost modern. In
a vast, beautifully restored 19th-century warehouse down a narrow lane, it's
replete with painted cast-iron pillars, soaring wrought-iron balconies, and oak
and marble tables with specially designed table settings, and has a granite mosaic

floor. Although maybe too conscious of its own sense of style, Pakhuis (which means "warehouse" in Dutch) is all stocked up in matters of taste and serves excellent Flemish cuisine. Main courses range from 9.60€ to 19€ ($11–$21.75).

Convivial and trendy, **Keizershof** 🐝, Vrijdagmarkt 47 (© **09/223-44-66**), situated on the garish market square, has an attractively informal ambience and a good menu of Continental fare. Behind its narrow, hard-to-spot facade are plain wood tables on multiple floors around a central stairwell. The decor beneath the timber ceiling beams is spare, tastefully tattered, and speckled with paintings by local artists. Service for office workers doing lunch is fast; in the evenings you're expected to linger. In summertime, you can dine alfresco in a courtyard at the back. An entree will set you back 8.50€ to 17.25€ ($9.75–$19.75).

Moments **Heading Out to Waterloo**

The Battle of Waterloo was Europe's Gettysburg, and the battlefield on which it was fought remains much as it was on June 18, 1815. To visit it, you don't actually go to the town of Waterloo, 6 miles (10km) south of Brussels. The Battle of Waterloo was not fought there. A stretch of rolling farmland dotted with stoutly built manor-farmhouses several miles to the south got that "honor." By bus from Brussels, take line W from Gare du Midi to the **Centre Visiteur (Visitor Center),** route du Lion 252–254 (© **02/385-19-12**), where an audiovisual presentation on the tactical background plus an extract from a fictional film version of the conflict will give you an idea of the battle's impressive scale.

The view of the theater of war from the top of the **Butte du Lion (Lion Mound)** beside the Visitor Center is worth the 226-step climb, though it takes an active imagination to fill the peaceful farmland with slashing cavalry charges, thundering artillery, and 200,000 color-fully uniformed, struggling soldiers. Across the road from the Visitor Center is the Waxworks Museum, where Napoleon, Wellington, Blücher, and others appear as rather tatty wax figures. Also next to the Center is the Battlefield Panorama (Panorama de la Bataille), featuring a painted diorama of the massive French cavalry charge led by Marshal Ney. It was a sensation in the pre-cinema era.

These three sites are open January to February and November to December, daily from 10:30am to 4pm; March, daily from 10:30am to 5pm; April to September, daily from 9:30am to 6:30pm; October, daily from 9:30am to 5:30pm. A combined ticket is 9.65€ ($11) for adults, 8€ ($9.25) for students and seniors, 6.15€ ($7) for children ages 6 to 12, and free for children under 6.

In Waterloo itself is the well-ordered **Musée Wellington (Wellington Museum),** chaussée de Bruxelles 147 (© **02/354-78-06**), in an old Bra-bant coaching inn that was the Duke's headquarters. It was from here that Wellington sent his historic victory dispatch. The museum is open April to September, daily from 9:30am to 6:30pm; November to March, daily from 10:30am to 5pm. Admission is 5€ ($5.75) for adults, 4€ ($4.50) for students and seniors, 1€ ($1.15) for children ages 6 to 12, and free for children under 6.

AN EXCURSION TO ANTWERP ⭐

Antwerp, the acknowledged "Diamond Center of the World," is one of western Europe's most hidden gems. Many people think of it only as a port and center of the diamond trade, yet it is also easygoing, stylish, and filled with the monuments of a wealthy medieval and Renaissance period. Only 48 minutes by rail from Brussels, and compact enough for walking, it's an ideal day trip out of the capital city.

ESSENTIALS

GETTING THERE   You can count on around four trains an hour from Brussels. Antwerp's two train stations are **Antwerpen Centraal Station,** 1 mile (1.5km) east of the Grote Markt, on the edge of the city center, in an area that's currently the focus of a great deal of construction activity; and **Berchem,** 2.5 miles (4km) south of the city center. Centraal Station is far more useful for visitors, so if you can, try to arrive at that station. Trains do connect the two stations, so the worst that will happen is you'll need to transfer at Berchem. For schedule and fare information, call ✆ **03/240-20-40.**

Antwerp is on the **Thalys** high-speed train network that connects Paris, Brussels, and Amsterdam (and Cologne via Brussels). All Thalys trains stop at Berchem. Reservations are required for Thalys (for more on high-speed trains, see p. 32); the local reservations number is ✆ **03/240-20-40.**

VISITOR INFORMATION   There is a small branch of the Antwerp Tourist Office on the Koningin Astridplein square just outside Antwerpen Centraal Station that is open daily from 9am to 6pm. Signs inside the train station will direct you there. Pick up a very useful map of the city at the office; it'll cost you about 1€ $1.15. The main branch of the **Antwerp Tourist Office,** Grote Markt 15, 2000 Antwerpen (✆ **03/232-01-03;** www.visitantwerpen.be; Tram: 2, 3, 4, 8, 15), is open Monday to Saturday from 9am to 5:45pm, and Sunday from 9am to 4:45pm.

TOP ATTRACTIONS & SPECIAL MOMENTS

Housed in an impressive neoclassical building, the **Koninklijk Museum voor Schone Kunsten Antwerpen (Antwerp Royal Museum of Fine Arts)** ⭐⭐⭐, Leopold de Waelplaats 2 (✆ **03/238-78-09**), has a collection of paintings by Flemish masters that is second to none in the world. Among them are more Rubens masterpieces in one place than anywhere else. To view them, pass through the ground-floor exhibits of canvases by modern artists (including works by Ensor, Magritte, Permeke, and Delvaux). Ascend to the second floor, where you'll find works by Rubens, Jan van Eyck, Rogier van der Weyden, Dirck Bouts, Hans Memling, the Brueghel family, and by the Dutch artists Rembrandt and Frans Hals. The museum is open Tuesday to Sunday from 10am to 5pm. Admission is 4€ ($4.50) for adults, 3€ ($3.50) for seniors and students, and free for children under 19.

A masterpiece of Brabant Gothic architecture, the towering **Onze-Lieve-Vrouwekathedraal (Cathedral of Our Lady)** ⭐⭐⭐, Handschoenmarkt (✆ **03/213-99-40**), off of the Grote Markt, is the largest church in the Low Countries. Begun in 1352 and completed by around 1520, it has 7 aisles and 125 pillars, but of the original design's five towers, only one was ever completed. This one is the tallest church spire in the Low Countries, 403 feet high. The cathedral's interior is a mix of baroque and neoclassical. It houses four Rubens

Moments **Cruising the Harbor**

Do take a cruise around Antwerp's awesome harbor, which handles 16,000 ships and 100 million tons of cargo a year. Most departures are from the Steen waterfront on the Scheldt. **Flandria Line** (*©* **03/231-31-00**) runs a 2½-hour harbor cruise for 11.50€ ($13.25) for adults and 6.50€ ($7.25) for children.

altarpieces. The cathedral is open Monday to Friday from 10am to 5pm, Saturday from 10am to 3pm, and Sunday and holidays from 1 to 4pm. Admission is 2€ ($2.25), free for children under 13.

To touch Antwerp's cultural heart, a visit to the **Rubenshuis (Rubens House)** 🐦🐦, Wapper 9–11 (*©* **03/201-15-55**), a short walk east of the center, is essential. Antwerp's most illustrious son, the artist Peter Paul Rubens (1577–1640), lived and worked here. Rubens amassed a tidy fortune from his paintings that allowed him to build this impressive mansion in 1610, along what was then a canal, when he was 33. Today, you can stroll past the baroque portico into its reconstructed period rooms and through a Renaissance garden, and come away with a good idea of the lifestyle of a patrician Flemish gentleman of that era. Examples of Rubens's works, and others by master painters who were his contemporaries, are scattered throughout. The museum is open Tuesday to Sunday from 10am to 4:45pm. Admission is 5€ ($5.75) for adults, and 2.50€ ($3) for students; admission on Friday is free.

De Steen 🐦, Steenplein 1 (*©* **03/232-08-50**), a medieval fortress on the banks of the Scheldt beside the Scheldt, is Antwerp's oldest building. The glowering fortress has served a number of purposes over the centuries. Today, it houses the **Nationaal Scheepvaartmuseum (National Maritime Museum).** There are exhibits about the development of the port, and maritime history in general. The most eye-catching are models of old-time sailing ships, like those of the Belgian East India Company clippers. The museum is open Tuesday to Sunday from 10am to 4:45pm. Admission is 4€ ($4.50) for adults, 2€ ($2.25) students, and free for children.

The Diamond Quarter

Some 85% of the world's rough diamonds, 50% of cut diamonds, and 40% of industrial diamonds—together valued at more than $12.5 billion—are traded here annually. The diamond cutters of Antwerp are world-renowned for their skill, which you can admire in the Diamond Quarter, a surprisingly down-at-the-heels-looking area, only steps away from Centraal Station. More than 12,000 cutters and polishers work inside 380 workshops, serving 1,500 firms and 3,500 brokers and merchants. Browsing the various shop windows in the quarter is a highly enjoyable activity and won't cost you a thing.

WHERE TO DINE

The attractive **In de Schaduw van de Kathedraal** 🐦, Handschoenmarkt 17–21 (*©* **03/232-40-14**), in the city center, features traditional Belgian cuisine gussied up just a bit. Mussels and eel assume several guises on the menu, and beef is also well represented. If the prices here seem a little inflated, it's probably because of the excellent location; after all, this restaurant lies, as its name says, "in the shadow of the cathedral." Main courses cost 20€ to 45€ ($23–$51.75).

A location amid the delightful 16th-century Vlaeykensgang courtyard's jumble of cafes, restaurants, and antique apartments, all but guarantees a pleasant atmosphere at **Sir Anthony Van Dijck** ✩✩, Oude Koornmarkt 16 (📞 **03/231-61-70**). This used to be a Michelin Star–rated restaurant, until owner and chef Marc Paesbrugghe got tired of staying on the Michelin treadmill. Reopened as a relaxed French brasserie-restaurant, in a sparely elegant setting that's flooded with light from the old-world Vlaeykensgang courtyard through big, arched windows, it retains a commitment to good food. Main courses run 14€ to 19.50€ ($16–$22.50).

3 Bruges ✩✩✩

The graceful small city of Bruges (Brugge) has drifted down the stream of time with all the self-possession of the swans that cruise its canals. To step into the old town is to be transported instantly back to the Middle Ages, when Bruges was among the wealthiest cities of Europe. UNESCO has recognized the cultural importance of the historic center by awarding it World Heritage status. The city is the pride and joy of all Flanders.

Medieval Gothic architecture is the big deal here. Sure, there's a layer of Romanesque; a touch of Renaissance, baroque, and rococo; a dab of neoclassical and neo-Gothic; and a smidgen of Art Nouveau and Art Deco. But Gothic is what Bruges provides, in quantities that come near to numbing the senses— and likely would do so if it weren't for the distraction of the city's contemporary animation.

GETTING THERE   Trains arrive every half hour or so from Brussels, Antwerp, and Ghent, and from the North Sea ports of Ostend (Oostende) and Zeebrugge. Journey time is about 1 hour by train from Brussels and Antwerp, 30 minutes from Ghent, and 15 minutes from Ostend and Zeebrugge.

A train to and from Lille in northern France connects there with the Eurostar trains through the Channel Tunnel from London to Paris and Brussels. From Paris, you can take the Thalys high-speed trains through Brussels to Bruges, or the slower and cheaper international trains, changing in Brussels. International trains from Cologne to London, via Ostend, stop in Bruges. From Amsterdam, you can go via Antwerp or Brussels, either on the Thalys, or the normal international and InterCity trains. Although the city is called Bruges in English and French, in Dutch it's "Brugge," and that's what the train station destination boards say. The station is on Stationsplein, about 1 mile (1.6km) south of town, a 20-minute walk to the town center or a short bus or taxi ride. For train information, call 📞 **050/38-23-82** between 6:30am and 10:30pm.

VISITOR INFORMATION   Toerisme Brugge, Burg 11, 8000 Brugge (📞 **050/44-86-86;** www.brugge.be), is the official dispenser of tourist information for the city. The office is open March to mid-November, Monday to Friday from 9:30am to 6:30pm, weekends from 10am to noon and 2 to 6:30pm; Mid-November to February, Monday to Friday from 9:30am to 5pm, weekends from 9:30am to 1pm and 2 to 5:30pm. In addition, there's a booth for tourist information and hotel bookings outside the train station.

TOP ATTRACTIONS & SPECIAL MOMENTS

In the **Markt (Market Square),** heraldic banners float from venerable facades. This square, along with the Burg (see below), is the heart of Bruges and the focal point of your sightseeing. Most major points of interest in the city are no more than a 5- or 10-minute walk away.

Bruges

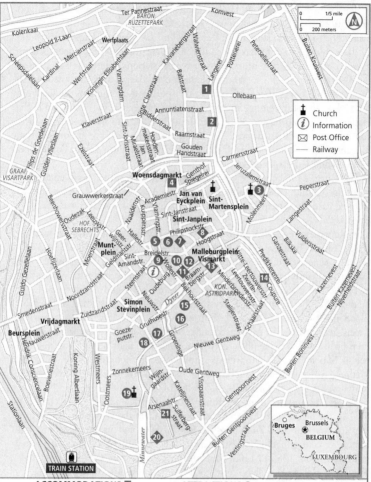

ACCOMMODATIONS ■
Dante **14**
Egmond **21**
Fevery **2**
Relais Oud Huis Amsterdam **4**
Ter Duinen **1**

DINING ◆
Brasserie Erasmus **11**
Breydel-de-Coninck **13**
De Gouden Meermin **7**
Kasteel Minnewater **20**
Lotus **8**

ATTRACTIONS ●
Basiliek van het Heilig Bloed
(Basilica of the Holy Blood) **10**
Belfort en Hallen (Belfry and Market Halls) **9**
Burg **6**
Groeninge Museum **15**
Gruuthuse Museum **16**
Kantcentrum (Lace Center) **3**
Markt **5**
Memling Museum **18**
Onze-Lieve-Vrouwekerk
(Church of Our Lady) **17**
Prinselijk Begijnhof ten Wijngaarde
(Princely Beguinage of the Vineyard) **19**
Stadhuis (Town Hall) **12**

A part of the **Belfort en Hallen (Belfry and Market Halls)** ✦✦, Markt (② **050/44-87-11**), the bell tower was, and is, the symbol of Bruges's civic pride. The tower itself stands 272 feet high. Its lower section dates from around 1240, with the corner turrets added in the 14th century and the upper, octagonal section in the 15th century. If you have the stamina, climb the 366 steps to the Belfry's summit for a panoramic view over Bruges and the surrounding countryside. Its magnificent 47-bell carillon peals out every quarter hour. From the 13th to the 16th century, much of the city's commerce was conducted in the Hallen. These halls have recently been brought back into use for exhibits by a consortium of local art dealers. The complex is open Tuesday to Sunday from 9:30am to 5pm. Admission is 5€ ($5.75) for adults, 2.50€ ($3) for visitors ages 13 to 26 and seniors, and free for children under 13.

The **Burg,** a public square just steps away from the Markt, holds an array of beautiful buildings. On this site, Baldwin Iron Arm, Count of Flanders, built a fortified castle (or "burg"), around which a village grew up that developed into Bruges.

A Romanesque basilica with a Gothic upper floor, the **Basiliek van het Heilig Bloed (Basilica of the Holy Blood)** ✦✦, Burg 10 (② **050/33-67-92**), houses a venerated relic of Christ. Since 1149, it has been the repository of a fragment of cloth embedded in a rock-crystal vial and stained with what is said to be the coagulated blood of Christ, wiped from his body by Joseph of Arimathea after the crucifixion. Every year, in the colorful Procession of the Holy Blood on Ascension Day, the bishop of Bruges carries the relic through the streets, accompanied by costumed residents acting out biblical scenes. The basilica is open April to September, daily from 9:30am to noon and 2 to 6pm; October to March, Thursday to Tuesday from 10am to noon and 2 to 4pm, and Wednesday from 10am to noon. Admission to the basilica is free; to the museum, 1€ ($1.15) for adults, and .50€ (60¢) for children.

Bruges's beautiful Gothic **Stadhuis (Town Hall)** ✦, Burg 12 (② **050/44-87-11**), the oldest town hall in Belgium, dates from the late 1300s. Don't miss the upstairs **Gotische Zaal (Gothic Room)** ✦✦ and its ornate decor, wall murals depicting highlights of the town's history, and the illuminated vaulted oak ceiling from 1385 to 1402, which features scenes from the New Testament. The Town Hall is open daily from 9:30am to 5pm. Admission is 1.50€ ($1.75) for adults, and .50€ (60¢) for children.

The **Groeninge Museum** ✦✦✦, Dijver 12 (② **050/44-87-11**), ranks among Belgium's leading traditional museums of fine arts, with a collection that covers painting in the Low Countries from the 15th to the 20th century. The Gallery of Flemish Primitives holds some 30 works by painters such as Jan van Eyck, Rogier van der Weyden, Hieronymus Bosch, and Hans Memling. Works by Magritte and Delvaux also are exhibited. The museum is open Tuesday to Sunday from 9:30am to 5pm. Admission is 6.25€ ($7.25) for adults, 3.75€ ($4.25) for children ages 5 to 18, and free for children under 5.

Lodewijk Van Gruuthuse, a Flemish nobleman and herb merchant who was a counselor to the Dukes of Burgundy in the 1400s, lived in this ornate Gothic mansion, now the **Gruuthuse Museum** ✦, Dijver 17 (② **050/44-87-11**). Among the 2,500 antiques in the house are paintings, sculptures, tapestries, lace, weapons, glassware, and richly carved furniture. The museum is open Tuesday to Sunday from 9:30am to 5pm. Admission is 3.25€ ($3.75) for adults, 1.75€ ($2) for children ages 5 to 18, and free for children under 5.

In the former Sint-Janshospitaal (Hospital of St. John), where the earliest wards date from the 13th century, is housed the **Memling Museum** ⭐⭐, Mariastraat (✆ **050/44-87-11**). Visitors come primarily for the magnificent collection of paintings by the German-born artist Hans Memling (ca. 1440–94), who moved to Bruges from Brussels in 1465 and became one of the city's most prominent artists. You'll find Memling masterpieces such as the three-paneled altarpiece of St. John the Baptist and St. John the Evangelist. The museum is open April to September daily from 9:30am to 5pm; October to March, Tuesday to Sunday from 9:30am to 12:30pm and 2 to 5pm. Admission is 3€ ($3.50) for adults, and 1.50€ ($1.75) for children.

It took 2 centuries (from the 13th–15th) to build the **Onze-Lieve-Vrouwekerk (Church of Our Lady)** ⭐⭐, Onze-Lieve-Vrouwekerkhof Zuid (✆ **050/34-53-14**), whose soaring 396-foot spire can be seen from miles around. Among the many art treasures within is a beautiful Carrara marble sculpture of the *Madonna and Child* ⭐⭐⭐, by Michelangelo. This statue, made in 1504, was the only one of Michelangelo's works to leave Italy during his lifetime. It was bought by a Bruges merchant, Jan van Mouskroen, and donated to the church in 1506. The church also holds a painting of the *Crucifixion* by Anthony Van Dyck, and the impressive side-by-side bronze **tomb sculptures** ⭐ of the Duke of Burgundy, Charles the Bold, who died in 1477, and his daughter, Mary of Burgundy, who died at age 25 in 1482. The church is open Monday to Friday from 9am to 12:30pm and 1:30 to 5pm, Saturday from 9am to 12:30pm and 1:30 to 4pm, and Sunday from 1:30 to 4pm. Admission to the Church and *Madonna and Child* altar is free; to the chapel of Charles and Mary and the museum, 2.50€ ($3) for adults, and 1.50€ ($1.75) for children.

A combination workshop, museum, and sale room, the **Kantcentrum (Lace Center)** ⭐⭐, Peperstraat 3A (✆ **050/33-00-72**), is where the ancient art of making lace by hand gets passed on to the next generation. The center is open Monday to Friday from 10am to noon and 2 to 6pm, Saturday from 10am to noon and 2 to 5pm. Admission is 1.50€ ($1.75) for adults, and 1€ ($1.15) for children.

Through the centuries, since it was founded in 1245 by the Countess Margaret of Constantinople, the **Prinselijk Begijnhof ten Wijngaarde (Princely Beguinage of the Vineyard)** ⭐⭐⭐, Wijngaardstraat (✆ **050/33-00-11**), at the Lake of Love, has been one of the most tranquil spots in Bruges, and so it remains today. *Begijns* were religious women, similar to nuns, who accepted vows of chastity and obedience, but drew the line at poverty, preferring to earn a living by looking after the sick and making lace. The begijns are no more, but the Begijnhof is occupied by the Benedictine nuns of the Monasterium De Wijngaard, who try to keep their traditions alive. This beautiful little cluster of 17th-century whitewashed houses surrounding a lawn with poplar trees and flowers makes a marvelous escape from the hustle and bustle of the outside world. The Begijnhof courtyard is always open and admission is free.

WHERE TO STAY

Dante   This ultramodern brick hotel is set alongside a lovely canal, a short walk west from the center of Bruges. The hotel is an artful combination of old Bruges style and modern amenities and fittings. Its spacious guest rooms are restfully decorated in warm colors like peach and furnished with bamboo and rattan beds. Most have a view of the canal at Coupure. The Dante's vegetarian restaurant Toermalijn is highly regarded locally.

Coupure 29, 8000 Brugge. ℭ **050/34-01-94**. Fax 050/34-35-39. www.hoteldante.be. 22 units. 106€–131€ ($122–$151) double. Rates include buffet breakfast. AE, DC, MC, V. **Amenities:** Restaurant; laundry; non-smoking rooms. *In room:* Hair dryer.

Egmond ⭐⭐   The Egmond has just eight rooms, housed in a rambling mansion next to the Minnewater Park, but the lucky few who stay here will find ample space, plenty of family ambience, abundant local color, and lots of peace and tranquillity. All rooms have recently been redecorated and are furnished in an individual style; all have views of the garden and the Minnewater Park. Every afternoon, free coffee and tea are served in the new garden terrace or in the lounge.

Minnewater 15, 8000 Brugge. ℭ **050/34-14-45**. Fax 050/34-29-40. www.egmond.be. 8 units. 100€–120€ ($115–$138) double. Rates include buffet breakfast. No credit cards. *In room:* Hair dryer.

Fevery ⭐   A family-owned hotel, the Fevery is on a quiet side street off of Langerei in a quiet part of town. The modern and comfortably furnished guest rooms, enlarged through a rebuilding program that ended in 2002, are cheery and immaculate, with new bathrooms and monogrammed pressed sheets. The proprietor Mr. Asselman is a wealth of local information and clearly takes great pride in his establishment.

Collaert Mansionstraat 3, 8000 Brugge. ℭ **050/33-12-69**. Fax 050/33-17-91. www.hotelfevery.be. 10 units. 60€–80€ ($69–$92) double. Rates include buffet breakfast. AE, MC, V. **Amenities:** Lounge.

Relais Oud Huis Amsterdam ⭐⭐   Rooms in this large canal-side building, parts of which date back to the 1300s, are large and sumptuously furnished. Some of the bathrooms feature whirlpool tubs. The elegant guest rooms in the front overlook the canal; those in back overlook the garden and picturesque rooftops. In the rear, there's a charming little courtyard with umbrella tables and a garden off to one side—the setting for Sunday concerts in June.

Spiegelrei 3, 8000 Brugge. ℭ **050/34-18-10**. Fax 050/33-88-91. www.oha.be. 34 units. 207€–329€ ($238–$378) double. AE, DC, MC, V. **Amenities:** Bar; laundry; nonsmoking rooms. *In room:* Hair dryer.

Ter Duinen ⭐   This charming hotel is an ideal marriage of classical style and modern conveniences. Guest rooms are ample in size, brightly decorated, and have modern furnishings. Some rooms have wooden ceiling beams, and some have a great view overlooking the tranquil Langerei canal, just north of the town center and an easy walk away. Proprietors Marc and Lieve Bossu-Van Den Heuvel take justified pride in their hotel and extend a friendly welcome to guests.

Langerei 52, 8000 Brugge. ℭ **050/33-04-37**. Fax 050/34-42-16. www.terduinenhotel.be. 20 units. 98€–148€ ($113–$170) double. Rates include full breakfast. AE, DC, MC, V. **Amenities:** Lounge; laundry. *In room:* A/C, hair dryer.

WHERE TO DINE

Brasserie Erasmus ⭐ FLEMISH   Small but popular, this is a great stop after viewing the cathedral and nearby museums. It serves a large variety of Flemish dishes, all prepared with beer. Try the typically Flemish souplike stew dish *waterzooï,* which is very good here and is served with fish, as it's supposed to be, although they also make it with chicken, a style that has become the norm elsewhere.

Wollestraat 35. ℭ **050/33-57-81**. Main courses 15€–25€ ($17.25–$28.75); fixed-price menus 20€–30€ ($23–$34.50). MC, V. Tues–Sun noon–4pm (summer also Mon) and 6–11pm.

Breydel-de-Coninck ⭐ SEAFOOD   The wood beam ceilings and plaid upholstery here are cheerful but the real attraction is the seafood. The specialties are mussels, eels, and lobsters prepared with white wine, cream, or garlic sauces that enhance the flavor of the seafood without overwhelming it. Try a pail full of plain mussels, or go for something with a little more zest, such as the *moules Provençal* (mussels in a light red sauce with mushrooms, peppers, and onions).

Breidelstraat 24. ✆ **050/33-27-46**. Main courses 9.50€–19.50€ ($11–$22.50); fixed-price meals 14.50€–35€ ($16.75–$40.25). AE, MC, V. Thurs–Tues noon–3pm and 6–9:30pm.

De Gouden Meermin ✰ FLEMISH   The best of the many brasseries, tea-rooms, and cafes that line the Markt, this one has both outdoor dining and a glassed-in room that overlooks the square. The Flemish dishes are made with local ingredients, and the bowls of homemade soup are delicious. Sandwiches, snacks, and crêpes (a large variety, and all good) are available.

Markt 31. ✆ **050/33-37-76**. Main courses 12€–32€ ($13.75–$36.75); fixed-price menu 32€ ($36.75). AE, DC, MC, V. Daily 10am–10pm.

Kasteel Minnewater ✰✰ *Value* BELGIAN/FRENCH   Old paintings on the walls, a marble fireplace, chandeliers, and fine table linen, all complement this château-restaurant's superb location on the *Minnewater* (Lake of Love). It exudes an unstuffy charm that makes château dining not just something for lords and ladies, and though prices have been edging up, it still provides a good deal considering the setting.

Minnewater 4. ✆ **050/33-42-54**. Main courses 10.75€–24.50€ ($12.25–$28.25). V. Summer daily 11am–11pm; winter Mon–Fri noon–2:30pm and 6:30–11pm, Sat–Sun 11am–11pm.

Lotus ✰ VEGETARIAN   Even non-vegetarians will likely enjoy the delicious lunch here. There are just two menu options—but at least you can choose from a small, medium, or large serving—each with a hearty assortment of imaginatively prepared vegetables, served in a tranquil but cheery Scandinavian-style dining room.

Wapenmakersstraat 5. ✆ **050/33-10-78**. Fixed-price lunch menus 7.50€–9€ ($8.75–$10.25). No credit cards. Mon–Sat 11:45am–2pm.

EXCURSION TO OSTEND ✰

The "Queen of the Coast's" glitter has faded since its 19th-century heyday as a royal vacation spot and prestigious European watering hole, but plenty of reasons remain to justify a visit to Ostend (*Oostende* in Dutch; *Ostende* in French), 12 miles (20km) west of Bruges. Great sandy beaches, a casino, racetrack, art museums, spa, good shopping, an Olympic-size indoor swimming pool, outdoor pools filled with heated seawater, sailing and windsurfing, and last but by no means least, a legitimate reputation of being a seafood cornucopia, all draw visitors to Belgium's most popular beach resort.

ESSENTIALS

GETTING THERE   Trains depart from Bruges at least every half hour for the 15-minute trip to Oostende Station, Stationsplein (✆ **059/70-15-17**), an extravagant neo-baroque edifice from 1913, beside the harbor.

VISITOR INFORMATION   Toerisme Oostende, Monacoplein 2, 8400 Oostende (✆ **059/70-11-99;** www.oostende.be), is open May to October, Monday to Saturday from 9am to 7pm, and Sunday from 10am to 7pm; November to April, Monday to Saturday from 10am to 6pm, and Sunday 10am to 5pm. A **tourist information booth** at the train station is open July and August, daily from 9am to 1pm and 4 to 7:30pm.

TOP ATTRACTIONS & SPECIAL MOMENTS

The long beach west of the harbor has stretches that are under lifeguard surveillance in summertime from 10:30am to 6:30pm and some stretches where swimming is not permitted at any time. Look out for the signs that indicate both of these, and for the green, yellow, or red flags that tell you whether the sea conditions permit swimming.

The **Casino-Kursaal Oostende** ☆, Monacoplein (𝄞 **059/70-51-11**), has an opulent interior, with a concert hall, panoramic rooftop restaurant (open 5pm–midnight), dance hall, and, of course, gaming rooms, where you can play roulette, blackjack, and punto banco. The gaming rooms are open daily from 3pm to 7am. Admission is 4€ ($4.50) and a passport is required.

The house where Anglo-Belgian artist James Ensor (1860–1949) lived between 1916 and his death has been transformed into a museum of his life, and restored to its condition when his aunt kept a ground-floor shells-and-souvenir store here. Ensor's studio and lounge are on the second floor of the **James Ensorhuis** ☆, Vlaanderenstraat 27 (𝄞 **059/80-53-35**), off Wapenplein. Little understood or appreciated during his lifetime for his fantastical, hallucinatory, and sexually ambiguous visions, the pre-Expressionist painter is now considered a founder of modern art. The museum is open June to September, Wednesday to Monday from 10am to noon and 2 to 5pm; November to May, Saturday and Sunday from 2 to 5pm; closed October. Admission is 1.50€ ($1.75) for adults, and free for children under 17.

WHERE TO DINE

Family-owned and with a high local reputation, **David Dewaele** ☆☆, Visserskaai 39 (𝄞 **059/70-42-26**), occupies a prime position on Ostend's "Fisherman's Wharf." A marine theme is maintained in the bright, elegant interior, with a decor of seashells, sailing photographs, and other nautical tokens. Most fish comes fresh from the North Sea and from the market across the street. Main courses cost 16€ to 35€ ($18.50–$40.25); fixed-price menus 25€ ($28.75) and 49.50€ ($57).

At **James Taverne** ☆☆, James Ensor Galerij 34 (off Vlaanderenstraat; 𝄞 **059/70-52-45**), an Old Flemish tavern in an Art Deco shopping gallery, tucking into a plate of two homemade *garnaalkroketten* (shrimp croquettes), accompanied by two slices of lemon and a sprig of crisply fried parsley, washed down with a glass of local Wieze beer, is something of an Ostend tradition. The James's cozy and friendly atmosphere is equally memorable. Main courses cost 9€ to 16.50€ ($10.25–$19).

4 Liège

Fervent, lively Liège—its nickname is *la Cité Ardente* (the Passionate City)—exudes the aura of an aging industrial gloom, but that seems to fade next to its gracefully down-at-the-heels 19th-century monuments and remnants from the time of its powerful prince-bishops.

GETTING THERE   There are between two and four trains an hour to Liège from Brussels and Antwerp, one an hour from Maastricht and Cologne, and one every 2 hours from Luxembourg. The Thalys high-speed train, goes via Brussels, from Paris and Amsterdam, and direct from Cologne. The main train station is **Gare des Guillemins,** rue des Guillemins (𝄞 **04/229-21-11**), just south of the city center. The smaller, more centrally located station **Liège Palais,** on rue de Bruxelles, is used by some local and connecting trains.

Liège

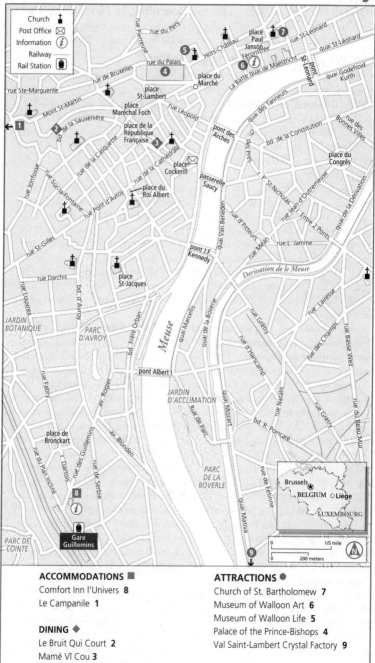

Map Legend
- Church ✝
- Post Office ✉
- Information ⓘ
- Railway —
- Rail Station 🚉

Map labels:

rue du Péry · rue du Palais · rue Pierreuse · rue de Bruxelles · rue Ste-Marguerite · Mont St-Martin · bd. de la Sauvenière · place St-Lambert · place Maréchal Foch · rue de la Casquette · place de la République Française · rue Jonfosse · rue Sur-la-Fontaine · rue St-Gilles · rue Pont d'Avroy · place du Roi Albert · rue de la Cathédrale · place Cockerill · rue Darchis · rue L'ouvrex · bd. d'Avroy · place St-Jacques · JARDIN BOTANIQUE · PARC D'AVROY · bd. Frère Orban · rue Fabry · place de Bronckart · rue du Plan Incliné · r. Dartois · rue des Guillemins · av. Rogier · av. Blonden · rue de Serbie · pont Albert · JARDIN D'ACCLIMATION · rue de Parc · quai Marcellis · quai de la Boverie · quai Mozart · bd. R. Poincaré · PARC DE LA BOVERIE · rue de Fétinne · quai Mativa · PARC DE COINTE · Gare Guillemins

Hors-Château · place du Marché · place Paul Janson · Féronstrée · rue St-Léonard · quai St-Léonard · quai Godefroid Kurth · La Batte · quai de Maestricht · pont St-Léonard · rue Léopold · pont des Arches · quai des Tanneurs · bd. de la Constitution · rue des Bonnes Villes · place du Congrès · Q. des Prés · passerelle Saucy · rue J. P. St-Nicholas · rue Jean d'Outremeuse · quai de la Dérivation · rue Van-Beneden · rue d'Harscamp · rue d'Patteus · rue Jean Entre 2 Ponts · rue Méan · rue L. Jamme · pont J.F. Kennedy · Derivation de le Meuse · rue L'airesse · rue Grétry · rue des Champs · rue Basse Wez · rue du Beau Mur · rue Natalis · Meuse

Locator map:
Brussels · BELGIUM · Liège · LUXEMBOURG

Scale: 0 – 1/5 mile · 0 – 200 meters

ACCOMMODATIONS ■
Comfort Inn l'Univers **8**
Le Campanile **1**

DINING ◆
Le Bruit Qui Court **2**
Mamé Vî Cou **3**

ATTRACTIONS ●
Church of St. Bartholomew **7**
Museum of Walloon Art **6**
Museum of Walloon Life **5**
Palace of the Prince-Bishops **4**
Val Saint-Lambert Crystal Factory **9**

VISITOR INFORMATION   The city **tourist office,** En Féronstrée 92, 4000 Liège (© **04/221-92-21;** www.liege.be), is open Monday to Friday from 9am to 6pm, Saturday from 10am to 4pm, and Sunday from 10am to 2pm.

TOP ATTRACTIONS & SPECIAL MOMENTS

A small but impressive collection of works by Walloon (French-speaking Belgian) artists from the 16th century to the present, graces the **Musée de l'Art Wallon (Museum of Walloon Art)** ⚐, En Féronstrée 86 (© **04/221-92-31**), by the river in the center. Among these are Paul Delvaux, Constant Meunier, Antoine Wiertz, Félicien Rops, René Magritte, Roger Somville, and Pierre Alechinsky. The museum is open Tuesday to Saturday from 1 to 6pm, and Sunday from 11am to 4:30pm. Admission is 1.25€ ($1.40) for adults, and .80€ (90¢) for children.

An incredible array of exhibits bring to life the days of 19th-century Walloons and their traditions and customs, at the **Musée de la Vie Wallonne (Museum of Walloon Life)** ⚐⚐, Cour des Mineurs (© **04/223-60-94**), in the city center, north of place Saint-Lambert. Housed in a 17th-century former Franciscan convent, the collection features examples of popular art, crafts, recreation, and even the workings of a coal mine. Here, too, is a marvelous puppet collection, which includes the city's beloved Tchantchès. The museum is open Tuesday to Saturday from 10am to 5pm, and Sunday from 10am to 4pm. Admission is 2.50€ ($3) for adults, 1.50€ ($1.75) for children ages 6 to 18, and free for children under 6.

The twin-towered Romanesque **Eglise St-Barthélemy (Church of St. Bartholomew),** place St-Barthélemy (© **04/221-89-44**), dates from 1108. Its **Fonts Baptismaux (Baptismal Font)** ⚐ is counted among "Belgium's Magnificent Seven" most important historical treasures. The copper-and-brass font, cast in the early 1100s by master metalsmith Renier de Huy, a masterpiece of the Mosan Art style that flourished in the Meuse Valley during the Middle Ages, rests on the backs of ten sculpted oxen and is surrounded by five biblical scenes. The church is open to visitors Monday to Saturday from 10am to noon and 2 to 5pm, and Sunday from 2 to 5pm. Admission is 2.50€ ($3) for adults, and 1€ ($1.15) for children.

The prince-bishops, who ruled the city and the surrounding territory from 980 to 1794, constructed for themselves the largest secular Gothic structure in the world. Of primary interest at the **Palais des Prince-Evêques (Palace of the Prince-Bishops)** in place Saint-Lambert are the two inner courtyards, one lined with 60 carved columns depicting the follies of human nature, and the other housing an ornamental garden. Today, this historic building is Liège's Palace of Justice, housing courtrooms and administrative offices. The palace is open Monday to Friday from 10am to 5pm. Admission to the courtyards is free; contact the tourist office for guided tours.

A visit to the **Val Saint-Lambert Crystal Factory,** rue de Val 245, Seraing (© **04/337-39-60**), southwest of Liège, beside the Meuse, on N90, would be interesting enough even if only to watch the company's craftsmen at work making the renowned, hand-blown Val Saint-Lambert crystal. But you can also buy the finished product—including slightly flawed pieces at a considerable price reduction—from the factory store. The workshop is sited within a complex that contains the remains of a 13th-century Cistercian abbey, a 16th-century Mosan Renaissance–style house, and examples of industrial archaeology from the 18th and 19th centuries. You can also visit the on-site **Musée du Cristal (Crystal**

Museum), which is open daily from 9am to 5pm; admission is 5€ ($5.75) for adults, 3€ ($3.50) for children ages 5 to 16, and free for children under 5.

WHERE TO STAY & DINE

There's good value for money at the 51-room **Comfort Inn l'Univers** ⚘, rue des Guillemins 116 (✆ **04/254-55-55;** www.comfortinn.com/hotel/be010), close to Gare des Guillemins, where the guest rooms are modest in decor but quite comfortable. Though there's no restaurant on the premises, several are within walking distance. A major renovation program, including all-new bathrooms, has recently been completed. Rates here are 57€ to 75€ ($65.50–$86.25) double.

Guest rooms at **Le Campanile,** rue Jules de Laminne 18 (✆ **04/224-02-72;** www.campanile.fr), are spacious and comfortable, if not much inflected with character, at this modern hotel, which has a reputation for its value. The suburban setting won't appeal to anyone who wants to be in the heart of town, but it's just 5 to 10 minutes by bus to the city center. Rates run 55€ to 70€ ($63.25–$80.50) double and include a buffet breakfast.

An imposing 19th-century building, formerly a bank, confers a certain class on **Le Bruit Qui Court,** bd. de la Sauvenière 142 (✆ **04/232-18-18**), which is matched by a refined cuisine. Light menu dishes, such as salads and quiches, predominate and mix flavors in a manner that often is unexpected. By contrast, you can dine in the ground-floor strong room, behind the original heavily armored door. A main course will set you back 9€ to 18€ ($10.25–$20.75).

Mamé Vî Cou, rue de la Wache 9 (✆ **04/223-71-81**), is Walloon dialect for "A Nice Old Lady," and though I would never call Madame Dupagne old, her welcome is certainly nice enough. Her character-filled, oak-beamed restaurant is a Liège institution, serving traditional Walloon specialties such as chicken in beer, and hot black pudding with acid cherries. Main courses cost 9.50€ to 16.50€ ($11–$19).

SHOPPING

On Sunday mornings, this **street market** is strung out for about a mile along the quai de la Batte on the bank of the Meuse. You'll find brass, clothes, flowers, foodstuffs, jewelry, birds, animals, books, radios, and . . . the list is simply endless. Shoppers from as far away as Holland and Germany join what seems to be at least half the population of Liège.

AN EXCURSION TO NAMUR ⚘

A handsome riverside town, 31 miles (50km) southwest of Liège at the confluence of the Meuse and Sambre rivers, the bustling capital of Belgium's French-speaking Wallonia region has fine museums and churches, a casino, and an abundance of cafes and restaurants. The town is dominated by its vast hilltop Citadel.

GETTING THERE   There are two trains an hour on average from Liège, and three from Brussels. The **train station** is at square Léopold (✆ **081/25-22-22**).

VISITOR INFORMATION   The main **Tourist Office,** Hôtel de Ville (Town Hall), rue de Fer 42, 5000 Namur (✆ **081/24-64-44;** fax 081/24-65-54; tourisme@ville.namur.be), is open Monday to Saturday from 9am to 12:30pm and 1:30 to 6pm. There are two smaller **Tourist Information Centers,** one adjacent to the train station in square Léopold (✆ **081/24-64-49**), and one at the confluence of the rivers Meuse and Sambre, at place du Grognon (✆ **081/ 24-64-48**).

TOP ATTRACTIONS & SPECIAL MOMENTS

There has been a fortification atop this bluff since Celtic times, but the Dutch in the 19th century are responsible for the present shape of the **Citadelle (Citadel)** ★★, route Merveilleuse (© 081/22-68-29). Today, the structure is part of a wooded estate that includes museums, playgrounds, restaurants, cafes, and craft shops. The intriguing underground caverns can be explored (by torchlight) with a guide on a 45-minute tour. There's an interesting museum of the forest. The Citadel is open June to September, daily from 11am to 5pm; and Easter to May, Saturday, Sunday, and holidays from 11am to 5pm. Admission to the Citadel and museums (includes a 20-min film) is 6€ ($7) for adults, and 3€ ($3.50) each for the first 2 children, thereafter 2€ ($2.25) per child from the same family. To reach the Citadel, you can take either a cable car from rue Notre-Dame, for 5€ ($5.75) for adults, and 2.50€ ($3) for children, or one of two scenic roads that wind up the steep cliff side.

Namur sometimes seems unsure about what to make of one of its best-known sons, the bizarre and erotic 19th-century painter and engraver Félicien Rops. The **Musé Félicien Rops (Félicien Rops Museum)**, rue Fumal 12 (© 081/22-01-10), is tucked away in a narrow side street, near the artist's birthplace in the old quarter of town—but inside, exposure is the name of the game. The perfection of Rops's soft-ground etchings and drypoint work is internationally recognized, and he was indisputably one of the most outstanding engravers of the late 19th century. The museum is open July to August, daily from 10am to 6pm; September to June, Tuesday to Sunday from 10am to 5pm. Admission is 3€ ($3.50) for adults, and 1.50€ ($1.75) for children.

A variety of **river cruise** (© 082/22-23-15) options is available from Namur, including trips to Dinant, cruises on the Meuse and Sambre rivers, and a cruise called "Namur by Night." All of these depart from the junction of the Meuse and Sambre rivers, beside bd. Baron Louis Huart.

WHERE TO DINE

The trendy, informal **Brasserie Henry's Bar** ★★, Place Chanoine Descamps 5 (© 081/22-02-04), in one of Namur's nicest squares is a good place to get a feel for the new Namurois style. You can pick up nine Normandy oysters, or go for Belgian specialties such as *asperges à la flamande* (asparagus served in the Flemish style) and *waterzooï* (souplike Flemish stew). In addition to the long and elegant main dining room, there's a plant-bedecked outdoor terrace at the back. Main courses cost 5.50€ to 16.50€ ($6.25–$19); fixed-price menus 20€ to 25€ ($23–$28.75).

La Petite Fugue ★, place Chanoine Descamps 5 (© 081/23-13-20), is an intimately atmospheric little place in the heart of old Namur. Set inside a converted 18th-century presbytery, it has an interior typical of bourgeois Namur houses of the time, with a wood staircase and all-wood fixtures and fittings. Prices are reasonable considering the fine French food and service, and the restaurant's 20 or so places tend to fill up fast. Main courses cost 7.50€ to 13.50€ ($8.75–$15.50); a fixed-price menu 22.50€ ($26).

5 An Excursion to Luxembourg City

Luxembourg City occupies a location that is a natural fortress in the first place, and the immensely powerful fortifications built here over the centuries by a parade of invaders gave warmongers and peacemakers alike sleepless nights, until they were finally dismantled in 1867. Today, beautiful parks that so distinguish the face of the city cover ground once occupied by forts. Luxembourg City is an attractive mixture of reminders of Europe's constant battles for power, Luxembourgers' own equally vigorous determination to create a comfortable lifestyle for themselves, and modern Europe's search for peaceful cooperation between nations.

GETTING THERE   Luxembourg is linked by train through Belgium, Germany, and France to most major European countries. **Gare Centrale** (✆ **49-90-49-90**), the main train station, is in the southern part of town. The Luxembourg National Tourist Office operates a **Bureau d'Acceuil (Welcome Desk)** at Gare Centrale (✆ **42-82-82-20;** fax 42-82-82-30). This information desk is open June to September, Monday to Saturday from 9am to 7pm, and Sunday from 9am to 12:30pm and 2 to 6pm; October to May, daily from 9:15am to 12:30pm and 1:45 to 6pm.

VISITOR INFORMATION   **Luxembourg City Tourist Office,** place d'Armes, B.P. 181, 2011 Luxembourg-Ville (✆ **22-28-09;** www.lcto.lu), is open January to March and October to December, Monday to Saturday from 9am to 6pm, and Sunday and holidays from 10am to 6pm; April to September, Monday to Saturday from 9am to 7pm, and Sunday and holidays from 10am to 6pm.

TOP ATTRACTIONS & SPECIAL MOMENTS

Luxembourg City grew up around Count Sigefroi's 10th-century castle at Montée de Clausen on the Bock promontory. In time, there came to be 3 rings of battlements around the city, 15 forts, and an exterior wall interspersed with 9 more forts, 3 of them cut right into the rock. Even more impressive than these above-ground fortifications were the 15½ miles (25km) of underground tunnels that sheltered troops by the thousands, as well as their equipment, horses, workshops, artillery, arms, kitchens, bakeries, and even slaughterhouses. Legend says that within these tremendous rocky walls of the fortress sits a beautiful maiden named Mélusine, whose knitting needles control the fate of Luxembourg. In 1867, the Treaty of London ordered the dismantling of all these battlements, and what you see today represents only about 10% of the original works. The **Casemates** (✆ **22-28-09**) are open March to October, daily from 10am to 5pm. Admission is 1.50€ ($1.75) for adults, and 1€ ($1.15) for children.

The oldest part of the **Palais Grand-Ducal (Palace of the Grand Dukes)** ✪, rue du Marché-aux-Herbes (✆ **46-70-70**), dates back to 1572. Its "new" right wing was built in 1741. Next-door is the Chamber of Deputies (Luxembourg's Parliament). Guided tours are conducted mid-July to August, Monday to Friday from 2:30 to 5pm (in English at 4:30pm only), and Saturday from 10 to 11am (not in English). Admission is 5.45€ ($6.25) for adults, and 2.75€ ($3.15) for children; tickets are available from the Luxembourg City Tourist Office in place d'Armes.

The **Musée National d'Histoire et d'Art (National Museum of Art and History)** ✪, Marché-aux-Poissons (✆ **47-93-301;** www.mnha.lu), in the oldest part of the city, holds fascinating archaeological, geological, and historical exhibits. In addition, there's the exquisite Bentinek-Thyssen Collection of works of art by Low Countries artists from the 15th to the 18th century, among them Rubens, Van Dyck, Breughel, and Rembrandt. The museum is open Tuesday to Sunday from 10am to 5pm. Admission is 5€ ($5.75) for adults, 3€ ($3.50) for seniors, students, and children ages 12 to 18, and free for children under 12.

A magnificent Gothic structure built between 1613 and 1621, the **Cathédrale de Notre-Dame (Notre-Dame Cathedral)** ✪, bd. Roosevelt (entrance on

Luxembourg City

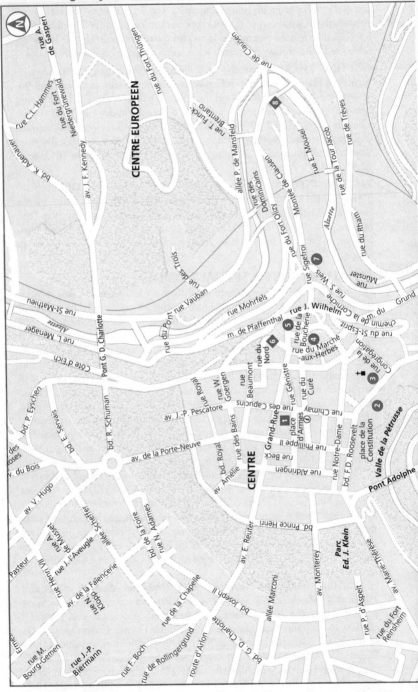

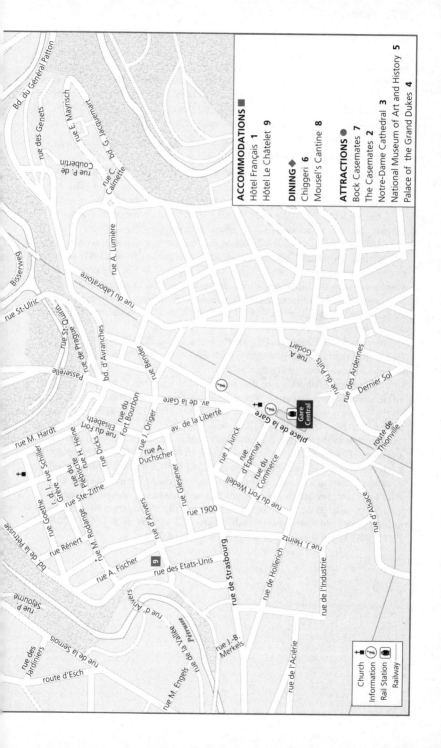

ACCOMMODATIONS ■
Hôtel Français **1**
Hôtel Le Châtelet **9**

DINING ◆
Chiggeri **6**
Mousel's Cantine **8**

ATTRACTIONS ●
Bock Casemates **7**
The Casemates **2**
Notre-Dame Cathedral **3**
National Museum of Art and History **5**
Palace of the Grand Dukes **4**

Church
Information
Rail Station
Railway

153

rue Notre-Dame), contains the royal family's vault and a remarkable Treasury (it can only be viewed on request). This is the scene of the **Octave of Our Lady of Luxembourg,** an annual ceremony on the fifth Sunday following Easter, when thousands of pilgrims arrive to pray to the miraculous statue of the Holy Virgin for protection. They then form a procession to carry the statue from the Cathedral through the streets to an alter covered with flowers in av. de la Porte Neuve, north of place d'Armes. The Cathedral is open daily from 10am to noon and 2 to 6pm. Admission is free.

WHERE TO STAY & DINE

Small and central, the **Hôtel Français** ✦, place d'Armes 14 (© **47-45-34;** hfinfo@pt.lu) is one of the nicest moderately priced hotels in town. The 21 guest rooms have been recently refurbished and redecorated in a bright, modern style, though some are on the small side. The hotel is in a pedestrian-only zone, but cars and taxis are allowed to drop off and pick up people and baggage. Rates run 115€ to 125€ ($132–$144) double and include continental breakfast.

The small **Hôtel Le Châtelet** ✦, bd. de la Pétrusse 2 (© **40-21-01;** www. chatelet.lu), close to the Pétrusse Valley on the edge of the new city center, is a longtime favorite of visiting academics and businesspeople. Its rooms are divided between two lovely old Luxembourg homes; all have modern, comfortable, and attractive furnishings. Rates are 85€ to 120€ ($97.75–$138) double and include a buffet breakfast.

The remarkable **Chiggeri** ✦✦, rue du Nord 15 (© **22-99-36**), off Grand-Rue is in a rambling mansion on a quiet side street. The main dining room employs African-influenced decorative motifs and has a friendly but professional style. The menu changes seasonally, and the Mediterranean dishes with Asian influences are always inventive. When the weather's good, you may want to dine on the outdoors terrace. Main courses cost 9€ to 12€ ($10.25–$13.75); fixed-price menus run 10€ to 56€ ($12.75–$64.50).

Next door to the Mousel Brewery, down beside the Alzette River, the excellent **Mousel's Cantine** ✦, Montée de Clausen 46 (© **47-01-98**), is a great place to sample regional treats. The decor is rustic, with plain wooden tables and oil paintings in the back room, and the front room overlooks the quaint street outside. The menu features hearty portions of Luxembourg favorites such as sauerkraut with sausage, potatoes, and ham. To wash this down, try a stein of the unfiltered local Mousel brew. A main course will set you back 15€ to 20€ ($17.25–$23) and there's a plat du jour for 9€ ($10.25).

The Czech Republic

The Czech Republic, comprising the ancient kingdoms of Bohemia, Moravia, and Silesia, is the westernmost of the former Soviet satellite countries and probably the easiest way to explore what used to be the other side of the Iron Curtain. The Republic is actually a lot more modernized than most of its former East Bloc neighbors. As proof, nearly 15 years after 1989's bloodless "Velvet Revolution" over Communism, and over a decade after the peaceful split with the Slovak part of the former Czechoslovakia, the European Union put the Czechs at the head of its new intake of states in May 2004.

For rail travelers, however, the Republic still has some work to do in the modernizing department. Putting the words luxury and Czech Railways in the same phrase together would be an oxymoron. With the exception of a handful of international trains crisscrossing the country, most local routes in the country are served by ubiquitous, prompt, and cheap-but-oh-so-grungy trains. And the Republic isn't covered by a Eurailpass—a negative if you plan on covering a number of countries on your trip. Nevertheless, once at your destination, few countries in Europe can match the mix of history of this one. And the Republic is renowned as a value destination, so rail travelers' dollars will go a lot farther here than in many other countries.

HIGHLIGHTS OF THE CZECH REPUBLIC

The capital, **Prague,** is widely regarded as one of the most beautiful cities in Europe. This quirky and compact heart of Bohemia is a jumble of architecture. Gothic bestrides baroque, Renaissance adjoins Cubist, with a splash of Socialist Realism and post-modern kitsch thrown in for good measure. It's also, unquestionably, the first stop on any rail traveler's itinerary. Most international trains arrive here and it's the only city that welcomes direct flights from North America.

But Prague isn't the Czech Republic's only draw. For castle-hoppers, the majestic **Karlštejn Castle** (p. 178) is an easy day trip by train from Prague and one of the country's most popular destinations. And visitors are venturing more and more into West Bohemia where one of the world's best-known spas **(Karlovy Vary)** has been restored to its Victorian-era splendor, and where castles abound in the surrounding countryside. These are old-world spas—not New Age health farms—villages where you get your system replenished by drinking the waters, strolling the promenades, and soaking up the ambience. And though much of the Czech Republic isn't efficiently accessed by rail—hence the absence of Moravia from this chapter—the cities in this region generally make for easy rail trips out of Prague. In addition to the spa towns, if you have the time in your schedule, don't pass up the opportunity to visit Southern Bohemia's jewel of cities, **Český Krumlov,** named a "World Heritage Site" by UNESCO for its magnificent old-world architecture and atmosphere. You can reach this town on your way through **České Budějovice,** the hometown of the original Budweiser brand and a convenient rail base for exploring southern Bohemia.

Moments Festivals & Special Events

The world famous **Prague Spring International Music Festival** is a 3-week series of classical music performances and concerts that usually takes place the last 3 weeks of May. Details on the festival can be found online at **www.festival.cz**. There is also an autumn version of the festival in September **(www.pragueautumn.cz)** with a similarly impressive mix of internationally recognized orchestras, conductors, and soloists.

After being banned during communism, **The Festival Of The Five-Petaled Rose** in Český Krumlov has made a triumphant comeback and is now in its 18th year. It's held each year on the summer solstice. Residents of Český Krumlov dress up in Renaissance costume and parade through the streets. Afterward, the streets become a stage with plays, chess games with people dressed as pieces, music, and even duels "to the death." Information is available online at **www.ckrumlov.cz**.

1 Essentials

GETTING THERE
BY PLANE   **CSA Czech Airlines (www.csa.cz/en),** the national airline offers flights to Prague from a number of U.S. cities, including New York, Atlanta, Chicago, Dallas, and Washington, D.C. From Canada, you can fly to Prague out of Toronto and Montreal.

To make a reservation in North America, call toll-free © **800/223-2365** (9am–8pm only). For more information, in the U.S. call © **212/765-6545** (New York); in Canada, call © **416/363-3174** (Toronto).

The only major U.S. airline that flies to Prague (though always with a stopover somewhere in Europe) is **Delta Airlines** (© **800/241-4141;** www.delta.com). Other airlines that service Prague out of Europe and that offer connecting services to several major U.S. airlines include **Lufthansa** (© **800/ 645-3880;** 01/803-803-803; www.lufthansa.com) and **British Airways** (© **0845/773-3377;** www.britishairways.com).

All flights arrive in the newly rebuilt **Ruzyně Airport** (© **220/111-111;** **www.csl.cz**), which is 12 miles (19km) west of the city center. At the airport, you'll find a bank for changing money (usually open daily 7am–11pm), telephones, and several car-rental offices.

THE CZECH REPUBLIC BY RAIL
PASSES
Note: The Czech Republic is not covered by the Eurailpass though the **European East Pass** and the **Czech Flexipass** (chapter 2) are accepted. The Republic does have two country-specific pass options. The new **Prague Excursion Pass** provides one round-trip excursion on the Czech National Railways from any Czech border to Prague (note that you don't have to return to the same border town on the way out from Prague). It is valid for 7 days and stops in other places in the Czech Republic are allowed on the way to and from Prague, but

The Czech Republic

your entire journey must be completed within 1 calendar day. The pass costs $55 for first class or $40 for second class. Travelers under 26 years old can get a **Prague Excursion Youth Pass,** which costs only $45 for first class and $35 for second class. Children ages 4 to 11 pay $28 in first class or $20 in second class.

All of the passes above must be purchased in North America before you leave on your trip. You can buy them on the phone or online from **Rail Europe** (© 877/272-RAIL in the U.S., 800/361-RAIL in Canada; www.raileurope.com).

FOREIGN TRAIN TERMS

In Prague, many of the international ticket window agents at the main train station will speak English. It may not be the most pleasant experience—Czech sales assistants in any trade tend to be surly—but you should get along fairly well.

As you get farther afield from Prague, you may not find such convenience, but with a little patience and a bit of preparation before you join the line, you should be able to be understood enough in English to get to where you want to go, and at the appropriate fare. Many destinations are often hard to pronounce, so be sure to write them down clearly on a piece of paper to show to the agent, or to circle your end station in this guide book or on a train timetable.

Note that you will see signs bearing the following terms in train terminals and major attractions: **Vchod (entrance); Východ (exit); Informace (information); Odjezd/Odlet (Departures);** and the all-important **Toalety (restrooms).**

Useful Czech Train & Travel Terms

Where is the . . . ?	**Kde je . . . ?**	*gde* yeh . . .
train station	**nádraž'**	nah-drah-zhee
How much is the fare?	**Kolik je j'zdné?**	*koh*-leek yeh yeesd-neh
I am going to . . .	**Pojedu do . . .**	*poh*-yeh-doo doh . . .
I would like . . .	**Chci . . .**	khtsee . . .
One-way ticket	**J'zdenka**	yeez-den-kah
Round-trip ticket	**Zpátečn' j'zdenka**	zpah-tech-nee jeez-den-kah
I'm looking for . . .	**Hledám . . .**	hleh-dahm . . .
the city center	**centrum**	tsent-room
the tourist office	**cestovn' kancelář**	tses-tohv-nee kahn-tseh-larsh
Where is the nearest telephone?	**Kde je nejbližš' telefon?**	gde yeh *nay-*bleesh-ee *tel*-oh-fohn
I would like to buy . . .	**Chci koupit . . .**	khtsee *koh*-peet . . .
a map	**mapu**	*mahp*-oo

PRACTICAL TRAIN INFORMATION

The train network in the Czech Republic is run by **Czech Railways (České dráhy),** which uses a number of trains of different quality. For a list of the trains, their abbreviations on timetables, and an explanation of their features, see "Train Designations in the Czech Republic," below. Ordinary passenger trains (marked Os for *osoboní* on timetables) don't require reservations or supplements and offer first- and second-class seating. They are also slow as molasses and usually very uncomfortable—avoid them if you can. If you get stuck, splurge on first-class to make the trip as painless as possible.

The train network itself is pretty extensive and connects to a number of major cities in both eastern and western Europe. Major cities with InterCity or EuroCity connections to Prague include Vienna, Munich, Berlin, Cologne, Frankfurt, and Paris. Locally, the routings are a little odd and getting to some of the country's smaller towns and out of the way spots is, as a result, often faster by bus. Stick to the major cities and towns we discuss in this chapter and you'll be fine. To find out about timetables of all connections within the Czech Republic and from/to abroad go to **www.jizdnirady.cz.**

RESERVATIONS   Reservations on Czech trains are mandatory only if an R surrounded by a box is listed on the timetable next to your departure, or if you are traveling on an SC train. That said, trains can get very crowded, and if you plan on traveling in high season or on weekends, make a reservation way in advance so you can assure yourself of a seat and avoid standing in lines at the station. Reservations on express trains must be made at least an hour before departure and can be made inside almost all of the Republic's train stations. A reservation costs 20Kč (75¢). Note that reservations on local trains in the Czech

Train Designations in the Czech Republic

Name	Abbreviation	Explanation
SuperCity	SC	Czech trains with a high standard of quality and consist of modernized first-class coaches only and a restaurant car. A reservation is necessary and special prices apply (see "Reservations" in this section for more on pricing).
EuroCity	EC	European trains that are guaranteed to meet an international standard. These have first- and second-class coaches and a restaurant car. A supplement is required and reservations are possible but not mandatory.
InterCity	IC	These trains offer a certain level of guaranteed quality, and have first- and second-class coaches, and a restaurant car. A supplement is required and reservations are possible but not mandatory.
Express	Ex or R	*Expresní* or *rychlík* trains offer fast connections between selected Czech cities, and have first- and second-class coaches. These trains are indicated by the letter **R** in a timetable. Reservations are only mandatory on these trains if the R is boxed on the timetable. There is no supplement.

Republic cannot be made in North America, though you can buy open tickets through Rail Europe.

Reservations for sleeper accommodations on night trains in the Czech Republic and on international night trains to and from Prague are a must. Reserve these as soon as you can (most international trains allow you to reserve up to 3 months in advance). You can reserve most international sleepers and couchettes through Rail Europe before you depart North America. Sleeper supplement prices are variable; a couchette costs 728Kč ($28).

Note: Even if you have a rail pass of any type, you'll still have to pay a travel supplement of 60Kč ($2.30) one-way, when traveling on IC and EC trains.

You pay a fixed price for any route taken on an SC train, regardless of distance or time. The fee is 600Kč ($22.80) one-way or 1,000Kč ($38.50) return in July and August; 800Kč ($30.40) one-way or 1,200Kč ($45.60) return September to June.

SERVICES & AMENITIES   Generally, Czech trains do not have a very good reputation in terms of comfort and cleanness. They are old, lack most creature

Trains & Travel Times in the Czech Republic

From	To	# of Trains	Frequency	Travel Time
Prague	Karlovy Vary	4	Daily	4 hr.
Prague	Český Krumlov	7	Daily	3 hr. 26 min.–4 hr. 10 min.
Český Krumlov	České Budějovice	9	Daily	55 min.
Prague	České Budějovice	10	Daily	2 hr. 10 min.

comforts, and run on old-style single tracks. That said, they still run pretty reliably and for reasonable prices. First-class travel (the only way to go) in the Republic is far less expensive than in western European countries.

Sleeping accommodations—ranging from simple couchettes to private single rooms—are available on long-haul trains within the Czech Republic and on international trains running through or terminating in Prague. Sleepers tend to be expensive (though often less than a hotel room) and the quality of the accommodations varies widely. *Warning:* Theft is common from couchette compartments, so if you opt for a couchette, keep a close eye on your belongings.

Restaurant cars are available on SC, EC, and IC trains. They are not available, however, on Express trains, so bring lots of food—and lots of bottled water. (Do not drink tap water on trains, or anywhere else for that matter.)

In Prague's main station, České Budějovice's station, and in other selected cities' train stations the Czech railways has a "ČD center," providing complete services—reservations and ticket sale, timetable info, international train connections info, hotel booking, currency exchange, and so on.

You also can check their website on **www.cd.cz** (so far, only the timetable section is in English, though the railway company is working on putting up a more extensive English site) or call ✆ **840/112-113** for more information.

FAST FACTS: The Czech Republic

Area Codes The **country code** for the Czech Republic is **420**. The Czech telephone network has undergone a massive overhaul and all telephone numbers have changed. In all cases, the **city codes** are now connected to the local number in front so that the entire 9-digit number must be dialed locally. For directory assistance in English and for information on services and rates calling abroad, dial ✆ **1181**.

Business Hours Most **banks** are open Monday to Friday 8am to 6pm. Pubs are usually open daily 11am to midnight. Most restaurants open for lunch noon to 3pm and for dinner 6 to 11pm; only a few stay open later.

Climate Prague's average summer temperature is about 63°F (18°C), but some days can be quite chilly and others uncomfortably sultry. In winter, the temperature remains close to freezing. During an average January, it's sunny and clear for only 50 hours the entire month. Pollution, heaviest in the winter, tends to limit the snowfall in Prague; however, the city's been blanketed for quite a long period of winter the last couple of years.

Currency The basic unit of currency is the koruna (plural, koruny) or crown, abbreviated Kč. Each koruna is divided into 100 haléřů or hellers. At this writing, $1 = approximately 26Kč or 1Kč = 3.8¢, and £1 = 45Kč.

Documents Required American citizens need only passports and no visas for stays under 90 days. Canadians need a visa. For more information go to **www.czech.cz**.

Electricity Czech appliances operate on 220 volts and plug into two-pronged outlets that differ from those in America and the United Kingdom. Appliances designed for the U.S. or U.K. markets must use an adapter and a transformer.

Embassies The **U.S. Embassy** is at Tržiště 15, Praha 1 (© **257-530-663**). The **Canadian Embassy** is at Mickiewiczova 6, Praha 6 (© **272-101-811**).

Health & Safety You will likely feel safer in Prague than in most Western cities, but always take common-sense precautions. Don't walk alone at night around Wenceslas Square—one of the main areas for prostitution. All visitors should be watchful of pickpockets in heavily touristed areas, especially on Charles Bridge, in Old Town Square, and in front of the main station. Be wary in crowded buses, trams, and trains.

If you need any medicine of common use, you can purchase it from a pharmacist. Czech pharmacies are called *lékárna* and are recognized by a green cross on a white background. The most centrally located one is at Václavské nám. 8, Praha 1 (© **224-227-532**), open Monday to Friday from 8am to 6pm. If you need a doctor or dentist and your condition isn't life-threatening, you can visit the **Polyclinic at Národní,** Národní 9, Praha 1 (© **222-075-120;** for the emergency operator © 140-533; Metro: Můstek), during walk-in hours, from 8am to 5pm. For emergency medical aid, call the **Foreigners' Medical Clinic,** Na Homolce Hospital, Roentgenova 2, Praha 5 (© **257/272-146** or 257/272-191 after hours; Metro: Anděl, then bus 167).

Holidays Official holidays are observed on January 1 (New Year's Day), Easter Monday, May 1 (Labor Day), May 8 (Liberation Day from Fascism), July 5 (Introduction of Christianity), July 6 (Death of Jan Hus), September 28 (St. Wenceslas Day), October 28 (Foundation of the Republic), November 17 (Day of student movement in 1939 and 1989), December 24 and 25 (Christmas), and December 26 (St. Stephen's Day). On these holidays, most business and shops (including food shops) are closed, and buses and trams run on Sunday schedules.

Mail Post offices are plentiful and are normally open Monday to Friday from 8am to 6pm. Mailboxes are orange and are usually attached to the side of buildings. If you're sending mail overseas, make sure it's marked "Par Avion" so it doesn't go by surface. If you mail your letters at a post office, the clerk will add this stamp for you. Mail can take up to 10 days to reach its destination. For a regular letter to a European country you need a 9Kč (35¢) stamp, and you need a 14Kč (55¢) stamp to send a regular letter to America.

Police & Emergencies You can reach Prague's police and fire services by calling © **158** from any phone. For an ambulance, call © **155.**

Telephone The **country code** for the Czech Republic is **420.** The **city codes** are connected to the local number in front so the entire number is dialed locally and has nine digits. For directory assistance in English and for information on services and rates for calling abroad, dial © **1181.**

There are two kinds of pay phones. One accepts coins and the other operates only with a phone card, available from post offices and newsagents in denominations ranging from 50Kč to 500Kč ($1.90–$19). The minimum cost of a local call is 4Kč (15¢) in coin-op phones. The more efficient phone card telephones deduct the price of your call from the card. If you're calling home, get a phone card with plenty of cash on it, as calls run about 20Kč (75¢) per minute to the United States and 15Kč (35p) to the United Kingdom. Charging to your phone credit card from a public telephone is often the most economical way to call home.

A fast, convenient way to call home from Europe is via services that bypass the foreign operator and automatically link you to an operator with your long-distance carrier in your home country. The access number in the Czech Republic for **AT&T USA Direct** is ☎ **00-420-00101**, for **MCI Call USA** ☎ **00-420-00112**, and for **Sprint Global One** ☎ **00-420-87187**. Canadians can connect with **Canada Direct** at ☎ **00-420-00151**, and Brits with **BT Direct** at ☎ **00-420-04401**. From a pay phone in the Czech Republic, your local phone card will be debited only for a local call.

Tipping   At most restaurants and pubs, locals just round the bill up to the nearest few crowns. When you're given good service at tablecloth places, a 10% tip is proper. Washroom and cloakroom attendants usually demand a couple of koruny, and porters in airports and rail stations usually receive 20Kč (75¢) per bag. Taxi drivers should get about 10%, unless they've already ripped you off.

2 Prague

Exactly 80 years after native-son Franz Kafka's death, Prague's mix of the melancholy and the magnificent, set against some of Europe's most spectacular architecture, still confounds all who live or visit here. Its tightly wound brick paths have felt the hooves of kings' horses, the jackboots of Hitler's armies, the heaving tracks of Soviet tanks, and the shuffle of students in passive revolt. Fate tested the city once again in August 2002 when record floodwaters from the River Vltava engulfed much of Lesser Town and part of Old Town putting many restaurants and attractions near the riverfront out of business for months. But the city has rebuilt and renovated and in 2003 was back open for business. The 6-centuries-old Charles Bridge is today jammed with visitors and venture capitalists looking for memories or profits from a once-captive city now enjoying yet another renaissance.

For the rail traveler, Prague is *the* city to visit in the Czech Republic—if you can visit only one place in the country, this is the one you want to see. And it's also the one you most likely *will* see. The central hub for most of the country's trains, the city is also a convenient stop on rail routes heading from the west into eastern Europe. It's about 5 hours by train from Berlin and Vienna, and 7 hours from Frankfurt and Budapest.

If the Czech Republic is the first stop on your rail trip, it's also home to the only airport that serves direct flights from the U.S. And on the convenience front, though it's cheaper than many other European capitals, it's the most modern of the eastern European cities, so you'll have access to most of the creature comforts of home, even while surrounded by centuries of medieval architecture.

If your schedule allows it, plan on spending at least 2 days here, though you could spend more than a week and not discover all of the city's treasures.

STATION INFORMATION
GETTING FROM THE AIRPORT TO THE TRAIN STATION
Plenty of taxis line up in front of Ruzyně Airport (p. 156). **CEDAZ** (© 220-114-296) operates an airport shuttle bus to náměstí Republiky in central Prague and from that point you can take the Metro to all of Prague's train stations. It leaves the airport daily every 30 minutes from 6am to 9pm and stops near the náměstí Republiky Metro station (Line B; trip time: 30 min.). The shuttle costs 90Kč ($3.45). You can also take **city bus 119** from the airport to the Dejvická Metro station (Line A) for 12Kč (45¢; trip time: 30 min.).

INSIDE THE STATIONS
Prague has two central rail stations: Hlavní nádraží and Nádraží Holešovice.

Of the two, **Hlavní nádraží (Main Train Station),** Wilsonova třída 80, Praha 2 (© 224-614-071), is the grander and more popular; however, it's also seedier. On the second floor, about 55 yards to the left, just next to the arrivals table, is the **train information** office (marked by a lowercase "i"); it's open daily from 3:15am to 12:40am. Tickets for domestic and international trains are available at the windows located in the main hall on the ground level.

There are also several visitor and accommodation information windows situated in the main hall. Useful is the **ČD center** (© 840-112-113) run by the Czech Railways. It provides domestic and international train information as well as exchange and accommodation services. It is open daily from 6am to 7pm. The **Prague Information Service (PIS)** office helps with accommodations, tickets for events, city tours, and excursions. It is open April to October, Monday to Friday 9am to 7pm, and Saturday and Sunday 9am to 4pm; and from November to March Monday to Friday, 9am to 6pm and Saturday from 9am to 3pm. Another helpful travel and accommodation agency in the station is **AVE Travel** (© 224-223-226), which is open daily from 6am to 10pm.

The station's basement has a 24-hour luggage-storage counter, which charges 15Kč (60¢) per bag over 33 pounds per day (counted from midnight). The nearby lockers aren't secure and should be avoided.

The main train station is reachable by Metro line C, station Hlavní nádraží. **Nádraží Holešovice (North Train Station),** Partyzánská at Vrbenského, Praha 7 (© 224-615-865) is usually the terminus for trains from points north, especially international trains arriving from Germany. It's not as centrally located as the Main Train Station, but its more manageable size and convenient location at the end of Metro line C make it a popular choice. The **AVE Travel** office (© 266-710-514) here is open daily from 7am to 9pm.

Prague also has two smaller rail stations. **Masaryk Station,** Hybernská, Praha 1 (© 221-111-122; Metro: nám. Republiky) is primarily for travelers arriving on trains from other Bohemian and Moravian cities. It's about 10 minutes by

---

⌜Warning Beware the Taxi Driver
Most of Prague's taxi drivers will take advantage of you; getting an honestly metered ride from the airport is close to impossible. The fare from the airport to Hlavní nádraží (the main train station) should be no more than about 700Kč ($27).

Prague

Prague Castle

See inset above

HRADČANSKÁ

HRADČANY

Prague Castle

MALOSTRANSKÁ

MALÁ STRANA

Loretánské nám.

LOBKOVICKÁ ZAHRADA

STRAHOVSKÁ ZAHRADA

SEMINÁŘSKÁ ZAHRADA

Petřín Tower

PETŘÍNSKÉ SADY

Funicular

STŘELECKÝ OSTROV

Spartakiádní Stadion

KINSKÉHO ZAHRADA

Prague
CZECH
REPUBLIC

ANDĚL

SMÍCHOV STATION

SMÍCHOV

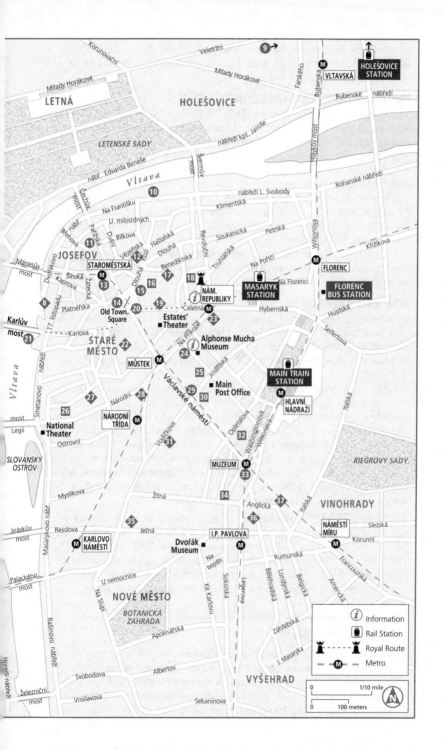

foot from the main station. **Smíchov Station,** Nádražní ulice, Praha 5 (© **224-617-686;** Metro: Smíchovské Nádraží), is used mainly for commuter trains from western and southern Bohemia.

INFORMATION ELSEWHERE IN THE CITY

The **Prague Information Service (PIS),** Na Příkopě 20, Praha 1 (© **12444;** www.pis.cz; Metro: nám. Republiky or Můstek) makes lodging reservations, gives touring tips, and sells tickets for cultural events and tours. It's website offers regularly updated tourism information in English. It's open April to October Monday to Friday 9am to 7pm, Saturday and Sunday 9am to 5pm; November to March Monday to Friday 9am to 6pm, Saturday 9am to 3pm, closed on Sunday.

The city's **Cultural and Information Center,** on the ground floor of the Municipal House (Obecní dům), nám. Republiky 5, Praha 1 (© **222-002-100;** fax 222-002-636; Metro: nám. Republiky), offers advice, tickets, souvenirs, refreshments, and restrooms. It's open daily 9am to 5pm.

On the Web, the well-designed **www.czechsite.com** offers tips on getting around, attractions, museums, galleries, and restaurants. You can book your lodging on the site.

GETTING AROUND

In order to easily get around town, you'll first need a quick explanation of the city's layout. The River Vltava bisects Prague. **Staré Město (Old Town)** and **Nové Město (New Town)** are on the east (right) side of the river, while the **Hradčany (Castle District)** and **Malá Strana (Lesser Town)** are on the west (left) bank.

Bridges and squares are the most prominent landmarks. **Charles Bridge,** the oldest and most famous of those spanning the Vltava, is at the epicenter and connects Old Town with Lesser Town and the Castle District. Several important streets radiate from Old Town Square, including fashionable **Pařížská** to the northwest, historic **Celetná** to the east, and **Melantrichova,** connecting to Wenceslas Square (Václavské nám.) to the southeast. On the west side of Charles Bridge is **Mostecká,** a 3-block-long connection to **Malostranské náměstí,** Malá Strana's main square. **Hradčany,** the Castle District, is just northwest of the square, while a second hill, **Petřín,** is just southwest.

BY PUBLIC TRANSPORTATION Prague's public transport network is a vast system of subways, trams, and buses. You can ride a maximum of four stations on the Metro or 15 minutes on a tram or bus, without transfers, for 8Kč (30¢); children 5 and under ride free. This is usually enough for trips in the historic districts. Rides of more than four stops on the Metro, or longer tram or bus rides, with unlimited transfers for up to 1 hour after your ticket is validated, cost

---

Tips Reading Maps

When reading maps or searching for addresses, keep in mind that *ulice* (abbreviated ul.) means "street," *třída* means "avenue," *náměstí* (abbreviated nám.) is a "square" or "plaza," a *most* is a "bridge," and *nábřeží* is a "quay." In Czech, none of these terms are capitalized. In addresses, street numbers usually follow the street name (like Václavské nám. 25). Each address is followed by a district number, such as Praha 1 (Praha is "Prague" in Czech).

12Kč (45¢). You can buy tickets from coin-operated orange machines in Metro stations or at most newsstands. Hold on to your ticket (which you must validate at the orange or yellow stamp clocks in each tram or bus when you get on board or at the entrance to the Metro) during your ride—you'll need it to prove you've paid if a ticket collector asks. If you're caught without a valid ticket, you have to pay a 400Kč ($15.20) fine to a ticket controller on the spot.

Warning: Oversize luggage (larger than carry-on size) requires a single trip ticket for each piece. You may be fined 50Kč ($1.90) for not having tickets for your luggage.

Metro trains operate daily from 5am to midnight and run every 3 to 8 minutes. The most convenient stations are Můstek, at the foot of Václavské náměstí (Wenceslas Sq.); Staroměstská, for Old Town Square and Charles Bridge; and Malostranská, serving Malá Strana and the Castle District.

The electric **tramlines** run practically everywhere. You never have to hail trams; they make every stop. The most popular, **no. 22** and **no. 23,** run past top sights such as the National Theater and Prague Castle. Regular bus and tram service stops at midnight, after which selected routes run reduced schedules, usually only once per hour. If you miss a night connection, expect a long wait for the next bus.

Passes   You can purchase discounted transport passes for the public transport system. A 1-day pass good for unlimited rides is 70Kč ($2.65), a 3-day pass 200Kč ($7.60), a 7-day pass 250Kč ($9.50), and a 15-day pass 280Kč ($10.65). You can buy the day passes at the "DP" windows at any Metro station.

BY FUNICULAR   A cog railway makes the scenic run up and down Petřín Hill every 15 minutes or so from 9:15am to 8:45pm, with an intermediate stop at the Nebozízek Restaurant in the middle of the hill overlooking the city. It requires the same 12Kč (45¢) ticket as other public transportation, and discounted transport passes are accepted. The funicular departs from a small house in the park just above the middle of Újezd in Malá Strana.

BY TAXI   *Avoid taxis!* If you must, hail one in the streets or in front of train stations, large hotels, and popular attractions, but be forewarned that many drivers simply gouge tourists. The best fare you can hope for is 17Kč (65¢) per kilometer, but twice or three times that isn't rare. The rates are usually posted on the dashboard, making it too late to haggle once you're in and on your way. Negotiate a price and have it written down before getting in. Better yet, go on foot or by public transport. Somewhat reputable companies with English-speaking dispatchers are **AAA Taxi** (© **140 14** or **222-333-222**) and **SEDOP** (© **271-726-666**).

WHERE TO STAY

Prague's full-service hotels have had to tighten efficiency in the face of heavier international competition, but due to low supply, room rates still top those of many similar or better-quality hotels in western Europe. Pensions with limited services are cheaper than hotels, but compared with similar Western B&Bs, they're pricey. The best budget accommodations are rooms in private homes or apartments.

All kinds of private housing are offered by several local agencies. The leader now is Prague-based **E-TRAVEL.CZ,** which offers all types of accommodations at their main website, or you can tap their large pictured database of apartments at **www.apartments.cz**. The office is near the National Theater at Ostrovní 7, Praha 1 (© **224-990-990;** www.travel.cz; Metro: Národní třída). Another agency, especially for those arriving late by train or air, is **AVE Travel Ltd.** (© 224-223-226; www.avetravel.cz). It has outlets at the airport (7am–10pm), at the Main Train Station (6am–10pm), and at the North Train Station (7am–9pm).

Andante (Value) One of the best value choices near Wenceslas Square, the understated Andante is tucked away on a dark side street, about 2 blocks off the top of the square. Despite its less than appealing neighborhood (women traveling alone might feel more comfortable staying elsewhere), this is the most comfortable property in the moderate range. It lacks the character of the old Hotel Evropa (see below), but also the neglect.

Ve Smečkách 4, Praha 1. © 222-210-021. Fax 222-210-591. www.andante.cz. 32 units. 3,450Kč ($131) double; 4,560Kč ($173) suite. Rates include breakfast. AE, MC, V. Metro: Muzeum. **Amenities:** Restaurant; bar; laundry. In room: Hair dryer.

Hotel Cloister Inn ★ (Value) Between Old Town Square and the National Theater (a 3-min. walk from the Charles Bridge), the Cloister Inn occupies a building that the secret police once used to hold prisoners. It sounds ominous, but it offers sparse, clean accommodations at an unbeatable price for the location. The hotel's new owner has refurbished the property and installed comfortable Scandinavian furniture in the guest rooms.

Bartolomějská 9, Praha 1. © 224-211-020. Fax 224-210-800. www.cloister-inn.cz. 73 units with ensuite showers. 4,200Kč ($160) double. Rates include breakfast. AE, MC, V. Metro: Národní třída. **Amenities:** Breakfast room. In room: Hair dryer.

Hotel Esplanade Located on a side street at the top of Wenceslas Square and across from the Main Train Station, the Esplanade began life as a bank and the offices of an Italian insurance company. Rooms are bright and airy, some with standard beds, others with French provincial headboards, and others with extravagant canopies.

Washingtonova 19, Praha 1. © 224-501-172. Fax 224-229-306. www.esplanade.cz. 74 units. 4,500Kč ($171) double; from 7,230Kč ($275) suite. Rates include breakfast. AE, MC, V. Metro: Muzeum. **Amenities:** Restaurant; cafe, bar; laundry. In room: Hair dryer.

Hotel Evropa The hotel's statue-studded exterior is still one of the most striking landmarks on Wenceslas Square, but unlike other early-20th-century gems, it hasn't been polished and continues to get duller. Rooms are aging and most don't have baths; some are just plain shabby. The best choice is a room facing the square with a balcony, but all are falling into various levels of disrepair. Still, this is an affordable chance to stay in one of Wenceslas Square's once-grand addresses, and it's a short walk to the Main Train Station.

Václavské nám. 25, Praha 1. © 224-228-117. Fax 224-224-544. 90 units, 23 with bathroom. 2,600Kč ($100) double without bathroom, 3,990Kč ($152) double with bathroom; from 4,700Kč ($179) suite. Rates include continental breakfast. AE, MC, V. Metro: Můstek. **Amenities:** Restaurant; cafe. In room: No phone.

Hotel Paříž ★★ At the edge of náměstí Republiky (very close to the Metro) and across from the Municipal House, the Paříž provides a rare glimpse back into the gilded First Republic. Each light fixture, etching, and curve at this Art Nouveau landmark recalls the days when Prague was one of the world's richest cities. For a glimpse of the hotel's atmosphere, rent the film *Mission Impossible;* you can see Tom Cruise plotting his revenge from within one of the fine suites. The high-ceilinged guest rooms are comfortable, with modern Art Deco accents.

U Obecního domu 1, Praha 1. © 222-195-195. Fax 224-225-475. www.hotel-pariz.cz. 94 units. 9,000Kč ($342) double; from 12,300Kč ($467) suite. Rates include breakfast. AE, DC, MC, V. Metro: nám. Republiky. **Amenities:** Restaurant; cafe; laundry. In room: Hair dryer.

Hotel Ungelt *(Value)*   It's not very opulent, but the Ungelt offers airy, spacious suites. Each contains a living room, a full kitchen, and a bathroom. Rooms have standard-issue beds; some have hand-painted ceilings. The Old Town Square is just around the corner and the train station is less than half a mile away.

Štupartská 1, Praha 1. ℭ **224-828-686.** Fax 224-828-181. www.ungelt.cz. 10 units. 4,431Kč ($168) 1-bedroom suite for 2; 6,540Kč ($249) 2-bedroom suite for 3 or 4. Rates include breakfast. AE, MC, V. Metro: Staroměstská or nám. Republiky. **Amenities:** Bar; laundry. *In room:* Hair dryer.

Palace Hotel *⭐*   The Palace is a top, upscale property, a block from Wenceslas Square and within walking distance of the Main Train Station, although we think the nearby Paříž (see above) has far more character. The 1903 Art Deco property is nevertheless a favorite with visiting dignitaries (from Caruso to Steven Spielberg) and offers excellent service. Guest rooms are some of the largest and most modern luxury accommodations in Prague, each with an Italian marble bathroom.

Panská 12, Praha 1. ℭ **224-093-111.** Fax 224-221-240. www.palacehotel.cz. 124 units. 6,000Kč ($228) double; from 9,630Kč ($366) suite. Rates include breakfast. AE, DC, MC, V. Metro: Můstek. **Amenities:** 2 restaurants; 2 lounges; laundry; rooms for those with limited mobility (2). *In room:* Hair dryer.

U Krále Karla *⭐*   This Castle Hill property does so much to drive home its Renaissance roots, King Charles's heirs should be getting royalties. Replete with period-print, open-beamed ceilings and stained-glass windows, the atmosphere is almost Disneyesque in its pretense, but somehow appropriate for this location at the foot of Prague Castle. This is a fun, comfortable choice, with heavy period furniture and colorful angelic accents everywhere, though it is pretty far from the train station.

Nerudova-Úvoz 4, Praha 1. ℭ **257-532-869.** Fax 257-533-591. www.romantichotels.cz. 19 units. 5,500Kč ($209) double; 7,900Kč ($300) suite. Rates include breakfast. AE, MC, V. Tram: 22 or 23 to Malostranské nám. **Amenities:** Restaurant; cafe; bar; laundry. *In room:* Hair dryer.

TOP ATTRACTIONS & SPECIAL MOMENTS

Most of Prague's special features are best viewed while slowly wandering through the city's heart. Except for the busy main streets, where you may have to dodge traffic, Prague is ideal for walking. Actually, walking is really the only way to explore Prague. Most of the town's oldest areas are pedestrian zones, with motor traffic restricted. If you have the time and energy, absorb the grand architecture of Prague Castle and the Old Town skyline (best from Charles Bridge) at sunrise and then at sunset. You'll see two completely different cities.

Prague Castle (Pražský Hrad) *⭐⭐⭐ (Moments)*   The huge hilltop complex known collectively as Pražský Hrad encompasses dozens of towers, churches, courtyards, and monuments. A visit could easily take an entire day or more. Still, you can see the top sights in the space of a morning or an afternoon. Make sure not to miss **St. Vitus Cathedral (Chrám sv. Víta)** *⭐* constructed in A.D. 926 as the court church of the Premyslid princes. It was named for a wealthy 4th-century Sicilian martyr and has long been the center of Prague's religious and political life. The cathedral's architecture is a mix of Gothic, baroque, and neo-Gothic elements.

The **Royal Palace (Královský palác)** *⭐*, in the third courtyard of the castle grounds, served as the residence of kings between the 10th and the 17th centuries. Vaulted Vladislav Hall, the interior's centerpiece, was used for coronations and still serves for inauguration of the Czech presidents and special occasions. You'll find a good selection of guidebooks, maps, and other related

> **Tips   Prague in a Day**
>
> If you are doing a quick stopover in Prague and have only 1 day to see the city, do what visiting kings and potentates do on a short visit: Walk the **Royal Route** from the top of the Hradčany hill (tram 22 or 23 or a taxi is suggested for the ride up unless you're very fit). Tour **Prague Castle,** and then stroll across Charles Bridge on the way to the winding alleys of **Old Town (Staré Město).**

information at the entrance. Other must-sees include **St. George's Basilica (Kostel sv. Jiří),** which houses a museum of historic Czech art. **Golden Lane (Zlatá ulička),** a picturesque, fairy-tale street of tiny 16th-century servants' houses; and the **Powder Tower (Prašná věž,** aka Mihulka), a laboratory for the 17th-century alchemists serving the court of Emperor Rudolf II.

Tickets are sold at the **Prague Castle Information Center** (© 224-373-368), in the second courtyard after passing through the main gate from Hradčanské náměstí. The center also arranges tours in various languages and sells tickets for individual concerts and exhibits.

Hradčanské nám., Hradčany, Praha 1. © 224-373-368. Fax 224-310-896. www.hrad.cz. Grounds free. Combination ticket to 5 main attractions (St. Vitus Cathedral, Royal Palace, St. George's Basilica, Powder Tower, Golden Lane), 220Kč ($8.35) adults, 110Kč ($4.20) students without guide; 300Kč ($11.40) adults, 190Kč ($7.20) students with English-speaking guide. Guided tours for groups of 5 and more. (Tues–Sun 9am–4pm). Ticket valid 1 day. Castle daily 9am–5pm (to 4pm Nov–Mar). Metro: Malostranská, then tram 22 or 23, up the hill 2 stops.

THE JEWISH MUSEUM

The Jewish Museum manages all the Jewish landmarks in Josefov, the Jewish Quarter, which is the northwest quarter of Old Town. The museum offers guided package tours with an English-speaking guide as part of a comprehensive admission price. The package includes the Ceremonial Hall, Old Jewish Cemetery, Pinkas Synagogue, Klaus Synagogue, Maisel Synagogue, and Spanish Synagogue.

Maisel Synagogue   Maisel Synagogue is used as the exhibition space for the Jewish Museum. Most of Prague's ancient Judaica was destroyed by the Nazis during World War II. Ironically, those same Germans constructed an "exotic museum of an extinct race," thus salvaging thousands of objects, such as the valued Torah covers, books, and silver now displayed here.

Maiselova 10 (between Široká and Jáchymova 3), Praha 1. © 222-317-191. Fax 222-317-181. www.jewish museum.cz. Admission to museum sites listed above is 290Kč ($11) adults, 200Kč ($7.60) students. Apr–Oct tours for groups of 10 or more on the hr. starting 9am (last tour 5pm). Nov–Apr tours leave whenever enough people gather in same language, open 9am–4:30pm Sun–Fri. Metro: Staroměstská.

Old Jewish Cemetery (Starý židovský hřbitov) ✪   Dating from the mid–15th century and a block away from the Old-New Synagogue, this is one of Europe's oldest Jewish burial grounds. It's also one of the most crowded because the city restricted Jewish burials—a 1-block zone is filled with more than 20,000 graves. The most renowned occupant: Rabbi Yehuda Loew (d. 1609), who created the legendary Golem (clay creature) to protect the Jews of Prague.

U Starého hřbitova 3A. © 222-317-191. Fax 222-317-181. www.jewishmuseum.cz. Admission to all Jewish Museum sites 290Kč ($11) adults, 200Kč ($7.60) students. Sun–Fri 9am–6pm. Metro: Staroměstská.

Old-New Synagogue (Staronová synagoga) ✪   First called the New Synagogue to distinguish it from an even older one that no longer exists, the

Old-New Synagogue, built around 1270, is Europe's oldest Jewish house of worship. Note that this is the one site in Josefov not included in the Jewish Museum tour package.

Červená 3. ⓒ 222-317-191. Admission 200Kč ($7.60) adults, 140Kč ($5.30) students. Sun–Thurs 9am–6pm; Fri 9am–5pm. Metro: Staroměstská.

THE NATIONAL GALLERY

The national collection of fine art is grouped for display in the series of venues known collectively as the **National Gallery** (**Národní Galerie; www.ng prague.cz**).

St. Agnes Convent (Klášter sv. Anežky české)
This complex of early Gothic buildings and churches dates from the 13th century. The convent, tucked in a corner of Staré Město, is appropriately home to a collection of medieval and Renaissance art.

U milosrdných 17, Praha 1. ⓒ 224-810-628. Admission 100Kč ($3.85) adults, 50Kč ($1.90) children. Tues–Sun 10am–6pm. Metro: Staroměstská.

Šternberk Palace (Šternberský palác)
The jewel in the National Gallery crown, the gallery at Šternberk Palace, adjacent to the main gate of Prague Castle, was overhauled in 2002 and 2003. It now has an exhibition of ancient Greek and Roman art, though the primary collection still features European artworks from the 14th through the 18th centuries. You'll find small sculptures mixed along with Renaissance oils from Dutch masters. Pieces by Rembrandt, El Greco, Goya, Dürer, and Van Dyck are mixed among numerous pieces from Austrian imperial-court painters.

Hradčanské nám. 15, Praha 1. ⓒ 220-514-634. Admission 100Kč ($3.85) adults, 50Kč ($1.90) students and children. Tues–Sun 10am–6pm. Metro: Malostranská or Hradčanská; Tram: 22 or 23.

St. George's Convent at Prague Castle (Klášter sv. Jiří na Pražském hradě)
Dedicated to displaying traditional Czech art, the castle convent is especially packed with Gothic and baroque Bohemian iconography as well as portraits of patron saints. The most famous among the unique collection of Czech Gothic panel paintings are those by the Master of the Hohenfurth Altarpiece and the Master Theodoricus. There's also a noteworthy collection of Czech Mannerist and baroque paintings from the 17th and 18th centuries.

Jiřské nám. 33. ⓒ 257-531-644. Admission 50Kč ($1.90) adults, 20Kč (75¢) students. Tues–Sun 10am–6pm. Metro: Malostranská or Hradčanská; Tram: 22 or 23.

Kinský Palace (Palác Kinských)
This rococo palace houses graphic works from the National Gallery collection, including pieces by Georges Braque, André Derain, and other modern masters. Pablo Picasso's 1907 *Self-Portrait* is here and has virtually been adopted as the National Gallery's logo.

Staroměstské nám. 12, Praha 1. ⓒ 224-810-758. Admission 100Kč ($3.85) adults, 50Kč ($1.90) students. Tues–Sun 10am–6pm. Metro: Line A to Staroměstská.

Veletržní Palace
This 1925 constructivist palace, built for trade fairs, holds the bulk of the National Gallery's collection of 20th- and 21st-century works by Czech and other European artists. Three atrium-lit concourses provide a comfortable setting for some catchy and kitschy Czech sculpture and multimedia works. Alas, the best cubist works from Braque and Picasso, Rodin bronzes, and many other primarily French pieces have been relegated to the second floor. In 2000, the museum's 19th-century collection was moved here as well.

Moments   Charles Bridge

Dating from the 14th century, the **Charles Bridge (Karlův most)** ★★★, Prague's most celebrated structure, links Prague Castle to Staré Město. For most of its 600 years, the 1,700-foot-span has been a pedestrian promenade, although for centuries walkers had to share the concourse with horse-drawn vehicles and trolleys. Today, the bridge is filled with hordes walking among folksy artists and street musicians. Strolling the bridge is a quintessential Prague experience and should not be missed.

Veletržní at Dukelských hrdinů 47, Praha 7. © **224-301-111.** Admission 200Kč ($7.60) adults, 100Kč ($3.85) students to all 3 floors; 150Kč ($5.70) adults, 70Kč ($2.65) for 2 floors; 100Kč ($3.85) adults, 50Kč ($1.90) for visiting only 1 floor of the Palace. 1st Wed of each month free admission. Tues–Sun 10am–6pm. Metro: Vltavská or tram 5, 12, or 17 to Veletržní stop.

FAMOUS SQUARES

The most celebrated square, **Old Town Square (Staroměstské nám.),** is surrounded by baroque buildings and packed with colorful craftspeople, cafes, and entertainers. In ancient days, the site was a major crossroad on central European merchant routes. In its center stands a memorial to Jan Hus, the 15th-century martyr who crusaded against Prague's German-dominated religious and political establishment. Unveiled in 1915, on the 500th anniversary of Hus's execution, the monument's most compelling features are the asymmetry of the composition and the fluidity of the figures.

The **Astronomical Clock (orloj)** at **Old Town Hall (Staroměstská radnice)** performs a glockenspiel spectacle daily on the hour from 8am to 8pm. Originally constructed in 1410, the clock has long been an important symbol of Prague. **Wenceslas Square (Václavské nám.),** a former horse market, has been the focal point of riots, revolutions, and national celebrations.

MORE ATTRACTIONS

Cathedral of St. Nicholas (Chrám sv. Mikuláše) ★ *Moments*   This church is critically regarded as one of the best examples of the high baroque north of the Alps. K. I. Dienzenhofer's 1711 design was augmented by his son Kryštof's 260-foot dome, which has dominated the Malá Strana skyline since its completion in 1752. Prague's smog has played havoc with the building's exterior, but its gilded interior is stunning. Gold-capped, marble-veneered columns frame altars packed with statuary and frescoes.

Malostranské nám., Praha 1. © **257-534-215.** Free admission. Daily 9am–5pm, concerts are usually held at 5pm. Metro: Malostranská, then tram 12, 22, or 23 1 stop to Malostranské nám.

PARKS & GARDENS

From **Vyšehrad,** Soběslavova 1 (© **224-920-735;** tram 3 from Karlovo nám. to Výtoň south of New Town), legend has it that Princess Libuše looked out over the Vltava valley toward the present-day Prague Castle and predicted the founding of a great state and capital city. Vyšehrad was the seat of the first Czech kings of the Premyslid dynasty before the dawn of this millennium. Today, within the confines of the citadel, lush lawns and gardens are crisscrossed by dozens of paths, leading to historic buildings and cemeteries. From here you'll see one of the city's most panoramic views.

The **Royal Garden (Královská zahrada)** at Prague Castle, once the site of the sovereigns' vineyards, was founded in 1534. Dotted with lemon trees and surrounded by 16th-, 17th-, and 18th-century buildings, the park is laid out with abundant shrubbery and fountains. Enter from U Prašného mostu street north of the castle complex.

In Hradčany, the **Garden on the Ramparts (Zahrada na Valech),** a park below the castle with a gorgeous city panorama, was reopened in spring 1995 after being thoroughly refurbished. The park is open from Tuesday to Sunday 9am to 5pm.

WHERE TO DINE

The true Czech dining experience can be summed up in three native words: *vepřo, knedlo, zelo*—pork, dumplings, cabbage. If that's what you want, try most any *hostinec* (Czech pub). Most offer a hearty *guláš* or pork dish with dumplings and cabbage for about 80Kč to 150Kč ($3–$5.70). After you wash it down with Czech beer, you won't care about the taste—or your arteries.

At most restaurants, menu prices include VAT. Tipping has become more commonplace in restaurants where the staff is obviously trying harder; rounding up the bill to about 10% or more is usually adequate.

Warning: Some restaurants gouge customers by charging exorbitant amounts for nuts or other seemingly free pre-meal snacks left on your table. Ask before you eat.

Bohemia Bagel *(Value* BAGELS/SANDWICHES   The roster of golden-brown, hand-rolled, stone-baked bagels at this restaurant near the Jewish Quarter, at the base of Petřín Hill, is stellar. Plain, cinnamon raisin, garlic, or onion provides a sturdy but tender frame for Scandinavian lox and cream cheese or jalapeño-cheddar cheese (on which you can lop Tex-Mex chili for the Sloppy Bagel). The cushioned wooden booths in an earthy contemporary setting are comfortable.

Újezd 16, Praha 1. *©* **257-310-694.** Bagels and sandwiches 25Kč–145Kč (95¢–$5.50). No credit cards. Mon–Fri 7am–midnight; Sat–Sun 8am–midnight. Tram: 6, 9, 12, 22, or 23 to Újezd.

Café-Restaurant Louvre CZECH/INTERNATIONAL   This big, breezy upstairs dining hall in New Town is great for a coffee, an inexpensive pre-theater meal, or an upscale game of pool. A fabulous Art Nouveau interior with huge original chandeliers buzzes with shoppers, businessmen, and students. Main dishes range from trout with horseradish to beans with garlic sauce. Avoid the always-overcooked pastas and stick to the basic meats and fish. In the snazzy billiards parlor in back, you can have drinks or a light meal.

Národní třída 20, Praha 1. *©* **224-930-949.** Reservations not accepted. Main courses 100Kč–300Kč ($3.85–$11.40). AE, DC, MC, V. Daily 8am–11:30pm. Metro: Národní třída.

Creperie Café Gallery Restaurant FRENCH   This convenient and affordable French eatery rests at the foot of Charles Bridge on the Old Town side. Occupying a wing of the St. Francis church complex, the Creperie creates the feel of a cozy farmhouse with old wooden chairs and hand-stitched pillows thrown on sturdy benches. The savory galettes are filled with spinach, tangy niva cheese, or chicken and make a good light lunch after a heavy morning of trudging. The sweet crepes with chocolate, fruit compote, or whipped cream are good for an afternoon break or for dessert following an evening stroll across the bridge.

Křížovnické nám. 3, Praha 1. *©* **221-108-240.** Crepes and galettes 75Kč–129Kč ($2.85–$4.90). AE, MC, V. Daily 10am–midnight. Metro: Staroměstská.

Jarmark *☆ (Value* CZECH   This is Bohemia's answer to those endless cafeteria lines your parents would drag you through, except this one, a quarter of a mile from the Main Tran Station, serves a really tasty variety of meats, sides, and salads, and, of course, beer. And this one is not all-you-can-eat-for-one-price despite its convenient come-and-shove-it-in system. Everyone gets a ticket upon entering, which will be validated at each stop you make among the various rows of steaming hot tables, veggie carts, and drink dispensers.

Vodičkova 30, Dům "U Nováků".℃ 224-233-733. Reservations not accepted. Main courses 70Kč–150Kč ($2.65–$5.70). No credit cards. Daily 11am to 10pm; Mon–Fri breakfast 8am–10am. Metro: Můstek.

Kogo ★★ (Value ITALIAN   This ristorante-pizzeria in the middle of Old Town is very trendy and popular. Fresh and well-prepared salads, pizza, pasta, and Italian specialties are served by an above-average waitstaff in a pleasant atmosphere. Beyond the standard and tasty pasta roster, the roasted veal is a good choice or try the rare (for Prague) and tasty mussels in white wine and garlic.

A second Kogo restaurant is located at Na Příkopě 22, Praha 1 (℃ 221-451-259; Metro: Můstek).

Havelská 27, Praha 1. ℃ 224-214-543. Reservations recommended. Main courses 130Kč–400Kč ($4.95–$15.20). AE, MC, V. Daily 11am–11pm. Metro: Můstek.

Pivnice Radegast CZECH   The raucous Radegast dishes up Prague's best pub guláš in a single narrow vaulted hall, where the namesake Moravian brew seems to never stop flowing from its taps. Around the corner from a bunch of popular bars and close to Old Town Square, the Radegast attracts a good mix of visitors and locals and a young, upwardly mobile crowd.

Templová 2, Praha 1. ℃ 222-328-069. Main courses 60Kč–240Kč ($2.30–$9.10).AE, MC, V. Daily 11am–midnight. Metro: Můstek or nám. Republiky.

Pizzeria Rugantino ★ PIZZA   This restaurant's wood-fired stoves and handmade dough result in a crisp, delicate crust, a perfect platform for a multitude of cheeses, vegetables, and meats. The Diabolo with fresh garlic bits and very hot chiles goes nicely with a cool iceberg salad and a pull of Krušovice beer. The constant buzz, nonsmoking area, and heavy childproof wooden tables make this place near the Jewish Quarter a family favorite.

Dušní 4, Praha 1. ℃ 222-318-172. Individual pizzas 100Kč–300Kč ($3.85–$11.40). No credit cards. Mon–Sat 11am–11pm; Sun 5–11pm. Metro: Staroměstská.

Ponte ★ (Value INTERNATIONAL   Our favorite choice above Wenceslas Square in Vinohrady, Ponte is one of the best values in Prague and especially great for shunning the cold of an autumn or winter evening near the roaring fire in the brick cellar dining room. As its name suggests, this place is a bridge between Italian cuisine and other Continental foods. Beyond the penne and pesto, there are several vegetarian and low-calorie, chicken-based selections. Jazz combos play on most nights from a small stage in the corner.

Anglická 15, Praha 2. ℃ 224-221-665. Reservations recommended. Main courses 195Kč–695Kč ($7.40–$26.40). AE, MC, V. Daily 12am–11pm. Metro: I. P. Pavlova or nám. Míru.

Radost FX ★★ VEGETARIAN   In vogue and vegetarian, Radost is a clubhouse for hip New Bohemians that's a short walk from the Main Train Station. The veggie burger is well seasoned and substantial on a grain bun, and the soups, such as lentil and onion, are light and full of flavor. The dining area is a dark rec room of upholstered armchairs, chaise lounges, couches from the 1960s, and coffee tables on which you eat. It serves as an art gallery as well.

Bělehradská 120, Praha 2. ℃ 224-254-776. Main courses 100Kč–250Kč ($3.85–$9.50). MC, V. Daily 10am–5am. Metro: I.P. Pavlova.

Moments Kavárna Society

Cafe life is back in a big way in Prague. From dissident blues to high society, these are the places where non-pub Praguers spend their afternoons and evenings, sipping coffee and smoking cigarettes while reading, writing, or talking with friends.

The **Kavárna (Cafe) Slavia** 🟡, Národní at Smetanovo nábřeží 2, Praha 1 (© **224-218-493;** Metro: Národní třída), reopened in 1997, after a half-decade sleep. The restored crisp Art Deco room recalls the Slavia's 100 years as the meeting place for the city's cultural and intellectual crowd. You'll still find a relatively affordable menu of light fare served with the riverfront views of Prague Castle and the National Theater. It's open daily 8am to midnight.

The quaint **Café Milena,** Staroměstské nám. 22, Praha 1 (© **221-632-602;** Metro: Staroměstská), is managed by the Franz Kafka Society and named for Milena Jesenská, one of the writer's lovers. The draw is a great view of the Orloj, the astronomical clock with the hourly parade of saints on the side of Old Town Square's city hall. It's open daily 10am to 8pm.

Of all the beautifully restored spaces in the Municipal House, the **Kavárna Obecní dům** 🟡, nám. Republiky 5, Praha 1 (© **222-002-763;** Metro: nám. Republiky), might be its most spectacular room. Lofty ceilings, marble accents and tables, an altarlike mantle, huge windows, and period chandeliers provide the awesome setting for coffees, teas, and other drinks, along with pastries and light sandwiches. It's open daily 7:30am to 11pm.

In the neighborhood behind the National Theater is **Angel Café** 🟡, Opatovická 3, Praha 1 (© **224-930-019;** Metro: Národní třída). This cafe best reflects the light-and-bright 1990s restaurant movement captured by Pret a Manger in Britain. Unlike the cash-and-carry Pret, you can sit comfortably in the relaxing Angel atmosphere and linger over tasty sandwiches served with quality cheeses, spreads, and vegetables on fresh bread. French pastries highlight the breakfast lineup along with properly stiff espressos. Who needs Starbucks?

A New Age alternative to the clatter of the kavárnas is **Dahab** 🟡🟡, Dlouhá 33, Praha 1 (© **224-827-375;** Metro: nám. Republiky). This tearoom was founded by Prague's king of tea, Luboš Rychvalský, who introduced Prague to Eastern and Arabic tea cultures soon after the 1989 revolution. Here you can choose from about 20 varieties of tea and more than 10 kinds of coffee. Arabic soups, hummus, tahini, couscous, pita, and tempting sweets are also on the menu. It's open daily from noon to midnight.

Restaurant U Čížků 🟡 *Value* CZECH   One of the city's first private restaurants, this cozy cellar-cum-hunting lodge on Charles Square is still an excellent value. The fare is purely Czech, and the massive portions of game, smoked pork, and other meats will stay with you for a while. The traditional *Staročeský talíř* (local pork meat, dumplings, and cabbage) is about as authentic Czech as it gets.

Karlovo nám. 34, Praha 2. (✆ **222-232-257**. Reservations recommended. Main courses 170Kč–320Kč ($6.45–$12.15). AE, MC, V. Daily noon–10pm.

U medvídků ✰✰ CZECH   Bright and noisy, the House at the Little Bears serves a better-than-average vepřo, knedlo, and zelo with two-color cabbage. The pub, on the right after entering, is much cheaper and livelier than the bar to the left. It's a hangout for locals, German tour groups, and foreign journalists in search of the original Czech Budweiser beer, Budvar. In high season, an oompah band plays in the beer wagon.

Na Perštýně 7, Praha 1. (✆ **224-211-916**. Main courses 90Kč–250Kč ($3.40–$9.50). AE, MC, V. Daily 11am–11pm. Metro: Národní třída.

SHOPPING

Czech porcelain, glass, and cheap but well-constructed clothing draw hordes of day-trippers from Germany. Private retailers have been allowed to operate here only since late 1989, but many top international retailers have already arrived. Shops lining the main route from Old Town Square to Charles Bridge are also great for browsing. For clothing, porcelain, jewelry, garnets, and glass, stroll around Wenceslas Square and Na Příkopě, connecting Wenceslas Square with náměstí Republiky.

For glass and crystal, try **Moser,** at Na Příkopě 12, Praha 1 (✆ **224-228-686;** Metro: Můstek), or at Malé nám. 11, Praha 1 (✆ **221-611-520;** Metro: Můstek). The Moser family began selling Bohemia's finest crystal in central Prague in 1857, drawing customers from around the world. It's open from Monday to Friday 9am to 8pm, Saturday and Sunday 10am to 6pm at Na Příkopě; from Monday to Friday 10am to 7pm, Saturday and Sunday 10am to 6pm at Malé nám.

Celetná Crystal, Celetná 15, Praha 1 (✆ **224-811-376;** Metro: nám. Republiky), has a wide selection of world-renowned Czech crystal, china, arts and crafts, and jewelry displayed in a spacious three-floor showroom right in the heart of Prague. At **Cristallino,** Celetná 12, Praha 1 (✆ **224-223-027;** Metro: nám. Republiky), you'll find a good selection of stemware and vases in traditional designs. The shop's central location belies its excellent prices.

Havelský trh (Havel's Market), Havelská ulice, Praha 1 (Metro: Můstek), is on a short street running perpendicular to Melantrichova, the main route connecting Staroměstské náměstí with Václavské náměstí. This open-air market (named well before Havel became president in 1989) features dozens of private vendors selling seasonal homegrown fruits and vegetables. Other goods, including flowers and cheese, are also for sale. Since this place is designed primarily for locals, the prices are exceedingly low by western European standards. The market is open Monday to Friday 7am to 6pm.

NIGHTLIFE

Prague's nightlife has changed completely since the Velvet Revolution—for the better if you plan to go clubbing, for the worse if you hope to sample the city's classical offerings. Still, seeing *Don Giovanni* in the Estates' Theater, where Mozart first premiered it, is worth the admission cost. Ticket prices, while low by Western standards, have become prohibitively high for the average Czech. You'll find, however, the exact reverse in the rock and jazz scene. Dozens of clubs have opened, and world-class bands are finally adding Prague to their European tours.

Turn to the ***Prague Post*** (www.praguepost.cz) for listings of cultural events and nightlife around the city; it's available at most newsstands in Old Town and Malá Strana. Once in Prague, you can buy tickets at theater box offices or from any one of dozens of agencies throughout the city center. Large, centrally located agencies (take the Metro to Můstek for all) are the **Prague Tourist Center,** Rytířská 12, Praha 1 (© **224-212-209**), open daily 9am to 8pm; **Bohemia Ticket International,** Na Příkopě 16, Praha 1 (© **224-215-031**); and **Čedok,** Na Příkopě 18, Praha 1 (© **224-197-640**).

THE PERFORMING ARTS   Although there's plenty of music year-round, the symphonies and orchestras all come to life during the **Prague Spring Music Festival** (see "Festivals & Special Events," on p. 156). Tickets for festival concerts run from 250Kč to 2,000Kč ($9.50–$76).

The **Czech Philharmonic** and **Prague Symphony** orchestras usually perform at the **Rudolfinum,** náměstí Jana Palacha, Praha 1 (© **227-059-352;** Metro: Staroměstská). The Czech Philharmonic is the traditional voice of the country's national pride, often playing works by native sons Dvořák and Smetana; the Prague Symphony ventures into more eclectic territory. Tickets are 100Kč to 600Kč ($3.85–$22.80). Ticket orders and purchases can be made in advance (and you are advised to book well in advance) through the agency **TICKET-PRO,** Salvátorská 10, 110 00 Praha 1, Czech Republic (© **296-329-999;** www. ticketpro.cz). All major credit cards are accepted. Any remaining tickets are sold at the venues of the performances, which have various opening hours, but usually few seats remain within a month of the festival.

In a city full of spectacularly beautiful theaters, the massive pale-green **Estates'** Theater (Stavovské divadlo), Ovocný trh 1, Praha 1 (© **224-215-001;** Metro: Můstek), is one of the most awesome. Built in 1783 and the site of the premiere of Mozart's *Don Giovanni* (conducted by the composer), the theater now hosts many of the classic productions of European opera and drama. Simultaneous English translation, transmitted via headphone, is available for most plays. Tickets cost 200Kč to 1,000Kč ($7.60–$38). Lavishly constructed in the late-Renaissance style of northern Italy, the gold-crowned **Národní divadlo (National Theater),** Národní třída 2, Praha 1 (© **224-901-448;** Metro: Národní třída), overlooking the Vltava River, is one of Prague's most recognizable landmarks. Completed in 1881, the theater was built to nurture the Czech National Revival—a grassroots movement to replace the dominant German culture with that of native Czechs. Today, classic productions are staged here in a larger setting than at the Estates' Theater, but with about the same ticket prices.

The **National Theater Ballet** performs at the National Theater. The troupe has seen most of its top talent go west since 1989, but it still puts on a good show. After critics complained that Prague's top company has grown complacent, choreographer Libor Vaculík responded with humorous and quirky stagings of off-the-wall ballets such as *Some Like It Hot* and *Psycho.* Tickets cost 200Kč to 600Kč ($7.60–$22.80). **Laterna Magika,** Národní třída 4, Praha 1 (© **224-931-482;** Metro: Národní třída), is a performance-art show in the new wing of the National Theater. The multimedia show, which combines live theater with film and dance, was once considered radical and is not for those easily offended by nudity. Tickets are 400Kč ($15.20).

JAZZ CLUBS   Upscale by Czech standards, **AghaRTA Jazz Centrum,** Krakovská 5, Praha 1 (© **222-211-275;** Metro: Muzeum), regularly features some of the best music in town, from standard acoustic trios to Dixieland, funk, and fusion. Bands usually begin at 9pm. The club is open Monday to Friday 5pm to 1am and Saturday and Sunday 7pm to 1am. Cover is 100Kč ($3.85). **Reduta Jazz Club,** Národní třída 20, Praha 1 (© **224-933-487;** Metro:

Moments An Excursion to Karlštejn Castle

By far the most popular day trip from Prague is to **Karlštejn Castle,** 18 miles (30km) southwest of Prague, which was built by Charles IV in the 14th century to safeguard the crown jewels of the Holy Roman Empire and has been restored to its original state.

As you approach the castle by train from the Prague, little will prepare you for your first view: a spectacular castle perched high on a hill, surrounded by lush forests and vineyards. The Holy Rood Chapel is famous for the more than 2,000 precious and semiprecious inlaid gems that adorn its walls, and the Chapel of St. Catherine was King Karel IV's private oratory. Both the Audience Hall and the Imperial Bedroom are impressive, despite being stripped of their original furnishings. To see the Holy Rood Chapel you need to make a reservation (© **274-008-154;** www.spusc.cz or www.hradkarlstejn.cz).

Admission for a shorter tour is 200Kč ($7.60) adults and 100Kč ($3.85) students, and the longer one with the Holy Rood Chapel is 300Kč ($11.40) adults, 100Kč ($3.85) students. It's open Tuesday through Sunday: May, June, and September 9am to noon and 12:30 to 5pm; July and August 9am to noon and 12:30 to 6pm; April and October 9am to noon and 1pm to 4pm; November, December, and March 9am to noon and 1pm to 3pm; closed January, February.

Most trains leave from Prague's Hlavní nádraží to the castle on an hourly basis throughout the day (trip time: 43 min.) and less frequently from Smíchov Station (Metro: Smíchovské nádraží), from which the trip time is only 34 minutes. One-way, second-class fare is 46Kč ($1.75) from the Main Train Station or 40Kč ($1.55) from Smíchov station. For train schedules, go to **www.jizdnirady.cz.** The castle is a 1.2-mile (1.9km) walk from the train station, though the stroll uphill to the castle—and the views that come with it—is one of the main highlights of the experience.

There is no official tourist center in Karlštejn, but the ticket and castle information booth can help you. On the main street heading up to the castle itself you will find a number of stores and a restaurant. Take a break in **Restaurace Blanky z Valois,** where pizzas range from 80č to 190Kč ($3.05–$7.20). It is open daily from 11am to 10pm.

Národní třída), is a smoky subterranean room that looks exactly like a jazz cellar should. An adventurous booking policy, which even included a saxophone gig with a U.S. president in 1994, means that different bands play almost every night. Music usually starts around 9pm. It's open from 9pm to midnight. Cover is usually 100Kč ($3.85).

PUBS & BARS   You'll experience true Czech entertainment in only one kind of place—a smoky local pub serving some of the world's best beer. Remember to put a cardboard coaster in front of you to show you want a mug, and never wave for service, as the typically surly waiter will just ignore you.

Originally a brewery dating from 1459, **U Fleků,** Křemencova 11, Praha 2 (© **224-934-019;** Metro: Národní třída), is Prague's most famous beer hall, and one of the only pubs that still brews its own beer. This huge place has a myriad of timber-lined rooms and a large, loud courtyard where an oompah band performs. Tourists come here by the busload, so U Fleků is avoided by disparaging locals who don't like its German atmosphere anyway. The pub's special dark beer is excellent, however, and not available anywhere else. It's open daily 9am to 11pm.

One of the most famous Czech pubs, **U Zlatého tygra (At the Golden Tiger),** Husova 17, Praha 1 (© **222-221-111;** Metro: Staroměstská or Můstek), was a favorite watering hole of ex-president Havel and the late writer Bohumil Hrabal. Particularly smoky, and not especially tourist friendly, it is nevertheless a one-stop education in Czech culture. Then-presidents Havel and Clinton joined Hrabal for a traditional Czech pub evening here during Clinton's 1994 visit to Prague. It's open daily from 3 to 11pm.

3 Western & Southern Bohemia

The Czech Republic is composed of two regions: Bohemia and Moravia. The larger of the two, Bohemia, occupying the central and western areas of the country, has for centuries been caught between a rock (Germany) and a hard place (Austria). Bohemia was almost always in the center of regional conflicts, both secular and religious. But the area also flourished, as witnessed by the wealth of castles that dot the countryside and the spa towns that were once the playgrounds of the rich and famous. The good news for the rail traveler is that the region is small enough that you can visit these towns as separate day trips from Prague, or once in the region, you can hop from one place to the other.

KARLOVY VARY (CARLSBAD)

The discovery of Karlovy Vary (Carlsbad), 75 miles (120km) west of Prague, by Charles IV reads something like a 14th-century episode of *The Beverly Hillbillies.* According to local lore, the king was out huntin' for some food when up from the ground came a-bubblin' water (though discovered by his dogs, not an errant gunshot). Knowing a good thing when he saw it, Charles immediately set to work building a small castle, naming the town that evolved around it Karlovy Vary (Charles's Boiling Place). The first spa buildings were built in 1522, and before long, notables such as Russian Czar Peter the Great, and later Bach, Beethoven, Freud, Goethe, and Marx all came to take the waters.

After World War II, East Bloc travelers (following in the footsteps of Marx, no doubt) discovered the town, and Karlovy Vary became a destination for the proletariat. On doctors' orders, most workers enjoyed regular stays of 2 or 3 weeks, letting the mineral waters ranging from 110.3°F to 161.6°F (43.5°C–72°C) from the town's 12 spas heal their tired and broken bodies. Even now, most spa guests are there by doctor's prescription.

GETTING THERE   There is no fast rail connection from Prague to Karlovy Vary and train travel takes much longer than a trip by bus, so although it's the most popular of the towns to visit (and thus the one we mention first), it's actually easier to get here by bus or by train from one of the other Bohemian towns.

The train from Prague goes through the northern region of Bohemia and reaches the spa town in about 4 hours. There are two trains leaving from Prague's main station and nádraží Holešovice in the morning and two from Masaryk station in the late afternoon. The fare runs 224Kč to 274Kč ($8.50–$10.40).

Karlovy Vary's **Horní (upper) train station** is connected to the town center by city bus 11. If you are coming via Mariánské Lázně, there are about seven trains daily. The 1½ hour-trip costs 76Kč ($2.90) and you will end up at

Karlovy Vary's **Dolní (lower) nádraží.** Just a 5-minute walk from this station is the main stop for all city buses (**Městská tržnice**) and city center.

By Bus   Taking a bus to Karlovy Vary is much more convenient if you're leaving from Prague. Frequent express buses leave from Prague's Florenc bus station and arrive in Karlovy Vary in 2¼ hours. The trip costs 130Kč ($4.95). Take a 10-minute walk or local bus 4 into Karlovy Vary's spa center. Note that you must have a ticket to board local transport. You can buy tickets for 8Kč (30¢) at the bus station stop, or, if you have no change, the kiosk across the street sells tickets during regular business hours. For timetable information go to **www. jizdnirady.cz**.

VISITOR INFORMATION   **Infocentrum města Karlovy Vary** is located near the main Mlýnská kolonáda, on Lázeňská 1 (✆ **353-224-097**), and is open April to October Monday to Friday from 7am to 5pm, Saturday and Sunday from 9am to 3pm; and November to March on Monday to Friday from 7am to 4pm. The office also has a window at the terminal of the **Dolní (lower) nádraží** bus and train station, Západní ulice (✆ **353-232-838**). These are the official town's information centers, which will answer your questions and help you make hotel reservations, sell you tickets for entertainment in the city, and so on.

Another option is **Kur-Info,** inside the Vřídelní kolonáda (✆ **353-229-312**), which is open April to October Monday to Friday 7am to 5pm, Saturday and Sunday 9am to 3pm, November to March Monday to Friday 7am to 4pm. It provides accommodation services, arranges guided tours and spa treatments, and sells tickets for some events. Be sure to pick up the *Promenáda* magazine, a comprehensive collection of events with a small map of the town center.

For Web information on festivals and events in the city, go to **www.karlovy vary.cz**.

TOP ATTRACTIONS & SPECIAL MOMENTS

The town's slow pace and pedestrian promenades, lined with Art Nouveau buildings, turn strolling into an art form. Nighttime walks take on an even more mystical feel as the sewers, river, and many major cracks in the roads emit steam from the hot springs underneath. A good place to start is the **Hotel Thermal** at the north end of the old town's center, an easy walk from the bus station. The 1970s glass, steel, and concrete structure, between the town's eastern hills and the Ohře River, sticks out like a sore communist thumb amid the 19th-century architecture. Nonetheless, you'll find three important places here: its outdoor pool, the only centrally located outdoor public pool; its upper terrace, boasting a spectacular view of the city; and its cinema, Karlovy Vary's largest, which holds many of the local film festival's premier events.

As you enter the heart of the town on the river's west side, you'll see the renovated ornate white wrought-iron **Sadová kolonáda** adorning the beautifully manicured park **Dvořákovy sady.** Continue following the river, and about 110 yards later you'll encounter the **Mlýnská kolonáda,** a long, covered walkway housing several Karlovy Vary springs, which you can sample 24 hours a day. Each spring has a plaque beside it telling which mineral elements are present and the temperature of the water. Bring your own cup or buy one just about anywhere to sip the waters; most are too hot to drink from your hands.

When you hit the river bend, the majestic **Church of St. Mary Magdalene** sits perched atop a hill, overlooking the **Vřídlo,** the hottest spring in town. Built in 1736, the church is the work of Kilian Ignac Dientzenhofer, who also created two of Prague's more notable churches—both named St. Nicholas. Housing

⌒ *Moments* Spa Cures & Treatments

Most visitors to Karlovy Vary come specifically to get spa treatments, and therapy programs usually last 1 to 3 weeks. After consulting with a spa physician, guests are given a regimen of activities that may include mineral baths, massages, waxings, mudpacks, electrotherapy, and pure oxygen inhalation. After spending the morning at a spa, guests are then usually directed to walk the paths of the town's surrounding forest.

The common denominator of all the cures is an ample daily dose of hot mineral water, which bubbles up from 12 springs. This water definitely has a distinct odor and taste. You'll see people chugging it down, but it doesn't necessarily taste very good. Some thermal springs actually taste and smell like rotten eggs. You might want to take a small sip at first.

You'll also notice that almost everyone in town seems to be carrying "the cup," basically a mug with a built-in straw that runs through the handle. Young and old alike parade through town with their mugs, filling and refilling them at each new thermal water tap. You can buy these mugs everywhere for as little as 100Kč ($3.85) or as much as 500Kč ($19); they make a quirky souvenir. *Warning:* None of the mugs can make the hot springs taste any better!

Most rail travelers won't have the 1-week minimum most major spas demand, but many of the local hotels also offer spa and health treatments, so ask when you book your room. Most will happily arrange a treatment if they don't provide it directly. Visitors to Karlovy Vary for just a day or 2 can experience the waters on an "outpatient" basis. The **Sanatorium Baths III-VESO,** Mlýnské nábřeží 7 (© **353-223-473**), welcomes day-trippers with mineral baths, massages, saunas, and a cold pool. It's open Monday to Friday 7am to 2pm for spa treatments; swimming pool and sauna Monday to Friday 3pm to 6pm, Saturday 1 to 5pm.

For more information and reservations for spa packages contact **Čedok,** Na Příkopě 18, Praha 1 (© **224-197-777;** www.cedok.cz), in Prague.

Vřídlo, which blasts water some 50 feet into the air, is the glass building called the **Vřídelní kolonáda.** It was built in 1974 and houses several hot springs you can sample for free. The building also holds the Kur-Info information center and several kiosks selling postcards, stone roses, and drinking cups. Heading away from the Vřídelní kolonáda are Stará and Nová Louka streets, which line either side of the river. Along **Stará (Old) Louka** you'll find several fine cafes and glass and crystal shops. Crystal and porcelain are Karlovy Vary's other claims to fame. Dozens of places throughout town sell everything from plates to chandeliers. **Nová (New) Louka** is lined with hotels and the historic **Town's Theater.**

Both streets lead to the **Grandhotel Pupp.** After a massive reconstruction that erased nearly 50 years of communism (it was temporarily called the Grand Hotel Moskva), the Pupp is once again the crown jewel of the town. Regardless of capitalism or communism, the Pupp remains what it always was: the grande dame of hotels in the area. Once catering to nobility from all over central

Europe, the Pupp still houses one of the town's finest restaurants, the Grand, and its grounds are a favorite with the hiking crowd.

If you still have the energy, atop the hill behind the Pupp stands the **Diana Lookout Tower.** Footpaths leading through the forests eventually spit you out at the base of the tower, as if to say, "Ha, the trip is only half over." If you are not up to the five-story climb, you can use the lift and enjoy the view of the town from above. Alternatively, a cable car runs to the tower every 15 minutes or so from the base located right next to the Grandhotel Pupp. A one-way ticket on the cable car is 30Kč ($1.15); round-trip, it's 50Kč ($1.90). The cable car runs every 15 minutes daily from 9am to 7pm.

WHERE TO STAY & DINE

Some of the town's major spa hotels accommodate only those who are paying for complete treatment, unless their occupancy rates are particularly low. The hotels listed below accept guests for stays of any length.

One of Karlovy Vary's best hotels, the 116-room **Grandhotel Pupp** ✮✮✮, Mírové nám. 2 (✆ **353-109-631;** www.pupp.cz), was built in 1701 and is also one of Europe's oldest. While the hotel's public areas ooze with splendor and charm, guest rooms aren't as consistently enchanting. The best tend to be on the upper floors facing the town center; only some rooms have air-conditioning. The Grand Restaurant serves up as grand a dining room as you'll find, with the food to match. The hotel's rates are quoted in euros to combat the volatility of the crown and run 230€ ($265) double; from 320€ ($368) for a suite. Breakfast costs 13€ ($15) extra.

Parkhotel Pupp ✮, Mírové nám. 2 (✆ **353-109-111;** www.pupp.cz), is housed within the same complex as its five-star cousin, but a world apart in terms of frills—and price. Still, rooms are large and all the same facilities are available; the views are just less spectacular. Rates are 115€ ($132) double; 155€ ($178) suite. Breakfast costs 10€ ($11.50) extra.

Less stylish but still in a great location is **Hotel Dvořák,** Nová Louka 11 (✆ **353-102-111;** www.hotel-dvorak.cz). Now part of the Vienna International hotel/resort chain, the Dvořák has improved immensely, especially in terms of service. If the Pupp has the history and elegance, the Dvořák has the facilities. However, the rooms, for all their creature comforts, lack the Old World charm found at the Pupp. Rates run 116€ to 166€ ($133–$191) double, including buffet breakfast. A daily exchange rate is used for those who want to pay in hard Czech currency.

Family-run hotel **Embassy** ✮✮, Nová Louka 21 (✆ **353-221-161;** www. embassy.cz), manages to evoke the turn of the last century with elegantly decorated rooms. Although smaller than those at the Pupp, they're impeccably furnished and overlook the river. The restaurant downstairs is where a lot of movers and shakers at the Karlovy Vary film festival get away from the glitz and get down to business. You can stay here for 2,980Kč to 3,290Kč ($113–$125) double; 3,830Kč ($146) suite. Rates include breakfast. On the ground floor of the hotel is the **Embassy** restaurant (✆ **353-221-161**), which has a pub on one side and an intimate dining room on the other. On a cold day, the pub works wonders with a hearty goulash soup. But the dining room is the Embassy's hidden treasure. What the meals lack in flair, they make up for with sophistication. Main courses cost 145Kč to 895Kč ($5.50–$34).

Look for the restaurant **Promenáda** ✮, Tržiště 31 (✆ **353-225-648**), if you'd like to dine in an intimate atmosphere. Across from the Vřídelní kolonáda, the

Tips **Avoiding the Crowds**

Consider yourself warned: Word has spread about Český Krumlov. The summer high season can be unbearable, as thousands of visitors blanket its medieval streets. If possible, try to visit in the off season—we suggest autumn to take advantage of the colorful surrounding hills—when the crowds recede, the prices decrease, and the town's charm can really shine. Who knows? You might even hear some Czech!

Note: The city suffered damage during the floods that plagued the Republic in August 2002. Most of its venues, however, were cleaned and renovated by the end of 2003. For more details about the town go to **www.ckrumlov.cz.**

Promenáda serves the best food around, offering a wide selection of generous portions. The daily menu usually includes well-prepared wild game, but the mixed grill for two and the chateaubriand, both flambéed at the table, are the chef's best dishes. Main courses run 210Kč to 599Kč ($8–$22.75).

ČESKÝ KRUMLOV

If you have time for only one day trip, consider making it Český Krumlov, 96 miles (155km) south of Prague. One of Bohemia's prettiest towns, Krumlov is a living gallery of elegant Renaissance-era buildings housing charming cafes, pubs, restaurants, shops, and galleries. In 1992, UNESCO named Český Krumlov a World Heritage Site for its historic importance and physical beauty.

Bustling since medieval times, the town, after centuries of embellishment, is exquisitely beautiful. In 1302, the Rožmberk family inherited the castle and used it as their main residence for nearly 300 years. Looking out from the Lazebnický bridge, with the waters of the Vltava below snaking past the castle's gray stone, you'll feel that time has stopped. At night, with the castle lit up, the view becomes even more dramatic.

GETTING THERE   The only way to reach Český Krumlov by train from Prague is via České Budějovice (see below), a slow ride that deposits you at a station relatively far from the town center (trip time ranges from 3 hr. 26 min.–4 hr. 10 min.). Seven trains leave daily from Prague's Hlavní nádraží, and the fare is 224Kč ($8.50).

If you are already in České Budějovice and you want to make a trip to Krumlov, numerous trains connecting these two cities run throughout the day. It takes about 57 minutes and costs 46Kč ($1.75).

For timetables go to **www.jizdnirady.cz.**

The Český Krumlov train station is situated in northern suburb of the city. You can take a city taxi (parked in front of the station building) to get to the town center. The 10- to 15-minute ride costs about 100Kč ($3.85).

VISITOR INFORMATION   On the main square, in a renovated Renaissance building, the **Infocentrum,** nám. Svornosti 2, 381 01 Český Krumlov (*©* and fax **380-704-621**), offers a complete array of services from booking accommodations to ticket reservations for events, as well as a phone and fax service. It's open daily 9am to 6pm. For more information about Český Krumlov visit its well organized website, **www.ckrumlov.cz**, which features a very cool interactive map of the city.

TOP ATTRACTIONS & SPECIAL MOMENTS

Bring a good pair of walking shoes and be prepared to wear them out. Český Krumlov not only lends itself to hours of strolling, but its hills and alleyways demand it. No cars, thank goodness, are allowed in the historic town, and the cobblestones keep most other vehicles at bay. The town is split into two parts—the Inner town and Latrán, which houses the city's famous castle. They're best tackled separately, so you won't have to crisscross the bridges several times.

Begin at the **Okresní Muzeum (Regional Museum;** ℭ **380-711-674)** at the top of Horní ulice and to the right of the Main Square. Once a Jesuit seminary, the three-story museum now contains artifacts and displays relating to Český Krumlov's 1,000-year history. The highlight of this mass of folk art, clothing, furniture, and statues is a giant model of the town that offers a bird's-eye view of the buildings. Admission is 35Kč ($1.35), and it's open from Tuesday to Sunday from 10am to 12:30pm and 1 to 6pm.

Across the street is the **Hotel Růže (Rose),** which was once a Jesuit student house. Built in the late 16th century, the hotel and the prelature next to it show the development of architecture in the city—Gothic, Renaissance, and rococo influences are all present. Continue down the street to the impressive late Gothic **St. Vitus Cathedral.** Be sure to climb the church tower, which offers one of the most spectacular views of both the Inner Town and the castle across the river. It's open daily from 8am to 8pm.

As you continue down the street, you'll come to **náměstí Svornosti.** For such an impressive town, the main square is a little disappointing, with few buildings of any character. The **Radnice (Town Hall),** at nám. Svornosti 1, is one of the few exceptions. Its Gothic arcades and Renaissance vault inside are exceptionally beautiful in this otherwise run-down area. From the square, streets fan out in all directions. Take some time just to wander through them.

One of Český Krumlov's most famous residents was Austrian-born, 20th-century artist Egon Schiele. He was a bit of an eccentric who, on more than one occasion, raised the ire of the town's residents (many were distraught with his use of their young women as his nude models); his stay was cut short when residents' patience ran out. But the town readopted the artist in 1993, setting up the **Egon Schiele Foundation** and the **Egon Schiele Centrum** in Inner Town, Široká 70–72, 381 01, Český Krumlov (ℭ **380-704-011;** fax 380-711-191). The center documents his life and work, housing a permanent selection of his paintings as well as exhibitions of other 20th-century artists. Admission depends on the exhibitions being displayed. It's open daily from 10am to 6pm.

For a different perspective on what the town looks like, take the stairs from the **Městské divadlo (Town Theater)** on Horní ulice down to the riverfront and rent a boat from **Maleček boat rentals** at Rooseveltova 28 (ℭ **380-712-508;** www.malecek.cz) at 400Kč ($15.40) per half hour. Always willing to lend his advice, the affable Pepa Maleček will tell you what to watch out for and where the best fishing is (no matter how many times you say that you don't want to fish!).

WHERE TO STAY & DINE

Hotels are sprouting up, or are getting a "new" old look; PENSION AND ZIMMER FREI signs line Horní and Rooseveltova streets and offer some of the best values in town. For a comprehensive list of area hotels and help with bookings, call or write the Infocentrum listed above.

We recommend **Hotel Konvice,** Horní ul. 144 (ℭ **380-711-611**), as a good value choice. If you can get a room with a view out the back, take it immediately. Rooms themselves are small but clean and comfortable, with nice parquet

Moments Seeing the Český Krumlov Chateau

Reputedly the second-largest castle in Bohemia (after Prague Castle), the **Český Krumlov Château** was constructed in the 13th century as part of a private estate. Throughout the ages, it has passed to a variety of private owners, including the Rožmberk family, Bohemia's largest landholders, and the Schwarzenbergs, the Bohemian equivalent of *Dynasty's* Carrington family. Perched high atop a rocky hill, the château is open from April to October only, exclusively by guided tour.

Follow the path at the entrance for the long climb up to the castle, and first to greet you is a round 12th-century tower—painstakingly renovated—with a Renaissance balcony. You'll pass over the moat, now occupied by two brown bears. Beyond it is the **Dolní Hrad (Lower Castle)** and then the **Horní Hrad (Upper Castle).** Guided visits begin in the rococo **Chapel of St. George,** continue through the portrait-packed **Renaissance Hall,** and end with the **Royal Family Apartments,** outfitted with ornate furnishings that include Flemish wall tapestries and European paintings. Tours last 1 hour and depart frequently. Most are in Czech or German, however. If you want an English-language tour, arrange it ahead of time (© 380-704-721; www.ckrumlov.cz). The guided tour costs 140Kč ($5.30) adults and 70Kč ($2.65) students. The castle hours are from Tuesday to Sunday: June to August 9am to noon and 1pm to 6pm; April, May, September, and October 9am to noon and 1pm to 5pm. The last entrance is 1 hour before closing.

Tip: Once past the main castle building, you can see one of the more stunning views of Český Krumlov from **Most Na Plášti,** a walkway that doubles as a belvedere over the Inner Town. Even farther up the hill lies the castle's riding school and gardens.

floors and well-appointed baths. As you overlook the river and the castle on the opposite bank, you'll wonder why people would stay anywhere else. Rates are 1,600Kč ($60.80) double; 1,700Kč to 2,600Kč ($64.60–$98.80) suite. Breakfast is included.

Along "pension alley," **Pension Anna** Rooseveltova 41 (© **380-711-692**), is a comfortable and rustic choice. What makes this a favorite is the friendly management and the homey feeling you get as you walk up to your room. Forget hotels—this is the kind of place where you can relax. The owners even let you buy drinks and snacks at the bar downstairs and take them to your room. Rates include breakfast and run 1,500Kč ($57) double; 2,100 ($79.80) suite.

For a typical Czech dining experience visit **Hospoda Na louži** Kájovská 66 (© **380-711-280**), which offers diners good value for their money. The large wooden tables encourage you to get to know your neighbors in this Inner Town pub, located in a 15th-century house near the Main Square. The atmosphere is fun and the food above average. If no table is available, stand and have a drink; the seating turnover is pretty fast, and the staff is accommodating. Main courses cost 49Kč to 129Kč ($1.85–$4.90).

Located in the former cooling room of the local Eggenberg Brewery near the castle, **Restaurant Eggenberg,** Latrán 27 (© **380-711-917**), is one of the few big beer halls in town, with some of the freshest drafts anywhere. Traditional meat-and-dumplings-style Czech food is augmented by vegetarian dishes. Main courses cost 80Kč to 195Kč ($3.05–$7.40).

ČESKÉ BUDĚJOVICE

This fortress town was born in 1265, when Otakar II decided that the intersection point of the Vltava and Malše rivers would be the perfect site to protect the approaches to southern Bohemia. Although Otakar was killed at the battle of the Moravian Field in 1278, and the town was subsequently ravaged by the rival Vítkovic family, the construction of the city continued, eventually taking the shape originally envisaged.

Today, České Budějovice, hometown of the original Budweiser brand beer, is more a bastion for the beer drinker than a protector of Bohemia. But its slow pace, relaxed atmosphere, and interesting architecture make it a worthy stop for the rail traveler, especially as a base for exploring southern Bohemia or as a quick stopover for those heading on to Austria.

GETTING THERE   By Train   Ten express trains from Prague's Hlavní nádraží make the trip to České Budějovice in about 2½ hours. The fare is 204Kč ($7.75). From the train station, take city bus 1, 3, or 4 to the city center; the ride costs 8Kč (30¢). For timetable information go to **www.jizdnirady.cz.**

VISITOR INFORMATION   The **ČD Center** (© **387-854-361**) at the train station is open non-stop (except the lunch break 12:30–1pm) and provides train information, makes hotel bookings, and sells event tickets.

Tourist Infocentrum, nám. Přemysla Otakara II 2 (© and fax **386-359-480**), in the Main Square, sells maps and guidebooks, and finds lodging.

TOP ATTRACTIONS & SPECIAL MOMENTS

You can comfortably see České Budějovice in a day. At its center is one of central Europe's largest squares, the cobblestone **náměstí Přemysla Otakara II.** The square contains the ornate **Fountain of Sampson,** an 18th-century water well that was once the town's principal water supply, plus a mishmash of baroque and Renaissance buildings. On the southwest corner is the **town hall,** an elegant baroque structure built by Martinelli between 1727 and 1730. On top of the town hall, the larger-than-life statues by Dietrich represent the civic virtues: justice, bravery, wisdom, and diligence.

One block northwest of the square is the **Černá věž (Black Tower),** visible from almost every point in the city. Its 360 steps are worth the climb to get a bird's-eye view in all directions. The most famous symbol of České Budějovice, the 232-foot, 16th-century tower was built as a belfry for the adjacent **St. Nicholas Church.** This 13th-century church, one of the town's most important sights, was a bastion of Roman Catholicism during the 15th-century Hussite rebellion. You shouldn't miss the flamboyant white-and-cream, 17th-century baroque interior. Admission to the tower is 20Kč (75¢); admission to the church is free. The tower is open Tuesday to Sunday 10am to 6pm; the church is open daily 9am to 8pm.

WHERE TO STAY & DINE

Several agencies can locate reasonably priced private rooms. Expect to pay about 500Kč ($19) per person, in cash. Tourist Infocentrum (see "Visitor Information," above) can point you toward a wide selection of conveniently located rooms and pensions.

Location is everything for the city's most elegant hotel, **Grandhotel Zvon,** nám. Přemysla Otakara II 28 (© **387-311-384;** www.hotel-zvon.cz), which occupies several historic buildings on the Main Square. Upper-floor rooms have

Moments **For Beer Lovers: Touring a Beer Shrine**

On the town's northern edge sits a shrine for those who pray to the gods of the amber nectar. This is where it all began, where **Budějovický Budvar,** the original brewer of Budweiser brand beer, has its one and only factory. Established in 1895, Budvar draws on more than 700 years of Bohemian brewing tradition to produce one of the world's best beers. For information, contact Budvar n.p., Karolíny Světlé 4, České Budějovice (℗ 387-705-341; exkurse@budvar.cz).

Tours can be arranged by phoning ahead, but only for groups. If you're traveling alone or with only one or two other people, ask a hotel concierge at one of the bigger hotels (we suggest the Zvon) if he or she can put you in with an already scheduled group. Failing that, you might want to take a chance and head up to the brewery, where, if a group has arrived, another person or two won't be noticed.

Trolley buses 2, 4, 6, and 8 stop by the brewery; this is how it ensures that its workers and visitors reach the plant safely each day. The trolley costs 8Kč (30¢) to the brewery. You can also hop a cab from the town square for about 100Kč to 150Kč ($3.85–$5.70).

been renovated and tend to be more expensive, especially those with a view of the square, which aren't only brighter, they're larger and nicer, too. Others are relatively plain and functional. There's no elevator, but if you don't mind the climb, stay on the fourth floor. One of the biggest improvements here in recent years has been the staff, which seem to be learning that guests like respect and quality treatment. Rooms cost 1,600Kč to 3,080Kč ($60.80–$117) double; 2,420Kč to 4,030Kč ($91.95–$153) suite.

Around the corner from the Zvon you can find **Hotel Malý Pivovar (Small Brewery)** ⭐⭐, Ulice Karla IV 8–10 (℗ **386-360-471;** budvar.hotel@cbu. pvtnet.cz). A renovated 16th-century microbrewery combines the charms of a B&B with the amenities of a modern hotel. Rooms are bright and cheery, with antique-style wooden furniture. It's definitely worth consideration if being only 100 feet from the sometimes-noisy Main Square isn't a problem. Rates are 1,890Kč to 2,450Kč ($71.80–$93.10) double; 1,690Kč to 2,750Kč ($64.20–$105) suite. Breakfast is included.

If you've pledged not to go to any restaurant "tourist traps," you might make an exception for this one housed in a historic building. Labyrinthine **Masné Krámy (Meat Shops)** ⭐, Krajinská 29 (℗ **387-318-609**), located just northwest of náměstí Přemysla Otakara II, occupies a series of drinking rooms on either side of a long hall, and is a must for any serious pubgoer. The inexpensive and filling food is pure Bohemian, including several pork, duck, and trout dishes. Come for the boisterous atmosphere, or for what's possibly the best goulash in the Czech Republic. Main courses run 85Kč to 180Kč ($3.25–$6.85).

Usually crowded, **U paní Emy,** Široká 25 (℗ **387-312-846**), has an extensive menu and reasonable prices. The chicken and fish dishes are the most popular. The pan-fried trout tastes very light, not oily as most Czech restaurants tend to make it. A wine bar here stays open to the wee hours. Main courses cost 69Kč to 200Kč ($2.60–$7.60).

6

Denmark

With one of Europe's best rail networks, the maritime nation of Denmark is easily viewed from the window of a train. It may not offer the dramatic and often hair-raising train trips of nearby Norway, but you'll pass by attractive fishing villages, hamlets with half-timbered houses, Renaissance castles, Viking ruins, and sand dunes along the North Sea. And attractive waterscapes will greet you at practically every turn.

And since 1997, touring Denmark by rail has been that much easier because of the opening of the tunnel and bridge crossing The Great Belt. This body of water separates the island of Zealand (on which Copenhagen sits), with the island of Funen. Funen is the island between Zealand and the peninsula of Jutland. Jutland is connected geographically to Germany and the rest of continental Europe. These new rail links mean that the three landmasses of Denmark, including Copenhagen, can be reached without having to take ferry crossings, as was the case in the past. In the past decade, high-speed diesel trains have linked the major cities of Denmark, such as Copenhagen and Århus, at faster speeds than ever before.

The county's international rail links were also dramatically improved in the summer of 2002 when a 10-mile (16km) rail and motorway tunnel and bridge complex linked the northeast of Denmark (including Copenhagen) with southern Sweden (through Malmö).

Price-wise, Denmark is not a cheap destination for the rail traveler, but because of its small size and the country's extensive and efficient rail system, you'll only need 3 to 4 days to take in its scenic highlights.

HIGHLIGHTS OF DENMARK

All visitors to Denmark seem to arrive in **Copenhagen,** the capital, as it's not only the gateway to the country—both by rail and air—but also the country's major attraction. Travel guru Arthur Frommer once wrote that after Copenhagen, Europe will become a footnote. High praise indeed for this lively, bustling city, home to a quarter of all Danes, with a population toppling one-and-a-half million.

The city is filled with entertainment and sightseeing possibilities, containing a virtual treasure trove of art, museums of all kinds, imposing Renaissance castles, and old churches. Allow at least 2 to 3 days here and know that you will have only scratched the surface of a city founded in 1167 by Bishop Absalon.

If time remains, another day can be spent taking a side trip 25 miles (40km) north of Copenhagen to **Helsingør,** which is easily reached by frequent train service. The world, it seems, comes to pay its respect to Hamlet's Castle. Does it really matter that there may never have been a Hamlet and that Shakespeare never visited this castle? **Kronborg Slot,** nonetheless, is one of Europe's grand pilgrimages.

With yet another day to spare, visitors can take the train to the neighboring island of Funen and the city of **Odense,** 97 miles (156km) west of Copenhagen. This ancient town, third largest in Denmark, was the birthplace of Hans Christian Andersen, and his fans can see his humble boyhood home and a house and museum devoted to the master storyteller.

Scandinavia

Moments **Festivals & Special Events**

The **Funen Festival** in Odense is an annual musical extravaganza held in mid-June and frequently draws big international headliners. The festival's music is often hard-core rock, but gentler, classical melodies are presented as well. For more information, call the Odense Tourist Bureau (© **66-12-75-20**).

If jazz appeals more to your musical tastes, international jazz musicians play in the streets, squares, and theaters during the **Copenhagen Jazz Festival** in early July. Pick up a copy of *Copenhagen This Week* to find the venues. For information, call © **33-93-20-13** or check out **www.festival.jazz.dk**. Early July.

At **Århus Festival Week** in early September, a wide range of cultural activities—including opera, jazz, classical, and folk music, ballet, and theater—is presented. It's the largest cultural festival in Scandinavia. Sporting activities and street parties abound as well. For more information, contact Århus Tourist Office, Rådhuset, Århus C, DK-8000 Århus (© **89-31-82-70**).

For most visitors, Odense will mark the end of a rail tour of Denmark. Those with more time can continue by rail into Jutland, a peninsula of heather-covered moors, fjords, farmland, lakes, and sand dunes.

On Jutland, the most interesting city to visit is **Århus,** 109 miles (175km) west of Copenhagen and easily reached by train. Århus is the capital of Jutland and Denmark's second largest city, as well as a cultural center of renown and a university town with a lively port life.

After a visit to Jutland, many visitors return to Copenhagen and go on to their next rail adventure. Or else they continue north of Aalborg to the port of **Frederikshavn,** 238 miles (381km) northwest of Copenhagen, where they can make overnight ferry connections to Oslo, and continue their Scandinavian rail travels in the far northern country of Norway.

1 Essentials

GETTING THERE

From North America, nonstop flights to Copenhagen from the greater New York area take about 7½ hours to reach Copenhagen; from Chicago, 8½ hours, and from Seattle, 9½ hours.

SAS (© **800/221-2350** in the U.S.; www.scandinavian.net) has more non-stop flights to Scandinavia from more North American cities than any other airline, and more flights to and from Denmark and within Scandinavia than any other airline in the world. North American carriers flying to Copenhagen include **Air Canada** (© **888/247-2262;** www.aircanada.ca), **American Airlines** (© **800/433-7300;** www.aa.com), **Delta Airlines** (© **800/221-1212;** www. delta.com), and **United Airlines** (© **800/538-2929;** www.united.com).

In the United Kingdom, **British Airways** (© **800/AIRWAYS,** or 08457/733-377 in the U.K.; www.ba.com) offers convenient connections through Heathrow to Copenhagen. Other European airlines with connections through their home countries to Copenhagen include **Icelandair** (© **800/223-5500** in the U.S. or 020/7874-1000 in the U.K.; www.icelandair.com), **Northwest/ KLM** (*©* **800/374-7747** in the U.S. or 0870/507-4074 in the U.K.; www. klm.com), and **Lufthansa** (*©* **800/645-3880** in the U.S. or 0845/773-7747 in the U.K.; www.lufthansa-usa.com). Be aware, however, that unless you make all your flight arrangements in North America before you go, you might find some of these flights prohibitively expensive.

DENMARK BY RAIL
PASSES
For information on the **Eurailpass, Eurailpass Flexi,** and **Scanrail Pass** see chapter 2. Note that if you will be confining your travel to Denmark and the other Scandinavian countries, the Scanrail Pass is your best option.

All Denmark train passes must be purchased in North America and are available from **Rail Europe** (*©* **877/272-RAIL** in the U.S., 800/361-RAIL in Canada; www.raileurope.com) or **ScanAm World Tours,** 108 N. Main St., Cranbury, NJ 08512 (*©* **800/545-2204;** www.scandinaviantravel.com).

FOREIGN TRAIN TERMS
Almost everyone in Denmark, where school children start learning English in grade school, speaks English, so there's no need to worry about a language barrier.

PRACTICAL TRAIN INFORMATION
Flat, low-lying Denmark, with its hundreds of bridges and absence of mountains, has a large network of railway lines that connect virtually every hamlet with the largest city, Copenhagen. For **information, schedules,** and **fares** anywhere in Denmark, call *©* **70-13-14-15.** Waiting times for a live person on this telephone line range from long to very long. An alternative way to gather schedules and prices, and even reserve a seat on specific trains, involves surfing over to the website maintained by the **Danish State Railways (www.dsb.dk).**

A word you're likely to see and hear frequently is *Lyntog* (Express Trains), which are the fastest trains presently operational in Denmark. Be warned in advance that the most crowded times on Danish trains are Fridays, Sundays, and national holidays, so plan your reservations accordingly.

The Danish government offers dozens of discounts on the country's rail networks—depending on the age of a traveler, days or hours traveled, and destination. On any train within Denmark, children between the ages of 12 and 15 are charged half price if they're accompanied by an adult, and up to two children under 12 can travel for free with any adult on any train in Denmark. Seniors (age 65 or older) receive a discount of between 25% for travel on Fridays, Sundays, and holidays, and discounts of 50% every other day of the week.

Trains & Travel Times in Denmark

From	To	Type of Train	# of Trains	Frequency	Travel Time
Copenhagen	Odense	InterCity	2	Daily	1 hr. 30 min.
Copenhagen	Odense	InterCity	Every 30 min.	Sun	1 hr. 32 min.
Copenhagen	Odense	InterCity	Every 30 min.	Mon–Sat	1 hr. 32 min.
Copenhagen	Århus	InterCity	16	Daily	3 hr. 8 min.
Copenhagen	Helsingør	DSB	Every 30 min.	Daily	55 min.
Århus	Aalborg	InterCity	Every hour	Daily	1 hr. 45 min.
Aalborg	Frederikshavn	InterCity	Every hour	Daily	1 hr.

No identification is needed when you buy your ticket, but the conductor who checks your ticket may ask for proof of age.

RESERVATIONS The **Danish State Railways (DSB)** runs all train services except for a few private lines and the outfit is one of the best and most reliable in Europe. Reservations, costing $11 per person, are required on the new, sleek **InterCity (IC)** trains unless you board after 8pm or are traveling on the line from Aalborg to Frederikshavn where overnight ferries leave for Norway.

You can reserve both first-class or second-class cars on all IC trains. In Denmark, second-class travel is generally quite comfortable, so you may not want to pay the extra money for a first-class seat.

The other major type of train, the **Regional (R),** is more antiquated, runs slower, and consists entirely of second-class seating. Seat reservations are optional on these slower trains, which don't tend to be crowded except at major holidays or during peak travel periods, especially July—the single biggest travel month in Denmark. In most cases, you'll be able to find a seat without a reservation, but you may not want to take that chance. Note that reservation fees aren't covered by railpasses, so you'll have to pay extra for them.

SERVICES & AMENITIES Because Denmark is so small, long overnight hauls aren't usually a factor. There are, however, overnight trains running between Copenhagen and two port cities in Jutland, Esbjerg, and Frederikshavn. In both cases, sleepers must be reserved in advance. In addition to the price of the regular rail fare or your railpass, you can reserve a six-person cabin, a two-person cabin, or, most expensive of all, a private cabin for one. In general, a *couchette* on an IC train costs $28. As there are no dining cars on trains, plan accordingly and take extra provisions if you think you'll need them. Most trains do, however, offer trolleys selling snacks and drinks. "Snacks" are usually expensive *smørrebrød* or open-faced sandwiches, though the coffee is reasonably priced.

FAST FACTS: Denmark

Area Code The country code for Denmark is **45**. It precedes any call made to Denmark from another country. There are no city area codes. Every telephone number has eight digits.

Business Hours Most **banks** are open Monday to Friday from 9:30am to 4pm (Thurs to 6pm), but outside Copenhagen, banking hours vary. **Stores** are generally open Monday to Thursday from 9am to 5:30pm, Friday 9am to 7 or 8pm, and Saturday noon to 2pm; most are closed Sunday.

Climate Denmark's climate is mild for Scandinavia—New England farmers experience harsher winters. Summer temperatures average 61° to 77°F (16°C–25°C). Winter temperatures seldom go below 30°F (–1°C), thanks to the warming waters of the Gulf Stream. From a weather perspective, mid-April to November is a good time to visit.

Currency The basic unit of currency is the krone (crown), or DKK, made up of 100 øre. At this writing, $1 = approximately 6.67DKK.

Documents Required Americans and Canadians need a valid passport for travel in Denmark.

Electricity Voltage is generally 220 volts AC, 50 to 60 cycles. In many camping sites, 110-volt power plugs are also available. Adapters and transformers may be purchased in Denmark. It's always best to check at your hotel desk before using an electrical outlet.

Embassies All embassies are in Copenhagen. The embassy of the **United States** is at Dag Hammärskjölds Allé 24, DK-2100 København (𝄯 **35-55-31-44**). **Canada**'s embassy is at Kristen Berniskows Gade 1, DK-1105 København K (𝄯 **33-48-32-00**).

Health & Safety You will have few health issues to worry about in Denmark, although problems can, of course, occur. You don't need to get shots; most foodstuffs are safe, and the water in cities and towns is potable. If you're concerned, order bottled water. It is easy to get a prescription filled in towns and cities (make sure your doctor fills out any prescriptions using generic and not brand names), and nearly all places have English-speaking doctors in hospitals with well-trained medical staffs.

Denmark is one of the safest European countries for travelers. Copenhagen, the major population center, naturally experiences the most crime. Muggings have been reported in the vicinity of the railway station, especially late at night, but crimes of extreme violence are exceedingly rare. Exercise the usual precautions you would when traveling anywhere.

Holidays Some of the dates below may vary slightly each year, so check with a local tourist office. Danish public holidays are New Year's Day (Jan 1), Maundy Thursday, Good Friday, Easter Sunday, Easter Monday, Labor Day (May 1), Common Prayers Day (4th Fri after Easter), Ascension Day (mid-May), Whitsunday (late May), Whitmonday, Constitution Day (June 5), Christmas Day (Dec 25), and Boxing Day (Dec 26).

Legal Aid While traveling in Denmark, you are, of course, subject to that country's laws. If arrested or charged, you can obtain a list of private lawyers from the U.S. Embassy to represent you.

Mail Most post offices are open Monday to Friday from 9 or 10am to 5 or 6pm and Saturday from 9am to noon; they're closed Sunday. All mail to North America is sent airmail without extra charge. The cost for mail weighing 20 grams (.175 oz.) is 5.50DKK (85¢). Mailboxes are painted red and display the embossed crown and trumpet of the Danish Postal Society.

Police & Emergencies Dial 𝄯 **112** for the fire department, the police, or an ambulance, or to report a sea or an air accident. Emergency calls from public telephone kiosks are free (no coins needed).

Telephone The country code of **45** should precede any call made to Denmark from another country. Danish phones are fully automatic. Dial the eight-digit number; there are no city area codes. Don't insert any coins until your party answers. At public telephone booths, use two 50-øre coins or a 1-krone or 5-krone coin only. You can make more than one call on the same payment if your time hasn't run out. Emergency calls are free.

Tipping Tips are seldom expected. Porters charge fixed prices, and tipping hairdressers or barbers is not customary. Service is built into the system, and hotels, restaurants, and even taxis include a 15% service charge in their rates. Consider tipping only for special services—some Danes would feel insulted if you offered them a tip.

2 Copenhagen ⊛⊛⊛

The capital of Denmark, home to more than a fifth of the country's population, is booming, bustling, and cosmopolitan. In summer—the time to visit—the entire city seems to flock outdoors to enjoy precious sunshine after bitter, cold months of a lingering winter. Cafe culture flourishes, and locals flood the Strøget (the pedestrian-only mall in the heart of town) or go boating on the city's lakes. But mainly they bike. At night, the Tivoli Gardens explode into a burst of light with entertainment for the masses. All this makes Copenhagen a summer festival before it settles down once more in September for a long winter's nap.

For the rail passenger, Copenhagen is the virtual gateway to all of Scandinavia, including Norway and Sweden. Trains will carry you from Copenhagen to Stockholm in just 5½ hours and to Oslo in 9 hours. If you're traveling by train throughout Europe, be advised that Copenhagen's connections to Germany are great, especially to Hamburg and Berlin.

Copenhagen is also the rail hub of Denmark even though it lies in the far eastern section of the country. The city offers easy rail links to all major attractions on the island of Zealand (on which Copenhagen lies) and to the eastern island of Funen, which is most often visited by those wishing to explore Odense, the birthplace of Hans Christian Andersen. You'll also find convenient connections to the major cities and towns on the peninsula of Jutland, including Århus.

STATION INFORMATION
GETTING FROM THE AIRPORT TO THE TRAIN STATION
Flights into Copenhagen land at **Kastrup Airport** (✆ **70-10-30-30**), 7¼ miles (12km) from the center of Copenhagen. Since 1998, trains have linked the airport with Copenhagen's Central Railway Station, in the center of the hotel zone, and the trip now takes a mere 11 minutes and costs 22.50DKK ($3.40). Note that rail passes do not cover this trip. The Air Rail Terminal is underneath the airport's arrivals and departure halls, just a short escalator ride from the gates in Terminal 3. It has more than 30 check-in counters, ticketing offices (where you can validate a rail pass), information desks, restaurants, and fast-food chains.

You can also take an SAS bus to the city terminal; the fare is 24DKK ($3.60). A taxi to the city center costs around 128DKK ($19). Even cheaper is a local bus, no. 250S, which leaves from the international arrivals terminal every 15 or 20 minutes for Town Hall Square in central Copenhagen near the rail station and costs 22.50DKK ($3.40).

INSIDE THE STATION
Trains arrive at the **København Hoved Banegaard (Central Rail Station),** Copenhagen's main train hub, in the center of Copenhagen near the Tivoli Gardens and Rådhuspladsen (Town Hall Square). It's frequently abbreviated København H on train schedules. Call ✆ **70-13-14-15** for local rail information.

Visitor information and hotel reservations are not available inside the rail station but you'll find both at the Tourist Information Center, just 2-minutes away (see below). Several ATMs can be found on the streets outside the station. Inside the Central Station is a currency exchange kiosk open daily 8am to 9pm, which charges 25DKK ($3.75) commission on cash or 15DKK ($2.25) on a traveler's check. There is also an on-site luggage storage kiosk, charging 25DKK to 35DKK ($3.75–$5.25) per bag for 24 hours; service is Monday to Saturday 5:30am to 1am, Sunday 6am to 1am. Several restaurants and a few shops are also located in the station. From the Central Station, you can easily connect with the local sub-way system, the **S-tog.** Trains depart from platforms within the terminal.

INFORMATION ELSEWHERE IN THE CITY

The **Copenhagen Tourist Information Center,** Bernstorffsgade 1 (℃ **33-25-38-44**), is across from the main entrance to the Tivoli and around the corner from the rail station. In July and August, it's open Monday to Saturday 9am to 8pm; Sunday 9am to 6pm. In May, June, and early September, daily 9am to 8pm; mid-September to April Monday to Friday 9am to 4:30pm and Saturday 9am to 1:30pm. The staff here will make hotel reservations in various classifica-tions for 50DKK ($7.50). While here, pick up a copy of *Copenhagen This Week;* its Events Calendar has good listings for sightseeing and entertainment.

GETTING AROUND

A joint zone fare system includes Copenhagen Transport buses and State Rail-way and S-tog trains in Copenhagen and North Zealand, plus some private rail-way routes within a 25-mile (40km) radius of the capital. You can transfer from train to bus and vice versa with the same ticket.

A *grandbillet* (basic ticket) for both buses and trains costs 15DKK ($2.25). You can buy 10 tickets for 90DKK ($14). Children under 12 pay half price; those under 5 ride free on local trains, and those under 7 go free on buses. For 90DKK ($14), you can purchase a ticket good for 24 hours of bus and train travel through nearly half of Zealand—it's worth it for a heavy day of sightsee-ing. It's half price for children 7 to 11, free for children under 7.

Copenhagen's well-maintained buses are the least expensive method of get-ting around. Most buses leave from Rådhuspladsen. Buses run along the major routes every 10 to 15 minutes. The city is divided into different bus zones. You purchase a ticket for the number of zones in which you wish to travel—for example, traveling in 2 zones (the central city area) costs 15DKK ($2.25) for 1 hour. For information, call ℃ **36-13-14-15.**

The S-tog connects central Copenhagen with its suburbs. The tickets are the same as on buses (see above), and you can transfer from a bus line to an S-tog train on the same ticket. For more information, call ℃ **33-14-17-01** at any time.

In 2001, Copenhagen launched its first Metro line, taking passengers from east to west across the city or vice versa. Operating around the clock, the Metro runs as far west as Vanløse and as far south as Vestamager. Nørreport is the trans-fer station to the S-tog system. Metro trains run every 2 minutes during rush hours and every 15 minutes at night. Fares are integrated into the existing zonal system (see above).

Watch for the FRI **(free)** sign or green light to hail a taxi. Be sure the taxi has a meter. Fares run as follows: 23DKK ($3.45) when the flag drops, then 11DKK

Value Discount Pass

The **Copenhagen Card** entitles you to free and unlimited travel by bus and rail throughout the metropolitan area (including North Zealand), 25% to 50% discounts on crossings to and from Sweden, and free admission to many sights and museums, including Tivoli. The card is available for 1 or 3 days and costs 215DKK ($32) or 495DKK ($74), respectively. Children under 12 pay half price. For more information, contact the Copenhagen Tourist Information Center (see above).

Copenhagen

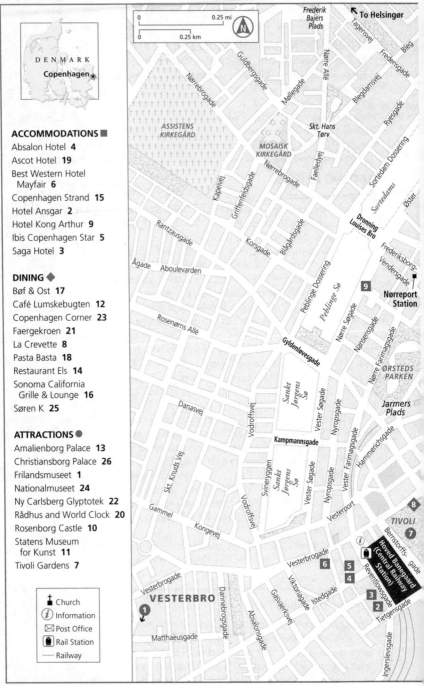

ACCOMMODATIONS ■
Absalon Hotel **4**
Ascot Hotel **19**
Best Western Hotel
  Mayfair **6**
Copenhagen Strand **15**
Hotel Ansgar **2**
Hotel Kong Arthur **9**
Ibis Copenhagen Star **5**
Saga Hotel **3**

DINING ◆
Bøf & Ost **17**
Café Lumskebugten **12**
Copenhagen Corner **23**
Faergekroen **21**
La Crevette **8**
Pasta Basta **18**
Restaurant Els **14**
Sonoma California
  Grille & Lounge **16**
Søren K **25**

ATTRACTIONS ●
Amalienborg Palace **13**
Christiansborg Palace **26**
Frilandsmuseet **1**
Nationalmuseet **24**
Ny Carlsberg Glyptotek **22**
Rådhus and World Clock **20**
Rosenborg Castle **10**
Statens Museum
  for Kunst **11**
Tivoli Gardens **7**

✝ Church
ⓘ Information
✉ Post Office
🏠 Rail Station
---- Railway

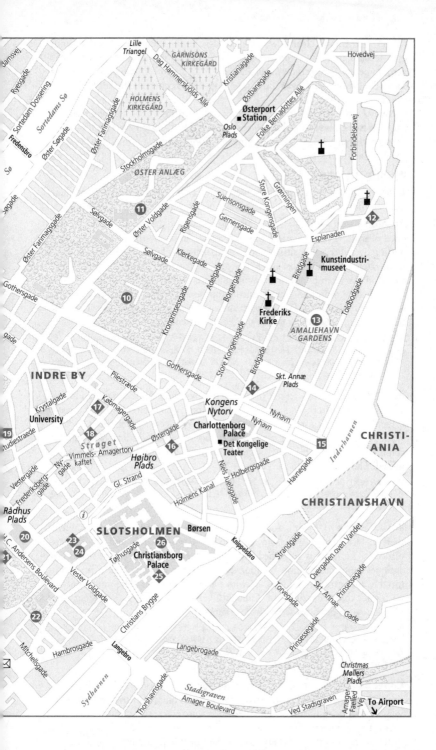

($1.65) per .6-mile (1km), Monday through Friday from 6am to 6pm. From 6pm to 6am, and all day on Saturday and Sunday, the cost is 15DKK ($2.25) per kilometer. *Tips are included in the meter price, so don't tip extra!* Many drivers speak English. **Københavns Taxa** (© **35-35-35-35**) operates the largest fleet in the city.

Many Copenhageners ride bicycles. For 75DKK ($11) per day, you can rent a bike at **Københavns Cykler,** Reventlowsgade 11 (© **33-33-86-13**). Hours are Monday through Friday from 8:30am to 5:30pm, Saturday from 9am to 1pm, and Sunday from 10am to 1pm.

WHERE TO STAY

Note: Air-conditioning is not a standard amenity in Scandinavia, where it rarely gets very hot in summer. So, unless noted below, your hotel won't have any.

Absalon Hotel ⭐ *Value*   Long the most popular and most affordable budget hotel near the Central Station, this well-managed, family-run lodging has been putting up rail travelers since 1938. It is actually two hotels in one: the government-rated three-star Absalon Hotel and the one-star Absalon Annex. The rooms in the main building are more comfortable and spacious. Best of all are the 19 luxury rooms and suites on the top floor, with such extra amenities as soundproof windows and a refrigerator with complimentary drinks. Both the three-star and the one-star annex share the same entrance and reception.

Helgølandsgade 15, DK-1653 København. © 32-24-22-11. Fax 33-24-34-11. www.absalon-hotel.dk. 165 units. 1,125DKK–1,380DKK ($169–$207) double; from 1520DKK ($228) suite. Rates include buffet breakfast. AE, DC, MC, V. Closed Dec 14–Jan 2. Bus: 6, 10, 16, 27, or 28. **Amenities:** Breakfast room; nonsmoking rooms. *In room:* Hair dryer in some.

Ascot Hotel ⭐ *Value*   In the very heart of town, near the Central Station and a 2-minute walk from Rådhuspladsen, this is one of the better midsize hotels of Copenhagen. Dating from 1902, it's seen many changes and alterations over the years. Many architectural graces of yesterday remain, including black-marble columns and interior bas-reliefs. The bedrooms all beautifully kept and well furnished. There's also a fitness center.

Studiestraede 61, DK-1554 København. © 33-12-60-00. Fax 33-14-60-40. www.ascothotel.dk. 163 units. 1,490DKK ($224) double; from 1,930DKK ($290) suite. AE, DC, MC, V. Bus: 14 or 16. **Amenities:** Restaurant; bar; laundry. *In room:* Hair dryer.

Best Western Mayfair   A short walk from the Central Station, this is one of the best-located hotels in town, close to the Tivoli Gardens and the Rådhuspladsen. The hotel is furnished in a classical English style supplemented by antiques from the Far East. Bedrooms are midsize for the most part, and comfortably and attractively furnished with marble bathrooms. The most desirable units offer an extra sitting area. Thoughtful extras abound here, including complimentary tea or coffee served in the lounge.

Helgølandsgade 3, DK-1653 København. © 800/528-1234 in the U.S. or 33-31-48-01. Fax 33-23-96-86. www.themayfairhotel.dk. 106 units. 1,325DKK–1,525DKK ($199–$229) double; from 1,900DKK ($285) suite. Rates include breakfast. AE, DC, MC, V. Bus: 6, 16, 28, 29, or 41. **Amenities:** Breakfast room; bar; laundry; nonsmoking rooms. *In room:* Hair dryer.

Copenhagen Strand ⭐   On the waterfront, a warehouse built of brick and timber has been skillfully converted into a modern hotel of charm and grace. No longer a paper mill, the Strand welcomes you today with a rustic, maritime decor. The architects planned the hotel so that most of the bedrooms open onto views of the waterfront. The well-furnished bedrooms are cozily midsize, and each has a well-kept bathroom with a tub (some have showers). The preferred Executive Rooms offer extras such as bathrobes.

Havnegade 37, DK-1058 København. © **33-48-99-00.** Fax 33-48-99-01. www.copenhagenstrand.dk. 174 units. 1,613DKK ($242) double; from 2,858DKK ($429) executive room or suite. Tram: 1 or 6. **Amenities:** Breakfast room; bar; laundry; nonsmoking rooms; rooms for those with limited mobility. *In room:* Hair dryer.

Hotel Ansgar Only a 3-minute walk from the Central Station, this hotel lies in the heart of Copenhagen but on a fairly tranquil one-way street. The five-story building dates from 1885 but has recently been upgraded and extensively modernized, and is a family favorite because of its two dozen spacious rooms with extra beds. Rooms are comfortable, cozy, and modern with Danish designs and a marble, shower-only bathroom.

Colbjørnsensgade 29, DK-1652 København. © **33-21-21-96.** Fax 33-21-61-91. www.ansgar-hotel.dk. 81 units. 875DKK–1,095DKK ($131–$164) double. Rates include buffet breakfast. AE, DC, MC, V. Bus: 6, 10, 28, or 41. **Amenities:** Breakfast room; lounge; laundry.

Hotel Kong Arthur ★ *(Value)* This 1882 hotel, a former orphanage enjoys a tranquil residential setting and opening onto a string of city lakes. Completely renovated and modernized over the years, it is a very welcoming and intimate choice with its small atrium garden, where breakfast is served in summer. The comfortable guest rooms have spacious tiled bathrooms. The helpful staff will do anything from cleaning shoes to getting theater tickets.

Nørre Søgade 11, DK-1370 København. © **33-11-12-12.** Fax 33-32-61-30. www.kongarthur.dk. 107 units. 1,400DKK–1,600DKK ($210–$240) double; from 2,900DKK ($435) suite. Rates include buffet breakfast. AE, DC, MC, V. Bus: 5, 7, or 16. **Amenities:** 3 restaurants; bar; laundry; nonsmoking rooms. *In room:* Hair dryer.

Ibis Copenhagen Star Hotel An easy walk from the Central Station, this hotel hides behind a neoclassical facade from 1880. It opened as a hotel in 1990 when two buildings were combined, modernized, and extensively upgraded. Grace notes inside include teakwood tables, granite columns, and leather chairs. Bedrooms are midsize and traditionally and comfortably furnished, each with a well-maintained bathroom. The best deals, if you can afford them, are the suites equipped with Jacuzzis.

Colbjørnsensgade 13, DK-1652 København. © **33-22-11-00.** Fax 33-21-21-86. www.ibis.dk. 134 units. 970DKK ($146) double; from 1,395DKK ($209) suite. Rates include breakfast. AE, DC, MC, V. Bus: 6, 16, 28, 29, or 41. **Amenities:** Breakfast room; bar; laundry; nonsmoking rooms.

Saga Hotel Close to the Central Station, this long-time budget favorite of foreign visitors and students was created in 1947 by combining two late-19th-century apartment buildings. Only 31 of the comfortably but simply furnished bedrooms have private bathrooms. The shared hallway bathrooms are adequate. Many of the bedrooms are spacious, with three to four beds—great for friends traveling together. *Warning:* The five-story building has no elevator.

Colbjørnsensgade 18-20, DK-1652 København. © **33-24-49-44.** Fax 33-24-60-33. www.sagahotel.dk. 79 units. 470DKK–720DKK ($71–$108) double without bathroom, 550DKK–920DKK ($83–$138) double with bathroom. Rates include breakfast. AE, DC, MC, V. Bus: 6, 10, 16, 28, or 41. **Amenities:** Breakfast room.

TOP ATTRACTIONS & SPECIAL MOMENTS

Like many rail travelers, you may have only 1 day to spend in Copenhagen. That's far too little time, but start the day off by strolling the old city's cobble-stone streets and along its many canals. Spend the afternoon at **Christiansborg Palace,** on Slotsholmen, where the queen receives guests. Early in the evening, head to the **Tivoli.** If it's winter, then explore **Kongens Nytorv (King's New**

Finds **A "Free City" Within Copenhagen**

Not for everybody, but worth a look, is a trip to the **Free City of Christia-nia,** on the island of Christianshavn (take bus no. 8 from Rådhuspladsen). Since 1971, some 1,000 squatters have taken over 130 former army bar-racks (spread across 20 acres) and declared themselves a free city. You can shop, dine, and talk to the natives about the experimental community, which has its own doctors, clubs, and stores. It even flies its own flag. Exer-cise caution here, however, as it's a favorite of pickpockets.

Square) and the charming old sailor's quarter called Nyhavn. At some point in the day, be sure to climb the Rundetårn (Round Tower) for a glorious panorama of Copenhagen.

If you have a second day, visit **Amalienborg Palace,** the queen's residence. Try to time your visit so that you can see the changing of the guard. It doesn't have the precision or pomp of the changing of the guard at Buckingham Palace (p. 402), but nonetheless remains a Kodak moment. Continue beyond the palace to the city's beloved statue, *The Little Mermaid,* perched upon a rock in the harbor. In the afternoon, see the art treasures of **Ny Carlsberg Glyptotek.**

Amalienborg Palace 🎬🎬   The 18th-century French-style rococo home of the Danish royal family since 1794, Amalienborg opens onto Copenhagen's most beautiful square and is the setting for the changing of the guard ceremony at noon. The ceremony only takes place when the queen is in residence, which is signaled by the raising of a swallowtail flag. Since 1994, certain rooms of Amalienborg have been opened to the public, revealing lavish private and state rooms, all of which were refurbished over a period lasting from 1863 to 1972. Two of the most interesting rooms are the **study of Christian IX** (1863–1906) and the **drawing rooms of Queen Louise** (1817–98). These rooms are fur-nished with gifts from their far-flung children in honor of their unofficial status as "parents-in-law to Europe." You can also see the **study of King Frederik VIII** with its original antiques, plus galleries devoted to costumes and royal gems.

Christian VII's Palace. 📞 **33-12-21-88.** Admission 40DKK ($6) adults, 25DKK ($3.75) students and seniors, 5DKK (75¢) children 5–12. Free for children under 5. Jan 2–Apr Tues–Sun 11am–4pm; May–Oct daily 10am–4pm; Nov–Dec 17 Tues–Sun 11am–4pm; Dec 27–30 daily 11am–4pm. Closed Dec 18–26 and Jan 1. Bus: 1, 6, 9, or 10.

Christiansborg Palace 🎬🎬🎬   Since 1167, five royal palaces have stood on this site on Slotsholmen, a small island separated from the heart of the city by a moatlike canal, pierced by several bridges. The present granite-and-copper palace dates from 1928. For 8 centuries, this has been the center of political power in Denmark, and the Christiansborg complex today is home to the houses of parliament, the prime minister's offices, and the Danish Supreme Court. Of more interest to visitors is a tour of the lushly decorated Royal Recep-tion Salons, taking in such attractions as the Throne Room, the Banqueting Hall, and the Queen's Library.

In the courtyard, an equestrian statue of Christian IX (1863–1906) guards the grounds, and on the north end you'll find the **Kongeliege Stalde & Kareter (Royal Stables & Coaches).** Especially interesting here are the regal coaches and the grand carriages used in days of yore. There's a separate admission charge to the stables of 10 DKK ($1.50) adults, 5DKK (75¢) children.

Christiansborg Slotsplads. ℂ **33-92-64-92**. Royal Reception Rooms, 45DKK ($6.75) adults, 10DKK ($1.50) children; parliament, free; castle ruins, 20DKK ($3) adults, 5DKK (75¢) children. Guided tours of reception rooms May–Sept daily 11am, 1pm, and 3pm; Oct–Apr Tues, Thurs, Sat, and Sun 3pm. English-language tours of Parliament daily 11am, 1pm, and 3pm. Castle ruins May–Sept daily 9:30am–3:30pm; Oct–Apr Tues–Thurs and Sat–Sun 9:30am–3:30pm. Royal Stables May–Sept Fri–Sun 2–4pm; Oct–Apr Sat–Sun 2–4pm. Bus: 1, 2, 6, 8, 9, 42, or 43.

Frilandsmuseet (Open-Air Museum) ★★   Covering 90 acres in Lyngby, on the fringe of the city, this museum, re-creates rural Denmark and does so exceedingly well. It's a 2-mile (3.2km) walk around the entire compound where you'll come across cottages once inhabited by fishermen, a farmstead from the 1700s on a remote Danish island, a primitive longhouse from the remote Faeroe Islands, and even tower windmills and a potter's workshop from the 1800s. Buildings were shipped from all over Denmark and reassembled here. Organized activities often take place here on summer afternoons. Sometimes dancers perform Danish folkloric shows, or you might see demonstrations of lace-making and loom-weaving. The park is a 9-mile (14km) ride from the Central Station, and there is a restaurant serving lunch on the grounds.

Kongevejen 100. ℂ **33-13-44-11**. Admission 50DKK ($7.50) adults, free for children under 16. Easter–Sept Tues–Sun 10am–5pm; Oct 1–19 Tues–Sun 10am–4pm. Closed Oct 21–Easter. S-tog: Copenhagen Central Station to Sorgenfri (trains leave every 20 min.). Bus: 184 or 194.

Nationalmuseet (National Museum) ★★★   One of the great museums of Scandinavia, this is the treasure trove of Denmark, a gigantic repository of artifacts that allows visitors to stroll through 10,000 years of history. The vast complex takes in the Prinsens Palae or prince's palace constructed in 1744. There are six different departments in all, beginning with Danish prehistory, spanning the period from 13,000 B.C. to A.D. 1000. Among the stunning exhibits is the "Sun Chariot" found in a bog and dating from 1200 B.C. Finds from the Viking epoch include runic stones from Jutland in the 10th century. Religious objects and other exhibits such as a 12th-century golden altar from Århus, fill a lot of the rooms devoted to the Middle Ages and the Renaissance. Lesser rooms feature the Danish collections of 1660 to 1830 (mainly antiques), Near Eastern and Classical Antiquities, the Ethnographical Collections (among the finest in the world), and the Royal Collection of Coins and Medals.

Ny Vestergade 10. ℂ **33-13-44-11**. Admission 50DKK ($7.50) adults, 40DKK ($6) students, free for children under 16. Tues–Sun 10am–5pm. Closed Dec 24, 25, and 31. Bus: 1, 2, 5, 6, 8, 10, or 41.

Ny Carlsberg Glyptotek ★★★   Carl Jacobsen, Mr. Carlsberg Beer himself, opened this major art museum behind the Tivoli more than a century ago. Jacobsen was a feverish collector of classical art, and the museum still reflects his 19th-century taste. The beer baron's original collection of classical art has been beefed up considerably over the years, including a treasure trove of French Impressionists that started with a gift of some three dozen works of Paul Gauguin. You'll see art by Monet, Manet, Degas, and Renoir and such French sculpture as Rodin's *Burgers of Calais*. Cézanne's much reproduced *Portrait of the Artist* also hangs here.

The antiquities collection is one of the greatest in the north of Europe, filled with sculpture and art from ancient Greece and Egypt as well as Italy in the Etruscan and Roman eras. The most notable prize in the Egyptian collection is a prehistoric rendering of a hippopotamus. Impressive Greek originals such as a headless Apollo or Niobe's tragic children are on view with Roman copies of

Moments   **The Old Sailor's Port at Nyhavn**

Nothing quite captures the spirit of maritime Copenhagen the way **Nyhavn** ★★★ does. This colorful canal was dug in the late 1600s to permit seafaring vessels to go right up to Kongens Nytorv, the city's largest square, with an equestrian statue of Christian IV in the center. Here mariners would unload their cargo from the remote corners of the globe at the old warehouses once located here. Because so many sailors were in the area at night, a series of rowdy bars, cafes, and bordellos were opened to serve them.

In time, the area became gentrified and many of the most famous Copenhageners preferred to live here, including Hans Christian Andersen who resided at various addresses: 20, 67, and 18 Nyhavn in that chronological order. Today, charming little restaurants and cafes, with a scattering of bars, line the canal, and this is one of the most favored places for absorbing Copenhagen's unique flavor. The northern side of Nyhavn is a pedestrian area crowded with locals and visitors alike. High-speed craft come and go from here all day, linking Copenhagen with Malmö, Sweden.

original Greek bronzes such as a 4th-century Hercules. The Etruscan art display is especially notable, with its sarcophagi, winged lions, bronzes, and pottery.

Dantes Plads 7. ⒸⒸ **33-41-81-41.** Admission 40DKK ($6) adults, free for children; free for all Wed and Sun. Tues–Sun 10am–4pm. Bus: 1, 5, 10, 550S, 650S.

Rådhus (Town Hall and World Clock)   The city hall building, constructed in an ornate architectural style in 1905, stands in the very heart of Copenhagen "guarded" by statues of storyteller Hans Christian Andersen and Niels Bohr, the Nobel Prize–winning physicist. You can climb the tower for an impressive **panoramic view** of the old city, taking in all its architecture, canals, lakes, and harborfront setting. The second attraction here is the **World Clock,** the famous timepiece created by Jens Olsen and open to view on the ground floor Monday to Friday from 10am to 4pm and Saturday from 10am to 1pm. Frederik IX set the clock on December 15, 1955, and the timepiece is so precise, it's calibrated to lose just 0.4 seconds every 3 centuries.

Rådhuspladsen. ⒸⒸ **33-66-25-82.** Rådhus, 30DKK ($4.50); clock, 10DKK ($1.50) adults, 5DKK (75¢) children. Guided tour: Rådhus, Mon–Fri 3pm, Sat 10am; tower, Mon–Sat noon. Bus: 1, 6, or 8.

Rosenborg Castle ★★   Inspired by Dutch Renaissance architecture, this *slot* (castle) was constructed of red brick and decorated with sandstone and is rather the same as it was in 1633 except for the absence of the original moat. First laid out in 1606, *Kongens Have* or the king's garden remains a delightful oasis of tranquillity within the bustling city. Danish royals used Rosenborg as their summer house until 1710 when King Frederik IV pronounced it "too small for a king." The castle is filled with royal treasures ranging from Narwhal tusk and ivory coronation chairs to Frederik VII's baby shoes. The **crown jewels and regalia**—the single most impressive treasure—is on exhibit in the Treasury. In the Knights Hall you can see the coronation seat and other royal relics from the 18th century. The most lavish royal bedroom, Room 3, is decorated with Asian lacquer art with a stucco ceiling. Christian IV died in this room surrounded by mourners.

Øster Voldgade 4A. ⓒ **33-15-32-86.** Admission 60DKK ($9) adults, 40DKK ($6) students and seniors, 10DKK ($1.50) children 5–12, free for children 4 and under. Palace and treasury (royal jewels), June–Aug daily 10am–4pm; May and Sept to mid-Oct daily 11am–3pm; mid-Oct to Apr Tues–Sun 11am–2pm. S-tog: Nørreport. Bus: 5, 10, 14, 16, 31, 42, 43, 184, or 185.

Statens Museum for Kunst ★★★   The Royal Museum of Fine Arts is the largest in Denmark and one of the great art museums of Northern Europe. Its collection of Flemish and Dutch paintings from the 15th to the 18th centuries is especially impressive: an era of golden age landscapes and marine paintings by Rubens and his school, and remarkable portraits by every artist from Rembrandt to Frans Hals. The European art section is rich in works from the Italian school from the 14th to the 18th centuries and the French school from the 17th and 18th centuries. The Statens is also one of the grandest showcases for showing the development of Danish painting in the 19th century. Notable paintings, each a world masterpiece, displayed here include *Workers Coming Home* by Edvard Munch, *Interior with a Violin* by Matisse, *Alice* by Modigliani, *The Guitar Player* by Juan Gris, and *The Judgement of Paris* by Harald Giersing. The museum also houses an impressive collection of Viking artifacts and has a sculpture garden filled with both classical and contemporary works. In 1998, a concert hall, Children's Art Museum, and a glass wing were added, the latter devoted to temporary shows.

Sølvgade 48-50. ⓒ **33-74-84-94.** www.smk.dk. Admission 50DKK ($7.50) adults, free for children under 16. Tues and Thurs–Sun 10am–5pm; Wed 10am–8pm. Bus: 10, 14, 43, or 184.

Tivoli Gardens ★★★   This miniature pleasure "city" was inspired by the fabled pleasure gardens of London, Paris, and Vienna in the 1700s. Ride a roller coaster or take a flying-trunk tour of Hans Christian Andersen's fairy tales

---

Moments   **Meetin' the Mermaid**

Scandinavia's *The Little Mermaid* ★ is the most famous statue in Scandinavia, and every visitor wants to see her. The life-size bronze of *Den Lille Havfrue* was inspired by Hans Christian Andersen's *The Little Mermaid,* one of the world's most famous fairy tales. Edvard Eriksen's sculpture, unveiled in 1913, rests on rocks right off the shore. In spite of its small size, the statue is as important a symbol to Copenhageners as the Statue of Liberty is to New Yorkers. The mermaid has fallen prey to vandals over the years. In the early 1900s, her arm was cut off and later recovered. She was decapitated on April 25, 1964, and the head was never returned. (The original mold exists, so missing body parts can be recast.) In January 1998, she lost her head again, and most of the city responded with sadness. "She is part of our heritage, like the Tivoli, the queen, and stuff like that," said local sculptor Christian Moerk.

Although not taking blame for the attack, the Radical Feminist Faction sent flyers to newspapers to protest "the woman-hating, sexually fixated male dreams" allegedly conjured by the statue's nudity. The head mysteriously turned up at a TV station, delivered by a masked figure. Welders restored it, making the seam invisible.

amidst a setting of restaurants, cafes, pavilions, and beautiful gardens with fountains. Tivoli is also the setting for free outdoor music and drama performances.

Europe's most famous recreational area was built on the south side of Rådhuspladsen (Town Hall Square) in 1843 on top of the ancient ramparts that once enveloped Copenhagen. It's illuminated at night by more than 100,000 colored lights, and has four times that many flowers. The gardens sprawl across 20 acres in the center of the city. It's not all beauty—witness the slot machines, shooting galleries, and pinball arcades—but there is much to savor here, ranging from an Arabian-style palace to a beer garden opening onto a lake with ducks, swans, and boats.

A parade of the red-uniformed Tivoli Boys Guard takes place on Saturday and Sunday at 6:30pm and again at 8:30pm, and their regimental band presents concerts on Saturday at 3pm on an open-air stage. The oldest building at Tivoli, the Chinese-style Pantomime Theatre, with its famous peacock curtain, stages pantomimes in the evening. Expect fireworks, brass bands, orchestras, vaudeville-like acts, dance clubs—and a hell of a good time.

Vesterbrogade 3. *C* 33-15-10-01. Admission 11am–1pm 55DKK ($8.25) adults, 30DKK ($4.50) children under 14; combination ticket including admission and all rides 100DKK ($15). May to mid-Sept, daily 11pm–midnight. Partial Christmastime opening from mid-Nov until Christmas Eve (reduced admission). Closed mid-Sept to Apr. Bus: 1, 16, or 29.

WHERE TO DINE

Bøf & Ost FRENCH/DANISH   Popular with university students, this affordable restaurant—Beef & Cheese in English—is housed in an 18th-century building with an outdoor terrace overlooking Greyfriars Square, one of the landmark plazas in Copenhagen's Old Town. Its cellars were created out of the ruins of a monastery that stood here in the Middle Ages. You don't get a lot of surprises here, but you do get good, solid, home-style cooking based on fresh ingredients, most obtained from the countryside of Denmark.

Gråbrødretorv 13. *C* 33-11-99-11. Reservations required. Main courses 149DKK–189DKK ($22–$28). Fixed-price lunch 118DKK ($18). DC, MC, V. Mon–Sat 11:30am–10:30pm. Bus: 5.

Café Lumskebugten *Finds* DANISH   The menu at this restaurant, established in 1854 as a rowdy tavern for sailors, hasn't changed in more than 100 years though the clientele has. As the tavern's reputation improved over the decades, even royal family members started turning up for dinner. Still going strong today, and decorated with antique ship models, it is one of the best places for authentic Danish cuisine. Try the fish cakes with mustard sauce and minced beetroot.

Esplanaden 21. *C* 33-15-60-29. Reservations recommended. Main courses 178DKK–225DKK ($27–$34). AE, DC, MC, V. Mon–Fri 11am–10:30pm; Sat 5–10:30pm. Bus: 1, 6, or 9.

Copenhagen Corner SCANDINAVIAN   Close to the Central Station and just around the corner from the Tivoli Gardens, this is arguably the most conveniently located restaurant in the center of the city. It serves well-prepared and unpretentious meals, including some of the Danes' most famous dishes, and does so exceedingly well at moderate prices. Authentic Scandinavian dishes appear on the menu every day, including filet of deer, Norwegian salmon, and three kinds of herring, the latter a special delight for the locals.

H.C. Andersens Blvd. 1A. *C* 33-91-45-45. Reservations recommended. Main courses 98DKK–228DKK ($15–$34); 3-course, fixed-price menu 298DKK ($45). AE, DC, MC, V. Daily 11:30am–11pm. Bus: 1, 6, or 8.

Faergekroen DANISH   Tivoli is not a place for cheap dining, which makes this popular and affordable restaurant at the edge of the lake, housed in a pink half-timbered Danish cottage, all the more delightful. While sitting on its out-door terraces on a sunny day, you can enjoy honest, straightforward fare, with-out a lot of fancy trimmings. The chef is justifiably proud of his repertoire of classic dishes from Mother Denmark's collection of recipes.

Vesterbrogade 3, Tivoli Gardens. © **33-12-94-12.** Reservations recommended for outdoor terrace tables. Main courses 85DKK–185DKK ($13–$28). Fixed-price lunch 115DKK–140DKK ($17–$21). AE, DC, MC, V. Daily 11am–midnight.

La Crevette ✺✺ SEAFOOD/CONTINENTAL   For a really big splurge in Copenhagen, reserve a table at this classic restaurant, housed in a 1909 pavilion with an outdoor terrace in the middle of Tivoli Gardens. Some of the freshest and best seafood in the city is served at this restaurant by chefs who dare to be innovative while still adhering to classic culinary principles. Most dishes here are "sure bets," including such Danish delights as marinated slices of salmon with oyster flan and egg cream with chives or grilled sea bass and scampi on crispy spinach and sautéed eggplant.

Vesterbrogade 3, Tivoli Gardens. © **33-14-68-47.** Reservations required. Main courses 225DKK–315DKK ($34–$47); 4-course, fixed-price dinner 445DKK ($67). AE, DC, MC, V. Daily noon–10pm.

Restaurant Els DANISH/FRENCH   With its original 1854 decor, including murals by 19th-century Danish artist, Christian Hitsch, intact, this is one of the city's most respected and traditional restaurants. Hans Christian Andersen regu-larly dined here. If you're dropping in for lunch, you might make an entire meal out of the delectable open-faced Danish sandwiches, but in the evening the mar-ket-fresh menu is based on an expanded, mainly French-inspired repertoire. Try the breast of wild duck with blackberry sauce or one of the other tasty delights.

Store Strandstraede 3, off Kongens Nytorv. © **33-14-13-41.** Reservations recommended. Main courses 45DKK–115DKK ($6.75–$17) lunch; 178DKK–225DKK ($27–$34) dinner. AE, DC, MC, V. Mon–Sat noon–3pm; daily 5:30–10pm. Bus: 1, 6, or 10.

Sonoma California Grille & Lounge ✺ *Finds* CALIFORNIAN/PACIFIC RIM   A sign of changing times, this new restaurant has opened on the site of Den Gyldne Fortun (Golden Fortune), a dining room that, since 1796, attracted the likes of Hans Christian Andersen and Jenny Lind. Today the kitchen turns out a cuisine heavily influenced by the kitchens of California, Hawaii, Japan, and Mexico, with farm-raised seasonal produce prepared in the healthiest and tastiest of fashion. For dessert, try the passion fruit soufflé or, get this, grilled pineapple lasagna. Naturally, California wines are heavily featured.

Ved Stranden 18. © **33-12-20-11.** Reservations recommended. Main courses 176DKK–205DKK ($26–$31); 4-course, fixed-price menu 369DKK ($55). AE, DC, MC, V. Daily 11am–midnight. Bus: 1, 6, or 10.

Søren K ✺ INTERNATIONAL   This finely honed restaurant, named to honor the country's most famous philosopher, opened in 1999 on the ground level of the Royal Library with a minimalist decor and windows overlooking the sea. As the chefs rarely cook with such high cholesterol ingredients as butter, cream, or cheese, a meal here is both a health-conscious and savory experience. The menu is seasonally adjusted, but might include such delights as venison roasted with nuts or the freshest of Norwegian salmon.

On the ground floor of the Royal Library's Black Diamond Wing, 1 Søren Kierkegaards Plads. © **33-47-49-49.** Reservations recommended. Main courses 65DKK–125DKK ($9.75–$19) at lunch; 195–225DKK ($29–$34) at dinner; 3-course, fixed-price dinner 350DKK ($53). DC, MC, V. Mon–Sat noon–midnight. Bus: 8.

SHOPPING

Much of the action takes place on **Strøget,** the pedestrian street in the heart of the capital. Strøget begins as Frederiksberggade, north of Rådhuspladsen, and winds to Østergade, which opens onto Kongens Nytorv. The jam-packed street is lined with stores selling everything from porcelain statues of *Youthful Boldness* to Greenland shrimp to Kay Bojesen's teak monkeys. The hurried visitor searching for Danish design might head first for **Illum,** Ostergade 52 (© **33-14-40-02**), one of Copenhagen's leading department stores filled with top-notch Danish designs as well as those from other Scandinavian countries. Another elegant department store and the largest in Scandinavia is **Magasin,** Kongens Nytorv (© **33-11-44-33**), which offers the tops in Scandinavia fashion, plus lots of elegant glass and porcelain along with handcrafts.

Those seeking the best of top-grade Scandinavian sweaters or Icelandic cardigans will find a vast selection at the **Sweater Market,** Frederiksberggade 15 (© **33-15-27-73**). The hand-knits are made of 100% Danish wool. Those who flock to flea markets will find **Det Blå Pakhus,** Holmbladsgade 113 (© **32-95-17-07**), to their liking. Charging an entrance fee of 15DKK ($2.25), "The Blue Warehouse" (its English name) is the country's largest indoor market, with 325 vendors, hawking everything from antiques and carpets to assorted bric-a-brac.

For Copenhagen's world-renowned glassware, porcelain, and crystal, head for **Holmegaards Glasvaerker,** in the Royal Scandinavian retail center, Amagertorv 4 (© **33-12-44-77**), in business for 2 centuries. Some of their patterns go back to the mid–19th century. A prestigious name, **Rosenthal Studio-haus** is found at Frederiksberggade 21 (© **33-14-21-01**), which has good buys in lead crystal (especially Orrefors) along with many limited editions of exquisite glassware. Founded in 1775, **Royal Copenhagen Porcelain,** in the Royal Scandinavia retail center, Amagertorv 4 (© **33-13-71-81**), attracts the serious collector. The company's trademark of three wavy blue lines is now a world-famous symbol.

A legend for its fine silver, **Georg Jensen,** in the Royal Scandinavian retail center, Amagertorv 4 (© **33-11-40-80**), offers the largest and most impressive collection of Jensen holloware in Europe along with gold and silver jewelry in both traditional and contemporary Danish design.

NIGHTLIFE

For the visitor to Copenhagen in summer, nothing competes with the **Tivoli Gardens** (p. 203) after dark. On an open-air stage in the center of the garden, vaudeville-like acts such as aerialists perform nightly at 7pm and again at 10:30pm (also Sat at 5pm). These performances are free, and are often a venue for jazz or folkloric entertainment. More than a dozen *commedia dell'arte* productions are performed at the **Pantomime Theater,** with a Chinese stage and peacock curtain. The free shows are staged Tuesday to Sunday at 6:15pm and at 8:30pm.

Grand concerts, everything from symphony to opera, are presented in the 2,000-seat **Tivolis Koncertsal** or concert hall, with tickets costing from 200DKK to 400DKK ($30–$60). Major artists from all over the world perform here Monday to Saturday at 7pm (sometimes at 9pm, depending on the event). For more information and to book tickets, call © **33-15-10-12.**

Copenhagen is also filled with music clubs featuring jazz, rock, and blues, and has many dance clubs. Some of the best jazz artists in the United States or Europe, even Africa, perform at **Copenhagen JazzHouse,** Niels Hemmingsensgade 10 (© **33-15-26-00**), with shows beginning at 8:30pm nightly, costing a cover that can range from 70DKK to 360DKK ($11–$54), depending on the artists booked.

Small and cozy, **La Fontaine,** Kompagnistraede 11 (℃ **33-11-60-98**), presents jazz artists Friday and Saturday beginning around 11:30pm. Otherwise, it's a lively bar open daily from 8pm to 5am. When music is presented, there's a cover charge of 45DKK ($6.75). A short stroll over from the Tivoli, **Baron & Baroness,** Vesterbrogade 2E (℃ **33-16-01-01**), is an upscale nightclub that's good for dinner and dancing. A dinner costs 150DKK to 250DKK ($23–$38), with a cover of 40DKK ($6) imposed for those who show up just for the disco above, which is open only Thursday to Saturday 10pm until dawn. The bar is open nightly, however, from 6pm to at least 3am.

A long-enduring favorite is **Den Røde Pimpernel,** Vesterbrogade 3 (℃ **33-11-12-41**). At "The Scarlet Pimpernel," live bands play dance music Tuesday to Saturday from 9pm. The club is open Tuesday to Saturday 9pm to 8am, but the 50DKK ($7.50) cover is imposed only on Friday and Saturday.

A trendy joint, **NASA,** Gothersgade 8F, Boltensgaard (℃ **33-93-74-15**), is the best club at a three-floor entertainment complex. Live groups, often from London, appear here at what is technically a private club but open to most newcomers Thursday to Sunday from midnight to 5am, charging a cover of 100DKK ($15). A so-called "Design Disco" **Subsonic,** Skindergade 45 (℃ **33-13-26-25**), is one of Copenhagen's hippest clubs. Some of the hottest young men and women in Copenhagen show up here to dance the night away, but only on Friday and Saturday from 11pm to 5:30am, when a cover ranging from 50DKK to 70DKK ($7.50–$11) is imposed.

Copenhagen also has a number of atmospheric old bars, of which our favorite is **Det Lille Apotek,** Stor Kannikestraede 15 (℃ **33-12-56-06**), which offers an antique atmosphere and is a student favorite. Open daily 11am to midnight. Although spruced up today, **Nyhavn 17,** Nyhavn 17 (℃ **33-12-54-19**), is one of the remaining honky-tonks left over from the days when this increasingly patrician quarter was a sailors' haunt. Open Sunday to Thursday 10am to 2am, Friday and Saturday until 3am. For drinking in a more elegant and peaceful atmosphere, try the cozy, traditional **Queen's Pub,** in the Kong Frederik Hotel, Vester Voldgade 25 (℃ **33-12-59-02**), open daily from noon to midnight.

EXCURSION TO HELSINGØR (HAMLET'S CASTLE) ♠

Located 25 miles (40km) north of Copenhagen, the town of Helsingør is the most popular 1-day trip from the Danish capital. It's visited chiefly because of so-called Hamlet's Castle, although we must point out that there was no Hamlet and Shakespeare never visited Helsingør.

The Danish Riviera with its sandy but windy and cold beaches separates Helsingør from Copenhagen. To the east, a fleet of ferries links Helsingør across a 2½ mile (4km) strait with the town of Helsingborg, Sweden. Helsingør came into fame because of its strategic position at the entrance to the Øresund, a narrow strip of water that connects the Baltic Sea to the North Sea.

GETTING THERE   Helsingør lies at the end of the northern line of trains heading from Copenhagen into the final reaches of North Zealand. A one-way trip takes 50 minutes, and trains leave frequently throughout the day from Copenhagen's Central Station.

Ferries, covered by the Eurailpass, ply the waters of the narrow channel separating Helsingør in Denmark and Helsingborg in Sweden, taking 25 minutes. Ferries are operated by **Scandlines** (℃ **33-15-15-15**) around the clock. Between 6am and 11pm daily, departures are every 20 minutes. During the slow period, daily 11pm to 6am, departures are timed at intervals of between 40 and 80 minutes.

Border formalities between the two countries are perfunctory, and although you must carry a passport, it might not even be requested.

VISITOR INFORMATION The **Helsingør Tourist Office,** Havnepladsen 3 (© **49-21-13-33**), is open Monday to Friday 9am to 6pm, and Saturday 10am to 1pm. It's directly across the street from the rail station.

TOP ATTRACTIONS & SPECIAL MOMENTS

For most visitors there is only one site here worthy of making the trip: **Kronborg Slot** ✸✸✸, Kronborg (© **49-21-30-78**), a sandstone-and-copper Dutch Renaissance castle known in English as "Elsinore Castle." The most famous castle in Scandinavia lies on a peninsula jutting out into the Øresund, and it's said to be the home of Holger Danske (Holger the Dane), a mythological hero who sleeps beneath the castle. Though he never saw it, the Bard chose this dank and gloomy place for his equally gloomy Elizabethan drama, *Hamlet,* which has been staged at the castle on several occasions. Dating from 1426, the castle was completely rebuilt in 1585 and restored again after a fire gutted it in 1629. Several rooms, including the state apartments, are open to the public, although the place is rather starkly furnished. The **Great Hall** is the largest in northern Europe, but only 7 of its original 40 tapestries—each commissioned by Frederik II in 1585—remain.

Also on the premises is the **Danish Maritime Museum** (© **49-21-30-52**), exploring the history of Danish shipping and seen on guided tours leaving every half hour from October to April. In summer you can explore on your own. The castle is a half mile (.8km) north of the Helsingør train depot.

Admission is 40DKK ($6) for adults, 15DKK ($2.25) for ages 6 to 14 (free for ages under 6). Open May to September daily 10:30am to 5pm; April and October Tuesday to Sunday 11am to 4pm; November to March Tuesday to Sunday 11am to 3pm; Bus: 340, 347, 801, 802, and 803.

WHERE TO DINE

If you're in Helsingør for lunch, as most visitors are, head for **Anno 1880,** Kongensgade 6 (© **49-21-54-80**), serving good Danish food in a narrow, half-timbered structure that used to be an old grocery store. The cuisine is appropriate to the setting—mostly time-tested Danish recipes such as fried steak with sautéed onions and boiled potatoes. Main courses cost 168DKK to 218DKK ($25–$33).

You might also try the appealing **Ophelia Restaurant,** in the Hotel Hamlet, Bramstraede 5 (© **49-21-05-91**), named for the Shakespeare heroine. The chef combines his Danish recipes with classics from French and Italian kitchens, and does so rather well. Main courses cost 148DKK to 185DKK ($22–$28).

Finally, for a change of pace and excellent value, try **Samos,** Stengade 81 (© **49-21-39-46**), which dishes out good, hearty Greek food. The location is in a 1770 Customs House near Kronborg Castle that today is a complex of international restaurants. An all-you-can-eat buffet is offered for 39DKK ($5.85), with main courses costing 110DKK to 185DKK ($17–$28).

AN EXCURSION TO ODENSE ✸✸

After Helsingør, the second most popular rail trip from Copenhagen is to the ancient town of Odense, third largest in Denmark, situated 97 miles (156km) west of Copenhagen. This was the birthplace of Hans Christian Andersen (1805–75), Scandinavia's most famous storyteller, still as popular today as he was more than a century ago.

Odense

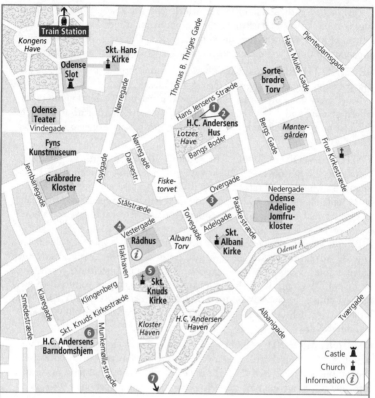

ATTRACTIONS ●
Den Fynske Landsby/Funen Village **7**
H.C. Andersen's Barndomshjem
  (Andersen's childhood home) **6**
H.C. Andersens Hus **12**
St. Canute's Cathedral **5**

DINING ◆
Den Gamle Kro **3**
Marie Louise **4**
Under Lindetaeet **2**

Odense lies on the island of Funen, which separates Zealand (site of Copenhagen) from Jutland, attached to the European mainland. Even without the spinner of white swan and ugly duckling fairy tales, Odense is a lively little town of pedestrian streets and quaint charm, worth a look on its own merits.

GETTING THERE   From Copenhagen's Central Station, a dozen trains per day make the 2-hour trip west to the city of Odense.

Note: Every hotel in Odense is located within a 1-mile (1.6km) radius of the railway station, and even the main shopping streets (Kongensgade and Vestergade) are on the opposite side of a verdant downtown park (Kongens Have) near the railway station.

VISITOR INFORMATION   The **Odense Tourist Bureau,** at Rådhuset, Vestergade 2A (© **66-12-75-20;** www.visitodense.com), is open June 15 to August 31 Monday to Friday 9:30am to 7pm, Saturday and Sunday 10am to 4pm; September to June 14 Monday to Friday 9am to 4:30pm, Saturday 10am to 1pm. Should you wish to stay overnight, the staff here will reserve you a hotel room for 35DKK ($5.25).

Besides helping arrange excursions, the tourist bureau sells the value-laden **Odense Adventure Pass.** It gives you access to 18 of the city's museums, the Odense Zoo, six indoor swimming pools, and unlimited free travel on the city buses and DSB trains within the municipality. It also entitles you to discounts on river cruises. Passes are valid for 1 or 2 days. A 1-day pass is 110DKK ($17) for adults, 60DKK ($9) for children under 14; 2-day passes cost 150DKK ($23) and 80DKK ($12).

GETTING AROUND   All Odense buses originate or terminate at the railway station. You can hop aboard a bus at various stops and buy your ticket once you're aboard. Buses cost 12DKK ($1.55) per ride within Odense and most of its suburbs, and tickets are valid for transfers within a 90-minute period of their issue.

Buses bound for the center (inner) city are painted red, and have two-digit ID numbers; numbers 42 and 52 are the most-used by people headed to the center of town. Buses bound for the suburbs of Odense or small towns throughout Funen usually opt for the off-white buses, which have three-digit ID numbers. These also stop at downtown destinations en route to the suburbs.

You can also rent a bike from **City Cykler,** Vesterbvro 27 (© **66-13-97-83**), for prices ranging from 99DKK to 150DKK ($15–$23) per day, depending on the type of cycle.

TOP ATTRACTIONS & SPECIAL MOMENTS

Odense Tourist Bureau (see above) offers **2-hour walking tours** from mid-June through August. They leave every Tuesday, Wednesday, and Thursday at 11am from a meeting place behind the tourist office and cover the town's major sights. Tours are given in English, and advance reservations are recommended. Tours cost 40DKK ($6) per adult, 20DKK ($3) per child.

Other than the Hans Christian Andersen monuments (see below), you can visit the chief attraction, **Funen Village/Den Fynske Landsby** ✹✹, Sejerkovvej 20 (© **65-51-47-01**), a large open-air museum of regional artifacts and buildings 1½ miles (2.4km) south of the historic center and reached by bus 21 or 22 from Flakhaven. This is really a living museum to Funen in the 18th and 19th centuries. Old structures from all over Funen were brought here and reassembled, including a village school, vicarage, jail, windmill, farmstead, and weaver's shop among other attractions. Everything is authentically furnished, and you can visit workshops to see craftspeople at work, later enjoying plays and folkloric dances at the Greek-style theater. Admission is 55DKK ($8.25) for adults or 15DKK ($2.25) for children. Open April to May and September to October Tuesday to Sunday 11am to 3pm; June to August daily 9:30am to 7pm, and November to March Sunday 11am to 3pm.

H.C. Andersen's Hus 𝕬𝕬, Bangs Border 29 (🕾 **65-51-47-01**), is the goal of most pilgrims to Odense. Popular with children of all ages, this museum is devoted to keeping alive the memory of Andersen. Precious memorabilia include his top hat, battered suitcase, and even his celebrated walking stick. Rare artifacts include letters to fellow writer Charles Dickens in London, and to "the Swedish nightingale," Jenny Lind, on whom Andersen had developed a crush. Reprints of his books in countless languages are on view. Admission is 40DKK ($6) for adults, 15DKK ($2.25) for children (free for ages 4 and under). Open June 16 to August daily 9am to 7pm; September to June 15 daily 10am to 4pm.

The other site associated with the writer is the **H.C. Andersen's Barndomshjem (Andersen's Childhood Home),** Munkememøllerstraede 3 (🕾 **65-51-47-01**). The house is modest but this is where the fairy-tale writer lived from age 2 to 14. He was a gawky boy, a true ugly duckling, made fun of by his schoolmates. Life didn't get better after school, when he went home at night to a drunken, superstitious mother who worked as a washerwoman. But all is serene at the cottage today, and the "garden still blooms," as it did in *The Snow Queen.* Admission is 10DKK ($1.50) for adults and 5DKK (75¢) for children; hours in July and August are daily 10am to 4pm; September to June Tuesday to Sunday 11am to 3pm.

Before bidding adieu to Odense, head for **St. Canute's Cathedral** 𝕬, Klosterbakken 2 (🕾 **66-12-61-23**), the most impressive Gothic style building in Denmark. Work on this cathedral began in the 13th century, but it wasn't until the 15th century that it was completed. Note the gold altar screen with an elegant **triptych** 𝕬𝕬𝕬 carved by Claus Berg in 1526 at the request of Queen Christina. The admission-free church stands opposite City Hall. Open May 15 to 30 and September 1 to 14, Monday to Saturday 10am to 5pm; April to May 14 and September 15 to 30, Monday to Saturday 10am to 4pm; June to August Monday to Saturday 10am to 5pm, Sunday noon to 3pm; and October to March Monday to Friday 10am to 4pm, and Saturday 10am to 2pm.

WHERE TO DINE

While you're in the center of the historic core of Odense exploring, you'll find a number of atmospheric restaurants serving good food, including **Den Gamle Kro,** Overgade 23 (🕾 **66-12-14-33**). A refined French and Danish cuisine based on fresh ingredients from the surrounding countryside is served at this old town center inn, which dates back to1683. Dine in one of two intimate and antique-filled rooms, or have a drink in the cellar bar. Main courses cost 169DKK to 258DKK ($25–$39), with fixed-price menus going for 158DKK to 348DKK ($24–$52).

The landmark **Under Lindetraeet,** Ramsherred 2 (🕾 **66-12-92-86**), a centuries-old inn across from the much-visited H.C. Andersen's Hus, is noted for its fresh, top-quality ingredients and skillfully prepared Danish dishes. It serves some of the best meat and shellfish dishes in the area but is not so pretentious that it can't also dish out *lobscouse,* the fabled sailors' hash. Main courses cost 225DKK to 495DKK ($34–$74); a fixed-price lunch goes for 238DKK ($36).

3 Highlights of Jutland

From the islands of Zealand, on which Copenhagen sits, and Funen, whose heart is Odense, we move to the largest land mass of Denmark: Jutland. It's a peninsula of heather-covered moors, fjords, lakes, sandy dunes, and farmland. For your final look at Denmark, head via fast train to Jutland's major city—Århus.

ÅRHUS ★★

The capital of Jutland and Denmark's second-largest city, Århus lies 109 miles (175km) west of Copenhagen. A university town with a lively port, it is the cultural center of Jutland and a major industrial center as well. Pronounced *Ore-hoos*, Århus is self-styled "the world's smallest big city," and it's filled with some notable attractions and architectural gems of yesteryear. Its well-preserved historic core deserves at least a half day of your time. The city is fairly compact, and it's easy to walk around.

GETTING THERE   Sixteen fast trains leave Copenhagen's Central Station each day, reaching Århus in 3 hours, 8 minutes. The city's railway station, Århus Hovedbanegard, lies on the south side of the town center.

VISITOR INFORMATION   Tourist Århus is in the Rådhuset (Town Hall) on Park Allé (© 89-40-67-00), and is a few minutes' walk from the train station. It's open mid-June to mid-September Monday to Friday 9:30am to 6pm, Saturday 9:30am to 5pm, Sunday 9:30am to 1pm; off season Monday to Friday 9am to 4pm. Should you wish to stay overnight, the staff here will arrange hotel rooms for a fee of 25DKK ($3.75).

GETTING AROUND   A regular bus ticket, valid for one ride, can be purchased on the rear platform of all city buses for 14DKK ($2.10). You can buy a **tourist ticket** for 97DKK ($15) at the tourist office or at newstands (kiosks) throughout the city center. The 24-hour ticket covers an unlimited number of rides within the central city and includes a 2½-hour guided tour of Århus.

The value-filled **Århus Pass** allows unlimited travel by public transportation, free admission to many museums and attractions, and also includes a 2½-hour guided tour. A 2-day pass costs 121DKK ($18) for adults and 55DKK ($8.25) for children; 1-week passes are 171DKK ($26) for adults and 83DKK ($12) for children. The Århus Pass is sold at the tourist office, many hotels, camping grounds, and kiosks throughout the city.

TOP ATTRACTIONS & SPECIAL MOMENTS

For the best introduction to Århus, head for the town hall's tourist office, where a 2½-hour **sightseeing tour** leaves daily at 10am from June 24 to August 31. It costs 50DKK ($7.50) per person, unless you have an Århus Pass.

The late Gothic **Cathedral of St. Clemens (Århus Domkirke),** Bispetorvet (© 86-12-38-45), is the longest in Denmark, with a 305-foot nave. Begun in the 13th century in the Romanesque style, it was completely overhauled in the 15th century into a rather Flamboyant Gothic overlay. The original structure is best seen by looking at the Romanesque chapels in each arm of the transept. This red brick cathedral is covered in copper roofing and crowned by a 315-foot spire. Inside the chief treasures are a 15th-century triptych, a Renaissance pulpit, and an 18th-century pipe organ. Admission is free and the cathedral is open May to September 9:30am to 4pm; October to April Monday to Saturday 10am to 3pm.

The town's other crowning achievement is its **Rådhuset (Town Hall),** Rådhuspladsen (© 89-40-20-00), built from 1936 to 1941 to commemorate the

500th anniversary of the town charter. Arne Jacobsen, the famous architect, was one of the designers of this marble-plated building. You face an elevator or else 346 steps if you want to go to the top of the 197-foot tower, which opens onto a panoramic view of Århus and the countryside around it. A guided tour costs 10DKK ($1.50); otherwise, admission to the tower is 5DKK (75¢). Guided tours are offered Monday through Friday at 11am; additional tours of the tower take place at noon and 2pm. Closed September to June 23.

The biggest attraction of all, **Den Gamle By** ✮✮✮, an open-air museum, is located 1½ miles (2.4 km) west of the train station, just outside of town, at Viborgvej 2 (© **86-12-31-88**). The little community of more than 75 buildings lies in a park west of the town center and is the best of the open-air museums of Denmark. Re-created in a botanical garden, urban life from the 16th- to the 19th-centuries lives again here. You can wander at leisure through workshops watching craftspeople at work, including carpenters, hatters, bookbinders, and so on. You can also explore old-fashioned buildings such as a schoolhouse, pharmacy, or post office, as well as the Burgomaster's House, the half-timbered 16th-century home of a rich merchant. Various rooms show the evolution of interior decorating over the centuries in Denmark. On-site is a museum filled with artifacts ranging from delftware to antique clocks. Summer music programs are staged, and on the grounds you'll find a tea garden, bakery, beer cellar, and full-service restaurant. Admission is 75DKK ($11) for adults, 25DKK ($3.75) for children. Open September and October and April and May, daily 10am to 5pm; November to December and February to March, daily 10am to 4pm; January, daily 11am to 3pm; and June to August, daily 9am to 6pm. To get here, take bus 3, 14, or 25 (trip time: 3–5 min.) or walk (about 15–20 min.) from the train station. The bus takes 3 to 5 minutes. Otherwise, you can walk over to Den Gamle from the station in 15 to 20 minutes.

WHERE TO STAY & DINE

"The Inn in the Corner," or **Kroen I Krogen,** stands at Banegårdspladsen 4 (© **86-19-24-39**), and has attracted a devoted following since it was established across from the train depot in 1934. Its Danish menu is one of the town's finest, and the setting is atmospheric, with walls decorated by hand-painted panels. The food is simple, straightforward, and good, and the herring and fish dishes are especially inviting. All main courses cost 198DKK ($30), with fixed-price menus going for 228DKK to 258DKK ($34–$39).

With a history going back to 1907, **Teater Bodega,** Skolegade 7 (© **86-12-19-17**), is still going strong, serving excellent Danish meals, including delectable open-faced sandwiches at lunch, across from the Århus Cathedral. Theater buffs and art lovers, among others, are drawn to the atmosphere of thespian memorabilia and the Danish country-style cooking, including hash, Danish roast beef, and freshly caught fish. Lunch *smørrebrød* costs 43DKK to 83DKK ($6.45–$12), and main courses run 80DKK to 170DKK ($12–$26).

For the finest food in town, eat at **Prins Ferdinand** ✮✮✮, Viborgvej 2 (© **86-12-52-05**), on the periphery of the historic center and established in 1988 by Peter Brun and Lotte Norrig, who offer an applause-worthy repertoire of dishes. Flickering candles and fresh flowers set a romantic atmosphere as you dine on turbot with Russian caviar, sea devil with lobster Thai style with lemongrass, or a boneless pigeon marinated in hoisin sauce. Main courses cost 150DKK to 235DKK ($23–$35); fixed-price menus at lunch run 170DKK to 235DKK ($26–$35).

Ferries to Sweden & Norway

Stena Line (© 96-20-02-00), one of Europe's largest and most reliable ferryboat operators, runs the two most popular routes in and out of town. Passengers heading to Norway can take a daily, 9-hour ferryboat between Frederikshavn and Oslo. Depending on the season, passengers pay between 165DKK to 365DKK ($25–$55) each. Be warned in advance that southbound boats originating in Oslo depart after dark, and, consequently, all passengers are required to rent an overnight cabin for the 9-hour transit. Cabins, each suitable for two passengers, rent for between 300DKK to 1,300DKK ($45–$195) each. Stena also operates five ferryboats a day between the Swedish port of Gothenburg and Frederikshavn. Transit time is between 2 and 3 hours, depending on the boat. Passengers pay between 90DKK and 180DKK ($14–$27) each way, though Eurail passholders get a 30% reduction on this ferry. Stena also operates three catamaran crossings every day that are much faster than the ferries.

The city of Larvik is yet another ferry gateway into Norway, although it's less used. **Color Line** (© 99-56-19-77) operates one or two daily ferry services between Frederikshavn and Larvik (trip time: 6¼ hr.), which cost 160DKK–340DKK ($21–$45) per person. Passholder discounts are given on this ferry route as well.

Should you wish to stay overnight, the first-class **Scandic Plaza** ⊛, Banegårdsplads 14, DK-8100 (© 87-32-01-00), is in the very center of town, close to the Town Hall and major attractions. A remake of an original 1930s hotel, the 162-room property was vastly renovated and overhauled in 1997 and is better than ever, with tastefully decorated and comfortably furnished bedrooms. Rates, which include breakfast, are 795DKK to 1,495DKK ($119–$224) double; 1,995DKK ($299) for a suite.

FREDERIKSHAVN

The embarkation ferry departure point for Norway, the coastal town of Frederikshavn, 238 miles (381km) northwest of Copenhagen, is the final stop for rail passengers in North Jutland.

In lieu of major attractions, you get stores loaded with Danish goods. Swedes and Norwegians arrive by sea in droves to shop for Danish food products that are much cheaper than back in their hometowns.

GETTING THERE   Frederikshavn is the northern terminus of the DSB rail line. About 20 trains leave daily from Århus to Frederikshavn; travel time is roughly 2¾ hours. Trains leaving out of Copenhagen take 6 hours.

VISITOR INFORMATION   The **Frederikshavn Turistbureau,** Brotorvet 1 (© 98-42-32-66), near the ferry dock and a short walk down Havnepladsen from the train station, is open in summer daily from 8:30am to 5pm. In the off season, hours are Monday to Friday 9am to 4pm, Saturday 11am to 2pm. *Note:* Though the bureau will make hotel arrangements for you, they charge a fee of 20% of your total room cost, so it's best to make arrangements on your own.

TOP ATTRACTIONS & SPECIAL MOMENTS

Worth exploring, the oldest part of Frederikshavn, **Fiskerkylyngen,** lies to the north of the fishing harbor and is filled with well-preserved homes, many dating from the 1600s. Otherwise, attractions are minor except for the **Bangsbo Museum** ⚓, Dronning Margrethesvej (© 98-42-31-11), one of the best openair museums in the north of Jutland, lying 2 miles (3.5km) south of the town center in a deer park. Several 18th-century buildings lie near the ruins of a 14th-century manor house. Many mementos of Denmark of yesterday are found here, including a barn from 1580 (one of the oldest in Denmark), farm equipment, and a large display of World War II relics. An ancient ship, similar to vessels used by the Vikings, is also displayed. Admission is 30DKK ($4.50) for adults, 5DKK (75¢) for children. Open June to October daily 10:30am to 5pm; November to May Tuesday to Sunday 10:30am to 5pm.

WHERE TO STAY & DINE

Near the harbor in an 1850s building, **Restaurant Baachus,** Lodsgade 8A (© **98-43-29-00**), is an unpretentious bistro serving respectable Danish food at affordable prices. Its 40-seat, old-fashioned dining room turns out such treats as a creamy fish soup—the house specialty—along with the best catch of the day, perhaps turbot from icy waters. For the carnivore, there is also a selection of succulent meat dishes. Main courses cost 90DKK to 150DKK ($14–$23) with set menus going for 69DKK to 199DKK ($10–$30).

Another good choice, **Vinkaelderen,** Havnegade 8 (© **98-42-02-70**), lies midway between the harbor and the center of town. Built in the post-war era, it's been popular ever since with both locals and transients heading for the ferries. Good and affordable Danish cuisine is served, mostly fresh fish and Danish beef dishes. Main courses go for 98DKK to 200DKK ($15–$30), with a fixed-price menu costing 178DKK ($27). Open daily 10am to midnight.

If you're staying overnight while waiting for a ferry, check into the 95-room **Hotel Jutlandia,** Havnepladsen, DK-9900 (© **98-42-42-00**), the biggest and best-rated place to stay in town, situated close to the embarkation point for the boats to Gothenburg. Scandinavian design and first-class comfort are found here, especially in the midsize and comfortably furnished bedrooms. The on-site restaurant, Gray Duck, is one of the town's best. Rates, including breakfast, are 1,135DKK ($170) double; 2,435DKK ($365) suite.

A more affordable choice is the 28-room **Hotel 1987,** Damsgaards Plads 8E, DK-9900 (© **98-43-19-87**), carved out of a 130-year-old marine warehouse in 1987. Completely modernized, the intimate and cozily furnished bedrooms are comfortable and equipped with shower-only bathrooms. Doubles cost 600DKK to 750DKK ($90–$113), including breakfast.

7

Finland

Finland is the last frontier country of western Europe, and it is one of the northernmost countries in the world, with nearly a third of its land, Lapland, north of the Arctic Circle. Despite the confiscation of nearly a tenth of its territory following the Winter War with Russia, in 1939 and 1940, Suomi (its Finnish name) is still one of the largest countries of Europe, about the size of Italy. But it is also one of the least populated, having some five million people.

Of the Scandinavian countries sitting on the "roof" of Europe, Finland is the most difficult to reach by rail. But once arriving in Helsinki, the Finnish capital, you'll have access to two unique travel opportunities. From Helsinki, you can take one of two daily trains to St. Petersburg in Russia where you can visit the Hermitage, one of the world's greatest depositories of art. Helsinki is also the gateway to the newly emerging Baltic countries, especially Estonia, which is only a short boat ride from the Finnish capital.

And even though Finland has few connections to European rail networks, it nonetheless is an easy ferry trip away from Stockholm, which enjoys excellent rail links to other Scandinavian capitals and, as a result, the rest of continental Europe. With a Eurailpass, you can, for example, get on a train in Rome and ride the rails all the way to Stockholm where you can make the final run by ferry into Helsinki. Once in Helsinki, you can hook up with efficient rail lines in what is increasingly emerging as the "crossroads" between the east and west of Europe.

Finland also possesses a number of other pluses as a rail destination. The Finnish rail system is one of the most modern in the world, linking all the country's major towns and cities except those in the remote north. Even though Finland is a large country, it is easy to get about by rail. And, in what may be the most literate country in the world, there is no language barrier as almost all Finns speak English, and rather fluently at that.

Summer is the best season to visit, when the country's endless scenic vistas of vast green forests and blue lakes can be seen from your train window. Many rail passengers visit in summer just to enjoy the Midnight Sun, best seen from Rovaniemi, the capital of Finnish Lapland.

HIGHLIGHTS OF FINLAND

Of course, an entire book could be written on the lakes and untamed wilderness of Finland, which contrast nicely with the country's small, ultramodern cities. But the remoteness of the country's location means a rail visitor who makes it to this part of the world (most often by boat or air from Stockholm), usually descends on Helsinki for a visit of only 2 or 3 days before moving on to other points on the continent.

Now that the Iron Curtain is long gone, many adventurous travelers also stop off in Finland before ferrying over to Tallin, the capital of Estonia, or taking the

Finland

Moments Festivals & Special Events

After a long, cold winter, most Helsinki residents turn out to celebrate the arrival of spring at the **Walpurgis Eve Celebration,** held on April 30. Celebrations are held at Market Square, followed by May Day parades and other activities the next morning.

A major Scandinavian musical event, the **Helsinki Festival** presents orchestral concerts by outstanding soloists and ensembles, chamber music and recitals, exhibitions, ballet, theater, and opera performances, along with jazz, pop, and rock concerts. For complete information about the program, contact the Helsinki Festival, Lasipalatsi Mannerheimintie 22–24 Finland–00100 Helsinki (© **09/6126-5100;** www.helsinkifestival.fi). The festival takes place from mid-August to early September.

Since the 1700s, the annual **Baltic Herring Market** has taken place along the quays of Market Square in early October. Fishermen continue the centuries-old tradition of bringing their catch into the city and selling it from their boats. Prizes and blue ribbons go to the tastiest herring.

train to Russia's St. Petersburg (the former Leningrad) to see the treasures of the Hermitage.

As the capital of Finland, **Helsinki** lies at the crossroads between eastern and western Europe. It's also the country's rail hub. You can begin your adventure in this city by heading for **Market Square** to test the pulse rate of the capital, followed by visits to two of the most important attractions, the **Finnish National Gallery** and the **Mannerheim Museum,** the latter the former home of field marshal Baron Carl Gustaf Mannherheim. The following morning you can spend in the **National Museum of Finland,** followed by an afternoon at the **Seurasaari Open-Air Museum** and **Suomenlinna Fortress,** the "Gibraltar of the North." At some point in your journey, avail yourself of the opportunity to enjoy an authentic Finnish sauna in the land where the institution was invented.

1 Essentials

GETTING THERE

With more flights to Helsinki from more parts of the world (including Europe, Asia, and North America) than any other airline, **Finnair** (© **800/950-5000** in the U.S.; www.finnair.com) is the only airline that flies nonstop from North America to Finland (an 8-hr. trip). Departures take place from New York and Miami.

Several other airlines fly from North America to gateway European cities and then connect to Helsinki. Foremost among these is **British Airways (BA;** © **800/247-9297** in the U.S., or 08457/733-377 in London; www.ba.com). **Finnair** (© **0870/241-4411** in London; www.finnair.com) also offers more frequent service to Helsinki from several airports in Britain.

If you're stopping in Finland after traveling by train through the continent, it's likely that you'll head here via modern ferry service from Stockholm on **Silja**

Line (www.silja.com) or **Viking Line** (www.vikingline.fi). Eurail passholders ride free on the ferry, though if you wish to stay in a cabin for the 9- to 14-hour journey (depending on whether you travel to Turku or Helsinki), there is a supplement ranging from 36€ to 388€ ($41.50–$446) per person based on double occupancy. Prices depend on class of cabin, the number of passengers per room, and the line you take.

If you take the ferry from Stockholm to Turku, the county's former capital on the west coast of Finland, you can catch one of the seven daily trains (including a high-speed Pendolino) that take you across southern Finland to Helsinki. The trip takes 2¼ hours. Most passengers, however, take a ferry directly from Stockholm to Helsinki without making any extra rail travel. Ferry service is also available from Rostock, Germany to Helsinki, but we do not recommend this option as it takes more than 22 hours to make the crossing.

FINLAND BY RAIL
PASSES

For information on the **Eurailpass,** the **Eurailpass Flexi,** the **Scanrail Pass,** and other multicountry options, see chapter 2.

Finland has its own **Finnrail Pass** for use on the country's elaborate network of railroads. The pass entitles holders to unlimited travel for any 3, 5, or 10 days within a 1-month period on all passenger trains of the VR Ltd. Finnish Railways. Travel days may be used either consecutively or nonconsecutively. Prices run from $143 in second class and $214 in first class for 3 days of travel to $259 in second class and $387 in first class for 10 days of travel. Travelers over 65 and children 2 to 15 are charged half the full fare (proof of age required); children 5 and under ride free when accompanied by a full-fare adult (they do not, however, get a seat).

The Finnrail Pass should be purchased before you leave home and can be obtained from **Rail Europe** (© **877/272-RAIL** in the U.S., **800/361-RAIL** in Canada; www.raileurope.com) or through your travel agent. Rail Europe also offers a Finnrail Pass with a choice of two popular excursions out of Helsinki: a boat trip to Talinn, Estonia (p. 220) or a round-trip fare on the luxurious *Sibelius* train to St. Petersburg, Russia, with any pass that includes Finland (p. 233). Depending on the class of service and the option you choose, prices run from $279 for second-class travel and the ferry excursion to Talinn, and from $145 for the trip to St. Petersburg.

Note: Second-class trains in Finland are comparable to first-class trains in many other countries, so splurging on a first-class ticket or pass is unnecessary.

FOREIGN TRAIN TERMS

Forget trying to learn Finnish; to speak it, you pretty much need to be born there, as it's one of the world's most difficult languages. The good news for English-speakers is that Finnish "train lingo" is hardly a consideration because school

Trains & Travel Times for Finland

From	To	Type of Train	# of Trains	Frequency	Travel Time
Stockholm	Helsinki	Ferry	2	Daily	14 hr.
Helsinki	St. Petersburg	*Sibelius*	1	Daily	7 hr.
Helsinki	St. Petersburg	*Repin*	1	Daily	7 hr.
Helsinki	Tallinn	Jet Boat	12	Mon–Sat	1 hr. 40 min.

Moments   Speeding to Estonia

One of the added advantages of traveling as far east as Helsinki is the chance to take a day trip to the city of Tallinn, capital of Estonia. You can't get to Tallinn by train, but Nordic Jet Line's high-speed catamarans, launched in the spring of 2003, run quickly and efficiently between Helsinki and the Estonian city.

Tallinn, with its German spires, Russian domes, and Scandinavian towers, is quickly becoming a top choice for offbeat travel in Europe, and you can easily spend a day here exploring **Vanalinn (Old Town),** which is home to Europe's oldest town hall. The suds flow in its outdoor cafes, and local troupes will entertain you all summer.

Both the HSC *Baltic Jet* and HSC *Nordic Jet* zip you to Tallin in only 1 hour, 40 minutes. Boat tickets can be purchased at both rail stations and travel agents in Finland or by calling ℂ **09/681-700** or 06/137-000 for reservations. For more information, check out the company's website at **www-eng.njl.fi.**

Depending on the time of departure, one-way jet-class tickets range from 19€ to 38€ ($21.75–$43.75); business-class tickets range from 51€ to 59€ ($58.75–$67.75). You can also purchase these tickets from Rail Europe.

children in Finland start learning English in grade school, and you won't have problems finding someone at any of the major stations who speaks English.

PRACTICAL TRAIN INFORMATION

Finland's extensive and reliable rail network is run by Finnish Railways, and all major Finnish cities are linked by rail to Helsinki. Most trains are new (or close to it) and operate on a timely basis. And Finland's rail engineers now offer some of the most modern and high-speed trains in Europe. For example, the new high-tech Pendolino (they "tilt" as they take corners) trains have cut traveling time between Helsinki, the present capital, to Turku, the ancient capital, to just 2 hours. There are a total of four types of trains that operate in the country: **InterCity (IC)** trains, high-speed **Pendolino (EP)** express trains, regular express trains, and slower local and commuter trains.

The good news for travelers on a budget: Finnish trains are cheaper than those in the rest of Scandinavia. And if you choose to purchase open round-trip (return) tickets, they are valid for 1 month.

For a Finnish Railways journey planner, check **www.vr.fi.**

RESERVATIONS   Because Finnish trains tend to be crowded, you should reserve a seat in advance—in fact, seat reservations are obligatory on all express trains marked "IC" or "EP" on the timetable. The charge for seat reservations, which depends on the class and the length of the journey, ranges from 3€ to 6€ ($3.45–$6.90). If you want, you can also make a reservation before you leave North America through Rail Europe for $11. *Warning:* Reserved seats are not marked so you'll never know if you're taking someone's seat or not unless the passenger shows up to evict you.

SERVICES & AMENITIES   It's not possible to reserve *couchettes* on Finnish trains as there are none. You can reserve two- and three-berth compartments, however. These sleepers should be reserved as far in advance as possible, especially during the peak months of July and August. To reserve in advance, contact Rail Europe or your travel agent. Prices for accommodations vary, so ask when you make the reservation.

Most express trains are air-conditioned, and offer nonsmoking sections, music channels, and facilities for those with mobility issues. Many Finnish trains have outlets peddling snacks and drinks. Prices, however, are lethal. If you're watching your euros, it's far better to pick up a supply of food and drink for your journey at the rail station before boarding the train.

FAST FACTS: Finland

Area Code The international country code for Finland is **358**. The city area code for Helsinki is **09**.

Business Hours Most **banks** are open Monday to Friday from 9:15am to 4:15pm. You can also exchange money at the railway station in Helsinki daily from 8am to 9pm, and at the airport daily from 6:30am to 11pm. **Store** hours vary. Most are open Monday to Friday from 9am to 6pm and Saturday from 9am to 3pm. Nearly everything is closed on Sunday. An exception are **R-kiosks,** which sell candy, tobacco, toiletries, cosmetics, and souvenirs all over Helsinki and elsewhere; they're open Monday to Saturday 8am to 9pm and Sunday from 9 or 10am to 9pm.

Climate Spring arrives in May and the summers are short—a standing joke in Helsinki claims summer lasts from Tuesday to Thursday. July is the warmest month, with temperatures averaging around 59°F (15°C). The coldest months are January and February, when the Finnish climate is comparable to that of New England. Snow usually arrives in December and lasts until April.

Documents Required American and Canadian citizens need only a valid **passport** to enter Finland. You need to apply for a visa only if you want to stay more than 3 months.

Electricity Finland operates on 220 volts AC. Plugs are usually of the continental type with rounded pins. Always ask at your hotel desk before plugging in any electrical appliance. Without an appropriate transformer or adapter, you'll destroy the appliance.

Embassies & Consulates The Embassy of the **United States** is at Itäinen Puistotie 14A, FIN-00140 Helsinki (© **09/171-931**); and the Embassy of **Canada** is at Pohjoisesplanadi 25B, FIN-00100 Helsinki (© **09/228-530**). If you're planning to visit Russia after Finland and need information about visas, the **Russian Embassy** is at Tehtaankatu 1B, FIN-00140 Helsinki (© **09/ 661-877**). However, it's better to make all your travel arrangements to Russia before you leave home.

Health & Safety Finland's national health plan does not cover U.S. or Canadian visitors. Any medical expenses that arise must be paid in cash. (Medical costs in Finland, however, are generally more reasonable than elsewhere in western Europe.) British and other European Union (EU) citizens can ask their insurer for an E111 form, which will cover emergencies in Finland and all other EU countries.

Finland is one of the safest countries in Europe, although the recent arrival of desperately poor immigrants from former Communist lands to the south means the situation is not as tranquil or as safe as before.

Holidays The following holidays are observed in Finland: January 1 (New Year's Day), Epiphany (Jan 6), Good Friday, Easter Monday, May 1 (Labor Day), Ascension Day (mid-May), Whitmonday (late May), Midsummer Eve and Midsummer Day (Fri and Sat of the weekend closest to June 24), All Saints' Day (Nov 6), December 6 (Independence Day), and December 25 and 26 (Christmas and Boxing Days).

Mail Airmail letters take about 7 to 10 days to reach North America; surface mail—sent by boat—takes 1 to 2 months. Parcels are weighed and registered at the post office, which may ask you to declare the value and contents of the package on a preprinted form. Stamps are sold at post offices in all towns and cities, at most hotels, sometimes at news kiosks, and often by shopkeepers who offer the service for customers' convenience. In Finland, mailboxes are bright yellow with a trumpet embossed on them. Airmail letters cost .60€ (70¢) for up to 20 grams. For postal information, call ✆ 09/9800-7100.

Police & Emergencies In Helsinki, dial ✆ 112; for the police, call ✆ 100-22.

Telephone To make **international calls** from Finland, first dial the international prefix of 990, 994, or 999, then the country code, then the area code (without the general prefix 0), and finally the local number. For information on long-distance calls and tariffs, call ✆ 0800/9-0999. To place calls to Finland, dial whatever code is needed in your country to reach the international lines (for example, in the United States, dial **011** for international long distance), then the country code for Finland **(358)**, then the area code (without the Finnish long-distance prefix 0), and finally the local number. To make long-distance calls within Finland, dial 0 to get a long-distance line (the choice of carrier is at random), the area code, and the local number. (Note that all area codes in this guide are given with the prefix 0.) For phone number information, dial ✆ 02-02-02. Besides phone booths and hotels, calls can be made from local post and telephone offices.

Tipping It's standard for **hotels** and **restaurants** to add a service charge of 15%, and usually no further tipping is necessary. In restaurants, however, it's customary to also leave the small change. **Taxi drivers** don't expect a tip. It is appropriate to tip **doormen** at least 1€ ($1.15), and **bellhops** usually get 1€ ($1.15) per bag (in most Finnish provincial hotels, guests normally carry their own luggage to their room). At railway stations, **porters** are usually tipped 1€ ($1.15) per bag. Hairdressers and barbers don't expect tips. **Coat check charges** are usually posted; there's no need for additional tipping.

2 Helsinki ✶✶✶

A rail hub situated at the crossroads of eastern and western Europe, Helsinki is the capital of the Independent Republic of Finland and is home to some 500,000 people. Although Helsinki is most often reached by a boat cruise from Stockholm, the city is connected to a vast network of rail lines running throughout Finland and even extending south to Russia for those who want to go either to Moscow or St. Petersburg. You can visit every major town or city in Finland via Helsinki.

The city was founded in 1550 at the mouth of the Vantaa River by Swedish King Gustav Vasa, when Finland was a part of Sweden, and was later relocated on the Vironniemi peninsula in the place now known as Kruununhaka. It was not the capital of Finland until after the Napoleonic Wars. Russia, concluding a peace with the French, annexed Finland to its empire and moved the capital from Turku to Helsinki, which was closer to St. Petersburg.

Perhaps the city's greatest allure for the rail traveler is its individuality—it is distinct from all other European capitals and has a flavor all its own. Unlike Athens, you'll find no ancient temples here, for Finland is a decidedly modern nation with granite neoclassical structures. And, unlike Vienna, Helsinki is not full of unicorns, gargoyles, palaces, and tombs that testify to architectural splendor and the glory of empire. All the kings who've ruled the city have been foreigners; instead of glorifying monarchy, the Finns are more likely to honor an athlete or a worker in their sculpture. As proof, just take a look at the figures standing proudly, even defiantly, in front of Stockmann's Department Store: three nude blacksmiths.

STATION INFORMATION

GETTING FROM THE AIRPORT TO THE TRAIN STATION

Helsinki–Vantaa Airport (✆ **0200/14-636;** www.helsinki-vantaa.fi) is 12 miles (19km) north of the center of town, about a 30-minute bus ride from there. Bus 615 goes back and forth from the airport and Railway Square, site of the main train terminal. A bus departs 2 to 3 times per hour between 5:30am and 10:20pm, and the fare is 3€ ($3.50) one-way. A conventional taxi ride from the airport to the rail station in the center of Helsinki costs 20€ to 25€ ($23–$28.75) one-way.

INSIDE THE STATION

Trains arrive in the center of the city at the **Central Helsinki Railway Station,** Kaivokatu (✆ **03/072-0900**). Designed by Eliel Saarinen, the station itself is a national monument and a classic example of the Art Nouveau style. And it's an especially good station for English speakers: All information in the station is posted in both Finnish and English.

Trains heading to St. Petersburg and ultimately to Moscow, the latter a 15-hour journey from Helsinki, depart from here. Trains also leave from this station for all major cities in Finland, including Tampere and Turku (both just 2 hr. away). Trains also depart from this station heading north to Rovaniemi, the capital of Finnish Lapland (about five to eight trains leave daily). The Lapland trip takes 10 to 13 hours, depending on the train.

If you don't want to go to the tourist office (see below), you'll find a hotel booking service, **Hotellikeskus** (✆ **09/2288-1400;** www.helsinkiexpert.fi), right in the station on the righthand side of the building as you exit from the trains. The staff charges a fee of 5.05€ ($5.80) per person if you show up; the service is free by phone or if you e-mail **hotel@helsinkiexpert.fi.**

Helsinki

- - - - Ferry
.... Rail Station
🏠 Railway

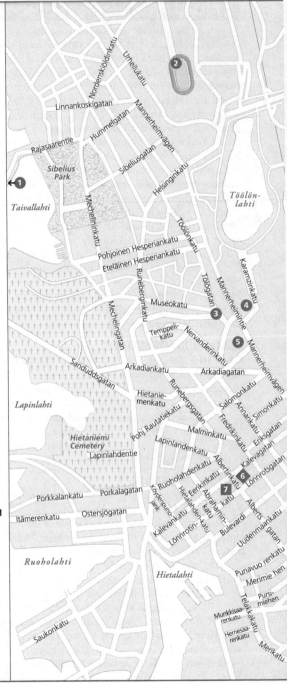

Aleksis Kivisgata
Lautatarhank
Sturenkatu
Helsinginkatu
Helsingegatan
Sörnasstrand väg
Castréninkatu
Agricolankatu
Hämeentie
Sörnäistenrantatie
Siltasaarenkatu
K. Porthanink
Kolmaslinja
Eläintar-
hanlahti
Säästöpankin-
ranta
Hakanranta
Pitkänsillanranta
Siltavuoren-
salmi
Kaisan-
iemen-
lahti
Kaisaniemenranta
Siltavuorenranta
Nora Kajan
Maurinkatu
Meritullinkatu
Unioninkatu
Snellmaninkatu
Elisabetsgatan
15
Central Railway
Station
Fabianinkatu
Mariankatu
Pohjoisranta
Pohjoissatama
Kaisaniemenkatu
Snellmansgatan
Kirkkokatu
14
16
Hallituskatu
Mariegatan
Laivas tokatu
Katajan
8
Aleksanterinkatu
Unionsgatan
17
19
Luotsikatu
Merikasaminkatu
9
13
Pohjois esplanadi
N. esplanaden
18
Yrjönkatu
Market
Square
Kanavakatu
Kanalgatan
Eteläranta
■ **Tallinn
Ferry
Terminal**
Bulevarden
10
Fabianinkatu
11
Iso
Roobertinkatu
Hogbergsgatan
Kaserngatan
12
Eteläsatama
Fredriksgatan
katu
Laivasillankatu
Tähtitornik
Observgatan
Valksaari
To Suomenlinna Fortress
& Helsinki Zoo
Sepänkatu
Jääkärinkatu
Bergmansgatan
Luoto
Ryssasaari
Vuorimiehenkatu
Fabriksgatan
Itainen Puistotie Ostra Allen
Ehrenströmsvägen
Tehtaankatu
Puistokatu
Iso Puistotie
Stora Allen
20
Puolimatkansaari
Pietarinkatu
21
Juhani
Ahontie
Kaivopuisto
Havsgatan
Merisatamaranta
Ehrenströmintie
Merisatama

0   0.25 mi
0   0.25 km

You can store your luggage at the office seen on the far right of the main hall as you emerge from the trains. Lockers cost 3€ ($3.50) per day. A money exchange kiosk is also located in the main hall and is open daily from 7am to 9pm. For rail information, you can visit **Train Information Center** (℗ **0307/ 29-900**) on the righthand side of the main hall. It's possible to make seat reservations on Finnish trains at counters 1 through 10 Monday to Friday 8am to 9:30pm and Saturday and Sunday 9:30am to 9:30pm. To validate a rail pass, go to counters 14 through 17.

INFORMATION ELSEWHERE IN THE CITY

From the train station, walk 2 blocks down Keskuskatu turning left onto Pohjoisesplanadi, and you'll arrive at the **Helsinki City Tourist Office,** Pohjoisesplanadi 19 (℗ **09/169-3757**). It's open May 2 to September 30 Monday to Friday 9am to 8pm and Saturday and Sunday 9am to 6pm; off season Monday to Friday 9am to 6pm and Saturday 9am to 4pm.

Tourshop (℗ **09/2288-1400**), a service at the Helsinki Tourist Office, is your best bet for booking tours once you reach Helsinki. The staff here will make hotel reservations for 5€ ($5.75). The tourist office also sells air, bus, and cruise tickets; event tickets; and the money-saving **Helsinki Card** (see below).

GETTING AROUND

Helsinki is small enough to be explored on foot, but some of it's best attractions lie outside the city center, and you'll need to take a taxi or public transportation to get to them.

Visitors to Helsinki can purchase the **Helsinki Card,** which offers unlimited travel on the city's public buses, trams, subway, and ferries, and a free guided sightseeing bus tour (in summer daily, off season on Sun), as well as free entry to about 50 museums and other sights in Helsinki. The Helsinki Card is available for 1-, 2-, or 3-day periods. The price of the card for adults is 24€ ($27.60) for 1 day, 34€ ($39.10) for 2 days, and 42€ ($48.30) for 3 days. A card for children costs 9.50€ ($10.95) for 1 day, 12.50€ ($14.40) for 2 days, and 15€ ($17.25) for 3 days. The cards can be bought at 50 sales points in the Helsinki area, including the Helsinki City Tourist Office, travel agencies, and hotels.

You can also buy a **Tourist Ticket** for travel over a 1-, 3-, or 5-day period. This ticket lets you travel as much as you like within the city limits on all forms of public transportation except regional buses. A 1-day ticket costs 4.80€ ($5.50) for adults, 2.40€ ($2.75) for children 7 to 16; a 3-day ticket 14.40€ ($16.55) for adults, 7.20€ ($8.30) for children 7 to 16. Children under 7 travel free. Tickets can be purchased at many places throughout Helsinki, including the Helsinki City Tourist Office and transportation service depots, such as the Railway Square Metro Station, which is open Monday to Thursday 7:30am to 6pm and Friday 7:30am to 4pm.

The **City Transport Office** is at the Rautatientori metro station (℗ **09/472-2454**), open Monday to Thursday 7:30am to 6pm and Friday 7:30am to 4pm. The transportation system operates daily from 5:30am to 1:35am. A single ticket with transfer costs 2€ ($2.30) for adults, 1€ ($1.15) for children; a tram ticket is 1.70€ ($1.95) from the driver or 1.20€ ($1.40) if prepaid, with no right of transfer.

You can order taxis by telephone (℗ **0100/0700**), find them at taxi ranks, or hail them on the street. All taxis have an illuminated yellow sign that reads: TAKSI/TAXI. The basic fare costs 5€ ($5.75) and rises on a per-kilometer basis, as indicated on the meter. Surcharges are imposed in the evening (6–10pm) and on

Saturday after 4pm. There's also a surcharge at night from 10pm to 6am and on Sunday.

WHERE TO STAY

Cumulus Seurahuone ✪   Directly across the street from the railway station in the heart of Helsinki, this stylish and up-to-date hotel's origins go back to 1833, though the present building dates from 1913, when it was custom-built as an Art Nouveau, five-story apartment house. Some of the bedrooms are completely contemporary; other units retain some of the allure of their old-fashioned past, often with the original furnishings and such details as brass headboards.

Kaivokatu 12. FIN-00100. Helsinki. ✆ **09/69-141.** Fax 09/691-4010. 118 units. Sun–Thurs 206€ ($237) double; Fri–Sat 115€ ($132) double, 257€ ($296) suite. Rates include breakfast. AE, DC, MC, V. Tram: 3B, 3T, or 4. **Amenities:** Restaurant; bar; laundry; nonsmoking rooms. *In room:* Hair dryer.

Hotel Arthur *Value*   In high-priced Helsinki, the Arthur is an affordable stopover for the frugal rail traveler. A 4-minute walk from the rail station, this privately owned hotel is run by the local YMCA in a turn-of-the-20th-century building with an annex dating from 1950. The rooms are small and furnished in a standard motel fashion, but the cramped bathrooms have full plumbing. The hotel is known for its tasty breakfasts and its generous and reasonably priced lunch buffets.

Vuorikatu 19, FIN-00100 Helsinki. ✆ **09/173-441.** Fax 09/626-880. www.hotelarthur.fi. 143 units. June 15–Aug 18 and some weekends (Fri–Sun) in winter 88€ ($101) double; rest of year 110€ ($127) double. Year-round 148€–170€ ($170–$196) suite. Rates include breakfast. Additional bed 10€ ($11.50). AE, DC, MC, V. Tram: 1, 2, 3, 6, or 7. **Amenities:** Restaurant; bar; laundry; nonsmoking rooms. *In room:* Hair dryer.

Hotelli Finn *Value*   This small hotel is less than 1,000 feet from the rail station, set on the fifth and sixth floors of a dignified but rather austere city office building. It's a welcoming place, however, and has been in the hands of the same family owners since 1960. Rooms can comfortably house 2 to 4 guests; furnishings are rather basic but better than the average college dorm lodgings. The Finn's owners pride themselves on being one of the least expensive hotels in central Helsinki.

Kalevankatu 3B, FIN-00100 Helsinki. ✆ **09/684-4360.** Fax 09/6844-3610. www.hotellifinn.fi. 27 units. 65€ ($74.75) double without bathroom; 80€ ($92) double with bathroom. AE, DC, MC, V. Tram: 3, 4, 7, or 10. **Amenities:** Breakfast room; lounge.

Lord Hotel ✪ *Finds*   Opened in 1990 and a half mile (.8km) from the rail station, this hotel is a bit of an oddity and an atmospheric place to stay. A 1903 student center and university dormitory was combined with a newer annex and turned into an inviting hotel. The older building is intriguing architecturally in that it suggests a *faux* medieval fortress complete with tower and crenellations along with heavy ceiling beams. The well-furnished bedrooms are midsize, often boasting hardwood floors, Jacuzzi tubs in the bathrooms, and beautiful Finnish textiles covering the upholstery.

Lonnrotinkatu 29. FIN-00180 Helsinki. ✆ **09/615-815.** Fax 09/680-1315. www.lordhotel.fi. 48 units. Sun–Thurs 170€ ($196) double, Fri–Sat 93€ ($107) double; daily 270€ ($311) suite. Rates include breakfast. AE, DC, MC, V. Tram: 3B or 3T. **Amenities:** Restaurant; laundry; nonsmoking rooms; 1 room for those with limited mobility. *In room:* Hair dryer.

Rivoli Jardin ✪✪   This recently renovated and well-managed hotel is one of the best boutique hotels in Helsinki, and is just over ¼ mile (.4km) from the rail station. Custom designed as a hotel in 1984, it has stayed abreast of the times with frequent refurbishing, and a warm welcome awaits you in its stone- and

Moments Paying Homage to Finlandia & Sibelius

Jean Sibelius (1865–1957), composer of *Finlandia,* lived for more than half a century at Ainola Ainolantie (© 09/287-322) in Järvenpää, 24 miles (39km) from Helsinki. Few countries seem as proud of one of their native composers as the Finns are of Jean Sibelius. In 1903, while he was skiing with his brother-in-law, Sibelius discovered a forested hill, which inspired him to commission construction of what would eventually become his family home. He named it after his wife, Aino, and from 1904 maintained a residence there with his children for many years. Today, he and his wife are buried on the property, which has become a shrine for music lovers. Some claim that they can hear the beginning of his violin concerto as they approach the house on a still day.

Visitors can tour the interior of the Art Nouveau house, which remains as the maestro left it. There are no great antiques or art—in fact, Ainola is simplicity itself—just as Sibelius preferred it. In many places, the log walls remain in their natural state, and traditional tiled heating stoves are visible. The highlight of the exhibit is the grand piano. Some of the walls are decorated with the private paintings of the composer.

To get to the house, hop on a train from Central Helsinki Railway Station to Järvenpää. Admission is 5€ ($5.75) adults, 1€ ($1.15) children. Open June to August Tuesday to Sunday 10am to 5pm, May and September Wednesday to Sunday 10am to 5pm.

marble-clad lobby. All the midsize bedrooms are individually decorated, for the most part with water hyacinth furniture and exquisite woodcarvings. Rooms have wall-to-wall carpeting or Asian rugs placed on hardwood floors, and each has an attractively tiled bathroom.

Kasarmikatu 40, FIN-00130 Helsinki. © **09/681-500.** Fax 09/656-988. www.rivoli.fi. 55 units. 227€ ($261) double; 325€ ($374) suite. Rates include breakfast. AE, DC, MC, V. Tram: 10. **Amenities:** Breakfast room; bar; laundry; nonsmoking rooms; 1 room for those with limited mobility. *In room:* Hair dryer.

Sokos Hotel Klaus Kurki ⭐   Today a choice hotel, this 1912 brick structure was originally a small inn for out-of-town merchants who coveted a stay behind its romantic Art Nouveau facade. Sensitively modernized, it was last renovated in 2002 when all the midsize and well-furnished bedrooms were handsomely decorated and given more atmosphere and style with Finnish hand-woven rugs, French Belle Epoque poster art, and Tiffany-style lamps. Each guest room has a fully tiled bathroom. The hotel is about ¼ mile (.4km) from the rail station.

Bulevardi 2, FIN-00120 Helsinki. © **09/618-911.** Fax 09/4334-7100. www.sokoshotels.fi. 136 units. June 15–Aug 15 and selected weekends (Fri–Sat only), 89€ ($102) double; rest of year 215€ ($247) double. Rates include breakfast. AE, DC, MC, V. Tram: 3B, 3T, 6, or 10. **Amenities:** Restaurant; bar; laundry; nonsmoking rooms. *In room:* Hair dryer.

TOP ATTRACTIONS & SPECIAL MOMENTS

Eduskuntatalo (Finnish Parliament)   Near the post office and only a few blocks from the rail station, this building of pink Finnish granite (built in 1931) houses the 200 members of the one-chamber parliament (40% of whose members are women). The building looks austere on the outside, but it's much warmer inside. Members meet in a domed interior (Parliament Hall), decorated with sculpture by Wäinö Aaltonen. The architect, J. S. Sirén, who wanted to celebrate the new republic, chose a modernized neoclassic style.

Mannerheimintie 30. ℂ 09/4321. Free admission. Tours given Sat at 11am and noon, Sun at noon and 1pm; July–Aug also Mon–Fri at 2pm. Tram: 3B or 3T.

Finnish National Gallery ⊛⊛   Finland's largest selection of sculpture, painting, and graphic art is displayed at this museum. The Finnish National Gallery is host to three independent museums: the **Museum of Finnish Art,** the **Kiasma (Museum of Contemporary Art),** and the **Sinebrychoff Art Museum (Museum of Foreign Art).** The first museum is housed in the Ateneum building across from the railway station. More than a century old, it was designed by Theodore Höijer. The Museum of Finnish Art has the largest collection of Finnish artists, from the mid-1700s to 1960, as well as the works of some 19th- and 20th-century international artists.

Kaivokatu 2. ℂ 09/173-361. www.fng.fi/fng/rootnew/en/vtm/etusivu.htm. Admission 5.50€ ($6.35) adults, 4€ ($4.60) students and seniors, free for children under 18. Special exhibits, 6€–10€ ($6.90–$11.50). Free admission every Wed from 5–8pm. Tues and Fri 9am–6pm; Wed–Thurs 9am–8pm; Sat–Sun 11am–5pm. Tram: 3 or 6.

Helsinki City Museum   At Villa Hakasalmi, about ¼ mile (.4km) from the railway station, the museum presents the history of Helsinki from its founding up to modern times. A small-scale model of the town in the 1870s is on display. There is also an exhibit of home decorations from the 18th and 19th centuries, glass, porcelain, and toys.

Sofiankatu 4 (by Senate Sq.). ℂ 09/169-3933. Admission 3€ ($3.45), free for children under 18, free for everyone on Thurs. Mon–Fri 9am–5pm; Sat–Sun 11am–5pm. Tram: 1, 2, 3B, 3T, 4, 7A, or 7B.

Kiasma (Museum of Contemporary Art) ⊛   Part of the Finnish National Gallery (see above), this museum opened in 1998 and houses Finland's finest collection of contemporary art. An American architect, Steven Hall, designed the stunning 14,400-square-foot structure, which is ideally lit for displaying modern art. The permanent collection exhibits post-1960 Finnish and international art, but also features changing exhibitions. Based on the word *chiasma,* for crossovers in genetics and rhetoric, the name for the new museum suggests Finland's special ability to achieve crossovers between the worlds of fine art and high technology. A "mediatheque" concentrates on displaying the museum's media collections.

Mannerheiminaukio 2. ℂ 09/1733-6501. www.kiasma.fi. Admission 5.50€ ($6.25) adults, 4€ ($4.50) students and seniors, free for those under 18. Free admission every Friday from 5–8:30pm. Tues 9am–5pm; Wed–Sun 10am–8:30pm. Tram: 3B or 3T.

Lutheran Cathedral (Tuomiokirkko) ⊛   Dominating the city's skyline is one of the city's most visible symbols, a green-domed cathedral erected between 1830 and 1852. Built during the Russian administration of Helsinki in a severe, almost stark interpretation that reflected the glory of ancient Greece and Rome, the Lutheran Cathedral was designed by German-born architect Carl Ludvig Engel. It was inaugurated as part of the 19th-century reconstruction of Helsinki—usually in the neoclassical style—after a fire had destroyed most of the city. Today, the rites celebrated inside conform to the Evangelical Lutheran denomination. Extensive renovations, both to the cathedral and to its crypt, brought it back to its original beauty in 1998.

Senaatintori. ⓒ 09/709-2455. Free admission. June–Aug Mon–Sat 9am–6pm, Sun noon–8pm; Sept–May Mon–Fri 10am–4pm, Sat 10am–6pm, Sun noon–6pm. Tram: 1, 2, 3B, or 3T.

Mannerheim Museum ⭐⭐   You can visit the home of Baron Carl Gustaf Mannerheim, Finland's former field marshal and president—a sort of George Washington in this country. Now a museum, his former residence houses his collection of European furniture, Asian art and rugs, and personal items (uniforms, swords, decorations, gifts from admirers) that he acquired during his long career as a military man and statesman. The house remains the same as it was when he died in 1951. It's quite a hike from the train station and close to the water, so take the tram here.

Kallionlinnantie 14. ⓒ 09/635-443. Admission (including guided tour) 7€ ($8) adults, 5€ ($5.75) children 12–16, free for children under 12. Fri–Sun 11am–4pm. Tram: 3B or 3T.

National Museum of Finland ⭐⭐   This museum was designed in the style called National Romantic. Opened in 1916, it contains three major sections—prehistoric, historic, and ethnographic. The country's prehistory in the light of archaeological finds may be seen, revealing that after the Ice Age and at the dawn of the Stone Age humans made their homes in Finland. Of particular interest are the Finno–Ugric collections representing the folk culture of the various peoples of northeastern and eastern Europe as well as northwestern Siberia who speak a language related to Finnish. Church art of the medieval and Lutheran periods, folk culture artifacts, folk costumes and textiles, furniture, and an important coin collection are exhibited.

Mannerheimintie 34. ⓒ 09/4050-9544. www.nba.fi/NATMUS/Kmeng.html. Admission 5€ ($5.75) adults, 3.50€ ($4) students, free for children under 18. Free admission on Tues from 5:30–8pm. Tues–Wed 11am–8pm; Thurs–Sun 11am–6pm. Tram: 4, 7A, 7B, or 10.

Seurasaari Open-Air Museum ⭐⭐   In a national park on the island of Seurasaari (a short boat trip from the mainland) is clustered a miniature preview of Old Finland—about 100 buildings (authentically furnished), a 17th-century

---

Moments **Olympic Memories & a Flying Finn**

Way back in 1952 Helsinki hosted the Olympic Games at its **Olympia-stadion,** Paavo Nurmi tie 1 (ⓒ 09/440-363). Today a tower at that impressive sports stadium remains, and an elevator whisks passengers up to the top for a panoramic view of the city and the archipelago. The stadium, 1¼ miles (2km) from the city center, was originally built in 1938, but the Olympic Games scheduled for that year were cancelled due to the hostilities in Europe that eventually led to World War II. The seating capacity of the stadium is 40,000, larger than any other arena in the country. The stadium was closed and rebuilt between 1992 and 1994, and today is a first-rate sports venue. Outside the stadium is a statue by Wäinö Aaltonen of the great athlete Paavo Nurmi, "The Flying Finn." The runner is depicted in full stride and is completely nude, a fact that caused considerable controversy when the statue was unveiled in 1952. Admission is 2€ ($2.30) adults, 1€ ($1.15) children under 16. Open Monday to Friday 9am to 8pm, Saturday and Sunday 9am to 6pm. Tram: 3B, 3T, 4, or 10.

⟨Moments⟩ Exploring the Fortress of Finland

The 18th-century **Suomenlinna Fortress** ★★ (✆ **09/684-1880**; www.suomenlinna.fi/english/eng_entry.php3) is known as the "Gibraltar of the North," and lies on the archipelago, guarding the approach to Helsinki. With its walks and gardens, cafes, restaurants, and old frame buildings, the island makes for one of the most interesting outings from Helsinki. Originally built in the mid–18th century when Finland was a part of Sweden, the fortress was taken over by the Russians in 1808. After Finland gained independence in 1917, the fortress was given its present name, Suomenlinna, which means "the fortress of Finland." It served as part of the nation's defenses until 1973. The fortification work involved six islands, but today the main attraction is the part of the fortress on **Susisaari** and **Kustaanmiekka** islands, now joined as one body of land. Kustaanmiekka is a small, well-preserved bastioned fort with defense walls and tunnels. The main fortress is on Susisaari, which is also home to a number of parks and squares.

You can take a **ferry** from Market Square to Suomenlinna year-round beginning at 6:20am daily. The boats run about once an hour, and the last one returns from the island at 1:45am. The round-trip ferry ride costs 2€ ($2.30) for adults and 1€ ($1.15) for children.

The island has no "streets," but individual attractions are sign-posted. During the peak summer months (June–Sept), Suomenlinna maintains two information kiosks, one at Market Square (by the departure point for the Suomenlinna ferryboat) and a second on the island itself (near Tykistolahti Bay). The latter kiosk serves as the starting pont for **guided tours**—offered in English—of the fortress with a focus on its military history. Tours are scheduled between June and August (otherwise by appointment) daily at 10:30am, 1pm, and 3pm, and cost 6€ ($6.90) for adults and 3€ ($3.45) for children. The rest of the year, the guided tours, which must be reserved in advance, are offered on an as-needed basis and priced at 130€ ($150) for up to 16 participants.

church, and a gentleman's manor dating from the 18th century and containing period furnishings. In addition, visitors can see one of the "aboriginal" saunas, which resemble a smokehouse. The fire and verve associated with this collection of historic, freestanding buildings are most visible during the summer months, when you can visit the interiors, and when an unpretentious restaurant serves coffee, drinks, and platters of food. Although the buildings are locked during the winter months, you can still view the exteriors and explore the parkland that surrounds them. A wintertime walk through this place is not as far-fetched an idea as you might think—it's a favorite of strollers and joggers, even during snowfalls.

Seurasaari Island. ✆ **09/4050-9660.** www.nba.fi/MUSEUMS/SEURAS/Seurseng.htm. Admission 4.50€ ($5.20), free for children under 18. May 15–31 and Sept 1–15 Mon–Fri 9am–3pm and Sat–Sun 11am–5pm; June 1–Aug 30 Thurs–Tue 11am–5pm, Wed 11am–7pm. Closed Sept 16–May 14. Bus: 24 from the Erottaja bus stop, near Stockmann Department Store, to the island. The 3-mile (4.8km) ride takes about 15 min., and costs 2€ ($2.30) each way.

Sinebrychoff Art Museum (Museum of Foreign Art) ✦ *Finds*   Part of the Finnish National Gallery (see above), this museum was built in 1840 and still displays its original furnishings. It houses an extensive collection of foreign paintings from the 14th to the 19th centuries and has a stunning collection of foreign miniatures. The collection originated from the wealthy Sinebrychoff dynasty, a family of Russians who owned a local brewery and occupied this yellow-and-white neo-Renaissance mansion. They were great collectors of antiques, their taste leaning toward the opulent in furnishings. Their art collection was wide ranging, especially noted for its Dutch and Swedish portraits of the 17th and 18th centuries. There is also a stunning collection of porcelain. Outdoor concerts in summer are often staged in their formerly private park surrounding the estate.

Sinebrychoff, Bulevardi 40. ☎ 09/1733-6460. www.sinebrychoffintaidemuseo.fi. Admission 4€ ($4.60) adults, children under 18 free. Special exhibits 4€–8€ ($4.60–$9.20). Free admission every Thurs from 5–8pm. Tues and Fri 10am–6pm; Wed and Thurs 10am–8pm; Sat and Sun 11am–5pm. Tram: 6.

WHERE TO DINE

Bellevue RUSSIAN   Immensely popular, this restaurant dates from 1913 and is still serving the time-tested specialties that put it on the Helsinki culinary map in the first place. With Russian wines as a side offering, the menu offers all those favorites that delighted Finland's former tsarist rulers, including blinis, caviar, Russian-style herring, stuffed cabbage, and the inevitable chicken Kiev. The Bellevue is located in the center of the city, near the Uspenski Orthodox Cathedral. Most main courses are priced at the lower end of the scale.

Rahapajankatu 3. ☎ 09/179-560. Reservations required. Main courses 16€–57€ ($18.40–$65.55). AE, DC, MC, V. Mon–Fri 11am–midnight; Sat–Sun 5pm–midnight. Tram: 4.

Kellarikrouvi ✦ FINNISH/INTERNATIONAL   Built at the turn of the 20th century, this restaurant is installed in a former storage cellar for firewood and "winter potatoes." When it opened in 1965, it became the first restaurant in Helsinki to serve beer from a keg, which it still does today in great abundance. The cuisine is inspired, combining local Finnish recipes with innovative Continental influences.

Pohjoinen Makasiinikatu 6. ☎ 09/686-0730. Reservations recommended for dinner. Main courses 13.60€–26.50€ ($15.65–$30.50); fixed-price lunch (11am–2pm) 36€–39€ ($41.40–$44.85). AE, DC, MC, V. Mon–Fri 11am–midnight; Sat 4pm–midnight; Sun (upstairs section only) noon–midnight. Tram: 3B.

König ✦ SCANDINAVIAN   The great Finnish architect, Eliel Saarinen, who designed Helsinki's rail station, also designed this 1892 restaurant in the cellar of what used to be one of the largest banks in Finland. Many of the country's greatest artists, including the composer Jean Sibelius, made this their favorite dining

---

Moments **The Art of Crayfish Eating**

Every Finn looks forward to the crayfish season, which runs between July 20 and mid-September. Some 225,000 pounds of this delicacy are caught yearly in inland waters and you'll find it in virtually every restaurant in Helsinki. Called *rapu*, the crayfish is usually boiled in salt water and seasoned with dill. For Finns, the eating of crayfish is an art form, and they suck out every morsel of flavor. Of course, with all this slurping and shelling, you'll need a bib. After devouring half a dozen, Finns will down a glass of schnapps, but unless you're accustomed to schnapps, we suggest you order a beer or glass of white wine instead.

room. The grand culinary tradition still goes on today, and chefs continue to offer traditional dishes such as red deer chops but also keep abreast of modern cooking techniques.

Mikonkatu 4. ℂ **09/6844-0713.** Reservations required. Main courses 13€–32€ ($14.95–$36.80). AE, DC, MC, V. Winter Mon–Sat noon–midnight; summer Mon 7pm–1am, Tues–Sat 7pm–4am. Tram: 3B or 3T.

Ravintola Rivoli SEAFOOD/FRENCH/FINNISH   Visit this Art Nouveau restaurant, especially one of its dining sections called "Fish Rivoli," for some of the best and freshest tasting Finnish seafood, such as the grilled rainbow trout or freshly caught salmon from very chilly local rivers. The tasty dishes are

(Moments Traveling On to St. Petersburg

Known as Leningrad in its communist heyday, St. Petersburg is hailed as one of the most beautiful cities on the globe. Home of the famous Hermitage museums, the city is only a 7-hour train ride from Helsinki and is a popular destination with rail travelers. For 50€ ($57.50) one-way, you can head out daily from Helsinki on either a Finnish morning train, *Sibelius,* or a Russian afternoon train, *Repin,* to St. Petersburg. (**Note:** Russian rail improvements should, by 2005, have the trip time on the *Repin* down to 4 hr.)

Both trains offer first- and second-class service. The *Repin* uses old-style compartment seating with sleeping berths in the first-class section, while the *Sibelius* uses the modern style used on most trains in Europe. Note that only the *Sibelius* has nonsmoking sections (very large ones, at that). Both the Russian and Finnish trains have first-class restaurant cars, and the *Sibelius* also has a coffee bar.

Border formalities when traveling between the two countries are now at a minimum, and currency exchange and tax-free refunds are all smoothly handled on the trains. You don't even have to clear Customs unless you have something to declare.

Tip: Bring along your own supply of drinking water and a personal supply of toilet tissue for both the train and for use in St. Petersburg.

You no longer have to purchase tickets through a designated Intourist agency to get to St. Petersburg. Any travel agent in Helsinki can sell you a ticket. Note that reservations are mandatory and must be made at least 48 hours in advance of departure. Rail Europe sells *Sibelius* tickets for $145 in second class, $225 in first class.

Arrivals in St. Petersburg are at the rail station, **Findlandskhy Vokzal** on Ploschad Lenina (ℂ **812/168-7687**), where you can catch a taxi to your hotel. You can arrange your hotel through a Helsinki travel agent before leaving Finland. For more information on train service to St. Petersburg, head online to **www.vr.fi.**

Note: You will need a visa to enter Russia. Visas are issued by the nearest Russian embassy or consulate. Some agencies advertising travel to Russia can also help you obtain a visa. For information about visa assistance, check **www.visatorussia.com.** In the United States, contact the Russian Embassy, 2650 Wisconsin Ave. NW, Washington, DC 20007 (ℂ **202/298-5700**; www.russianembassy.org).

prepared with market-fresh ingredients, and some are inspired by French cooking techniques.

Albertinkatu 38. ℂ 09/643-455. Reservations recommended. Main courses 15€–38€ ($17.25–$43.70). AE, DC, MC, V. Mon–Fri 11am–midnight; Sat 5pm–midnight. Closed Sat June–Aug and bank holidays. Tram: 6. Bus: 14.

Ravintola Sipuli ★★ FINNISH   In the 1800s this was a warehouse, taking its name of *Sipuli* (onion) from the onion-shaped domes of the Orthodox Upenski Cathedral in the vicinity. Architects successfully turned the structure into a restaurant of atmosphere and charm, with thick beams, paneling, and brick walls. Today, the chef is known for his robust flavors and clever use of Finnish products, especially reindeer meat shipped down from Lapland.

Kanavaranta 3. ℂ 09/622-9280. Reservations recommended. Main courses 18€–29€ ($20.70–$33.35). AE, DC, MC, V. Mon–Fri noon–2pm and 6–midnight. Tram: 2, 4.

Wellamo ★ *Finds* FINNISH/FRENCH/RUSSIAN   On the residential island of Katajanokka, but easily reached by tram from the heart of the city, this elegant restaurant draws a steady stream of habitués. The menu features many dishes evocative of a Paris bistro, but also heads east to chilly Siberia for such delights as a regional ravioli stuffed with minced lamb, fresh herbs, mushrooms, and sour cream. The chef is also known for his many game dishes.

Vyäkatu 9. ℂ 09/663-139. Reservations recommended. Main courses 12€–19€ ($13.80–$21.85). AE, MC, V. Tues–Fri 11am–2pm and 5–11pm; Sat 5–11pm; Sun 1–8pm. Tram: 4.

SHOPPING

Most stores are open Monday to Friday 9am to 6pm and on Saturday 9am to 1pm. A new government regulation allows shopping on Sunday in June, July, August, and December. As a result, Forum and Stockmann (see below) are open during those months on Sunday from noon to 4pm.

The most important shopping neighborhoods are in the center of the city. They include **Esplanadi,** for those seeking the finest of Finnish design—but at high prices. Even if you don't buy anything, it's a delightful promenade in summer, and loaded with shops filled with the best of Finnish crafts, as well as a number of art galleries.

Esplanadi leads from the commercial heart of town all the way to the waterfront. Bordering the water is **Market Square (Kauppatori),** a fresh open-air market that's open Monday to Saturday. In summer, peddlers set up trolleys and tables to display their wares. Most of the goods for sale are produce (some of them ideal for picnic food), but there are souvenir and gift items as well.

The other main shopping section is called simply **Central,** beginning at Esplanadi and extending to the famous Central Helsinki Railway Station. Many of the big names in Finnish shopping are located here. One of the main shopping streets is **Aleksanterinkatu,** which runs parallel to Esplanadi, stretching from the harborfront to Mannerheimintie.

Other shopping streets, all in the center, include **Iso Roobertinkatu** and **Bulevardi,** lying off Esplanadi. Bulevardi starts at the Klaus Kurki Hotel and winds its way to the water.

Helsinki's largest department store, **Stockmann,** Aleksanterinkatu 52 (ℂ 09/ 1211; Tram: 3B), is also Finland's finest and oldest. Stockmann has a little bit of everything, the most diversified sampling of Finnish and imported merchandise of any store: glassware, stoneware, ceramics, lamps, furniture, furs, contemporary jewelry, clothes and textiles, handmade candles, reindeer hides—everything.

The **Forum Shopping Center,** Mannerheimintie 20 (Tram: 3B, 3T, 7A, or 7B), covering an entire block, houses 120 shops, a seven-story atrium, restaurants, and service enterprises—making it the number-one shopping center in Finland. You'll find a wide array of merchandise here, including art, gold, jewelry, food, clothing, yarns, leather, glasses, rugs, and watches.

NIGHTLIFE

The ballet and opera performances of the **Finnish National Opera,** Helsinginkatu 58 (© **09/4030-2211;** Tram: 3B), are internationally acclaimed. The ticket office is open Monday to Friday 9am to 6pm and Saturday 3 to 6pm. On performance nights, the ticket office stays open until the performance begins. The opera and ballet season runs from late August to May and tickets are 14€ to 80€ ($16–$92).

Although it has been reconfigured, redecorated, and reincarnated many times since it was established in 1915, **Baker's Family,** Mannerheimintie 12 (© **09/ 612-6330;** Tram: 3B), is the most deeply entrenched, long-lived drinking and dining complex in Helsinki. It sprawls across three floors, and on a busy night is often crammed with clubbers—many of them single. Most people come for the cafe, open daily 7am to 4am, or for one of the bars, open Monday to Saturday 11am to 2am.

Club Cream, Erottajan 7 (© **09/680-2665;** Tram: 3B, 3T), is one of the newest dance clubs in Helsinki, and offers two floors of space, two animated bars, lots of night owls under 35 from all Finnish subcultures, and powerful references to whatever's happening in the nightlife circles of London and Los Angeles. It's open Wednesday to Sunday from 9pm to 4am. The cover is 5€ ($5.75).

Storyville, Museokatu 8 (© **09/408-007;** Tram: 4, 7, or 10), is one of the busiest and most active live music venues in Helsinki and was named after the fabled red-light district of New Orleans; as such, it offers a menu of Créole and Cajun specialties to match. Full meals average 20€ to 30€ ($23–$34.50) each, and more important, live music—blues, jazz, Dixieland, soul, or funk—is featured Wednesday to Saturday from 6pm to 4am. The cover is 6€ to 8€ ($7–$9.25).

8

France

The civilization and history of France and the French way of life—the *savoir-faire* of its people—lure rail travelers from all over the world to this country that covers an area smaller than Texas. And the fact that it is among the easiest countries to travel by train doesn't hurt either. France leads all nations on the planet in rail technology, including the United States. Its TGV trains hold the world's friction rail speed record at 320 mph (514kmph). Rail lines, stretching some 24,000 miles (39,000km), go almost anywhere. In nearly all cases, visitors to France will find that a train will speed you quickly and rapidly to your destination, often at alarming speeds.

But France, often referred to as "the garden of Europe," is—perhaps more than any country in the world—a land to be savored, not sped through. Each region of the country is so intriguing and varied that you may immerse yourself in one province for so long that you'll never get back on the train to go see what's on the other side. It's better to get to know intimately one, two, or three regions than trying to explore them all. This is not a country to rush through on one of those quick rail tours ("If it's Tuesday, it must be Nice").

Of course, the primary language of the country is French, which might intimidate non-speakers, though it shouldn't—most tourism officials and nearly all rail personnel speak at least some English. So you should have little trouble riding the rails and making your requests known or getting your questions answered. And, as a final plus, though train travel is not cheap in France when compared to other countries, it's unquestionably the least expensive way to see the country.

HIGHLIGHTS OF FRANCE

On the tightest of schedules, particularly if you're traveling by rail to other European capitals such as London or Rome, you'll need 3 days for Paris—the logical starting point for any journey in France as it's the country's rail hub and one of the great rail hubs of Europe. While in Paris, see the world-class museums (including the **Musée du Louvre** and **Musée d'Orsay**); tour famous monuments, such as the **Eiffel Tower** and **Arc de Triomphe;** and bask in the glorious architecture of the city's magnificent churches, including **St-Chapelle** and, of course, the cathedral of **Notre-Dame.** But the city is also full of marvelous and evocative neighborhoods just waiting to be explored: Like Sartre, have a coffee and croissant on the **Left Bank,** then explore **St-Germain-des-Prés,** the ancient **Ile de la Cité,** the glamorous **Ile St. Louis,** the historic **Le Marais,** and, an absolute must-do—stroll down the famous **Champs-Elysées.**

Set aside a 4th day to journey south by rail to the magnificent palace of **Versailles,** an easy train trip from the French capital.

But don't make the mistake of limiting your visit to Paris, unless you'd call a trip to New York a look at America. France has a number of scenic and sight-filled provinces (enough to fill a whole book—*Frommer's France,* for example) just waiting to be explored. Note, however, that we've limited ourselves in this

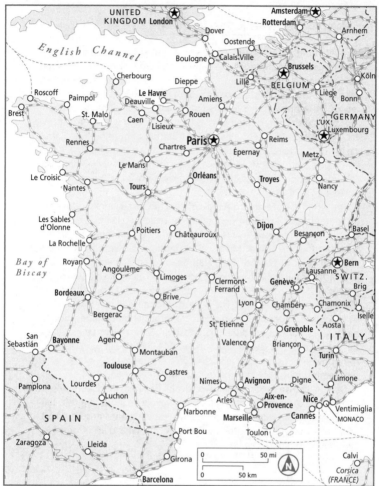

chapter to the most popular regions that are also easily reached by rail out of Paris. So you will find plenty about the Loire Valley, Provence, and the Riviera, but you won't see Brittany or Normandy (including the famous abbey of Mont-St-Michel) because it's very difficult to get to some of those places solely by train.

About 120 rail miles (113km) southwest of Paris stretches the "green heart of France," the breathtakingly beautiful region of the **Loire Valley.** The towns of this area have magic names, but they also read like Joan of Arc's battle register—Orléans, Blois, Tours. Every hilltop has a castle or palace, there are vineyards as far as your eye can see, the Loire winds like a silver ribbon, and walled cities cluster around medieval churches. It is estimated that the average visitor spends only 3 nights in the Loire Valley. A week would be better. Even then, you will have only skimmed the surface. If you're severely hampered by lack of time, then try at least to see the following châteaux: **Chenonceaux, Amboise, Azay-le-Rideau, Chambord, Chaumont,** and **Blois.**

Moments **Festivals & Special Events**

Parades, boat races, music, balls, and fireworks are all part of the ancient **Carnival of Nice,** which draws visitors from all over Europe and North America. This "Mardi Gras of the Riviera" begins sometime in February, usually 12 days before Shrove Tuesday, celebrating the return of spring with 3 weeks of parades, *corsi* (floats), *veglioni* (masked balls), confetti, and battles in which young women toss flowers. The climax is the century-year-old tradition of burning King Carnival in effigy, after *Les Batailles des Fleurs* (Battles of the Flowers), when teams pelt each other with flowers. Make reservations well in advance. For information, contact the Nice Convention and Visitors Bureau (© 08-92-70-74-07).

The world-class **Festival d'Avignon,** held the first 3 weeks in July, has a reputation for exposing new talent to critical acclaim. The focus is usually on avant-garde works in theater, dance, and music by groups from around the world. Much of the music is presented within the 14th-century courtyard of the Palais de l'Ancien Archeveché (the Old Archbishop's Palace). Other events occur in the medieval cloister of the Cathédral St-Sauveur. Part of the fun is the bacchanalia that takes place nightly in the streets. The prices for rooms and meals skyrocket, so make reservations far in advance. For information on dates, tickets, and venues, contact the **Bureaux du Festival,** Espace Saint-Louis, 20 rue du portail Boquier, 84000 Avignon (© 04-90-27-66-50; www.festival-avignon.com). Tickets cost 13€ to 30€ ($14.95–$34.50). Make hotel reservations early. For information, call © 04-90-27-66-50.

One of France's most famous festivals, the **Festival d'Automne** in Paris, is one of its most eclectic, focusing mainly on modern music, ballet, theater, and modern art. Contact the Festival d'Automne (© 01-53-45-17-00; www.festival-automne.com). Events take place from mid-September to late December.

The best center for touring, and the place with the best rail connections, is the ancient city of **Tours.** Many visitors also like to pay a rail visit first to the city of **Orléans,** with its evocative memories of Joan of Arc.

To continue your rail journey through France, head for **Provence,** where you'll need at least 3 days. High-speed TGV trains have put the south of France within an easy commute of Paris, speeding you to where you want to go in record times. The chief centers of the region are **Avignon,** seat of the popes during the 14th century; **Arles,** which once cast a spell over van Gogh and which inspired some of his greatest paintings; and **Aix-en-Provence,** home to Provence's most celebrated son, the artist Paul Cézanne.

To conclude your French rail trip, head to France's vacation hot spot par excellence for 2 to 3 days. Known to the world as the **Cote d'Azur** (the French name, of course, for its Riviera), this is a short stretch of curving coastline near the Italian border with a veritable bounty of hotels and resorts. It's also a land drenched in sunshine, sprinkled with vineyards and olive groves, and dotted with some of the world's most fascinating tourist meccas.

For the rail traveler, the resort of **Cannes** in the west and the city of **Nice** in the east make the best centers. Both have high-speed train connections to Paris. For a more sophisticated beach-style ambience, head to Cannes for at least 2 days, enjoying its glamour and style. But for a more typically Provençal city, make it Nice, which is also the best for sightseeing as it has far more museums and monuments, and is the better center for day excursions to hill towns such as **St-Paul-de-Vence,** and especially to **Monaco.**

1 Essentials

GETTING THERE

The French national carrier, **Air France** (© **800/237-2747;** www.airfrance. com), offers daily or several-times-a-week flights out of several North American cities to Paris.

Other major carriers offering direct flights to Paris out of North America include **American Airlines** (© **800/433-7300;** www.aa.com); **Continental Airlines** (© **800/525-0280;** www.continental.com); **Delta Air Lines** (© **800/ 241-4141;** www.delta.com); **US Airways** (© **800/428-4322;** www.usairways. com), and **Air Canada** (© **888/247-2262;** www.aircanada.ca).

British Airways (© **800/AIRWAYS;** www.britishairways.com) offers connecting flights to Paris from 18 U.S. cities, with a stop in either Heathrow or Gatwick airports in England. Other carriers offering connecting flights to Paris include **Aer Lingus** (© **866/IRISH-FLY;** www.aerlingus.com) and **Northwest/ KLM** (© **800/374-7747;** www.klm.com).

Flight time to Paris varies according to the departure city, but it generally takes 7 to 11 hours to get to France's capital from most major North American cities.

FRANCE BY RAIL

The *Société Nationale des Chemins de Fer* **(SNCF),** the French National Railway (and the parent company of Rail Europe), runs more than 3,000 train stations, supervises more than 21,000 miles (33,600km) of track, and is fabled for its on-time performance. About 50 of the country's cities are linked by some of the world's fastest trains and you can get from Paris to just about anywhere in a matter of hours. For information about train schedules in France, check out **www.sncf.com**.

France is also well connected to the major international rail lines running through Europe. High-speed **Artesia** trains connect Paris and Lyon to Milan in Italy; **Eurostar** connects Paris with London; **Thalys** trains link Paris with several cities in Belgium, the Netherlands, and Cologne in Germany; **TGV** trains connect a whole bunch of French cities with Brussels and a whole bunch of destinations in Switzerland; and **Elipsos** overnight hotel trains connect Paris with both Madrid and Barcelona. Regular EuroCity trains also connect major cities in France to other countries' rail networks. Paris is one of Europe's busiest rail junctions, with trains arriving at and departing from its six stations every few minutes from all over France and Europe.

PASSES

For information on the **Eurailpass, Eurailpass Flexi, France Railpass, France Rail 'n Drive Pass,** the new **France 'n Switzerland Pass,** and other multi-country options, see chapter 2.

The railpasses mentioned above, as well as point-to-point rail tickets within France are available through most travel agencies or through **Rail Europe**

(© **877/272-RAIL** in the U.S., **800/361-RAIL** in Canada; www.rail europe.com).

FOREIGN TRAIN TERMS

Welcome officers (called *Agents d'accueil*) wear orange caps and armbands and are found at major rail stations to help answer your questions. They are English speaking. In French, *résa* is a reservation, and before boarding a train in France, you must validate your ticket by having it *composté*—that is, stamped with the date and time—at one of the orange- or yellow-colored machines near the loading platform.

Ticket windows are marked *guichets,* and a lost items office is called *consigne manuelle.* SNCF's time schedules are *horaires.* Sleepers are known as *voitures-lits,* and in second-class sections you can often request *sièges inclinables* (reclining seats) for an extra fee.

A *supplement,* is a supplement, and these supplements are color coded. SNCF calendars designate days for rail travelers as *période bleue* or *période rouge.* Trips in the blue period get many discounts; trips in the red period are peak periods where you get no discounts. There is also a *période blanche* or white, when moderate discounts are available. To be eligible for a discount, each leg of your rail trip must begin during a period of the appropriate color. For a complete list of these red, white, and blue periods, request a *Calendrier Voyageurs* at any rail station information office. You can also buy point-to-point tickets in North America from Rail Europe.

PRACTICAL TRAIN INFORMATION

SNCF-operated, the heavily state-subsidized French rail system is one of the world's greatest. Trains radiate out from Paris like the spokes of a wheel, taking you to all parts of France, though service may not be as extensive in some regions as in others. The high-speed TGV *(Trains à Grande Vitesse)* trains are the pride of the SNCF, traveling 186 miles (300km) per hour.

The country also has regional express **Corail (TRN)** trains that offer modern comfort, are air-conditioned, and travel at speeds of about 60 mph. These trains are used on many major city links. T.E.R. trains are regional trains linking smaller cities to such transportation hubs as Paris, Nimes, and Toulouse. Comfort is marginal—no air-conditioning, for example—and trains are slow.

Tickets are most often valid for up to 2 months following purchase. In some very large train stations, such as those in Paris, separate ticket windows are set aside for different types of trains: Long haul is *grandes-lignes, banlieue* is for suburban lines. You can, of course, purchase tickets on board a train but you'll be hit with a hefty surcharge; and travel agents will sell you a rail ticket, but will charge you a stiff handling fee. This is one country where rail travel can get very expensive, so if you plan to travel quite a bit, a railpass makes sense. Railpasses should be hand-stamped at a designated rail station ticket window before you get on the first leg of your journey.

We'll admit that there is great freedom in seeing France by car, but the high price of gasoline or petrol, the never-ending high *autoroute* tolls, and the stiff car-rental fees in the country make driving super expensive. Trains are a whole lot cheaper. If you want to drive, even a little, consider the **France Rail 'n Drive Pass** (see above).

For one-way travel, request *un billet aller-simple;* for round-trip journeys, ask for *un billet aller-retour.* In all cases, round-trips are less expensive than two one-way tickets.

For SNCF routes, timetables, and information check **www.sncf.com** or **www.raileurope.com**.

RESERVATIONS   Although you can travel on most French trains without reservations, they are compulsory on Eurostar, Thalys, Artesia, EuroCity, Elipsos, and TGVs, as well as many regional *Rapide* trains. You have until noon to reserve seats on lines running between 5pm and the following day. If you're heading into or out of Paris on an international train, make reservations at least 2 to 3 days in advance. Reservations can be made as early as 60 days in advance of departure online at SNCF's website or through Rail Europe. During holiday periods, at Easter, and in July and August (especially Aug), reservations should be made as far in advance as possible.

If you're taking an overnight train, be sure to reserve your sleeping accommodations (see "Services & Amenities," below) as far in advance as possible.

Having a railpass does not exempt you from reservations fees or supplements. ***Insider's tip:*** If you're on a tight budget, instead of taking the overnight train from Paris to Nice and paying supplements and *couchette* (a sleeping berth sort of like a fold-out bunk bed) fees, take a day train with unreserved seats. You'll get a nice view of the countryside and save a lot of euros.

SERVICES & AMENITIES   Nearly all the country's trains, including the TGV, offer both first- or second-class seating, the first-class carriages designated with the number 1. Second-class travel on French trains is the equivalent of first-class travel in many parts of the world.

On overnight trains, you can reserve a couchette, although you must reserve one in advance (up to 1¼ hr. before departure) and pay a supplement, usually about 20€ ($23) per passenger in Europe, approximately $28 if done in North America before you leave home. The second-class couchette compartments are crowded with six berths; there are only four in the first-class couchette compartments.

The elegant and expensive (and more comfortable) way to go is with a sleeper (called *voitures-lits*), filled with real beds. Second-class sleepers hold two to three passengers; first-class sleepers hold one to two people. Sleeper prices start at 40€ ($46) per person and go way up. Hotel trains that run in France include the Trenhotel Ellipsos running between Spain and France and the Artesia Nuit that runs between France and Italy.

A special feature for frugal travelers on many French trains is known as *Cabine 8*. This is available in second-class coach travel where you'll find compartments with 8 bunk beds that are free for your use. You can reserve these bunks for a standard seat reservation fee.

Although food and drink are served aboard most French trains, especially long-haul ones, if you want to guard your euros, board a French train with enough bottled water and food for the length of your journey as the prices are very high indeed. Sometimes "minibar trolleys" are wheeled through the carriages, selling food and drink, but the charges are similarly lethal (equivalent to buying a drink in a New York theater at intermission). Most main major rail stations have restaurants and bars, but the prices at these establishments are also often ridiculously high. There's a great shortage of station delis serving wines, pâtés, cheese, and fresh bread. If you have time, you can often leave the station and search for a local deli or grocery store where the prices are far more reasonable.

SNCF operates a special telephone line (© **0800/154-753**) for rail travelers with disabilities who might face accessibility issues.

Train Schedules & Travel Times in France

From	To	Type of Train	# of Trains	Frequency	Travel Time
Paris	Tours	TRN	5	Daily	2 hr. 16 min.–2 hr. 30 min.
Paris	Tours	TGV	1	Daily	1 hr. 10 min.
Paris	Orleans	TRN	6	Daily	1 hr. 3 min.–1 hr. 41 min.
Paris	Avignon	TGV	14	Daily	2 hr. 31 min.–3 hr. 41 min.
Paris	Arles	TGV	1	Daily	3 hr. 58 min.
Paris	Aix-en-Provence	TGV	3	Daily	3 hr.
Paris	Cannes	TGV	5	Daily	5 hr. 11 min.–5 hr. 43 min.
Paris	Nice	TGV	5	Daily	5 hr. 3 min.–5 hr. 43 min.
Nice	Monaco	TRN	24	Daily	17 min.–32 min.

FAST FACTS: France

Area Code All French telephone numbers now consist of 10 digits, the first two of which are like an area code. If you're calling anywhere in France from within France, just dial all 10 digits—no additional codes are needed. If you're calling from the United States, drop the initial 0 (zero).

Business Hours Business hours are erratic, as befits a nation of individualists. Most banks are open Monday through Friday from 9:30am to 4:30pm. Many, particularly in small towns, take a lunch break at varying times. Hours are usually posted on the door. Most museums close 1 day a week (often Tues), and they're generally closed on national holidays. Usual hours are from 9:30am to 5pm. Refer to the individual listings.

Generally, offices are open Monday to Friday 9am to 5pm, but always call first. In Paris or other big French cities, stores are open from 9 or 9:30am (but often 10am) to 6 or 7pm without a break for lunch. Some shops, particularly those operated by foreigners, open at 8am and close at 8 or 9pm. In some small stores, the lunch break can last 3 hours, beginning at 1pm. This is more common in the south than in the north.

Climate France's weather varies from region to region and even from town to town as few as 12 miles (19km) apart. Despite its northern latitude, Paris never gets very cold—snow is a rarity. Rain usually falls in a kind of steady, foggy drizzle and rarely lasts more than a day. May is the driest month. The Mediterranean coast in the south has the driest climate. When it does rain, it's heaviest in spring and autumn. (Cannes sometimes receives more rainfall than Paris.) Summers are comfortably dry. Provence dreads *le mistral* (an unrelenting, hot, dusty wind), which most often blows in winter for a few days but can last up to 2 weeks.

Documents Required All foreign (non-French) nationals need a valid passport to enter France. The French government no longer requires visas for U.S. citizens, providing they're staying in France for less than 90 days. Citizens of Canada do not need visas.

Electricity In general, expect 200 volts or 50 cycles, though you'll encounter 110 and 115 volts in some older places. Adapters are needed to fit sockets. Many hotels have two-pin (in some cases, three-pin) sockets for razors. It's best to ask your concierge before plugging in any appliance.

Embassies & Consulates If you have a passport, immigration, legal, or other problem, contact your consulate. Call before you go, as they often keep odd hours and observe both French and home-country holidays. The Embassy of the **United States,** at 2 rue St-Florentin (℃ **01-43-12-22-22;** Métro: Concorde), is open Monday through Friday from 9am to 6pm. Passports are issued at its consulate at 2 rue St-Florentin (℃ **01-43-12-22-22;** Métro: Concorde). The Embassy of **Canada** is at 35 av. Montaigne, 8e (℃ **01-44-43-29-00;** Métro: F.D.-Roosevelt or Alma-Marceau), open Monday through Friday from 9am to noon and 2 to 5pm.

Health & Safety In general, France is viewed as a "safe" destination. You don't need to get shots; most food is safe and the water in France is potable. If you're concerned, order bottled water. It is easy to get a prescription filled in French towns and cities, and nearly all places contain English-speaking doctors at hospitals with well-trained staffs. In other words, France is part of the civilized world.

The most common menace, especially in large cities, particularly Paris, is the plague of pickpockets and gangs of Gypsy children who surround you, distract you, and steal your purse or wallet (especially in Métro stations). Likewise, one should protect one's valuables on French trains, where most robberies occur while passengers are asleep. Much of the country, particularly central France, remains relatively safe, though no place in the world is crime-free. Those intending to visit the south of France, especially the Riviera, should exercise caution—robberies and muggings here are commonplace.

Holidays In France, holidays are *jours feriés.* The main holidays include New Year's Day (Jan 1), Easter Sunday and Monday, Labor Day (May 1), V-E Day in Europe (May 8), Whit Monday (May 19), Ascension Thursday (40 days after Easter), Bastille Day (July 14), Assumption of the Blessed Virgin (Aug 15), All Saints' Day (Nov 1), Armistice Day (Nov 11), and Christmas (Dec 25).

Mail Most post offices are open Monday through Friday from 8am to 7pm and Saturday from 8am to noon. Allow 5 to 8 days to send or receive mail from your home. Airmail letters within Europe cost .45€ (50¢); to the United States and Canada, .65€ (75¢). Airmail letters to Australia and New Zealand cost .80€ (90¢). You also can exchange money at post offices. Many hotels sell stamps, as do local post offices and cafes displaying a red TABAC sign outside.

Police & Emergencies If your wallet gets stolen, go to the police station in person (ask at your hotel's front desk for a close location). Otherwise, you can get help anywhere in France by calling ℃ **17** for the police or ℃ **18** for the fire department *(pompiers).*

Telephone The French use a Télécarte, a phone debit card, which you can purchase at rail stations, post offices, and other places. Sold in two versions, it allows you to use either 50 or 120 charge units (depending on the card) by inserting the card into the slot of most public phones. Depending on the type of card you buy, the cost is 7.45€ ($8.55).

If possible, avoid making calls from your hotel, as some French establishments will double or triple the charges.

To call France from North America, dial 011, then 33 (the country code for France), the area code, and the eight-digit number. Although French area codes are two digits (the 1st digit is always a 0), you do not dial the zero when calling from abroad. For example, the Hôtel Négresco (℡ **04-93-16-64-00**) contains the area code for southeastern France (04). **To call long-distance within France,** you simply dial this 10-digit number. But if you call from North America, you would dial ℡ 011-33-4-93-16-64-00.

To call North America from France, a relatively inexpensive way is to use a telephone credit card. Access codes for the major U.S.-based carriers are as follows: **AT&T,** ℡ **0800-99-00-11; MCI,** ℡ **0800-99-00-19; Sprint,** ℡ **0800-99-00-87.**

Tipping The law requires all bills to say *service compris,* which means the tip has been included. But French diners often leave some small change as an additional tip, especially if service has been exceptional.

Some general guidelines: For hotel staff, tip 1.05€to 1.50€ ($1.20–$1.75) for every item of baggage the porter carries on arrival and departure, and 1.50€ ($1.75) per day for the maid. In cafes, service is usually included. Tip taxi drivers 10% to 15% of the amount on the meter. In theaters and restaurants, give cloakroom attendants at least .75€ to 1.20€ (85¢–$1.40) per item. Give restroom attendants about .30€ (35¢) in nightclubs and such places. Give cinema and theater ushers about .30€ (35¢). For guides for group visits to museums and monuments, .75€ to 1.50€ (85¢–$1.75) is a reasonable tip.

2 Paris ★★★

Paris has been celebrated in such a torrent of songs, poems, stories, books, paintings, and movies that for millions of people the capital of France is an abstraction rather than a city. To most North American visitors, the city is still "Gay Paree," the fairy-tale town inviting you for a fling, the hub of everything "European," and the epitome of that nebulous attribute known as "chic." Paris remains the metropolis of pleasure, the picture postcard of blooming chestnut trees and young couples kissing by the Seine.

Paris is the glamour capital of the globe, by day a stone mosaic of delicate gray and green, by night a stunning, unforgettable sea of lights—white, red, orange. Broad, tree-lined boulevards open up before you, the mansions flanking them looming tall, ornate, and graceful. Everywhere you look are trees, squares, and monuments—and train stations. For Paris is also the center of France's extensive web of rail networks and a major international rail hub. Because of its far-reaching connections—by train to all of continental Europe and by air to North America—the city is a natural spot to begin a multi-country rail tour of Europe. Name a major city in Europe and you can almost assuredly get there from Paris without too much hassle. And the same holds true for most of the major cities of France as well.

STATION INFORMATION
GETTING FROM THE AIRPORTS TO THE TRAIN STATIONS

Paris has two international airports: **Aéroport d'Orly,** 8½ miles (14km) south of the city, and **Aéroport Roissy–Charles de Gaulle,** 14¼ miles (23km) northeast of the city. A shuttle, which is 15.50€ ($17.85), makes the 50- to 74-minute journey between the two airports about every 30 minutes.

At **Charles de Gaulle** (© 01-48-62-22-80), foreign carriers use Aérogare 1, while Air France wings into Aérogare 2. From Aérogare 1, you take a moving walkway to the checkpoint and Customs. The two terminals are linked by a *navette* (shuttle bus). The shuttle also transports you to the **Roissy rail station,** from which fast **RER** (Réseau Express Régional) trains leave every 15 minutes heading to such Métro stations as Gare du Nord (see below), Châtelet, Luxembourg, Port-Royal, and Denfert-Rochereau. A typical fare from Roissy to any point in central Paris is 14€ ($16.10) in first class, 9.80€ ($11.25) in second class.

Note: Underneath Aérogare 2 is a TGV rail station. If you're headed for Avignon, Tours, or Brussels, you can catch a train here, but trains running through this station *do not go to Paris!*

You can also take an **Air France Coach** (© 08-92-35-08-20) to central Paris for 10€ ($11.50). It stops at the Palais des Congrès (Port Maillot), and then continues on to place Charles-de-Gaulle-étoile, where subway lines can carry you to any point in Paris. That ride, depending on traffic, takes between 45 and 55 minutes. The shuttle departs about every 15 minutes between 5:30am and 11pm.

Another option is the **Roissybus** (© 08-92-68-77-14), departing from the airport daily from 5:45am to 11pm and costing 8.80€ ($10.10) for the 45- to 50-minute ride. Departures are about every 15 minutes, and the bus will take you near the corner of rue Scribe and place de l'Opéra in the heart of Paris.

A **taxi** from Roissy to the central Paris rail stations will cost about 40€ to 45€ ($46–$51.75), but from 8pm to 7am the fares are 40% higher. Long lines for taxis form outside each of the airport's terminals and are surprisingly orderly.

Orly Airport (© 01-49-75-15-15) has two terminals—Orly *Sud* (South) for international flights and Orly *Ouest* (West) for domestic flights. They're linked by a free shuttle bus (trip time: 15 min.).

Air France Coaches leave from Exit E of Orly Sud and from Exit F of Orly Ouest every 15 minutes between 5:30am and 11pm for a major rail terminus, Gare des Invalides; the fare is 7.50€ ($8.65). Returning to the Airport, buses leave the Invalides terminal for Orly Sud or Orly Ouest every 15 minutes, taking about 30 minutes.

Another way to get to central Paris is via the free **shuttle bus** that leaves both of Orly's terminals about every 15 minutes for the nearby Métro and RER train station (Pont-de-Rungis/Aéroport-d'Orly). RER trains take 35 minutes for rides into the city center. A trip to Les Invalides, for example, is 9.50€ ($10.95).

A **taxi** from Orly to central Paris costs about 35€ to 40€ ($40.25–$46), more at night. Don't take a meterless taxi from Orly—it's much safer (and usually cheaper) to hire one of the metered cabs, which are under the scrutiny of a police officer.

INSIDE THE STATIONS

There are 6 major train stations in Paris. **Welcome Offices** in the city's rail stations (except Gare St-Lazare) and at the Eiffel Tower can give you free maps, brochures, and *Paris Selection,* a French-language monthly listing current events and performances. There is a Tourist Information Office that offers hotel

Paris

MONTMARTRE

Moulin Rouge **13**

bd. de Clichy

place Pigalle

bd. de Rochechouart

bd. de la Chapelle

Gare du Nord

av. Trudaine

rue Condorcet

rue de Magenta

rue de Dunkerque

La Fayette

rue du Faubourg St-Martin

rue Blanche

rue N.D. de Lorette

rue Pigalle

asino e Paris

Ste-Trinité

azare

St-Vincent de Paul

rue de Chabrol

Gare de l'Est

Notre-Dame de Lorette

La Fayette

Folies Bergère

rue de Paradis

St-Laurent

quai de Valmy

bd. Haussmann

Opéra Garnier

bd. des Italiens

place de l'Opéra

rue du 4 Septembre

bd. Montmartre

bd. de Bonne Nouvelle

rue du Faubourg St-Denis

rue de Strasbourg

rue du Faubourg St-Martin

place de la République

pucines

14 Bourse des Valeurs

rue de Richelieu

rue St-Augustin

lace des Petits Champs

ndôme

rue du Mail

rue d'Aboukir

rue Réaumur

bd. St-Martin

Conservatoire des Arts et Métiers

avenue de la République

St-Roch

Palais Royal

place A. Malraux

rue de Valois

Bourse du Commerce

Forum des Halles

bd. de Sébastopol

rue de Turbigo

rue Beaubourg

rue du Temple

bd. du Temple

bd. Voltaire

St-Ambroise

ILERIES

place du Carrousel

Musée du Louvre **15**

rue de Rivoli

rue St-Martin

30

31

rue des Archives

rue de Turenne

LE MARAIS

rue St-Martin

quai des Tuileries

Archives Nationales

St-Denis

bd. Beaumarchais

rue du Chemin Vert

Voltaire

quai Malaquais

28

Théâtre du Châtelet **27**

St-Merri

rue St-Antoine

St-Gervais

place des Vosges **36**

rue de la Roquette

cole Nationale es Beaux-Arts

32

Hôtel de Ville

St-Paul

Théâtre de la Bastille

16 ST-GERMAIN-DES-PRÉS

quai des Grands Augustins

ILE DE LA CITÉ

26

Cloître N.Dame

quai de l'Hôtel de Ville

place de la Bastille

bd. St-Germain

17

18

24

23

25

33 Notre-Dame

ILE ST-LOUIS

St-Louis

bd. Henry IV

Opéra Bastille

rue du Faubourg St–Antoine

22

quai de la Tournelle

pont de Sully

37

rue de Charenton

Sorbonne

21

rue Saint Jacques

rue des Ecoles

bd. St-Germain

Institut du Monde Arabe

avenue Daumesnil

Palais du Luxembourg

19

20

QUARTIER LATIN

quai Saint Bernard

bd. de la Bastille

av. L. Rollin

de Vaugirard

JARDIN DU LUXEMBOURG

Panthéon

Université Paris VII

Lyon

bd. Diderot

Gare de Lyon

rue d'Assas

rue Gay Lussac

rue d'Ulm

JARDIN DES PLANTES

quai de Bercy

Université Paris V

rue Claude Bernard

rue Buffon

Gare d'Austerlitz

quai d'Austerlitz

Seine

quai de la Rapée

d. du Montparnasse

net

U MONTPARNASSE

St-Médard

rue Censier

Université Paris III

pont d'Austerlitz

quai d'Austerlitz

pont de Bercy

bd. de Port Royal

bd. Saint Marcel

quai de Bercy

Observatoire de Paris

bd. Arago

bd. Raspail

bd. St-Jacques

place d'Italie

bd. de l'Hôpital

rue Jeanne d'Arc

bd. Vincent d'Arc

Auriol

(i) Information

✉ Post Offoce

— Railway

🚉 Rail Station

★ Paris

FRANCE

Avignon

⌐Tips The New Airport Shuttle

Cheaper than a taxi for one or two people but more expensive than airport buses and trains, the **Paris Shuttle** (ℂ **01-43-90-91-91;** www.paris shuttle.com) will pick you up in a minivan at Charles de Gaulle or Orly and take you to your hotel or rail station for 23€ ($26.45) for one person or 17€ ($19.55) per person for parties of two or more. It'll take you to the airports from your hotel for the same price. The **Blue Vans** (ℂ **01-30-11-13-00)** offers a similar service, charging 22€ ($25.30) for one passenger or 14€ ($16.10) per person for larger groups going to Charles de Gaulle. Both accept American Express, Diners Club, MasterCard, and Visa, but only if you book online.

---

reservations at the **Gare de Lyon** (see below). If you need a hotel room, and you arrive at another station, visit the city's main tourist office (see "Information Elsewhere in the City," below).

Paris' North Station or **Gare de Nord** (Métro: Gare du Nord), 18 rue de Dunkerque, is a major gateway to France. Passengers from the English Channel ports of Boulogne and Calais arrive here, as do trains from the Netherlands, Belgium, and Germany. It is also the termination point for Eurostar trains arriving from London and for Thalys trains from Brussels and Amsterdam. For rail information, go to the office across from platform #1 daily 6am to 11pm. Seat reservations on TGV trains and sleeping car reservations can be made here. Across from platform #3 is a kiosk that exchanges money daily 6:15am to 11:30pm. There are also ATMs scattered throughout the station. **Eurostar (www.eurostar.com)** has its own terminal and reservations offices in the building, and there's a special waiting room upstairs from the main terminal. For more on Eurostar, see chapter 10.

The East Station or **Gare de l'Est** (Métro: Gare de l'Est), place de 11 Novembre 1918, is the main terminal for departures into eastern France, with continuing service to such countries as Switzerland, Austria, Germany, and Luxembourg. The Rail Information Center here lies between platforms #6 and #7 and is open daily 8:45am to 8pm. You can make seat reservations here but only Monday to Saturday. A currency exchange kiosk, located in the main terminal opposite platforms #25 and #26, is open daily 6:45am to 10pm. ATMs are also available.

Gare de Lyon (Métro: Gare de Lyon), 20 blvd. Diderot, is the best equipped in Paris, and is the gateway station for passengers heading for Provence and the French Riviera, as well as Italy and western Switzerland. Train information and reservations are handled at an office in the exact center of the station, open Monday to Saturday 8am to 10pm, Sunday 8am to 7pm.

A most helpful Tourist Information and Hotel Reservations Office is located in the Paris Convention and Visitors Bureau, found in the station's main ticket hall. It's open Monday to Saturday 8am to 8pm. For hotel reservations fees, see "Information Elsewhere in the City," below. This station is also the site of **Restaurant Le Train Bleu** (ℂ 01-43-43-09-06; www.le-train-bleu.com), the most elegant train station restaurant in Europe. Open since 1901, the restaurant features good food in a fanciful Belle Epoque–style dining room.

Gare d'Austerlitz (Métro: Gare d'Austerlitz), 55 quai d'Austerlitz, is the arrival and departure point for trains heading into the central and southwestern sections of France and going on to Iberia (Spain and Portugal). The grand Train

Hotel Elipsos trains to Madrid *(Francisco de Goya)* and Barcelona *(Joan Miró)* depart from and arrive in this station. In the foyer of the station (not the main hall) is a Train Information Center open Monday to Saturday 7:30am to 7:45pm. Seat reservations can also be made here. A money exchange office in the main hall is open daily 6:30am to 11pm.

Two other minor stations are **Gare St-Lazare** (Métro: Gare St-Lazare), with trains departing for Normandy, and **Gare de Montparnasse** (Métro: Montparnasse-Bienvenue), with trains going to Brittany and TGV departures to southwestern France.

The stations above are not connected to each other by rail, but all are linked by bus, which is preferable to the Métro if you have luggage. Each of the stations above also contains luggage storage lockers, cafes, bars, washing facilities, and waiting rooms. You can call for train station information over the phone at (✆ **08-92-35-35-35** daily between 7am and 8pm. You can also make reservations at this number.

Warning: The stations and surrounding areas are usually seedy and frequented by pickpockets, hustlers, hookers, and addicts. Be alert, especially at night.

INFORMATION ELSEWHERE IN THE CITY

The **main Tourist Information Office** is at 127 av. Des Champs-Elysées, 8e ((✆ **08-92-68-31-12;** Métro: Georges-V), where you can get details about Paris and the provinces. It's open April through October, daily from 9am to 8pm (closed May 1), and November through March, daily from 11am to 6pm (closed Dec 25). The staff reserves hotel rooms but only on the same day, charging 3€ ($3.45) for a 1-star hotel, 4€ ($4.60) for a 2-star; 6€ ($6.90) for a 3-star, and 7.50€ ($8.65) for a 4-star.

There is also a branch of the tourist office in the base of the Eiffel Tower (open only May–Oct Mon–Sat 8am–8pm).

THE CITY LAYOUT

Paris is surprisingly compact and an excellent city for strollers. Occupying 432 square miles (696 sq. km), it's home to more than 10 million people. The River Seine divides Paris into the *Rive Droite* **(Right Bank)** to the north and the *Rive Gauche* **(Left Bank)** to the south. These designations make sense when you stand on a bridge and face downstream (west)—to your right is the north bank, to your left the south. A total of 32 bridges link the Right Bank and the Left Bank, some providing access to the two islands at the heart of the city—**Ile de la Cité,** the city's birthplace and site of Notre-Dame; and **Ile St-Louis,** a moat-guarded oasis of 17th-century mansions.

The "main street" on the Right Bank is, of course, **avenue des Champs-Elysées,** beginning at the Arc de Triomphe and running to place de la Concorde. Avenue des Champs-Elysées and 11 other avenues radiate like the arms of an asterisk from the Arc de Triomphe, giving it its original name, place de l'étoile (*étoile* means "star"). It was renamed place Charles-de-Gaulle following the general's death; today, it's often referred to as place Charles-de-Gaulle-Etoile.

ARRONDISSEMENTS IN BRIEF   The heart of medieval Paris was the **Ile de la Cité** and the areas immediately surrounding it. As Paris grew, it absorbed many of the once-distant villages, and today each of these *arrondissements* (districts) retains a distinct character. They're numbered 1 to 20 starting at the center and progressing in a clockwise spiral. The key to finding any address in Paris is to look for the arrondissement number, rendered either as a number followed by "e" or "er" (1er, 2e, and so on). If the address is written out more formally, you can tell what arrondissement it's in by looking at the postal code. For example, the address may be written with the street name, then "75014 Paris." The last two digits, 14, indicate that the address is in the 14th arrondissement, Montparnasse.

On the Right Bank, the **1er** is home to the Louvre, place Vendôme, rues de Rivoli and St-Honoré, Palais Royal, and Comédie-Française—an area filled with grand institutions and grand stores. At the center of the **2e** is the Bourse (Stock Exchange), making it the city's financial center. Most of the **3e** and the **4e** is referred to as the Marais, the old Jewish quarter that in the 17th century was home to the aristocracy—today, it's a trendy area of boutiques and restored mansions as well as the center of Paris's gay and lesbian community. On the Left Bank, the **5e** is known as the Latin Quarter, home to the Sorbonne and associated with the intellectual life that thrived in the 1920s and 1930s. The **6e,** known as St-Germain-des-Prés, stretches from the Seine to boulevard du Montparnasse. It is associated with the 1920s and 1930s and known as a center for art and antiques; it boasts the Palais and Jardin du Luxembourg. The **7e,** containing both the Tour Eiffel and Hôtel des Invalides, is a residential district for the well heeled.

Back on the Right Bank, the **8e** epitomizes monumental Paris, with the triumphal avenue des Champs-Elysées, the Elysées Palace, and the fashion houses along avenue Montaigne and the Faubourg St-Honoré. The **18e** is home to Sacré-Coeur and Montmartre and all that the name conjures of the Bohemian life painted most notably by Toulouse-Lautrec. The **14e** incorporates most of Montparnasse, including its cemetery, whereas the **20e** is where the city's famous lie buried in Père-Lachaise and where today the recent immigrants from North Africa live. Beyond the arrondissements stretch the vast *banlieue,* or suburbs, of Greater Paris, where the majority of Parisians live.

GETTING AROUND
BY METRO (SUBWAY)   The Métro (© **08-92-68-77-14**) is the fastest and most efficient means of transportation in Paris. All lines are numbered, and the final destination of each line is clearly marked on subway maps, in the underground passageways, and on the train cars. The Métro runs daily from 6:30am to around 1:15am. It's reasonably safe at any hour, but beware of pickpockets.

Note: To familiarize yourself with Paris's Métro, check out the **color map** on the inside front cover of this book.

To make sure you catch the correct train, find your destination on the map, then follow the rail line it's on to the end of the route and note the name of the final destination—this final stop is the direction. In the station, follow the signs labeled with your direction in the passageways until you see it labeled on a train.

Transfer stations are *correspondances*—some require long walks; Châtelet is the most difficult—but most trips require only one transfer. When transferring, follow the orange CORRESPONDANCE signs to the proper platform. Don't follow a SORTIE (exit) sign or you'll have to pay another fare to get back on the train.

Many of the larger stations have maps with push-button indicators that light up your route when you press the button for your destination.

On the urban lines, it costs the same to travel to any point: 1.30€ ($1.50). At the turnstile entrances to the station, insert your ticket and pass through. At some exits, tickets are also checked, so hold on to yours. There are occasional ticket checks on trains and platforms and in passageways, too.

Value **Saving on Travel**

When purchasing Métro tickets, a *carnet* (book of coupons) is the best buy—10 tickets for 10€ ($11.50). You can also purchase a **Paris-Visite,** a tourist pass valid for 1, 2, 3, or 5 days on the public transportation system, including the Métro, buses, and RER (Réseau Express Régional) trains (most not included on a Eurailpass). (The RER has both first- and second-class compartments, and the pass lets you travel in first class.) As a bonus, the funicular ride to the top of Montmartre is included. The cost ranges from 8.35€ ($9.60) for a 1-day pass to 26.65€ ($30.65) for 5 days. The card is available at RATP (Régie Autonome des Transports Parisiens), tourist offices, or the main Métro stations (© 08-36-68-77-14), and through Rail Europe.

Another discount pass is **Carte Mobilis,** which allows unlimited travel on all bus, subway, and RER lines during a 1-day period for 5.20€ ($6) depending on the zone. Ask for it at any Métro station.

Most economical, for anyone who arrives in Paris early in the week, is a **Carte Orange.** Sold at large Métro stations, it allows 1 week of unlimited Métro or bus transit within central Paris for 14.50€ ($16.70). These passes are valid from any Monday to the following Sunday, and are sold only on Mondays, Tuesdays, and Wednesdays. You'll have to submit a passport-size photo in order to buy the pass.

BY BUS Buses are much slower than the Métro, and the majority run from 7am to 8:30pm (a few operate until 12:30am, and 10 operate during early-morning hours). Service is limited on Sunday and holidays. Bus and Métro fares are the same; you can use the same tickets on both. Most bus rides require one ticket, but some destinations require two (never more than two within the city limits).

At certain stops, signs list the destinations and numbers of the buses serving that point. Destinations are usually listed north to south and east to west. Most stops are also posted on the sides of the buses. During rush hours, you may have to take a ticket from a dispensing machine, indicating your position in the line at the stop.

If you intend to use the buses a lot, pick up an RATP bus map at the office on place de la Madeleine, 8e, or at the tourist offices at RATP headquarters, 53 bis quai des Grands-Augustins, 6e. For detailed recorded information (in English) on bus and Métro routes, call © **08-92-68-77-14.**

BY TAXI It's impossible to get one at rush hour, so don't even try. Taxi drivers are organized into a lobby that keeps their number limited to 15,000.

Watch out for common rip-offs. Always check the meter to make sure you're not paying the previous passenger's fare. Beware of cabs without meters, which often wait outside nightclubs for tipsy patrons, or settle the tab in advance. You can hail regular cabs on the street when their signs read LIBRE. Taxis are easier to find at the many stands near Métro stations.

The flag drops at 1.50€ ($1.75), and from 7am to 7pm you pay 1€ ($1.15) per kilometer (.6 miles). From 7pm to 7am, you pay 1.10€ ($1.25) per kilometer. On airport trips, you're not required to pay for the driver's empty return ride.

You're allowed several pieces of luggage free if they're transported inside and are less than 11 pounds. Heavier suitcases carried in the trunk cost 1.50€ to 2€

($1.75–$2.30) apiece. Tip 12% to 15%—the latter usually elicits a *"Merci."* For radio cabs, call ℂ **01-44-52-23-58**—note that you'll be charged from the point where the taxi begins the drive to pick you up.

WHERE TO STAY

Although Paris hotels are quite expensive, there is some good news. Scores of lackluster Paris lodgings have been renovated and offer much better value in the moderate-to-inexpensive price range.

The nightmare summer of 2003 notwithstanding, hot weather doesn't last long in Paris, so most hotels don't have air-conditioning (we'll note in the reviews below if a hotel does). To avoid a noise problem when you have to open windows, request a room in the back when making a reservation.

Galileo Hotel ⭐ *Finds* This charming and elegant town house hotel is only a short walk from the Champs-Elysées and close to Gare St-Lazare. Owners Roland and Elisabeth Buffat have built up a good reputation with their attractively furnished and affordable bedrooms, which are filled with modern comforts (including air-conditioning). The most coveted and spacious are rooms 100, 200, 501, and 502, each opening onto a glass-covered veranda.

54 rue Galilée, 75008 Paris. ℂ **01-47-20-66-06**. Fax 01-47-20-67-17. www.galileohotel.com. 27 units. 163€ ($187) double. AE, DC, MC, V. Métro: George-V. **Amenities:** Laundry; rooms for those with limited mobility. *In room:* Hair dryer.

Grand Hôtel St-Michel Located in a 19th-century building in the heart of the Latin Quarter, this hotel has been tastefully and sensitively restored and decorated with antique reproductions and elegant fabrics. Its 6th-floor bedrooms open onto views over the rooftops of Paris; the most desirable rooms have balconies with views of the Sorbonne and the Pantheon. All but four rooms have both showers and tubs in the bathrooms (the rest have showers only).

19 rue Cujas, 75005 Paris. ℂ **01-46-33-33-02**. Fax 01-40-46-96-33. www.grand-hotel-st-michel.com. 45 rooms. 160€ ($184) double; 220€ ($253) triple. AE, DC, MC, V. Métro: Cluny–La Sorbonne. RER: Luxembourg or St-Michel. **Amenities:** Bar; laundry. *In room:* Hair dryer.

Hôtel Aviatic Deep in the heart of Montparnasse, this hotel has been completely remodeled although many of its old architectural touches remain, including an inner courtyard with a vine-covered wall lattice, and a lobby with marble columns, antiques, and crystal chandeliers. Its conservatory is an oasis of plants and natural light, and its Empire Lounge is a tasteful, relaxing retreat. Run by the same family for more than a century, Aviatic offers midsize bedrooms with lots of thoughtful extras such as air-conditioning and good reading lamps.

105 rue de Vaugirard, 75006 Paris. ℂ **01-53-63-25-50**. Fax 01-53-63-25-55. www.aviatic.fr. 43 units. 130€–170€ ($150–$196) double; 250€–297€ ($288–$342) suite. AE, DC, MC, V. Métro: Montparnasse-Bienvenue or St-Placide. **Amenities:** Laundry; nonsmoking rooms. *In room:* Hair dryer.

Hôtel Britannique This attractive and well-furnished boutique hotel enjoys a privileged position close to the Louvre and Saint-Chapelle. The French call it a *hotel de charme*, and so it is, with a slightly English aura as suggested by its name. The public rooms could be the setting for an Agatha Christie novel, and the immaculate and soundproof bedrooms in this renovated 19th-century town house are studies in taste and comfort.

20 av. Victoria, 75001 Paris. ℂ **01-42-33-74-59**. Fax 01-42-33-82-65. www.hotel-britannique.fr. 39 units. 157€–180€ ($181–$207) double; 280€ ($322) suite. AE, DC, MC, V. Métro: Châtelet. **Amenities:** Laundry. *In room:* Hair dryer.

Hôtel Burgundy ★ *Value*   Two British-born entrepreneurs took a former bordello and an adjacent 1830s boarding house where Baudelaire wrote poetry in the 1860s and turned them into this seamless and stylish hotel. Just off the place de Madeleine, this tastefully furnished town mansion is an exceptional value for its location and offers handsomely decorated bedrooms with modern conveniences. Bedrooms were completely renovated in 2001.

8 rue Duphot, 75001 Paris. ℂ **01-42-60-34-12.** Fax 01-47-03-95-20. www.burgundyhotel.com. 89 units. 165€–195€ ($190–$224) double; 300€–305€ ($345–$351) suite. AE, DC, MC, V. Métro: Madeleine or Concorde. **Amenities:** Restaurant; bar; laundry. *In room:* Hair dryer.

Hôtel de la Place des Vosges ★ *Value*   Built 350 years ago, this hotel is a 2-minute walk from the beautiful city square from which it takes its name. The author, Victor Hugo, lived around the corner from this well-managed and small-scale property, which was once a stable for the horses of Henri IV. Last renovated in 2002, the hotel offers cozy bedrooms with beamed ceilings and adjoining tile-clad bathrooms (with tub or shower).

12 rue de Birague, 75004 Paris. ℂ **01-42-72-60-46.** Fax 01-42-72-02-64. www.hotelplacedesvosges.com. 16 units. 101€–140€ ($116–$161) double. AE, MC, V. Métro: Bastille. **Amenities:** Laundry. *In room:* Hair dryer.

Hôtel de l'Université ★   This *hotel de charme* is popular with North American visitors and is installed in a restored 300-year-old town house. Its Left Bank location is much favored by the literati, and it is filled with atmospheric touches such as antiques-filled rooms, splendid staircases and fireplaces (evocative of its status as a former convent), rattan beds, vaulted ceilings, and oak pillars. Try for room no. 35, which has a fireplace and opens onto a courtyard with a fountain. All bedrooms have air-conditioning.

22 rue de l'Université, 75007 Paris. ℂ **01-42-61-09-39.** Fax 01-42-60-40-84. www.hoteluniversite.com. 27 units. 155€–255€ ($178–$293) double. AE, MC, V. Métro: St-Germain-des-Prés. **Amenities:** Bar; laundry. *In room:* Hair dryer.

Hôtel du Pas-de-Calais   This hotel is a good choice for those nostalgic for some of that old St-Germain-des-Prés bohemian atmosphere—in fact Jean-Paul Sartre worked on his play, *Dirty Hands,* in room no. 41. A much-needed renovation at the dawn of the millennium transformed the hotel's once-dowdy atmosphere into something a bit lighter and brighter. The inner bedrooms open onto a secluded courtyard with garden tables set out. All rooms have air-conditioning.

59 rue des Sts-Pères, 75006 Paris. ℂ **01-45-48-78-74.** Fax 01-45-44-94-57. 40 units. 145€–214€ ($167–$246) double; 275€ ($316) suite. AE, DC, MC, V. Métro: St-Germain-des-Prés or Sèvres-Babylone. **Amenities:** Laundry. *In room:* Hair dryer.

Hotel Le Tourville ★   Between the Eiffel Tower and Les Invalides, this small *luxe* hotel is located in a town house that dates from the Belle Epoque era of the 1890s. Today it's been renovated and tastefully furnished with old paintings, antiques, and contemporary chairs and sofas. The four best accommodations open onto a terrace. The air-conditioned bedrooms are light in color and have such homey touches as quilted bedspreads; the large bathrooms are clad in black marble and white tiles.

16 av. De Tourville, 75007 Paris. ℂ **01-47-05-62-62.** Fax 01-47-05-43-90. www.hotelletourville.com. 30 units. 145€–215€ ($167–$247) double; 310€ ($357) suite. AE, DC, MC, V. Métro: Ecole Militaire. **Amenities:** Bar; laundry; nonsmoking rooms. *In room:* Hair dryer.

Hôtel Queen Mary ★   A model of charm and homey comfort, this hotel is housed in a restored turn-of-the-20th-century building with an iron-and-glass canopy. All the midsize bedrooms and spacious suites are air-conditioned and have deep mahogany furnishings, comfortable beds, and luxurious fabrics. All but five bathrooms have both tubs and showers (others are shower only). Other grace notes include a flowery patio and a liberal sprinkling of antiques in the public rooms.

9 rue Greffulhe, 75008 Paris. ℰ **01-42-66-40-50.** Fax 01-42-66-94-92, www.hotelqueenmary.com. 36 units. 149€–178€ ($171–$205) double; 239€ ($275) suite. AE, DC, MC, V. Métro: Madeleine, Saint-Lazare, or Havre-Caumartin. **Amenities:** Bar; nonsmoking rooms; rooms for those with limited mobility. *In room:* Hair dryer.

Hôtel Saint-Merry ✦ *Finds*   This former bordello, with its 18th-century ceiling beams still intact, is today a little boutique hotel that's a choice address for an arts-oriented crowd. Rooms are a bit small but are handsomely furnished and comfortable, with a lot of atmosphere, including neo-Gothic architectural details. Once in total decay, the surrounding Marais quarter has now been completely gentrified, and is great for strolling about.

78 rue de la Verrerie, 75004 Paris. ℰ **01-42-78-14-15.** Fax 01-40-29-06-82. www.hotelmarais.com. 12 units. 160€–230€ ($184–$265) double; 335€ ($385) suite. Métro: Hôtel de Ville or Châtelet. **Amenities:** Laundry. *In room:* Hair dryer.

Hôtel St-Louis ✦ *Value*   Believe it or not, this most affordable hotel occupies some of the most expensive real estate in Paris. Filled with antiques and loaded with atmosphere, the restored 17th-century town house lies on the romantic Ile St-Louis, right between the Left and Right Banks. Admittedly, the bedrooms are small but they are cozy and filled with charm and tasteful appointments. If you opt for one of the top-floor rooms, you might get a small balcony opening onto some of Paris's best cityscapes.

75 rue St-Louis-en-l'Ile, 75004 Paris. ℰ **01-46-34-04-80.** Fax 01-46-34-02-13. www.hotelsaintlouis.com. 19 units. 130€–145€ ($150–$167) double; 210€ ($242) suite. AE, MC, V. Métro: Pont Marie or St-Michel. **Amenities:** Laundry. *In room:* Hair dryer.

TOP ATTRACTIONS & SPECIAL MOMENTS

The French capital contains some of the world's greatest museums and some of its most impressive monuments, but the main attraction of Paris remains Paris itself. You'll make that discovery yourself the moment you start sightseeing. For unless you're taking an organized tour, you are liable to become so ensnared by the vistas you find en route to a particular sight that you run the risk of never getting there.

No single palace, museum, church, or monument is as captivating as any of the dozen street settings of this city. They work like sirens' songs on a visitor's senses, luring you into hours of aimless rambling when you should be steering resolutely toward some three-star edifice.

There are people—and you well might agree with them—who find visiting museums in Paris redundant. Why sacrifice the sunshine to pursue art and culture through dim museum corridors when every Seine-side stroll brings you vistas the masters have painted and every city square is a model of architectural excellence?

If that is your view, stick with it. Of the almost 100 highly worthy Paris museums, only 2 or 3 are "required viewing" for the world traveler: the Louvre, Centre Pompidou, and the Musée d'Orsay. So, before we hit the must-see museums, here are the greatest districts for strolling and discovering, with monuments galore.

PLACE DE LA CONCORDE ★★★   Regarded by many as the most beautiful urban square in the world, this immense 85,000-square-yard expanse is so vast that your eye can't take it in at one glance. The center of the oval is swarming with cars, a motorist's nightmare, but the hugeness of the place seems to swallow them up.

In the middle, looking pencil-small, rises a 33-centuries-old obelisk from Egypt, flanked by cascading fountains. Grouped around the outer edges are 8 statues representing 8 French cities. Near the statue of Brest was the spot where the guillotine stood during the Revolution. On Sunday morning of January 21, 1793, King Louis XVI lost his royal head there, and was followed by 1,343 other victims, including Marie Antoinette and subsequently, Danton and Robespierre, the very men who lad launched the Terror.

The Place borders the Tuileries Gardens on the east, and on the west the second great showpiece of Paris, the . . .

CHAMPS-ELYSEES ★★★   You get a bit tired of repeating "the most famous in the world," but, of course, this *is* the world's most famous promenade. Pointing from the Place de la Concorde like a broad, straight arrow to the Arc de Triomphe at the far end, this avenue is at its best when lit at night.

The automobile showrooms and gift stores have marred the once-impeccable elegance of this stretch, but this is still the greatest vantage point from which to watch Paris roll and stroll by, preferably while sipping a cold drink at one of the many cafes that line the sidewalk.

TROCADERO   This is actually a series of adjoining sights, which a master touch of city planning has telescoped into one (a characteristic Parisian knack). From the Place du Trocadéro, you can step between the two curved wings of the **Palais de Chaillot** and gaze out on a view that is nothing short of breathtaking. At your feet lie the **Jardins de Trocadéro,** centered by fountains. Directly in front, **Pont d'Iéna** spans the Seine. Then, on the opposite bank, rises the iron immensity of the **Tour Eiffel.** And beyond, stretching as far as your eye can see, the **Champ de Mars,** once a military parade ground but now a garden landscape with arches and grottoes, lakes, and cascades.

THE SEINE ISLANDS ★★★   **Ile de la Cité,** the "egg from which Paris was hatched," lies quietly in the shadow of Notre-Dame. The home of French kings until the 14th century, the island still has a curiously medieval air, with massive gray walls rising up all around you, relieved by tiny patches of parkland.

Just behind Notre-Dame, sunken almost to the level of the river, is the **Memorial de la Déportation,** the monument to the thousands of French men, women, and children who perished in Nazi concentration camps from 1940 to1945. You step down into a series of granite chambers with narrow, iron-barred windows, horribly reminiscent of the actual killing pens—and just as bare. Hewn into the stone walls are the nightmarish names of the camps, each one like the tolling of a funeral bell: Auschwitz—Bergen—Belsen—Dachau—Buchenwald—Mathausen—Treblinka . . .

Back on the ground level, you'll see an iron bridge leading over to **Ile St-Louis.** This smaller and even quieter of the river islands has remained almost exactly as it was in the 17th century, after it had been divided up into private building lots. Sober patrician houses stand along the four quays, and the fever-beat of the city seems a hundred miles away.

PLACE VENDOME ★★★   This is *the* textbook example of classical French architecture, a pure gem set in the fashionable heart of the Right Bank. The pillared palaces encircling the square include the Ritz Hotel as well as the Ministry of Justice. The center is crowned by a 144-foot-high column, erected to commemorate Napoléon's greatest victory—Austerlitz. The actual column is stone, but the enclosing spiral band of bronze was cast from the 1,200 cannons (a fantastic number) captured by the emperor in the battle. The statue on top of the pillar is, of course, Napoléon, restored here after being pulled down twice: once by Royalist reactionaries, the second time by Communard revolutionaries.

A TOUR OF LE MARAIS ★★★ Very few cities on the earth boast an entire district that can be labeled a sight. Paris has several. The Marais or marshland is the vaguely defined maze of streets north of the **Place de la Bastille.**

During the 17th century, this was a region of aristocratic mansions, which lost their elegance when the fashionable set moved elsewhere. The houses lost status, but they remain standing. Le Marais is increasingly fashionable, and many artists and craftspeople have moved in and restored the once-decaying mansions.

Take the Métro to the place de la Bastille to begin your tour of the neighborhood. The actual Bastille, of course, is gone now (currently a hub of traffic), though it once housed such illustrious tenants as "The Man in the Iron Mask" and the Marquis de Sade. The mob attack on the fortress on July 14, 1789, touched off the French Revolution, and Bastille Day, a major French holiday, commemorates the storming of the prison.

If you don't mind risking your life, you can cross the square to look as the **Colonne de Juillet,** which, surprisingly, honors the victims of the July Revolution of 1830 that marked the supremacy of Louis-Philippe. The winged god of Liberty crowns the column.

From place de la Bastille, head up rue Saint-Antoine, cutting right on rue des Tournelles, with its statue honoring Beaumarchais *(The Barber of Seville).* Take a left again onto the Pas-de-la-Mule, "the footsteps of the mule," which will carry you to . . .

PLACE DES VOSGES ★★★ An enchanted island rather than a city square, this silent, serenely lovely oasis is the oldest square in Paris and the most entrancing.

Laid out in 1605 by order of King Henry IV, it was once called "Palais Royale" and was the scene of innumerable cavaliers' duels. The Revolutionary government changed its name but—luckily—left its structure intact. In the middle is a tiny park, and on 3 sides an encircling arcaded walk, supported by arches and paved with ancient, worn flagstones.

That's all, but the total effect is so harmonious, so delicately balanced between mellow stone and green trees, that it works like a soothing balm on the nerves. Spend half an hour there and you're ready to face the pedestrian traffic again.

At No. 6 on the square is the **Maison De Victor Hugo.** The house in which Victor Hugo lived and worked from 1832 to 1848 has been turned into a miniature museum. You probably know Hugo as a literary great, but here you'll also see the drawings, carvings, paintings, and pieces of furniture he made. The windows of his study overlook the square, and it's easy to see where he drew his inspiration.

QUARTIER LATIN ★★★ The Latin Quarter lies in the 5th Arrondissement on the Left Bank and consists of the streets winding around Paris University, of which the **Sorbonne** is only a part.

The logical starting point for touring this area is the **Place Saint-Michel,** right on the river, decorated by an impressive fountain. This was the scene of some of the most savage fighting during the uprising of the French Resistance in August 1944. Here—as in many, many other spots—you'll see the moving little name tablets, marking the place where a Resistance fighter fell: *"Ici est Tombé . . . le 19 Août 1944. Pour la Libération de Paris."*

Running straight south is the main thoroughfare of the quarter, the wide, pulsating **boulevard St-Michel** (called boul "Mich" by the locals). But turn left instead and dive into the warren of dogleg alleys adjoining the river—**rue de la Huchette, rue de la Harpe, rue St-Séverin.** Thronged with students; tingling with the spice smells of Arabian, African, and Vietnamese cooking; narrow, twisting, and noisy, the alleys resemble an Oriental bazaar more than a European city. This impression is aided by the incredibly garish posters advertising horror movies, belly dancers, and sticky Algerian sweets; the crush of humanity; the honking of cars bullying a path through the swarming crowds.

Emerge at the **Church of St-Séverin** and you're back in Paris again. Dating from the 13th century, this flamboyant Gothic edifice acts like a sanctuary of serenity at the edge of an ant heap.

Head down the **rue St-Jacques** and Paris reasserts herself completely. The next crossing is the **boulevard St-Germain,** lined with sophisticated cafes and some of the most avant-garde fashion shops in town.

MONTMARTRE ★★★ This name has caused chaos and confusion in many an unwary visitor. So just to make things clear—there are three of them in Paris.

The first is the **boulevard Montmartre,** a busy commercial street nowhere near the mountain. The second is the tawdry, expensive, would-be naughty, and utterly phony amusement belt along the **boulevard de Clichy,** culminating at **Place Pigalle** (the "Pig Alley" of World War II GIs). The third—*the* Montmartre we're talking about—lies on top, and on the slopes of the actual *Mont.*

The best way to get here is to take the Métro to **Anvers,** then walk to the nearby rue de Steinkerque, and ride the curious little funicular to the top. It operates between 6am and 11pm.

Montmartre used to be the city's artists' village, glorified by masters such as Utrillo, painted, sketched, sculpted, and photographed by ten thousand lesser lights. The tourists, building speculators, and nightclub entrepreneurs came and most of the artists went, but a few still linger. And so does some of the village charm that once drew them. Just enough to give you a few delightful hours, and leave you nostalgic for a past you wish you'd known.

The center point, **Place de Tertre,** looks like an almost-real village square, particularly when the local band is blowing and puffing oompah music. All around the square run terrace restaurants with dance floors and colored lights. Gleaming through the trees is the **Basilica of Sacré-Coeur.**

Behind the church and clinging to the hillside below are steep and crooked little streets that seem—almost—to have survived the relentless march of progress. **Rue des Saules** still has Montmartre's last vineyard. **Rue Lepic** still looks—almost—the way Renoir and the melancholy van Gogh and the dwarfish genius Toulouse-Lautrec saw it. This—almost—makes up for the blitz of portraitists and souvenir stores and postcard vendors up on top.

Arc de Triomphe ★★★ At the western end of the Champs-Elysées, the Arc de Triomphe is the third of the trio of great Paris symbols and the largest triumphal arch in the world, about 163 feet high and 147 feet wide. Its location in the center of it all is unequalled in the city, but that same location makes it pretty difficult to reach for the uninitiated. Don't try crossing the square to reach it! Take the underground passage. With a dozen streets radiating from the "Star," the traffic circle is vehicular roulette.

Commissioned by Napoléon in 1806 to commemorate his Grande Armée's victories, the arch wasn't completed until 1836, under Louis-Philippe. The arch is engraved with the names of the 128 victories of Napoléon and the 600 generals who participated in them. You can take an elevator or climb the stairway to the top, where there's an exhibition hall with lithographs and photos depicting the arch throughout its history. From the observation deck, you have a panoramic view of the Champs-Elysées as well as such landmarks as the Louvre, the Eiffel Tower, and Sacré-Coeur.

Underneath the arch burns the Flame of Remembrance that marks the tomb of France's unknown Soldier. The effect at night is magical—if only that light weren't burning for millions of young men who lost their lives in war.

Place Charles de Gaulle-Etoile, 16e. (℗ **01-55-37-73-77**. www.monuments.fr. Admission 7€ ($8.05) adults, 4.50€ ($5.20) ages 18–25, free for 17 and under. Apr–Sept daily 10am–11pm; Oct–Mar daily 10am–10:30pm. Métro: Charles de Gaulle-Etoile. Bus: 22, 30, 31, 52, 73, or 92.

Basilique du Sacré-Coeur ★★★   Montmartre's crowning achievement is a white church that, along with the Eiffel Tower, dominates the skyline of Paris, though its view of Paris takes precedence over the basilica itself. Its gleaming white domes and *campanile* (bell tower) tower over Paris like a Byzantine church of the 12th century. But it's not that old: After France's defeat by the Prussians in 1870, the basilica was planned as an offering to cure the country's misfortunes; rich and poor alike contributed. Construction began in 1873, but the church wasn't consecrated until 1919. The interior is decorated with mosaics, the most striking of which are the ceiling depiction of Christ and the mural of the Passion at the back of the altar. The crypt contains what some believe is a piece of the sacred heart of Christ—hence the church's name.

On a clear day, the vista from the dome can extend for 35 miles (56km). You can also walk around the inner dome of the church, peering down like a pigeon (one is likely to be keeping you company).

Place St-Pierre, 18e. (℗ **01-53-41-89-00**. www.paris.org/Monuments/Sacre.Coeur. Free admission to basilica; joint ticket to dome and crypt 5€ ($5.75) adults. Basilica open daily 7am–11pm; dome and crypt daily 9am–7pm. Métro: Abbesses; take the elevator to the surface and follow the signs to the *funiculaire*, which goes up to the church for the price of a Métro ticket.

Centre Pompidou ★★★   Dreamed up in 1969 by then–French president Georges Pompidou, this temple for 20th-century art was designed by Richard Rogers and Renzo Piano, opened in 1977, and became the focus of immediate controversy. Its bold exoskeletal architecture and the brightly painted pipes and ducts crisscrossing its transparent facade (green for water, red for heat, blue for air, and yellow for electricity) created a toy factory–like impression that was jarring in the old Beaubourg neighborhood. Relaunched in 2000, in what has been called "the most avant-garde building in the world," the newly restored Pompidou Centre is packing in the art-loving crowds again.

The **Musée National d'Art Moderne** ★★★ housed in the center offers a large collection of 20th-century art. With some 40,000 works, this is the big draw, although only some 850 works can be displayed at one time. Minor Cubists are represented alongside such giants as Braque and Picasso (many of his harlequins). The museum has beefed up its permanent collection considerably with many acquisitions. A large part of the collection is devoted to American artists.

> ## (Moments As Twilight Falls over Paris
>
> Even if you have only 24 hours in Paris and can't explore most of the sights recommended in this chapter, try to make it to Sacré-Coeur at dusk. Here, as you sit on the top steps, the church at your back, the Square Willette in front of you, nighttime Paris begins to come alive. First, a twinkle like a firefly; then all of the lights go on. One young American got carried away describing it all: "Here, away from the whirling taxis, concierges, crazy elevators, and tipping problems, the sound of Paris permeates by osmosis." Try to see it.

The permanent collection includes works ranging from the Fauves to Icelandic Conceptual art. Among the sculpture, which leans heavily on the use of 20th-century metals, is a walk-through Calder and his ironic wire portrayal of the late Josephine Baker. Other sculpture includes works by Henry Moore and Jacob Epstein. Seasonally, special exhibitions are organized.

Place Georges-Pompidou, 4e. ⓒ 01-44-78-12-33. www.centrepompidou.fr. Admission 10€ ($11.50) adults, 8€ ($9.20) students, free for under age 18. Special exhibits 8.50€ ($9.80) adults, 6.50€ ($7.50) students, free for under age 13. Wed–Mon 11am–10pm. Métro: Rambuteau, Hôtel de Ville, or Châtelet–Les Halles.

Conciergerie ⭐⭐ The most sinister building in France squats on the north bank of the Ile de la Cité (near the Pont au Change) and forms part of the huge Palais de Justice. Its name is derived from the title *concierge* (constable), once borne by a high official of the Royal Court. But its reputation stems from the Revolution.

Even on warm days, a chill wind seems to blow around its two bleak towers, and the massive walls feel eternally dank. Here, as nowhere else in Paris, you can see the tall, square shadow of the guillotine. For, after the fall of the Bastille, this became the country's chief prison. When the Reign of Terror got under way, the Conciergerie turned into a kind of stopover depot en route to the "National Razor."

There are the splendid remnants of a medieval royal palace in here, complete with refectory and giant kitchen. But the only features that imprint themselves on the mind are the rows of cells and the doghouse hovel in which prisoners—shorn and bound—sat waiting for their ride to the blade. Famous prisoners who had a brief stay here before an even briefer trip to the guillotine include Marie Antoinette (you can visit her cell), Madam du Barry, Danton, and Robespierre. Among the few who stayed here, but lived to write about it, was America's Thomas Paine, who remembered chatting in English with Danton.

1 quai de l'Horloge, 1er. ⓒ 01-53-73-78-50. www.monum.fr. Admission 5.50€ ($6.35) adults, 3.50€ ($4.05) ages 18–25, free for children under 18. Apr–Sept daily 9:30am–6:30pm; Oct–Mar daily 10am–5pm. Métro: Cité, Châtelet, or St-Michel. RER: St-Michel.

Eiffel Tower ⭐⭐⭐ Strangely enough, this symbol of Paris (one of the most recognizable in the world) wasn't meant to be a permanent structure at all. Gustave-Alexandre Eiffel erected it specifically for the Universal Exhibition of 1889, and it was destined to be pulled down a few years later. And some architects, who loathed it, wanted it torn down even sooner than that. But Parisians loved it, and, when wireless telegraphy and radio appeared on the scene, the 985-foot tower—the tallest on the earth—presented a handy signaling station.

During the German advance on Paris in 1914, the powerful beam from the top of the tower effectively jammed the enemy's field radios. Today, the tower has a TV antenna tacked on the top and is 1,056 feet tall.

But forget all of the statistics and just stand underneath the tower and look straight up. It's like a rocket of steel lacework shooting into the sky. If nothing else, it is a fantastic engineering achievement.

The view is the reason most people go to the third landing at the top of the tower, and this extends for 42 miles (68km), theoretically. In practice, weather conditions tend to limit it. Nevertheless, the view is fabulous, and the best time for visibility is about an hour before sunset.

Champ de Mars, 7e. ℂ 01-44-11-23-23. www.tour-eiffel.fr. Admission to first landing 3.65€ ($4.20), second landing 7€ ($8.05), third landing 10.20€ ($11.75). Stairs to second floor 3.30€ ($3.80). Sept–May daily 9:30am–11pm; June–Aug daily 9am–midnight. Fall and winter, stairs open only to 6:30pm. Métro: Trocadéro, Ecole Militaire, or Bir-Hakeim. RER: Champs de Mars–Tour Eiffel.

Hotel des Invalides ★★★   This is not a "hotel," rather a palace and a church combined, which today houses a great museum, dozens of military administration offices, and the tomb of Napoleon. The monumental ensemble was originally built by Louis XIV as a stately home for invalid soldiers (hence the name). Most of the enormous space is taken up by the military-themed **Musée de l'Armée,** whose collection includes Viking swords, Burgundian basinets, 14th-century blunderbusses, Balkan khandjars, American Browning machine guns, and suits of armor worn by kings and dignitaries. You can gain access to the **Musée des Plans-Reliefs** through the west wing. This collection shows French towns and monuments done in scale models (the model of Strasbourg fills an entire room), as well as models of military fortifications since the days of the great Vauban.

But it's the Tomb of Napoléon beneath the golden dome in the rear that makes this one of Paris's greatest showpieces. It's a shrine, and, like most shrines, impersonal. No trace of the man here—everything is in symbols. Napoléon rests in a sarcophagus of red granite on a pedestal of green granite. Surrounding the tomb are 12 figures of victories and 6 stands of captured enemy flags. The pavement of the crypt consists of a mosaic of laurel leaves. First buried at St. Helena, Napoléon's remains were returned to Paris in 1840. Also interred here are Napoléon's brothers, Joseph and Jerome, his son (who was never crowned), and Marshal Foch, who led the Allied armies to victory in 1918.

Place des Invalides, 7e. ℂ 01-44-42-37-72. Admission to Musée de l'Armée, Napoléon's Tomb, and Musée des Plans-Reliefs 6.50€ ($7.50) adults, 4.60€ ($5.30) children 12–17, free for children 11 and under. Oct–Mar daily 10am–5pm; Apr–May and Sept daily 10am–6pm; June–Aug daily 10am–7pm. Closed Jan 1, May 1, Nov 1, and Dec 25. Métro: Latour-Maubourg, Varenne, or Invalides.

Musée d'Orsay ★★★   Rail travelers will feel right at home in the neoclassical Gare d'Orsay train station, which has been transformed into one of the world's great museums. It contains an important collection devoted to the pivotal years from 1848 to 1914. Across the Seine from the Louvre and the Tuileries, it is a repository of works by the Impressionists as well as the Symbolists, Pointillists, Realists, and late Romantics. Artists represented include van Gogh, Manet, Monet, Degas, and Renoir. It houses thousands of sculptures and paintings across 80 galleries, plus Belle Epoque furniture, photographs, objets d'art, architectural models, and a cinema.

One of Renoir's most joyous paintings is here: *Moulin de la Galette* (1876). Another celebrated work is by James McNeill Whistler—*Arrangement in Gray and Black: Portrait of the Painter's Mother.* The most famous piece in the museum is Manet's 1863 *Déjeuner sur l'herbe* (Picnic on the Grass).

1 rue de Bellechasse or 62 rue de Lille, 7e. (©) **01-40-49-48-14**. www.musee-orsay.fr. Admission 7€ ($8.05) adults, 5€ ($5.75) ages 18–24 and seniors, free for children 17 and under. Tues–Wed and Fri–Sat 10am–6pm; Thurs 10am–9:45pm (June 20–Sept 20 from 9am–6:30pm); Sun 9am–6pm. Métro: Solférino. RER: Musée d'Orsay.

Musée du Louvre ⭐⭐⭐   The largest palace in the world (it was converted into a museum after the Revolution), The Louvre is also one of the world's largest and greatest museums, housing a collection of up to 208,500 works of art. The collection is both impressive and exhausting.

To enter the Louvre, you pass through the 71-foot **I. M. Pei glass pyramid** in the courtyard. Commissioned by Mitterrand and completed in 1989, it received mixed reviews. There's so much to see, so many endless nightmare hallways to get lost in, that—regardless of how much you may enjoy exploring a museum on your own—here we suggest you start with a **guided tour** (in English), which lasts about 90 minutes. These start under the pyramid at the station marked ACCEIL DES GROUPES. Once you've gotten the lay of the land, you can always go back and see what you missed.

The collections are divided into seven departments: Asian antiquities; Egyptian antiquities; Greek, Etruscan, and Roman antiquities; sculpture; paintings; prints and drawings; and objets d'art. Three items are standouts and usually top everybody's must-see list. To the left of the main entrance, at the crest of a graceful flight of stairs, stands *The Winged Victory*. In the Department of Greek Antiquities, on the ground floor, stands the supple statue of *Venus de Milo,* the warm marble subtly tinted by sunlight. Upstairs, in a room of her own, and covered with bulletproof glass and surrounded by art students, photographers, and awe-struck visitors, hangs the gently chiding portrait of the *Mona Lisa.*

Note: Though the $1.2-billion Grand Louvre Project, a 15-year-long project, is officially complete, refurbishment of individual galleries and paintings continues. For up-to-the-minute data on what is open or about to open, you can check out the Louvre's website at **www.louvre.fr**.

34–36 quai du Louvre, 1er. Main entrance in the glass pyramid, Cour Napoléon. (©) **01-40-20-53-17**, or 01-40-20-51-51 for recorded message. www.louvre.fr. Admission 7.50€ ($8.65) before 3pm, 5€ ($5.75) after 3pm and on Sun, free for children 17 and under, free first Sun of every month. Mon and Wed 9am–9:45pm (Mon short tour only); Thurs–Sun 9am–6pm. (Parts of the museum begin to close at 5:30pm.) 1½-hour English-language tours leave Mon and Wed–Sat at various times for 3€ ($3.45), free for children 12 and under with museum ticket. Métro: Palais Royal–Musée du Louvre.

Musée National Auguste Rodin ⭐⭐   Auguste Rodin, the man credited with freeing French sculpture of Classicism, once lived and had his studio in the charming 18th-century mansion **Hôtel Biron,** across the boulevard from Napoléon's Tomb in the Hôtel des Invaliders. Today the house and garden are filled with his works, a soul-satisfying feast for the Rodin enthusiast. In the cobbled Court of Honor, within the walls as you enter, you'll see *The Thinker* crouched on his pedestal to the right of you; *the Burghers of Calais* grouped off

---

Tips The Handy Museum Pass

La Carte Musées et Monuments (Museum and Monuments Pass) is available at any of the museums that honor it or at any branch of the Paris Tourist Office. It offers entrance to the collections of 70 monuments and museums in Paris and the Ile de France. A 1-day pass is 15€ ($17.25), a 3-day pass 30€ ($34.50), and a 5-day pass 45€ ($51.75).

to the left of you; and to the far left, the writhing *Gates of Hell,* atop which *The Thinker* once more meditates. There's a third *Thinker* inside the museum before the second-floor window. In the almost too-packed rooms, men and angels emerge from blocks of marble, hands twisted in supplication, and the nude torso of Balzac rises up from a tree. Wander back from the house through the long wooded garden where more sculptures await you under the trees.

In the Hôtel Biron, 77 rue de Varenne, 7e. ℂ **01-44-18-61-10.** www.musee-rodin.fr. Admission 5€ ($5.75) adults, 3€ ($3.45) ages 18–25, free for children 17 and under. Apr–Sept Tues–Sun 9:30am–5:45pm; Oct–Mar Tues–Sun 9:30am–4.45pm. Métro: Varenne.

Musée Picasso ★★★   When it opened in the beautifully restored Hôtel Salé in the Marais, the press hailed it as a "museum for Picasso's Picassos," meaning those he chose not to sell. The world's greatest Picasso collection, acquired by the state in lieu of $50 million in inheritance taxes, consists of 203 paintings, 158 sculptures, 16 collages, 19 bas-reliefs, 88 ceramics, and more than 1,500 sketches and 1,600 engravings, plus 30 notebooks. These works span some 75 years of Picasso's life and changing styles. Superior to a similar museum in Barcelona, it offers an unparalleled view of the artist's career and different periods, including his fabled gaunt blue figures and harlequins.

The range of paintings includes a 1901 self-portrait and embraces such masterpieces as *Le Baiser* (The Kiss). Other masterpieces are *Reclining Nude* and *Man with a Guitar.* It's easy to stroll through seeking your favorite work—ours is the delightfully wicked *Jeune garçon à la langouste* (Young Man with a lobster). The museum also owns several studies for *Les Demoiselles d'Avignon,* the painting that launched Cubism in 1907.

In the Hôtel Salé, 5 rue de Thorigny, 3e. ℂ **01-42-71-25-21.** www.musee-picasso.fr. Admission 5.50€ ($6.35) adults, 4€ ($4.60) ages 17–25 and seniors, free for children 18 and under. Apr–Sept Wed–Mon 9:30am–6pm; Oct–Mar Wed–Mon 9:30am–5pm. Métro: St-Paul, Filles di Calvaire, or Chemin Vert.

Notre-Dame ★★★   The Cathedral of Paris and one of civilization's greatest edifices, this is more than a building—it's like a book written in stone and wood and glass. And it can be read line by line, the Virgin's Portal alone telling four different picture stories. The doors of Notre-Dame did, in fact, take the place of religious textbooks during the ages when few of the faithful were literate.

The cathedral replaced two Romanesque churches (Ste. Mary and St. Stephen), which stood on the spot until 1160. Then Bishop Maurice de Sully, following the example of Suger, the abbot of St. Denis, undertook the new structure, and building continued for more than 150 years. The final result was a piece of Gothic perfection, not merely in overall design but in every detail. The rose window above the main portal, for instance, forms a halo 31 feet in diameter around the head of the statue of the Virgin. You'll have to walk around the entire structure to appreciate this "vast symphony of stone" with its classic flying buttresses. Better yet, cross the bridge to the Left Bank and view it from the quay.

More than any other building, Notre-Dame is the history of a nation. Here, the boy-monarch Henry VI of England was crowned king of France in 1422, during the Hundred Years War when—but for Joan of Arc—France would have become an English dominion. Here, Napoléon took the crown out of the hands of Pope Pius VII, and crowned himself and Josephine emperor and empress. Here, General de Gaulle knelt before the altar on August 26, 1944, to give thanks for the liberation of Paris—imperturbably praying while sniper bullets screeched around the choir galleries. Because of the beauty of its ornaments and of its symbolic meaning of redemption of all evil, Notre-Dame is a joyous church—though

Moments A Walk Among the Dead

When it comes to name-dropping, **Cimetière de Père-Lachaise,** 16 rue de Repos, 20e (© **01-55-25-82-10**), has been called the "grandest address in Paris." Everybody from Sarah Bernhardt to Oscar Wilde (his tomb by Epstein) was buried in this cemetery. So were Balzac, Delacroix, and Bizet. Colette was taken here in 1954 (legend has it that cats replenish the red roses found on her black granite slab). The "little sparrow," Edith Piaf, followed. The lover of George Sand, poet Alfred de Musset, was buried under a willow. Napoléon's marshals Ney and Masséna were entombed here, as were Chopin and Molière. Marcel Proust's black tombstone rarely lacks a bunch of violets. He wished to be buried with his friend and lover, composer Maurice Ravel, but their families wouldn't allow it.

Some tombs are sentimental favorites: That of rock star Jim Morrison reportedly draws the most visitors—and causes the most disruption. Dancer Isadora Duncan rests in a "pigeonhole" in the Columbarium, where bodies have been cremated and then "filed." If you search hard enough, you can find the tombs of Abélard and Héloïse, the ill-fated lovers of the 12th century. Other famous lovers rest here: One stone is marked Gertrude Stein on one side, Alice B. Toklas on the other.

Spreading over more than 110 acres, Père-Lachaise was acquired by the city in 1804. Nineteenth-century French sculpture abounds, each family trying to outdo the others in ornamentation and cherubic ostentation. Some French socialists still pay tribute at the Mur des Fédérés, the anonymous gravesite of the Communards who were executed on May 28, 1871. Several monuments also honor the French who died in the Resistance or in Nazi concentration camps.

Note: A free map is available at the newsstand across from the main entrance; it will help you find the well-known gravesites. Admission is free, and the cemetery is open Monday to Friday 8am to 6pm, Saturday 8:30am to 6pm, and Sunday 9am to 6pm. It closes at 5:30pm November to early March. Métro: Père-Lachaise.

those devils and gargoyles grinning from its ledges add a genuinely macabre touch. You can almost see Victor Hugo's hunchback peering from behind them.

There are many cathedrals larger than Notre-Dame, but the interior has a transcending loftiness that makes it seem immense. The flat-topped twin towers flanking the entrance rise to 225 feet. You can climb the 387 steps to a panoramic view of the city.

6 place de Parvis Notre-Dame, 4e. © **01-42-34-56-10.** www.paris.org/Monuments/NDame. Admission free to cathedral; towers 6.10€ ($7) adults, 4.10€ ($4.70) ages 18–25 and seniors, free for children under 18; treasury 2.50€ ($2.90) adults, 2€ ($2.30) ages 12–25 and seniors, free for children under 5. Cathedral open year-round daily 8am–6:45pm. Towers and crypt Apr–Sept daily 9:30am–6pm; Oct–Mar daily 10am–5:15pm. Museum Wed and Sat–Sun 2:30–5pm.

The Sewers of Paris (Les Egouts) ☆ Some say Baron Haussmann will be remembered mainly for erecting this vast, complicated network of Paris sewers. That these sewers have remained such a popular attraction is something of a curiosity in itself. They were made famous by Victor Hugo's *Les Misérables*. "All dripping with slime, his soul filled with a strange light," Jean Valjean in his desperate flight through the sewers of Paris is one of the heroes of narrative drama.

The *égouts* of the city are constructed around a quartet of principal tunnels, one of them 18 feet wide and 15 feet high. These underground passages are truly mammoth containing pipes bringing in drinking water and compressed air as well as telephone and telegraph lines. Furthermore, each branch pipe bears the number of a building to which it is connected (guides are fond of pointing out Maxim's). It's like an underground city, with the street names clearly labeled. Tours begin at Pont de l'Alma on the Left Bank. A stairway here leads into the bowels of the city. However, you often have to wait in line as much as 2½ hours.

Pont de l'Alma, 7e. © **01-53-68-27-82**. Admission 3.80€ ($4.35) adults, 3.05€ ($3.50) students, seniors, and children 5–12, free for children under 5. May–Oct Sat–Wed 11am–5pm; Nov–Apr Sat–Wed 11am–4pm. Closed 3 weeks in Jan. Métro: Alma-Marceau. RER: Pont de l'Alma.

Ste-Chapelle ✦✦✦ One of the oldest, most beautiful medieval churches in the world, La Sainte Chapelle was built in 1246 for the express purpose of housing the relics of the Crucifixion obtained from Constantinople. But the relics were later transferred to Notre-Dame, leaving La Saint Chapelle as an empty showcase, although a magnificent one.

The church actually has two levels: one humble, the other superb. You enter through the lower chapel, supported by flying buttresses and ornamented with fleurs-de-lis. This chapel was for servants. The upper chapel, reached by a spiral staircase, was used by the royal household. You can still see the small grated window from which Louis XI could participate in services without being noticed.

The outstanding feature of this chapel is its 15 magnificent stained-glass windows, flooding the church's interior with colored light—deep blue, ruby, and dark green—and depicting more than a thousand scenes from the Bible.

Ste-Chapelle stages concerts in summer, with tickets running 17€ to 25€ ($19.55–$28.75). Call © **01-42-77-65-65** from 11am to 6pm daily for details.

Palais de Justice, 4 bd. Du Palais, 1er. © **01-53-73-78-50**. www.monum.fr. Free admission. Apr–Sept daily 9:30am–6pm; Oct–Mar daily 10am–5pm. Métro: Cité, St-Michel, or Châtelet–Les Halles. RER: St-Michel.

WHERE TO DINE

Alcazar Bar & Restaurant ✦ MODERN FRENCH This is what the French Parisians call a *brasserie de luxe,* and it's the creation of the famous British restaurateur, Sir Terence Conran, featuring an avant-garde decor in its street-level dining room and chic bar upstairs. The menu is personal, creative, perfumed with herbs, and constantly changing with the addition of new taste sensations such as magret of duckling with white radishes and sesame oil.

62 rue Mazarine, 6e. © **01-53-10-19-99**. Reservations recommended. Main courses 16€–29€ ($18.40–$33.35); fixed-price lunch 16€–26€ ($18.40–$29.90). AE, DC, MC, V. Daily noon–3pm; Sun–Thurs 7pm–11pm); Fri–Sat 7pm–midnight. Métro: Odéon.

Allard ✦ TRADITIONAL FRENCH This is one of the most famous, most fashionable, and one of the best Left Bank bistros, with a tradition going back to 1931. Following a long decline, it has bounced back to reclaim its former prestige when it catered to Left Bank artists and even an occasional French prime minister. Here you can try those famous dishes that Americans and English people considered typically French in the past half century, or even before—foie gras, escargots, veal stew, cassoulet Toulousian, and, of course, the inevitable frogs' legs.

41 rue St-André-des-Arts, 6e. ✆ **01-43-26-48-23**. Reservations required. Main courses 15€–35€ ($17.25–$40.25); fixed-price menu 30.50€ ($35.10) lunch, 35€ ($40.25) dinner. AE, DC, MC, V. Mon–Sat noon–3pm and 7:30–11pm. Métro: St-Michel or Odéon.

L'Ambassade d'Auvergne ✦ AUVERGNAT/FRENCH   In an obscure district of Paris, this rustic tavern not only oozes charm but also dispenses the hearty *cuisine bourgeoise* of Auvergne, the heartland of France. You enter through a busy bar, with heavy oak beams, hanging hams, and ceramic plates. At the entrance is a display of the chef's specialties: jellied meats and fowls, pâté cakes, plus an assortment of regional cheese and fresh fruit of the season. Rough wheat bread is stacked in baskets, and rush-seated ladder-back chairs are placed at tables, along with stem glassware, mills to grind your own salt and pepper, and a jug of mustard to go with all those pork products.

22 rue de Grenier St-Lazare, 3e. ✆ **01-42-72-31-22**. Reservations recommended. Main courses 14€–19€ ($16.10–$21.85); fixed-price menu 28€ ($32.20). AE, MC, V. Daily noon–2pm and 7:30–11:30pm. Métro: Rambuteau.

Angélina TEA/TRADITIONAL FRENCH   This *salon de thé*, or tea salon, is the best known and most fashionable in Paris, serving you not only tea, but some of Paris's most elegant sandwiches and freshly made salads. In an elegant setting of carpets and high ceilings, Angélina features a constantly changing *plat du jour*, and offers those old French favorites, such as steak tartare or sole meunière, as main courses.

226 rue de Rivoli, 1er. ✆ **01-42-60-82-00**. Reservations accepted for lunch, not for teatime. Pot of tea for one 5.50€–6€ ($6.35–$6.90); sandwiches and salads 6€–9€ ($6.90–$10.35); main courses 14€–18€ ($16.10–$20.70). AE, MC, V. Daily 9am–7:30pm (lunch 11:45am–3pm). Métro: Tuileries or Concorde.

Aux Charpentiers ⓥalue TRADITIONAL FRENCH   In days of yore, it seemed that practically every frugal traveler to Paris made this notation: Visit the Louvre and dine at Aux Charpentiers. This St-Germain-des-Prés bistro, in business for a century and a half, is still going strong and still serving the *cuisine bourgeoise* (hearty but not effete) that made it such a legend in the '50s and '60s. Feast on one of the *plats du jour*, invariably an example of French home-style cookery, featuring the likes of stuffed cabbage or lentils flavored with salt pork.

10 rue Mabillon, 6e. ✆ **01-43-26-30-05**. Reservations required. Main courses 19€–35€ ($21.85–$40.25); fixed-price menu 19€ ($21.85) lunch, 25€ ($28.75) dinner. AE, DC, MC, V. Daily noon–3pm and 7–11:30pm. Métro: St-Germain-des-Prés.

Aux Lyonnais ✦ LYONNAIS/FRENCH   This bistro offers the finest Lyonnaise cuisine in Paris, and the cooking of Lyon is the best in France—especially the pork dishes. (The menu at Lyonnais proclaims that in Lyon *"le cochon est roi"*—pig is king.) The *fin de siècle* atmosphere is set by frosted globe chandeliers, floral tiled walls, and stuffed deer and boar heads. We invariably start things off with *la salade verte au lard avec de saucisson chaud* (a green salad with bacon and hot sausage). The chicken in a velvety-smooth cream sauce with tarragon and mushrooms is a classic.

32 rue St-Marc, 2e. ✆ **01-42-96-65-04**. Reservations required. Main courses 19€–29€ ($21.85–$33.35). AE, DC, MC, V. Mon–Sat 11:30am–3pm and 6:30–11:30pm. Métro: Bourse or Richelieu-Drouot.

Bofinger ✦ ALSATIAN/FRENCH   This is the oldest Alsatian brasserie in Paris, tracing its origins back to 1864. It successfully retains the palace style of that era: lots of leaded glass, creamy macramé curtains, lampshades shaped like tulips, antique mirrors, mahogany pieces, dark-gray benches, a revolving main door, and a central dome of stained glass—in other words, Emile Zola would

feel at home here. At night, many members of the Parisian slumming chic venture into the Bastille district to come here for beer and sauerkraut complete with sausages, smoked bacon, and pork chops.

5–7 rue de la Bastille, 4e. ⓒ **01-42-72-87-82.** Reservations recommended. Main courses 21€–35€ ($24.15–$40.25). AE, DC, MC, V. Mon–Fri noon–3pm and 6:30pm–1am; Sat–Sun noon–1am. Métro: Bastille.

Brasserie Balzar ⊛ TRADITIONAL FRENCH If they visited Paris, chances are your grandfather (maybe even your great-grandfather), your father, or your ancestors dined at this cheerful Left Bank bistro near the Sorbonne that Sartre, Camus, James Thurber, and a host of international journalists called their favorite. Count on the most traditional of French cookery—we're talking onion soup, pepper steak, sole meunière, fried calves' liver, and even pigs' feet.

49 rue des Ecoles, 5e. ⓒ 01-43-54-13-67. Reservations strongly recommended. Main courses 15€–18€ ($17.25–$20.70). AE, MC, V. Daily 6am–11:45pm. Métro: Odéon or Cluny–La Sorbonne.

Crémerie–Restaurant Polidor ⊛ TRADITIONAL FRENCH Along with the previously recommended Aux Charpentiers, this is one of the most famous and traditional of French bistros, serving a *cuisine familiale* (family cuisine) since the early 1900s. Over the years it has attracted the literati, including Hemingway and Kerouac, but today is likely to be filled with students and area artists. Nothing is as French as *boeuf bourguignonne* or *blanquette de veau,* and naturally these world-famous dishes are regularly featured. For dessert, get a chocolate, raspberry, or lemon tart—the best in all Paris.

41 rue Monsieur-le-Prince, 6e. ⓒ 01-43-26-95-34. Main courses 7€–12€ ($8.05–$13.80); fixed-price menu (Mon–Fri) 9€ ($10.35) lunch, 18€ ($20.70) dinner. No credit cards. Daily noon–2:30pm and 7pm–midnight; Sun 7–11pm. Métro: Odéon.

L'Ambroisie ⊛⊛⊛ MODERN & TRADITIONAL FRENCH One of Paris's most talented chefs, Bernard Pacaud, draws world attention (and three coveted Michelin stars) with his vivid flavors and expert skill. Expect culinary perfection but a cool reception at this early-17th-century town house in Le Marais, with three high-ceilinged salons whose decor recalls an Italian palazzo. Pacaud's tables are nearly always filled with satisfied diners who come back again and again. Dishes change seasonally; one of our favorite dishes in all Paris is this restaurant's *poulard de Bresse demi-deuil homage à la Mère Brazier* (chicken roasted with black truffles and truffled vegetables in a style invented by a Lyonnais matron after World War II).

9 place des Vosges. ⓒ 01-42-78-51-45. Reservations required far in advance. Main courses 68€–110€ ($78.20–$127). AE, MC, V. Tues–Sat noon–1:30pm and 8–9:30pm. Métro: St-Paul or Chèmin Vert.

La Petite Hostellerie ⊛Value TRADITIONAL FRENCH Since 1902, the fixed-price dinners here have kept many a struggling Left Bank artist from starvation. That is true even today, and the good news is that the old-fashioned cuisine—favorites such as duck a l'orange and *coq au vin*—is as good as it ever was. And where do you see a peach Melba (remember that dessert?) on the menu anymore? Select a table on the busting, ground floor or else head upstairs where the ambience with its 18th-century woodwork is more formal.

35 rue de la Harpe (a side street north of bd. St-Germain, just east of bd. St-Michel), 5e. ⓒ 01-43-54-47-12. All main courses 9.50€ ($10.95); fixed-price menu 10€–19.50€ ($11.50–$22.45). AE, DC, MC, V. Wed–Sun noon–2pm; Tues–Sun 6:30–11pm. Closed 2 weeks in Feb and 3 weeks in Aug. Métro St-Michel or Cluny–La Sorbonne.

Le Fumoir ⊛ INTERNATIONAL This is the place to dine after you've seen the masterpieces of the Louvre, as this bustling brasserie is only a few steps away.

If you want to dine light, you can do so here, partaking of the freshly made salads, the lavish pastries, and various snacks. But if you want more substantial and well-prepared fare based on market-fresh ingredients, you have come to the right place. Currently, it's one of the most fashionable places in Paris to be seen eating or drinking and the chefs will feed you well.

6 rue de l'Amiral-Coligny, 1er. ⓒ 01-42-92-00-24. Reservations recommended. Main courses 25€–30€ ($28.75–$34.50). Salads, pastries, and snacks daily 11am–2pm; full menu daily noon–3pm and 7–11:30pm. AE, V. Métro: Louvre-Rivoli.

SHOPPING

Perfumes and **cosmetics,** including such famous brands as Guerlain, Chanel, Schiaparelli, and Jean Patou, are almost always cheaper in Paris than in the United States. Paris is also a good place to buy Lalique and Baccarat **crystal.** They're expensive but still priced below international market value. **Lingerie** is another great French export. All the top lingerie designers are represented in boutiques as well as in the major department stores, Galeries Lafayette and Le Printemps.

Directly across from the Louvre, **Le Louvre des Antiquaires,** 2 place du Palais-Royal, 1er (ⓒ 01-42-97-29-86; Métro: Palais-Royal), is the largest repository of antiques in central Paris. More than 250 dealers display their wares on three floors, specializing in objets d'art and small-scale furniture of the type that might have been favored by Mme de Pompadour.

Viaduc des Arts, 9–147 av. Daumesnil (between rue de Lyon and av. Diderot), 12e (ⓒ 01-44-75-80-66; Métro: Bastille, Ledru-Rollin, Reuilly-Diderot, or Gare-de-Lyon), occupies the vaulted spaces beneath one of the 19th-century railway access routes into the Gare de Lyon. Around 1990, crafts artists, including furniture makers, potters, glassblowers, and weavers, began occupying the then-empty niches beneath the viaduct, selling their wares to homeowners and members of Paris's decorating trades.

Purveyor to kings and presidents of France since 1764, **Baccarat,** 30 bis rue de Paradis, 10e (ⓒ 01-47-70-64-30; Métro: Gare-de-l'Est), and 11 place de la Madeleine, 8e (ⓒ 01-42-65-36-26; Métro: Madeleine), produces world-renowned full-lead crystal in dinnerware, jewelry, chandeliers, and statuary. **Lalique,** 11 rue Royale, 8e (ⓒ 01-53-05-12-12; Métro: Concorde), famous for its clear- and frosted-glass sculpture, Art Deco crystal, and perfume bottles, has recently branched out into sales of other types of merchandise, such as silk scarves meant to compete with Hermès and leather belts with Lalique buckles.

One of the few regional handcrafts stores in Paris worth going out of your way to find, **La Tuile à Loup,** 35 rue Daubenton, 5e (ⓒ 01-47-07-28-90; Métro: Censier-Daubenton), carries beautiful pottery and faïence from many regions of France. Look for figures of Breton folk on the faïence of Quimper as well as garlands of fruits and flowers from the *terre vernissée* (varnished earth, a charming way to define stoneware) from Normandy, Savoy, Alsace, and Provence.

After you've admired the architecture of one of Europe's most famous department stores, step inside **Au Printemps,** 64 bd. Haussmann, 9e (ⓒ 01-42-82-50-00; Métro: Havre-Caumartin; RER: Auber), for a view of all it offers. Inside the main building is **Printemps de la Mode,** which occupies the bulk of the structure, and a housewares shop, **Printemps de la Maison.** Upstairs are wares of every sort, especially clothing. An affiliated store across the street is **Le Printemps de l'Homme,** the menswear division. Behind the main store is a branch of **Prisunic,** Printemps's workaday but serviceable dime store, which contains a grocery. At **Galeries Lafayette,** 40 bd. Haussmann, 9e (ⓒ 01-42-82-34-56; Métro:

Moments   The Famous Cafes of Paris

Whatever your pleasure—reading, meeting a lover, writing your memoirs, or drinking yourself into oblivion—you can do it at a French cafe.

Brasserie Lipp, 151 bd. St-Germain, 6e (℃ **01-45-48-53-91;** Métro: St-Germain-des-Prés), has an upstairs dining room, but it's more fashionable to sit in the back room. For breakfast, order traditional black coffee and croissants. At lunch or dinner, the specialty is pork and *choucroute* (sauerkraut)—the best in Paris. Open daily from noon to 2am, although restaurant service is available only from 11am to 1am—it's fashionable to arrive late.

Across from the Centre Pompidou, the avant-garde **Café Beaubourg,** 100 rue St-Martin, 4e (℃ **01-48-87-63-96;** Métro: Rambuteau or Hôtel-de-Ville), boasts soaring concrete columns and a minimalist decor by the architect Christian de Portzamparc. In summer, tables are set on the sprawling terrace, providing a panoramic view of the neighborhood's goings-on. Open Sunday through Thursday from 8am to 1am and Friday and Saturday from 8am to 2am.

Jean-Paul Sartre came to **Café de Flore,** 172 bd. St-Germain, 6e (℃ **01-45-48-55-26;** Métro: St-Germain-des-Prés). It's said he wrote his trilogy, *Les Chemins de la Liberté (The Roads to Freedom)* here. The cafe is still going strong, though the celebrities have moved on. Open daily 7am to 1:30am.

Next door, the legendary **Deux Magots,** 6 place St-Germain-des-Prés, 6e (℃ **01-45-48-55-25;** Métro: St-Germain-des-Prés), is still the hangout for sophisticated residents and a tourist favorite in summer. Inside are two Asian statues that give the cafe its name. Open daily from 7:30am to 1:30am.

Fouquet's, 99 av. des Champs-Elysées, 8e (℃ **01-47-23-50-00;** Métro: George-V), is the premier cafe on the Champs-Elysées. The outside tables are separated from the sidewalk by a barricade of potted flowers. Inside is an elegant grill room, private rooms, and a restaurant. The cafe and grill room are open daily from 8am to 2am; the restaurant daily from noon to 3pm and 7pm to midnight.

At **La Coupole,** 102 bd. Montparnasse, 14e (℃ **01-43-20-14-20;** Métro: Vavin), the crowd ranges from artists' models to young men dressed like Rasputin. Perhaps order a coffee or cognac VSOP at one of the sidewalk tables. The dining room serves food that is sometimes good, sometimes indifferent. But people don't come here for the cuisine; it's more on the see-and-be-seen circuit. Try the sole meunière or cassoulet. A buffet breakfast is served Monday through Friday from 8:30 to 10:30am. Open daily from 8:30am to 1am.

Chaussée-d'Antin; RER: Auber), stand under "the Dome"—a stained-glass cupola that towers above the arcaded store. Built in 1912, Galeries Lafayette is divided into several stores: **Galfa** men's store, **Lafayette Sports,** and two other general-merchandise stores, both known simply as **"GL."**

Anna Lowe, 104 rue du Faubourg St-Honoré, 8e (✆ **01-42-66-11-32;** Métro: Miromesnil), is one of the premier boutiques for the woman who wishes to purchase a little Chanel or perhaps a Versace at a discount, *bien sur.* Many clothes are runway samples; some have been gently worn. The inventory at **Réciproque,** 88–123 rue de la Pompe (between av. Victor-Hugo and av. Georges-Mandel), 16e (✆ **01-47-04-30-28;** Métro: Pompe), is scattered over five buildings. Everything is secondhand, clustered into sections devoted to Chanel, Versace, Lacroix, Hermès, and Mugler. Women will find gowns, suits, sportswear, and shoes.

At the place de la Madeleine stands one of the most popular sights in the city—not La Madeleine church but **Fauchon,** 26 place de la Madeleine, 8e (✆ **01-47-42-60-11;** Métro: Madeleine), which offers a wider choice of upscale gourmet products than any other store in the world.

Almost every working woman around place de la Madeleine shops at **Catherine,** 7 rue Castiglione, 1er (✆ **01-42-61-02-89;** Métro: Concorde). It resembles a high-volume pharmacy more than a boutique; *flacons* of perfume move in and out of the premises very fast. You get a 30% discount on most brands of makeup and perfume and a 20% discount on brands like Chanel and Dior.

NIGHTLIFE

Opéra Garnier, place de l'Opéra, 9e (✆ **08-92-89-90-90;** Métro: Opéra), is the premier stage for dance and opera. Painstaking restorations have returned the Garnier to its former glory: Its boxes and walls are again lined with flowing red and blue damask, the gilt gleams, the ceiling (painted by Marc Chagall) has been cleaned, and air-conditioning has been added. The box office is open Monday through Saturday from 11am to 6:30pm. The controversial building known as the **Opéra Bastille,** place de la Bastille, 120 rue de Lyon (✆ **08-92-89-90-90** or **01-40-01-19-70;** Métro: Bastille), was designed by the Canadian architect Carlos Ott, with curtains created by fashion designer Issey Miyake. The main hall is the largest of any French opera house, with 2,700 seats, but music critics have lambasted the acoustics. Both traditional opera performances and symphony concerts are presented here. There are sometimes free concerts on French holidays; call before your visit.

Conceived by the Mitterrand administration, **Cité de la Musique,** 221 av. Jean-Jaurès, 19e (✆ **01-44-84-45-00,** or 01-44-84-44-84 for tickets and information; Métro: Porte-de-Pantin), has been widely applauded. At the city's northeastern edge in what used to be a run-down neighborhood, the $120-million stone-and-glass structure, designed by Christian de Portzamparc, incorporates a network of concert halls, a library and research center, and a museum. The complex hosts a variety of concerts, ranging from Renaissance to 20th-century programs.

Picasso and Utrillo once patronized this cottage near the top of Montmartre, **Au Lapin Agile,** 22 rue des Saules, 18e (✆ **01-46-06-85-87;** Métro: Lamarck or Caulain Court), formerly known as the Café des Assassins. For decades, it has been the heart of French folk music. You'll sit at wooden tables in a dimly lit room with walls covered by bohemian memorabilia, listening to French folk tunes, love ballads, army songs, sea chanteys, and music-hall ditties. It's open Tuesday through Sunday nights from 9:15pm to 2am with a cover charge of 24€ ($27.60) that includes the first drink.

The **Crazy Horse Saloon,** 12 av. George-V, 8e (✆ **01-47-23-32-32;** Métro: George-V or Alma-Marceau), a sophisticated strip joint, has thrived for decades thanks to good choreography and a sly, flirty theme that celebrates and exalts the female form. Shows, which last 1¾ hours, are attended by menfolk and, to a lesser extent, women, from around Europe and the world. The cover (including 2 drinks) is 69€ to 80€ ($79.35–$92), with the dinner spectacle costing 120€ ($138). The **Folies-Bergère**, 34 rue Richer, 9e (*©* **01-44-79-98-98;** Métro: Grands-Boulevards or Cadet), is a Paris institution; foreign visitors have been flocking here since 1886. Don't expect the naughty and slyly permissive skin-and-glitter revue that used to be the trademark of this place—today, it's a conventional 1,600-seat theater devoted to a frequently changing roster of big-stage performances, in French, many of which are adaptations of Broadway blockbusters. Hours and days of spectacles vary according to the performance, but shows are usually Tuesday through Saturday at 9pm, Sunday at 3pm, and the cover is 20€ to 50€ ($23–$57.50); dinner and show 60€ to 90€ ($69–$104).

As it moves deeper into the millennium, **Lido de Paris,** 116 bis av. des Champs-Elysées, 8e (*©* **800/227-4884** in the U.S., or 01-40-76-56-10; Métro: George-V), has changed its feathers and modernized its shows. Its $15 million production, *C'est Magique,* reflects a dramatic reworking of the classic Parisian cabaret show, with eye-popping special effects, water technology using more than 60,000 gallons per minute, even aerial and aquatic ballet. Dinner dance is at 8pm and the show is at 10pm and costs 130€ to 145€ ($150–$167); seeing the show only (10pm and midnight) costs 90€ ($104).

Moulin Rouge, Place Blanche, 18e (*©* **01-53-09-82-82;** Métro: Blanche), is a camp classic. Try to get a table, as the view is much better on the main floor than from the bar. Handsome men and girls, girls, girls, virtually all topless, keep the place going. Dance finales usually include two dozen of the belles ripping loose with a topless can-can. Revues are nightly at 9 and 11pm. The cover charge, including champagne, is 82€ to 92€ ($94.30–$106); 7pm dinner and show 130€ ($150); for seats at the bar, the cover (including two drinks) is 63€ ($72.45).

Jazz lovers go to **Baiser Salé,** 58 rue des Lombards, 1er (*©* **01-42-33-37-71;** Métro: Châtelet), which is set within a cellar lined with jazz-related paintings, a large bar, and an ongoing roster of videos that show great jazz players (Charlie Parker, Miles Davis) of the past. Everything is mellow and laid-back, with an emphasis on the music. Hours are Wednesday to Sunday and the cover charge is 8€ ($9.20); free Monday and Tuesday. **Le Bilboquet/Club St-Germain,** 13 rue St-Benoît, 6e (*©* **01-45-48-81-84;** Métro: St-Germain-des-Prés), the restaurant/jazz club/piano bar where the film *Paris Blues* was shot, offers some of the best music in the city. Jazz is featured on the upper level in the restaurant. Under separate management, the downstairs disco, Club St-Germain, charges no cover—but drinks cost a staggering 15€ ($17.25). You can walk from one club to the other, but you have to buy a new drink each time you change venues.

If you are in the mood for dancing, go to **Batofar,** Facing 11 quai François Mauriac, 13e (*©* **01-56-29-10-33;** Métro: Quai de la Gare). Self-consciously proud of its status as a club that virtually everybody views as hip, Batofar sits within a converted barge that floats on the Seine, sometimes with hundreds of gyrating dancers, most of whom are in their 20s and 30s. House, garage, techno, and live jazz from groups that hail from (among other places) Morocco, Senegal, and Germany sometimes add to the mix. It's open Tuesday through Saturday from 6pm to 3 or 4am, depending on business; closed November through March. The cover charge is 10€–16€ ($11.50–$18.40).

Established in 1936, **La Balajo** 9 rue de Lappe, 11e (© **01-47-00-07-87;** Métro: Bastille), is the place where Edith Piaf won the hearts of Parisian music lovers. Sessions held three afternoons a week focus on tangos, *paso dobles,* and waltzes, and are more staid than their late-night counterparts. Then, you get a younger crowd, lots of merengue and salsa (Tues–Thurs nights), and disco (Fri–Sat). Hours are Monday, Thursday, and Sunday from 2:30 to 6:30pm; Tuesday through Saturday from 10:30pm to 5am. The cover is 8€ to 9€ ($9.20–$10.45) for afternoon sessions; 16€ to 18€ ($18.40–$20.70) for night-time sessions. The entrance fee includes the first drink. The name **Les Bains,** 7 rue du Bourg-l'Abbae, 3e (© **01-48-87-01-80;** Métro: Etiene Marcel), comes from this hot spot's former function as a Turkish bath. Dancing begins at midnight, and a supper club–like restaurant lies upstairs. Meals cost 38€ to 46€ ($43.70–$52.90). On certain nights this is the hottest party atmosphere in Paris, and Mondays are increasingly gay, although sexual preference is hardly an issue at this club. "We all walk the waterfront," one DJ enigmatically told us, as he played soul, house music, or whatever. It's open daily midnight to 6am and the cover is 20€ ($23).

Many Parisians now prefer the wine bar to the traditional cafe or bistro—the food is often better and the ambience more inviting. **Au Sauvignon,** 80 rue des Sts-Pères, 7e (© **01-45-48-49-02;** Métro: Sèvres-Babylone), is a tiny spot that has tables overflowing onto a covered terrace and a decor featuring old ceramic tiles and frescoes done by Left Bank artists. Wines range from the cheapest Beaujolais to the most expensive Puligny-Montrachet. A glass of wine costs 4.80€ to 5.50€ ($5.50–$6.35), with an additional charge of .50€ (60¢) to consume it at a table. It is closed in August. **Les Bacchantes,** 21 rue Caumartin, 9e (© **01-42-65-25-35;** Métro: Havre-Caumartin), prides itself on offering more wines by the glass—at least 50—than any other wine bar in Paris; prices range from 3€ to 6€ ($3.45–$6.90). It also does a hefty restaurant trade in well-prepared *cuisine bourgeoise.* Wines are mainly from France, but you'll also find examples from neighboring countries of Europe. **Willi's Wine Bar,** 13 rue des Petits-Champs, 1e (© **01-42-61-05-09;** Métro: Bourse, Louvre, or Palais-Royal), offers about 250 kinds of wine, including a dozen "wine specials" you can taste by the glass for 4€ to 15€ ($4.60–$17.25). Daily specials are likely to include lamb brochette with cumin or Lyonnais sausage in truffled vinaigrette, plus a spectacular dessert like chocolate terrine.

Barrio Latino, 46 rue du Faubourg St-Antoine, 12e (© **01-55-78-84-75;** Métro: Bastille), is a multi-story emporium of good times, Gallic flair, and Latino charm. Tapas bars and dance floors are located on the street level *(rez-de-chausée)* and third floor *(2eme étage);* a Latino restaurant is on the second floor *(1er étage).* Clientele is mixed, mostly straight, partly gay, and 100% blasé about matters such as an individual's sexuality. There is a cover charge of 8€ ($9.20) for non-diners Friday and Saturday after 9pm. **Harry's New York Bar,** 5 rue Daunou, 2e (© **01-42-61-71-14;** Métro: Opéra or Pyramides), is the most famous bar in Europe—quite possibly in the world. Opened on Thanksgiving Day 1911 by an expat named MacElhone, it's the spot where members of the World War I ambulance corps drank themselves silly. In addition to being Hemingway's favorite, Harry's is where the white lady and sidecar cocktails were invented; it's also the alleged birthplace of the Bloody Mary and the headquarters of a loosely organized fraternity of drinkers known as the International Bar Flies (IBF). A softer, somewhat less macho ambience reigns in the cellar, where a pianist provides music every night from 10pm to 4am. At **Le Fumoir,** 6 rue de l'Amiral-de-Coligny, 1er (✆ **01-42-92-00-24;** Métro: Louvre-Rivoli), the well-traveled crowd that lives or works in the district provides a kind of classy raucousness. The decor is a lot like that of an English library, with about 6,000 books providing an aesthetic backdrop to the schmoozing. The stiff mixed drinks are popular, as are the wines and beers and the dozen or so types of cigars for sale.

AN EXCURSION TO VERSAILLES

The town of Versailles, 13 miles (21km) southwest of Paris, is a stodgily formal place, but the palace here is the sight of a lifetime.

GETTING THERE   To get to Versailles, catch the **RER** line C at the Gare d'Austerlitz, St-Michel, Musée d'Orsay, Invalides, Ponte de l'Alma, Champ de Mars, or Javel stop, and take it to the Versailles Rive Gauche station, from which there's a **shuttle bus** to the château. Priced at 4.70€ ($5.40) round-trip, the transit takes 35 to 40 minutes; Eurailpass and any France Railpass holders travel free on the RER, but they'll need to show their pass at the ticket kiosk near any RER entrance, in exchange for which they'll receive an RER ticket. Or, you can take one of the regular **SNCF trains,** which make frequent runs from Gare St-Lazare and Gare Montparnasse in Paris to Versailles: Trains departing from Gare St-Lazare arrive at the Versailles Rive Droite railway station; trains departing from Gare Montparnasse arrive at the Versailles Chantiers station. Both stations are a 10-minute walk from the château, and we recommend the walk as a means of familiarizing yourself with the town, its geography, its scale, and its architecture. You can also take bus B, bus H, or (in midsummer) a shuttle bus marked CHATEAU from any of the three stations directly to the château for a fee of 2€ ($2.30) each way, per person. Because of the vagaries of the bus schedules, we highly recommend the walk. Directions to the château are clearly signposted from each of the three railway stations.

VISITOR INFORMATION   The **Office de Tourisme** is at 2 bis av. De Paris (✆ **01-39-24-88-88**), a short walk from the rail station and close to the main entrance to Versailles. Open daily 9am to 7pm (closes at 6pm in winter).

TOP ATTRACTIONS & SPECIAL MOMENTS

The unbelievably vast **Château de Versailles** ★★★ (✆ **01-30-83-78-00;** www. chateauversailles.fr) is as ornately artificial as a jewel box. Here, the kings of France built a whole glittering private world for themselves, as remote from the grime and noise and bustle of Paris as a gilded planet—a fact that helps to explain why there are no more kings of France. Begun in 1661, the construction of the château involved 32,000 to 45,000 workmen, some of whom had to drain marshes—often at the cost of their lives—and move forests. Louis XIV set out to create a palace that would awe all Europe, and the result was a symbol of pomp and opulence that was to be copied, yet never quite duplicated.

For viewing purposes, the palace is divided up into sections. The first section features the six magnificent **Grands Appartements** ★★★, done in the Louis XIV style; each takes its name from the allegorical painting on its ceiling. The most famous room in this section is the 236-foot **Hall of Mirrors** ★★★ (where the Treaty of Versailles was signed). Begun by Mansart in 1678 in the Louis XIV style, it was decorated by Le Brun with 17 large arched windows matched by beveled mirrors in simulated arcades.

Highlights in other sections include the **Opera House** designed by Gabriel for Louis XV in 1748, though it wasn't completed until 1770. Also of interest are the **apartments of Mme de Pompadour,** the queen's private suites, the salons, the **Royal Chapel,** and the **Museum of the History of France.**

The Grands Appartements, the Royal Chapel, and the Hall of Mirrors can be visited without a guide. To see other parts of the Château, you have to wait for certain opening times (there's a shortage of guards). Seeing all of it can take up an entire morning and leave you pretty exhausted.

For a little relaxation, head for the **Gardens of Versailles** ✿. This park is the ultimate in French landscaping perfection—every tree, shrub, flower, and hedge disciplined into a frozen ballet pattern and blended with soaring fountains, sparkling little lakes, grandiose steps, and hundreds of marble statues. It's more like a colossal stage setting than a park—even the view of the blue horizon seems embroidered on.

Try to save time to visit the **Grand Trianon,** which is a good walk across the park. In pink-and-white marble, it was designed by Hardouin-Mansart for Louis XIV in 1687. The Trianon is furnished mostly with Empire pieces. You can also visit the **Petit Trianon,** which was built by Gabriel in 1768 as a retreat for Louis XV and his mistress, Mme du Barry. Later on, it was the favorite residence of Marie Antoinette, who could escape the rigors of court here.

The latest attraction is the **Grande Ecourie,** the newly reopened stables of Louis XIV. For 2 centuries, these historic stables have been closed to the public. They once housed more than 600 horses of the king. Today, they are home to 20 cream-colored Lusitanian horses from Portugal. Visitors are taken on a brief guided tour and then witness morning dressage demonstrations. Ten advanced equestrian students direct the horses, and costumed riders demonstrate equestrian choreography performed to music.

The château is open from May 2 to September 30, Tuesday through Sunday from 9am to 6:30pm (5:30pm the rest of the year). It's closed December 25 and January 1. The grounds are open daily from dawn to dusk; the Trianons are open from noon to 6pm. Individual attractions may have earlier opening and closing times.

Call or visit the website for a complete fee schedule (which varies, depending on which attractions you visit). An unguided visit to the Grands Appartements costs 7.50€ ($8.65) adults, 5€ ($5.75) after 3:30pm, and the same price for ages 18 to 25 and 60 and over. Both Trianons charge 5€ ($5.75) adults, 3€ ($3.45) ages 18 to 25, seniors 60 and over, and adults after 3:30pm. The palace is free for children 17 and under.

3 The Loire Valley ✿✿✿

Val de Loire, the Loire Valley, is called "the garden of France," but known more popularly around the world as the "châteaux county." Bordered by vineyards, the winding Loire Valley cuts through the soft contours of the land of castles deep in the heart of France. When royalty and nobility built châteaux throughout this valley during the Renaissance, sumptuousness was uppermost in their minds. An era of excessive pomp reigned here until Henri IV moved his court to Paris.

The Valley of the Loire has also played a major part in the national consciousness. Joan of Arc, the maid of Orléans, came this way looking for her dauphin, finding him at Chinon. Carried from castle to castle were mistresses, the list now legendary, ranging from Agnés Sorel (the mistress of Charles VII) to Diane du Poitiers (the mistress of Henri II). In his heyday, the Chevalier King brought Leonardo da Vinci from Florence, installing him at Amboise.

Catherine de Médici and her "flying squadron" of beauties, Henry III and his handsome minions—the people and the events make a rich tapestry.

The Loire has a tale to tell, as even the most cursory visitor to its châteaux discovers. Its sights and curiosities are multifarious, ranging from Renaissance, medieval, and classical châteaux to residences where Balzac wrote or Rabelais lived, to Romanesque and Gothic churches, to Roman ramparts, to art treasures. There's even a castle that inspired the fairy tale *Sleeping Beauty.*

Attempts to explore the valley in 2 to 3 days are doomed, but that is all the time most rail passengers have to spare. If your schedule can accommodate it, allow at least a week. Autumn or spring is ideal for a visit, though most of the intriguing *son-et-lumiére* (sound-and-light) programs take place in summer when the châteaux are floodlit. First performed on the banks of the Loire, these pageants have become one of the main attractions of France.

The cities of **Orléans** or **Tours**, both within easy rail reach of Paris, are the major transportation hubs for the Loire Valley. Tours is more central and makes the best base because it is better connected by rail and public transport to the major châteaux: **Chenonceaux, Amboise, Azay-le-Rideau, Chambord, Chaumont,** and **Blois.**

ORLEANS ⍟

Orléans suffered heavy damage in World War II, so those visiting who hoped to see how it looked when the Maid of Orléans was here are likely to be disappointed. However, the reconstruction of Orléans has been judiciously planned, and there are many rewarding targets for visitors.

Orléans is the chief town of Loiret, on the Loire River, 74 miles (119km) southwest of Paris. Joan of Arc freed the city in 1429 from the attacks of the Burgundians and the English. That deliverance is celebrated every year on May 8, the anniversary of her victory. An equestrian statue of Joan of Arc stands in the **Place du Martroi,** which was created by Foyatier in 1855.

From that square, you can head down the **rue Royale**—rebuilt in the 18th-century style—across the **Pont George V,** erected in 1760. After crossing the bridge you'll have a good view of the town. A simple cross marks the site of the Fort des Tourelles, which Joan of Arc and her men captured.

GETTING THERE   Ten trains per day arrive from Paris's Gare d'Austerlitz (trip time: 1¼ hr.); there are also a dozen connections from Tours (trip time: 50 min.). The one-way fare from Paris is 15.50€ ($17.85); from Tours 15€ ($17.25). The Orléans station is about a 10 to 15 minute walk from the town center.

VISITOR INFORMATION   The **Office de Tourisme** is at 6 rue Albert, 1e (✆ **02-38-24-05-05;** www.ville-orleans.fr), just outside of the rail station. Hours are Tuesday to Saturday 9:30am to 1pm and 2 to 6pm. They will make free hotel reservations for you, but you have to be in the office in person and the reservation must be for that same day.

TOP ATTRACTIONS & SPECIAL MOMENTS

In the heart of town stands **Cathédrale Ste-Croix** ⍟, Place Ste-Croix (✆ **02-38-77-87-50**), begun in 1287 in the High Gothic style, although burned by the Huguenots in 1567. The first stone on the present building was laid by Henry IV in 1601, and work continued on the cathedral until 1829. Inside, the church of the Holy Cross contains a gigantic organ from the 17th-century, and some magnificent woodwork from the early 18th century in the chancel. You'll need a guide to tour the chancel and the crypt and to see the

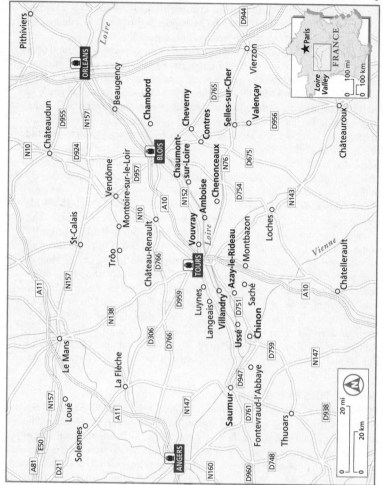

treasury with its Byzantine enamels and textiles, its goldwork from the 15th and 16th centuries, and its Limoges enamels. Admission is free, but you should tip the guide if you opt for one of the tours. Hours are daily 9:30am to noon and 2:15 to 5pm (May–Sept until 6pm). Guided visits can be arranged by the tourist office for 4€ ($4.60) adults, 2€ ($2.30) children 6 to 13. Tours are given June to September daily at 3, 4, and 5pm.

Hôtel Groslot, Place de l'Etape (northwest of the cathedral; ℂ **02-38-79-22-30**), is a Renaissance mansion begun in 1550 and embellished in the 19th century. François II (first husband of Mary Queen of Scots) lived in it during the fall of 1560 and died on December 5 the same year. Between the Revolution and the mid-1970s, it functioned as the town hall. Despite that, marriage ceremonies, performed by the town's magistrates, still occur here. Romance is nothing new to this building: It was here that Charles IX met his lovely Marie Touchet. The statue of Joan of Arc praying (at the foot of the flight of steps) was the work of Louis Phillipe's daughter, Princess Marie d'Orléans. In the garden, you can see remains of the 15th-century Chapelle St-Jacques. Admission is free and hours are Monday to Friday 9am to 7pm.

After visiting the Groslot, you can backtrack to the cathedral square and walk all the way down rue Jeanne-d'Arc, across rue Royale, to see a small museum dedicated to Orléans's favorite mademoiselle, the **Maison Jeanne-d'Arc,** 3 place de Gaulle (© **02-38-52-99-89**). The house is a 20th-century reproduction of the 15th-century house where Joan of Arc, the liberator and patron of Orléans, stayed during her local heroics. The original house was much modified, then destroyed by bombing in 1940. The first floor has temporary exhibitions, and the second and third floors contain Joan-related models and memorabilia. Admission is 2€ ($2.30) adults, 1.50€ ($1.75) seniors and students, free for children. Hours are May to October Tuesday to Sunday 10am to 12pm and 1:30 to 6pm; November to April Tuesday to Sunday 1:30 to 6pm.

The **Musée des Beaux-Arts** ★★, 1 rue Fernand-Rabier (© **02-38-79-21-55**), occupies the 16th-century town hall, known as Hôtel des Créneaux. This is mainly a picture gallery of French works from the 15th to the 19th centuries. Some of the art here once hung in Richelieu's château. Other pieces of art include busts by Pigalle and a fine array of portraits, including one of Mme de Pompadour, of whom, when she crossed the Pont George V, the people of the town remarked: "Our bridge has just borne France's heaviest weight." See also works by Georges de La Tour, Correge, Le Nain, Phillippe de Champaigne, La Hire, Boucher, Watteau, and Gauguin, as well as a salon of pastels by Perronneau. Several foreign works are also displayed, including a lovely Velásquez. Admission is 4€ ($4.60) adults, 2€ ($2.30) students and under 15. Hours are Sunday and Tuesday 11am to 6pm; Wednesday 10am to 8pm; Thursday to Saturday 10am to 6pm.

WHERE TO STAY & DINE

Hôtel d'Arc, 37 rue de la République, 45000 Orléans (© **02-38-53-10-94;** www.hoteldarc.fr), a 35-room hotel with an Art Deco facade, sits in the middle of the town center and is close to nearly everything, including the train station and the city's pedestrian-only shopping streets. The 1920s structure has been considerably modernized; its average-size bedrooms are tastefully and comfortably furnished. Avoid rooms facing rue de la République as they tend to be noisy. Rates are 65€ to 70€ ($74.75–$80.50) double.

If you seek more modern comfort, **Hôtel Mercure Orléans** ★, 44-46 quai Barentin, 45000 Orléans (© **02-38-62-17-39;** www.mercure.com), is the town's finest address. Along the river, adjacent to pont Joffre, this 109-room bandbox structure is within walking distance of place du Martroi and its Joan of Arc statue. The recently refurbished, air-conditioned bedrooms are done in a typical chain style but are comfortable and inviting. Rates are 104€ to 115€ ($120–$132) double.

La Vieille Auberge, 2 rue de Faubourg St-Vincent (© **02-38-53-55-81**), is one of the most dignified-looking and best restaurants in Orléans. Menu items include sophisticated treatments of Loire Valley whitefish, game, and local produce, all accompanied by regional Loire wines that blend well with the cuisine. Main courses cost 14€ to 29€ ($16.10–$33.35) and a fixed-price menu is offered at 28.50€ to 37€ ($32.80–$42.55).

Les Antiquaires ★★★, 2–4 rue au Lin (© **02-38-53-52-35**), the town's finest dining choice, is a rustically elegant, stone-sided, 14th-century mansion

Orléans

Orléans map with the following labels:

Gare · To Chartres & Paris · To Etampes · place de Gambetta · bd. de Verdun · Bus Station · PARC LOUIS PASTEUR · rue E. Vignat · rue du faubourg St-Vincent · Paris · Orleans · FRANCE · place Albert-1er · 1 · rue Bannier · rue de la République · rue d'Alsace-Lorraine · rue de la Bretonnerie · bd. de Aléxandre Martin · rue Jules Lemaître · 0 100 mi · 0 100 km · 0 1/4 mi · 0 0.25 km · rue R. Chollet · place de l'Etape · 8 · rue du Bourdon Blanc · bd. St-Euverte · place du Martroi · rue d'Escures · Hôtel Groslot 6 · rue Dupanloup · place Ste-Croix · 7 · Cathédrale Ste-Croix · place du Gén de Gaulle · rue Jeanne d'Arc · place Abbé Desnoyes · 2 · Maison de Jeanne d'Arc · Musée Historique · 5 · Musée des Beaux-Arts · rue de Bourgogne · rue de Bourgogne · To Sens & Gien · rue Royale · rue de la Tour Neuve · Eiglise St-Aignan · place du Châtelet · To Blois & Tours · quai Cypierre · 3 · Nouvelle Halle · quai du Châtelet · quai du Fort-Alleaume · Loire · pont George-V

Church · Information · Post Office · Rail Station

ACCOMMODATIONS ■
Hôtel d'Arc 1
Hôtel Mercure Orléans 3

DINING ◆
La Vieille Auberge 8
Les Antiquaries 4

ATTRACTIONS ●
Cathédrale Ste-Croix 7
Hôtel Groslot 6
Maison Jeanne-d'Arc 2
Musée des Beaux-Arts 5

on a narrow street near the river. The owners create a virtually flawless cuisine based on modern interpretations of traditional French recipes, each of which changes with the seasons. Main courses cost 18€ to 25€ ($20.70–$28.75) and a fixed-price menu is offered for 36€ ($41.40) Monday to Friday only, or 40€ to 60€ ($46–$69), any day of the week.

TOURS ★

With a population of 130,000, Tours is known for its fine food and wine. Although without a major château itself, this industrial and residential city is the traditional center for exploring the Loire Valley and is definitely the best base for a rail traveler touring the region because of its excellent train connections.

At the heart of the châteaux country, Tours is 144 miles (232km) southwest of Paris and 70 miles (113km) southwest of Orléans. At the junction of the Loire and Cher rivers, it was one of the great pilgrimage sites of Europe in the Middle Ages. The townspeople are fond of pointing out that Tours, not Paris, is actually the logical site for the capital of France. And it virtually *was* the capital in June of 1940, when Churchill flew here to meet with Paul Reynaud.

Because many of the city's buildings were bombed in World War II, 20th-century apartment towers have taken the place of stately châteaux. However, because Tours is at the doorstep of some of the most magnificent châteaux in France, it makes a good base from which to explore and its nightlife is the best in the area. Most Loire Valley towns are rather sleepy, but Tours is where the action is, as you'll see by its noisy streets and cafes. A quarter of the residents are students, who add a vibrant, active touch to the city.

GETTING THERE   **Trains** to Tours depart from Paris from two stations, Gare Montparnasse and Gare d'Austerlitz. The quickest transits are usually from Gare Montparnasse, departure point for up to 10 TGV trains per day, charging 35.10€ to 45.50€ ($40.35–$52.35) one-way for the 70-minute trip. Most of the conventional—slower—trains to Tours depart from the Gare d'Austerlitz. Transit time on these trains is about 2¼ hours, and they cost from 25€ to 40€ ($28.75–$46) one-way, based on the time of day and day of the week you travel.

Trains arrive in Tours at place du Maréchal-Leclerc, 3 rue Edouard-Vaillant (© 08-36-35-35-35 for information), just a stone's throw from most of the city's major attractions. The city itself is easily navigable on foot and most hotels are close to the train station.

VISITOR INFORMATION   The **Office de Tourisme** is at 78 rue Bernard-Palissy (© 02-47-70-37-37), just across the place du Géneral-Leclerc from the train station. Hotels can be reserved here but only if the client is in the office on the same day the room is needed. There is no charge for this service. Summer hours are Monday to Friday 8:30am to 7pm and Sunday 10am to 5pm. Off-season hours are Monday to Friday 9am to 12:30pm and 1:30 to 5pm; Sunday 10am to 4pm.

TOP ATTRACTIONS & SPECIAL MOMENTS
Cathédrale St-Gatien, 5 place de la Cathédrale (© 02-47-70-21-00), the chief attraction of Tours, honors an evangelist of the 3rd century. Its facade is in the flamboyant Gothic style, flanked by two towers, the bases of which date from the 12th century, although the lanterns are Renaissance. The choir was built in the 13th century, and each century up to and including the 16th produced new additions. Sheltered inside is the handsome 16th-century tomb of the children of Charles VIII. Some of the stained-glass windows, the building's glory, date from the 13th century. Admission is free and hours are daily 9am to 6pm.

The **Musée des Beaux-Arts,** 18 place François-Sicard (© 02-47-05-68-73), is housed in an archbishop's palace of the 17th and 18th centuries complete with Louis XVI woodwork and Tours silk-damask hangings. Among the foreign acquisitions, the most outstanding paintings are Mantegna's *Christ in the Garden of Olives* and *The Resurrection.* Other foreign works include an early Rembrandt *(Flight into Egypt),* plus canvases by Rubens, Luca Giordano, and Mattäus Günther. The French school is represented by Le Sueur, Fouquet, Boucher, Vernet, Vuillard, David, Ingres, Degas *(Calvary),* Delacroix *(Comedians and Buffoons),* and Monet. The most important sculpture is by Houdon and Lemoyne. You can tour the gardens for free daily from 7am to 8:30pm. Admission to the museum is 4€ ($4.60) adults, 2€ ($2.30) students and seniors, free for children under 13. Hours are Wednesday to Monday 9am to 12:45pm and 2 to 6pm.

WHERE TO STAY & DINE
The **Best Western Le Central,** 21 rue Berthelot, 37000 Tours (© 800/528-1234 in the U.S. or Canada, or 02-47-05-46-44; www.bestwestern.com), is within walking distance of the river and cathedral, surrounded by gardens, lawns, and trees. Built in 1850, this 41-room hotel is a more modest but economical choice, with family-style and homelike bedrooms that come in a variety of shapes and sizes, all of them renovated in 1999. About half the bathrooms have showers only. Rates are 80€ to 95€ ($92–$109) double.

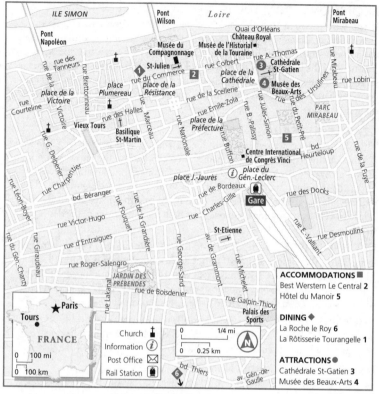

The following appears in the map legend:

ACCOMMODATIONS ■
Best Werstern Le Central **2**
Hôtel du Manoir **5**

DINING ◆
La Roche le Roy **6**
La Rôtisserie Tourangelle **1**

ATTRACTIONS ●
Cathédrale St-Gatien **3**
Musée des Beaux-Arts **4**

Church †
Information ⓘ
Post Office ✉
Rail Station ▤

The 19th-century **Hôtel du Manoir,** 2 rue Traversière, 37000 Tours (© 02-47-05-37-37; manoir37@aol.com), is situated on a quiet street near the train station, shops, and restaurants. This 20-room residence provides guests with a comfortable place to stay in small to midsize bedrooms; half the bathrooms have showers only. Rates run 39.50€ to 49€ ($45.45–$56.35) double.

One of the hottest chefs in town, Alain Couturier, blends new and old techniques at **La Roche le Roy** ★★, 55 rte. St-Avertin. © 02-47-27-22-00), in a steep-gabled, 15th-century manor south of the town center. Couturier's repertoire includes such delights as scalloped foie gras with lentils, cod with saffron cream, and pan-fried scallops with a truffle vinaigrette. Main courses are 15€ to 30€ ($17.25–$34.50). A fixed-price menu is offered for 32€ ($36.80) lunch only, and 45€ to 65€ ($51.75–$74.75) for dinner. To get here, follow av. de Grammot south from the town center until you pass over a bridge and the street becomes rte. St-Avertin.

La Rôtisserie Tourangelle, 23 rue du Commerce Tours (© 02-47-05-71-21), has been a local favorite since shortly after the end of World War II. It's better to concentrate on the ever-changing menu, which may include homemade foie gras and whitefish caught in the Loire and served with *beurre blanc* (white butter sauce). A fixed-price lunch costs 18€ ($20.70) and the fixed-price lunch or dinner is 32€ ($36.80) to 50€ ($57.50). It's a short walk from the cathedral.

EXCURSIONS FROM TOURS

If you wish to see at least five or six of the greatest châteaux in Europe (pre-viewed below), Tours is your best choice as a transportation hub, although some connections can be a bit difficult and are not always via a rail line. Be advised that none of the hometowns of these world-famous châteaux are of any particular tourist interest. So once you land on your feet in these Loire towns, you can go immediately to the châteaux without feeling you're missing out on a lot of other attractions.

AZAY-LE-RIDEAU

This sleepy little town, visited only for its château (see below), is 13 miles (21km) southwest of Tours. Now named after its chateau, the village was once known as Azay-le-Brûlé or "Azay the Burnt." Passing through with his court in 1418, the dauphin, later Charles VII, was insulted by the Burgundians. The result: A whole garrison was killed for the outrage, and the village and its fortress razed. The château standing here today was built upon the ruins of the destroyed structure.

GETTING THERE   To reach Azay-le-Rideau, take one of three daily trains from Tours. Trip time is about 30 minutes; the one-way fare is 4.80€ ($5.50). The local railway station is in an isolated spot 1¼ miles (2km) outside of town. There's no public transport, but visitors can call for a taxi (✆ **02-47-45-26-26**), which, after a brief delay, will arrive to haul them to the château.

VISITOR INFORMATION   **Syndicat d'Initiative** (tourist office) is on place de l'Europe (✆ **02-47-45-44-40**). Hours are Monday to Saturday 9am to 7pm and Sunday 10am to 6pm. The tourist office is in the city center near the château.

Top Attractions & Special Moments

Château d'Azay-le-Rideau ✭✭, 37190 Azay-le-Rideau (✆ **02-47-45-42-04**), despite its medieval appearance and defensive architecture, was actually created as a private residence during the Renaissance.

Giles Berthelot, the financial minister of François I, built the château begin-ning in 1518. Actually, his big-spending wife, Phillipe, supervised its construc-tion. Both of them should have known better. So elegant and harmonious, so imposing was their creation that the Chevalier King grew immensely jealous. In time Berthelot fled and the château reverted to the king. François I didn't live there, however, but started the custom of granting it to "friends of the crown." After a brief residency by Prince Frederick of Prussia in 1870, the château became the property of the state in 1905.

Before entering you can circle the mansion, enjoying its near-perfect propor-tions, the crowning achievement of the French Renaissance in Touraine. Architec-turally, its most fancifully ornate feature is a great bay enclosing a grand stairway with a straight flight of steps. The Renaissance interior is a virtual museum.

The largest room at Azay, the **Banqueting Hall,** is adorned with four 17th-century Flemish tapestries representing scenes from the life of Constantine (it took a crafts person 1 year just to weave 4 square feet. In the kitchen is a collec-tion of utensils, including a wooden mold capable of making 45 designs on cakes. The corner carvings are most unusual: One, for example, shows a dog bit-ing its own ear.

In the dining room is a trio of 16th-century Flemish tapestries. The fireplace is only a plaster molding of a chimneypiece made by Rodin for the Château of Mon-tal. The fireplace masterpiece, however, is in a ground-floor bedroom containing a 16th-century four-poster bed. Over the stone fireplace hovers a salamander, the symbol of François I.

The château is open daily during July and August from 9:30am to 7pm; April to June and September to October from 9:30am to 6pm; and November to March from 9:30am to 12:30pm and 2 to 5:30pm. Admission is 5.50€ ($6.35) for adults and 3.50€ ($4.05) for ages 18 to 25, free for children under 18. Allow 2 hours for a visit. From May to July, *son et lumière* (sound and light) performances, about an hour in length, with recorded music and lights beaming on the celebrated exterior of the château, begin at 10:30pm; during August they begin at 10pm; and during September at 9:30pm. Tickets are 9€ ($10.35) for adults and 5€ ($5.75) for ages 18 to 25; free for those under 18. Admission to *son-et-lumière* performances is free for persons under 18.

AMBOISE

On the banks of the Loire, Amboise is a real Renaissance town in the center of vineyards known as Touraine-Amboise. Leonardo da Vinci spent his last years in this ancient city. Dominating the town is the **Château of Amboise,** the first in France to reflect the impact of the Italian Renaissance. Amboise is the most important day trip from Tours. The town is 22 miles (35km) east of Tours and 136 miles (219km) southwest of Paris.

GETTING THERE   Amboise lies on the main Paris-Blois-Tours rail line, with 14 trains per day arriving from both Tours and Blois (see below). The trip from Tours takes 20 minutes and costs 4.50€ ($5.20) one-way; the trip from Blois also takes 20 minutes and costs 5.30€ ($6.10). About five conventional trains per day depart from Paris's Gare d'Austerlitz (trip time: 2½ hr.), and several high-speed TGV trains leave from the Gare Montparnasse for St-Pierre-des-Corps, less than .6 miles (1km) from Tours. From St-Pierre-des-Corps, you can transfer to a conventional train bound for Amboise. One-way fares from Paris to Amboise cost 22.05€ ($25.35). For more information and schedules, call ℭ **08-36-35-35-35.**

VISITOR INFORMATION   **Office de Tourisme,** quai du Général-de-Gaulle (ℭ **02-47-57-09-28;** www.amboise-valdeloire.com), is open Monday to Saturday 9am to 8pm, Sunday 10am to 6pm. To get here from the train station, walk across the bridge over the river and turn right. The château is a short walk away.

Top Attractions & Special Moments

The **Château d'Amboise** ✪✪ (ℭ **02-47-57-00-98**) is a combination of both Gothic and Renaissance architecture. This 15th-century château suffered during the Revolution (and as a result, only about a quarter of the original structure remains), and it is mainly associated with Charles VIII, who built it on a rock spur separating the valleys of the Loire and the Amasse. Born at Amboise on June 30, 1470, Charles returned to France at the age of 25 following an Italian campaign, and with him, he brought artists, designers, and architects from "that land of enchantment." In a sense, he brought the Italian Renaissance to France.

You visit first the flamboyant **Gothic Chapel of St. Hubert,** distinguished by its lacelike tracery. It allegedly contains the remains of da Vinci. Actually, the great artist was buried in the castle's Collegiate Church, which was destroyed between 1806 and 1810. During the Second Empire, excavations were undertaken on the site of the church, and bones discovered were "identified" as those of Leonardo.

The **Logis du roi** (the king's apartment), its facade pierced by large double mullioned windows and crowned by towering dormers and sculptured canopies, survived the Revolution intact. Alas, Charles VIII's own apartment caused his death: He died at Amboise on April 8, 1498, after accidentally banging his head against a wall. At the end of the terrace, near the room of his queen, Anne of Brittany, is a low doorway where it is said the mishap took place.

Adjoining the apartment are two squat towers, the Hurtalt and the Minimes, which contain ramps of huge dimensions so that cavaliers on horseback or nobles in horse-drawn chariots could ascend them.

Today, the walls of the château are hung with tapestries, the rooms furnished in the style of the *époque*. From the terraces are panoramic views of the town and the Loire Valley. Admission is 7€ ($8.05) adults, 6€ ($6.90) students, 4€ ($4.60) children, free for children 6 and under. Hours are July to August daily 9am to 8pm; April to June daily 9am to 6:30pm; September to October daily 9am to 6pm; November 1 to 15 daily 9am to 5:30pm; November 16 to January daily 9am to noon and 2 to 4:45pm; February to March daily 9am to noon and 1:30 to 5:30pm

Clos-Lucé ⭐, 2 rue de Clos-Lucé (*②* **02-47-57-62-88**), is a 15th-century manor house of brick and stone about a 2-mile (3.2km) walk from the Château d'Amboise. In what had been an oratory for Anne of Brittany, François I installed "the great master in all forms of art and science," Leonardo da Vinci. Loved and venerated by the Chevalier King, da Vinci lived there for 3 years, dying at the manor in 1519. (Incidentally, those deathbed paintings depicting Leonardo in the arms of François I are probably symbolic; the king was supposedly out of town when the artist died.)

From the window of his bedroom Leonardo liked to look out at the château where François lived. Whenever he was restless, the king would visit Leonardo via an underground tunnel.

Inside, the rooms are well furnished, some containing reproductions from the period of the artist. The downstairs is reserved for da Vinci's designs, models, and inventions, including his plans for a turbine engine, an airplane, and a parachute. Admission is 11€ ($12.65) adults, 9€ ($10.35) students, 6.50€ ($7.50) children 6–15, free for children 5 and under. Hours are daily 9am to 6pm.

BLOIS

Just 37 miles (60km) northeast of Tours and within easy rail reach of that city, the small town of **Blois** ("Blwah") is often called the center of the châteaux country. It lies on the right bank of the Loire and is often visited by rail passengers in the morning, who then spend the afternoon at the château nearby at Chambord (see below). In 1429, Joan of Arc launched her expeditionary forces from Blois to oust the English from Orléans.

GETTING THERE   The Paris-Austerlitz line via Orléans delivers six **trains** per day from Paris (trip time: 2 hr.), at a cost of 19.90€ ($22.90) one-way; from Tours, five trains arrive per day (trip time: 30 min.), at a cost of 8.40€ ($9.65) one-way. For information and schedules, call *②* **08-36-35-35-35.**

The train station is at place de la Gare. Once here, you can take a **bus** (*②* **02-54-90-41-41**) to tour various châteaux in the area, including Chambord. Buses depart from the train station from June to September only. The Château de Blois and tourist office are within an easy 5-minute walk southeast of the rail station.

VISITOR INFORMATION   The **Office de Tourisme** is in the Pavillon Anne-de-Bretagne, 3 av. Jean-Laigret (*②* **02-54-90-41-41;** www.loiredes chateaux.com). Off-season hours are Sunday and Monday 10:30am to 5pm and

Tuesday to Saturday 9am to 7pm. Summer hours are Sunday and Monday 10am to 7pm and Tuesday to Sunday 9am to 7pm. Closed in January.

Top Attractions & Special Moments

Château de Blois ★★★ (© 02-54-90-33-33) is forever linked to one of the most famous murders in French history, that of the Duke of Guise—called *Balafre* (Scarface) on December 23, 1588. His archrival, Henri III, ordered the murder. The château and scene of this famous assassination was begun in the 13th century by the counts of Blois. Charles d'Orléans, the "poet prince," lived at Blois after his release from 25 years of English captivity. He had married Mary of Cleves and brought a "court of letters" to Blois. In his 70s, Charles became father of the future Louis XII, who was to marry Anne of Brittany, and Blois was launched in its new role as a royal château. In time it was to be called the second capital of France, and Blois itself the city of kings.

However, Blois eventually became a palace of banishment. Louis XIII sent his interfering mother, Marie de Médici, here, but the plump matron escaped by sliding into the moat on a coat down a mound of dirt left by the builders. In 1626, the king sent his conspiring brother, Gaston d'Orléans here. He actually stayed put.

If you stand in the courtyard of the great château, you'll find it's like an illustrated storybook of French architecture. The **Hall of the Estates-General** is a beautiful work from the 13th century; the so-called **gallery of Charles d'Orléans** was actually built by Louis XII between 1498 and 1501, as was the **Louis XII wing.** The **François I** wing is a masterpiece of the French Renaissance; the **Gaston d'Orléans** wing was constructed by François Mansart between 1635 and 1637. Of them all, the most remarkable is the François I wing, which contains a spiral staircase with elaborately ornamented balustrades and the king's symbol, the salamander. In the Louis XII wing, seek out paintings by Antoine Caron, court painter to Henri III, depicting the persecution of Thomas More.

The château presents a *son-et-lumière* (sound-and-light) show in French from May to September, beginning in most cases at 10:30pm, but in rare instances, including throughout the month of May, at 9:30 or 10:15pm, depending on the school calendar. As a taped lecture is played, colored lights and dramatic readings evoke the age in which the château was built. The show costs 9.50€ ($10.95) for adults, 4.50€ ($5.20) for children 7 to 15. Admission to the château itself is 6€ ($6.90) adults, 4€ ($4.60) students ages 12 to 20, 2€ ($2.30) for children 6 to 11, free for children 5 and under. Hours are daily June 2 to April 4 and November 3 to December 31 9am to 12:30pm and 2 to 5:30 pm; April 5 to June 27 and September 1 to November 2 9am to 6pm; June 28 to August 31 9am to 7pm.

CHAMBORD

In the village of Chambord, 11 miles (18km) east of Blois (see above) and 118 miles (190km) southwest of Paris, stands a château where the French Renaissance in architecture reached its peak.

GETTING THERE   This is one place you can't get to by rail alone; you'll need to take a train to Blois (see above), then travel here by other means. From June 15 to September 15, **Transports du Loir et Cher** (© 02-54-58-55-61) operates bus service to Chambord, leaving Blois at 12:30pm with returns at 6:45pm. You can also rent a bicycle in Blois and ride the 11 miles (18km) to Chambord, or take one of the tours to Chambord leaving from Blois in summer.

VISITOR INFORMATION The **Office de Tourisme,** on place St-Michel
(© **02-54-33-39-16**), is open daily April through September from 10am to
7:30pm.

Top Attractions & Special Moments

Work on **Château de Chambord** ✹✹✹, 41250 Bracieux (© **02-54-50-40-00**),
was begun in 1519 with 2,000 laborers. After 20 years, the largest château in the
Loire Valley emerged. It was ready for the visit of Charles V of Germany, who
was welcomed by nymphets in transparent veils tossing wildflowers in the
emperor's path.

French monarchs—Henri II, Catherine de Medici, and Louis XIII—came
and went from Chambord, but it was the personal favorite of François I, the
Chevalier King (who is said to have carved the following on one of the window
panes with his diamond ring: "A woman is a creature of change; to trust her is
to play the fool.").

The château was restored in part by the brother of Louis XIII, Gaston d'Orléans. His daughter, "La Grand Mademoiselle" (Mademoiselle de Montpensier),
wrote that she used to force her father to run up and down Chambord's famous
double spiral staircase after her. Because of its corkscrew structure, he never
caught her (one person may descend at one end and another ascend at the other
without ever meeting.)

The château is set in a park of more than 13,000 acres, enclosed within a wall
stretching 20 miles (32km). At its lowest point the château was used as a munitions factory. The state acquired Chambord in 1932. Its facade is characterized
by four monumental towers. The keep contains a spectacular terrace, which the
ladies of the court used to stand on to watch the return of their men from the
hunt. From that platform, you can inspect the dormer windows and the richly
decorated chimneys, some characterized by winged horses. The apartments of
Louis XIV (the Sun King paid nine visits here), including his redecorated bedchamber, are also in the keep. A trio of rooms was restored by the government,
but not with the original furnishings, of course.

The château is open daily 9am to 6:15pm (last entrance at 5:45pm). Admission is 7€ ($8.05)for adults, 4.50€ ($5.20) for ages 18 to 25, and free for children 17 and under. The price is 12€ ($13.80). Allow 1½ hours to go through
the château.

CHAUMONT-SUR-LOIRE

The château in the village of Chaumont is 25 miles (40km) east of Tours and
124 miles (200km) southwest of Paris. It was built next to the Loire River during the reign of Louis XII by Charles d'Amboise. The castle is reached from the
village by a long walk through a wooded park. The original fortress was dismantled by Louis XI, and in 1560 Chaumont was acquired by Catherine de
Médici. Later, the château was privately owned until it was taken over by the
state in 1938.

GETTING THERE Seventeen **trains** per day travel to Chaumont from Blois
(trip time: 15 min.) and Tours (trip time: about 45 min.). One-way fares are
3.05€ ($3.50) from Blois or 7€ ($8.05) from Tours. The railway station servicing Chaumont is in Onzain, 1½ miles (2.4km) north of the château, a nice
walk. For transportation information, call © **08-36-35-35-35.**

VISITOR INFORMATION **Office de Tourisme,** rue du Maréchal-Leclerc
(© **02-54-20-91-73**), is open Monday to Saturday 9:30am to 10:30pm; Sunday

10am to 7pm. From the tourist office, it's a 5-minute (steeply uphill) walk to the Château de Chaumont. There's no public transportation available.

Top Attractions & Special Moments

Château de Chaumont ★★ (℗ 02-54-51-26-26) was home to Diane de Poitiers, mistress of Henry II. Not that she wanted it. The king had given her Chenonceau (see below), which she loved, but Catherine de Médici had her banished from that favored château and shipped her off to Chaumont. At the time, the château of Chaumont probably looked grim. Its battlements, its pepper-pot turrets crowning the towers—the whole effect resembled a prison.

Inside, portraits reveal the king's mistress to have truly lived up to her reputation as forever beautiful. Another portrait—that of Catherine de Médici, wife of Henri II, looking like a devout nun—invites unfavorable comparison.

Architecturally, the castle spans the intermediate period between the Middle Ages and the Renaissance. Inside, the prize exhibit is a rare collection of **medallions by Nini,** an Italian artist. A guest of the château for a while, he made medallion portraits of kings, queens, nobles, and even Benjamin Franklin, who once visited Chaumont.

In the bedroom occupied by Catherine de Médici is a portrait of a witty-looking cardinal who wanted to become the pope. There is also a rare portrait of Catherine, painted when she was young, wearing many jewels, including a ruby later owned by Mary, Queen of Scots. Catherine was superstitious, always keeping her astrologer, Cosino Rugieri, at beck and call. She had him housed in one of the tower bedrooms (a portrait of him remains). It is reported that he foretold the disasters awaiting her sons, including Henri III. In the astrologer's bedroom is a most unusual tapestry depicting Medusa with a flying horse escaping from her head.

The château is open April to September 9:30am to 6pm and October to March daily 10am to 4:30pm. Admission is 5.50€ ($6.35) for adults, 3€ ($3.45) for students and children 18 and under. Allow 2 hours to see Chaumont.

CHENONCEAUX

Only 16 miles (26km) east of Tours is the tiny village called Chenonceaux, home to the château Chenonceau (notice the missing "x" in the castle's name).

GETTING THERE   There are four daily **trains** from Tours to Chenonceaux (trip time: 30 min.), costing 5.20€ ($6) one-way. The train deposits you at the base of the château.

VISITOR INFORMATION   The **Syndicat d'Initiative** (tourist office; 1 rue Bretonneau; ℗ 02-47-23-94-45), is open from Easter to September. Monday to Saturday 9:30am to 1pm and 2:30 to 7:30pm; Sunday 2:30 to 6:30pm.

Top Attractions & Special Moments

The Renaissance masterpiece, **Château de Chenonceau** ★★★ (℗ 02-47-23-90-07), has essentially orbited around the series of famous *dames de Chenonceau* who have occupied it. François I seized the château in 1524 from a wealthy Tours family and in 1547, Henri II gave Chenonceau to his mistress, Diane de Poitiers, who was 20 years his senior. For a time, this remarkable woman was virtually the queen of France. But when Henri died in a jousting tournament in 1559, his jealous wife, Catherine de Médici became regent of France and immediately forced Diane de Poitiers to abandon her beloved Chenonceau in exchange for Chaumont (see above). Catherine added her own touches to the château, building a two-story gallery across the bridge—obviously inspired by her native Florence.

The long gallery running along the Cher River contains a black-and-white diamond floor.

It was at Chenonceau that Catherine received a pair of teenage honeymooners: her son, François II, and his bride, Mary Stuart (aka Mary, Queen of Scots). And it was here, in the 18th century that Rousseau declared his undying love for the mistress of the château, Madame Dupin, the grandmother of George Sand, and was promptly rebuffed.

Many of the château's walls today are covered with Gobelins tapestries, including one depicting a woman pouring water over the back of an angry dragon, another of a three-headed dog and a seven-headed monster. The chapel contains a delicate marble Virgin and Child, plus portraits of Catherine de Médici in her traditional black and white. There's even a portrait of the stern Catherine in the former bedroom of her rival, Diane de Poitiers. But in the Renaissance-style bedchamber of François I, the most interesting portrait is that of Diane de Poitiers as the huntress Diana, complete with a sling of arrows on her back. *The Three Graces* are by Van Loo. The château is open daily 9am to 7pm. Admission is 6.50€ ($7.50) for adults and 6.10€ ($7) for students and children 7 to 15. A *son-et-lumière* show, *The Era of the Ladies of Chenonceaux*, is staged daily in July and August at 10:15pm; admission is 7.60€ ($8.75) for adults, 6.10€ ($7) for students and ages 7 to 15, free for 6 and under. Allow 2 hours to see this château.

4 Provence & the Riviera

The French Riviera, known to the world as the fashionable *Côte d'Azur*, is actually part of the greater region of sunny Provence that sweeps across the southern tier of France and is an easy train ride from Paris.

Provence has its own language and customs. The region is bounded on the north by the Dauphine, the west by the Rhône, the east by the Alps, and the south by the Mediterranean. In this section we cover the northern area of this region, what's traditionally thought of as Provence (and whose most evocative cities include **Avignon, Aix-en-Provence,** and **Arles**), and then head down to French Riviera and its two grandest resorts, **Cannes** and **Nice.** The good news for rail travelers is that no matter what section you choose, you'll have very few problems getting around by train and from the south, you can even make an easy rail excursion to the principality of **Monaco.**

Of course, easy rail access isn't necessarily the big draw in this region. The weather isn't bad either. The winter temperature is higher in the Riviera than the rest of France, mainly because of the Alpine chain that protects the Côte d'Azur from cold, continental winds. The Riviera's high season used to be winter and spring only. However, with changing tastes, July and August have become the most crowded months, and reservations are imperative. The average summer temperature is 75°F (24°C); the average winter temperature, 49°F (10°C). If you can, we recommend coming here in May or October when crowds thin, prices drop, but the weather remains lovely and the Riviera and the countryside of Provence can give you exactly what the travel posters promise.

If the weather isn't enough, perhaps the most compelling endorsement of the Riviera has been the number of artists drawn to its shores and hillside villas, leaving behind a rich legacy. At Cagnes, Renoir praised the "light effects" of the region. Nice was selected by Matisse as the spot in which to spend the remaining years of his life (you can visit his remarkable Chapel of Saint Dominique at

Vence). For the fishermen of Villefranche, Cocteau decorated a chapel. Picasso left an art legacy from one end of the Riviera to the other.

Or maybe it's the food. After all, so many visitors come to Provence specifically to dine, so do try some of the region's specialties, especially the *salade niçoise,* which essentially includes fresh vine-ripened tomatoes, small radishes—either red or black—green peppers, and often potatoes, and green beans. The thick, saffron-flavored fish soup of the Mediterranean, the bouillabaisse, is eagerly ordered by diners all over Provence, as is *ratatouille* (a mixture of small eggplants, tomatoes, miniature squash, and red peppers simmered in olive oil).

AVIGNON ⭐⭐⭐

In the 14th century, Avignon was the capital of Christendom; the popes lived here during what the Romans called "the Babylonian Captivity." The legacy left by that "court of splendor and magnificence" makes Avignon even today one of the most interesting and beautiful of Europe's cities of the Middle Ages.

Today, this walled city of some 100,000 residents is a major stopover on the rail route from Paris to the Mediterranean and it's the transportation hub for inland Provence. It is increasingly known as a cultural center. Artists and painters have been moving here, especially to rue des Teinturiers. Experimental theaters, galleries, and cinemas have brought diversity to the inner city. The popes are long gone, but life goes on exceedingly well.

GETTING THERE   From Paris, TGV Med trains frequently depart from Gare de Lyon, the trip taking 2 hours and 38 minutes. A one-way fare costs 113€ ($130) in first class, 82.20€ ($94.55) in second class. Trains also arrive frequently from Marseille (trip time: 30 min.), with a ticket costing 22.60€ ($26); and from Arles (trip time: 15 min.), with a fare of 7.40€ ($8.50). For train information and reservations, call ℂ **08-36-35-35-39.**

VISITOR INFORMATION   The **Office de Tourisme** is at 41 cours Jean-Jaurès (ℂ **04-32-74-32-74;** www.ot-avignon.fr), about 200 yards north of the train station. Off-season hours are Monday to Friday 9am to 6pm, Saturday 9am to 5pm, and Sunday noon to 3pm. Summer hours are Monday to Saturday 9am to 6pm and Sunday noon to 5pm. This office does not reserve hotel rooms.

TOP ATTRACTIONS & SPECIAL MOMENTS

Even more famous than the papal residency is the ditty *"Sur le pont d'Avignon, l'on y danse, l'on y danse,"* echoing through every French nursery and around the world. Ironically, **pont St-Bénézet** ⭐⭐ was far too narrow for the *danse* of the rhyme. Spanning the Rhône and connecting Avignon with Villeneuve-lèz-Avignon, the bridge is now a ruin, with only 4 of its original 22 arches. According to legend, it was inspired by a vision that a shepherd named Bénézet had while tending his flock. The bridge was built between 1177 and 1185 and suffered various disasters from then on. (In 1669, half the bridge fell into the river.) On one of the piers is the two-story **Chapelle St-Nicolas**—one story in Romanesque style, the other in Gothic. The remains of the bridge are open daily from 9am to 6:30pm. Admission is 3.50€ ($4.05) for adults and 3€ ($3.45) for students and seniors, free for ages 7 and under.

The **Palais des Papes** ⭐⭐⭐, place du Palais (ℂ **04-90-27-50-00**), dominates Avignon. In 1309, a sick man, nearing the end of his life, arrived in Avignon. His name was Clement V, and he was the leader of the Christian world. Lodged as a guest of the Dominicans, he died in the spring of 1314 and was succeeded by John XXII. The new pope, unlike the popes of Rome, lived modestly in the Episcopal Palace. When Benedict XII took over, he greatly enlarged and rebuilt the palace. Clement VI, who followed, built an even more elaborate extension called the New Palace. After Innocent VI and Urban V, Pope Gregory XI did no building. Inspired by Catherine of Siena, he was intent upon returning the papacy to Rome, and he succeeded. In all, seven popes reigned at Avignon. Under them art and culture flourished, as did vice. Prostitutes blatantly went about peddling their wares in front of fat cardinals, rich merchants were robbed, and innocent pilgrims from the hinterlands were brutally tricked and swindled.

From 1378, during the Great Schism, one pope ruled in Avignon, another in Rome. The reign of the pope and the "anti-pope" continued, one following the other, until both rulers were dismissed by the election of Martin V in 1417. Rome continued to rule Avignon until it was joined to France at the time of the French Revolution.

You're shown through the palace today on a guided 50-minute tour, taking in the Chapelle St-Jean, known for its 14th-century frescoes, and the Grand Tinel or banquet hall, about 135 feet (41 km) long. The pope's bedroom is on the second floor of the Tour des Anges, and other attractions include the Great Audience Hall containing frescoes attributed to Giovanetti and painted in 1352.

The on-site **Musée du Petit Palais** contains an important collection of paintings from the Italian schools from the 13th through the 16th centuries, including works from Florence, Venice, Sienna, and Lombardy. In addition, salons display paintings done in Avignon in the 15th century. Several salons are devoted to Roman and Gothic sculptures from Avignon.

The ramparts (still standing) around Avignon were built in the 14th century, and are characterized by their machicolated battlements, turrets, and old gates. They are squat and very thick, like huge children's blocks placed there according to a playful up-and-down design. The fortifications were rebuilt in the 19th century by Viollet-le-Duc, the busiest man in France, who restored Notre-Dame in Paris and the fortified walls at Carcassonne.

Admission (including a tour with a guide or cassette recording) is 9.50€ ($10.90) adults, 7.50€ ($8.60) students and seniors, free for ages 7 and under. Hours are daily November to March 9:30am–5:45pm; April to June and August to October daily 9am to 7pm; July daily 9am to 8pm.

Nearby is **Cathédrale Notre-Dame des Doms,** place du Palais (© 04-90-86-81-01), dating from the 12th century and containing the flamboyant Gothic tomb of John XXII, who died at the age of 90. Benedict XII is also buried there. Crowning the top is a gilded statue of the Virgin from the 19th century. From the cathedral, you can enter the **Promenade du Rocher des Doms,** strolling through its garden and enjoying the view across the Rhône to Villeneuve-lés-Avignon. Admission is free. Hours vary according to religious ceremonies, but are generally daily 9am to noon and 2 to 6pm.

It's been decades since the death of Jacques Doucet (1853–1929), the Belle Epoque dandy, dilettante, and designer of Parisian haute couture, but his magnificent art collection is on view to the general public at **La Fondation Angladon-Dubrujeaud** ✦✦, 5 rue Laboureur (© 04-90-82-29-03). When not designing, Doucet collected the early works of a number of artists, among them Picasso, Max Jacob, and van Gogh. Today, you can wander through Doucet's former abode, viewing rare antiques; 16th-century Buddhas; Louis XVI chairs designed by Jacob; and canvases by Cézanne, Sisley, Degas, and Modigliani. Doucet died in 1929 at 76, his fortune so diminished that his nephew paid for his funeral, but his rich legacy lives on here. Admission is 5€ ($5.75) adults, 3€

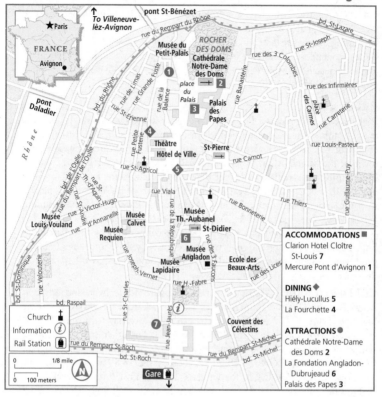

The map includes the following labels:

- To Villeneuve-lèz-Avignon
- pont St-Bénézet
- ★ Paris
- FRANCE
- Avignon
- rue du Rempart du Rhône
- bd. St-Lazare
- rue St-Joseph
- Musée du Petit-Palais
- ROCHER DES DOMS
- rue des 3 Colombes
- Cathédrale Notre-Dame des Doms
- rue des Infirmières
- rue de Limas
- rue Grande Fusterie
- place du Palais
- rue Banasterie
- rue St-Pierre
- place des Carmes
- rue Carreterie
- pont Daladier
- bd. du Rhône
- rue St-Étienne
- rue de la Balance
- Palais des Papes
- Rhône
- rue Petite Fusterie
- Théâtre
- Hôtel de Ville
- St-Pierre
- rue Louis-Pasteur
- rue Carnot
- bd. de l'Oulle
- bd. du Rempart de l'Oulle
- rue St-Dominique
- rue St-André
- rue d'Annanelle
- rue Victor-Hugo
- rue St-Agricol
- rue Viala
- Musée Louis-Vouland
- Musée Requien
- Musée Calvet
- Musée Th.-Aubanel
- St-Didier
- rue Bonneterie
- rue Thiers
- rue Guillaume-Puy
- rue de la République
- Musée Lapidaire
- Musée Angladon
- Ecole des Beaux-Arts
- rue des 3 Faucons
- rue H.-Fabre
- rue des Lices
- rue Joseph-Vernet
- rue St-Charles
- bd. St-Dominique
- rue Velouterie
- bd. Raspail
- Church
- Information
- Rail Station
- rue du Rempart St-Roch
- rue Jean-Jaurès
- Couvent des Célestins
- rue du Rempart St-Michel
- bd. St-Roch
- bd. St-Michel
- Gare
- 0 1/8 mile
- 0 100 meters

ACCOMMODATIONS ■
Clarion Hotel Cloître St-Louis **7**
Mercure Pont d'Avignon **1**

DINING ◆
Hiély-Lucullus **5**
La Fourchette **4**

ATTRACTIONS ●
Cathédrale Notre-Dame des Doms **2**
La Fondation Angladon-Dubrujeaud **6**
Palais des Papes **3**

($3.45) students and teens 14 to 18, 1.50€ ($1.75) children 7 to 13. Hours are Tuesday to Sunday 1 to 6pm.

WHERE TO STAY & DINE

Clarion Hotel Cloître St-Louis ⚐, 20 rue Portail Boquier, 84000 Avignon (② **800/CLARION** in the U.S., or 04-90-27-55-55; www.cloitre-saint-louis. com), is housed in a former Jesuit school built in the 1580s. Outbuildings and new construction include a wing designed by world-class architect Jean Nouvel. Ranging from medium to large, the 80 bedrooms don't have much style but are tastefully and comfortably furnished. Rates are 107€ to 250€ ($123–$288) double; 275€ ($316) suite.

Mercure Pont d'Avignon, Quartier de la Balance, rue Ferruce, 84000 Avignon (② **04-90-80-93-93;** www.mercure.com), is one of the best in Avignon, and is a good value for what it offers. The 87 midsize bedrooms are well-maintained and simply though comfortably furnished, with small bathrooms that have a tub and a shower. It lies within the city walls, at the foot of the Palace of the Popes. Rates are 110€ ($127) double, 200€ ($230) suite.

Hiély-Lucullus ⚐⚐, 5 rue de la République (② **04-90-86-17-07**), is a Relais Gourmand reigning supreme in Avignon. The chef, André Chaussy, offers reasonable fixed-price menus (no a la carte)—the best in town. The pièce de résistance is *agneau des Alpilles grillé* (grilled Alpine lamb). Fixed-price menu prices are 30€ to 38€ ($34.50–$43.70) and reservations are a must.

La Fourchette, 7 rue Racine (📞 **04-90-85-20-93;** Bus: 11), offers creative French cooking at a moderate price, although it shuts down on the weekends. The dining rooms are light and airy thanks to large windows. For a main course, we recommend the blanquette of monkfish with endive or daube of beef with a gratin of macaroni. Main courses run 16€ to 28€ ($18.40–$32.20); set-price dinners cost 30€ ($34.50).

ARLES 🐸🐸🐸

It's been called "the soul of Provence," though it was known as "the little Rome of the Gauls," when Constantine the Great named it the second capital in his empire in A.D. 306. Art lovers, archaeologists, and historians are attracted to this town on the Rhône. Many of its scenes, painted so luminously by van Gogh in his declining years, remain to delight. The great Dutch painter left Paris for Arles in 1888. It was in that same year that he cut off part of his left ear. But he was to paint some of his most celebrated works in the Provençal town, including *Starry Night, The Bridge at Arles, Sunflowers,* and *L'Arlésienne.*

Befitting its glorious past, Arles is still well connected—by rail that is. It's linked to both Paris and Avignon (where you usually need to change trains to get here) by high-speed lines and also offers connections to other cities in Provence.

GETTING THERE   Trains leave from Paris's Gare de Lyon and arrive at Arles's **Gare SNCF** (av. Paulin-Talabot), a short walk from the town center. One high-speed direct TGV travels from Paris to Arles each day (trip time: 4½ hr.; 107€/$123 for 1st class, 78€/$89.70 for 2nd). For other trains, you must change in Avignon. There are hourly connections between Arles and Avignon (trip time: 15 min.; 8.60€/$9.90 for 1st class, 7.70€/$8.85 for 2nd), Marseille (trip time: 1 hr.; 17.40€/$20 for 1st class, 11.60€/$13.35 for 2nd), and Aix-en-Provence (trip time: 1¾ hr. with a stop in Marseilles; 22.90€/$26.35 for 1st class; 15.40€/$17.70 for 2nd). For rail schedules and information, call 📞 **08-36-35-35-39.**

VISITOR INFORMATION   The Office de Tourisme, where you can buy a *billet global* (see below), is on the esplanade Charles-de-Gaulle (📞 **04-90-18-41-20**). Summer hours (Mar 31–Sept 28) are daily 9am to 6:45pm. Off-season hours (Sept 29–Mar 30) are Monday to Saturday 9am to 5:45pm and Sunday 10:30am to 2:30pm.

TOP ATTRACTIONS & SPECIAL MOMENTS

At the tourist office, buy a ***billet global*** 🐸, a pass that admits you to the town's museums, Roman monuments, and major attractions, at a cost of 12€ ($13.80) for adults and 5€ ($5.75) students and ages 17 and under.

The town is full of Roman monuments. The general vicinity of the old Roman forum is occupied by **place du Forum,** shaded by plane trees. Once, the Café de Nuit, immortalized by van Gogh, stood on this square. Two Corinthian columns and pediment fragments from a temple can be seen at the corner of the Hôtel Nord-Pinus. South of here is **place de la République** (also known as the place de l'Hôtel de Ville), the principal plaza, dominated by a 50-foot blue porphyry obelisk. On the north is the impressive Hôtel-de-Ville (town hall) from 1673, built to Mansart's plans and surmounted by a Renaissance belfry.

One of the city's great classical monuments is the Roman **Théâtre Antique** 🐸🐸, rue du Cloître (📞 **04-90-49-36-25**). Begun by Augustus in the

1st century, only two Corinthian columns remain. The theater was where the *Venus of Arles* was discovered in 1651. Take rue de la Calade from city hall. The theater is open daily, as follows: November through February from 10 to 11:30am and 2 to 4:30pm; March and April from 9 to 11:30am and 2 to 6:30pm; May through September from 9am to 6:30pm; and during October from 9am to 11:30pm and 2 to 5:30pm. Admission costs 3€ ($3.45) for adults, 2.20€ ($2.55) for students and ages 12 to 18. It's free for children under 12.

Nearby is the **Amphitheater (Les Arènes)** ✸✸, rond-point des Arènes (✆ **04-90-49-36-86**), also built in the 1st century. It seats almost 25,000 and still hosts bullfights in summer. Visit at your own risk, as the stone steps are uneven, and much of the masonry is worn. For a good view, you can climb the three towers that remain from medieval times, when the amphitheater was turned into a fortress. Hours are daily as follows: November to February 10am to 4:30pm; March, April, and October 9am to 5:30pm; and May to September 9am to 6:30pm. Admission costs 4€ ($4.60) for adults, 3€ ($3.45) for students and persons age 18 and under.

Perhaps the most memorable sight in Arles, **Les Alyscamps** ✸, rue Pierre-Renaudel (✆ **04-90-49-36-87**), was once a necropolis established by the Romans. After being converted into a Christian burial ground in the 4th century, it became a setting for legends and was even mentioned in Dante's *Inferno*. Today, it's lined with poplars and the remaining sarcophagi. Arlesiens escape here to enjoy a respite from the heat. Admission is 3.50€ adults, 2.60€ ages 12 to 18, free for ages 11 and under. Hours are mid-September to mid-June daily 9am to 12:30pm and 2 to 7pm; mid-June to mid-September daily 9am to 7pm.

Half a mile (.8km) south of the town center, you'll find **Musée de l'Arles Antique** ✸✸, Presqu'île du Cirque Romain (✆ **04-90-18-88-88**), one of the world's most famous collections of Roman Christian sarcophagi, plus a rich ensemble of sculptures, mosaics, and inscriptions from the Augustinian period to the 6th century A.D. Eleven detailed models show ancient monuments of the region as they existed in the past. Admission is 5.50€ ($6.35) adults, 3€ ($3.45) students and children under 12. Hours are February 11 to November 1 daily 9am to 7pm; November 2 to February 10 daily 10am to 5pm.

Museon Arlaten ✸, 29 rue de la République (✆ **04-90-96-08-23**), was founded by poet Frédéric Mistral, leader of a movement to establish modern Provençal as a literary language, using the money from his Nobel Prize for literature in 1904. This is a folklore museum, with regional costumes, portraits, furniture, dolls, a music salon, and one room devoted to mementos of Mistral. Among its curiosities is a letter (in French) from Theodore Roosevelt to Mistral, bearing the letterhead of the Maison Blanche in Washington, D.C. Admission is 4€ ($4.60) adults, 2.70€ ($3.10) students and children under 18. Hours are July to August 9:30am to 1pm and 2 to 6:30pm; October to March 9:30am to 12:30pm and 2 to 5pm; April, May, and September 9:30am to 12:30pm and 2 to 6pm.

WHERE TO STAY & DINE

Because of its reasonable rates, **Hôtel Calendal** ✸, 5 rue Porte de Laure, 13200 Arles (✆ **04-90-96-11-89;** www.lecalendal.com), is a bargain hunter's favorite. On a quiet square near the arena, this 38-unit hotel offers recently renovated rooms with bright colors, high ceilings, and a sense of spaciousness. The restaurant has a limited menu featuring omelets, soups, and platters. Rates run 45€ to 97€ ($51.75–$112) double.

Hôtel d'Arlatan ✿, 26 rue du Sauvage, 13100 Arles (© **04-90-93-56-66;** www.hotel-arlatan.fr), the former residence of the comtes d'Arlatan de Beaumont, has been managed by the same family since 1920. It was built in the 15th century on the ruins of an old palace. Rooms are furnished with authentic Provençal antiques and walls covered by tapestries. Rates are 95€ to 173€ ($109–$199) double; 243€ ($279) suite.

A few steps from the Arena, **Chez Gigi,** 49 rue des Arènes (© **04-90-96-68-59**), offers home-cooking at reasonable prices. Noteworthy dishes are the *soupe des poisons* (fish soup served with crusty breads and cheese) and the authentic *dorade Provençal* (an ocean fish grilled with Provençal herbs). Main courses run 7€ to 14€ ($8.05–$16.10).

Lou Marquès ✿✿, at the Hôtel Jules-César, 9 bd. Des Lices (© **04-90-52-52-52**), part of a Relais & Châteaux hotel, has the highest reputation in town for its creative twists on Provençal specialties. As a main course try *pave de loup en barigoule d'artichaut et à la sauge* (a thick slice of wolf fish with sage-stuffed artichokes) or *filet mignon de veau et ragout fin de cèpes et salsifis* (veal with a stew of mushrooms and oyster plant). Main courses run 17€ to 34€ ($19.55–$39.10); fixed price menus run 18€ ($20.70) at lunch, from 56€ ($64.40) at dinner.

AIX-EN-PROVENCE ✿✿✿

The celebrated son of this old capital city of Provence, Paul Cézanne, immortalized the countryside nearby. Just as he saw it, Montagne Sainte-Victoire still looms over the town, although a string of high-rises have now cropped up on the landscape. The most charming center in all of Provence, this faded university town was once a seat of aristocracy, its streets walked by counts and kings. Aix still has much of the atmosphere it acquired in the 17th and 18th centuries before losing its prestige to Marseille, 20 miles (32km) to the south.

GETTING THERE The city is easily accessible, with 21 trains arriving from Marseille, taking 35 minutes and costing 6€ ($6.90) one-way. Eight trains arrive daily from Nice, the trip taking 3 to 4 hours, and costing 29.90€ ($34.40) one-way. There are also 8 trains per day from Cannes (trip time: 3½ hr.), costing 27.30€ ($31.40) one-way. A newer train station designed for the high-speed TGV Med trains, is at Vitroll, 9 miles (5.5km) to the west of Aix. There are bus links, costing 3.60€ ($4.15) one-way, from Vitroll into the center of Aix. For more information, call © **08-36-35-35.**

VISITOR INFORMATION The **Office de Tourisme** is at 2 place du Général-de-Gaulle (© **04-42-16-11-61;** www.aixenprovencetourism.com). To get here from the train station, stroll up av. Victor-Hugo (bearing towards your left) and you'll eventually see it on your left. The office will reserve hotel rooms for you at no charge. Summer hours are Monday to Saturday 8:30am to 9pm and Sunday 10am to 8pm. Off-season hours are Monday to Saturday 9am to 6pm and Sunday 10am to 4pm.

TOP ATTRACTIONS & SPECIAL MOMENTS

Aix's main street, **cours Mirabeau** ✿✿, is one of Europe's most beautiful. Plane trees stretch their branches across the top like an umbrella, shading it from the hot Provençal sun and filtering the light into shadows that play on the rococo fountains below. Shops and sidewalk cafes line one side of the street; sandstone *hôtels particuliers* (mansions) from the 17th and 18th centuries fill the other. The street begins at the 1860 fountain on place de la Libération, which honors Mirabeau, the revolutionary and statesman.

> **Moments Aix Through the Eyes of Cézanne**
>
> The best experience in Aix is a walk along the *route de Cézanne* (D17), which winds eastward through the countryside toward Ste-Victoire. From the east end of cours Mirabeau, take rue du Maréchal-Joffre across boulevard Carnot to boulevard des Poilus, which becomes avenue des Ecoles-Militaires and finally D17. The stretch between Aix and the hamlet of Le Tholonet is full of twists and turns where Cézanne often set up his easel to paint. The entire route is a lovely 3½-mile (5.5km) stroll. Le Tholonet has a cafe or two where you can refresh yourself while waiting for one of the frequent buses back to Aix.

Cézanne was the major forerunner of Cubism. **Atelier de Cézanne,** 9 av. Paul-Cézanne (outside town; © **04-42-21-06-53**), surrounded by a wall and restored by American admirers, is where he worked. Admission is 5.50€ ($6.35) adults, 2€ ($2.30) students and children. Hours are April to September Wednesday to Monday 10am to noon and 2:30 to 6pm; October to March Wednesday to Monday 10am to noon, 2 to 5pm.

Cathédrale St-Sauveur ★, place des Martyrs de la Résistance (© **04-42-23-45-65**), is dedicated to Christ under the title St-Sauveur (Holy Savior or Redeemer). Its baptistery dates from the 4th and 5th centuries, but the complex as a whole has seen many additions. It contains a 15th-century Nicolas Froment triptych, *The Burning Bush.* Masses are conducted every Sunday at 9am, 10:30am, and 7pm. Admission is free and hours are daily 9am to noon and 2 to 6pm.

Three series of tapestries from the 17th and 18th centuries line the gilded walls of **Musée des Tapisseries** ★, 28 place des Martyrs de la Résistance (© **04-42-23-09-91**), a former archbishop's palace. *The History of Don Quixote,* by Natoire; *The Russian Games,* by Leprince; and *The Grotesques,* by Monnoyer were paintings collected by archbishops to decorate the palace. Admission is 2€ ($2.30) adults, free for ages 25 and under. Hours are Wednesday to Monday 10 to 12:30pm and 2 to 5pm.

WHERE TO STAY & DINE

Grand Hôtel Nègre Coste, 33 cours Mirabeau, 13100 Aix-en-Provence (© **04-42-27-74-22;** www.hotelnegrecoste.com), a former 18th-century town house, is popular with the dozens of musicians who flock to Aix for the summer festivals. The higher floors of this 37-room hotel overlook cours Mirabeau and the old city. Room rates are 65€ to 160€ ($74.75–$184) double.

Not everything is state of the art, but to many, **Hôtel Cardinal,** 24 rue Cardinale (© **04-42-38-32-30**), is still the best value in Aix. Guests stay in the 29 simply furnished rooms either in the main building or in the high-ceilinged 18th-century annex up the street, site of most of the hotel's suites. Bathrooms tend to be small but each has a good shower. Rates are 65€ to 70€ ($74.75–$80.50) double; 76€ ($87.40) suite.

Antoine Côte Cour, 19 rue Mirabeau (© **04-42-93-12-51**), is in an 18th-century town house a few steps from place Rotonde. A simple wine, such as Côtes-du-Rhône, goes nicely with the hearty Mediterranean fare, which may include a memorable pasta Romano flavored with calves' liver, flap mushrooms, and tomato sauce; ravioli with goat cheese; osso buco; and at least half a dozen kinds of fresh fish. Main courses run 15€ to 32€ ($17.25–$36.80).

Aix-en-Provence

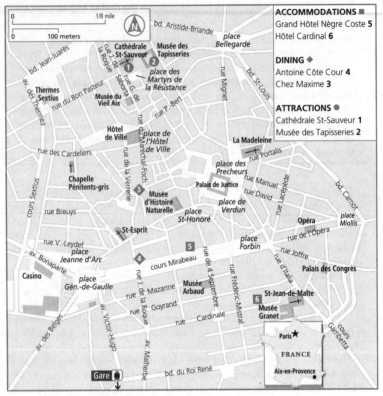

ACCOMMODATIONS ■
Grand Hôtel Nègre Coste 5
Hôtel Cardinal 6

DINING ◆
Antoine Côte Cour 4
Chez Maxime 3

ATTRACTIONS ●
Cathédrale St-Sauveur 1
Musée des Tapisseries 2

Chez Maxime, 12 place Ramus (© **04-42-26-28-51**), located in the pedestrian zone, reflects the skills and personality of its owner, Felix Maxime. Eat on the side-walk terrace or in the wood-trimmed stone dining room. Specialties include as many as 19 kinds of grilled meat or fish, cooked over an oak-burning fire, and several preparations of lamb. Main courses run 10€ to 15€ ($11.50–$17.25); fixed-price menus 17.50€ ($20.15) lunch, 29.10€ ($33.45) dinner.

CANNES ✦✦✦

Popular with celebrities, Cannes is at its most frenzied during the **International Film Festival** at the **Palais des Festivals** on the promenade de la Croisette. Held in May, it attracts not only film stars but those with similar aspirations. On the seafront boulevards flashbulbs pop as the starlets emerge—usually wearing what women will be wearing in 2010 (maybe). International regattas, galas, *concours d'élégance,* even a Mimosa Festival in February—something is always happening at Cannes, except in November, which is traditionally a dead month.

Sixteen miles (26km) southwest of Nice, Cannes is sheltered by hills. For many it consists of only one street, **promenade de la Croisette** ✦✦ (or just La Croisette), curving along the coast and split by islands of palms and flowers. It is said that the Prince of Wales (before he became Edward VII) contributed to its original cost. But he was a Johnny-come-lately to Cannes. Setting out for Nice in 1834, Lord Brougham, a lord chancellor of England, was turned away because of an outbreak of cholera. He landed at Cannes and liked it so much he decided to build a villa there. Returning every winter until his death in 1868, he proselytized it in London, drawing a long line of British visitors. In the 1890s, Cannes became popular with Russian grand dukes (it is said more caviar was consumed there than all of Moscow). One French writer claimed that when the Russians returned as refugees in the 1920s, they were given the garbage-collection franchise.

A port of call for cruise liners, the seafront of Cannes is lined with hotels, apartment houses, and chic boutiques. Many of the bigger hotels, some dating from the 19th century, claim part of the beaches for the private use of their guests, but there are public areas as well.

GETTING THERE   Cannes is connected to Nice, Paris, and the rest of France by rail. **Trains** arrive frequently throughout the day. Cannes is only 15 minutes by train from Antibes and only 35 minutes from Nice. The TGV from Paris via Marseille also services Cannes. (Transit from Paris to Cannes via TGV takes only about 6 breathless hr.) For rail information and schedules, call ✆ **08-36-35-35-35.**

In case you want to fly into Nice and begin your rail journey on the Riviera instead of Paris, the Nice **international airport** (✆ **08-20-42-33-33**) is a 20-minute drive northeast of Cannes. **Buses** pick up passengers at the airport every 30 minutes during the day, delivering them in Cannes to the rail station, Gare Routière, place de l'Hôtel de Ville (✆ **04-93-45-20-08**).

VISITOR INFORMATION   The **Office de Tourisme** is in the Palais des Festivals, esplanade Georges-Pompidou (✆ **04-93-39-24-53**; www.cannes.fr), a short walk along the harbor quays from the trains station. Hours are daily 9am to 8pm. This office doesn't make hotel reservations. If you need one, call the town's **Centrale de Reservation** at ✆ **04-93-99-99-00** daily 9am to 7pm.

TOP ATTRACTIONS & SPECIAL MOMENTS

Above the harbor, the old town of Cannes sits on Suquet Hill, where you'll see the 14th-century **Tour de Suquet,** which the English dubbed the Lord's Tower.

Nearby is the **Musée de la Castre** ★, in the Château de la Castre, Le Suquet (✆ **04-93-38-55-26**), with paintings, sculpture, the decorative arts, and a section on ethnography, which includes objects from all over: from the Pacific islands to Southeast Asia, including Peruvian and Mayan pottery. There's also a gallery devoted to relics of Mediterranean civilizations, from the Greeks to the Romans, from the Cypriots to the Egyptians. Five rooms display 19th-century paintings. The museum is open Tuesday to Sunday: April to June 10am to noon and 2 to 6pm, July to September 10am to noon and 3 to 7pm, and October to March 10am to noon and 2 to 5pm. Admission is 3€ ($3.45), free for students and children 14 and under.

FERRYING TO THE ILES DE LERINS ★★

Across the bay from Cannes, the Lérins Islands are the most interesting excursion from the port. Ferryboats depart at 30-minute intervals throughout the day, beginning at 7:30am and lasting until 30 minutes before sundown. The largest of the ferryboat companies in Cannes is **Compagnies Estérel-Chanteclair** (✆ **04-93-39-11-82**), but other contenders include **Compagnie Maritime Cannoise** (✆ **04-93-38-66-33**) and **Trans-Côte d'Azur** (✆ **04-92-98-71-30**). Departures are from the Gare Maritime des Iles, 06400 Cannes. Round-trip passage costs 10€ ($11.50) per adult and 5€ ($5.75) for children 5 to 10, free for children under 5.

> ### *Moments* Celebrity-Watching in Cannes
>
> At the end of May, the **International Film Festival** is held at the Palais des Festivals on promenade de la Croisette. It attracts not only film stars but seemingly every photographer in the world. You've got a better chance of being named prime minister of France than you do of attending one of the major screenings. (Hotel rooms and tables at restaurants are equally scarce during the festival.) But the people-watching is fabulous. If you find yourself here at the right time, you can join the thousands of others who line up in front of the Palais des Festivals, aka "the bunker," where the premieres are held. With *paparazzi* shouting and *gendarmes* holding back the fans, the guests parade along the red carpet, stopping for a moment to strike a pose and chat with a journalist. *C'est Cannes!*
>
> *Tip:* You may also be able to get tickets for some of the lesser films, which play 24 hours.

ILE STE-MARGUERITE This island was named after St-Honorat's sister, Ste-Marguerite, who lived here with a group of nuns in the 5th century. Today it is a youth center whose members (when they aren't sailing and diving) are dedicated to the restoration of the fort. From the dock, you can stroll along the island (signs point the way) to the Fort de l'Ile, built by Spanish troops from 1635 to 1637. Below is the 1st-century B.C. Roman town where the *The Man in the Iron Mask* was imprisoned. You can visit his cell.

Musée de la Mer, Fort Royal (© **04-93-38-55-26**), traces the history of the island, displaying artifacts of Ligurian, Roman, and Arab civilizations, plus the remains discovered by excavations, including paintings, mosaics, and ceramics. It's open July to September Wednesday to Monday 10:30am to 12:15pm and 2:15 to 6:30pm; October to June it closes at sundown (4:30–5:30pm). Admission is 3€ ($3.45) for adults and free for students and children ages 17 and under.

ILE ST-HONORAT 🏛🏛 Only a mile (1.6km) long, but richer in history than its sibling islands, Ile St-Honorat is the site of a monastery whose origins go back to the 5th century. Today, **Abbaye de St-Honorat** 🏛, Les Iles de Lérins, 06400 Cannes (© **04-92-99-54-00**), boasts a combination of medieval ruins and early-20th-century ecclesiastical buildings, and a community of about 30 Cistercian monks. Under controlled circumstances, if space is available, well-intentioned outsiders can visit and spend the night, but only for prayer and meditation. Most visitors opt to avoid the monastery, wandering through the pine forests on the island's western side, and sunbathing on its beaches.

WHERE TO STAY & DINE

On a quiet street about 4 blocks from the seafront, **Hôtel Brimer,** 6 rue Lecerf (© **04-93-38-69-54**), occupies the second floor of a four-story building constructed in the 1970s. The 15 bedrooms are well maintained, furnished unpretentiously but comfortably, and are relatively affordable in high-priced Cannes. Rates are 70€ to 110€ ($80.50–$127) double; 120€ to 150€ ($138–$173) suite.

Hôtel le Fouquet's 🏛, 2 rond-point Duboys-d'Angers (© **04-92-59-25-00**), is an intimate 10-room hotel drawing a discreet clientele, often from Paris, who'd never think of patronizing the grand palace hotels. Very "Riviera French"

Cannes

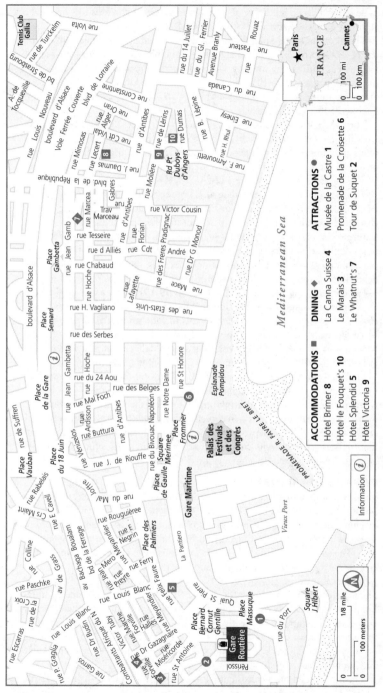

ATTRACTIONS ●
Musée de la Castre **1**
Promenade de la Croisette **6**
Tour de Suquet **2**

DINING ◆
La Canna Suisse **4**
Le Marais **3**
Le Whatnut's **7**

ACCOMMODATIONS ■
Hôtel Brimer **8**
Hôtel le Fouquet's **10**
Hôtel Splendid **5**
Hôtel Victoria **9**

Information ⓘ

Mediterranean Sea

in design and decor, it lies several blocks from the beach and feels very much like an intimate B&B. Rates are 80€ to 200€ ($92–$230) double.

The 64-room **Hotel Splendid** ⚜, Allée de la Liberté (4 and 6 rue Félix-Faure; ✆ **04-97-06-22-22**), is an ornate white building with wrought-iron accents looking out onto the sea, the old port, and a park. The rooms boast antique furniture and paintings as well as videos; about half have kitchenettes. It's a favorite of actors, musicians, and politicians. Rates are 122€ to 246€ ($140–$283) double; 250€ ($288) suite.

The **Hôtel Victoria** ⚜, rond-point Duboys-d'Angers (✆ **04-92-59-40-00;** www.hotel-victoria-cannes.com), a stylish modern hotel in the heart of Cannes, offers accommodations with period reproductions and refrigerators. Nearly half of the 25 rooms have balconies overlooking the small park and the hotel pool (worth the extra cost). Rates are 142€ to 182€ ($163–$209) double.

Two sisters own **La Canna Suisse** ⚜, 23 rue Forville (le Suquet; ✆ **04-93-99-01-27**), a 30-year-old restaurant in Vieux Cannes that's decked out like a Swiss chalet and specializes in the cheese-based cuisine of Switzerland's Alps. The menu features only two kinds of fondue—a traditional version concocted from six kinds of cheese and served in a bubbling pot with chunks of bread on skewers, plus another that adds either morels or cèpes (flap mushrooms) to the blend, depending on your wishes. Main courses run 15€ to 22€ ($17.25–$25.30).

Le Marais, 9 rue du Suquet (✆ **04-93-38-39-19**), draws a chic crowd from the worlds of fashion and entertainment. Its terrace is one of the most sought-after outdoor venues in town. Menu items include sea bream filet with olive-based tapenade sauce; and a "triptych" of meats that includes magret of duck, beef filet, and shoulder of lamb with mint sauce. Main courses cost 19€ to 32€ ($21.85–$36.80); fixed-price menus run 29€ to 35€ ($33.35–$40.25).

Le Whatnut's, 7 rue Marceau (✆ **04-93-68-60-58**), is a sophisticated, urbane, and permissive restaurant that also features a bar and a dance floor where patrons can dance and drink until long after the usual dinner hour. The menu isn't terribly long but is well chosen with examples such as a diet-conscious array of grilled fish, perhaps sea bass; a platter with shrimp and scallops; and filets of beef garnished with morels or foie gras. Main courses run 16€ to 26€ ($18.40–$29.90); fixed-price menus run 30€ ($34.50).

CANNES AFTER DARK

Palm Beach Casino, Place F.D.-Roosevelt (Pointe de la Croisette; ✆ **04-97-06-36-90**), lies on the southeast edge of La Croisette. The casino maintains slot machines that operate daily from 11am to 5am; plus suites of rooms devoted to *les grands jeux* (blackjack), roulette, and baccarat that are open nightly 8pm to 5am. The cover charge is 11€ ($12.65) for access to les grands jeux, where presentation of a passport or an identity card is required.

In the cellar of the Hotel Grey d'Albion is the long-term nightlife staple, the disco, **Jane's,** 38 rue des Serbes (✆ **04-92-99-79-79**). It isn't considered ultra-hip or even particularly cutting edge, but you can have a lot of fun here, merely because of the exoticism of the diverse crowd of single people who mill through the place. There's a cover of between 10€ to 15€ ($11.50–$17.25), depending on the night of the week, and a policy of allowing women in free every Friday and Saturday before midnight.

The hippest and most consistently in-demand club is **Le Cat-Corner,** 22 rue Macé (✆ **04-93-39-31-31**), where a multicultural blend of night owls, mostly under 35, come to dance, drink, talk, and flirt. It opens every night from 11:30pm till 4am, and charges 16€ ($18.40) for admission.

NICE ★★★

The Victorian upper class and czarist aristocrats loved Nice in the 19th century, but it is solidly middle class today. In fact, of all the major resorts of France, from Deauville to Biarritz to Cannes, Nice is the least expensive. It is also the best excursion center on the Riviera and has the best rail connections along the Côte d'Azur. For example, you can go by rail to San Remo, the queen of the Italian Riviera, returning to Nice by nightfall. And from the Nice Airport, the second largest in France, you can travel by rail along the entire coast to such other resorts as Cannes.

Nice is the capital of the Riviera, the largest city between Genoa and Marseille (also one of the most ancient, having been founded by the Greeks, who called it "Nike," or victory). Because of its brilliant sunshine and relaxed living, artists and writers have been attracted to Nice for years. Among them were Matisse, Dumas, Nietzsche, Appollinaire, Flaubert, Victor Hugo, Guy de Maupassant, George Sand, Stendhal, Chateaubriand, and Mistral.

GETTING THERE   Trains arrive at **Gare Nice-Ville,** avenue Thiers (© **08-36-35-35-35**). From here you can take trains to Cannes, Monaco, and Antibes, with easy connections to anywhere else along the Mediterranean coast. There's a small-scale tourist center (© **08-92-70-74-07**) at the train station, open Monday through Saturday from 8am to 6:30pm and Sunday from 8am to noon and 2 to 5:30pm. Hotel reservations can be made by the staff for no charge. If you face a long delay, you can eat at the cafeteria and even take showers at the station.

Transatlantic and inter-continental flights land at **Aéroport Nice–Côte d'Azur** (© **08-20-42-33-33**). From here, conventional municipal bus number 98 departs at 20-minute intervals from the airport for Nice's train station, charging 3.50€ ($4.05) per person, each way. A somewhat more luxurious mode of transport involves a specially conceived yellow-sided shuttle bus *(la navette de l'aéroport)* that also charges 3.50€ ($4.05) for a ride between the airport and Nice's train station. A **taxi** ride from the airport to the station will cost at least 25€ to 30€ ($28.75–$34.50) each way. Trip time is about 30 minutes.

VISITOR INFORMATION   Of the city's three tourist offices, the largest and most central is at 5 promenade des Anglais (© **08-92-70-74-07;** fax 04-93-16-85-16), near place Massena (about a ¾-mile/1.2km walk from the train station). The staff can make a hotel reservation (but only for the night of the day you happen to show up) at no charge. Hours are Monday to Saturday 8am to 8pm; Sunday 9am to 7pm.

GETTING AROUND   Most of the local buses in Nice create connections with one another at their central hub, the **Station Central,** 10 av. Félix-Faure (© **04-93-13-53-13**), a very short walk from place Masséna. Municipal buses each charge 1.30€ ($1.50) for a ride within Greater Nice. To save money, consider buying a five-ticket *carnet* for 16€ ($18.40). Bus number 8 makes frequent trips to the beach.

TOP ATTRACTIONS & SPECIAL MOMENTS

There's a higher density of museums in Nice than in many comparable French cities. If you decide to skip the beach and devote your time to visiting some of the most impressive museums in the south of France, you can buy a **Carte**

Passe-Musée that costs 15€ ($17.25) for 3 days or 25€ ($28.75) for 7 days. It allows you admission into seven of the city's largest museums and you can buy it at any of the museums or from the tourist office. There are no reductions for students or children. For more information, call ✆ **04-97-03-82-20.**

In 1822, the orange crop at Nice was bad and the workers faced a lean time. So the English residents put them to work building the **promenade des Anglais** 😷😷, a wide boulevard fronting the bay, split by "islands" of palms and flowers and stretching for about 4 miles (6.5km). Fronting the beach are rows of grand cafes, the Musée Masséna, villas, and hotels—some good, others decaying.

Crossing this boulevard in the briefest of bikinis or thongs are some of the world's most attractive bronzed bodies. They're heading for the **beach**—"on the rocks," as it's called here. Tough on tender feet, the beach is made not of sand but of pebbles (and not-too-small ones). It's one of the least attractive aspects of the cosmopolitan resort city. Many bathhouses provide mattresses for a fee.

In the east, the promenade becomes **quai des Etats-Unis,** the original boulevard, lined with some of the best restaurants in Nice, all specializing in bouillabaisse. Rising sharply on a rock is the site known as **Le Château,** the spot where the ducs de Savoie built their castle, torn down in 1706. All that remains are two or three stones—even the foundations have disappeared in the wake of Louis XIV's destruction of what was viewed as a bulwark of Provençal resistance to his regime. The hill has been turned into a garden of pines and exotic flowers. To reach the site for the view, you can take an elevator; many prefer to take the elevator up, and then walk down. The park is open daily from 8am to dusk.

At the north end of Le Château is the famous old **graveyard** of Nice, visited primarily for its lavish monuments that form their own enduring art statement. It's the largest one in France. To reach it, you can take a small, canopied **Train Touristique de Nice** (✆ **06-16-39-53-51**), which departs from the Jardin Albert-1er. It makes a 40-minute sightseeing transit past many of Nice's most heralded sites, including place Masséna, promenade des Anglais, and quai des Etats-Unis. With departures every 30 to 60 minutes, the train operates daily from 10am to 5pm (until 6pm Apr–May and Sept, until 7pm June–Aug). There's no service between mid-November and mid-December and during most of January. Train rides last about 45 minutes. The price is 6€ ($6.90) per person.

Cathédrale Orthodoxe Russe St-Nicolas à Nice 😷, av. Nicolas-II (off bd. du Tzaréwitch; ✆ **04-93-96-88-02**), was ordered built by none other than Tsar Nicholas II. This is the most beautiful religious edifice of the Orthodoxy outside Russia and is a perfect expression of Russian religious art abroad. It dates from the Belle Epoque, when some of the Romanovs and their entourage turned the Riviera into a stamping ground (everyone from grand dukes to ballerinas walked the promenade). The cathedral is richly ornamented and decorated with icons. You'll spot the building from afar because of its collection of ornate onion-shaped domes. Admission is 2.50€ ($2.90) adults, 2€ ($2.30) students, free for children under 12. Hours are May to September daily 9am to noon and 2:30 to 6pm; October to April daily 9:30am to noon and 2:30 to 5:30pm. It's closed to purely touristy visits on Sunday mornings. From the central rail station, head west along av. Thiers to bd. Gambetta; then go north to av. Nicolas-II.

The villa housing the **Musée des Beaux-Arts** 😷😷, 33 av. des Baumettes (✆ **04-92-15-28-28**), was built in 1900 in the style of the First Empire as a residence for Victor Masséna, the prince of Essling and grandson of Napoléon's marshal. The city of Nice has converted the villa into a museum of local history

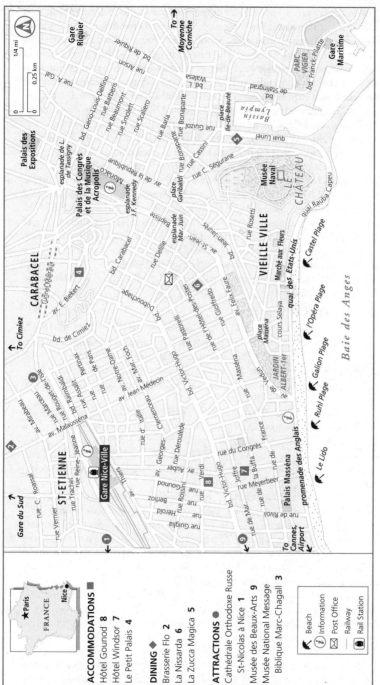

Nice

ACCOMMODATIONS ■
Hôtel Gounod **8**
Hôtel Windsor **7**
Le Petit Palais **4**

DINING ◆
Brasserie Flo **2**
La Nissarda **6**
La Zucca Magica **5**

ATTRACTIONS ●
Cathédrale Orthodoxe Russe
St-Nicolas à Nice **1**
Musée des Beaux-Arts **9**
Musée National Message
Biblique Marc-Chagall **3**

Beach
ℹ Information
⊠ Post Office
— Railway
🚉 Rail Station

★ Paris
FRANCE
Nice ●

Gare du Sud
To Cimiez
To Cimiez
To Cannes, Airport
To Moyenne Corniche

ST-ETIENNE
CARABACEL
VIEILLE VILLE
LE CHÂTEAU

Gare Nice-Ville
Gare Riquier
Gare Maritime

Palais des Expositions
Palais des Congrès et de la Musique Acropolis

Musée Naval

Marché aux Fleurs
place Masséna
JARDIN ALBERT-1er
Palais Masséna

Bassin Lympia
PARC VIGIER

Baie des Anges

Castel Plage
l'Opéra Plage
Galion Plage
Ruhl Plage
Le Lido

301

and decorative art. A First Empire drawing room furnished in the opulent taste of that era, with mahogany-veneer pieces and ormolu mounts, is on the ground floor. There's a representation of Napoléon as a Roman Caesar and a bust by Canova of Maréchal Masséna. The first-floor gallery exhibits a collection of Niçoise primitives and also has a display of 14th- and 15th-century painters, as well as a collection of 16th- to 19th-century masterpieces of plates and jewelry decorated with enamel (Limoges). There also are art galleries devoted to the history of Nice. Admission is 4€ ($4.60) adults, 2.50€ ($2.90) students, free for children under 18. Hours are Tuesday to Sunday 10am to 6pm.

Musée National Message Biblique Marc-Chagall ✸✸, av. du Dr.-Ménard (© **04-93-53-87-20**), is the first state museum in France built to house the works of a single living artist. In the hills of Cimiez above Nice, the single-story museum is devoted to Marc Chagall's treatment of biblical themes. The handsome museum is surrounded by shallow pools and a garden planted with thyme, lavender, and olive trees. Born in Russia in 1887, Chagall became a French citizen in 1937. The artist and his wife donated the works—the most important collection of Chagall ever assembled—to the French state in 1966 and 1972. Displayed are 450 of his oil paintings, gouaches, drawings, pastels, lithographs, sculptures, ceramics, a mosaic, three stained-glass windows, and a tapestry. Admission is 6.80€ ($7.80) adults, 5.20€ ($6) students, free for children under 18. Hours are Wednesday to Monday 10am to 6pm.

WHERE TO STAY & DINE

The 46-room **Hôtel Gounod** ✸, 3 rue Gounod, 06000 Nice (© **04-93-16-42-00;** www.gounod-nice.com), is situated in the city center, a 5-minute walk from the sea. The high-ceilinged guest rooms are quiet and usually overlook the gardens of private homes. There aren't many amenities, but guests have free unlimited use of the pool and Jacuzzi at the Hôtel Splendid next door. Rates are 135€ ($155) double; 200€ ($230) suite.

The 57-room **Hôtel Windsor,** 11 rue Dalpozzo, 06000 Nice (© **04-93-88-59-35;** www.hotelwindsornice.com), one of the most arts-conscious hotels in Provence, is set within a *maison bourgeoise* (near the Negresco and the promenade des Anglais), built by disciples of Gustav Eiffel in 1895. Inside, you'll find an artsy ambience and comfortable, individually furnished, midsize bedrooms. Rates are 115€ to 145€ ($132–$167) double.

The 25-room **Le Petit Palais,** 17 av. Emile-Bieckert, 06000 Nice (© **04-93-62-19-11;** www.hotel-petit-palais.com), occupies a mansion built around 1890; in the 1970s it was the home of the actor and writer Sacha Guitry, a name that's instantly recognized in millions of French households. The preferred rooms, and the most expensive, have balconies for sea views during the day and sunset watching at dusk. Rooms are Art Deco and Italianate in style; the shower-only bathrooms are small. Rates are 87€–144€ ($100–$166) double.

Brasserie Flo, 2–4 rue Sacha-Guitry (© **04-93-13-38-38**), is the town's most bustling brasserie. The place is brisk, stylish, reasonably priced, and fun. Menu items include an array of grilled fish, *choucroute* (sauerkraut) Alsatian style, steak with brandied pepper sauce, and fresh oysters and shellfish. Main courses run 15€ to 29€ ($17.25–$33.35); fixed-price menus run 29€ ($33.35).

In the heart of town, about a 10-minute walk from place Masséna, **La Nissarda,** 17 rue Gubernatis (© **04-93-85-26-29**), is maintained by a Normandy-born family who work hard to maintain the aura and the traditions of Nice. The place serves a fixed-price menu of local versions of ravioli, spaghetti carbonara, lasagna, and fresh-grilled salmon with herbs. A handful of Norman-based specialties also manage to creep into the menu, including escallops of veal with cream sauce and apples. The fixed-price menu runs 16€ to 21.50€ ($18.40–$24.75).

The chef at **La Zucca Magica** 🍴, 4 bis quai Papacino (© **04-93-56-25-27**), was recently selected as the best Italian chef in Nice. Chef Marco serves refined cuisine at reasonable prices, using recipes from Italy's Piedmont region and updating them with no meat or fish. You can count on savory cuisine using lots of herbs, Italian cheeses, beans, and pasta. Lasagna is a specialty. Fixed menus run 18€ ($20.70) at lunch, 27€ ($31.05) at dinner.

NICE AFTER DARK

OPERA   The major cultural center on the Riviera is the **Opéra de Nice,** 4 rue St-François-de-Paule (© 04-92-17-40-40), built in 1885 by Charles Garnier, fabled architect of the Paris Opéra. A full repertoire is presented, with emphasis on serious, often large-scale operas. In one season you might see *Tosca, Les Contes de Hoffmann,* Verdi's *Macbeth,* Beethoven's *Fidelio,* and *Carmen,* as well as a *saison symphonique,* dominated by the Orchestre Philharmonique de Nice. The opera hall is also the major venue for concerts and recitals. Tickets are available (to concerts, recitals, and full-blown operas) up to about a day or 2 prior to any performance. You can show up at the box office (Tues–Fri 10am–5:30pm) or buy tickets in advance with a major credit card by phoning © **04-92-17-40-40.** Tickets run 10€ ($11.50) for nosebleed (and we mean it) seats to 60€ ($69) for front-and-center seats on opening night.

BARS & CLUBS   Near the Hôtel Ambassador, **L'Ambassade,** 18 rue des Congrès (© **04-93-88-88-87**), was designed in a mock-Gothic style that includes the wrought-iron accents you'd expect to find in a château; it has two bars and a dance floor. At least 90% of its clients are straight and come in all physical types and age ranges. The cover is 15€ to 16€ ($17.25–$18.40) and includes the first drink.

One of the newest and most charming discos in Nice is **Niel's Club,** 10 rue Cité du Parc (© **04-93-80-49-84**), in a location on an all-pedestrian zone just inland from the quai des Etats-Unis. The setting is a 19th-century cellar whose stone and brick vaulting used to shelter horses, goats, and sheep. It's filled with hipster music much appreciated by the crowds of extroverted Niçoise who pile in here for drinking and dancing. Expect to pay a cover charge of up to 11€ ($12.65), which includes the first drink, especially on its busiest nights, Friday and Saturday.

Cabaret du Casino Ruhl, in the Casino Ruhl, 1 promenade des Anglais (© 04-97-03-12-77), is Nice's answer to the cabaret glitter that appears in more ostentatious forms in Monte Carlo and Las Vegas. It includes just enough flesh to titillate; lots of spangles, feathers, and sequins; a medley of cross-cultural jokes and nostalgia for the old days of French *chanson;* and an acrobat or juggler. The cover of 22€ ($25.30) includes the first drink; dinner and the show, complete with a bottle of wine per person, costs 65€ ($74.75). Shows are presented every Friday and Saturday at 10:30pm. No jeans or sneakers.

AN EXCURSION TO ST-PAUL-DE-VENCE 🍴🍴

Of all the perched hill towns of the Riviera, St-Paul-de-Vence, 19 miles (31km) north of Nice, is the best known. It was popularized in the 1920s when many noted artists lived here, occupying the little 16th-century houses that flank the narrow cobblestone streets. The hill town was originally built to protect its inhabitants from Saracens raiding the coast. The feudal hamlet grew up on a bastion of rock, almost blending into it. Its ramparts (allow 30 min. to encircle them) overlook a peaceful setting of flowers and olive and orange trees. As you make your way through the warren of streets you'll pass endless souvenir shops, a charming old fountain carved in the form of an urn, and a Gothic church from the 13th century.

GETTING THERE   The nearest rail station is in Cagnes-sur-Mer, from which buses depart every 30 minutes for St-Paul-de-Vence. Rail passengers who arrive in Nice usually rent a car or opt for 1 of about 20 buses a day, departing from Gare Routière, near the Nice railway station. For bus information, call **Cie SAP** (© **04-93-58-37-60**). Buses stop in St-Paul near the post office, on the Route de Vence, about a quarter-mile (.4km) from the town center.

VISITOR INFORMATION   The **Office de Tourisme** is at Maison Tour, 2 rue Grande (© **04-93-32-86-95;** www.riviera.fr/tourisme.htm), is open June to September daily 10am to 7pm; October to May 1 daily 10am to 6pm.

Top Attractions & Special Moments

Foundation Maeght 👉👉👉, outside the town walls (© **04-93-32-81-63**), is the most important attraction of St-Paul. On the slope of a hill in pine-studded woods, the Maeght Foundation is like a Shangri-la. Not only is the architecture daringly avant-garde, but the building itself houses one of the finest collections of contemporary art on the Riviera. Nature and the creations of men and women blend harmoniously in this unique achievement of the architect, José Luis Sert. Its white concrete arcs give the impression of a giant pagoda.

A stark Calder rises like some futuristic monster on the grassy lawns. In a courtyard, the elongated bronze works of Giacometti (one of the finest collections of his works in the world) form a surrealistic garden, creating a hallucinatory mood. Sculpture is also displayed inside, but it's at its best in the naturalistic setting of the surrounding terraces and gardens. The museum is built on several levels, its many glass walls providing an indoor-outdoor vista. Everywhere you look, you see 20th-century art: mosaics by Chagall and Braque, Miró ceramics in the "labyrinth," and Ubac and Braque stained glass in the chapel. Bonnard, Kandinsky, Léger, Matisse, Barbara Hepworth, and many other artists are well represented.

The foundation, a gift "to the people" from Aimé and Marguerite Maeght, also provides a showcase for new talent. Exhibitions are always changing.

Admission is 11€ ($12.65) adults, 9€ ($10.35) students and ages 10–25, free for children under 10. Hours are July to September daily 10am to 7pm; October to June daily 10am to 12:30pm and 2:30 to 6pm.

AN EXCURSION TO VENCE 👉👉

Travel up into the hills northwest of Nice—across country studded with cypresses, olive trees, and pines, where bright flowers, especially carnations, roses, and oleanders, grow in profusion—and Vence comes into view. Outside the town, along boulevard Paul-André, two old olive presses carry on with their age-old duties. But the charm lies in the **Vieille Ville** (Old Town).

GETTING THERE   It's easier to reach Vence by bus then by train. Frequent **buses** (no. 400 or 410) originating in Nice take about an hour to reach Vence, and cost 4.50€ ($5.20) each way. For bus information, contact the **Compagnie SAP** at © **04-93-58-37-60** for schedules. The nearest **rail station** is in Cagnes-sur-Mer, about 4.5 miles (7km) from Vence. From here, call © **08-36-35-35-35.**

VISITOR INFORMATION   The **Office de Tourisme** is on place Grand-Jardin © **04-93-58-06-38.** It's open July and August Monday to Saturday 9am to 7pm, Sunday 9 am to 1pm; September to June Monday to Saturday 9am to 12:30pm and 2 to 6pm.

TOP ATTRACTIONS & SPECIAL MOMENTS

Visitors invariably have themselves photographed on **place du Peyra** in front of the urn-shaped **Vieille Fontaine** (Old Fountain), a background shot in several motion pictures. The 15th-century **square tower** is also a curiosity.

If you're wearing the right kind of shoes, the narrow, steep streets of the old town are worth exploring. Dating from the 10th century, the **cathedral** on place Godeau is unremarkable except for some 15th-century Gothis choir stalls. But if it's the right day of the week, most visitors quickly pass through the narrow gates of this once-fortified walled town to where the sun shines more brightly, at the Chapelle du Rosaire.

The **Chapelle du Rosaire** ★★, av. Henri-Matisse (✆ **04-93-58-03-26**), was built by the great Henri Matisse at age 77. After a turbulent personal search, the artist set out to create "the culmination of a whole life dedicated to the search for truth." Just outside Vence, Matisse created a Chapel of the Rosary for the Dominican nuns of Monteils. From the front you might find it unremarkable and pass it by—until you spot a 40-foot, crescent-adorned cross rising from a blue-tiled roof.

Matisse wrote: "What I have done in the chapel is to create a religious space . . . in an enclosed area of very reduced proportions and to give it, solely by the play of colors and lines, the dimensions of infinity." The light picks up the subtle coloring in the simply rendered leaf forms and abstract patterns: sapphire-blue, aquamarine, and lemon-yellow. In black-and-white ceramics, St. Dominic is depicted in only a few lines. The most remarkable design is the black-and-white-tiled Stations of the Cross with Matisse's self-styled "tormented and passionate" figures. The bishop of Nice came to bless the chapel in the late spring of 1951, and, his masterpiece completed, Matisse died 3 years later.

Admission is 2.50€ ($2.90) adults, 1€ ($1.15) persons 16 and under; contributions to maintain the chapel are welcomed. Hours are December to September Tuesday and Thursday 10 to 11:30am and 2 to 5:30pm; Monday, Wednesday, and Saturday 2 to 5:30pm. Sunday mass is at 10am, followed by visit at 10:45am.

WHERE TO DINE

If you, like most rail passengers, visit both St-Paul-De-Vence and Vence in a single day, one of the best and most affordable places for lunch in the area is in Vence.

La Farigoule, 15 rue Henri-Isnard (✆ **04-93-58-01-27**), is set within a century-old house in Vence that opens onto a rose garden, where tables are set out during summer. This restaurant specializes in Provençal cuisine, including a conservative but flavor-filled array of dishes that feature a *bourride Provençal* (a bouillabaisse with a dollop of cream and lots of garlic); shoulder of roasted lamb with a ragout of fresh vegetables, served with fresh thyme; aioli; and fresh fish selections. The fixed-price menu runs 25€ to 45€ ($28.75–$51.75) at lunch, and 30€ to 45€ ($34.50–$51.75) at dinner.

AN EXCURSION TO MONACO ★★★

The outspoken Katharine Hepburn called it "a pimple on the chin of the south of France." She wasn't referring to the principality's lack of beauty but rather to the preposterous idea of having a little country, a feudal anomaly, taking up some of the choicest coastline along the Riviera. Hemmed in by France on three sides and facing the Mediterranean, Monaco staunchly maintains its independence. Even Charles de Gaulle couldn't force Prince Rainier to do away with his tax-free policy. As almost everybody in an overburdened world knows by now, the Monegasques do not pay taxes. Part of their country's revenue comes from tourism and gambling.

Monaco, or rather its capital of Monte Carlo, has for a century been a symbol of glamour. Its legend was further enhanced by the marriage in 1956 of the world's most eligible bachelor, Prince Rainier, to an American film star, Grace Kelly. She met the prince when she attended the Cannes Film Festival to promote the Hitchcock movie she made with Cary Grant, *To Catch a Thief.*

Monaco became the property of the Grimaldi clan, a Genoese family, as early as 1297. With shifting loyalties, it has maintained something resembling independence ever since. In a fit of impatience, the French annexed it in 1793, but the ruling family recovered it in 1814, although the prince at the time couldn't bear to tear himself away from the pleasures of Paris for "dreary old Monaco."

The second-smallest state in Europe (Vatican City is the tiniest), Monaco consists of the old town, **Monaco-Ville,** sitting on a promontory, the Rock, 200 feet high—the seat of the royal palace and the government building, as well as the famous Oceanographic Museum (see below). On the west of the bay, **La Condamine,** the home of the Monegasques, is at the foot of the old town, forming its harbor and port sector.

Up from the port (walking is steep in Monaco) is **Monte Carlo,** once the playground of European royalty and still the center for the wintering wealthy, and the setting for the casino and its gardens and the deluxe hotels, such as the Hôtel de Paris. The fourth part of Monaco, **Fontvieille,** is an industrial suburb, surprisingly neat; but this entire principality is kept tidy.

Ironically, **Monte Carlo Beach,** at the far frontier, is on French soil. It attracts a chic, well-heeled crowd, including movie stars in bikinis so perishable they would disappear should they get wet. The resort consists of a freshwater swimming pool, an artificial beach, and sea-bathing establishment.

GETTING THERE   Monaco has rail connections to other coastal cities, especially Nice. **Trains** arrive every 30 minutes from Cannes, Nice, Menton, and Antibes. For more rail information and schedules, call ✆ **08-36-35-35-35.** Monaco's railway station (Gare SNCF) is on avenue Prince Pierre. It's a long steep walk uphill from the train station to Monte Carlo. If you'd rather take a **taxi** but can't find one at the station, call ✆ **377/93-50-56-28** or 93-15-01-01. There are no border formalities for anyone entering Monaco from mainland France.

VISITOR INFORMATION   The **Direction du Tourisme** office is at 2A bd. des Moulins (✆ **92-16-61-16;** www.monaco.net). They do not reserve rooms for visitors. Hours are Monday to Saturday 9am to 7pm and Sunday 10am to noon.

TOP ATTRACTIONS & SPECIAL MOMENTS

During summer, most day-trippers from Nice head to **Les Grands Appartements du Palais** ⭐, place du Palais (✆ **93-25-18-31**), wanting to see the home of Monaco's royal family, the Palais du Prince, which dominates the principality from "the Rock." A tour of the Grands Appartements allows you a glimpse of the Throne Room and some of the art (including works by Brueghel and Holbein) as well as the late Princess Grace's state portrait. The palace was built in the 13th century, and part of it dates from the Renaissance. The ideal time to arrive is 11:55am to watch the 10-minute **Relève de la Garde (Changing of the Guard).**

In a wing of the palace, the **Musée du Palais du Prince (Souvenirs Napoléoniens et Collection d'Archives),** place du Palais (✆ **93-25-18-31**), has a collection of mementos of Napoléon and Monaco itself. When the royal residence is closed, this museum is the only part of the palace the public can visit.

A single ticket to the Grands Appartements costs 6€ ($6.90) for adults, 3€ ($3.45) for children aged 8 to 16 and students. A single ticket to the Musée du

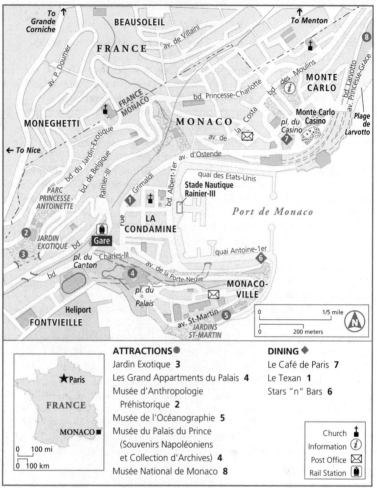

To Grande Corniche ↑

BEAUSEIL

av. de Villaini

To Menton ↑

FRANCE

av. P. Doumer

des Moulins

8

MONTE CARLO

bd. Princesse-Charlotte

bd. Lavotto

av. Princesse-Grace

FRANCE MONACO

MONEGHETTI

MONACO

la Costa

Monte Carlo Casino

pl. du Casino

Plage de Larvotto

av. de

7

← To Nice

bd. du Jardin-Exotique

bd. de Belgique

Rainier-III

Grimaldi

av. d'Ostende

quai des Etats-Unis

Stade Nautique Rainier-III

Port de Monaco

PARC PRINCESSE ANTOINETTE

bd. Albert-1er

rue

1

LA CONDAMINE

2

JARDIN EXOTIQUE

bd.

Gare

3

pl. du Canton

Charles-III

bd.

av. de la Porte-Neuve

4

pl. du Palais

quai Antoine-1er

6

MONACO-VILLE

Heliport

FONTVIEILLE

5

av. St-Martin

JARDINS ST-MARTIN

0   1/5 mile
0   200 meters

★ Paris

FRANCE

MONACO ■

0   100 mi
0   100 km

ATTRACTIONS ●

Jardin Exotique **3**
Les Grand Appartments du Palais **4**
Musée d'Anthropologie
  Préhistorique **2**
Musée de l'Océanographie **5**
Musée du Palais du Prince
  (Souvenirs Napoléoniens
  et Collection d'Archives) **4**
Musée National de Monaco **8**

DINING ◆

Le Café de Paris **7**
Le Texan **1**
Stars "n" Bars **6**

Church ✝
Information ⓘ
Post Office ✉
Rail Station 🚉

Palais is 4€ ($4.60) for adults, 2€ ($2.30) for children aged 8 to 16 and students. A combination ticket is 8€ ($9.20) for adults, 4€ ($4.60) children 8 to 16, free for children under 8. Grands Appartements hours are June to September daily 9:30am to 6pm; October daily 10am to 5pm. Museum hours are June to September Tuesday to Sunday 9:30am to 6:30pm; October and from November 1-10 Tuesday to Sunday 10am to 5pm; Dec 18 to May Tuesday to Sunday 10:30am to 12:30pm and 2 to 5pm. Closed November 11 to December 17, December 25, and January 1.

Built on the side of a rock, the **Jardin Exotique** ★★, bd. du Jardin-Exotique (℃ **93-15-29-80**), is known for its cactus collection. It was begun by Prince Albert I, who was a naturalist and scientist. He spotted some succulents growing in the palace gardens and created this garden from them. You can also explore the grottoes here, as well as the **Musée d'Anthropologie Préhistorique** (℃ **93-15-80-06**). The view of the principality is splendid. Admission to the garden is 6.60€ ($7.60) adults, 3.30€ ($3.80) children 6 to 18, free for children under 6.

> ### (*Finds*   Fabulous & Fake
>
> **Bijoux Marlene,** Les Galeries du Metropole, 207 av. des Spélugues (© **93-50-17-57**), sells only imitation gemstones. They're shamelessly copied from the real McCoys sold by Cartier and Van Cleef & Arpels. Made in Italy of gold-plated silver, the fake jewelry (the staff refers to it as *Les Bijoux Fantaisies*) costs between 10€ ($11.50) and 300€ ($345) per piece.

It's open mid-May to mid-September daily 9am to 7pm; mid-September to mid-May daily 9am to 6pm or until sunset, whichever comes first.

The **Musée de l'Océanographie** ☆☆, av. St-Martin (© **93-15-36-00**), was founded in 1910 by Albert I, great-grandfather of the present prince. In the main rotunda is a statue of Albert in his favorite costume: that of a sea captain. Displayed are specimens he collected during 30 years of expeditions. The aquarium, one of the finest in Europe, contains more than 90 tanks. Some of the exotic creatures you'll see were unknown before he captured them. Skeletons of specimens are located on the main floor, including a whale that drifted ashore at Pietra Ligure in 1896. The skeleton is remarkable for its healed fractures—sustained when a vessel struck the animal as it was drifting on the surface. Admission is 11€ ($12.65) adults, 6€ ($6.90) children 6 to 18, free for children under 6. Hours are April to June and Sept daily 9am–7pm; July to August daily 9am–8pm; October to March daily 10am–6pm.

In a villa designed by Charles Garnier (architect of Paris's Opéra Garnier), the **Musée National de Monaco** ☆ 17 av. Princesse-Grace (© **93-30-91-26**), houses a magnificent collection of antique mechanical toys and dolls. See the 18th-century Neapolitan crib, which contains some 200 figures. This collection, assembled by Mme de Galea, was presented to the principality in 1972; it stemmed from the 18th- and 19th-century trend of displaying new fashions on doll models. Admission is 6€ ($6.90) adults, 3.50€ ($4.05) students and children 6 to 14, free for children under 6. It's open Easter to September daily 10am to 6:30pm; October to Easter daily 10am to 12:15pm and 2:30 to 6:30pm.

WHERE TO DINE

Le Café de Paris ☆, place du Casino (© **92-16-20-20**), provides you with a front-row view of the comings and goings of the nerve center of Monte Carlo. Menu items change frequently, and platters, especially at lunchtime, are appreciated by local office workers because they can be served and consumed relatively quickly. Main courses run 16€ to 49€ ($18.40–$56.35).

Le Texan, 4 rue Suffren-Reymond (© **93-30-34-54**), lies on a sloping street leading down to the harbor—a world away from the casinos and nightlife of the upper reaches. Menu items include T-bone steak, barbecued ribs, pizzas, nachos, tacos, a Dallasburger (*avec* guacamole), and the best margaritas in town. Main courses run 14€ to 22€ ($16.10–$25.30).

Stars 'n' Bars, 6 quai Antoine-1er (© **97-97-95-95**), is modeled on the sports bars popular in the U.S. It features two dining and drinking areas devoted to American-style food, as well as a disco ("Le Club") Friday and Saturday nights (cover is 10€/$11.50). No one will mind if you drop in just for a drink, but if you're hungry, menu items read like an homage to the American experience. Steaks run 19€ to 47€ ($21.85–$54.05) and other items cost 7€ to 19€ ($8.05–$21.85).

Germany

Although it's only about half the size of Texas, Germany is a large country by European standards. Yet thanks to it being decked out with one of the continent's most comprehensive, efficient, and speedy rail networks, coming to grips with the place by train is easy.

Many German city centers today share, on the surface at least, a similar trait of bland modernity; that's due to most of them having been blown to bits in World War II bombings, and rebuilt in haste in the post-war period. But an impressive array of the finest of the lost architectural and cultural treasures has been re-created, and this work continues apace.

In many smaller towns that were spared the hard hand of war, historic cores of astonishing harmony and beauty are there to be discovered. And the natural beauty of landscapes that range from Alpine peaks to low-lying coastal plains, and across rivers, lakes, and seas, make Germany in many ways western Europe's great undiscovered country. It's also one of the easiest to reach by rail, thanks to its comprehensive links to every major European nation on the continent. In other words, Germany is both an easy and a fascinating stop on any rail traveler's journey throughout Europe.

HIGHLIGHTS OF GERMANY

To cover all of the fascinating towns and sights of Germany could easily take an entire book, and several months. Because most rail travelers won't have more than a week or so to visit the country, in this chapter, we stick to the regions and cities we feel will give the visitor a good look at the best Germany has to offer, from the Bavarian charm of the south to an ancient city of the north. We've also stuck to places that can easily be reached by rail or in conjunction with a rail trip. So, for example, although many people fly into the commercial cities of Hamburg and Frankfurt, we don't cover them beyond telling you how to board a train out of each city because there are far better places for travelers on a limited timetable to explore.

To say that Germany's capital, **Berlin,** had its ups and downs during the century just past would be to make an understatement of monumental proportions. From proud imperial capital, through defeat in World War I, '20s instability and decadence, Hitler and the Holocaust, total destruction and total defeat in World War II, occupation, partition by the Cold War "iron curtain" of the Berlin Wall, and ultimately peaceful reunification, to national capital once again—Berlin has seen it all. And guess what? Berlin is back! As the capital city and a major rail junction in the North, it's usually the starting point of many a visitor and we rank it first on our tour of the country as well. While you can get a quick glimpse of Berlin in a couple of hours from the top deck of an open-top tour bus, as with all of the world's great cities you need to take some time to explore, to settle in, and to allow a little of the city's unique atmosphere to seep into your psyche. You can't do this in less than 2 days, and 3 would be better, setting that

Germany

as an upper limit for travelers on limited time and with a desire to see more of Germany.

Down south is another great city, one that has always been a favorite. **Munich,** capital of the highly independent state of Bavaria, has plenty of attractions all by itself, and sits on the doorstep of the **Alps,** a winter wonderland that has summer highs, too. Should altitude not be your thing, you can instead chill out on the beautiful lake called variously the **Bodensee** and **Lake Constance.** You can do this in 2 to 3 days if you limit the time spent in Munich and make a difficult choice of just one of the possible side trips.

Germany may not be exactly noted as a land of Romance, but it does have its own **Romantic Road,** a route that connects some of Europe's best preserved medieval towns and monuments. As an alternative to visiting Munich and Bavaria, you can visit two or three of the Romantic Road highlights, or, if you have only a spare day or 2, try to fit in just one or at most two. From here, if you have a little more time, you can take a kind of pot-luck selection of day trips

Moments **Festivals & Special Events**

Mozart aficionados flock to the **Mozart Festival,** a major cultural event held in the baroque city of Würzburg from May to the first week in July. For more information, contact **Tourismus Zentrale** in Würzburg-Palais, am Congress-Centrum (© **0931/37-33-35**).

One of Europe's two or three major opera events, the **Richard Wagner Festival** takes place in the composer's Festspielhaus in Bayreuth, the capital of upper Franconia. The festival is held from late July to late August and opera tickets must often be booked years in advance. For information, contact Festival Administration, **Bayreuther Festspiele,** Am Festspiele, 95445 Bayreuth (© **0921/7-87-80;** www.festspiele.de).

Oktoberfest, Germany's most famous festival takes place in Munich from mid-September to the first Sunday in October. Millions show up, and hotels are packed. Most activities are at Theresienwiese, where local breweries sponsor gigantic tents that can hold up to 6,000 beer drinkers. Contact the **Munich Tourist Bureau** (© **089/2-33-03-00**) or surf the Web to **www.muenchen-tourist.de** for particulars, or just show up. Always reserve hotel rooms well in advance.

or overnight visits to three other highlights of the country, each of which has been selected from an over-full field for having some special interest or character: **Bayreuth,** the renowned center of Wagnerian opera; **Heidelberg,** a medieval jewel; **Lübeck,** an ancient trading town that is just filled with northern charm.

1 Essentials

GETTING THERE

Flughafen Frankfurt/Main (© 069/69-00; www.frankfurt-airport.de) lies 7 miles (11km) from the city center at the Frankfurter Kreuz, the intersection of two major expressways, A3 and A5. This airport, continental Europe's busiest, is Germany's major international gateway. From here, all important German airports can be reached. Flying time from Frankfurt to Berlin and Hamburg is 70 minutes, and to Munich, 60 minutes.

At the **Airport Train Station** beneath Terminal 1, you can connect to German InterCity trains and S-Bahn commuter trains to Frankfurt and nearby cities. Terminal 2 is linked to Terminal 1 by a people-mover system, Sky Line, which provides quick transfers (the airport's standard connection time is 45 min. maximum). From Frankfurt's main rail station, the **Hauptbahnhof,** trains depart hourly for most major cities of Germany.

Lufthansa (© 800/645-3880; 01/803-803-803; www.lufthansa.com) operates the most frequent service and flies to the greatest number of Germany's airports, from around 16 gateway cities in the U.S. and Canada.

Other major North American carriers that fly to Germany include **American Airlines** (© 800/443-7300; www.aa.com), **Continental Airlines** (© 800/231-0856; www.continental.com), **Delta Airlines** (© 800/241-4141; www.delta.com), **United Airlines** (© 800/241-6522; www.ual.com), **US Airways** © 800/428-4322; www.usairways.com), and **Air Canada** (© 888/247-2262; www.aircanada.com).

GERMANY BY RAIL

The national rail corporation in Germany, **Deutsche Bahn (German Railways)—DB** for short—spreads its silvery tentacles into the remotest corners of the land, and manages more than 25,000 miles (40,250km) of rail track. The rail system is renowned for its timeliness and reach; German trains even crank their way up more than a few Alpine mountainsides. The busiest stations, in places such as Berlin, Munich, and Frankfurt, see hundreds of arrivals and departures, local, regional, national, and international, every day. No matter where you end up in the country, you'll never be stuck for a choice of destination. For more information, to order tickets, and for the best European train timetables on the Web, check out DB's website at **www.bahn.de**.

TICKETS & PASSES

For details on purchasing multi-country options, such as the **Eurailpass,** and for information on the **German Rail Pass** see chapter 2. In addition to the German Rail Pass, DB also offers a **Twinpass,** for two adults traveling together, that's a real bargain. This pass costs $390 for 4 days in 1 month for first class or $270 for second class (price is for two, not per person). The passes above must be purchased in North America through your travel agent or **Rail Europe** (✆ **877/272-RAIL** in the U.S., 800/361-RAIL in Canada; www.raileurope.com).

Other discount fares and tickets available in Germany at most rail stations include:

BahnCard A range of cards—BahnCard 25, 50, and 100—offer reduced-rate travel for people who intend to do a lot of traveling by train in Germany over an extended period of time.

Gruppe&Spar Tickets for groups of six or more people traveling together, with savings of 50%–70%, depending on how far in advance you buy them (up to 14 days).

Länder-Tickets In some of the German *länder* (states) a range of reduced-rate tickets is offered on particular routes for families and groups of up to five people.

FOREIGN TRAIN TERMS

The rail network as a whole is known as *Die Bahn*. A *Zug* is a train. A fast regional train is known as a *schnellzüg* or *eilzüge*. Night trains are known as *nachtzüge*. A *Zuschlag* is a supplement, which you'll need to pay on some of the high-speed German trains.

Class is *Klasse*. *Zweite (2.) Klasse* is second class and *Erste (1.) Klasse* is first class. A station is a *Bahnhof.* In towns and cities that have more than one station, the main station is often called the *Hauptbahnhof (HBF)*. The German term for platform is *Gleis* or *Bahnsteig*. The bigger stations have separate counters for selling domestic tickets *(Inlandsreisen)* and international tickets (*Auslandsreisen,* or just plain International). A *Fahrkarte* or *Fahrschein* is a ticket. A timetable is a *Fahrplan*. Platforms are generally subdivided into sections—A, B, C, D, and so on—and you are often informed of what section *(Abschnitt)* you will board or vacate the train at. If you have baggage you want to store for a time, look for the *Gepäckaufbewahrung*. Arrival and Departure are *Ankunft* and *Abfahrt,* respectively. And if you need to change trains, the word for transfer is *umsteigen*.

PRACTICAL TRAIN INFORMATION

As Berlin strengthens its role as capital, increasing numbers of trains are speeding their way into town. All points of the country, especially Frankfurt, Munich, and Bonn, maintain excellent rail connections, with high-tech, high-speed improvements being made to the country's railway system virtually all the time. One recent major improvement is that Berlin and the great port of Hamburg are now 15 minutes closer thanks to high-speed (155 mph/250kmph) InterCity Express service (the trip is now 2 hr. 8 min.).

Unlike many other European countries whose rail service is highly centralized, Germany uses a multi-hub system, which means you rarely have to wait as long for a train. About 20,000 **InterCity (IC)** passenger trains offer express service every hour between most large and medium-size German cities. IC trains have adjustable cushioned seats and individual reading lights, and often offer telephone services. Bars, lounges, and dining rooms are available, too. A network of **EuroCity (EC)** trains connecting Germany with 13 other countries offers the same high standards of service as those of IC.

Germany's high-speed **InterCity Express (ICE)** trains are sleek, comfortable, and among the fastest in Europe, reaching speeds of 165 mph (265kmph). These trains run on several major rail corridors in the country (and a limited number of international routes as well), and each train makes a few stops along the way. There are actually several different types of ICE trains, ranging from the older but incredibly spacious domestic ICE 1 trains to the newer ICE T trains that use tilting technology and travel internationally. All ICE trains offer state-of-the-art amenities, which may include electronic seat reservation displays, personal audio systems, luggage storage lockers, and computer ports. Many ICE trains also have "family" cars with play areas for kids. Some ICE 3 and ICE T trains have panoramic lounges that offer excellent views of the surrounding landscape. The ICE network significantly reduces travel time, making transits north to south across the country easily possible in the course of a single day. Some 200 east-west connections have been added to the German Rail timetable to link the *Deutsche Bundesbahn* (west) and the *Deutsche Reichsbahn* (east).

Interregio (IR) trains handle inter-regional service and stop at more stations than the InterCity trains. *Regionalverkehr* (RV, RE, and SE) trains are local trains that stop at every station on their route.

InterCity Night (ICN)—one of the most comfortable night trains in Europe and occasionally known as DB Nachtzug—operates on several domestic and international routes, including Berlin to Munich or Paris, and Munich to Florence or Copenhagen. Passholders get discounted prices on sleeping accommodations on these trains. **CityNightLine (CNL)** trains are exceptionally comfortable double-decker night trains that run between Germany, Austria, and Switzerland. Note, however, that CNL trains don't offer passholder discounts, and accommodations can be very expensive. For more information on CNL trains, check out **www.citynightline.ch**.

Thalys (www.thalys.com) international trains run from Paris, Brussels, and Amsterdam to Cologne and Düsseldorf.

RESERVATIONS   German trains are invariably crowded, and even though reservations aren't required on most IC or ICE routes, many people reserve seats. We strongly recommend that you do, too, if you don't want to end up standing. Reservations on all night trains are mandatory and should be made as far in advance as possible, especially if you're traveling on an international route. Seat reservations can be made at all German train stations or can be reserved in

Trains & Travel Times in Germany

From	To	Type of Train	# of Trains	Frequency	Travel Time
Frankfurt	Berlin	ICE	27	Daily	4 hr. 4 min.
Berlin	Potsdam	SE	29	Daily	23 min.
Berlin	Würzburg	ICE	15	Daily	3 hr. 48 min.
Berlin	Munich	ICE	23	Daily	6 hr. 30 min.
Berlin	Bayreuth	ICE	7	Daily	5 hr. 24 min.
Berlin	Lübeck	ICE	20	Daily	3 hr. 41 min.
Munich	Berchtesgaden	IC	12	Daily	1 hr. 30 min.
Munich	Chiemsee	IC	10	Daily	1 hr.
Munich	Würzburg	ICE	30	Daily	2 hr. 30 min.
Munich	Bayreuth	ICE	16	Daily	3 hr. 07 min.
Munich	Heidelberg	IC	7	Daily	3 hr. 04 min.

North America through Rail Europe starting at $11; couchettes on night trains can be reserved starting at $28. Sleeper reservations are normally included in the price of the ticket or pass supplement that you pay.

SERVICES & AMENITIES   All German trains, even the smallest, have a first-class section or cars (offering more leg space and comfier seats), and there are smoking and nonsmoking compartments. Trains are generally clean and comfortable.

ICE trains have a buffet or restaurant car (called *BordBistro* or *BordRestaurant*) that sells drinks and snacks, and the quality is usually good. IC trains generally have an attendant who pushes around a small cart, from which coffee, tea, mineral water, sandwiches, potato chips, and other snacky items are dispensed. These are more expensive than the same things bought from a supermarket, so if you are on a tight budget, buy them before boarding the train.

ICN trains offer first and tourist class. Sleeping accommodations in first class include single or double compartments with shower and toilet, and they are equipped with key cards, phones for wake-up service, luggage storage, and other amenities. Tourist class offers open seating with *sleeperettes* (reclining seats). The ICN is equipped with a restaurant and bistro car, and a breakfast buffet is included in the first-class fare. For an extra cost, a limited menu for dinner is offered.

CNL trains offer roomy deluxe single- and double-sleeper cabins with private bathrooms and showers, as well as economy four-bed cabins with shared bathrooms. All cabins have electronic locks and are air-conditioned. CNL trains have a dining car that offers both a restaurant (full-service) and bistro (self-service). Breakfast is included in the price of all sleepers and is delivered to your door. There's also a bar car (the only place on the train where smoking is allowed).

DB will arrange assistance for travelers with disabilities in getting to and boarding trains, among other things, provided you call their Mobility Assistance Centre (© **01805/512-512**) at least a day in advance.

FAST FACTS: Germany

Area Codes   The country code for Germany is **49**. To call Germany from North America, you would dial 011 (the international access code), followed by the country code, the local area code (see below), and the telephone number.

When making local calls in Germany, you won't need to use the area codes shown in this book. You do need to use an area code between towns and cities. The area code for Berlin is 030. Other area codes used in this book include: Munich 089, Augsburg 0821, Bayreuth 0921, Heidelberg 06221, and Lübeck 0451.

Business Hours Most **banks** are open Monday to Friday 8:30am to 1pm and 2:30 to 4pm (Thurs to 5:30pm). Money exchanges at airports and border-crossing points are generally open daily from 6am to 10pm. Exchanges at border railroad stations are kept open for arrivals of all international trains. Most **businesses** are open Monday to Friday from 9am to 5pm and on Saturday from 9am to 1pm. Store hours can vary from town to town, but **shops** are generally open Monday to Friday 9 or 10am to 6 or 6:30pm (to 8:30pm on Thurs). Saturday hours are generally from 9am to 1 or 2pm, except on the first Saturday of the month, when stores may remain open until 4pm.

Climate The most popular tourist months are May to October, although winter travel to Germany is becoming increasingly popular, especially to the ski areas in the Bavarian Alps. Germany's climate varies widely. In the north, winters tend to be cold and rainy; summers are most agreeable. In the south and in the Alps, it can be very cold in winter, especially in January, and very warm in summer, but with cool, rainy days even in July and August. Spring and fall are often stretched out.

Documents Required For stays of up to 3 months, citizens of the U.S., Canada, the U.K., Ireland, Australia, and New Zealand need only have a valid passport. A visa is required for stays of longer than 3 months.

Electricity Germany operates on 220 volts electricity (North America uses 110 volts). So you'll need a small voltage transformer that plugs into the round-holed European electrical outlet for any small appliance up to 1,500 watts. When in doubt, ask your hotel's front desk for advice before plugging anything in.

Embassies The following embassies are all in Berlin. **United States:** Clay-allee 170, Dahlem (© **030/832-92-33;** U-Bahn: Dahlem-Dorf). **Canada:** Friedrichstrasse 95 (© **030/20-31-20;** U-Bahn: Friedrichstrasse).

Health & Safety Should you get ill while in Germany, hotels and tourist offices usually keep a list of English speaking doctors and dentists, and the country's medical system is excellent. At least one pharmacy in every major city is open all night. Water is safe to drink in all major cities, but you should not drink any mountain stream water, no matter how pure it looks.

Germany is a reasonably safe country in which to travel, although neo-Nazi skinheads, especially in the eastern part of the country, have sometimes attacked black or Asian travelers. One of the most dangerous places, especially at night, is around the large railway stations in such cities as Frankfurt, Munich, Berlin, and Hamburg. Some beer halls get especially rowdy late at night.

Holidays January 1 (New Year's Day), Easter (Good Friday and Easter Monday), May 1 (Labor Day), Ascension Day (10 days before Pentecost/Whitsunday, the 7th Sun after Easter), Whitmonday (day after Pentecost/Whitsunday), October 3 (Day of German Unity), November 17

(Day of Prayer and Repentance), and December 25 to 26 (Christmas). In addition, the following holidays are observed in some German states: January 6 (Epiphany), Corpus Christi (10 days after Pentecost), August 15 (Assumption), and November 1 (All Saints' Day).

Mail General delivery—mark it POSTE RESTANTE—can be used in any major town or city in Germany. You can pick up your mail upon presentation of a valid identity card or passport. Street mailboxes are painted yellow. It costs 1.50€ ($1.75) for the first 5 grams (about ⅕ oz.) to send an airmail letter to the United States or Canada, and 1€ ($1.15) for postcards. To mail a package, go to one of the larger post offices, preferably the main branch in the area.

Police & Emergencies Throughout Germany the emergency number for **police** is ☎ **110**; for fire or to call an ambulance, dial ☎ **112.**

Telephone Local and long-distance calls may be placed from all post offices and coin-operated public telephone booths. The unit charge is .15€ (20¢). More than half the phones in Germany require an advance-payment telephone card from **Telekom,** the German telephone company.

If you're going to make a lot of phone calls or wish to make an international call from a phone booth (don't make these calls from a hotel, where rates are often quadruple the standard), you'll probably want to purchase a **phone card.** Phone cards are sold at post offices and newsstands. The 6.15€ ($7.10) card offers about 40 minutes, and the 26€ ($29.90) card is useful for long-distance calls. Simply insert them into the telephone slot.

German phone numbers are not standard and come in various formats. Germans also often hyphenate their numbers differently. But because all the area codes are the same, these various configurations should have little affect on your phone usage once you get used to the fact that numbers are inconsistent and vary from place to place.

To make a **collect or calling-card call to North America,** dial one of the following access numbers to reach an operator or an English-language voice prompt: **AT&T** is ☎ **0800-888-00-10;** for **MCI** ☎ **0800-888-8000;** and for **Sprint** ☎ **0800-888-0013. USA Direct** can be used with all telephone cards and for collect calls. The number from Germany is ☎ **01-30-00-10. Canada Direct** can be used with Bell Telephone Cards and for collect calls. This number from Germany is ☎ **01-30-00-14.** To call the U.S. or Canada direct, dial **001** followed by the area code and phone number.

If you're calling from a public pay phone in Germany, you must deposit the basic local rate.

Tipping If a restaurant bill says *Bedienung,* that means a service charge has already been added, so just round up to the nearest euro.

If not, add 10% to 15%. Round up to the nearest euro for taxis. Bellhops get 1€ ($1.15) per bag, as does the doorperson at your hotel, restaurant, or nightclub. Room-cleaning staffs get small tips in Germany, as do concierges who perform some special favors such as obtaining hard-to-get theater or opera tickets. Tip hairdressers or barbers 5% to 10%.

2 Berlin ⋆⋆⋆

With its field of new skyscrapers and hip clubs and fashion boutiques, Berlin is positioning itself as the continent's new capital of cool. As one hip young Berliner, Joachim Stressmann, put it: "We don't know where we're going, but we know where we've been, and no one wants to go back there."

Before the war, the section of the city that became East Berlin had been the cultural and political heart of Germany, where the best museums, the finest churches, and the most important boulevards lay. The walled-in East Berliners turned to restoring their important museums, theaters, and landmarks (especially in the Berlin-Mitte section), while the West Berliners built entirely new museums and cultural centers. This contrast between the two parts of city is still evident today, though east and west are coming together more and more within the immense, fascinating whole that is Berlin.

Given its history and its wide range of attractions, hotels, and restaurants, the city is a natural starting point for a rail tour of the country, even if you end up flying into a more popular airport, such as Frankfurt. Situated in the northeast of Germany, Berlin offers excellent rail connections to all of the major cities of Germany and is an especially good international hub for those traveling west to the east. It has direct rail connections to many major cities, including Paris, Brussels, Vienna, Florence, Zurich, Budapest, and Prague.

STATION INFORMATION
GETTING FROM THE AIRPORT TO THE TRAIN STATION
Note: If you fly into Frankfurt, a popular airport for flights out of North America, follow the directions listed under "Getting There" above for getting to the Frankfurt train station and then hop a train to Berlin. It takes approximately 4 hours by train to get to Berlin's train stations from Frankfurt.

Berlin-Tegel Airport (© 01805/00-01-86; www.berlin-airport.de) is 5 miles (8km) northwest of the city center and is the city's busiest. Public transportation by bus, taxi, or U-Bahn (see "Getting Around," below) is convenient to all points in the city. BVG buses X9 and 109 run every 10 to 15 minutes from the airport to Bahnhof Zoo station in Berlin's center, departing from outside the arrival hall; a one-way fare is 2.40€ ($2.75). A taxi to the city center costs 20€ to 22€ ($23–$25.30) and takes 20 minutes. No porters are available for luggage handling, but pushcarts are free.

Historic **Berlin-Tempelhof Airport** (© 01805/00-01-86; www.berlin-airport.de/PubEnglish), made famous as the city's lifeline during the Berlin Airlift, has declined in importance. And **Berlin-Schönefeld Airport** (© 01805/00-01-86; www.berlin-airport.de/PubEnglish) is used mostly for Russian flights. Both airports are well connected to the city by public transportation, should you happen to end up at them.

INSIDE THE STATIONS
Most arrivals from western European and western German cities are at the **Bahnhof Zoologischer Garten** (© 0810/599-66-33), the main train station, called "Bahnhof Zoo," in western Berlin. In the center of the city, close to the Kurfürstendamm, it's well connected for public transportation. Facilities include a bank for currency exchange, ATMs, a train information office *(Reisezentrum)* off the station's Main Hall, luggage storage lockers, restaurants, and digital train information boards. A tourist information counter dispensing free maps and tourist brochures is open daily from 5am to 11pm. The staff will make same-day hotel reservations for 2.55€ ($2.95).

Western Berlin

ACCOMMODATIONS ■

Art Nouveau **6**
Bleibtreu Hotel **7**
Hotel Crystal **10**
Hotel Domus **12**
Hotel Kronprinz Berlin **4**
Hotel Sylter Hof Berlin **16**
Sorat Art'otel **13**

ATTRACTIONS ●

Ägyptisches Museum
  (Egyptian Museum) **2**
Brandenburger Tor
  (Brandenburg Gate) **18**
Gemäldegalerie **17**
Jüdisches Museum Berlin
  (Jewish Museum Berlin) **20**

Kaiser-Wilhelm Gedächtniskirche
  (Kaiser Wilhelm
  Memorial Church) **14**
Reichstag (Parliament) **19**
Schloss Charlottenburg
  (Charlottenburg Palace) **1**
The Story of Berlin **11**
Zoologischer Garten Berlin
  (Berlin Zoo) **15**

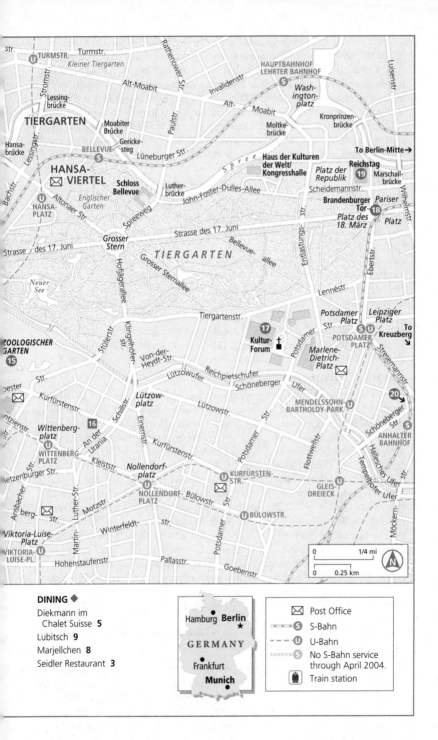

str. ⓤTURMSTR. Turmstr. Turmstr.
Kleiner Tiergarten

Stromstr.

Lessing-
brücke

Alt-Moabit

Invalidenstr.

Rathenower Str.

Paulstr.

Alt-

Moabit

HAUPTBAHNHOF
LEHRTER BAHNHOF

ⓢ Wash-
ington-
platz

Luisenstr.

Kronprinzen-
brücke

Moltke-
brücke

TIERGARTEN

Lessingstr.

Bachstr.

Hansa-
brücke

Moabiter
Brücke

Gericke-
steg

BELLEVUE ⓢ

**HANSA-
VIERTEL** ✉

Altonaer Str.

Englischer
Garten

ⓤ
HANSA-
PLATZ

Lüneburger Str.

**Schloss
Bellevue**

Luther-
brücke

S p r e e

Haus der Kulturen
der Welt/
Kongresshalle

John-Foster-Dulles-Allee

Platz der
Republik

Scheidemannstr.

To Berlin-Mitte →

Reichstag
⑲ Marschall-
brücke

Brandenburger Pariser
Tor ⑱
Platz des Platz
18. März

Wilhelmstr.

Ebertstr.

Spreeweg

Strasse des 17. Juni

**Grosser
Stern**

Bellevue-

allee

Strasse des 17. Juni

Hofjägerallee

T I E R G A R T E N

Grosser Sternallee

Entlastungs-

Neuer
See

ⓏOOLOGISCHER
GARTEN
⑮

Stülerstr.

Klingelhofer-
str.

Von-der-
Heydt-Str.

Tiergartenstr.

Lennéstr.

Potsdamer Leipziger
Platz Platz
Str. ⓢⓤ
POTSDAMER
PLATZ

To
→ Kreuzberg

⑰
**Kultur-
Forum** ✝

Potsdamer

Marlene-
Dietrich-
Platz ✉

Streemannstr.

ester Str.

Kurfürstenstr. ✉

Lützowufer

Reichpietschufer

Schöneberger

Ufer

MENDELSSOHN-
BARTHOLDY-PARK ⓤ

⑳

tzienstr.

Wittenberg-
platz ⓤ
WITTENBERG-
PLATZ

etzenburger Str.

**Lützow-
platz**

Schillstr.

An der
Urania

⑯

Einemstr.

Lützowstr.

Kurfürstenstr.

Potsdamer

Str.

Flottwellstr.

Schöneberger Str. ⓢ

ANHALTER
BAHNHOF

Hallesches Ufer

Kleiststr.

**Nollendorf-
platz** ⓤ
NOLLENDORF-
PLATZ

Bülowstr.

ⓤ KURFÜRSTEN-
STR. ✉

GLEIS-
DREIECK ⓤ

Tempelhofer Ufer

Ansberg-
er
Str.

Luther-Str.

Motzstr.

Martin-

Winterfeldt-

str.

ⓤ BÜLOWSTR.

Möckern-

Viktoria-Luise-
Platz ✉
VIKTORIA- ⓤ
LUISE-PL.

Hohenstaufenstr.

Pallasstr.

Goebenstr.

0 —————— 1/4 mi
0 —————— 0.25 km

Ⓝ

DINING ◆

Diekmann im
 Chalet Suisse **5**
Lubitsch **9**
Marjellchen **8**
Seidler Restaurant **3**

Hamburg **Berlin**
★

GERMANY

Frankfurt

Munich

✉ Post Office
ⓢ S-Bahn
ⓤ U-Bahn
ⓢ No S-Bahn service
through April 2004.
🚆 Train station

Berlin's other major international train station is the **Berlin Ostbahnhof** (© **0810/599-66-33**), or East Station, where most long-distance trains usually stop. You can easily get to the Bahnhof Zoo from here by the public S-Bahn train system. Facilities here include a currency exchange desk on the street level of the station, a train information office open 5:30am to 11pm, luggage storage facilities, a large supermarket, and some fast-food restaurants.

One other station is **Berlin Lichtenberg** (© **0810/599-66-33**), on the far eastern edge of the city, though most visitors will never use it. It services mostly regional trains and trains heading into Poland, and is also connected to the S-Bahn network.

Note: A new central station for Berlin is currently under construction, but isn't scheduled to open until 2006.

INFORMATION ELSEWHERE IN THE CITY

The **Berlin Tourist Information Center** (www.berlin-tourism.de), Europa Center (near Memorial Church), entrance on Budapesterstrasse, is just a few minute's walk from the Bahnhof Zoo station. It's open Monday to Saturday 10am to 7pm and Sunday 10am to 6pm. The office dispenses advice and maps, and will make hotel reservations for you for a charge of 3€ ($3.45).

There's also a branch of the office at the south wing of the Brandenburg Gate, open daily 10am to 6pm. Neither branch accepts phone calls from the general public. Instead, dial © **030/25-00-25** for hotel reservations within Germany. If you're calling from outside of Germany, you'll have to access a different number: © **1805/75-40-40.** For information online, check out **www.berlin-tourism.de**.

GETTING AROUND

The Berlin public transportation system consists of buses, trams, and **U-Bahn** (underground) and **S-Bahn** (elevated) trains. The network is run by the **BVG** (© **030/29-71-9843;** www.bvg.de), which operates an information booth outside the Bahnhof Zoo on Hardenbergplatz. Public transportation throughout the city operates from about 4:30am to 12:30am daily (except for 62 night buses and trams, and U-Bahn lines U-9 and U-12).

The **BVG standard ticket** *(Einzelfahrschein)* costs 2.40€ ($2.75) and is valid for 2 hours in all directions, transfers included. A 24-hour ticket for the whole city costs from 6.30€ ($7.25). Only standard tickets are sold on buses. Tram tickets must be purchased in advance. All tickets should be kept until the end of the journey; otherwise, you'll be liable for a fine of 40€ ($46). Unless you buy a day pass, don't forget to time-punch your ticket at one of the small red boxes prominently posted at the entrance to city buses and underground stations.

Taxis are available throughout Berlin. The meter starts at 3.05€ ($3.50), plus 1.55€ ($1.80) per kilometer after that. Visitors can flag down taxis that have a T-sign illuminated. For a taxi, call © **21-02-02,** 69-41-099, or 24-63-25-63.

Value **The Welcome Card**

If you're going to be in Berlin for 3 days, you can purchase a **WelcomeCard** for 19€ ($21.85), entitling holders to 72 free hours on public transportation in Berlin and Brandenburg. You also get free admission or price reductions of up to 50% on sightseeing tours, museums, and other attractions. Reductions of 25% are granted at 10 of the city's theaters as well. It's valid for one adult and up to three children 13 or younger.

Berlin Mitte

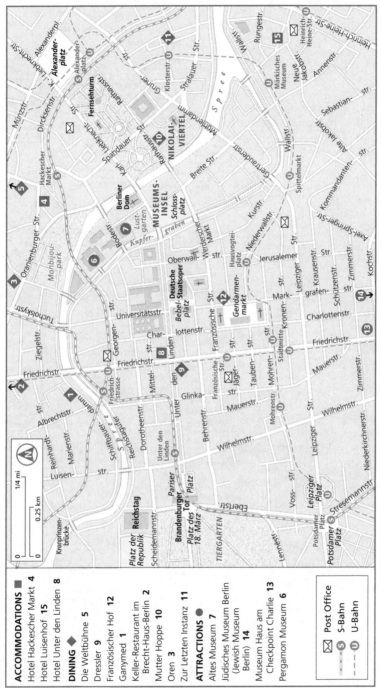

ACCOMMODATIONS ■
Hotel Hackescher Markt **4**
Hotel Luisenhof **15**
Hotel Unter den Linden **8**

DINING ◆
Die Weltbühne **5**
Dressler **9**
Französischer Hof **12**
Ganymed **1**
Keller-Restaurant im
Brecht-Haus-Berlin **2**
Mutter Hoppe **10**
Oren **3**
Zur Letzten Instanz **11**

ATTRACTIONS ●
Altes Museum **7**
Jüdisches Museum Berlin
(Jewish Museum
Berlin) **14**
Museum Haus am
Checkpoint Charlie **13**
Pergamon Museum **6**

⊠ Post Office
Ⓢ S-Bahn
Ⓤ U-Bahn

Berlin U-Bahn & S-Bahn

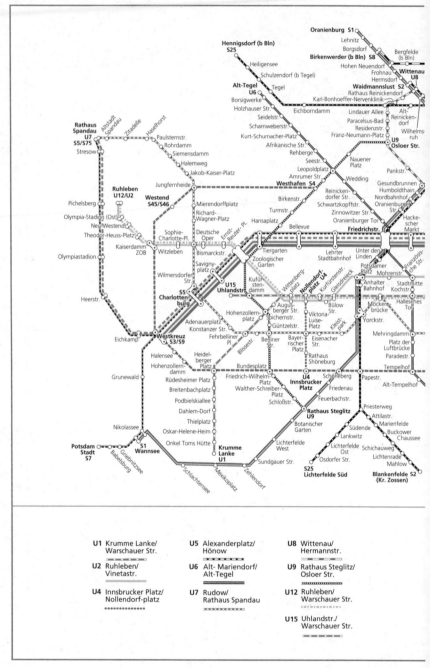

U1 Krumme Lanke/ Warschauer Str.

U2 Ruhleben/ Vinetastr.

U4 Innsbrucker Platz/ Nollendorf-platz

U5 Alexanderplatz/ Hönow

U6 Alt- Mariendorf/ Alt-Tegel

U7 Rudow/ Rathaus Spandau

U8 Wittenau/ Hermannstr.

U9 Rathaus Steglitz/ Osloer Str.

U12 Ruhleben/ Warschauer Str.

U15 Uhlandstr./ Warschauer Str.

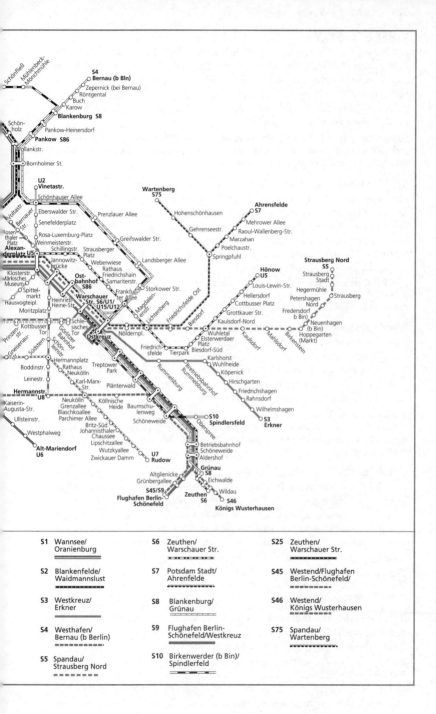

S1   Wannsee/
      Oranienburg

S2   Blankenfelde/
      Waidmannslust

S3   Westkreuz/
      Erkner

S4   Westhafen/
      Bernau (b Berlin)

S5   Spandau/
      Strausberg Nord

S6   Zeuthen/
      Warschauer Str.

S7   Potsdam Stadt/
      Ahrenfelde

S8   Blankenburg/
      Grünau

S9   Flughafen Berlin-
      Schönefeld/Westkreuz

S10   Birkenwerder (b Bln)/
       Spindlerfeld

S25   Zeuthen/
       Warschauer Str.

S45   Westend/Flughafen
       Berlin-Schönefeld/

S46   Westend/
       Königs Wusterhausen

S75   Spandau/
       Wartenberg

WHERE TO STAY

Art Nouveau   On the fourth floor of an Art Nouveau apartment house, this little known hotel is an atmospheric choice. The well-furnished and comfortable rooms are pleasantly decorated and high ceilinged and are filled with excellent beds and well-kept bathrooms. Rooms in the rear are more tranquil except when the schoolyard is full of children at play. There's an honor bar in the lobby where guests keep track of their own drinks.

Leibnizstrasse 59, D-10629 Berlin. ℂ **030/327-74-40**. Fax 030/327-74-40. www.hotelartnouveau.de. 16 units. 110€–165€ ($127–$190) double; 175€–230€ ($201–$265) suite. Rates include continental breakfast. AE, MC, V. U-Bahn: Adenauerplatz. *In room:* Hair dryer.

Bleibtreu Hotel ⭐   Hidden away from the bustle of Berlin, this is a trend-conscious choice. Its tiny lobby is accessible via an alleyway that leads past a garden and a big-windowed set of dining and drinking facilities. The setting is the labyrinthine premises of what was built long ago as a Jugendstil-era apartment house. Rooms are small, minimalist, and furnished in carefully chosen natural materials. The shower-only bathrooms are cramped but well designed.

Bleibtreustrasse 31 (1 block south of Ku'damm). ℂ 800/223-5652 for reservations in the U.S. and Canada, or 030/88-47-40. Fax 030/88-47-44-44. www.bleibtreu.com. 60 units. 192€–242€ ($221–$278) double; 302€–352€ ($347–$405) suite. Rates include continental breakfast. AE, MC, V. S-Bahn: Savignyplatz. **Amenities:** Restaurant; bar; cafe; lounge; laundry, rooms for those with limited mobility. *In room:* Hair dryer.

Hotel Crystal   In a 19th-century building, this six-story hotel is off Savigny-platz, a few minutes walk north of Kurfürstendam. Quiet and unassuming, it's owned and operated by American John Schwarzrock and his German wife, Dorothée, who are always glad to welcome North American visitors. The very basic rooms are comfortable and extremely clean, with a varied collection of plain, simple furnishings that you might think was gathered piecemeal.

Kantstrasse 144, 10623 Berlin. ℂ **030/312-90-47**. Fax 030/312-64-65. 33 units, 21 with bathroom (5 with shower only). 47€ ($54.05) double without bath; 62€ ($71.30) double with shower only; 66.50€ ($76.50) double with bath. Rates include continental breakfast. AE, MC, V. S-Bahn: Savignyplatz. **Amenities:** Bar. *In room:* Hair dryer.

Hotel Domus (*Value*)   Clean, streamlined, and unpretentious, this hotel dates from 1975 and was created from an older core whose elaborate detailing couldn't be salvaged. The result is a stylish, uncluttered piece of architecture that rises from a prestigious neighborhood a few blocks from Ku'damm. It's a favorite of business travelers. Rooms are well designed, well scrubbed, and though not particularly large, very comfortable, each with a neat, shower-only bathroom. Overall, it's a worthy, albeit simple choice, a good value and with helpful staff.

Uhlandstrasse 49, D-10719 Berlin. ℂ **030/880-34-40**. Fax 030/88-03-44-44. www.hotel-domus-berlin.de. 71 units. 120€–145€ ($138–$167) double; 140€–150€ ($161–$173) suite. AE, DC, MC, V. U-Bahn: Hohen-zollernplatz. **Amenities:** Lounge. *In room:* Hair dryer.

Hotel Hackescher Markt ⭐   You'd never know this nugget of charm was newly built in 1998, as everything about it evokes a late-19th-century landmark. Inside, there's a quiet, flagstone-and-ivy covered courtyard that clients use for reading. Rooms are soothing, partially oak-paneled, and outfitted with comfortable and practical furniture. Bathrooms have heated floors. Some guests appreciate the romantic overtones of rooms on the uppermost floor, whose walls are angled due to the building's mansard roof. The staff is polite and very helpful.

Grosse Präsidentenstrasse 8, D-10178 Berlin. (✆) **030/28-00-30.** Fax 030/28-00-31-11. www.hackeschermarkt.com. 31 units. 135€–170€ ($155–$196) double; 175€–202€ ($201–$232) suite. AE, MC, V. U-Bahn: Hackescher Markt. **Amenities:** Restaurant; bar; laundry. *In room:* Hair dryer, no A/C.

Hotel Kronprinz Berlin

For all its many discreet charms and features, this fine boutique hotel—at the far western edge of the Ku'damm—remains relatively little known or publicized. All of the individually decorated rooms have balconies and fine appointments (often tasteful reproductions of antiques). All units are equipped with compact bathrooms with either tubs or showers. Many guests congregate in the garden under the chestnut trees in summer.

Kronprinzendamm 1, 10711 Berlin. (✆) **030/89-60-30.** Fax 030/893-12-15. www.kronprinz-hotel.de. 80 units. 145€–180€ ($167–$207) double; 220–250€ ($253–$288) suite. Buffet breakfast is 10€ ($11.50) extra. AE, DC, MC, V. U-Bahn: Adenauerplatz. **Amenities:** Bar; laundry, nonsmoking rooms, rooms for those with limited mobility. *In room:* Hair dryer.

Hotel Luisenhof ⚜

One of the most desirable small hotels in Berlin's eastern district, the Luisenhof occupies a dignified house, built in 1822. Its five floors of high-ceilinged rooms will appeal to those desiring to escape modern Berlin's sterility. Rooms range greatly in size, but each is equipped with good queen or twin beds. Bathrooms, though small, are beautifully appointed, most with a tub and shower.

Köpenicker Strasse 92, 10179 Berlin. (✆) **030/241-59-06.** Fax 030/279-29-83. www.luisenhof.de. 27 units. 136€ ($156) double; from 195€ ($224) suite. Rates include breakfast. AE, DC, MC, V. U-Bahn: Märkisches Museum. **Amenities:** Restaurant; laundry. *In room:* Hair dryer.

Hotel Sylter Hof Berlin

This hotel, built in 1966, offers rich trappings at good prices. The main lounges are warmly decorated in Louis XV style, with chandeliers, provincial chairs, and antiques. The well-maintained rooms, most of which are singles, may be too small for most tastes, but the staff pays special attention to your comfort. The compact tiled bathrooms are a bit cramped. The staff is warm and welcoming.

Kurfürstenstrasse 114–116, 10787 Berlin. (✆) **030/2-12-00.** Fax 030/214-28-26. www.sylterhof-berlin.de. 161 units. 125€–140€ ($144–$161) double; from 180€ ($207) suite. Rates include buffet breakfast. Rates include buffet breakfast. AE, DC, MC, V. U-Bahn: Wittenbergplatz. **Amenities:** Bar; lounge; nightclub. *In room:* Hair dryer.

Hotel Unter den Linden

An architectural fright erected during the Cold War, this hotel is softening under capitalist control. The location, at the corner of Unter den Linden and Friedrichstrasse, is almost unbeatable for Berlin Mitte convenience. You can walk out the door and stroll over to the Reichstag or the Brandenburger Tor. It's banal but affordable. Its guest rooms are comfortable and a bit small, each with newly installed plumbing including shower-only bathrooms.

Unter den Linden 14, 10117 Berlin. (✆) **030/23-81-10.** Fax 030/23-81-11-00. 331 units. 98€–143€ ($113–$164) double. Rates include continental breakfast. AE, DC, MC, V. U-Bahn: Friedrichstrasse. **Amenities:** Bistro bar with summer terrace; laundry. *In room:* TV.

Sorat Art'otel ⚜

Chic, discreet, and avant-garde, the Sorat is unlike any other Berlin hotel. Rooms, all medium size, have a minimalist decor that includes touches from top designers. Although they will not please clients seeking a traditional Berlin hotel, modernists will be at home with the pedestal tables evoking cable spools and chrome-legged furnishings; and everyone will appreciate the large beds, soundproofing, and good lighting. Bathrooms are generous in size. The service here is among Berlin's finest.

Joachimstalerstrasse 28–29 (near Ku'damm), 10719 Berlin. ⓒ **030/88-44-70.** Fax 030/88-44-77-00. www.
sorat-hotels.com. 133 units. 147€–267€ ($169–$307) double. Rates include buffet breakfast with champagne. AE, DC, MC, V. U-Bahn: Kurfürstendamm. **Amenities:** Restaurant; lounge; laundry. *In room:* Hair dryer.

TOP ATTRACTIONS & SPECIAL MOMENTS

The great art collections of old Berlin suffered during and after World War II.
Although many paintings were saved by being stored in salt mines, many larger
works were destroyed by fire. Part of the surviving art stayed in the east, including a wealth of ancient treasures that remind us of the leading role played by
German archaeologists during the 19th and early 20th centuries. The paintings
that turned up in the west and were passed from nation to nation in the late
1940s have nearly all been returned to Berlin.

CHARLOTTENBURG PALACE & MUSEUMS

Charlottenburg lies just west of the Tiergarten. Plan on spending the day here
because the area contains several museums and the royal apartments. After seeing the main attractions, you can enjoy a ramble through **Schlossgarten Charlottenburg.** These formal gardens look much as they did in the 18th century.
A grove of cypresses leads to a lake with swans and other waterfowl. North of
the palace stands the **Mausoleum,** which holds the tombs of King Friedrich
Wilhelm II and Queen Luise, sculptured by Rauch, and several other interesting funerary monuments of the Prussian royal family.

Ägyptisches Museum (Egyptian Museum) ✦   The western Berlin branch
of the Egyptian Museum is housed in the east guardhouse built for the king's
bodyguard. It's worth the trip just to see the famous colored bust of **Queen
Nefertiti** ✦✦✦, dating from about 1340 B.C. The bust, stunning in every way,
is housed all by itself in a dark first-floor room, illuminated by a spotlight. It is
believed that the bust never left the studio in which it was created but served as
a model for other portraits of the queen. The left eye was never drawn in. In
addition, look for the head of Queen Tiy and the world-famous head of a priest
in green stone. The monumental **Kalabasha Gateway** was built by Emperor
Augustus around 30 B.C. Other displays feature jewelry, papyrus, tools, and
weapons, as well as objects relating to the Egyptian belief in the afterlife.

Schlossstrasse 70. ⓒ **030/32-09-11.** Admission 6€ ($6.90) adults, 3€ ($3.45) children; free admission 1st
Sun of each month. Tues–Fri 10am–6pm; Sat–Sun 11am–6pm. U-Bahn: Sophie-Charlotte-Platz or Richard-
Wagner-Platz. Bus: 109, 110, or 145.

Schloss Charlottenburg (Charlottenburg Palace) ✦✦   Napoléon exaggerated a bit in comparing Schloss Charlottenburg to Versailles when he invaded
Berlin in 1806, but in its heyday this palace was the most elegant residence for
Prussian rulers outside the castle in Potsdam. Begun in 1695 as a summer palace
for the Electress Sophie Charlotte, patron of philosophy and the arts and wife of
King Frederick I (Elector Frederick III), the little residence got out of hand until
it grew into the massive structure you see today.

The main wing contains the apartments of Frederick I and his "philosopher
queen." Of special interest in this section is the **Reception Chamber.** This large
room is decorated with frieze panels, vaulted ceilings, and mirror-paneled
niches. The **new wing,** known as the Knobelsdorff-Flügel, was built from 1740
to 1746, and contains the apartments of Friedrich the Great. Today, these rooms
serve as a museum of paintings, the finest of which are on the upper floor. Works
by Watteau include *The Trade Sign of the Art Dealer Gersaint,* purchased by
Friedrich in 1745 for the palace's music hall. Also note the decoration on the
walls and ceilings.

Luisenplatz. ⓒ **030/320-91-275.** Combined ticket for all buildings and historical rooms 7€ ($8.05) adults, 5€ ($5.90) children under 14 and students. Palace, Tues–Fri 9am–5pm, Sat–Sun 10am–5pm; museum, Tues–Fri 10am–6pm; gardens (free admission) daily 6:30am–8pm. U-Bahn: Sophie-Charlotte-Platz or Richard-Wagner-Platz. Bus: 109, 121, 245, or 204.

OTHER TOP MUSEUMS & SIGHTS

Altes Museum ⭐ Karl Friedrich Schinkel, the city's greatest architect, designed this structure, which resembles a Greek Corinthian temple, in 1822. On its main floor is the **Antikensammlung** (aka the Museum of Greek and Roman Antiquities). This great collection of world-famous works of antique decorative art was inaugurated in 1960. It's rich in pottery; Greek, Etruscan, and Roman bronze statuettes and implements; ivory carvings, glassware, objects in precious stone, and jewelry of the Mediterranean region, as well as gold and silver treasures; mummy portraits from Roman Egypt; wood and stone sarcophagi; and a few marble sculptures. The collection includes some of the finest Greek vases of the black- and red-figures style dating from the 6th century to the 4th century B.C. The best known is a large Athenian wine jar (amphora) found in Vulci, Etruria, dating from 490 B.C., which shows a satyr with a lyre and the god Hermes.

Bodestrasse 13, Museumsinsel. ⓒ **030/20-90-55-55.** Admission 6€ ($6.90) adults, 3€ ($3.45) children. Tues–Sun 10am–6pm. U-Bahn/S-Bahn: Friedrichstrasse. Bus: 100 to Lustgarten, 147, 157, 257.

Brandenburger Tor (Brandenburg Gate) ⭐⭐ This triumphal arch stood for many years next to the Wall, symbolizing the divided city. Today it represents the reunited German capital. Six Doric columns hold up an entablature inspired by the Propylaea of the Parthenon at Athens. Surrounded by the famous and much photographed Quadriga of Gottfried Schadow from 1793, the gate was designed by Carl Gotthard Langhans in 1789. Napoléon liked the original Quadriga so much he ordered them taken down and shipped to Paris, but they were returned to Berlin in 1814. In Berlin's heyday before World War II, the gate marked the grand western extremity of the "main street," Unter den Linden. In the Room of Silence, visitors still gather to meditate and reflect on Germany's past.

Pariser Platz. Free admission. Room of Silence daily 11am–6pm. S-Bahn: Unter den Linden. Bus: 100.

Dahlemer Museen ⭐⭐ After extensive reorganizing, this complex of museums, occupying one mammoth structure in the heart of Dahlem's Freie Universität, contains institutions devoted to everything from ethnological collections to Far Eastern Art.

Occupying most of the main building is the **Ethnologisches Museum** ⭐⭐⭐, the greatest ethnological collection on earth, totaling some 500,000 artifacts from all continents, even prehistoric America. Art and artifacts are displayed from Africa, the Far East, the South Seas, and South America. Many of the figures are ritualistic masks and are grotesquely beautiful. The Incan, Mayan, and Aztec stone sculptures alone equal the collections of some of the finest museums of Mexico. The best part is the collection of authentic boats from the South Pacific. The museum displays an intriguing assemblage of pre-Columbian relics, including gold objects and antiquities from Peru. The museum's Department of Music allows visitors to hear folk music recordings from around the globe.

In the same complex, the **Museum für Ostasiatische Kunst (Museum of Far Eastern Art)** ⭐⭐ is a gem of a museum devoted primarily to Japan, Korea, and China, with artifacts dating back to as far as 3000 B.C. Launched in 1906 as the first Far Eastern museum of art in Germany, this museum is one of

Europe's finest in presenting an overview of some of the most exquisite ecclesiastical and decorative art to come out of the Far East.

Germany's greatest collection of Indian art is on exhibit in the same building at the **Museum für Indische Kunst,** covering a span of 40 centuries. It's an international parade of some of the finest art and artifacts from the world of Buddhism, representing collections from such lands as Burma, Thailand, Indonesia, Nepal, and Tibet.

Lansstrasse 8. ℭ 030/83-011. Admission 3€ ($3.45) adults, 1.50€ ($3.95) students and children. Tues–Fri 9am–6pm; Sat–Sun 11am–6pm. U-Bahn: Dahlem-Dorf.

Gemäldegalerie ★★★   This is one of Germany's greatest art museums. Several rooms are devoted to early German masters, with altarpieces dating from the 13th to 15th centuries. Note the panel of *The Virgin Enthroned with Child* (1350), surrounded by angels that resemble the demons so popular in the later works of Hieronymus Bosch. Eight paintings make up the Dürer collection in adjacent rooms.

Another gallery is given over to Italian painting. Here are five Raphael Madonnas, and works by Titian *(The Girl with a Bowl of Fruit),* Fra Filippo Lippi, Botticelli, and Correggio *(Leda with the Swan).* There are also early Netherlandish paintings from the 15th and 16th centuries (van Eyck, Van der Weyden, Bosch, and Bruegel). Several galleries are devoted to Flemish and Dutch masters of the 17th century, with no fewer than 20 works by Rembrandt, including the *Head of Christ.*

Stauffenbergstrasse (entrance is at Mattäiskirchplatz 4). ℭ 030/20-90-55-55. Admission 6€ ($6.90) adults, 3€ ($3.45) children. Tues–Sun 10am–6pm (Thurs to 10pm). U-Bahn: Potsdamer Platz, then bus 148. Bus: 129 from Ku'damm (plus a 4-min. walk).

Jüdisches Museum Berlin (Jewish Museum Berlin) ★★   The most talked-about museum in Berlin, the Jewish Museum (Europe's largest) is housed in a building that is one of the most spectacular in Berlin. Called "the silver lightning bolt," it was designed by architect Daniel Libeskind. To some viewers, the building suggests a shattered Star of David by its building plan and the scarring in the zinc-plated facade. Odd-shaped windows are haphazardly embedded in the building's exterior.

Inside, the spaces are designed to make the visitor uneasy and disoriented, simulating the feeling of those who were exiled. A vast hollow cuts through the museum to mark what is gone. When the exhibits reach the rise of the Third Reich, the hall's walls, ceiling, and floor close in as the visitor proceeds. A chillingly hollow Holocaust Void, a dark, windowless chamber, evokes much that was lost.

(*Moments* **Strolling the Historic Nikolai Quarter**

The historic **Nikolaiviertel** (U-Bahn: Klosterstrasse), a symbol of Berlin's desire to bounce back after war damage, was restored in time for the city's 750th anniversary in 1987. Here, on the banks of the Spree River, is where Berlin was born. Many of the 16th-century neighborhood's medieval and baroque buildings were completely and authentically reconstructed after World War II. Subsequently, some of the city's old flavor has been recaptured here. Period taverns and churches make it ideal for a leisurely stroll down narrow streets illuminated by gas lanterns.

> **Moments   A New Wall**
>
> Berliners aren't likely to forget the **Berlin Wall** any time soon, but just in
> case, their government has reconstructed a partial stretch of the wall at
> Bernauer Strasse and Ackerstrasse (U-Bahn: Bernauer Strasse), at a cost of
> 1.43 million€ ($1.64 million). The 230-foot-long memorial consists of two
> walls that include some of the fragments of the original wall (those frag-
> ments not bulldozed away or carried off by souvenir hunters). The memo-
> rial is mostly made of mirrorlike stainless steel. Slits allow visitors to peer
> through. A steel plaque reads "In memory of the division of the city from
> 13 August 1961 to 9 November 1989." Critics have called the construction
> "a sanitized memorial," claiming it does little to depict the 255 people
> shot trying to escape its predecessor.

The exhibits concentrate on three themes: Judaism and Jewish life, the devastating effects of the Holocaust, and the post–World War II rebuilding of Jewish life in Germany. The history of German Jewry is portrayed through objects,
works of art, and documentation. The on-site Liebermanns Restaurant features
world cuisine, with an emphasis on Jewish recipes—all strictly kosher.

Lindenstrasse 9–14. ✆ **030/25-99-33.** Admission 5€ ($5.75); free for kids 5 and under. Family ticket 10€
($11.50) for 2 adults, 4 children. Mon 10am–10pm; Tues–Sun 10am–8pm. U-Bahn: Hallesches Tor or
Kochstrasse.

Kaiser-Wilhelm Gedächtniskirche (Kaiser Wilhelm Memorial Church)
The massive red sandstone church that originally stood here was dedicated in
1895 as a memorial to Kaiser Wilhelm II. In 1945, during the closing months
of World War II, a bomb dropped by an Allied plane blasted it to pieces,
leaving only a few gutted walls and the shell of the neo-Romanesque bell tower.
After the war, West Berliners decided to leave the artfully evocative ruins as a
reminder of the era's suffering and devastation. In 1961, directly at the base of
the ruined building, they erected a small-scale modern church. Its octagonal hall
is lit solely by thousands of colored glass windows set into a honeycomb frame-
work. On its premises, you can visit a small museum with exhibits and photographs documenting the history of the original church and the ravages of war.

Breit-Scheidplatz. ✆ **030/218-50-23.** Free admission. Ruined church Mon–Sat 10am–4pm; new church
daily 9am–7pm. U-Bahn: Zoologischer Garten.

Museum Haus am Checkpoint Charlie   This small building houses exhibits
depicting the tragic events leading up to and following the erection of the former Berlin Wall. You can see some of the instruments of escape used by East
Germans. Photos document the construction of the wall, escape tunnels, and
the postwar history of both parts of Berlin from 1945 until today, including the
airlift of 1948 and 1949. One of the most moving exhibits is the display on the
staircase of drawings by schoolchildren who, in 1961 and 1962, were asked to
depict both halves of Germany in one picture.

Friedrichstrasse 44. ✆ **030/253-72-50.** Admission 7€ ($8.05) adults, 4€ ($4.60) children. Daily 9am–10pm.
U-Bahn: Kochstrasse or Stadtmitte. Bus: 129.

Reichstag (Parliament)   The night of February 17, 1933, was a date that
lives in infamy in German history. On that night, a fire broke out in the seat of
the German house of parliament, the Reichstag. It was obviously set by the

Moments **In Memory of . . .**

At the corner of Lewetzov and Jagow streets is a **Jewish War Memorial** to the many Berliners who were deported—mostly to their deaths—from 1941 until the end of the war in 1945. The memorial is a life-size sculpture of a freight car with victims being dragged into it. Behind it is a 50-foot structure listing the dates of the various death trains and the number of prisoners shipped out. The memorial stands on the site of a former synagogue destroyed by the Nazis.

Nazis on orders of Hitler, but the German Communist Party was blamed. That was all the excuse Hitler's troops needed to begin mass arrests of "dissidents and enemies of the lawful government." During World War II, the Reichstag faced massive Allied bombardment. Today it's once again the home of Germany's parliament. A new glass dome, designed by English architect Sir Norman Foster, now crowns the neo-Renaissance structure originally built in 1894. You can go through the west gate for an elevator ride up to the dome, where a sweeping vista of Berlin awaits you. There's both an observation platform and a rooftop restaurant (the view is better than the food).

Platz der Republik 1. ☎ 030/2273-2152. Free admission. Daily 8am–midnight (last entrance at 10pm). S-Bahn: Unter den Linden. Bus: 100.

Pergamon Museum ✹✹✹   The Pergamon Museum houses several departments, but if you have time for only one exhibit, go to the central hall of the U-shaped building to see the **Pergamon Altar** ✹✹✹. This Greek altar (180–160 B.C.) has a huge room all to itself. Some 27 steps lead up to the colonnade. Most fascinating is the frieze around the base, tediously pieced together over a 20-year period. Depicting the struggle of the Olympian gods against the Titans as told in Hesiod's *Theogony,* the relief is strikingly alive, with figures projecting as much as a foot from the background. This, however, is only part of the collection of Greek and Roman antiquities housed in the north and east wings. You'll also find a Roman market gate discovered in Miletus, and sculptures from many Greek and Roman cities, including a statue of a goddess holding a pomegranate (575 B.C.), found in southern Attica.

The **Near East Museum** ✹, in the south wing, contains one of the largest collections anywhere of antiquities discovered in the lands of ancient Babylonia, Persia, and Assyria. Among the exhibits is the Processional Way of Babylon with the Ishtar Gate, dating from 580 B.C., and the throne room of Nebuchadnezzar.

Kupfergraben, Museumsinsel. ☎ 030/2090-55-55. Admission 6€ ($6.90) adults, 3€ ($3.45) children; free the 1st Sun of the month. Tues, Wed, Fri, Sat, and Sun 10am–6pm, Thurs 10am–10pm. U-Bahn/S-Bahn: Friedrichstrasse. Tram: 1, 2, 3, 4, 5, 13, 15, or 53.

The Story of Berlin   This multimedia extravaganza portrays 8 centuries of the city's history through photos, films, sounds, and colorful displays. Beginning with the founding of Berlin in 1237, it chronicles the plague, the Thirty Years' War, Frederick the Great's reign, military life, the Industrial Revolution and the working poor, the Golden 1920s, World War II, divided Berlin during the Cold War, and the fall of the Wall. Lights flash in a media blitz as you enter the display on the fall of the Wall, making you feel like one of the first East Berliners to cross over to the West. Conclude your tour on the 14th floor with a panoramic view of today's Berlin. Though the displays are a bit jarring and the historical information is too jumbled to be truly educational, the museum does leave a lasting impression. Allow at least 2 hours.

Ku'damm-Karree, Kurfürstendamm 207–208 (at the corner of Uhlandstrasse). ℭ **01805/99-20-10.** Admission 9.30€ ($10.70) adults, 7.50€ ($8.60) students/children, 21€ ($24.15) families. Daily 10am–8pm (visitors must enter by 6pm). S-Bahn: Uhlandstrasse.

A PARK & A ZOO

Tiergarten ⚐   Tiergarten, the largest green space in central Berlin, covers just under 1 square mile (1.6 sq. km), with more than 14 miles (23km) of meandering walkways. Late in the 19th century, partially to placate growing civic unrest, it was opened to the public, with a layout formalized by one of the leading landscape architects of the era, Peter Josef Lenné. The park was devastated during World War II, and the few trees that remained were chopped down for fuel as Berlin shuddered through the winter of 1945 and 1946. Beginning in 1955, trees were replanted and alleyways, canals, ponds, and flowerbeds rearranged in their original patterns through the cooperative efforts of many landscape architects.

The park's largest monuments include the Berlin Zoo, described below, and the **Siegessäule (Victory Column),** which perches atop a soaring red-granite pedestal from a position in the center of the wide boulevard (Strasse des 17 Juni) that neatly bisects the Tiergarten into roughly equivalent sections.

From the Bahnhof Zoo to the Brandenburger Tor. Bus: 100, 141, or 341 to Grosser Stern.

Zoologischer Garten Berlin (Berlin Zoo) ⚐ *Kids*   Occupying most of the southwest corner of Tiergarten is Germany's oldest and finest zoo. Founded in 1844, it's a short walk north from the Ku'damm. Until World War II, the zoo boasted thousands of animals of every imaginable species and description—many familiar to Berliners by nicknames. The tragedy of the war struck here as well, and by the end of 1945, only 91 animals remained. Since the war, the city has been rebuilding its large and unique collection; today more than 13,000 animals are housed here. The zoo has Europe's most modern birdhouse, featuring more than 550 species. The most valuable inhabitants here are giant pandas.

The **Aquarium** is as impressive as the adjacent zoo, with more than 9,000 fish, reptiles, amphibians, insects, and other creatures. Crocodiles, Komodo dragons, and tuataras inhabit the terrarium within. You can walk on a bridge over the reptile pit. There's also a large collection of snakes, lizards, and turtles. The "hippoquarium" is a new attraction.

Hardenbergplatz 8. ℭ **030/25-40-10.** Zoo, 9€ ($10.35) adults, 4.50€ ($5.20) children. Zoo and aquarium, 14€ ($16.10) adults, 7€ ($8.05) children. Zoo, Apr–Oct daily 9am–5pm; Nov–Mar daily 9am–5:30pm. Aquarium, year-round, daily 9am–6pm. S-Bahn/U-Bahn: Zoologischer Garten.

WHERE TO DINE

Diekmann im Chalet Suisse ⚐ NEW GERMAN/SWISS   Should you have the urge to breathe fresh air in the extensive Grünewald park, close to the U.S. embassy, you'll find this fine restaurant a great place to dine. Its timber, farmhouse-style Swiss setting suits the forested surroundings down to the roots. You can choose from an extensive list of German and Swiss dishes, and sit either indoors in one of four sparely decorated but elegant wood-floored rooms, or, in fine weather, outdoors on the rustic terrace.

Clayallee 99, in the Grünewald, Dahlem. ℭ **030/832-63-62.** Main courses 9.80€–21.50€ ($11.25–24.70); menus 20€–40€ ($23–$46). AE, DC, MC, V. Daily 11:30am–around midnight. U-Bahn: Dahlem-Dorf.

Die Weltbühne INTERNATIONAL/MEDITERRANEAN   You're likely to get so distracted with visual input at the long bar here that you might find it hard to eventually move into dinner. The dining room is divided into semiprivate banquette areas outlined in hardwood paneling, forest-green upholstery, elaborate Murano-glass chandeliers, and vague references to Bauhaus. Cuisine is sophisticated and superb, based on a changing set of international dishes influenced by the season and the inspiration of the chef.

Gormannstrasse 14. ℂ 030/28-00-94-40. Reservations recommended on weekends. Main courses 14.50€–22€ ($16.70–$25.30). AE, MC, V. Daily 6pm–12:30am. U-Bahn: Rosenthalerplatz.

Dressler CONTINENTAL   Resembling an arts-conscious bistro of the sort that might have entertained tuxedo-clad clients in the 1920s, Dressler is set behind a wine-colored facade, and outfitted with leather banquettes, black-and-white tile floors, mirrors, and film memorabilia from the great days of early German cinema. Waiters scurry around with vests and aprons, carrying trays of everything from caviar to strudel, as well as three kinds of oysters and hefty portions of lobster salad.

Unter den Linden 39. ℂ 030/204-44-22. Main courses 13.80€–23€ ($15.90–$26.45). AE, DC, MC, V. Daily 8am–midnight. S-Bahn: Unter den Linden.

Französischer Hof *Value* GERMAN   If you want a reasonable meal in a relaxed atmosphere, this is the place. It fills two floors connected by a Belle Epoque staircase, evoking a century-old Parisian bistro. The kitchen may not be the finest, but ingredients are fresh and deftly handled. There's a delectable selection of fish canapés, and the saddle of lamb is always admirably done.

Jagerstrasse 56. ℂ 030/204-35-70. Reservations recommended on weekends. Main courses 10€–18€ ($11.50–$20.70). AE, DC, MC, V. Daily noon–midnight. U-Bahn: Hausvogteiplatz.

Ganymed GERMAN/INTERNATIONAL   There's nothing trendy or immediately fashionable about this restaurant, started up in 1929, and which stalwartly continued doing business within East Berlin throughout the Cold War. The setting includes two formal dining rooms, one with an ornate plaster ceiling of great beauty; the other a more modern, big-windowed affair that overlooks the Spree. Food arrives in worthy portions, with plenty of flavor, albeit without too much concern for modern culinary fancies or trends.

Schiffbauerdamm 5. ℂ 030/285-90-46. Reservations recommended on weekends. Main courses 10€–17€ ($11.50–$19.55). Fixed-price menus 25€–48€ ($28.75–$55.20). AE, MC. Mon–Sat 5pm–1am; Sun noon–1am. U-Bahn: Friedrichstrasse.

Keller-Restaurant im Brecht-Haus-Berlin SOUTH GERMAN/AUSTRIAN   From 1953 until his death in 1956, Bertolt Brecht lived in this building (the top floor is a museum dedicated to the playwright). The restaurant, with white plaster and exposed stone, is decorated with photographs of the playwright's family, friends, and theatrical productions. Traditional south German and Austrian food is served, such as an Austrian recipe for *Fleisch Laberln* (meatballs made from minced pork and served with dumplings). In good weather, the seating area includes an enclosed courtyard upstairs.

Chausseestrasse 125. ℂ 030/282-38-43. Main courses 8€–15€ ($9.20–$17.25). AE, DC, MC, V. Daily 6pm–midnight, and from May–Oct 11am–3pm and 6pm–midnight. U-Bahn: Zinnowitzer Strasse.

Lubitsch CONTINENTAL   Deeply entrenched in the consciousness of many local residents, Lubitsch is considered in some quarters to have a degree of conservative chic. Expect platters of chicken curry salad with roasted potatoes, Berlin-style potato soup, braised chicken with salad and fresh vegetables, a roulade of suckling pig, and Nürnberger-style *wursts*. Count on a not so friendly staff, a black-and-white decor with Thonet-style chairs, and a somewhat arrogant environment that despite its drawbacks, is very, very *Berliner.*

Bleibtreustrasse 47. (*C*) **030/882-37-56.** Main courses 6€–21€ ($6.90–$24.15). AE, DC, MC, V. Mon–Sat 9am–midnight. U-Bahn: Kurfürstendamm.

Marjellchen ★ EAST PRUSSIAN   This is the only restaurant in Berlin specializing in the cuisine of Germany's long-lost province of East Prussia, along with those of Pomerania and Silesia. Amid a Bismarckian ambience of vested waiters and oil lamps, you can enjoy savory old-fashioned fare (marinated elk, for example), of a type that Goethe and Schiller favored. Marjellchen isn't the place to go, however, if you want to keep tabs on your cholesterol intake.

Mommsenstrasse 9. (*C*) **030/883-26-76.** Reservations required. Main courses 10.20€–20.45€ ($11.75–$23.50). AE, DC, MC, V. Mon–Sat 5pm–midnight. U-Bahn: Adenauerplatz or Uhlandstrasse.

Mutter Hoppe *Value* GERMAN   This cozy, wood-paneled restaurant still serves the solid Teutonic cuisine favored by a quasi-legendary matriarch (Mother Hoppe) who used to churn out vast amounts of food to members of her extended family and entourage. Within a quartet of old-fashioned dining rooms, you'll enjoy heaping portions of such rib-sticking fare as sauerbraten with roasted potatoes, and braised filet of pork in mushroom-flavored cream sauce.

Rathausstrasse 21, Nikolaiviertel. (*C*) **030/241-56-25.** Main courses 8.20€–17.90€ ($9.45–$20.60). MC, V. Daily 11:30am–midnight. U-Bahn/S-Bahn: Alexanderplatz.

Oren ISRAELI/ARABIC   Next door to the massive reconstruction of the Oranienburger synagogue, these cream-colored, high-ceilinged premises are owned by Berlin's Jewish community. The savory aromas of old-fashioned Jewish cooking permeate the restaurant, and the vegetarian and fish platters are wholesome, affordable, and plentiful. The menu includes cream of garlic soup; smoked trout; falafel with hummus, tahini, olives, and pita; and cold gefilte fish with red-beet salad.

Oranienburgerstrasse 28. (*C*) **030/282-82-28.** Main courses 9€–25€ ($10.35–$28.75). AE, MC, V. Mon–Thurs noon–1am; Fri–Sat 10am–2am; Sun 10am–1am. S-Bahn: Oranienburger Tor.

Seidler GERMAN   Ensconce yourself in a restaurant that enjoys a reputation as a select dining spot and social center, with a devoted local following among theater and media personalities. The ambience is that of a Berlin bistro, charmingly cluttered with kitsch from all over the world. The chef believes in strong flavors and good hearty cooking, typified by the savory *Kohlroulade,* a stuffed cabbage roll. Another highlight is the rack of lamb with honey onions and rosemary potatoes.

Damaschkestrasse 26. (*C*) **030/323-14-04.** Reservations required. Main courses 7€–19€ ($8.05–$21.85). MC. Mon–Sat 5pm–midnight. U-Bahn: Adenauerplatz.

Zur Letzten Instanz GERMAN   Reputedly, this is Berlin's oldest restaurant, dating from 1525, and has supposedly been frequented by everybody from Napoléon to Beethoven. The place is located on two floors of a baroque building just outside the crumbling brick wall that once ringed medieval Berlin. Double doors open on a series of small woodsy rooms. The menu is old-fashioned, mainly limited to good, hearty fare in the best of the Grandmother Berlin tradition of staples.

Waisenstrasse 14–16 (near Alexanderplatz). (*C*) **030/242-55-28.** Main courses 11€–16€ ($12.65–$18.40); fixed-price dinner 19€–27€ ($21.85–$31.05). AE, DC, MC, V. Mon–Sat noon–1am; Sun noon–11pm. U-Bahn: Klosterstrasse.

SHOPPING

The **Ku'damm** (or Kurfürstendamm) is the Fifth Avenue of Berlin. It's filled with quality stores but also has outlets hustling cheap souvenirs and T-shirts. Although Berliners themselves shop on the Ku'damm, many prefer the specialty stores on the side streets, especially between **Breitscheidplatz** and **Olivaer Platz.** You may also want to check out **Am Zoo** and **Kantstrasse.**

Another major shopping street is the **Tauentzienstrasse** and the streets that intersect it: **Marburger, Ranke,** and **Nürnberger.** This area offers a wide array of stores, many specializing in German fashions for women. Stores here are often cheaper than on the Ku'damm. Also on Tauentzienstrasse (near the Ku'damm) is Berlin's major indoor shopping center, the **Europa Center** (© **030/348-0088**), with around 75 shops, as well as restaurants and cafes.

A new, upmarket version of the Europa Center is the **Uhland-Passage,** at Uhlandstrasse 170, which has some of the best boutiques and big-name stores in Berlin. Shoppers interested in quality at any price should head to **Kempinski Plaza,** Uhlandstrasse 181–183, a pocket of posh with some of the most exclusive boutiques in the city. Haute-couture women's clothing is a special feature here. More trendy and avant-garde boutiques are found along **Bleibtreustrasse.**

If you're looking for serious bargains, head to **Wilmersdorferstrasse,** with a vast number of discount stores, although some of the merchandise is second-rate. Try to avoid Saturday morning, when it's often impossibly overcrowded.

In eastern Berlin, not that long ago, you couldn't find much to buy except a few souvenirs. All that is changed now. The main street, **Friedrichstrasse,** offers some of Berlin's most elegant shopping. Upmarket boutiques—selling everything from quality women's fashions to Meissen porcelain—are found along **Unter den Linden.** The cheaper stores in eastern Berlin are around the rather bleak-looking **Alexanderplatz.** Many specialty and clothing shops are found in the **Nikolai Quarter.** The largest shopping mall in eastern Berlin, with outlets offering a little bit of everything, is at the **Berliner Markthalle,** at the corner of Rosa-Luxemburg-Strasse and Karl-Liebknecht-Strasse.

Most stores in Berlin are open Monday to Friday from 9 or 10am to 6 or 6:30pm. Many stay open late on Thursday evenings, often to 8:30pm. Saturday hours are usually from 9 or 10am to 2pm. Most stores are not open on Sunday.

The prestigious emporium **KPM (Königliche Porzellan-Manufaktur [Royal Porcelain Factory]),** in the Kempinski Hotel Bristol, Kurfürstendamm 27 (© **030/88-67-21-10;** U-Bahn: Kurfürstendamm), was founded in 1763. Since then, KPM's exquisite hand-painted, hand-decorated items have become world-famous for their artistry and delicacy. Stiff competition for KPM emanates from **Meissener Porzellan,** Kurfürstendamm 26A (© **030/88-68-35-30;** U-Bahn: Kurfürstendamm), one of the most famous porcelain outlets in Europe. It offers the finest array of exquisite Meissen dinner plates in Berlin, and displays and sells sculptures and chandeliers.

Kaufhaus des Westens, Tauentzienstrasse 21 (© **030/21-210;** U-Bahn: Kurfürstendamm or Wittenbergplatz), a huge luxury department store (the largest in continental Europe), known popularly as **KaDeWe** (pronounced *kah*-day-vay), is best known for its food department, where more than 1,000 varieties of German sausages are displayed along with delicacies from all over the world. Sitdown counters are available. After fortifying yourself here, you can explore the six floors of merchandise.

MARKETS

You might want to check out the finds at the flea market **Antik & Flohmarkt,** Friedrichstrasse S-Bahn station, Berlin-Mitte (© **030/208-26-45;** U-Bahn/ S-Bahn: Friedrichstrasse), inside the S-Bahn station. Some 60 vendors try to tempt buyers with assorted bric-a-brac, including brassware and World War II mementos. The favorite weekend shopping spot of countless Berliners, the flea market **Berliner Trödelmarkt,** Strasse des 17 Juni (© **030/26-55-00-96;** S-Bahn: Tiergarten), lies near the corner of Bachstrasse and Strasse des 17 Juni, at the western edge of the Tiergarten, adjacent to the Tiergarten S-Bahn station. They come here to find an appropriate piece of nostalgia, a battered semi-antique, or used clothing. The market is held every Saturday and Sunday from 10am to 5pm.

NIGHTLIFE

In Berlin, nightlife runs around the clock, and there's plenty to do at any time. The English-language monthly *Checkpoint Berlin* lists happenings in the city and is available for free at hotel reception desks and tourist offices and sold at news kiosks.

PERFORMING ARTS One of the world's premier orchestras, the **Berlin Philharmonic Orchestra (www.berlin-philharmonic.com)** is home-based at the Philharmonie, Herbert-von-Karajan-Strasse 1 (© **030/254-88-132;** S-Bahn: Potsdamer Platz), a concert hall noted for its excellent acoustics. The box office is open Monday to Friday from 3 to 6pm, and Saturday and Sunday from 11am to 2pm. Tickets for most performances cost 15€ to 51€ ($17.25–$58.65). You can't place orders by phone, but if you're staying in a first-class or deluxe hotel, the concierge can usually get seats for you. An 1821 building, the **Konzerthaus Berlin,** in the Schauspielhaus, Gendarmenmarkt. © **030/203-09-21-01;** U-Bahn: Französische Strasse), offers two venues for classical concerts: the Grosser Konzertsaal for orchestra and the Kammermusiksaal for chamber music. The Deutsches Sinfonie-Orchester is also based here.

The **Deutsche Oper Berlin** opera company performs in Charlottenburg in one of the world's great opera houses, Bismarckstrasse 35 (© **030/343-84-01;** U-Bahn: Deutsche Oper and Bismarckstrasse). The company tackles Puccini favorites, Janácek rarities, or modern works, and has a complete Wagner reper-toire. A ballet company performs once a week. Concerts, including *Lieder* evenings, are also presented on the opera stage. Tickets are 15€–102€ ($17.25–$117). The **German State Opera** performs in the Staatsoper, Unter den Lin-den 7 (© **030/20-35-45-55;** www.staatsoper-berlin.org; U-Bahn: Französische Strasse), originally constructed in 1743 and rebuilt in the 1950s. The box office is open Monday to Friday from 10am to 6pm, and Saturday and Sunday from noon to 6pm. Tickets cost 11€ to 82€ ($12.65–$94.30). The opera closes from mid-June to late August.

CLUBS The top Berlin jazz club is **Quasimodo,** Kantstrasse 12A (© **030/ 312-80-86;** U-Bahn: Zoologischer Garten). Although many different styles of music are offered here, including rock and Latin, jazz is the focus. Local acts are featured on Tuesday and Wednesday, when admission is free (otherwise the cover is 8€–22€/$9.20–$25.30). The club is open Tuesday to Saturday 9pm to 3am, with shows beginning at 10pm. A small and smoky jazz house, **A Trane,** Bleibtreustrasse 1 (© **030/313-25-50;** S-Bahn: Savignyplatz), features musi-cians from around the world. It's open Monday to Thursday 8pm to 4am, Fri-day and Saturday 9pm to 4am. Music begins around 10pm. There's a cover of 8€ to 15€ ($9.20–$17.25).

Moments   The Love Parade

The **Love Parade** is the techno-rave street party to end all parties. During the second weekend of July, around 1 million (mostly) young people converge in the center of Berlin for 48 decidedly hedonistic hours. What began in 1988 as a DJ's birthday party with about 150 friends has grown into an immense corporate event that wreaks havoc on the rest of the city's usually impeccable organization (particularly the public transportation system).

The center of Berlin turns into one giant party and is awash with litter and good-natured debauchery. It's the techno version of New Orleans' Mardi Gras. Because of the frenzied jiggling, gyrating, and very noisy good times, anyone wanting an even remotely peaceful weekend should follow the little old ladies and rock fans on the fast train out of town. The event starts off on Saturday afternoon, when a booming caravan of floats carries the best DJs in Europe from Ernst-Reuter-Platz to the Brandenburg Gate. If you want to see the procession, come early and grab as high a view as possible.

Knaack-Klub, Greifwalderstrasse 224 (✆ **030/442-70-60;** S-Bahn: Alexanderplatz), features a live-music venue, two floors of dancing, and a games floor. There are usually four live rock shows a week, with a fairly even split between German and international touring bands. Hours are Monday to Friday 10pm to 4am, Saturday and Sunday 10pm to 7am. Cover ranges from 2.50€ to 5€ ($2.90–$5.75). Top DJs play the latest international hits at **Big Eden,** Kurfürstendamm 202 (✆ **030/882-61-20;** U-Bahn: Uhlandstrasse), which accommodates 1,000 dancers on its huge floor. The club is open Sunday to Thursday from 9pm to 5am, and Friday and Saturday from 9pm to 6am. The cover ranges from 5€ to 10€ ($5.75–$11.50) and includes a drink. **Café Keese,** Bismarckstrasse 108 (✆ **030/312-91-11;** U-Bahn: Ernst-Reuther-Platz), caters to a more traditional clientele, most aged 35 to 40. Here women can ask the men to dance. The orchestra plays a lot of slow music, and the place is often jammed, especially on Saturday nights. Formal attire is requested. It's open Tuesday to Thursday 8pm to3am, Friday to Saturday from 8pm to 4am, Sunday to Monday from 4pm to 1am. There's no cover, but there is a one-drink minimum on weekends. A renewed interest in ballroom dancing has kept **Clärchen's Ballhaus,** Auguststrasse 24–25 (✆ **030/282-92-95;** U-Bahn: Rosenthaler), going. It's schmaltzy enough to remind sentimental newcomers of the nostalgic old days. On Wednesday, women are encouraged to ask men to the dance floor. Open Tuesday, Wednesday, Friday, and Saturday from 8:30pm to around 3am. The cover is 8€ ($9.20).

BARS & CAFES   Squat and unpretentious, the **Historischer Weinkeller,** Alt-Pichelsdorf 32 (✆ **030/361-80-56;** U-Bahn: Olympia-Stadion), is a highly atmospheric vaulted cellar. During summer months, an outdoor rustic beer garden is open. A cozy pub, **Joe's Wirthaus zum Löwen,** Hardenbergstrasse 29 (✆ **030/262-10-20;** U-Bahn: Zoologischer Garten), is attractively decorated with traditional Teutonic accessories. Even in winter, when you're snug and warm inside, you get the feeling you're sitting out under the chestnut trees.

Many hip locals cite **Bar am Lützowplatz,** Lützowplatz 7 (© **030/262-68-07;** U-Bahn: Nollendorferplatz), as their favorite bar, partly because it manages to be beautiful, chic, breezy, and artsy, and partly because it provides a concentrated kind of conviviality within a prosperous but staid neighborhood. It presents an almost reverential portrait of Mao Tse-tung as its visual focal point, the humor of which cannot be lost on the devoted capitalists and *bons vivants* who come here to see, be seen, and flirt. You might be rejected at the door by a bouncer who disapproves of your sense of style at **Newton Bar,** Tharlogginstrasse 57 (© **030/20-61-29-99;** U-Bahn: Stadtmitte). Here's what you get if you're admitted: a high-ceilinged, well-proportioned room that evokes 1960s modernism at its best. You can't help but be intrigued by a huge black-and-white mural that sweeps an entire runway of naked fashion models across your field of vision, and by service rituals inspired by Old Prussia.

A *Kneipe* is a cozy rendezvous place, the equivalent of a Londoner's local pub. The typical Berliner has a favorite Kneipe for relaxing after work and visiting with friends. There are hundreds in Berlin. **Gaststätte Hoeck,** Wilmersdorferstrasse 149 (© **030/341-81-74;** U-Bahn: Bismarckstrasse), the oldest Kneipe in Charlottenburg (1892) still sports original wood panels with inlaid glass on the walls. It also has a brightly illuminated facade jammed with local beer slogans. More than a dozen kinds of beer are offered and wine by the glass. At **Lutter und Wegner 1811,** Schlüstrasse 55 (© **030/881-34-40;** S-Bahn: Savignyplatz), the wide selection of drinks ranges from single-malt Scottish whiskeys to Italian grappas. In summer, you can sit on a terrace and observe the passing parade.

AN EXCURSION TO POTSDAM

The best day trip from Berlin is to the baroque town of Potsdam, 15 miles (24km) southwest of the city, on the Havel River. It's often been called Germany's Versailles. The town has many historic sights, and was beautifully planned, with large parks and a beautiful chain of lakes formed by the river.

GETTING THERE   Potsdam Hauptbahnhof is on the major Deutsche Bundesbahn rail lines, with 29 daily connections to the rail stations in Berlin (travel time is 23 min. to Bahnhof Zoo and 54 min. to Ostbahnhof). There are also 14 trains daily to and from Hannover (trip time: 3–3½ hr.), and 15 daily trains to and from Nürnberg (trip time: 6–6½ hr.). For rail information and schedules, call © **1805/99-66-33.**

VISITOR INFORMATION   Potsdam–Information, Friedrichstrasse 5 (© **0331/27-55-80**), is the place to go for information and maps. The office is open April to October, Monday to Friday from 9am to 7pm, Saturday from 10am to 6pm, and Sunday from 10am to 4pm; November to March, Monday to Friday from 9am to 6pm, and Saturday and Sunday from 10am to 2pm.

GETTING AROUND   By Public Transportation   Ask at the tourist office about a **Potsdam Billet,** costing 5€ ($5.75) and good for 24 hours on the city's public transportation system. In Potsdam, **bus no. A1,** leaving from the rail station, will deliver you to the Potsdam palaces. Call © **0331/2-80-03-09** for more information.

TOP ATTRACTIONS & SPECIAL MOMENTS

With its palaces and gardens, **Sans Souci Park** ✦✦✦ was the work of many architects and sculptors (Sans Souci means "free from care"). The park covers an area of about 1 square mile (1.6 sq. km). Its premier attraction is the palace of Frederick I ("the Great"), one of the most liberal and farsighted of the Prussian monarchs. He was a great general, but he liked best to think of himself as an enlightened patron of the arts. Here he could get away from his duties, indulge his intellectual interests, and entertain his friend Voltaire. The style of the buildings he had constructed is called "Potsdam rococo."

Sans Souci Palace ☆☆☆, with its terraces and gardens, was inaugurated in 1747. The long one-story building is crowned by a dome and flanked by two round pavilions. The elliptically shaped **Marble Hall** is the largest in the palace, but the **music salon** is the supreme example of the rococo style. A small bust of Voltaire commemorates the writer's sojourns here. The palace can only be visited with a guide. *Tip:* It is best (especially in summer) to show up before noon to buy your tickets for the palace tour. The palace is open April to October, Tuesday to Sunday from 9am to 5pm; November to March, Tuesday to Sunday from 9am to 4pm; closed Monday. Guided tours (in English) of the palace are 8€ ($9.20) for adults, 5€ ($5.75) for children ages 8 to 18 and students, and is free for children under 8.

Built between 1755 and 1763, the **Bildergalerie (Picture Gallery),** Östlicher Lustgarten (© **0331/96-94-181**), has a facade similar to that of Sans Souci Palace, a flamboyant interior, and it's usually a lot less crowded than the palace. The collection of some 125 paintings features works by Italian Renaissance and baroque artists along with Dutch and Flemish masters. Concerts at the Potsdam Park Festival take place here. The Bildergalerie is open May 15 to October 15, Tuesday to Sunday, from 10am to 5pm. Admission is 2€ ($2.30) for adults, 1.50€ ($1.75) for students and children ages 8 to 18, and free for children under 8. Guided tours cost 3€ ($3.45) for adults, 2.50€ ($2.90) for students and people under 18, and is free for children under 8.

The largest building in the park is the extravagant **Neues Palais** (© **0331/ 969-42-55**), built between 1763 and 1769, at the end of the Seven Years' War. Crowning the center is a dome. The rococo rooms, filled with paintings and antiques, were used by the royal family. The most notable chamber is **the Hall of Shells,** with its fossils and semiprecious stones. At the palace theater, concerts take place every year April to November. The palace is open April to October, Saturday to Thursday from 9am to 5pm; November to March, Saturday to Thursday from 9am to 4pm. Admission is 5€ ($5.75) for adults, 4€ ($4.60) for children ages 8 to 18, and free for children under 8. It, too, is usually less crowded than Sans Souci.

On Heiliger See, or "Holy Lake," in the northern part of Potsdam, lies the **Neuer Garten** (© **0331/23-141;** bus: 695), about a mile (1.6km) northwest of Sans Souci. The nephew and successor to Frederick the Great, Frederick William II, had these gardens laid out. Set between the park and the palace, this lovely baroque garden is well maintained, and it's a delight to take a walk into it, enjoying the flowerbeds, the well-trimmed hedges and arbors, and the fountains in decorated basins. The hours are the same as those for Sans Souci (see above). Admission is free.

Built in the style of an English country house, **Schloss Cecilienhof** ☆, inside the Neuer Garten (© **0331/969-42-44;** bus: 695), was intended by Kaiser Wilhelm II between 1913 and 1917 for Crown Prince Wilhelm. The palace was occupied as a royal residence until March 1945, when the crown prince and his family fled to the West. Cecilienhof was the headquarters of the 1945 Potsdam Conference, attended by the heads of the Allied powers, including Truman, Stalin, and Churchill. You can visit the studies of the various delegations and see the large round table, made in Moscow, where the actual agreement was signed. The palace is open Tuesday to Sunday from 9am to 12:30pm and 5 to 7pm. Admission is 9€ ($10.35) for adults, 5.50€ ($6.35) for students, and free for children under 6.

WHERE TO DINE

The most romantic dining choice in town is **Juliette** ⭐, Jägerstrasse 39 (② **0331/ 270-17-91;** tram: 94 or 96). The cozy and intimate restaurant is set inside a restored old house, with blazing fireplace, low ceilings, and tiny windows. The excellent waiters—many of them hail from France—expertly serve a traditional French menu, which features some wonderful chicken dishes. Main courses cost 21€ to 26€ ($24.15–$29.90). Reservations are required.

   Villa Kellerman ⭐, Mangerstrasse 34–36 (② **0331/29-15-72;** S-Bahn: Potsdam Stadt), one of the most talked-about restaurants in Potsdam, is located in an 1878 villa once occupied by author Bernhardt Kellerman. The fine Italian cuisine attracts a diverse clientele from the financial and art worlds. Your meal might include marinated carpaccio of sea wolf; ravioli stuffed with cheese, spinach, and herbs; or an array of veal and beef dishes. The wine list is mostly Italian. Main courses cost 14€ to 24€ ($16.10–$27.60).

3 Munich ⭐⭐

The people of Munich never need much of a reason for celebrating. If you arrive here in late September, you'll find them in the middle of the **Oktoberfest,** which draws more than 7 million people every fall and lasts for 16 days, ending on the first Sunday in October. Although Oktoberfest, when beer flows as freely as water, is the most famous of Munich's festivals, the city is actually less inhibited during the more interesting pre-Lenten **Fasching.** Even the most reserved Germans get caught up in this whirl of colorful parades, masked balls, and revelry.

   Munich is a lively place all year long—fairs and holidays seem to follow one on top of the other. But this is no "oompah" town. Here you'll find an elegant and tasteful city with sophisticated clubs and restaurants, wonderful theaters, fine concert halls, and fabulous museums. According to various polls, it's also the Germans' first choice as a place to live.

   Munich is a prime rail destination, and though we rate Berlin first in importance, Munich is definitely more picturesque and, in some ways, easier to reach. Its train connections to the rest of Germany are superb, and its position on several high-speed international rail lines makes it an easy stop for anyone on a multi-country tour of Europe. If you plan on concentrating on the Bavaria region of Germany, it should be your unequivocal starting point. And Munich also makes a good starting or stopping point for any European rail trip as its international airport offers a number of flight connections to North America.

STATION INFORMATION
GETTING FROM THE AIRPORT TO THE TRAIN STATION
About 17 miles (27km) northeast of central Munich at Erdinger Moos, the **Munich International Airport** (② **089/97-52-13-13**), inaugurated in 1992, is among the most modern, best-equipped, and most efficient airports in the world. A second terminal was begun in 2000 and should be completed by the time you read this. The airport handles more than 400 flights a day, serving at least 65 cities worldwide. Passengers can fly nonstop from New York, Miami, Chicago, and Toronto, among other places.

Munich

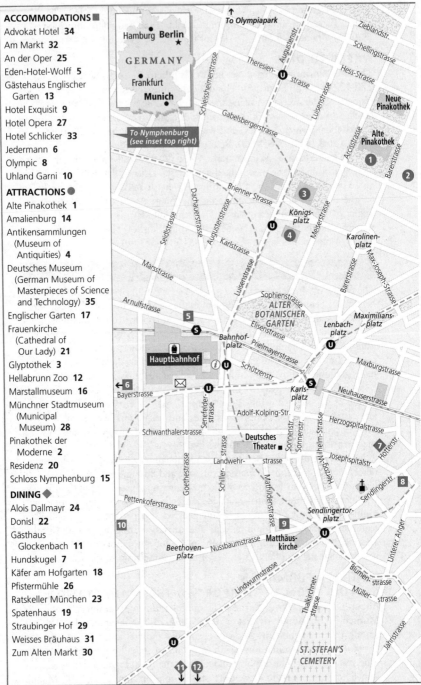

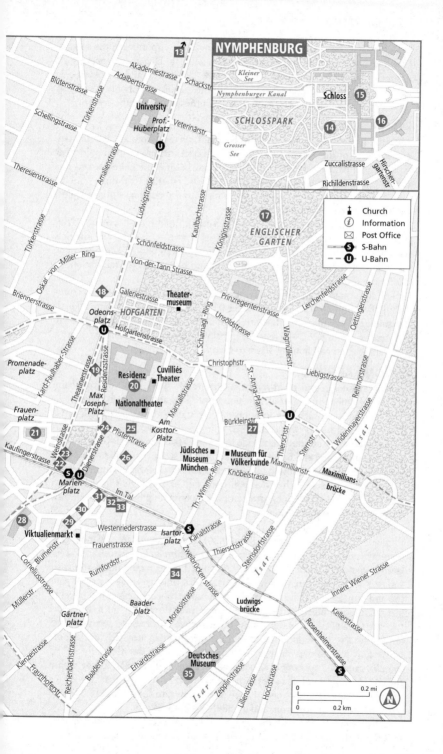

NYMPHENBURG

Kleiner See

Nymphenburger Kanal

Schloss **15**

SCHLOSSPARK

14

16

Grosser See

Zuccalistrasse

Richildenstrasse

Akademiestrasse

Adalbertstrasse

Schackstr.

13

Blütenstrasse

Türkenstrasse

Schellingstrasse

University

Prof.- Huberplatz

Veterinärstr.

Amalienstrasse

Theresienstrasse

Ludwigstrasse

Kaulbachstrasse

Königinstrasse

ENGLISCHER GARTEN

17

Schönfeldstrasse

Von-der-Tann Strasse

Türkenstrasse

Oskar -von -Miller- Ring

Brienerstrasse

18

Galeriestrasse

Theater- museum

Prinzregentenstrasse

Lerchenfeldstrasse

Oettingenstrasse

Odeons- platz

HOFGARTEN

Hofgartenstrasse

K. Scharnagl- Ring

Unsöldstrasse

Wagmüllerstr.

Reitmorstrasse

Promenade- platz

Kard-Faulhaber-Strasse

Theatinerstrasse

Residenzstrasse

19

Residenz

Cuvilliés Theater

Marstallstrasse

Christophstr.

St.-Anna-Pfarrstr.

Liebigstrasse

Widenmayerstrasse

I s a r

Frauen- platz

20

Max Joseph- Platz

Nationaltheater

Am Kosttor- Platz

Bürkleinstr.

Thierschstr.

Sternstr.

21

Weinstrasse

24

Pfisterstrasse

25

27

Kaufingerstrasse

23

22

Dienerstrasse

26

Jüdisches Museum München

Museum für Völkerkunde

Maximilianstr.

Maximilians- brücke

Marien- platz

Im Tal

Knöbelstrasse

Th.-Wimmer-Ring

31

32

33

30

28

29

Viktualienmarkt

Westenriederstrasse

Frauenstrasse

Isartor- platz

Kanalstrasse

Thierschstrasse

Steinsdorfstrasse

Zweibrückenstrasse

Innere Wiener Strasse

Cornelliusstrasse

Blumenstr.

Rumfordstr.

34

I s a r

Müllerstr.

Gärtner- platz

Reichenbachstrasse

Baaderstrasse

Baader- platz

Morassistrasse

Ludwigs- brücke

Kellerstrasse

Klenzestrasse

Fraunhoferstr.

Erhardtstrasse

Deutsches Museum

35

I s a r

Zepplinstrasse

Lilienstrasse

Hochstrasse

Rosenheimerstrasse

✝	Church
ⓘ	Information
⊠	Post Office
Ⓢ	S-Bahn
Ⓤ	U-Bahn

0   0.2 mi

0   0.2 km

S-Bahn (℅ **089/414-243-44**) trains connect the airport with the Hauptbahnhof (main railroad station) in downtown Munich. Departures are every 20 minutes for the 40-minute trip. The fare is 8€ ($9.20); Eurailpass holders ride free. A taxi into the center costs about 50€ ($57.50). Airport buses, such as those operated by Lufthansa, also run between the airport and the center.

INSIDE THE STATION

Munich's main rail station, the **Hauptbahnhof,** on Bahnhofplatz near the city center, is one of Europe's largest. It contains a hotel, restaurants, shopping, car parking, and banking facilities. All major German cities are connected to this station. Some 20 daily trains connect Munich to Frankfurt (trip time: 3¾ hr.), and 23 to Berlin (trip time: 6¾ hr.). For information about long-distance trains, call ℅ **01805/99-66-33.**

The rail station is connected with the **S-Bahn** rapid-transit system, a 260-mile (418km) network of tracks, providing service to various city districts and outlying suburbs. For S-Bahn information, call ℅ **089/4142-43-44.** The **U-Bahn** (subway) system serving Munich is also centered at the rail station. In addition, buses fan out in all directions.

The city's main tourist office, **Fremdenverkehrsamt,** is located at the Hauptbahnhof, Bahnhofplatz 2 (℅ **089/2-33-03-00;** www.muenchen-tourist.de), at the south exit opening onto Bayerstrasse. It offers a free map of Munich and will also reserve rooms (see "Where to Stay," below). Its hours are Monday to Saturday 9am to 8pm and Sunday 10am to 6pm.

GETTING AROUND

The city's underground rapid-transit system, the **U-Bahn** or Untergrundbahn network, is modern and relatively noise-free. The aboveground **S-Bahn,** or Stadtbahn, services suburban locations. At the transport hub, Marienplatz, U-Bahn and S-Bahn rails cross each other.

The same ticket entitles you to ride both the U-Bahn and the S-Bahn, as well as **trams (streetcars)** and **buses.** The U-Bahn is the system you will probably use most frequently. You're allowed to use your Eurailpass on S-Bahn journeys, as it's a state-owned railway. Otherwise, you must purchase a single-trip ticket or a strip ticket for several journeys at one of the blue vending machines positioned at the entryways to the stations.

If you're making only one trip, a **single ticket** will average 2€ ($2.30), although it can reach as high as 8€ ($9.20) to an outlying area. A more economical option is the **strip ticket,** called *Streifenkarte* in German. It's good for several rides and sells for 9€ ($10.35). A trip within the metropolitan area costs you two strips, which are valid for 2 hours. In that time, you may interrupt your trip and transfer as you like to any public transportation, as long as you travel in one continuous direction. When you reverse your direction, you must cancel two strips again. Children 6 to 14 use the red *Kinderstreifenkarte,* costing 3.50€ ($4.05) for five strips; for a trip within the metropolitan area, they cancel only one strip. Children over the age of 15 pay adult fares. A **day ticket** for 4.50€ ($5.20), called a *Tageskarte,* is also a good investment if you plan to stay within the city limits. If you'd like to branch out to Greater Munich—that is, within a 50-mile (80km) radius—you can purchase a day card for 10€ ($11.50). For public transport information, dial ℅ **089/41-42-43-44.**

Cabs begin at 2.55€ ($2.95), plus an additional 1.35€ ($1.55) per kilometer (.6 miles). Call ℅ **089/2161** or 089/194-10 for a radio-dispatched taxi.

Munich U-Bahn & S-Bahn

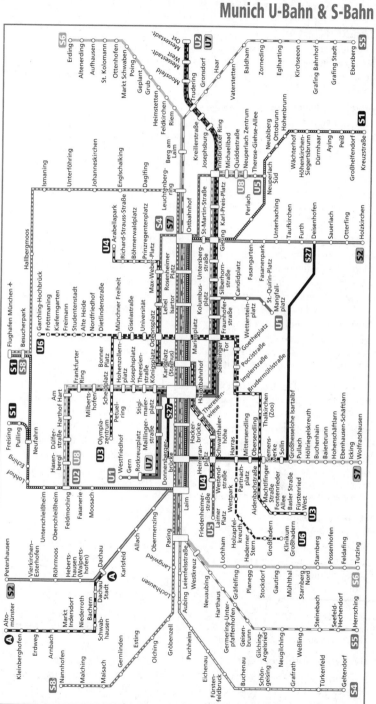

WHERE TO STAY

The area surrounding the Bahnhoff doesn't have many recommendable hotels, but hotels in the center of town tend to be very expensive. We list the best hotels in the vicinity of the train station, as well as some of our favorite value selections for the rest of the city.

Advokat Hotel This hotel occupies a six-story apartment house originally constructed in the 1930s. Its stripped-down, streamlined interior borrows in discreet ways from Bauhaus and minimalist models. The result is an aggressively simple, clean-lined, and artfully spartan hotel with few facilities, though each room comes with a well-equipped, compact bathroom, most with both tub and shower. A delightful rooftop breakfast is served.

Baaderstrasse 1, 80469 München. ℂ **089/21-63-10.** Fax 089/21-63-190. www.hotel-advokat.de 50 units. 185€ ($213) double; from 195€ ($224) suite. Rates include continental breakfast. S-Bahn: Isartor. **Amenities:** Bar. *In room:* No hair dryer.

Am Markt This popular Bavarian hotel lies in the heart of the city's older section and is a good choice for the rail traveler on a tight budget. Owner Harald Herrler has maintained a nostalgic decor in the lobby: Behind his reception desk is a wall of photographs of friends or former guests, including the late Viennese chanteuse Greta Keller. Rooms are quite small, but modern and neat. Mattresses are well worn but comfortable. Only 12 rooms have private bathrooms, but all have sinks with hot and cold running water.

Heiliggeistrasse 6, 80331 München. ℂ **089/22-50-14.** Fax 089/22-40-17. 32 units, 12 with bathroom. 66€ ($75.90) double without bathroom; 87€–92€ ($100–$106) double with bathroom. Rates include continental breakfast. S-Bahn: Marienplatz. **Amenities:** Lounge. *In room:* No hair dryer.

An der Oper This five-floor hotel, just steps from the Bavarian National Theater, is superbly located for sightseeing or shopping in the traffic-free malls. In spite of its basic decor, there are touches of elegance. Rooms, which range from small to medium, have double-glazed windows, a small sitting area with armchairs, and a table for those who want breakfast in their rooms. Bathrooms tend to be small, but are well organized and come mainly with just a shower.

Falkenturmstrasse 11 (just off Maximilianstrasse, near Marienplatz), 80331 München. ℂ **089/2-90-02-70.** Fax 089/29-00-27-29. www.hotelanderoper.com. 68 units. 150€–215€ ($173–$247) double. Rates include buffet breakfast. AE, MC, V. Tram: 19. **Amenities:** Lounge. *In room:* Hair dryer.

Eden-Hotel-Wolff ⭐ If you must stay in the train station area, this is your best bet, despite the fact that it's often booked by tour groups. The interior is richly traditional, with chandeliers and dark-wood paneling. Most rooms are spacious, and all are tastefully furnished in a decor that runs the gamut from extremely modern to rustic. Bathrooms are large. Some units are hypoallergenic, with special beds and a private ventilation system.

Arnulfstrasse 4–8, D-80335 München. ℂ **089/55-11-50.** Fax 089/551-15-555. www.ehw.de. 216 units. 169€–282€ ($194–$324) double; 256€–358€ ($294–$412) suite. 1 child up to age 6 stays free in parent's room. Rates include buffet breakfast. AE, DC, MC, V. Parking 14€ ($16.10). U-Bahn/S-Bahn: Hauptbahnhof. **Amenities:** Restaurant; bar; laundry. *In room:* TV, minibar, hair dryer, safe.

Gästehaus Englischer Garten ⭐⭐ This is an oasis of charm and tranquillity, close to the Englischer Garten. The decor of the small to medium rooms has been called "Bavarian grandmotherly"; furnishings include genuine antiques, old-fashioned but exceedingly comfortable beds, and Oriental rugs. The shower-only bathrooms are small, but their maintenance is first-rate. In fair weather, breakfast is served in a rear garden.

Liebergesellstrasse 8, 80802 München-Schwabing. © **089/3-83-94-10**. Fax 089/38-39-41-33. 25 units, 20 with bathroom. 70€–103€ ($80.50–$118) double without bathroom; 103€–115€ ($118–132) double with bathroom. Breakfast 8.50€ ($9.80) extra. AE, MC, V. Parking 5.10€ ($5.85). U-Bahn: Münchener Freiheit. **Amenities:** Lounge. *In room:* No hair dryer.

Hotel Exquisit ⭐

One of the most appealing hotels in the Sendlinger Tor neighborhood lies behind a wine-colored facade on a quiet residential street near the theater district. It has a paneled lobby whose focal point is a lounge that gets busy around 6 or 7pm. Rooms are spacious and comfortable. About half overlook an ivy-draped garden; others look over the street. The shower-only bathrooms have adequate shelf space. The staff is especially cordial.

Pettenkoferstrasse 3, D-80336 München. © **089/55-19-900**. Fax 089/55-199-499. www.augustiner-restaurant. com. 50 units. 160€–195€ ($184–$224) double; 195€–240€ ($224–$276) suite. Rates include buffet breakfast. AE, DC, MC, V. U-Bahn: Sendlinger Tor. **Amenities:** Bar. *In room:* Hair dryer.

Hotel Opera ⭐ *Finds*

This charming little gem is filled with comfort and an authentic Bavarian atmosphere. Each room is beautifully and individually decorated, often with antiques from the countryside. Those overlooking the courtyard contain French doors leading to small balconies. Those at the rear on the third and fourth floors are more tranquil, although they're slightly smaller than those fronting the street. Bathrooms are relatively small but well maintained.

St-Anna Strasse 10, 80538 München. © **089/22-55-33**. Fax 089/21-04-09-77. www.hotel-opera.de. 25 units. 150€–210€ ($173–$242) double; 265€–295€ ($305–$339) suite. AE, MC, V. Parking nearby. U-Bahn: Lehel. **Amenities:** Bar; laundry. *In room:* Hair dryer.

Hotel Schlicker *Finds*

In spite of its location between a McDonald's and a Burger King, this is a hotel of charm and tradition, with a pedigree going back to 1544. It's in the heart of Munich, just steps away from the landmark Marienplatz. Only the breakfast room suggests that this was once an ancient inn; the rest of the hotel has been modernized. The midsize bedrooms are comfortable and traditional, each with a tiled bathroom.

Tal 74, 80331 München. © **089/2428870**. Fax 089/296059. www.hotel-schlicker.de. 69 units. 105€–156€ ($121–$179) double; 180€–215€ ($207–247) suite. AE, DC, MC, V. U-Bahn: Marienplatz. *In room:* No hair dryer.

Jedermann *Value*

Those in awe of the high prices of Munich hotels find comfort at this pleasant and deftly run hotel, just a 10-minute walk from the Hauptbahnhof. Its central location and good value make it a desirable choice, especially for travelers on a budget. The old-fashioned Bavarian rooms are generally small, but cozy and comfortable, each with a shower-only bathroom. A generous breakfast buffet is served.

Bayerstrasse 95, 80335 München. © **089/54-32-40**. Fax 089/54-32-41-11. www.hotel-jedermann.de. 56 units. 67€–149€ ($77.05–$171) double; 102€–179€ ($117–$206) triple. Rates include buffet breakfast. MC, V. 10-min. walk from Hauptbahnhof (turn right on Bayerstrasse from south exit). **Amenities:** Lounge. *In room:* No hair dryer.

Olympic ⭐

Built as a private villa around 1900, this hotel represents one of Munich's most appealing conversions of an antique building into a hip and attractive hotel. The comfortable all-white rooms are minimalist in design and more modern than the reception areas. Most of the midsize bathrooms come with shower only. The hotel has earned an increasing number of gay clients, due to its location within a neighborhood that's loaded with gay bars.

Hans Sachs Strasse 4, D-80469 München. © **089/231-89-0**. Fax 089/231-89-199. www.hotel-olympic.de. 38 units. 130€ ($150) double; 150€ ($173) suite. Rates include continental breakfast. AE, DC, MC, V. U-Bahn: Sendlinger Tor. **Amenities:** Lounge. *In room:* No hair dryer.

Uhland Garni   Located in a residential area, just a 10-minute walk from the Hauptbahnhof, the Uhland could easily become your home in Munich. The stately town mansion, built in Art Nouveau style, stands in its own small garden. The hotel offers friendly, personal service, and rooms are soundproof, snug, traditional, and cozy. Bathrooms contain showers. Only breakfast is served.

Uhlandstrasse 1, 80336 München. ℂ 089/54-33-50. Fax 089/54-33-52-50. www.hotel-uhland.de. 25 units. 77€–165€ ($88.55–$190) double. Rates include buffet breakfast. AE, DC, MC, V. Bus: 58. **Amenities:** Lounge. *In room:* Hair dryer.

TOP ATTRACTIONS & SPECIAL MOMENTS

Munich is stocked with so many treasures that any visitor who plans to "do" the city in a day or 2 will not only miss out on many major sights but will also fail to grasp the city's spirit and absorb its special flavor. Below you'll find a few vital highlights to help you make the best of your time in the city.

Alte Pinakothek ✦✦✦   This is one of the most significant art museums in the world. The nearly 900 paintings on display in this huge neoclassical building represent the greatest European artists of the 14th through the 18th centuries. Begun as a small court collection by the royal Wittelsbach family in the early 1500s, the artistic treasure trove grew and grew. The museum is immense; we do not recommend that you try to cover it all in a single day. Pick up a floor plan to guide you through the dozens of rooms.

The landscape painter *par excellence* of the Danube school, Albrecht Altdorfer, is represented by six monumental works. Works of Albrecht Dürer include his final, and greatest, *Self-Portrait* (1500). Also displayed is Dürer's last great painting, a two-paneled work called *The Four Apostles* (1526). Works by Lucas Cranach the Elder include his *Venus.* Several galleries are given over to Dutch and Flemish masters. There are more Rubens here than in any other museum in Europe. Roger van der Weyden's *St. Columbia Altarpiece* (1460–62) measures nearly 10 feet across, a triumph of his subtle linear style. Rembrandts and Van Dycks are also displayed. French, Spanish, and Italian artists can be found in both the larger galleries and the small rooms lining the outer wall. Note Raphael's *Holy Family* and Leonardo da Vinci's *Madonna.*

Barerstrasse 27. ℂ 089/23-80-52-16. Admission 5€ ($5.75) adults, 3.50€ ($4.05) students, free for children 14 and under. Tues–Sun 10am–5pm (until 10pm Thurs). U-Bahn: Königsplatz.

Antikensammlungen (Museum of Antiquities) ✦   This collection grew around the vase collection of Ludwig I, who had fantasies of transforming Munich into a second Athens. Many pieces are small in size but not in value or artistic significance. The museum's five main-floor halls house more than 650 Greek vases. The oldest, the pre-Mycenaean "goddess from Aegina" (3000 B.C.), carved from a mussel shell, is in room I. The upper level of the Central Hall is devoted to large Greek vases discovered in Sicily and to Etruscan art. On the lower level is Greek, Roman, and Etruscan jewelry. Also on this level are rooms devoted to ancient colored glass, Etruscan bronzes, and Greek terra-cottas.

Königsplatz 1. ℂ 089/59-83-59. Admission 3.50€ ($4.05) adults, 2€ ($2.30) students and seniors, free for children 14 and under, and free for everyone on Sun. Tues and Thurs–Sun 10am–5pm; Wed 10am–8pm. U-Bahn: Königsplatz.

Deutsches Museum (German Museum of Masterpieces of Science and Technology) ✦✦✦   The world's largest technological museum contains a huge collection of artifacts and historic originals, including the first electric dynamo, the first automobile (Benz, 1886), and the first diesel engine. There are hundreds of buttons to push, levers to crank, and gears to turn. Among the most popular displays are those on mining, with a series of model coal, salt, and iron mines, and the electrical power hall, with high-voltage displays that actually produce lightning. There are exhibits on transportation, printing, photography, and textiles, and halls devoted to air-and-space and high-tech themes. Activities include glassblowing and paper-making demonstrations. The astronomy exhibit is the largest in Europe.

Museumsinsel 1. ⓒ 089/2-17-91. www.deutsches-museum.de. Admission 7.50€ ($8.65) adults, 5€ ($5.75) seniors, 3€ ($3.45) students, free for children 6 and under. Daily 9am–5pm (closes at 2pm the 2nd Wed in Dec). Closed major holidays. S-Bahn: Isartor. Tram: 18.

Frauenkirche (Cathedral of Our Lady) ⭐

When the smoke cleared from the 1945 bombings, only a fragile shell remained of Munich's largest church. Workmen and architects who restored the 15th-century Gothic cathedral used whatever remains they could find in the rubble, along with modern innovations. The overall effect of the rebuilt Frauenkirche is strikingly simple, yet dignified. The twin towers with their onion domes, which remained intact, have been the city's landmark since 1525. Instead of the typical flying buttresses, huge props on the inside, which separate the side chapels, support the edifice. Twenty-two simple octagonal pillars support the Gothic vaulting over the nave and chancel. Entering the main doors, your first impression is that there are no windows (most of them are hidden by the enormous pillars). According to legend, the devil laughed at the notion of hidden windows and stamped in glee at the stupidity of the architect—you can still see the strange footlike mark called "the devil's step" in the entrance hall.

Frauenplatz 12. ⓒ 089/29-00-82-0. Free admission. Sat–Thurs 7am–7pm; Fri 7am–6pm. U-Bahn/S-Bahn: Marienplatz.

Glyptothek ⭐

The ideal neighbor for the Museum of Antiquities, the Glyptothek supplements the pottery and smaller pieces of the main museum with the country's largest collection of ancient Greek and Roman sculpture. Included are the famous pediments from the temple of Aegina, two marvelous statues of *kouroi* (youths) from the 6th century B.C., the colossal figure of a *Sleeping Satyr* from the Hellenistic period, and a splendid collection of Roman portraits.

Königsplatz 3. ⓒ 089/28-61-00. Admission 3€ ($3.45) adults, 2€ ($2.30) students and seniors, free for children 13 and under. Tues–Wed and Fri–Sun 10am–5pm; Thurs 10am–8pm. U-Bahn: U2 to Königsplatz.

Münchner Stadtmuseum (Municipal Museum) ⭐

Munich's Municipal Museum offers insight into the city's history and people's daily lives. A wooden model shows Munich in 1572. Special exhibits about popular arts and traditions are presented frequently. The museum's most important exhibit is its Moorish Dancers *(Moriskentanzer)* on the ground floor. These 10 figures, each 2 feet high, carved in wood, and painted in bright colors by Erasmus Grasser in 1480, are among the best examples of secular Gothic art in Germany. The historical collection of musical instruments on the fourth floor is one of the greatest of its kind in the world.

St. Jacobs-Platz 1. ⓒ 089/233-22370. Admission 2.50€ ($2.90) adults, 1.50€ ($1.75) students and children 6–15 (free 5 and under); Sun free for everyone. Tues–Sun 10am–6pm. U-Bahn/S-Bahn: Marienplatz.

Pinakothek der Moderne ⭐⭐

In 2002, one of the world's largest museums devoted to the visual arts of the 19th and 20th centuries opened in Munich, just minutes from the Alte and Neue Pinakothek. The collection of this large museum includes works by artists such as Picasso, Magritte, Klee, Kandinsky, even Francis Bacon, de Kooning, and Warhol. It owns 400,000 drawings and prints from Leonardo da Vinci to Cézanne up to contemporary artists. The architectural galleries hold some 350,000 drawings, 100,000 photographs, and 500 models, and the applied arts section features more than 50,000 items. You're taken from the beginnings of the Industrial Revolution via Art Nouveau, up Bauhaus and today's computer culture.

Barerstrasse 40. ⓒ **089/23805-360.** www.pinakothek-der-moderne.de. Admission 9€ ($10.35) adults, 5€ ($5.75) students and seniors. Combination ticket to Neue Pinakothek, Alte Pinakothek, Pinakothek der Moderne, and Schack-Galerie 12€ ($13.80) adults, 7€ ($8.05) students and seniors. Tues–Sun 10am–5pm; until 8pm Thurs–Fri. U-Bahn: Odeonsplatz.

Residenz ★ This enormous palace, completely restored since its almost total destruction in World War II, was the official residence of the rulers of Bavaria from 1385 to 1918. Added to and rebuilt over the centuries, the complex is a conglomerate of various styles, including German Renaissance, Palladian, and Florentine Renaissance. In the **Ancestral Gallery** are portraits of the Wittelsbach family, set into gilded, carved paneling. The largest room in the museum is the **Antiquarium,** possibly the finest example of interior Renaissance secular styling in Germany. Frescoes adorn nearly every inch of space on the walls and ceilings. The central attraction is the two-story chimneypiece of red stucco and marble, completed in 1600, adorned with Tuscan pillars and the coat of arms of the dukes of Bavaria. On the second floor, is an enormous collection of Far Eastern porcelain.

If you have time to view only one item in the **Schatzkammer (Treasury)** ★★, make it the 16th-century Renaissance statue of *St. George Slaying the Dragon.* This equestrian statue is made of gold, but you can barely see the precious metal for the thousands of diamonds, rubies, emeralds, sapphires, and semiprecious stones embedded in it. The **Alte Residenztheater** or **Cuvilliés Theater** ★ is Germany's most outstanding example of a rococo tier-boxed theater. François de Cuvilliés designed the theater in the mid–18th century. During World War II, the interior was dismantled and stored. After the war, it was reassembled in the reconstructed building. In summer, the theater hosts concerts and opera performances.

Max-Joseph-Platz 3. ⓒ **089/29-06-71.** Combination ticket for Residenzmuseum and Schatzkammer 7.15€ ($9.40) adults, 3.05€ ($3.50) students/seniors, free for ages 15 and under. Ticket for either Schatzkammer or Residenzmuseum 4.10€ ($4.70) adults, 2.55€ ($2.95) seniors/students, free for ages 16 and under. Daily 10am–4pm. U-Bahn: Odeonsplatz.

A PARK & A ZOO

Munich's city park, the 18th-century **Englischer Garten** ★, was the brainchild of Sir Benjamin Thompson, an English scientist who spent most of his life in the service of the Bavarian government. You can wander for hours along the walks and among the trees, flowers, and sunbathers. Nude sunbathing is permitted in certain areas of the park (some claim these areas are Munich's most popular tourist attraction). For a break, stop for tea on the plaza near the Chinese pagoda, or have a beer at the nearby beer garden. You might also take along a picnic.

Hellabrunn Zoo stands in Tierpark Hellabrunn, about 4 miles (6km) south of the city center, at Tierparkstrasse 30 (ⓒ **089/62-50-80;** www.zoo-munich.de; U-Bahn: Thalkirchen; bus: 52). It's one of the largest zoos in the world, with hundreds of animals roaming in a natural habitat. A walk through the attractive park is recommended even if you're not a zoo buff. There's a big children's zoo, as well as a large aviary. You can visit the zoo daily 8am to 6pm (in winter,

9am–5pm); admission is 7€ ($8.05) for adults, 5.50€ ($6.35) for students and seniors, 4€ ($4.60) for children ages 4 to 14, and free for children 3 and under.

A NEARBY PALACE

Schloss Nymphenburg ★★   Five miles (8km) north of the city, this sophisticated summer palace was begun in 1664 by Elector Ferdinand Maria in Italian-villa style and took more than 150 years to complete. The final palace plan was created mainly by Elector Max Emanuel, who in 1702 decided to enlarge the villa by adding four large pavilions connected by arcaded passageways. Gradually the French style took over, and today the facade is a subdued baroque. The palace interior is less subtle, however. Upon entering the main building, you're in the **great hall,** decorated in rococo colors and stuccos. The frescoes by Zimmermann (1756) depict incidents from mythology, especially those dealing with Flora, goddess of nymphs, for whom the palace was named. Concerts are still presented here in summer.

To the south of the palace buildings, in the rectangular block of low structures that once housed the court stables, is the **Marstallmuseum.** In the first hall, look for the glass coronation coach of Elector Karl Albrecht, built in Paris in 1740. From the same period comes the hunting sleigh of Electress Amalia, with the statue of Diana, goddess of the hunt; even the sleigh's runners are decorated with shellwork and hunting trophies. The coaches and sleighs of Ludwig II are displayed in the **third hall.** Don't miss the ornately gilded **state coach.**

Nymphenburg's park ★ stretches for 500 acres. A canal runs through it from the pool at the foot of the staircase to the cascade at the far end of the English-style gardens. A number of delightful pavilions are in the park: the Badenburg Pavilion, a bathing pavilion near the lake of the same name; the Pagodenburg, decorated in chinoiserie style; and the Magdalenenklause (Hermitage), meant to be a retreat for prayer and solitude; and the **Amalienburg pavilion** ★★, whose plain exterior belies the rococo decoration (including rich carvings, and wall paintings) inside.

Schloss Nymphenburg 1. ℰ **089/17-908-668.** Admission to all attractions 7.65€ ($8.80) adults, free for children 6 and under. Separate admissions: 3.60€ ($4.15) Schloss Nymphenburg or 2.55€ ($2.95) to either Marstallmuseum, Amalienburg, or Porzellansammlung porcelain. Free for children 15 and under. Mon–Fri 8am–6pm. Parking beside the Marstallmuseum. U-Bahn: Rotkreuzplatz, then tram no. 17 to Botanischer-garten. Bus: 41.

WHERE TO DINE

Alois Dallmayr ★★ CONTINENTAL   Alois Dallmayr, which traces its history back to 1700, is the most famous delicatessen in Germany. Its tempting array of delicacies from around the globe has been sampled by many a royal court. The upstairs dining room serves a subtle German version of continental cuisine, owing a heavy debt to France. The food array is dazzling, ranging from herring and sausages to tomatoes from Morocco and papayas from Brazil, and the famous French poulet de Bresse.

Dienerstrasse 14–15. ℰ **089/2-13-51-00.** Reservations required. Main courses 14€–36€ ($16.10–$41.40); fixed-price menus 32€ ($36.80) for 3 courses, 45€ ($51.75) for 4 courses. AE, DC, MC, V. Mon–Wed 9:30am–7pm; Thurs–Fri 9:30am–8pm; Sat 9am–4pm. Tram: 19.

Donisl BAVARIAN/INTERNATIONAL   Munich's oldest beer hall, dating from 1715, is *gemütlich,* with a relaxed and comfortable atmosphere, though the seating capacity is 550. In summer, you can dine in the garden area out front. The restaurant has two levels, the second of which is a gallery. The standard menu offers traditional Bavarian food and a weekly changing specials menu. A specialty is *Weisswürste,* the little white sausage that has been a decades-long tradition of this place.

Weinstrasse 1. ☎ **089/22-01-84.** Reservations recommended. Main courses 8€–15€ ($9.20–$17.25). DC, MC, V. Daily 9am–midnight. U-Bahn/S-Bahn: Marienplatz.

Gästhaus Glockenbach ✹✹✹ MODERN CONTINENTAL   There's a good chance you'll have one of your finest meals in Munich at this restaurant, which more than holds its own against more expensive establishments. The setting is a 200-year-old building close to the Südbahnhof train station. The dignified country-baroque interior is accented with vivid modern paintings and the most elegant table settings in town. Cuisine changes with the season. You'll find imaginative preparations of venison and pheasant in autumn, lamb and veal dishes in springtime, and shellfish whenever in season. Ultrafresh vegetables are imported from local farms and from sophisticated purveyors worldwide.

Kapuzinerstrasse 29, corner of Maistrasse. ☎ **089/53-40-43.** Reservations recommended. Main courses 24€–29€ ($27.60–$33.35); fixed-price lunch 29€ ($33.35); fixed-price dinner 79€ ($90.85). AE, MC, V. Tues–Sat noon–2pm (last order) and 7–10pm (last order). Closed 1 week at Christmas. U-Bahn: Goetheplatz.

Hundskugel BAVARIAN   The city's oldest tavern dates from 1440 and apparently serves the same food it did back then. Why mess with success? Perhaps half the residents of Munich at one time or another have made their way here. The cookery is honest Bavarian with no pretensions. Although the chef makes a specialty of *Spanferkel* (roast suckling pig with potato noodles), you might prefer *Tafelspitz* (boiled beef) in dill sauce or roast veal stuffed with goose liver. To begin, try one of the hearty soups, made fresh daily.

Hotterstrasse 18. ☎ **089/26-42-72.** Reservations required. Main courses 9€–20€ ($10.35–$23). No credit cards. Daily 10:30am–midnight. U-Bahn/S-Bahn: Marienplatz.

Käfer am Hofgarten ITALIAN/FRENCH   This likable and stylish bistro and bar is a replica of something you might find in Paris or Lyon. There are outdoor terraces in front and back, and a live pianist bashes out cabaret and jazz tunes every night. Tables are spaced close to one another, which enhances the restaurant's sense of intimacy, though your conversation is likely to be overheard by your immediate neighbors. Menu items change daily according to the season and the inspiration of the chefs.

Odeonsplatz 6–7. ☎ **089/290-75-30.** Main courses 12€–16€ ($13.80–$18.40). AE, MC, V. Daily 10am–1am. U-Bahn: Odeonsplatz.

Pfistermühle BAVARIAN   The country comes right into the heart of Munich at this authentic and old-fashioned place, a series of charmingly decorated dining rooms in a converted old mill. Many of the dishes would be familiar to your Bavarian grandmother, and portions are generous. Come here for some of the most perfectly prepared roasts in the city, always served with a selection of fresh vegetables. You can also opt for a fine array of fresh fish from the lakes and rivers of Bavaria, especially the delectable salmon trout or brown trout.

In the Platz Hotel, Pfistermühle 4. ☎ **089/2370-3865.** Reservations recommended. Main courses 13€–20€ ($14.95–$23); set menus 34€–45€ ($39.10–$51.75). AE, DC, MC, V. Mon–Sat noon–midnight. U-Bahn: Marienplatz.

Ratskeller München BAVARIAN   Throughout Germany, you'll find *Ratskellers,* traditional cellar restaurants in Rathaus (city hall) basements, serving good inexpensive food and wine. Munich is proud of its Ratskeller restaurant. The decor is typical: dark wood and carved chairs. The most interesting tables

Moments Beer Gardens

If you're in Munich anytime between the first sunny spring day and the last fading light of a Bavarian-style autumn, you should head for one of the city's celebrated beer gardens *(Biergartens)*. Traditionally, beer gardens were simply tables placed under chestnut trees planted above the storage cellars to keep beer cool in summer. (Lids on beer steins, incidentally, were meant to keep out flies.) It's estimated that today Munich has at least 400 beer gardens and cellars. Food, drink, and atmosphere are much the same in all of them. A beer will generally run you about 3€ ($3.45).

are in the semiprivate dining nooks in the rear, under the vaulted painted ceilings. The menu, generally a showcase of regional fare, also includes some international dishes, many of them vegetarian, and some lighter fare.

Im Rathaus, Marienplatz 8. © **089/219-98-90.** Reservations required. Main courses 9€–22€ ($10.35–$28.75). AE, MC, V. Daily 10am–midnight. U-Bahn/S-Bahn: Marienplatz.

Spatenhaus BAVARIAN/INTERNATIONAL   One of Munich's best-known beer restaurants offers wide windows overlooking the opera house. You can sit in an intimate, semiprivate dining nook or at a big table. Spatenhaus has old traditions, typical Bavarian food, and generous portions at reasonable prices. If you want to know what this fabled Bavarian gluttony is all about, order the "Bavarian plate," which is loaded down with various meats, including pork and sausages. You should order the restaurant's own beer, Spaten-Franziskaner-Bier.

Residenzstrasse 12. © **089/2-90-70-60.** Reservations recommended. Main courses 13€–25€ ($14.95–$28.75). AE, MC, V. Daily 10:30am–2:30pm and 5:30pm–midnight. U-Bahn: Odeonsplatz or Marienplatz.

Straubinger Hof BAVARIAN   Consistently crowded, this restaurant in the Altstadt is a well-managed, unpretentious, traditional place sponsored by the brewers of Paulaner beer. Stop in for a brew in the morning and afternoon, though during peak lunch and dinner hours, it's good form to order at least a steaming platter of *Tafelspitz* (boiled beef with horseradish) or roasted knuckle of pork. The food here caters to nostalgia—you may see the term *Grossmutter Art* ("in the style of grandmother") on the menu. Portions are ample and prices are reasonable. In summer, seating spills out onto the pavement.

Blumenstrasse 5. © **089/2-60-84-44.** Reservations recommended. Main courses 12€–18€ ($13.80–$20.70). No credit cards. Mon–Fri 9am–11pm; Sat 8am–4pm. U-Bahn/S-Bahn: Marienplatz.

Weisses Bräuhaus BAVARIAN/RHENISH   Big, bustling, and Bavarian with a vengeance, this is not for the pretentious. It's an informal place that does what it's been doing for centuries: serving home-brewed beer. The front room, with smoke-blackened, dark-wood paneling and stained glass, is for drinking and informal eating; the back room has white tablecloths and black-outfitted waiters. You can sample typical Bavarian dishes. You'll have to share your table, but that's part of the fun.

Tal 7. © **089/29-98-75.** Reservations recommended, especially for the back room. Main courses 12€–20€ ($13.80–$23). No credit cards. Daily noon–midnight. U-Bahn/S-Bahn: Marienplatz.

Zum Alten Markt *Value* BAVARIAN/INTERNATIONAL   Snug and cozy, Zum Alten Markt serves beautifully presented fresh cuisine at a good price. Located on a tiny square just off Munich's outdoor food market (where its fish and vegetables are bought fresh every day), the restaurant has a mellow charm. The interior decor, with its intricately coffered wooden ceiling, came from a 400-year-old Tyrolean castle. In summer, tables are set up outside. The chef makes a great Tafelspitz.

Am Viktualienmarkt, Dreifaltigkeitsplatz 3. © 089/29-99-95. Reservations recommended. Main courses 12€–17€ ($13.80–$19.55). No credit cards. Mon–Sat 10am–midnight. U-Bahn/S-Bahn: Marienplatz. Bus: 52.

SHOPPING

The most interesting shops are concentrated on Munich's pedestrians-only street, between Karlsplatz and Marienplatz. Store hours in Munich are generally Monday to Friday 9 or 9:30am to 6pm and Saturday 9 or 9:30am to 1 or 2pm.

Formerly Munich's exclusive distributor of Meissen and Dresden china, **Kunstring Meissen,** Briennerstrasse 4 (© 089/28-15-32; U-Bahn: Odeonsplatz), still contains one of Munich's largest inventories of the elegant porcelain. One of Germany's most famous porcelain factories, **Porzellan-Manufaktur-Nymphenburg,** based on the grounds of Schloss Nymphenburg (see above), has a sales outlet in Munich's center at Odeonsplatz 1 (© 089/28-24-28; U-Bahn: Odeonsplatz).

At **Bayerischer Kunstgewerbeverein (Bavarian Association of Arts & Crafts),** Pacellistrasse 6–8 (© 089/290-14-70; U-Bahn: Karlsplatz), a showcase for Bavarian artisans, you'll find excellent handcrafts: ceramics, glasses, jewelry, woodcarvings, pewter, and seasonal Christmas decorations. **Otto Kellnberger Holzhandlung,** Heiliggeiststrasse 8 (© 089/22-64-79; U-Bahn/S-Bahn: Marienplatz), is a small but choice emporium of traditional woodcarvings that evoke all the folkloric charm and much of the folkloric kitsch of remote Alpine Bavaria.

Stylish **Dirndl-Ecke,** Am Platzl 1/Sparkassenstrasse 10 (© 089/22-01-63; U-Bahn/S-Bahn: Marienplatz), specializes in high-grade dirndls, feathered Alpine hats, and all clothing associated with the Alpine regions. Everything sold is of fine quality. Established in 1907, **Frankonia,** Maximiliansplatz 10 (© 089/290-00-20; tram: 19), has Munich's most prestigious collection of traditional Bavarian dress (called *Tracht*). Go to **Loden-Frey,** Maffeistrasse 7–9 (© 089/21039-0; U-Bahn/S-Bahn: Marienplatz), for the world's largest selection of *Loden* clothing and traditional Bavarian costumes.

The original founders of the conservative jeweler's store **Hemmerle,** Maximilianstrasse 14 (© 089/24-22-60-0; U-Bahn/S-Bahn: Marienplatz), made their fortune designing bejeweled fantasies for the Royal Bavarian Court of Ludwig II. All pieces are limited editions, designed and made in-house by Bavarian craftspeople. The company also designs its own wristwatch.

Germany's oldest miniature pewter foundry, the **Münchner Poupenstuben und Zinnfiguren Kabinette,** Maxburgstrasse 4 (© 089/29-37-97; U-Bahn: Karlsplatz), dates from 1796. The store is a great source for miniature houses, furniture, birdcages, and people, all cunningly crafted from pewter or carved wood. Some of the figures are made from 150-year-old molds that are collector's items in their own right.

NIGHTLIFE

To find out what's happening in Munich, go to the tourist office on Platform 12 at the Hauptbahnhof (© 089/2-33-03-00) and ask for *Monatsprogramm* (a monthly program guide), costing 1.50€ ($1.75). It contains a complete cultural guide, telling you not only what's being presented—including concerts, opera, special exhibits, and museum hours—but also how to purchase tickets.

THE PERFORMING ARTS   The **Bayerischen Staatsoper** is one of the world's great companies and the company's roster includes some of the world's greatest singers. Their productions at the **Bavarian State Opera,** National-theater, Max-Joseph-Platz 2 (✆ **089/21-85-19-20;** www.bayerische.staatsoper. de; U-Bahn/S-Bahn: Marienplatz), are beautifully presented. Hard-to-get tickets may be purchased at the box office Monday to Friday from 10am to 6pm and Saturday from 10am to 1pm, plus 1 hour before each performance. The National-theater is also the home of the **Bavarian State Ballet.** Tickets for ballet and opera performances cost 15€ to 130€ ($17.25–$150).

An attraction in itself, the **Altes Residenztheater (Cuvilliés Theater),** Residenzstrasse 1 (✆ **089/21-85-19-20;** U-Bahn: Odeonplatz.), is also an important performance venue. The **Bavarian State Opera** (✆ **089/21-85-19-19**) and the **Bayerisches Staatsschauspiel** (✆ **089/21-85-19-20**), perform smaller works here, in keeping with the tiny theater's more intimate character. Box-office hours are the same as those for the Nationaltheater (see above). Opera tickets are 15€ to 150€ ($17.25–$173); theater tickets are 13€ to 55€ ($14.95–$63.25).

Musicals, operettas, ballets, and international shows are all performed at the **Deutsches Theater,** Schwanthalerstrasse 13 (✆ **089/55-23-44-44;** U-Bahn/S-Bahn: Karlsplatz/Stachus). During Carnival in January and February, the theater becomes a ballroom. Tickets are 15.50€ to 85€ ($17.85–$97.75), and higher for special events.

The famous **Münchner Philharmoniker (Munich Philharmonic Orchestra)** was founded in 1893. Its home is the **Gasteig Kulturzentrum,** Rosen-heimerstrasse 5 (✆ **089/54-81-81-81;** www.muenchnerphilharmoniker.de; S-Bahn: Rosenheimerplatz). The box office is open Monday to Friday from 10am to 8pm and Saturday from 10am to 4pm. Tickets are 12€ to 60€ ($13.80–$69).

BEER HALLS   A *Bierhalle* (Beer Hall) is a traditional Munich institution, offering food, entertainment, and, of course, beer. The state-owned **Hof-bräuhaus** ⚑, Am Platzl 9. ✆ **089/22-16-76.** U-Bahn/S-Bahn: Marienplatz), is the world's most famous beer hall. The present structure was built in 1897, but the tradition of a beer house on this spot dates from 1589. This one was the set-ting for the notorious meeting where Hitler took control of the tiny German Workers' Party in 1920. Today, 4,500 beer drinkers can crowd in here. Several rooms, including a top-floor room for dancing, are spread over three floors. The ground-floor Schwemme has a brass band. In the second-floor restaurant, strolling musicians entertain, and dirndl-clad servers offer mugs of beer between singalongs. Every night from 8pm to midnight the Hofbräuhaus presents a typi-cal Bavarian show in its Fest-Hall. The hall is open daily from 9am to midnight. Admission is 5€ ($5.75).

A popular summertime rendezvous, **Waldwirtschaft Grosshesselöhe** George-Kalb-Strasse 3 (✆ **089/74-99-40-30;** S-Bahn: Isartal Bahnhof), located above the Isar River near the zoo, has seats for some 2,000 drinkers. Music rang-ing from Dixieland to English jazz to Polish is played throughout the week. It's open daily from 11am to 11pm

CLUBS & BARS   Munich's leading jazz club, attracting artists from through-out Europe and North America, is **Jazzclub Unterfahrt,** Einsteinstrasse 42 (✆ **089/448-27-94;** U-Bahn: Max-Weber-Platz). Reaching it requires wander-ing down a labyrinth of underground cement-sided corridors that might remind you of a bomb shelter during the Cold War. Once inside, the space opens to reveal flickering candles, a convivial bar, high ceilings, and clusters of smallish tables facing a stage and whatever singers and musicians happen to be emoting at the time. The bar opens daily at 7:30pm; live music is Monday to Thursday from 9pm to midnight, and Friday to Saturday from 7:30pm to 3am. The cover is 9€ to 15€ ($10.35–$17.25).

In the sprawling premises of what used to be a factory, **Kunstpark Ost,** Grafingerstrasse 6 (*C* **089/49-00-27-30;** S-Bahn: Ostbahnhof), is Munich's newest complex of bars, restaurants, and dance clubs. People tend to move randomly from venue to venue, without any particular loyalty to one or the other. Your best bet is to show up sometime after 8pm, when all the bars will be functioning. The discos don't get going until at least 10:30pm. There's a cover of 5€ to 7€ ($5.75–$8.05).

Master's Home, Frauenstrasse 11 (*C* **089/22-99-09;** S-Bahn: Marienplatz), is one of the historic core's most animated and convivial bars. The setting is the ground floor of an imposing 19th-century building, within a large room outfitted with antiques and warm colors. Located on Munich's most desirable shopping street, **Schumann's,** Maximilianstrasse 36 (*C* **089/22-90-60;** tram: 19), doesn't have to waste any money on decor. The local *beau monde* keep it fully fashionable. Schumann's is known as a "thinking man's bar," and is popular with the film, advertising, and publishing worlds (closed Sat).

4 The Bavarian Alps & Lakes ★★

The mountainous region of Germany along the Austrian border is a world unto itself. Its hospitality is famous, and the picture of the plump, rosy-cheeked innkeeper with a constant smile is no myth. Many travelers think of the Alps as a winter vacationland, but you'll find that nearly all the Bavarian resorts and villages boast year-round attractions.

The Bavarian Alps are both a winter wonderland and a summer playground. The **skiing** here is the best in Germany. A regular winter snowfall in January and February usually measures from 12 to 20 inches. This leaves about 6 feet of snow in the areas served by ski lifts. In summer, **Alpine hiking** is a major attraction— climbing mountains, enjoying nature, and watching animals in the forest.

The Alpine region is a good place for all travelers! It's one of the most scenic regions not just in Europe, but in the entire world, and has surprisingly good (and frequent) rail connections, considering the terrain. Not every mountaintop and valley can be explored by train, but there are selected places of strong interest that can be reached easily by rail that are outlined in this section. Of course, it takes longer to get to some places here than it would around Berlin or Hamburg, where connections by high-speed ICE train are intensive, so readers on limited time budgets will have to limit themselves to just a few choice spots.

BERCHTESGADEN ★★

Berchtesgaden is a quiet old Alpine village 98 miles (158km) southeast of Munich with ancient winding streets and a medieval marketplace and castle square. It is situated below the many summits of Watzmann Mountain—8,901 feet at its highest point. According to legend, the mountain peaks were once a royal family who were so evil that God punished them by turning them into rocks. It makes an excellent stop on a tour of the Alps because of its frequent and good connections to many of the major cities in the area.

ESSENTIALS

GETTING THERE   **Berchtesgaden Station** lies on the Munich–Freilassing rail line. Twelve trains a day arrive from Munich (trip time: 1½ hr.). For rail information and schedules, call ✆ **01805/99-66-33.** Berchtesgaden has three mountain rail lines—the Obersalzbergbahn, Jennerbahn, and Hirscheckbahn—going to the mountain plateaus around the resorts. These mountain lines are not covered by railpasses and tickets cost 18.50€ ($21.30). For more information, contact **Berchtesgadener Bergbahn AG** (✆ **08652/9-58-10**) and **Obersalzbergbahn AG** (✆ **08652/25-61**).

VISITOR INFORMATION   Information is available at the **Kurdirektion,** Königsseerstrasse 2 (✆ **08652/967-0**), across from the train station, to your left. It's open Monday to Friday from 8am to 5pm and Saturday from 9am to noon.

TOP ATTRACTIONS & SPECIAL MOMENTS

In the Middle Ages, Berchtesgaden grew up around a powerful Augustinian monastery. Its monks introduced the art of woodcarving, for which the town is still noted. When the town became part of Bavaria in 1809, the abbey was secularized and eventually converted to a palace for the royal Wittelsbach family. Now the **Königliches Schloss (Royal Palace) Berchtesgaden,** Schlossplatz 2 (✆ **08652/947-980;** bus: 9539), is a museum, mostly devoted to the royal collection of sacred art, including wood sculptures. There's also a gallery of 19th-century art, a collection of Italian furniture from the 16th century, and a display of 17th- and 18th-century pistols and guns. The palace is open June through October, Sunday to Friday from 10am to 1pm and 2 to 5pm; and November through May, Monday to Friday from 11am to 2pm. Admission is 7€ ($8.05) adults, 3€ ($3.45) for children ages 6 to 17, and free for children under 6.

The **Stiftskirche (Abbey Church),** from 1122, adjacent to the palace, is mainly Romanesque, with Gothic additions. One of its ancient twin steeples was destroyed by lightning and rebuilt in 1866. The interior contains many fine works of art; the high altar has a painting by Zott dating from 1669. In the vestry is a small silver altar donated by Empress Maria Theresa of Austria.

The **Schlossplatz** ⊛, partially enclosed by the castle and Stiftskirche, is the most attractive plaza in town. On the opposite side of the square from the church is a 16th-century arcade that leads to **Marktplatz,** with typical Alpine houses and a wooden fountain from 1677 (restored by Ludwig I in 1860). Some of Berchtesgaden's oldest inns and houses border this square. Extending from Marktplatz is the **Nonntal,** lined with more old houses, some built into Lockstein Mountain, which towers above the town.

A minor but interesting museum, **Heimatmuseum,** Schloss Aldelsheim, Schroffen-Bergallee 6 (✆ **08652/44-10**), is devoted to Alpine woodcarving. The craft here predates the more fabled woodcarving at Oberammergau, and some of the best examples in Germany are on display in this museum. Admission is by guided tour only Monday through Friday at 10am and 3pm for a charge of 3€ ($3.45).

WHERE TO STAY & DINE

The modest 40-room **Hotel Fischer** ⊛, Königsseerstrasse 51 (✆ **08652/95-50;** www.hotel-fischer.de), is the town's leading inn. This hotel, overlooking the town and a short uphill walk from the railway station, was built in the late 1970s in the Bavarian style. Fronted with dark-stained wooden balconies against a cream-colored facade, it rambles pleasantly along the hillside and is notable for its indoor swimming pool. Rooms are cozy and traditional, each with a regional theme. Some bathrooms have showers only. Rates, including buffet breakfast cost 98€ to 140€ ($113–$161) double.

Vier Jahreszeiten, Maximilianstrasse 20 (℃ **08652/95-20;** www. berchtesgaden.com/vier-jahreszeiten), is an old inn with modern extensions in the heart of the village. The inn has been remodeled and improved over the years and now offers a good level of comfort to its guests, almost rivaling the Fischer. Some of the newer units, with tiny sitting rooms and balconies, resemble suites. Each accommodation comes with a compact, tiled bathroom with shower. There's a terrace for your summer viewing pleasure. A double costs 78€ to 140€ ($89.70–$161).

You'll get an undeniable sense of Bavarian *Gemütlichkeit* in the richly paneled **Hubertusstube,** Maximilianstrasse 20 (℃ **08652/95-20**), where a trio of old-fashioned dining rooms, each with a century-old history of hospitality, offers well-prepared German food and a view of the Alps. Menu items include rich servings of such game dishes as roasted venison with red wine sauce, as well as perfectly prepared pepper steaks, roasted pork shank, and salmon-trout. Main courses cost 8€ to 20€ ($9.20–$23).

The decor at the **Panorama Restaurant,** in the Alpenhotel Kronprinz, Am Brandholz (℃ **08652/60-70**), includes lots of blond birch paneling and touches of pale blue, but virtually no one notices it because the windows encompass a sweeping view of Obersalzberg and the nearby mountains. Good-tasting menu items include braised trout with almonds; pepper steak; and a savory version of the traditional rib-sticker, *Schweinshaxen* (pork shank). An entree will set you back 10€ to 25€ ($11.50–$28.75).

CHIEMSEE ✪

Chiemsee, known as the "Bavarian Sea," is one of the most beautiful lakes in the Bavarian Alps. The lake is about 53 miles (85km) southeast of Munich and is surrounded by a serene landscape. In the south, the mountains reach almost to the water. Resorts line the shores of this large lake, but the main attractions are its two islands, **Frauenchiemsee** and **Herrenchiemsee,** where Ludwig II built his palace, Neues Schloss. The good news for rail travelers is that these two scenic destinations are just a short boat ride away from an ideally located town on a major rail line, making them easily accessible.

GETTING THERE **Prien Bahnhof** is on the Munich–Salzburg rail line, with frequent connections in all directions. Ten trains arrive daily from Munich (trip time: 1 hr.). For information, call ℃ **01805/99-66-33.**

VISITOR INFORMATION Contact the **Kur- und Verkehrsamt,** Alte Rathaus-Strasse 11, in Prien am Chiemsee (℃ **08051/6-90-50**). It's open Monday to Friday 9am to 7pm and Saturday 9am to 1pm. The office is a 5-minute walk from the station, along Seestrasse; follow the signs for the "Ortszentrum."

GETTING AROUND From the liveliest resort, Prien, on the lake's west shore, you can reach either Frauenchiemsee or Herrenchiemsee via lake steamers that make regular trips throughout the year (cost is 6.80€/$7.80 round-trip to either resort). The steamers, operated by **Chiemsee-Schiffahrt Ludwig Fessler** (℃ **08051/60-90**), make round-trips year-round covering the entire lake.

TOP ATTRACTIONS & SPECIAL MOMENTS

Herrenchiemsee (or Herreninsel) is home to the fantastic **Neues Schloss,** Herrenchiemsee 3 (℡ **08051/68-870**), begun by Ludwig II in 1878. Never completed due to the king's death in 1886, the castle was to have been a replica of Versailles, which Ludwig admired.

The palace **entrance** is lit by a huge skylight over the sumptuously decorated staircase. Frescoes depicting the four states of existence alternate with Greek and Roman statues in niches on the staircase and in the gallery above. The vestibule is adorned with a pair of enameled peacocks, Louis XIV's favorite bird.

The **Great Hall of Mirrors** ★★ is unquestionably the most splendid room, and most authentic replica of Versailles. The 17 door panels contain enormous mirrors reflecting 33 crystal chandeliers and 44 gilded candelabra. The vaulted ceiling is covered with 25 paintings depicting the life of Louis XIV.

Practically every inch of the **state bedroom** ★ has been gilded. On the dais, instead of a throne, is a richly decorated bed, its purple-velvet draperies weighing more than 300 pounds. Separating the dais from the rest of the room is a carved wooden balustrade covered with gold leaf. On the ceiling, a huge fresco depicts the descent of Apollo, surrounded by the other gods of Olympus. The sun god's features bear a strong resemblance to those of Louis XIV.

You can visit Herrenchiemsee year-round. April to October, tours run daily 9am to 6pm; off season, daily 10am to 4:45pm. Admission (in addition to the round-trip boat fare) is 5.50€ ($6.35) for adults, 4.50€ ($5.20) for students, and free for children under 16.

Frauenchiemsee (or Fraueninsel) is the smaller of the lake's two major islands. On its sandy shore stands a fishing village that holds an elaborate festival at Corpus Christi (usually in late May). The island is also home to a Benedictine convent, **Frauenchiemsee Abbey,** founded in 782, which makes it the oldest in Germany. You can walk around the island in about 30 minutes to enjoy panoramic views of the lake. **Torhalle** (℡ **08054/72-56**), a summer-only art gallery, is installed in the ancient hall that used to be the gatehouse of the Frauenwörth convent. Admission is 2€ ($2.30) for adults and 1.50€ ($1.75) for children.

WHERE TO STAY & DINE

The rustic decor at the 46-room **Bayerischer Hof,** Bernauerstrasse 3 (℡ **08051/ 60-30;** www.bayerischerhof-prien.de), creates the illusion that this relatively severe modern hotel is older than it is. Of particular note is the painted ceiling in the dining room. The rest of the hotel is more streamlined—modern, efficient, and quite appealing. The rooms are very comfortable and the shower-only bathrooms are well equipped. Rates run 82€ to 110€ ($94.30–$127) double, including buffet breakfast.

Just a 2-minute drive (or a 5-min. walk) from the center of Prien, **Restaurant Mühlberger** ★★, Bernauerstrasse 40 (℡ **08051/966888**), is housed in a relatively modern building whose exposed pine and coziness makes you think it might be older. The thoughtful and hospitable staff will present menu items that reflect the diversity of local culinary traditions, and although lots of imagination is shown in the kitchens, some of the recipes evoke strong memories of their childhoods in many of the patrons. Main courses run 23€ to 25€ ($26.45–$28.75); a fixed-price dinner costs 49€ ($56.35).

GARMISCH-PARTENKIRCHEN ★★★

Sixty miles (97km) southwest of Munich, the twin villages of Garmisch and Partenkirchen make up Germany's top Alpine resort (it's also great in summer for strolling or hiking). In spite of their urban flair, the towns maintain the charm of an ancient village, especially Partenkirchen. Even today, you occasionally see country folk in traditional dress, and you may be held up in traffic while the cattle are led from their mountain-grazing grounds down through the streets of town. This is an excellent spot for the rail traveler to take a break from the rails and get a breath of fresh air while enjoying marvelous views.

ESSENTIALS

GETTING THERE   The **Garmisch-Partenkirchen Station** lies on the Munich–Innsbruck rail line, with frequent connections to many major cities in the region. Twenty trains per day arrive from Munich (trip time: 1 hr. 22 min.). For information and schedules, call ℂ **01805/99-66-33.**

Mountain rail service to several plateaus and the Zugspitze, the tallest mountain in Germany, is offered by the **Bayerische Zugspitzbahn** at Garmisch (ℂ **08821/79-70**). The mountain line is not covered by railpasses; the price depends on your final destination.

VISITOR INFORMATION   Contact the **Verkehrsamt,** Richard-Strauss-Platz (ℂ **08821/180-700**). It's open Monday to Saturday 8am to 6pm and Sunday and holidays 10am to noon. It's about a 5-minute walk from the train station to the tourist office; head left along Bahnhofstrasse, then left on Chamonixstrasse.

TOP ATTRACTIONS & SPECIAL MOMENTS

Garmisch-Partenkirchen is a center for winter sports, summer hiking, and mountain climbing. The symbol of the city's growth and modernity is the **Olympic Ice Stadium,** built for the 1936 Winter Olympics and capable of holding nearly 12,000 people. The World Cup Ski Jump is held every New Year on the slopes at the edge of town in the **Ski Stadium.** The town and its environs offer some of the most panoramic views and colorful buildings in Bavaria. The pilgrimage **Chapel of St. Anton,** on a pinewood path at the edge of Partenkirchen, is all pink and silver, inside and out. Its graceful lines are characteristic of the 18th century, when it was built. In the park surrounding the chapel, the **Philosopher's Walk** ★ is a delightful spot to wander, just to enjoy the views of the mountains around the low-lying town.

To the Top of the Zugspitze ★★★

From Garmisch-Partenkirchen, you can see the tallest mountain in Germany, the **Zugspitze,** 9,720 feet above sea level. Ski slopes begin at a height of 8,700 feet. For a panoramic view of both the Bavarian and the Tyrolean (Austrian) Alps, go all the way to the summit. There are two different ways to reach the Zugspitze from the center of Garmisch. The first begins with a trip on the cog railway, the **Zugspitzbahn,** which departs from the back of Garmisch's main railway station daily every hour from 8:35am to 2:35pm. The train travels uphill, past lichen-covered boulders and coursing streams, to a high-altitude plateau, the Zugspitzplatte, where views sweep out over all Bavaria. At the Zugspitzplatte, you'll transfer onto a cable car, the Gletscher Sielbahn, for a 4-minute ride uphill to the top of the Zugspitze. There, far-reaching panoramas, a cafe and restaurant, a gift shop, and many Alpine trails await. Total travel time for this itinerary is about 55 minutes.

Moments A Dramatic Alpine Fantasy

Hiking is Bavaria's favorite pastime. Locals believe firmly in the emotional and spiritual benefits of walking and hill climbing and tend to hit the trails the moment the snows melt.

The tourist office in Garmisch-Partenkirchen will point you to hiking trails of varying degrees of difficulty, all clearly marked with signs. The office also offers a brochure outlining the half-dozen best trails. You don't have to be an Olympic athlete to enjoy them. Most hikes will take an energetic person 4 to 5 hours, but some of them are shorter and easy enough for children.

An interesting hike is through the **Partnachklamm Gorge** ★★, a canyon with a roaring stream at the bottom and sheer cliff walls rising on either side of the hiking trail. Take the Graseck Seilbahn from its departure point at the bottom of the gorge, less than a half mile (1km) south of Garmisch's ski stadium, and get off at the first station, which is adjacent to a cozy hotel, the **Forsthaus Graseck** (© 08821/5-40-06). The 3-minute cable-car ride costs 3.50€ ($4.05) per person each way (free for hotel guests) and operates from 7am to 10pm, midnight on weekends. You may want to get a meal or drink at the hotel first.

Afterward descend on foot along narrow paths by the sides of the stream, as it cascades downhill. The path crosses the gorge and returns you to the point where you entered. Many readers have found this one of their most memorable adventures in Bavaria. The experience of walking along a rocky ledge just above a rushing river and often behind small waterfalls, while looking up at 1,200 feet of rocky cliffs, is truly awesome (and sometimes wet).

The other way to get to the summit is to take the Zugspitzbahn for a briefer trip, disembarking 9 miles (14km) southwest of Garmisch at the lower station of the Eibsee Sielbahn (Eibsee Cable Car), next to a clear Alpine lake. The cable car will carry you from there directly to the summit of the Zugspitze, for a total transit time of about 38 minutes. The Eibsee Sielbahn makes its run at least every half hour 8:30am to 4:30pm (5:30pm in July and Aug).

Round-trip tickets allow you to ascend one-way and descend the other, in order to enjoy the widest range of spectacular views. May to October, round-trip fares are 43€ ($49.45) for adults, and 25€ ($28.75) for children ages 6 to 15. In winter, round-trip fares are reduced to 34€ ($39.10) for adults, and 21€ ($24.15) for children ages 5 to 15. Railpasses don't cover the cog railways and cable cars, but the Zugspitzbahn gives a 5€ ($5.75) reduction to travelers holding a valid train ticket to Garmisch-Partenkirchen. For more information, contact the Bayerische Zugspitzbahn, Olympiastrasse 27, Garmisch-Partenkirchen (© 08821/7-97-0; www.zugspitze.de).

WHERE TO STAY & DINE

Founded in 1542, **Posthotel Partenkirchen** ★, Ludwigstrasse 49 (© 08821/9-36-30; www.post-hotel.de), is one of the town's most prestigious hotels. Here you'll experience old-world living and personalized service. The 57 U-shaped guest rooms are stylish, with antiques and elaborately carved furnishings. The sunny balconies overlook a garden and offer a view of the Alps. Rooms are generally medium in size, though some are quite spacious. Rates include continental breakfast and run 110€ to 130€ ($127–$150) double; 150€ ($173) suite. The hotel's **restaurant** (✖) is renowned throughout Bavaria for its distinguished continental cuisine. The interior dining rooms are rustic, with a mellow, old-fashioned atmosphere. Everything seems comfortably subdued, including the diners. Main courses cost 10€ to 29€ ($11.50–$33.35).

Reindl's Partenkirchner Hof (✖), Bahnhofstrasse 15 (© **08821/5-80-25;** www.reindls.de), opened in 1911, and this special Bavarian retreat has always attracted a devoted following. The four-story building has a high level of luxury and hospitality and wraparound verandas, giving each room an unobstructed view of the mountains and town. The 63 guest rooms are among the most attractive in town. The best are the suites opening onto panoramic views of mountains or the garden. Fine carpeting and rustic pine furniture add to the allure. Rates run 110€ to 140€ ($127–$161) double; 161€ to 192€ ($185–$221) suite.

A bit of the Bavarian Alps always seems to flower in the intimate **Flösserstuben,** Schmiedstrasse 2 (© **08821/28-88**), close to the town center. On most evenings, the weathered beams above the dining tables reverberate with laughter and good cheer. You can select a seat at a colorful wooden table or on an ox-yoke-inspired stool in front of the spliced saplings that decorate the bar. Hungarian goulashes, sauerbraten, and all kinds of Bavarian dishes are abundantly available. It's a real find! Main courses cost 5€ to 17€ ($5.75–$19.55).

OBERAMMERGAU (✖)

59 miles (95km) SW of Munich, 12 miles (20km) N of Garmisch-Partenkirchen

In the summer of 2000, Oberammergau (59 miles/95km southwest of Munich) staged its famous Passion Play, which is performed only 1 year out of every 10. Surely the world's longest-running show, it began in 1634 when the town's citizens took a vow to give dramatic thanks after they were spared from the devastating plague of 1633. In many ways, it's an authentic re-creation of a medieval morality play. The town is packed to the gills all summer for this major event.

However, a rail visit to Oberammergau, which is just 2 hours by train from Munich, is ideal at any time, even without the performance. The town is in a wide valley surrounded by forests, green meadows, and mountains, and has long been known for the skill of its woodcarvers. Numerous hiking trails lead through the nearby mountains to hikers' inns. You can also simply go up to the mountaintops on the Laber cable railway or the Kolben chairlift.

ESSENTIALS

GETTING THERE The **Oberammergau Bahnhof** is on the Murnau-Bad Kohlgrum-Oberammergau rail line, with frequent connections in all directions. Through Murnau, all major German cities can be reached. Daily trains arrive from Munich in 2 hours and from Frankfurt in 7 hours. For rail information and schedules, call © **01805/99-66-33.**

VISITOR INFORMATION Contact the **Oberammergau Tourist Information Office,** Eugen-Papst-Strasse 9A (© **08822/9-23-10**). It's open Monday to Friday 9am to 6pm and on Saturday 9am to noon. To get here from the train station, exit the station and go straight ahead for about ⅓ mile (.5km), then head left at the V+R Bank for about ⅕ mile (.3km).

TOP ATTRACTIONS & SPECIAL MOMENTS

Aside from the Passion Play actors, Oberammergau's most respected citizens are its **woodcarvers,** many of whom have been trained in the village woodcarvers' school. In the **Pilatushaus,** Ludwig-Thoma-Strasse (© **08822/16-82**), you can watch local carvers, as well as painters, sculptors, and potters, as they work. May to October, their hours are Tuesday to Friday from 1:30 to 6pm. You'll see many examples of their art throughout the town, on the painted cottages and inns and in the churchyard.

When strolling through the village, note the frescoed houses named after fairy-tale characters, such as the "Hansel and Gretel House" and "Little Red Riding Hood House." Most often, these frescoes are based on scenes from fairy tales. The most famous frescoed house is **Pilatushaus** on Ludwig-Thoma-Strasse, where the fresco is based on a depiction of Jesus Christ coming before Pilate.

Heimatmuseum, Dorfstrasse 8 (© **08822/9-41-36**), has a notable collection of 18th-, 19th-, and 20th-century Christmas crèches, all hand carved and painted. It's open mid-April to mid-October, Tuesday to Sunday 2 to 6pm; off season, Saturday only 2 to 6pm. Admission is 2.50€ ($2.90) for adults, 1.50€ ($1.75) for students.

WHERE TO STAY & DINE

Note: The cost of accommodation in Oberammergau includes a universally imposed *Kurtaxe* (special tax) of 1.30€ ($1.50). This entitles visitors to a card providing small discounts at local attractions.

Alte Post, Dorfstrasse 19 (© **08822/91-00;** www.ogau.de), is a chalet-style provincial inn with a wide overhanging roof, green-shuttered windows painted with decorative trim, and tables set on a sidewalk under a long awning. The interior has a storybook charm, with a ceiling-high green ceramic stove, Alpine chairs, and shelves of pewter plates. The 32 rustic rooms range in size from cozy to spacious and have wood-beamed ceilings and wide beds with giant posts (no hair dryers, though); most have views. All the small, shower-only bathrooms are tiled. Rates are 68€ to 86€ ($78.20–$98.80) double and include continental breakfast.

A cozy 18th-century Bavarian inn, the **Turmwirt,** Ettalerstrasse 2 (© **08822/ 9-26-00;** www.turmwirt.de), offers 22 small, snug rooms, many with private balconies opening onto mountain views. Each comes with a small but well-maintained shower-only bathroom (no hair dryer). The present building, an intricately painted country house with a homey interior, was constructed in 1889 and has been altered and renovated many times. The owners are three generations of the same family, who often present Bavarian folk evenings. Rooms cost 77€ to 98€ ($88.55–$113) double, including a buffet breakfast

SIDE TRIP TO SCHLOSS LINDERHOF ★★

Until the late 19th century, a modest hunting lodge, owned by the Bavarian royal family, stood on a large piece of land 8 miles (13km) west of the village. But in 1869, "Mad" King Ludwig struck again, this time creating a French rococo palace, Schloss Linderhof, in the Ammergau Mountains. This is his most successful creation. Unlike his palace at Chiemsee (see "Chiemsee," earlier in this chapter), Schloss Linderhof was not meant to copy any other structure. And unlike the Neuschwanstein palace (p. 377), its concentration of fanciful projects and designs was not limited to the palace interior.

Ascending the winged staircase of Carrara marble, you'll find yourself at the **West Gobelin Room** (music room), with carved and gilded paneling and richly colored tapestries. This room leads directly into the **Hall of Mirrors,** where the mirrors are set in white-and-gold panels, decorated with gilded woodcarvings. The hall's ceiling is festooned with frescoes depicting mythological scenes. The **king's bedchamber,** the largest room in the palace, overlooks the Fountain of Neptune and the garden cascades.

In the popular style of the previous century, Ludwig laid out the **gardens** ★★ in formal parterres with geometrical shapes, baroque sculptures, and elegant fountains. The front of the palace opens onto a large pool where, from a gilded statue in its center, a jet of water sprays 105 feet into the air.

Schloss Linderhof, 82488 Ettal-Linderhof (⟨© **08822/920-321;** www. linderhof.de), is open to the public throughout the year, and makes a good day trip from Munich, as well as from Oberammergau. It's open March to October daily 9am to 6pm. From October to March, the grotto and Moorish Kiosk are closed, but the castle is open daily 9:30am to noon and 1 to 4pm. Admission in the summer is 6€ ($6.90) for adults, 5€ ($5.75) for students, and free for children 14 and under. In winter, admission is 4.50€ ($5.20) for adults, 3.50€ ($4.05) for students, and free for children 14 and under.

Buses run between Oberammergau and Schloss Linderhof seven times per day (there's no train service), beginning at 9am; the last bus leaves Linderhof at 5:35pm. Round-trip fare is 6€ ($6.90).

5 Lake Constance (Bodensee) ★★★

Mild climate and plentiful sunshine make Lake Constance (*Bodensee* in German) a top vacation spot for lovers of sun and sand, as well as for sightseers and spa-goers. The hillsides that slope to the water's edge are covered with vineyards and orchards and are dotted with colorful hamlets and busy tourist centers. Cruise ships and ferries link every major center around the lake. The 162-mile (260km) shoreline is shared by Germany, Austria, and Switzerland.

Lake Constance is actually divided into three lakes, although the name is frequently applied only to the largest of these, the Obersee. The western end of the Obersee separates into two distinct branches: One, the Überlingersee, is a long fjord; the other, the Untersee, is more irregular, jutting in and out of marshland and low-lying woodland. The two branches are connected by a narrow channel—which is actually the upper Rhine.

Lake Constance offers a wealth of **activities,** including swimming, sailing, windsurfing, diving, and rowing. Local tourist offices will connect you with various outfitters.

It's a beautiful region and there are plenty of rail connections, in particular to Konstanz and Friedrichshafen, but also to many other points around the lakeshore, and to Munich, making this place a good scenic stopover point when traveling by train either to or from Munich and Bavaria.

LINDAU ★

A unique setting on an island at the eastern end of Lake Constance made Lindau, 111 miles (179km) southwest of Munich, a prime tourist attraction. Today, this garden city is under landmark protection and has outgrown its boundaries and spread to the shores of the mainland. This charming city now caters to the tourist's every whim, from bathing to baccarat. It's one of the most important resort towns in the Bodensee area and a must for rail travelers touring the region.

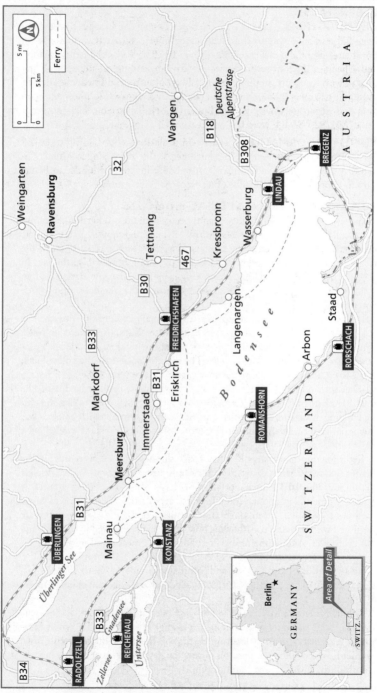

Lake Constance

ESSENTIALS

GETTING THERE   Lindau is on the Basel–Lindau and Lindau–Buchloe **rail** lines and it's about 3 hours from Munich by train. Lindau's train station is on the island in the old town center. Call ℘ **01805/99-66-33** for information and schedules. Five to seven **ferries** per day (depending on the season) link Lindau with Konstanz, stopping at Meersburg, Mainau, and Friedrichshafen en route; the trip takes 3 hours and is not covered by a railpass. For information on fares and departure times, contact **Bodensee-Schiffsbetriebe,** Hafenstrasse 6 (℘ **07531/923-83-89;** www.bsb-online.com).

VISITOR INFORMATION   **Tourist-Information** is at Ludwigstrasse 68 (℘ **08382/26-00-30**). April 1 to September 5, the office is open Monday to Saturday 9am to 7pm, and Sunday 9am to noon; in winter, Monday to Friday 9am to noon and 2 to 5pm. The office faces the train station.

TOP ATTRACTIONS & SPECIAL MOMENTS

A tour of this *Ferieninsel* (Holiday Island) begins with the **old harbor,** seen from the lakeside promenade. The **Mangturm,** the old lighthouse, stands on the promenade as a reminder of the heavy fortifications that once surrounded the city. The entrance to the harbor is marked by the 108-foot **New Lighthouse.** To get here from the train station, make a right upon exiting the station and go straight for a few minutes; you'll eventually arrive at the lakeshore, from which you can see the lighthouse.

In the center of the town, **Hauptstrasse** is the main street of the Altstadt. The most easily recognizable building here is the **Altes Rathaus,** erected in 1422. The stepped gables are typical of the period, but the building's facade also combines many later styles of architecture. The interior, once used as a council hall, is the town library. Frescoes represent scenes from a session of the 1496 Imperial Diet. Just north of Hauptstrasse is the town's most familiar landmark, the round **Diebsturm (Thieves' Tower),** with a turreted roof. Next to it is the oldest building in Lindau, the 11th-century **St. Peter's Church,** which houses a war memorial chapel. In the church is a group of frescoes by Hans Holbein the Elder.

Returning to Hauptstrasse, which cuts through the exact center of the island, follow the street eastward to the **Haus zum Cavazzen,** Am Marktplatz (℘ **08382/94-40-73**), the handsomest patrician house on Lake Constance. It houses the municipal art collection. Included are exhibits of sculpture and painting from the Gothic, Renaissance, and baroque periods. Some of the rooms are furnished with period pieces showing how wealthy citizens lived in the 18th and 19th centuries. Among the rarities is a collection of mechanical musical instruments. This attraction can be visited by guided tour only, April to October, Tuesday to Friday 11am to 5pm, and Saturday to Sunday noon to 5pm. Admission is 2.50€ ($2.90) adults, 1€ ($1.15) students and children; children under 10 enter free.

Passing across Am Marktplatz and by the Collegiate Church and St. Stephen's Church, both baroque, you come to the strange pile of rocks known as **Heathen's Wall,** dating from Roman times. Beyond this is the **Stadtgarten (Town Garden),** which, although peaceful during the day, livens up at night when the wheels of the town's casino begin to spin.

WHERE TO STAY & DINE

The old-world **Bayerischer Hof** ★★★, Seepromenade (℘ **800/223-5652** in the U.S. and Canada, or 08382/91-50; www.bayerischerhof-lindau.de), clearly outdistances all others in Lindau. It opens onto the lakeside promenade and looks almost like a hotel on the Mediterranean. The atmosphere and service here are first-rate. The 100 large rooms are the finest in Lindau, each well furnished with traditional styling. Most have good views; the less desirable units overlook a narrow thoroughfare. Rates are 140€ to 232€ ($161–$267) double; 259€ to 417€ ($298–$480) suite. Rates include buffet breakfast.

The modest, charming little **Hotel-Garni Brugger,** Bei der Heidenmauer 11 (© **08382/9-34-10;** www.hotel-garni-brugger.de), is the best affordable choice in Lindau. It's pleasingly proportioned, with a gabled attic, French doors that open onto the balconies in the back, and a winter garden filled with potted plants. The 23 small rooms are up-to-date, furnished in a functional modern style, with lots of light; and each comes with a small, shower-only tiled bathroom. The location is an easy walk from the lake and casino. Rooms cost 80€ to 88€ ($92–$101) double; rates include continental breakfast.

From the beautifully decorated inner room of **Hoyerberg Schlüssle** ★★★, Hoyerbergstrasse 64 (© **08382/2-52-95**), a superb cafe-restaurant, you get a view of the mountains and lake. You can also dine on two terraces. Continental delicacies include cream of scampi soup, Bodensee pike-perch stuffed with champagne-flavored herbs, and Allgäuer saddle of venison with small flour dumplings and French beans. Meals here are memorable; the chef has great flair and style, and doesn't over-sauce the food. Reservations required for the restaurant; not for the cafe. Main courses cost 22€ to 28€ ($25.30–32.20); a fixed-price menu costs 56€ to 74€ ($64.40–$85.10).

Zum Sünfzen, Maximilianstrasse 1 (© **08382/58-65**), is an old, all-wood, family-owned restaurant serving good Bavarian food at reasonable prices. Dishes range from roast pork with vegetables to filet of venison. Fresh fish from Lake Constance is a specialty. The food is the type you might be served in a middle-class private home along the lake. Main courses run 7€ to 16€ ($8.05–$18.40).

FRIEDRICHSHAFEN

Fourteen miles (22km) west of Lindau, Friedrichshafen is set at the northeastern corner of the Bodensee, near the lake's widest point. It's graced with one of the longest waterfront exposures of any town along the lake.

By Train   Friedrichshafen is the largest railway junction along the northern edge of the Bodensee and is a major transfer point for rail passengers going on to other cities and resorts along the lake. The town has two railway stations, the **Stadtbahnhof,** in the town center, and the **Hafenbahnhof,** along the Seestrasse, about ¾ mile (1km) away. Both of these stations are interconnected by bus nos. 1, 2, 3, 4, 5, 6, and 7. For information and schedules, call © **01805/99-66-33.**

From April to October, about eight lake steamers travel between Friedrichshafen and Lindau, Bregenz (Austria), and Konstanz. These ferries are not covered by a railpass. For departure times and details, call © **07541/ 923-83-89.**

VISITOR INFORMATION   The city's **Tourist Information Office** is right outside the train station at Bahnhofplatz 2 (© **07541/30010;** www. friedrichshafen.de). It's open May to September, Monday to Friday 9am to 5pm, Saturday 10am to 2pm; October to April, Monday to Thursday 9am to noon and 2 to 5pm, and Friday 9am to 1pm.

TOP ATTRACTIONS & SPECIAL MOMENTS

The best thing to do in town is to stroll the lake-fronting **Seepromenade,** with its sweeping view that extends on clear days all the way to the Swiss Alps.

Cycling along the broad Seestrasse is also a delight. A kiosk within the Stadt-bahnhof rents bikes for 7€ to 9€ ($8.05–$10.35) a day. Contact the tourist office for details.

The town's architectural highlight is the 17th-century **Schlosskirche,** Schlossstrasse 33 (© **07541/21422**). The palatial ecclesiastical buildings that were once part of the church's monastery were converted in the 1800s into a palace for the kings of Württemberg. Today, they are privately owned and can't be entered, but the church is well worth a visit. It's open only Easter to October, daily 8am to 6pm.

Zeppelin-Museum (© **07541/38010;** www.zeppelin-museum.de), in the Hafenbahnhof, Seestrasse 22, is a tribute to Count Ferdinand von Zeppelin. Around 1900, this native of Konstanz invented and tested the aircraft that bore his name. The museum has a re-creation of the giant and historic zeppelin *Hindenburg,* including a full-scale replica of its passenger cabins. The famous blimp exploded in a catastrophic fire in New Jersey in 1937, possibly due to sabotage. The museum also has memorabilia associated with zeppelins and their inventor. May to October, it's open Tuesday to Sunday 10am to 6pm; November to April, Tuesday to Sunday 10am to 5pm. Admission is 6.50€ ($7.50) for adults and 3€ ($3.45) for children 16 and under.

WHERE TO STAY & DINE

The charming lakeside **Buchhorner Hof** ✦, Friedrichstrasse 33 (© **07541/20-50**), provides a compromise between the luxurious, modern comfort of larger hotels and the traditional hospitality of smaller inns. It's housed in the oldest building in town. Each of the 98 rooms is well furnished and comes with a midsize modern bathroom. The bar is a cozy retreat. Rates run 99€ to 139€ ($114–$160) double; 180€ ($207) suite.

The 132-room **Seehotel Friedrichshafen** ✦, Bahnhofplatz 2 (© **07541/30-30;** www.seehotelfn.de), is beside the Seepromenade, right near the rail station. It's one of the newest and most appealing hotels in town. The small guest rooms are sensibly, even stylishly, decorated. Some have air-conditioning; most have views of the water. All the bedrooms have midsize bathrooms; some have showers only. The staff is sensitive and well trained. Rates include buffet breakfast and run 126€ to 157€ ($145–$181) double; 171€ ($197) suite.

Diners at the **Hotel-Restaurant Maier** ✦, Poststrasse 1–3 (© **07541/40-40**), in the center of Fischbach appreciate the generous, well-prepared portions of German cuisine, the attentive service, and the sweeping views over the lake. One dining room is contemporary and modern; the other a re-creation of a traditional *Stube* in the mountains. Menu items include venison in red wine sauce with mushrooms, schnitzels, and elaborate pastries for dessert. Main courses cost 10€ to 20€ ($11.50–$23).

Depending on the time of day, **Restaurant Kurgarten,** Olgastrasse 20 (© **07541/3-20-33**), might look like a cafe, a bar, or a restaurant. It has a beautiful view over its own garden and the lake, and there's a wide range of tasty international menu items, including Argentine beefsteak. Vegetarian choices are also available. Main courses cost 9€ to 18€ ($10.35–$20.70).

KONSTANZ (CONSTANCE) ✦

Crowded against the shores of Lake Constance by the borders of Switzerland (it's only 47 miles/76km north of Zurich), the medieval town of Konstanz had nowhere to grow but northward across the river. Today this resort city lies on both banks of the Rhine, as the river begins its long journey to the North Sea.

It's a beautiful and interesting city, though, admittedly, it should be visited primarily as part of a rail tour of the Bodensee because it's harder to reach Konstanz from Germany's major cities than it is to travel here via rail and ferry from other towns on the lake.

GETTING THERE   Konstanz is on the Konstanz–Offenburg **rail** line, the Schwarzwaldbahn, with frequent connection to most German cities. For information, call © **01805/99-66-33.**

Ferry service and lake cruises operate between Konstanz, Mainau Island, Meersburg, Lindau, and Bregenz. These ferries are not covered by a railpass. The ferry operator is **Bodensee-Schiffsbetriebe,** Hafenstrasse 6 (© **07531/ 923-83-89**).

VISITOR INFORMATION   For information, go to **Verkehramt,** Bahnhofplatz 13 (© **07531/13-30-30**), near the rail station. The office is open April to July, Monday to Friday from 9am to 6pm, Saturday from 9am to 4pm, and Sunday from 10am to 1pm; August to September, Monday to Friday from 9am to 8pm, and Saturday and Sunday from 10am to 4pm; November to March, Monday to Friday from 9am to noon and 2 to 6pm (and the 1st four Sat of Dec from 9am–4pm).

TOP ATTRACTIONS & SPECIAL MOMENTS

The best way to see Konstanz is from the water. The **shoreline** ✪ is fascinating, with little inlets that weave in and out around ancient buildings and city gardens. Several pleasure ships offer tours along the city shoreline and across the lake to Meersburg and several other destinations. Contact **Bodensee-Schiffsbetriebe,** Hafenstrasse 6 (© **07531/28-13-89;** www.bsb-online.com). Ferries from Konstanz to Meersburg leave every 15 minutes from 6am to 8pm; then one per hour from 8pm to 6am. The cost is 1.70€ ($1.95). For information, contact **Stadtwerke Konstanz** (© **07531/80-33-66;** http://sw.konstanz.de).

During the summer, outdoor concerts are presented in the **city gardens.** Below the gardens is the **Council Building,** where the Council of Constance met. Originally constructed as a storehouse in 1388, the hall came to be used for meetings, and was restored in 1911 and decorated with murals depicting the history of the town. On the harbor in front is an obelisk erected in memory of Count Ferdinand von Zeppelin, the citizen of Konstanz who invented the dirigible in the late 19th century.

The unusual, almost tropical island of **Mainau,** 4 miles (6km) north of Konstanz, is located in the arm of the Bodensee known as the Überlingersee. Here, palms and orange trees grow and fragrant flowers bloom year-round, practically in the shadow of the snow-covered Alps. In the center of this botanical oasis is an ancient castle, once a residence of the Teutonic Knights. Only the island's gardens and parks can be visited. They're open March to October, daily from 7am to 10pm; November to February, daily from 9am to 5pm.

You can reach Mainau either by tour boat from Konstanz or by walking across the small footbridge connecting the island to the mainland, north of the city. Admission is 11€ ($12.65) for adults, 5€ ($5.75) for students, and 3€ ($3.45) for children. For more information, call © **07531/3030** or visit **www. mainau.de**.

Strandbad Horn, at the tip of the peninsula, is the largest and most popular beach in the area. You can rent Windsurfers for 7€ ($8.05) per hour. From the town center, bus no. 4 runs here about every 30 minutes; the fare is 1.80€ ($2.05).

WHERE TO STAY & DINE

Though located in Petershausen, the **Buchner Hof,** Buchnerstrasse 6 (© **07531/8-10-20;** www.buchner-hof.de), is just a short walk from most points of interest and is across the Rhine from Konstanz. The 13 pleasantly furnished rooms range from small to medium, and have tiny bathrooms. The hotel is named after composer Hans Buchner, who became organist at the town cathedral in 1510 and was one of the first musicians to arrange and catalog the wealth of Gregorian chants found in the region. Rates include buffet breakfast and run 90€ to 100€ ($104–$115) double; 110€ ($127) suite. It's closed Dec 23 to Jan 7.

If you happen to lose at roulette on one of your casino outings in Konstanz, you can revive your spirits (and drink a few, too) on the lakeside terrace of the **Casino Restaurant am See** 🍴, Seestrasse 21 (© **07531/81-57-65**). The view is lovely, and the food first-rate. The restaurant offers a good choice of international dishes; try the fresh fish or saddle of lamb. The food is backed up by a good wine cellar. A jacket and tie are required for men and reservations are a must. Main courses cost 11€ to 28€ ($12.65–$32.20).

6 Highlights of the Romantic Road

The aptly named Romantic Road, or *Romantische Strasse,* is one of Germany's most popular tourist routes. The road stretches for 180 miles (290km) between Würzburg in the north and Füssen in the foothills of the Bavarian Alps. Strung along the way is a series of medieval villages and 2,000-year-old towns. Frankfurt and Munich are convenient gateways for exploring the road by rail. The entire length of the Romantic Road is best done by car or bus and could take days to see in its entirety. That said, many of the top cities along the route can easily be reached by rail, and we highlight the best of those cities in this section.

Note: The Romantic Road Association will provide information on sights and attractions and mail information packs in English. Contact the **Romantische Strasse Arbeitsgemeinschaft,** Marktplatz, 91550 Dinkelsbühl (© **09851/9-02-71;** www.romantischestrasse.de).

WÜRZBURG 🍴🍴

For Germans, the south begins at Würzburg, one of the loveliest baroque cities in the country. Würzburg, 174 miles (280km) northwest of Munich, is the best starting point for the Romantic Road. Not only is it an interesting town in and of itself, but it also has excellent rail connections to most of Germany's major cities and to the cities along the Romantic Road route. It's also the jumping-off point for the Romantic Road Europabus tour (see "Traveling the Romantic Road by Bus," above), for which railpass holders get a discount. This young and lively city on the Main is often crowded in summer.

GETTING THERE **Würzburg Hauptbahnhof** is connected to several major rail lines. From Frankfurt, 30 trains arrive per day (trip time: 1½ hr.); from Munich, 20 trains (trip time: 2½ hr.); and several trains from Berlin (trip time: 3 hr. 50 min.). For rail information and schedules, call © **01805/99-66-33.** The main train station is just outside and to the north of the old town center.

VISITOR INFORMATION Contact the **Verkehrsbüro tourist office** at Am Marktplatz 9 (© **0931/37-23-35**). It's open April to December Monday to Friday 10am to 6pm, Saturday to Sunday 10am to 2pm, January to March Monday to Friday 10am to 4pm, Saturday 10am to 1pm. The tourist office is in the central square, at the heart of the old town.

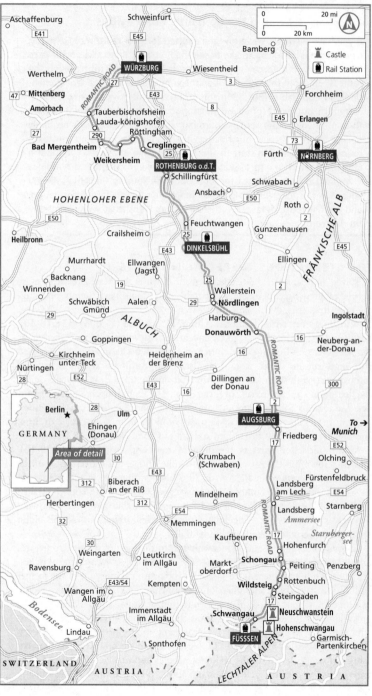

The Romantic Road

> **(Moments** Traveling the Romantic Road by Bus
>
> If you have plenty of vacation time allotted for your rail trip to Germany, have a railpass, and would like to see the Romantic Road at a slower pace than a train would provide, there is a secondary option for traveling the route. From April through October, the comfortable and modern Romantic Road Europabus (Bus 190) runs from Würzburg (it actually starts in Frankfurt, but we recommend starting in Würzburg) to Füssen, passing through many of the route's charming villages and towns. It's probably one of the most scenic bus rides on the planet. The one-way trip takes roughly 11 hours from start to finish. If you have a railpass, you'll get a 60% discount off the fare. Seats should be reserved on either bus at least 2 working days in advance through **Deutsche Touring GmbH** (**(C) 49697/ 90-32-56;** fax 49697/90-32-81). For more timetables, fare information, and further route details, see the company's website at **www.deutsche-touring.com**.

TOP ATTRACTIONS & SPECIAL MOMENTS

In spring and summer, the liveliest place in town is the **Markt (central marketplace).** Here street performers entertain and vendors hawk their wares, ranging from fresh fruit to souvenir trinkets.

Würzburg's cathedral, **Dom St. Kilian,** Domstrasse (**(C) 0931/321-18-30**), begun in 1045 and dedicated to a 7th-century Irish missionary to Franconia, is the fourth-largest Romanesque church in Germany. The interior was adorned with high-baroque stucco work done after 1700. An imposing row of bishops' tombs begins with that of Gottfried von Spitzenberg (ca. 1190), who was one of the first prince-bishops to rule over the town. The Dom is open Easter to October, Monday to Saturday from 10am to 5pm, and Sunday from 1 to 6pm; November to Easter, Monday to Saturday from 10am to noon and 2 to 5pm, and Sunday from 12:30 to 1:30pm and 2:30 to 6pm. Admission is free.

Mainfränkisches Fortress (Festung Marienberg) ★ (**(C) 0931/4-30-16**), located across from the Altstadt, over the stone bridge, was the residence of the local prince-bishops from 1253 to 1720. Although portions of the stronghold have been restored, the combination of age and wartime destruction has taken a serious toll on its thick walls and once-impenetrable ramparts. But what remains is worth a visit. The 8th-century **Marienkirche,** one of the oldest churches in Germany, stands within its walls.

In the former arsenal and Echter bulwark, to the right of the first courtyard, is the **Mainfränkisches Museum** (**(C) 0931/4-30-16;** www.mainfraenkisches-museum.de), housed here since 1946. It's the historical museum of the former Bishopric of Würzburg and Dukedom of Franconia and the provincial museum of lower Franconia. On display is a collection of important sculptures by the great flamboyant Gothic master, Tilman Riemenschneider (1460–1531), called "the master of Würzburg." The sculptor came to live here in 1483 and was the town's mayor in 1520 and 1521. Never a totally decorative artist, Riemenschneider concentrated on the reality of people's appearance, highlighting their hands, faces, and clothing. The museum also displays paintings by Tiepolo and sandstone figures from the rococo gardens of the prince-bishops' summer palace. A tribute to one of the few industries of the city, winemaking, is paid in the press house, which contains historic casks and carved cask bases and a large collection of glasses and goblets. Admission is 4€ ($4.60) adults; children 14 and under are free. Open Tuesday through Sunday 10am to 5pm. To get here, take bus no. 9.

Fürstenbaumuseum (© 0931/4-38-38) is situated in the restored princes' wing of the fortress. Here the visitor gets a glimpse of the living quarters and living conditions of the prince-bishops up to 1718. The urban-history section offers a stroll through 1,200 eventful years of Würzburg's history, including an exhibit relating to the discovery of X-rays by Wilhelm Conrad Röntgen in 1895. A model of the town shows its appearance in 1525, and another shows the destruction after the bombing of 1945. Admission is free for the fortress. Museum admission and hours are the same as for the Mainfränkisches Museum.

A baroque horseshoe-shaped castle, the **Residenz (Schloss und Gartenverwaltung Würzburg)** ★★, Residenzplatz 2, Tor B (© 0931/355-51-70; tram: 1 or 5), was begun in 1720 to satisfy Prince-Bishop Johann Philipp Franz von Schönborn's passion for elegance and splendor. At its center is the masterful Treppenhaus (staircase), above which a high, rounded ceiling is decorated with a huge fresco by Tiepolo depicting Apollo ascending to the zenith of the vault. The surrounding themes represent the four corners of the world, the seasons, and signs of the zodiac. In the court chapel, a rectangular room divided into five oval sections, three with domed ceilings, window arches are placed at oblique angles to coordinate the windows with the oval sections. Colored marble columns define the sections, their gilded capitals enriching the ceiling frescoes by Johann Rudolf Byss. At the side altars, Tiepolo painted two important works: *The Fall of the Angels* on the left and *The Assumption of the Virgin* on the right. During the summer, a **Mozart festival** is held in the upper halls. The castle is open April to October, daily from 9am to 6pm; November to March, daily from 10am to 4:30pm. Admission is 4€ ($4.60) for adults, 3€ ($3.45) for students, and free for seniors and children under 15.

WHERE TO STAY & DINE

For homespun cleanliness, the **Franziskaner,** Franziskanerplatz 2 (© 0931/3-56-30; fax 0931/3-56-33-33; tram: 1), is a winner—and the price is right, too. You'll receive a hearty welcome from the staff. The lobby has attractive black panels surrounded with natural wood; the breakfast room has fine large windows looking out to the greenery beyond. All of the rooms are well furnished, each with an immaculate bathroom (some have showers only); some nonsmoking rooms are available. Rates run 102€ to 123€ ($117–$141) double and include a buffet breakfast.

St. Josef ★, Semmelstrasse 28 (© 0931/30-86-80; fax 0931/3-08-68-60), is the best inexpensive accommodation in the Altstadt. Its owner has been successful in bringing it up-to-date. The 35 rooms, though small, are pleasantly furnished and well maintained, each equipped with an efficiently organized bathroom with shower unit. Breakfast is the only meal offered, but there are many Weinstuben and restaurants in the area. Fresh flowers add a personalized touch to this well-run establishment. Rates run 82€ to 90€ ($94.30–$104) double and include a buffet breakfast.

The 500-year-old **Ratskeller Würzburg,** Langgasse 1 (© 0931/1-30-21; tram: 1, 2, 3, or 5), part of the Rathaus, is not only an interesting place to visit, but also serves tasty Franconian fare at reasonable prices. Country cookery is an art here, as you'll discover if you order the boiled breast of beef with horseradish sauce and noodles. The English-speaking host will help you with menu selections. Game is featured in season. They also specialize in local beer and

Franconian white wines. Reservations are required Saturday and Sunday. Main courses 6€ to 15€ ($6.90–$17.25).

One of the best dining spots in the region is **Wein- und Fischhaus Schiff-bäuerin** ✦, Katzengasse 7 (© **0931/4-24-87;** tram: 3 or 4), a combined wine house/fish restaurant, across the river in an old half-timbered building on a narrow street, about 1 minute from the old bridge. The house specializes in freshwater fish, such as pike, carp, trout, and eel. Most of these dishes are priced per 100g. Soup specialties are fish, snail, lobster, and French onion. Main courses cost 14€ to 20€ ($16.10–$23) and credit cards are not accepted.

ROTHENBURG OB DER TAUBER ✦✦✦

If you have time for only one town on the Romantic Road, make it Rothenburg, the best-preserved medieval city in Germany. Inside its undamaged 13th-century city walls the old center is seemingly untouched by the passage of time from its heyday as a free imperial city in the 14th century. The only drawback is that Rothenburg, about 32 miles (52km) southeast of Würzburg, suffers from serious overcrowding, in summer.

ESSENTIALS

GETTING THERE   You can reach Rothenburg via a daily train from Frankfurt (trip time: 3 hr.), from Hamburg (trip time: 5½ hr.), or from Berlin (trip time: 7 hr.). Rothenburg lies on the Steinach–Rothenburg rail line, with frequent connections to all major German cities. For information, call © **01805/99-66-33.**

VISITOR INFORMATION   Contact **Stadt Verkehrsamt,** Rathaus (© **09861/40-492).** November to March, it's open Monday to Friday 9am to noon and 1 to 5pm and Saturday 10am to 1pm; April to October, it's open Monday to Friday 9am to 6pm and Saturday 10am to 3pm.

TOP ATTRACTIONS & SPECIAL MOMENTS

For an excellent view, take a walk on the **town ramparts** ✦. The wall tour, from the massive 16th-century Spitaltor (at the end of the Spitalgasse) to the Klingentor, takes about a half hour.

Rothenburg's **Rathaus (Town Hall)** ✦, Marktplatz (© **09861/40-40**), consists of an older Gothic section from 1240 and a newer Renaissance structure facing the square. From the 165-foot tower of the Gothic hall you get a great **view** ✦ of the town below. The new Rathaus, built in 1572 to replace a portion destroyed in the fire, is decorated with intricate friezes and a large stone portico opening onto the square. The octagonal tower at the center of the side facing the square contains a grand staircase leading to the upper hall. The Rathaus is open Monday to Friday from 8am to 6pm; the tower April to October, daily from 9:30am to 12:30pm and 1 to 5pm. Admission to the Rathaus is free; to the tower 1€ ($1.15) for adults, and .50€ (60¢) for children.

The historical collection of Rothenburg is housed at the **Reichsstadtmuseum,** Klosterhof 5 (© **09861/93-90-43;** www.reichsstadtmuseum.rothenburg.de), in a 13th-century Dominican nunnery. The cloisters are well preserved, and you can visit the convent hall, kitchen, and apothecary. The museum collection includes period furniture and art from Rothenburg's more prosperous periods, and a section of archaeological objects from prehistoric times up to the Middle Ages. Among the artistic exhibits is the 1494 *Rothenburg Passion* series, 12 pictures by Martinus Schwartz that depict scenes from the suffering of Christ. An interesting object is a historic tankard that holds more than 6 pints. The museum is open April to October, daily from 10am to 5pm; November to March, daily from 1 to 4pm. Admission is 3€ ($3.45) for adults, and 2€ ($2.30) for children and students.

The choir of the Gothic **St. Jakobskirche (Church of St. Jacob),** Klostergasse 15 (© **09861/7006-20**), dates from 1336. In the west gallery is the **Altar of the Holy Blood** 🟊🟊, a masterpiece by the famous Würzburg sculptor Tilman Riemenschneider (ca. 1460–1531). The work was executed between 1499 and 1505, to provide a worthy setting for its Reliquary of the Holy Blood. This relic, venerated in the Middle Ages, is contained in a rock-crystal capsule set in the reliquary cross (ca. 1270) in the center of the shrine. The church is open April to October, Monday to Friday from 9am to 5:30pm, Sunday from 11am to 5:30pm; December, daily from 9am to 5pm; November and January to March, daily from 10am to noon and 2 to 4pm. Admission is 1.55€ ($1.80) for adults, and .75€ (85¢) for children.

WHERE TO STAY & DINE

The **Goldener Hirsch** 🟊, Untere Schmiedgasse 16–25 (© **09861/70-80**), is one of the leading inns of Rothenburg. It looks a bit more austere than some of the other inns in town and lacks a certain coziness, but it's nevertheless extremely pleasant and well maintained. In spite of the age of the building, the 72 rooms are very modern, with built-in furniture, evoking Scandinavia more than Bavaria. Try for one of the older units, which are larger and furnished in a more Bavarian motif. Rates are 100€–215€ ($115–$247) double and include buffet breakfast.

The 72-room **Hotel Reichs-Küchenmeister** 🟊, Kircheplatz 8 (© **09861/ 97-00;** www.reichskuechenmeister.com), is one of the town's oldest structures and was salvaged from a World War II firestorm through a massive, thoroughly sensitive restoration. It's both stylish and well equipped. Rooms are furnished with regional wooden furniture; some contain minibars. Bathrooms are a bit small, but maintenance is tidy and each comes with a tiled shower. Seventeen rooms are available in the less desirable annex across the street. Rates include a buffet breakfast and cost 75€ to 135€ ($86.25–$155) double; 130€ to 215€ ($150–$247) suite.

The **Baumeisterhaus** 🟊, Obere Schmiedgasse 3 (© **09861/9-47-00**), is housed in an ancient patrician residence, built in 1596. It contains Rothenburg's most beautiful courtyard (you can dine here if you reserve in advance). The patio has colorful murals, serenely draped by vines. Frankly, although the Franconian menu is good, the romantic setting is the main attraction. One of the chef's best dishes is sauerbraten (braised beef marinated in vinegar and served with *Spätzle,* small flour dumplings). The food, for the most part, is the rib-sticking fare beloved by Bavarians. Main courses cost 9€ to 24€ ($10.35–$27.60).

The **Ratsstube,** Marktplatz 6 (© **09861/92411**), enjoys a location right on the market square, one of the most photographed spots in Germany. It's a bustling center of activity throughout the day, beginning when practically every Rothenburger stops by for a cup of morning coffee. Inside, a true tavern atmosphere prevails, with hardwood chairs and tables, vaulted ceilings, and pierced copper lanterns. On the a la carte menu are many Franconian dishes, including sauerbraten and venison, both served with fresh vegetables and potatoes. Main courses cost 10€ to 22€ ($11.50–$25.30).

AUGSBURG

Augsburg's 2,000 years of history (it's one of the country's oldest cities and was founded by the Roman emperor Augustus) have made it one of southern Germany's major sightseeing attractions. The city is especially noteworthy for its picture-perfect Renaissance and baroque architecture. About 42 miles (68km) northwest of Munich, it's the Romantic Road's largest town and serves also as a gateway to the Alps and the south. It's also well connected to area rail lines and has especially good connections to Munich, so if you can't travel the entire Romantic Road, you can do it as an easy day trip out of Munich.

GETTING THERE   About 90 Euro and InterCity trains arrive here daily from all major German cities. There are 60 trains a day from Munich (trip time: 30–50 min.), 35 from Frankfurt (trip time: 3–4½ hr.), and 1 train per hour from Würzburg (trip time: 2 hr.). For information, call ℭ **01805/99-66-33.** There are 60 trains a day from Munich (trip time: 30–50 min.) and 35 from Frankfurt (trip time: 3–4½ hr.). The main station is ⅔ mile (1km) west of the center of town; you can walk into town or take the bus (see below).

VISITOR INFORMATION   Contact **Tourist-Information,** Bahnhafstrasse 7 (ℭ **0821/50-20-70**), open October 15 to May, Monday to Friday 9am to 5pm, and Saturday at Rathausplatz, 10am to 2pm. The office is right near the train station.

GETTING AROUND   Public transportation in Augsburg consists of four tram lines and 31 bus lines. They operate from 5am to midnight daily; fare is 1.90€ ($2.20). Once you're in town, however, it's quite easy to get around on foot, so you won't need to spend too much time on trams and buses.

TOP ATTRACTIONS & SPECIAL MOMENTS

Extending southward from the Rathaus is the wide **Maximilianstrasse** ⟨, lined with shops and old burghers' houses and studded with fountains by the Renaissance Dutch sculptor Adrien de Vries.

The cathedral of Augsburg, **Dom St. Maria,** Hoher Weg (ℭ **0821/316-63-53;** tram: 2), contains the oldest stained-glass windows in the world. These Romanesque windows, dating from the 12th century, are in the south transept and depict Old Testament prophets in a severe but colorful style. They are younger than the cathedral, which was begun in 944. The 11th-century bronze doors, leading into the three-aisle nave, are adorned with bas-reliefs of a mixture of biblical and mythological characters. The cathedral is open Monday to Saturday from 7am to 6pm; Sunday from 9:30am to 6pm. Admission is free.

Jakob Fugger, a scion of the powerful Fugger banking family, set up the **Fuggerei,** Vorderer Lech (ℭ **0821/31-98-810;** www.fuggerei.de; tram: 1), in 1519 to house poorer Augsburgers. A nominal annual rent of 1€ ($1.15, formerly one Rhenish guilder) has not changed in more than 450 years. The only obligation is that tenants pray daily for the souls of their founders. The Fuggerei is a miniature, self-contained town with its own gates, which are shut from 10pm to 5am and guarded by a night watchman. A house at Mittlere Gasse 13 is now the Fuggerei's museum. The rough 16th- and 17th-century furniture, wood-paneled ceilings and walls, and cast-iron stove, and other objects of everyday life, show what it was like to live here in earlier times. The museum is open March to December daily from 9am to 6pm. Admission is 1€ ($1.15) for adults, and .50€ (60¢) for students and children.

The **Schaezlerpalais,** Maximilianstrasse 46 (℗ **0821/3244102;** tram: 1), a 60-room mansion facing the Hercules Fountain and constructed between 1765 and 1770, contains an amazing art collection. Most of the works are by German artists of the Renaissance and baroque periods, including Hans Holbein the Elder and Hans Burgkmair. Albrecht Dürer's famous portrait of Jakob Fugger is here. Rubens, Veronese, Tiepolo, and others are also represented. The palace contains a rococo ballroom, with gilded and mirrored wall panels and a ceiling fresco, *The Four Continents.* The gallery is open Wednesday to Sunday from 10am to 5pm. Admission is 3€ ($3.45) for adults, and 1.50€ ($1.75) for children over 10 and students.

Napoléon visited the Augsburg **Rathaus (Town Hall),** Am Rathausplatz 2 (℗ **0821/324-9180;** tram: 1 or 2), built by Elias Holl in 1620. After a costly restoration following World War II damage, the public can again visit the Rathaus on walking tours that offer a view of the "golden chamber" and other rooms. The building is open daily from 10am to 6pm. Admission is 1.55€ ($1.80) for adults, .75€ (85¢) for children ages 7 to 14, and free for children under 7.

WHERE TO STAY & DINE

The 15th-century half-timbered structure of the appealing **Dom Hotel,** Frauentorstrasse 8 (℗ **0821/34-39-30;** www.domhotel-augsburg.de; tram: 2), rises imposingly beside Augsburg's famous cathedral. You don't get a lot of style, but you do get comfort—and a pool. Rooms on most floors are medium in size and nicely appointed. In the smaller attic accommodations you can rest under a beamed ceiling and enjoy a panoramic sweep of the rooftops of the city. Each of the 43 rooms comes with a neatly tiled shower-only bathroom. Rates run 73€ to 117€ ($83.95–$135) double, and include a buffet breakfast.

The Romantik Hotel Augsburger Hof ⭐, Auf dem Kreuz 2 (℗ **0821/34-30-50;** tram: 2), is a favorite for its traditional and romantic atmosphere. The 36-room hotel was originally built in 1767 in a solid, thick-walled design with exposed beams and timbers. Rooms are completely up-to-date but not as romantic as the hotel's name suggests. They range from small to spacious. Some bathrooms seem crowded in as an afterthought, but each is beautifully maintained and contains a shower. Some rooms overlook the tranquil inner courtyard. Rooms cost 90€ to 133€ ($104–$153) double, and include a buffet breakfast.

Die Ecke ⭐, Elias-Holl-Platz 2 (℗ **0821/51-06-00;** tram: 2), is the town's finest dining choice. This restaurant's guests have included Hans Holbein the Elder, Wolfgang Amadeus Mozart, and, in more contemporary times, Rudolf Diesel, of engine fame, and Bertolt Brecht. The Weinstube ambience belies the skilled cuisine of the chef. Breast of duckling might be preceded by a pâté or pheasant. The filet of sole in Riesling is a classic, and venison dishes in season, a specialty, are the best in town. Reservations are a must. Main courses cost 15€ to 30€ ($17.25–$34.50); a fixed-price dinner is 40€ ($46) for four courses, 60€ (70¢) for 6 courses.

The affordable **Fuggerei Stube,** Jakoberstrasse 26 (℗ **0821/3-08-70**), can fit 60 persons at a time into its large, *gemütlich* dining room. Expect generous portions of well-prepared German food such as sauerbraten, pork schnitzel, game, and fish dishes. The beer foaming out of the taps here is Storchenbräu; most visitors find that it goes wonderfully with the conservative German specialties that are this establishment's forte. Main courses cost 8.50€ to 18€ ($9.80–$20.70); a fixed-price menu 22€ ($25.30).

FÜSSEN ✿

Füssen, in the foothills of the Bavarian Alps and 74 miles (119km) southwest of Munich, is the end of the Romantic Road. The town is mainly a base for those going on to the castles at Neuschwanstein and Hohenschwangau, but it has a number of attractive buildings, including a 15th-century castle once used by the bishops of Augsburg as a summer palace. Füssen is also ideally located for excursions into the surrounding countryside.

ESSENTIALS

GETTING THERE   Trains from Munich and Augsburg arrive frequently throughout the day. For information, call ✆ **01805/99-66-33.** Train time from Munich is 2½ hours; from Frankfurt, 6 to 7 hours. The train station is just north of the town center.

VISITOR INFORMATION   Contact the **Füssen-Tourismus,** Kaiser-Maximilian-Platz 1 (✆ **08362/93-85-0**). Hours vary but are usually summer Monday to Friday 8:30am to 6:30pm and Saturday 9am to 2:30pm; and winter Monday to Friday 9am to 5pm and Saturday 10am to noon. The office is just east of the train station, along Bahnhofstrasse and across Augsburgerstrasse.

TOP ATTRACTIONS & SPECIAL MOMENTS

Füssen's main attraction is the **Hohes Schloss,** Magnusplatz (✆ **08362/90-31-64**), one of the finest late-Gothic castles in Bavaria. It was once the summer residence of the prince-bishops of Augsburg. Inside you can visit the Rittersaal or "Knight's Hall," known for its stunning coffered ceiling. There's also a collection of Swabian art work from the 1400s to the 1700s. The castle is open April to November Tuesday to Sunday 11am to 4pm and December to March 2pm to 4pm, and charges 2.55€ ($2.95) for admission, free for children under 14.

Immediately below the castle lies the 8th-century **St. Mangkirche** and its **abbey** (✆ **08362/48-44**), which was founded by the Benedictines and grew up on the site where St. Magnus died in 750. In the 18th century it was reconstructed in the baroque style, and in 1803 it was secularized. Free tours of the abbey are given July to September on Tuesday and Thursday at 4pm and on Saturday at 10:30am; May, June, and October on Tuesday at 4pm and Saturday at 9:30am; and January to April on Saturday at 10:30am.

WHERE TO STAY & DINE

The hotel staff at **Christine,** Weidachstrasse 31 (tel] **08362/72-29;** fax 08362/94-05-54), spends the winter months refurbishing the rooms so they'll be sparkling for spring visitors. Breakfast, the only meal served, is presented on beautiful regional china as classical music plays in the background. A Bavarian charm pervades the hotel, and the 13 small- to medium-size rooms are very cozy, though hardly fit for King Ludwig were he to return. The shower-only bathrooms are a bit cramped. Rates include a continental breakfast and run 95€ to 130€ ($109–$150) double. Credit cards are not accepted. To get here from the train station, go past the tourist office and continue on Sebastianstrasse to Schwedenstrasse, where you turn left and keep going into Weidachstrasse.

A conservative yet flavorful blend of Swabian and Bavarian specialties is served to the loyal clients of the small, attractively old-fashioned **Zum Schwanen,** Brotmarkt 4 (✆ **08362/61-74**). Specialties include homemade sausage, roast pork, lamb, and venison. Service is always helpful and attentive, and you get good value here, along with generous portions. Main courses cost 6€ to 15€ ($6.90–$17.25). Reservations are required.

TWO NEARBY CASTLES

Just 2 miles (3km) east of Füssen are the two "Royal Castles" of Hohenschwangau and Neuschwanstein, among the finest in Germany. Hohenschwangau, the more sedate of the two, was built by Maximilian II in 1836; Neuschwanstein was the brainchild of his son, "Mad" King Ludwig II. Ten buses a day travel to the castles from Füssen's train station. The bus fare is 2.90€ ($3.35) round-trip. Be prepared for very long lines (sometimes up to an incredible 4 or 5 hr.) at the castles in the summer, especially in August.

Not as glamorous or spectacular as Neuschwanstein, neo-Gothic **Hohenschwangau Castle** ⟨★⟩, Alpseestrasse, Hohenschwangau (© **08362/8-11-27**), has a richer history. The original structure dates from the days of the 12th-century knights of Schwangau. When the knights faded away, the castle began to fade, too. When Ludwig II's father, Crown Prince Maximilian (later Maximilian II), saw the castle in 1832, he purchased it and in 4 years had it completely restored. The rooms are styled and furnished in a heavier Gothic mode than those in Neuschwanstein. Among the most attractive chambers is the **Hall of the Swan Knight,** named for the wall paintings depicting the saga of Lohengrin.

Hohenschwangau, Alpseestrasse (© **08362/8-11-27**), is open March 15 to October 15, daily 8:30am to 5:30pm; October 16 to March 14, daily 9:30am to 4pm. Admission is 8€ ($9.20) for adults and 7€ ($8.05) for students and children 6 to 15; children under 6 enter free.

Construction of King Ludwig II's fairy-tale castle, **Neuschwanstein** ⟨★★★⟩, lasted 17 years until the king's death, when all work stopped. The **study,** like most of the rooms, is decorated with wall paintings showing scenes from Nordic legends. The only fabric in the room is hand-embroidered silk, used in curtains and chair coverings, all designed with the gold-and-silver Bavarian coat of arms. From the vestibule, you enter the **throne room.** This Byzantine-style hall was never completed. The floor is a mosaic, depicting the animals of the world. The circular apse where the king's throne was to have stood is reached by a stairway of white Carrara marble.

The **king's bedroom** took 4½ years to complete. The walls are decorated with panels carved to look like Gothic windows, and with a mural depicting the legend of Tristan and Isolde. The ornate bed is on a raised platform with an elaborately carved canopy. On the fourth floor is the **Singer's Hall,** decorated with marble columns and elaborately painted designs interspersed with frescoes depicting the life of Parsifal.

The castle, located at Neuschwansteinstrasse 20 (© **08362/8-10-35**), is open year-round. In September, visitors have the additional treat of hearing Wagnerian concerts along with other music in the Singer's Hall. For information and reservations, contact the tourist office, **Verkehrsamt,** at the Rathaus in Schwangau (© **08362/93-85-23**). Tickets go on sale in early June, and sell out rather quickly. The castle can only be visited on one of the guided tours (offered in English), which are given year-round, except November 1; December 24, 25, and 31; January 1; and Shrove Tuesday. April to September, tours are given 9am to 6pm; October to March, 10am to 4pm. Admission is 8€ ($9.20) for adults, 7€ ($8.05) for students and seniors over 65, and free for children 14 and under.

Reaching Neuschwanstein involves a steep ½-mile (1km) climb from Hohenschwangau Castle. This can be a 25-minute walk for the athletic, an eternity for those less so. To cut down on the climb, you can take a bus to Marienbrücke, a bridge that crosses over the Pöllat Gorge at a height of 305 feet. From that vantage point, you, like Ludwig, can stand and meditate on the glories of the castle and its panoramic surroundings. If you want to photograph the castle, don't wait until you reach the top, where you'll be too close for a good shot. It costs 2.05€ ($2.35) for the bus ride up to the bridge or 1€ ($1.15) if you'd like to take the bus back down the hill. From Marienbrücke, it's a 10-minute walk to Neuschwanstein castle. This footpath is very steep.

The most traditional way to reach Neuschwanstein is by horse-drawn carriage; this costs 5.50€ ($6.35) for the ascent and 3€ ($3.45) for the descent. Some readers have complained about the rides being overcrowded and not at all accessible for visitors with disabilities.

7 More Highlights of Germany

Germany has no shortage of historic towns and other places of interest. The following are just three of the many that would justify a closer look. We chose these three specifically because of their unique character. Bayreuth is a baroque city renowned for its connections to the composer Wagner; Heidelberg is a quintessential university town with buildings that date back to its founding in the Middle Ages; and Lubeck, the former capital of the Hanseatic League, still has the artistic and architectural treasures it accumulated during its years as a center for trade. All three of these cities are also known for their excellent train connections, making them easily accessible to the rail traveler.

BAYREUTH ⚜

Bayreuth lies in a wide valley on the upper basin of the Roter Main River, 143 miles (230km) north of Munich, in the Franconia region of Germany. It is forever associated with the memory of **Richard Wagner** (1813–83). The town is worth a visit for its baroque and rococo architectural treasures even if you're not interested in its favorite son, but most people come here because it's the premier location for Wagnerian performances in the world. Bayreuth is Valhalla to Wagner enthusiasts.

ESSENTIALS

GETTING THERE   **Bayreuth Hauptbahnhof** is on the main Nürnberg–Bayreuth and the Bayreuth–Weiden rail lines. Express trains arrive from Berlin (trip time: 5½–6 hr.) every hour or 2, and from Munich (trip time: 3 hr.) every hour. For rail information and schedules, call ✆ **1-94-19.** The train station is just north of the city center, which you can reach by walking for a few minutes along Bahnhofstrasse and Luitpoldplatz.

VISITOR INFORMATION   Contact **Tourist-Information,** Luitpoldplatz 9 (✆ **0921/885-88;** www.bayreuth-tourismus.de), Monday to Friday 9am to 6pm and Saturday 9:30am to 1pm. The office is only a few minutes' walk from the train station.

GETTING AROUND   Many streets within the historic core of Bayreuth are exclusively reserved for pedestrians, and that, coupled with the city's small size, makes walking between points of interest both easy and efficient. The centerpiece of the old town is the Marktplatz, from which bus nos. 1, 7, 8, 9, and 16 make frequent runs to and from Bayreuth's modern neighborhoods around the Hauptbahnhof. One-way bus fare is 1.50€ ($1.75).

THE BAYREUTHER FESTSPIELE

The town's claim to fame is that it's the site of the Richard Wagner opera festival, which takes place between mid-July and the end of August. If you arrive in

Bayreuth then, you may think that the whole town has turned out to pay homage to the great composer, who built his opera house here, lived here, and was buried here following his death in Venice.

Visitors should know that tickets to the festival operas are almost impossible to obtain (there's a 5-year waiting list) but can sometimes be booked as part of a package tour (see chapter 2). Tickets cost 50€ to 200€ ($57.50–$230). *Warning:* During the 5 weeks of the festival, hoteliers raise their rates quite a bit. Always firmly establish the rate before booking a room, and make reservations far in advance.

TOP ATTRACTIONS & SPECIAL MOMENTS

Wagner's operas are performed at the **Festspielhaus,** Am Festspielhügel 2–3 (© **0921/7-87-80;** bus: 2), at the northern edge of town. The theater, designed by the composer himself, is not beautiful, but it's an ideal Wagnerian facility, with a huge stage capable of swallowing up Valhalla, and excellent, beautifully balanced acoustics throughout the auditorium. The festival was opened here in 1876 with the epic *Ring* cycle. Guided tours are available only in German and are not offered during rehearsals and at festival time. Tours are given April to September, Tuesday through Sunday at 10, 10:45am, 2:15, and 3pm; October and December to March, Tuesday to Sunday at 10:45am and 2:30pm. Tours are 2.50€ ($2.90).

Wagner's residence from 1874 until his death in 1883 is now the **Richard-Wagner-Museum (Wahnfried),** Richard-Wagner-Strasse 48 (© **0921/757-28-16;** www.wagnermuseum.de; bus: 2), south of the town center. Only the front of the original Wahnfried—which means "illusory peace"—remains intact. On display is a wide range of Wagner memorabilia, including manuscripts, pianos, furnishings, artifacts, and even a death mask. If you walk to the end of the garden, fronting the rotunda, you'll see the graves of the composer and his wife. The museum is open April through October, daily from 9am to 5pm (to 8pm Tues and Thurs); November through March, daily from 10am to 5pm (to 8pm Thurs). Admission is 4€ ($4.60), and 4.50€ ($5.20) at festival time.

Wagner's father-in-law was Franz Liszt (1811–86), the Hungarian-born composer and piano virtuoso, who is buried in Bayreuth cemetery. His daughter, Cosima, married Wagner. The **Franz-Liszt-Museum,** Wahnfriedstrasse 9 (© **0921/5-5-16-64-88;** bus: 2), shows the room where the composer died and displays memorabilia related to his life and work. The museum is open September through June, daily from 10am to noon and 2 to 5pm; July through August, daily from 10am to 5pm. Admission is 1.60€ ($1.85).

WHERE TO STAY & DINE

Right in front of the train station, the **Bayerischer Hof,** Bahnhofstrasse 14 (© **0921/7-86-00;** www.bayerischer-hof.de), offers a convenient location, some of the best service in town, and a pool. The hotel's 50 bedrooms range from mid-size to spacious and are furnished with both modern and traditional pieces, usually reproductions of antiques. Each bedroom comes with a tiled, compact shower-only bathroom. The hotel's three fine restaurants offer both French and Franconian cooking. Rates include a buffet breakfast and run 89€ to 155€ ($102–$178) double; 240€ ($276) suite.

HEIDELBERG ✦✦✦

Heidelberg, 55 miles (88km) south of Frankfurt, on the Neckar River is one of the few German cities that was not leveled by air raids in World War II, and therefore still has original buildings from the later Middle Ages and early Renaissance. It is, above all, a university town and has been since 1386. Students make up much of the population of the city. The colorful atmosphere that university life imparts to the town is felt especially in the old student quarter, with its narrow streets and lively inns.

ESSENTIALS

GETTING THERE   Heidelberg's **Hauptbahnhof** is an important railroad station, lying on the Mannheim line, with frequent service to both regional towns and major cities. From Frankfurt, 40 trains arrive per day (trip time: 1 hr.); travel time to and from Munich is about 3½ hours. For information, call ⓒ **01805/99-66-33.** The station is 1⅔ miles (2.7km) southwest of the old heart of town; take the bus to get to the town center (see "Getting Around," below).

VISITOR INFORMATION   Contact **Tourist-Information,** Pavillon am Hauptbahnhof (ⓒ **06221/1-94-33**), right next to the train station. It's open Monday to Saturday 9am to 7pm and Sunday 10am to 6pm. Here visitors can purchase a Heidelberg Card, which provides discounts on attractions and free use of public transportation. It costs 12€ ($13.80) for an adult for up to 2 days.

GETTING AROUND   Heidelberg is crisscrossed with a network of trams and buses, many of which intersect at the Bismarckplatz in the town center. Bus nos. 41 and 42 travel at frequent intervals between the railway station and the Universitätsplatz. The Altstadt stretches on either side of the Hauptstrasse between the Bismarckplatz and the Universitätsplatz. Bus or tram fares cost 1.90€ ($2.20) for a single ride, although a 24-hour pass, valid for up to five persons traveling within a group, costs 6€ ($6.90).

TOP ATTRACTIONS & SPECIAL MOMENTS

You can reach the huge red-sandstone **Heidelberg Castle** (ⓒ **06221/53-84-31**), set amid woodlands and terraced gardens, by a 2-minute cable-car ride, or by foot (it's a very steep climb, though). The cable car leaves from the platform near the Kornmarkt and costs round-trip 3.50€ ($4.05) for adults and 2.50€ ($2.90) for children. The Klingentor, the much easier walk, takes about 20 minutes.

The castle is a dignified ruin, but is still one of the finest Gothic-Renaissance castles in Germany. Entering at the main gate, you first come upon the huge **Gun Park** to your left, from which you can gaze down upon Heidelberg and the

---

Moments Boating in the Neckar

Heidelberg is a good point from which to explore the romantic Neckar Valley. From April to early October, you can take a boat tour along the river as far as Neckarsteinach. There are usually four or five round-trips daily, and you need not return on the same boat. Boats are operated by the **Rhein-Neckar-Fahrgastschiffahrt GmbH,** Stadthalle, Heidelberg (ⓒ **06221/ 2-01-81**). Trips between Heidelberg and Neckarsteinach cost 9.50€ ($10.95) round-trip, and those between Heidelberg and Hirschhorn (which operate June 17–Sept 30) cost 13€ ($14.95) round-trip. You can order drinks or snacks on the boat. Some of the people operating the boats are descended from the Neckar fishers who helped Mark Twain when he rafted down from Hirschhorn. The same families have been working the Neckar since the early 1600s.

Neckar Valley. Along the north side of the courtyard stretches the stern **Palace of Friedrich IV** ★★, erected from 1601 to 1607. The palace is less damaged than other parts of the castle, and its rooms, including the gallery of princes and kings of the German empire, have been almost completely restored.

At the west end of the terrace, in the castle cellars, is the late-16th-century **Wine Vat Building** ★, worth a visit for a look at the **Great Cask.** This huge barrel-like monstrosity, built in 1751, is capable of holding more than 55,000 gallons of wine. To the east, connecting the palace of Friedrich IV to the **Ottheinrich Building,** itself an outstanding example of German Renaissance architecture, is the **Hall of Mirrors Building,** constructed in 1549, a Renaissance masterpiece. Only the shell of the original building remains, enough to give you an idea of its former glory.

A 1-hour guided tour of the castle costs 3.50€ ($4.05) for adults and 1.70€ ($1.95) for children. Tours are frequent, especially in summer. Admission to the grounds is free; admission to the entrance courtyard and Great Cask is 2.50€ ($2.90) for adults, 1.20€ ($1.40) for children. It's open daily from 8am to 6pm.

All the important sights of Heidelberg lie on or near the south bank of the Neckar. However, you should cross to the north side of the river (via the 18th-c. Karl Theodore Bridge) for the best overall view.

In the town itself, a tour of the main attractions begins with **Marktplatz** in front of the Rathaus. On market days, the square is filled with stalls of fresh flowers, fish, and vegetables. At the opposite end of the square is the late-Gothic **Heiliggeistkirche,** built around 1400, the largest Gothic church in the Palatinate.

Housed in a baroque palace, the **Kurpfälzisches Museum (Museum of the Palatinate),** Hauptstrasse 97 (© **06221/58-34-02;** bus: 11, 12, 35, or 42), contains a large collection of painting and sculpture from 6 centuries. Notable is the Riemenschneider Altar from Windsheim (1509), showing Christ and the 12 Apostles. There's also an archaeological collection with a cast of the jawbone of the 500,000-year-old Heidelberg Man and a section on the history of the Palatinate. The museum is open Tuesday and Thursday to Sunday from 9am to 5pm, and Wednesday from 10am to 8pm. Admission is 2.50€ ($2.90) adults, 1.50€ ($1.75) children under 18.

WHERE TO STAY & DINE

The grand **Parkhotel Atlantic** ★, Schloss-Wolfsbrunnen-Weg 23 (© **06221/ 60-42-0;** www.parkhotel-atlantic.de), on the wooded outskirts of Heidelberg, near the castle, offers modern comfort in annexes built around the core of an older villa. Visitors are assured calm and comfort. This hotel's setting makes it the best in its price range; hotels in the city center, unless soundproofed, get a lot of traffic noise. The 24 guest rooms are decorated in 1965-ish modern style but are quite comfortable. A double costs 95€ to 145€ ($109–$167); the rates include a buffet breakfast

A glorious old inn right out of the German Renaissance, the **Zum Ritter St. Georg** ★, Hauptstrasse 178 (© **06221/13-50;** www.ritter-heidelberg.de; bus: 10, 11, or 12), is a well-preserved rarity, although it's not entirely notable for comfort and antique charm. Built in 1592 by Frenchman Charles Bèlier, it's now listed among the major sightseeing attractions of this university town. There are no public lounges. Many of the 40 rooms are somewhat cramped, but the beds are most comfortable and the bathrooms have been refurbished. Rates include a buffet breakfast and cost 160€ to 220€ ($184–$253) double; 260€ ($299) suite.

No other place in Heidelberg captures bygone days quite like the **Mensur-stube** ✿, in the Hotel Hirschgasse, Hirschgasse 3 (✆ **06221/454165;** bus: 34). In this rustic and cozy spot, you sit at tables more than 2 centuries old—you can still see where Bismarck and others carved their names. Swords hang from the ceiling—in the past, when dueling was the regular sport of the student fraternities, duels were fought in what is now the dining room. Traditional recipes are served, from a limited menu. Main courses run 18€ to 21€ ($20.70–$24.15).

The **Zum Ritter St. Georg** ✿, Hauptstrasse 178 (✆ **06221/1-35-0;** bus: 10, 11, or 12), is located in one of Heidelberg's most famous Renaissance buildings and is popular with both students and professors, who know that they can get good German cooking here. You dine in the elegant Great Hall (the Ritterstube), with its sepia ceilings, wainscoting, and Oriental rugs; the equally classy Belier, with wood paneling and fresh flowers; or in the smaller Councillors' Chamber (Ratsherrenstube), which is less formal. The house specialty is saddle of Odenwald venison for two (in season). Main courses cost 10.50€ to 21.50€ ($12.10–$24.75); fixed-price menus 14€ to 35€ ($16.10–$40.25).

LÜBECK ✿✿✿

Lübeck, 41 miles (66km) north of Hamburg, was made a free imperial city in 1226. From the 13th century on, it was the capital of the Hanseatic League, the association of merchants that controlled trade along the Baltic as far as Russia. Today Lübeck is a city of high-gabled houses, massive gates, and strong towers. The Hanseatic merchants decorated their churches with art treasures and gilded the spires to show off their wealth. Many of these survivors of nearly 900 years of history still stand.

Many travelers from North America may not have heard of this city, yet it's almost as historic and pretty as Belgium's famed Bruges (see "Bruges," in chapter 3) and is also a UNESCO World Heritage Site. It's got a kind of relaxed charm that's sort of un-German and impressed us immensely. Head here and you'll avoid the tourist rush that many of Germany's other small towns are plagued with. It's a real find and a wonderful place for a short rail visit, as it has excellent rail connections to many of Germany's major cities.

ESSENTIALS

GETTING THERE The **Lübeck Hauptbahnhof** lies on major rail lines linking Denmark and Hamburg, and on the Hamburg-Lüneburg-Lübeck-Kiel-Flensburg and Lübeck-Rostock-Stralsund lines, with frequent connections. From Hamburg, 40 trains arrive daily (trip time: 40 min.), 7 from Berlin (trip time: 4 hr. 40 min.). For information, call ✆ **01805/99-66-33.** The station is ¾ mile (1.2km) west of the city center; to get into town, take a bus from the station. The fare is 2€ ($2.30).

VISITOR INFORMATION For tourist information, contact **Travemünde Tourismus,** Breitestrasse 62 (✆ **0451/1-22-54-19;** www.luebeck-tourism.de), in a pedestrian mall in the heart of town. The office is open Monday to Friday 9:30am to 6pm and Saturday and Sunday 10am to 2pm. Hours are usually extended in summer, and the office is open then on Sundays from 10am to 2pm.

TOP ATTRACTIONS & SPECIAL MOMENTS

Lübeck's **Altstadt** ✿✿✿ is surrounded by the Trave River and its connecting canals, giving it an islandlike appearance. It's estimated that within an area of 2 square miles (5 sq. km) around the Marktplatz stand 1,000 medieval houses. Nearby is **Petersgrube,** the finest street in Lübeck, lined with restored houses. A walk through the old streets of Lübeck reveals a continuing use of brick (the city insisted on this after fires in the 13th c.). The effect is one of unity among all the houses, churches, shops, and guildhalls.

Just across the west bridge from the Altstadt, the **Holstentor (Holsten Gate)** ⭐⭐ is the first monument to greet visitors emerging from the train station. At one time it was the main town entrance, built in the 15th century as much to awe visitors with the power and prestige of Lübeck as to defend it against intruders. To the outside world, the towers look simple and defiant, rather like part of a great palace. But on the city side, they contain a wealth of decoration, with windows, arcades, and rich terra-cotta friezes. Within the gate is the **Museum Holstentor** (℡ 0451/1-22-41-29), housing a model of Lübeck as it appeared in the mid–17th century. The museum is open Tuesday to Sunday 10am to 5pm (to 4pm in winter). Admission is 4€ ($4.60) for adults and .50€ (60¢) for children 17 and under.

The **Rathaus** ⭐, Rathausplatz (℡ 0451/1221005), traces its origins from 1230. It has been rebuilt several times, but there are remains of the original structure in the vaulting and Romanesque pillars in the cellar and the Gothic south wall. The towering walls have been made with open-air medallions to relieve the pressure on the Gothic-arcaded ground floor and foundations. Tours are Monday to Friday at 11am, noon, and 3pm, costing 2.60€ ($3) for adults and 1.50€ ($1.75) for children.

Across Marktplatz from the Rathaus, the **Marienkirche (St. Mary's Church:** ℡ **0451/30-77-00)**, is the most outstanding church in Lübeck, possibly in northern Germany. Built on the highest point in the Altstadt, it has flying buttresses and towering windows that leave the rest of the city's rooftops at its feet. Organ concerts take place during the summer months, carrying on the tradition established by St. Mary's best-known organist and composer, Dietrich Buxtehude (1668–1707).

On Breitestrasse, is one of the last of the elaborate guild houses of Hanseatic Lübeck, the **Haus der Schiffergesellschaft (Seamen's Guild House)** ⭐, built in 1535 in Renaissance style, with stepped gables and High Gothic blind windows. It's worth seeing just for the medieval furnishings and the beamed ceilings in the main hall, now a restaurant.

WHERE TO STAY & DINE

Ringhotel Jensen, An der Obertrave 4–5 (℡ 0451/70-24-90; www.ringhotel-jensen.de), is one of Lübeck's best moderately priced hotels, a good value if your expectations aren't too high. The 42 small to medium rooms are modestly furnished in modern style and were recently renovated and had their plumbing upgraded. Some have fine views of the Hanseatic architecture across the canal. The buffet breakfast is served in a delightful room with picture windows overlooking the canal. Rates run 98€ to 108€ ($113–$124) double; from 164€ ($189) suite. Rates include buffet breakfast.

The Kaiserhof ⭐, Kronsforder Allee 11–13 (℡ 0451/70-33-01; www.kaiserhof-luebeck.de; bus: 2, 7, 10, 16, or 32), could probably demand a higher price for its rooms. Two former patrician town houses outside the city center on a tree-lined boulevard have been remodeled into this hotel. The owner has created a fashionable yet homelike environment, with a pool. The 60 guest rooms come in various shapes and sizes and are individually furnished, with compact bathrooms. Some overflow guests are housed in a more sterile but still quite comfortable annex. Rates include buffet breakfast and run 89€ to 121€ ($102–139) double; 194€ to 250€ ($223–$288) suite. Rates include buffet breakfast.

A classic example of Hanseatic architecture on a medieval street, **Das Schabbelhaus** ✧✧, Mengstrasse 48–52 (© **0451/7-20-11;** bus: 5, 7, 11, 12, 14, or 16), is installed in two patrician buildings from the 16th and 17th centuries. A wooden staircase and balcony lead to two rooms devoted to author Thomas Mann memorabilia. In the restaurant, ceiling-high studio windows overlook the small gardens. It's easy to get the impression that the setting competes with the food, but that's not entirely true as the Northern German and Italian dishes served here are prepared quite skillfully. Main courses cost 14€ to 22€ ($16.10–$25.30); fixed-price 4-course menu 39€ ($44.85); menu for two including wine 96€ ($110).

Entering **Haus der Schiffergesellschaft** ✧, Breite Strasse 2 (© **0451/7-67-76;** bus: 1 or 2), with ship models hanging from the ceiling and other nautical memorabilia, is like going inside a museum of Hanseatic architecture. The restaurant, which dates back to 1535, was once patronized exclusively by sailors. Today, good food (and lots of it) is served on scrubbed-oak plank tables with high-backed wooden booths carved with the coats of arms of Baltic merchants. Often, you must share a table. Many northern regional dishes are offered. Main courses cost 9.50€ to 26€ ($10.95–$29.90). Reservations are required and credit cards are not accepted.

10

Great Britain

Great Britain is made up of England, Scotland, and Wales, three ancient kingdoms that are today part of the United Kingdom. Although it's the largest island in western Europe, sea-girt Great Britain is a relatively small country, covering some 88,150 square miles (228,300 sq. km). Thanks to its history, landscape, and overall appeal, it consistently ranks among the top destinations for travelers the world over.

HIGHLIGHTS OF GREAT BRITAIN

You could spend weeks exploring this fascinating country and still have plenty more to see. Mighty castles, stately homes, magnificent gardens, soaring cathedrals, romantic landscapes, and historic cities are flung across the far corners of Great Britain like so many jewels. But if time is an issue, you couldn't do any better than to limit yourself to London and Edinburgh, the great capital cities of England and Scotland. **London** is a dizzying delight, full of pomp and pedigree, a place where high culture and cutting-edge trends feed off one another. London is sedate and raucous, a time-tested background for legendary sites that hark back to the earliest days of the kingdom. **Edinburgh,** crowned by its famous castle, is just as royal as London, and far more dramatically situated, but it's much smaller and easier to digest in a short period. With its unique combination of medieval and neoclassical towns, Edinburgh invites exploration. Scotland's greatest national museums and collections are concentrated here. The town is suffused with creative energy that blossoms during the famed Edinburgh International Festival.

1 Essentials

GETTING THERE

The main international airports serving the U.K. are Heathrow and Gatwick, both near London.

Heathrow   Heathrow (© **020/8759-4321;** www.baa.co.uk), the main international airport, is 15 miles (24km) west of Central London. It's served by **Air Canada** (© **888/247-2262;** www.aircanada.ca), **American Airlines** (© **800/ 433-7300;** www.aa.com), **British Airways** (© **800/AIRWAYS;** www.british airways.com), **Continental Airlines** (© **800/231-0856;** www.continental. com), **Icelandair** (© **800/223-5500** in the U.S.; www.icelandair.com), **United Airlines** (© **800/538-2929;** www.united.com), and **Virgin Atlantic Airways** (© **800/862-8621;** www.virgin-atlantic.com).

The vast majority of flights from North America, Australia, and New Zealand arrive at Terminals 3 and 4. The London Tourist Board has a **Tourist Information Centre** in the Tube station concourse that connects with **Terminals 1, 2, and 3,** open daily from 8am to 6pm (to 7pm Mon–Sat June–Sept). There are **British Hotel Reservation Centre** desks (© **020/7340-1616;** www.bhrc.co.uk) in the arrivals area of every terminal, open daily.

(Moments   Festivals & Special Events

On the Saturday closest to her official birthday in mid-June, Elizabeth II inspects her regiments from an open carriage and receives the salute during the **Trooping the Colour.** It's quintessential English pageantry and draws big crowds—many of them waiting to see a wretched young soldier faint in the heat under his ridiculous bearskin hat. Tickets are free and are allocated by ballot. Apply in writing between January and the end of February, enclosing an International Reply Coupon (available at most post offices) to: The Ticket Office, HQ Household Division, Chelsea Barracks, London SW1H 8RF. Canadians should apply to Royal Events Secretary, Canada House, Trafalgar Square, London SW1Y 5BJ.

The Henry Wood Promenade Concerts, the famous summer musical season at London's Royal Albert Hall, dates back to 1895. It runs the gamut from ancient to modern classics, and jazz, too. It's only £3 ($4.80) to rough it with the promenaders on the floor of the hall (© **020/ 7589-8212;** www.royalalberthall.com or www.bbc.co.uk/proms). The season runs from mid-July to mid-September.

The Edinburgh International Festival is the highlight of the Edinburgh year and turns the city into a non-stop celebration. The festival attracts artists and companies of the highest international standard in all fields of the arts, including music, opera, dance, theater, poetry, and prose. One of the festival's most exciting spectacles is the **Military Tattoo** on the floodlit esplanade in front of Edinburgh Castle, high on its rock above the city. The city is jammed during this period, and it's essential to book a hotel in advance. For more details on the festival, see "The Edinburgh Festival: Art & Tattoos" on p. 427.

Gatwick   Gatwick (© **08700/002468;** www.baa.co.uk) is a smaller airport about 25 miles (40km) south of London. It's served by American, British Airways, Delta, Continental, Northwest, Qantas, and Virgin Atlantic.

BRITAIN BY TRAIN

It used to be that to get to London from the continent by train, involved at least one ferry transfer, but no longer. With the 1994 opening of the Chunnel, running underneath the English Channel from England to France, one can now get to London with relative ease. The wonderful **Eurostar** (www.eurostar.com) train offers direct service from Paris's Gare Du Nord (trip time 2½ hr.) and Brussels' Central Station (trip time 2¼ hr.) to Waterloo International in London in just 3 hours, making London (or Paris) an easy day-trip destination for those wanting to add another European city to their itineraries. More than a dozen Eurostar trains travel both to and from the Continent daily. **Rail Europe** (© **877/ 272-RAIL** in the U.S., **800/361-RAIL** in Canada; www.raileurope.com) sells Eurostar tickets, allowing you to combine a trip to London with a rail tour of the Continent. Eurailpass-holders do get a discount when purchasing a Eurostar ticket.

Should you wish to go the slow train route from the Continent to London, you'll need to get off your train in France near the English Channel and take a ferry or hovercraft across the water (sometimes the trains will cross on the ferry).

You'll disembark at one of the U.K channel ports—those closest to London are Dover, Ramsgate, and Folkestone to the east, and Southhampton, Portsmouth, and Newhaven to the south—and from there you'll board a British train for the journey onward to London.

PASSES

The **Eurailpass** is not accepted on British trains. If you're going to be traveling by train around England, Wales, and Scotland—perhaps taking a few train excursions out of London—then consider buying a **BritRail** pass. If you're going to Great Britain in winter, these may be a very economical option as the passes are often discounted if you're traveling November through February. For information on the various BritRail pass options available, including the **BritRail Classic Pass,** the **BritRail Flexipass,** and the **BritRail England Pass,** see chapter 2.

Note that BritRail passes are not for sale in the U.K., so you must obtain them before you leave home. You can purchase BritRail passes on the phone or online through **Rail Europe** (© 877/272-RAIL in the U.S., 800/361-RAIL in Canada; www.raileurope.com); and in person at the **British Travel Shop** next to the VisitBritain office in Manhattan, 551 Fifth Ave., 7th floor, New York, NY (© 212/490-6688).

Note: If you plan only to travel for a day or 2 to Edinburgh out of London, it may be more economical to purchase Rail Europe's Edinburgh Overnight or Daytrip excursion packages instead of a pass. For more information on these, and a host of other rail excursions to locations all over Great Britain, call Rail Europe or check out their website.

SPECIAL TRAIN TERMS

You won't encounter any incomprehensible train terms in England, but there are several ticket types used there that you might be unfamiliar with. These are the fares you'll most likely use on an excursion from London.

Cheap day returns   For round-trip journeys under 50 miles (81km), leaving London after 9:30am. No need to book specific train times. An ordinary **day-return** ticket allows travel during peak times.

Network Away Break   No need to book specific trains, but not available on some peak services. Return journey must be within 5 days.

Super APEX   Selected services only, off-peak. Must be bought 14 days before departure with fixed dates and times for both halves of the journey.

APEX   Selected services only, mostly off-peak. Must be purchased a week in advance with fixed dates and times for departure and return.

Super Advance   Must be bought by 6pm the day before departure with fixed times and dates, mostly off-peak.

Supersaver return   Walk on, but not within the morning (after 9:30am) and evening rush hours. Not available on a Friday.

Standard return   A no-restriction splurge.

PRACTICAL TRAIN INFORMATION

The entire British railway system was privatized under Margaret Thatcher, so there are now 26 companies that operate trains to specific parts of the country. Virgin, Connex, and GNER are three of the major names you might encounter. The sleek high-speed **InterCity** trains that run between London and heavily traveled main-line routes (such as Edinburgh) are the most dependable and the most comfortable. For shorter trips, such as to Brighton and Cambridge, **commuter trains** are used. In some cases you might need to transfer to a **local train** to reach your destination. The local trains connect small towns between larger towns and are very basic. The local stations are small and sometimes (particularly on Sun) there's no one to help with information or ticket sales. You will always find train schedules posted in the local stations, and if there is no window service, you can buy your ticket on the train. There is no smoking on local trains. Smoking is confined to strictly designated areas in the other trains.

An announcement is made before the train arrives at each station. Station stops are short, so be ready to disembark when the train comes to a halt. In newer trains there will be a well-marked button to push that will open the door automatically. In older trains, you'll need to open the door yourself. It may open from the inside, or you may have to open the window and reach outside to turn the door handle.

The trains have a two-tiered ticket system: first class and standard (2nd) class. First-class tickets cost about one-third more than standard class. The first-class cars have roomier seats and fewer people, so they're less crowded. But you can travel quite comfortably in standard class. There is no first-class service on local trains. There are toilets on board all but the local trains.

First-class service on InterCity trains (such as those between London and Edinburgh) includes free coffee, tea, beverages, and snacks served at your seat; some trains offer a free newspaper and a higher standard of personal service. Standard class passengers can buy sandwiches and drinks in a cafe car. On most lines an employee comes through with a food and beverage trolley. There is no food service on local trains.

Tickets & Reservations   You can purchase your ticket with cash or credit card at a ticket window in any British train station and can get your BritRail passes validated there as well. You can also buy a ticket on the train with cash. If you have a validated BritRail Pass (see "Passes," above), just board your train. Seat reservations are not required on most trains, but they are a good idea on some fast InterCity trains, especially if you're traveling on a weekend. They are pretty much a must on the night and weekend trains between Edinburgh and London if you're traveling in summer. Reservations can be purchased (usually for about £2/$3.20, though they are often free if you have a BritRail Pass) at the same time you buy your ticket, or you can make them inside the train station up to a couple of hours before departure. Should you wish to reserve a seat on a British train before arriving, you can do so through Rail Europe (see "Passes," above) for $11.

FAST FACTS: Great Britain

Area Codes Every telephone number in England and Scotland is prefaced by an area code that must be used if you are dialing long distance (London's area code, for example, is **20**; Edinburgh's is **131**). If you're calling long distance but within the United Kingdom, preface the area code with a zero (in other words, London would be 020), followed by the number. See "Telephone" below.

Business Hours Banks are usually open Monday through Friday 9:30am to 3:30pm. Business offices are open Monday through Friday 9am to 5pm. Pubs are allowed to stay open Monday through Saturday 11am to 11pm. and Sunday noon to 10:30pm. Some bars stay open past midnight. Stores generally open at 9am and close at 5:30pm. Monday through Saturday, staying open until 7pm on Wednesday or Thursday. Outside of the large cities, stores may be open for only a half day on Saturday. Larger stores in London and Edinburgh are usually open on Sunday as well.

Climate Unpredictable is the best that can be said about the weather in England and Scotland. Great Britain is an island and its climate is influenced by the often-stormy North Atlantic. Precipitation is frequent; so are gray skies. Year-round, it tends to be wetter, windier, and colder in Edinburgh than in London. Without question, the best times to visit here are late spring and summer.

Currency Britain's decimal monetary system is based on the pound (£), which is made up of 100 pence (written as "p"). The exchange rate used in this chapter is £1=$1.60. You'll find currency exchanges (bureaux de change) in railway stations, at most post offices, and in many tourist information centers.

Documents Required All U.S. citizens and Canadians must have a passport with at least 2 months validity remaining. No visa is required. The immigration officer may also want proof of your intention to return to your point of origin (usually a round-trip ticket) and visible means of support while in Britain.

Electricity British current is 240 volts, AC cycle, roughly twice the voltage of North American current, which is 115-120 volts, AC cycle. You won't be able to plug the flat pins of your appliance's plugs into the holes of British or Scottish wall outlets without suitable converters or adapters (available from an electrical supply shop). Be forewarned that you'll destroy the inner workings of your appliance (and possibly start a fire) if you plug an American appliance directly into a European electrical outlet without a transformer.

Embassies & High Commissions All embassies, consulates, and high commissions are located in London, the capital of the U.K. In case you lose your passport or have some other emergency, here's a list of addresses and phone numbers: The **U.S. Embassy** is at 24 Grosvenor Sq., W1 (② 020/7499-9000; Tube: Bond St.), open Monday to Friday from 8:30am to noon and 2 to 4pm (there are no afternoon hours on Tues). The **Canadian High Commission** is at MacDonald House, 38 Grosvenor Sq., W1 (② 020/7258-6600; Tube: Bond St.), open Monday through Friday 8am to 11am.

Health & Safety There are no major health risks associated with traveling in Britain. Pharmacies are called chemists in the United Kingdom; **Boots** is a chain that has outlets all over the country. Any prescriptions you bring with you should use generic, not brand names. In general, England and Scotland are very safe countries. In London, as in any large metropolis, use common sense and normal caution when you're in a crowded public area or walking alone at night. For police, fire, or an ambulance, dial ② **999.**

Holidays Americans may be unfamiliar with some British and Scottish holidays, particularly the spring and summer **Bank Holidays** (the last Mon in May and Aug), when everyone takes off for a long weekend. Most banks and many shops, museums, historic houses, and other places of interest are closed then and public transport services are reduced. The same holds true for other major British holidays: New Year's Day, Good Friday, Easter Monday, May Day (the 1st Mon in May), Christmas, and Boxing Day (Dec 26). Crowds swell during school holidays: mid-July to early September, 3 weeks at Christmas and at Easter, and a week in mid-October and in mid-February.

Legal Aid Your consulate, embassy, or high commission (see above) will give you advice if you run into trouble. They can advise you of your rights and even provide a list of attorneys (for which you'll have to pay if services are used), but they can't interfere on your behalf in the legal processes of Great Britain. For questions about American citizens arrested abroad, including ways of getting money to them, call the **Citizens Emergency Center of the Office of Special Consulate Services,** in Washington, D.C. (② **202/647-5225**). Other nationals can go to their nearest consulate or embassy.

Mail Post offices and sub-post offices throughout England and Scotland are open Monday through Friday 9am to 5pm and Saturday 9am to noon.

Many sub-post offices and some main post offices close for an hour at lunchtime. Post offices are identified by a red sign. An airmail letter to North America costs 47p (75¢) for 10 grams, and postcards require a 42p (67¢) stamp. Mail within the U.K. can be sent first- or second-class.

Police & Emergencies The best source of help and advice in emergencies is the police. For non-life-threatening situations, dial "0" (zero) and ask for the police; dial ℰ **999** for emergencies only (no coin required). If the local police can't assist, they'll have the address of a person who can. Losses, thefts, and other crimes should be reported immediately.

Telephone If you don't know the phone number of the party you want to call, you can dial **National Directory Enquiries** at ℰ **192**; the call is free. You can access **International Directory Enquiries** at ℰ **192,** but it will cost 25p (40¢) a shot.

The country code for the United Kingdom is **44.** To call England or Scotland from the United States, dial **011-44,** the area or city code, and then the 6, 7, or 8-digit phone number. If you're in England or Scotland and dialing a number within the same area code, the local number is all you need.

Two types of public pay phones are generally available: those that take only coins, and those that accept coins, credit cards, and phone cards. **Phone cards** are available in four values—£2 ($3.20), £4 ($6.40), £10 ($16), and £20 ($32)—and are reusable until the total value has expired. You can buy the cards from newsstands and post offices. At coin-operated phones, insert your coins before dialing. The minimum charge is 20p (32¢).

To make an international call from the U.K., dial the international access code **(00),** then the country code, then the area code, and finally the local number. Or call through one of the following long-distance access codes: **AT&T USA Direct** (ℰ 0800/890-011) and **Canada Direct** (ℰ 0800/890-016). The country code for the **U.S.** and **Canada** is 1.

Tipping In restaurants, **service charges** of 15% to 20% are often added to the bill. Sometimes this is clearly marked; at other times it isn't. When in doubt, ask. If service isn't included, it's customary to add 15% to the bill. **Sommeliers** get about £1 ($1.60) per bottle of wine served. Tipping in pubs isn't done, but in **cocktail bars** the server usually gets about £1 ($1.60) per round of drinks. It's standard to tip **taxi drivers** 10% to 15% of the fare. **Barbers and hairdressers** expect 10% to 15%. **Tour guides** expect £2 ($3.20), though it's not mandatory. **Theater ushers** are not tipped.

2 London

London is one of the world's great cities and it appeals to visitors of every age. It has a 2,000-year-old history and yet it's as cutting-edge as tomorrow. There's no end of things to do and ways to enjoy the pulsating capital of the United Kingdom. Famous monuments like the Tower of London and Westminster Abbey draw crowds every day. Pomp and ceremony still define Royal London, with its palaces and protocols. London's museums, nothing short of fabulous, are unrivaled in the scope and quality of their collections. And when it comes to nightlife, London is unbeatable: theater, dance, music of every kind, pubs, and late-night clubs—take your pick. Most important of all for the rail traveler, London's the major transit point to and from the Continent, and Great Britain's largest rail hub.

STATION INFORMATION
GETTING FROM THE AIRPORT INTO TOWN

The odds are that you will arrive in London at either Heathrow or Gatwick, London's two main international airports. The other airports—Luton, Stansted, and London City—do not service scheduled international flights, only charters and European destinations.

From Heathrow   There are several ways to get into London from Heathrow. The cheapest way into town is the **Underground** or **Tube,** London's subway system. There are two airport Tube stations on the Piccadilly Line: one for Terminals 1, 2, and 3, and one for Terminal 4. The journey into Central London takes 40 to 50 minutes. A one-way fare to Central London is £3.70 ($5.90).

The quickest and most comfortable way into town is via **Heathrow Express** (© 0845/600-1515; www.heathrowexpress.co.uk), the luxury nonstop rail service to Paddington Station, which takes 15 minutes from Terminals 1, 2, and 3, and 20 to 25 minutes from Terminal 4. Trains leave Heathrow from 5:10am to 11:40pm and arrive there from 5:30am to midnight. Standard-class one-way tickets cost £11.70 ($18.70) and BritRail passes may be used on the Heathrow Express. For more information, see the website or contact Rail Europe.

Finally, the **Airbus** (© 08705/747777; www.gobycoach.com), operated by National Express, leaves twice an hour from just outside every Heathrow terminal and goes to 23 stops in Central London. Ask your hotel or B&B if there's one close by because this may be the most convenient option. One-way tickets cost £8 ($12.85). **Black taxis** are always available at Heathrow. The approximate fare to London is £45 ($72).

From Gatwick   There are four ways of making the 25-mile (40km) trek into London from Gatwick. The most popular is the **Gatwick Express** train, which takes around 30 minutes to reach Victoria station, and costs £11 ($17.60) one-way. The station is below the airport, and trains depart every 15 minutes from 6:50am to 10:50pm. A slightly cheaper option is **South Central Trains,** which charges £8.20 ($13.10) one-way for a train that takes 35 to 45 minutes, depending how often it stops between Victoria station and the airport. BritRail passes can be used on both trains. For information on both, call National Rail Enquiries (© 08457/484950), or Rail Europe.

Hotelink (© 01293/552251; www.hotelink.co.uk) runs a minibus service and charges £20 ($32) to take you directly to your hotel. **Checker Cars** (© 01923/502808 from South Terminal, or 01923/569790 from North Terminal) provides 24-hour taxi service between Gatwick and Central London; expect to pay about £65 ($104) for the 90-minute journey.

INSIDE THE STATIONS

The British Rail train network connects London to all the major cities, and most towns within the U.K. (and some European destinations; see "Britain by Train," later in this chapter). There are seven major British Rail train stations in London, each serving different parts of the U.K. For more information on the destinations each station serves, see "London's Major Train Stations" below. The station you travel to or from will be determined by where you're coming from or where you want to go.

All train stations are also part of the London Underground public transport network, making it fairly easy to travel from one station to another. In addition, London Transport runs two express buses, routes 205 and 705, between the

London's Major Train Stations*

Station	Destinations Served
Charing Cross	Trains travel southeast to Canterbury, Hastings, Dover, and English Channel ports that connect with ferry service to the Continent.
Euston	Trains head northwest to the Lake District and up to Scotland (overnight service to Edinburgh).
King's Cross	Trains travel to destinations in the east and north of England, including York, and up to Edinburgh.
Liverpool Street	Trains head east to English Channel ports with continuing service to the Netherlands, northern Germany, and Scandinavia.
Paddington	Trains travel to Heathrow airport and southwest to Bath, the West Country, South Wales, and the Midlands.
Victoria	Trains head for Gatwick airport and the southeast, including Canterbury and Brighton.
Waterloo	Trains go primarily to the south of England; Waterloo International, connected to Waterloo Station, is the arrival and departure point for Eurostar trains to Paris and Brussels.

In addition to the mainline stations, there are also numerous regional stations, including Blackfriars, Charing Cross, London Bridge, Marylebone, St. Pancras, Stratford, and Clapham Junction.

major London British Rail stations. You can obtain 24-hour train information by calling **National Rail Enquiries** ✆ **0845/484950.**

Facilities and amenities at each station differ but most include ATMs, currency exchange desks, shops, cafes, and pubs. Most stations have large information boards with arrival and departure information for all the destinations they service. Tickets can be purchased at each station (ticket desks and machines) or aboard the train.

The London Tourist Board operates several **Tourist Information Centres (TIC)** inside London's train stations and at Heathrow Airport. At a TIC, you can get maps, brochures, and information about booking a hotel room. The following stations in London have a TIC:

- **Liverpool Street**   The **Tourist Information Centre** is in the Underground station at Liverpool Street Station and is open Monday through Friday 8am to 6pm and Saturday and Sunday 9am to 5:30pm.
- **Victoria**   The main London Tourist Board **Tourist Information Centre** is located in the forecourt of Victoria Station. It's open Monday to Saturday from 8am to 8pm Easter through May, to 9pm June through September, and from 8am to 6pm on Sundays and during the winter. The Centre can help you book a hotel room in any price category.
- **Waterloo**   The **Tourist Information Centre** is in the Arrivals Hall and is open from 8am to 10:30pm daily.

If all you need is a hotel room, the simplest way to get one is to call the reliable **British Hotel Reservation Centre** (✆ **020/7340-1616;** www.bhrc.co.uk); they book hotel rooms in all price categories.

INFORMATION ELSEWHERE IN THE CITY

The **Britain Visitor Centre,** 1 Regent St., SW1 (no phone) is open Monday 9:30am to 6:30pm, Tuesday to Friday 9am to 6:30pm, Saturday and Sunday 10am to 4pm (June–Oct Sat 9am–5pm). It brings together the English, Welsh,

London

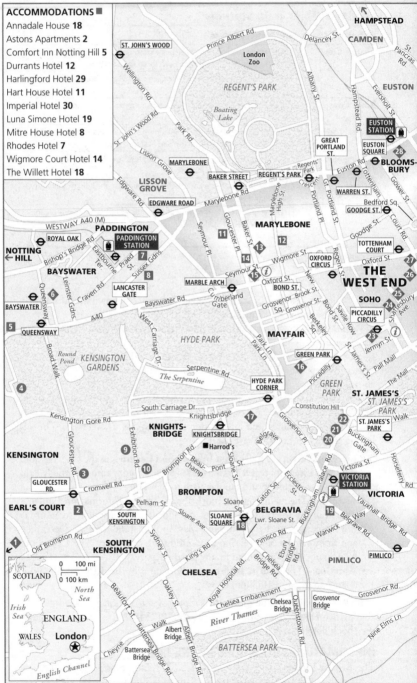

ACCOMMODATIONS ■
Annadale House **18**
Astons Apartments **2**
Comfort Inn Notting Hill **5**
Durrants Hotel **12**
Harlingford Hotel **29**
Hart House Hotel **11**
Imperial Hotel **30**
Luna Simone Hotel **19**
Mitre House Hotel **8**
Rhodes Hotel **7**
Wigmore Court Hotel **14**
The Willett Hotel **18**

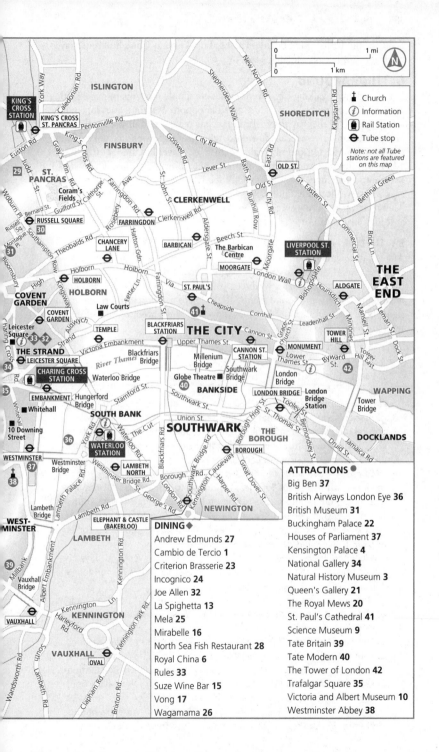

ISLINGTON

SHOREDITCH

KING'S CROSS STATION

KING'S CROSS ST. PANCRAS
Pentonville Rd.

York Way
Caledonian Rd.

Euston Rd.
Gray's Inn Rd.

FINSBURY

OLD ST.

29 ST. PANCRAS

Coram's Fields

CLERKENWELL

RUSSELL SQUARE

Clerkenwell Rd.

FARRINGDON

31

CHANCERY LANE

BARBICAN

The Barbican Centre

LIVERPOOL ST. STATION

COVENT GARDEN

HOLBORN

HOLBORN

MOORGATE

London Wall

ALDGATE

THE EAST END

Law Courts

ST. PAUL'S

Cheapside

Cornhill

COVENT GARDEN

Leicester Square

TEMPLE

BLACKFRIARS STATION

THE CITY

Cannon St.

TOWER HILL

THE STRAND

33 32

Strand

Upper Thames St.

CANNON ST. STATION

MONUMENT

Lower Thames St.

34

LEICESTER SQUARE

Victoria Embankment

Blackfriars Bridge

Millenium Bridge

Byward St.

42

CHARING CROSS STATION

River Thames

Waterloo Bridge

Globe Theatre

Southwark Bridge

London Bridge

WAPPING

35

EMBANKMENT

Hungerford Bridge

Stamford St.

40 BANKSIDE

LONDON BRIDGE

London Bridge Station

Tower Bridge

Whitehall

SOUTH BANK

Union St.

Tooley St.

DOCKLANDS

10 Downing Street

36

WATERLOO STATION

SOUTHWARK

THE BOROUGH

WESTMINSTER

37

Westminster Bridge

LAMBETH NORTH

BOROUGH

38

WEST-MINSTER

Lambeth Bridge

LAMBETH

ELEPHANT & CASTLE (BAKERLOO)

NEWINGTON

39

Vauxhall Bridge

VAUXHALL

KENNINGTON

VAUXHALL

OVAL

Scale: 0 — 1 mi / 0 — 1 km

Legend:
✝ Church
ⓘ Information
🚉 Rail Station
⊖ Tube stop

Note: not all Tube stations are featured on this map

DINING ◆

Andrew Edmunds 27
Cambio de Tercio 1
Criterion Brasserie 23
Incognico 24
Joe Allen 32
La Spighetta 13
Mela 25
Mirabelle 16
North Sea Fish Restaurant 28
Royal China 6
Rules 33
Suze Wine Bar 15
Vong 17
Wagamama 26

ATTRACTIONS ●

Big Ben 37
British Airways London Eye 36
British Museum 31
Buckingham Palace 22
Houses of Parliament 37
Kensington Palace 4
National Gallery 34
Natural History Museum 3
Queen's Gallery 21
The Royal Mews 20
St. Paul's Cathedral 41
Science Museum 9
Tate Britain 39
Tate Modern 40
The Tower of London 42
Trafalgar Square 35
Victoria and Albert Museum 10
Westminster Abbey 38

Scottish, and Irish Tourist Boards. There's also a **Thomas Cook** hotel and travel-reservations office on the premises.

GETTING AROUND

London's a great walking city, but distances are simply too large to make getting everywhere on your own two feet a viable option. Without question, public transportation is the way to go. Tube and bus maps are available at all Underground stations, or you can download them from the website, **www.london transport.co.uk**. You can also call the 24-hour **travel hot line** ✆ **020/7222-1234** for information on how to get from one point to another. There are **LT Information Centres** at several major Tube stations: Euston, King's Cross, Liverpool Street, Piccadilly Circus, Victoria, St. James's Park, and Oxford Circus. They're all open daily—except for the last two, which close on Sundays—from at least 9am to 5pm.

BY UNDERGROUND

The London Underground or Tube is easy to use and is the fastest and best way to move around this enormous city. Station signs in the subway tunnels and on the different platforms clearly direct you to eastbound and westbound, or northbound and southbound trains. Route maps are posted everywhere, and signs above the tracks will let you know how long you'll need to wait before your train arrives.

⟨Value⟩ Discount Transportation Passes

Anyone planning to use public transport should check out the range of money-saving passes that can be used on both the Tube and buses. You can buy all of them at Tube stations, tobacconists, and newsagents with a **Pass Agent** sticker in their window. Here's a sample of the most useful passes for visitors to London:

One-Day Travelcards can be used for unlimited trips before 9:30 am (peak) or after 9:30am (off-peak) Monday to Friday, and all day on Saturday, Sunday, and holidays, and on N-prefixed night buses. Adults traveling within Zones 1 and 2 pay £4.10 ($6.55) off-peak and £5.10 ($8.15) peak. In contrast, the **One-Day LT Card** is available for all zones at peak travel times; it costs £8 ($12.85).

Weekend Travelcards are valid for 2 consecutive weekend days or public holidays, and on night buses. They cost £6.10 ($9.75) for zones 1 and 2.

One-Week Travelcards are good for any number of trips, any hour of the day, and on night buses. The One-Week Travelcard for Zone 1 costs £16.50 ($26.40).

The London Visitor Travelcard is a special tourist deal that includes discount vouchers for some major attractions. It isn't available in the United Kingdom and can be purchased before you go from **Rail Europe** (✆ **877/272-RAIL** in the U.S., 800/361-RAIL in Canada; www.raileurope. com). All-zone adult passes cost $35 for 3 days, $46 for 4 days, and $69 for 7 days. Zone 1 and 2 passes cost $24, $29, and $36. An extra bonus: There are no time restrictions, and you can use them on night buses.

Except for Christmas Day, Tube trains run every few minutes from about 5:30am Monday to Saturday and 7am or so on Sunday. Nearly all lines stop running at 11:45pm.

There are two ways to buy tickets for the Tube: at the station ticket window or using one of the push-button machines (many of which accept credit cards). Queuing at the window can be phenomenally time-consuming, particularly at West End stations during the summer and during rush hour. You will have to go to the window, though, if you want to buy a pass valid for longer than 2 days (see "Discount Transportation Passes," above). Ticket machines take coins, bank notes, and sometimes credit cards. Hold onto your ticket throughout your ride because you'll need it to exit and London Transport inspectors make random checks. No excuse, however imaginative or heart-rending, will get you out of the rigidly imposed £10 ($16) penalty fare.

The London Underground operates on a system of six fare zones. These radiate out in concentric rings from the central Zone 1, which is where visitors spend most of their time. Zone 1 covers an area from the Tower of London in the east to Notting Hill in the west, and from Waterloo in the south to Baker Street, Euston, and King's Cross in the north. Single (one-way) tickets within Zone 1 on the Underground cost £1.60 ($2.60) for adults and 60p ($1) for children. The price of a book of 10 single tickets, a **Carnet,** is £11.50 ($18.40).

BY BUS

Traveling by bus is a great way to see London, but it can be frustratingly slow, particularly in rush hour traffic and the Tube is far more efficient. Normal buses run until around midnight when night buses, with an N in front of the number, take over for the next 6 hours. On most routes, there's one night bus every half hour or hour, and those to, from, and through the West End all go via Trafalgar Square, so if in doubt, head there.

Making sense of bus routes can be bewildering, however, even if you have a bus map. You'll find routes posted at most bus stops. If you are unsure about where to get off, ask the driver or conductor to let you know when the bus has reached your destination.

To stop a bus when you're on it, press the bell (or tug the wire running the length of the ceiling in an old bus). Without any signal, the driver won't stop unless passengers are waiting to get on at the next stop. If you're the one waiting, make sure to note whether it is a compulsory (white background on the sign) or a request stop (red background). If the latter, give a big wave or the bus won't stop.

You can buy single-trip bus tickets on the bus itself. On older buses, a conductor comes around, but most new buses are now driver-only, so you pay when you board. Drivers do not change banknotes, so have some £1 ($1.60) coins handy. If inspectors find you without a ticket, the on-the-spot fine is £5 ($8).

For ticket-buying purposes, there's just Zone 1, and then the rest of London. Adult bus fares are £1 ($1.60) within Central London Zone 1, 70p ($1.10) outside Zone 1, £1.50 ($2.40) on night buses. A **Saver 6** gives you six journeys for the price of five Zone 1 adult fares (£3.90/$6.25).

WHERE TO STAY

Annadale House   This late Victorian brick-fronted town house on a safe, quiet street close to Sloane Square is decorated with an eclectic mix of English antiques and modern furniture. Bedrooms are cozy and comfy rather than grand

and have small shower-only bathrooms. Number 14 is a large pleasant double, and no. 15 looks into the back garden and has a soft, romantic feel. There's no bar or public area but guests can use the small kitchen and are welcome to enjoy the charming back garden. The continental breakfast costs extra, but is served in your room. Single women will feel comfortable here.

39 Sloane Gardens, London SW1W 8EB. ✆ **020/7730-6291.** Fax 020/7730-2727. info@annadale-hotel. co.uk. 15 units. £95–£110 ($152–$176) double. Continental breakfast £5 ($8). AE, DC, MC, V. Tube: Sloane Sq. *In room:* Hair dryer, no A/C.

Astons Apartments 🅐🅐   Behind the red brick facades of three Victorian town houses just a couple of minutes from the Gloucester Road Tube station, you'll find this modern and impeccably maintained apartment hotel. Astons is a great choice for those who want to be in charge of their own cooking. Most of these fully equipped studios were recently refurbished and daily maid service is included. The executive doubles are larger and have some extra amenities, including larger bathrooms. All the studios have kitchenettes and there's a big supermarket nearby where you can stock up on supplies.

31 Rosary Gardens, London SW7 4NH. ✆ **800/525-2810** or 020/7590-6000. Fax 020/7590-6060. www. astons-apartments.com. 54 units. £90 ($144) standard double; £125 ($200) executive double. Discount available for Frommer's readers; inquire when booking. Children stay free in parent's room. AE, DISC, MC, V. Tube: Gloucester Rd. **Amenities:** Nonsmoking rooms. *In room:* Hair dryer, no A/C.

Comfort Inn Notting Hill 🅐 (Value)   Located on a quiet, pretty street off Notting Hill Gate, the Comfort Inn stretches across five terrace houses. The rooms are on the three upper floors (there is an elevator) and are a fair size for London. Rear windows look across fire escapes and rooftops, while second-floor rooms on the front have access to an east-facing balcony. Rooms have been redecorated with a nice business feel and equipped with firm new beds; bathrooms are also newly renovated.

6–14 Pembridge Gardens, London W2 4DU. ✆ **020/7229-6666.** Fax 020/7229-3333. www.lth-hotels.com. 64 units. £58–£94 ($92.80–$150) double. Rates include continental breakfast. AE, DC, MC, V. Tube: Notting Hill Gate. **Amenities:** Bar; laundry; nonsmoking rooms. *In room:* Hair dryer, no A/C.

Durrants Hotel 🅐   Opened in 1789 off Manchester Square, this 92-room hotel makes for an atmospheric London retreat. It's quintessentially English, with pine- and mahogany-paneled public areas, a wonderful Georgian room that serves as a restaurant, and even an 18th-century letter-writing room. The wood-paneled guest rooms are generously proportioned (for the most part) and nicely furnished, with decent-size bathrooms.

George St., London W1H 6BJ. ✆ **020/7935-8131.** Fax 020/7487-3510. www.durrantshotel.co.uk. 92 units. £145–£165 ($232–$264) double. AE, MC, V. Tube: Bond St. **Amenities:** Restaurant; bar; lounge; laundry. *In room:* TV, hair dryer, no A/C.

Harlingford Hotel 🅐🅐   Andrew Davies is the third generation of his family to run this Bloomsbury B&B, a dignified, dove-gray, Georgian-era building not far from Russell Square. He recently oversaw a designer-aided overhaul of the hotel's rooms. The bathrooms are small but adequate. With their gracious arched windows and high ceilings, the lounge and breakfast room are a real asset. Guests can get a key and enjoy the communal gardens opposite the hotel. The only downside: no elevator.

61–63 Cartwright Gardens, London WC1H 9EL. ✆ **020/7387-1551.** Fax 020/7387-4616. www.harlingford hotel.com. 44 units. £90 ($144) double. Rates include full English breakfast. AE, DC, MC, V. Tube: Euston, Russell Sq. **Amenities:** Lounge. *In room:* TV, no A/C.

Moments   A Stroll Through the City

You may not be able to get around the city by shoe leather alone, but London's still a great walking town when taken in small doses. Stroll in London's great parks: Kensington Gardens, Hyde Park, Green Park, St. James's Park, and Regent's Park offer beautiful paths, fountains, trees, flowers, and meadows. Or pick a neighborhood and stroll down the historic streets, admiring the architecture, the hidden mews, and the garden squares. One of the most pleasant London walks is along the Thames on the South Bank: starting at Westminster Bridge you can follow a riverside path all the way down to Tower Bridge.

Hart House Hotel ★★   One of the most welcoming and professionally run B&Bs in London, Hart House occupies a Georgian town house built in 1782. It still retains its dignified entrance hall and polished paneling. The rooms (all nonsmoking) are attractive and comfortable with small but immaculate bathrooms. Double-glazing screens out the traffic roar on Gloucester Place, the busy road from Oxford Street to Baker Street. There's no elevator.

51 Gloucester Place, London W1H 3PE. © 020/7935-2288. Fax 020/7935-8516. www.harthouse.co.uk. 15 units, all with bathroom (some with shower only). £95 ($152) double. Rates include full English breakfast. Discounts for 6 nights or more. AE, MC, V. Tube: Marble Arch, Baker St. **Amenities:** Laundry; nonsmoking rooms. *In room:* Hair dryer, no A/C.

Imperial Hotel ★ *(Value)*   This affordable, full-service hotel on the eastern side of Russell Square is just a stone's throw from Covent Garden and Soho. There are nine floors of bedrooms, one of them nonsmoking. The hotel does a lot of tour-group business, but the rooms have stood up well to the traffic. They're all a decent size, have unusual triangular-shaped bay windows, and good storage space. In most of the doubles and twins, the toilet and tub/shower are handily separate.

Russell Sq., London WC1B 5BB. © 020/7278-7871. Fax 020/7837-4653. www.imperialhotels.co.uk. 448 units. £98 ($157) double. Rates include full English breakfast. AE, DC, DISC, MC, V. Tube: Russell Sq. **Amenities:** Restaurant; cafe/bar; laundry; nonsmoking rooms. *In room:* No A/C.

Luna Simone Hotel ★★   Among the dozens of hotels near Victoria Station, this family-run hotel—renovated from top to bottom in 2002—stands out by a mile. The rooms vary widely in size, but with their fresh decor and newly tiled bathrooms, they beat all the dowdy, badly designed hotels and B&Bs for miles around. The look throughout is light, simple, and modern, a refreshing change from the interiors of so many Victorian buildings. The breakfast room is totally nonsmoking.

47–49 Belgrave Rd., London SW1V 2BB. © 020/7834-5897. Fax 020/7828-2474. www.lunasimonehotel. com. 36 units. £60–£80 ($96–$128) double. Rates include full English breakfast. MC, V. Tube: Victoria, Pimlico. **Amenities:** Lounge; breakfast room. *In room:* Hair dryer, no A/C.

Mitre House Hotel ★★   This fine hotel near Paddington Station stretches across four Georgian town houses and is kept in tiptop shape by the Chris brothers, who recently took over management from their parents. It's a great family hotel because of the assortment of accommodations. All the rooms are above average size for London; those at the back are quieter. Hair dryers are available at the reception desk. There's a big and very pleasant lounge and bar, and an elevator.

178–184 Sussex Gardens, London W2 1TU. ✆ 020/7723-8040. Fax 020/7402-0990. www.mitrehouse hotel.com. 69 rooms. £80 ($128) double. Rates include full English breakfast. AE, DC, MC, V. Tube: Paddington. **Amenities:** Bar; laundry. *In room:* No A/C.

Rhodes Hotel 🏠🏠 The owner of the Rhodes, located on a busy street near Paddington Station, recently spruced up the entire hotel. The velvet-curtained lounge and the downstairs dining room now boast hand-painted Greek-inspired murals, and painted angels gaze down from the ceiling. Other improvements include air-conditioning in the main part of the hotel (though not in the annex, which is why the rooms are cheaper there). The bedroom decor is quite simple and comfortable, and all rooms have refrigerators. Number 220 has its own little private roof terrace with table and chairs.

195 Sussex Gardens, London W2 2RJ. ✆ 020/7262-0537. Fax 020/7723-4054. www.rhodeshotel.com. 18 units. £75–£85 ($120–$136) double. Rates include continental breakfast. MC, V. Tube: Paddington. **Amenities:** Breakfast room; lounge. *In room:* Hair dryer, no A/C in annex rooms

Wigmore Court Hotel 🏠 *Finds* The owner of this appealing Georgian-era B&B near Marble Arch, knows the long climb to the fifth floor is a turn-off for a lot of guests, even though they get help with their bags, so she's introduced a reward system. Anyone who does make it to the top can sink into a four-poster bed to recover. There are two more, one each on the second and third floors. Budget travelers can get a very good deal here. The decor is a pleasant mix of traditional styles. Guests can use the kitchen and laundry facilities, a big bonus normally restricted to budget B&Bs.

23 Gloucester Place, London W1H 3PB. ✆ 020/7935-0928. Fax 020/7487-4254. www.wigmore-hotel.co.uk. 18 units, 16 with bathroom (some with shower only). £89 ($142) double. Rates include full English breakfast. Discount of 10% for 1-week. stays. MC, V. Tube: Marble Arch. **Amenities:** Laundry. *In room:* Hair dryer, no A/C.

The Willett Hotel 🏠🏠 Noteworthy for its mansard roof, bay windows, and a host of the other Victorian architectural details, the Willet is a dream location for shopaholics, just off Sloane Square and a 5-minute walk to Chelsea's King's Road. The hotel has been completely refurbished in a heavily traditional style to match the building. All the rooms are different, but each meets very high standards and has a refrigerator. Deluxe rooms have canopies over the beds, voluptuous swagged curtains, and nice but not terribly large bathrooms.

32 Sloane Gardens, London SW1 8DJ. ✆ 800/270-9206 in the U.S., or 020/7824-8415. Fax 020/7730-4830. www.eeh.co.uk. 19 units, all with bathroom (most with shower only). £90–£145 ($144–$232) double. Rates do not include 17.5% VAT. Rates include full English breakfast. AE, DC, MC, V. Tube: Sloane Sq. **Amenities:** Laundry. *In room:* Hair dryer, no A/C.

TOP ATTRACTIONS & SPECIAL MOMENTS

British Airways London Eye 🏠🏠 At 443 feet high, this is the world's tallest observation wheel. Located on the south bank, across from the Houses of Parliament, the Eye gives you a half-hour "flight" with stunning 25-mile (40km) views over the capital. Each enclosed "pod" of the wheel holds about 25 passengers and is large enough so that you can move around or sit on a bench in the middle. Book your "boarding ticket" in advance to avoid standing in line; all tickets use a timed-entry system. The Eye opened for the millennium and will keep spinning at least through 2004 because it's such a popular attraction.

Jubilee Gardens, SE1. ✆ 0870/500-0600. www.ba-londoneye.com. Admission £11 ($17.60) adults, £10 ($16) seniors, £5.50 ($8.80) children 5–15. Open daily 9:30am; last admission varies seasonally (May 8 or 9pm, June 9 or 10pm, July–Aug 10pm, Oct–Dec 8pm). Tube: Waterloo, Westminster.

British Museum ★★★   The British Museum showcases countless treasures of ancient and modern civilizations. The museum is so vast (with 2½ miles/4km of galleries) that you might want to take one of the 1½ hour tours offered daily at 10:30am, 1pm, and 3pm for £8 ($12.85).

The **Great Court,** designed by Lord Norman Foster and completed in 2000, realigned access to the galleries. The inner courtyard is now canopied by a glass roof and houses a bookshop and restaurants. The famous Round Reading Room in the center of the court has been restored to its original Victorian splendor.

Massive winged and human-headed stone bulls and lions that once guarded the gateways to the palaces of Assyrian kings line the **Assyrian Transept** on the ground floor. The star attraction in the angular hall of Egyptian sculpture is the **Rosetta stone,** whose discovery led to the deciphering of hieroglyphs. Also on the ground floor is the Duveen Gallery, housing the **Parthenon sculptures** (formerly known as the Elgin Marbles) from the Parthenon on the Acropolis in Athens. The Department of Medieval and Later Antiquities has its galleries on the first floor (second floor to Americans). One exhibit, the **Sutton Hoo Anglo-Saxon burial ship** discovered in Suffolk, is a treasure trove of gold jewelry, armor, weapons, bronze bowls and cauldrons, silverware, and a drinking horn.

The featured attractions of the upper floor are the Egyptian Galleries, especially the **mummies.** The galleries of the City of Rome and its empire include exhibits of art before the Romans.

The **Sainsbury African Galleries,** one of the finest collections of African art and artifacts in the world, features changing displays selected from more than 200,000 objects.

Great Russell St., WC1. © 020/7323-8000. www.thebritishmuseum.ac.uk. Free admission. Galleries: Sat–Wed 10am-5:30pm, Thurs–Fri 10am–8:30pm. Great Court: Sun–Weds 9am–6pm, Thurs–Sat 9am–11pm. Closed Jan 1, Good Friday, Dec 24–26. Tube: Holborn, Tottenham Court Rd., or Goodge St.

Buckingham Palace ★   This massive building is the Queen's official London residence and one of the most famous buildings in the capital. You can tell that Her Majesty is at home when the Royal Standard flies at the masthead. The palace was originally built as a country house for the duke of Buckingham. In 1762, George III bought it and from then on the building was expanded, remodeled, faced with Portland limestone, and bombed twice during the Blitz. Today, contained within a 42-acre garden, it stands 360 feet long and has 600 rooms. The Queen's family occupies a mere 12 of them; the rest are used as offices and reception rooms.

The palace is open to the public for 8 weeks in August and September, when the royal family is away on vacation in Scotland. Nothing that you actually see on the self-guided tour, which includes 19 of the state apartments, justifies the exorbitant admission price, although you do get to wander in the famous gardens and see Queen Victoria's enormous ballroom. Keep in mind that these are not the rooms where the Royals live, only where they entertain and carry out official duties. Timed-entry tickets are available in advance or on the day of at the ticket kiosk near the palace. You can avoid the long queues (sometimes up to an hour) by purchasing tickets in advance by credit card (© 020/7321-2233), and visitors with disabilities can reserve tickets directly through the palace by calling © 020/7930-5526.

The **Royal Mews** ★, also on Buckingham Palace Road, is one of the finest working stables in the world today. Gilded and polished state carriages, such as the gold state coach used at every coronation since 1831, are housed here, along with the horses that draw them.

⌒Moments   Changing of the Guard

Buckingham Palace's most famous spectacle, the **Changing of the Guard,** is one of the finest examples of military pageantry you'll ever see. The ceremony begins at 11:15am and lasts for half an hour. The new guard, marching behind a band, comes from either the Wellington or Chelsea barracks and takes over from the old guard in the forecourt of the palace. The guard changes daily from April through July, and every other day for the rest of the year. The ceremony may be abruptly canceled during "uncertain" weather conditions. Always consult tourist information offices or local publications for schedules before arriving.

In 2002, as part of her Golden Jubilee celebrations, Queen Elizabeth reopened the **Queen's Gallery** ⭐, whose entrance is right next door to the Royal Mews. In the newly redesigned galleries you can see paintings and precious objects from the enormous Royal art collection. Items on display change throughout the year.

The Mall, SW1. ✆ **020/7389-1377.** 020/7799-2331 recorded info, 020/7321-2233 credit-card bookings, 020/7839-1377 for visitors with disabilities. www.royalresidences.com. State Rooms £12 ($19.20) adults, £10 ($16) seniors, £6 ($9.60) under 17, £30 ($48) family ticket. Aug 1 Sept 28 daily 9:30am–4:15pm (last admittance 3:15pm). Royal Mews £5 ($8) adults, £4 ($6.40) seniors, £2.50 ($4) under-17s, £12.50 ($20) family ticket. March–July 11am–4pm (last admission 3:15pm); Aug–Sept 10am–5pm (last admission 4:15pm). Queen's Gallery £6.50 ($10.40), £5 ($8) over 60 and students, £3 ($4.80) under 17. Daily 10am–5:30pm (last admittance 4:30pm). Changing of the Guard free (call ✆ **020/7799-2331** for recorded information). Tube: St. James's Park, Green Park, or Victoria.

Houses of Parliament ⭐   The Houses of Parliament, along with their trademark clock tower, are quintessential symbols of London. They're the stronghold of Britain's democracy, the assemblies that effectively trimmed the sails of royal power. Both the House of Commons and the House of Lords are in the former royal Palace of Westminster, the king's residence until Henry VIII moved to Whitehall. The current Gothic Revival buildings date from 1840 and were designed by Charles Barry. (The earlier buildings were destroyed by fire in 1834.) Assisting Barry was A. W. N. Pugin, who designed the paneled ceilings, tiled floors, stained glass, clocks, fireplaces, umbrella stands, and even the inkwells. There are more than 1,000 rooms and 2 miles (3.2km) of corridors. The clock tower at the eastern end houses the world's most famous timepiece. **"Big Ben"** refers not to the clock tower itself, but to the largest bell in the chime, which weighs close to 14 tons.

You may observe parliamentary debates from the Stranger's Galleries in both houses. Sessions usually begin in mid-October and run to the end of July, with recesses at Christmas and Easter. The debates in the House of Commons are usually lively and contentious, but your chances of getting into the House of Lords, when it's in session, are generally better. Under Tony Blair's New Labour government, the 600 peers in the House of Lords lost their hereditary posts and were replaced by "people's peers"—considered by many Londoners to be as useless as the old peers. If you want to attend a session, line up at Stephen's Gate, heading to your left for the entrance into the Commons or to the right for the Lords. The London daily newspapers announce sessions of Parliament.

Both houses are open to the general public for 75-minute **guided tours** only during a limited period each year (July 26–Aug 30 and Sept 19–Oct 5). Tickets can be booked through Firstcall (℡ **0870/906-3838;** www.firstcalltickets.com), and cost £7 ($11.20). You must be there 10 minutes before your timed-entry tour begins.

Westminster Palace, Old Palace Yard, SW1. House of Commons ℡ 020/7219-3000. House of Lords ℡ 020/7219-3107. www.parliament.uk. Free admission, subject to recess and sitting times. House of Commons: Mon 1:30–8:30pm, Tues–Wed 11:30am–7:30pm, Thurs–Fri 9:30am–3pm. House of Lords: Mon–Weds from 2:30pm, Thurs and occasionally Fri from 11am. Queue at St. Stephen's entrance, near the statue of Oliver Cromwell. Tube: Westminster.

Kensington Palace ✦   Located at the western edge of Kensington Gardens, Kensington Palace was acquired by William and Mary in 1689 and remodeled by Sir Christopher Wren. George II, who died in 1760, was the last king to use it as a royal residence. Princess Diana lived here when in London; the area in front of the palace drew tens of thousands of mourners after her death, a sea of flowers and tributes testifying to a nation's grief.

You can tour the main **State Apartments** of the palace, but many rooms are private and still lived in by lesser Royals. One of the more interesting chambers to visit is Queen Victoria's bedroom, where, on the morning of June 20, 1837, she was roused from her sleep with the news that she had succeeded to the throne, following the death of her uncle, William IV. She was 18 years old. As you wander through the apartments, you'll see many fine paintings from the Royal Collection. A special attraction is the **Royal Ceremonial Dress Collection,** set in several restored rooms from the 19th century—including Victoria's birth room—where you'll find a series of settings with the appropriate court dress of the day. Several of Diana's famous frocks are on display, as are the dowdier dresses worn by Queen Elizabeth II.

The Broad Walk, Kensington Gardens, W8. ℡ 020/7937-9561. www.hrp.org.uk. Admission £10 ($16) adults, £7.50 ($12) seniors and students, £6.50 ($10.40) children 5–16, £28 ($44.80) family. Mar–Oct daily 10am–5pm; Nov–Feb daily 10am–4pm. Tube: Queensway or Bayswater on the north side of the gardens; High St. Kensington on the south side; then you'll have a long walk.

National Gallery ✦✦✦   One of the finest art museums in the world, Britain's national art collection comprises more than 2,300 paintings dating from 1260 to 1900, supplemented by masterpieces on loan from private collectors. The gallery is arranged in four time bands. The **Sainsbury Wing** shows work from 1260 to 1510 by such artists as Giotto, Botticelli, Leonardo da Vinci, Piero della Francesca, and Raphael. The **West Wing** takes on the next 90 years, with El Greco, Holbein, Bruegel, Michelangelo, Titian, and Veronese. The **North Wing** holds the 17th-century masters, Rubens, Poussin, Velázquez, Rembrandt, and Vermeer. Van Dyck's *The Abbé Scaglia* entered the collection in 1999, given by a private owner in lieu of inheritance tax. Works by Stubbs, Gainsborough, Constable, Turner, Canaletto, van Gogh, Corot, Monet, Manet, Renoir, and Cézanne are all in the **East Wing.** From May to September, the National Gallery lets natural daylight illuminate many of the paintings, particularly in the Sainsbury Wing, to magical effect—the colors are truer, and it cuts down on glare and shadow from the frames. You'll need to choose a sunny day for your visit, though, because artificial help steps in if it gets too gloomy. Weekday mornings and late on Wednesday are the quietest times.

There's a free (donation invited) audio guide to every painting on the main floor, and free, guided tours start at 11:30am and 2:30pm every day, plus at 6:30pm on Wednesday evenings. Most of the gallery talks are also free. There are two eateries: the Crivelli's Garden Restaurant and Italian Bar (℡ **020/7747-2869**) on the first floor of the Sainsbury Wing, and the Gallery Cafe sandwich cafe in the basement of the main building.

Trafalgar Sq., WC2. ℂ 020/7747-2885. www.nationalgallery.org.uk. Free admission. Daily 10am–6pm, Wed 10am–9pm. Free guided tours daily 11:30am and 2:30pm. Closed Jan 1, Dec 24–26. Tube: Charing Cross, Embankment, or Leicester Sq.

Natural History Museum ⚑⚑ It roars. It opens its jaws and moves its head. And it's the biggest hit the museum has ever had: a **robotic Tyrannosaurus Rex** hovering over a fresh dino-kill. It's worth a trip just to watch the 12-feet-tall toothy beast, driven by motion sensors, react to the appearance of each new human meal (not suitable for young kids). Before you see "T" you'll encounter two cunning-looking animatronic raptors eyeing you from atop a perch. All this takes place in a Victorian hall full of **dinosaur skeletons** and exhibitions about the life of the 'saurs. Head to the **Earth Galleries** for the earthquake and volcano simulations that hint at the terror of the real thing. Kids also love the slithery and slimey critters in the **Creepie-Crawlies** exhibit.

Sir Hans Sloane was such a prolific collector that his treasures overflowed the British Museum. Hence the decision to build this palatial building (1881), with its towers, spires, and navelike hall, fit "for housing the works of the Creator." Yet it, too, can display only a fraction of its animal, vegetable, and mineral specimens. An exciting project is set to revolutionize all that, opening both the storerooms and the science labs, with their 300 white-coated experts, to public view. The £28 million ($45 million) first phase of the Darwin Centre opened in summer 2002.

Cromwell Rd., S. Kensington, SW7. ℂ 020/7938-9123. www.nhm.ac.uk. Free admission. Mon–Sat 10am–5:50pm, Sun 11am–5:50pm. Closed Dec 23–26. Guided 45-min. tours daily, £3 ($4.80) adults, £1.50 ($2.40) children. Tube: South Kensington.

St. Paul's Cathedral ⚑ During World War II, newsreel footage showed the famous classical dome of St. Paul's Cathedral standing amidst the rubble caused by German bombings. That it survived at all is a miracle: It was badly hit twice during the early years of the Blitz. Then again, St. Paul's is accustomed to calamity, having been burned down three times and destroyed once by invading Norsemen. After the Great Fire of 1666, the old St. Paul's was razed, making way for a new Renaissance structure designed by Sir Christopher Wren and built between 1675 and 1710. It is an Anglican cathedral, and was the site of Princess Diana's wedding to Prince Charles in 1981.

Inside, the cathedral is laid out like a Greek cross. With the exception of Grinling Gibbons' magnificent choir stalls, the cathedral houses few art treasures. There are, however, many monuments, including one to the Duke of Wellington and a memorial chapel to American service personnel who lost their lives in World War II while stationed in the United Kingdom. Encircling the dome is the Whispering Gallery. You can climb to the very top of the dome for a spectacular 360-degree view of London. Wellington and Lord Nelson both lie in the crypt, as does London's most famous architect, Sir Christopher Wren.

Guided "Supertours" last 1½ hours and include parts of the cathedral not open to the general public. They take place Monday through Saturday at 11am, 11:30am, 1:30pm, and 2pm and cost £2.50 ($4) adults, £2 ($3.20) seniors and students, and £1 ($1.60) children, plus the regular admission fee. Audio tours lasting 45 minutes are available until 3pm; they cost £3.50 ($5.60) for adults, £3 ($4.80) seniors and students.

St. Paul's Churchyard, EC4. ℂ 020/7236-4128. www.stpauls.co.uk. Cathedral £6 ($9.60) adults, £5 ($8) seniors and students, £3 ($4.80) children 6–16; free for children 5 and under. Sightseeing Mon–Sat 8:30am–4pm. No sightseeing Sun (services only). Tube: St. Paul's.

Science Museum ★★★   This is one of the best science museums in the world. The striking new £45 million ($72 million) **Wellcome Wing** houses six new exhibitions presenting the latest developments in science, medicine, and technology. Find out what the kids might look like in 30 years in the *Who am I?* gallery. For a more intimate portrait, check out the gory digital cross sections in *The Visible Human Project.* This is fantasyland for gadget geeks, who'll love all the interactivity. There's a 450-seat IMAX cinema on the first floor and another huge new gallery, **Making the Modern World,** links the Wellcome Wing to the old museum. Using some of the most iconic treasures of the permanent collection—the Apollo 10 space capsule, an early train known as Stephenson's Rocket, and a fleece from famous Scottish clone, Dolly the Sheep—it charts 250 years of technological discoveries and their effects on our culture.

The new galleries are stunning, but don't let them dazzle you into forgetting the rest of this marvelous museum. It is home to many pioneering machines: Arkwright's spinning machine, for instance, and the Vickers "Vimy" aircraft, which made the first Atlantic crossing in 1919. The basement is dedicated to children, with water, construction, sound and light shows, and games. Although the museum introduced free admission in December 2001, it does still charge for shows at the IMAX and rides on its two simulators.

Exhibition Rd., SW7. ✆ 020/7938-8000. www.sciencemuseum.org.uk. Free admission. Daily 10am–6pm. Tube: South Kensington.

Tate Britain ★★★   The new Tate Modern (see below) at Bankside hogs most of the limelight, but the shifting around of the Tate collections has also seen a huge overhaul at the original gallery, founded in 1897. The refurbished Tate Britain reopened in November 2001 with more exhibition space and a suite of airy new galleries. Having handed International Modernism over to Bankside, Tate Britain now concentrates on British work dating back to 1500. It ditched the chronological displays for a thematic approach. **Art Now** focuses on new media and experimental work by foreign artists living in London and Brits based here and abroad; **Private and Public** includes portraits and scenes of daily life; **Artists and Models** explores nudes and self-portraiture; **Literature and Fantasy** is for visionary artists such as William Blake and Stanley Spencer; and **Home and Abroad** looks at the landscape artist at home and abroad. Juxtaposing very different kinds of work isn't always successful, but the vibrancy of the place can't help but give you a rush. Important artists, like Gainsborough, Constable, Hogarth, and Hockney, get their own rooms, which should pacify the traditionalists.

Millbank, SW1. ✆ 020/7887-8000. www.tate.org.uk. Free admission. Daily 10:30am–5:50pm. Closed Dec 24–26. Tube: Vauxhall.

Tate Modern ★★★   The Tate Modern, London's new and wildly popular cathedral of modern art, occupies the defunct Bankside Power Station on the South Bank of the Thames opposite St. Paul's Cathedral. You enter the huge old turbine hall, left empty, and three floors of galleries where the work is arranged thematically rather than chronologically: **Landscape/Matter/Environment, Still Life/Object/Real Life, History/Memory/Society,** and **Nude/Action/Body.** In some rooms, paintings are next to sculptures next to installations. Others are devoted to a single artist—like the marvelous Joseph Beuys sculptures. The display concept is certainly challenging, but the themes often seem spurious, lacking the quirky spirit of a mixed private collection where one person's taste is the guide.

There's no such thing as a flash visit to Tate Modern. Set aside half a day if you can. Free guided tours start daily at 10:30, 11:30am, 2:30, and 3:30pm, each focusing on one of the four themes. Be sure to go up to the glass-roofed level seven to see the spectacular views across the Thames. The cafe there is often mobbed so time your visit for early mealtimes and during the week. It is also open for dinner until 9:30pm on Friday and Saturday but doesn't take bookings.

25 Sumner St., SE1. ✆ 020/7887-8000. www.tate.org.uk. Free admission. Temporary exhibitions £5.50–£8.50 ($8.80–$13.60). Sun–Thurs 10am–6pm, Fri–Sat 10am–8pm. Tube: Southwark, Mansion House, or St. Paul's (cross over the Millennium Bridge).

The Tower of London ✿✿✿　This is the most perfectly preserved medieval fortress in Britain and you'll need at least 2 or 3 hours for your visit. Over the centuries, the Tower has served as a palace and royal refuge; a prison, military base, and supplies depot; home to the Royal Mint and the Royal Observatory; and finally a national monument. The oldest part is the massive **White Tower,** built in 1078 by the Norman king, William the Conqueror, to protect London and discourage rebellion among his new Saxon subjects. Every king after him added to the main structure, so that when Edward I completed the outer walls in the late 13th century, they enclosed an 18-acre square. Walk round the top of the walls for a bird's-eye view of how the Tower of London would have looked when it was in use.

The **Crown Jewels,** glittering in the Jewel House in Waterloo Barracks, are the real must-see. Here you'll see the Imperial State Crown, encrusted with 3,200 precious stones, including a 317-carat diamond. **The Chapel Royal of St. Peter ad Vincula** contains the graves of all the unfortunates executed at the Tower. The Scaffold Site, where the ax man dispatched seven of the highest-ranking victims, including Henry VIII's wives, Anne Boleyn and Catherine Howard, is just outside. Everyone else met their end on **Tower Green** after arriving by boat at **Traitors' Gate.** The **Bloody Tower** was where Richard of Gloucester locked up his young nephews while he usurped his crusading brother Edward IV. The princes' bodies were later mysteriously found by the White Tower. Today, an exhibit re-creates how Sir Walter Raleigh might have lived during his 13-year imprisonment after the Gunpowder Plot against James I.

The royal menagerie moved out in 1834 to form the new London Zoo—all except the **ravens.** Legend has it that Charles II was told that if they ever left the Tower, the monarchy would fall. Ever since, a few birds with clipped wings have been kept in a lodging next to Wakefield Tower, looked after by a yeoman warder. The **yeoman warders,** or Beefeaters, have guarded the Tower for centuries. Now usually retired soldiers, they lead tours every half hour from 9:30am to 3:30pm and give vivid talks at 9:30, 10:15, 11:30am, 2:15, 4:30, and 5:15pm (the 1st one Sun is at 10:30am). Costumed guides also re-create historic happenings.

Tower Hill, EC3. ✆ 0870/756-6060 or 0870/756-7070 (box office). www.hrp.org.uk. Admission £11.50 ($18.40) adults, £8.75 ($14) seniors and students, £7.50 ($12) children, free for children under 5, £34 ($54.40) family. Mar–Oct Tues–Sat 9am–6pm, Sun–Mon 10am–6pm; Nov–Feb Tues–Sat 9am–5pm, Sun–Mon 10am–5pm. Last tickets sold 1 hr. before closing. Closed Dec 24–26, Jan 1. Tube: Tower Hill.

Trafalgar Square ✿　One of London's greatest landmarks, Trafalgar Square honors England's great military hero Horatio, Viscount Nelson (1758–1805). Lord Nelson was a hero of the Battle of Calvi, where he lost an eye; the Battle of Santa Cruz, where he lost an arm; and the Battle of Trafalgar, where he lost his life. A statue of Nelson stands atop a 145-foot granite column, created by E. H. Baily in 1843, in the center of the square. The column looks down Whitehall toward the Old Admiralty, where Nelson's body lay in state. The figure of the naval hero towers 17 feet high—not bad for a man who stood 5 feet

4 inches. Queen Victoria's favorite animal painter, Sir Edward Landseer, added the four lions at the column base in 1868. The pools and fountains, Sir Edwin Lutyens' last work, were added in 1939.

Sir Charles Barry, designer of the Houses of Parliament, created the present square in the 1830s. It has just received a much-welcomed makeover that connects it to the National Gallery so that visitors no longer have to cross a street roaring with traffic to reach it. Still a favorite spot for political demonstrations, it's also the site of two London traditions: the giant Christmas tree installed every December (an annual gift from Norway to the British people, as thanks for sheltering its royal family during World War II) and the raucous celebrations on New Year's Eve.

To the southeast of the square, at 36 Craven St., stands a house Benjamin Franklin occupied when he was a general of the Philadelphia Academy (1757–74). To the north rises the National Gallery and, behind it, the National Portrait Gallery, a collection of British greats (and not-so-greats). Also on the square is the landmark church, **St. Martin-in-the-Fields,** with its towering steeple.

At the intersection of Pall Mall and Charing Cross Rd. Tube: Charing Cross.

Victoria and Albert Museum ★★ (Moments)

The Victoria and Albert (V&A) is the greatest museum in the world devoted to the decorative arts. The medieval holdings include such treasures as the early-English Gloucester Candlestick; the Byzantine Veroli Casket, with its ivory panels based on Greek plays; and the Syon Cope, a highly valued embroidery made in England in the early 14th century. An area devoted to Islamic art houses the Ardabil Carpet from 16th-century Persia. The V&A houses the largest collection of **Renaissance sculpture** outside Italy and the greatest collection of **Indian art** outside India. One room displays Raphael's giant cartoons for tapestries for the Sistine Chapel. There are suites of English furniture, metalwork, and ceramics, and a superb collection of portrait miniatures, including the one Hans Holbein the Younger made of Anne of Cleves for the wife-hunting Henry VIII. The **Dress Collection** includes a collection of corsetry through the ages that's sure to make you wince, and the quintessential "little black dress." There's also a remarkable collection of musical instruments.

In 2001, the V&A opened 15 new galleries—called The **British Galleries**—dedicated to British design from 1500 to 1900. From Chippendale to Morris, all of the top British designers are featured in exhibits ranging from 19th-century furniture by Charles Rennie Mackintosh to the "Great Bed of Ware," mentioned in Shakespeare's *Twelfth Night,* and the wedding suite of James II.

Cromwell Rd., SW7. © 020/7942-2000. www.vam.ac.uk. Free admission. Thurs–Tues 10am–5:45pm; Wed and last Fri each month 10am–10pm. Closed Dec 24–26. Tube: South Kensington.

Westminster Abbey ★★★

This ancient building is neither a cathedral nor a parish church, but a "royal peculiar," under the jurisdiction of the dean and chapter, and subject only to the sovereign. Mostly dating from the 13th to 16th centuries, Westminster Abbey has played a prominent part in British history, most recently with the funeral of Princess Diana and, in 2002, of the Queen Mother. All but two coronations since 1066 have taken place here. The oak **Coronation Chair,** made in 1308 for Edward I, can be seen in the **Chapel of Edward the Confessor.** Five kings and four queens, including half-sisters Queen Elizabeth I and Mary Tudor and Elizabeth's rival for the throne, Mary Queen of Scots, are buried in the beautiful, fan-vaulted **Chapel of Henry VII.**

In 1400, Geoffrey Chaucer became the first literary celebrity to be buried in **Poets' Corner**—in his case, though, it was because he worked for the abbey. Ben Jonson is there, as well as Dryden, Samuel Johnson, Sheridan, Browning, and Tennyson.

Guided tours of the abbey cost £3 ($4.80) and start at 10, 10:30, 11am, 2, 2:30, and 3pm during the week April through October; at 10, 11am, 2, and 3pm on winter weekdays; and at 10, 10:30, and 11am on Saturday year-round. Audio guides are £2 ($3.20). With both, you get discounted entry to the **Chapter House** (1245–55) in the east cloister, the nearby **Pyx Chamber,** and the **Abbey Museum.**

Dean's Yard, SW1. ☎ 020/7222-5152, 020/7222-5897 Chapter House, or 020/7233-0019 Pyx Chamber and Abbey Museum. www.westminster-abbey.org. Admission £5 ($8) adults, £3 ($4.80) seniors and students, £2 ($3.20) under 16, £10 ($16) family ticket. Chapter House, Pyx Chamber, and Abbey Museum £2.50 ($4) adults, £1.90 ($3.05) seniors and students, £1.30 ($2.10) under 16; reduced with Abbey admission, free with guided and audio tour. Cloisters, College Garden, St. Margaret's Church free. Abbey Mon–Fri 9:30am–4:45pm; Sat 9:30am–2:45pm; last admission 1hr. before closing, Sun for worship. Chapter House Apr–Sept 9:30am–5:30pm; Oct 10am–5pm; Nov–Mar 10am–4pm. Pyx Chamber and Abbey Museum daily 10:30am–4pm. Cloisters 8am–6pm. College Garden Apr–Sept 10am–6pm; Oct–Mar 10am–4pm. St. Margaret's Church Mon–Fri 9:30am–3:45pm; Sat 9:30am–1:45pm; Sun 2–5pm. Tube: Westminster.

WHERE TO DINE

Andrew Edmunds ⭐ *Finds* MODERN BRITISH   This charming Soho restaurant started life as a wine bar and is attached to the print gallery next door. Popular for business lunches by day, at night it becomes the haunt of romantic young couples eating dinner by candlelight. They have to whisper their sweet nothings because the tables are pretty close together. The handwritten menu changes frequently but always offers modern European cuisine in healthy portions and delicious desserts.

46 Lexington St., W1. ☎ 020/7437-5708. Reservations recommended. Main courses £8.25–£13.50 ($13.20–$21.60). AE, MC, V. Mon–Sat 12:30–3pm and 6–10:45pm; Sun 1–3pm and 6–10:30pm. Tube: Oxford Circus, Piccadilly Circus.

Cambio de Tercio ⭐⭐ SPANISH   Several changes of chef have done nothing to dent the standards or popularity of the stylish Cambio de Tercio. The dramatic Spanish-style interior is home to a charming staff, who'll guide you through a menu of Iberian delights. Ham is the house specialty. You should dress up a bit for this place and starve yourself beforehand.

163 Old Brompton Rd., SW5. ☎ 020/7244-8970. Reservations required for dinner. Main courses £10.50–£15 ($16.80–$24). AE, MC, V. Daily noon–2:30pm; Mon–Sat 7–11:30pm; Sun 7–11pm. Tube: Gloucester Rd., South Kensington.

Criterion Brasserie ⭐ MODERN FRENCH   Here's a spot to sample the cooking of Michelin three-star bad boy Marco Pierre White without having to remortgage your house. Right on Piccadilly Circus, the inside is like a Byzantine palace with its fantastic gold vaulted ceiling. The staff is often pressed for time, but the cuisine is superb. Save the Criterion for a lunchtime blowout. Big favorites are ballottine of salmon with herbs and *fromage blanc,* and risottos are always real star performers.

224 Piccadilly, W1. ☎ 020/7930-0488. Reservations essential. Main courses £12–£15 ($19.20–$24); fixed-price lunch £14.95–£17.95 ($23.90–$28.70); fixed-price dinner £14.95 ($23.90), order before 6:30pm. AE, DC, MC, V. Mon–Sat noon–2:30pm; 5:30–11:30pm. Tube: Piccadilly Circus.

Incognico ⭐⭐ MODERN FRENCH   Owned by Michelin-star-winning Nico Ladenis, this brasserie serves up superlative French cooking for relatively non-astronomic prices. The fish is delicious, and there are great vegetarian choices, such as Parmesan risotto with mushrooms. Unlike many of London's eateries, where the food is only part of the entertainment, eating here feels like a very special gastronomic experience. The fixed-price menus offer especially good value.

117 Shaftesbury Ave., WC2 ✆ 020/7836-8866. Reservations essential. Main courses £12.50–£18.50 ($20–$29.60). Fixed-price lunch and pre-theater meal £12.50 ($20). AE, DC, MC, V. Daily noon–3pm; Mon–Sat 5:30–midnight. Tube: Leicester Sq., Tottenham Ct. Rd.

Joe Allen AMERICAN   This dark wood-paneled basement, with its ridiculously discreet entrance, is a Theatreland institution where Londoners dining late rub shoulders with the cream of West End talent. You'll have to splurge to join them or stick to starters and salads where the portions are pretty generous. The menu changes daily, except for the perennial bowl of chili, and the cuisine is a mix of classic down-home dishes and modern British cooking. The service is sometimes perfunctory, and the tables are too close together, but the lively atmosphere and live jazz on Sunday nights compensate.

13 Exeter St., WC2. ✆ 020/7836-0651. Reservations essential at weekends. Main courses £9–£15 ($14.40–$24); fixed-price lunch and pre-theater menu £14–£16 ($22.40–$25.60); weekend brunch menu £17.50–£19.50 ($28–$31.20). AE, MC, V. Mon–Fri noon–1am; Sat 11:30am–1am; Sun 11:30am–midnight. Tube: Covent Garden.

La Spighetta ★★ PIZZA & PASTA   This little basement eatery was created by Giorgio Locatelli, who is chef and part owner of Knightsbridge's illustrious and molto pricey Zafferano. The menu is as authentic and uncomplicated as the decor, using an Italian wood-fired oven for the pizzas. There are nine main pasta dishes and lots of meat and fish main courses. This place is justly popular for working lunches and for R&R after the day is done.

43 Blandford St., W1. ✆ 020/7486-7340. Reservations recommended. Main courses £7–£11 ($11.20–$17.60). AE, MC, V. Mon–Sat noon–2:30pm; Mon–Sat 6:30–11:30pm; Sun 6:30–10:30pm. Tube: Baker St.

Mela ★★ INDIAN   This festive restaurant—it's name means fair—won the 2001 Moët & Chandon award as best Indian restaurant in London. It claims to take its inspiration from Delhi's famous Wali Gali street's food stalls, where workers go to refuel at midday. Lunch here is a fantastic deal: curry or dal of the day, with bread, pickle, and chutney for under £2 ($3.20). This is a great way for curry novices to have a cheap taster—and to see it being made in the open kitchen. But do come back in the evening for a proper go at the innovative Indian country cuisine, when you can choose from more than 10 different dishes.

152–156 Shaftesbury Ave., WC2. ✆ 020/7836-8635. Main courses £7.95–£18.95 ($12.70–$30.30); light lunches £1.95–£4.95 ($3.10–$7.90); fixed-price meal for 2 people £24.95–£34.95 ($39.90–$55.90). AE, MC, V. Mon–Sat noon–11:30pm; Sun noon–10:30pm. Tube: Leicester Sq.

Mirabelle ★★ MODERN EUROPEAN   This brasserie-style restaurant is the best value mouthful of Marco Pierre White's cooking you will ever eat. The seasonally changing menu is sensational, and dishes are made with tricky ingredients timed perfectly. On sunny days, you can sit out on the terrace. If you're on a tight budget, the lower priced, two-course, fixed-price lunch may be a splurge but it costs less than most of his main courses.

56 Curzon St., W1. ✆ 020/7499-4636. Reservations essential. Main courses £14.50–£28.50 ($23.20–$45.60); fixed-price lunch £16.50–£19.95 ($26.40–$31.90). AE, DC, MC, V. Daily noon–2:30pm; 6–11:30pm. Tube: Green Park.

North Sea Fish Restaurant FISH AND CHIPS   Locals love North Sea's version of what is, of course, the national dish. Here the look is country-cozy, even down to the stuffed fish on the walls. The best deal is the enormous seafood platter, which comes with bite-size, battered pieces of lots of different sorts of fish and seafood. You can go for straight cod, of course, or skate, haddock, or plaice, all brought in fresh from Billingsgate every morning. And after all that I'll salute any diner who's got room for one of the traditional desserts.

7–8 Leigh St., WC1. © 020/7387-5892. Reservations recommended for dinner. Main courses £8.30–£16.95 ($13.30–$27.10). AE, DC, MC, V. Mon–Sat noon–2:30pm; 5:30–10:30pm. Tube: Russell Sq., King's Cross.

Royal China ⭐⭐ CHINESE   The plaudits keep rolling in for Royal China's dim sum, which is reckoned by many to be the best in London. The decor is marvelously over-ornate, with Hong Kong casino-style, black-and-gold paneling. But you don't have to be a high roller to dine here: A dim sum extravaganza is unlikely to set you back much more than £10 ($16). The most popular dish, and deservedly so, is the roast pork puff. Come during the week when it's a lot more peaceful, and the staff are more likely to have their happy faces on.

13 Queensway, W2. © 020/7221-2535. Reservations recommended. Main courses £6–£40 ($9.60–$64); fixed-price dinner £28–£36 ($44.80–$57.60). AE, DC, MC, V. Mon–Thurs noon–11pm; Fri–Sat noon–11:30pm; Sun 11am–10pm; dim sum to 5pm daily. Tube: Bayswater, Queensway.

Rules ⭐⭐ TRADITIONAL BRITISH   Lillie Langtry and Edward VII used to tryst at this ultra-British restaurant, but despite the hammy quaintness, Rules is a very modern restaurant operation. It markets the house specialty, "feathered and furred game," as healthy, free range, additive-free, and low in fat. The food is delicious: traditional yet innovative, until you get to the puddings (desserts), which are a mix of nursery and dinner-dance classics. The wine list is pricey, but Rules does have three brown ales, so try one of those instead.

35 Maiden Lane, WC2. © 020/7836-5314. Reservations essential. Main courses £16.95–£22.50 ($27.10–$36); weekday fixed-price menu (served 3–5pm) £19.95 ($31.90). AE, DC, MC, V. Mon–Sat noon–11:15pm; Sun noon–10:15pm. Tube: Charing Cross, Covent Garden.

Suze Wine Bar ⭐ PACIFIC RIM   There's a comfortable bistrolike ambience at this charming Mayfair wine bar; the walls are maroon and hung with modern art. The food is Australasian with some international crossovers and always simply and well prepared. Try the succulent New Zealand green-tipped mussels, a house specialty, or the New Zealand scallops. There are several sharing platters to choose from: Italian antipasti, vegetarian, Greek, seafood, and cheese. And, of course, you can get a fine glass of wine.

41 N. Audley St., W1. © 020/7491-3237. Reservations recommended. Main courses £5.95–£13.50 ($9.50–$21.60); platters to share £5.95–£10.95 ($9.50–$17.50). AE, DC, MC, V. Mon–Sat 11am–11pm. Tube: Green Park.

Vong ⭐⭐ THAI-FRENCH   This is the London outpost of famous chef Jean-Georges Vongerichten, though you probably won't find him in the kitchen. Make sure to dress up for the occasion because you'll have to make an entrance from the reception area down into the chic basement dining room where single-stem orchids decorate the tables. The Thai-French cuisine includes a delicious lobster daikon roll with rosemary ginger dip. Vegetarian options are available. If you can, add on the divine warm Valrhona chocolate cake with lemongrass ice cream.

Berkeley Hotel, Wilton Place, SW1. © 020/7235-1010. Reservations essential. Main courses £16–£32 ($25.60–$51.20); fixed-price lunch £18.50–£20 ($29.60–$32); black plate menu pre-/post-theater £22.50 ($36). AE, DC, DISC, MC, V. Mon–Fri noon–2:30pm; Sat–Sun 11:30am–2pm; Mon–Sat 6–11:30pm; Sun 6–10pm. Tube: Hyde Park Corner, Knightsbridge.

Moments The Delectable Delights of Soho

The French had to show them how to do it, but Londoners have taken to sweet flaky pastries, tarts, and cakes with a vengeance. There are patisseries all over the city, but it's most fun to go to Soho and people-watch while you eat. The most venerable patisserie is **Maison Bertaux,** 28 Greek St., W1 (② 020/7437-6007), and I defy you to pass by its delectable window without wanting to dunk a brioche in a cup of coffee.

Patisserie Valerie, 44 Old Compton St., W1 (② 020/7437-3466), is *the* place to gawk at greedy film and theater types who've fallen for its chocolate truffle cake. The crowds are smaller at **Amato,** 14 Old Compton St., W1 (② 020/7734-5733), but its alcoholic chocolate-and-coffee mousse cake is to die for.

Wagamama 🏶 JAPANESE NOODLES   I eat at a Wagamama every time I'm in London, and crave the yaki soba when I'm away. At this branch, the dining room is set up with ranks of long shared tables like a traditional Japanese noodle bar. The thread noodles come in soups, pan-fried, or served with various toppings. For a hearty dish, try the chili beef ramen—chargrilled sirloin, chiles, red onion, parsley, and spring onions served in a chili-soup base. Each dish is cooked and served immediately, and don't expect to linger too long in the bus-station bustle.

Wagamama also has branches at 10a Lexington St., W1 (② **020/7292-0990**); 101a Wigmore St., W1 (② **020/7409-0111**); 26a Kensington High St., W8 (② **020/7376-1717**); and 11 Jamestown Rd., Camden Town, NW1 (② **020/ 7428-0800**). All are nonsmoking.

4a Streatham St. (off Coptic St.), WC1. ② 020/7323-9223. Main courses £5.20–£8.50 ($8.30–$13.60). AE, DC, MC, V. Mon–Sat noon–11pm; Sun 12:30–10pm. Tube: Tottenham Court Rd.

SHOPPING

London is one of the world's great shopping cities, with a vast and enticing array of department stores, boutiques, small shops, and markets. Major shopping areas are found in the West End, Knightsbridge, and Chelsea. Most stores are open Monday through Saturday from 9:30 or 10am to 5:30 or 6pm and stay open until 8 or 9pm at least 1 night a week. Major sales are held in January and June.

WEST END SHOPPING   Most of the department stores, designer shops, and multiples (chain stores) have their flagships in the West End. **Oxford Street** is home of many large stores with prices that are more affordable than other areas in the West End. Two of the department stores you might want to check out are **Marks & Spencer,** 458 Oxford St. (② **020/7935-7954;** Tube: Marble Arch), where you find basics of all kinds and styles, and more upscale **Selfridges,** 400 Oxford St. (② **020/7629-1234;** Tube: Marble Arch), one of the largest department stores in Europe.

Bond Street (Tube: Bond St.) is the address for all the hot international designers. Here and on adjacent streets, you find a large conglomeration of very expensive fashion boutiques. For books, head to **Charing Cross Road** where, among other booksellers, you find **W & G Foyle, Ltd.,** 113–119 Charing Cross Rd., WC2 (② **020/7440-3225;** Tube: Tottenham Court Rd.), which claims to be the world's largest bookstore and carries an impressive array of hardcovers and paperbacks, as well as travel maps, records, and sheet music.

The **Covent Garden Market** (© 020/7836-9136; Tube: Covent Garden), in the restored Covent Garden fruit and vegetable market, has different market areas with stalls selling "collectible nostalgia," crafts, clothes, and all manner of whatnot. The streets around the market are chockablock with shops selling everything from clothes and books to aromatherapy and food. **Penhaligon's,** 41 Wellington St., WC2 (© 020/7836-2150; Tube: Covent Garden), is an exclusive-line, Victorian perfumery with a large selection of perfumes, after-shaves, soaps, candles, and bath oils for women and men.

Curving **Regent Street,** just off Piccadilly Circus, is a major shopping street for all sorts of goods. **Liberty,** 214–220 Regent St., W1 (© 020/7734-1234: Tube: Oxford Circus), is a six-floor emporium famous for its fine quality fabrics. If you're after English bone china, stop in at **Royal Doulton Regent Street,** 154 Regent St., W1 (© 020/7734-3184; Tube: Piccadilly Circus or Oxford Circus), which carries Royal Doulton, Minton, and Royal Crown Derby. **Scotch House,** 84–86 Regent St., W1 (© 020/7734-0203; Tube: Piccadilly Circus), has a worldwide reputation for its comprehensive selection of cashmere and wool knitwear for men, women, and children; the shop also sells tartan garments and accessories, as well as Scottish tweed classics. If you're looking for toys or children's gifts, check out **Hamleys,** 188–196 Regent St., W1 (© 020/7494-2000; Tube: Piccadilly Circus), which stocks more than 35,000 toys and games on seven floors.

KNIGHTSBRIDGE SHOPPING   London has plenty of department stores to choose from, but **Harrods,** 87–135 Brompton Rd., SW1 (© 020/7730-1234; Tube: Knightsbridge), is the most famous. As firmly entrenched in London life as Buckingham Palace, this enormous store has some 300 departments, delectable Food Halls, and several cafes. **Beauchamp Place,** running south from Brompton Road, is known for its trendy, upscale shops.

CHELSEA SHOPPING   Chelsea's **King's Road** (Tube: Sloane Sq.) became world-famous during the Swinging Sixties and is still popular with younger shoppers, but it's becoming more and more a lineup of chain stores, markets, and *multistores* (large or small conglomerations of indoor stands, stalls, and booths within one building). The area is also known for its design-trade showrooms and stores of household wares. King's Road begins on the west side of Sloane Square tube station.

PORTOBELLO ROAD MARKET   Portobello Road in Notting Hill (Tube: Notting Hill Gate) is London's most famous street market. The market, held on Saturdays from 6am to 5pm, is a magnet for collectors of everything from overpriced junk to valuable antiques. If you're a serious collector, return on a weekday to check out the antiques and art shops that line Portobello Road.

NIGHTLIFE

London is one of the world's great cultural capitals and renowned for its nightlife. Theater, music, and dance performances of all kinds take place every night. You can also spend an evening in a pub or dancing at one of London's many clubs. To find out what's happening, buy a copy of *Time Out,* an invaluable listings magazine published weekly and sold at all newsagents.

In general, you should be able to buy tickets for almost any show or performance once you arrive by going directly to the theater's box office or by calling the theater directly. Many London theaters accept telephone credit-card bookings at regular prices plus a minimal fee. By buying directly from the box office, you don't have to pay the commission fee (up to 30%) charged by ticket agencies. A **half-price ticket booth** in Leicester Square (no phone; Tube: Leicester Sq.) sells seats for shows available that day. The booth is open Monday through Saturday noon to 6:30pm and noon to 2pm for matinees (which may be on Wed, Thurs, Sat, or Sun).

THEATER   Plays and musicals are staged all over the city in approximately 100 theaters, but the commercial hits are centered in the **West End.** The West End theater district is concentrated in the area around Piccadilly Circus, Leicester Square, and Covent Garden. The prestigious **Royal Shakespeare Company** (✆ **01789/403404;** www.rsc.org.uk) uses the **Barbican Centre** (Silk St., EC2; ✆ **020/7382-7297;** Tube: Barbican), a multi-arts center in The City, as one of its London venues and also mounts productions in West End theaters. The **South Bank Arts Centre** (South Bank, SE1; Tube: Waterloo) is home to the **Royal National Theatre** (✆ **020/7452-3000;** www.nt-online.org), which stages performances in three theaters.

BALLET, OPERA & CLASSICAL MUSIC   London is home base to two major opera and dance companies. The **Royal Opera** and **Royal Ballet** perform at the **Royal Opera House** (Covent Garden, WC2E; ✆ **020/7304-4000;** www.royalopera.org; Tube: Covent Garden). The **English National Opera** and **English National Ballet** perform at the **London Coliseum** (St. Martin's Lane, WC2N; ✆ **020/7632-8300;** www.eno.org; Tube: Leicester Sq.).

The home base for the **London Symphony Orchestra** (www.lso.co.uk) is **Barbican Hall** at the Barbican Centre, Silk Street, EC2Y (✆ **020/7638-8891;** Tube: Barbican). You may also catch a performance there by the **Royal Philharmonic Orchestra** (www.rpo.co.uk), which plays concerts at the Barbican and at the **Royal Albert Hall,** Kensington Gore SW7 (✆ **020/7589-8212;** Tube: High St. Kensington), an enormous circular domed concert hall that has been a landmark in South Kensington since 1871. The **South Bank Centre,** South Bank, SE1 (✆ **020/7960-4242;** www.sbc.org.uk; Tube: Waterloo), presents approximately 1,200 classical music and dance concerts per year in three separate auditoriums.

PUBS   Most pubs adhere to strict hours governed by Parliament: Monday through Saturday 11am to 11pm and Sunday noon to 10:30pm. Americans take note: In a pub, you never tip the bartender; the best you can do is offer to buy him or her a drink. Ten minutes before closing a bell rings, signaling that it's time to order your last round. There are hundreds of pubs in London; the following is a very selective list.

Cittie of Yorke, 22 High Holborn, WC1 (✆ **020/7242-7670;** Tube: Holborn or Chancery Lane), has the longest bar in Britain and looks like a great medieval hall—an appropriate appearance because a pub has existed at this location since 1430. **Seven Stars,** 53 Carey St., WC2 (✆ **020/7242-8521;** Tube: Holborn), is tiny and modest except for its collection of Toby mugs and law-related art. The pub is located at the back of the law courts, so lots of barristers drink here. **Black Friar,** 174 Queen Victoria St., EC4 (✆ **020/7236-5650;** Tube: Blackfriars), is an Edwardian wonder made of marble and bronze Art Nouveau. The interior features bas-reliefs of mad monks, a low-vaulted mosaic ceiling, and seating carved out of gold marble recesses. **Churchill Arms,** 119 Kensington Church St., W8 (✆ **020/7727-4242;** Tube: Notting Hill Gate or High St. Kensington), is loaded with Churchill memorabilia. The pub hosts an entire week of celebration leading up to Sir Winston's birthday on November 30. Visitors are often welcomed like regulars here, and you'll find the overall ambience to be down-to-earth and homey.

DANCE CLUBS   Cover charges vary according to day of the week and/or what band is playing. For more options, check out the music and clubs listings in *Time Out*. The big dance clubs don't really start hopping until after 10pm and typically stay open until 3 or 4am on weekends.

The **Complex,** 1–5 Parkfield St., N1 (✆ 020/7288-1986; Tube: Angel), frequently books live bands and has four floors with different dance vibes on each. **Equinox,** Leicester Square, WC2 (✆ 020/7437-1446; Tube: Leicester Sq.), boasts London's largest dance floor and one of the largest lighting rigs in Europe. A diverse crowd dances to equally diverse music, including dance hall, pop, rock, and Latin. The **Hippodrome,** Cranbourn Street and Charing Cross Road, WC2 (✆ 020/7437-4311; Tube: Leicester Sq.), is a cavernous place with a great sound system and lights to match. This club was a favorite of Princess Diana during her early club-hopping days; now the place is tacky, touristy, and packed on weekends. **Venom Club/The Zoo Bar,** 13–17 Bear St., WC2 (✆ 020/7839-4188; Tube: Leicester Sq.), features a trendy Euro-androgynous crowd and music so loud you have to use sign language. The club boasts the slickest, flashiest, most psychedelic decor in London.

Bar Rumba, 36 Shaftesbury Ave., W1 (✆ 020/7287-2715; Tube: Piccadilly Circus), is all over the map musically; every night this club features a different type of music, including jazz fusion, phat funk, hip-hop, soul, R&B, and swing. **Hanover Grand,** 6 Hanover St., W1 (✆ 020/7499-7977; Tube: Oxford Circus), is funky and down and dirty on Thursday, but otherwise cutting-edge and always crowded.

BARS   If you want to slip into an elegant mode and mood, head for one of these classy hotel bars for your favorite cocktail.

The **American Bar** in the Savoy Hotel, The Strand, WC2 (✆ 020/7836-4343; Tube: Charing Cross Rd. or Embankment), is one of London's most sophisticated gathering places and reputedly serves the best martini in town. **The Library** in the Lanesborough Hotel, 1 Lanesborough Place, SW1 (✆ 020/7259-5599; Tube: Hyde Park Corner), one of London's poshest drinking retreats, is famous for its unparalleled collection of ancient cognacs. At the **Lillie Langtry Bar** in the Cadogan Hotel, Sloane Street, SW1 (✆ 020/7235-7141; Tube: Sloane Sq. or Knightsbridge), you can go back in time to the charm and elegance of the Edwardian era, when Lillie Langtry, an actress and a society beauty (mistress of Edward VII and friend of Oscar Wilde), lived here.

3 Edinburgh

Edinburgh (pronounced *Edin*-burra) is one of the most beautiful and fascinating cities in Europe. Located near the Firth of Forth, an inlet from the North Sea, and surrounded by rolling hills, lakes, and forests, Scotland's capital enjoys an unparalleled setting with panoramic views from every hilltop. The looming presence of Edinburgh Castle lends a romantic, historic air to this fair city, but Edinburgh is also very much an international city of today, where you'll find chic cafes and aggressively modern architecture within the city's medieval core. Edinburgh is divided into two distinct areas: Old Town, where the city began, and New Town, an elegant example of 18th-century urban planning. It's a wonderfully strollable city full of fine museums, galleries, historic attractions, and real character.

GETTING THERE

BY PLANE   **Edinburgh Airport** (© 0131/333-1000), 6 miles (10km) west of the city center, receives flights from within the British Isles and the rest of Europe. An **Airlink** bus (© 0131/555-6363; www.lothianbuses.co.uk) makes the 25-minute trip from the airport to the city center every 10 minutes, letting you off near Waverley Station; the fare is £3.30 ($5.30) one-way or £5 ($8) round-trip. A taxi into the city costs about £14 ($22.40), depending on traffic, and also takes about 25 minutes.

BY RAIL   Fast trains operated by **GNER** (© 08457/225225; www.gner. co.uk) link London with Edinburgh's **Waverley Station,** at the east end of Princes Street, right in the middle of the city. The station is the central rail hub for all of Scotland and has a train information center, a couple of restaurants, and a luggage storage facility. All fast trains to Waverly provide restaurant, buffet, and at-seat trolley service; complimentary beverages and snacks are available in First Class. BritRail Passes (but not Eurailpasses) may be used for the trip between London and Edinburgh.

All trains depart from London **King's Cross** Station, except for the **overnight train,** which departs from London **Euston.** The journey takes 4½ hours and costs from £85 ($136) for an advance purchase Standard Class round-trip ticket to £270 ($432) for a same-day First Class ticket. Overnight trains take 7¼ hours and have couchettes, which you can reserve for an extra £17.50 ($28). Seat reservations are recommended but not required on all London–Edinburgh trains. If you're traveling around the same time as the Edinburgh Festival or on a summer weekend, we advise getting a seat reservation in advance.

VISITOR INFORMATION & ROOM RESERVATIONS

Edinburgh & Scotland Information Centre, 3 Princes St. (© 0131/473-3800; www.edinburgh.org), in the Waverley Shopping Centre next to Waverley Station, can give you sightseeing information, exchange currency, and also book hotels in all price categories. The center sells bus tours and theater tickets as well. It's open Monday through Saturday from 9am to 6pm (to 7pm June–July and Sept, to 8pm Aug) and Sunday from 10am to 6pm (to 7pm June–July and Sept, to 8pm Aug). There's also an information and accommodations desk at Edinburgh Airport.

GETTING AROUND

ON FOOT   Edinburgh is divided into a New Town and an Old Town, and walking is the best way to see both. Most of the city's major attractions lie along or near the **Royal Mile,** the main thoroughfare of the **Old Town,** which begins at Edinburgh Castle and runs all the way to the Palace of Holyroodhouse. Because of its narrow lanes and passageways, you can only explore the Old Town in any depth on foot. Lying below the Old Town and separated from it by a deep leafy ravine (that's home to Waverly station and has a river called the Water of Leith flowing through it) is the **New Town,** an extraordinary adventure in urban planning built between 1766 and 1840. It takes in most of the northern half of the heart of the city and is made up of a network of squares, streets, terraces, and circuses, reaching from Haymarket in the west to Abbeyhill in the east. **Princes Street,** famed for its shopping, is the New Town's main artery. Expect to do some climbing because parts of Edinburgh are quite hilly.

Edinburgh

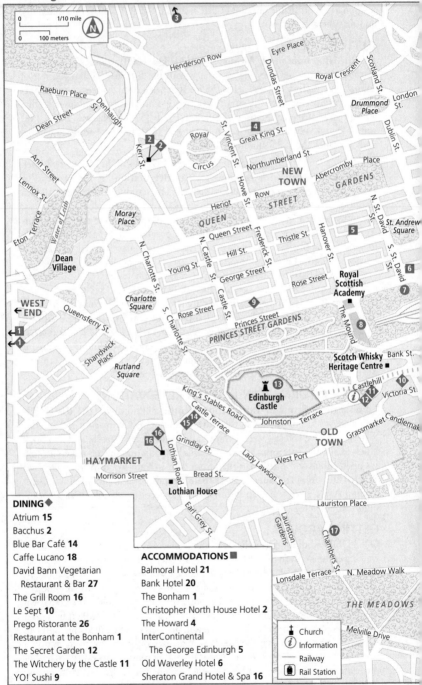

✝ Church
ⓘ Information
— Railway
🏛 Rail Station

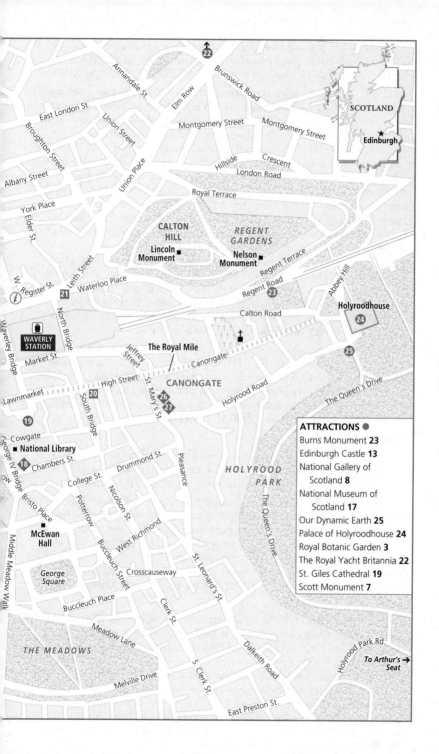

SCOTLAND

★ Edinburgh

East London St.

Annandale St.

Elm Row

Brunswick Road

Union Street

Montgomery Street

Montgomery Street

Broughton Street

Union Place

Hillside

Crescent

London Road

Albany Street

York Place

Royal Terrace

Elder St.

CALTON HILL

REGENT GARDENS

Lincoln Monument ■

Nelson Monument ■

W. Register St.

Leith Street

Waterloo Place

Regent Terrace

ⓘ

21

Regent Road

23

Abbey Hill

Holyroodhouse

24

North Bridge

Calton Road

WAVERLY STATION

Waverley Bridge

Market St.

Jeffrey Street

The Royal Mile

Canongate

25

High Street

St. Mary's St.

CANONGATE

Holyrood Road

The Queen's Drive

Lawnmarket

20

South Bridge

26
27

19

Cowgate

■ National Library

George IV Bridge

18

Chambers St.

College St.

Drummond St.

Nicolson St.

Pleasance

HOLYROOD PARK

Bristo Place

Potterrow

West Richmond

The Queen's Drive

■ McEwan Hall

Buccleuch Street

Crosscauseway

St. Leonard's St.

George Square

Buccleuch Place

Clerk St.

Meadow Lane

THE MEADOWS

S. Clerk St.

Dalkeith Road

Holyrood Park Rd.

**To Arthur's →
Seat**

Middle Meadow Walk

Melville Drive

East Preston St.

ATTRACTIONS ●

Burns Monument **23**
Edinburgh Castle **13**
National Gallery of
  Scotland **8**
National Museum of
  Scotland **17**
Our Dynamic Earth **25**
Palace of Holyroodhouse **24**
Royal Botanic Garden **3**
The Royal Yacht Britannia **22**
St. Giles Cathedral **19**
Scott Monument **7**

If you want a qualified professional guide to show you around, contact (in advance) the **Scottish Tourist Guides Association** (© **01786/451953;** www. stga.co.uk). The rate for a half day is £65 ($104); for a full day it's £100 ($160).

BY BUS   If you're traveling any distance, the bus will be your least expensive mode of transport. **Lothian Buses** (© **0131/555-6363** for schedules; www. lothianbuses.co.uk) operates a comprehensive system of double-decker buses throughout Edinburgh. The fare depends on the distance you ride, with a minimum fare of 60p ($1) for one or two stages and a maximum fare of £1 ($1.60) for nine or more stages. A stage isn't a stop, but a distance of about half a mile (.8km). Exact change is required if you're paying your fare on the bus. The **Daysaver** ticket allows 1 day of unlimited travel on city buses for £2.50 ($4) and can be purchased from the bus driver. A **GoSmart Ridacard** allows unlimited travel on all buses for £11 ($17.60) for 1 week. For an introduction to the principal attractions in and around Edinburgh, consider the same company's **Edinburgh Tour** (www.edinburghtour.com), which allows you to get on and off at any of the 15 stops. Buses start from the Waverley Bridge near the Scott Monument daily at 9:15am, departing every 15 minutes in summer and about every 30 minutes in winter; if you remain on the bus without getting off, the trip will take about 2 hours. The cost is £8.50 ($13.60) for adults, £7.50 ($12) for seniors. You can buy tour tickets and Ridacards and obtain further information at the **Waverley Bridge Travel Shop,** beside Waverley Station.

BY TAXI   You can hail a taxi or pick one up at a taxi stand. Meters begin at £1.40 ($2.25) and increase 22p (35¢) every 52 seconds. Taxi ranks are at Hanover Street, North Street, Andrew Street, Waverley Station, Haymarket Station, and Lauriston Place. Fares are displayed on the meter and charges posted, including extra charges for night drivers or destinations outside the city limits. To call for a taxi, try **City Cabs** (© **0131/228-1211**).

WHERE TO STAY

Edinburgh offers a full range of accommodations throughout the year. Hotels fill up during the 3-week period of the Edinburgh International Festival in August, so if you're coming at that time, be sure to reserve far in advance.

Balmoral Hotel ★★★   Located almost directly above the Waverley Rail Station, this legendary Edinburgh landmark opened in 1902 as the grandest hotel in the north of Britain. The spacious guest rooms with their large windows are a graceful reminder of an earlier age but there's nothing old-fashioned about the stylish furnishings and unusually roomy bathrooms.

1 Princes St., Edinburgh EH2 2EQ. © 800/225-5843 in the U.S., or 0131/556-1111. Fax 0131/557-8747. www.roccofortehotels.com. 188 units. £220–£330 ($352–$528) double. AE, DC, MC, V. **Amenities:** 2 restaurants; bar; lounge. *In room:* Hair dryer.

Bank Hotel ★ *Value*   This unusual hotel is located right in the heart of Old Town and offers better value than all of its competitors along the Royal Mile. Built in 1923 as a branch of the Royal Bank of Scotland, it now offers a handful of individually decorated theme rooms (each named for a famous Scotsman) above Logie Baird's Bar, a lively (and smoky) ground-floor bar and restaurant. There are delightful touches throughout, and the bathrooms are as nice and comfortable as the rooms.

Royal Mile at 1–3 S. Bridge St., Edinburgh EH1 1LL. © 0131/622-6800. Fax 0131/622-6822. www.festival-inns.co.uk. 9 units. £70–£130 ($112–$208) double. Rates include breakfast. AE, DC, MC, V. Bus: 4, 15, 31, or 100. **Amenities:** Bar; laundry. *In room:* Hair dryer, no A/C.

The Bonham ★★★ Style is pumped up to a very high level at this New Town hotel occupying three Victorian town houses. The high-ceilinged, large-windowed guest rooms feature the best of contemporary furnishings against a bold palette of colors. Beds are huge and bathrooms as fine as you'll find. The hotel is very techno-friendly and every room has its own communication and entertainment center. The excellent Restaurant at the Bonham is reviewed on p. 424.

35 Drumsheugh Gardens, Edinburgh EH3 7RN. ℂ **0131/623-6060.** Fax 0131/226-6080. www.thebonham. com. 48 units. £165–£240 ($264–$384) double. AE, MC, V. Bus: 41 or 42. **Amenities:** Restaurant; bar; lounge; laundry; nonsmoking rooms. *In room:* Hair dryer, no A/C.

Christopher North House Hotel ★★ *Finds* The welcome you get at this charming boutique hotel, set in a neoclassical town house in New Town, is the friendliest in Edinburgh. Room furnishings are modern but the decor is full of dramatic and period accents. Some of the rooms are rather small; suites are large and comfortably luxurious. Bathrooms throughout are ample and well equipped. Bacchus, the hotel's intimate restaurant (p. 423), is one of Edinburgh's best-kept secrets.

6 Gloucester Place, Edinburgh EH3 6EF. ℂ **0131/225-2720.** Fax 0131/220-4706. www.christophernorth. co.uk. 15 units. £120 ($192) double; £200 ($320) suite. Includes full breakfast. Check the website for special offers. AE, DC, MC, V. Bus: 19 or 80 to Northwest Circus Pl. **Amenities:** Restaurant; bar; lounge; nonsmoking rooms. *In room:* Hair dryer, no A/C.

The Howard ★★★ Classic elegance, impeccable service, and gorgeous furnishings combine to make this one of Edinburgh's finest small deluxe hotels. Occupying three Georgian terrace houses in New Town, the Howard is refined but relaxed about it. The spacious guest rooms are impeccable, the bathrooms fabulous (some have freestanding "roll top" Georgian-style bathtubs). Your "dedicated butler" is on call 24/7.

34 Great King St., Edinburgh EH3 6QH. ℂ **800/323-5463** in the U.S., or 0131/315-2220. Fax 0131/557-6515. www.thehoward.com. 18 units. £235–£255 ($376–$408) double. Rates include breakfast. AE, DC, MC, V. Bus: 13, 23, 27, or C5. **Amenities:** Restaurant; bar; laundry. *In room:* Hair dryer, no A/C.

InterContinental The George Edinburgh ★ Originally designed as a bank by famed architect Robert Adam over 200 years ago, the George stands only yards from St. Andrew Square, the city's financial center. The public rooms have been designed with old-fashioned elegance and comfort in mind. The guest rooms, contained in an older and a newer wing, are good size and traditionally furnished; those on the upper floors have marvelous views of Edinburgh and the Firth of Forth. Bathrooms are on the small side.

19–21 George St., Edinburgh EH2 2PB. ℂ **800/327-0200** in the U.S., or 0131/225-1251. Fax 0131/226-5644. http://edinburgh.intercontinental.com. 195 units. £205–£240 ($328–$384) double. AE, DC, MC, V. Bus: 41 or 42. **Amenities:** 2 restaurants; bar; lounge; laundry; nonsmoking rooms. *In room:* Hair dryer.

Old Waverley Hotel ★ Opposite Waverley Station, the Old Waverley dates from 1843 and was built to celebrate a revolutionary new form of transportation: the railroad. The lounges have been given a contemporary look with bright splashes of color. The recently refurbished guest rooms are well maintained and comfortable (but lack air-conditioning), with good-size bathrooms; some look onto Princes Street and the castle.

43 Princes St., Edinburgh EH2 2BY. ℂ **0131/556-4648.** Fax 0131/557-6316. www.paramount-hotels.co.uk/ oldwaverley. 66 units. £160 ($256) double. Rates include breakfast. AE, DC, MC, V. **Amenities:** Restaurant; bar; laundry. *In room:* Hair dryer; no A/C.

Sheraton Grand Hotel & Spa ✰✰   A short walk from Princes Street and directly across from the Lyceum Theatre, this upscale hotel offers spacious, traditionally furnished guest rooms that are extremely comfortable and have nice bathrooms; the castle-view rooms on the top floors are the best. What really makes this hotel stand out, however, is its new spa—one of Europe's greatest—which contains a state-of-the-art gym, gorgeous indoor and outdoor pools, steam room and sauna, and a complete array of spa treatments.

1 Festival Sq., Edinburgh EH3 9SR. ℂ 800/325-3535 in the U.S. and Canada, or 0131/229-9131. Fax 0131/228-4510. www.sheraton.com. 278 units. June–Sept £220–£260 ($352–$416) double. Children under 17 stay free in parent's room. AE, DC, MC, V. Bus: 4, 15, or 44. **Amenities:** 2 restaurants; bar; laundry; nonsmoking rooms. *In room:* Hair dryer.

THE TOP ATTRACTIONS & SPECIAL MOMENTS

Old Town's **Royal Mile** ✰✰✰ stretches from Edinburgh Castle all the way to the Palace of Holyroodhouse and bears four names along its length: Castlehill, Lawnmarket, High Street, and Canongate. Walking along it, you'll see some of the most interesting old structures in the city, with turrets, gables, and towering chimneys.

Edinburgh Castle ✰✰   No place in Scotland is filled with as much history, legend, and lore as Edinburgh Castle. Its early history is vague, but it's known that in the 11th century, Malcolm III (Canmore) and his Saxon queen, later venerated as St. Margaret, founded a castle on this spot; the oldest structure in Edinburgh is **St. Margaret's Chapel,** a small stone structure on the castle grounds dating from the 12th century. The somber and sparsely furnished **State Apartments** include Queen Mary's Bedroom, where Mary Queen of Scots gave birth to James VI of Scotland (later James I of England). Scottish Parliaments used to convene in the **Great Hall.** For most visitors, the highlight is the **Crown Chamber,** housing the Honours of Scotland (Scottish Crown Jewels), used at the coronation of James VI, along with the scepter and sword of the state of Scotland. The storerooms known as the **French Prisons** were used to incarcerate captured French soldiers during the Napoleonic wars. Many of them made wall carvings you can see today. **Mons Meg,** a 15th-century cannon weighing more than 5 tons, is the most famous of the batteries of cannons that protected the castle.

⟨ Moments   Great Scott!

Looking more like a neo-Gothic church spire than a monument to a famous writer, the **Scott Monument** in the East Princes St. Gardens (ℂ 0131/529-4068) is Edinburgh's most famous landmark. In the center of this 200-foot spire completed in the mid–19th century is a large seated statue of novelist Sir Walter Scott and his dog, Maida. Some of Scott's characters are carved as small figures in the monument. You can climb 287 steps to the top for a spectacular view. From here, clearly visible along Regent Road, you can see the **Burns Monument,** dedicated to poet Robert Burns and designed by Thomas Hamilton in 1830. Admission to the Scott Monument is £2.50 ($4). The monument is open March through May and October Monday through Saturday from 9am to 6pm, Sunday 10am to 6pm; June through September Monday through Sat 9am to 8pm, Sunday 10am to 6pm; November through February Monday through Saturday 9am to 4pm, Sunday 10am to 6pm. It's an easy walk from Waverley station, or take any city center bus along Princes Street.

Castlehill. ✆ **0131/225-9846**. Admission £8 ($12.85) adults, £6.50 ($10.40) seniors. Apr–Sept daily 9:30am–5:15pm; Oct–Mar daily 9:30am–4:15pm. Bus: Traveline.

National Gallery of Scotland ☆☆

In the center of Princes Street Gardens, this gallery is small as national galleries go, but the collection contains several important works. Italian paintings include Verrocchio's *Ruskin Madonna,* Andrea del Sarto's *Portrait of a Man,* Domenichino's *Adoration of the Shepherds,* and Tiepolo's *Finding of Moses,* plus works by Raphael and Titian. Also worth seeking out are works by El Greco, Velázquez, and notable paintings by Rubens and Rembrandt. The Maitland Collection includes one of Cézanne's *Mont St-Victoire* series, an early Monet (*Shipping Scene—Night Effects*), as well as works by Degas, van Gogh, Renoir, Gauguin, and Seurat. Look for the stunning landscape, *Niagara Falls, from the American Side,* by 19th-century American painter Frederic Church, and Henry Raeburn's famous *The Rev. Robert Walker Skating on Duddingston Loch.*

The Mound. ✆ **0131/624-6200**. www.nationalgalleries.org. Free admission. Mon–Sat 10am–5pm; Sun noon–5pm; open an hour later during the Edinburgh Festival in Aug. Bus: 3, 21, or 26.

National Museum of Scotland ☆☆

Scotland's premier museum, built of pale Scottish sandstone, opened in 1998 to house the nation's greatest national treasures. There are many beautiful objects on display here but the museum in some ways overwhelms the collections. You can follow a chronological trail through the centuries in galleries called "Beginnings," "Early People," "Industry and Empire," and so on up to the "Twentieth Century Gallery." Highlights include wonderful examples of ancient jewelry displayed in modern sculptures by Sir Eduardo Paolozzi; the Trappan treasure horde of silver objects found buried in East Lothian; the 12th-century Lewis chessmen; and, gruesomely, the "Maiden"—an early guillotine. There are great views from the roof terrace.

Chambers St. ✆ **0131/247-4422**. www.nms.ac.uk. Free admission. Mon–Sat 10am–5pm; Tues 10am–8pm; Sun noon–5pm. Bus no. 23, 27, 28, 41, 42.

Our Dynamic Earth

A former brewery was converted into this multimedia amphitheater capped by a translucent tentlike roof. Its galleries explain the natural diversity of the earth, elaborating on the seismological and biological processes that led from the Big Bang to the world we know today. The presentation features audio and video clips; buttons you can push to simulate earthquakes, meteor showers, and views of outer space; replicas of the slimy green primordial soup; time capsules winding their way back through the eons; and a series of specialized aquariums, some with replicas of primordial life forms, some with living sharks, dolphins, and coral. Visitors wander through simulated terrains—polar ice caps, tundras, deserts, grasslands, and tropical rainforest. Also on the premises are a restaurant, a cafe, and a gift shop.

Holyrood Rd. ✆ **0131/550-7800**. Admission £7.95 ($12.70) adults, £4.50 ($7.20) seniors. Apr–Oct daily 10am–6pm; Nov–Mar Wed–Sun 10am–5pm (last entry 3:30pm). Bus: 30, 35.

Palace of Holyroodhouse ☆☆

Early in the 16th century, this palace was built by James IV adjacent to a 12th-century Augustinian abbey. The nave of the abbey church still remains, but only the north tower of James's palace is left. Most of what you see today was built by Charles II after Scotland and England were united in the 17th century. The palace, which serves as the Queen's official residence in Scotland, is open to visitors when she's not in town.

One of the more dramatic incidents at Holyroodhouse occurred in 1566 when David Rizzio, the Italian secretary of Mary Queen of Scots, was stabbed

56 times in front of her eyes by her jealous husband, Lord Darnley, and his accomplices. A plaque marks the spot. And one of the more curious exhibits is a piece of needlework done by Mary depicting a cat-and-mouse scene—her cousin, Elizabeth I, happens to be the cat. Mary lived on the second floor of King James' Tower, the oldest surviving section of the palace, with Lord Darnley's rooms below. Some of the rich tapestries, paneling, massive fireplaces, and antiques from the 1700s are still in place. The Throne Room and other drawing rooms are still used for state occasions. In the rear of the palace is the richly furnished King's Bedchamber. The Picture Gallery contains many dubious portraits of Scottish monarchs painted by Dutch artist Jacob De Witt, who in 1684 signed a contract to turn them out at the rate of one a week for 2 years.

Behind Holyroodhouse begins **Holyrood Park,** Edinburgh's largest. With rocky crags, a loch, sweeping meadows, and the ruins of a chapel, it's a wee bit of the Scottish countryside in the city, and a great place for a picnic. From the park you can climb up a treeless, heather-covered crag called **Arthur's Seat** ★★★ for breathtaking panoramas of the city and the Firth of Forth.

Canongate, at the eastern end of the Royal Mile. ℂ 0131/556-7371. www.royal.gov.uk. Admission £6.50 ($10.40) adults, £5 ($8) seniors. Nov–Mar daily 9:30am–4:30pm; Apr–Oct daily 9:30am–6pm (last admissions 45 min. before closing). Bus: 30, 35.

The Royal Yacht *Britannia* ★★★

Used by Queen Elizabeth II and the royal family since 1952, this luxurious 412-foot yacht was decommissioned in 1997, berthed in Leith (2 miles/3 km from Edinburgh's center), and opened to the pubic. You reach the famous vessel by going through a rather dreary shopping mall to a visitor center where you collect a portable audio guide keyed to the major staterooms and working areas on all five decks. You can walk the decks where Prince Charles and Princess Diana strolled on their honeymoon, visit the drawing room and the little-changed Royal Apartments, and explore the engine room, the galleys, and the captain's cabin.

Ocean Terminal, Leith. ℂ 0131/555-5566. www.royalyachtbritannia.co.uk. £7.75 ($12.40), £5.95 ($9.50) seniors. Apr–Sept daily 9:30am–4:30pm; Oct–Mar 10am–3:30pm. Bus: 11, 22, 34, 35, 36, 49.

Royal Botanic Garden ★★★

One of the grandest gardens in Great Britain, the Royal Botanic Garden sprawls across 70 acres on the north side of the Water of Leith. It dates from the late 17th century, when it was originally used to grow and study medicinal plants. The collection grew dramatically between 1904 and 1932 with plants collected in southwestern China and brought to Edinburgh by George Forrest. Today, the new Chinese Garden contains the largest collection of Chinese plants outside of China. The gardens are particularly famous for their rhododendrons, at their most spectacular in April and May. Rare orchids and huge Amazonian water lilies are on view in a group of hothouses, and a 2-centuries-old palm tree grows in the glass-roofed Palm House. Plant enthusiasts should consider taking one of the guided tours that leave from the West Gate on Arboretum Place at 11am and 2pm April through September. You can enjoy fabulous views of Edinburgh's Old Town skyline from the Terrace Café.

Entrances at 20A Inverleith Row and Arboretum Place. ℂ 0131/552-7171. Free admission. Guided tours £2 ($3.20). Apr–Aug daily 9:30am–7pm (to 6pm Mar and Sept; to 5pm Feb and Oct; to 4pm Nov–Jan). Guided tours: Apr–Sept daily 11 am, 2pm. Bus: 8, 17, 23, 27.

St. Giles Cathedral

A short walk downhill from Edinburgh Castle, this dark and somewhat grim-looking stone church is one of the principal landmarks along the Royal Mile. Dating mostly from the late 15th century, but with sections that date back to the 12th century, it is usually referred to as a cathedral but is more officially a "high kirk" of Scottish Presbyterianism. It was from here that the famous Scottish minister John Knox preached and directed the Scottish Reformation in the 16th century. The interior is not particularly noteworthy except for the four massive Norman-era pillars. The walls are covered with funerary monuments, including one to Edinburgh-born Robert Louis Stevenson. Thistle Chapel houses beautiful stalls and notable heraldic stained-glass windows from 1911.

High St. ℂ **0131/225-9442.** Free admission. Easter–Sept Mon–Fri 9am–7pm, Sat 9am–5pm, Sun 1–5pm; Oct–Easter Mon–Sat 9am–5pm, Sun 1–5pm. Guides are available at all times to conduct free tours. Bus: 23, 27, 28, 35, 41, 42.

WHERE TO DINE

Edinburgh boasts the finest restaurants in Scotland. If you can't stomach the idea of dining on regional fare such as haggis (spicy intestines), you'll find an array of top restaurants serving Scottish, French, Modern European, and ethnic cuisines. The Scottish-French culinary connection dates back to the time of Mary Queen of Scots, though it's been much refined over the centuries. More and more restaurants are catering to vegetarians, too. Some of the dishes Edinburgh is known for include fresh salmon and seafood, game from Scottish fields, and Aberdeen Angus steaks. Some restaurants have sections reserved for non-smokers; others don't. If smoking and dining (or nonsmoking and dining) are very important to you, inquire when making your reservation.

Atrium ⟨⟨ MODERN SCOTTISH/INTERNATIONAL   This trend-setting restaurant next to the Traverse Theatre has been one of top dining spots in Edinburgh since 1993. Chef Neil Forbes draws inspiration from Scotland and all over the world and has won numerous awards for the fresh, inventive dishes on his daily-changing menu. Rosemary crème brûlée with mascarpone sorbet is one delectable dessert worth trying. The restaurant stocks a wide array of wines.

Cambridge St., next to Traverse Theatre. ℂ **0131/228-8882.** www.atriumrestaurant.co.uk. Reservations recommended. Main courses £14.50–£20 ($23.25–$32); fixed-price dinner £48 ($76.80). AE, DC, MC, V. Mon–Fri noon–2pm and 6:30–10pm; Sat 6:30–10pm. Bus: 1, 10, 11, 15.

Bacchus ⟨ (Finds) SCOTTISH/INTERNATIONAL   This intimate restaurant is used mostly by lucky guests of the Christopher North Hotel and doesn't really look elsewhere to fill its few tables, but it's open to non-guests and makes for a romantic evening out. It's also far more reasonably priced than most restaurants of its caliber. You can order an Aberdeen Angus steak with peppercorn sauce; homemade spinach and ricotta ravioli; or fish, pheasant, and chicken dishes. A nice selection of wines is available.

In the Christopher North House Hotel, 6 Gloucester Place. ℂ **0131/225-2720.** Reservations required. Main courses £7.50–£15 ($12–$24). AE, MC, V. Mon–Sat 6–10pm. Bus: 19 or 80 to Northwest Circus Pl.

Blue Bar Café INTERNATIONAL   In a cool circular room on the second floor of the Traverse Theatre, this hip bistro is a less expensive alternative to the Atrium (see above). The sophisticated menu changes monthly. You might find pipperade risotto with eggplant caviar; succulent breast of duck with bubble and squeak; or a perfect pan-roasted cod with mussels, cockles, and clams. On theater nights, this is a crowded, fun place to dine.

Cambridge St., on the second floor of the Traverse Theatre. ℂ **0131/228-1222.** Reservations recommended. Light menu £5.25–£6.50 ($8.40–$10.40); main courses £10.50–£15.50 ($16.80–$24.80). AE, DC, MC, V. Daily 11:30am–3pm and 6–10:45pm. Bus: 1, 10, 11, 15.

Caffe Lucano *(Finds)* PASTA/CAFE   Just around the corner from the Museum of Scotland, this pleasant, nonsmoking cafe is a good spot for lunch or afternoon coffee or tea. All fresh ingredients are used to make their Italian specialties: risotto, spaghetti, ravioli, and tortellini. You can get the soup of the day and bread for £2.80 ($4.50). There's also a good array of fresh sandwiches for takeout.

37–39 George IV Bridge. (©) 0131/225-6690. Main courses £5.95–£14.95 ($9.50–$23.90). MC, V. Mon–Fri 7am–10pm; Sat 8am–10pm; Sun 9am–8pm. Bus: 23, 27, 41.

David Bann Vegetarian Restaurant & Bar *(Finds)* VEGETARIAN   All the current trends in vegetarian cooking are wonderfully summarized in this hip new vegetarian restaurant around the corner from a the new Scottish Parliament building. With its stylish decor and smooth jazzy background, it's a place where you want to linger. The chef creates vegetarian dishes inspired and influenced by the foods of India, China, Italy, and the Mediterranean. The menu changes often, but possible choices include Malaysian vegetable curry or baked polenta with Gorgonzola. This is a good spot to come for a meatless Sunday brunch.

56–58 St. Mary's St. (©) 0131/556-5888. Reservations recommended weekend dinner. Light meals £6.50–£7 ($10.40–$11.20); main meals £8.80–£10.50 ($14.10–$16.80). AE, DC, MC, V. Daily 11am–"late." Bus: 30, 35.

The Grill Room *(★★)* FRENCH/SCOTTISH   For a very fine and memorable meal, The Grill Room in the Sheraton Grand Hotel is a standout. You can expect impeccably high standards and attentive service, but the restaurant is also pleasantly relaxed. Nicolas Laurent, the French-born head chef, uses high-quality French and Scottish produce to create his flavorful dishes. The delectable Degustation Menu lets you taste a bit of everything. The desserts are captivating.

In the Sheraton Grand Hotel, 1 Festival Sq. (©) 0131/221-6422. Reservations required. Fixed-price lunch £21–£24 ($33.60–$38.40); degustation menu £45 ($72); menu saison £27.50–£30.50 ($44–$48.80). AE, DC, MC, V. Mon–Fri noon–2:30pm, Mon–Sat 7–10:30pm. Bus: 1, 10, 11, 15.

Le Sept *(★ Finds)* FRENCH/SCOTTISH   You have to turn off the Royal Mile and make your way down a narrow lane to find this wonderfully romantic restaurant. It has a simple French bistro look, with a tile floor and low ceilings, and offers a small but satisfying array of traditional French and Scottish dishes (plus a vegetarian choice). You can try rack of lamb or one of the daily fish dishes, such as grilled salmon. The steaks are good, and so are the dessert crepes. One side of the restaurant is reserved for nonsmokers.

7 Old Fishmarket Close. (©) 0131/225-5428. Reservations recommended dinner. Main courses £10–£16 ($16–$25.60). AE, DC, MC, V. Mon–Thurs noon–2pm and 6–10:30pm; Sat noon–11pm; Sun 12:30–10pm. Bus: 3, 7, 14, 21.

Prego Ristorante *(★ Finds)* ITALIAN   Heavenly smells emanate from the kitchens of this handsome new restaurant near the new Scottish Parliament building. The cooking, billed as *"cucina rustica italiana"* (country Italian cooking), re-creates regional specialties from different parts of Italy. You can dine on *osso buco alla Milanese* (braised veal shinbone), or a fish dish such as *pesce spada alla Siciliana* (chargrilled swordfish with capers and oregano). Pasta dishes are also delicious. Italian wines are featured, *naturalmente*.

38 St. Mary's St. (©) 0131/557-5754. Reservations recommended. Main courses £6.75–£14.95 ($10.80–$23.90). DC, MC, V. Mon–Sat noon–2pm and 5:30–10pm. Bus: 30, 35.

Restaurant at the Bonham *(★)* SCOTTISH/CONTINENTAL   The dining room at the chic Bonham Hotel combines 19th-century oak paneling and deep ceiling coves with modern paintings and oversize mirrors. Chef Michel Bouyer, classically trained in Paris, has created a stimulating menu in his own style. On the oft-changing menu you might encounter butternut squash soup with pumpkin oil, pan-fried Scottish beef, or roasted wild sea bass. If you're a chocoholic, finish with the hot milk chocolate soufflé with white chocolate sorbet.

In the Bonham Hotel, 35 Drumsheugh Gardens. ℂ **0131/623-9319.** Reservations recommended. Main courses £15–£18.50 ($24–$29.60); fixed-price lunches £12.50–£15 ($20–$24). AE, DC, MC, V. Mon–Sat 12:30–2:30pm and 6:30–10pm; Sun 12:30–3pm and 6:30–10pm. Bus: 13, 19, 29, 35.

The Secret Garden *Finds* SCOTTISH/FRENCH   This charming restaurant is associated with The Witchery by the Castle (see below), but you have to walk down a narrow lane behind that restaurant to find it. The dining room is lighter and airier than The Witchery's, and the whole setup is not quite so posh, making it a better pick for a casual night out. The menus are basically the same at both places, relying on well-prepared versions of French and Scottish favorites and daily specials.

The Witchery by the Castle, Castlehill, The Royal Mile. ℂ **0131/220-4392.** Reservations recommended. Main courses £13.95–£19.95 ($22.30–$31.90). AE, MC, V. Daily noon–4pm and 5:30–11:30pm. Bus: 23, 27, 28.

The Witchery by the Castle ✿ SCOTTISH/FRENCH   This pretty and popular place, with a subterranean dining room and dining by candlelight, bills itself as the oldest restaurant in town and is said to be haunted by one of the many victims burned as a witch on nearby Castlehill between 1470 and 1722. It's a good place for a romantic dinner. The chef uses creative flair to prepare unfussy Scottish food, such as filet of Aberdeen Angus beef, chargrilled veal cutlet, and—most delectable and expensive of all—a platter of Scottish seafood and crustaceans. Some 550 wines and 40 malt whiskies are available.

352 Castlehill, Royal Mile. ℂ **0131/225-5613.** Reservations recommended. Main courses £13.95–£19.95 ($22.30–$31.90); fixed-price lunch and pre-theater supper £9.95 ($15.90). AE, DC, MC, V. Daily noon–4pm and 5:30–11:30pm. Bus: 23, 27, 28.

YO! Sushi SUSHI/JAPANESE   If you're wandering around Rose Street, one of Edinburgh's lively nightlife streets, and you want a not-very-expensive meal, try this sushi chain. Customers sit at a curving counter and fresh sushi selections circle around on a conveyer belt. Each selection is on a color-coded plate, which indicates the price. You can get sashimi, *nigri, maki,* hand rolls, inside-out rolls, and *gunkan,* plus an array of other hot Japanese dishes, such as yakitori, teriyaki, tempura, and noodles. If you have any questions, just press the "help" button.

Moments **Oh, Give It a Try!**

Haggis, the much-maligned national dish of Scotland, is certainly an acquired taste. But you've come all this way—why not be brave and give it a try? **Macsween of Edinburgh Haggis** is a long-established family business specializing in haggis. Macsween haggis includes lamb, beef, oatmeal, onions, and a special blend of seasonings and spices cooked together. There's also an all-vegetarian version. Both are sold in vacuum-packed plastic bags that require only reheating in a microwave or regular oven. You can find this company's product at food stores and supermarkets throughout Edinburgh. Two central distributors are **Peckham's Delicatessen,** 155–159 Bruntsfield Place (ℂ **0131/229-7054**), open daily from 8am to 8pm, and **Jenner's Department Store,** 2 E. Princes St. (ℂ **0131/260-2242**), open Monday through Saturday from 9am to 6pm and Sunday from noon to 5pm.

66 Rose St. (© **0131/220-6040**. Individual plates £1.50–3.50 ($2.40–$5.60). AE, MC, V. Daily noon–10pm. Bus: 12, 26, 44.

SHOPPING

New Town's **Princes Street** is the main shopping artery. **George Street** and Old Town's **Royal Mile** are also major shopping areas. The best buys are in tartans and woolens, along with bone china and Scottish crystal. Shopping hours are generally Monday through Saturday from 9am to 5 or 5:30pm and Sunday from 11am to 5pm. On Thursdays, many shops remain open to 7 or 8pm.

James Pringle Woolen Mill, 70–74 Bangor Rd., Leith (© **0131/553-5161**), produces a large variety of top-quality wool items, including cashmere sweaters, tartan and tweed ties, travel rugs, tweed hats, and tam-o'-shanters. In addition, it boasts one of Scotland's best Clan Tartan Centres, with more than 5,000 tartans accessible. A free audiovisual presentation shows the history and development of the tartan. You can visit for free, and there's even a free taxi service to the mill from anywhere in Edinburgh (ask at your hotel). **Shetland Connection,** 491 Lawnmarket (© **0131/225-3525**), promotes Shetland Island knitwear, and is packed with sweaters, hats, and gloves in colorful Fair Isle designs; the shop also sells hand-knitted mohair, Aran, and Icelandic sweaters. A large range of Celtic jewelry and gifts makes this shop a top-priority visit.

Geoffrey (Tailor) Highland Crafts, 57–59 High St. (© **800/566-1467** in the U.S. and Canada, or 0131/557-0256; www.geoffreykilts.co.uk), is the most famous kiltmaker in the Scottish capital. It stocks 200 of Scotland's best-known tartan patterns and is revolutionizing the kilt by establishing a subsidiary called 21st Century Kilts, which makes them in fabrics ranging from denim to leather. Geoffrey is also one of the few kiltmakers to actually weave the object, and you can watch the process at the **Edinburgh Old Town Weaving Company,** 555 Castlehill (© **0131/557-0256;** bus: 35), Monday through Friday from 9am to 5pm. Note that the factory doesn't sell kilts directly to visitors. Some of the most stylish tartans are found at **Anta,** 32 High St. (© **0131/557-8300**), where Lachian and Anne Stewart, the creative design team behind Ralph Lauren's home tartan fabrics, present a series of tartans newly invented in unique styles. The woolen blankets with hand-purled fringe are woven on old-style looms. **Clan Tartan Centre,** 74 Bangor Rd., Leith (© **0131/553-5100**), is one of the leading tartan specialists in Edinburgh, regardless of which clan you claim as your own. If you want help in identifying a particular tartan, the staff will assist you. **Tartan Gift Shops,** 54 High St. (© **0131/558-3187**), has a chart indicating the Scottish place of origin of family names, accompanied by a bewildering array of hunt and dress tartans for men and women, sold by the yard. There's also a line of lambswool and cashmere sweaters and all the accessories.

NIGHTLIFE

For 3 weeks in August, the **Edinburgh International Festival** brings world-class cultural offerings to the city, but year-round there are plenty of choices, whether you prefer theater, opera, ballet, symphony concerts, or other diversions. The waterfront district, featuring many jazz clubs and restaurants, is especially lively in summer, and students flock to the pubs and clubs around Grassmarket. Discos are found off High and Princes streets, and in the city's numerous pubs you can often hear traditional Scottish folk music for the price of a pint. For a thorough list of entertainment options during your stay, pick up a copy of *The List,* a free biweekly paper available at the tourist office.

Moments The Edinburgh Festival: Art & Tattoos

The brightest highlight of Edinburgh's year comes in August during the **Edinburgh International Festival,** whose main information and ticket office is The Hub, Castle Hill, Edinburgh EH1 7ND (© **0131/473-2000;** www.eif.co.uk), open Monday through Friday from 9:30am to 5:30pm. Since 1947, the festival has attracted artists and companies of the highest international standard in all fields of the arts, including music, opera, dance, theater, poetry, and prose. One of the festival's most exciting spectacles is the **Military Tattoo** on the floodlit esplanade in front of Edinburgh Castle, high on its rock above the city. First performed in 1950, the Tattoo features the precision marching of the British Army's Scottish regiments and performers from some 30 countries, including bands, dancers, drill teams, gymnasts, and motorcyclists, even horses, camels, elephants, and police dogs. The music ranges from ethnic to pop and from military to jazz. Schedules are released each year about 6 months before the festival. Tickets are available from the Edinburgh Military Tattoo Office, 32 Market St., Edinburgh EH1 1QB (© **0131/225-1188;** www.edintattoo.co.uk).

Less predictable in quality but greater in quantity is the **Edinburgh Festival Fringe** (© **0131/226-0026;** www.edfringe.com), an opportunity for anybody—professional or nonprofessional, an individual, a group of friends, or a whole company—to put on a show wherever they can find an empty stage or street corner. Ticket prices vary from £5 to £50 ($8–$80).

THE PERFORMING ARTS

THEATER   Edinburgh has a lively theater scene. In 1994, the **Festival Theatre,** 13–29 Nicolson St. (© **0131/529-6000;** bus: 3, 31, 33), opened on the eastern edge of Edinburgh; it has the largest stage in Britain and is used for theater, dance, opera, and presentations of all kinds. Tickets are £6 to £50 ($9.60–$80). Another major theater is the **King's Theatre,** 2 Leven St. (© **0131/529-6000;** bus: 10, 11), a 1,600-seat Victorian venue offering a wide repertoire of classical entertainment, including ballet, opera, and productions from London's West End. The resident company of the **Royal Lyceum Theatre,** Grindlay Street (© **0131/248-4848;** bus: 11, 15), also presents everything from Shakespeare to new Scottish playwrights. The **Traverse Theatre,** Cambridge Street (© **0131/228-1404;** bus: 11, 15), is one of the few theaters in Britain funded solely to present new plays by British writers and first translations into English of international works.

BALLET, OPERA & CLASSICAL MUSIC   The **Scottish Ballet** and the **Scottish Opera** perform at the **Edinburgh Playhouse,** 18–22 Greenside Place (© **0870/606-3424;** bus: 7, 10), the city's largest theater. The **Scottish Chamber Orchestra** makes its home at the **Queen's Hall,** Clerk Street (© **0131/668-2019;** bus: 3, 33, 31), also a major venue for the Edinburgh International Festival.

11

Greece

Think of Greece, and ancient temples and sun-baked islands are likely the first images that will cross your mind. But Greece has a different side as well, and a train ride is just the way to see it. Greek rail voyages offer travelers spectacular views as trains cross charming stone bridges and seemingly endless stretches of track on tall mountains, low valleys, near gorges and waterfalls. The country's track system runs almost the entire perimeter of the Peloponnese, offering a permanent view of the sea on one side of the train and alternating scenes of rugged mountains or peaceful plains on the other.

Trains bear witness to the surprising variety of landscapes present in a country as small as Greece, usually providing views that cars, the preferred means of transportation in Greece, can't possibly offer. In addition to providing a safe means of transport in a country with one of the poorest road safety records in Europe, rail rides beat the traffic jams that inevitably clog Greece's main roads, especially during a mass exodus on a summer weekend or following a long holiday.

Like most everything in Greece, its trains are either (sometimes charmingly) old, brand new, or in the process of being renewed. New stations are being added to an ever-extending Athens subway system; existing national lines and stations are being upgraded. Many of the changes are scheduled to coincide with the 2004 Summer Olympics in Athens, including a suburban railway extension to Athens's airport that will link to the city's subway system. Other projects are slated for completion at a later date. What is definite is that with all the improvements, there has never been a better time to trek through Greece by train.

Note: The information in this chapter is accurate as of August 2003. Much is expected to change as far as pricing and hours are concerned in advance of the 2004 Olympic Games. We strongly advise you to call anything and everything to confirm operating hours and costs before you go.

HIGHLIGHTS OF GREECE

If you're flying into Greece, like it or not, your first stop will probably be **Athens,** as it's the major airport hub for all of Greece. Rail travelers are limited to the mainland, as the islands have no train service, and it is the treasures of the mainland that we cover in this chapter. Of course, taking a boat or a plane is an option once you are in the country, especially if you're holding a Greece Rail 'n Fly Flexipass (see below), so don't think you have to limit yourself solely to the options outlined in this chapter—they are just more convenient and accessible for the rail traveler with limited time. And one more thing to keep in mind: Where it exists, the rail network offers hidden treasures at unassuming stops; but it is also noticeably absent in some parts of the country, namely the southernmost tips of the Peloponnese and the western mainland.

Athens offers a perfect base from which to explore Greece as it's the hub of the country's North-South rail network. The new underground **metro** lines have

made it easy to explore the city's ancient glory on modern transport. Hop on the metro and a quick ride will take you to the ancient **Acropolis** hill and the renowned monuments that adorn it, including its crown jewel, the 2,500-year-old **Parthenon.** In the shadow of the ancient hill, the touristy Plaka and Monastiraki districts provide ample opportunities to shop, eat, and relax amid scattered antiquities. A new pedestrian walkway that currently loops around the Acropolis and links some of the ancient sites is expected to expand even farther in 2004 with plans to add the city's most ancient cemetery, **Kerameikos,** to the promenade. In the summer, enjoy a concert or theatrical performance at the **Herodion Atticus Theater** at the foot of the Acropolis.

Had enough of the hustle and bustle of Greece's largest city, home to half the country's 11 million people? Get out of town!

Grab a train and head southwest, enjoying a bird's-eye-view of the impressive **Isthmus of Corinth** as you head toward **Nafplion.** The charming seaside town with its castle and fortress is a great travel hub for a mini tour of some of southern Greece's ancient sites: **Argos** by train, **Epidaurus** and **Mycenae** by bus.

If natural scenery is more to your liking, head west from Athens to Patras, stopping over at **Diakofto** for a swim and for one of the oldest and most scenic train rides in Greece via the rack-and-pinion railroad up the mountain to **Kalavryta.** If you come in the winter, you can put skiing on your agenda as well.

The port town of **Patras** will be the starting point of your rail trip if you come to Greece via ferry from Italy, or it can be one of your travel options from Athens

Moments Festivals & Special Events

Carnival *(Karnavali)* is celebrated all over the country with parades, marching bands, costumes, drinking, dancing, and more or less loosening of inhibition, depending on the locale. The city of Patras shows its support of the latter theory with its famous parade. Masked revels are also widely held in Macedonia. In Athens' Plaka district people bop each other on the head with plastic hammers. Celebrations last the 3 weeks preceding Lent.

Independence Day and the **Feast of the Annunciation** are celebrated on the same day, March 25; the former with military parades, especially in Athens. March 25.

From June to September, the **Athens Festival** features superb productions of ancient drama, opera, orchestra performances, ballet, modern dance, and popular entertainers in the Herodion Atticus Theater, at the foot of the Acropolis. For information, contact the **Greek Festival Office,** Panepistimiou 39 (in the arcade; © **210/322-1459,** or the theater at 210/323-2771). Right around the same time period, the **Epidaurus Festival** of classical Greek drama is staged in that town's famous theater and continues to early September. For information, contact the Greek Festival Office or call © **27530/22-026** in Epidaurus.

as you continue past Kalavryta. From here you can head south to the **beaches** dotting the western Peloponnesian coast, or take a detour from **Pyrgos** to **Ancient Olympia,** birthplace of the Olympic Games. The archaeological site and museum are being upgraded to receive the flood of visitors expected for the 2004 Olympics.

If you keep riding the main line north, you'll come to **Thessaloniki,** Greece's co-capital, which is also accessible by plane, and serves as a rail base for east–west excursions in Greece.

Southwest of Thessaloniki, **Mount Olympus,** where Zeus and the other mythological gods dwelled, can prove a challenge to hikers and a rewarding escape for nature lovers. Travel east from Thessaloniki to **Xanthi** and you'll be treated to the rare opportunity of seeing Muslim mosques and Christian churches coexisting in harmony, as well as a breathtaking train ride through the **Nestos river valley,** which looks even better when hiked.

1 Essentials

GETTING THERE
BY PLANE Athens International Airport Eleftherios Venizelos (© 210/ 353-0000; www.aia.gr), 17 miles (27km) northeast of Athens at Spata. It is a destination airport for all major European airlines. Only **Delta Air Lines** (www.delta.com) and Greece's **Olympic Airways** (www.olympic-airways.gr) operate direct flights from the United States, both from New York's John F. Kennedy International Airport. Flights are daily in the summer and reduced to three or four weekly trips in the winter months. All other European airlines departing the United States make a stop before arriving in Athens, usually at their national hub.

Makedonia Airport (© **23104/73-212**), 10 miles (16 km) in the northern city of Thessaloniki receives flights from more than a dozen European cities. Charter flights also link various European cities with regional airports throughout the country.

BY TRAIN   Reaching Greece directly from western Europe by train is a long and difficult adventure that we cannot recommend. Greece is, however, connected to the Balkan countries and Turkey by rail. Two trains a day leave Thessaloniki for Skopje, Macedonia and beyond to Belgrade, Serbia. One of the two continues to Zagreb, Croatia and Ljubljana, Slovenia. A train to Sofia, Bulgaria that continues to Bucharest, Romania and Budapest, Hungary also departs daily from Thessaloniki. Daily routes to Istanbul, Turkey are possible from Greece's eastern border station of Pythio, accessible by train from Thessaloniki.

Note: Eurailpasses are not accepted in the Balkans, Turkey, or Russia. The Balkan Flexipass (see chapter 2) covers rail travel in Bulgaria, Greece, Macedonia, Romania, Turkey, and Serbia and Montenegro.

BY BOAT   Ironic or not, most rail travelers coming from the Continent will head to Greece not by train but via ferry service from Italy. Ferries from Ancona, Bari, and Brindisi arrive daily at the ports of Patras and Igoumenitsa. Trip times vary depending on the ferry you take and your departure and arrival points. The three major ferry companies that accept the Eurailpass or offer discounts to passholders on the Italy/Greece routes are **Blue Star Ferries, Hellenic Mediterranean Lines** (HML), and **Superfast Ferries.** Depending on the season and company, you may have to pay a port charge or high-season surcharge, both between 6€ and 20€ ($6.90–$23).

For detailed information on ferry crossings between Greece and Italy (including routes, prices, passholder discounts, and contact information for the ferry lines), see p. 575.

Trains from Patras will take you around the Peloponnese or, if you prefer, straight to Athens to continue your rail journey from there. There is no direct rail service out of Igoumenitsa, but you can take one of the town's public buses (KTEL) to the train station at Kalambaka for 14€ ($16.10) and continue your journey from there. There are two daily buses that make the 4-hour journey from the Igoumenitsa bus station (© **26650/22-309**) to Kalambaka, which is one of the stops on the 7½-hour Igoumenitsa–Thessaloniki line. Tell the driver in advance of your desire to disembark at Kalambaka. Avoid making the journey in winter because bad weather may close the mountain pass it crosses.

GREECE BY RAIL
PASSES
If your rail journey will be limited to the Greece mainland, then we recommend buying point-to-point tickets instead of a pass as train travel in Greece is quite inexpensive. For information on the **Eurailpass, Eurailpass Flexi, Eurailpass Saver,** and **Balkan Flexipass,** see chapter 2. For information on the Balkan Flexipass, see the Appendix.

Greek Flexipass Rail 'n Fly   This pass provides 3 days of unlimited travel, plus two one-way air coupons on Olympic Airways to any of 34 domestic destinations, including 25 Aegean and Ionian islands. The coupons have to be exchanged and flights reserved at the **Ionian Travel Organization,** 4 Pireos St., Athens (© **210/523-9609**), and can't be exchanged at the airport. The pass costs $251 for adults over age 26 and $244 for adults under 26.

All of the passes above must be purchased in North America before you leave on your trip. You can buy them on the phone or online from **Rail Europe** (© **877/272-RAIL** in the U.S., 800/361-RAIL in Canada; www.raileurope.com).

The **Hellenic Railway Organization** (**OSE** in Greek), in conjunction with Italian companies, offers discounted train and ferry travel from Athens to Rome, Bologna, Florence, Milan, and Venice via the Italian ports of Ancona and Bari. Costs range from 131€ to 168€ ($150–$193). For more information on available discounts, check out the company's website at **www.ose.gr**.

FOREIGN TRAIN TERMS

All signs on the train system are in both Greek and English, but with the exception of the Athens metro system and major airports, all announcements are only in Greek. Most Greeks have basic knowledge of English, but trying to communicate in English by phone with locals in a smaller city might be a hassle. That

Useful Greek Train Terms

Pou ine (ee-nay) . . .	Where is . . .
o stathmos	the station
to treno	the train
to grafeio pliroforio	the information desk
to skevofylakio	the baggage car
i (ee) *apovathra*	the platform
Isitiria (ee-sit-ee-ria)	tickets
Ena isitirio gia . . .	A ticket to . . .
Dyo isitira gia . . .	Two tickets to . . .
Poso kani?	How much does it cost?
Aplo isitirio	one-way ticket
Isitirio me epistrofi	round-trip ticket
Proti thesi	first class
Defteri thesi	second class
Mia thesi sto parathiro	A window seat
Mia thesi sto diadromo	An aisle seat
Deksia/aristeri plevra tou trenou	Right/left side of the train
Prepi na allakso treno?	Do I have to change trains?
Yparhi ekptosi gia . . .	Is there a discount for . . .
ikogenies	families
pedia	children
fitites (fi-ti-tes)	students
Ehi kilikio sto treno?	Is there a snack bar on the train?
Pote (po-teh) *fevgi to treno?*	When does the train leave?
Ti ora ftani to treno?	What time does the train arrive?
Epitrepete to kapnisma?	Is smoking allowed?
Tha ithela thesi mi kapnizonton.	I would like a seat in the non-smoking section.
Ehei to treno klinamaksa?	Does the train have a sleeper car?

includes calls to a local station where employees can even be abrupt with Greek speakers. See "Useful Greek Train Terms" above for a short list of phrases that will come in handy while you are riding the Greek rail system.

PRACTICAL TRAIN INFORMATION

There are a few different types of trains in Greece, notably the fast and modern **InterCity (IC)** trains connecting the country's urban centers and the old, slow **InterRegio (IR)** and **Regional (R)** trains that serve local and regional routes. Noteworthy are the new speedy and ultracomfortable **InterCity Express (ICE)** trains that travel between Athens and Thessaloniki. Train travel is generally pleasant, ridiculously inexpensive, and offers unforgettable scenic views throughout the country.

Apart from the backbone Athens–Thessaloniki line and few major cities where schedules are more frequent, other destinations are served with just two or three trains a day. The **Hellenic Railway Organization (www.ose.gr)** publishes a convenient pamphlet listing all timetables, but as of this writing it is solely in Greek and available only if you ask for it.

Tickets are available at all stations and the three main **Hellenic Railways Organization (OSE)** ticket offices: Karolou 1, Athens (© **210/529-7777**); Sina 6, Athens (© **210/362-4402**); Aristotelous 18, Thessaloniki (© **23105/ 17-517**). Tickets can also be purchased and received through OSE's **Courier service** by calling © **210/529-7313** in Athens and © **23105/99-143** in Thessaloniki from 8am to 2:30 p.m. Monday through Friday. The tickets and a small fee can be paid on delivery in cash or by credit card.

Tickets should be purchased ahead of time. Inspectors board the train to hole-punch tickets for validation. If you don't have one, the inspector will sell you a ticket and charge you a fine, ranging from 50% of the ticket's cost for long-distance trips to 20 times as much for regional travel. Advance ticket purchases also guarantee you a seat: Some routes are packed with passengers, especially in the busier summer months, weekends, and holidays. If you're sure of your trip, opt for a round-trip ticket and save 20% over the cost of two one-ways.

Greek Train Station Phone Numbers

Argos	27510/67-212
Athens	
Peloponnisou Station	210/513-1601
Larissis Station	210/529-8829
Diakofto	26910/43-206
Isthmos	27410/49-070
Kalavryta	26920/22-245
Korinthos	27410/22-522
Nafplion	27520/29-380
Olympia	26240/22-677
Patras	26106/39-102
Pyrgos	26210/22-525
Thessaloniki	23105/98-112
Toxotes	25410/93-290
Xanthi	25410/22-581

Announcements at train stations are only made in Greek. They're almost always inaudible, anyway, so the language really doesn't matter. Even though the train might have a sign saying where it's headed, just to be safe, ask and make sure it's the one you want to get on. Impressively for Greek standards, the trains run pretty much on time; and if there are two trains at the station leaving a few minutes apart, you don't want to get on the wrong one.

Your ticket will indicate whether you have a first- or second-class seat, the car number your seat is in (in other words, 1, 2, 3, and so on, usually indicated on each car by a small square plate placed next to the door), and your actual seat number. In major cities, the announcement before the train arrives includes the order of the cars. Pay attention or ask, because they don't always come in numeric order.

RESERVATIONS   Greece is one of the few countries that doesn't offer the option of making train reservations before leaving North America (except for the few international lines that travel to the country), though you can buy tickets up to a month in advance from either Rail Europe or The Hellenic Railways Office in Athens.

SERVICES & AMENITIES   Where available, first-class travel is worth the extra cost, with seats being more comfortable and cars less crowded. On an InterCity train, a first-class ticket will also give you the opportunity to rent movies on DVD for 8€ ($9.20) and carry extra luggage. Overhead rails for duffle bags and small suitcases are available; larger baggage should be checked in.

There are currently two sleeper services on the Athens–Thessaloniki route. There is also a sleeper car on the Thessaloniki–Ormenio line that crosses into Bulgaria. Brand new compartment cars are expected in 2004. Sleeper compartment prices change according to the number of people staying in them. Single-sleepers range in cost from 21€ to 29.50€ ($24.15–$33.95); it's 16€ to 18.50€ ($18.40-$21.30) per person for doubles, and 9.75€ ($11.20) per person for a three-bed compartments. Four-bed and six-bed cars cost 12€ and 8€ ($13.80, $9.20) per person respectively.

InterCity trains have a food stand run by one of the country's top snack shops or attendants selling overpriced sandwiches, chips, and refreshments. Some InterCity trains also have restaurant coaches with fairly good and inexpensive food.

Trains & Travel Times in Greece

From	To	Type of Train	# of Trains	Frequency	Travel Time
Athens	Kalambaka	IC	2	daily	4 hr. 30 min.
Athens	Corinth	IC	5	daily	1 hr. 39 min.
Athens	Thebes	IC	6	daily	1 hr. 2 min.
Athens	Patras	IC	6	daily	3 hr. 15 min.
Athens	Nafplion	R	2	daily	2 hr. 58 min.
Athens	Olympia	IC	2	daily	5 hr. 37 min.
Athens	Diakofto	IC	6	daily	2 hr. 50 min.
Athens	Thessaloniki	IC	6	daily	4 hr. 57 min.– 5 hr. 34 min.
Nafplion	Argos	R	3	daily	16 min.
Patras	Olympia	IC	2	daily	1 hr. 55 min.
Thessaloniki	Litohoro	R	4	daily	1 hr. 6 min.
Thessaloniki	Xanthi	IC	3	daily	3 hr. 44 min.

IC = InterCity; R = Regional. Trains listed above are InterCity only, unless the route doesn't offer InterCity service. Routes with IC service listed may offer additional regional service.

FAST FACTS: Greece

Area Code The international country code for Greece is 30. To call Greece from abroad, dial the international access code from your base country plus 30, followed by the new Greek city codes launched in 2002 (all begin with 2 and end with 0), then the number:

Argos **27510**; Athens/Piraeus **210**; Diakofto **26910**; Isthmos **27410**; Kalavryta **26920**; Korinthos **27410**; Litohoro **23520**; Nafplion **27520**; Olympia **26240**; Patras **2610**; Pyrgos **26210**; Thessaloniki **2310**; Toxotes, **25410**; Xanthi **25410**.

Business Hours Work hours in Greece vary by season, day of the week, and type of business. Banks are generally open Monday to Thursday 8am to 2:30pm and Friday 8am to 2pm. Although business hours can vary by up to an hour depending on the season, shops are generally open Monday, Wednesday, Saturday from 8:30am to 2pm; Tuesday, Thursday, Friday from 8:30am to 2pm and again from 5:30pm to 8:30pm. Supermarkets remain open through the mid-day siesta. In tourist areas, stores are generally open longer as well as on Sundays, when other shops are closed. It is rumored that store hours may be extended in light of the 2004 Olympics and may finally become uniform throughout the country.

Climate The weather in Greece is generally mild in the winter and hot in the summer. Rain is more frequent in western and northern Greece in the winter months. In recent years, torrential rainstorms that last all of 10 minutes have become more common, especially in Thessaloniki, but also in Athens, and usually in the summer. In the mountainous part of the country, which covers most of the mainland, snowfall can cause disruption of road and rail travel, though this is infrequent. Spring and fall are the best times to visit Greece if sightseeing is your purpose: Archaeological sites and museums are not crowded, and the temperatures are pleasant enough to walk in without breaking into a huge sweat. Prices for travel and accommodations are also relatively low, compared to the peak–summer season from mid-June to mid-September. If you're looking to beat the heat at the beach, head to Greece from mid-June to late August.

Documents Required A valid passport is required for entry to Greece. No visa is needed for most foreigners, including North Americans who stay for less than 3 months; authorization must be obtained from the Aliens Bureau for visits exceeding 3 months. A passport or other form of identification may be required when registering in a hotel.

Electricity Electric current in Greece is 220 volts AC, alternating at 50 cycles. Appliances from North America that are not dual voltage will require a transformer and a round two-prong adapter plug.

Embassies & Consulates The embassies for the U.S. and Canada are in Athens: **United States,** Vas. Sofias 91 (✆ 010/721-2951; emergency number 010/729-4301); **Canada,** Ioannou Yenadiou 4 (✆ **210/727-3400** or 210/725-4011).

Health & Safety Make sure to bring a hat and your sunscreen to protect yourself from the much-touted Greek sun. Aside from that, there are no specific health concerns you'll need to worry about in Greece. Should you get sick, embassies can provide information on English-speaking physicians.

Except for emergencies, hospital admittance is possible through a doctor. Major hospitals rotate emergency duty daily; call ✆ **106** to hear recorded information in Greek on whose turn it is. Pharmacies *(pharmakio)*, identified by their green crosses, are usually open 8am to 2pm but always post a list of those pharmacies (they rotate) that stay open after closing hours, again in Greek.

While Greece is considered to be a safe country, reports of pickpocketing and purse snatching, mostly in Athens, have increased.

Holidays Greece celebrates the following national holidays: **New Year's Day,** January 1; **Epiphany** (Baptism of Christ), January 6; **Clean Monday** *(Kathari Deftera),* day before **Shrove Tuesday,** about 40 days before Easter; **Independence Day,** March 25; **Good Friday** to **Easter,** including Easter Monday; **May Day** (Labor Day), May 1; **Whit Monday** (Holy Spirit Monday), day after Pentecost, the seventh Sunday after Easter; **Assumption of the Virgin,** August 15; *Ochi* **Day,** October 28; **Christmas and the following day,** December 25 and 26.

Legal Aid Foreigners should contact their embassies or consulates for legal assistance while in Greece.

Mail Mail boxes and signs denoting post offices are usually bright yellow. Stamps are most easily found at kiosks scattered around Greece as well as shops that sell postcards. In Athens the main **post offices** are at Aeolou 100, just south of Omonia Square and in Syntagma Square on the corner of Mitropoleos Street. They're open Monday to Friday 7:30am to 8pm, Saturday 7:30am to 2pm, and Sunday 9am to 1pm. All other post offices close at about 2pm and do not open on Sundays. A postcard to the U.S. costs .65€ (75¢).

Police & Emergencies For emergencies throughout Greece dial ✆ **100** for fast **police** assistance and ✆ **171** for the **Tourist Police.** Dial ✆ **199** to report a **fire** and ✆ **166** for an **ambulance** and **hospital.**

Telephone The country code for Greece is **30.** Most public phones accept only phone cards, available at kiosks. Local phone calls cost .06€ (7¢). Domestic and international calls can be expensive, especially at hotels. International calling cards have become widely available and are a cheaper option. The phone numbering system has recently been overhauled in Greece. Beware of outdated phone directories. All new mobile phone numbers start with **69** and all fixed–line numbers with a prefix starting with **2** (see "Area Codes," above).

Phone cards that you can slide into the slot of a public phone cost between 3€ and 24€ ($3.45–$27.60). International calls with these cards cost .25€ (30¢) per minute. Other calling cards that can be used on public and regular telephones, where you dial a number and then the code you scratch off behind the card, cost between 5€ and 25€ ($5.75–$28.75), but each carries a value that is slightly higher. International calls to the United States with these cards cost .44€ (50¢) per minute

Tipping Restaurants include a service charge in the bill, but many visitors add a 10% tip. Hotel chambermaids should get at least 1€ ($1.15) per day and bellhops 1€ to 2€ ($1.15–$2.30), depending on the service. Most Greeks don't give a percentage tip to taxi drivers but instead round the fare up to the nearest euro.

2 Athens

Since antiquity, the face of Athens has changed many times. Its latest transformation comes with good reason—and a deadline: the 2004 Summer Olympics. Construction crews have taken over the city, from work on Olympic venues to ambitious transportation projects—including adding stations to the relatively new underground metro system and completing a ring road that links the airport to the country's main north–south highway. It may not cure the capital of its concrete monstrosities, but efforts to beautify the city by restoring numerous neoclassical structures and creating a pedestrian walkway linking Athens' major archaeological sites have made the city—home to half of Greece's 11 million inhabitants—just a bit more easy on the eyes. The pollution is still there. So are the thousands of taxis. But now there are options to make a visit here more pleasant, and the government is promising that by the time the Opening Ceremonies kick off in August 2004, there will be even more reasons to visit this historic city.

STATION INFORMATION
GETTING FROM THE AIRPORT TO THE TRAIN STATION
A rail link to the city center from **Athens International Airport Eleftherios Venizelos** is scheduled for completion shortly before Athens hosts the Olympics in August 2004. Until then, a taxi into Athens will cost about 20€ ($23), and is your best bet for reaching the city's train stations, especially if you have a lot of luggage. Note that some cab drivers at the airport have been known to try and overcharge obvious tourists. When you get into a taxi, check to see that the meter is turned on and set on "1" rather than "2"; the meter should be set on "2" (double fare) only between midnight and 5am, or if you take a taxi outside the city limits (if you plan to do this, try to negotiate a flat rate in advance). Also note that the following rate add-ons are standard when traveling to and from the airport: a 2€ ($2.30) airport surcharge, all tolls between the airport and Athens proper (currently 1.80€/$2.05 but expected to rise after the Olympics), and a .29€ (35¢) charge for each piece of luggage weighing over 10 pounds.

Public bus service from the airport to the city center (bus E95) is also available every 20 minutes for about 3€ ($3.45). If you wish to take public transportation to the train station, take the E95 bus to its final stop at Syntagma Square and from there take the Metro to Stathmos Larissis, the fourth stop on the red line towards Sepolia. Metro tickets cost .70€ (80¢) and can be purchased at the stations.

INSIDE THE STATION
Athens has two major train stations that are just a short distance from each other. The **Larissis Station** *(Stathmos Larissis)* serves the standard rail lines leading to and from northern Greece. A currency exchange kiosk and a luggage storage office are pretty much all the amenities the station has to offer.

Less than a 10-minute walk away, the city's second train station, **Peloponnissou Station** *(Stathmos Peloponnissou)* is the departure and arrival point for the country's southern and western rail lines. Rail connections from Patras arrive here, so if you arrived in Greece on the ferry to Patras, you'll end up at this station. Aside from a rail information booth and some ticket windows, there are few amenities at Peloponnissou, so if you need currency exchange, you'll have to walk over to Larissis.

Neither station has a visitor information desk or a place where you can make hotel reservations. Note also that if you wait to make a reservation inside the

Athens

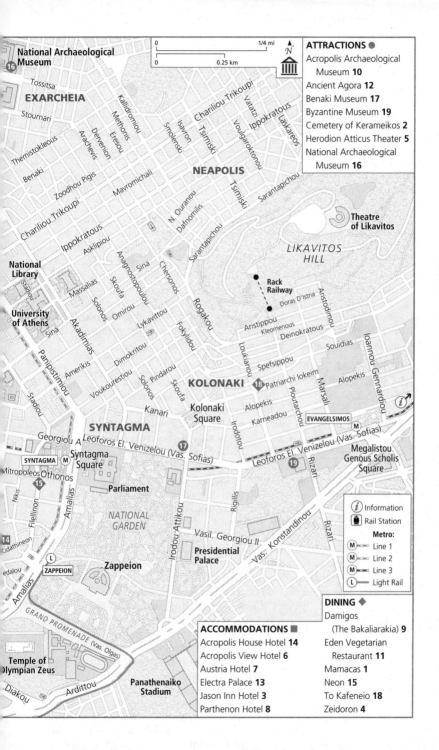

National Archaeological Museum **16**

Tossitsa

EXARCHEIA

Stournari

0   1/4 mi
0   0.25 km

N

Themistokleous

Benaki

Kallidromiou

Methonis

Arachovis

Dervenion

Eresou

Zoodhou Pigis

Mavromichali

Chariliou Trikoupi

Isavron

Smolenski

Tsimiski

Voulgaroktonou

Ippokratous Laskareos

Vatatzi

NEAPOLIS

Tsimiski

Sarantapichou

Chariliou Trikoupi

Ippokratous

N Ouranou

Dafnomilis

Asklipiou

Sina

Chersonos

Sarantapichou

Rogakou

**National
Library**

Massalias

Skoufa

Solonos

Omirou

Lykavittou

Fokylidou

Anagnostopoulou

Stadiou

**University
of Athens**

Sina

Akadimias

Panipistimiou

Amerikis

Dimokritou

Voukourestiou

Solonos

Pindarou

Skoufa

KOLONAKI

18 Patriarchi Iokeim

*LIKAVITOS
HILL*

Theatre
of Likavitos

Rack
Railway

Doras D'Istria

Aristippou
Kleomenous

Deinokratous

Loukianou

Spefsippou

Ploutarchou

Aristodimou

Marsali

Souidias

Ioannou Gennadiou

Alopekis

(i)

Kanari

**Kolonaki
Square**

Alopekis

Karneadou

Irodotou

EVANGELISMOS (M)

SYNTAGMA

Georgiou A

Leoforos El. Venizelou (Vas. Sofias)

17

Leoforos El. Venizelou (Vas. Sofias)

19

Rizari

**Megalistou
Genous Scholis
Square**

SYNTAGMA (M)

**Syntagma
Square**

Mitropoleos

Othonos

15

Nikis

Filellinon

Amalias

Parliament

*NATIONAL
GARDEN*

Irodou Attikou

Vasil. Georgiou II

Rigillis

Vas. Konstandinou

Rizari

Kidathineon

14

(L)

ZAPPEION

edalou

Zappeion

**Presidential
Palace**

Amalias

GRAND PROMENADE (Vas. Olgas)

**Temple of
Olympian Zeus**

Diakou

Ardittou

**Panathenaiko
Stadium**

train stations just before you depart, you may find yourself without a seat on the train. Instead, make reservations at the Hellenic Railway Office at 1 Karolou (℡ **210/524-0647**); at 17 Filellinon, off Syntagma Square (℡ **210/323-6747**); or at most travel agents. Information (in theory in English) on timetables is available by dialing ℡ **145** or 147.

INFORMATION ELSEWHERE IN THE CITY

Unfortunately, for a country so heavily dependent on tourism, Greece's visitor information desks are virtually non-existent, though there are two notable exceptions.

A visitor information booth at the arrivals terminal of **Athens International Airport** (℡ **210/353-0445**), is open from 9am to 7pm on weekdays; 10am to 3 p.m. on Saturdays.

The **Greek National Tourism Organization** (known by its Greek initials *EOT*), Tsoha 7 (℡ **210/870-7000;** www.gnto.gr), just moved to a new location outside of the city center. It's open Monday through Friday from 7:30am to 2:30pm and is near the Ambelokipi Metro station on the blue line. There, you should be able to get information, including maps, transportation schedules, and booklets on other parts of Greece.

Perhaps the best source of visitor information is a hotel—most have stands with various brochures and maps. Another option is to call the **Tourist Police** (℡ **171**), who are on-call 24 hours a day. They speak English, among other languages, and will help with problems or emergencies.

GETTING AROUND

BY PUBLIC TRANSPORTATION   Public transportation in the city is cheap if not exactly speedy. The city's **blue-and-white buses** run regular routes in Athens and its suburbs daily from around 5am to midnight, depending on the line. Bus frequency also varies from route to route but one should hit a stop about every 15 minutes, a bit more on Sundays. The orange or yellow-and-purple **trolley buses** serve the city center daily 5am to midnight.

Tickets for both types of buses cost .45€ (50¢) and must be bought in advance from kiosks *(periptera)* or special bus ticket booths scattered around town. The tickets are sold individually and in packets of 10; they are good for a ride anywhere on the system. When you board, validate your ticket in the automatic machine. ***Hold onto it:*** Uniformed and plainclothes inspectors periodically check tickets and levy a basic fine of 4.80€ ($5.50), or a more punitive fine of 20€ ($23), on the spot if you don't have a valid ticket.

When Athens' new Metro subway system is completed, there will be easy public transportation available in much of central Athens and beyond. Right now there are three lines up and running. A century-old urban rail that links the northern suburbs to the port of Piraeus **(green line)** also stops at the Olympic stadium (Maroussi station). In 2000, two new subway lines were added. The **blue line** connects the Defense Ministry on Messogion Avenue with the central Monastiraki station in the heart of Athens' archaeological and tourist district. The north–south **red line** crosses the Acropolis and the central squares of Syntagma and Omonia. Additional stations were under construction as of this writing with expected completion dates shortly before the Olympics.

Metro tickets, which can also be used on the older green line, cost .70€ (80¢). A ticket valid only for the green line is .60€ (70¢). Trains on the red and blue lines run about every 5 to 15 minutes daily from 5:30am to midnight; green line trains start a half hour earlier and run a half hour later. Validate your ticket at the machines as you enter and hang on to it or risk a fine. You can use the same ticket to travel on the blue, red, and green lines interchangeably, but only if you're heading in one direction within 90 minutes of validation. Metro and bus tickets aren't interchangeable, but a 24-hour ticket that allows unlimited rides on all public transport, including a single ride to the airport, is available for 2.90€ ($3.35) and can be purchased on one of the buses servicing the airport or at any metro station. For information on the Metro system, check out **www.ametro.gr.**

BY TAXI   The more than 15,000 taxis in Athens are famous—or infamous, if you wish—for their poor service. Efforts to change this reputation before the Olympics have even resulted in the sending of drivers to charm school. It is not unusual for cabs to double up on passengers. In fact, if you're in a hurry, try and hail one with a passenger; if your stop is on the way, get in.

There're about 15 radio taxi companies, which you can call and reserve ahead of time. Some established companies include **Athina-1** (✆ **210/921-7942**), **Ikaros** (✆ **210/515-2800**), and **Parthenon** (✆ **210/532-3300**). If you're trying to make travel connections during rush hours, the service will be well worth the 1.30€ ($1.50) surcharge for an on-the-spot call or the 2.20€ ($2.55) surcharge for an appointment. Your hotel can make the call for you and make sure that the driver knows where you want to go. Most restaurants will call a taxi for you without charge.

At press time, the meter starts at .75€ (85¢), the minimum fare is 1.50€ ($1.75), and the "1" meter rate is .26€ (30¢) per kilometer, with a surcharge of .70€ (80¢) for service *from* (not to) a port or rail or bus station; a luggage surcharge of .29€ (35¢) is charged for each piece of luggage weighing over 10 lbs. Note that riders pay all tolls where applicable.

Warning: There were reports during the summer of 2003 that some cab drivers were charging extra for turning on the air conditioner. That's illegal. If a cabbie tries this tactic on you, protest or find yourself another taxi.

ON FOOT   Even before the pedestrian walkway that loops around the Acropolis was completed, most of Athens' must-see sites were best seen on foot. Now with the walkway expanding to ancient sites farther away from the archaeological district, visitors have one more reason to walk about town. But walkers beware: A red traffic light or stop sign is no guarantee that cars will stop for you. The (supposedly) car-free pedestrian zones in sections of the **Plaka,** the **Commercial Center,** and **Kolonaki** do, however, make strolling, window-shopping, and sightseeing infinitely more pleasant.

WHERE TO STAY

Warning: Nearly all the city's best hotel rooms, in addition to several cruise ships, have been reserved to host sports officials and sponsors during the 2004 Olympics. This will pose a problem during much of the time surrounding the 2004 Games (in Aug) for people not part of the Olympic family. It is also expected that hotel prices will skyrocket in advance of the Olympics. Unless you're specifically coming for the Games, your best bet is to avoid Athens during the Olympics and in the month preceding it.

Acropolis House Hotel   For a view of the Acropolis, try to get room 401 or 402 at this small hotel, located in a renovated 150-year-old villa. The location, off a relatively quiet pedestrian-only side street in the Plaka, is a real plus, although motorcycle noise can be a problem. The newer wing (only 65 years old) isn't particularly special though corridor bathrooms (one for each room, located across the hall) are fully tiled and modern. Guests can use a washing machine for a small fee and air-conditioning is available for a small surcharge.

Kodrou 6–8, 105 58 Athens. ✆ **210/322-2344.** Fax 210/324-4143. 25 units, 15 with bathroom. 53.80€ ($61.90) double without bathroom; 67.20€ ($77.30) double with bathroom. 1.12€ ($1.30) surcharge for A/C. Rates include continental breakfast. V. Walk 2 blocks out of Syntagma Sq. on Mitropoleos St. and turn left on Voulis, which becomes pedestrianized Kodrou. Metro: Syntagma (red and blue lines), 5-min. walk to train station.

Acropolis View Hotel   This nicely maintained hotel with a helpful staff is on a residential side street off Rovertou Galli, not far from the Herodion Atticus theater. The usually quiet neighborhood, at the base of Filopappou Hill, is a 10- to 15-minute walk from the heart of the Plaka and the ancient sites. Rooms (most freshly painted each year) are small but clean and pleasant, with good bathrooms; 16 have balconies. Some, like no. 405, overlook Filopappou Hill, and others, like no. 407, face the Acropolis.

Rovertou Galli and 10 Webster St., 117 42 Athens. ✆ **210/921-7303.** Fax 210/923-0705. 32 units. 127€ ($146) double. Rates include generous buffet breakfast. Substantial reductions Nov–Apr 1. AE, MC, V. From Syntagma Sq. take Amalias Ave. to Dion. Areopagitou; head west past Herodion Atticus theater to Rovertou Galli St. Webster is the little street intersecting Rovertou Galli St. between Propilion and Garabaldi. Metro: Acropolis (red line), 10-min. walk to train station. **Amenities:** Breakfast room; bar.

Austria Hotel ✦   This well-maintained hotel at the base of wooded Filopappou Hill is operated by a Greek-Austrian family, who offer great service and can point you to all the local sites, only a stone's throw away. The Austria's rooms and bathrooms are rather spartan but tidy. There's a great view of the nearby Parthenon and the rest of Athens, including Piraeus and the neighboring islands, from the rooftop, where you can sunbathe or sit under an awning.

Mousson 7 Filopappou, 117 42 Athens. ✆ **210/923-5151.** Fax 210/924-7350. Austria@austriahotel.com. 36 units (11 with shower only). 120€ ($138) double. Rates include breakfast. AE, DC, MC, V. Follow Dionyssiou Areopagitou St. around south side of Acropolis to where it meets Rovertou Galli St.; take Garibaldi around base of Filopappou Hill until reaching Mousson St. Metro: Acropolis (red line), 10-min. walk to train station. **Amenities:** Breakfast room; rooftop terrace.

Electra Palace ✦   The Electra, just a few blocks southwest of Syntagma Square, is the most modern and stylish hotel in the Plaka. Rooms are of good size and have balconies. The top floors are where you want to be, both for the Acropolis view and to escape traffic noise. The problem: The Electra won't guarantee you a top-floor room when you reserve, and if you sit on a lower-floor balcony, you'll inhale lots of fumes, hear lots of traffic noise—and have a view of the building across the street. Still, you can always retreat to the rooftop pool (a real bonus!) and take in the Acropolis view from there.

Nikodimou 18 Plaka,105 57 Athens. ✆ **210/324-1401.** Fax 210/324-1875. 106 units. 129€–168€ ($148–$193) double. Rates include breakfast. AE, DC, MC, V. Metro: Syntagma (red and blue lines), 5-min. walk to train station. **Amenities:** Restaurant; bar. *In room:* hair dryer.

Jason Inn Hotel *(Value)*   If you don't mind walking a few extra blocks to Syntagma, this is one of the best values in Athens, with a staff that's usually very helpful. You're just out of the Plaka, around the corner from the newly fashionable Psirri district and steps from bustling Athinas Street. The hotel is redecorated on a regular basis and has bright, attractive rooms with modern amenities and double-paned windows to keep out traffic noise. *Note:* If the Jason Inn Hotel is full, the staff may be able to find you a room in one of its other hotels: the similarly priced **Adrian,** in the Plaka, or the slightly less expensive **King Jason** or **Jason,** both a few blocks from Omonia Square.

Agion Assomaton 12, 105 53 Athens. © **210/325-1106.** Fax 210/324-3132. Douros@hotelnet.gr. 57 units. 89.60€ ($103) double. Rates include American buffet breakfast. AE, MC, V. From Monastiraki Sq., head west on Ermou, turn right at Thissio Metro station, pass small below-ground-level church and bear left. Metro: Monastiraki (blue and green lines), 10-min. walk to train station.

Parthenon Hotel   This recently redecorated hotel has an excellent location just steps from the Plaka and the Acropolis. The carpeted bedrooms have bright, cheerful bedspreads and decent-size bathrooms. The Parthenon is a member of the AirOtel Athenian hotel group; if it's full, management will try to get you a room in the **Christina,** a few blocks away, or at the **Riva** or **Alexandros,** near the Megaron (the Athens Concert Hall). *One warning:* On occasion we have found the desk staff less than helpful and infuriatingly vague about room prices.

Odos Makri 6, 115 27 Athens. © **210/923-4594.** Fax 210/644-1084. 79 units. 85€ ($97.75) double. MC, V. From Syntagma, take Amalias into Dionyssiou Areopagitou; Makri is the second street on the left. Metro: Acropolis (red line), 5-min. walk to train station. **Amenities:** Restaurant; bar. *In room:* TV (some rooms).

TOP ATTRACTIONS & SPECIAL MOMENTS

Studying or even simply glancing at Athens' many antiquities is an unavoidable must. Whether they be open-air attractions such as the Acropolis or Agora or items enclosed in the glass cases of one of the city's three dozen museums, Athens has endless treasures to showcase, enough that a single trip can't fit them in. Below are the highlights—admittedly a mere drop in the ocean of what the city has to offer—that a rail traveler to the city shouldn't miss.

The Acropolis ★★★   When you climb up the Acropolis, you'll realize why people seem to have lived here as long ago as 5000 B.C. The sheer sides of the Acropolis make it a superb natural defense, just the place to avoid enemies and to be able to see invaders coming across the sea or the plains of Attica. Athens's civic and business center, the **Agora,** and its cultural center with several theaters and concert halls, bracketed the Acropolis; when you peer over the sides of the Acropolis at the houses in Plaka and the remains of the ancient Agora and the Theater of Dionysos, you'll see the layout of the ancient city. The **Parthenon** dedicated to Athena Parthenos (the Virgin), patron goddess of Athens, was the most important religious monument. Climbing up, you first pass through the **Beule Gate,** built by the Romans, but known by the name of the French archaeologist who discovered it in 1852. Next comes the **Propylaia,** the monumental 5th-century B.C. entranceway. The little **Temple of Athena Nike (Athena of Victory),** a beautifully proportioned Ionic temple built in 424 B.C., is perched above the Propylaia; it was restored in the 1930s. Off to the left of the Parthenon is the **Erechtheion,** which the Athenians honored as the tomb of Erechtheus, a legendary king of Athens. Be sure to see the original Caryatids (the monumental female figures who served as columns on the Erechtheion's porch) in the Acropolis Museum.

The Parthenon's entire roof and much of the interior were blown away in 1687, when a party of Venetians attempted to take the Acropolis from the Turks. A shell fired from a nearby hill struck the Parthenon—where the Turks were storing gunpowder and munitions—and caused appalling damage to the building and its sculptures. Most of the remaining sculptures were carted off to London by Lord Elgin in the first decade of the 19th century. Those surviving sculptures—known as the **Elgin Marbles**—are on display in the British Museum, and are a seemingly eternal point of friction between Greeks and Britons. A new Acropolis Museum is under construction—slated like most other works in

Moments **Traveling to the Ancient City of Thebes**

The setting of many ancient tragedies and one of ancient Greece's most powerful cities, **Thebes** *(Thiva)* is an hour's train ride from Athens on the Athens–Thessaloniki line. The city itself is nothing to write home about, but if you're an archaeology buff, its **Archaeological Museum,** Pindarou Street (② **22620/27-913**), is well worth visiting on a morning excursion. Although the collection includes a wide range of pottery, inscriptions, and sculpture, the Mycenaean objects are the highlight. There are several painted Mycenaean sarcophagi, some fine gold jewelry, and handsome body armor. The scant remains of ancient Thebes—the unexcavated ancient city lies under the modern one—are signposted at the museum. Allow an hour for your visit.

Admission is 2€ ($2.30). The museum is open 8:30am to 7pm, Tuesday through Sunday; on Mondays it opens at 12:30pm and closes at 7pm.

Several InterCity and regional trains run from Athens to Thebes every day. Depending on which train you take, the cost of a first-class ticket is 4.70€ to 12€ ($5.40–$13.80), and 3.20€ to 8.50€ ($3.70–$9.80) for a second-class ticket. To get from the station to the museum, you can walk (it's about 10–15 min. on foot) or you can take a short taxi ride. Call ② **22620/27-077** from the station for a taxi.

progress for a pre-Olympic completion date—and is said to include a room that will await the Elgin Marbles' return. The Parthenon originally had sculpture on both its pediments, as well as a frieze running around the entire temple. Only a few fragments of any of the sculptures remain in place. Four of the original **Caryatids** from the Erechtheion are on display at the **Acropolis Archaeological Museum** (one disappeared during the Ottoman occupation, and one is in the British Museum). Other delights here include sculpture from the Parthenon burnt by the Persians, statues of **korai (maidens)** dedicated to Athena, figures of **kouroi (young men),** and a wide range of other finds from the Acropolis.

Dionysiou Areopagitou St. ② **210/321-0219.** Admission 12€ ($13.80) adults, 6€ ($6.90) seniors, students. Free Sun. This ticket, which is valid for 1 week, includes admission to the Acropolis, Acropolis Museum, Ancient Agora, Theater of Dionysos, Karameikos Cemetery, Roman Forum, Tower of the Winds, and Temple of Olympian Zeus. It is still possible to buy individual tickets at the other sites. Open in summer daily 8am–7pm; winter daily 8:30am–3pm. The ticket booth, along with a small post office and a snack bar, are slightly below the Acropolis entrance. From Syntagma Sq., take Amalias Ave. into pedestrian-only Dionysiou Areopagitou St., and follow marble path up to the Acropolis. Metro: Acropolis (red line).

Ancient Agora ⭐⭐   The Agora was Athens's commercial and civic center, its buildings used for a wide range of political, educational, philosophical, theatrical, and athletic purposes. This is a nice place to wander and enjoy the views up toward the Acropolis. Be sure to take in the herb garden and flowers planted around the 5th century B.C. **Temple of Hephaistos** *(Thisseion);* peek into the heavily restored 11th-century Byzantine **Church of the Agii Apostoli (Holy Apostles);** and admire the 2nd-century B.C. **Stoa of Attalos,** a monument built by King Attalos of Pergamon and totally reconstructed in the 1950s.

The **museum** in the Stoa's ground floor has finds from 5,000 years of Athenian history, including sculpture and pottery, as well as a voting machine and a child's potty seat, all with labels in English. The museum (which has excellent modern restrooms) closes 15 minutes before the site.

You'll want to spend at least 3 hours exploring all of the Agora attractions.

Below the Acropolis on the edge of Monastiraki. ✆ **210/321-0185.** Admission (includes museum) 4€ ($4.60) adults, 2€ ($2.30) seniors and students. Free Sun. Summer daily 8am–7pm; winter daily 8:30am–3pm. Metro: Monastiraki, Acropolis.

Benaki Museum   You'll find all of Greek history under one roof at this museum. This stunning private collection includes treasures from the Neolithic era to the 20th century. The folk art collection (including magnificent costumes and icons) is superb, as are the two entire rooms from 18th-century northern Greek mansions, the ancient Greek bronzes, gold cups, Fayum portraits, and rare early Christian textiles. A new wing has doubled the exhibition space of the original 20th-century neoclassical town house that belonged to the wealthy Benaki family. It's a very pleasant place to spend several hours. *Note:* The Benaki's massive collection of Islamic Art will be housed in another museum (no name has been announced yet) slated to open before the Olympics in 2004 near Kerameikos.

Koumbari 1 (at Leoforos Vasilissis Sofias, Kolonaki, 5 blocks east of Syntagma Sq.). ✆ **210/367-1000.** www.benaki.gr. Admission 6€ ($6.90) adults, 3€ ($3.45) students; free Thurs. Mon, Wed, Fri, Sat 9am–5pm; Thurs 9am–midnight; Sun 9am–3pm; closed Tues. From Syntagma Sq., walk along Vas. Sofias Ave. for about 5 min. The museum is on your left. Metro: Syntagma or Evangelismos.

Byzantine Museum   Anything and everything you every wanted to know about icons (paintings, usually of saints, usually on wood) can be found here. As its name makes clear, this recently renovated museum, in a 19th-century Florentine-style villa, is devoted to the art and history of the Byzantine era (roughly A.D. 4th–15th c.). Selections from Greece's most important collection of icons and religious art—along with sculptures, altars, mosaics, religious vestments, Bibles, and a small-scale reconstruction of an early Christian basilica—are exhibited on several floors around a courtyard.

Note: At press time, the permanent collection is closed for renovations; expected to open by year's end. Currently open for rotating temporary exhibits.

Vasilissis Sofias 22 ✆ **210/721-1027.** Free admission. Tues–Sun 8:30am–3pm. From Syntagma Sq., walk along Vas. Sofias Ave. for about 10 min. The museum is on your right. Metro: Evangelismos (blue line).

Cemetery of Kerameikos ✦   A cemetery may not be your first choice for sightseeing, but the Kerameikos is a pleasant spot to sit and read or soak up the historical atmosphere because it's seldom crowded. This ancient cemetery, where Pericles gave his famous **funeral oration** for the Athenian soldiers killed during the first year's fighting in the Peloponnesian War, is a short walk from the Ancient Agora and not far from the presumed site of Plato's Academy. There are a number of well-preserved funerary monuments and the remains of the colossal **Dipylon Gate,** the main entrance to the ancient city of Athens. You can also see substantial remains of the 5th-century B.C. fortifications known as the "Long Walls" that ran from Athens to Piraeus.

If you like cemeteries, ancient and modern, be sure to also take in Athens's enormous **First Cemetery,** near the all-marble Panathenaic Stadium *(Kallimarmaro),* where notables such as former Prime Minister George Papandreou are buried beneath elaborate monuments. You can easily spend a couple of hours exploring both cemeteries.

Note: At press time, the Kerameikos cemetery was closed for renovations and is scheduled to re-open in time for the 2004 Olympics.

148 Ermou. (℃ **210/346-3553**. Admission 2€ ($2.30). Expected re-opening in advance of August 2004 Olympics. Walk west from Monastiraki Sq. on Ermou past Thisio Metro station; cemetery is on the right. Metro: Monastiraki or Theseion.

National Archaeological Museum Home to some of Greece's most precious treasures, this museum was shut down in 2002 for major renovations ahead of the 2004 Olympics. It is scheduled to re-open before the August 2004 Games, though no concrete date has been set. The museum's second floor was closed in 1999 after a deadly earthquake caused significant damage. At press time, it was not clear whether the restored 3500 B.C. Thira frescoes (displayed on the 2nd floor before the earthquake) would remain in the museum when it reopens or be sent back to the island of Thira (Santorini). In addition, it was not known at press time where (and what) objects would be displayed.

44 Patission. (℃ **210/821-7717**. Fax 210/821-3573. Admission 6€ or 12€ ($6.90, $13.80) with admission to the Acropolis. Anticipated hours Mon 12:30–5pm; Tues–Fri 8am–5pm; Sat–Sun and holidays 8:30am–3pm. (The museum is sometimes open to 7pm, but you cannot count on this.) The museum is ¹/₃ of a mile (.5km/10 min. on foot) north of Omonia Sq. on the road named Leoforos 28 Oktovriou (Oct 28) but usually called Patission. Metro: Omonia.

Moments **The Athens Festival**

From early June through September, the **Athens Festival** (which, along with the Epidaurus Festival in the ancient theater at Epidaurus makes up the Hellenic Festival) features famous Greek and foreign artists from Elton John to Placido Domingo performing on the slopes of the Acropolis. The atmosphere makes this a truly special and unforgettable experience: You may catch an opera, concert, drama, or ballet in the ancient and majestic Herodion theater—and, usually, see the Acropolis illuminated over your shoulder or the moon through one of the open arches hovering over the stage at the same time. To enjoy the performance to the fullest, bring some kind of cushion to sit on (the cushions available are often minimal). Schedules are usually available at the **Hellenic Festival Office,** 39 Panepistimiou (in the arcade; (℃ **210/ 322-1459** or the theater at 210/323-2771).

Theatrical performances are mostly in Greek though foreign companies also take the stage (In 2003, for example, the schedule included a production by the Washington, D.C.–based Shakespeare Theatre.) And, of course, you won't face a language barrier at the music and dance performances.

The office is usually open Monday through Saturday from 8:30am to 2pm and 5 to 7pm, Sunday from 10am to 1pm; you will have better luck coming here in person than trying to reach the office by phone. If available—and that's a big if—tickets can also be purchased at the **Herodion Atticus Theater** ((℃ **210/323-2771** or 210/323-5582) several hours before the performance. Again, you will probably have better luck going to the ticket office than phoning there, although if your hotel has a concierge, you may be able to arrange for tickets over the phone. Shows usually begin at 9pm. For online information on the Hellenic Festival, check out **www.hellenicfestival.gr**.

WHERE TO DINE

Damigos (The Bakaliarakia) ★★★ GREEK   This basement taverna has been serving delicious deep-fried codfish and eggplant, as well as chops and stews for inveterate meat-eaters, since 1865. The wine hails from the family vineyards and if you like it, you can usually buy a bottle to take away. There are few pleasures greater than sipping the white or rosé retsina while watching the cook turn out unending meals in his absurdly small kitchen. Don't miss the delicious *skordalia* (garlic sauce), equally good with cod, eggplant, bread—well, you get the idea.

Kidathineon 41🕐 **210/322-5084.** Main courses 3.90€–9€ ($4.50–$10.35). No credit cards. Daily 7pm–anywhere from 11pm–1am. Usually closed July–Sept. From Syntagma Sq., head south on Filellinon or Nikis St. to Kidathineon; Damigos is downstairs on left just before Andrianou St.

Eden Vegetarian Restaurant ★ VEGETARIAN   You can find vegetarian dishes at almost every Greek restaurant, but if you want to experience organically grown products, soy (rather than eggplant) moussaka, mushroom pie with a whole-wheat crust, freshly squeezed juices, and salads with bean sprouts, join the young Athenians and Europeans who patronize the Eden. The prices are reasonable if not cheap, and the decor is engaging, with 1920s-style prints and mirrors and wrought-iron lamps.

Lissiou 12 🕐 and fax **210/324-8858.** Main courses 6.70€–15€ ($7.35–$17.25). AE, MC, V. Daily noon–midnight. Closed Tues and usually closed Aug. From Syntagma Sq., head south on Filellinon or Nikis St. to Kidathineon, which intersects Andrianou St.; turn right on Andrianou and take Mnissikleos up 2 blocks toward Acropolis to Lissiou.

Mamacas ★ MODERN GREEK   One of the new-generation "modern tavernas," Mamacas gives traditional Greek dishes a contemporary twist. Customary lentil soup? At Mamacas make it a salad. And peppers usually stuffed with rice or ground meat are filled with cheese and spices. In just a few years, Mamacas has managed to sprawl from a single building onto much of the block surrounding the quiet Gazi neighborhood, where a former gas factory has been turned into a cultural center. Seating is available inside or out and there's a view of the Acropolis from the enclosed rooftop, open only in the winter.

Persefonis 14, Gazi, 🕐 **210/346-4984.** Reservations recommended. Main courses 20€–25€ ($23–$28.75). Daily 2pm–2 am. No credit cards. Tucked behind the Gazi factory on Pireos St. As of this writing the pedestrian walkway linking Kerameikos was under construction, limiting vehicle access from Ermou St.

Neon ★ *Value* GREEK/INTERNATIONAL   If you're tired of practicing your restaurant Greek, Neon chain restaurants are a good place to eat, as most things are self-service. This centralized location of the chain is convenient, although not as charming as the original on Omonia Square. There is also a Neon a block north of Kolonaki Square at Tsakalof and Iraklitou. You're sure to find something to your taste—maybe a Mexican omelet, spaghetti Bolognese, the salad bar, or sweets ranging from Black Forest cake to tiramisu.

3 Mitropoleos St. (on the southwest corner of Syntagma Sq.). 🕐 **210/322-8155.** Snacks .80€–2.20€ (90¢–$2.55); sandwiches 2.20€–5.60€ ($2.55–$6.45); main courses 3.40€–13.40€ ($3.90–$15.40). No credit cards. Daily 9am–midnight.

To Kafeneio ★★ GREEK/INTERNATIONAL   This is hardly a typical *kafeneio* (coffee shop/cafe). If you relax, you can easily run up a substantial tab ($50 for lunch or dinner for two is easy), but you can also eat more modestly and equally elegantly. Have something light, such as the artichokes a la polita, or onion pie, washed down with draft beer or the house wine, and topped off with profiteroles, and you won't put too big a dent in your budget. I've always found this an especially congenial spot when I'm eating alone (perhaps because I love people-watching and profiteroles).

26 Loukianou St. (②) 210/722-9056. Reservations recommended. 6.70€–22.40€ ($7.70–$25.75). No credit cards. Mon–Sat 11am–midnight or later. Closed Sun and most of Aug. From Kolonaki Sq., follow Patriarhou Ioakim St. several blocks uphill to Loukianou and turn right on Loukianou.

Zeidoron ⭐ GREEK/TAPAS   This *mezedopolio* (Greek version of tapas) is one of a number of restaurants springing up in the old warehouse district of Psirri. There are lots of delicious mezedes to choose from, including vegetable croquettes, several eggplant dishes, and some heartier meat dishes, such as pork in mustard. You can have a varied and delicious meal—and keep the price tab reasonable—by avoiding the more expensive mezedes such as shrimp. A wide variety of wines, beers, and ouzos is available.

10 Taki and Agion Anargiron. (②) 210/321-5368. Reservations recommended. Main courses 7.80€–21€ ($9–$24.15); appetizers 5.60€–16.80€ ($6.45–$19.30). No credit cards. Mon–Sat 11am–at least midnight. Closed Aug. From Syntagma Sq. take Ermou to Navarhou Apostoli, which runs into Taki, and intersects Agion Anargiron.

SHOPPING

Between the **Plaka** and **Monastiraki,** you'll find everything Greece is known for—from the stunning to the utterly kitsch—and that you might want to buy: from modern Greek art to replicas of ancient masterpieces and ouzo bottles that look like temples. Generally speaking, you'll get sick of seeing the same things over and over again as you stroll down both streets. Be careful of prices: The operative word here is bargain, and haggling is expected. You'll almost never pay the quoted price. That's especially true at the flea market between Plaka and Monastiraki, which draws huge crowds on Sundays when all other shops are closed. Bargaining is less acceptable outside the Plaka and Monastiraki, where you won't find a ton of 5€ ($5.75) plaster busts of Athena.

Stavros Melissinos, Athens' **Poet-Sandalmaker,** Pandrossou 89 ((②) 210/321-9247), is an international favorite, whose elderly proprietor plays himself up as a poetry-writing sandalmaker. Some two-dozen strappy leather designs are available to choose from.

Seeking a small copper pot to make Greek coffee or a copper mug for your wine? Try **Nikolaos Paschalidis'** shop in Monastiraki, Hephestou 9 ((②) 210/321-0064), which specializes in all things copper. **Pelekanos,** Andrianou 155 ((②) 210/331-0968), also has traditional objects made of metal, but carries other folk art as well.

Handmade jewelry and ceramics line the walls of **Archipelagos,** Andrianou 142 ((②) 210/323-1321), while hand-painted seascapes on wood adorn the **Coracle Shop,** Nikodimou 41 ((②) 210/324-9573). **Vergina,** Kidathineon 24 Plaka ((②) 210/324-5304), carries artwork and stunning contemporary jewelry by

---

(**Tips** **Insider Tip**

Serious shoppers should keep an eye out for the "Best of Athens" issue of the English language magazine *Odyssey.* The issue, usually published in July or August, and available at many book stores and kiosks, is filled with shopping tips—as well as lots of scoops on what's in and what's out in Athens.

> **Tips Skipping the Harbor**
>
> Many guidebooks tout Greece's largest passenger and cargo harbor, **Piraeus,** as a must-do day trip for its seafood and shopping. We think it's highly overrated and that a rail traveler pressed for time won't miss much by skipping it. Yes, its seafood is good, but you can also find great seafood in Athens and other parts of Greece. So unless you're taking a ferry to the islands, your time is better spent elsewhere.

---

modern Greek artists. The **Center of Hellenic Tradition,** 3 Mitropoleos and 36 Pandrossou in the Plaka (✆ **210/321-3023**), is a wonderful place for quality traditional Greek art, including icons, pottery, woodcarvings, embroideries, and prints. Best of all, you can take a break from shopping and look at the Acropolis while you have coffee and a snack at the cafe here.

NIGHTLIFE

Greece's nightlife isn't limited to the nighttime; it actually runs through the early hours of the morning. And that's true all year-round. In Athens, the only thing that changes is the locale: the city center and northern suburbs in the winter; the seaside restaurants and bars in the summer. Many bars and clubs move their operations from one locale to the other depending on the time of year. Some clubs feature DJs, others live performers. The choices—no matter what the season—are endless.

Check the daily *Athens News* or the daily *Kathimerini* insert in the *International Herald Tribune* for current cultural and entertainment events, including films, lectures, theater, music, and dance. The weekly *Hellenic Times* and monthly *Now in Athens* list nightspots, restaurants, movies, theater, and much more. If you plan on attending the theater, note that most plays will be in Greek.

THE PERFORMING ARTS   The acoustically marvelous new **Megaron Mousikis Concert Hall,** Vas. Sofias 89 (✆ **210/729-0391** or 210/728-2333), hosts a wide range of classical-music programs that include quartets, operas in concert, symphonies, and recitals. On performance nights, the box office is open Monday through Friday from 10am to 8:30pm, Saturday from 10am to 2pm and 6 to 8:30pm, and Sunday from 6 to 8:30pm. Tickets are also sold Monday through Friday from 10am to 5pm in the Megaron's convenient downtown kiosk at Omirou 8 (✆ **210/324-3297**), open Monday through Friday from 10am to 4pm. Ticket prices run from 5€ ($5.75) to as much as 100€ ($115), depending on the performance. The Megaron has a limited summer season, but is in full swing the rest of the year.

The **Greek National Opera** performs at the **Olympia Theater,** 59 Akadimias, at Mavromihali (✆ **210/361-2461**). The summer months are usually off season.

The **Hellenic American Union,** 22 Massalias between Kolonaki and Omonia squares (✆ **210/368-0000**), often hosts performances of English-language theater and American-style music (tickets are usually about 10€/$11.50 and up). If you arrive early, check out the art shows or photo exhibitions in the adjacent gallery.

The **Athens Center,** 48 Archimidous (✆ **210/701-2268**), often stages free performances of ancient Greek and contemporary international plays in June and July.

Since 1953, the **Dora Stratou Folk Dance Theater** has been giving performances of traditional Greek folk dances on Filopappos Hill. At present, performances take place May through September, Tuesday through Saturday at 9:30pm, Sunday at 8:15pm. Closed Monday. You can buy tickets at the **box office,** 8 Scholio, Plaka, from 8am to 2pm (© 210/324-4395). Prices are 13€ ($14.95). Tickets are also usually available at the theater before performances.

TRADITIONAL MUSIC   Walk the streets of the Plaka on any night and you'll find plenty of tavernas offering pseudo-traditional live music. As noted, many are serious clip joints, where if you sit down and ask for a glass of water, you'll be charged 100€ ($115) for a bottle of scotch. At most of these places, there's a cover (usually at 10€/$11.50). We've had good reports on **Taverna Mostrou,** 22 Mnissikleos (© 210/324-2441), which is large, old, and best known for traditional Greek music and dancing. Open Thursday through Sunday, its shows begin around 11pm and usually last until 2am. The cover of 30€ ($34.50) includes a fixed-menu supper. A la carte fare is available but expensive (as are drinks). Nearby, **Palia Taverna Kritikou,** 24 Mnissikleos (© 210/322-2809), is another lively open-air taverna with music and dancing.

Several appealing tavernas that usually offer low-key music include fashionable **Daphne's,** 4 Lysikratous (© 210/322-7971); **Nefeli,** 24 Panos (© 210/321-2475); **Dioyenis,** 4 Sellei (Shelley; © 210/324-7933); **Stamatopoulou,** 26 Lissiou (© 210/322-8722); and longtime favorite **Xinos,** 4 Agelou Geronta (© 210/322-1065).

3 Highlights of the Peloponnese

What's special about the Peloponnese, the southwestern section of Greece's mainland? It's tempting to answer, "Everything." Many of the most famous ancient sites in Greece are in the Peloponnese, from the magnificent classical temples at Corinth, Nemea, and Olympia; to the monumental theaters at Argos and Epidaurus, still used for performances today.

The good news for rail travelers is that while many of the Aegean islands sag under the weight of tourists from May until September, the Peloponnese is still relatively uncrowded, even in midsummer. That doesn't mean that you're going to have Olympia all to yourself if you arrive at high noon in August, but it does mean that if you get to Olympia early in the morning, you may have a quiet hour under the pine trees.

The bad news for rail travelers is that seeing all the sights requires careful planning and good timing because rail service in the region is not particularly quick or plentiful. Still, one of the great delights of seeing the Peloponnese comes from the quiet hours spent in seaside cafes, watching fishermen mend their nets while Greek families settle down for a leisurely meal. *Leisurely* is the word to remember in the Peloponnese, an ideal place to make haste slowly—even if the trains run slowly here, the scenery outside your window will keep you entranced enough that you won't mind.

CORINTH *(KORINTHOS)*

Just 55 miles (89km) west of Athens, Corinth, is the major gateway to the Peloponnese for those traveling by train out of Athens. For the rail traveler, this city makes an excellent day trip out of Athens or a good stopover point on the way to Nafplion. It is not, however, a good base city, so don't think about spending the night here.

Tips Learning the Lingo

You'll probably be pleasantly surprised at how very impressed Peloponnesian locals will be if you master the linguistic basics of hello *(ya-sas)* and thank you *(efcharisto)*. If you have trouble pronouncing "efcharisto," here's a suggestion: It sounds a lot like the name "F. Harry Stowe." If you're still having trouble, try *merci* (French for "thank you"), which most Greeks use interchangeably with *efcharisto*.

Modern Corinth—rebuilt after a series of earthquakes destroyed most of the city and remarkably bland—is a far cry from ancient Corinth, which was famously splendid and lively. As one Greek proverb had it, "See Corinth and die," suggesting that there was nothing to look forward to after visiting the splendid monuments (and fleshpots) of the city that dominated trade in Greece for much of the 7th and 8th centuries B.C. and had a second golden age under the Romans in the 2nd century A.D. It is for the remnants of this ancient Corinth and some dramatic train views that a visitor should make the trek here.

GETTING THERE   More than a dozen trains a day make the trip from Athens's Stathmos Peloponnissou (Train Station for the Peloponnese) to the Corinth station off Demokratias (© **27410/22-522**), heading just past the canal that separates the Peloponnese from mainland Greece. The 4-mile- (6km-) long **Corinth Canal,** built by French engineers at the end of the 19th century, revolutionized shipping in the Mediterranean, allowing vessels that would circle the Peloponnese for days to instead cut through the canal in hours. Check out the dramatic view of the 87-meter-tall rocks flanking the canal either as the train slows while it crosses the bridge over them or by stopping off at **Isthmos,** one station away from Corinth.

A ticket for the 2-hour trip between Athens and Corinth is 3.80€ ($4.35) in first class, 2.60€ ($3) in second. The InterCity train surcharge is 2.60€ ($3), though you don't have to pay it if you hold a valid railpass. Two trains make the trip between Corinth and Nafplion each day and travel time is a little over an hour. Fares cost 2.90€ ($3.35). For more information on schedules and fares, call © **210/512-4913.**

VISITOR INFORMATION   There is no visitor information office in Corinth, though you can reach the tourist police at 51 Ermou (© **27410/ 23-282**), near the Athens bus station, if you need immediate assistance.

TOP ATTRACTIONS & SPECIAL MOMENTS

A 20-minute bus ride or a 10-minute cab ride from the train station will take you to **Ancient Corinth** ✦✦. The most noteworthy feature of the archaeological site includes the handsome 6th-century B.C. **Temple of Apollo,** which stands on a low hill overlooking the extensive remains of the **Roman Agora (marketplace).** Only 7 of the temple's 38 monolithic Doric columns are standing, the others having long since been toppled by earthquakes. The *Vima* **(public platform),** located in the Agora, is the spot where St. Paul had to plead his case when the Corinthians, irritated by his constant criticisms, hauled him up in front of the Roman governor Gallo in A.D. 52.

The **Archaeological Museum** (© **27410/31-207**), on the site of Ancient Corinth, has a fine collection of the famous Corinthian pottery that is often decorated with charming red and black figures of birds and animals. There are also a number of statues of Roman worthies and several mosaics, including one in which Pan is shown piping away to a clutch of cows. Admission to the museum and archaeological site is 6€ ($6.90). Both are open in summer Monday through Sunday from 8am to 7pm; winter Monday through Sunday from 8am to 5pm.

Last but not least among important Corinth sites is the imposing castle of **Acrocorinth** (© 27410/31-966), on a natural acropolis towering 1,885 feet above the plain of Corinth. On a clear day, the views from the summit are superb. The Acrocorinth features ancient and medieval fortifications built by Greeks, Byzantines, Franks, Venetians, and Turks. Today, there are three courses of outer walls, massive gates with towers, and a jumble of ruined houses, churches, and barracks. Admission is free.

WHERE TO DINE

Restaurants near the ancient sites and the Corinth Canal tend to have high prices and mediocre food. That said, here are some suggestions if you find yourself hungry in Corinth.

Locals speak well of the grandly named **Splendid** restaurant across from the Archaeological Museum; a lunch or dinner of simple stews, chops, and salads costs around 10€ ($11.50). The **Ancient Corinth** on the main square offers much the same food at similar prices.

In the modern town, a light meal goes for around 10€ ($11.50) at the following two places: The **Pantheon Restaurant,** Ethniki Antistaseos (© 274/102-5780), serves standard Greek fare such as chops, salads, and moussaka. If you're tired of struggling with Greek menus, try the branch of the popular cafeteria-style chain **Neon** (© 274/102-3337), where much of the food is on display.

NAFPLION

Located 90 miles (145km) southwest of Athens on the Gulf of Argos' northeast coast, Nafplion is a popular destination among Greeks and visitors alike. Keep in mind that *lots* of Athenians head here on weekends, when it's best not to arrive without a hotel reservation. With a landscape that features looming castles, an island fortress, and opportunities for endless strolls through stepped streets and on a seaside promenade, it's no wonder Nafplion is one of the most charming towns not only in the Peloponnese but in all of Greece.

Combining evidence of the historical periods that touched it—from the Venetian canons, Turkish fountains, and mosques and buildings used during its term as modern Greece's first capital following the 1821 War of Independence—Nafplion has managed to preserve a charm unlike that of other Greek towns.

GETTING THERE   Two regional trains make the trip to Nafplion from Stathmos Peloponnissou in Athens daily (via Argos) and an additional one commutes between Nafplion and Argos once a day. The trip from Athens lasts 3 hours, much less time than it would take by bus (at least 4 hr.). A second-class ticket (the only option) with direct service to Nafplion out of Athens costs 4.80€ ($5.50). The 15-minute ride between Argos and Nafplion costs .60€ (70¢).

The train station in Nafplion is a tad inconveniently located near the water's edge on the side of town where practically nothing else is located. From the station call © 27520/24-120 for a cab to get you where you want to go, or at least as close as possible. Nafplion is small enough that getting anywhere by cab takes less than 5 minutes, but for many locations, including hotels, you'll have to lug luggage up some steps. The minimum charge for a cab is 3€ ($3.45).

VISITOR INFORMATION   The **municipal tourist office** is at 25 Martiou 2 (© **27520/24-444**), kitty-corner from the bus station, and it's one of the most helpful offices in all of Greece. It's usually open Monday through Friday from 9am to 1pm and 5 to 8pm (although it is often mysteriously closed during work hours). If you arrive in town without a hotel reservation (not recommended), the staff here will often find rooms in local pensions. Ask for the useful brochure *Nafplion Day and Night.* From the train station, the office is a very walkable 218 yards, located on the route to the Palamidi.

TOP ATTRACTIONS & SPECIAL MOMENTS

Nafplion is a stroller's delight, and is so small that you can't get seriously lost, so have fun exploring. No trip to the town would be complete without a visit to its two fortresses: the Acronafplia and the Palamidi, both of which dominate the city's skyline. If you're here in the summer, try to visit the fortresses in the relative cool of either morning or evening.

Getting to the remains of the Greek, Frankish, and Venetian fortresses on **Acronafplia** is a challenge, so if you don't feel like walking, take a cab. Start inside the town, where a glass encasement on a wall of the **Church of St. Spyridon** displays a bullet that killed Ioannis Kapodistrias, the first governor of modern Greece, who was assassinated in 1828. A bit farther uphill is the **Catholic Church of the Metamorphosis,** built by the Venetians, turned into a mosque by the Turks, and re-consecrated as a church after 1821. Its doorway displays an inscription featuring Philhellenes, including nephews of Lord Byron and George Washington, who died for Greece in the war for independence.

In the days before the Greek historical preservation movement dug in its tentacles, hotels were built over the Acronafplia's fortifications, one reason that the original structures have been obscured. Unless you are a military historian, you may have to take it on faith that what you're looking at here is a Frankish castle and Venetian defense tower to the east and a Byzantine castle to the west. Wandering around the Acronafplia is free.

As tough as it is getting to the Acronafplia, it's still a much simpler walk than climbing the near 1,000 steps required to get to the **Palamidi** (© **27520/28-036**). We recommend taking a cab to the top and then walking down. The Venetians spent 3 years building the Palamidi, only to be conquered the next year by the Turks in 1715. You'll enter the fortress the way the Turkish attackers did, through the main gate to the east. Once inside, you can trace the course of the massive wall that encircled the entire summit and wander through the considerable remains of the five defense fortresses that failed to stop the Turkish attack. The tour and the view from the summit of the Palamidi is worth its 4€ ($4.60) admission fee. It is open weekdays 8am to 7 pm in the summer, 8:30am to 5pm in the winter. *Note:* The swimming at Arvanitia beach below the Palamidi is excellent and won't require your leaving town. After you pass the harbor-side cafes with the sea on your right and come to the end of the promenade, follow the rocky pier to your left and just keep going; it's about a 15-minute walk.

Back down in the town harbor, boats are available for a brief visit to the **Bourtzi,** a Venetian-built island fortress in the harbor, or you can just look down on the structure when you climb the Acronafplia.

The **Archaeological Museum** ✦ (© **27520/27-502**), is housed in the 18th-century Venetian arsenal that dominates Syntagma Square, and features artifacts, including pottery and jewelry, from excavations in the area. The thick walls make this a deliciously cool place to visit on even the hottest day. It's open Tuesday to Sunday 8:30am to 3pm; admission is 3€ ($3.45).

WHERE TO STAY & DINE

You'll have to take a cab or a short, steep hike past the main town square to get to the beautifully restored **Byron Hotel** ☆☆, 2 Platonos St., Plateia Agiou Spiridona (© **27520/22-351;** www.byronhotel.gr). Make sure you ask for one of the rooms with a view—you'll pay an extra but very worthwhile 10€ ($11.50) for the privilege—as they are larger than the tiny rooms without one. The quiet, 17-room hotel overlooks the Church of Agios Spiridonas, and is a favorite among the floods of Greeks who take a summer weekend break to Nafplion; be sure to reserve well in advance if you'll be here in July or August. Rooms cost 50€ to 70€ ($57.50–$80.50) double; price depends on the size of the room and how many steps you'll have to climb to get there (there's no elevator). Breakfast is 6€ ($6.90) extra. To get to the hotel, take a cab from the train station; the short ride should run you about 4€ ($4.60).

Don't want an uphill hike to your hotel? Try the well-priced **Hotel Agamemnon** ☆, Akti Miaouli 3 (© **27520/28-021**), situated on the beachfront off the harbor. The hotel's 40 guest rooms are generic but comfortable. Request a sea view and you'll be gazing at the Bourtzi; otherwise, you'll end up facing the building on the narrow back street. It's located just past a string of cafes, but the bustle from below is almost unnoticeable from your balcony. Cost is about 78€ ($89.70) for a double room.

Eating in Nafplion presents a dilemma: dine on seafood at the seaside or on traditional cuisine inland? Oddly enough, not all the restaurants in and just off **Plateia Syntagma** (Syntagma Sq.) are the tourist traps you'd expect. Prices are pretty uniform in Nafplion, ranging from 5€ to 10€ ($5.75–$11.50) for a main course at dinner, depending on how much meat or seafood you order. If fish is on your plate, the price will be much higher; check prices or ask your waiter before ordering.

The competing taverns on Staikopoulou Street (just one street farther in from the main square) are all overshadowed by **Taverna Vassilis,** Staikopoulou 22 (© **27520/25-334**), one of the oldest in town and renowned for its traditional Greek cuisine. Eat inside in the winter; there's outdoor sidewalk seating in summer, though the narrow street may make passing pedestrians annoying or pleasant to watch, depending on your mood.

On the square, the relatively inexpensive **Hellas Restaurant** ☆ (© **27520/ 27-278**) is another reliable, established restaurant with traditional food. Sitting outside is a less-crowded experience here because of its location on the square as opposed to a side street.

A string of well-regarded fish taverns line the waterfront, with **Savouras** ☆, Bouboulinas 79 (© **07520/27-704**), and neighboring **Arapakos** ☆, Bouboulinas 81 (© **27520/27-675**), topping the list. You get your pick of the day's catch for fish, but traditional Greek cuisine, of course, is also available. Be prepared for slightly poor service at both restaurants when it gets crowded, especially during the weekends.

For coffee or dessert, pick any one of the cafes along **Akti Miaouli** on the waterfront and you won't go wrong.

DAY EXCURSIONS TO MYCENAE & EPIDAURUS

Although there is no connecting rail service to either spot, while in Nafplion it would be a shame to miss the citadel and massive tomb known as the Treasury of Atreus at **Mycenae** as well as the sanctuary, museum, and ancient theater at **Epidaurus.** Your options are a bus ride (2€/$2.30 to Mycenae, 2€/$2.30 to Epidaurus) or taking an organized tour. The municipal tourist office's recommended

Moments A Side Trip to Argos

Argos was one of ancient Greece's greatest strongholds. There should be lots of impressive remains to visit here, but because modern Argos (pop. 20,000) is built precisely on top of the ancient city, little remains of its former glory. There are, however, a few notable exceptions that make this a good excursion out of Nafplion or Athens.

The Museum at Argos, Elgas St. off Plateia Ayiou Petrou (🕿 27510/68-819), is a small archaeological museum that has a handful of superlative pieces, including the fragment of a 7th-century B.C. clay *krater* (vessel) showing a determined Ulysses blinding the one-eyed Cyclops. Outside, in the museum's shady courtyard, are some terrific Roman mosaics showing the god Dionysos and the seasons. It's open Tuesday through Sunday 8:30am to 3pm.

Argos's **4th-century theater** ✮ was probably the largest in classical Greece. Twenty thousand spectators could sit here, in 89 tiers of seats, many of which were carved from the hillside itself. Near the theater are the minimal remains of the ancient **agora,** as yet largely unexcavated, as it lies under today's Argos. Joint admission to the theater, agora, and the archaeological museum is 3€ ($3.45).

Just outside of town, Argos' citadels **Aspis** and **Larissa** (🕿 27510/22-810), provide stunning views of the region, including the Gulf of Nafplion. Admission is free, and they're usually open from sunrise to sunset. You can climb up to the Larissa from Argos's ancient theater (allow at least 1 hr.), and then hike across the ridge called the Deiras to the Aspis.

Three trains a day leave from Nafplion to Argos. It costs .60€ (70¢) for the 15-minute trip, but the schedule isn't the best and you're probably better off taking a bus (trip time: 30 min.) from the Nafplion station on Plateia Kapodistrias (🕿 275/202-8555) and then catching a train back. The bus ride costs .90€ ($1.05). About five trains a day make the 3-hour trip from Station Peloponnissou in Athens to Argos. The Argos train station, on Leoforos Vas. Sofias (🕿 275/106-7212), is about ⅔ mile (1km) from the central square.

day trips are jointly organized by Zafeiris Tours (🕿 27520/22-221) and Dialogos Tours (🕿 27520/59-130). At press time, during the tourist high season, which runs from April to October, tours to Tyrins, Mycenae, and Nemea run on Mondays, leaving Nafplion at 8:45am and returning at 5pm. The 45€ ($51.75) cost includes entrance to all sites. On Wednesdays, the companies offer a tour to Epidaurus, Corinth, and the Isthmus. Departure from Nafplion is at 7:45am with a 6pm return. Cost is 50€ ($57.50). Both excursions feature English-guided tours and include about 2 hours of free time for lunch (not included in the price).

Mycenae

Ancient legend calls Mycenae the home of King Agamemnon, the most powerful leader in Greece during the Trojan War. In today's reality, all that is left are the impressive remnants of what might have been: the palace where

Agamemnon may have lived, the tub where he may have met his death, and the tomb where he may have been buried.

Agamemnon led the Greeks in the 10-year fight to reclaim his brother's wife, Helen, from the Trojan prince who took her away. Homer, who tells the story in *The Iliad,* calls Mycenae "rich in gold," a fact later confirmed by archaeological digs. The German archaeologist Heinrich Schliemann, who found and excavated Troy, began excavating at Mycenae in 1874.

Enter through the **Lion Gate** and on the other side of the ancient citadel's defense walls, you'll see **Grave Circle A,** where Schliemann found graves containing some 31 pounds of gold treasure. Remains on the site include those of **houses** and a **palace.** A small **bathtub** in the palace may have been where Agamemnon was stabbed to death by his wife, Clytemnestra. If you're not claustrophobic, bring a flashlight and climb down into the enormous **cistern** on the citadel's northeast corner. The most impressive of the Mycenean sites is the massive tomb known as the **Treasury of Atreus** ★★★, considered to be Agamemnon's tomb. While many *tholos* (beehive) tombs are scattered around Mycenae, this is the largest. About a 5-minute walk from the citadel, it was probably built around 1300 B.C. along with the Lion Gate.

The enormous tomb, with its 118-ton lintel, is 43 feet high and 47 feet wide. Look up toward the ceiling, and you'll see why these are called beehive tombs. Once your eyes get accustomed to the poor light, you can make out the bronze nails that once held hundreds of bronze rosettes in place in the ceiling. This tomb was robbed in antiquity, so we'll never know what it contained, although the contents of Grave Circle A provide an idea of what riches must have been here.

A new archaeological museum opened in Mycenae in July 2003 and houses more than 2,500 of Schliemann's finds from the archaeological site and the surrounding areas. Many of the treasures, including the ceramics, gold, and ivory works, are on public view for the first time since their discovery at the end of the 19th century.

Admission to the Treasury of Atreus, archaeological site, and museum is 6€ ($6.90). For more information, call © **27510/76-585.** The attractions are open in summer daily from 8am to 7pm; in winter daily from 8am to 5pm. On Mondays, the museum opens at 12:30pm.

Four daily buses shuttle between Nafplion's bus station (© **27520/28-555**) and Mycenae. The hour-long trip costs 2€ ($2.30). The bus stops right outside the archaeological site.

Epidaurus

The **Theater of Epidaurus** is one of the most impressive sights in Greece. Probably built in the 4th century, this theater seats some 14,000 spectators. Unlike so many ancient buildings, the theater was not pillaged for building blocks in antiquity. As a result, it is astonishingly well preserved; restorations have been both minimal and tactful.

Climb up to the top of the **ancient theater** ★★★ and you'll tower over 55 rows of seats: The lower, original section has 34 rows; the upper section of 21 rows was added in a 2nd-century B.C. expansion. The theater's acoustics are famous—you'll almost certainly see someone demonstrating how a whisper can be heard all the way from the round orchestra pit to the top row of seats. Epidaurus is considered a living monument, and hosts the summer-long Epidaurus Festival, consisting mostly of performances of classical Greek plays on Friday and Saturday nights. Performances are staged in Greek only, and translations aren't offered, though most visitors don't mind the language barrier and come to see them anyway; visitors can usually follow along because the plays are almost always well-known ancient Greek tragedies or comedies.

The new **Epidaurus Festival Museum,** near the entrance to the theater, with its displays of props, costumes, programs, and memorabilia from past performances is a great supplement to a tour of the theater. It's usually open when the site is open, daily from May 1 until September 30 (and until 9pm on performance nights); entrance is free.

A stop at the site's other museum before roaming through the rest of the location will help to put some flesh on the bones of the sanctuary's scant remains. The **excavation museum** features architectural fragments from the sanctuary, votive offerings of terra-cotta body parts, and surgical implements.

The **Sanctuary of Asklepios,** who was worshipped in other parts of Greece as well, served as a religious center for his cult and as a spa, where the sick would come to be cured and the healthy to relax. Accommodations for visitors, **bathhouses,** a **gymnasium, stadium, temples,** and **shrines** are among the ruins. It is unclear why the round **tholos** has labyrinthine foundations, but scholars suspect Asklepios's healing serpents lived there. Two long **stoas** nearby provided a sleeping spot for patients hoping to see Asklepios in a dream. Those cured dedicated the votive offerings and inscriptions on display at the museum.

Combined admission to the site, theater, and museums (✆ **27530/22-009**) is 6€ ($6.90). The hours for all the attractions in summer are Monday through Friday from 8am to 7pm; in winter, Monday through Friday from 8am to 5pm, and Saturday and Sunday from 8: 30am to 3: 15pm.

Five buses leave the Nafplion bus station (✆ **27520/28-555**) daily to and from Epidauros, with extra buses during the summer-long **Epidaurus Festival.** Buses stop just outside the archaeological site. For theater tickets call ✆ **210/ 322-1459** in Athens or ✆ **27530/22-026** in Epidaurus. It's also possible to buy tickets at most of the travel agencies in Nafplion and at the theater itself, starting at 5pm on the day of a performance. The bus trip costs only 2€ ($2.30) and normally takes about 45 minutes, but allow more time if you're heading to a performance.

DIAKOFTO/KALAVRYTA ★★★

The scenic seaside rail route from Athens to the coastal port village of Diakofto in the northern Peloponnese is nothing compared to the view from the main line's mountainous branch from Diakofto to Kalavryta. Forget Greece, it's one of the best rail excursions in all of Europe. The famous **rack-and-pinion railroad** *odontotos,* literally "toothed" track in Greek, travels up the mountain to Kalavryta as it offers stunning views of the steep rocks and rich vegetation engulfing the gorge through which the Vouraikos river winds below. The narrowest narrow-gauge rail in Greece, odontotos was completed in 1896 for the practical purpose of transporting ore down from Kalavryta. Today, the rail is considered a masterpiece by engineering standards, and provides a scenic journey through the region's thick vegetation, caves, and waterfalls as the train weaves along either side of the Vouraikos, navigating through roughly cut tunnels, picturesque bridges, and hanging cliffs. You may even pass a few hikers along the way. A steam car originally rode the 14-mile (22.5km) track until it was replaced around 1960 by a diesel one. An original, known as *Moutzouris,* or smudgy, can be seen at the Diakofto train station. On the line's 100th anniversary in 1996, it rode the route successfully.

GETTING THERE Eight trains a day, including six InterCity trains, run from Athens to Diakofto on the Patras line. A one-way, first-class ticket costs 5.90€ ($6.80); second class is 3.80€ ($4.35). There is an additional 4.70€ ($5.40) surcharge on InterCity routes. Depending on the type of train, the trip can last anywhere from just under 3 to about 4 hours. The cost of the 1-hour trip from Diakofto to Kalavryta is 1.60€ ($1.85). Railpasses are good on all of the above trains, but travelers with passes will still have to pay a "special" odontotos surcharge of 2.10€ ($2.40). Though there used to be five trains that ran the Diakofto–Kalavryta route daily, as of this writing, the line was closed to allow for upgrades in advance of the 2004 Olympics and its expected increase in tourism. It's expected to reopen early in 2004. To find out if the line has reopened, call the station at **Diakofto** (𝄐 **26910/43-206**) or **Kalavryta** (𝄐 **26920/22-245**).

VISITOR INFORMATION There are no tourist information centers in either Diakofto or Kalavryta, but the municipality information lines can be helpful to tourists. The Kalavryta municipality number is 𝄐 **26920/22-390;** Diakofto's municipality number is 𝄐 **26910/43-350.**

TOP ATTRACTIONS & SPECIAL MOMENTS

Just past the halfway mark on the train route from Diakofto to Kalavryta, around 8 miles (12.5km) into the trip, you'll be able to spot the pretty village of **Zahlorou** on the banks of the Vouraikos river. If you get off at the nearby **Mega Spilaio** station (the only one on the route) about 45 minutes into the trip, a short walk will reward you with the sight of the **Monastery of the Great Cave,** or *Moni Megalou Spilaiou* (𝄐 **26920/22-401**). Built into the steep walls of the **Mount Helmos,** tradition holds that the monastery was founded in the 4th century by two brothers on the site where an icon of the Virgin Mary, said to have been painted by St. Luke, was found. The monastery was destroyed and rebuilt many times throughout history, with the most recent structure dating to a reconstruction following a 1934 fire. Sacred relics, gospels with Byzantine craftsmanship, and intricately carved icon stands from all periods of Christianity can be seen at the monastery, for an admission fee of 2€ ($2.30). The monastery is open daily from 7am to 1pm and 2pm to 7:30pm. *Note:* Only one of the five daily trains on the route will definitely stop at the Mega Spilaio station; the other four will only make optional stops. Make sure to inform the engineer of your desire to stop. For a return trip out of the station, inform a station attendant that you wish to board and then stand on the platform and hail the train. The train always stops if there is a passenger on the platform.

Get back on the train and about 20 minutes later you will arrive at Kalavryta, located 2,461 feet up the mountain. A historic city that maintains its traditional character with stone houses and well-kept old buildings, **Kalavryta** (𝄐 **26920/ 22-390** for city hall) left its mark on Greece's history as the cradle of the country's revolution. Just a few kilometers outside of town, the celebrated 10th-century **monastery of Agia Lavra** (𝄐 **26920/22-363**), showcases the **banner** that was raised to launch the **1821 independence struggle** from the Ottoman Turks and marks the spot where the fighters took their oath. Like the Monastery of the Great Cave, Agia Lavra also was destroyed throughout its history, most recently by the Germans during World War II. The mark of the Nazi occupying forces is still vivid in Kalavryta today: A **monument** marks the execution site of nearly 1,500 men over the age of 13 in 1943, and the main church's clock still reads 2:34, the time of the massacre, one of the country's biggest during World War II.

Agia Lavra is open 10am to 1pm and 4pm to 5pm (afternoon hours change to 3pm–4pm after the end of daylight savings time in Oct). Admission is 1€ ($1.15). The monastery is about 3 miles (5km) from the train station and you should take a cab to get there. Locals say cabbies usually charge "whatever they want," but the price generally hovers around 10€ ($11.50). You can ask the cab to wait for you (the meter runs), have them come back to pick you up at an agreed-upon time, or give them a ring when you're ready to leave. To get a taxi, call © 26920/31-537.

About 11 miles (17km) outside of town, but well worth the trip, is the **Cave of the Lakes,** or *Spilaio ton Limnon* (© 26920/31-001). A natural wonder with stalactites and stalagmites adorning it, the cave features more than a dozen lakes on three levels. Excavations and explorations have limited public access to only a part of the cave. A walking tour that lasts just over 30 minutes costs 7€ ($8.05). The cave has two faces depending on the season: Rivers and waterfalls gush in the winter and spring when there's more water from snow and rain, and there are still lakes in the summer and fall. Ongoing excavations since its redis-covery in 1964 have yielded finds dating to prehistoric times. There is no pub-lic transportation from the station to the caves. They are open Monday through Friday from 9am to 4pm and Saturdays, Sundays, and holidays from 9:30am to 5:30pm. Taxis are the only option; to get one, call © 26920/31-537.

WHERE TO STAY & DINE

Note: Unlike many other places in Greece, in Kalavryta and Diakofto, peak sea-son is winter and prices are lower in summer.

You'll probably want to stay in Diakofto for the beach, and the beach alone. Just 1,604 feet from the sea and very close to the train station, the two-floor **Chris Paul Hotel** (© 26910/41-715) is a good place for a swim and overnight stop before heading to Kalavryta. The air-conditioned guest rooms are simply and efficiently furnished. The price for a double is 50€ ($57.50) in off season, up to 65€ ($74.75) in peak season.

If the beach isn't your thing, take the train to Zahlorou (see above), where you'll find the **Romantzo Hotel** (© 26920/22-758), right next to the pictur-esque train station. Located in a forested gorge and surrounded by natural beauty, the old wooden hotel is, as its name suggests, romantic. There are sev-eral hiking trails nearby; a trail that goes to the nearby Monastery of the Great Cave is just a few steps away. The hotel has few rooms and they go fast, so reserve well in advance. The hotel's restaurant offers great home-cooked meals, though if you wish to dine elsewhere, many tavernas are located in the village. Rooms run 30€ ($34.50) double in summer but are a bit more expensive in the winter because of heating costs.

In Kalavryta, one of the top housing options is the **Xenonas Fanara** (© 26920/23-665), a guesthouse built in 1995 that has nine apartments, each suitable for two to four people. It is open year-round. Rooms have all the expected amenities, including kitchens, heating and television, as well as bal-conies with views. The hotel is only about 330 yards and an easy walk from the train station. Quoted prices are for 3-night stays (Fri–Sat): 95€ ($109) double during the off season; 145€ ($167) in peak season.

OLYMPIA

The birthplace of the ancient Olympic Games, Olympia hosted the top athletic event for more than 1,000 years beginning in 776 B.C. Various venues, temples, and other structures were constructed throughout its history, the remains of which can be seen at the archaeological site today, including the Games' original stadium, gymnasium, and temple of Hera, where the Olympic flame is lit for the modern Olympics.

Olympia's museum has been closed for renovations in advance of the upcoming Athens Games and is scheduled to re-open shortly before the August 2004 Olympics begin.

GETTING THERE   At press time, the train station at Olympia was temporarily closed due to the construction of a bridge. Under normal circumstances, two InterCity trains depart Athens in the morning for a direct, 5-hour trip to Olympia. A first-class ticket to Olympia is 12€ ($13.80) and a second-class ticket is 8.20€ ($9.45), plus an additional 6.20€ ($7.15) for the InterCity surcharge. Otherwise, you have to take one of several trains a day from Athens or Patras to the nearby town of Pirgos, where three daily regional trains shuttle the half-hour distance to Olympia. Information on schedules and fares is available from the Peloponnissou station in Athens (© 210/513-1601), the station in Olympia (© 26240/22-670), and the station at Pirgos (© 26210/22-525). Tickets from Pirgos to Olympia cost .70€ (80¢). The ancient site of Olympia is less than a 15-minute walk from the village and train station. Olympia is a walkable town with no public transportation, so you can stroll to all the attractions or take a taxi (© 26240/22-555).

VISITOR INFORMATION   The municipality's tourism information office at © 26240/23100 rarely picks up. Try the tourist police instead at © 26240/22-550; they are most helpful.

TOP ATTRACTIONS & SPECIAL MOMENTS
Between the museum and archaeological site, you'll need the better part of a day to tour ancient Olympia. At press time, the **Archaeological Museum** (© 26240/22-529 and 26240/22742) was closed for renovations in advance of the 2004 Athens Olympics; expected reopening time is Spring 2004 though the exact date and planned admission fees were not yet available. To give you an idea of what to expect, the collection had been organized chronologically from the Neolithic to Roman times. In addition to ancient athletic paraphernalia including bronze and stone discuses and bronze weights used for balance by long jumpers, the museum collection features bronze and marble statues of victorious athletes, donated to ancient Olympia by their cities of origin. Two of antiquity's major statues, Paionios' **winged victory** and Praxiteles' **Hermes** were on display as well. Call the museum before you head out to get information on hours and admission fees.

Across the road, the **Ancient Site** (© 26240/22-517) is divided into two distinct parts: the religious sanctuary and the athletic facilities. The **religious sanctuary** is dominated by the Temple of Hera and the massive Temple of Zeus. With its three standing columns, the **Temple of Hera** is the older of the two, built around 600 B.C. The Hermes of Praxiteles statue was found here, buried under the mud that covered Olympia for so long due to the repeated flooding of the Alfios and Kladeos rivers. The **Temple of Zeus,** which once had 34 massive Doric columns, was built around 456 B.C. Inside the temple stood one of the Seven Wonders of the Ancient World: an enormous gold-and-ivory statue of Zeus on an ivory-and-ebony throne. Not only do we know that Phidias made the 43-foot-tall statue, we know where he made it: The **Workshop of Phidias** was on the site of the well-preserved brick building clearly visible west of the temple, just outside the sanctuary. A cup with the inscription "I belong to Phidias" was found inside that building.

On the sporting side in addition to the famed stadium, there are also the remains of the **gymnasium** and **palestra,** where foot racing and boxing skills were practiced. The remains of a shrine to Philip of Macedon, father of Alexander the Great, and Roman baths and fountains can also be seen. Admission to the ancient site costs 6€ ($6.90). It's open 8am to 7pm daily.

The **Museum of the Olympic Games** (*©* 26240/22-544), back in the town of Olympia, displays victors' medals, commemorative stamps, and photos of winning athletes, such as former King Constantine of Greece and the great American athlete Jesse Owens. Admission is 2€ ($2.30) and it's open daily from 8am to 3:30pm.

WHERE TO STAY & DINE

For a village, the nearly two-dozen hotels around Olympia may seem excessive, and they probably would be if not for the massive influx of tourists the city sees in July and August, as well as the expected surge of visitors expected in 2004 because of the Athens Olympics. Note that some hotels in town close in the winter, though both the hotels we mention below are open year-round.

Perhaps the best hotel in town, **Hotel Europa** ★★, *©* 26240/22-650, part of the Best Western chain, is a 3-minute cab ride from the station, and sits high on a hill overlooking both the modern village and the ancient site. Most of the large rooms look out onto a large pool and garden, and several have small views of the ancient site. All have balconies and unstocked refrigerators. The 110€ ($127) rate for a double includes breakfast.

With a pleasant rooftop cafe, **Hotel Neda,** Odos Praxiteles (*©* 26240/ 22-563) is on the quieter end of the noisy hotel scale. The air-conditioned rooms are large; some of the doubles have double beds, but most have twins, so specify which you prefer. All units have balconies. Double rooms run 50.40€ ($58). The hotel is about 330 yards from the train station—an easy walk.

The excellent and reasonably priced restaurant, **Taverna Praxiteles** ★, Spiliopoulou 7 (*©* 26240/23-570), is all that remains of the now-defunct Hotel Praxiteles. It's packed almost every evening, first by visitors eating unfashionably early, then with locals, who start showing up around 10pm. Although the entrees are good, it's easy to make a meal of the delicious and varied appetizers. A sampling plate costs about 6.20€ ($7.15) and might include octopus, eggplant salad, *taramosalata* (fish-roe salad, though locals jokingly call it cheap caviar), fried cheese, and a handful of olives. In good weather, tables are outside on the sidewalk; the rest of the year, meals are served in the pine-paneled dining room.

The charming **Taverna Kladeos** ★★ (*©* 26240/23-322) is situated just behind the train station. A traditional taverna in the midst of Olympia's increasing throng of tourist traps, it has the best food in town. The menu changes according to what's in season. The house wine, a light rose, is heavenly. If you want to buy some to take with you, give an empty water bottle to your waiter and ask him to fill it with *krasi* (wine). Main courses cost 5.60€ to 11.20€ ($6.45–$12.90).

PATRAS

Greece's third-biggest city, the port of Patras is a busy transit point, providing ferry connections to Italy and the islands of the Ionian Sea. It would seem that, like Piraeus outside of Athens, the only reason to come to Patras is to catch a ferry. But at least once a year, Patras offers visitors a different incentive to visit. The city is famous for its annual **Carnival** (*©* 26102/22-157), celebrated annually during the 3 weeks before Lent. It's not New Orleans, but it is the closest thing to it in Greece and there are parades, costumes, and floats. If you're considering a trip to Patras around Carnival time, make sure to reserve a hotel room well in advance, as there are usually no last-minute rooms available.

The city also has some notable projects in the works. In 2004, one of the world's largest suspension bridges (7,382 ft.) at Rio just outside Patras is slated for completion. The bridge will link the Peloponnese to mainland Greece at Antirio, possible now only by a ferry shuttle service or roundabout rail service via Athens. Patras is also one of the "Olympic Cities" as it will host the preliminary rounds of soccer competition for the Athens Games. The city's soccer stadium is being revamped for that purpose.

And Patras has also been designated Europe's cultural capital for 2006, when dozens of cultural events—including exhibitions, live performances, and street art displays—will complement its annual Carnival. Established in 1985, the European Capital of Culture aims at highlighting the richness and diversity of European cultures. Thessaloniki had the distinction in 1997.

GETTING THERE   Eight direct trains leave daily from the Peloponnissou Station in Athens (© **210/513-1601**) to Patras, including five InterCity trains, which take almost 4 hours, as opposed to the slower ones, which take about 5. A first-class, one-way ticket costs 7.90€ ($9.10) and a second-class one is 5.30€ ($6.10). There's an additional surcharge of 4.70€ ($5.40) if you take the InterCity train.

The Patras train station, Othonos Amalias 14 (© **261/027-3694**), is on the waterfront near the boat departure piers. Patras is one of the arrival and departure points for ferry service between Greece and Italy. *Note:* If you are taking the train to Patras for the sole purpose of catching the ferry, be sure to leave plenty of time to get to the city and your boat in case of a train delay.

VISITOR INFORMATION   An information center run by the municipality is located at Othonos-Amalias 6, less than 545 yards from the train station, across the pier (© **26104/61-740**). It's open daily from 8am to 10pm.

TOP ATTRACTIONS & SPECIAL MOMENTS

Hovering above the city, the **Achaia Clauss Winery** (© **2610/325051**) is a gem waiting to be polished. Maker of some of the most loved wine to come out of Greece, Achaia Clauss offers free tours of the place where Europe's oldest wines sit in massive barrels, some carved with works of art. Tours of the winery founded by the German vintner Clauss are given daily except for Good Friday and Easter. At the end of the tour, you can sample a bit of the local product. Don't miss a taste of the winery's famed Mavrodafni sweet red or the view of the city below. The winery is accessible by taxi from the train station (the ride costs about 7€/$8.05), or by bus no.7 from the city bus station (4 blocks away) for 1€ ($1.15). Only one bus per hour travels up to the winery and you should call the bus station (© **26104/53-930**) to confirm times. To return from the winery call a radio taxi (© **26103/46-700** or 26104/25-201) to come pick you up.

Closer to the city, the **Castle at Chlemoutsi** is an astonishingly well-preserved 13th-century Frankish fort with crenellated walls, cavernous galleries, and an immense hexagonal keep. It changed hands many times, from the Franks, Venetians, and Turks, to the Greeks. The gaps in the outer wall were caused by Ibrahim Pasha's cannon during the Greek War of Independence. The castle is open most days from sunrise to sunset; admission is free. The city's **Archaeological Museum,** Mezonos 42 (© **26102/20-829** or 26102/75-070), features artifacts uncovered from the area with finds spanning the period from

Patras

ACCOMMODATIONS ■
Astir Hotel **10**
Primarolia **8**

DINING ◆
Café Stathmos **7**
Pharos Fish Taverna **6**
Pitssi **2**

ATTRACTIONS ●
Achaia Clauswinery **3**
Archaeological Museum **9**
Castle at Chlemoutsi **5**
Cathedral of St. Andrew **1**
Roman Odeion **4**

Greece

Aegean Sea

Patras ● ✪ Athens

Peloponnese

Mediterranean Sea **CRETE**

International Ferry Terminal
Ionian Ferry Terminal

Sarandaporou
Faviero
Norman
Karolou
Satovriandou
Athenon

Bus Station

Train Station

Plateia Olgas

Maizonos
Kolokotroni
Korinthou
Zaimi

UPPER TOWN

Amalias
Ayiou Andreas
Othonos
Riga Feraou
Ayiou Nikolaou

Acropolis/ Patras Fortress

Fishing Harbor

Plateia Vas. Yioryiou A'

Votsi
Kanakari
Yrokostopulou
Ypsilantou

Maizonos
Korinthou
Sachturi
Trion Navarchon
Koran
Dimitriu Gunari
Alexandrou

Ayios Yioryios

Pantokratoros
Lontou
Nikita
Germanou
Ayiou Dimitriou

Papaviessa

0   200 m
0   200 y

N

3000 B.C. to 800 B.C. as well as the city's first Roman finds. It's open Tuesday through Friday from 8:30am to 3pm; Friday through Sunday 8am to 7 pm; closed Mondays. Admission is free.

Much like the Herodion Atticus Theater in Athens, the ancient **Roman Odeion** in Patras hosts summer-long cultural events (② **26102/76-207**). The **Cathedral of St. Andrew,** the city's patron saint, is a major pilgrimage site thanks to the presence of St. Andrew's skull in an ornate gold reliquary to the right of the altar. The church is on the waterfront, a 10-minute walk from the train station.

WHERE TO STAY & DINE

Conveniently located on the waterfront across from the rail station, **Primarolia** ★★, Othonos Amalias 33 (② **26106/24-900**), is within easy walking distance of almost everything you'd want to see in Patras. One of Greece's first

---

Tips **Watching the Scenery**

When traveling out of Athens to Patras, you'll have a view of the sea on your left and rugged mountains on your right until the Isthmus of Corinth. Once you pass that landmark, the scenery swaps, with the coast following you on your right all the way to Patras's train station. Pick the side you prefer accordingly.

boutique hotels, it showcases artwork and furniture by well-known artists and designers throughout the premises, and all of its 14 rooms sport a different decor scheme. The rooms' little touches make all the difference, especially the extra fluffy towels in the bathrooms. Some guest rooms overlook the harbor, others the back street; either way you'll want to look at your own room instead. Prices begin at 118€ ($136) double and go up to 177€ ($204) for the largest rooms and suites. Specify if you want a sea view.

Its guest room decor may be stuck in the 1970s, but the 120-room **Astir Hotel,** Agiou Andrea 16 (© **26102/77-502**), has a central location, with views of the harbor and a rooftop terrace, that makes it worth an overnight stay, especially if you've got an early ferry or train to catch. It's within easy walking distance of the train station. Rates run 130€ to 150€ ($150–$173) double and include breakfast.

Back in the center of town, you won't have to look further than the train station for a great meal. **Café Stathmos** (© **26106/22-550**) puts all other station cafeterias and snack bars to shame. Its grilled sandwiches and salads can compete with any bistro, and it will cost you under 7€ ($8.05) for a complete meal including appetizers.

Got time for a slow, easy, and ridiculously cheap meal the real Greek way? Opt for **Pitsi** (© **26103/31-644**) at Trion Navarhon 72, a wide street with a huge pedestrian walkway running down the middle. Pitsi features lamb and other meat perfectly cooked on a rotating spit. Even the chicken burger patties are great. Main courses cost 4€ to 7€ ($4.60–$8.05), unless you order a kilo (2.2 lb.) of pork or lamb, each priced at 18€ ($20.70).

If seafood is what you're after, try **Pharos Fish Taverna,** Amalias 48. © **26103/36-500,** a local favorite where you can choose your own fish. Prices depend on the size of the fish and the day's market rate, but figure a main course will cost about 10€ ($11.50).

4 Thessaloniki & the Northeast

History has left its mark on Greece's second largest city, Thessaloniki, in more ways than one. Traces of its Greek, Roman, Byzantine, Turkish, and Jewish past are visible on virtually every corner of this bustlingly modern city of one million people. Thessaloniki's multicultural past is legendary: from housing one of the largest Jewish populations in eastern Europe before the Holocaust to being the birthplace of Kemal Ataturk, founder of modern Turkey.

Today's Thessaloniki offers locals and tourists alike a rich nightlife; good and relatively inexpensive traditional and multiethnic cuisine; cultural treasures, such as an unparalleled collection of Byzantine churches; and a 2.5-mile- (4km-) long seaside boardwalk. And, in 2004, if you can't get into Athens, Thessaloniki will host some of the preliminary soccer events at the Olympic Games. Most important of all for the rail traveler, the city is the springboard for rail excursions to the whole of northern Greece as well as the country's gateway to the Balkans.

STATION INFORMATION
GETTING FROM THE AIRPORT TO THE TRAIN STATION
From the U.S., there are no direct flights to Thessaloniki. Connections can be made at a number of European cities, including London, Amsterdam, Brussels, Frankfort, Stuttgart, Munich, Zurich, and Vienna. From London, there are direct flights on **Olympic.** Located 10 miles (16km) from the city center, **Makedonia Airport** (© **23104/73-212**), is linked to the city center by a public bus line.

Taking a taxi, however, will get you to the train station on the other side of town far quicker, and costs just 5 to 10€ ($5.75–$11.50), depending on traffic.

INSIDE THE TRAIN STATION

Most visitors to the city will arrive by train. Nearly a dozen trains a day run from Athens to Thessaloniki on newly laid tracks. Service on this line has been vastly improved and we've traveled the route more than a dozen times and never run into any time delays. The InterCity trains on this route are air-conditioned, clean, roomy, and almost soundproof; they are definitely preferable to the older, regional ones—some of which may be in dubious condition. Depending on the type of train, the trip can take from 5 to 7 hours. The overnight sleeper train has sleeper compartments that hold four to six passengers. Reservations for sleeping compartments should be made many days in advance at Larissus Station in Athens (© **210/323-6747**). Because of the variety of trains operating the route, the cost of a second-class seat can run from 14.10€ to 45.20€ ($16.20–$52) and a first-class seat from 20.80€ to 59.30€ ($24–$68.20).

The Thessaloniki train station (© **23105/17-517**), Greece's largest, is at the edge of the city on Monastiriou, which is the extension of Egnatia west of Vadari Square, the site of numerous shady bars. There is a tourist information desk, but not much more than maps and general information are provided. Some not-very-exciting restaurants, cafes, shops, and newsstands are also housed in the premises. Beware of pickpockets while inside and around the station.

A taxi ride to Aristotelous Square from the station takes about 10 minutes and costs about 5€ ($5.75). To avoid the trek to the train station to get information and buy tickets, use the OSE (train) office at Aristotelous Square 18 (© **23105/ 98-120**), open Monday to Friday 9am to 9pm, and Saturday 9am to 3pm.

INFORMATION ELSEWHERE IN THE CITY

The main office of the **Greek National Tourism Organization (EOT)** has moved to a new location at Georgikis Scholis 46 (© **23102/71-888**). It's open Monday through Friday from 7:30am to 2:30pm and Saturday from 8:30am to 2pm. From the train station, take bus no. 3 to the Kalamari station. A useful magazine to buy at virtually any newspaper kiosk is the quarterly *Pillotos,* which lists in Greek all of the cultural and entertainment goings-on in the city. *Pillotos* has an English-language "Blue Pages" section with all the important addresses and phone numbers you could want, from the police and radio taxis to consulates, banks, bars, and cinemas.

GETTING AROUND

In the city center, most of the attractions, restaurants, and shops are easily reached on foot in no more than 20 minutes. Otherwise, you'll need to use public transportation or take a taxi (probably your best option).

By Bus Unlike Athens, Thessaloniki has only one public transportation option: the bus. Although the city has a pretty good bus network, the actual buses are impossible to board with backpacks or slightly large luggage during rush hour. Tickets can be purchased from kiosks or on board the bus from machines. On buses, exact fare is required, so try to have a variety of change with you. Validate your ticket and hold on to it in case a conductor boards the bus to check. The price for a ticket purchased before boarding is .45€ (50¢); if bought on the bus, tickets are .50€ (60¢).

By Taxi Cabs are slightly easier to hail here than they are in Athens. Take along a map or have someone write out your destination in Greek, so that you can

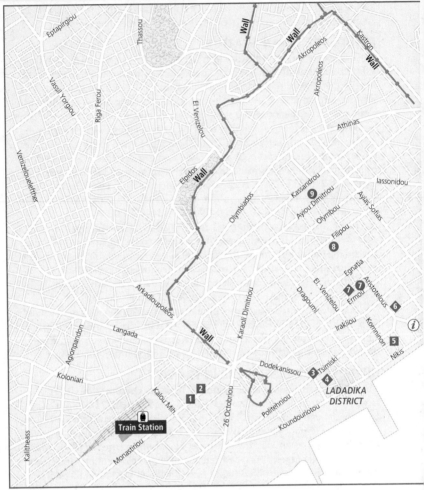

show the driver where you want to go. Rates are moderate when compared to those in the U.S.; tips are not expected—rounding up the fare as a modest tip is appreciated. Make sure, however, that the driver turns on his meter and that, within the city limits, the rate that it uses is number 1. Rate number 2 is for outside the city limits. There's an extra 2€ ($2.30) charge for trips from the airport. After midnight, all fares on the meter are doubled.

WHERE TO STAY

Note: The hotel prices below vary depending on whether it's peak or off-peak season. In Thessaloniki, that translates into whether it's convention or international fair time. Conventions are held at various times throughout the year; the international fair is in September.

Capsis Hotel A stone's throw away from the city's train station, the Capsis was recently renovated and also houses a convention center. It attracts many business travelers, but its location on busy Monastiriou is just as good for leisure visitors,

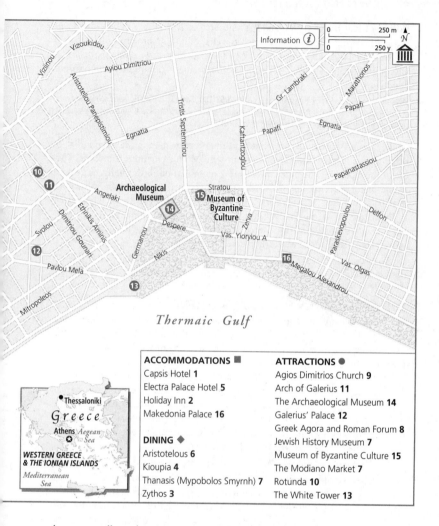

Information (i)
0 ——————— 250 m
0 ——————— 250 y
N

ACCOMMODATIONS ■	ATTRACTIONS ●
Capsis Hotel **1**	Agios Dimitrios Church **9**
Electra Palace Hotel **5**	Arch of Galerius **11**
Holiday Inn **2**	The Archaeological Museum **14**
Makedonia Palace **16**	Galerius' Palace **12**
	Greek Agora and Roman Forum **8**
DINING ◆	Jewish History Museum **7**
Aristotelous **6**	Museum of Byzantine Culture **15**
Kioupia **4**	The Modiano Market **7**
Thanasis (Mypobolos Smyrnh) **7**	Rotunda **10**
Zythos **3**	The White Tower **13**

who can stroll to the city center and sightsee along the way. The elaborate entrance bears no resemblance to the mediocre rooms, but at least those are clean and air-conditioned. The rooftop pool is one of the hotel's best features.

Monastiriou Street 18, 54629 Thessaloniki. ℂ 23105/21-321. Fax 23105/10-555. 422 units. www. capsishotel.gr. 129€–196€ ($148–$225) double (peak vs. off-peak season). Rates include breakfast. AE, DC, MC, V. **Amenities:** Restaurant; 2 bars. *In room:* Hair dryer.

Electra Palace Hotel   Overlooking Thessaloniki's main square, the Electra Palace, with its handsome, curved, arcaded façade, has the nicest location in town—except when there are noisy demonstrations in Aristotle Square. It has recently reopened as a government-rated five-star hotel after a long-overdue renovation. All the guest rooms are air-conditioned; insist on one of the fourth- or fifth-floor rooms with balcony overlooking the square.

Aristotelous Sq. 9A, 54624 Thessaloniki. ℂ 231/023-2221, ext. 229. Fax 231/023-5947. electrapalace@ the.forthnet.gr. 70 units. 180€–280€ ($207–$322) Rates include American-style buffet breakfast. AE, DC, MC, V. **Amenities:** 2 restaurants; 2 bars; nonsmoking rooms. *In room:* Hair dryer.

Holiday Inn   Built in 1968 and last renovated in 2000, this hotel, like the Capsis, is an obvious choice for the train traveler, due to its proximity (about 660 ft.) to the city's train station. Its 177 rooms include new, modern furniture; air-conditioning; satellite TV; and, perhaps most importantly, soundproof windows.

Monastiriou Street 8, 54629 Thessaloniki. ℂ **23105/63-100.** Fax 23105/63-101. www.holiday-inn.com/ thessaloniki. 177 units. 140€ to 168€ ($139-$193) double. Rates include breakfast. **Amenities:** Restaurant; coffee shop; bar; laundry; nonsmoking rooms. *In room:* Hair dryer.

Makedonia Palace   A large hotel on the promenade, the Makedonia Palace offers a view of the entire city's sea front with Mount Olympus sometimes visible in the distance. The hotel was recently renovated but little change is evident in the bland guest rooms, which don't compare to the glitzy lobby. All rooms have balconies, but be sure to ask for a room with a sea view, or you'll get a relatively boring one of the city. On the plus side, the hotel offers the most elaborate breakfast I've found in Greece, with a spread ranging from waffles and vegetables to cold cuts and nearly a dozen variety of sweets.

Megalou Alexandrou 2, ℂ **23108/97-197.** Fax 23108/67-210. 284 units Off-peak double 185€ ($213) city view, 225€ ($259) sea view; peak season 260€ ($299) city view, 300€ ($345) sea view. Breakfast 16€ ($18.40) extra. **Amenities:** 2 restaurants; 2 bars. *In room:* No hair dryer.

TOP ATTRACTIONS & SPECIAL MOMENTS

The attractions in Thessaloniki are a mosaic of the city's rich historic past. Just like any other Greek town, Thessaloniki is dominated by ugly flat blocks, but the monuments woven into the city's architecture manage to evoke distant memories of a more beautiful past.

There are way too many things to see in Thessaloniki and no matter how much time you have, it still won't be enough. But if you're planning on a small stint in the city on your rail tour of Greece, consider the attractions listed below, and you'll at least get a taste of almost all of the different cultural and historical offerings in Thessaloniki: from Greek and Roman antiquities to relics of the Byzantium and Ottoman ages to today's marketplace.

Agios Dimitrios Church   A small church was built on the site of a former Roman bath to commemorate Dimitrios, the city's patron saint, in the 4th century. Some 100 years later the church was expanded to its current five-aisled basilica form, but a 1917 fire burned down the original, prompting the construction of the church you'll find today. Almost all the mosaics here are restorations of what was lost in the fire, but a cluster of mosaics survive from the 5th to 7th centuries A.D. The **crypt** ✦ (ℂ **23102/70-591**), which you enter down a narrow, twisting staircase, is pleasantly mysterious, with several small anterooms and remains of the **Roman baths.** Particularly venerated is the place where Dimitrios is believed to have been martyred and the spot with a holy water font.

Corner of Odos Agiou Dimitriou and Odos Agiou Nikolaou (1 block north of the Roman market, at the base of the Upper City). ℂ **23102/13-627.** Free admission. Church and crypt open Mon 12:30–7pm; Tues–Sat 8am–8pm; Sun 10:30am–8pm.

The Archaeological Museum ✦✦✦   Home to the priceless treasures found at the Royal Tombs at Vergina, the Archaeological Museum is worth a visit for these artifacts alone. Most Greek (and fewer non-Greek) archaeologists think that the gold *larnax* (box) with the 16-pointed star held the bones of Philip II of Macedon, the father of Alexander the Great, that the small ivory head is his portrait, and that the bronze greaves were part of his armor. Some spoilsport foreign scholars think these finds belonged to another royal Macedonian—but just try telling that to any Greek! The 4th-century bronze crater from Derveni, with wild scenes of a Dionysiac revel, is less controversial, and absolutely superb.

Other exhibits at the museum showcase Thessaloniki's history from prehistoric days through the Roman period. These rooms are usually not crowded, and the delicate Hellenistic glass—how did these paper-thin vessels survive?—and Roman mosaics from private houses are quite wonderful. You'll need a few hours to see it all.

Manoli Andronikou 6 (opposite the south side of the International Fairgrounds). (© **23108/30-538**. Free admission. Open Tues–Sun 8:30am–3pm; Mon 10:30am–5pm.

Galerian Complex   The Roman Tetrach Galerius went on a construction spree in the 4th century A.D., but it wasn't until about 2 decades ago that many were re-discovered. **The Arch of Galerius** was built in A.D. 305 by, of course, Galerius to commemorate a victory over the Persians a few years earlier. Known as the *kamara* by the locals, only a part of the original structure, which has carvings depicting Galerius's battles, remains. The arch, located right next to a busy avenue, was recently restored after traffic pollution began eroding some of the details.

Nearby stands the **Rotunda** ((© **23102/04-414;** aka *Agios Georgios* or St. George), a typical round-shaped Roman construction. Some think it was built as Galerius's mausoleum, others as a temple. It eventually became the church of St. George under Byzantine rule, when its mosaic ornamentation was commissioned. The Turks turned it into a mosque in the 15th century. The structure was restored over the course of a decade to repair damage from a 1978 earthquake and was opened to the public in 1999. Visit on a Wednesday and you'll catch the neighborhood street market as well.

Take the pedestrian walkway to Navarinou Square, flanked by a flurry of eateries, small boutiques, and book and record shops, and you'll see what remains of Galerius' **palace.** The best-preserved part of the complex is the **Octagon,** a mysterious building that some archaeologists think may have been Galerius's throne room.

The arch is located on Egnatia and Dimitriou Gounari sts.; the Rotonda behind it on Agios Georgios Square at Filippou St. Free admission. Open daily 8:30am–3pm.

Greek Agora and Roman Forum (★   Formerly the ancient Greek agora, or marketplace, it was expanded by the Romans and became their forum. It was discovered in the 1960s by accident when work crews were digging the foundations for the city's courts. You can see the arched remains of the **cryptoporticus,** a retaining wall that supported part of the upper forum. The best-preserved site here is the large **Odeum,** or Odeon, a theater where Romans enjoyed watching both musical performances and fights to the death between gladiators and wild beasts. Today, the Odeum is used for concerts in the summer.

Dikasterion Sq., bounded by Filippou, Agnostou Stratiotou, Olimbou, and Makedonikis Amnis sts.

Jewish History Museum (aka The Museum of the Jewish Presence in Thessaloniki)   This small museum in the heart of the **Modiano Market** uses photographs and artifacts to portray Jewish life in Thessaloniki. Thessaloniki Jews established the city's first printing press in the early 1500s, and founded the city's first newspaper, *El Lunar,* in 1865. The community, which came to Thessaloniki after its persecution in 15th-century Spain, thrived under the Ottoman Empire, and in 1900, 80,000 of Thessaloniki's 173,000 inhabitants were Jews. Just before World War II, there were 60,000 Jews here; 2,000 survived the death camps. Today there are almost none. Allow at least an hour for your visit to the museum.

Agios Minas 13; ℂ **23102/50-406.** Free admission. Open Tues, Fri, Sun 11am–2pm; Wed–Thurs 5pm to 8pm. Closed Mon and Sat. Groups of more than 3 people are asked to call ahead.

Museum of Byzantine Culture ★★★   At present, this is the only museum in the world entirely devoted to Byzantine art and civilization. Spanning history from the Roman empire to the fall of Constantinople in 1453, this museum perfectly compliments the Archeological Museum located next door. Exhibits on three topics have been installed: Early Christian Churches, the Early Christian City and Private Homes, and Burials and Cemeteries in the Early Christian World. Byzantine art, including 15th- through 19th-century icons, mosaics, and jewelry are on display. The museum shop usually has a range of books on Byzantine culture as well as museum reproductions and postcards.

2 Stratou Ave. ℂ **23108/68-570.** Admission 4€ ($4.60). Open Tues–Sun 8:30am–7pm; Mon 12:30–7pm.

The Modiano Market ★★   You could easily spend a morning in the glass-roofed market that covers an entire square block, happily wandering from stall to stall and eyeing the fish, meat, fruit, vegetables, flowers, spices, and baked goods on sale. A number of cafes and tavernas are located in and around it so browse, buy, and binge at leisure.

The block bounded by Aristotelous, Ermou, Vassileos Irakleiou, and Komninon sts. Open Mon–Sat 7am–5pm.

The White Tower   This 98-foot tower is the city's most famous landmark. The cylinder-shaped stone structure was built by the Ottoman Turks in the 16th century as part of the city's walls but was later used as a place of execution. In the 1980s, it was restored and turned into a museum during celebrations for the 2,300th anniversary of the city's founding. Its steep winding staircase goes up six floors and offers terrific views of the city and harbor. Each floor has a round room with alcoves, some of which were once prison cells. At the very end of the staircase, a rooftop cafe rewards you for the climb. Allow an hour here.

Nikis St. and Pavlou Mela St. (on the seaside promenade just south of the Archaeological Museum). ℂ **23102/67-832.** Free admission. Open Tues–Sun 8am–6:45 pm; Mon 12:30–7pm.

WHERE TO DINE

Note: Most Thessaloniki restaurants do not accept credit cards.

Aristotelous ★★★ GREEK/TAPAS   Situated in a small arcade on the city's magnificent square of the same name, Aristotelous specializes in creative variations on traditional Greek cuisine. Considered one of the best ouzo places in town, it's no wonder it's always packed. Seating creeps out of the restaurant and onto the space between two office buildings, which is charming and quiet. And because it doesn't accept reservations, expect to wait for a table. Delicious traditional Greek mezedes such as fried zucchini, feta cheese mashed with hot peppers, and the *pastitsio* (Greek lasagna) will have you asking for recipes.

Aristotelous 8, In a cul-de-sac between office buildings on the east side of Odos Aristotelous, just north of Odos Tsimiski. ℂ **23102/33-195.** Reservations not accepted. Mezedes 12€–30€ ($13.80–$34.50). No credit cards. Open Mon–Sat 10am–2am; Sun 11am–6pm.

Kioupia ★ GREEK   There are more than 65 items on the menu at this taverna with brick walls and a wood floor in the old warehouse district. There's excellent *stifada* (stews), *keftadakia* (meat balls), and spicy *gardoubitsa* (liver and garlic). A number of dishes including eggplant, zucchini, lamb and cheese, and minced beef and cheese are wrapped in crisp layers of *filo* (pastry). Dessert brings a range of Greek and Turkish sweets. The house *retsina* is excellent, and there's an extensive wine list.

Note: The same management runs the nearby **Amorgos,** 4 Panaiou and Doxis, Ladadika (⊘ **231/055-7161**), which specializes in fresh fish.

3–5 Morihovou Sq., Ladadika. ⊘ **231/055-3239.** Fax 231/055-3579. www.kioupia.gr. Reservations recommended after 9pm. Main courses 10€–15€ ($11.50–$17.25). AE, MC, V. Open Mon–Sat 1pm–1am.

Thanasis (Mypobolos Smyrnh) ★★★ GREEK   For nearly 50 years, Thessalonians have been beating a path to this small family-owned taverna, which serves Greek home-style cooking—including stuffed squid and mussels, both fried and steamed—with zest. During the day, local workers, especially from the market located on the other side of the same building complex, fill the restaurant. At night, get ready to grab a tambourine and dance on the table. The music—Greek, of course—gets very loud, especially in winter when seating is solely indoors.

Komninon 32 (just inside the Modiano Market). ⊘ **231/027-4170.** Fax 231/034-7062. Reservations necessary after 10pm. Main courses 6€–12€ ($6.90–$13.80). No credit cards. Open Mon–Sat 8am–3am.

Zythos ⊛ GREEK/CONTINENTAL   This was one of the first restaurants to open in Thessaloniki's restored warehouse district, and it's still very popular with ladies who lunch, young lovers, and harried businessmen. The decor is lots of wood and brick, just as you'd expect in a former warehouse. There are usually two daily specials, including one vegetarian choice, on the menu.

Katouni 5, Ladadika. ⊘ **23105/40-284.** Main courses 8€–15€ ($9.20–$17.25). No credit cards. Open daily 11am–1am.

SHOPPING

Thessaloniki has one of the country's best shopping districts, with a wide variety of shops located in a relatively small area, compared to Athens at least.

Stroll along **Tsimiski, Mitropoleos,** and **Proxenou Koromila** streets between **Pavlou Mela** (the diagonal street connecting the church of Ayia Sofia with the White Tower) and the north–south vertical of **Venizelou.** In this area are the city's few department stores, many boutiques selling the latest in expensive haute couture, shops selling jeans and casual clothing, *lots* of shoe stores, jewelry and antiques stores, and a number of confectioneries.

Fear not: You have left the kitsch souvenir shops of Athens' Plaka behind. That void is filled instead by a number of shops selling the works of local artisans, such as coppersmiths and jewelers, often at bargain prices. Not surprisingly, most of the shops are near the church of the Panayia Chalkeon (The Virgin of the Copper Makers) in **Dikasterion Square.**

Copperware items such as wine carafes and trays are made on-site at the family-run **Adelphi Kazanzidi,** 12 Klissouras off the western side of Dikasterion Square, a block north of Egnatia (⊘ **23102/62-741**). The copper-working skills here have been passed down from generation to generation. At **Skitso,** 11 Grigori Palama (⊘ **23102/69-822**), handmade wooden objects are the highlight, including puppets, ships, crosses, and children's toys. It's a block west of the intersection of Pavlou Mela and Tsimiski. **Ergasterio Kouklis,** 2 Mitropolitou Gennadiou (⊘ **23102/36-890**), has wonderful dolls—for collectors, as well as for children.

At **Tanagrea,** on Vogatsikou (a block east of the Metropolitan Cathedral between Mitropoleos and Proxenou Koromila), you'll find a wide selection of handcrafted items by a stable of artisans employed by this well-known chain of

Moments **Scaling Mount Olympus**

The mythical home of Greece's ancient gods, **Mount Olympus** is actually a range of peaks that includes **Mytikas,** the country's tallest at 9,750 feet. It rises above the plains of Thessaly and Macedonia. The whole area is a national park that features more than 1,500 plant species, many particular to the area, and lots of wildlife.

If you're daring, the hike straight to the top will take about 6 hours. It's an ambitious effort to do all at once. Instead it is recommended to spend the night at one of the mountain's shelters, **Stavros** (3,096 ft.) or **Spilios Agapitos** (✆ 23520/81-800; 6,888 ft.) for about 10€ ($11.50). The **Greek Mountaineering Club (GMC;** ✆ **210/323-4555** in Athens, 2310/278-288 in Thessaloniki, or 0352/81-944 in Litochoro) can provide information about Olympus, from weather conditions to shelter reservations. Information is also available from the **SEO (Association of Greek Climbers;** ✆ **23520/82-300),** or the **EOS (Hellenic Alpine Association;** ✆ **23520/81-944).**

On the Larissa–Thessaloniki line, get off at the **Litohoro** station (✆ **23520/22-522).** The Litohoro station (you might see it on a timetable as Litochoron) is on the coast 5.6 miles (9km) away from the base of the mountain; when you arrive, call ✆ **23520/82-333** for a cab, which are always hovering around the town square and will arrive quickly.

stores, which also has outlets in Athens, Crete, and Spetsai. Offerings include ceramics, pewter, silver, leather goods, paintings, glassware, and jewelry.

Relics, 3 Yioryio Lassani (✆ **23102/26-506**), offers high-quality antiques, from silver- and glassware to jewelry, ceramics, and prints. This is a serious shop with serious prices. Located a block east of the Mitropoleos Cathedral off Mitropoleos, it's closed on Sundays.

NIGHTLIFE
Within the grounds of an old, wonderfully restored flour-mill complex, the **Milos** (*mee*-los) complex, Andreadou Yioryiou 56 (✆ **23105/51-838**), contains a club for blues, folk, jazz, and pop groups; a nightclub featuring Greek singers and comedians; a bar/disco; an outdoor concert stage and movie theater; several exhibition rooms and art galleries; a cafe; and an ouzeri serving more than 30 kinds of *mezedes.* Almost as soon as it opened in 1990, Milos became one of the top musical venues in the country and is a permanent fixture of Thessaloniki nightlife year-round. The ouzeri, cafe, and galleries open from about 11am on. The clubs open at 10pm

AN EXCURSION TO XANTHI
The rare site of church crosses filling the landscape alongside Muslim minarets can be seen in Xanthi, one of the few places in Greece where Greek and Turkish influences and populations coexist. Tobacco has historically been the dominant industry here with the Thracean plain's tobacco producers and the Muslim cattle growers from the northern mountain range meeting in this town's bustling marketplace.

GETTING THERE   Daily trains leave Thessaloniki directly for Xanthi six times a day and include the option of InterCity travel. A second-class ticket costs 7€ ($8.05) plus 4.70€ ($5.40) for the InterCity surcharge. The trip is 3 hours and 45 minutes on InterCity.

If you need to take a cab when you arrive in town, call ✆ **25410/72-803.** You can call one and negotiate a price for an hour or 2 if you want to visit the Pomaks (see below).

VISITOR INFORMATION   The only information available is an automated information line at ✆ **25410/24-444,** but that's all in Greek. The good news: Hotels, including the Z Palace below, will provide English-speaking visitors helpful information on where to go and what to see.

TOP ATTRACTIONS & SPECIAL MOMENTS

A trip north into the mountains, only doable by car, leads to the almost unspoiled **villages of the Pomaks,** Muslims of Slavic ethnic origin. Women and young girls wearing scarves on their heads still wash their clothes in the river. Numerous mosques dot these villages in a country that is predominantly Greek Orthodox. The largest of the villages is that of **Echinos,** with a handful of mosques that can be visited. Make sure to leave a contribution if you do.

As the train approaches Xanthi from Thessaloniki, it winds its way through the **Nestos river valley** on a breathtaking ride, ducking in and out of tunnels and trees. Make sure you sit on the right side of the train for a better view of Nestos as you head towards Xanthi from Thessaloniki; on the opposite side for the return route.

Tourists can hike into the valley starting at the village of **Toxotes,** 9 miles (15km) away from Xanthi. One train makes the 10-minute run from Xanthi to Toxotes at 11:25am, and two return from Toxotes at 12:15pm and 7:10pm. If you're going to hike Nestos, you might want to starting walking from Toxotes if the train travel times aren't right for you. The Nestos delta, a few miles down the river, was declared a special protection area by the European Union. It features freshwater lakes, rare plant species, and birds. You can also see the tunnels the train goes through as it runs past the river valley.

WHERE TO STAY & DINE

The newly built government-rated four-star **Z Palace hotel,** Terma Geroghiou Kondyli (✆ **25410/64-414;** www.z-palace.gr), is a short walk from the Xanthi train station. Ask for a room on a higher floor for a better view of the city. The hotel features an outdoor pool. For rough and ready food tossed onto wax paper instead of plates, **Ladokolla** serves Greek grill like you've never had it before. Located at 90 28 Oktovriou St. (✆ **25410/68-970**), Ladokolla serves mainly souvlakia, gyros, and pita bread in a narrow, split-level eatery.

At the mouth of the Nestos river valley, superb food at laughably low prices is to be found at the open-air **Nestos Restaurant** (✆ **25410/93-838**), just outside the village of Toxotes. The hors d'oeuvres are as filling and delicious as a main dish and offer a greater sample of the splendid tastes available.

12

Hungary

Awakened from its long slumber behind the Iron Curtain, Hungary is one of Europe's hottest destinations. Poised between East and West, both geographically and culturally, it's at the center of the region's rebirth. Once the seat of a sprawling multi-national empire, Hungary today is a small country on the verge of accession to the European Union. Though a significant number of Hungarians still hanker for their lost empire, a growing majority prefer to look forward to their place in a more unified and peaceful Europe. And its placement makes it a perfect stopover for the train traveler crisscrossing the continent and for visitors looking for more bang for their buck—the country is still a good deal cheaper than most of its Western counterparts if not the true budget destination it once was. Still, in a land of expensive gasoline and hefty highway tolls, trains are the principal means of long-distance travel for most of the population and the best way to see this remarkable little country is by rail.

HIGHLIGHTS OF HUNGARY

All rails in Hungary lead into and out of Budapest, lively capital and undisputed transportation hub, a proud city sitting astride the Danube River in the middle of the country. Savor Budapest, one of Europe's most appealing cities. But you should also go beyond the capital and explore the smaller cities and the countryside. Hop a train up the Danube to the "Danube Bend" towns of Szentendre, Esztergom, or Visegrád. In the artists' village of Szentendre, wander the winding streets and drop in on the wonderful museums and galleries; in Visegrád don't miss the ruins of King Matthias's Renaissance Palace; ascend the steep stairs to the cupola at Esztergom's cathedral from where you can see deep into the Slovak countryside across the Danube. Take a trip to Lake Balaton, Hungary's summer playground, to the southwest of the capital. Explore the little villages around the lake, neatly tucked away in the rolling countryside, with grapes of the popular Balaton wines ripening in the strong southern sun. Swim in the hot thermal waters of Hévíz outside Keszthely. On your way to the lake, stop for a day or 2 in Veszprém, a delightful little city with a rich past.

1 Essentials

GETTING THERE

BY PLANE The Hungarian airline **Malév** (**© 800/877-5429,** 800/262-5380 or 800/223-6684) is the principal carrier from North America to Budapest. Other airlines offering service to the area include **Delta, Lufthansa,** and **British Airways.**

All flights arrive at **Ferihegy II** (**© 1/296-7155** for general info, 1/296-5052 for arrivals, 1/296-5883 for departures), located in the XVIII district in southeastern Pest.

> ### *Moments* Festivals & Special Events
>
> The 2-week **Budapest Spring Festival** features opera, ballet, classical music, and drama performances in all the major halls and theaters of Budapest. Simultaneously, temporary exhibitions open in many of Budapest's museums. Tickets are available at the Festival Ticket Service, V. 1081 Rákóczi út 65 (© **1/333-2337**), and at the individual venues. The action happens in mid- to late March.
>
> Every year on the second weekend in July, the ancient town of **Visegrád**, on the Danube, hosts the **International Palace Tournament,** authentic medieval festival replete with dueling knights on horseback, early music, and dance.
>
> On **St. Stephen's Day,** August 20, the country's patron saint is celebrated nationwide with cultural events and a dramatic display of fireworks over the Danube at 9pm. Hungarians also celebrate their Constitution on this day, as well as ceremoniously welcome the first new bread from the recent crop of July wheat.
>
> In celebration of the opening of the fall season, special classical music and dance performances are held for 3 weeks in all the city's major halls during **Budapest Art Weeks.** For information, contact the Hungarian Arts Festivals Federation (© **36/1-318-8165;** www.arts festivals.hu). The festival's traditional start is September 25, the day of Béla Bartók's death.

HUNGARY BY RAIL
PASSES
For information on the **Eurail Pass, Eurail Flexipass,** and **European East Pass,** and other multicountry options, see chapter 2.

The **Hungarian Flexipass,** which must be purchased before you leave for Europe, offers first-class travel within Hungary for either 5 non-consecutive days in a 15-day period or 10 non-consecutive days in a 1-month period. The 5-day pass costs $76 and the 10-day pass is $95. You can purchase a pass from **Rail Europe** (© **877/272-RAIL** in the U.S., **800/361-RAIL** in Canada; www. raileurope.com) or through your travel agent.

FOREIGN TRAIN TERMS
Hungarian ticket agents speak little English, so you will need to know some basic terminology in Hungarian. For a list of the most useful words for train travelers, see "Useful Hungarian Train Terms" below.

PRACTICAL TRAIN INFORMATION
Timetables for arrivals are displayed in stations on big white posters, while departures are on yellow posters.

Train service in Hungary is extremely reliable and usually runs according to schedule, though it's somewhat slower than in western Europe. The country's rail network is extensive, totaling more than 4,800 miles (7,740km), but you should keep in mind that the network is extremely centered on Budapest, so that

Hungary

city will almost always be both your arrival and your departure point from Hungary. Numerous international trains stop in Budapest, and several daily trains arrive in the city from Vienna, Prague, and Berlin.

Aside from international express trains, your best bet within Hungarian borders are the **InterCity (IC)** express trains, which stop only once or twice en route between major cities. These modern trains are state-of-the-art, clean—and the only trains in Hungary with air-conditioning. If you can't stand cigarette smoke, they're also your best bet for getting a nonsmoking seat as they have only one car designated for smoking (while the opposite is often the case on most European trains).

After the InterCity trains come the *gyors* fast trains, which are almost as fast as the IC trains, but are older and grittier. Avoid the slow *személy* and *sebes* trains as they stop at all local stations, making a ride seem interminable.

You can access a timetable on the Web at **www.elvira.hu**, where you can search in English. Other rail information can be found at **www.mav.hu/eng**.

RESERVATIONS   You must reserve a seat on all international express trains and on all InterCity trains. Note that Hungarian trains are often crowded during the summer high season, and that lines for reservations can get very long, so be sure to reserve a seat several days in advance (or better yet, do it before you leave home through Rail Europe for $11). If you wait to make a reservation in

ESSENTIALS 477

Useful Hungarian Train Terms

Indul	departure
Érkezik	arrival
Honnan	from where
Hova	to where
Vágány	platform
Munkanap	weekdays
Hétvége	weekend
munkaszüneti nap	Saturday
ünnepnap	holiday
gyors	fast train or express
jegy	ticket
oda	one-way
oda-vissza	round-trip
helyjegy	reservation
első osztály	first class
másodosztály	second class
nem dohányzó	non-smoking
ma	today
holnap	tomorrow

Hungary, you'll pay 750 Ft ($3.40) per reservation on an international trains and 440 Ft ($2) for a regional or local train reservation.

SERVICES & AMENITIES Generally speaking, most trains in Hungary do not have as many amenities as their western European counterparts. You will find a snack bar on InterCity and international express trains but not on other trains in Hungary. Occasionally, on trains other than IC trains you will encounter a snack cart—no more than a grocery wagon pushed from car to car—but you shouldn't count on that. Hungarians love to eat on trains, so don't find yourself the only one with nothing to nosh! Fill up with drinks and eats before you depart on your trip; every station has snack bars. Note also that trains do not have potable water, so you'll need to bring your own.

Some international trains that pass through Hungary have sleeping cars, but none of the local trains or regional trains have sleeper options of any sort.

Trains & Travel Times in Hungary

From	To	Type of Train	# of Trains	Frequency	Travel Time
Budapest	Esztergom	R	14	Daily	1 hr. 28 min.–1 hr. 55 min.
Budapest	Visegrád	R	20	Daily	1 hr. 4 min.
Budapest	Veszprém	IC*	3	Daily	1 hr. 35 min.
Budapest	Visegrád	R	19	Daily	1 hr. 4 min.
Budapest	Keszthely	IC*	2	Daily	2 hr. 50 min.

* *Reservations compulsory on InterCity trains between Budapest and Veszprém and Budapest and Keszthely. Numerous Regional trains also travel these routes.*

FAST FACTS: Hungary

Area Codes See "Telephone" below.

Business Hours **Banks** are usually open from Monday to Thursday 8am to 3pm and Friday 8am to 1pm. Most **stores** are open from Monday to Friday 10am to 6pm (except shopping malls which remain open until 7pm) and Saturday 9 or 10am to 1 or 2pm. Smaller shops close for an hour at lunch, and as a general matter only stores in central tourist areas are open Sunday. Many shops and restaurants close for 2 weeks in August.

Climate Hungary's climate is fairly mild—the annual mean temperature is 50°F (10°C). That said, summers can get sweltering hot and humid, especially in July, and winters can be damp and chilly. Fall and spring are generally pleasant and mild, though it can get wet in May and June.

Currency The basic unit of currency in Hungary is the **forint (Ft)**. The rate of exchange used to calculate the dollar values given in this chapter is $1 = about 220 Ft (or 100 Ft = 45¢). Though Hungary is to become a member of the European Union (EU) in 2004, it will not adopt the euro until 2007.

Documents Required A valid passport is the only document required for citizens of the U.S., Canada and all EU countries. Citizens of Australia and New Zealand need a visa as well.

Electricity The voltage is 220V/50Hz with European two-prong plug. Electrical equipment of 110V/60Hz requires the use of an adapter and/or voltage converter.

Embassies & Consulates The embassy of the **United States** is at V. Szabadság tér 12 (© **1/475-4400**; Metro: Kossuth tér); the embassy of **Canada** at XII. Budakeszi út 32 (© **1/392-3360**; Metro: Moszkva tér, then tram 22).

Health & Safety For medical treatment, try the **American Clinic,** across from the Mammut shopping center at I. Hattyu u. 14 (© **1/224-9090**; Metro: Moszkva tér).

By U.S. standards, Hungary is a relatively safe country—muggings and violent attacks are rare. Nevertheless, foreigners are always prime targets. Beware of pickpockets, especially on crowded trams, Metros, and buses. Avoid being victimized by wearing a money belt under your clothes instead of wearing a fanny pack or carrying a wallet or purse. No valuables should ever be kept in the outer pockets of a backpack.

Holidays National holidays include: January 1, March 15 (National Holiday, Easter Sunday & Monday, May 1 (May Day), Pentecost (Whitsun), August 20 (St. Stephen's Day), October 23 (Remembrance Day), November 1 (All Saints' Day), and December 25 (Christmas).

Legal Aid Contact your embassy for legal assistance.

Mail Mail can be received at American Express, V. Deák Ferenc u. 10, 1052 Budapest (© **1/235-4330** or 235-4300). In summer, it's open Monday through Saturday from 9am to 7:30pm, Sunday from 9am to 2pm. In winter, it's open 9am to 5:30pm Monday through Saturday, and 9am to 2pm on Sunday. One can also receive mail c/o Poste Restante, Magyar Posta, Petőfi Sándor u. 17–19, 1052 Budapest, Hungary (© **1/318-3947** or 487-1100). This office, not far from Deák tér (all metro lines), is open Monday through Friday from 8am to 8pm and on Saturday from 8am to 2pm.

At press time, an airmail postcard costs 100 Ft (45¢); an airmail letter costs 150 Ft (70¢), depending on its size and weight.

Police & Emergencies Call ✆ **1/438-8080** to reach a new 24-hour hot line service in English, or call ✆ **104** for an ambulance, ✆ **105** for the fire department, or ✆ **107** for the police.

Telephone The **country code** for Hungary is **36.** The **city code** for Budapest is **1;** use this code when you're calling from outside Hungary. If you're within Hungary but not in Budapest, first dial **06;** when you hear a tone, dial the city code and phone number. If you're calling within Budapest, simply leave off the code and dial only the regular seven-digit phone number. Dial **198** for domestic directory assistance and **199** for international queries.

Numbers beginning with **06-20, 06-30, 06-70, or 06-80,** followed by a seven-digit number, are **mobile phone numbers.** If the mobile number you've been given has only six digits, it's incorrect; try adding a **9** before the other six digits. Be aware that you pay for a long-distance call when you call a mobile phone (except 06-80, which is toll-free).

Public **pay phones** charge varying amounts for local calls depending on the time of day you place your call. It's cheapest in the evenings and on weekends. Public phones operate with 20 Ft (10¢), 50 Ft (20¢) and 100 Ft (45¢) coins or with phone cards (in 50 or 120 units) you can buy from post offices, newsstands, travel agencies, and any MATÁV customer service office (MATÁV Pont).

You can reach the **AT&T** operator at ✆ **00/800-01111,** the **MCI** operator at ✆ **00/800-01411,** and the **Sprint** operator at ✆ **00/800-01877.**

Tipping The general tipping rate is usually 10%. Among those who welcome tips are waiters, taxi drivers, hotel employees, barbers, cloakroom attendants, toilet attendants, masseuses, and tour guides.

2 Budapest

Budapest came of age in the 19th century, at the start of which the two towns of Buda and Pest were little more than provincial outposts on the Danube. Indeed, Budapest, notwithstanding its long and tattered history of Roman, Mongol, and Turkish conquest, is very much a late-19th-century city, with its characteristic coffeehouse and music hall culture. But, along with its extraordinary ambience, the city also has most of the modern conveniences one expects of a European capital.

As the central rail hub of Hungary (indeed the entire Hungarian rail network revolves around this city) and the home of the region's major airport, this remarkably unpretentious city is a must-stop location on any rail tour of the country. And on a rail journey that spans Europe's eastern and western halves, Budapest is an ideal stopover—a city that combines the best of both worlds. And, as if that weren't enough to recommend it, it's also one of the cheapest of Europe's major metropolises, making it a boon for budget hunters.

STATION INFORMATION

GETTING FROM THE AIRPORT TO THE TRAIN STATIONS

The **Airport Minibus** (✆ 1/296-8555 or fax 1/296-8993), a service of the **LRI** (Budapest Airport Authority), leaves **Ferihegy II** (✆ 1/296-7155 for general info, 1/296-5052 for arrivals, 1/296-5883 for departures), located in the XVIII district in southeastern Pest, every 10 or 15 minutes throughout the day. It will take you directly to any city address and costs 2,100 Ft ($9.45).

MÁV (Hungarian State Railway company) also operates a **minibus** from the airport to any of the city's three main train stations for 2,100 Ft ($9.45). Call **1/353-2722** or 1/357-2617 for more information.

We strongly *discourage* the use of cabs from the **Airport Taxi** fleet (✆ 1/296-6534), which is notoriously overpriced. Alas, for reasons no one has been able to explain to us with a straight face, these cabs are the only ones permitted to wait for fares on the airport grounds. Dozens of cabs from the cheaper fleets we recommend, however, are stationed at all times on roadside pullouts just off the airport property, waiting for radio calls from their dispatchers. If you want to take a cab, you can phone from the terminal to any of these fleets and a cab will be there for you in a matter of minutes. For two people traveling together, a taxi from a recommended fleet to the city will be comparable in price to the combined minibus fares, at about 4,500 Ft ($20.25). The ride should take 20 to 30 minutes.

The cheapest way into the city is by public transportation; the bus-to-Metro-to-town trip takes about an hour total. Take the red-lettered **bus 93** to the last stop, Kőbánya-Kispest. From there, the Blue Metro line runs to the Inner City of Pest and Nyugati pályaudvar, one of the city's major train stations. The trip takes two transit tickets, which costs 240 Ft ($1.10).

INSIDE THE STATIONS

Budapest has three major train stations: Keleti pályaudvar (Eastern Station), Nyugati pályaudvar (Western Station), and Déli pályaudvar (Southern Station). The stations' names, curiously, correspond neither to their geographical location in the city nor to the origins or destinations of the trains serving them. Each has a Metro station beneath it and an array of accommodations booking offices (see "Information Elsewhere in the City," below), currency-exchange booths, and other services.

Most international express trains pull into and depart from bustling **Keleti Station** (✆ 1/314-5010; Metro: Keleti pu.), a classic steel-girdered station originally built in 1884 and located in Pest's seedy Baross tér. In addition to the Metro (the Red line), numerous bus, tram, and trolleybus lines serve Baross tér. There are a few digital information boards that will keep you apprised of arrivals and departures at the platforms.

Some international trains call at **Nyugati Station** (✆ 1/349-0115; Metro: Nyugati pu.), another classic designed by the Eiffel company and built in the 1870s. Numerous tram and bus lines serve busy Nyugati tér, and the Blue Metro line stops underneath the station. This is the only train station with an official **Tourinform** visitor information office (✆ 1/302-8584; www.tourinform.hu), which dispenses advice, free brochures, maps, and will make hotel reservations. It's located in the station's main hall.

Two major hotel reservation services have offices here. **Cooptourist,** Nyugati Station (℡ 36/1-458-6200), is open 9am to 4:30pm Monday through Friday and does not accept credit cards. **Budapest Tourist,** Nyugati Station (℡ **36/ 1-318-6552**), is open 9am to 5pm Monday through Friday, 9am to 12pm Saturday, and does not accept credit cards.

Few international trains arrive at **Déli Station** (℡ 1/375-6293; Metro: Déli pu.), an ugly modern building in central Buda. The Red Metro line terminates just beneath the station. In addition to the usual tourist amenities, the station has an immense supermarket that is a good place to stock up on food before your train journey.

The train station phone numbers listed above are good from 8pm to 6am. During the day, obtain **domestic train information** at ℡ **1/461-5400** and **international train information** at ℡ **1/461-5500.**

Purchase **tickets** at station ticket windows or (a better idea) from the **Hungarian State Railways (MÁV) Service Office,** VI. Andrássy út 35 (℡ **1/322- 8082**), open Monday to Friday 9am to 5pm.

INFORMATION ELSEWHERE IN THE CITY

The city's best source of visitor information is **Tourinform,** V. Liszt Ferenc tér 11, in Pest (℡ **1/322-4098;** www.hungarytourism.hu; Metro: Opera, Yellow line; Tram: Oktogon, no. 4–6). It's open daily in winter from 10am to 6pm, in summer from 9am to 7pm. Another source is the **Vista Visitor Center,** V. Paulay Ede u. 7 (℡ **1/267-8603;** www.vista.hu; Metro: Deák tér). It's open from Monday to Friday 9am to 8pm and Saturday 10am to 4pm.

The most established hotel reservation agencies are the former state-owned travel agents **Ibusz, Cooptourist,** and **Budapest Tourist.** These tend to have the greatest number of rooms listed and all have offices in the airport. The main **Ibusz reservations office** is at Ferenciek tere 10 (℡ **1/485-2700;** fax 1/318- 2805; Metro: Ferenciek tere), open year-round from Monday to Friday 8:15am to 5pm. All major credit cards are accepted. The other agencies have offices at Nyugati Station (see above).

It's a good idea before you even arrive in Budapest to consult one of the many websites that offer tourist information in English. The site **www.gotohungary. com** has a wealth of tourist information, as does **www.hungarytourism.hu.** Current local news, entertainment listings, and the like can be found at either or **www.budapestweek.com.**

GETTING AROUND

Budapest has an extensive and inexpensive public transportation system; it's the best way to get around town. Bear in mind, however, that except for 17 well-traveled bus and tram routes, all forms of transport shut down nightly at around 11:30pm.

All forms of public transportation require the self-validation of pre-purchased **tickets** *(vonaljegy),* costing 120 Ft (55¢) apiece (children under 6 travel free). Single tickets can be bought at Metro ticket windows and newspaper kiosks or automated machines in most Metro stations and at major transportation hubs. For 1,070 Ft ($4.80) you can get a **10-pack** *(tizes csomag),* and for 2,100 Ft ($9.45) a **20-pack** *(huszas csomag).* During the process of validating tickets you must keep the stack intact. Do not tear the individual tickets off as you use them.

Your best bet is to buy a day pass or multiday pass. Passes are inexpensive and need be validated only once. **Day passes** *(napijegy)* cost 925 Ft ($4.15) and

Budapest

ACCOMMODATIONS ■
Charles Apartment House **16**
Hotel Astra Vendégház **8**
Hotel Kulturinnov **7**
Hotel MEDOSZ **29**
Hotel Victoria **12**
King's Hotel **23**
Peregrinus ELTE Hotel **19**
Radio Inn **31**

DINING ◆
Angelika Cukrászda **6**
Central Kávéház **18**
Gerbeaud's **14**
Gundel **32**
Kacsa Vendéglő **2**
Kádár Étkezde **24**
Le Jardin de Paris **9**
Lou Lou **5**
Marquis de Salade **28**
Művész Kávéház **27**
Ruszwurm Cukrászda **10**

ATTRACTIONS ●
Bazilika
    (St. Stephen's Church) **25**
Budapesti Történeti
    Múzeum **15**
Chain Bridge **13**
Dohány Synagogue **22**
Gellért Hegy **17**
Hungarian State Opera
    House **26**
Károly Kert **21**
Mátyás Templom **11**
Nemzeti Galéria **15**
Nemzeti Múzeum **20**
Néprajzi Múzeum **4**
Parliament **3**
Vidám Park **29**
Zeneakadémia (Ferenc Liszt
    Academy of Music) **30**

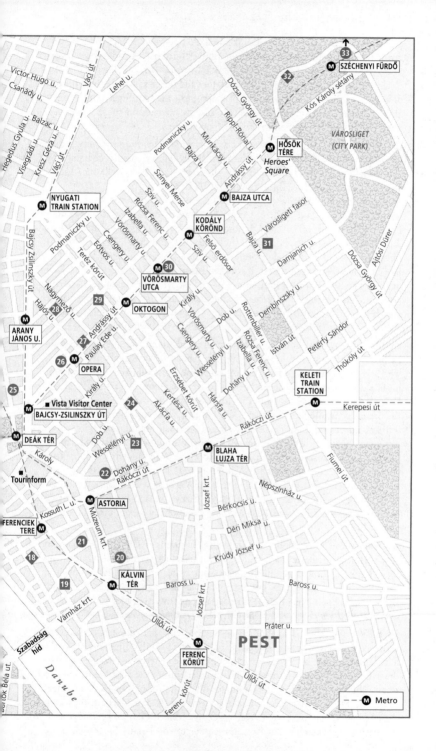

are valid until midnight of the day of purchase. Buy them at Metro ticket windows; the clerk validates the pass at the time of purchase. A **3-day pass** *(turistajegy)* costs 1,850 Ft ($8.30) and a **7-day pass** *(hétibérlet)* 2,250 Ft ($10.10).

Uniformed inspectors frequently check for valid tickets, particularly at the top or bottom of the escalators to Metro platforms. On-the-spot fines (2,000 Ft/$9) are assessed to fare dodgers. All public transport operates on rough schedules, posted at bus and tram shelters and in Metro stations.

By Metro The Metro is clean and efficient, with trains running every 3 to 5 minutes from about 4:30am until about 11:30pm. The three lines are known by color—Yellow, Red, and Blue. Officially they have numbers as well, but all signs are color-coded. All three lines converge at **Deák tér.**

The **Yellow (1) line,** the oldest Metro on the European continent, lies just a few steps underground, and runs from Vörösmarty tér in the heart of central Pest, out the length of Andrássy út, and past the Városliget (City Park). Tickets for the Yellow line are validated on the train itself. The **Red (2)** and **Blue (3) lines** are modern Metros, deep underground and accessible by escalator. The Red line runs from eastern Pest, through the center, across the Danube to Déli Station. The Blue line runs from southeastern Pest, through the center, to northern Pest. Tickets must be validated at the automated time-stamp boxes before you descend the escalator. When changing lines at Deák tér, you must validate a new ticket at the orange machines in the hallway between lines.

By Bus Many parts of the city, most notably the Buda Hills, are best accessed by bus *(busz).* Most lines are in service from about 4:30am to about 11:30pm, with less frequent weekend service on some. You must validate your bus ticket on board at the mechanical red box found by each door. Tickets for Budapest buses cannot be purchased from the driver (though in smaller cities and towns the drivers generally do sell tickets). You can board the bus by any door.

Black-numbered local buses constitute the majority of bus lines. Red-numbered buses are express. If the red number on the bus is followed by an *E,* the bus runs nonstop between terminals (whereas an *É*—with an accent—signifies *éjszaka,* meaning night). A few buses are labeled by something other than a number; one you'll probably use is the **Várbusz** (Palace Bus), a minibus that runs between Várfok utca, off Buda's Moszkva tér, and the Castle District; other buses labeled "V" (for *villamos*/tram) occasionally run in place of a tram that is down.

By Tram You'll find Budapest's bright-yellow trams *(villamos* in Hungarian) very useful, particularly the **4** and **6,** which travel along the city's Outer Ring (Nagykörút) section. You must validate your ticket on board. As with buses, tickets are valid for one ride, not for the line itself. Trams stop at every station, and all doors open, regardless of whether anyone is waiting to get on. *The buttons near the tram doors are for emergency stops, not stop requests.*

By HÉV The HÉV is a suburban railway network that connects Budapest to various points along the city's outskirts. There are four HÉV lines; only one, the **Szentendre line,** is of serious interest to tourists. The terminus for the Szentendre HÉV line is Buda's Batthyány tér, also a station of the Red Metro line. To reach Óbuda's Fő tér (Main Square), get off at the Árpád híd (Árpád Bridge) stop. The HÉV runs regularly between 4am and 11:30pm. For trips within the city limits, you need one transit ticket, available at HÉV ticket windows at the Batthyány tér Station or from the conductor on board. These tickets are different from the standard transportation tickets and are punched by conductors on board. If you have a valid day pass, you do not need to buy a ticket for trips within the city limits.

By Taxi Budapest taxis are largely unregulated, so fares vary tremendously. Perhaps because there are more taxi drivers than the level of business can support, many drivers are experts at fleecing foreigners. If you're careful, however, taxis are still a bit cheaper than in the West. Several fleet companies have good reputations, honest drivers, and competitive rates. There is no standard rate across the various companies but each should have its own rate displaced on the meter. So take the front seat (which is the standard practice in Hungary) and check the rates before you start your journey. We particularly recommend **Fő Taxi** (*©* 1/222-2222). Other reliable fleets are **Volántaxi** (*©* 1/466-6666), **City Taxi** (*©* 1/211-1111), **Tele5** (*©* 1/355-5555), and **6×6** (*©* 1/266-6666).

WHERE TO STAY

In recent years Budapest has seen a proliferation of new pensions and small hotels. The better choices among these—and the less expensive—are usually outside the city center, but all the places we list can easily be reached by public transportation. Notwithstanding the arrival of these new places, Budapest retains its reputation as a city without enough guest beds. Indeed, in high season it can be difficult to secure a room, so make reservations and get written confirmation well ahead if possible.

Note that hotels and pensions in Budapest divide the year into three seasons. **High season** is roughly from March or April to September or October and the week between Christmas and New Year's. **Midseason** is usually considered March, October, and November. **Low season** is roughly from November to February, except Christmas week. Some hotels discount as much as 50% in low season, while others offer no winter discount; be sure to inquire.

Charles Apartment House *©* *Value* Owner Károly (Charles) Szombati has gradually amassed 70 apartments (for 1–4 people) in a group of apartment buildings in a dull but convenient Buda neighborhood. All are average Budapest apartments with full kitchens, but the furnishings are comfortable and clean and the price is right. Hegyalja út is a very busy street, but only a few of the apartments face out onto it; the rest are in the interior of the buildings or on side streets. The downside: It's not near a Metro station, so you'll need to take a taxi or bus to get to and from the rail stations.

I. Hegyalja út 23, 1016 Budapest. *©* **1/212-9169.** Fax 1/202-2984. www.charleshotel.hu. 70 units. 44€–120€ ($50.60–$138) apt in low season; 48€–136€ ($55.20–$156) in high season. Rates include breakfast. AE, DC, MC, V. Bus: 78 from Keleti pu. to Mészáros utca. **Amenities:** Restaurant, bar; laundry. *In room:* Hair dryer.

Hotel Astra Vendégház *©©* *Finds* This little gem of a hotel opened in 1996 inside a renovated 300-year-old building on a quiet side street in Buda's lovely and quiet Watertown neighborhood just two stops on the Metro from Déli Station. The rooms are large, with wood floors and classic Hungarian-style furniture; the overall effect is a far more homey and pleasant space than that found in most Budapest hotel rooms. Indeed, the hotel is tasteful through and through, and the staff are friendly. Some rooms overlook the inner courtyard, while others face the street.

I. Vám u. 6, 1011 Budapest. *©* **1/214-1906.** Fax 1/214-1907. www.hotelastra.hu. 12 units. 105€ ($121) double. Rates include breakfast. Rates 10% lower in low season. Metro: Batthyány tér (Red line). **Amenities:** Restaurant; bar.

Hotel Kulturinnov ★★ *Finds*　This is the guesthouse of the Hungarian Culture Foundation, dedicated to forging ties with ethnic Hungarians in neighboring countries. It's open to the public, but few travelers know about it. The rooms are small and simple; nothing is modern, but everything works and the bathrooms are clean. The hotel can be a bit hard to find; the entrance is unassuming and practically unmarked. Go through the iron grille door and pass through an exhibition hall, continuing up the grand red-carpeted staircase to the right. You'll need to take a bus or taxi to get to the Metro from here.

I. Szentháromság tér 6, 1014 Budapest. © **1/355-0122** or 1/375-1651. Fax 1/375-1886. 16 units. 80€ ($92) double. Rates almost 50% lower in low season. Rates include breakfast. AE, DC, MC, V. Bus: "Várbusz" from Moszkva tér or 16 from Deák tér. **Amenities:** 2 restaurants; 2 bars.

Hotel MEDOSZ ★ *Value*　Formerly a trade-union hotel for agricultural workers, the MEDOSZ is located on Jókai tér, in the heart of Pest's theater district, a few blocks from the Opera House and very close to the Metro. This is as good as it gets off the river in central Pest. Although the hotel has not been renovated since it was privatized, it remains a great value given its location. The rooms are simple but clean. Next door is one of Budapest's special treats for children: a puppet theater *(bábszínház).*

VI. Jókai tér 9, 1061 Budapest. © **1/374-3000.** Fax 1/332-4316. www.medoszhotel.hu. 67 units. 59€ ($67.85) double. Rates are 20% lower in low season. Rates include breakfast. No credit cards. Metro: Oktogon. No amenities.

King's Hotel ★★ *Finds*　King's Hotel opened for business in 1995 in a beautifully renovated and restored *fin-de-siècle* building in the heart of Pest's Jewish district, a quick Metro ride away from Keleti Station. The reception is uniformly friendly and helpful. Despite the somewhat drab modern furnishings, rooms retain a 19th-century atmosphere, many with small balconies overlooking the quiet residential street. Most, but not all, have a private bathroom. The kosher hotel restaurant is the only one of its kind in Budapest. *Note:* Meals are served on weekends and Jewish holidays in the hotel's restaurant by prior arrangement only.

VII. Nagydiófa u. 25–27 Budapest. © and fax **1/352-7675.** 80 units. 13,200 Ft–17,600 Ft ($60–$80) double; $140 suite. Rates include breakfast. AE, DC, MC, V. Metro: Astoria (Red line). **Amenities:** Restaurant (kosher).

Peregrinus ELTE Hotel ★★ *Value*　This is the guesthouse of Pest's ELTE University, ideally located in the heart of the Inner City and close to the Metro. While many guests are affiliated with the university, the hotel is open to the public as well. The building dates from the turn of the 20th century and was renovated when it was opened in 1994. Rooms are simple but comfortable. Reserve well in advance. Payment must be in cash in Hungarian forints.

V. Szerb u. 3, 1056 Budapest. © **1/266-4911.** Fax 1/266-4913. 26 units. 22,000 Ft ($99) double; 18,000 Ft ($81) in low season. Rates include breakfast. No credit cards. Metro: Kálvin tér (Blue line). No amenities.

Radio Inn ★★ *Value*　As the official guesthouse of Hungarian National Radio, the Radio Inn houses many visiting dignitaries, and also offers large apartments to individual tourists (all comfortably furnished and painstakingly clean with fully equipped, spacious kitchens). The inn is in an exclusive embassy neighborhood (next door to the Chinese embassy), a stone's throw from City Park, and a block from Pest's grand Andrássy út. The Metro's Yellow line takes you into the center of Pest in 5 minutes. Behind the building, there's an enormous private courtyard full of flowers.

VI. Benczúr u. 19, 1068 Budapest. ℂ **1/342-8347** or 1/322-8284. Fax 1/322-8284. www.hotels.hu/
radio_inn_budapest. 36 units. In high season 43€ ($49.45), 65€ ($74.75), and 84€ ($96.60) for 1, 2, and
3-person apts; 43€ ($49.95), 48€ ($55.20), and 61€ ($70.15) in low season. Breakfast 5€ ($5.75) extra.
MC, AE, MC, V. Metro: Bajza utca (Yellow line). **Amenities:** Restaurant, bar; laundry; nonsmoking rooms.

Hotel Victoria 🏆🏆 The Hotel Victoria, located in Buda's lovely Watertown
district, is separated from the Danube bank by the busy road that runs alongside
the river. The narrow building has only three rooms on each of its nine floors.
Two-thirds are corner rooms with large double windows providing great views
over the river to Pest. Rooms are quite large, with spacious bathrooms. Middle
rooms, though smaller than corner ones, also have windows facing the river.
Unfortunately, noise from the busy road beneath your window may disturb your
rest. It's a quick tram ride to the nearest Metro stop.

I. Bem rakpart 11, 1011 Budapest. ℂ **1/457-8080.** Fax 1/457-8088. www.victoria.hu. 27 units. 102€ ($117)
double. Rates include breakfast. Rates 25% lower in low season. AE, DC, MC, V. Tram: 19 from Batthyány tér
to the 1st stop. **Amenities:** Bar; laundry. *In room:* Hair dryer.

TOP ATTRACTIONS & SPECIAL MOMENTS

Budapesti Történeti Múzeum (Budapest History Museum) This
museum, also known as the Castle Museum, is the best place to get a sense of
the once-great medieval Buda. Even though the museum's descriptions are written in English, it's probably worth splurging for a guided tour—the history of
the palace's repeated cycles of destruction and reconstruction is so arcane it's difficult to understand what you're really seeing.

I. In Buda Palace, Wing E, on Castle Hill. ℂ **1/225-7815** or 1/355-8849. Admission 700 Ft ($3.15). Guided
tours by qualified staff in English for serious history buffs, 6,000 Ft ($27; open to negotiation), available on
advance request. 10 am–6pm daily, closed Tuesday. Metro: Moszkva tér, then bus "Várbusz"; or Deák tér, then
bus 16. Funicular: From Clark Ádám tér to Castle Hill.

Nemzeti Galéria (Hungarian National Gallery) 🏆 Hungary has produced some fine artists, particularly in the late 19th century, and this is the place
to view their work. The giants of the time are the brilliant but moody Mihály
Munkácsy; László Paál, a painter of village scenes; Károly Ferenczy, a master of
light; and Pál Szinyei Merse, the plain-air artist and contemporary of the early
French Impressionists.

I. In Buda Palace, Wings B, C, and D, on Castle Hill. ℂ **1/375-5567.** Admission 600 Ft ($2.70). Tues–Sun
10am–4pm. Metro: Moszkva tér, then bus "Várbusz"; or Deák tér, then bus 16. Funicular: From Clark Ádám
tér to Castle Hill.

Nemzeti Múzeum (Hungarian National Museum) 🏆🏆 This enormous
neoclassical structure, built from 1837 to 1847, played a major role in the beginning of the Hungarian Revolution of 1848 and 1849; on its wide steps on
March 15, 1848, poet Sándor Petőfi and other young radicals are said to have
exhorted the people of Pest to revolt against the Hapsburgs. The two main
museum exhibits on view are "The History of the Peoples of Hungary from the
Paleolithic Age to the Magyar Conquest" and "The History of the Hungarian
People from the Magyar Conquest to 1989."

VIII. Múzeum krt. 14. ℂ **1/338-2122.** Admission 600 Ft ($2.70). Tues–Sun 10am–6pm (to 5pm in winter).
Metro: Kálvin tér.

Néprajzi Múzeum (Ethnographical Museum) Directly across from Parliament, the vast Ethnographical Museum features an ornate interior equal to that
of the Opera House. A ceiling fresco of Justitia, the goddess of justice, by artist

Károly Lotz, dominates the lobby. Although a third of the museum's holdings are from outside Hungary, most concentrate on the items from Hungarian ethnography. The fascinating permanent exhibition, "From Ancient Times to Civilization," features everything from drinking jugs and razor cases to chairs and clothing.

V. Kossuth tér 12. ℂ 1/473-2440. Admission 500 Ft ($2.25). Tues–Sun 10am–5pm. Metro: Kossuth tér.

Vidám Park (Amusement Park) ★★★   This is a must if you're traveling with kids. Two rides in particular aren't to be missed. The 100-year-old **Merry-Go-Round** *(Körhinta)*, constructed almost entirely of wood, was recently restored to its original grandeur, though it still creaks mightily as it spins. The riders must actively pump to keep the horses rocking, and authentic Würlitzer music plays. The **Ferris wheel** *(Óriáskerék)* is also wonderful, though it has little in common with rambunctious modern Ferris wheels. A gangly bright-yellow structure, it rotates at a liltingly slow pace, gently lifting you high in the sky for a remarkable view. The Vidám Park also features Europe's longest wooden roller coaster.

XIV. Állatkerti krt. 14–16. ℂ 1/363-2660. www.vidampark.hu. Admission 300 Ft ($1.35) adults, 100 Ft (45¢) children; rides 200 Ft–600 Ft (90¢–$2.70). Apr–Sept Monday–Friday 11am–7pm, and Saturday–Sunday 10am–8pm; Oct–Mar Monday–Friday noon–6pm and Saturday–Sunday 10am–6:30pm. Metro: Széchenyi fürdő.

HISTORIC BUILDINGS

Magyar Állami Operaház (Hungarian State Opera House) ★   Completed in 1884, Budapest's Opera House boasts a fantastically ornate interior featuring frescoes by two of the best-known Hungarian artists of the day, Bertalan Székely and Károly Lotz. Home to both the State Opera and the State Ballet, the Opera House has a rich and evocative history.

VI. Andrássy út 22. ℂ 1/331-2550. Admission (by guided tour only) 1,500 Ft ($6.75). Tours daily at 3 and 4pm. Metro: Opera.

Parliament   Budapest's great Parliament, an eclectic design mixing the predominant neo-Gothic style with a neo-Renaissance dome, was completed in 1902. Standing proudly on the Danube bank, visible from almost any riverside point, it has from the outset been one of Budapest's symbols, though until 1989 a democratically elected government had convened here only once (just after World War II, before the Communist takeover). The Parliament is home to the legendary crown jewels of St. Stephen.

V. Kossuth tér. ℂ 1/441-4415. Admission (by guided tour only): 30-min. tour in English, 1,700 Ft ($7.65) adults, 800 Ft ($3.60) students. Tickets available at gate XII on weekdays and gate VI on weekends. Tours year-round Wed–Sun at 10 am and 2pm, the latter in summer only. Closed when Parliament is in session, usually on Wednesdays. Metro: Kossuth tér.

CHURCHES & SYNAGOGUES

Bazilika (St. Stephen's Church)   The country's largest church, this basilica took more than 50 years to build (the 1868 collapse of the dome caused significant delay) and was finally completed in 1906. Szent István Square, a once-sleepy square in front of the church, was elegantly renovated in the autumn of 2002, converted along with several neighboring streets into a pedestrian-only zone.

V. Szent István tér 33. ℂ 1/332-0873. Church, free; treasury, 200 Ft (90¢); tower, 400 Ft ($1.80). Church, daily 7am–7pm, except during services; treasury, daily 9am–5pm (10am–4pm in winter); Szent Jobb Chapel, Mon–Sat 9am–5pm (10am–4pm in winter) and Sun 1–5pm; tower, daily Apr–May 10am–4:30pm, June–Aug 9:30am–6pm, and Sept–Oct 10am–5:30pm. Metro: Arany János utca or Bajcsy-Zsilinszky út.

Dohány Synagogue ⟨★★⟩   Built in 1859 and recently restored, this is said to be the largest synagogue in Europe and the second largest in the world. The architecture has striking Moorish and Byzantine elements. The synagogue has a rich but tragic history. There's a Jewish museum next door that traces the origins of Hungarian Judaism and features exhibits of ceremonial Judaica throughout the centuries.

VII. Dohány u. 2–8. ⟨©⟩ 1/342-8949. Admission 600 Ft ($2.70). Open Tues–Thurs 10am–5pm; Fri 10am–2pm; Sun 10am–2pm. Metro: Astoria or Deák tér.

Mátyás Templom (Matthias Church) ⟨★★★⟩   Officially named the Church of Our Lady, this symbol of Buda's Castle District is popularly known as Matthias Church after the 15th-century king who was twice married here. Though it dates from the mid–13th century, like other old churches in Budapest it has an interesting history of destruction and reconstruction, always being refashioned in the architectural style of the time. Current plans for renovation have been put on hold due to financial constraints.

I. Szentháromság tér 2. ⟨©⟩ 1/355-5657. Entrance 400 Ft ($1.80). Daily 9am–6pm (to 5pm in winter). Metro: Moszkva tér, then bus "Várbusz"; or Deák tér, then bus 16. Funicular: From Clark Ádám tér to Castle Hill.

PARKS & PANORAMAS

Gellért Hegy (Gellért Hill), towering 750 feet above the Danube, offers the city's best panorama (Bus: 27 from Móricz Zsigmond körtér). It's named after the Italian Bishop Gellért, who assisted Hungary's first Christian king, Stephen I, in converting the Magyars. Gellért became a martyr when vengeful pagans, outraged at the forced and violent nature of Stephen's proselytism, rolled him in a barrel to his death from the side of the hill on which his enormous statue now stands. On top of Gellért Hill you'll find the Liberation Monument, built in 1947 to commemorate the Red Army's liberation of Budapest from Nazi occupation. Also atop the hill is the Citadella, built by the Austrians shortly after they crushed the Hungarian uprising of 1848–49.

City Park (Városliget) ⟨★⟩ is an equally popular place to spend a summer day (Metro: Hósök tere/Heroes' Square and Széchenyi Fürdó). Heroes' Square, at the end of Andrássy út, is the most logical starting point for a walk in City Park. The lake behind the square is used for boating in summer and ice-skating in winter. The park's Zoo Boulevard (Állatkerti körút), the favorite street of generations of Hungarian children, is where the **zoo,** the **circus,** and the **amusement park** are all found. **Gundel,** Budapest's most famous restaurant, is also here, as are the **Széchenyi Baths.**

Károly kert (Charles Garden) ⟨★★★⟩, a little enclosed park in the southern half of the Inner City (Metro: Astoria [Red line]), is the location of what we consider to be Budapest's most charming playground. To enter the park, you must pass through a gigantic wrought-iron gate. The equipment here might not be as modern or as varied as at some of the city's other playgrounds, but the place has a distinct old-world charm and its location in the Inner City makes it a convenient destination.

WHERE TO DINE

Étterem is the most common Hungarian word for restaurant and is used for everything from cafeteria-style eateries to first-class restaurants. A *vendéglő,* or guesthouse, is a smaller, more intimate restaurant, often with a Hungarian folk motif; a *csárda* is a countryside vendéglő. An *étkezde* is an informal lunchroom open only in the daytime. An *önkiszolgáló* is a self-service cafeteria, typically open only for lunch. Stand-up *bufes* are often found in bus stations and near busy transport hubs. A *cukrászda* or *kávéház* is a central European coffeehouse, where coffee and sweets are served. A *borozó* is a wine bar, a *söröző* a beer bar; sandwiches are usually available at both. Finally, a *kocsma* is a sort of roadside tavern; the Buda Hills are filled with them. Most kocsmas serve full (if greasy) dinners, but their kitchens close very early.

Gundel ★★ (Moments) HUNGARIAN/INTERNATIONAL   Budapest's fanciest and most famous historic restaurant, Gundel was reopened a decade ago by the Hungarian-born New York restaurateur George Lang. Located in City Park, Gundel has an opulent dining room and a large, carefully groomed garden. Lamb and wild-game entrees are house specialties, and the menu highlights fruits and vegetables in season. In late spring, don't miss out on the asparagus served in hollandaise with grilled salmon. Homemade fruit ice cream served in the shape of the fruit makes for a delectable dessert, as does the famous Gundel torta, a decadently rich chocolate layer cake.

XIV. Állatkerti út 2. © 1/468-4040. www.gundel.hu. Reservations highly recommended. Main courses 3,000 Ft–15,500 Ft ($13.50–$69.75). AE, DC, MC, V. Daily noon–4pm and 7pm–midnight. Metro: Hősök tere.

Kacsa Vendéglő ★ HUNGARIAN   Kacsa (meaning "duck") is located on the main street of Watertown, the Buda neighborhood that lies between Castle Hill and the Danube. Here you'll find an intimate, elegant, and understated dining atmosphere, though the service seems overly attentive and ceremonious. Enticing main courses include roast duck with Morello cherries and haunch of venison with grapes. The vegetarian plate is the best we've had anywhere.

I. Fő u. 75. © 1/201-9992. Reservations recommended. Main courses 1,900 Ft–3,600 Ft ($8.55–$16.20). MC, V. Mon–Fri noon–3pm and 6pm–1am; Sat–Sun just 6pm–1am. Metro: Batthyány tér.

Kádár Étkezde ★★★ (Finds) HUNGARIAN   From the outside the only sign of the place is a very small red sign saying KÁDÁR ÉTKEZDE. No more than a lunchroom, this place, in the heart of the Jewish district, has a great atmosphere: high ceilings, wood-paneled walls with photos (many autographed) of actors and athletes, and old-fashioned seltzer bottles on every table. Everyone is personally greeted by Uncle Kádár himself, a neighborhood legend. The food is simple but hearty, and the service friendly. Table sharing is the norm.

VII. Klauzál tér 9. © 1/321-3622. Main courses 500 Ft–750 Ft ($2.25–$3.40). No credit cards. Tues–Sat 11:30am–3:30pm. Metro: Astoria or Deák tér.

Le Jardin de Paris ★★ FRENCH   This wonderful little French bistro is in the heart of Buda's Watertown, aptly located just across the street from the monstrous Institut Français. A cozy cellar space, it's decorated with an eclectic collection of graphic arts, and a jazz trio plays nightly. The menu contains nouvelle French specialties, and the wine list features French as well as Hungarian vintages. In summer there's outdoor seating in a garden area.

I. Fő u. 20. © 1/201-0047. Reservations recommended. Main courses 1,650 Ft–2,750 Ft ($7.40–$12.40). AE, DC, MC, V. Daily noon–midnight. Metro: Batthyány tér.

Lou Lou ★ FRENCH   Located on a quiet side street in the financial district not far from Parliament, this is a handsome addition to the Budapest dining scene. The decor is rustic and tasteful, with Roman yellow walls and a vaulted ceiling. They specialize in fresh fish dishes, and feature an extensive wine list; a very good house wine is also available by the carafe.

V. Vigyázó F. u. 4. © 1/312-4505. Reservations recommended. Main courses 2,100 Ft–4,500 Ft ($9.45–$20.25). AE, MC, V. Mon–Fri noon–3pm and 7pm–11pm; Sat 7pm–midnight. Closed Sun. Metro: Kossuth tér.

Coffeehouse Culture

Imperial Budapest, like Vienna, was famous for its coffeehouse culture. Literary movements and political circles alike were identified in large part by which coffeehouse they met in. You can still go to several classic coffeehouses, all of which offer delicious pastries, coffee, and more in an atmosphere of splendor.

Try **Gerbeaud's** ✰✰✰, in the Inner City at V. Vörösmarty tér 7 (📞 1/429-9000); **Művész Kávéház** ✰, across the street from the Opera House at VI. Andrássy út 29 (📞 1/352-1337; Metro: Opera); **Central Kávéház**, V. Károlyi Mihály u. 9. (📞 1/266-2110; Metro: Ferenciek tere, Blue line); **Ruszwurm Cukrászda** ✰, in the Castle District at I. Szentháromság u. 7 (📞 1/375-5284; Várbusz [Castle Bus] from Moszva tér); or **Angelika Cukrászda** ✰✰, also in Buda, at I. Batthyány tér 7 (📞 1/201-4847; Metro: Batthyány tér).

Marquis de Salade ✰✰✰ RUSSIAN/MIDDLE EASTERN   On the edge of Pest's theater district and just one Metro stop from Nyugati Station, this funky little restaurant employs an eclectic mix of eight cooks from Russia, Bangladesh, Hungary, Italy, and the Caucasus Mountains, who turn out an amazing and far-ranging assortment of exceptional dishes. Try the lamb with rice (Azerbaijan) or the borscht (Russian). Tablecloths and tapestries are for sale.

VI. Hajós u. 43. 📞 1/302-4086. Main courses 1,500 Ft–2,800 Ft ($6.75–$12.60). V. Daily 11am–midnight. Metro: Arany János u.

SHOPPING

Shoppers fill the pedestrian-only **Váci utca,** from the stately Vörösmarty tér, the center of Pest, across the roaring Kossuth Lajos utca, all the way to Vámház krt. The **Castle District** in Buda, with many folk-art boutiques and galleries, is another popular (if somewhat overpriced) area for souvenir hunters. Locals (and budget travelers) might window-shop in these two neighborhoods, but they do their serious shopping elsewhere. One popular street is Pest's **Outer Ring** (Nagykörút); another bustling street is Pest's **Kossuth Lajos utca,** off the Erzsébet Bridge, and its continuation **Rákóczi út,** extending all the way out to Keleti Station.

Hungary's famous folkloric objects are the most popular souvenirs among foreign visitors. The state-owned Folkart shops (Népművészeti Háziipar) have a great selection of handmade goods. Popular items include pillowcases, pottery, porcelain, dolls, dresses, skirts, and sheepskin vests. The main store, **Folkart Centrum,** is at V. Váci u. 58 (📞 1/318-5840), and is open daily from 10am to 7pm. One outstanding private shop on Váci utca is **Vali Folklór,** in the courtyard of Váci u. 23 (📞 1/337-6301). This cluttered shop is run by a soft-spoken man named Bálint Ács, who travels the villages of Hungary and neighboring countries in search of authentic folk items and, as a recent addition, communist-era badges, pins, and medals.

Holló Folkart Gallery, at V. Vitkovics Mihály u. 12 (📞 1/317-8103), is an unusual gallery selling handcrafted reproductions of folk-art pieces from various regions of the country. It is open Monday through Friday from 10am to 6pm; Saturday 10am to 1pm.

Another popular Hungarian item is **porcelain,** particularly from the country's two best-known producers, Herend and Zsolnay. Although both brands are available in the West, here you'll find a better selection and lower prices. At the **Herend Shop,** V. József nádor tér 11 (© **1/317-2622**), you'll find the widest Herend selection in the capital. Delightfully gaudy Zsolnay porcelain from the southern city of Pécs is Hungary's second-most celebrated brand of porcelain; visit **Zsolnay Márkabolt,** V. Kígyó u. 4 (© **1/318-3712**).

Budapest also has a handful of **vintage market halls** (vásárcsarnok), wonders of steel and glass, built in the 1890s in the ambitious grandiose style of the time. Three are still in use and provide a measure of local color you won't find in the grocery store. The **Központi Vásárcsarnok** (Central Market Hall), on IX. Vámház körút (on the Pest side of the Szabadság Bridge), is the largest and most spectacular market hall. Other vintage market halls include the **Belvárosi Vásárcsarnok** (Inner City Market Hall), on V. Hold utca, behind Szabadság tér in central Pest; and the **Józsefváros Vásárcsarnok,** on VIII. Rákóczi tér. Other active and lively markets include the **Fehérvári úti Vásárcsarnok,** on XI. Fehérvári út, in front of the Buda Skála department store, just a block from the Móricz Zsigmond körtér transportation hub; the **Fény utca Piac,** on II. Fény utca, just off Moszkva tér in Buda; and **Lehel Piac,** XIII. Váci út, right behind the West End Shopping Centre at Nyugati Train Station.

NIGHTLIFE

The most complete schedule of mainstream performing arts is found in the free bimonthly *Koncert Kalendárium* at the Central Philharmonic Ticket Office in Vörösmarty tér. The *Budapest Sun* also is a good source, as is the new magazine *Look,* and the *Budapest Week* website (**www.budapestweek.com**).

The **Central Theater Ticket Office** (Színházak Központi Jegyiroda), VI. Andrássy út 18 (© **1/267-1267; Metro: Opera**), sells tickets to just about everything, from theater and operetta to sports events and rock concerts; it's open from Monday to Friday 10am to 6pm. For **classical performances,** go to

---

(Moments **Music for a Summer Evening**

During the warm lazy days of summer, you'll find several special venues for classical music. Tickets are available at the **National Philharmonic Ticket** Office (see above).

The historic outdoor Dominican Courtyard, inside the Castle District's Hilton Hotel, I. Hess András tér 1–3 (© **1/488-6600**; Metro: Moszkva tér, then bus "Várbusz"; or Deák tér, then bus 16), is the site of a series of classical recitals during the summer. The District's beautiful **Matthias Church** (Mátyás Templom), next door at I. Szentháromság tér 2, holds a regular Tuesday- and Friday-night series of organ concerts from June to September. Concerts start at 7:30pm. Tickets can be purchased before the performance at the church entry.

Organ concerts are also held Monday evenings at 7pm during July and August at **St. Stephen's Church** (Bazilika), Hungary's largest church, V. Szent István tér 33 (© **1/317-2859**; Metro: Arany János utca or Bajcsy-Zsilinszky út). You can buy tickets at the church entry before the performance.

the National Philharmonic Ticket Office (Filharmónia Nemzeti Jegyiroda), V. Vörösmarty tér 1 (© **1/318-0281;** Metro: Vörösmarty tér). For **opera and ballet,** go to the **Hungarian State Opera Ticket Office** (Magyar Állami Opera Jegyiroda), VI. Andrássy út 20 (entrance inside the courtyard; © **1/353-0170;** Metro: Opera). For **rock and jazz concert** tickets, try Ticket Express, VI. Jókai u. 40 (© **1/353-0692;** Metro: Opera).

THE PERFORMING ARTS   Completed in 1884, the **Magyar Állami Operaház** (Hungarian State Opera House), VI. Andrássy út 22 (© **1/331-2550;** Metro: Opera), is Budapest's most famous performance hall. Hungarians adore opera, and a large percentage of seats are sold on a subscription basis; buy your tickets a few days ahead, if possible. The box office is open from Monday to Friday 11am to 6pm. Ticket prices range from 2,900 Ft to 9,800 Ft ($13.05–$44.10).

The Great Hall (Nagyterem) of the **Zeneakadémia** (Ferenc Liszt Academy of Music), VI. Liszt Ferenc tér 8 (© **1/341-4788,** ext. 179; Metro: Oktogon), is the premier music hall. Box-office hours are from 2pm to show time on the day of performance. Tickets range from 1,000 Ft to 6,000 Ft ($4.50–$27).

LIVE-MUSIC CLUBS   **Fat Mo's Music Club,** always a hot place, is at V. Nyári Pál u. 11 (© **1/267-3199;** Metro: Kálvin tér [Blue line]). There's no cover charge. The live jazz concerts start at 9pm and dancing starts at 11pm. The best night is definitely Sunday, with *Hot Jazz Band* performing in the style of the '20s and '30s. Make sure you book a table if you wish to enjoy their superb food as well, steak being the specialty. **TRAFO,** XI. Liliom u. 41 (© **1/215-1600;** Tram: 4 or 6 to Üllöi út), is an old electric power station recently renovated and transformed into a cultural center for young artists. It also hosts the hippest disco in town. *The* nights are Wednesday and Sunday with DJ Palotai, with the party starting at 10pm, but you can have a great time on Fridays dancing to the '60s and '70s greatest hits. **Old Man's,** VIII. Akácfa u. 13 (© **1/322-7645;** Metro: Blaha Luzja tér), is the place to take in the best jazz and blues in Hungary. Hobo, the legendary figure of Hungarian beat music since the late 1960s, regularly plays here with his blues band. This very hip spot is open daily from 3pm to 3am.

BARS   The **Irish Cat Pub,** V. Múzeum krt. 41 (© **1/266-4085;** Metro: Kálvin tér), is an Irish-style pub with Guinness on tap and a whiskey bar. It's a popular meeting place for expatriates and travelers, serving a full menu, and is open from Monday to Saturday 10am to 2 am and Sunday 5pm to 2am. **Morrison's Music Pub,** VI. Révay u. 25 (© **1/269-4060;** Metro: Opera), is a casual place packed by an almost-20-something crowd. There's a small dance floor, an eclectic variety of loud live music, and a number of beers on tap. It's open from Wednesday to Saturday 11am to 4am, Sunday from 5pm to 2am.

EXCURSIONS TO THE DANUBE BEND

The delightful towns along the Danube Bend—Szentendre, Esztergom, and Visegrád—are easy day trips from Budapest. The great natural beauty of the area, where forested hills loom over the river, makes it a welcome departure for the city weary.

SZENTENDRE

Peopled in medieval times by Serbian settlers, **Szentendre** (pronounced *Sen*-tendreh), 13 miles (21km) north of Budapest, counts half a dozen Serbian churches among its rich collection of historical buildings. Since the turn of the century, Szentendre has been home to an artist's colony and has a wealth of museums and galleries. The town is an extremely popular tourist destination.

GETTING THERE   The HÉV suburban railroad connects Budapest's Batthyány tér with Szentendre. Trains leave daily, year-round, every 20 minutes or so from 4am to 11:30pm (trip time: 45 min.). The one-way fare is 320 Ft ($1.45); subtract 120 Ft (55¢) if you have a valid Budapest public transportation pass.

VISITOR INFORMATION   The information office **Tourinform** is at Dumtsa Jenő u. 22 (© **26/317-965**). It is open April through October daily from 9:30am to 4:30pm; in the off season it's open Monday to Friday from 9:30am to 4:30pm. To get here, just follow the flow of pedestrian traffic into town on Kossuth Lajos utca.

Top Attractions & Special Moments

The **Margit Kovács Museum** ✸✸✸, Vastagh György u. 1 (© **2/631-0244**), is a must-see, displaying the exceptional and highly original work of Hungary's best-known ceramic artist. Her sculptures of elderly women and friezes of village life are particularly moving. The museum is open April to October Tuesday to Sunday 9am to 5pm (Nov–Mar to 4pm). Admission is 400 Ft ($1.80). At Fő tér 6 (© **2/631-0244**) is the **Ferenczy Museum** ✸✸, dedicated to the art of the prodigious Ferenczy family. The paintings of Károly Ferenczy, one of Hungary's leading Impressionists, are featured. It's open from April to October Wednesday to Sunday 10am to 5pm; from November to March Friday to Sunday 10am to 4pm. Admission is 300 Ft ($1.35).

Where to Dine

If you get hungry, **Aranysárkány Vendéglő (Golden Dragon Inn)** ✸, Alkotmány u. 1/a (© **2/630-1479**, www.aranysarkany.hu), just east of Fő tér on Hunyadi utca, is always crowded. Choose from such enticing offerings as spicy leg of lamb, roast leg of goose, and venison ragout. A tasty vegetarian plate is also offered. Various traditional Hungarian beers are on tap. Be sure to stop in at the **Dobos Museum & Café** ✸, Bogdányi u 2, for a slice of authentic *dobos torta,* a sumptuously rich layer cake named after pastry chef József Dobos, who experimented with butter frostings in the 19th century and was appointed the Habsburg emperor's official baker because of his success.

ESZTERGOM

Formerly a Roman settlement, **Esztergom** (pronounced *Ess*-tair-gome), 29 miles (46km) northwest of Budapest, was the seat of the Hungarian kingdom for 300 years. Hungary's first king, István I (Stephen I), crowned by the pope in A.D. 1000, converted Hungary to Catholicism, and Esztergom became the country's center of the early church. Although its glory days are long gone, the quiet town remains the seat of the archbishop-primate—the "Hungarian Rome."

GETTING THERE   Seventeen trains daily make the run between Budapest's Nyugati Station and Esztergom (trip time: 1¼ hr.). Train tickets cost 436 Ft ($1.95).

VISITOR INFORMATION   **Gran Tours,** Széchenyi tér 25 (© **3/350-2001**), is the best source of information. Summer hours are from Monday to Friday 8am to 4pm and Saturday 9am to noon; winter hours are from Monday to Friday 8am to 4pm. The station is on the outskirts of town, while the tourist info center is in the city center. Take bus 1 or 6 to Széchenyi tér. Local buses depart from outside the train station.

Top Attractions & Special Moments

The massive, neoclassical **Esztergom Cathedral** (© 3/341-1895), in Szent István tér on Castle Hill, is Esztergom's most popular attraction and one of Hungary's most impressive buildings. It was built in the last century to replace the cathedral ruined during the Turkish occupation. The cathedral **Treasury (Kincstár)** 🎯 contains a stunning array of ecclesiastical jewels and gold works. If you brave the ascent of the cupola, you're rewarded at the top with unparalleled views of Esztergom and the surrounding Hungarian and Slovak countryside. The cathedral is open daily, summer from 8am to 6pm, winter from 9am to 4pm. The treasury, crypt, and cupola are open daily, summer from 9am to 5pm, winter from 11am to 4pm. Admission to the cathedral and the crypt are free, but it costs 300 Ft ($1.35) to see the treasury and 200 Ft (90¢) to see the cupola. To get here, take bus 6 from the train station and get off at the cathedral.

Where to Dine

The food at **Szalma Csárda** 🎯🎯🎯, Nagy-Duna sétány 2 (© 3/331-5336), is absolutely first-rate, with everything made to order and served piping hot. The excellent house soups—fish soup *(halászlé),* goulash *(gulyásleves),* and bean soup *(babgulyás)*—constitute meals in themselves. It's open daily from noon to 10pm and doesn't accept credit cards. Main courses cost 950 Ft to 1,800 Ft ($4.25–$8.10). You'll need to take a taxi from the train station to get to the restaurant, but it won't cost you more than 1,000 Ft ($4.50).

VISEGRÁD

Halfway between Szentendre and Esztergom, **Visegrád** (pronounced *Vee*-sheh-grod) is a sparsely populated, sleepy riverside village, which makes its history all the more fascinating and hard to believe. The Romans built a fort here, which was still extant when Slovak settlers gave the town its present name (meaning "High Castle") in the 9th or 10th century. After the Mongol invasion (1241–42), construction began on both the present ruined hilltop citadel and the former riverside palace. Eventually, Visegrád could boast one of the finest royal palaces ever built in Hungary. Only one king, Charles Robert (1307–42), actually used it as his primary residence, but monarchs from Béla IV, in the 13th century, through Matthias Corvinus, in the late 15th century, spent time in Visegrád and contributed to its development, the latter expanding the palace into a great Renaissance center known throughout Europe.

GETTING THERE   There's no direct train service to Visegrád. Instead, take 1 of 20 daily trains departing from Nyugati Station for Nagymaros (trip time: 1 hr.). From Nagymaros, take a ferry across the river to Visegrád. The ferry dock (RÉV, © 06-8/040-6611) is a 5-minute walk from the train station. A ferry leaves every hour throughout the day. The train ticket to Nagymaros costs 436 Ft ($1.95); the ferryboat ticket to Visegrád costs 200 Ft (90¢).

VISITOR INFORMATION   **Visegrád Tours,** RÉV u. 15 (© 2/639-8160), is located across the road from the RÉV ferryboat landing. It is open from April to October, daily 9am to 6pm; from November to March, weekdays 10am to 4pm.

Top Attractions & Special Moments

The **Royal Palace** covered much of the area where the boat landing and Fő utca (Main St.) are now found. The entrance to its open-air ruins, the **King Matthias**

Museum ★★, is at Fő u. 27 (© **2/639-8026**). Admission is 400 Ft ($1.80). The museum is open Tuesday to Sunday from 9am to 4:30pm. The buried ruins of the palace, having achieved a near-mythical status, were not discovered until this century. Almost all of what you see is the result of ongoing reconstruction.

The **Citadel** ★★★ (© **2/639-8101**) on the hilltop above Visegrád affords one of the finest views you'll find over the Danube. Admission to the Citadel is 400 Ft ($1.80). It is open daily from 9am to 6pm. There are three buses a day to the Citadel, departing from the RÉV ferryboat terminal at 9:26am, 12:26pm, and 3:26pm, respectively. Otherwise, "City Bus," a van taxi that awaits passengers outside Visegrád Tours, takes people up the steep hill for the steep fare of 2,000 Ft ($9) apiece. Note that it is not a casual walk to the Citadel; consider it a day hike and pack accordingly.

Where to Dine

In keeping with its name, **Renaissance Restaurant,** at Fő u. 11, across the street from the MAHART boat landing (© **2/639-8081**), specializes in authentic medieval cuisine. Food is served in clay crockery without silverware (only a wooden spoon) and guests are offered paper crowns to wear. The menu meal is 4,000 Ft ($18), but is available for groups only. It's open daily, from noon to 10pm. If you're big on the medieval theme, come for dinner on a Thursday (July and Aug only), when a six-course "Royal Feast" is celebrated following a 45-minute duel between knights. No vegetarians, please! Tickets for this special evening are handled by Visegrád Tours (see above). The duel gets underway at 6pm sharp.

3 The Lake Balaton Region

An excellent spot for rail travelers of all ages looking for some fun and sun in Hungary, **Lake Balaton** may not be the Mediterranean, but don't tell that to the Hungarians. Throughout the long summer, swimmers, windsurfers, sailboats, kayaks, and cruisers fill the warm and silky smooth lake, Europe's largest at 50 miles (80km) long and 10 miles (15km) wide at its broadest stretch. Around the lake's 315 miles (197km) of shoreline, vacationers cast their reels for pike; play tennis, soccer, and volleyball; ride horses; and hike in the hills.

Teenagers and students tend to congregate in the hedonistic towns of the south shore, where huge 1970s-style beachside hotels are filled to capacity all summer long, and disco music pulsates into the early morning hours. We think the area's noisy, crowded, and overrated.

Our personal preference (and the choice of most post-college travelers and families) is for the hillier, more graceful north shore, and it's the region we cover in this section. *Note:* As you head to this region from Budapest by rail, the northern shore of the lake will first appear every bit as built up and crowded as the southern shore. Beyond Balatonfüred, this impression begins to fade. Here, little villages are neatly tucked away in the rolling countryside, where the grapes of the popular Balaton wines ripen in the strong sun. The best way to see the area is to move westward along the coast, passing from one lakeside settlement to the next, and making the occasional foray inland into the rolling hills of the Balaton wine country. After a quick trip to the charming town of **Veszprém,** move on and stop for a swim—or the night—in the small town of **Szigliget.** The city of **Keszthely,** sitting at the lake's western edge, marks the end of its northern shore and is your final stop on a tour of this lovely region.

GETTING THERE   From Budapest, trains to the various towns along the lake depart from Déli Station. A few express trains run from Keleti Station and hook around the southern shore to Keszthely only. All towns on the lake are within 1½ to 4 hours of Budapest by a *gyors* (fast) train, though the trip will take much longer on a *sebes* (local). The *sebes* trains are interminably slow, stopping at each village along the lake. Unless you're going to one of these little villages (sometimes a good idea, though we cover only the major towns in this section), try to get on an *gyors*.

HOTEL INFORMATION   Because hotel prices are unusually high (for Hungary, anyway) in the Balaton region, and because just about every local family rents out a room or two in summer, we especially recommend **private rooms** as the lodging of choice in this area. Most are clean and will give you the opportunity to get to know the local population. You can reserve a room through a local tourist office (addresses are listed below under each town) or you can just look for the ubiquitous SZOBA KIADÓ (or ZIMMER FREI) signs that decorate most front gates in the region. When you take a room without using a tourist agency as the intermediary, prices are generally negotiable. In the height of the season, you shouldn't have to pay more than 6,000 Ft ($27) for a double room within reasonable proximity of the lake.

EN ROUTE TO LAKE BALATON: VESZPRÉM

Just 10 miles (16km) from Lake Balaton, **Veszprém** (pronounced *Vess*-praym) surely ranks as one of Hungary's most charming and vibrant small cities, and it's the ideal starting point for a rail tour of Lake Balaton's northern shore. Here you'll find a harmonious mix of old and new: A delightfully self-contained and well-preserved, 18th-century baroque Castle District spills effortlessly into a typically modern city center, distinguished by lively, wide-open, pedestrian-only plazas.

The history of Veszprém, like the scenic Bakony countryside that surrounds it, is full of peaks and valleys. The city was first established as an episcopal see in the time of King Stephen I, Hungary's first Christian king, but was completely destroyed during the course of the long Turkish occupation, the Habsburg-Turkish battles, and the subsequent Hungarian-Austrian independence skirmishes. The reconstruction of Veszprém commenced in the early 18th century, though the castle itself, blown up by the Austrians in 1702, was never rebuilt. The baroque character of that era today attracts thousands of visitors who pass through each year.

GETTING THERE   Ten daily **trains** depart Budapest's Déli Station for Veszprém, including two direct InterCity trains that make the trip in only an hour and 35 minutes. (It's a 2-hr. trip if you snag a regular fast train, a lot longer if you don't.) Tickets cost 882 Ft ($3.95), plus a reservation supplement for the IC train.

VISITOR INFORMATION   **Tourinform,** Vár utca 4 (© **8/840-4548**), just moved to a new address in the center of the Castle District. It's open Monday through Friday 9am to 5pm, Saturday and Sunday 9am to 4pm (only weekdays in winter). To get here from the train station, take bus 4 or 1 to the bus station at the foot of the castle hill; from here, it's a 10-minute walk to the office.

TOP ATTRACTIONS & SPECIAL MOMENTS

Most of Veszprém's main sights are clustered along Vár utca, the street that runs the length of the city's small but lovely Castle District.

Housed inside the 18th-century canon's house, the **Exhibition of Religious Art,** Vár u. 35, has a fine collection of religious (Roman Catholic) art. Admission is 100 Ft (45¢). Open daily from 9am to 5pm; closed October to April.

At Vár u. 16, the vaulted **Gizella Chapel,** named for King Stephen's wife, was unearthed during the construction of the adjoining Bishop's Palace in the 18th century. Today, it houses a modest collection of ecclesiastical art, but is best known for the 13th-century frescoes that, in various states of restoration, decorate its walls. Admission is 40 Ft (20¢). Open daily from 9am to 5pm; closed October to April.

For a wonderful view of the surrounding Bakony region, climb up the steps to the narrow observation deck at the top of the **Fire Tower** at Óváros tér. Though the foundations of the tower are medieval, the structure itself was built in the early 19th century. Enter via the courtyard of Vár u. 17, behind Óváros tér. Admission is 150 Ft (65¢). Open daily from 10am to 6pm.

WHERE TO STAY & DINE

Péter-Pál Panzió ☆ (© **8/856-7790** or 88/328-091; www.hotels.hu/peter_pal_panzio), is conveniently located on Dózsa György u. 3; it's a 5-minute walk from the center of town. Don't be put off by the grungy building facade. Inside are 12 tidy but very small rooms, all with twin beds, shower-only bathroom, and television. Insist on a room in the rear of the building, as the pension sits close to the busy road. Rates are 38€ to 54€ ($44–$62) double. Breakfast is included and is served in the garden in summer. Call ahead for reservations.

Hotel Villa Medici ☆☆ (© and fax **8/859-0070;** www.villamedici.hu), at Kittenberger u. 11, is a modern, full-service hotel set in a small gorge on the edge of the city, next to Veszprém's zoo-park. There are 24 double rooms and two suites; each has a bathroom with shower and the usual hotel amenities. Rates are 17,600 Ft–18,700 Ft ($79.20–$84.15) for a double room; 24,500 Ft ($110) for a suite. Breakfast is included. The hotel also features a sauna, a small indoor swimming pool, and a beauty salon. The reception staff speaks English and will make tour arrangements for you. Major credit cards are accepted. Take Bus 4 from the train station to the stop in front of Veszprém Hotel, and then change to Bus 3, 5, or 10. These buses will take you as far as the bridge overlooking the gorge. You can walk from there.

Cserhát Étterem ☆ (© **8/842-5441**), housed in the huge structure at Kossuth u. 6, is an old-style *önkiszólgáló* (self-service cafeteria). You'll find this very popular cafeteria behind the Nike store; go up the winding staircase inside the building. Hearty traditional meals are available for less than 600 Ft ($2.70). The menu changes daily; it's posted on a bulletin board at the bottom of the stairs. Open Monday through Friday from 9am to 6pm and Saturday 9am to 3pm.

For something more upscale, **Villa Medici Étterem** (owned by the same people who own the hotel), at Kittenberger u. 11 (© **8/859-0072**), is *the* place. It's expensive for Hungary but worth it. Main courses here are between 2,200 Ft and 3,000 Ft ($9.90–$13.50). Villa Medici serves Hungarian/continental cuisine daily from 12am to 11pm.

SZIGLIGET ☆☆

Halfway between the Tihany peninsula and Keszthely is the lovely village of Szigliget (pronounced *Sig*-lee-get), a picturesque Hungarian lake village with some magnificent castle ruins and an easy stopover point for rail travelers. If you

⌒ Moments Herend: Home of Hungary's Finest Porcelain

About 10 miles (16km) west of Veszprém lies the sleepy village of Herend. What distinguishes this village from other villages in the area is the presence of the Herend Porcelain factory, where Hungary's finest porcelain has been made since 1826.

Herend Porcelain began to establish its international reputation as far back as 1851, when a dinner set was displayed at the Great Exhibition in London. Artists hand paint every piece, from tableware to decorative accessories. Patterns include delicate flowers, butterflies, and birds.

The recently opened **Porcelanium Visitors Center** features the newly expanded **Herend Museum** (© 8/826-1801; www.museum.herend. com), which displays a dazzling collection of Herend porcelain. It is open daily from April to October, 9am to 5:30pm; weekdays only from November to March, 9am to 4:30pm. Admission is 300 Ft ($1.35).

At the **factory store** (© 8/852-3223), you might find patterns that are unavailable in Budapest's Herend Shop. The factory store is open Monday through Saturday, 9:30am to 6pm; in winter, Monday through Friday 9:30am to 4pm, Saturday 9:30am to 2pm. The Porcelanium Visitors Center also has a coffeehouse and upscale restaurant. Food is served on Herend china, naturally. Herend is easily accessible via bus from the Veszprém bus station—the destination "Herend" should be indicated on the front of the bus you want. It leaves every half hour. The trip takes 20 minutes and costs 263 Ft ($1.20) one-way.

are as taken as we were by the thatched-roof houses, the lush vineyards, and the sunny Mediterranean feel of Szigliget, you might consider spending the night.

GETTING THERE   Five daily trains leave from Veszprém's rail station that will get you to **Badacsonytördemic-Szigliget Station.** The trip can take as short as 3¼ hours or as long as 4½ depending on the train you catch and how many connections you need to make (there is no direct train service). InterCity trains (you must make a reservation!) are available for at least part of the route, but, in this case, won't get you to Szigliget any faster than some of the *gyors* trains because you have to make a number of connections.

It is a 20-minute bus ride to Szigliget from the train station. Each arriving train is met by a bus, which stops on the platform right outside the station building. The destination of the buses is "Tapolca." You get off the bus at the stop near the beach in the village center (the village itself is tiny and easily traversed on foot).

VISITOR INFORMATION   Natur Tourist (© 8/746-1197), in the village center, is open daily from 9am to 7pm (closing earlier in winter) and can help book private rooms. There are also ubiquitous ZIMMER FREI signs along the roads.

TOP ATTRACTION & SPECIAL MOMENTS

Szigliget is marked by the fantastic ruins of the 13th-century **Szigliget Castle,** which stand above the town on **Várhegy (Castle Hill).** In the days of the

Turkish invasions, the Hungarian Balaton fleet, protected by the high castle, called Szigliget home. You can hike up to the ruins for a splendid view of the lake and the surrounding countryside; look for the path behind the white 18th-century church, which stands on the highest spot in the village.

If you really enjoy hiking, you might take a local bus from Szigliget (the station is in the village center) to the nondescript nearby village of **Hegymagas,** about 3 miles (4.8km) to the north along the Szigliget-Tapolca bus route. The town's name means "Tall Hill," and from here you can hike up **Szent György-hegy (St. George Hill).** This marvelous vineyard-covered hill has several hiking trails, the most strenuous of which goes up and over the rocky summit.

The lively **beach** at Szigliget provides a striking contrast to the quiet village. In summer, buses from neighboring towns drop off hordes of beachgoers. The beach area is crowded with fried food and beer stands, ice cream vendors, a swing set, and a volleyball court. Admission to the beach is 300 Ft ($1.35).

Szigliget is also home to the **Eszterházy Wine Cellar,** the largest wine cellar in the region. After a hike in the hills or a day in the sun, a little wine tasting just might be in order. Natur Tourist can provide you with the best directions, as getting here can be a bit confusing. Tours of the cellar are offered only for organized groups; others can drop-in and sample the wares. It's open Monday through Friday noon to 8pm, Saturday 3pm to 10pm. There's no admission charge.

WHERE TO STAY & DINE

Szőlőskert Panzió (© 8/746-1264) on Vadrózsa utca, might be the best option for a stay, given its close proximity to the beach, which is just 430 yards away. Situated on the hillside amidst lush terraces of grapes, the pension is open only in summer. A double is 7,500 Ft ($33.75).

A good place to fortify yourself before or after a hike is the **Vár Csárda** ★★, Kisfaludy u. 30 (© **8/746-1990**), on the road up to the castle. It's a casual restaurant with plenty of outdoor seating, serving traditional Hungarian fare. Main courses run from 800 Ft to 1,500 Ft ($3.60–$6.75). Open daily 11am to 11pm.

KESZTHELY

Keszthely (pronounced *Kest*-hay), which sits at the western edge of Lake Balaton, is one of the largest towns on the lake, and is easily reached by rail from both Budapest and other lake towns. Though Keszthely was largely destroyed during the Turkish wars, the town was rebuilt in the 18th century by the Festetics family, an aristocratic family who made Keszthely their home through World War II. The town's main sites all date from the days of the wealthy Festetics clan.

GETTING THERE   Nine daily trains depart Budapest's Déli Station for Keszthely; several InterCity trains also make the journey each week. If the only city you plan to visit on Lake Balaton is Keszthely, snagging a ride on the IC (which only takes 2 hr. 50 min.) is a great timesaver. You will, of course, need to reserve a seat on these trains well in advance and can do so through Rail Europe for $11. A few daily express trains also leave Budapest out of Keleti Station and hook around the southern lakeshore, offering direct service to Keszthely. Trip time on these trains is about 3 hours and 30 minutes. Otherwise, the trip takes about 4 hours and costs 1,482 Ft ($6.65).

If you're heading to Keszthely Station out of Szigliget, you can hop on any of the four daily trains and numerous weekday trains that depart from Szigliget's rail station. Make sure, however, to consult a timetable before leaving, as there's no direct service and where you choose to transfer can seriously affect your journey time. Depending on the train you select, the trip can take anywhere from a very reasonable 47 minutes to a ridiculous 2 hours and 10 minutes.

The train station is on the southeastern edge of the town.

VISITOR INFORMATION   For information, stop in at **Tourinform,** at Kossuth u. 28 (*©* and fax **8/331-4144;** www.keszthely.hu), in the city's former town hall. From the train station, walk up Mártírok u. and then turn right onto Kossuth u. and walk north until you get to the city's Main Square. It's open daily, Monday through Friday from 9am to 5pm; and on Saturday and Sundays in high season only from 9am to 1pm.

TOP ATTRACTION & SPECIAL MOMENTS

The highlight of a visit to Keszthely is the splendid **Festetics Mansion** *⚔*, at Szabadság u. 1 (*©* **8/331-2190** or 83/312-191), in the center of the city, a short walk north of the Tourinform office. Part of the mansion, a baroque 18th-century home (with 19th-c. additions) for generations of the Festetics family, is now open as a museum. The main attraction is the ornate Helikon library, which features magnificent floor-to-ceiling oak bookcases—hand-carved by a local master, János Kerbl. The museum also features hunting gear and trophies of a bygone era. The museum is open in summer, daily from 9am to 6pm; in winter, it closes at 5pm and is closed on Monday. Admission for foreigners is 1,400 Ft ($6.30), only 400 Ft ($1.80) for Hungarians.

The mansion's lovely concert hall, the Mirror Gallery, is the site of **classical music concerts** almost every night throughout the summer (just two or three times a month Sept–May). Concerts usually start at 8pm; tickets, ranging all the way from 900 Ft to 5,000 Ft ($4.05–$22.50) apiece, are available at the door or earlier in the day at the museum cashier.

Another Keszthely museum worth a visit is the **Balaton Museum** *⚔*, on the opposite side of the town center from the Festetics Mansion, at Múzeum u. 2 (*©* **8/331-2351;** www.museum.hu). This museum features exhibits on the geological, archaeological, and natural history of the Balaton region. It's open from May to October Tuesday to Sunday from 10am to 6pm; November to April Tuesday to Saturday 9am to 5pm. Admission is 200 Ft (90¢).

Located down the hill from Fő tér (Main Sq.), off Bem u., is Keszthely's **open-air market.** Vendors line the street daily. While dawn to mid-afternoon is the busiest time, some vendors stay open into early evening. You'll find fruit and vegetables, spices, preserves, and honey, as well as household appliances, handmade baskets, and children's clothing.

WHERE TO STAY & DINE

The center of Keszthely's summer scene, just like that of every other settlement on Lake Balaton, is down by the water on the *"strand."* Keszthely's **beachfront** is dominated by several large hotels. Regardless of whether or not you're a guest, you can rent windsurfers, boats, and other water-related equipment from these hotels.

A good hotel bet is the 232-room **Danubius Hotel Helikon** (*©* **8/331-1330;** www.danubiusgroup.com). The small but comfortable guest rooms offer balconies overlooking Lake Balaton and have all the necessary amenities. The resort also has an indoor swimming pool, sauna, massage parlor, and outdoor sun deck. Rates run 56€ to 110€ ($64.50–$127) double, including breakfast. Numerous special packages are available.

Moments   An Excursion to the Lake at Hévíz

If you think the water of Lake Balaton is warm, just wait until you jump into the lake at **Hévíz** ⭐⭐, a resort town (pronounced *Hay*-veez) about 5 miles (8km) northwest of Keszthely. Here, you'll find the largest thermal lake in Europe and the second largest in the world (the largest being in New Zealand), covering 60,000 square yards.

The lake's water temperature seldom dips below 85° to 90°F—even in the most bitter spell of winter. Consequently, people swim in the lake year-round. Hévíz has been one of Hungary's leading spa resorts for over 100 years, and it retains a distinct 19th-century atmosphere.

While the lakeside area is suitable for ambling, no visit to Hévíz would be complete without a swim (© 8/334-0587). An enclosed causeway leads out into the center of the lake where locker rooms and the requisite services, including massage, float rental, and a *palacsinta* (crepe) bar are housed. *Note:* There is no shallow water in the lake, so take care.)

Hévíz is an easy 10 minutes by bus from Keszthely (there's no train service). Buses (labeled "Heviz") depart every half hour or so from the bus station adjacent to the train station (conveniently stopping to pick up passengers in front of the church on Fő tér). The bus trip costs 158 Ft (70¢), one-way. The entrance to the lake is just opposite the bus station. You'll see a whimsical wooden facade and the words tó fürdő (Bathing Lake). Tickets cost 490 Ft ($2.20) for up to 3 hours or 990 Ft ($4.45) for a day pass; however, the latter is not available from November through March. Your ticket entitles you to a locker; insert the ticket into the slot in the locker and the key will come out of the lock. Keep the ticket until exiting, as the attendant needs to see it to determine whether you've stayed a half day or a full day.

Oázis Reform Restaurant, at Rákóczi tér 3 (© **8/331-1023**), is a self-service salad bar featuring adequate (if uninspired) vegetarian fare. There are cold and hot options and you can combine any salads you want. Go at lunch time, when the food is freshest. Oázis is open Monday to Friday, 11am to 4pm; Saturday only in summer. All salads cost 2000 Ft ($9) per 2.2 pounds. You can combine any salads.

Csiga Kisvendéglő (Little Snail Guest House) ⭐, at Tessedik u. 30 (© **8/331-4799**), a good 15-minute walk from the center, is a small neighborhood restaurant serving a variety of meat and fish dishes. At 750 Ft to 1,500 Ft ($3.40–$6.75) for main dishes, prices are more than reasonable. Csiga is open Monday through Friday 11am to 9pm; Saturday and Sunday (Sun only in summer) 11am to 10pm. It's a 20-minute walk from the Main Square (Fő tér); from the train station, you'll need to take a taxi.

Ireland

Ireland is one of the most beautiful and richly textured destinations, from the "40 shades of green" fields, to the buzz of Dublin, Galway, and Cork. Moreover, Ireland presents a familiar face. The language is the same, if more lyrical; the faces and surnames seem familiar; the food is recognizable; the stout legendary; and the hospitality genuine. Indeed, for many Irish Americans a trip to Ireland is experienced as a kind of homecoming. It takes a while for this superficial reverie to wear off. And when it does, a less sentimental, truer face of Ireland shows itself. And this is when the country becomes truly exciting.

Traveling in Ireland by train is easy and relatively stress-free, especially if you have a phobia about driving on the left (you aren't alone if you do). Getting around and soliciting train information is obviously easy for English speakers. Moreover, Eurail passholders get significant discounts on the ferries running to and from the Continent, though the trip wastes a day of vacation time each way. Also, be aware that, while rail routes are extensive in the eastern part of the country, you still may want a car to visit more remote pockets of the west. As you'll see later in this chapter, two of our recommended itineraries make use of a rail-drive pass and combine train travel with driving. But there's no doubt that Ireland is a truly gorgeous country with a mostly agricultural landscape, and train travel is one of the most pleasant ways to experience that beauty.

HIGHLIGHTS OF IRELAND

For many rail travelers, Ireland is just one country in a multinational journey, so we've chosen to focus on those areas of Ireland that are particularly accessible by rail or can be easily experienced with a rail-drive itinerary. As a result, we've focused the attentions of this chapter on the sunny east coast city of Wexford, the foodie haven that is West Cork and Kerry, and the spectacular Galway region. We feel that these areas combine to offer a little something for everyone and are not only immensely doable, but also show you a side of the country that will more than likely leave you breathless. Here are a few of the highlights:

With 40% of the Republic's population living within 61 miles (97km) of **Dublin,** the capital is by far the largest and most workaday of all Irish cities. It's also home to great shopping, wonderful restaurants and pubs, historic treasures like Dublin Castle and the Book of Kells, the National Museum, and the bucolic pleasures of St. Stephen's Green and Phoenix Park.

Boasting the best (warmest and driest) weather in Ireland, the **southeast** is often one alternative to a pub for getting out of the rain. Besides its weather, the southeast offers sandy beaches and the Viking streets of **Wexford.** And it's all extremely accessible via the east's extensive rail route network. For Eurail passholders, **Rosslare** is the jumping off point for ferries to France.

Cork City is Dublin's rival in sport and stout. It feels more like an exciting university town than a city, and provides a congenial gateway to the south and west of Ireland, which many consider the country's ultimate destinations. Plan

Moments Festivals & Special Events

The most up-to-date listings of events in Ireland can be found at **www.ireland.travel.ie** and **www.entertainment.ie**.

St. Patrick's Dublin Festival is a massive 4-day fest (Mar 15–18) that's open, free, and accessible to everyone. Street theater, carnival acts, sports, music, fireworks, and other festivities culminate in Ireland's grandest parade, with marching bands, drill teams, floats, and delegations from around the world. For information, call ℂ **01/676-3205** or surf the Web to **www.stpatricksday.ie**.

Killarney SummerFest is a (mainly rock) music festival, held June 26 to July 6, that gets bigger every year and is now one of the highlights of the Irish summer of music. Fringe events include street entertainment and art workshops. The action takes place in Fitzgerald Stadium, Killarney. For tickets, check out **www.ticketmaster.ie**.

The 2-week **Galway Arts Festival and Races** (ℂ **091/566577;** www.galwayartsfestival.ie), is a shining star on the Irish arts scene, featuring international theater, big-top concerts, literary evenings, street shows, arts, parades, music, and more. The famous Galway Races follows, with 5 more days of racing and merriment, music, and song. The action happens from July 15 to August 2 in Galway City.

to spend a couple of days here. Within arm's reach of Cork are the truly impressive Blarney Castle (with its less impressive stone), the culinary and scenic delights of **Kinsale,** the **Drombeg Stone Circle,** Sherkin and Clear islands, and **Mizen Head.** This region holds the spectacular landscape of **West Cork,** one of the truly gorgeous pockets of Ireland. You can spend as little as a few days or as long as a week here. Its remoteness adds to its charm, but also results in less convenient rail travel options. That's why we recommend a rail-drive itinerary (see section 4 of this chapter) to see this part of the country.

The once-remote splendors of County Kerry have long ceased to be a secret, so at least during high season, visitors must be prepared to share the view. Some highlights of this region are the Dingle Peninsula, the Skellig and the Blaskett islands, the truly lovely town of **Kenmare,** Tralee and its annual international and folk festivals, and dazzling views of sea, shore, and mountains—a new one, it seems, at every bend in the road. The **"Ring of Kerry"** (less glamorously known as N70 and N71), a 110-mile (178km) circuit of the Iveragh Peninsula, is the most visited attraction in Ireland next to the Book of Kells. Though not doable by train, you can tour the Ring by car or bus, and it's included in our foodie's itinerary of West Cork and Kerry found on p. 538. Because of its relative inaccessibility by rail, figure on renting a car for at least some of your trip if you want to include Kerry in your plans. **Killarney** is easily reached by train and was put on the map by its surrounding natural beauty—serene lakes, mountain peaks (the tallest in Ireland), and the ever-present sea—and is now synonymous with souvenir shops and tour buses.

The west of Ireland, once a land of last resort, today offers a first taste of Ireland's beauty and striking diversity. **Galway** just may be the perfect small city. It is without a doubt the most vibrant, colorful place in Ireland—a youthful,

prospering port and university city, and the self-acclaimed arts capital of Ireland with theater, music, dance, and a vibrant street life to prove it. And it's rail friendly, right on a major connecting line to Dublin. You'll want to spend at least a few days soaking up its unique atmosphere.

1 Essentials

GETTING THERE
BY PLANE

About half of all visitors from North America arrive in Ireland on direct transatlantic flights to Dublin Airport, Shannon Airport, or Belfast International Airport. The other half fly first into Britain or Europe, then "backtrack" into Ireland by air or sea. In the Republic, there are seven smaller regional airports, all of which (except Knock) offer service to Dublin and several of which receive some European traffic. They are Cork, Donegal, Galway, Kerry, Knock, Sligo, and Waterford. The routes and carriers listed below are provided to suggest the range of possibilities for air travel to Ireland.

FROM NORTH AMERICA   The Irish national carrier, **Aer Lingus** (✆ 800/ 474-7424; www.aerlingus.com) is the traditional leader in providing transatlantic flights to Ireland. Other carriers that fly directly to Ireland from the U.S. are **American Airlines** (✆ 800/433-7300; www.aa.com), **Delta Airlines** (✆ 800/ 241-4141; www.delta.com), and **Continental Airlines** (✆ 800/231-0856; www.continental.com).

FROM BRITAIN   The following carriers offer direct flights from London to Ireland: **Aer Lingus** (✆ 800/474-7424 in the U.S.; 020/8899-4747 in Britain); British Airways' short-flight sister, **City Flyer Express** (✆ 0345/222111; www. british-airways.com); **Lufthansa** (✆ 800/645-3880 in the U.S.; www.lufthansa. co.uk); and **British Midland** (✆ 800/788-0555 in the U.S. or 0870/607-0555 in Britain; www.iflybritishmidland.com).

Two low-cost airlines making the London-Dublin hop are **CityJet** (✆ 0345/ 445588 in Britain) and **Ryanair** (✆ 0541/569569 in Britain; www.ryanair. com). The budget-minded **Virgin Express** (✆ 01293/747747; www.virgin-atlantic.com) flies from London Gatwick to Shannon.

FROM THE CONTINENT   Major direct flights into Dublin from the Continent include service from Amsterdam on **KLM** (✆ 800/374-7747 in the U.S.; www.klm.com); Madrid and Barcelona on **Iberia** (✆ 800/772-4642 in the U.S.; www.iberia.com); Brussels on **Sabena** (✆ 800/952-2000 in the U.S.; www.sabena.com); Copenhagen on **Aer Lingus** and **SAS** (✆ 800/221-2350 in the U.S.; www.scandinavian.net); Frankfurt on **Aer Lingus** and **Lufthansa** (✆ 800/645-3880 in the U.S.; www.lufthansa.com); Paris on **Aer Lingus** and **Air France** (✆ 800/237-2747 in the U.S.; www.airfrance.com); Prague on **CSA Czech Airlines** (✆ 212/765-6588 in the U.S.; www.csa.cz); and Rome on **Aer Lingus.**

BY FERRY

The Eurailpass offers a 50% discount on ferry passage to or from Ireland and the Continent. The Irish Sea has a reputation for making seafarers woozy, so it's always a good idea to consider an over-the-counter pill or patch to guard against seasickness if you choose to take this route.

Irish Ferries (www.irishferries.ie) sails from Roscoff and Cherbourg, France, to Rosslare. Transit time between the two ports is 18 hours. For reservations, call **Scots-American Travel** (✆ 561/563-2856 in the U.S.; info@scotsamerican.

⌒Tips Point to Point: Britain to Ireland

If you're visiting both Britain and Ireland but really just want to get between A and B, Irish Ferries offers **"SailRail,"** round-trip travel between any rail station in Ireland and 2,400 stations in Britain via its Dublin–Holyhead ferry route. The fares are calculated *for two adults* by zone, depending on distance (a single traveler pays a supplement of €15–€32/ $17.25–$36.80 round-trip depending on the zones traveled). A sample round-trip fare for two adults from Dublin to London is €125 ($144). For more information, see **www.irishferries.ie**. For reservations, call **Scots-American Travel** (✆ 561/563-2856 in the U.S.; info@scotsamerican.com) or **Irish Ferries** (✆ 08705/171717 in the U.K. or ✆ 1890/313131 in Ireland).

com) or **Irish Ferries** (© **08705/171717** in the U.K. or 01/638-3333 in Ireland).

P&O European Ferries operates from Cherbourg, France, to Rosslare. For reservations, call Scots-American Travel (© **561/563-2856** in the U.S. or 01/638-3333 in Ireland; www.poferries.com). **Brittany Ferries** (© **021/427-7801** in Cork; www.brittany-ferries.com) connects Roscoff, France, to Cork (crossing time is about 19 hr.). For prices and more on these ferries, see the "Ferry Routes & Railpass Discounts" chart on p. 62.

If, like most travelers, you're only going to travel one-way to the Continent, the ferry ride is a huge time-waster, and the Irish Sea does not make for the smoothest ride on the planet. So we have to recommend that you skip the ferries and head to the Continent on a budget carrier, such as **Ryanair** (© **353/1249-7851,** with toll-free numbers in many European countries; www.ryanair.com), if you're doing a multi-country rail itinerary.

IRELAND BY RAIL
MULTI-COUNTRY PASSES
For information on the **Eurailpass, Eurailpass Flexi, BritRail Pass + Ireland,** and other multi-country options, see chapter 2. If you hold either of the multi-country rail-drive passes—the **EurailDrive Pass** or the **Eurail Selectpass Drive** (p. 53 and 54)—you may designate Ireland one of your country options. Some of the routes mentioned later in this chapter require driving and were designed with these passes in mind. *Note:* Rail Europe does not offer any rail-drive pass that's specific to the Republic of Ireland.

IRELAND RAILPASSES
And if your rail travels won't extend past The Republic? These Ireland-only passes are available from booking offices of **Iarnrod Eireann** (© **1850/366222,** or 01/836-6222; www.irishrail.ie) and the Dublin Tourism office on Suffolk Street (p. 514). *Note:* Discounted passes are available for children.

Irish Explorer Rail Only   For use only in the Republic of Ireland, this pass is good for 5 days of rail-only travel within 15 consecutive days for €105 ($121). It's valid for unlimited travel on InterCity, DART, and Suburban Rail.

Emerald Card   Valid for second-class rail and bus service throughout Ireland and Northern Ireland, this pass costs €310 ($357) for 15 days of travel within a 30-day period, or €180 ($207) for 8 days of travel within a 15-day period.

Irish Explorer Rail and Bus   For use only in the Republic of Ireland, this pass is good for 5 days of rail and bus travel within 15 consecutive days for €160 ($184).

READY-MADE RAIL GETAWAYS
Iarnrod Eireann (© **1850/366222;** 01/836-6222; www.irishrail.ie), the Irish rail network, also offers a variety of ready-made day tours and getaways that depart by train from Dublin. They can be purchased at booking offices of Iarnrod Eireann and at the Dublin Tourism office on Suffolk Street (see "Information Elsewhere in the City," below).

RailTours   These 1-day tours are a convenient way to see a hefty portion of the country. The fare includes reserved seats on InterCity rail services with full dining facilities (meals, however, are not included). For some itineraries, special coaches with qualified driver/guides take you where rail lines don't. There are a dozen itineraries available, including Glendalough and the Wicklow Mountains

Trains & Travel Times in Ireland

From	To	Type of Train	# of Trains	Frequency	Travel Time
Dublin Heuston	Cork	IC	5	Mon–Sat	2 hr. 41 min.
Dublin Heuston	Cork	IC	6	Sun	2 hr. 41 min.
Dublin Heuston	Killarney	IC	2	Daily	3 hr. 30 min.
Dublin Heuston	Galway	IC	4	Daily	2 hr. 42 min.
Dublin Connolly	Rosslare Europort	IC	3	Daily	3 hr. 30 min.
Dublin Connolly	Wexford	IC	3	Daily	2 hr. 41 min.

for €29 ($33.35); The Ring of Kerry for €99 ($114); The Cliffs of Moher, Burren, and Galway Bay for €89 ($102); and Waterford Crystal, Kilkenny Castle, and the Nore Valley for €89 ($102).

RailBreaks   These ready-made 2- or 3-day holidays include train travel and accommodation and let you take in a specific region. There are about a dozen options to choose from, with rates starting as low as €105 ($121) per person for a 3-day break in the Aran Islands, including rail travel, B&B accommodation, and breakfast daily. A 3-day entertainment break in Killarney, including rail travel, hotel accommodation, breakfast daily, plus 2 dinners, costs €177 ($204) per person.

FOREIGN TRAIN TERMS

Booking tickets in Ireland is self-explanatory for English speakers, aside from the occasional variance in vocabulary. *One piece of useful information:* The Irish use the term "return" instead of round-trip, and "single" instead of one-way.

PRACTICAL TRAIN INFORMATION

Iarnrod Eireann (© **1850/366222,** or 01/836-6222; www.irishrail.ie), aka Irish Railways, runs all of the train routes in the Republic of Ireland. The company's website is loaded with valuable information and has timetables, route maps, station information, and tips for rail travelers with disabilities.

RESERVATIONS   Holders of Eurail, BritRail + Ireland, Emerald Card, Irish Explorer, and Irish Rover passes do not need to make reservations on trains. Ireland is a small country, and there are no overnight trains or sleeper coaches. But be aware, however, that trains on the more popular routes can be very crowded, with standing room only, especially on Bank Holiday weekends. It's a good idea to arrive at least 45 minutes before departure time to ensure that you get a seat.

Note: Don't worry if a station's booking office is closed or if there is a long line as your train readies for departure should you decide to make a spur-of-the-moment trip and haven't got a pass; you can always buy your ticket on board the train.

SERVICES & AMENITIES   All InterCity train stations are staffed during rush hours and during the day Monday through Saturday; Dublin city stations are staffed around the clock daily, and stations in larger cities, such as Cork and Limerick, are staffed virtually around the clock. Tickets can be purchased during booking hours using cash or major credit cards. Stations in cities and larger towns have public restrooms, shops, telephones, lockers, luggage trolleys, and taxi ranks. Stations in smaller suburbs and small towns have public restrooms, telephones, and taxi ranks. You can view the list of amenities offered in each station on **www.irishrail.ie**.

The trains themselves tend to be on the clean-but-shabby side—some are old—but all are undergoing a years-long refurbishment. All InterCity trains offer some kind of food service, be it a restaurant car or a snack cart. If you're traveling in first class, you may even be able to get tableside meal service (albeit for a high price) on some routes. There are no sleeper trains in Ireland.

FAST FACTS: Ireland

Area Codes The area codes for major Irish cities are Dublin **01**, Cork **021**, Killarney **064**, Galway **091**.

Business Hours **Banks** are open 10am to 4pm Monday to Wednesday and Friday, and 10am to 5pm Thursday.

Post offices (known as **An Post**) in city centers are open from 9am to 5:30pm Monday to Friday and 9am to 1:30pm Saturday. Post offices in small towns often close for lunch from 1 to 2:30pm.

Museums and sights are generally open 10am to 5pm Tuesday to Saturday, and 2 to 5pm Sunday.

Shops are generally open 9am to 6pm, Monday to Friday with late opening on Thursdays until 7 or 8pm. In Dublin's city center most department stores and many shops are open 12 to 6pm Sundays.

Electricity The Irish electric system operates on 220 volts with a plug bearing three rectangular prongs. To use standard North American 110-volt appliances without destroying them or causing a fire, you'll need both a transformer and a plug adapter. Most new laptops have built-in transformers, but some do not, so beware.

Embassies & Consulates The **American Embassy** is at 42 Elgin Rd., Ballsbridge, Dublin 4 (✆ **01/668-8777**); the **Canadian Embassy** is at 65/68 St. Stephen's Green, Dublin 2 (✆ **01/678-1988**).

Health & Safety The Republic of Ireland has enjoyed a traditionally low crime rate, particularly when it comes to violent crime. Those days do regrettably seem to be passing, especially in the cities. By U.S. standards, Ireland is still very safe, but not safe enough to warrant carelessness. Travelers should take normal precautions to protect their belongings from theft and themselves from harm.

In recent years, the larger cities have been prey to pickpockets, purse-snatchers, car thieves, and drug traffickers. Dublin's busiest thoroughfares by day have been the scene of brutal, mindless beatings at night. To alert visitors to potential dangers, the Garda Siochana (Ireland's police) publishes a small leaflet, *A Short Guide to Tourist Security,* which is available at tourist offices and other public places. Take special care if you'll be out in Dublin when the pubs and nightclubs close for the night. Ask at your hotel about which areas are safe and which are not, and when. Take a taxi back to your hotel if you're out after midnight.

Ireland poses no major health risks to the rail traveler. As a rule, no health documents are required to enter Ireland from the United States, Canada, the United Kingdom, Australia, New Zealand, or most other countries. If, however, you have visited areas in the previous 14 days where a contagious disease is prevalent, proof of immunization may be required.

Mail In Ireland, mailboxes are painted green with the word POST on top. From the Republic, an airmail letter or postcard to the United States or Canada, not exceeding 25 grams, costs €.55 (65¢) and takes 5 to 7 days to arrive.

Telephone In the Republic, the telephone system is known as Eircom. Phone numbers in Ireland are currently in flux, as digits are added to accommodate expanded service. Every effort has been made to ensure that the numbers and information in this guide are accurate at the time of writing. If you have difficulty reaching a party, the Irish toll-free number for directory assistance is ☎ 11811. From the United States, the (toll) number to call is ☎ 00353-91-770220.

Local calls from a phone booth in the Republic require a **Callcard,** a prepaid computerized card that you insert into the phone instead of coins. They can be purchased in a range of denominations at phone company offices, post offices, and many retail outlets (such as newsstands). There's a local and international phone center at the General Post Office on O'Connell Street.

To place a call from your home country to Ireland, dial the international access code (011 in the U.S.), plus the country code (**353** for the Republic), and finally the number, remembering to omit the initial 0, which is for use only within Ireland (for example, to call the County Kerry number 066/00000 from the United States, you'd dial **011-353-66/00000**).

To place a direct international call from Ireland, dial the international access code (**00**) plus the country code (U.S. and Canada 1), the area or city code, and the number. For example, to call the U.S. number (212/000-0000) you'd dial (00-1-212/000-0000). The toll-free international access code for **AT&T** is ☎ 1-800-550-000, for **Sprint** it's ☎ 1-800-552-001, and for **MCI** it's ☎ 1-800-55-1001.

Tipping Most hotels and guesthouses add a service charge to the bill, usually 12.5% to 15%, although some smaller places add only 10% or nothing at all. Always check to see what amount, if any, has been added to your bill. If it is 12.5% to 15%, and you feel this is sufficient, then there is no need for more gratuities. If a smaller amount has been added, however, or if staff members have provided exceptional service, it is appropriate to give additional cash gratuities. For porters or bellhops, tip €1 ($1.15) per piece of luggage. For taxi drivers, hairdressers, and other providers of service, tip as you would at home, an average of 10% to 15%.

For restaurants, the policy is usually printed on the menu—either a gratuity of 10% to 15% is automatically added to your bill or it's left up to you. Always ask if you are in doubt. As a rule, bartenders do not expect a tip, except when table service is provided.

2 Dublin

One of Europe's trendiest cities, Dublin is home to more than a third of the entire population of Ireland. It's also the rail hub of the Republic and home to a major international airport, making it the logical first stop for rail travelers touring the country. Another plus: Compared to other European capitals,

Dublin is a relatively small metropolis and easily traversed. The city center—identified in Irish on bus destination signs as AN LAR—is bisected by the River Liffey flowing west to east into Dublin Bay. Canals ring the city center: The Royal Canal forms a skirt through the north half, and the Grand Canal the south half. True Dubliners, it is said, live between the two canals. The buzzing, prosperous hub of Dublin lies mostly south of the Liffey. The area containing most of the best hotels, restaurants, shops, and sights is a small, well-defined compound that can be easily walked in a half hour.

On the downside, Dublin's an expensive place to visit, but it's still cheaper than some other cities in Europe. And we'll give you a number of tips and options for the city that should keep even a frugal rail traveler on budget.

STATION INFORMATION
GETTING FROM THE AIRPORT TO THE TRAIN STATION
Dublin International Airport (✆ **01/814-1111;** www.dublin-airport.com) is 7 miles (11km) north of the city center. A Travel Information Desk located in the Arrivals Concourse provides information on public bus and rail services throughout the country.

If you need to connect immediately with the Irish rail service, the **Airlink Express Coach** (✆ **01/873-4222**) provides express bus service from the airport to the two main rail stations, **Connolly** and **Heuston.** Service runs daily from 7am until 11pm (Sun 7:30am–8:30pm), with departures every 20 to 30 minutes. A one-way fare is €5 ($5.75) for adults and €2 ($2.30) for children under age 12.

An excellent airport-to-city bus service called **AirCoach** operates 24 hours a day, making runs at 15-minute intervals. AirCoach runs direct from the airport to Dublin's city center and south side, servicing O'Connell Street, St. Stephen's Green, Fitzwilliam Square, Merrion Square, Ballsbridge, and Donnybrook—that is, all the key hotel and business districts. The one-way fare is €6 ($6.90); you buy your ticket from the driver. Although AirCoach is slightly more expensive than the Dublin Bus (see below), it is faster because it makes fewer intermediary stops and it brings you right into the hotel districts. To confirm AirCoach departures and arrivals, call ✆ **01/844-7118** or find it on the Web at **www.aircoach.ie**.

Dublin Bus (✆ **01/872-0000;** www.dublinbus.ie) service runs between the airport and the city center between 6am and 11:30pm. The one-way trip takes about 30 minutes, and the fare is €5 ($5.75). The 16a, 33, 41, 41a, 41b, 41c, 46x, 58x, 746, 747, and 748 all serve the city center from Dublin Airport. Consult the Travel Information Desk located in the Arrivals Concourse to figure out which bus will bring you closest to your hotel.

For speed and ease—especially if you have a lot of luggage—a **taxi** is the best way to get directly to your hotel or guesthouse. Depending on your destination in Dublin, fares average between €13 and €19 ($14.95–$21.85). Surcharges include €.50 (60¢) for each additional passenger and for each piece of luggage. Depending on traffic, a cab should take between 20 to 45 minutes to get into the city center. Taxis are lined up at a first-come, first-served taxi stand outside the arrivals terminal.

Passenger and car ferries from Britain arrive at the **Dublin Ferryport** (✆ **01/855-2222**), on the eastern end of the North Docks, and at the **Dun Laoghaire Ferryport.** Call **Irish Ferries** (✆ **01/661-0511;** www.irishferries.ie) for bookings and information. There is bus and taxi service from both ports.

Dublin

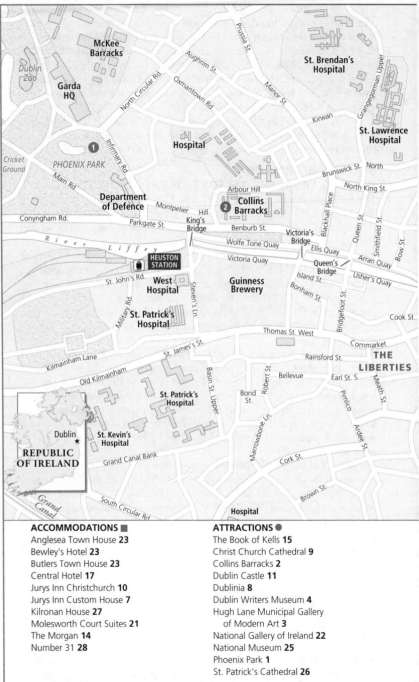

ACCOMMODATIONS ■
Anglesea Town House **23**
Bewley's Hotel **23**
Butlers Town House **23**
Central Hotel **17**
Jurys Inn Christchurch **10**
Jurys Inn Custom House **7**
Kilronan House **27**
Molesworth Court Suites **21**
The Morgan **14**
Number 31 **28**

ATTRACTIONS ●
The Book of Kells **15**
Christ Church Cathedral **9**
Collins Barracks **2**
Dublin Castle **11**
Dublinia **8**
Dublin Writers Museum **4**
Hugh Lane Municipal Gallery
   of Modern Art **3**
National Gallery of Ireland **22**
National Museum **25**
Phoenix Park **1**
St. Patrick's Cathedral **26**

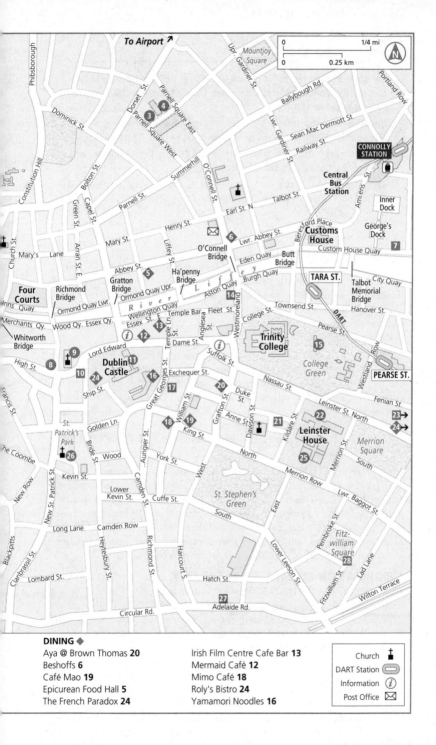

To Airport ↗

Mountjoy Square

0 ___ 1/4 mi
0 ___ 0.25 km

Phibsborough

Dominick St.

Constitution Hill

Upr. Gardiner St.

Ballybough Rd.

Portland Row

Dorset St.

Parnell Square East
Parnell Square West

❸ ❹

Lwr. Gardiner St.

Sean Mac Dermott St.

Railway St.

CONNOLLY
STATION

Church St.
Mary's Lane

Bolton St.
Green St.
Capel St.
Arran St. E

Parnell St.

Summerhill

O'Connell St.

Earl St. N.

Talbot St.

Central
Bus
Station

Amiens St.

Inner
Dock

Henry St.

Beresford Place

Customs
House

George's
Dock

❼

Mary St.

✉

Lwr. Abbey St.

Custom House Quay

Custom House Quay

O'Connell
Bridge

❻

Eden Quay

Butt
Bridge

City Quay

Abbey St.

Gratton
Bridge

❺

Ha'penny
Bridge

Burgh Quay

TARA ST.

Talbot
Memorial
Bridge

Hanover St.

Four
Courts

Richmond
Bridge

Ormond Quay Upr.

L i f f e y

River Liffey

Wellington Quay

Aston Quay

Westmoreland

College St.

Townsend St.

DART

Inns Quay

Ormond Quay Lwr.

Essex Qy.

Temple Ln.
Temple Bar

Fleet St.

Pearse St.

Merchants Qy.

Wood Qy.

Essex St.

Anglesea

PEARSE ST.

Whitworth
Bridge

❾

Dame St.

ⓘ

ⓘ

Trinity
College

❶❺

High St.

❽

❿

Lord Edward

Dublin
Castle

❶❶

❶❷

❶❸

❶❹

Suffolk St.

College
Green

Westland Row

❷❹

❶❻

Great Georges St.

Exchequer St.

Nassau St.

Fenian St.

Ship St.

❶❼

❷⓿

Duke St.

Leinster St. North

❷❷

❷❸→
❷❹→

Francis St.

St.
Patrick's
Park

Golden Ln.

William St.

❶❽

❶❾

King St.

Aungier St.

Anne St.

Dawson St.

❷❶

Kildare St.

Leinster
House

Merrion
Square

The Coombe

❷❻

Bride St.

Wood

York St.

West

North

Merrion Row

Merrion St.

South

New Row

New St.

St. Patrick St.

Lower
Kevin St.

Camden St.

Cuffe St.

St. Stephen's
Green

East

Lwr. Baggot St.

Kevin St.

Lower Leeson St.

Blackpitts

Clanbrassil St.

Long Lane

Camden Row

Heytesbury St.

Richmond St.

Harcourt S.

South

Pembroke St.

Fitz-
william
Square

❷❽

Lad Lane

Lombard St.

Hatch St.

❷❼

Adelaide Rd.

Circular Rd.

Fitzwilliam St.

Wilton Terrace

DINING ◆

Aya @ Brown Thomas **20**
Beshoffs **6**
Café Mao **19**
Epicurean Food Hall **5**
The French Paradox **24**

Irish Film Centre Cafe Bar **13**
Mermaid Café **12**
Mimo Café **18**
Roly's Bistro **24**
Yamamori Noodles **16**

Church ✝
DART Station ⬭
Information ⓘ
Post Office ✉

513

Which Dublin Station?

Connolly Station   InterCity routes to Sligo, Belfast; Rosslare; Longford; DART service to Malahide, County Dublin (north) and Greystones, County Wicklow (south).

Heuston Station   InterCity routes to Cork, Tralee, Limerick, Waterford, Ballina/Westport, Galway, Kildare, Clonmel; No DART service.

Pearse Street   DART service to Malahide, County Dublin (north) and Greystones, County Wicklow (south).

Tara Street   DART service to Malahide, County Dublin (north) and Greystones, County Wicklow (south).

INSIDE THE STATIONS

Dublin has two major train stations—**Heuston Station,** Kingsbridge, off St. John's Road; and **Connolly Station,** Amiens Street—and an additional two minor ones. To determine which station works best for your rail itinerary, see "Which Dublin Station?," above. Both stations are staffed 24 hours daily and will book tickets Monday through Saturday 6:30am to 10:30pm and Sunday 7:45am to 10:30pm.

CONNOLLY STATION   The major train station for points north of Dublin, Connolly is on the eastern side of Dublin, just a block away from the city's Central Bus Station. Station facilities include a left-luggage office, fast-food restaurants and cafes, public telephones, a taxi rank, ATMs, public bathrooms, newsagents, and ticket vending machines. A visitor information desk is located at track level in the station. There are maps and brochures, but no room reservation service. For more information about this station, call ℂ **01/703-2358** or see **www.irishrail.ie.**

HEUSTON STATION   On the western side of Dublin, Heuston appropriately handles a lot of the trains heading west out of the city. A visitor information desk is located at track level in the station. Station facilities include a left-luggage office, fast-food restaurants and cafes, public telephones, a taxi rank, ATMs, public bathrooms, newsagents, and ticket vending machines. There are maps and brochures, but no room reservation service. For more information about this station, call ℂ **01/703-3299** or see **www.irishrail.ie.**

INFORMATION ELSEWHERE IN THE CITY

Dublin Tourism (ℂ **01/605-7700;** www.visitdublin.com) operates six walk-in visitor centers in greater Dublin that are open every day except Christmas. The principal center is in the wonderfully restored Church of St. Andrew on Suffolk Street, Dublin 2, open from June to August Monday to Saturday from 9am to 8:30pm, Sunday and Bank Holidays 10:30am to 2:30pm, and the rest of the year Monday to Saturday 9am to 5:30pm, Sunday and bank holidays 10:30am to 3pm. The Suffolk Street office is about a half mile (.8km) from Connolly Station and includes a currency exchange counter, a car-rental counter, an accommodation reservations service, bus and rail information desks, a gift shop, and a cafe.

   The five other centers are in the **Arrivals Hall** of Dublin Airport; **Exclusively Irish,** O'Connell Street, Dublin 1; **Baggot Street Bridge,** Baggot Street, Dublin 2; **The Square Towncentre,** Tallaght, Dublin 24; and the ferry terminal at **Dun**

Laoghaire Harbor (all telephone inquiries should be directed to the number listed above). All centers are open year-round with at least the following hours: Monday to Friday 9am to 5:30pm and Saturday 9am to 1pm.

For accommodation reservations throughout Ireland by credit card, contact Dublin Tourism.

GETTING AROUND

Getting around Dublin is not at all daunting. Public transportation is good and getting better, taxis are plentiful and reasonably priced, and there is always your own two feet. In fact, with its current traffic and parking problems, it's a city where the foot is mightier than the wheel. If you plan on renting a car for one of the rail-drive itineraries in this chapter, don't do it until you're ready to leave the city!

ON FOOT Small and compact, Dublin is ideal for walking, as long as you remember to look right and then left (in the direction opposite your instincts) for oncoming traffic before crossing the street, and to obey traffic signals. Each traffic light has timed "walk–don't walk" signals for pedestrians. Pedestrians have the right of way at specially marked, zebra-striped crossings; as a warning, there are usually two flashing lights at these intersections.

BY BUS Dublin Bus operates a fleet of green double-decker buses, single-deck buses, and minibuses (called "imps") throughout the city and its suburbs. Most buses originate on or near O'Connell Street, Abbey Street, and Eden Quay on the north side, and at Aston Quay, College Street, and Fleet Street on the south side. Bus stops are located every 2 or 3 blocks. Destinations and bus numbers are posted above the front windows; buses destined for the city center are marked with the Irish Gaelic words AN LAR.

Bus service runs daily throughout the city, starting at 6am (10am Sun), with the last bus at 11:30pm. On Thursday, Friday, and Saturday nights, Nitelink service runs from the city center to the suburbs from midnight to 3am. Buses operate every 10 to 15 minutes for most runs; schedules are posted on revolving notice boards at each bus stop.

Inner-city fares are calculated based on distances traveled. The minimum fare is €.80 (92¢); the maximum fare is €2 ($2.30). The Nitelink fare is a flat €4 ($4.60). Buy your tickets from the driver as you enter the bus; exact change is required, so have your loose change available. Notes of €5 or higher may not be accepted. Discounted 1-day, 3-day, 5-day, and 7-day passes are available. The 1-day bus-only pass costs €5 ($5.75), the 3-day pass costs €9.50 ($10.90), the 5-day pass goes for €14.50 ($16.70), and the 7-day pass costs €17.50 ($20.10).

Moments **Late-Night Crime**

Crime in Dublin—and most specifically late-night crime—has been on the ascent in recent years. Most alarming are the random, senseless acts of violence that can occur on any street in Dublin after dark. Forget muggings: We're talking about unprovoked, serious beatings of innocent passersby by gangs of hooligans. These attacks are often booze-fueled and happen on streets that are perfectly safe during the day. Be especially on your guard in the areas around O'Connell Street and Grafton Street after pubs' closing time (particularly the areas around the train stations). Never walk back to your hotel alone after this hour.

For more information, contact **Dublin Bus,** 59 Upper O'Connell St., Dublin 1 (✆ **01/872-0000;** www.dublinbus.ie).

BY DART While Dublin has no subway in the strict sense, there is an electric rapid-transit train known as the **DART** (Dublin Area Rapid Transit). It travels mostly at ground level or on elevated tracks, linking the city-center stations at **Connolly Station, Tara Street,** and **Pearse Street** with suburbs and seaside communities as far as Malahide to the north and Greystones to the south. Service operates roughly every 10 to 20 minutes Monday to Saturday from 7am to midnight and Sunday from 9:30am to 11pm. The minimum fare is €1 ($1.15). One-day and 10-journey passes, as well as student and family tickets, are available at reduced rates. For further information, contact **DART,** Pearse Station, Dublin 2 (✆ **1850/366222** in Ireland, or 01/836-6222; www.irishrail.ie).

BY TRAM The newest addition to Dublin's public transportation network is the sleek light-rail tram known as **LUAS,** set to debut in 2004 (though cynical locals doubt it will open before 2005). Traveling at a maximum speed of 45 mph (70kmph) and departing every 5 minutes in peak hours, LUAS aims to appease Dublin's congestion problems and bring the city's transportation into the 21st century. Three lines will link the city center at **Connolly Station** and **St. Stephen's Green** with the suburbs of Tallaght in the southwest and Dundrum and Sandyford to the south. Fares were not yet set as of press time. For further information, contact **LUAS** (✆ **01/703-2029;** www.luas.ie).

BY TAXI It's very difficult to hail a taxi on the street; instead, they line up at ranks. Ranks are located outside all of the leading hotels, at bus and train stations, and on prime thoroughfares such as Upper O'Connell Street, College Green, and the north side of St. Stephen's Green near the Shelbourne Hotel. You can also phone for a taxi. Some of the companies that operate a 24-hour radiocall service are **Co-Op** (✆ **01/676-6666**), **Shamrock Radio Cabs** (✆ **01/855-5444**), and **VIP Taxis** (✆ **01/478-3333**). If you need a wake-up call, VIP offers that service, along with especially courteous dependability.

Taxi rates are fixed by law and posted in each vehicle. A 2002 survey found the following to be typical travel costs in the city center: A 2-mile (3.2km) journey costs €4.95 ($5.70) by day and €6.85 ($7.90) at night, a 5-mile (8km) journey runs €10 ($11.50) by day and €12.25 ($14.10) at night, and a 10-mile (16km) journey costs €16.25 ($18.70) by day and €21.25 ($24.40) at night. There's an additional charge for each extra passenger and for each suitcase of €.50 (60¢). And it costs an extra €1.50 ($1.70) for a dispatched pickup. *Be warned:* Some hotel staff members will tack on as much as €4 ($4.60) for calling you a cab, although this practice violates city taxi regulations.

WHERE TO STAY

Anglesea Town House ⟨✦⟩ Everyone who stays at this 1903 Edwardian-style B&B raves about the same thing: the extraordinary breakfasts served by Helen Kirrane. The place is full of old-world comforts—rocking chairs, settees, a sun deck, and lots of flowering plants—and guest rooms are pretty and very comfortable. But it's the breakfasts that you'll remember long after you leave Dublin. It's a 20-minute walk to the city center.

63 Anglesea Rd., Ballsbridge, Dublin 4. ✆ **01/668-3877.** Fax 01/668-3461. 7 units. €130 ($150) double. No service charge. Rates include full breakfast. AE, MC, V. DART: Lansdowne Rd. Bus: 10, 46A, 46B, 63, or 84. **Amenities:** Breakfast room. *In room:* Hair dryer, no A/C.

Bewley's Hotel ⚜ Bewley's Hotel occupies what was once a 19th-century brick Masonic school building next to the British Embassy. Public lounges and reception areas are grand, with mahogany wainscoting, marble paneling, and polished bronze. Rooms, too, are spacious and appointed with a writing desk, an armchair, and either a king-size bed or a double and a twin bed. The hotel is an excellent value for families and groups; the downside is its location a 20-minute walk from the city center.

Merrion Rd., Ballsbridge, Dublin 4. ℂ **01/668-1111.** Fax: 01/668-1999. www.bewleyshotels.com. 220 units. €99 ($114) double. Rate includes service charge and taxes. AE, DC, MC, V. DART: Sandymount (5-min. walk). Bus: 7, 7A, 7X, 8, or 45. **Amenities:** Restaurant. *In room:* Hair dryer, no A/C.

Butlers Town House ⚜⚜ *Value* This beautifully restored and expanded Victorian town house B&B feels like a grand family home. The atmosphere is semiformal yet invitingly elegant, classy without the starched collar. Rooms are richly furnished with four-poster or half-tester beds, using top-quality fabrics and an eye for blending rich colors. The sheets are of two-fold Egyptian cotton, the water pressure is heavenly, and the staff is gracious. There's free tea and coffee all day.

44 Lansdowne Rd., Ballsbridge, Dublin 4. ℂ **800/44-UTELL** in the U.S., or 01/667-4022. Fax 01/667-3960. www.butlers-hotel.com. 20 units. €140–€190 ($161–$219) double. Rates include full breakfast. AE, DC, MC, V. Closed Dec 23–Jan 8. DART: Lansdowne Rd. Bus: 7, 7A, 8, or 45. **Amenities:** Breakfast room; laundry. *In room:* Hair dryer.

Central Hotel ⚜ Between Grafton Street and Dublin Castle, this century-old five-story hotel is now part of the Best Western chain. The public areas retain a Victorian atmosphere, enhanced by an impressive collection of contemporary Irish art. Guest rooms are high-ceilinged, with cheerful and colorful fabrics, and sturdy, Irish-made furnishings. The tucked-away Library Bar is a cozy haven for a drink and a moment's calm.

1–5 Exchequer St. (at the corner of Great Georges St.), Dublin 2. ℂ **800/780-1234** in the U.S., or 01/679-7302. Fax 01/679-7303. www.centralhotel.ie. 70 units. €160 ($184) double. Rates include full Irish breakfast and service charge. AE, DC, MC, V. Bus: 22A. **Amenities:** Restaurant; bar; lounge; nonsmoking rooms. *In room:* Hair dryer, no A/C.

Jurys Inn Christchurch ⚜ *Value* A good location in Old City, facing Christ Church cathedral, makes this a solid choice in the budget category. Totally refurbished in 1998, the rooms are larger than you'd expect and bright, though the decor has the same floral bedspreads and framed watercolors as every other chain hotel you've ever visited. Request a fifth-floor room facing west for a memorable view of Christ Church. *Tip:* Rooms 501, 507, and 419 are especially spacious.

Christ Church Place, Dublin 8. ℂ **800/44-UTELL** in the U.S., or 01/454-0000. Fax 01/454-0012. www. jurys.com. 182 units. €112 ($129) double. Breakfast €9.50 ($11). Service charge included. AE, MC, V. Bus: 21A, 50, 50A, 78, 78A, or 78B. **Amenities:** Restaurant; pub; laundry; nonsmoking rooms. *In room:* Hair dryer.

Jurys Inn Custom House ⚜⚜ *Value* Ensconced in the new financial services district and facing the quays, this Jurys Inn follows the successful formula of affordable comfort without frills. Double rooms offer both a double and a twin bed. Twenty-two especially spacious rooms, if available, cost nothing extra. Rooms facing the quays also enjoy vistas of the Dublin hills, but those facing the financial district are quieter. Book well in advance.

Custom House Quay, Dublin 1. ℂ **800/44-UTELL** in the U.S., or 01/607-5000. Fax 01/829-0400. www.jurys.com. 239 units. €103–€112 ($118–$129) double. Rates include service charge. Full Irish breakfast €8 ($9.20). AE, DC, MC, V. Discounted parking available at adjacent lot. DART: Tara Street. Bus: 27A, 27B, or 53A. **Amenities:** Restaurant; bar; laundry; nonsmoking rooms. *In room:* Hair dryer, no A/C.

Kilronan House ★★ This extremely comfortable B&B is set on a peaceful, leafy road just a 5-minute walk from St. Stephen's Green. Much of the Georgian character remains, such as the ceiling cornicing, hardwood parquet floors, and the fine staircase. The rooms are brightly inviting in white and yellow, and those facing the front have big bay windows. There's no elevator, so get a room on a lower floor. Breakfast here is especially good, featuring homemade breads.

70 Adelaide Rd., Dublin 2. ℂ **01/475-5266.** Fax 01/478-2841. www.dublinn.com/kilronan.htm. 15 units, 13 with private bathroom (shower only). €152 ($175) double. Rates include full breakfast. AE, MC, V. Bus: 14, 15, 19, 20, or 46A. *In room:* Hair dryer, no A/C.

Molesworth Court Suites ★ Hate hotels? Tucked away behind Mansion House, Molesworth Court is a 5-minute walk to Stephens Green. These tastefully decorated, comfortable apartments offer everything you need to set up your own base in Dublin, whether for a night or a month. They all have kitchens, small balconies, and the bi-level penthouses have spacious verandas. The staff is helpful, and there's daily maid service. The internal phone system provides you with your own voice mail.

Schoolhouse Lane (off Molesworth St.), Dublin 2. ℂ **01/676-4799.** Fax 01/676-4982. www.molesworth court.ie. 12 units. €160 ($184) 1-bedroom apt, €200 ($230) 2-bedroom apt. Nonrefundable booking deposit of €110 ($127) due 4 weeks before arrival. AE, MC, V. DART: Pearse. Bus: 10, 11A, 11B, 13, or 20B. **Amenities:** Laundry. *In room:* No A/C.

The Morgan ★★ In just a few short years, this stylized little boutique hotel in Temple Bar has developed a cult following among folks in fashion and music. Rooms are airy and minimalist, featuring light beechwood furnishings and crisp, white bedspreads against creamy neutral tones, with modern artwork adding visual punch. The overall effect is understated elegance, with a modern, luxurious twist. It manages to be both trendy and a classic at the same time.

10 Fleet St., Dublin 2. ℂ **01/679-3939.** Fax 01/679-3946. www.themorgan.com. 66 units. €215 ($247) double. AE, DC, MC, V. Bus: 78A or 78B. **Amenities:** Cafe; bar; laundry; nonsmoking rooms. *In room:* No A/C.

Number 31 ★★ This award-winning town house B&B, in the heart of Georgian Dublin, is actually two beautifully renovated architectural show houses featuring a fabulous sunken fireside seating area with mosaic tiles in the main lounge. In the main house, rooms vary from grand, high-ceilinged affairs to cozier nests. The smaller coach house has lower ceilings, but some rooms have their own patios. All the rooms are a triumph of quiet, good taste. Breakfast is magnificent.

31 Leeson Close, Lower Leeson St., Dublin 2. ℂ **01/676-5011.** Fax 01/676-2929. www.number31.ie. 20 units (all with bathroom). €140–€230 ($161–$265) double. Rates include breakfast. AE, MC, V. Free parking. Bus: 11, 11A, 11B, 13, 13A, or 13B. **Amenities:** Bar; lounge. *In room:* Hair dryer.

Waterloo House ★ Waterloo House (actually not one, but two Georgian town houses) is one of the most popular B&Bs in Dublin. The place is charming in an old-world kind of way, with classical music wafting through the lobby, and the elegant, high-ceilinged drawing room looking like a parlor out of an Agatha Christie novel. Guest rooms are comfortable and large (some have two double beds) but the decor (red-patterned carpet, box-pleated bedspreads) is a tad dated. Breakfast is a high point.

8–10 Waterloo Rd., Ballsbridge, Dublin 4. ℂ **01/660-1888.** Fax 01/667-1955. www.waterloohouse.ie. 17 units. €78–€175 ($90–$201) double. Rates include full breakfast. MC, V. Closed Christmas week. DART: Lansdowne Rd. Bus: 5, 7, or 8. **Amenities:** Breakfast room; all rooms are nonsmoking. *In room:* Hair dryer, no A/C.

TOP ATTRACTIONS & SPECIAL MOMENTS

The Book of Kells ★★★   The jewel in Ireland's tourism crown is the Book of Kells, a magnificent manuscript of the four Gospels, around A.D. 800, with elaborate scripting and illumination. It's the most majestic work of art to survive from the early centuries of Celtic Christianity, and has often been described as "the most beautiful book in the world." Its fascination derives from the digni-fied but elusive character of its main motifs, and the astonishing variety and complexity of the linear ornamentation that adorns every one of its 680 pages. This famous treasure and other early Christian manuscripts are on permanent public view at Trinity College, in the Colonnades, an exhibition area on the ground floor of the Old Library. The oldest university in Ireland, Trinity was founded in 1592 by Queen Elizabeth I. It occupies a beautiful 40-acre site just south of the River Liffey, with cobbled squares, gardens, a picturesque quadran-gle, and buildings dating from the 17th to the 20th centuries.

College Green, Dublin 2. ✆ **01/608-2320.** www.tcd.ie/library/kells.htm. Free admission to college grounds. €6 ($6.90) adults, €5 ($5.75) seniors/students, €11 ($13.80) families, free for children under 12. Mon–Sat 9:30am–5pm; Sun noon–4:30pm (opens at 9:30am June–Sept). Bus: All city buses stop here.

Christ Church Cathedral ★★   Standing on high ground in the oldest part of the city, this cathedral is one of Dublin's finest historic buildings. It dates from 1038, when Sitric, Danish king of Dublin, built the first wooden Christ Church here. In 1171, the original simple foundation was extended into a cruciform and rebuilt in stone by Strongbow. The present structure dates mainly from 1871 to 1878, when a huge restoration took place. Highlights of the interior include magnificent stonework and graceful pointed arches, with delicately chiseled sup-porting columns. This is the mother church for the diocese of Dublin and Glen-dalough of the Church of Ireland. The Treasury in the crypt is open to the public, and you can hear bells pealing in the belfry.

Christ Church Place, Dublin 8. ✆ **01/677-8099.** cccdub@indigo.ie. Suggested donation €5 ($5.75) adults, €2.50 ($2.90) students and children under 15. Daily 10am–5:30pm. Closed Dec 26. Bus: 21A, 50, 50A, 78, 78A, or 78B.

Collins Barracks   Officially part of the National Museum, Collins Barracks is the oldest military barracks in Europe. Even if it were empty, it would be well worth a visit for the structure itself, a splendidly restored early-18th-century masterwork by Colonel Thomas Burgh, Ireland's Chief Engineer and Surveyor General under Queen Anne. The collection housed here focuses on the decora-tive arts. Most notable is the extraordinary display of Irish silver and furniture. Until the acquisition of this vast space, only a fraction of the National Museum's collection could be displayed, but that is changing, and more and more treasures find their way here. It is a prime site for touring exhibitions, so consult *The Event Guide* for details. There is also a cafe and gift shop on the premises.

Benburb St., Dublin 7. ✆ **01/677-7444.** Free admission. Tours (hours vary) €1.50 ($1.70) adults, free for sen-iors and children. Tues–Sat 10am–5pm; Sun 2–5pm. Bus: 34, 70, or 80.

Dublin Castle ★★   Built between 1208 and 1220, this complex represents some of the oldest surviving architecture in the city. It was the center of British power in Ireland for more than 7 centuries, until the new Irish government took it over in 1922. Film buffs might recognize the castle's courtyard as a setting in the Neil Jordan film *Michael Collins*. Highlights include the 13th-century Record Tower; the State Apartments, once the residence of English viceroys; and the Chapel Royal, a 19th-century Gothic building with particularly fine plaster decoration and carved oak gallery fronts and fittings. The newest developments are the Undercroft, an excavated site on the grounds where an early Viking fortress stood, and the Treasury, built between 1712 and 1715 and believed to be the oldest surviving office building in Ireland. Also here are a craft shop, heritage center, and restaurant.

Palace St. (off Dame St.), Dublin 2. ℂ **01/677-7129.** dublincastle@eircom.net. Admission €4.25 ($4.90) adults, €3.25 ($3.75) seniors and students, €1.75 ($2) children under 12. No credit cards. Mon–Fri 10am–5pm; Sat–Sun and holidays 2–5pm. Guided tours every 20–25 min. Bus: 50, 50A, 54, 56A, 77, 77A, or 77B.

Dublinia 🍀   What was Dublin like in medieval times? This historically accurate presentation of the Old City from 1170 to 1540 is re-created through a series of theme exhibits, spectacles, and experiences. Highlights include an illuminated Medieval Maze, complete with visual effects, background sounds, and aromas that lead you on a journey through time from the arrival of the Anglo-Normans in 1170 to the closure of the monasteries in the 1530s. Another segment depicts everyday life in medieval Dublin with a diorama, as well as a prototype of a 13th-century quay along the banks of the Liffey. The medieval Fayre displays the wares of merchants from all over Europe. You can try on a flattering new robe, or, if you're feeling vulnerable, stop in at the armorer's and be fitted for chain mail.

St. Michael's Hill, Christ Church, Dublin 8. ℂ **01/679-4611.** www.dublinia.ie. Admission €5.75 ($6.60) adults, €4.50 ($5.20) seniors, students, and children, €15 ($17.25) family. AE, MC, V. Apr–Sept daily 10am–5pm; Oct–Mar Mon–Sat 11am–4pm, Sun 10am–4:30pm. Bus: 50, 78A, or 123.

Dublin Writers Museum 🍀🍀   Housed in a stunning 18th-century Georgian mansion with splendid plasterwork and stained glass, the museum is itself an impressive reminder of the grandeur of the Irish literary tradition. A fine collection of personal manuscripts and mementos that belonged to Yeats, Joyce, Beckett, Behan, Shaw, Wilde, Swift, and Sheridan are among the items that celebrate the written word. One of the museum's rooms is devoted to children's literature.

18–19 Parnell Sq. N., Dublin 1. ℂ **01/475-0854.** Admission €6 ($6.90) adults, €5 ($5.75) seniors, students and children, €16.50 ($19) families (2 adults and up to 4 children). AE, DC, MC, V. Mon–Sat 10am–5pm (6pm June–Aug); Sun and holidays 11am–5pm. DART: Connolly Station. Bus: 11, 13, 16, 16A, 22, or 22A.

Hugh Lane Municipal Gallery of Modern Art 🍀   Housed in a finely restored 18th-century building known as Charlemont House, this gallery is situated next to the Dublin Writers Museum. It is named after Hugh Lane, an Irish art connoisseur who was killed during the sinking of the *Lusitania* in 1915 and who willed his collection (including works by Courbet, Manet, Monet, and Corot) to be shared between the government of Ireland and the National Gallery of London. With the Lane collection as its nucleus, this gallery also contains paintings from the Impressionist and post-Impressionist traditions, sculptures by Rodin, stained glass, and works by modern Irish artists. In 2001, the museum opened the studio of Irish painter Francis Bacon; it was moved piece by piece from Bacon's original studio and reconstructed at the museum. The bookshop is considered the best art bookshop in the city.

Parnell Sq. N., Dublin 1. ℂ **01/874-1903.** Fax 01/872-2182. www.hughlane.ie. Free admission to museum; Francis Bacon studio €7 ($8.05) adults, €3.50 ($4) students. MC, V. Tues–Thurs 9:30am–6pm; Fri–Sat 9:30am–5pm; Sun 11am–5pm. DART: Connolly or Tara stations. Bus: 3, 10, 11, 13, 16, or 19.

Kilmainham Gaol Historical Museum 🍀   This is a key sight for anyone interested in Ireland's struggle for independence from British rule. Within these walls political prisoners were incarcerated, tortured, and killed from 1796 until

1924, when President Eamon de Valera left as its final prisoner. To walk along these corridors, through the exercise yard, or into the main compound is a moving experience that lingers hauntingly in the memory.

Kilmainham, Dublin 8. ℂ **01/453-5984.** www.heritageireland.ie. Guided tour €5 ($5.75) adults, €3.50 ($4) seniors, €2 ($2.30) children, €11 ($12.65) family. AE, MC, V. Apr–Sept daily 9:30am–4:45pm; Oct–Mar Mon–Fri 9:30am–4pm, Sun 10am–4:45pm. Bus: 51B, 78A, or 79 at O'Connell Bridge.

National Gallery of Ireland ✶✶✶   This museum houses Ireland's national art collection, as well as a superb European collection of art spanning from the 14th to the 20th centuries. Every major European school of painting is represented, including fine selections by Italian Renaissance artists (especially Caravaggio's *The Taking of Christ*), French Impressionists, and Dutch 17th-century masters. The highlight of the Irish collection is the room dedicated to the mesmerizing works of Jack B. Yeats, brother of the poet W. B. Yeats. All public areas are wheelchair accessible. The museum has a fine gallery shop and an excellent self-service restaurant.

Merrion Sq. W., Dublin 2. ℂ **01/661-5133.** Fax 01/661-5372. www.nationalgallery.ie. Free admission. Mon–Sat 9:30am–5:30pm; Thurs 9:30am–8:30pm; Sun noon–5pm. Free guided tours (meet in the Shaw Room) Sat 3pm, Sun 2, 3, and 4pm. Closed Good Friday and Dec. 24–26. DART: Pearse. Bus: 5, 6, 7, 7A, 8, 10, 44, 47, 47B, 48A, or 62.

National Museum ✶✶✶   Established in 1890, this museum is a reflection of Ireland's heritage from 2000 B.C. to the present. It is the home of many of the country's greatest historical finds, including the Treasury exhibit, which toured the United States and Europe in the 1970s with the Ardagh Chalice, Tara Brooch, and Cross of Cong. Other highlights range from the artifacts from the Wood Quay excavations of the Old Dublin Settlements to "Or," an extensive exhibition of Irish Bronze Age gold ornaments dating from 2200 to 700 B.C. The museum has a shop and a cafe. *Note:* The National Museum also encompasses the Collins Barracks (see above).

Kildare St. and Merrion St., Dublin 2. ℂ **01/677-7444.** Free admission. Tours (hours vary) €1.50 ($1.70) adults, free for seniors and children. MC, V. Tues–Sat 10am–5pm; Sun 2–5pm. DART: Pearse. Bus: 7, 7A, 8, 10, 11, or 13.

Phoenix Park ✶✶   Just 2 miles (3.2km) west of the city center, the Phoenix Park, the largest urban park in Europe, is the playground of Dublin. A network of roads and quiet pedestrian walkways traverses its 1,760 acres, which are informally landscaped with ornamental gardens and nature trails. Avenues of trees, including oak, beech, pine, chestnut, and lime, separate broad expanses of grassland. The homes of the Irish president and the U.S. ambassador are on the grounds, as is the Dublin Zoo. Livestock graze peacefully on pasturelands, deer roam the forested areas, and horses romp on polo fields. The **Phoenix Park Visitor Centre,** adjacent to Ashtown Castle, offers exhibitions and an audiovisual presentation on the park's history. The cafe/restaurant is open 10am to 5pm weekdays, 10am to 6pm weekends.

Phoenix Park, Dublin 8. ℂ **01/677-0095.** www.heritageireland.ie. Visitor Centre: Admission €2.75 ($3.15) adults, €2 ($2.30) seniors and students, €1.25 ($1.45) children, €9 ($10.35) families. June–Sept 10am–6pm (call for off-season hours). Bus: 37, 38, or 39.

St. Patrick's Cathedral ✶   It is said that St. Patrick baptized converts on this site, and consequently a church has stood here since A.D. 450, making it the oldest Christian site in Dublin. The present cathedral dates from 1190, but because of a fire and 14th-century rebuilding, not much of the original foundation remains. It is mainly early English in style, with a square medieval tower that houses the largest ringing peal bells in Ireland, and an 18th-century spire. The 300-foot interior makes it the longest church in the country. St. Patrick's is closely associated with Jonathan Swift, who was dean from 1713 to 1745 and whose tomb lies in the south aisle. Others memorialized within the cathedral include Turlough O'Carolan, a blind harpist and composer and the last of the great Irish bards; Michael William Balfe, the composer; and Douglas Hyde, the first president of Ireland. St. Patrick's is the national cathedral of the Church of Ireland.

21–50 Patrick's Close, Patrick St., Dublin 8. ℂ 01/475-4817. Fax 01/454-6374. www.stpatrickscathedral.ie. Admission €4 ($4.60) adults, €3 ($3.45) students and seniors, €9 ($10.35) family. MC, V. Mon–Fri 9am–6pm year-round; Nov–Feb Sat 9am–5pm and Sun 9am–3pm. Closed except for services Dec 24–26 and Jan 1. Bus: 65, 65B, 50, 50A, 54, 54A, 56A, or 77.

WHERE TO DINE

Aya @ Brown Thomas ✮✮✮ JAPANESE   This buzzing, fashionable annex to Dublin's poshest department store (actually, it's just across the street on Clarendon St.) is very much a good-time destination for chic Dubliners, with its conveyor belt sushi bar. The good news is that, beyond the trendiness, the food here is damn good. Lunch offers all the classics—tempura, gyosa, toritatsuta, and, of course, plenty of sushi—while the dinner menu expands to include yakitori, steaks, and noodle salads. Come for dinner Sunday through Tuesday for the Sushi55 special: all you can eat, including one complimentary drink, for €24 ($27.60).

49–52 Clarendon St., Dublin 2. ℂ 01/677-1544. Reservations recommended for dinner. Lunch avg. €11 ($12.65), dinner avg. €32 ($36.80). AE, DC, MC, V. Mon–Sat 10:30am–11pm; Sun noon–10pm. DART: Tara St. Bus: 16A, 19A, 22A, 55, or 83.

Beshoffs ✮ FISH AND CHIPS   The Beshoff name is synonymous with fresh fish in Dublin. Recently renovated in Victorian style, the restaurant has an informal atmosphere and a simple self-service menu. Crisp chips are served with a choice of fresh fish, from the original recipe of cod to classier variations using salmon, shark, prawns, and other local sea fare—some days as many as 20 varieties. The potatoes are grown on a 300-acre farm in Tipperary and freshly cut each day. A second shop is just south of the Liffey at 14 Westmoreland St., Dublin 2 (ℂ **01/677-8026**).

6 Upper O'Connell St., Dublin 1. ℂ **01/872-4400**. All items €3–€7 ($3.45–$8.05). No credit cards. Mon–Sat 10am–9pm; Sun noon–9pm. DART: Tara St. Bus: Any city-center bus.

Café Mao ✮✮✮ ASIAN   Dubliners have beaten a path to this place since it opened a few years back, and it's already become something of an icon. This is where to go when you feel like Asian cooking laced with a fun and exhilarating attitude. An exposed kitchen lines an entire wall, and the rest of the space is wide open—fantastic for people-watching on weekends. The menu reads like a "best of Asia": Thai fish cakes, nasi goreng, chicken hoi sin, salmon ramen. Everything is well prepared and delicious, so you can't go wrong.

2 Chatham Row, Dublin 2. ℂ 01/670-4899. Reservations recommended. Main courses €13–€18 ($14.95– $20.70). AE, MC, V. Mon–Thurs noon–11pm; Fri–Sat noon–11:30pm; Sun noon–10pm. DART: Pearse. Bus: 10, 11A, 11B, 13, or 20B.

Epicurean Food Hall ✮✮ GOURMET FOOD COURT   This wonderful food hall houses a wide variety of gourmet produce. Favorites include: **Caviston's,** Dublin's premier deli, for smoked salmon and seafood; **Itsabagel,** for its delicious bagels, imported from H&H Bagels in New York City; **Crème de la Crème,** for its French-style pastries and cakes; **Nectar,** for its plethora of healthy juice drinks; and **Aroma Bistro** for Italian paninis. There is limited seating but this place gets uncomfortably jammed during lunchtime midweek, so go mid-morning or afternoon.

Middle Abbey St., Dublin 1. No phone. All items €2–€12 ($2.30–$13.80). No credit cards. Mon–Sat 10am–6pm. Bus: 70 or 80.

The French Paradox ★★ *Value* WINE BAR This price-conscious, darling little bistro-cum-*bar de vin* has endeared itself to everyone in the city. The wine's the thing here, so relax with a bottle of Bordeaux or Côte du Rhone and whatever nibbles you like from the menu. There's a lovely cheese plate named for West Cork cheesemaker Bill Hogan, superb Iberico hams from Spain, or, if you're more hungry, the delicious bistro stalwart of confit of duck with vegetables. Simply delicious.

53 Shelbourne Rd., Dublin 4. ℂ **01/660-4068.** www.thefrenchparadox.com. Reservations recommended. All items €6–€15 ($6.90–$17.25). Main dishes come with glass of wine. AE, MC, V. Mon–Sat 12–3pm and 2 evening sittings at 6pm and 9pm. DART: Lansdowne Rd. Bus: 5, 6, 7, 8, 18, or 45.

Irish Film Centre Cafe Bar ★ IRISH/INTERNATIONAL One of the most popular drinking spots in Temple Bar, the hip Cafe Bar (in the lobby of the city's coolest place to grab a movie) features an excellent, affordable menu that changes daily. A vegetarian and Middle Eastern menu is available for both lunch and dinner. The weekend entertainment usually includes music or comedy.

6 Eustace St., Temple Bar, Dublin 2. ℂ **01/677-8788.** Lunch and dinner €6–€10 ($6.90–$11.50). MC, V. Mon–Fri 12:30–3pm; Sat–Sun 1–3pm; daily 6–9pm. Bus: 21A, 78A, or 78B.

Mermaid Café ★★★ MODERN Chef Temple Garner's cooking is downright terrific—think classic cooking with a fresh, eclectic twist. The New England crab cakes, grilled swordfish with mango relish, and roast duck breast on curried noodles are all flawlessly prepared and quite memorable. On top of all that, the wine list is one of the best in Ireland, and the desserts—especially the pecan pie—are divine.

70 Dame St., Dublin 2. ℂ **01/670-8236.** www.mermaid.ie. Reservations required. Dinner main courses €19–€30 ($21.85–$34.50). Sun brunch €9–€15 ($10.35–$17.25). MC, V. Mon–Sat 12:30–2:30pm and 6–11pm; Sun brunch 12:30–3:30pm and dinner 6–9pm. Bus: 50, 50A, 54, 56A, 77, 77A, or 77B.

Mimo Cafe ★★ *Value* MODERN CONTINENTAL This chic little cafe in the tony Powerscourt Townhouse shopping mini-mall is a classy and surprisingly budget-minded place to stop for terrific salads, pasta dishes, and inventive sandwiches. Grab one of the leather sofas or armchairs, and order the warm goat's cheese crostini with caramelized figs, wild honey, and beetroot dressing. A piano player is a civilized touch on Thursday and Friday afternoons.

Powerscourt Townhouse, Dublin 2. ℂ **01/674-6712.** Main courses €8–€10 ($9.20–$11.50). MC, V. Mon–Sun noon–5:30pm. Bus: Any city-center bus.

Roly's Bistro ★★ IRISH/INTERNATIONAL This two-story shop-front restaurant is a Dublin institution for the kind of excellent, tummy-warming food you never get tired of: confit of duck with garlic mash, roasted venison, chicken-and-bean sprout spring roll, game pie with chestnuts, wild mushroom risotto. The main dining room, with a bright and airy decor and lots of windows, can be noisy when the house is full, but the nonsmoking section has a quiet enclave of booths laid out in an Orient Express style for those who prefer a quiet tête-à-tête.

7 Ballsbridge Terrace, Dublin 4. ℂ **01/668-2611.** Reservations required. Main courses €19–€26 ($21.85–$29.90). Set-price lunch €18 ($20.70). AE, DC, MC, V. Daily noon–3pm and 6–10pm. DART: Lansdowne Rd. Station. Bus: 5, 6, 7, 8, 18, or 45.

Yamamori Noodles ★★ JAPANESE   If you're still skeptical about Japanese cuisine, Yamamori will make you an instant believer. In a pop, casual, and exuberant atmosphere, you may just be startled by how good the food is here. The splendid menu is a who's who of Japanese cuisine, and the prices range from budget to splurge. On a raw, drizzly Dublin day, the chile chicken ramen is a pot of bliss, while the Yamamori Yaki Soba offers, in a mound of wok-fried noodles, a well-rewarded treasure hunt for prawns, squid, chicken, and roast pork.

71–2 S. Great George's St., Dublin 2. ℂ 01/475-5001. Reservations only for parties of 4 or more persons. Main courses €11–€18 ($12.65–$20.70). MC, V. Sun–Wed 12:30–11pm; Thurs–Sat 12:30–11:30pm. Bus: 50, 50A, 54, 56, or 77.

SHOPPING

Ireland is known the world over for its handmade products and fine craftsmanship, and Dublin is a one-stop source for the country's best wares. For Irish crafts, head to the **Craft Centre of Ireland** (ℂ 01/475-4526), perched on the top floor of the St. Stephen's Green Centre, at the top of Grafton Street, which offers an exquisite collection of ceramics, wood turning, glassware, and more— all by top Irish artisans. Also check out **Tower Craft Design Centre** (ℂ 01/ 677-5655), on Pearse Street, alongside the Grand Canal. This beautifully restored 1862 sugar refinery now houses a nest of craft workshops where you can watch the artisans at work. The merchandise ranges from fine-art greeting cards and hand-marbled stationery to pewter, ceramics, pottery, knitwear, hand-painted silks, copper-plate etchings, all-wool wall hangings, silver and gold Celtic jewelry, and heraldic gifts. Finally, **Kilkenny Design Centre** (6–10 Nassau St., ℂ 01/677-7066) is a one-stop shop for original Irish designs and quality products, including pottery, glass, candles, woolens, pipes, knitwear, jewelry, books, and prints. For knitwear and tweeds, go to **Dublin Woollen Mills** (41–42 Lower Ormond Quay; ℂ 01/677-5014) on the north side of the River Liffey next to the Halfpenny Bridge. Since 1888, this shop has been a leading source of Aran sweaters, vests, hats, jackets, and scarves, as well as lamb's-wool sweaters, kilts, ponchos, and tweeds at competitive prices.

There are many good shopping malls in Dublin, but our favorite is the **Powerscourt Townhouse Centre,** 59 S. William St. (ℂ 01/679-4144), housed in a restored 1774 town house. This four-story complex consists of a central skylit courtyard and more than 60 boutiques, craft shops, art galleries, cafes, and restaurants. The wares include all kinds of crafts, antiques, paintings, prints, ceramics, leather work, jewelry, clothing, hand-dipped chocolates, and farmhouse cheeses.

The Temple Bar area has two excellent weekend markets. **Book Market Temple Bar** is held weekends from 11am to 4pm in Temple Bar Square and has enough of everything to make for excellent browsing—old and new titles, classics and contemporary novels, science fiction and mysteries, serious biographies, and pulp fiction. **Food Market Temple Bar** is held weekends from 10 am to 5pm in Meeting House Square and is a great picnic shopping spot. Everything here is organic, from fruits and veggies to a delicious selection of homemade cheeses, chutneys, breads, and jams.

NIGHTLIFE

One general fact to keep in mind concerning Dublin's nightlife is that there are very few fixed points. Apart from a handful of established institutions, venues come and go, change character, open their doors to ballet one night and cabaret the next. *In Dublin* and *The Event Guide* offer the most thorough and up-to-date listings. They can be found on almost any magazine stand.

The award-winning website of the *Irish Times* (**www.ireland.com**) offers a "what's on" daily guide to cinema, theater, music, and whatever else you're up for. The **Dublin Events Guide,** at **www.dublinevents.com**, also provides a comprehensive listing of the week's entertainment possibilities. *Time Out* now covers Dublin as well; check their website at **www.timeout.com/Dublin**.

PUBS   The mainstay of Dublin social life is unquestionably the pub. More than 1,000 specimens spread throughout the city, on every street, at every turn. In *Ulysses,* James Joyce referred to the puzzle of trying to cross Dublin without passing a pub; his characters quickly abandoned the quest as fruitless, preferring to sample a few in their path. Below we list a few the city's most distinctive pubs.

For conversation and atmosphere, head for the **Brazen Head,** 20 Lower Bridge St. (© **01/679-5186**). This brass-filled, lantern-lit pub claims to be the city's oldest, and it might very well be, considering that it was licensed in 1661 and occupies the site of an even earlier tavern dating from 1198. Nestled on the south bank of the River Liffey, it is at the end of a cobblestone courtyard and was once the meeting place of Irish freedom fighters such as Robert Emmet and Wolfe Tone. **The Long Hall,** 51 S. Great George's St. (© **01/475-1590**), is one of the city's most photographed pubs, with a beautiful Victorian decor of fili-gree-edged mirrors, polished dark woods, and traditional snugs. The hand-carved bar is said to be the longest counter in the city. The choice of trendsetters is **The Mercantile,** Dame Street, Dublin 2 (© **01/679-0522**). Try for one of the comfy booths in the back of this watering hole, which draws a mixed crowd of locals and in-the-know out-of-towners. Despite being very big, it's always buzzing and tends to get overjammed on weekends, so mid-week nights are the best. U2 members The Edge and Larry Mullen are regulars.

If you like Irish traditional music, **Chief O'Neill's,** Smithfield Village (© **01/817-3838;** www.chiefoneills.com), is one of the city's best haunts for gim-mick-free traditional music, in the hotel of the same name. Tucked between St. Stephen's Green and Merrion Street, **O'Donoghue's,** 15 Merrion Row (© **01/ 676-2807**), is a much-touristed, smoke-filled enclave that's widely heralded as the granddaddy of traditional music pubs. A spontaneous session is likely to erupt at almost any time of the day or night. **Oliver St. John Gogarty,** 57–58 Fleet St. (© **01/671-1822**), in the heart of Temple Bar, has an inviting old-world atmos-phere, with shelves of empty bottles, stacks of dusty books, a horseshoe-shaped bar, and old barrels for seats. There are traditional music sessions most every night from 9 to 11pm, as well as Saturday at 4:30pm, and Sunday from noon to 2pm.

THEATER   Dublin has a venerable and vital theatrical tradition, in which imagination and talent have consistently outstripped funding. The online book-ing site Ticketmaster (**www.ticketmaster.ie**) is an excellent place to get a quick look at what's playing where and also buy tickets.

For more than 90 years, the **Abbey Theatre,** Lower Abbey Street (© **01/878-7222;** www.abbeytheatre.ie), has been the national theater of Ireland. The origi-nal theater, destroyed by fire in 1951, was replaced in 1966 by the current unin-spired, 600-seat house. The box office is open Monday to Saturday 10:30am to 7pm; shows run Monday to Saturday at 8pm, and also at 2:30pm on Saturday. Tickets cost €15 to €26 ($17.25–$29.90). There are senior, student, and chil-dren's discounts available Monday to Thursday evening and for the Saturday matinee.

Just north of O'Connell Street off Parnell Square, the restored 370-seat **Gate Theatre,** 1 Cavendish Row (© **01/874-4368**), was founded in 1928 to provide a venue for a broad range of plays. That policy prevails today, with a program that includes a blend of modern works and the classics. Although less known by visitors, The Gate is easily as distinguished as the Abbey. The box office is open Monday to Saturday 10am to 7pm; shows run Monday to Thursday at 8pm. Tickets cost €21 to €25 ($24.15–$28.75) or €15 ($17.25) for previews.

AN EXCURSION TO GREYSTONES

You can easily spend a day or afternoon in Wicklow and return to the city for dinner and the theater. One accessible, charming gateway to County Wicklow is the small harbor town of **Greystones,** which you may not want to tell your friends back home about for fear of spoiling the secret. It is hands-down one of the most unspoiled and attractive harbor towns on Ireland's east coast. It has no special attractions except its lovely waterfront and small-town buzz, but that's enough to make it a perfect day out.

GETTING THERE   There is **InterCity** (© **01/836-6222;** www.irishrail.ie) and **DART** (© **1850/366222** in Ireland, or 01/836-6222; www.irishrail.ie) service daily between Dublin's Connolly Station and Greystones. DART trains are by far the most plentiful, running every 10 to 20 minutes on weekdays during rush hours. Even during off-peak times, DART trains are less than an hour apart. The **Greystones Station** (© **01/287-4160**) is a 5-minute walk from the beach.

TOURIST INFORMATION   There is no tourist office in Greystones, but you can obtain information from the **Wicklow Tourist Office,** Fitzwilliam Square, Wicklow Town, County Wicklow (© **0404/69117;** www.wicklow.ie),

---

(Moments   Off to the Races

Ireland's County Kildare is synonymous with horse racing. It's the heartland of the country's flourishing bloodstock industry and the National Stud. In this panorama of open grasslands and limestone-enriched soil, you'll find many of Ireland's 300 stud farms. Kildare is home to **The Curragh** (pronounced ker-ah), sometimes called the Churchill Downs of Ireland, the country's best-known racetrack. Just 30 miles (48km) west of Dublin, it makes for a great excursion out of the capital. Majestically placed at the edge of Ireland's central plain, The Curragh plays host to the **Irish Derby,** held in late June. Horses race at least one Saturday a month from March to October. A couple of years ago, the main stand was extensively renovated, a new betting hall added, and dining facilities (bars, restaurants, and food court) greatly expanded.

Getting to the track is easy—it is connected by rail to all major towns in the area. And **Irish Rail** (© 01/836-6222; www.irishrail.ie) offers a round-trip "Racing by Rail" package from Dublin's Heuston Station for €15 ($17.25), including a courtesy coach from the train station to the main entrance.

For more information on The Curragh, call © **045/441205** or check out its website at **www.curragh.ie**. Admission is €15 ($17.25) for most days of racing; €20 to €50 ($23–$57.50) on Derby days. Hours vary; the first race usually starts at 2pm but check the local newspaper sports pages to be sure.

open Monday to Friday year-round, Saturday during peak season. The Wicklow station is two stops beyond Greystones on the Dublin-Rosslare rail line.

Before returning to Dublin, grab dinner or a Sunday lunch at the **Hungry Monk Wine Bar,** on Church Road (© **01/287-5759**). It's been around for a long time, but it continues to pull new fans because of its no-nonsense approach to good food and wine. If you're in the mood for a nice, three-course meal, then head upstairs to the upscale restaurant. Downstairs, at the wine bar, is where you come for a one-plate dinner and a bottle of good wine. Think seafood chowder, vegetarian spring rolls, or Bombay chicken curry. The wines are well chosen and affordable, the service unobtrusive and correct, the crowd cheerful and enthusiastic. Main courses run €12 to €18 ($13.80–$20.70).

3 Wexford

The Irish national rail network is far more developed along the east coast, where historically the population has been concentrated, and subsequently it's easier to explore this side of the country on a rail holiday. The route from Dublin's Connolly Station to the Rosslare Europort, in County Wexford, runs along the scenic eastern seaboard part of the way, and you can jump off in any number of scenic towns (such as **Greystones;** see "An Excursion to Greystones," above) and then take in the Viking streets of **Wexford Town.** From the Rosslare Europort, Eurailpass holders can hook up with the ferry that makes the crossing to France.

The modern English name of Wexford evolved from *Waesfjord,* which is what the Viking sea-rovers called it when they settled here in the 9th century. It means "the harbor of the mud-flats." Like the rest of Ireland, Wexford was under Norman control by the 12th century, and some stone reminders of their dominance in this region survive. With a population of about 10,000, Wexford is a hardworking Irish harbor town with a surprisingly sophisticated social calendar, highlighted by the opera festival in late October. It's a good place to stay when you're making a ferry crossing that arrives or departs from Rosslare Harbor, just a quick 12-mile (19km) hop by train away.

Rimmed by the River Slaney, Wexford is a compact and congested town with many narrow streets—successors of the 9th-century market trails—lined with 18th-century houses and shop fronts. You'll want to explore it on foot, not behind the wheel. Four quays (Custom House, Commercial, Paul, and the semicircular Crescent) run beside the water. Crescent Quay marks the center of town. One block inland is Main Street, a long, narrow thoroughfare that you can easily walk.

GETTING THERE   Irish Rail provides daily train service from Dublin's Connolly Station to Wexford and Rosslare Pier. Three trains daily leave Connolly Station and serve **O'Hanrahan Station,** Redmond Square, Wexford (© **053/ 22522;** www.irishrail.ie); check with the booking office for times, as they can fluctuate according to season. The journey from Dublin to Wexford takes approximately 3¼ hours by InterCity train. The station is about 220 yards from the town center.

VISITOR INFORMATION   The **Wexford Tourist Office,** Crescent Quay, Wexford (© **053/23111;** www.wexfordtourism.com), is open year-round Monday to Saturday 9am to 6pm. To get to the office from the train station, turn left as you exit the station and then keep walking along the harbor.

TOP ATTRACTIONS & SPECIAL MOMENTS

The best way to see the town is by walking the entire length of North and South Main Street, taking time to detour up and down the alleys and lanes that cross the street. To get to Main Street, walk up Slaney Street from the train station, then turn left onto Selskar and keep going until it becomes Main.

You may want to start out by visiting the **Westgate Heritage Tower**, on Westgate Street (© **053/46506**), which will provide you with valuable context and background information before you explore the rest of the city. Westgate once guarded the western entrance of Wexford Town. Sir Stephen Devereux built it in the 13th century, on instructions from King Henry. Like other town gates, it consisted of a toll-taking area, cells for offenders, and accommodations for guards. Fully restored and reopened in 1992 as a Heritage center, it presents artifacts, displays, and a 27-minute audiovisual display, titled *In Selskar's Shadow,* which provides an informative introduction to Wexford's complex and turbulent history. The audiovisual show costs €2 ($2.30) adults, €1 ($1.15) children and students. It's open May to August Monday to Friday 10am to 6pm, Saturday and Sunday noon to 6pm; September to April Monday to Friday 10am to 5pm.

Nearby, off Temperance Row at Westgate Street, **Selskar Abbey** is said to be one of the oldest sites of religious worship in Wexford, dating from at least the 12th century. It was often the scene of synods and parliaments. The first Anglo-Irish treaty was signed here in 1169, and it's said that Henry II spent the Lent of 1172 at the abbey doing penance for having Thomas à Becket killed. Although the abbey is mostly in ruins, its choir is part of a Church of Ireland edifice, and a portion of the original tower is a vesting room.

As you walk through Wexford Town, keep an eye out for several notable landmarks. The first is the **Bull Ring** ⚔, off North Main Street, where a statue memorializes the Irish pikemen who fought for the cause. In 1798, the first declaration of an Irish Republic was made here. Earlier, in the 17th century, the town square was a venue for bull-baiting, a sport introduced by the butcher's guild. Tradition has it that, after a match, the hide of the ill-fated bull was presented to the mayor and the meat used to feed the poor. Today, activity at the ring is much tamer: a weekly outdoor market, open Friday and Saturday from 10am to 4:30pm.

Nearby is **St. Iberius Church,** on North Main Street (© **053/43013**). Erected in 1660, St. Iberius was built on hallowed ground—the land has been used for houses of worship since Norse times. The church has a lovely Georgian facade and an interior known for its superb acoustics. It's open May to September daily 10am to 5pm; October to April Tuesday to Saturday from 10am to 3pm. Free guided tours are given according to demand.

Finally, the **John Barry Monument,** on Crescent Quay, was a gift from the American people in 1956. The bronze statue facing out to the sea is a tribute to John Barry, a favorite son who became the father of the American Navy. Barry emigrated to the colonies while in his teens and volunteered to fight in the American Revolution. One of the U.S. Navy's first commissioned officers, he became captain of the *Lexington.* In 1797, George Washington appointed him commander-in-chief of the U.S. Navy.

If you feel like shopping, head to Main Street. At **Wexford Silver,** 115 N. Main St. (© **053/21933**), one of Ireland's leading silversmiths, Pat Dolan, plies his craft. He and his sons create gold, silver, and bronze pieces by hand using traditional tools and techniques. **The Wool Shop**, 39 S. Main St. (© **053/22247**), is Wexford's long-established best source for hand-knit items. The selection runs from caps and tams to sweaters and jackets, as well as tweeds, linens, mohairs, and knitting yarns. Shops in Wexford are open Monday to Thursday 9am to 5:30pm, Friday and Saturday 9am to 6pm; some shops stay open until 8pm on Friday.

Moments Wexford's Old-Time Pubs

Long a favorite with photographers, the pub called **Con Macken's, The Cape of Good Hope,** at the Bull Ring off North Main Street (© 053/ 22949), is unique for the trio of services it offers, aptly described by the sign outside the door: BAR-UNDERTAKER-GROCERIES. Hardly any visitor passes by without a second look at the windows; one displays beer and spirit bottles, the other plastic funeral wreaths. An alehouse for centuries, the Cape has always been at the center of Wexford political events, and rebel souvenirs, old weapons, and plaques line the bar walls.

Another pub with a history is **The Crown Bar,** on Monck Street (© 053/21133). Once a stagecoach inn, this tiny pub in the center of town has been in the Kelly family since 1841. Besides its historical overtones, it is well known for its museum-like collection of antique weapons. You'll see 18th-century dueling pistols, pikes from the 1798 Rebellion, powder horns, and blunderbusses, as well as vintage prints, military artifacts, and swords. Unlike most pubs, it's not always open during the day, so it's best to visit here in the evening.

The Wren's Nest, on Custom House Quay (© 053/22359), near the John Barry Memorial on the harbor, has redesigned its front bar to restore an old-style wood floor and ceiling. The varied pub grub includes Wexford mussel platters, house pâtés, soups, salads, and vegetarian entrees. There is free traditional Irish music on Tuesday and Thursday nights.

WHERE TO STAY & DINE

Dating from 1779, **White's** (© **800/528-1234** in the U.S., or 053/22311; www.bestwestern.com) is a vintage hotel right in the middle of town, with its older section facing North Main Street. The Best Western affiliate has been expanded and updated over the years, resulting in lots of connecting corridors and guest rooms of varying size and standards. Some have four-poster or canopy beds, others a more contemporary feel with blond-wood furnishings. The public rooms reflect the aura of an old coaching inn, complete with two lively bars: the Shelmalier, where jazz and folk music often plays on weekends, and Speakers, a popular lounge-style watering hole. Rooms cost €135 ($155) double, including breakfast.

A terrific budget option is **McMenamin's Townhouse** ★★ (© 053/46442), a feel-good, Victorian-style B&B that has a well-deserved reputation for taking good care of its guests, and subsequently does a huge amount of repeat business. It's ideally located for train travelers at the western end of town, opposite the railroad station. Guest rooms are individually furnished with local antiques, including brass beds and caned chairs. All the guest rooms are nonsmoking and have orthopedic beds. Rooms cost €70 ($80.50) double, including a copious breakfast.

For a moderately priced dinner, **Mange2** ★★, 100 S. Main St. (© 053/ 44033), offers French cooking with global flair—inventive without any wild antics, and quite eclectic, while retaining the subtlety and attention to detail that seems to be part of the French genetic code. The roast red pepper and fennel samosa with baby beets and yogurt dressing is delicately crisp, as is the pine-nut fritter that accompanies the filets of sole. Portions are generous. Main courses run €15 to €21 ($17.25–$24.15). **Bohemian Girl,** 2 Selskar St. (© **053/ 24419**), is a Tudor-style pub named for an opera written by one-time Wexford resident William Balfe. Its mood is definitely casual, thanks to lantern lights, barrel-shaped tables, and matchbook covers on the ceiling. Its excellent pub lunches (12:30pm–3pm year-round) include fresh oysters, pâtés, sandwiches, and homemade soups. Main courses cost €7 to €13 ($8.05–$15).

4 West Cork & Kerry: A Haven for Foodlovers

This rail-drive itinerary takes you through the southwest, the culinary hotbed of Ireland and one of its most interesting regions, but not necessarily the easiest place to get around in by rail. Take the train from Dublin's Heuston station to **Cork City,** known for its plethora of excellent eateries. Then rent a car and drive from Cork City through the vibrant little villages and towns of West Cork, including **Kinsale,** which is home to a Gourmet Festival each October. Over the border in County Kerry, discover beautiful **Kenmare,** home to an astonishing number of terrific restaurants and cafes, and a gateway to the **Ring of Kerry.** Continue from Kenmare to **Killarney,** where you can pick up the train back to Dublin.

CORK CITY

Cork City (pop. 240,000, including environs) may be far smaller than Dublin, but to a Corkman there isn't even the remotest possibility for comparison; Cork is simply superior. Any native will tell you that his beloved Cork provides all the conveniences of a city but retains its small-town, leisurely pace of life. And don't let the size mislead you. Cork is a busy commercial hub for the south of Ireland and also has a thriving arts culture. Here you'll find the Crawford Art Gallery, the most important gallery outside the capital, and the refurbished Cork Opera House, packing sell-out seasons.

But Cork's real draw is its fabulous dining scene. It is a foodie's paradise, with more good restaurants per capita than anywhere else in Ireland. (Now that we mention it, that's true for the entire county of Cork. Nearby Kinsale has its own gourmet food festival; in West Cork, seemingly every little hamlet possesses a wonderful little place to dine; and East Cork boasts the internationally acclaimed Ballymaloe House cooking school.) Though you can find Guinness drinkers everywhere in Ireland, many would argue that a true Corkonian will only drink Murphy's or Beamish, the two locally brewed stouts.

Be warned that the traffic moves fast here, and the locals talk even faster in their lovely singsong accent. They are also known for their particularly dry sense of humor. Cork slang is so rich, and so particular to Cork, that it makes even other Irish feel out of the loop.

GETTING THERE   Iarnrod Eireann (© **1850/366222** or 01/836-6222; www.irishrail.ie) links a number of prominent Irish cities and towns with Cork. At least nine trains daily leave Dublin's Heuston Station and serve **Kent Station,** Lower Glanmire Road, Cork (© **021/450-4777**), on the city's eastern edge. Most are direct, though some require that you change trains in Mallow. Check times with the booking office of Irish Rail.

VISITOR INFORMATION   For brochures, maps, and other information, visit the **Cork Tourist Office,** Tourist House, 42 Grand Parade, Cork (© **021/ 427-3251;** www.corkkerry.ie). Its hours are Monday to Saturday 9:15am to

5:30pm all year. For online information, consult **Local Cork** (http://cork. local.ie) or the **Cork Guide** (www.cork-guide.ie).

GETTING AROUND   Because of the problem finding street parking, the best way to see Cork is on foot (so wait to rent that car until your last day here), but don't try to do it all in a single day. The South Bank and the central part, or flat, of the city can easily take a day to explore; save the Cork Hills and the North Bank for another day. You might want to follow the signposted Tourist Trail to guide you to all the major sights.

   Bus Eireann operates bus service from Parnell Place Bus Station (© 021/ 450-8188; www.buseireann.ie) to all parts of the city and its suburbs, including Blarney and Kinsale. The flat fare is €.90 ($1.05). Buses run frequently from 7am to 11pm Monday to Saturday, with slightly shorter hours on Sunday.

TOP ATTRACTIONS & SPECIAL MOMENTS

There are lots of bridges in Cork, which can be quite confusing, when you're touring the city. Before you start thinking you're going around in circles, realize that central Cork is actually on an island that lies between two limbs of the River Lee. The South Bank encompasses the 17th-century city walls and the grounds of **St. Finbarr's Cathedral** 𝕱, the site of St. Finbarr's 6th-century monastery. The cathedral's interior features some unique mosaic work. Admission to the cathedral is free and though the hours vary, it's generally open Monday through Saturday from 10am to 5:30pm.

   The downtown core of the city is surrounded on the north and south by channels of the River Lee. This area includes the **Grand Parade,** a spacious thoroughfare that blends 18th-century bow-fronted houses and the remains of the old city walls with modern offices and shops. Extending from the northern tip of the Grand Parade is the city's main thoroughfare, **St. Patrick Street.** Referred to simply as Patrick Street by Corkonians, this broad avenue was formed in 1789 by filling in an open channel in the river. It is primarily a street for shopping, but it is also a place for folks to stroll, be seen, and greet friends. Patrick Street is also the site of the **statue** of 19th-century priest Fr. Theobald Matthew, a crusader against drink who is fondly called the "apostle of temperance." The statue stands at the point where Patrick Street reaches St. Patrick's Bridge and is the city's central point of reference.

   The city's antiques row is **Paul's Lane,** an offshoot of Paul Street, between Patrick Street and the Quays in the Huguenot Quarter. There are three shops along this lane, each brimming with old Cork memorabilia and furnishings: **Anne McCarthy,** 2 Paul's Lane (© 021/427-3755); **Mills,** 3 Paul's Lane (© 021/427-3528); and **O'Regan's,** 4 Paul's Lane (© 021/427-2902). All are open Monday to Saturday 10am to 6pm. Pop into the covered **Old English Market** 𝕱𝕱 (Mon–Sat 9am–6pm), off Patrick's Street and the Grand Parade, and sample the fare, but leave room for a superb meal in one of the city's many top-flight restaurants.

   Crawford Municipal Art Gallery 𝕱𝕱𝕱, Emmet Place (© 021/427-3377), is the best gallery outside of Dublin. Works by such well-known Irish painters as Jack B. Yeats, Nathaniel Grogan, William Orpen, Sir John Lavery, James Barry, and Daniel Maclise are the focal point in Cork's 18th-century former customs house. It's open Monday to Saturday, 10am to 5pm, and admission is free.

   St. Patrick's Bridge (or Patrick's Bridge) leads over the river to the north side of the city, a hilly, terraced section where Patrick Street becomes **St. Patrick's Hill,** with an incline so steep that it is nearly San Franciscan. If you climb the stepped sidewalks of St. Patrick's Hill, you will be rewarded with a sweeping view of the Cork skyline. St. Anne's Church, on Church Street, is Cork's prime landmark and better known as **Shandon Church** ⚬⚬. It's famous for its giant pepper pot steeple and its eight melodious bells. Virtually no matter where you stand in the downtown area, you can see the stone tower, crowned with a gilt ball and a unique fish weather vane. Up to recently it was known as "the four faced liar" because each of its four clock faces used to show a different time, except on the hour, when they all managed to synchronize. Somewhat sadly, that charming quirk was fixed a few years ago. Climb to the top of the church's belfry and you'll be rewarded with a spectacular view of the city. Admission to the church costs €3 ($3.45) and it's open Monday through Saturday 8:30am to 6pm.

Opposite the church is the **Old Butter Exchange** ⚬, on John Redmond Street (① **021/430-0600**). Started in 1770, it became the largest exporter of salted butter in the world, exporting around 500,000 casks of butter a year by 1892. Although the exchange closed in 1924, it's become a popular museum in this city of good food. The exchange now houses the Shandon Craft Centre and the Firkin Crane Centre, a hot venue for contemporary dance performances.

In July and August, **Bus Eireann,** Parnell Place Bus Station (① **021/450-8188**), offers narrated tours to all of Cork's major landmarks and buildings, including nearby Blarney Castle. Fares start at €8 ($9.20). While aspects of **Blarney Castle** ⚬⚬⚬ (① **021/438-5252**) are very touristy, it is still one of the most haunting and striking castles in Ireland. What remains of this impressive castle is a massive square tower, with a parapet rising 83 feet. The infamous Blarney Stone is wedged far enough underneath the battlements to make it uncomfortable to reach, but not far enough that countless tourists don't literally bend over backwards, hang upside down in a parapet, and kiss it. It's customary to tip the attendant who holds your legs (you might want to do it before he hangs you over the edge). After bypassing the stone, take a stroll through the gardens and a nearby dell beside Blarney Lake. The Badger Cave and adjacent dungeons, penetrating the rock at the base of the castle, can be explored by all but the claustrophobic with the aid of a flashlight. Admission is €7 ($8.05) for adults, €5

Moments Cork's Traditional Music Pubs

You'll find some of the best traditional Irish music played in **An Bodhran,** 42 Oliver Plunkett St. (① **021/427-4544**), every night starting at 9:30pm. Named for the traditional goat-skin drum, this pub's old-world decor includes stone walls, dark woods, and a huge stained-glass window with Book of Kells–inspired designs depicting Irish monks playing traditional Irish instruments.

Its name may mean the "migrant worker," but **An Spailpin Fanac** (① **021/427-7949**) is a permanent fixture in Cork. Its address at 28–29 S. Main St. is opposite the Beamish Brewery. It dates from 1779, making it one of Cork's oldest pubs. It is a lovely, soothing place—as all the best pubs are—with low ceilings, exposed brick walls, flagstone floors, open fireplaces, a simple wooden bar, and woven rush seats. Oh, and there's a darling, authentic snug. There is traditional Irish music Sunday to Thursday, starting at 9:30pm.

($5.75) for seniors and students. It's open May and September Monday to Saturday 9am to 6:30pm, Sunday 9:30am to 5:30pm; June to August Monday to Saturday 9am to 7pm, Sunday 9:30am to 5:30pm; October to April Monday to Saturday 9am to sundown, Sunday 9:30am to 5:30pm.

WHERE TO STAY & DINE

Built in 1810 on the north bank of the River Lee for Murphy's Brewery, **D'Arcy's,** 7 Sydney Place, Wellington Road (© 021/450-4658), is much bigger inside than it appears from outside. And for a place right in the middle of the city's hubbub, D'Arcy's is amazingly peaceful and calm. The guest rooms are spacious and bright, though a bit dated, with the odd abstract painting adding a mod touch. The higher up you go, the better the view, but be warned: There are 92 steps from the basement breakfast room to the top floor and no elevator, so booking a room on the top floor is a good way to stay in shape. Breakfasts are excellent. Rooms cost €80 to €90 ($92–$104) for a double, including breakfast.

Jurys Cork Inn ⚘, on Anderson's Quay (© 021/427-6444), is a comfortable if functional hotel overlooking the River Lee and an excellent choice for rail travelers on a budget. The flat-rate room price covers up to three adults—exceptional value for a city-center location. The brick facade and mansard-style roof blend in with Cork's older architecture, yet the interior is bright and modern, with contemporary light-wood furnishings. Rooms cost €80 to €89 ($92–$102) for a double. Breakfast costs €9 ($10.35) extra.

Seven North Mall Guesthouse ⚘, at 7 North Mall (© 021/439-7191), is a lovely waterside guesthouse that's attained cult status among travelers who know Ireland well. The town house dates from 1750 and looks out on the River Lee from the north bank. Angela Hegarty is obviously a detail-oriented person; every furnishing is carefully chosen, every accoutrement perfectly timbered, right down to the eating utensils. The result is an atmosphere of relaxation and elegant understatement. Up the narrow stairs, the rooms with river views are very appealing, but those in the back of the house are more spacious. The one ground-floor room is popular with travelers who have trouble with stairs. Rooms cost €90 ($104) for a double, including breakfast.

Isaacs ⚘⚘, 48 MacCurtain St. (© 021/450-3805), is so integral to the fabric of Cork's dining scene that we can hardly imagine the city without it. The dining room itself is quite beautiful and contemporary, with soaring warehouse-style ceilings and exposed brick walls. Chef Canice Sharkey's signature is modern, understated International cuisine: Think simple, fresh pasta dishes; hearty stews; mouthwatering grilled meats; and interesting salads. Daily blackboard specials add to the variety. The best-value deal is at lunchtime, when you can easily get out of here for €14 ($16.10) a head, but there can be a lackluster atmosphere. Dinnertime is far more convivial. Main courses run €14 to €22 ($16.10–$25.30).

Jacob's on the Mall ⚘⚘, 30A South Mall (© 021/425-1530), is the talk of the town. Chef Mercy Fenton doesn't so much cook as compose meals using fresh ingredients and side dishes to heighten the taste of her main dishes. Her grilled mackerel comes with buttery new potatoes and the licoricey hint of fennel, her crispy salmon is served with Chinese greens and noodles, and her breast of chicken with a dollop of lemon aioli. The place is truly lovely, with tall windows flooding the dining room with light. Main courses cost €14 to €30 ($16.10–$34.50).

The **Crawford Art Gallery Café** ⚘ (© 021/427-4415), on the ground floor of the gallery on Emmet Place, is decorated with oil paintings and statuary. The menu includes such traditional country dishes as lamb braised with vegetables and rosemary, and more contemporary open-faced sandwiches such as a wonderful smoked salmon, cheese, and pickle combination. All fish are brought in fresh daily from Ballycotton Bay, and breads and baked goods are from Ballymaloe kitchens. All items cost €4 to €12 ($4.60–$13.80).

Finally, every hometown should have a darling, perfect little eatery like the **Idaho Cafe,** at 19 Caroline St. (*ⓒ* **021/427-6376**). It's tiny, with patrons squeezed in together like sardines, and the pretentious quotient is zero. Needless to say, the food is to die for. Lunchtime specials often feature Ummero bacon with minty new potatoes and cashews. Everything is made from fresh ingredients by people who obviously understand that a bit of care in preparing even an inexpensive meal is much appreciated. To find this wee place, turn off Patrick Street, directly behind the Brown Thomas department store.

WEST CORK

Cork is often called "The Rebel County" for the independent spirit of those that reside here, both past and present. It is the largest of the 32 Irish counties, and one of the most diverse. The landscape has hardly been tamed, either, and West Cork holds some of Ireland's most beautifully remote and wild coastal regions, with long sandy beaches (called "strands" in Ireland), high rugged cliffs, and a scattering of offshore islands. There are rocky, heather-clad mountains, subtropical gardens (thanks to the congenial Gulf Stream), and still, dark lakes. You can find dark forests, old walled villages, deserted mining towns, colorful spinnakers of racing yachts, and plenty of seafaring folklore about shipwrecks. Little bays and harbors are indented all along the county's 680-mile-long (1,095km) coastline (one-fifth of the national coastline).

West Cork is known for its enticing and colorful towns. These little towns are great for exploring; there aren't many landmarks or historic sights of note, but they are the genuine article of Irish life. A cluster of artists gives **Ballydehob** a creative flair. At the local butcher, colorful drawings of cattle, pigs, and chickens indicate what's available, and a mural on the outside wall of a pub depicts a traditional music session. Other notable enclaves include the buzzing, seaside town of **Skibbereen** (meaning "little boat harbor"), where live, impromptu traditional music sessions are commonplace in its 22 pubs; the immaculate, flower-box-on-every-sill town of **Clonakilty;** the yachting town **Schull;** and **Barleycove,** a remote, windswept resort that's the last stop before Mizen Head and the sheer cliffs at the island's southernmost tip.

There's no better place to start a tour of County Cork than **Kinsale,** a small harbor town 18 miles (29km) directly south of Cork City. It's a small fishing village with a sheltered semicircular harbor rimmed by hilly terrain and is one of the most darling harbor towns in Europe. Kinsale fits the picture-postcard image of what a charming Irish seaport should look like—narrow, winding streets; well-kept 18th-century houses; imaginatively painted shop fronts; window boxes and street stanchions brimming with colorful flowers; and a harbor full of sailboats. The downside of all this is that the secret is out: Kinsale is a tourist mecca, so add parking problems and tour buses to the list of the city's sights. Considered the gateway to the western Cork seacoast, this compact town of 2,000 residents has also made a big name for itself as the "gourmet capital of Ireland." Home to more than a dozen award-winning restaurants and pubs, Kinsale draws food lovers year-round, particularly in October during the 4-day Gourmet Festival, when the atmosphere in town is especially convivial.

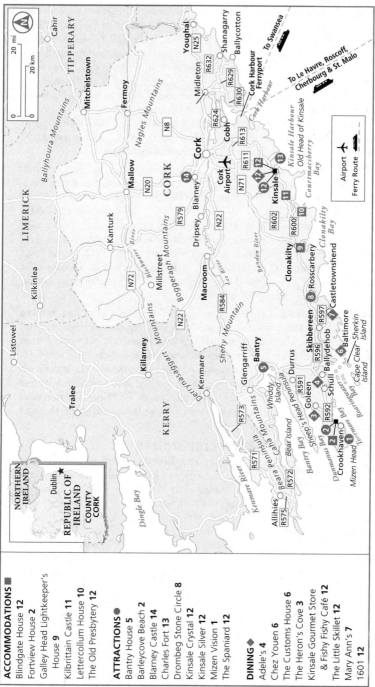

West Cork

ACCOMMODATIONS ■
Blindgate House **12**
Fortview House **2**
Galley Head Lightkeeper's House **9**
Kilbrittain Castle **11**
Lettercollum House **10**
The Old Presbytery **12**

ATTRACTIONS ●
Bantry House **5**
Barleycove Beach **2**
Blarney Castle **14**
Charles Fort **13**
Drombeg Stone Circle **8**
Kinsale Crystal **12**
Kinsale Silver **12**
Mizen Vision **1**
The Spaniard **12**

DINING ◆
Adele's **4**
Chez Youen **6**
The Customs House **6**
The Heron's Cove **3**
Kinsale Gourmet Store & Fishy Fishy Café **12**
The Little Skillet **12**
Mary Ann's **7**
1601 **12**

535

Kinsale is also noteworthy in the history department and shares a special connection to North America. In 1601, the town was the scene of the Battle of Kinsale, a turning point in Irish history. The defeat of the Irish helped to establish English domination. After the battle, a new governor representing the British crown was appointed. His name was William Penn. Ring any bells? For a time, Penn's son (also named William) served in Kinsale as clerk of the admiralty court, but Penn Jr. did not stay long; he was soon off to the New World to found the state of Pennsylvania.

Just off the coast of the Old Head of Kinsale—about 5 miles (8km) west of the town—a German submarine sank the *Lusitania* in 1915. More than 1,500 people were killed, and many are buried in a local cemetery.

VISITOR INFORMATION   The **Kinsale Tourist Office,** Pier Road, Kinsale (✆ 021/477-2234; www.kinsale.ie), is open March through November, Monday to Friday, 9:30am to 5:30pm. The **Skibbereen Tourist Office,** North Street, Skibbereen, County Cork (✆ 028/21766), is open year-round Monday to Friday 9:15am to 5:30pm, with weekend and extended hours May through September. There are seasonal tourist offices operating from May or June through August or September in the Square, **Bantry** (✆ 027/50229); and Rossa Street, **Clonakilty** (✆ 023/33226). The **Beara Tourism & Development Association,** the Square, **Castletownbere** (✆ 027/70054; www.bearatourism. com), is also open during the summer.

GETTING THERE   There's no rail service to West Cork. **Bus Eireann** (✆ 021/450-8188; www.buseireann.ie) operates regular daily service from Cork City to Kinsale and the principal towns in West Cork, but in the interest of time and convenience you're better off renting a car and driving. From Cork City, Kinsale is 18 miles (29km) south on the Airport Road. N71 is the main road into West Cork, and runs through the colorful towns of Clonakilty and Skibbereen. The N71 is the fastest way to get through West Cork, but your journey will be more rewarding and scenic if you take the coastal roads whenever possible.

TOP ATTRACTIONS & SPECIAL MOMENTS

In **Kinsale,** two craft shops not to miss are **Kinsale Crystal,** on Market Street (✆ 021/477-4493; www.kinsalecrystal.ie), and **Kinsale Silver,** on Pearse Street (✆ 021/477-4359; www.iol.ie/~dolan). The former was started in 1991 by a former Waterford Crystal master craftsman, who produces traditional full-lead, mouth-blown, and hand-cut crystal, with personalized engraving. Visitors are welcome to watch the entire fascinating process and admire the sparkling results, which are only sold in this shop; you'll find it nowhere else in Ireland. Kinsale Silver traces its origins back more than 300 years. The Dolan family runs this silversmith workshop where each piece is wrought and forged by hand, using tools of yesteryear.

Try the Murphy's in **1601,** also on Pearse Street (✆ 021/477-2529), named after the year of the Battle of Kinsale. This vintage pub is popular with locals and visitors alike, with three sections: pub, restaurant, and coffeehouse. If you've come to have a pint, head into the intimate back room, where there's a fireplace and seating for only about 50 people. **The Spaniard** (✆ 021/477-2436) is set high on Compass Hill overlooking the harbor and is perhaps Kinsale's most atmospheric pub. Its exterior, with its whitewashed walls and thatched roof is much photographed, and you can have your pint outside at a table while watching the sun set. Inside, low ceilings and seafaring memorabilia create an intimate feel, and there's a fireplace in the main room. Named for Don Juan de Aguila, who rallied his fleet with the Irish in a historic but unsuccessful attempt to defeat the British in 1601, this old pub draws large crowds for live music nightly in the summer, and on weekends at other times of the year. On Sunday year-round, there is a jazz-blues session at 5pm.

Southeast of Kinsale, at the head of the harbor, the coastal landmark of **Charles Fort,** off the Scilly Road, in Summer Cove (© **021/477-2263**), dates from the late 17th century. A classic star-shaped fort, it was constructed to pre-vent foreign naval forces from entering the harbor of Kinsale, then an important trading town. Additions and improvements were made throughout the 18th and 19th centuries, and the fort remained garrisoned until 1921. Across the river is James Fort (1602). Admission is €3.50 ($4) adults, €2.50 ($2.90) seniors and students, €1.25 ($1.45) children, €8.25 ($9.50) family. Tours are available on request. It's open mid-April to mid-October daily 9am to 6pm; mid-October to mid-March weekends 10am to 5pm.

On the R597 between Rosscarbery and Glandore, watch for signs for the **Drombeg Stone Circle.** This ring of 17 standing stones is the finest example of a megalithic stone circle in County Cork. Hills slope gently toward the sea nearby, and the builders could hardly have chosen a more picturesque spot. The circle dates from sometime between 153 B.C. and A.D. 127, but little is known about its ritual purpose. Just west of the circle are the remains of two huts and a cooking place; it is thought that heated stones were placed in a water trough (which can be seen adjacent to the huts), and the hot water was used for cook-ing. The cooking place dates from between the years 368 and 608.

Take the R592 through **Ballydehob,** an artist's haven, and down to **Mizen Head,** the southernmost point on mainland Ireland. On the way out, you'll pass **Barleycove Beach,** one of the most beautiful beaches in southwest Ireland, and a great place to explore. At Mizen Head, the land falls precipitously into the Atlantic breakers in a procession of spectacular 700-foot sea cliffs. A suspension bridge permits access to the old signal station, now a visitor center called **Mizen Vision** (© **028/35115;** www.mizenvision.com), on a small rock promontory. It affords pinch-yourself-it-can't-be-real views of the surrounding cliffs, open sea, and nearby Three Castle Head. Whales, seals, dolphins, porpoises, and daredevil seabirds contribute to the spectacle. No matter what the weather, it's worth a trip. On wild days, tremendous Atlantic waves assault the cliffs; on a clear day, seals bask on the rocks and gannets wheel over the sea and dive into the tranquil waters. Admission costs €4.50 ($5.20) for adults, €3.50 ($4) seniors and stu-dents, €2.50 ($2.90) children, free for children under 5, €14 ($16.10) family. Open April, May, and October daily 10:30am to 5pm; June to September daily 10am to 6:30pm; November to March Saturday to Sunday 12 to 6pm. Closed weekdays November to March.

The town of **Bantry** is on the main Cork-Killarney road through West Cork, the N71. You can't miss it as you drive the road. On the edge of town, the most prominent house in West Cork, **Bantry House** (© **027/50047;** www.bantry house.ie), was built around 1750 for the earls of Bantry. It has a mostly Georgian facade with Victorian additions. Its interior contains many items of furniture and *objects d'art* from all over Europe, including four Aubusson and Gobelin tapes-tries said to have been made for Marie Antoinette. The gardens, with original statuary, are beautifully kept and well worth a stroll. Climb the steps behind the building for a panoramic view of the house, gardens, and Bantry Bay. Admission costs €10 ($11.50) adults, €8 ($9.20) students and seniors, free for children under 14. It's open March 17 to October daily 9am to 6pm. In both the east and west wings of Bantry House, bed-and-breakfast rooms are available; each room is tastefully furnished with reproductions in keeping with the period and style of the house. Prices for bed-and-breakfast, including a tour of the house and gardens, run €220 to €240 ($253–$276) for a double room with private bathroom.

WHERE TO STAY & DINE

Blindgate House ★★, Blind Gate (© 021/477-7858; www.blindgatehouse. com), is a Zen haven amid the bustle of Kinsale town—immensely stylish, inarguably luxurious, and decidedly low-stress. Owner Maeve Coakley and designer Beatrice Blake have combined contemporary dark-wood furnishings, natural fabrics, wood flooring, and serene lighting to achieve an effect that feels wonderfully indulgent and calming. The 11 guest rooms are spacious and elegantly simple, while providing modern conveniences such as satellite TV. Rates are €135 to €160 ($155–$184) double, including breakfast. To get to the inn, follow Pearse Street to Church Street, then turn left at St. Multoge church and go up about 300 yards.

Nearby at 43 Cork St., **The Old Presbytery** ★★ (© 021/477-2027; www. oldpres.com) is a downright darling little guesthouse with an eye for detail and a passion for hospitality. The house is a charming labyrinth of half-staircases and landings, giving each room a private feel (though it can be tricky to trace your way back down to breakfast in the morning). Guest rooms are winningly decorated with brass and cast-iron beds, old armoires, and other auction finds. Breakfasts are especially fabulous. Rooms cost €80 to €140 ($92–$161) for a double, including breakfast.

Open daily for lunch and dinner, **The Little Skillet,** Main Street (© 021/ 477-4202), always makes you feel that you stumbled upon a terrific little find. For starters, it's got a feel-good atmosphere, with a big open hearth and rough stone walls. The kitchen serves up some of the tastiest Irish food you'll find anywhere—stews, Shepherd's pies, champ (mashed potatoes and onions), fresh steamed vegetables, but not a French fry in sight. Main courses run between €15 to €18 ($17.25–$20.70). When they're busy, you wait in the bar across the street and they call you when your table is ready. (You can bring your pint back with you.)

Meanwhile, the **Kinsale Gourmet Store & Fishy Fishy Café** ★★ (© 021/ 477-4453), next to St. Multoge Church in the center of town, is the "It" lunch spot in Kinsale—exactly the sort of hip, relaxed place you wish you had in your hometown. The food is outstanding, prices are fair, and the only apparent drawback is that it's not open for dinner. There's nothing complicated about its success: fresh seafood from the very best local sources, perfectly prepared fresh vegetables, yummy farmhouse cheeses, imaginative salads, and homemade breads. The cold dishes at the counter are wonderful, but Shanahan's culinary talents really shine through with his hot dishes. Be forewarned that the dozen-or-so tables are so very much in demand that a typical lunchtime wait is 30 minutes—go for an early or late lunch to avoid the rush. An average lunch costs €16 to €20 ($18.40–$23) per person.

Three West Cork roads (R600, R601, and R602) converge in Timoleague, which is also where you'll find **Lettercollum House** ★ (© 023/46251; www.lettercollum.ie). In this county overflowing with excellent places to eat, Lettercollum is one of the standard bearers. Owner and chef, Con McLoughlin, creates simple, original Irish Country dishes based on organic produce from the adjacent walled garden, pigs raised on the premises, and locally caught fish. His menu changes daily, and there are always several vegetarian choices. The dining room was once a convent's chapel and a lovely stained-glass window remains. The service is informal in the best way possible, the desserts worth saving room for, and the crowd duly appreciative. The fixed-price 4-course dinner costs €40 ($46) and must be booked several days ahead. It's open daily mid-March to November for dinner 7:30 to 9:30pm, and Sunday lunch 1 to 3pm. In the winter, it's open the same hours but only on weekends.

If you're looking for a moderately priced, honest-to-goodness castle in which to spend the night, **Kilbrittain Castle** ⚔ (© 023/49601), just outside Bandon, fits the bill. Built by the grandson of Brian Boru, high king of Ireland, in 1035, this is the oldest habitable castle in Ireland. Kilbrittain looks and feels like an authentic castle because that's exactly what it is. Climb the steep, winding tower staircase to the great Medieval hallway, and then up another staircase to your room. The history in these walls is the history of Ireland, and spending the night here—in surprising comfort and absolute peace—is a unique experience. The public rooms are full of historical gems, while the guest rooms are spacious, the views enchanting, and the breakfasts generous. Rooms cost €140 ($161) double, including breakfast. It's closed November to April.

Fortview House ⚔⚔, on R591 between Durrus and Goleen (© 028/35324), is a former winner of the Irish Agritourism Award for "best B&B in the South." It boasts pristine country-style rooms, with antique pine furniture, wood floors, iron and brass beds, and crisp Irish linens. Beamed ceilings and a warm color palette add to the comfortable feeling, and the spacious, inviting sitting room, equipped with tea and coffee facilities and an honor-system bar, completes the welcome. Violet Connell's copious breakfasts are legendary. Rooms cost €80 ($92) for a double, including breakfast. It's closed November to February.

Who says pub grub is low on the food chain? **Mary Ann's** ⚔⚔ (© 028/36146), in the adorable, one-lane village of Castletownshend (take R596 from Skibbereen), is one of those darling little places for which you'll thank yourself for making the effort to stop by. Dating from 1844, this rustic pub perched halfway down a hill is decorated with ships' wheels, lanterns, and bells—but you don't go to Mary Ann's for the cute decor. You go for the superlative-inspiring menu of seafood salads and West Cork cheese plates, as well as more ambitious dishes, such as scallops meunière, and sirloin steak with garlic butter. Weather permitting, you can sit outside in the attractive courtyard. Main dishes cost €15 to €20 ($17.25–$23).

The sailing mecca of **Baltimore** is a hot stop on any foodie's tour of West Cork. **The Customs House** ⚔⚔ (© 028/20200), about 150 feet from the Pier, may be the best fish restaurant in Ireland, and is certainly in the top three. Susan Holland is a truly talented chef (not to mention artist—check out her paintings on the walls) who finds inspiration in Mediterranean ingredients but is restrained enough to heighten the fish's flavors without overpowering them. The blackboard menu lists mouthwatering choices such as red mullet with tapenade, grilled squid with hot salsa, and John Dory with spinach, soy, and ginger. Duck also appears on the menu, though it would be a pity to dine here on anything other than fish. Desserts are elegant and simple. The dress code is smart casual, with the emphasis on smart. The fixed-price 3-course dinner costs €25 ($28.75), and the fixed-price 4-course dinner costs €35 ($40.25). It's closed October to mid-March.

> **Moments Living in a Lighthouse**
>
> If you've got 4 days or more to explore West Cork, consider staying in one of the most unique properties we know of. The **Galley Head Light-keepers House** ✦✦ stands next to the lighthouse on the tip of breathtaking Galley Head, just south of Clonakilty. It's actually two connecting houses, which can be rented separately or together. In the first house, the first level has a fully equipped kitchen, sitting room, and lounge/bedroom with bathroom. Upstairs, there are two bedrooms (one double, one twin) and a bathroom. The second house has the same basic floor plan, minus the downstairs lounge and bathroom. Both houses are chockablock with old-world charms—sturdy mahogany furnishings, oversized sofas and armchairs, quality Irish linens, a fireplace in every room, wide plank floors, and deep windowsills with wooden interior shutters.
>
> Its location is idyllic: As remote as you'd hope for from a lighthouse, and still only a 20-minute drive to bustling Clonakilty, a little jewel in West Cork. One of the property's best assets is its caretaker, Gerald Butler, a third-generation lightkeeper (on both sides of his family!) who actually grew up in this house. He's a marvelous storyteller and history buff and can give you a private tour of the lighthouse.
>
> The house can be rented through the **Irish Landmark Trust** (© 01/670-4733; www.irishlandmark.com) for €295 ($339) for 4 nights in low season, sliding up to €800 ($920) per week in high season.

Another pierside institution overlooking the marina of this picturesque harbor town, **Chez Youen** ✦✦ (© 028/20136) has been wooing West Cork since 1978. The decor evokes chef Jacob Youen's native Brittany and is tremendously relaxing, with beamed ceilings, candlelight, colorful pottery, and an open copper fireplace. Lobster is the specialty, fresh from local waters. The chef's signature dish—the one that commands the €40 ($46) price tag—is a mountainous gourmet shellfish platter, which includes Galley Head prawns, Baltimore shrimp, and velvet crab, as well as local lobster and oysters, all served in the shell. The fixed-price dinner costs €30 ($34.50). If you order a la carte, dinner main courses cost €18 to €40 ($20.70–$46). It's closed October to March.

On the Mizen Peninsula, in yet another harbor town called Schull, the tiny establishment **Adele's** ✦✦, on Main Street (© 028/28459), is a hip tearoom by day, serving up delicious baked goods, teas, and excellent sandwiches (the ciabatta with tomato and slabs of local Gubbeen cheese is a real treat). But the place really takes off in the evening, when the upstairs dining room opens and Simon Connor prepares meals with his creative use of basic, local ingredients. The menu changes daily and each dish is so enticing that it's always a challenge to choose: perhaps fresh mussels with angel-hair pasta and leeks, or tagliatelle with rosemary and parsley pesto. Panzanella, a marinated salad with red peppers, capers, and soaked bread crumbs, is a delicious summer appetizer. Lunch averages €10 to €14 ($11.50–$16.10). For dinner, main courses cost €14 to €20 ($16.10–$23). It's closed December to March.

In nearby Goleen, locals know **The Heron's Cove** ★ (© 028/35225; www. westcorkweb.ie/heron), signposted in the center of Goleen, as a terrific seafood restaurant, but it's really what the Irish call a "restaurant with rooms" and a very inviting place to stay. Its three sea-view rooms, with balconies overlooking a beautiful, sheltered cove, are tremendously appealing. The rooms are comfortably furnished, and the atmosphere of the entire B&B is so friendly, it's almost familial. Enjoying a wonderful dinner with wine over sunset and then scampering upstairs to your room for a moonlit view of the harbor is paradise found. Rooms cost €70 ($80.50) double, including full breakfast.

THE RING OF KERRY & KENMARE

For the majority of the literally millions of annual tourists to County Kerry whose explorations follow the turn of a bus driver's wheel, the Iveragh Peninsula is synonymous with the Ring of Kerry, a panorama of seacoast, mountain, and lake-land vistas. It's important to realize, however, that the Ring is a two-lane strip of road measuring roughly 110 miles (178km), tracing the peninsula's shores and missing its tip altogether, while the Iveragh Peninsula itself is nearly 700 square miles (1,813 sq. km) of wild splendor, which you'll notice once you get off the tourist strip. For the most part, the Ring follows N70 and circles the Iveragh Peninsula.

GETTING THERE   There is no InterCity train service within the Ring of Kerry. **Bus Eireann** (© 064/34777; www.buseireann.ie) provides limited daily service from Killarney to Caherciveen, Waterville, Kenmare, and other towns on the Ring. The best way to see the Ring, however, is by car, on the N71, N72, and N70 highways.

TOURIST INFORMATION   The **Kenmare Tourist Office,** Market Square, Kenmare (© 064/41233), is open daily Easter through September, 9:15am to 5:30pm, with extended hours in July and August. The rest of the year (from Oct–Easter), it's open Monday to Saturday.

TOP ATTRACTIONS & SPECIAL MOMENTS

The main reason why so many people "do" the Ring of Kerry is simply the scenery. It's a heartstoppingly gorgeous, magical drive. Most people start and finish at the largest hub, Killarney (see "Killarney," below), but Kenmare makes for a more charming, more classy, and more peaceful base. It's also a hub of great little eateries, so we're including in it our foodie's tour of West Cork and Kerry. The Ring of Kerry drive runs in either direction, but we strongly recommend a counterclockwise route for the most spectacular views. Although it's possible to circle the peninsula in as little as 4 hours, the only way to get a feel for the area and the people is to leave the main road, get out of your car, and explore some of the inland and coastal towns.

Originally called Neidin (pronounced Nay-*deen,* meaning "little nest" in Irish), **Kenmare** is indeed a little nest of verdant foliage nestled between the River Roughty and Kenmare Bay. It's an ideal base for Kerry sightseeing because it is well laid out and immaculately maintained—flower boxes in the windows, litter-free sidewalks—and full of excellent restaurants and places to stay.

Seafari's Eco-nature Cruises and **Seal-Watching Trips** (© 064/83171; www.seafariireland.com) are the very best way to see the Kenmare Bay, on board a 50-foot covered boat. The 2-hour cruises cover 10 miles (16km) and are narrated by well-versed guides who provide information on local history, geography, and geology. The guides frequently point out dolphins, sea otters, gray seals, herons, oyster catchers, and kingfishers. Boats depart from the pier next to the Kenmare suspension bridge. Tickets cost €20 ($23) for adults, €15 ($17.25) students, €10 ($11.50) children under 12, €50 ($57.50) family. It's open May to October 4.

From Kenmare to **Killarney,** the Ring road takes you on N71 through a scenic mountain stretch known as **Moll's Gap.** Don't miss the branch of the **Avoca Handweavers** (℃ **064/34720**), a knitwear and tweed shop spectacularly set on this high mountain pass, 960 feet above sea level. The wares range from colorful hand-woven capes, jackets, throws, and knitwear to pottery and jewelry. It's open mid-March to October.

Killarney is best known for the scenic beauty surrounding the town, and in particular for the spectacular 25,000-acre **Killarney National Park,** which includes the famous **Killarney Lakes** and the scenic **Gap of Dunloe.** The town itself, while colorful and bustling, has become a victim of its own success in recent years. Tourism is more in-your-face here than perhaps anywhere else in Ireland, with generic souvenir shops and overpriced restaurants chockablock.

Departing Killarney, follow the signs on N72 for Killorglin. Once you pass this little town, you're on N70 and vistas of Dingle Bay will soon appear on your right. **Carrantuohill,** at 3,414 feet, Ireland's tallest mountain, is to your left. The open bogland constantly comes into view. From it, the local residents dig pieces of peat, or turf, to burn in their fireplaces. Formed thousands of years ago, the boglands are mainly composed of decayed trees. They tend to be bumpy if you attempt to drive over them too speedily, so be cautious. The Ring winds around cliffs and the edges of mountains, with nothing but the sea below— another reason you will probably average only 30 mph (48kmph), at best. As you go along, you'll notice the remains of many abandoned cottages. They date from the famine years, in the mid-1840s, when the Irish potato crop failed and millions of people starved to death or were forced to emigrate. This peninsula alone lost three-fourths of its population.

The next town on the Ring is **Glenbeigh,** a palm-tree-lined fishing resort with a lovely duned beach called Rossbeigh Strand. You might want to stop here or continue the sweep through the mountains and along the sea's edge to **Cahirciveen.**

From here, you can make a slight detour to partake in **The Skellig Experience** (℃ **066/947-6306**) on Valentia Island (which you may also see spelled "Valencia"). The offshore island is 7 miles (11km) long and one of Europe's westernmost points. Connected to the mainland by a bridge at Portmagee, this was the site from which the first telegraph cable was laid across the Atlantic in 1866. In the 18th century, the Valentia harbor was famous as a refuge for smugglers and privateers; it's said that John Paul Jones, the Scottish-born American naval officer in the War of Independence, also anchored here quite often. The Skellig Experience blends right into the terrain, with a stark stone facade framed by grassy mounds. Inside, through a series of displays and audiovisual presentations, the center offers a detailed look at the area's birds and plant life. In particular, it tells the story of the Skellig Rocks, Skellig Michael, and Little Skellig, islands rising precipitously from the sea, about 8 miles (14km) off the coast of the Iveragh Peninsula. The experience isn't complete without the sea cruise, which circuits the islands. The fee for the exhibition and audiovisual is €4.50 ($5.20) for adults, €4 ($4.60) seniors and students, €2 ($2.30) children under 12. The exhibition, audiovisual, and sea cruise costs €21.50 ($24.70) for

County Kerry

0 ___ 10 mi
0 ___ 10 km

NORTHERN IRELAND

Dublin ★

REPUBLIC OF IRELAND

COUNTY KERRY

CLARE

Shannon Airport ✈

Kilrush

Limerick →

River Shannon

Tarbert Ferryport

Ballybunion

Tarbert

R551

R552

Mouth of the Shannon

Kerry Head

Listowel

LIMERICK

Ballyheige

N69

Ballyheige Bay

R551

N21

Mt Brandon ▲

Tralee Bay

Fenit Spa

Tralee

KERRY

Connor Pass

R560

Blennerville ⑪

Camp

Slieve Mish Mountains

N23

Ballyferriter

DINGLE PENINSULA

Dunquin

Ventry

Annascaul

R561

Castlemaine

Farranfore Airport ✈

R559

Dingle

Inch

Killorglin

Farranfore

Slea Head

Dingle Bay

Caragh Lough

R563

N22

Killarney ①

N72

Gt. Blasket Island

Glenbeigh

R562

Lough Leane

⑩ ⑧ ⑦

Killarney National Park

Ring of Kerry

⑨

⑥

Velentia Island

N70

Carrauntoohil ▲

IVERAGH PENINSULA

⑤

Lough Guitane

N22

Cahirciveen

N71

R569

Macroom

Portmagee ①

R565

N567

MacGillycuddy's Reeks

Kilgarvan

Ballinskelligs

R566

Lough Currane

Ring of Kerry

Kenmare

④

Skellig Rock

Waterville

③

Sneem

Parknasilla

N571

CORK

Caherdaniel ②

Kenmare River

Lauragh

Ballinskelligs Bay

Caha Mountains

Bantry

Clonakilty

Skibbereen

---

adults, €19.40 ($22.30) seniors and students, €12 ($13.80) children under 12. It's open April to October 10am to 6pm.

Head next for **Waterville,** an idyllic spot wedged between Lough Currane and Ballinskelligs Bay off the Atlantic. For years, it was the favorite retreat of Charlie Chaplin. If you follow the sea road north of town out to the Irish-speaking village of **Ballinskelligs,** at the mouth of the bay, you can also catch a glimpse of the two Skellig Rocks.

Continuing on N70, the next point of interest is **Derrynane House National Historic Park** (© 066/947-5113), a 320-acre site between Waterville and Caherdaniel, where Daniel O'Connell, remembered as "the Great Liberator" who freed Irish Catholics from English Penal Laws in 1829, lived for most of his life. The Irish government maintains the house as a museum. It's filled with documents, illustrations, and memorabilia related to O'Connell's life. Admission is €2.75 ($3.15) for adults, €2 ($2.30) seniors, €1.25 ($1.45) students and children. It's open November to March Saturday to Sunday 1 to 5pm; April and October Tuesday to Sunday 1 to 5pm; May to September Monday to Saturday 9am to 6pm, Sunday 11am to 7pm.

Watch for signs to **Staigue Fort,** about 2 miles (3.2km) off the main road. One of the best preserved of all ancient Irish structures, this circular fort is constructed of rough stones without mortar of any kind. The walls are 13 feet thick at the base, and the diameter is about 90 feet. Not much is known of its history, but experts think it probably dates from around 1000 B.C.

Sneem, the next village on the circuit, is a colorful little hamlet with twin parklets. Its houses are painted in vibrant shades of blue, pink, yellow, purple, and orange, like a little touch of the Mediterranean plunked down in Ireland.

As you continue on the Ring, the foliage becomes lusher, thanks to the warming waters and winds of the Gulf Stream. When you begin to see lots of palm trees and other subtropical vegetation, you'll know you are in Parknasilla, once a favorite haunt of George Bernard Shaw. From here, the N70 runs back to Kenmare.

WHERE TO STAY & DINE

Iskeroon ★★ (© 066/947-5119; www.iskeroon.com), David and Geraldine Hare's wonderfully light B&B near the pier in Caherdaniel, is as good as it gets for this price. The place has an arrestingly beautiful setting in a 4.5-acre tropical garden overlooking the sailboats of Derrynane Harbour and the Skelligs beyond. And if the views don't convince you, just step inside. The Hares have renovated their circa-1930s villa in a modern, fresh, Cape Cod style: Think stone floors, a sea-blue and sand palette, baskets and assorted *objets d'art.* It's got the best of both worlds: tranquil and yet just short walk away to the beach or a lovely pub or the pier, for island cruises. Breakfasts are excellent, here, too. With only three rooms, this place gets sold out long in advance, so book early. Rooms cost €110 ($127) for a double, including breakfast. It's open mid-April to September.

In Kenmare, **Shelburne Lodge** ★★, on the Cork Road (© 064/41013), is a fabulous, reasonably priced place to ink into your travel journal. It's a Georgian farmhouse that owners Maura and Tom Foley have transformed into one of the most original, stylish, and comfortable B&Bs on the island. Every room in the house has polished wood parquet floors, truly beautiful (and beautifully arranged) antique furnishings, contemporary artwork, and boldly colored walls. The guest rooms are all large and gorgeously appointed, with particularly sumptuous bathrooms (heated towel racks and handmade mirrors). The breakfasts are nothing short of decadent. Rooms cost €95 to €120 ($109–$138) for a double, including breakfast. It's open May to October.

Hawthorn House ⭐⭐, located on quiet Shelbourne Street in Kenmare (© **064/41035;** www.hawthornhousekenmare.com), is an excellent-value town house B&B that's attracted a huge following over the years. Mary O'Brien is a congenial, gifted hostess; and her guest rooms all have a pretty, feminine feel, with floral bedspreads and pastel walls. Rooms here may be slightly smaller than you'd find at rural B&Bs that were built for this purpose, but they are certainly comfortable. Breakfasts are bountiful and delicious. Rooms cost €70 ($80.50) double, including breakfast. It's open year-round, except Christmas.

Kenmare is truly a foodie's town, and **Mulcahy's** ⭐⭐⭐, 16 Henry St. (© **064/42383**), is a wonderful example of why. Bruce Mulcahy's restaurant is an out-of-the-box experience, from the moment you walk into the postmodern, avant-garde interior through the meal itself, a celebration of imaginative, but serious, fusion cooking. This is that rare combination of style and substance, folks. Starters might include anything from pea soup to sushi. Zingy Asian influences may come to bear on European classics, but everything is done with just the right amount of restraint. Good service and an affable clientele add to the fabulous dining experience. Main courses cost €18 to €23 ($20.70–$26.45).

Innovative continental cuisine is also the focus at **The Lime Tree** ⭐ (© **064/41225**), in an 1821 landmark renovated schoolhouse on Shelbourne Road next to the Park Hotel. Paintings by local artists line the stone walls, and the menu offers such dishes as oak-planked wild salmon, filet of Irish beef with colcannon (mashed potatoes with spring onions), and oven-roasted Kerry lamb. Main courses cost €17 to €25 ($19.55–$28.75). It's open only from April to November.

At **Café Indigo** ⭐⭐ (© **064/42356**), on The Square (above the Square Pint pub), Vanessa Falvey is one of Ireland's hottest young chefs. Her cooking is a model of sophistication and simplicity, using a combination of fresh, local ingredients to bring one strong flavor to the fore. She's especially good with fish and seafood; try the oven-baked salmon complimented by sun-dried-tomato tapenade. The dining room is understated, the food is classy and memorable, the crowd happy. Main courses cost €18 to €23 ($20.70–$26.45). It's open mid-March to mid-January for dinner only.

If you're looking for a stylish place to have a great meal that won't break the bank, **Packie's** ⭐⭐, on Henry Street (© **064/41508**), is it. The smart crowd fits in perfectly with the bistro look—colorful window boxes, stone walls filled with contemporary art, and dark oak tables and chairs. Everyone comes for the food, and chef-owner Maura Foley is known for never serving a bad meal. Her menu includes tried-and-true favorites such as Irish stew, and crab claws in garlic butter. But there are also more creative combinations, such as gratin of crab and prawns, and beef braised in Guinness with mushrooms. Desserts are terrific, too. Main courses cost €14 to €25 ($16.10–$28.75). It's open only from Easter to mid-November.

And, last but not least on your foodie tour, at midday, the **Purple Heather** ⭐⭐, also on Henry Street (© **064/41016**), is *the* place to lunch in Kenmare. The food is all about tearoom classics with a gourmet twist—wild smoked salmon or prawn salad, smoked trout pâté, vegetarian omelets, and Irish cheese platters, as well as homemade soups. All items cost €4 to €17 ($4.60–$19.55). It's closed Christmas week.

5 Killarney

Killarney is the busiest beehive of tourism in Ireland—the Grand Central Station of the southwest, with all the positive and negative connotations that this implies. The town becomes one giant traffic jam of battling tour buses every summer, and a Mecca for pushy jaunting-car (horse-and-buggy) drivers. The locals are well practiced at dispensing a professional brand of Irish charm, and accommodation and restaurant prices are hiked up to capitalize on the hordes descending from the motor coaches. If that's not your scene, it's easy enough to resist Killarney's gravitational pull and instead explore the incredibly picturesque hinterlands that border the town on all sides. You might sneak into town at some point to sample the best of what this tourist megalopolis has to offer.

It's important to remember that the reason Killarney draws millions of visitors a year has nothing to do with the town. It's all about the valley in which the town is nestled, a landscape of lakes and mountains that's so truly spectacular that Brendan Behan once said, "even an ad man would be ashamed to eulogize it." And entering these wonders is ever so easy. Walk from the town car park toward the cathedral, and turn left into **Killarney National Park.** In a matter of minutes, you'll see the reason for all the fuss. During the summer, the evenings are long, the twilight is often indescribable, and you needn't share the lanes. Apart from deer and locals, the park is all yours until dark.

GETTING THERE   **Irish Rail** trains from Dublin's Heuston Station (on the Dublin-Tralee line), Limerick, Cork, and Galway arrive daily at the **Killarney Railway Station,** Railway Road, off East Avenue Road (© **064/31067;** www.irishrail.ie). Check with the booking office for travel times.

Kerry folk like to say that all roads lead to Killarney, and at least a half-dozen major national roads do. They include N21 and N23 from Limerick, N22 from Tralee, N22 from Cork, N72 from Mallow, and N70 from the Ring of Kerry and West Cork. You'll need a car to drive from town to Killarney National Park on the Muckross and Kenmare roads (N71). But once you've done that, this a good place to ditch the rental before returning by train to Dublin.

VISITOR INFORMATION   The **Killarney Tourist Office** is at the Town Centre Car Park, Beech Road (© **064/31633**). To get here from the train station, make a left as you exit and head down Park Road. Keep walking until you hit Main Street; make a left and walk until you spot the office on your left-hand side. It's open October to April Monday to Saturday 9:15am to 1pm and 2:15 to 5:30pm; May Monday to Saturday 9:15am to 5:30pm; June Monday to Saturday 9am to 6pm, Sunday 10am to 1pm and 2 to 6pm; July to August Monday to Saturday 9am to 8pm, Sunday 10am to 1pm and 2 to 6pm; September Monday to Saturday 9am to 6pm, Sunday 10am to 1pm and 2:15 to 6pm. It offers many helpful booklets, including the *Tourist Trail* walking-tour guide and the *Killarney Area Guide,* with maps.

TOP ATTRACTIONS & SPECIAL MOMENTS

Killarney is small, with a full-time population of approximately 7,000. The town is so compact that it has no local bus service. It's built around one central thoroughfare, Main Street, which changes its name to High Street at midpoint. The principal offshoots of Main Street are Plunkett Street, which becomes College Street, and New Street, which, as its name implies, is still growing. The Deenagh River edges the western side of town, and East Avenue Road rims the eastern side. It's all very walkable in an hour or 2. The busiest section of town is at the southern tip of Main Street, where it meets East Avenue Road. Here the road curves and heads southward out to Muckross Road and the entrance to the Killarney National Park.

Killarney's main attraction is the national park and its three storied lakes—the **Lower Lake** (or Lough Leane), the **Middle Lake** (or Muckross Lake), and the **Upper Lake**—myriad waterfalls, rivers, islands, valleys, mountains, bogs, woodlands, and lush foliage and trees, including oak, arbutus, holly, and mountain ash. Large areas of the park are infested with rhododendron bushes, which have grown rampantly to the delight of visitors but the dismay of park rangers, because these runaway rhododendrons thwart the growth of indigenous plant life. There's also a large variety of wildlife, including a rare herd of red deer. You can't explore the park by car, so plan on hiking, biking, or hiring a horse-drawn jaunting car. The park offers four nature trails along the lakeshore.

There's access to the park from several points along the Kenmare road (N71). The main entrance is at **Muckross House & Gardens** (© **064/31440;** www.muckross-house.ie), a focal point of the Middle Lake and, in many ways, of the entire national park. It consists of a gracious ivy-covered Victorian mansion, Muckross House, and its elegant surrounding gardens. Dating from 1843, the 20-room Muckross House has been converted into a museum of County Kerry folk life, showcasing locally carved furniture, prints, maps, paintings, and needlework. Imported treasures such as Oriental screens, Venetian mirrors, Chippendale chairs, Turkish carpets, and curtains woven in Brussels are on display. Also on-site are a restaurant and crafts workshops, where local artisans demonstrate traditional trades such as bookbinding, weaving, and pottery. The adjacent mature gardens, known for their fine collection of rhododendrons and azaleas, are also worth exploring. Very near the Muckross House estate, the 70-acre **Muckross Traditional Farm** is home to displays of traditional farm life and artisans' shops. The farmhouses and buildings are so authentically detailed that visitors feel they are dropping in on working farms and lived-in houses. The animals and household environments are fascinating for visitors of all ages. Farmhands work in the fields and tend the animals, while the blacksmith, carpenter, and wheelwright ply their trades in the old manner. Women draw water

---

Moments Chugging Down the Tracks in Tralee

The commercial center of County Kerry, Tralee, is more a functioning town than a tourist center, but it has one tourist attraction that's of special interest to the rail traveler and makes for an easy excursion out of Killarney. The **Tralee Steam Railway** ⟨⟩⟨⟩, Ballyard (tel] **066/712-1064**), is Europe's westernmost railway. This restored steam train offers narrated, scenic 2-mile (3.2km) trips from Tralee's Ballyard Station to Blennerville. It uses equipment that was once part of the Tralee and Dingle Light Railway (1891–1953), one of the world's most famous narrow-gauge railways.

Round-trip fare costs €5 ($5.75) adults, €3.50 ($4) students and seniors, €2.50 ($2.90) children. Trains depart Blennerville on the half hour (1st departure 10:30am) and depart Tralee on the hour (last departure 5pm) daily from May through October. *Note:* Near the end of every month, the trains are off-track and serviced for a day or 2; call before you visit. To get to Tralee, grab one of the many trains that depart from Killarney (trip time: 40 min.) every day except Sunday.

⎛Moments A Boat Tour of the Lakes

There is nothing quite like seeing the sights from a boat on the lakes of Killarney. Two companies operate regular boating excursions, with full commentary. **M.V. Lily of Killarney Tours** (© 064/31068) and **M.V. Pride of the Lakes Tours** (© 064/32638) both depart from the pier at Ross Castle. Both are enclosed water buses that offer very similar hour-long cruises on the lakes. Tickets cost €8 ($9.20) for adults, €4 ($4.60) for children, €20 ($23) for a family. Each boat has five departures daily, so there's nearly always a cruise about to depart.

---

from the wells and cook meals in traditional kitchens with authentic utensils, crockery, and household items. The ruins of the 15th-century **Muckross Abbey,** founded about 1448 and burned by Cromwell's troops in 1652, are also near the house. The abbey's central feature is a vaulted cloister around a courtyard that contains a huge yew tree, said to be as old as the abbey itself. Admission to the house and garden costs €5.50 ($6.35) for adults, €4.25 ($4.90) seniors, €2.25 ($2.60) students and children. A combination house/garden/farm ticket costs €2.50 ($2.90) extra per person. It's open July and August daily 9am to 7pm; mid-March to June and September to October daily 9am to 6pm; November to mid-March daily 9am to 6pm.

Ross Castle (© **064/35851**) is a 15th-century fortress guarding the edge of the Lower Lake, 2 miles (3.2km) outside Killarney. Built by the O'Donoghue chieftains, the castle distinguished itself in 1652 as the last stronghold in the region to surrender to Cromwell's forces. All that remains today is a tower house, surrounded by a fortified *bawn* (walled garden) with rounded turrets. The tower has been furnished in the style of the late 16th and early 17th centuries, and offers a magnificent view of the lakes and islands from its top. Access is by guided tour only. A lovely lakeshore walk stretches for 2 miles (3.2km) between Killarney and the castle. Admission costs €5 ($5.75) for adults, €3.50 ($4) seniors, €2 ($2.30) students and children. It's open April daily 10am to 5pm; May and September daily 10am to 6pm; June to August daily 9am to 6:30pm; October Tuesday to Sunday 10am to 5pm. Closed November to March.

The most noteworthy of Killarney's islands is **Innisfallen,** or "Fallen's Island," which seems to float peacefully in the Lower Lake. You can reach it by rowboat, available for rental at Ross Castle. St. Fallen founded a monastery here in the 7th century, and it flourished for 1,000 years. It's said that Brian Boru, the great Irish chieftain, and St. Brendan the Navigator were educated here. From 950 to 1320, the "Annals of Innisfallen," a chronicle of early Irish history, was written at the monastery; it's now in the Bodlein Library at Oxford University. Traces of an 11th-century church and a 12th-century priory can still be seen today.

Amid mountains and lakelands, the winding, rocky, incredibly scenic **Gap of Dunloe** is about 6 miles (9.7km) west of Killarney. The route through the Gap passes a kaleidoscope of craggy rocks, massive cliffs, meandering streams, and deep gullies. The road ends at Upper Lake. No trip to the Gap is complete without visiting **Kate Kearney's Cottage** (© **064/44146**), a place of pilgrimage in Killarney and worth a stop if only for tradition's sake. Almost everyone who ventures through the famous Gap pops into this former coaching inn, and it's been that way for more than a century. Elegantly attired Victorians were served illegal poteen (potato moonshine) by Kate herself, who was believed by some to be a witch. From this point on, all cars are left behind and it's into the Gap on foot, horseback, bike, or horse-and-buggy. Today, this outpost 9 miles (15km) west of town is more than a little touristy—a glorified refreshment stop with souvenirs for sale. But from May through September, very good traditional music is performed here on Sunday, Tuesday, and Wednesday from 9 to 11:30pm.

WHERE TO STAY & DINE

Set on its own parklands between the Lower Lake and surrounding mountains, **Castlerosse Hotel and Leisure Centre** (© **800/528-1234** in the U.S., or 064/31114; www.towerhotelgroup.ie), located 2 miles (3.2km) from the heart of town on the Killorglin Road, is a modern, rambling, ranch-style inn next to Killarney's two golf courses. The rooms offer bright, contemporary furnishings and views of the lake, and the notable leisure center has an indoor pool, tennis courts, gym, sauna/steam room, and a 9-hole golf course. Rooms usually cost €130 ($150) double, including breakfast, but special rates are often exclusively available on the hotel's website.

One of Killarney's most attractive guesthouses, the award-winning **Earl's Court House,** Muckross Road (© **064/34009;** www.killarney-earlscourt.ie), is just a 5-minute walk from the town center. On arrival, guests are greeted with tea and scones in a lovely, old-fashioned lounge. The rooms are spacious and furnished with a distinct Victorian flair. Some have half-tester beds, others have sitting areas, and nearly all have balconies. The second-floor rooms, in particular, have clear views of the mountains. Rooms cost €90 to €150 ($104–$173) double, including breakfast.

Coopers Café and Restaurant, Old Market Lane (© **064/37716**), has clearly broken the mold here in Killarney, with its chic, urban, nightclub decor, making the most of glass, stone, aluminum, and sharp black-and-white contrasts. Overhead, the many-tendrilled wire-sculpture chandeliers with flower-cup lights cast a magical fairylike illumination. The total effect is as captivating as the inventive and varied menu, which focuses on local Irish seafood and wild game. Main courses cost €14 to €22 ($16.10–$25.30).

At the **Killarney Manor Banquet,** Loreto Road (© **064/31551**), you can have a five-course dinner in 19th-century style with a complete program of songs, ballads, and dance. It's held in a stately 1840s stone-faced mansion that was built as a hotel and later served as a convent and school. Of course, it's in the nature of these shows to be touristy, which doesn't mean the Irish don't enjoy them every now and then. The performers are talented and really get into it, and people have a good time. The mansion is on a hillside 2 miles (3.2km) south of town overlooking the Killarney panorama. From April through October, the banquet is staged 6 nights a week (usually closed on Sun) starting at 7:45pm. The price is €40 ($46) per person for complete banquet and dinner. If you don't want to eat there, the entertainment-only segment costs €15 ($17.25) and runs from 9 to 10:30pm. Reservations are required; most credit cards accepted.

14

Italy

This boot-shaped peninsula is called *La Bell'Italia* (Beautiful Italy), and so it is, stretching from the Alpine peaks in its north to the offshore island of Sicily. The works left by Leonardo da Vinci, Raphael, Michelangelo, and all the gang are waiting to dazzle you, including the ruins of Rome, the decaying but still magnificent *palazzi* of Venice, or the Renaissance treasures of Florence. You'll find enough Duomos, Madonnas, masterpieces, and scenery to dazzle the eye. And that's not all: Italy is a citadel of style and fashion and serves, at least in the view of Italians, the world's greatest cuisine. Each of the country's 20 regions has its own distinctive kitchen.

In our very limited space, we can only preview some of the highlights of this vast, diversified land, with its more than 5,000 miles (8,046km) of coastline, from the Ligurian Sea in the northwest to the Adriatic Sea washing eastward. The most hurried visitor with a railpass usually confines their itinerary to Rome, Florence, and Venice, and that's not a bad idea, as this trio of cities ranks among the top ten in the world for attractions. Just seeing those cities will easily eat up a week's vacation. And if you have extra time, you can venture into other major cities, such as Milan or Naples, or explore some of Italy's charming towns, such as Pisa and Turin, or the scenic Lake Como. The good news is that visiting these cities by rail is a breeze thanks to a thoroughly improved rail network. And though the cities themselves may not be cheap, rail travel in Italy is relatively inexpensive, making it a good destination for travelers trying to conserve their euros.

HIGHLIGHTS OF ITALY

On international flights, chances are you'll fly into **Rome** to begin your rail journey through Italy, though some people will find themselves flying into Milan (from which you can easily connect to Rome by train or plane). Rome deserves as much of your time as your schedule allows. It is one of the planet's great historical cities and is filled with museums, monuments, and a Roman *joie de vivre* unlike any other city in Italy.

Allow at least 3 or 4 days to skim the highlights. You can divide your time among the ancient, papal, and modern attractions the city has to offer. Visit the Colosseum, the Roman Forum, and Palatine Hill; then take in St. Peter's Basilica and the Sistine Chapel before tossing in a few coins at the Trevi Fountain. And these are just a tiny few of the sights the city has to offer.

After Rome, if you have time for the south, you can take the train to Naples for a day of exploring. If you can spare an extra day, stay overnight and spend the following day wandering around the ruins of **Pompeii** or **Herculaneum.**

Once back in Rome, grab a train north to **Florence,** where a minimum of 3 days is needed to explore the glories of the city of the Renaissance. Here are all the churches, museums, galleries, historic squares, panoramic views, and galleries you would ever want to see, beginning with the masterpieces of the Uffizi

Gallery, one of the world's largest and greatest repositories of art. Other highlights include the multi-colored Duomo or cathedral, Giotto's bell tower, the Palazzo Pitti, Michelangelo's *David* in the Galleria dell'Accademia, the massive Palazzo Vecchio (another Medici residence) opening onto Piazza della Signoria (where you'll want to have a coffee in a cafe), and the Medici Chapels. Walk the Ponte Vecchio, shop at San Lorenzo Market, and look into some of the world's greatest churches to occupy your final day or hours.

From Florence, head northeast by train to **Venice,** the queen of the Veneto and one of the world's most dazzling cities, built on 118 islets linked by 400 bridges with 150 canals cut through the maze. Venice is filled with attractions, including *palazzi* and churches but it is the glorious city itself that is its major allure. It shouldn't exist but does, like a preposterous dream.

After Venice, your rail journey takes you northwest to the sprawling metropolis of **Milan.** You'll need a full day for Milan, capital of Lombardy and a city of glitz and glamour. It doesn't have the attractions of the "royal trio," but is rich

Moments Festivals & Special Events

At the riotous **Carnevale,** theatrical presentations and masked balls take place throughout Venice and on the islands in the lagoon. The balls are by invitation only (except the Doge's Ball), but the street events and fireworks are open to everyone. The festivities take place the week before Ash Wednesday, the beginning of Lent. Contact the **Venice Tourist Office,** San Marco, Giardinetti Reali, Palazzo Selva, 30124 Venezia (© **041/5298711**).

Processions and age-old ceremonies—some from pagan days, some from the Middle Ages—are staged during the **Holy Week observances** held nationwide. The most notable procession is led by the pope, passing the Colosseum and the Roman Forum up to Palatine Hill; a torch-lit parade caps the observance. The events kick off 4 days before Easter Sunday, sometimes at the end of March but often in April.

Palio fever grips the Tuscan hill town of Sienna from early July to mid-August for a wild and exciting horse race that originated in the Middle Ages. Pageantry, costumes, and the celebrations of the victorious *contrada* (sort of a neighborhood social club) mark the spectacle. It's a "no rules" event: Even a horse without a rider can win the race. For details on Il Palio, contact the **Azienda di zienda di Promozione Turistica,** Piazza del Campo 56, 53100 Siena (© **0577/280551**).

in sights, nonetheless, highlighted by its Gothic Duomo, its famous opera house of La Scala; Leonardo's masterpiece, *The Last Supper,* in Santa Maria delle Grazie, and the Brera Palace and Art Gallery, one of northern Italy's greatest showcases of art.

After Milan, all of Italy's lake district, especially Como, is at your doorstep. You can also take the train northwest to the Piedmontese city of **Turin,** famous as the resting place of the controversial Holy Shroud, or else go to the port city of **Genoa,** birthplace of Columbus, to survey its many monuments and to tour its port facilities.

1 Essentials

GETTING THERE

High season on most airlines' routes to Italy is usually June to the beginning of September. This is the most expensive and most crowded time to travel. **Shoulder season** is April to May, early September to October, and December 15 to 24. **Low season** is November 1 to December 14 and December 25 to March 31.

Alitalia (© **800/223-5730;** www.alitalia.com) is the Italian national airline, with nonstop flights to Rome from a number of North American cities. Most flights arrive in either Milan or Rome.

Major North American carriers offering direct flights to Italy include **American Airlines** (© **800/433-7300;** www.aa.com), **Delta** (© **800/241-4141;** www.delta.com), **United** (© **800/241-6522;** www.united.com), **US Airways** (© **800/428-4322;** www.usairways.com), **Continental** (© **800/525-0280;** www.continental.com), and **Air Canada** (© **800/247-2262;** www.aircanada.ca).

British Airways (© 800/AIRWAYS; www.britishairways.com), **Virgin Atlantic Airways** (© 800/862-8621; www.virgin-atlantic.com), **Air France** (© 800/237-2747; www.airfrance.com), **Northwest/KLM** (© 800/374-7747; www.klm.com), and **Lufthansa** (© 800/645-3880; www.lufthansa-usa.com) offer some attractive deals for anyone interested in combining a trip to Italy with a stopover in, say, Britain, Paris, Amsterdam, or Germany.

Depending on your departure city, flying time to Italy ranges from 8 to 12 hours.

ITALY BY RAIL
PASSES
For information on the **Eurailpass, Eurailpass Flexi,** and other multi-country options, see chapter 2. Information on the Italy Flexi Rail Card and **Italy Rail 'n Drive** options is also available in chapter 2. All of these pass options must be purchased in North America and are available through **Rail Europe** (© 877/ 272-RAIL in the U.S., 800/361-RAIL in Canada; www.raileurope.com).

Italy also has a number of other railpasses that can be purchased at most of the country's major train stations. Seniors 60 and over can avail themselves of the **Carta d'Argento** if they present proof of age. Costing 25.80€ ($29.70), this card can be purchased only in Italy, and grants a 15% discount off the price of any first-class or second-class ticket. It's valid for 1 year.

For the same price, a similar pass, **Cartaverde,** also valid for 1 year, grants persons up to 26 years of age a 15% discount in either first- or second-class seats.

Another enticement is the **Carta Club Eurostar,** which costs 77.47€ ($89.10) for a 15% discount on the price of first-class tickets on all trains. It's valid for a year from the date of purchase.

FOREIGN TRAIN TERMS
A station is a *stazione,* and trains are *Espresso,* meaning an express, or *Diretto,* meaning direct. Additional charges are referred to as *supplemento.* These *Diretto* and *Espresso* trains can also be called *Regionali* or *Interregionali.* The train to avoid, especially on long-distance journeys, is a *locali,* which stops at all stations.

Tickets are called *biglietti,* with a single ticket labeled an *andata* or a round-trip *andata e ritorno.* First class is *prima;* second class is *seconda classe.* Ticket offices are called *la biglietteria.* For journeys up to 155 miles (250km), you can often make ticket purchases at newsstands or even a station tobacconist. Such a ticket is called *un biglietto a fascia chilometrica.*

PRACTICAL TRAIN INFORMATION
The train is the way to go in Italy. Train travel is inexpensive, the service is frequent, and the trains among the most modern in Europe. Most Italian trains have been integrated into the state system, and are operated by **Ferrovie dello Stato (FS).** Information on the rail network is available online at **www. ferrovie.it,** but be aware that the website is mainly in Italian. Most trains, except in deep rural areas of the south, are modern and air-conditioned.

Trains provide an excellent means of transport, even if you don't buy the Eurailpass or one of the special Italian Railway tickets (see above). As a rule of thumb, second-class travel usually costs about two-thirds the price of an equivalent first-class trip. That said, unless you're riding Eurostar Italia, you're better off opting for first class when traveling by rail in Italy. The relatively new **Inter-City (IC)** trains are modern, air-conditioned trains that make limited stops when compared to the far slower direct or regional trains (which should be avoided). The best of the Italian trains are unquestionably the high-speed **Eurostar Italia (ES)** trains (don't confuse these with the Eurostar trains that run from Britain to France—they aren't the same!). Using the same tilting technology as the German ICE T and Pendolino trains, these trains are modern, exceptionally comfortable, and though passholders pay a supplement to ride them, they are definitely the way to go in Italy.

Children 4 to 11 receive a discount of 50% off adult fares, and children 3 and under travel free with their parents. Seniors and travelers under age 26 can also purchase discount cards. Contact Rail Europe for more details.

New electric trains (known collectively as **Artesia** trains) have made travel between France and Italy faster and more comfortable than ever. **France's TGVs** travel at speeds of up to 185 miles (297km) per hour and have cut travel time between Paris and Turin from 7 to 5½ hours and between Paris and Milan from 7½ to 6¾ hours. **Italy's ETRs** travel at speeds of up to 145 miles (233km) per hour and currently run between Milan and Lyon (5 hr.), with a stop in Turin.

Tilting **Cisalpino** (*Chee*-sahl-peeno) trains are some of the world's most advanced and speed from northern Italy (primarily Venice, Florence, and Milan) to major cities in Switzerland and Germany. Though aimed mostly at business travelers, they're a great way to get from Italy to Switzerland. Passholders pay a small supplement (worth it!) to ride these trains.

A luxurious **Trenhotel Ellipsos** overnight train (the Salvador Dalí), connects Milan and Turin with Barcelona in Spain. **Artesia de Nuit** trains connect Paris to various cities in Italy. And **EuroNight (EN)** trains service both international and domestic routes.

RESERVATIONS   When you purchase either a single or a round-trip ticket, the validity is for a period of 2 months from the date you bought the ticket. The date you want to travel is stamped on the ticket at the time of purchase, providing you make a seat reservation. Undated tickets purchased at newsstands or from tobacconists need to be validated on the day you plan to take the journey.

Even though reservations are optional on most rail journeys, it's still wise to book a ticket and a seat on runs between such major cities as Florence and Venice, Rome and Naples, or Rome and either Florence or Milan. Italian trains are very crowded on public holidays, and reservations are almost mandatory during these peak periods. Big rail depots, such as the Stazione Termini in Rome, often have separate windows for making reservations—labeled *prenotazioni*. Reservations are mandatory on all ES, Artesia, Cisalpino, and night trains.

If you're traveling at night, it's wise to reserve a *couchette,* especially for long distances, such as the train that goes from Paris to Rome or vice versa. A wide variety of sleeping accommodations are available depending on the night trains that you choose. If you ask for *Superiore* or *Finestrino* when booking, you'll get a top bunk giving you more legroom and greater privacy. When reserving, try not to get a seat next to the corridor, as passengers here are the most likely to get robbed.

If you reserve in advance through Rail Europe, a *couchette* generally costs $28 in either first or second class, whereas a seat reservations goes for $11, unless you're traveling **Eurostar Italia (ES),** which costs $20 in first class or $16 in second class.

Note: Seat reservations are not always marked on seats and some people may try and claim your reserved seat as their own. Firmly but politely insist they

Trains & Travel Times in Italy

From	To	Type of Train	# of Trains	Frequency	Travel Time
Rome	Brindisi	Eurostar Italia	3	Daily	5 hr. 53 min.–6 hr.
Rome	Florence	Eurostar Italia	15	Daily	1 hr. 35 min.
Rome	Milan	Eurostar Italia	13	Daily	4 hr. 30 min.
Rome	Naples	Eurostar Italia	9	Daily	1 hr. 35 min.
Rome	Palermo	InterCity	1	Daily	11 hr.
Rome	Venice	Eurostar Italia	7	Daily	4 hr. 32 min.
Naples	Pompeii	InterCity	1	Daily	23 min.

vacate (and if you haven't reserved and sit in an apparently unreserved seat, be advised that you may actually be sitting in someone else's seat).

SERVICES & AMENITIES   Most InterCity trains have facilities for persons with limited mobility. There are dining facilities on all major trains; however, prices are lethal. If you're on a strict budget, do as the Italians do and pack your own picnic for consumption while riding the rails and taking in the scenery. It's a great way to travel. ES trains offer better seating and are one of the only domestic trains in Italy where second-class travel won't be a less-grand experience than first class. First-class passengers on ES trains get a free drink and snack served at their seats; second-class passengers get a free snack.

Overnight accommodations on Italian trains range from "Gran Class" single-sleeper cabins with private bathrooms and showers on the Ellipsos hotel train from Milan to Barcelona, to 6-berth economy couchettes on the Artesia de Nuit trains from Paris to Rome, to reclining sleeperette seats on EuroNight trains from Rome to Venice. Note that although sleeper cabins are segregated by sex (except for families taking a whole cabin), couchettes are not segregated by sex. Almost all night trains have a dining car that offers full restaurant service or sells snacks. First-class sleeper cabins usually include a meal in their rates. All sleeping accommodations (except for sleeperette seats on many EN trains) require additional supplements in addition to your railpass—and must be reserved well in advance. We recommend reserving before you leave home if possible. Note that to reserve some classes of sleeper cabins, you'll need to have a first-class railpass.

Warning: Theft on some Italian trains is a problem. If you opt for a couchette or sleeperette on an Italian train, make sure your belongings are well secured.

FAST FACTS: Italy

Area Code   The country code for Italy is **39**. Today, city codes (or area codes for cities) have been folded into each phone number. Therefore, you must dial the whole number, whether you're calling from outside or inside Italy or even within a city such as Rome itself.

Climate   It's warm all over Italy in summer; it can be very hot in the south, especially inland. The high temperatures (measured in Italy in degrees Celsius) begin in Rome in May, often lasting until sometime in October. Winters in the north of Italy are cold, with rain and snow, but in the south the weather is warm year-round, averaging 50°F (10°C) in winter. For the most part, it's drier in Italy than in North America, so high temperatures don't seem as bad because the humidity is lower. In Rome, Naples, and the south, temperatures can stay in the 90s for days, but nights are most often comfortably cooler.

Documents Required U.S. and Canadian citizens with a **valid passport** don't need a visa to enter Italy if they don't expect to stay more than 90 days and don't expect to work there. If after entering Italy you want to stay more than 90 days, you can apply for a permit for an extra 90 days, which as a rule is granted immediately. Go to the nearest *questura* (police headquarters) or to your home country's consulate. If your passport is lost or stolen, head to your consulate as soon as possible for a replacement.

Electricity The electricity in Italy varies considerably. It's usually alternating current (AC), varying from 42 to 50 cycles. The voltage can be anywhere from 115 to 220. It's recommended that any visitor carrying electrical appliances obtain a transformer. Check the exact local current at the hotel where you're staying. Plugs have prongs that are round, not flat; therefore, an adapter plug is also needed.

Embassies & Consulates In case of an emergency, embassies have a 24-hour referral service.

The **U.S. Embassy** is in Rome at Via Vittorio Veneto 119A (✆ **06/46741;** fax 06/46742217). **U.S. consulates** are in Florence, at Lungarno Amerigo Vespucci 38 (✆ **055/2398276;** fax 055/284088), and in Milan, at Via Principe Amedeo 2-10 (✆ **02/29035141**). There's also a consulate in Naples on Piazza della Repubblica 1 (✆ **081/5838111**). The consulate in Genoa is at Via Dante 2 (✆ **010/584492**). For consulate hours, see individual city listings.

The **Canadian Consulate** and passport service is in Rome at Via Zara 30 (✆ **06/445981**). The **Canadian Embassy** in Rome is at Via G. B. de Rossi 27 (✆ **06/445981**). The Canadian Consulate in Milan is at V.V. Pisani 19 (✆ 02/67581).

Health & Safety Italy has a low rate of violent crime, little of which is directed toward tourists. Petty crimes such as pickpocketing, theft from parked cars, and purse snatching, however, are serious problems, especially in large cities. Most reported thefts occur at crowded tourist sites, on public buses or trains, or at the major railway stations: Rome's Termini, Milan's Centrale, Florence's Santa Maria Novella, and Naples' Centrale. Clients of Internet cafes in major cities have been targeted. Elderly tourists who have tried to resist petty thieves on motor scooters have suffered broken arms and collarbones.

On trains, a commonly reported trick involves one or more persons who pretend to befriend a traveler and offer drugged food or drink. Also, thieves have been known to impersonate police officers to gain the confidence of tourists. The thief shows the prospective victim a circular plastic sign with the words "police" or "international police." If this happens, the tourist should insist on seeing the officer's identification card *(documento)*, as impersonators tend not to carry forged documents.

Tourists should immediately report thefts or other crimes to the local police.

Medical facilities are available, but may be limited outside urban areas. Public hospitals sometimes do not maintain the same standards as hospitals in the United States, so travelers are encouraged to obtain insurance that would cover a stay in a private Italian hospital or clinic. It is almost impossible to obtain an itemized hospital bill from public hospitals, as required by many U.S. insurance companies, because the Italian National Health Service charges one inclusive rate (care services, bed, and board).

Holidays Offices and shops in Italy are closed on the following **national holidays:** January 1 (New Year's Day), Easter Monday, April 25 (Liberation Day), May 1 (Labor Day), August 15 (Assumption of the Virgin), November 1 (All Saints' Day), December 8 (Feast of the Immaculate Conception), December 25 (Christmas Day), and December 26 (Santo Stefano).

Closings are also observed in the following cities on **feast days** honoring their patron saints: Venice, April 25 (St. Mark); Florence, Genoa, and Turin, June 24 (St. John the Baptist); Rome, June 29 (Sts. Peter and Paul); Palermo, July 15 (St. Rosalia); Naples, September 19 (St. Gennaro); Bologna, October 4 (St. Petronio); Cagliari, October 30 (St. Saturnino); Trieste, November 3 (St. Giusto); Bari, December 6 (St. Nicola); and Milan, December 7 (St. Ambrose).

Legal Aid The consulate of your country is the place to turn for legal aid, although offices can't interfere in the Italian legal process. They can, however, inform you of your rights and provide a list of attorneys. You'll have to pay for the attorney out of your pocket—there's no free legal assistance. If you're arrested for a drug offense, about all the consulate will do is notify a lawyer about your case and perhaps inform your family.

Mail Mail delivery in Italy is notoriously bad. Your family and friends back home might receive your postcards in 1 week, or it might take 2 weeks (sometimes longer). Postcards, aerogrammes, and letters weighing up to 20 grams sent to the United States and Canada cost .75€ (85¢). Stamps *(francobolli)* can be bought at *tabacchi* (tobacco stores) as well as post offices. You can buy special stamps at the **Vatican City Post Office,** adjacent to the information office in St. Peter's Square; it's open Monday through Friday from 8:30am to 7pm and Saturday from 8:30am to 6pm. Letters mailed at Vatican City reach North America far more quickly than mail sent from elsewhere for the same cost.

Police & Emergencies Dial ℂ **113** for ambulance, police, or fire. In case of a breakdown on an Italian road, dial ℂ **800/116800** at the nearest telephone box; the nearest Automobile Club of Italy (ACI) will be notified to come to your aid.

Telephone To call Italy from the United States, dial the **international prefix, 011;** then Italy's **country code, 39;** and then the the actual **phone number** (which has a city code built in).

A **local phone call** in Italy costs around .08€ (10¢). **Public phones** accept coins, precharged phone cards (*scheda* or *carta telefonica*), or both. You can buy a *carta telefonica* at any *tabacchi* (tobacconists; most display a sign with a white *T* on a brown background) in increments of 5€ ($5.75), 10€ ($11.50), and 20€ ($23). To make a call, pick up the receiver and insert .10€ (15¢) or your card (break off the corner first). Most phones have a digital display that will tell you how much money you've inserted (or how much is left on the card). Dial the number, and don't forget to take the card with you after you hang up.

To make a **collect or calling-card call** from a public phone, drop in .10€ (10¢) or insert a phone card (see above) and dial one of the following access numbers to reach an American operator or an English-language voice prompt: **AT&T** ✆ **1721011** (if calling a country other than the United States, after the access code dial 01, the country code of country you are calling, city code, and local number), **MCI** ✆ **172-10-22**, and **Sprint** ✆ **1721877**.

To call the free **national telephone information** (in Italian) in Italy, dial ✆ **12. International information** is available at ✆ **176** but costs .60€ (70¢) a shot.

Tipping In **hotels,** the service charge of 15% to 19% is already added to a bill. In addition, it's customary to tip the chambermaid .50€ (60¢) per day, the doorman (for calling a cab) .50€ (60¢), and the bellhop or porter 1.50€ to 2.50€ ($1.75–$2.90) for carrying your bags to your room. A concierge expects about 15% of his or her bill, as well as tips for extra services performed, which could include help with long-distance calls.

In **restaurants and cafes,** 15% is usually added to your bill to cover most charges. If you're not sure whether this has been done, ask, *"È incluso il servizio?"* (ay een-*cloo*-soh eel sair-*vee*-tsoh?). An additional tip isn't expected, but it's nice to leave the equivalent of an extra couple of dollars if you've been pleased with the service. Checkroom attendants expect .75€ (85¢), and washroom attendants should get .50€ (60¢). Restaurants are required by law to give customers official receipts. Taxi drivers expect at least 15% of the fare.

2 Rome

The city of Rome is simultaneously strident, romantic, and sensual. And although the romantic poets would probably be horrified at today's traffic, pollution, overcrowding, crime, political discontent, and barely controlled chaos of modern Rome, the city endures and thrives in a way that is called "eternal."

It would take a lifetime to know a city filled with 27 centuries of artistic achievement. A cradle of Western civilization, Rome is timeless with its ancient history, art, and architecture, containing more treasures per square foot than any other city in the world. Caesar was assassinated here, Charlemagne crowned, and the list of the major events goes on and on.

In between all that absorption of culture and history, take time to relax and meet the Romans. Savor their succulent pastas while enjoying a fine glass of wine on one of the city's splendid squares where one of the reigning Caesars might have gone before you, or perhaps Michelangelo or Raphael.

For the rail traveler, Rome, though too far south to be considered truly central, is easily reached by rail, and its ultra modern **Stazione Termini** is well connected to most other Italian cities, as well as several major European destinations. It's unquestionably the best starting point for a rail trip of Italy and makes an excellent starting or terminal point for a rail tour of Europe.

STATION INFORMATION
GETTING FROM THE AIRPORT TO THE TRAIN STATION
The gateway for most visitors beginning a rail journey of Italy is **Leonardo da Vinci Airport** (✆ **06/65951**), also called Fiumicino.

After you leave Passport Control, you'll see two **information desks** (one for Rome, one for Italy). At the Rome desk, you can pick up a general map and some pamphlets Monday to Saturday 8:30am to 7pm; the staff can also help you find a hotel room if you haven't reserved ahead. A *cambio* (money exchange) operates daily 7:30am to 11pm, offering surprisingly good rates.

There's a **train station** in the airport. To get into the city, follow the signs marked TRENI for the 30-minute shuttle to Rome's main station, **Stazione Termini** (arriving on Track 22). The shuttle runs 7am to 11:30pm for 8.80€ ($10.10) one-way. On the way, you'll pass a machine dispensing tickets, or you can buy them in person near the tracks if you don't have small bills on you. When you arrive at Termini, get out of the train quickly and grab a baggage cart. (It's a long schlep from the track to the exit or to the other train connections, and baggage carts can be scarce.)

A **taxi** from Da Vinci airport to the city costs 45€ ($51.75) and up for the 1-hour trip, depending on traffic. The expense might be worth it if you have a lot of luggage or just don't want to be bothered with the train trip. Call ✆ **06/6645,** 06/3570, or 06/4994 for information.

INSIDE THE STATION
Trains and buses (including trains from the airport) arrive in the center of old Rome at the silver **Stazione Termini,** Piazza dei Cinquecento (✆ **800/431784**); this is the train, bus, and subway transportation hub for all Rome and is surrounded by many hotels (especially cheaper ones). If you're taking the **Metropolitana (subway),** follow the illuminated red-and-white M signs. To catch a bus, go straight through the outer hall and enter the sprawling bus lot of **Piazza dei Cinquecento.** You'll also find **taxis** there.

The Roma Termini is a virtual city within a city. On the lower level of the two-level station is a vast array of services such as a drugstore, ATMs, clothing shops, fast food, lounges, hairdressers, a bookstore, barbershops, and even public showers. On site is a **tourist office** (✆ **06/48906300**), open daily 8:15am to 7:15pm. You can get minor data here, but for hotel reservations go to the kiosk across from track no. 20, open daily 7am to 10pm. A deposit is taken from you (the amount based on your selection of hotel), and you're supposed to arrive at your selected hotel within the hour. There's always a line but you can pick up one of the nearby phones and make a reservation for free by dialing ✆ **06/6991000.**

A **24-hour luggage storage** office is located near track no. 1. **Train information** is available from three computer touch screens at tracks 1, 9, and 22 in the center of the station. Train reservations are made at ticket windows no. 30 to no. 45. Windows no. 30 to no. 38—*Prenotazioni Posti–WL–Cuccette–Pendolino*—make reservations and arrange sleeper and *couchette* reservations. Windows no. 7 to no. 29—*biglietti Ordinari e Ridotti*—actually sell tickets. **Informazioni ferroviarie** (in the outer hall) dispenses information on rail travel to other parts of Italy.

Rome

ACCOMMODATIONS ■
Albergo Santa Chiara **4**
Casa Howard **16**
Hotel Adriano **6**
Hotel Columbia **34**
Hotel des Artistes **21**
Hotel dei Mellini **10**
La Residenza **17**
Medici **20**
Villa delle Rose **22**

DINING ◆
Césarina **14**
Colline Emiliane **18**
Dal Bolognese **11**
F.I.S.H. **24**
Girarrosto Toscano **9**
Hostaria Nerone **25**
La Cisterna **1**
L'Eau Vive **3**
Piperno **2**
Taverna Flavia **19**
Trattoria San Teodoro **27**

ATTRACTIONS ●
Arch of Constantine **30**
Basilica di San Giovanni in Laterano **33**
Basilica di San Pietro **7**
Campidoglio, Palazzo dei
      Conservatori and Museo Capitolino **26**
The Colosseum **31**
Domus Aurea **32**
Foro Imperiali (Imperial Forum) **28**
Foro Romano (Roman Forum)
      and Palatine Hill **29**
Galleria Borghese **13**
Museo Nazionale di Villa Giulia **12**
Musei Vaticani (Vatican Museums)
      and Sistine Chapel **8**
Pantheon **5**
Spanish Steps **15**
Trevi Fountain **23**

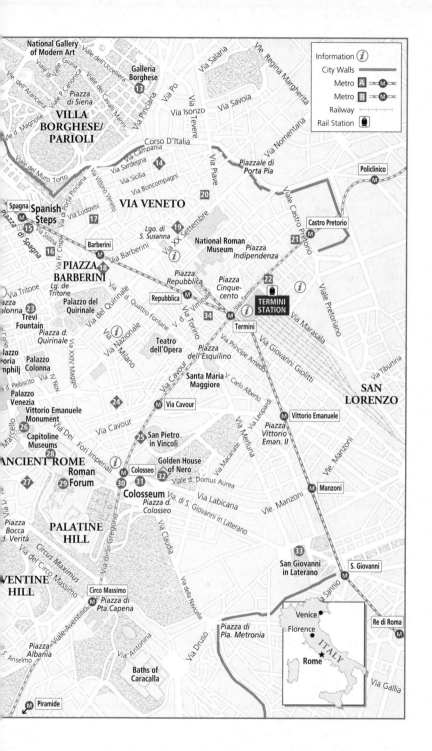

National Gallery
of Modern Art

Galleria
Borghese
13

Viale dell'Uccelliera

Via Salaria

Vle. Regina Margherita

Via Po

Via Savoia

Via Isonzo

Via Pinciana

*Piazza
di Siena*

**VILLA
BORGHESE/
PARIOLI**

Vle. d. Magnolie

Viale dell'Aranciera

Corso D'Italia

Via Nomentana

Via Campania

Via Sardegna

14

*Piazzale di
Porta Pia*

Policlinico
Ⓜ

Viale del Muro Torto

Via Sicilia

Via Boncompagni

Via Piave

Viale Castro Pretorio

Spagna
Ⓜ Spanish
Steps
15

VIA VENETO

20

Castro Pretorio
Ⓜ

Via Ludovisi

*Lgo. di
S. Susanna* **19**

*Piazza
di Spagna*

16

Barberini
Ⓜ

17

Via XX Settembre

**National Roman
Museum**

*Piazza
Indipendenza*

21

**PIAZZA
BARBERINI 18**

*Lg. de
Tritone*

Via Barberini

*Piazza
Repubblica*

*Piazza
Cinque-
cento*

22
ⓘ

Via Marasala

Via Tritone

Repubblica
Ⓜ

**Trevi
Fountain**

*Palazzo del
Quirinale*

34

**TERMINI
STATION**

Via Pretoriano

*Piazza
Colonna* **23**

*Piazza d.
Quirinale*

Via Nazionale

Via d. Quattro Fontane

Via Torino

Termini
Ⓜ

Via Giovanni Giolitti

*Palazzo
oria
mphilj*

*Palazzo
Colonna*

*Teatro
dell'Opera*

*Piazza
dell'Esquilino*

Via Principe Amedeo

**SAN
LORENZO**

Via Tiburtina

*Palazzo
Venezia*

**Vittorio Emanuele
Monument**

24

Via Cavour

**Santa Maria
Maggiore**

V. Carlo Alberto

Vittorio Emanuele
Ⓜ

Via Leopardi

26

Via Cavour
Ⓜ

*Piazza
Vittorio
Eman. II*

Vle. Manzoni

*Capitoline
Museums*

28

ANCIENT ROME

Roman
29 *Forum*
ⓘ

25 **San Pietro
in Vincoli**

Colosseo
Ⓜ

**Golden House
of Nero**

Viale d. Domus Aurea

Via Macanate

Via Merluna

Vle. Manzoni

Manzoni
Ⓜ

27

30 31

32

Colosseum *Via. di S. Giovanni in Laterano*

*Piazza d.
Colosseo*

Via Labicana

**PALATINE
HILL**

*Piazza
Bocca
d. Verità*

Circus Maximus

Via Claudia

Via della Navicella

33

**San Giovanni
in Laterano**

S. Giovanni
Ⓜ

**VENTINE
HILL**

Circo Massimo
Ⓜ

*Piazza di
Pta. Capena*

Via Sannio

*Piazza
Albania*

Viale Aventino

Via Antonina

*Piazza di
Pla. Metronia*

Via Druso

**Baths of
Caracalla**

Via Gallia

Ⓜ **Piramide**

Information ⓘ
City Walls ━━━
Metro Ⓐ ▬Ⓜ▬
Metro Ⓑ ▬Ⓜ▬
Railway ╂╂╂╂╂
Rail Station 🚉

Venice ●

Florence ●

Rome ★ **ITALY**

Re di Roma
Ⓜ

INFORMATION ELSEWHERE IN THE CITY

The chief tourist office is the **Azienda Provinciale di Turismo (APT)** at **Via Parigi 5** (℃ **06/36004399**). The headquarters are open Monday to Saturday 9am to 7:15pm.

More helpful are the offices maintained by the **Comune di Roma** at various sites around the city. They're staffed daily 9:30am to 7:30pm and dispense maps and brochures. Here are the addresses and phone numbers: in Piazza dei Cinquecento, outside Termini (℃ **06/47825194**); in Piazza Pia, near the Castel Sant'Angelo (℃ **06/68809707**); in Piazza San Giovanni, in Laterano (℃ **06/77203535**); along Largo Carlo Goldoni, near the intersection of Via del Corso and Via Condotti (℃ **06/68136061**); on Via Nazionale, near the Palazzo delle Esposizioni (℃ **06/47824525**); on Largo Corrado Ricci, near the Colosseum (℃ **06/69924307**); on Piazza Sonnino in Trastevere (℃ **06/58333457**); on Piazza Cinque Lune, near Piazza Navona (℃ **06/68809240**); and on Piazza Santa Maria Maggiore (℃ **06/4740955**).

GETTING AROUND

BY PUBLIC TRANSPORTATION   The **Metropolitana,** or **Metro,** for short, is the fastest means of transportation, operating daily 5:30am to 11:30pm. A big red M indicates the entrance to the subway. Tickets are .77€ (90¢) and are available from *tabacchi* (tobacco shops), many newsstands, and vending machines at all stations. Some stations have managers, but they won't make change. Booklets of tickets are available at tabacchi and in some terminals. *Tip:* Avoid riding the trains when the Romans are going to or from work or you'll be mashed flatter than fettuccine.

Roman buses are operated by **ATAC (Azienda Tramvie e Autobus del Comune di Roma),** Via Volturno 65 (℃ **06/46951** for information). For .77€ (90¢) you can ride to most parts of Rome, although it can be slow going in all that traffic and the buses are often very crowded. Your ticket is valid for 75 minutes, and you can get on many buses and trams during that time by using the same ticket. Buy bus tickets in tabacchi or bus terminals. You must have your ticket before boarding because there are no ticket-issuing machines on the vehicles.

Buses and trams stop at areas marked FERMATA. At most of these, a yellow sign will display the numbers of the buses that stop there and a list of all the stops along each bus's route in order, so you can easily search out your destination. Bus service runs from 5:30am to midnight, and the night service is from 12:10 to 5:30am; an N after the line number defines buses running at night. It's best, however, to take a taxi in the wee hours—if you can find one. At the **bus information booth** at Piazza dei Cinquecento, in front of the Stazione Termini, you can purchase a directory complete with maps summarizing the routes.

Although routes change often, a few old reliable routes have remained valid for years, such as **no. 27** from Stazione Termini to the Colosseum, **nos. 75 and 170** from Stazione Termini to Trastevere, and **no. 492** from Stazione Termini to the Vatican. But if you're going somewhere and are dependent on the bus, be

---

Value Traveler's Tip

At Stazione Termini, you can buy a special **tourist pass,** which allows you to ride on the ATAC network and the Metro. It costs 3.10€ ($3.55) for a day or 12.40€ ($14.25) for a week.

sure to carefully check where the bus stop is and exactly which bus goes there—
don't assume that it'll be the same bus the next day.

BY TAXI   Don't count on hailing a taxi on the street or even getting one at a
stand. If you're going out, have your hotel call one. At a restaurant, ask the
waiter or cashier to dial for you. If you want to phone for yourself, try one of
these numbers: © **06/6645,** 06/3570, or 06/4994. The meter begins at 3€
($3.45) for the first 3km (2 miles) and then rises .75€ (85¢) per kilometer.
Every suitcase costs 3€ ($3.45), and on Sunday a 1.05€ ($1.20) supplement is
assessed. There's another 2.50€ ($2.90) supplement 10pm to 7am.

WHERE TO STAY

Albergo Santa Chiara   This is one of the best located hotels in the inner core
of historic Rome, right in back of the Pantheon and opening onto the Piazza
della Minerva. In charge since 1838, the Corteggiani family has kept one of the
most ancient hotels in Rome up-to-date with extensive renovations. Marble
columns evoke the elegance of yesterday. The comfortable and well-maintained
bedrooms are furnished with classic simplicity and range in size from the very
small to the very large, the latter spacious enough to be classified as Roman
apartments. If you face Piazza della Minerva, you'll have a grand view, but you
can also anticipate noise late at night.

Via Santa Chiara 21, 00186 Roma. © **06/6872979.** Fax 06/6873144. www.albergosantachiara.com. 98
units. 178€–233€ ($205–$268) double; 365€–415€ ($420–$477) junior suite. Rates include breakfast. AE,
DC, MC, V. Metro: Piazza di Spagna. **Amenities:** Bar; laundry; room for those with limited mobility. *In room:*
Hair dryer.

Casa Howard ★★ *Finds*   It's rare to make a new discovery in the tourist-
trodden Spanish Steps area, which is why Casa Howard comes as a pleasant surprise. The little B&B occupies about two-thirds of the second floor of a historic
structure in an ideal location for shoppers. The welcoming family owners maintain beautifully furnished guest rooms, each with its own private bathroom
(although some bathrooms lie outside the bedrooms in the hallway). The Pink
Room is the most spacious, with its own en suite bathroom. Cristy at reception
can "arrange anything" in Rome for you and will also invite you to use the
house's private Turkish *hammam* (steam bath).

Via Capa le Case 18, 00187 Roma. © **06/69924555.** Fax 06/6794644. www.casahoward.com. 160€–190€
($184–$219) double. MC, V. Metro: Piazza di Spagna. **Amenities:** Bar; laundry. *In room:* Hair dryer.

Hotel Adriano ★   Stay here if you want affordable elegance and top-notch
living in a converted palace from the 15th century that's close to the Spanish
Steps, the Piazza Navona, and the Pantheon. Even some members of the Italian
Parliament, which is nearby, check in here. Bedrooms are simply furnished but
tasteful, with excellent beds usually resting on hardwood floors. You can enjoy
breakfast on the hotel's roof terrace.

Via di Pallacorda 2, 00186 Roma. © **06/68802451.** Fax 06/68803926. www.hoteladriano.com. 82 units.
190€ ($219) double, 220€ ($253) suite. Rates include breakfast. AE, DC, MC, V. Bus: 95, 175. **Amenities:**
Bar; laundry; 1 room for those with limited mobility.

Hotel Columbia ★★ *Finds*   This is one of the newest hotels in the neighborhood, with a hardworking multilingual staff. Originally built around 1900, the
hotel underwent a successful, radical renovation in 1997. The interior contains
Murano chandeliers and conservatively modern furniture. The compact and
cozy guest rooms have shower-only bathrooms and compare well against the

accommodations in the best hotels nearby. The appealing roof garden has a view over the surrounding rooftops.

Via del Viminale 15, 00184 Roma. © **06/4744289** or 06/4883509. Fax 06/4740209. www.venere.it/roma/columbia. 45 units. 144€–195€ ($166–$224) double. Rates include buffet breakfast. AE, DC, MC, V. Metro: Repubblica. **Amenities:** Bar; laundry; nonsmoking rooms. *In room:* Hair dryer.

Hotel des Artistes *(Value* A few steps from Termini Station, this hotel was completely renovated in 1997 and is still looking good. Asian carpets and velvet draperies along with spotless maintenance have made this one of the best values in the area. Mahogany furnishings, marble-clad bathrooms, and such extras as air-conditioning help make this a worthy choice. For the really frugal rail traveler, one part of the hotel is actually a hostel with dormitory-style rooms, bathrooms in the corridors, and a TV in each room. Charges for these units range from 65€ to 98€ ($74.75–$113) in a triple and are the best deal in the Termini area. The rooftop garden at night is a magnet to guests.

Via Villafranca 20, 00185 Roma. © **06/4454365.** Fax 06/4462368. www.hoteldesartistes.com. 45 units. 90€–165€ ($104–$190) double. Rates include buffet breakfast. AE, DC, MC, V. Metro: Castro Pretorio. Bus: 310. **Amenities:** Bar; nonsmoking rooms. *In room:* Hair dryer.

Hotel dei Mellini ✿ Pilgrims planning to explore the Vatican area can splurge on this hotel situated on the right bank of the Tiber between the Spanish Steps and St. Peter's Basilica. It's the most popular address in Rome for visiting actors and entertainers. The handsome public rooms are tastefully elegant. Guest rooms are spacious and have a classic Art Deco styling in their choice of furnishings and fixtures, including beautiful private bathrooms. Its roof terrace is one of the most charming in Rome, opening onto panoramic nighttime views of the floodlit city.

Via Muzio Clementi 81, 00193 Roma. © **06/324771.** Fax 06/32477801. www.hotelmellini.com. 80 units. 320€–350€ ($368–$403) double; from 420€ ($483) suite. Rates include breakfast. AE, DC, MC, V. Metro: Lepanto. **Amenities:** Restaurants for guests; bar; laundry; nonsmoking rooms. *In room:* Hair dryer.

La Residenza ✿✿ In a glamorous location (admittedly far from the Termini area) 10 minutes from the Spanish Steps, this little hotel successfully combines intimacy and elegance. A bit old-fashioned and homey, the converted villa has an ivy-covered courtyard and a series of grand public rooms with Empire divans, oil portraits, and rattan chairs. Terraces are scattered throughout. The guest rooms are generally spacious, containing bentwood chairs and built-in furniture, including beds. The dozen or so junior suites boast balconies. The bathrooms have robes and even come equipped with ice machines.

Via Emilia 22–24, 00187 Roma. © **06/4880789.** Fax 06/485721. www.hotel-laresidenza.com. 29 units. 180€–195€ ($207–$224) double; 207€–223€ ($238–$256) suite. Rates include buffet breakfast. AE, MC, V. Metro: Piazza Barberini. **Amenities:** Laundry; nonsmoking rooms. *In room:* Hair dryer.

Medici Near Termini and the shops along Via XX Settembre, this massively renovated hotel dates from 1906 when it was built to house passengers arriving by rail in Rome. Many of its better rooms overlook an inner patio garden. Rooms are a generous size and in a classic Roman style. The cheapest rooms are called standard; superior units offer air-conditioning, more antiques, and better furnishings.

Via Flavia 96, 00187 Roma. © 06/4827319. Fax 06/4740767. www.hotelmedici.com. 69 units (showers only). 150€–180€ ($173–$207) double. Rates include breakfast. AE, DC, MC, V. Metro: Piazza della Repubblica. **Amenities:** Bar; laundry; nonsmoking rooms. *In room:* Hair dryer.

Villa delle Rose Long a favorite with rail passengers, this palace is only 2 blocks from Termini Station and is an acceptable, if not exciting, choice. In the late 19th century it was a private villa but has been much altered and modified over the years to receive guests. Much of its old architectural allure is still in evidence, including the Corinthian-capped marble columns in the lobby and the luxuriant garden in back. Redecorating and upgrading of the bedrooms and the tiled bathrooms has made them more comfortable than ever.

Via Vicenza 5, 00185 Roma. ✆ 06/4451788. Fax 06/4451639. www.villadellerose.it. 38 units. 124€–170€ ($143–$196) double. Rates include buffet breakfast. AE, DC, MC, V. Metro: Termini or Castro Pretorio. **Amenities:** Breakfast garden. *In room:* Hair dryer.

TOP ATTRACTIONS & SPECIAL MOMENTS

Rome went all out to spruce up for the Jubilee year in 2000, and when you visit today, you'll benefit from the improvements made at the end of the 20th century. For the Jubilee, decades worth of grime from car exhaust and other pollution was scrubbed from the city's facades, revealing the original glory of the Eternal City (although Rome could still stand even more work on this front), and ancient treasures such as the Colosseum were shored up. Many of the most popular areas (such as the Trevi Fountain and Piazza Navona) are sparkling and inviting again.

Basilica di San Giovanni in Laterano ★★★ This church—not St. Peter's—is the cathedral of the diocese of Rome. Catholics all over the world refer to it as their "mother church." Originally built in A.D. 314 by Constantine, the cathedral has suffered many vicissitudes and was forced to rebuild many times. The present structure is characterized by its 18th-century facade by Alessandro Galilei (statues of Christ and the Apostles ring the top). Borromini gets the credit—some say blame—for the interior, built for Innocent X.

The most unusual sight is across the street at the "Palace of the Holy Steps," called the **Santuario della Scala Santa** ★, Piazza San Giovanni in Laterano (✆ 06/7726641). It's alleged that these were the actual steps that Christ climbed when he was brought before Pilate. These steps are supposed to be climbed only on your knees, which you're likely to see the faithful doing throughout the day. Visiting hours are daily from 6:15am to noon and 3:30 to 6:30pm. Admission is free.

Piazza San Giovanni in Laterano 4. ✆ 06/69886433. Basilica free; cloisters 2€ ($2.30). Summer daily 9am–6:45pm (off season to 6pm). Metro: San Giovanni. Bus: 4, 16, 30, 85, 87, or 174.

Basilica di San Pietro (St. Peter's Basilica) ★★★ As you stand in Bernini's **Piazza San Pietro (St. Peter's Square),** you'll be in the arms of an ellipse; like a loving parent, the Doric-pillared colonnade reaches out to embrace the faithful. Holding 300,000 is no problem for this square. Inside, the size of this famous church is awe-inspiring—though its dimensions (about two football fields long) are not apparent at first. St. Peter's is said to have been built over the tomb of the crucified saint. The original church was erected on the order of Constantine, but it threatened to collapse and the present structure is 17th-century Renaissance and baroque; it showcases the talents of some of Italy's greatest artists—Michelangelo and Raphael, among others.

In such a grand church, don't expect subtlety. But the basilica is rich in art. Under Michelangelo's dome is the celebrated **baldacchino** ★★★ by Bernini. In the nave on the right (the 1st chapel) is the best-known piece of sculpture, the *Pietà* ★★★ that Michelangelo sculpted while still in his early twenties. Just before the altar, and on the right, you'll see **a bronze statue of St. Peter** ★. It has been the custom for centuries for the faithful to kiss the saint's right foot, which today has literally been kissed smooth. You can visit the **treasury** ★, filled with jewel-studded chalices, reliquaries, and copes. One robe worn by Pius XII strikes a simple note in these halls of elegance. The sacristy now contains a **Museo Storico (Historical Museum)** displaying Vatican treasures, including the large 1400s bronze tomb of Pope Sixtus V by Antonio Pollaiuolo and several antique chalices. In addition you can visit the **Vatican grottoes** ★★ with their tombs, both ancient and modern (Pope John XXII gets the most adulation).

The grandest sight is yet to come: the climb to **Michelangelo's dome** ★★★, which towers about 375 feet high. Although you can walk up the steps, we recommend the elevator as far as it'll carry you. You can walk along the roof, for which you'll be rewarded with a panoramic view of Rome and the Vatican.

To tour the area around **St. Peter's tomb,** you must apply several days in advance to the excavations office (✆ **06/69885318**), open Monday through Saturday from 9am to 3:30pm. Pass under the arch to the left of the facade of St. Peter's to find it.

Piazza San Pietro. ✆ **06/69884676** or 06/69881662 (for information on celebrations). Basilica (including grottoes) free. Guided tour of excavations around St. Peter's tomb 9€ ($10.35); children younger than 15 are not admitted. Stairs to the dome 4€ ($4.60); elevator to the dome 5€ ($5.75); Sacristy (with Historical Museum) 5€ ($5.75). Basilica (including the sacristy and treasury) Oct–Mar daily 9am–5:15pm; Apr–Sept daily 8am–6:15pm. Grottoes daily 8am–5pm. Dome Oct–Mar daily 8am–5pm; Apr–Sept 8am–6pm. Metro: Ottaviano/San Pietro. Bus: 46.

Campidoglio ★★★**, Palazzo dei Conservatori** ★★★**, and Museo Capitolino** ★★   The Campidoglio stands on the summit of the Capitoline Hill, the most sacred of ancient Rome, where the Temples of Jupiter and Juno once stood. This was the spiritual heart of Rome, where triumphant generals made sacrifices to the gods who had given them their victories, and where the earthly homes of the king and queen of heaven stood.

One side of the piazza is open; the others are bounded by the **Senatorium (Town Council),** the statuary-filled **Palace of the Conservatori (Curators),** and the **Capitoline Museum.** These museums house some of the greatest pieces of classical sculpture in the world.

On the left is the **Capitoline Museum,** based on an architectural plan by Michelangelo, with an enormous collection of marble carvings from the ancient world. Many of them are just statues—notable for their age, but that's about it. In the first room is *The Dying Gaul* ★★, a work of majestic skill; in a special gallery all her own is *The Capitoline Venus,* who demurely covers herself—this statue (a Roman copy of the Greek original) has been a symbol of feminine beauty and charm down through the centuries. The famous statue of *Marcus Aurelius* ★★ is kept in the museum to protect it from pollution. This is the only bronze equestrian statue to have survived from ancient Rome, mainly because it was thought for centuries that the statue was that of Constantine the Great, and papal Rome respected the memory of the first Christian emperor.

Palace of the Conservatori, across the way, is rich in classical sculpture and paintings. In the courtyard are fragments of a colossal statue of Constantine. One of the most notable bronzes is the little boy picking a thorn from his foot, the *Spinario* ★★★, a Greek classic from the 1st century B.C. In addition, you'll find *Lupa Capitolina (Capitoline She-Wolf)* ★★★, a rare Etruscan bronze possibly from the 5th century B.C. (Romulus and Remus, the legendary twins that the she-wolf suckled, were added at a later date.) The entrance courtyard is lined with the remains (head, hands, a foot, and a kneecap) of an ancient colossal statue of Constantine the Great.

Moments **The Greatest View in Rome**

Before leaving the Campidoglio, walk around the right corner (as you face it) of the Senatorial Palace for a look at the Forum. This is a great vantage point for viewing the ruins below, and on a summer's evening you'll find small groups of visitors mixed with Roman couples leaning on the railing surveying the softly lit columns and crumbling temples.

Piazza del Campidoglio 1. © 06/67102071. Admission (to both museums) 7.80€ ($8.95). Tues–Sun 9am–8pm. Bus: 44, 81, 95, 160, 170, 715, or 780.

Colosseo (Colosseum) ★★★ In spite of the fact that it's a mere shell, the Colosseum remains the greatest architectural inheritance from ancient Rome. The completed stadium, called the Amphitheatrum Flavirum, was dedicated by Titus in A.D. 80 with a weeks-long bloody combat between gladiators and wild beasts. At its peak, the Colosseum could seat 80,000 spectators; exotic animals—humans also—were shipped in from the far corners of the empire to satisfy their jaded tastes. The games were quite an event, and everybody went. A day at the Colosseum was rather formal—the toga was *de rigueur* dress for men, even though many resented it much the way modern suburbanites hate to put on a tie on Saturday. The seating arrangement was a strictly social arrangement. The higher you were in society, the lower your seat was—even if you had the money, it was out of the question to "buy" a better seat, if your birth didn't warrant it.

Next to the Colosseum is the intricately carved **Arch of Constantine** ★★★, erected in honor of Constantine's defeat of the pagan Maxentius (A.D. 306). Many of the reliefs have nothing whatsoever to do with Constantine or his works, but tell of the victories of earlier Antonine rulers—they were apparently lifted from other, long-forgotten memorials.

Piazzale del Colosseo, Via dei Fori Imperiali. © 06/7004261. Admission 8€ ($9.20) all levels. Oct–Jan 15 daily 9am–3pm; Jan 16–Feb 15 daily 9am–4pm; Feb 16–Mar 17 daily 9am–4:30pm; Mar 18–Apr 16 daily 9am–5pm; Apr 17–Sept daily 9am–7pm. Guided tours in English with an archaeologist 3 times per morning on Sun and holidays 6€ ($6.90).

Domus Aurea (Golden House of Nero) ★ This bit of conspicuous consumption so embarrassed Vespasian that he spent the better part of his reign disassembling it. After the great fire of A.D. 64, Nero confiscated a square mile (2.5 sq. km) of the newly cleared land adjacent to the Forum and erected a palace of such sumptuous proportions and décor—including mother-of-pearl floors and golden fixtures—that it became a symbol of popular disaffection. Vespasian and his son, Titus, eliminated most of the palace's artifacts when they came to power. Out of its original 250 rooms, 30 are now open to the public, decorated with some of the sculptures, mosaics, and frescoes that have survived the past 2,000 years.

Via della Domus Aurea. © 06/39967700. Admission 5€ ($5.75), plus 1.50€ ($1.75) for a reservation. Wed–Mon 9am–7:45pm. Last admission 1 hr. before closing. Metro: Colosseo.

Fontana di Trevi (Trevi Fountain) ★★★ As you elbow your way through the summertime crowds around the Trevi Fountain, it's hard to believe that this little piazza was nearly always deserted before the film *Three Coins in a Fountain* brought the tour buses. Today, it's a must on everybody's itinerary. The fountain is an 18th-century extravaganza of baroque stonework ruled over by a large statue of Neptune. While some of the statuary is the work of other artists, the man who gets

Moments **I Left My Heart on the Piazza Navona**

One of the most beautifully baroque sites in all of Rome, **Piazza Navona** ★★★ is like an ochre-colored gem, unspoiled by new buildings, or even by traffic. The shape results from the Stadium of Domitian, the ruins of which lie underneath the present constructions. Great chariot races were once held here (some rather unusual, such as the one in which the head of the winning horse was lopped off as it crossed the finish line and was then carried by runners to be offered as a sacrifice by the Vestal Virgins atop the Capitoline). In medieval times, the popes used to flood the piazza to stage mock naval encounters. Today the piazza is packed with vendors and street performers, and lined with pricey cafes where you can enjoy a cappuccino or gelato and indulge in unparalleled people-watching.

Besides the twin-towered facade of 17th-century Santa Agnes, the piazza boasts several baroque masterpieces. The best known, in the center, is Bernini's **Fountain of the Four Rivers (Fontana dei Quattro Fiumi)** ★★★, whose four stone personifications symbolize the world's greatest rivers: the Ganges, Danube, della Plata, and Nile. It's fun to try to figure out which is which. (*Hint:* The figure with the shroud on its head is the Nile, so represented because the river's source was unknown at the time.) At the south end is the **Fountain of the Moor (Fontana del Moro),** also by Bernini. The **Fountain of Neptune (Fontana di Nettuno),** which balances that of the Moor, is a 19th-century addition; it was restored after a demented 1997 attack by two men who broke off the tail of one of its sea creatures.

the credit for the entire project is Nicola Salvi. The tradition of throwing coins into the fountain is an evolution of earlier customs. At one time, visitors drank water from the fountain, later they combined that with an offering to the spirits of the place. In our inflationary world, all we get to do is make the offering.

Piazza di Trevi. Metro: Barberini.

Foro Imperiali (Imperial Forums) ★★★   The Imperial Forums were constructed by a succession of emperors to make commerce more comfortable for the merchants of Rome, and to provide new libraries and more room for assembly, since the original Roman Forum had become too small.

With your back to the Colosseum, begin walking up the Via dei Fori Imperiali (built by the fascists in the '30s) keeping to the right side of the street. Those ruins across the street are what's left of the colonnade that once surrounded the **Temple of Venus and Roma.** Next to it, you'll recognize the back wall of the Basilica of Constantine. Shortly, you'll come to a large outdoor restaurant, where Via Cavour joins the boulevard you're on. Just beyond the small park across Via Cavour are the remains of the **Forum of Nerva,** built by the emperor whose 2-year reign (A.D. 96–98) followed that of the paranoid Domitian. Nerva's Forum is best observed from the railing that skirts it on the Via dei Fori Imperiali. The only really intelligible remnant is a wall of the Temple of Minerva with two fine Corinthian columns.

The next forum up was that of **Augustus** ⭐⭐, and was built before the birth of Christ to commemorate the emperor's victory over the assassins Cassius and Brutus in the Battle of Fillippi (42 B.C.). Continuing along the railing, you'll next see the vast semicircle of **Trajan's Market** ⭐⭐, Via Quattro Novembre 94 (✆ **06/6790048**), whose teeming arcades stocked with merchandise from the far corners of the Roman world have long collapsed, leaving only a few ubiquitous cats to watch after things. The shops once covered a multitude of levels, and you can still wander around many of them. It's open Tuesday through Sunday from 9am to 4:30pm. Admission is 8€ ($9.20).

You can enter the **Forum of Trajan** ⭐⭐ on Via Quattro Novembre near the steps of Via Magnanapoli. Once through the tunnel, you'll emerge into the newest and most beautiful of the Imperial Forums, built between A.D. 107 and 113. There are many statue fragments and pedestals bearing still-legible inscriptions, but more interesting is the great Basilica Ulpia, whose gray marble columns rise roofless into the sky. This forum was once regarded as one of the architectural wonders of the world.

Beyond the Basilica Ulpia is **Trajan's Column** ⭐⭐⭐, in magnificent condition, with intricate bas-relief sculpture depicting Trajan's victorious campaign (though, from your vantage point, you'll be able to see only the earliest stages). The next stop is the **Forum of Julius Caesar** ⭐⭐, the first of the Imperial Forums. It lies on the opposite side of Via dei Fori Imperiali. This was the site of the Roman stock exchange, as well as the Temple of Venus; restored columns stand cinematically in the middle of the excavations.

Via de Fori Imperiali. Free admission. Metro: Colosseo. On view 24 hours.

Foro Romano (Roman Forum) ⭐⭐⭐   The Roman Forum was built in the marshy land between the Palatine and the Capitoline hills (where legend has it that Romulus and Remus were suckled by the she-wolf). It flourished as the center of Roman life in the days of the Republic, before it gradually lost prestige to the Imperial Forum. By day the columns of now-vanished temples and the stones from which long-forgotten orators spoke are mere shells. But at night, when the Forum is silent in the moonlight, it isn't difficult to imagine that Vestal Virgins still guard the sacred temple fire.

If you want the stones to have some meaning, you'll have to purchase a detailed plan, as the temples can be hard to locate. Arm yourself with a good map sold at the entrance and allow at least 3 hours for wandering about. The best of the lot is the handsomely adorned **Temple of Castor and Pollux** ⭐⭐⭐, erected in the 5th century B.C. in honor of a battle triumph. The **Temple of Faustina** ⭐⭐, with its lovely columns and frieze (griffins and candelabra), was converted into the San Lorenzo in Miranda Church. The **Temple of the Vestal Virgins** ⭐⭐⭐ is a popular attraction; some of the statuary, mostly headless, remains.

A long walk up from the Roman Forum leads to the **Palatine Hill** ⭐⭐⭐, one of the seven hills of Rome; your ticket from the Forum will admit you to this attraction (it's open the same hours). The Palatine, tradition tells us, was the spot on which the first settlers built their huts, under the direction of Romulus. In later years, the hill became a patrician residential district that attracted citizens like Cicero. It's worth the climb for the panoramic, sweeping view of both the Roman and Imperial forums, as well as the Capitoline Hill and the Colosseum. Of the ruins that remain, none is finer than the so-called **House of Livia** ⭐⭐ (the "abominable grandmother" of Robert Graves's *I, Claudius*).

When the glory that was Rome has completely overwhelmed you, you can enjoy a respite in the cooling **Farnese Gardens** ✸, laid out in the 16th century, which incorporate some of Michelangelo's designs.

Largo Romolo e Remo. ✆ **06/6990110.** Forum free admission; Palatine Hill 8€ ($9.20). Apr–Sept daily 9am–7pm; Oct–Mar daily 9am–3:30pm. Last admission 1 hr. before closing. Closed holidays. Metro: Colosseo. Bus: 27, 81, 85, 87, or 186.

Galleria Borghese ✸✸✸   Most visitors come here to see Canova's famous **statue** ✸✸✸ of Pauline Bonaparte Borghese, the sister of Napoleon. But there are numerous other works of art worth seeing here. This treasure trove of art housed in a an opulent 17th-century palace includes such masterpieces as Bernini's *David, The Rape of Persephone,* and his *Apollo and Daphne.* Also on the ground floor of the palace are interesting 17th-century busts of Roman emperors, and a few pieces of Roman statuary from antiquity. Upstairs is a treasure house of painting including works of Raphael (*Young Woman with a Unicorn* and his famous *Deposition from the Cross* ✸✸✸), Pinturicchio, Botticelli, Correggio, Titian, Veronese, Bellini, and even some non-Italians, such as Bruegel and Albrecht Dürer. Two of the greatest paintings in all of Rome are showcased here—***Madonna del Palafrenieri*** ✸✸✸ by the "divine" Caravaggio, showing the Virgin, Jesus, and St. Anne; and Domenichino's ***Diana the Huntress*** ✸✸✸, with its rich, lush detail.

Important information: No more than 300 visitors at a time are allowed on the ground floor, and no more than 90 are allowed on the upper floor. Reservations are essential, so call ✆ **06/328101** (Mon–Fri 9am–6pm). However, the number always seems to be busy. If you'll be in Rome for a few days, try stopping by in person on your first day to reserve tickets for a later day. Better yet, before you leave home, contact **Select Italy** (✆ **847/8531661;** www.selectitaly.com).

Piazza Scipione Borghese 5 (off Via Pinciano). ✆ **06/8417645** for information. Admission 6.50€ ($7.50) plus 2€ ($2.30) for reservation fee. Tues–Sun 9am–7pm. Bus: 56 or 910.

Musei Vaticani (Vatican Museums) ✸✸✸   This is a repository of one of the world's greatest art collections, especially rich in treasures of antiquity and the Renaissance. Too many visitors try to squeeze the Vatican Museums into a day's itinerary that includes a half-dozen other sights. This is utter foolishness. There are many museums in the Vatican in addition to Michelangelo's Sistine Chapel, and several papal apartments you'll want to see. It would require much more time than a day to examine all that's here, so if you all you have is a day, pick a few spots to concentrate on.

Moments **A Lazy Afternoon at the Villa Borghese**

The **Borghese Gardens** (encompassing the Galleria Borghese), now a perfectly exquisite 17th-century estate, were developed by Cardinal Scipio Borghese, a high churchman belonging to another of Rome's mighty families. The most striking feature of the Borghese Gardens are its trees—stark and eerie looking, their trunks rising some 50 feet into the air without a single branch, only to burst forth in an evergreen canopy high above. Few activities are quite as pleasant as a slow stroll through the Villa Borghese on a sunny afternoon, pausing to admire carefully planned 17th-century vistas, ornamental fountains, and the magnificent trees.

The **Pinacoteca** ★★★, or picture gallery's art collection is arranged chronologically, starting with gilded polyptiques in the style of Byzantium, and progressing through the Renaissance up to the 21st century. There are some 15 rooms containing the works of such masters as Giotto, Beato Angelico, Raphael, da Vinci, Titian, Veronese, Caravaggio (the splendid *Deposition*), Murillo and Ribera. The gallery rooms are arranged in a circle, so you'll exit through the same door you entered.

The handsomely decorated rooms of the **Pius Clementine Museum** contain a vast collection of Greek and Roman sculpture. Of particular note are the porphyry sarcophagi of the mother and daughter of Constantine the Great (4th c.), Hercules (a gilded bronze of the 1st c.; note also the magnificent room it's in), the **Belvedere Apollo** ★★★ (a Roman copy of a 4th-c. B.C. Greek original), mosaics from the floor of the Villa Hadrian outside Tivoli, and the Belvedere Torso (a fragment of a Greek statue from the 1st c. B.C. that was carefully studied by Michelangelo). There are literally hundreds of other statues lounging in the halls.

The **Raphael Rooms** ★★ are one of the highlights of the museums. While still a young man, Raphael was given one of the greatest assignments of his short life: to decorate a series of rooms in the apartments of Pope Julius II. The decoration was carried out by Raphael and his workshop from 1508 to 1524. In these works, Raphael achieves the Renaissance aim of blending classic beauty with realism. In the important *Stanza della Segnatura,* the first room decorated by the artist, you'll find the majestic *School of Athens* ★★★, one of his best-known works, depicting such philosophers from the ages as Aristotle, Plato, and Socrates.

The majestic **Sistine Chapel** ★★★ was restored in the 1990s. Michelangelo devoted 4½ years to painting the beautiful ceiling frescoes of the chapel of Sistus IX (hence the name *Sixtine* or *Sistine*). The work was so physically taxing that it permanently damaged his eyesight. Glorifying the human body as only a sculptor could, Michelangelo painted nine panels taken from the pages of Genesis, and surrounded them with prophets and sibyls. Today, throngs of visitors walk around bumping into one another, faces pointed ceiling-ward, admiring the frescoes at the expense of a crick in the neck. Michelangelo not only did the ceiling but also the monumental fresco of *The Last Judgment* ★★★ on the altar wall.

Vatican City, Viale Vaticano (a long walk around the Vatican walls from St. Peter's Square). ℂ **06/69884341.** Admission is free for everyone. Mid-Mar to late Oct Mon–Fri 8:45am–3:45pm; Sat and last Sun of the month 8:45am–1:45pm. Off season Mon–Sat and last Sun of the month 8:45am–1:45pm. Closed all national and religious holidays (except Easter week) and Aug 15–16. Metro: Ottaviano/San Pietro, then a long walk.

Pantheon ★★★ Of all the great buildings of ancient Rome, only the Pantheon (All the Gods) remains intact today. It was built in 27 B.C. by Marcus Agrippa, and later reconstructed by the emperor Hadrian in the first part of the 2nd century A.D. This remarkable building is among the architectural wonders of the world because of its dome and its concept of space. The Pantheon was once ringed with niches containing white marble statues of Roman gods. Animals were sacrificed and burned in the center, and the smoke escaped through the only means of light, an opening at the top 27 feet in diameter. Michelangelo came here to study the dome before designing the cupola of St. Peter's, whose dome is only 2 feet smaller than the Pantheon's.

Piazza della Rotonda. ℂ **06/68300230.** Free admission. Mon–Sat 8:30am–7:30pm; Sun 9am–6pm. Bus: 46, 62, 64, 170, or 492 to Largo di Torre.

Scalinata di Spagna (Spanish Steps) ★★★ The Spanish Steps and the adjoining Piazza di Spagna both take their name from the Spanish embassy,

---

(*Moments* **Nostalgia for the Days of La Dolce Vita**

The posh, tree-lined Via Veneto still looks as elegant as it did in the 1950s when it reached its peak. Those *la dolce vita* days, when Middle East businessmen in *fez* and sunglasses lounged in sidewalk cafes surrounded by bevies of blonde beauties, and when movie stars promenaded with rich old men in monocles, are gone, although admittedly you can still see such scenes on rare occasions.

Via Veneto makes a large S-curve, and just where it straightens out for the last time, you'll see the swank American Embassy, whose Consular Division is in a rose-colored palace where the Queen of Italy once lived. From the Embassy on up to the Aurelian Wall are the most chic of the cafes, which still carry on a thriving business despite the depletion of the celebrity roster. These cafes, with their brightly colored umbrellas and awnings, are perfectly designed for people-watching. They straddle the sidewalk, and there's no way to stroll up Via Veneto without going through the middle of half a dozen of them.

The end of the Via Veneto is marked by a final burst of plush hotels and Harry's Bar. Right in front of you will be the hulking brickwork of the Aurelian Wall, begun in A.D. 271. The gate is a bit newer.

---

which was housed in a palace here during the 19th century. The Spanish, however, had nothing to do with the construction of the steps. They were built by the French, and lead to the French church in Rome, Trinita' dei Monti. The twin-towered church behind the obelisk at the top of the Steps is early 16th century. The Steps themselves are early 18th century.

Piazza di Spagna. Metro: Spagna.

Museo Nazionale di Villa Giulia (Etruscan) ★★★   Like the Palazzo Borghese, the Villa Giulia was built as a country house, and today it houses some of the greatest art left by the mysterious Etruscans, who appear to have sailed to Italy in large groups around 800 B.C., though little else is known of them.

If you have time only for the masterpieces, head for Sala 7, which has a remarkable *Apollo* from Veio from the end of the 6th century B.C. (clothed, for a change). Two other widely acclaimed pieces of statuary in this gallery are *Dea con Bambino (Goddess with a Baby)* and a greatly mutilated, but still powerful, *Hercules* with a stag. In the adjoining Sala 8, you'll see the lions' sarcophagus from the mid–6th century B.C., which was excavated at Cerveteri, north of Rome. Finally, in Sala 9, is one of the world's most important Etruscan art treasures, the bride and bridegroom coffin from the 6th century B.C., also from Cerveteri. Near the end of your tour, another masterpiece of Etruscan art awaits you in room 33: the *Cista Ficoroni*, a bronze urn with paw feet, mounted by three figures, dating from the 4th century B.C.

Piazzale di Villa Giulia 9. ☎ 06/3201951. Admission 4€ ($4.60). Tues–Sat 8:30am–7pm. Metro: Flaminio.

WHERE TO DINE

Césarina EMILIANA-ROMAGNOLA/ROMAN   This restaurant perpetuates the culinary traditions of the late Césarina Masi in a newer manifestation of the famous original hole-in-the-wall, which catered to Rome's fashionable set in the 1960s. Today, with three dining rooms and more than 200 seats, the restaurant serves excellent versions of *bollito misto* (an array of well-seasoned boiled meats), rolled from table to table on a cart; and *misto Césarina*—three kinds of pasta, each handmade and served with a different sauce. If anything, her food tastes better than ever.

Via Piemonte 109. ℂ **06/4880828.** Reservations recommended. Main courses 6€–15€ ($6.90–$17.25). AE, DC, MC, V. Mon–Sat 12:30–3pm and 7:30–11pm. Metro: Barberini. Bus: 52, 53, or 63.

Colline Emiliane ★★ EMILIANA-ROMAGNOLA   This small local favorite right off Piazza Barberini serves *classica cucina Bolognese* in a bustling, trattoria setting. It's a family-run place where everybody helps out. The owner is the cook and his wife makes the pasta, which, incidentally, is about the best you'll encounter in Rome. The enticing menu is loaded with old favorites and delicacies—none finer than an inspired *tortellini alla panna* (cream sauce) with truffles.

Via Avignonesi 22 (off Piazza Barberini). ℂ **06/4817538.** Reservations highly recommended. Main courses 7€–15€ ($8.05–$17.25). MC, V. Sat–Thurs 12:45–2:45pm and 7:45–10:45pm. Closed Aug. Metro: Barberini.

Dal Bolognese ★ BOLOGNESE   If *La Dolce Vita* were being filmed now, this restaurant would be used as a backdrop, its patrons photographed in their latest Fendi drag. It's one of those rare dining spots that's not only chic, but noted for its Bolognese cuisine as well. To begin your meal, we suggest *misto di pasta*—four pastas, each flavored with a different sauce, arranged on the same plate. Although almond cake is the house specialty, it's hard to resist the fresh strawberry tart.

Piazza del Popolo 1–2. ℂ **06/3611426.** Reservations required. Main courses 10€–20€ ($11.50–$23). AE, DC, MC, V. Tues–Sun 12:30–3pm and 8:15pm–midnight (last dinner order at 11:15pm). Closed 20 days in Aug. Metro: Flaminio.

F.I.S.H. ★ *(Finds* SEAFOOD   One of Rome's hottest new restaurants, F.I.S.H. stands for "Fine International Seafood House," and it definitely lives up to its billing. An array of beautifully executed pasta dishes is served nightly, but we prefer to stick to the market-fresh fish and shellfish dishes, which are among the finest served in Rome. The chic dining spot has a sleek but elegant décor, and it's tiny—reserve well in advance and count yourself lucky if you get a table.

Via dei Serpenti 16. ℂ **06/47824962.** Reservations imperative. Main courses 12€–18€ ($13.80–$20.70). AE, DC, MC, V. Tues–Sun noon–3pm and 7:45pm–1am. Closed: Aug 7–Sept 2 and Dec 25. Metro: Cavour.

Girarrosto Toscano ★ *(Value* TUSCAN   If you're calling on the Pope, you can stop off for lunch at this popular place near the Vatican, which serves some of the most memorable Tuscan dishes in Rome. The atmosphere is old, including a vaulted cellar ceiling in the dining room, but the food is market-fresh, especially the mammoth selection of antipasti. Oysters and fresh fish from the Adriatic are also served daily. Meat and fish dishes are priced according to weight, and costs can run considerably higher than the prices quoted below.

Via Germanico 58. ℂ **06/39725717.** Reservations required. Main courses 10€–16€ ($11.50–$18.40). AE, DC, MC, V. Tues–Sun 12:30–3:30pm and 8–11pm. Metro: Ottaviano.

Hostaria Nerone ★ ROMAN/ITALIAN   Opened in 1929 on the periphery of Park Colle Oppio, this affordable trattoria is unusually placed on the ruins of the Golden House of Nero. Instead of the depraved Roman dictator, you are welcomed by a member of the Santis family, who might offer you a table on a terrace overlooking the Baths of Trajan or the Colosseum. Palate-pleasing, robust regional fare is served, including a bountiful antipasti buffet, succulent pastas, and excellent market-fresh meat and fish dishes. The varied list of some of the best Italian wines is reasonably priced.

Via Terme di Tito 96. 📞 **06/4817952.** Reservations recommended. Main courses 7.50€–12.50€ ($8.65–$14.40). AE, DC, MC, V. Mon–Sat noon–3pm and 7–11pm. Metro: Colosseo. Bus: 75, 85, 87, 117, or 175.

La Cisterna ROMAN   Consider having at least one meal in the ancient district of Trastevere across the Tiber, as it's the most typical and atmospheric of all Roman districts. For some three-quarters of a century, the Simmii family have been turning out real Roman cookery—and serving it fresh from the ovens. In summer, guests opt for the restaurant's sidewalk tables as they devour fresh fish and other delectable dishes, including homemade pastas and well-flavored meats.

Via della Cisterna 13. 📞 **06/5812543.** Reservations recommended. Main courses 7€–13€ ($8.05–$14.95). AE, DC, MC, V. Mon–Sat 7pm–1:30am. Bus: 44, 75, 170, 280, or 710.

L'Eau Vive ⭐ *Finds* INTERNATIONAL   In a 17th century *palazzo*, this discovery, a favorite dining spot of Pope John Paul II, is run by lay missionaries who wear the dress of their native countries. In a formal atmosphere, a group of international nuns (who sing hymns at 10pm nightly) are the waitresses; tips are used for religious purposes. The beautifully balanced menu of well-prepared dishes is as international in flavor as the servers. Main dishes range from guinea hen with onions and grapes in a wine sauce to couscous.

Via Monterone 85. 📞 **06/68801095.** Reservations recommended. Main courses 15€–30€ ($17.25–$34.50); fixed-price menus 15€–30€ ($17.25–$34.50), AE, MC, V. Mon–Sat 12:30–2:30pm and 7:30–10:30pm. Closed Aug 1–20. Bus: 46, 62, 64, 70, or 115.

Piperno ⭐ ROMAN/JEWISH   In the heart of the old Jewish ghetto, this trattoria has been open and running since 1856, and every year it makes new fans of visitors to this historic part of old Rome. The featured Jerusalem artichokes (which isn't really an artichoke) are deep-fried but they appear on your plate flaky and dry—not greasy. The time-tested recipes are prepared with market-fresh ingredients—count yourself lucky if the stuffed squash blossoms appear on the menu. You'll be served by a uniformed crew of hardworking waiters, whose advice and suggestions are worth considering.

Via Monte de' Cenci 9. 📞 **06/68806629.** Reservations recommended. Main courses 17.50€–20€ ($20.15–$23). DC, MC, V. Tues–Sat noon–2:30pm and 8–10:30pm; Sun-Mon noon–2:30pm. Bus: 23.

Taverna Flavia ROMAN/INTERNATIONAL   This tavern is a robustly Roman restaurant, still serving the same food that once delighted the late Frank Sinatra and the "Hollywood on the Tiber" crowd in the 1950s. It's not chic anymore, but you can still enjoy the hearty classics served at this long-enduring favorite near Station Termini. Spaghetti cooked in champagne and other old-fashioned delights, such as fondue with truffles, are served here nightly.

Via Flavia 9 (a block from Via XX Settembre). 📞 **06/4745214.** Reservations recommended. Main courses 11€–17.50€ ($12.65–$20.15). AE, DC, MC, V. Mon–Fri 12:30–3pm and 7:30–11pm; Sat–Sun 7:30–11:30pm. Metro: Repubblica.

Trattoria San Teodoro ⭐ ROMAN   At last there's a good place to eat in the former gastronomic wasteland near the Roman Forum and Palatine Hill. The helpful staff at this top-rated trattoria welcomes visitors and locals to a shady terrace or to a dimly lit dining room. The market-fresh menu includes succulent homemade pastas, some excellent seafood (try the carpaccio made with tuna, turbot, or sea bass), and any number of well-flavored and tender meat dishes.

Brindisi: Gateway to Greece

The terminus of the ancient Appia Antica or Appian Way, traveled by everybody from Virgil to Marc Antony, is today the embarkation point for those crossing the Adriatic to Greece. The distance from Rome is 563 miles (906km) to the southeast.

For trains running between Rome and Brindisi, refer to "Trains & Travel Times" above. Brindisi's main station lies at Piazza Crispi, about 1½ miles (2km) from the ferry port. In summer, two trains from Rome go daily all the way to Brindisi Marittima station at the port, the embarkation for Greece-bound ferries. One-way rail fares between Rome and Brindisi cost 43.38€ to 47.74€ ($49.90–$54.90) if you don't have a pass.

The **Brindisi Tourist Office** is at viale Regina Margherita 43 (© 0831/523072), open July to August daily 9am to 1pm and 6 to 10pm; September to June daily 8am to 8pm. They do not make hotel reservations.

The easiest and quickest way to sail to Greece is aboard one of the hydrofoils operated by Italian Ferry from Brindisi to Corfu. In summer departures are daily at 2pm. Off season there are 5 hydrofoils a week. Trip time is 3 hours. Depending on the season, one-way passage is 64€ to 92€ ($73.60–$106). The most heavily traveled route from Brindisi, however, is the ferry service to Patras, gateway to Greece. Transit aboard one of these ferries takes 9 hours and costs from 30€ to 54€ ($34.50–$62.10) one-way. If you want a private cabin, the cost ranges from 97€ to 160€ ($112–$184) for a double. In addition, each person is assessed a port tax of 7€ ($8.05). *Note:* Eurailpasses are accepted on these ferries for passage only (cabins cost extra), though a small supplement is assessed during the summer high season. For more on ferries covered by the Eurailpass, see chapter 2; for more on the ferries to Greece, see chapter 11.

The best way to book a ticket is to contact one of the travel agencies that line each side of the Corso Garibaldi in Brindisi. The best is **Italian Ferry,** Corso Garibaldi 96 (© 0831/590840), which is not only a travel agency but the ferry line itself. It sells tickets on ferries and is the only agency that operates hydrofoils out of Brindisi.

For regular ferries, you can also arrange bookings through **Fragline,** via Spalato 31 (© 0831/548540), which is especially good in booking passage on car ferries between Brindisi and Corfu. **Medlink,** Corso Garibaldi 49 (© 0831/527667), also sells tickets between Brindisi and Corfu, as does **My Way,** Via Provinciale per Lecce 27A (© 0831/573800), specializing in bookings between Brindisi and both Corfu and Patras.

Via dei Fienili 49–51. © 06/6780933. Reservations recommended. Main courses 15€–25€ ($17.25–$28.75). AE, MC, V. Mon–Sat 12:30–3:30pm and 7:30pm–midnight. Metro: Circo Massimo.

SHOPPING

We won't pretend that Rome is Italy's finest shopping center (Florence and Venice are), nor that its shops are unusually inexpensive—many of them aren't.

But even on the most elegant of Rome's thoroughfares, there are values mixed in with the costly boutiques. On a short visit the best method is to stroll the major shopping streets (see below), ferreting out the best values.

The posh shopping streets **Via Borgognona** and **Via Condotti** begin near Piazza di Spagna. For the most part, the merchandise on both is chic and very, very expensive. Wise shoppers are advised to take a look at the goods displayed on the Spanish Steps before a tour of Via Condotti. Here, craftspeople good and bad lay out their wares on old velvet cloths—usually paintings, beads, silver and turquoise jewelry, some of it quite good—and bargain for the best offer. **Via Frattina** runs parallel to Via Condotti, its more famous sibling, and is the hippest and busiest shopping street in town. You'll frequently find it closed to traffic, converted into a pedestrian mall thronged with shoppers moving from boutique to boutique.

Beginning at the top of the Spanish Steps, **Via Sistina** runs to Piazza Barberini. It houses the city's densest concentration of boutiques and expensive dress shops. It's good for browsing, and women visitors will occasionally find exciting items on sale. Most shoppers reach **Via Francesco Crispi** by following Via Sistina 1 long block from the top of the Spanish Steps. Near the intersection of these streets are several shops full of unusual and not overly expensive gifts. Evocative of *La Dolce Vita,* **Via Veneto** is filled these days with expensive hotels and cafes and an array of relatively expensive stores selling shoes, gloves, and leather goods.

Traffic-clogged **Via Nazionale**—just crossing the street is no small feat—begins at Piazza della Repubblica and runs down almost to Piazza Venezia. Here you'll find an abundance of leather stores—more reasonable in price than those in many other parts of Rome—and a welcome handful of stylish boutiques.

Via dei Coronari, should be seen whether or not you buy. Buried in a colorful section of the Campus Martius (Renaissance Rome), Via dei Coronari is an antiquer's dream, literally lined with magnificent vases, urns, chandeliers, breakfronts, chaises, refectory tables, candelabra, you name it. You'll find the entrance to the street just north of the Piazza Navona.

Finds **Rome's Flea Market: Like an Oriental Bazaar**

Bus 75 travels the distance between Piazza Venezia and the Porta Portese, on the south side of Trastevere. Every Sunday from 7am to 1pm, this is the site of a **sprawling flea market,** noteworthy less for its bargains than for its perspectives into everyday Italian life. From the wide paved Piazzale Portuense, the market extends for block after block, looking more like an outlet store than a bazaar. Wooden stalls are crammed with transistor radios, clothing, bolts of brightly colored fabric, imitation antique globes, all sorts of gilded gimcrackery and cooking appliances. Men demonstrate how to broil a chicken over a tin of Sterno, an old circus performer draws a large crowd that watches him being wrapped in chains only to make a miraculous escape, strolling musicians play songs that everyone knows the words to. Farther down from the Portese Gate, there are stalls with 16th-century books in leather binders that have long lost their coloring, and a smattering of antiques, some good some not.

NIGHTLIFE

Evenings in Rome always begin at one of the cafes, the most famous of which line the **Via Veneto.** Two other popular gathering places for cafe-sitting are **Piazza della Rotonda** and **Piazza del Popolo.** For the cost of an espresso, the people-watching is free.

There are few evening diversions quite as pleasurable as a stroll past the solemn pillars of old temples or the cascading torrents of Renaissance fountains glowing under the blue-black sky. Of the **fountains,** the Naiads (Piazza della Repubblica), the Tortoises (Piazza Mattei) and, of course, the Trevi are particularly beautiful at night. The **Capitoline Hill** is magnificently lit after dark, with its Renaissance facades glowing like jewel boxes. Behind the Senatorial Palace is a fine view of the **Roman Forum.** If you're staying across the Tiber, **Piazza San Pietro,** in front of St. Peter's Basilica, is impressive at night without tour buses and crowds. And a combination of illuminated architecture, Renaissance fountains, and frequent sidewalk shows and art expositions is at **Piazza Navona.** If you're ambitious and have a good sense of direction, try exploring the streets to the west of Piazza Navona, which look like a stage set when lit at night.

The mini-magazines *Metropolitan* and *Wanted in Rome* have listings of jazz, rock, and such and give an interesting look at expatriate Rome. The daily *Il Messaggero* lists current cultural news, especially in its Thursday magazine supplement, *Metro.* And *Un Ospite a Roma,* available free from the concierge desks of top hotels, is full of details on what's happening. Even if you don't speak Italian, you can generally follow the listings featured in *TrovaRoma,* a special weekly entertainment supplement published in the newspaper *La Repubblica* on Thursday.

THE PERFORMING ARTS   If you're in the capital for the opera season, usually late December to June, you might want to attend the historic **Teatro dell'-Opera (Rome Opera House),** Piazza Beniamino Gigli 1, off Via Nazionale (© **06/481601;** Metro: Repubblica). Nothing is presented in August; in summer, the venue switches to the Baths of Caracalla. Call ahead or ask your concierge before you go. Tickets are 21€ to 119€ ($24.15–$137). The **Rome Opera Ballet** also performs at the Teatro dell'Opera. Look for announcements of classical concerts that take place in churches and other venues.

CAFES & BARS   Along the Via Veneto, **Harry's Bar,** at #150 (© **06/484643**) is the choicest watering hole. It has no connection with other famous Harry's bars, such as the one in Venice, and in many respects, the Roman Harry's is the most elegant of them all. **Caffè de Paris,** Via Vittorio Veneto 90 (© **06/4885284**), is a local landmark and a good place to get the night started. Tables spill out onto the sidewalk in summer, and the passing crowd walks through the maze.

The fashion-conscious descend on the Piazza de Popolo where there is always an aura of excitement, especially after midnight. The choicest place for a drink here is **Café Rosati,** Piazza del Popolo 5A (© **06/3225859**), in business since 1923. The preferred tables are out front where growling Maseratis cruise by while young Italian men in silk shirts hang from the car windows. Its rival, **Canova Café,** Piazza del Popolo 16 (© **06/3612231**), is another great place for people-watching. We also gravitate to the Piazza della Rotonda, across from the Pantheon, which is dramatically lit at night. The top cafe here is **Di Rienzo,** Piazza della Rotonda 8–9 (© **06/6869097**). The best coffee in Rome is brewed at **Caffè Sant'Eustachio,** Piazza Sant'Eustachio 82 (© **06/68802048**), where the water supply is funneled into the city by an aqueduct built in 19 B.C.

Alternately, you could try **Antico Caffè Greco,** 86 Via Condotti (© **06/ 6791700**), which has been serving drinks since 1760. Over the years it has attracted such habitués as Goethe, Stendhal, and D'Annunzio. Half a block from the foot of the Spanish Steps, it still retains a 19th-century atmosphere. The waiters wear morning coats—most effective looking—and seat you at small marble tables. Beyond the carved wooden bar, are a series of small elegant rooms hung with oil paintings in gilded frames.

CLUBS   Arciliuto, Piazza Monte Vecchio 5 (© **06/6879419;** bus: 42, 62, or 64), is a romantic candlelit spot within walking distance of the Piazza Navona that was reputedly once the studio of Raphael. From 10pm to 2am, Monday through Saturday, guests enjoy a musical salon ambience, listening to a guitarist, a pianist, and a violinist. The evening's presentation also includes live Neapolitan songs and new Italian madrigals, even current hits from Broadway or London's West End. The cover is 19€ ($21.85), including the first drink; it's closed July 15 to September 5.

In a high-tech, futuristic setting, **Alien,** Via Velletri 13–19 (© **06/8412212**), provides a bizarre space-age dance floor, bathed in strobe lights and rocking to the sounds of house/techno music. The crowd is young. It's open Tuesday to Sunday 11pm to 5am, with a cover of 16€ to 18€ ($18.40–$20.70) that includes the first drink.

If you're looking for a little counterculture edge, where you might find the latest Indie music from the U.K., head for **Black Out,** Via Saturnia 18 (© **06/ 70496791**), which occupies an industrial-looking site open only Thursday, Friday, and Saturday 10:30pm to 4am. The club lures a crowd, mainly Romans in their 20s and early 30s. The 5€ ($5.75) cover on Thursday and the 7.50€ ($8.65) cover on Saturday and Sunday include the first drink.

Big Mama, Vicolo San Francesco a Ripa 18 (© **06/5812551**), is a hangout for jazz and blues musicians where you're likely to meet the up-and-coming stars of tomorrow and sometimes even the big names. For big acts, the cover is 10€ to 30€ ($11.50–$34.50), plus 13€ ($14.95) for a seasonal membership fee.

AN EXCURSION TO TIVOLI ★★

An ancient town 20 miles (32km) east of Rome, Tivoli, known as Tibur to the ancient Romans, was the playground of emperors, who maintained lavish villas here near the famous woods and waterfalls. Today its reputation continues unabated: It's the most popular half-day jaunt from Rome.

GETTING THERE   From Rome, take Metro Line B to the end of the line, the Rebibbia Station. After exiting the station, board a Cotral bus for the rest of the way to Tivoli (it will drop you off in front of the tourist information office). A bus marked TIVOLI also leaves every 15 to 20 minutes during the day from Via Gaeta (west of Via Volturno), near the Stazione Termini. Both buses are part of the regular public transportation system. A one-way fare from Rome to Tivoli costs 1.60€ ($1.85).

VISITOR INFORMATION   For information about the town and its attractions, go to **Azienda Autonoma di Turismo,** Largo Garibaldi (© **0774/ 334522**), open Monday and Saturday 9am to 1pm, Tuesday to Friday 9am to 1pm and 3 to 6pm.

TOP ATTRACTIONS & SPECIAL MOMENTS

Four miles (6.5km) from the foothills on which Tivoli is built lies a gently sloping plain, the site of **Villa Adriana** or **Hadrian's Villa** ★★★, Via di Villa Adriana

(© **0774/530203**). Of all the Roman emperors dedicated to *la dolce vita,* the globe-trotting Hadrian spent the last 3 years of his life in the grandest style. Today the ruins of his estate cover 180 acres of rolling terrain. The estate was built as a heaven on earth in which to spend a long and luxurious retirement. Hadrian himself designed a self-contained world for a vast royal entourage, the guards required to protect them, and the hundreds of servants needed to bathe them, feed them, and satisfy their libidos. On the estate were theaters, baths, temples, fountains, gardens, and canals bordered with statuary. Much of the ruins are readily recognizable, and it's easy to wander around the hot baths and the cold baths and experience a real sense of the villa as it once was (though if you wish to see what it looked like during its heyday, see the plastic reconstruction at the entrance). Admission is 6.50€ ($7.50). It's open daily 9am to sunset (about 6:30pm in summer, 4pm Nov–Mar). To get here, take bus 2 or 4 from the center of Tivoli.

At Tivoli itself, the clutter and clamor of 21st-century Italy is forgotten in a perfect gem from the Renaissance: **Villa d'Este** 🌟🌟, Piazza Trento, Viale delle Centro Fontane (© **0774/312070**), so named after the 16th-century cardinal who transformed it from a government palace (it had been built in the 13th c. as a Benedictine Convent) into a princely residence that remained in the cardinal's family until 1918. The 16th-century frescoes and decorations of the place itself are attractive, but unexceptional. The garden on the sloping hill beneath is another story—a perfect fairy tale of the Renaissance, using water as a medium of sculpture, much the way the ancients used marble. Pathways are lined with 100 fountains of every imaginable size and shape. Admission is 6.50€ ($7.50). It's open Tuesday to Sunday at 9am; closing times vary according to the season (1 hr. before sunset). November to January it closes at 4pm; closing times may be as late as 6:45pm in summer.

3 Naples

Nestled by a blue bay in the shadow of Mount Vesuvius, Naples, just 136 miles (219km) southeast of Rome, has been known to seafarers since the 6th century B.C. It remains one of the Mediterranean's foremost port cities to this day, its streets teeming with life—shirtless dockworkers, prostitutes, scampering children, throngs of pedestrians, huge open markets, and apartment houses whose facades are all but obscured with laundry. It has its towering castles and elegant palaces, too, as befits a town whose past enthusiasts have included the Emperor Nero and the poet Virgil.

Naples is also an ideal jumping-off point for some of the most popular vacation and sightseeing attractions in southern Italy. From here you can explore the ruins of Pompeii and Herculaneum, or sail to the fabled Isle of Capri. But the city itself has its own impressive sights, including some excellent museums. We rank it behind Florence and Venice, but if you're in the area and can spare a day or 2, Naples has excellent rail connections to Rome and makes for a good 1- or 2-day rail excursion out of the capital city.

GETTING THERE The rail lines between Rome and Naples are among the most frequently used in Italy. You can take either a regular train or a Eurostar Italia train to go from Rome to Naples. Some nine express trains run daily from Rome's Stazione Termini to the **Stazione Centrale** in Naples, the trip taking only 1 hour and 35 minutes and costing 32.54€ ($37.40) one-way. Tickets may be booked by calling ℭ **892021.** Regular train service is slower but cheaper, taking about 2½ hours and costing 10€ ($11.50) one-way.

Trains from Rome usually pull into Stazione Centrale in the heart of Naples. Here you will find many services, including a 24-hour pharmacy, plus a train information and reservations office right off the main hall that's open daily from 7am to 9:15pm. There is also a money exchange kiosk here (charging very expensive rates) and various food services. The office for storing luggage is open daily from 8am to 8pm, and charges 2.58€ ($2.95) per bag for 12 hours.

On-site is a branch of **Ente Provinciale per il Turismo,** the local tourist office (ℭ **081/7612102**), open Monday to Saturday 9am to 1pm and 3 to 7pm, Sunday 9am to 1pm. It does not make hotel reservations.

Note: Most travelers will arrive at Stazione Central, but anybody with an Alitalia ticket can take the **Alitalia Airport Train by FS,** an express train that runs twice a day between Rome's Leonardo da Vinci International Airport (Fiumicino) and Naples's **Stazione Mergellina,** a secondary rail station outside the city center. For general rail information, call ℭ **892021** toll-free in Italy.

VISITOR INFORMATION   The main tourist office, **Ente Provinciale per il Turismo,** is at Piazza dei Martiri 56 (ℭ **081/4107211**); it's open Monday to Friday 9am to 2pm. The staff does not make hotel reservations, which you'll need to make by yourself or through a travel agency.

GETTING AROUND   The **Metropolitana** line will deliver you from Stazione Centrale in the east all the way to the suburb of Pozzuoli. Get off at Piazza Piedigrotta if you want to take the funicular to Vómero. The Metro uses the same tickets as buses and trams. It's dangerous to ride **buses** at rush hours— never have we seen such pushing and shoving. Many people prefer to leave the buses to the battle-hardened Neapolitans and take the subway or **tram** no. 1 or 4, running from Stazione Centrale to Stazione Mergellina. For a ticket valid for 75 minutes with unlimited transfers during that time, the cost is .80€ (90¢). A ticket for a full day of unlimited travel costs 2.32€ ($2.65).

If you survive the **taxi** driver's reckless driving, you'll have to do battle over the bill. Many cab drivers claim that the meter is broken and assess the cost of the ride, always to your disadvantage. Some legitimate surcharges are imposed, such as night drives and extra luggage. However, many drivers deliberately take the scenic route to run up costs. You can call a radio taxi at ℭ **081/5564444,** 081-5560202, or 081-5707070.

Funiculars take passengers up and down the steep hills of Naples. **Funicolare Centrale** (ℭ **081/6106400**), for example, connects the lower part of the city to Vómero. Departures, daily 7am to midnight, are from Piazzetta Duca d'Aosta, just off Via Roma. The same tickets valid for buses and the Metro are good for the funicular.

TOP ATTRACTIONS & SPECIAL MOMENTS

Charles III of Spain took over a 16th-century building and turned it into **Museo Archeologico Nazionale (National Archaeological Museum)** ✦✦✦, Piazza Museo Nazionale 18–19 (ℭ **081/440166**), when he became King of Naples in the mid–18th century; installed in the mansion was his exquisite Farnese collection. Since that time, the museum has added art and artifacts from the excavations at Pompeii and Herculaneum as well as the Borgia collection of Etruscan and Egyptian antiquities, making its contents the most valuable archaeological collection in Europe.

Among the outstanding works in the Farnese collection are the gigantic marble *Hercules,* dating from the 1st century B.C., and the *Farnese Bull,* a sculptured group from the Greek Apollonius of Tralles. The original dates from the 2nd century B.C., and this work, a copy, once stood in the Baths of Caracalla in Rome. Also from the collection is a bas-relief of Orpheus and Eurydice, whose original dates from the 5th century B.C.

Several galleries on the mezzanine level are given over to mosaics recovered from Pompeii and Herculaneum, the most magnificent of which depicts Alexander battling with the Persian forces. Admission is 6.50€ ($7.50), and hours are Monday and Wednesday to Sunday 9am to 7pm. Metro: Piazza Cavour.

Museo e Gallerie Nazionale di Capodimonte (National Museum & Gallery of the Capodimonte) ★★, in the Palazzo Capodimonte, Parco di Capodimonte lying off Amedeo di Savoia and entered at Via Miano 2 (© **081/ 7499111**), stands near the outskirts of the city. The Capodimonte Galleries are housed in an 18th-century palace, surrounded by its own attractive gardens. The State Apartments contain a rich collection of ivories, porcelains, glass, and china, as well as the **Farnese Armory.** The real attraction of the palace, however, is the National Gallery, which occupies the top floor. One of the finest galleries in Italy, it is especially rich in paintings of the 14th century and the early Italian Renaissance.

One of the best of the 14th-century group is a coronation scene painted by Simone Martini, a leader of the Sienese School. The Renaissance is well represented by the greatest artists of that period: Raphael *(The Holy Family and Saint John),* Filippino Lippi *(Annunciation and Saints),* Michelangelo, Botticelli, Titian, and Mantegna.

Museo Nazionale di San Martino (National Museum of San Martino) ★★, Largo San Martino 5 (© **081/5781769**), in the Vomero district, is worth the trip if you do nothing more than stand on the balcony overlooking the Bay of Naples and gaze in awe at the panorama that includes Vesuvius and Capri. Reconstructed in the 17th century in a Neapolitan baroque style on the site of a 14th-century monastery, the museum is on the grounds of the Castel Sant'Elmo, and houses a broad collection of costumes, armor, carriages, documents, and 19th-century Campania paintings. Of special interest is the elaborately decorated Nativity scene by Curiniello. Admission is 6€ ($6.90); it's open Tuesday to Sunday 9am to 6:30pm. Funicular: Stazione Centrale from Via Toledo or Montesanto.

Castelnuovo (New Castle) ★★, Piazza del Municipio (© **081/4201241**), is marked by three massive turrets towering above the square. Although it was begun in 1279 by Charles of Anjou, most of what you see today dates from its mid-15th-century restoration (after Alfonso the Magnanimous drove the House of Anjou from its premises). The castle's most celebrated feature is the Arch of Triumph by Francesco Laurana, commemorating Alfonso's victory. Among the rooms you can visit are the massive Hall of the Barons, now used by the Naples City Commission, and the 14th-century Palatine Chapel, at the core of the castle. Admission is 5€ ($5.75). Hours are Monday to Saturday 9am to 7pm. Tram: 1 or 4. Bus: R2.

WHERE TO STAY & DINE

Hotel Britannique, Corso Vittorio Emanuele 133, 80121 Napoli (© **081/ 7614145;** www.hotelbritannique.it), is known for its central location close to the satellite rail station of Mergellina, and for its attractive bedrooms overlooking the Bay of Naples. Personally managed by the owners, it remains charmingly old-fashioned, although it has been modernized. An oasis is the hotel's flower-filled garden. Many guest rooms, ranging from small to large, have some antiques, although most of the furnishings are functional. The bathroom plumbing is aging but still humming along. Doubles cost 170€ ($196), with a junior suite going for 190€ ($219); rates include breakfast. Metro: Piazza Amedeo. Bus: C16 or C28.

In the Santa Lucia area near the waterfront, the 10-floor **Hotel Royal** ★, Via Partenope 38-44, 80121 Napoli (© **081/7644800;** www.hotelroyal.it), has long been a favorite of Naples visitors. Because this is a noisy part of Naples, bedrooms are soundproof and have been recently refurbished. Each of the guest rooms has a balcony, though not all of them open onto the Bay of Naples. The hotel is especially noted for its "restaurant with a view," and for its well-stocked wine cellar. Facilities include a pool and a health club. Doubles cost from 185€ to 260€ ($213–$299), with a suite going for 380€ ($437); rates include breakfast. Tram: 4.

Near the seafront, **Don Salvatore** ★, Strada Mergellina 4A (© **081/681817**), naturally specializes in seafood and does so exceedingly well. The fish, which comes from the Bay of Naples, is then either grilled or shaped into an array of dishes including linguine with shrimp or squid. The wine cellar here is the best in Naples. Main courses cost 10€ to 14.50€ ($11.50–$16.70). Metro: Mergellina. Another favorite for seafood, **Giuseppone a Mare** ★, Via Ferdinando Russo 13 (© **081/5756002**), is known for serving some of the best and freshest seafood in Campania. Diners make their fishy choices—ranging from fresh crabs to eels—from a trolley wheeled by each table. Often the day's catch is deep-fried as many locals like it that way. Main courses cost 12€ to 15€ ($13.80–$17.25). Bus: 140. The grilled seafood is even better at the more highly rated **La Cantinella** ★★, Via Cuma 42 (© **081/7648684**), on a bustling street opening onto the bay in the romantic Santa Lucia area. The *antipasti* table is one of the most alluring in town, and you can include all sorts of other dishes—not just fish. Main courses cost 10€ to 24€ ($11.50–$27.60). Bus: 104, 140, or 150.

DAY EXCURSIONS FROM NAPLES

The most exciting sightseeing attractions in southern Italy lie within a 15-mile (24km) radius of Naples, making that city an ideal home base for many excursions into the surrounding countryside. We list the three most compelling places to visit below in order of their importance.

POMPEII ★★★

Buried in its heyday in A.D. 79 by the eruption of Mount Vesuvius, the city of Pompeii, 15 miles (24km) south of Naples, offers visitors a glimpse of life as it was lived 2,000 years ago. The volcanic ash and lava that destroyed the city also helped to preserve the ruins until their rediscovery in 1748.

GETTING THERE   The **Circumvesuviana Railway** (© **081/5368932**) departs Naples every half hour from Piazza Garibaldi. However, be sure you get on the train headed toward *Sorrento* and get off at Pompeii/Scavi (*scavi* means "ruins"). If you get on the Pompeii train, you'll end up in the town of Pompeii and will have to transfer to the other train to get to the ruins. A round-trip ticket costs 2.20€ ($2.55); trip time is 45 minutes each way. Circumvesuviana trains leave Sorrento several times during the day for Pompeii, costing 1.80€ ($2.05) one-way. There's an entrance about 50 yards from the rail station at the Villa dei Misteri. At the rail station in the town of Pompeii, **bus** connections take you to the entrance to the excavations.

VISITOR INFORMATION   The **tourist office** is at Via Sacra 1 (© **081/ 8507255**). It's open Monday through Friday from 8am to 3:40pm (until 7pm Apr–Sept), and Saturday from 8am to 2pm.

Top Attractions & Special Moments

Most people visit the **Ufficio Scavi di Pompeii,** Piazza Esedra (© **081/ 8610744**), the best-preserved 2,000-year-old ruins in Europe, on a day trip from Naples (allow at least 4 hr. for even a superficial look at the archaeological site). The ruins are open daily from 8:30am to 6pm, with a 3:30pm closing off season. Admission is 10€ ($11.50).

Of particular interest are the elegant patrician villas, some of which are in an amazing state of preservation. The finest of these is the **House of the Vettii (Casa dei Vettii)** ★★★, built around an attractive Etruscan courtyard and adorned with handsome statuary. The dining room, frescoed with Cupids, is decorated in the traditional Pompeiian black and red. Among the statues still remaining in the villa is a sculpture of Janus, the two-faced household god. The **House of the Mysteries (Villa dei Misteri)** ★★, near the Herculaneum Gate, just outside the city walls, is an unusual villa—in appearance and purpose. As a cult center for the mysterious sect of Dionysus, it is decorated with murals and frescoes depicting some of the sacred—and very secret—initiation rites of this popular, but strange religion.

The **Stabian Thermae (baths)** ★★★, near the center of town, are a surprisingly intact example of public baths in an early Roman town. If you miss seeing the small household accessories in the Pompeiian homes, you'll find them on display in the **Antiquarium,** where pottery, utensils, sculptures, and kitchen equipment are exhibited. Flanked by the Temples of Jupiter and Apollo and the huge Basilica is the physical and political core of Pompeii, the **Forum** ★. Damaged in the earthquake that crippled the city 16 years before Mount Vesuvius finished the job, this important edifice was never completely restored. As you wander through the ruins, you can try your hand at translating the graffiti and campaign slogans immortalized on the walls and columns.

VESUVIUS ★★★

It may not look as sinister as it did in A.D. 79 when it buried Pompeii, Herculaneum, and Stabiae in a flood of lava and volcanic ash, but Vesuvius is still an active volcano. It has erupted more than once since the dawn of the Christian era, including a tragic spouting of lava in 1631 that killed thousands, and a less fatal explosion in 1906 when it simply blew the ring off its crater. The last spectacular eruption was on March 31, 1944.

It might sound like a dubious invitation, but it's possible to visit the rim of the crater's mouth. As you look down into its smoldering core, you might recall that Spartacus, a century before the eruption that buried Pompeii, hid in the hollow of the crater, which was then covered with vines.

To reach Vesuvius from Naples, take the **Circumvesuviana Railway** from Piazza Vittoria, which hooks up with bus connections at Pugliano. You get off the train at the Ercolano station, the 10th stop. Three **Vesuviana Trasporti** (© **081/5592582**) buses per day go from Herculaneum to the crater of Vesuvius, costing 3€ ($3.45) round-trip. Once at the top, you must be accompanied by a guide, which will cost 6€ ($6.90). Assorted willing tour guides are found in the bus parking lot; they are available from early in the morning to about 4:30pm in winter, 6pm in the summer.

Moments   Sicily: Land of Myth & Legend

Sicily is the largest of Mediterranean islands, 110 miles (178km) north to south and 175 miles (282km) wide, and a land of dramatic intensity. For centuries, its beauty and charm have attracted the greedy eye of foreign invaders: the Greeks, Romans, Vandals, Arabs, Normans, Swabians, and the Houses of Bourbon and Aragon. Luigi Barzini wrote: "Sicily is the schoolroom model of Italy for beginners, with every Italian quality and defect magnified, exasperated and brightly colored." Of course, it is the people themselves—bound by tradition and local customs—that provide the greatest interest. Most rail travelers on their first journey to Italy won't have time to visit Sicily, but it's well worth exploring on subsequent excursions.

The best centers for touring are Palermo, Syracuse, and Taormina. If you're considering anchoring into Sicily for a holiday, then Taormina occupies the best site, with the finest choice of hotels in all price ranges. If you stick to the main road that skirts the coast, encircling the island, you'll get to see most of the major sights, veering inland for such attractions as the active volcano of Mount Etna.

Trains from all over Europe arrive at the port at Villa San Giovanni, near Reggio di Calabria on the Italian mainland, and roll onto enormous barges for the 1-hour crossing to Sicily. Passengers remain in their seats during the short voyage across the Strait of Messina, eventually rolling back onto the rail tracks at Messina, Sicily. From Rome, the trip to Palermo takes 11 to 12 hours, depending on the speed of the train; the rail route from Naples takes 9 to 11 hours. Aboard any of the trains pulling into Palermo, you can rent a *couchette*. For fares and information, call ✆ **892021**.

Palermo, the capital of Sicily and also its largest port lies 447 miles (721km) south of Naples and 579 miles (934km) south of Rome, and is reached by rail, part of it involving a sea crossing as outlined above. Its major attractions include the **Cathedral of Palermo** ✮✮, on the Corso Vittorio Emanuele (✆ **091/334376**), built in the 12th century on the foundation of an earlier basilica that had been converted by the Arabs into a mosque. The **Palace of the Normanni (Palace of the Normans)** ✮✮, at the Piazza Parlamento (✆ **091/7057003**), contains one

HERCULANEUM ✮✮

If you've a yen to explore more ruins, you can head for this seaside resort buried in the same eruption that doomed Pompeii. The site of Herculaneum is much smaller—only about one-fourth the size of Pompeii—and a portion of it remains unexcavated because it is covered by the sprawling slums of Resina. According to legend, Hercules himself founded the city, which was covered in A.D. 79 by much thicker volcanic mud than the lava layer that buried Pompeii. This mud acted as an excellent preservative until 1709 when Prince Elbeuf began "mining" the town for all the treasures he could carry away. In spite of the harm caused by this destructive looting, subsequent excavations have revealed a remarkably well-preserved town, whose buildings are frequently of a higher quality than those found in Pompeii.

of the greatest art treasures in Sicily, the **Cappella Palatina (Palatine Chapel)** ✹✹✹. Erected at the request of Roger II in the 1130s, it is the finest example of the Arabic-Norman style of design and building. In a former convent, **Museo Archeologico Regionale** ✹✹✹, Via Bara all'Olivella 24 (© 091/6116807), houses one of the greatest archaeological collections in Southern Italy. Many works displayed here were excavated from Selinunte, once one of the major towns in *Magna Graecia* (Greater Greece).

Taormina is the greatest holiday resort south of Capri lying 155 miles (250km) east of Palermo. Dating from the 4th century B.C., Taormina hugs close to the edge of a cliff overlooking the Ionian Sea. The sea, even the railroad track, lies down below, connected by bus routes. Looming in the background is Mount Etna, an active volcano. Noted for its mild climate, the town enjoys a year-round season. The **Taormina Tourist Office** is in the Palazzo Corvaja, Piazza Santa Caterina (© 0942/23243), open Monday to Saturday 8am to 2pm and 4 to 7pm.

Syracuse is 35 miles (56km) southeast of Catania, the leading city along the coast of eastern Sicily and a transportation hub for rail lines in the area. From other major cities in Sicily, Syracuse is best reached by **train**. It's 1½ hours from Catania, 2 hours from Taormina, and 5 hours from Palermo. Usually you must transfer trains in Catania. For information, call © 892021. Trains arrive in Syracuse at the station on Via Francesco Crispi, centrally located midway between the archaeological park and Ortygia.

The main **tourist office** is at Via San Sebastiano 45 (© 0931/67710), with a branch office at Via Maestranza 33 (© 0931/65201). Both are open Monday to Saturday 9am to 1:30pm and 3 to 6:15pm.

Syracuse's **Archaeological Park** ✹✹✹ lies west of the modern town reached along Viale Rizzo. It is peppered with the most important attractions, beginning with **Teatro Greco** ✹✹✹ or the Greek Theater on Temenite Hill. Although in ruins, this is one of the great Greek theaters remaining from the classical era. The **Roman Amphitheater** ✹ nearby was erected at the time of Augustus. It ranks among the top live amphitheaters left by the Romans in Italy.

Casa dei Cervi (House of the Stags) ✹, the finest house in Herculaneum., was named for the sculpture found inside it. Important private homes to seek out are the **House of the Bicentenary (Casa del Bicentenario)** ✹, the **House of the Wooden Cabinet (Casa a Graticcio)** ✹✹, and the **House of the Wooden Partition (Casa del Tramezzo di Legno)** ✹. Inside the **House of Poseidon and Amphitrite** is an excellent mosaic depicting the god and goddess of the sea.

In addition to the private homes and villas, Herculaneum contains some fascinating public buildings, including the large **Municipal Baths *(terme)*** ✹✹✹, and the more lavish **Suburban Baths (Terme Suburbane)** ✹, built near the elegant villas at the outskirts of the city.

You can visit the ruins daily 8:30am to 6pm. Admission is 10€ ($11.50). To reach the archaeological zone, take the regular train service from Naples on the Circumvesuviana Railway, a 20-minute ride that leaves about every half hour from Corso Garibaldi 387, just south of the main train station (you can also catch Circumvesuviana trains underneath Stazione Centrale itself; follow the signs). This train will also get you to Vesuvius (same stop), Pompeii, and Sorrento.

4 Florence & Tuscany

On the banks of the Arno, Florence had been a Roman stronghold since the 1st century B.C., but it was not until after A.D. 1200 that it began to come into its own as a commercial and cultural center. During the 13th century, the merchants and tradesmen organized the guilds, which were to control the economy and government of Florence for nearly 150 years. These guilds supervised the construction of several important buildings of the city, and, with their new-found wealth, commissioned works of art that were to adorn the churches and palaces.

This revival of interest in art and architecture brought about the Italian Renaissance, an amazing outburst of activity between the 14th and 16th centuries that completely changed the face of the Tuscan town. During its heyday under the benevolent eye (and purse) of the Medicis, the city was lavishly decorated with churches, palaces, galleries, and monuments, making it the world's greatest repository of art treasures. The list of geniuses who lived or worked here reads like a "who's who" in the world of art and literature: Dante (he "invented" the Italian language here), Boccaccio, Fra Angelico, Brunelleschi, Donatello, da Vinci, Raphael, Cellini, Michelangelo, Ghiberti, Giotto, and Pisano.

Smack in the middle of the country, Florence sits on one of the country's major high-speed rail lines and offers excellent connections to Rome, Milan, and Venice, as well as several foreign cities (Artesia de Nuit trains, for example, connect the city to Paris). It's the best spot to explore the Tuscany region by rail. Aside from its good train links, the city is a fabulous destination for rail travelers because of its compact nature—nearly everything, from the city's attractions to its hotels, are within walking distance of the city's train station.

STATION INFORMATION
GETTING FROM THE AIRPORT TO THE TRAIN STATION
If you fly into the Tuscany region (usually through a connection from another Italian city), you can take an express train into the city from **Galileo Galilei Airport** at Pisa (✆ **050/849111**), 58 miles (93km) west of Florence. It is not covered by railpasses and costs 6.51€ ($7.50) one-way into Florence.

There's also a small domestic airport, **Amerigo Vespucci,** on Via del Termine, near A-11 (✆ **055/30615**), 3½ miles (5.5km) northwest of Florence, a 15-minute drive. From the airport, you can reach Florence by ATAF bus 62, which stops at the main Santa Maria Novella rail terminal. The fare is 4€ ($4.60).

INSIDE THE STATION
If you're coming north by train from Rome, count on a trip time of 1 to 2¾ hours, depending on your connections. In Florence, **Santa Maria Novella rail station,** Piazza della Stazione, adjoins Piazza Santa Maria Novella. For railway information, call ✆ **848/892021.** Some trains into Florence stop at the **Stazione Campo di Marte,** on the eastern side of Florence. A 24-hour bus service (no. 12) runs between the two rail terminals and costs 1€ ($1.15).

Santa Maria Novella station has all the usual amenities. A train reservations office on-site is open daily from 7am to 8pm, and a money exchange center (open Mon–Sat 8:20am–7:20pm) is right inside the main station hall. A luggage storage facility is located at track #16, and charges 2.58€ ($2.95) per bag for 12 hours; it's open daily 4:15am to 1:30am. Also near track #16 is a 24-hour pharmacy, **Farmacia Comunale** (© 055/289435).

A small **Uffizio Informazioni Turistiche** (© 055/212245) at the station is located directly across the square from the main exit. It offers free maps and a listing of the hours for city attractions but doesn't make hotel reservations. It's open daily 8:30am to 7pm.

For hotel reservations, visit **Consorzio ITA** (© 055/282893) in the train station next to track #16, close to the pharmacy (see above). You can't reserve rooms over the phone but must show up in person daily 8:45am to 8pm. The staff here charges a commission ranging from 2.50€ to 7.75€ ($2.90–$8.90), depending on your choice of hotel. In the busy season, expect long lines.

INFORMATION ELSEWHERE IN THE CITY

The main tourist office is the **Azienda Promozione Turistica** at Via Manzoni 16 (© 055/23320) near the Uffizi galleries; it's open Monday through Saturday from 9am to 1pm. There is another branch at Via Cavour 1R (© 055/290832), open Monday through Saturday from 8:30am to 6:30pm and Sunday from 8:30am to 1:30pm. There is yet another branch just south of Piazza Santa Croce, at Borgo Santa Croce 29R (© 055/2340444), open the same hours as the Via Cavour branch. None of these information offices makes hotel reservations.

Two useful websites with information about Florence include **www.mega.it/florence** and **http://english.firenze.net**.

GETTING AROUND

Florence is a city designed for walking, with all the major sights in a compact area. The only problem is that the sidewalks are almost unbearably crowded in summer.

If you plan to use **public buses,** you must buy your ticket before boarding, but for 1€ ($1.15) you can ride on any public bus for a total of 60 minutes. A 3-hour pass costs 2€ ($2.30) and a 24-hour ticket costs 4.50€ ($5.20). You can buy bus tickets at *tabacchi* (tobacconists) and newsstands. Once on board, you must validate your ticket in the box near the rear door, or you stand to be fined 40€ ($35.70)—no excuses accepted. The local **bus station** (which serves as the terminal for ATAF city buses) is at Piazza della Stazione (© 055/56501), behind the train station.

Bus routes are posted at bus stops, but the numbers of routes can change overnight because of sudden repair work going on at one of the ancient streets—perhaps a water main broke overnight and caused flooding. We recently found that a bus route map printed only 1 week beforehand was already outdated. Therefore, if you're dependent on bus transport, you'll need to inquire that day for the exact number of the vehicle you want to board.

You can find **taxis** at stands at nearly all the major squares. Rates are a bit expensive: The charge is .75€ (85¢) per kilometer (.6 mile), with a 2.45€ ($2.80) minimum. If you need a **radio taxi,** call © 055/4390 or 055/4798.

WHERE TO STAY

Hotel Bellettini ⭑ *Value*   Midway between the Duomo (cathedral) and the rail station, this 32-room hotel was carved out of a 14th-century palace with a

Florence

ACCOMMODATIONS ■

Grand Hotel Cavour **23**
Hermitage Hotel **12**
Hotel Bellettini **3**
Hotel Monna Lisa **26**
Hotel Porta Rossa **19**
Hotel Tornabuoni Beacci **7**
Hotel Torre Guelfa **11**
Hotel Vasari **1**

DINING ◆

Buca dell'Orafo **15**
Cafaggi **32**
Cantinetta Antinori **6**
Da Ganino **21**
Il Latini **8**
Le Mossacce **24**
Osteria Numero Uno **10**
Paoli **20**
Sabatini **4**
Trattoria Garga **9**

ATTRACTIONS ●

Basilica di San Lorenzo **30**
Basilica di Santa Maria Novella **5**
Battistero San Giovanni **29**
Cappelle dei Medici **2**
Duomo (Cattedrale di Santa
   Maria del Fiore) **28**
Galleria degli Uffizi **16**
Galleria dell'Accademia **31**
Giardini di Boboli **14**
Giotto's Bell Tower
   (Campanile di Giotto) **25**
Museo dell'Opera del Duomo **27**
Museo di San Marco **33**
Museo Nazionale del Bargello **22**
Palazzo Pitti **13**
Palazzo Vecchio **17**
Piazza della Signoria **18**

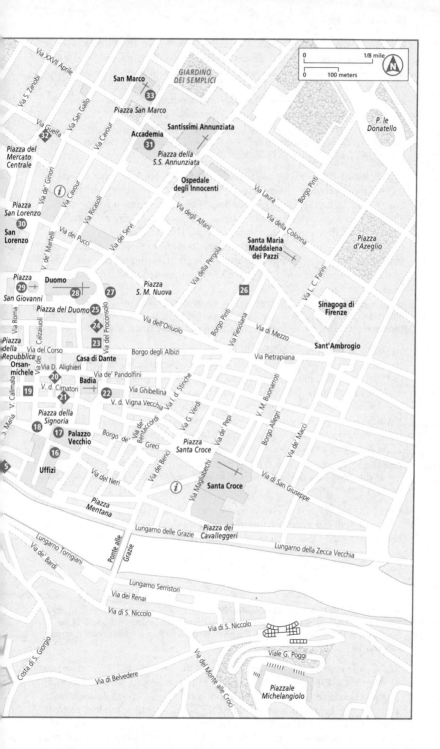

history of innkeeping going back 3 centuries. Run by two Tuscan-born sisters, it's one of the more traditional choices in the center of Florence, and filled with atmospheric trappings such as carved wood, wrought-iron beds, stained-glass windows, antiques, and terra-cotta tiles. The small to midsize bedrooms are furnished minimally but comfortably. Only two accommodations per floor share the corridor bathrooms, so you'll rarely have to wait in line.

Via di Conti 7, 50123 Firenze. ☎ 055/213561. Fax 055/283551. www.firenze.net/hotelbelletini.com. 26 units. 100€ ($115) double without bathroom, 130€ ($150) double with bathroom. Rates include buffet breakfast. AE, DC, MC, V. Bus: 1, 9, 14, 17, 23, 36, and 37. **Amenities:** Laundry.

Grand Hotel Cavour   Opposite the Bargello Museum, this hotel was converted from a private mansion and has retained much of the original pristine beauty, such as frescoed and coved ceilings. The hotel is known for its atmospherically decorated wine bar and restaurant, and for its roof terrace, "Michelangelo," which offers a panoramic sweep over the Duomo, Palazzo Vecchio, and more. The rooms, unlike the building, are contemporary in styling and comfort, although a bit small; the bathrooms are new. Regrettably, this hotel lies in a particularly noisy part of town, and even the soundproofed windows can't quite block out the sounds.

Via del Proconsolo 3, 50122 Firenze. ☎ 055/282461. Fax 055/218955. www.albergocavour.it. 110 units. 166€–198€ ($191–$228) double. Rates include buffet breakfast. AE, DC, MC, V. Bus: 14, 23, or 71. **Amenities:** Restaurant; laundry; nonsmoking rooms; rooms for those with limited mobility. *In room:* Hair dryer.

Hermitage Hotel ⭐   No hotel in Florence is better located than this offbeat charmer, situated right on the Arno at the foot of the Ponte Vecchio. Renovated in 1998, the hotel's rooms are pleasantly furnished with antiques from the 17th to the 19th centuries. Bathrooms are superb and contain lots of gadgets; some have hydro-massage tubs. Those rooms overlooking the Arno offer the most scenic view, and they've been fitted with double-glazed windows. The intimate lounge has a bar to one side and a fireplace for that nippy evening, but the main allure is the roof terrace planted with flowers, which offers wonderful views.

Vicolo Marzio 1, Piazza del Pesce I, 50122 Firenze. ☎ 055/287216. Fax 055/212208. www.hermitagehotel. com. 28 units. 195€–245€ ($224–$282) double. Rates include breakfast. MC, V. Bus: B. **Amenities:** Bar; laundry. *In room:* Hair dryer.

Hotel Monna Lisa ⭐   This privately owned Renaissance palazzo has been well preserved and tastefully furnished, and it's exceptionally located—just 4 blocks east of the Duomo. Most of the great old rooms overlook either an inner patio or a modest rear garden. Each of the salons is handsomely furnished. Many bedrooms have their original painted wooden ceilings, along with antiques and rich fabrics. Some of the accommodations are rather large, others a bit tiny. Each comes with a tiled bathroom. .

Borgo Pinti 27, 50121 Firenze. ☎ 055/2479751. Fax 055/2479755. www.monnalisa.it. 45 units. 181€–284€ ($208–$327) double; 232€–413€ ($267–$475) triple. Rates include breakfast. AE, DC, MC, V. Bus: A, 6, 31, or 32. **Amenities:** Laundry; nonsmoking rooms; rooms for those with limited mobility. *In room:* Hair dryer.

Hotel Porta Rossa ⭐   An inn on this spot has been putting up wayfarers to Florence since 1386, making Porta Rossa the second-oldest hotel in Florence. The hotel occupies the top three floors of a six-story structure. In spite of its antiquity, the hotel has kept abreast of the times, installing modern conveniences, good beds, and ample bathrooms, some with shower, others with tub. Most of the bedrooms are midsize to large. An attractive feature is a terrace with panoramic views of Florence.

Via Porta Rossa 19, 50123 Firenze. ℂ **055/287551**. Fax 055/282179. 79 units. 170€ ($196) double. Rates include breakfast. AE, DC, MC, V. Bus: A. **Amenities:** Bar; laundry; nonsmoking rooms; rooms for those with limited mobility. *In room:* Hair dryer.

Hotel Tornabuoni Beacci ⭐

Near the Arno and Piazza S. Trinità, on the principal shopping street, this near-century-old pensione occupies the top three floors of a 16th-century *palazzo*. The renovated hotel still bears an air of old-fashioned gentility and a lot of atmosphere. The rooms are moderately well furnished with period pieces in an old Florentine style. Rooms at the top are smaller but have better views. The roof terrace for breakfast or drinks is a delight, opening onto scenic vistas of the skyline of Florence.

Via Tornabuoni 3, 50123 Firenze. ℂ **055/212645**. Fax 055/283594. www.bthotel.it. 40 units. 185€–240€ ($213–$276) double; from 280€ ($322) suite. Rates include buffet breakfast. AE, DC, MC, V. Bus: B, 6, 11, or 36. **Amenities:** Restaurant; bar; laundry. *In room:* Hair dryer.

Hotel Torre Guelfa ⭐⭐

Only 164 feet from the Ponte Vecchio, this hotel is crowned with a 13th-century tower, offering panoramic views of the city. The structure dates from 1280 although there have been many alterations over the years, as recent as a renovation in 1998. The midsize accommodations are inviting and have pastel-washed walls, paisley carpeting, and good bathrooms; some have canopied cast-iron beds.

Borgo SS. Apostoli 8 (between Via dei Tornabuoni and Via Per Santa Maria), 50123 Firenze. ℂ **055/2396338**. Fax 055/2398577. www.hoteltorreguelfa.com. 39 units. 150€–180€ ($173–$207) double; 210€ ($242) suite. Rates include breakfast. AE, MC, V. Bus: D, 11, 36, 37, 68. **Amenities:** Bar; laundry. *In room:* Hair dryer.

Hotel Vasari ⭐ *Value*

Before it was completely revamped into an excellent hotel in 1993, this inn enjoyed a long history, having served as a monastery in the 16th century and as the town house mansion of the 19th century French poet, Alfonse de Lamartine. Much of the old charm remains, including ceiling frescoes and an original stone fireplace in the breakfast room. Bedrooms are small to midsize and are comfortably furnished but a bit minimalist. The tiled bathrooms are small but immaculate. The central location, just 1,000 feet from the Duomo is a plus.

Via B. Cennini 9–11, 50123 Firenze. ℂ **055/212753**. Fax 055/294246. www.hotelvasari.com. 27 units. 110€–155€ ($127–$178) double. Rates include breakfast. AE, DC, MC, V. Bus: 4, 7, 10, 13, 14, 23, or 71. **Amenities:** Bar; laundry. *In room:* Hair dryer.

TOP ATTRACTIONS & SPECIAL MOMENTS

To truly see the city at less than a breakneck pace, you need at least 3 days in Florence. If you have less time than that, make sure to see the **Uffizi** and the **Galleria dell'Accademia.** Don't forget to have a meal in one of the city's excellent Tuscan restaurants, and try to make time to view the city (especially the Ponto Vecchio) at sunset—it's a truly memorable experience.

One other noteworthy spot worth your attention is the **Piazza della Signoria** ⭐⭐. As the "front yard" of Florence's city hall, Palazzo Vecchio, Piazza della Signoria was the center of the city's political life from around A.D. 1300. Today the square is a favorite attraction, not only because of its historical significance, but for its wealth of artistic sights as well. On the piazza itself is the **Fountain of Neptune** ⭐, a massively detailed work by Ammannati. Created in the 16th century, it portrays the sea god surrounded by his following of water creatures and woodland nymphs. Also on the plaza is a copy of Michelangelo's *David*, substituted for the original after it was removed to the safety of the Academy Gallery in 1873. Opening onto the square is the **Loggia dei Lanzi** ⭐⭐, a spacious open hallway dating from the 14th century. It is lined with several important sculptures, all of them outshined by Cellini's brilliant masterpiece of *Perseus* 🟊🟊🟊 holding the head of Medusa.

Baptistery (Battistero San Giovanni) 🟊🟊🟊 Facing the Duomo, the octagonal Baptistery is a splendid example of Romanesque architecture as only the Florentines could interpret it. Dating from the 5th century, it was virtually rebuilt in the 11th and 12th centuries with particularly Florentine innovations. The facade is covered with green and white marble, and set into three sides are magnificent bronze doors decorated with gilded bas-reliefs. The greatest treasures here are the **East and West Doors** 🟊🟊🟊, artistically created by Ghiberti under a commission awarded him by the cloth guild of Florence. The enterprise, one of the curtain raisers on the Renaissance, cost the guild 22,000 florins (a 15th-c. Florentine could live in luxury on only 200 florins a year), and took Ghiberti a total of 52 years. After the second door was unveiled in 1452, Michelangelo adjudged it so beautiful that he dubbed it *The Gateway to Paradise.*

Piazza San Giovanni. ✆ **055/2302885.** Admission 3€ ($3.45). Daily noon–6:30pm. Bus: 1, 6, 17.

Bargello Museum (Museo Nazionale del Bargello) 🟊🟊 Begun in 1254, this medieval palace was once a powerful military fortress. Today, as a museum, it exhibits the arms and armor used during the more violent periods of its history, along with a fine collection of decorative art. But the real attraction at the Bargello is the splendid array of medieval and Renaissance sculpture. There's another *David* by Michelangelo here, though not nearly as virile as the famous one in the Accademia. Nor does it stand up to the most famous *David* 🟊🟊 here—Donatello's free-standing bronze creation, nude (except for boots and bonnet) atop the severed head of Goliath. Also by Donatello is his heroic and extremely lifelike interpretation of *St. George* 🟊. Michelangelo is represented in several works, including his *Bacchus,* a bust of *Brutus,* and a bas-relief of *Madonna and Child with John the Baptist.*

Via del Proconsolo 4. ✆ **055/294883.** Admission 4€ ($4.60). Daily 8:30am–1:50pm. Closed Jan 1, May 1, and Christmas. Bus: A, 14, or 23.

Basilica di San Lorenzo 🟊🟊 This church was begun in 1442 by Brunelleschi, and the interior completed by Manetti in 1460. Shaped like a Latin cross, the church was the favorite of the Medicis (the adjoining New Sacristy contains the tombs of the clan), so a great deal of money and artistic effort went into decorating it. The **Old Sacristy,** at the left of the nave, was partially decorated by Donatello, including some terra-cotta reliefs. The adjoining **Laurenziana Library** 🟊🟊 was designed by Michelangelo to contain the huge Medici collection of manuscripts. It boasts an unusual staircase and an intricately carved and paneled reading room.

Piazza San Lorenzo. ✆ **055/214443.** Free admission; 2.60€ ($3) for special exhibitions. Mon–Sat 8:30am–1:30pm. Bus: 1, 6, 7, 11, 17, 33, 67, or 68.

Basilica di Santa Maria Novella 🟊🟊 Right near the rail station, this landmark is a large Dominican edifice built between 1278 and 1350. On the Piazza Santa Maria Novella, its marble inlaid facade was added in the 15th century by Alberti. The church is especially interesting for its frescoes by Masaccio, Ghirlandaio, Orcagna, and Filippo Lippi. The adjoining cloisters are also worth a visit, especially the Spanish Chapel with frescoes by Andrea di Bonaiuto and his assistants.

Piazza Santa Maria Novella. (Ⓒ **055/215918**. Church free; Spanish Chapel and cloisters 2.70€ ($3.10). Church Mon–Fri 7am–noon and 3–6pm. Spanish Chapel and cloisters Sat–Thurs 8am–2pm; Sun 9am–1:30pm. Bus: A, 6, 9, 11, 36, 37, or 68.

Duomo Museum (Museo dell'Opera del Duomo) ✸✸   Across the street from but facing the apse of Santa Maria del Fiore, is this museum beloved by connoisseurs of Renaissance sculptural works. It shelters the sculptures removed from the campanile and the Duomo. A major reason for visiting the museum is to see the world-famous marble **choirs** ✸✸—*cantorie*—of Donatello and Luca della Robbia (both works face each other, and are housed in the first room you enter after climbing the stairs). One of Donatello's most celebrated works, *Magdalene* ✸✸, is in the room with the *cantorie*. A major attraction is an **unfinished *Pietà*** ✸✸, by Michelangelo, in the middle of the stairs. It was carved between 1548 and 1555, when the artist was in his 70s. The premier attraction, however, are the **restored panels of Ghiberti's Gates of Paradise** ✸✸✸, which were removed from the baptistery. In gilded bronze, each is a masterpiece of Renaissance sculpture, the finest low-relief perspective in all Italian art.

Piazza del Duomo 9. (Ⓒ **055/2302885**. Admission 6€ ($6.90). Year-round Mon–Sat 9am–6:30pm; Sun 8:30am–1pm. Bus: B, 14, 23, or 71.

Galleria degli Uffizi ✸✸✸   Outside the Prado and the Louvre, no art museum in the world can compare with the Uffizi, home to Italy's finest collection of art. The 16th-century building stretches from the Palazzo Vecchio to the Arno. In spite of its size and multitudinous works of art (about 2,500 paintings alone, plus miniatures, statues, and more than 100,000 drawings and prints), the museum is easily navigated, since the galleries are grouped by periods and schools. But don't expect to see everything in one day. Laid out progressively, the galleries begin with Room 1 (classical sculptures) and extend through Room 42 (Italian and French paintings of the 18th c.). The largest concentration of paintings is on Italian works of the 15th and 16th centuries (more than 400 of these alone). Room 10 is the most popular in the entire gallery. Here you'll find the works of Botticelli, including his ***Birth of Venus*** ✸✸✸ and *Primavera,* two of the most famous paintings in the world.

   Room 18, the octagonal Tribune, is the most splendid in the museum, even when it contains no exhibits. The floor is inlaid with marble in geometric

---

⌐Tips How to Avoid Those Endless Lines

Select Italy offers the possibility to reserve your tickets for the Uffizi, Boboli Gardens, Galleria dell'Accademia, and many other attractions in Florence. The cost varies from 12.50€ to 28€ ($14.40–$32.20), depending on the museum, and several combination passes are available. Contact **Select Italy** at (Ⓒ **847/853-1661**, or buy online at **www.selectitaly.com**.

   If you're already in Florence and don't want to waste a half day waiting to enter the Galleria degli Uffizi, Galleria dell'Accademia, Boboli Gardens, Pitti Palace, and many others, call **Firenze Musei** (Ⓒ **055/294883; www.firenzemusei.it**). The service operates Monday to Friday from 8:30am to 6:30pm, and Saturday to 12:30pm. Requests must be made a minimum of 5 days in advance; you pick up the tickets at the museum booth on the day your visit has been approved. There's a service charge of 3€ ($3.45), plus, of course, the regular price of the museum admission.

Moments **A Stroll Across Italy's Most Famous Bridge**

Miraculously spared by the Nazis in their bitter retreat from the Allied advance in 1944, the **Ponte Vecchio (Old Bridge)** ⭐⭐ is the last remaining medieval *ponte* that once spanned the Arno (the Germans blew up the rest). The existence of the Ponte Vecchio was again threatened in the flood of 1966—in fact, the waters of the Arno swept over it, washing away a fortune in jewelry from the famous goldsmiths' shops that flank the bridge.

Today the Ponte Vecchio is back in business, closed to traffic except the *pedoni* or foot passenger type. The little shops continue to sell everything from the most expensive of Florentine gold to something simple—say, a Lucrezia Borgia poison ring.

---

designs, and the domed ceiling studded with pearl shells. The room's most prominent spot is occupied by the **Medici Venus** ⭐⭐, a magnificent Greek sculpture, along with later copies of 4th-century Greek sculptures of *The Wrestler* and *Apollo.*

Piazzale degli Uffizi 6. ✆ 055/23885. www.uffizi.firenze.it. Admission 8.05€ ($9.25). Tues–Sun 8:15am–7pm (last entrance 45 min. before closing). Advance booking necessary. Bus: A, B, 23, or 71.

Galleria dell'Accademia ⭐⭐ This museum is visited mainly for one exhibit: Michelangelo's awesome statue of ***David*** ⭐⭐⭐. For years the 17-foot statue weathered the elements on the Piazza della Signoria, but was finally moved to the Accademia in 1873 and placed beneath the rotunda of a room built exclusively for its display. When he began work on *David,* Michelangelo was just 29. In the connecting picture gallery is a collection of Tuscan masters, such as Botticelli, and Umbrian works by Perugino (teacher of Raphael).

Via Ricasoli 60. ✆ 055/2388609. Admission 8.50€ ($9.80). Tues–Sun 8:15am–6:50pm. Bus: B, D, or 12.

Giotto's Bell Tower (Campanile di Giotto) ⭐⭐ Although better known for his great skill in fresco painting, Giotto left to posterity the most beautiful campanile (bell tower) in Europe, rhythmic in line and form. The 274-foot tower, a "Tuscanized" Gothic, with bands of colored marble, can be scaled for a truly memorable **panoramic view** ⭐⭐⭐ of the sienna-colored city and the blue-green Tuscan hills in the distance.

Piazza del Duomo. ✆ 055/2302885. Cathedral free; excavations 3€ ($3.45); cupola 6€ ($6.90). Mon–Fri 8:30am–6:30pm; Sat 8:30am–5pm. Bus: 1, 6, 17.

Il Duomo (Cattedrale di Santa Maria del Fiore) ⭐⭐⭐ The cathedral of Florence, called simply the *Duomo,* is the crowning glory of Florence. But don't rush inside too quickly, as the view of the exterior, with its geometrically patterned bands of white, pink, and green marble, is, along with **Brunelleschi's dome** ⭐⭐⭐, the best feature. One of the world's largest churches, the Duomo represents the flowering of the "Florentine Gothic" style. Begun in 1296, it was finally consecrated in 1436, yet finishing touches on the facade were applied as late as the 19th century. Inside, the overall effect is bleak, except when you stand under the cupola, frescoed in part by Vasari. Some of the stained-glass windows in the dome were based on designs by Donatello (Brunelleschi's friend) and Ghiberti (Brunelleschi's rival). The overall effect of the cathedral's famous dome atop its octagonal drum is one of the most striking sights of the city—and its most famous landmark. If you resist scaling Giotto's bell tower (below), you may want to climb Brunelleschi's ribbed dome. The view is well worth the trek.

Piazza del Duomo. (C) 055/2302885. Cathedral free; excavations 3€ ($3.45); cupola 6€ ($6.90). Mon–Fri 8:30am–6:30pm; Sat 8:30am–5pm. Bus: 1, 6, 17.

Medici Chapels (Cappelle dei Medici) ✹✹ Michelangelo left his mark on Florence in many places, but nowhere can you feel so completely surrounded by his works as in the Medici Chapels, adjoining the Basilica di San Lorenzo (see above). Working from 1521 to 1534, Michelangelo created the Medici tomb in a style that foreshadowed the baroque. Lorenzo the Magnificent was buried near Michelangelo's uncompleted *Madonna and Child* group. Ironically, the finest groups of sculpture were reserved for two of the lesser Medicis, who are represented as armored, idealized princes. The other two figures on Lorenzo's tomb are most often called *Dawn* (represented as woman) and *Dusk* (as man). The best-known figures are *Night* (chiseled as a woman in troubled sleep) and *Day* (a man of strength awakening to a foreboding world) at the feet of Giuliano, the duke of Nemours.

Piazza Madonna degli Aldobrandini 6. (C) 055/294883. Admission 6€ ($6.90). Mon–Sat 8:15am–5pm; Sun 8:30am–5pm. Closed 2nd and 4th Sun, and 1st, 3rd, and 5th Mon of each month. Bus: 1, 6, 7, 11, 17, 33, 67, or 68.

Palazzo Pitti and the Giardini di Boboli (Boboli Gardens) ✹✹ Just 5 minutes from the Ponte Vecchio, The Pitti, built in the mid–15th century (Brunelleschi was the original architect), was once the residence of the powerful Medici family. Today it contains several museums, the most important of which is the **Galleria Palatina** ✹✹, a repository of old masters. Devoted mainly to Renaissance works, the Palatine is especially rich in Raphaels, including his world-famous *Madonna of the Chair*. Other works by Titian, Botticelli, Fra Bartolomeo, Filippo Lippi, Tintoretto, Rubens, Van Dyck, and Velázquez round out the collection.

The **Royal Apartments (Appartamenti Reali)** ✹ boast lavish reminders of the time when the Pitti was the home of the Kings of Savoy. Reopened in 1993 after a restoration, these apartments in all their baroque sumptuousness, including a flamboyant decor and works of art by del Sarto and Caravaggio, can be viewed only on a guided tour, usually Tuesday and Saturday (also on an occasional Thurs) 9 to 11am and 3 to 5pm. Tours leave every hour. Reservations are needed, so call (C) **051/2388614.**

Other museums are the **Museo degli Argenti** ((C) **055-294883**), 16 rooms devoted to displays of the "loot" acquired by the Medici dukes; the **Coach and Carriage Museum;** the **Galleria d'Arte Moderna** ((C) **055-2388601**); the **Museo delle Porcellane** (porcelain); and the **Galleria del Costume.**

⟮ *Moments* A Garden Stroll

Behind the Pitti Palace are the extensive **Boboli Gardens** ✹, Piazza de'Pitti 1 ((C) **055/2651838**), designed and executed by Triboli, a landscape artist (on canvas and in real life), in the 16th century. Studded with fountains and statues, it provides an ideal setting for a relaxing break between museum visits. The gardens are also the setting for Fort Belvedere, an imposing structure that dominates the hillside and offers a spectacular view of Florence. For opening times see above.

Moments **One of the World's Greatest Views**

The best overall view of the city is from the **Piazzale Michelangelo** (bus 13 from the Central Station), an elevated plaza on the south side of the river. If you can ignore the milling crowds and souvenir peddlers who flood the square, you can enjoy a **spectacular view** ☆☆☆ of old Florence, circled by the hazy hills of Tuscany. It's like looking at a Renaissance painting. We prefer the view at dusk when the purple-fringed Tuscan hills form a frame for Giotto's bell tower, Brunelleschi's dome, and the towering hunk of stones that stick up from the Palazzo Vecchio. If you look up into the hills, you can also see the ancient town of Fiesole, with its Roman ruins and cathedral. Another copy of Michelangelo's famous statue *David* dominates Piazzale Michelangelo, giving the wide square its name. Crown your view with some of the delectable ice cream served on the square at **Gelateria Michelangelo** (✆ **055/2342705**), open daily 7am to 2am.

Piazza Pitti, across the Arno. ✆ **055/218741**. Palatina 8.50€; Modern Art Gallery 5€ ($5.75); 4€ ($4.60) for both Argenti and Boboli Gardens. Galleria Palatina and Appartamenti Reali Tues–Sun 8:15am–6:45pm. Museo degli Argenti and Modern Art Gallery daily 8:30am–1:30pm; closed the 1st and 5th Mon and the 2nd and 4th Sun of each month. Boboli Gardens June–Sept daily 8:30am–7:45pm; Apr–May and Oct daily 8:30am–6:45pm; Nov–Mar daily 9am–5:45pm; closed the 1st and last Mon of each month. Ticket office closes 1 hr. before the gardens. Bus: D, 11, 36, 37, or 68.

St. Mark's Museum (Museo di San Marco) ☆☆   This state museum is a handsome Renaissance palace whose cell walls are decorated with magnificent 15th-century **frescoes** ☆☆☆ by the mystical Fra Angelico. In the days of Cosimo dei Medici, San Marco was built as a Dominican convent. It originally contained bleak, bare cells, which Angelico and his students then brightened considerably. One of his better-known paintings here is *The Last Judgment* ☆☆, contrasting the beautiful angels and saints on the left with the demons and tortured sinners of hell on the right. Among his other works are a masterful *Annunciation* ☆☆☆, and a magnificently colorful *Virgin and Child.*

Piazza San Marco 1. ✆ **055/294883**. Admission 6€ ($6.90). Tues–Fri 8:30am–1:50pm; Sat–Sun 8:15am–6:50pm. Ticket office closes 30 min. before the museum. Closed 2nd and 4th Mon of the month; 1st, 3rd, 5th Sun of the month; Jan 1, May 1, and Christmas. Bus: 1, 6, 7, 10, 11, 17, or 20.

WHERE TO DINE

Buca dell'Orafo ☆ *Finds* FLORENTINE   This little dive is one of many cellars or *buca*-type establishments beloved by Florentines. The trattoria is usually stuffed with regulars, so if you want a seat, go early. Over the years the chef has made little concession to the foreign palate, turning out genuine Florentine specialties, like tripe and mixed boiled meats with a green sauce.

Via Volta dei Girolami 28R. ✆ **055/213619**. Main courses 10€–13€ ($11.50–$14.95). No credit cards. Tues–Sat 12:30–2:30pm and 7:30–10:30pm. Closed Aug and 2 weeks in Dec. Bus: B.

Cafaggi TUSCAN/SEAFOOD   In a converted palace, this 100-seat trattoria has been a Florentine tradition since 1922, its tables spread across two antique dining rooms. This charming and atmospheric eatery is securely ensconced on the Florentine dining circuit, its kitchen adhering to time-tested Tuscan recipes, including some of the town's best seafood. Some of the recipes appear a bit startling at first but can quickly become addictive as exemplified by the spaghetti with sardines, pine nuts, and raisins.

Via Guelfa 35R. ℂ **055/294989**. Reservations recommended. Main courses 9€–17€ ($10.35–$19.55). AE, MC, V. Mon–Sat noon–3pm and 7–10pm. Bus: 1, 6, 7, 11, 17, 33, 67, or 68.

Cantinetta Antinori ⭐ *(Finds* FLORENTINE/TUSCAN   The menu at one of Florence's most highly rated wine bars changes with the seasons, and is it ever good. You can visit this 15th-century *palazzo* for complete meals or else snacks. Regardless of what you order, your food is most often accompanied by one of the best-stocked cellars in town from a company that has been hawking wines for 6 centuries. The food is standard but satisfying, and many of the ingredients come directly from the Antinori farms.

Piazza Antinori 3. ℂ **055/292234**. Reservations recommended. Main courses 13€–22€ ($14.95–$25.30). AE, DC, MC, V. Mon–Fri 12:30–2:30pm and 7–10:30pm. Closed Aug and Dec 24–Jan 6. Bus: 6, 11, 14, 36, 37, or 68.

Da Ganino ⭐ FLORENTINE/TUSCAN   Both the *New York Times* and the Paris *Herald Tribune* have lavished justified praise on this intimate little trattoria, which is run by the Ganino family across from an American Express office midway between the Uffizi and the Duomo. Succulent pastas, well-flavored and perfectly cooked meats, classic T-bone *Fiorentina* steaks, and some of the best of regional ingredients, such as white truffles, keep foodies and locals coming back for more.

Piazza dei Cimatori 4R. ℂ **055/214125**. Reservations recommended. Main courses 6€–15€ ($6.90–$17.25). AE, DC. Mon–Sat 1–3pm and 7:30–10:30pm. Bus: 14, 23, or 71.

Il Latini ⭐ TUSCAN/FLORENTINE   Latini is loud and claustrophobic, and the service borders on hysterical. Still, this is an enduringly popular place with locals and visitors, who pack the place for the enormous portions served at communal tables. A waiter will arrive to recite a list of items corresponding to antipasti, pasta, main course, and dessert. If you insist on seeing a printed menu, someone will probably find one, but it's more fun just to go with the flow. We can't pretend the food is subtle—it isn't—but it's filling, relatively cheap, and made with fresh ingredients.

Via del Palchetti 6R (off Via Vigna Nuova). ℂ **055/210916**. Reservations recommended. Main courses 10€–17€ ($11.50–$19.55). AE, DC, MC, V. Tues–Sun 12:30–2:30pm and 7:30–10:30pm. Closed Dec 24–Jan 7. Bus: C, 6, 11, 36, or 37.

Le Mossacce *(Value* TUSCAN/FLORENTINE   Near the Duomo, this small *osteria* is known for serving tasty, affordable home cooking in generous portions to hungry Florentines. Many of the delights of the Florentine menu appear here, including such classics as *ribollita* (a thick vegetable soup) or those justly celebrated slices of *bistecca* (beefsteak) *alla fiorentina*. A tradition since 1942, Le Mossacce hires waiters who prefer to tantalize you with the offerings of the day instead of presenting you with a menu—we had a great meal following their advice.

Via del Proconsolo 55R. ℂ **055/294361**. Reservations unnecessary. Main courses 8€–15€ ($9.20–$17.25). AE, DC, MC, V. Mon–Fri noon–2:30pm and 7–9:30pm. Closed Aug. Bus: 14.

Osteria Numero Uno ⭐ INTERNATIONAL/FLORENTINE   Near the train station, this is a winning choice installed in a palace dating from the 1400s. Under vaulted ceilings with a décor of musical instruments and original paintings, you are served well-prepared Florentine and international dishes based on market-fresh ingredients. Most diners come here to order big slabs of the tender and well-flavored beefsteak, which will usually feed at least two people.

Via del Moro 22R. ☎ 055/284897. Reservations recommended. Main courses 8€–25€ ($9.20–$28.75). AE, DC, MC, V. Mon 7pm–12:30am; Tues–Sat noon–3pm and 7pm–midnight. Closed 3 weeks in Aug. Bus: C, 6, 9, 11, 36, 37, or 68.

Paoli ★★ TUSCAN/ITALIAN   Paoli, between the Duomo and Piazza della Signoria, is one of Florence's finest restaurants. It turns out a host of specialties, but could be recommended almost solely for its atmospheric medieval-tavern atmosphere. All pastas are homemade, and the fettuccine alla Paoli is served piping hot and full of flavor. The chef also does a superb *rognoncino trifolato* (thinly sliced kidney cooked with oil, garlic, and parsley) and sole meunière. It's worth saving room for one of the yummy desserts.

Via dei Tavolini 12R. ☎ 055/216215. Reservations required. Main courses 11€–19€ ($12.65–$21.85). AE, DC, MC, V. Wed–Mon noon–2:30pm and 7–10:30pm. Closed 3 weeks in Aug. Bus: A.

Sabatini ★★ FLORENTINE   In an antique house only 200 yards from the Duomo, this restaurant is said to serve the most classic Tuscan cuisine in Florence. Understated and traditional, it offers all the old-time favorites Florentines have grown to love, including *bistecca alla fiorentina*—arguably the finest in the city—and classics such as boiled Valdarno chicken in a savory green sauce. The wine cellar is particularly notable here for both its Tuscan and Umbrian vintages—one habitué called it "seductive."

Via de'Panzani 9A. ☎ 055/211559. Reservations recommended. Main courses 12.50€–24€ ($14.40–$27.60). AE, DC, MC, V. Tues–Sun 12:30–2:30pm and 7:30–10:30pm. Bus: 1, 6, 14, 17, or 22.

Trattoria Garga ★★ TUSCAN/FLORENTINE   Some of the most creative cuisine in Florence is served here, about midway between the Ponte Vecchio and Santa Maria Novella. This local favorite's postage-size kitchen turns out dishes based on old Tuscan recipes that have been given a new twist. The walls are from the days of the Renaissance, and they are decorated with contemporary paintings. Save room for dessert: The chef prepares a cheesecake so well known in Florence that even New Yorkers give it a thumbs-up.

Via del Moro 48R. ☎ 055/2398898. Reservations required. Main courses 20€–27€ ($23–$31.05). AE, DC, MC, V. Tues–Sun 7:30–11pm. Bus: 6, 9, 11, 36, 37, or 68.

SHOPPING

Florence is a city of high fashion, and it's also known for its leather goods, straw products, and magnificently crafted gold jewelry, much of the latter sold at the pint-sized shops along the Ponte Vecchio. Note, however, that it's not a city for bargains—prices are almost always appropriately up there.

Located away from the Ponte Vecchio, **Mario Buccellati,** Via dei Tornabuoni 69-71R (☎ **055/2396579**), a branch of the Milan store that opened in 1919, specializes in exquisite handcrafted jewelry and silver.

Intrepid shoppers head for the **Mercato della Paglia** or **Mercato Nuovo (Straw Market** or **New Market),** 2 blocks south of Piazza della Repubblica. (It's called Il Porcellino by the Italians because of the bronze statue of a reclining wild boar, a copy of the one in the Uffizi.) Tourists pet its snout (which is well worn) for good luck. The market stands in the monumental heart of Florence, an easy stroll from the Palazzo Vecchio. It sells not only straw items but also leather goods (not the best quality), along with typical Florentine merchandise: frames, trays, hand-embroidery, table linens, and hand-sprayed and -painted boxes in traditional designs.

Even better bargains await those who make their way through the pushcarts to the stalls of the open-air **Mercato Centrale (Mercato San Lorenzo),** in and around Borgo San Lorenzo, near the rail station. If you don't mind bargaining, which is imperative, you'll find an array of merchandise such as raffia bags, Florentine leather purses, sweaters, gloves, salt-and-pepper shakers, straw handbags, and art reproductions.

For one-stop shopping the best outlet is **La Rinascente,** Piazza della Repubblica 2 (*©* **055/219113**), right in the heart of Florence. This is where frugal but taste-conscious Florentines go to shop. Their clothing for men and women features some of the big names but also talented and lesser-known Italian designers. You'll also find good buys in china, perfumes, and jewelry, along with a "made in Tuscany" department that sells everything from terra-cotta vases to the finest virgin olive oils.

NIGHTLIFE

For theatrical and concert listings, pick up a free copy of **_Welcome to Florence,_** available at the tourist office. This helpful publication contains information on recitals, concerts, theatrical productions, and other cultural presentations.

THE PERFORMING ARTS   From May to July, the city welcomes classical musicians for its **Maggio Musicale** festival of cantatas, madrigals, concertos, operas, and ballets, many of which are presented in Renaissance buildings. The main venue for the festival is the **Teatro Comunale di Firenze/Maggio Musicale Fiorentino,** Corso Italia 16 (*©* **055/211158**), which also presents opera and ballet from September to December and a concert season from January to April. Schedule and ticket information for the festival is available from **Maggio Musicale Fiorentino/Teatro Comunale,** Corso Italia 16, 50123 Firenze (*©* **055/27791**). Tickets to theatrical productions and the festival cost 20€ to 100€ ($23–$115). For further information, visit the theater's website, at **www. maggiofiorentino.com**.

CAFES & CLUBS   **Café Rivoire,** Piazza della Signoria 4R (*©* **055/214412**), offers a classy and amusing old-world ambience with a direct view of the statues on one of our favorite squares in the world. You can sit at one of the metal tables on the flagstones outside or at one of the wooden tables in a choice of inner rooms filled with marble detailing and unusual oil renderings of the piazza outside.

The oldest and most beautiful cafe in Florence, **Gilli's,** via Roma 1, adjacent to Piazza Repubblica 39R, Via Roma 1 (*©* **055/213896**), is a few minutes' walk from the Duomo. It was founded in 1789, when Piazza della Repubblica had a different name. You can sit at a brightly lit table near the bar or retreat to an intricately paneled pair of rooms to the side and enjoy the flattering light from the Venetian-glass chandeliers.

May Day Club, Via Dante Alighieri 16R (*©* **055/2381290**), defines itself as a pub with recorded music that's about as hip and cutting edge as anything else in Tuscany. Its mostly white walls are adorned with a collection of antique radios and television sets (its owners refer to it as a museum of antique radios) and party-colored lights that constantly change the predominant colors. Entrance is free, and clients range in age from around 23 to 45.

Rio Grande, Viale degli Olmi 1 (*©* **055/331371**), is Florence's best, biggest, and most international disco. A 15-minute cab ride from Piazza del Duomo, near Parco della Cascine, it has an indoor/outdoor setting that includes century-old trees, a terrace, and three dance floors. The music includes everything from punk to rock to funk to garage. Gays mix with the mostly straight crowd with ease, and the typical age range is 18 to 32. For the disco only, a cover of 11€ to 16€ ($12.65–$18.40) is imposed.

AN EXCURSION TO PISA ★★

No longer the powerful port it was in the western Mediterranean in the 12th century, Pisa is still visited for its magnificent buildings, especially the Leaning Tower of Pisa, a building that is one of the most recognizable on earth. The silting up of its harbor marked Pisa's decline in 1284, and it suffered even greater devastation in the Allied bombings of 1944. Nonetheless, there is much here to celebrate at a point lying 47 miles (76km) west of Florence and easily visited on a day trip from that city.

GETTING THERE   Chances are you might land in Pisa to begin your descent on Florence. Both domestic and international flights land at Pisa's **Galileo Galilei Airport** (© 050/849300). From the airport, trains depart every 15 to 30 minutes, depending on the time of day, for the 5-minute ride into Pisa, costing 1€ ($1.15) each way. As an alternative, bus 3 leaves the airport every 20 minutes heading for Pisa, costing .80€ (90¢) one-way.

Trains make the 1-hour journey between Pisa and Florence every 1½ hours; the ride costs 4.95€ ($5.70) one-way. Trains running along the coast link Pisa with Rome, a trip of 3 hours. Depending on the time of day and the speed of the train, one-way fares are 13.96€ to 14.06€ ($16.05–$16.15). In Pisa, trains arrive at the **Stazione Pisa Centrale** (© 892021), about a 10- to 15-minute walk from the Leaning Tower. Otherwise, you can take bus 1 from the station into the heart of the city.

TOURIST INFORMATION   The **tourist office** at Via Cammeo 2 (© 050-560464) is open April to September Monday through Saturday from 9:30am to 6pm, Sunday from 10:30am to 4:30pm (the rest of the year Mon–Sat 9am–5pm, and Sun 10am–2pm). A second branch is at Piazza della Stazione, next to the train station (© 050/42291); it's open April to September Monday through Saturday from 9:30am to 7pm, and Sunday 9:30am to 3:30pm (the rest of the year Mon–Sat 9am–5pm, and Sun 9am–1pm).

TOP ATTRACTIONS & SPECIAL MOMENTS

Seemingly every visitor heads first for the **Leaning Tower of Pisa (Campanile)** ★★★, Piazza del Duomo 17 (© 050/560547). Construction began on the eight-story campanile in 1174 by Bonanno, and there has been a persistent legend that the architect deliberately intended that the bell tower lean (that claim is undocumented). If it stood up straight, the tower would measure about 180 feet. The tower was closed for many years as Pisans worked to stabilize it. Tons of soil were removed from under the foundation, and lead counterweights were placed at the monument's base. Admission is 15€ ($17.25), and hours in summer are daily 8am to 8pm (daily 8am–5:50pm off season). Only 40 people are admitted at one time. It's necessary to phone for a reservation or to do so online at **www.duomo.pisa.it**.

Tips A Money-Saving Deal

An 8€ ($9.20) **combination ticket** (you can buy it at any of the included attractions) allows you to visit two of these three sights: the baptistery, the cemetery, and the Duomo Museum. For 10€ ($11.50), you can visit the five major attractions: the baptistery, the Duomo, the cemetery, Duomo Museum, and the Museum of Preliminary Frescoes.

Also at the Piazza del Duomo, the **Baptistery (Battistero)** ✹✹✹ (✆ **050/560547**), is circular in shape, dating from 1152 when it was constructed along Romanesque lines, the work taking 100 years. It was finished in a more ornate Gothic style by Nicola and Giovanni Pisano. Its greatest treasure is the **hexagonal pulpit** ✹✹, designed by Nicola Pisano. Supported by pillars, it rests on the backs of a trio of marble lions, containing bas-reliefs of the *Crucifixion,* the *Adoration of the Magi,* the *presentation of the Christ Child at the Temple,* and *The Last Judgment.*

The **Duomo** ✹✹ itself, dominating the so-called Campo dei Miracoli (Field of Miracles), was begun by Buscheto in 1064, and is today one of the finest Pisan-Romanesque buildings in Tuscany, with a **west front** ✹✹✹ that is light and graceful with three tiers of marble columns. The south transept door has impressive Romanesque **bronze panels** ✹✹ from the late 12th century, the work of Bonanno Pisano. Yet another **impressive pulpit** ✹✹✹ found here was the creation of Giovanni Pisano who worked on it from 1302 to 1311. Admission is 5€ ($5.75). It's open April to September daily from 8am to 8pm; March and October daily from 9am to 5:30pm, and November to February daily from 9am to 4:30pm.

Camposanto ✹✹, Piazza del Duomo (✆ **050/560547**), is a cemetery that was begun in 1277 by Giovanni di Simone, one of the architects of the Leaning Tower. Called the Holy Field, the vast marble arcades of this long building, or so legend has it, contain soil brought back from the Holy Land. Allied bombings in 1944 destroyed most of its once-lavish frescoes, although scenes depicting *The Triumph of Death* remain (1360–80). Admission costs 5€ ($5.75). Hours are April to September daily from 8am to 7:30pm; March and October daily from 9am to 5:30pm, and November to February daily from 9am to 4:30pm.

WHERE TO DINE

One of Pisa's best restaurants, **Al Ristoro dei Vecchi Macelli,** Via Volturno 4 (✆ **050/20424**), is housed in a 1930s building near Piazzetta di Vecchi Macelli, and is known for its international and Pisan cuisine. It has the best seafood *antipasti* in town, with two dozen different offerings. Pasta is homemade and the fish-stuffed ravioli in cauliflower sauce is a sure winner. Main courses cost 11€ to 13€ ($12.65–$14.95), with 2 fixed-price menus going for 50€ to 65€ ($57.50–$74.75). Open Thursday to Sunday noon to 3pm and 8 to 10:30pm.

Another good choice for Pisan cuisine is **Antica Trattoria Da Bruno,** Via Luigi Bianchi 12 (✆ **050/560818**), which has been in business for some 50 years at its location close to the Leaning Tower. The recipes may be old-fashioned but the food is completely fresh and well prepared. Local favorites include *zuppa pisana,* a minestrone made with black cabbage, or wild boar with olives and polenta. Main courses cost 8€ to 15€ ($9.20–$17.25). It's open Monday noon to 2:30pm, Wednesday to Sunday noon to 3pm and 7 to 10:30pm.

AN EXCURSION TO SIENA

Although such a point of view may be heretical, one can almost be grateful that Siena lost its medieval battles with Florence. Had it continued to expand and change after reaching the zenith of its power in the 14th century, chances are it would be remarkably different today, influenced by the rising tides of the Renaissance and the baroque (represented today only in a small degree). But Siena retained its uniqueness (certain Sienese painters were still showing the influence of Byzantium in the late 15th c.) and is a showplace of the Italian Gothic.

GETTING THERE   A rail journey between Florence and Siena can be a bit inconvenient because it often requires a change of trains at an intermediary station, such as the one at the town of Empoli. Trains do arrive every hour from Florence, however, and cost 5.40€ ($6.20) one-way. Trains pull in at Siena's station at Piazza Fratelli Rosselli (© **0577/280115**), a difficult 30-minute climb uphill to the monumental center unless you take buses 2, 4, 6, or 10, depositing you at Piazza Gramsci in the heart of Siena.

TOURIST INFORMATION   The **Siena Tourist Office** at Piazza del Campo 56 (© **0577/280551**), is open daily 9am to 7pm, and dispenses information and good, free maps.

TOP ATTRACTIONS & SPECIAL MOMENTS

The Town Hall of Siena, **Palazzo Comunale,** stands in the virtual heart of Siena at the shell-shaped **Piazza del Campo** ✿✿✿, described by Montaigne as "the finest of any city in the world." Pause to enjoy **Fonte Gaia,** which locals sometimes call the Fountain of Joy because it was inaugurated to great jubilation throughout the city, with embellishments by Jacopo della Quercia (the present sculptured works are reproductions—the badly beaten-up original ones are found in the town hall). The square is truly stunning, designed like a sloping scalloped shell; you'll want to linger in one of the cafes along its edge. You'll hardly be able to miss the lithe **Torre (tower) del Mangia** ✿✿✿, dating from the 14th century, which soars to a height of 335 feet over the skyline of the city.

   The brick-built **Palazzo Pubblico** (1288–1309) on the square is filled with important art works by some of the leaders of the Sienese school of painting and sculpture. Upstairs in a museum is the *Sala della Pace,* frescoed from 1337-39 by Ambrogio Lorenzetti, and showing allegorically the idealized effects of good government and bad government. In this depiction, the most notable figure of the Virtues surrounding the King is *La Pace* (Peace). To the right of the King and the Virtues is a representation of Siena in peaceful times. The tower and museum at Piazza del Campo (© **0577/292263**) are open mid-March to October daily from 10am to 7pm; November to mid-March daily from 10am to 5pm, charging an admission of 6.50€ ($7.50).

   Southwest of Piazza del Campo stands **Il Duomo** ✿✿✿, Piazza del Duomo (© **0577/283048**), from 1136 to 1382, one of the great cathedrals of Italy, with a Pisan-influenced Romanesque-Gothic architecture. The impressive facade is from the 13th century, as is the Romanesque *campanile* or bell tower. The interior is a series of black-and-white zebralike striped designs. Black-and-white marble pillars support the vault. The chief treasure is the **octagonal pulpit** ✿✿✿ of the 13th century, the work of Nicola Pisano. The pillars of the pulpit are held up by a quarter of marble lions, evocative of the Pisano pulpit at Pisa.

   On Piazza San Giovanni, the **Battistero (Baptistery)** ✿ (© **0577/283048**) lies behind the Duomo. Its Gothic facade left unfinished by Domenico di Agostino, it is nonetheless an impressive site. Inside its chief attraction is the **baptismal font** ✿✿ from 1417, the work of Jacopo della Quercia, containing some bas-reliefs by such Tuscan masters as Donatello and Lorenzo Ghiberti. It is a Renaissance work of superb design and craftsmanship. Admission is 2.50€ ($2.90). It's open April to September daily from 9am to 7:30pm; October daily from 9am to 6pm; November to March daily from 9am to 1pm and 2 to 5pm.

   Pinacoteca Nazionale ✿✿, in the Palazzo Buonsignori, Via San Pietro 29 (© **0577/281161**), displays an amazing and extensive collection from the Sienese school ranging from the 13th to the 16th century, everything housed in a 15th-century *palazzo.* Displayed here are many of the Italian masters of the pre-Renaissance era. The principal treasures are found on the second floor, where you'll contemplate the artistry of Duccio in the early salons. The gallery is rich in the art of the two Lorenzetti brothers, Ambrogio and Pietro, who painted in the 14th century. Ambrogio is represented by an *Annunciation* and a *Crucifix.* But one of his most celebrated works, carried out with consummate skill, is an almond-eyed Madonna and her bambino surrounded by saints and angels. Pietro's most important entry here is an altarpiece—*Madonna of the Carmine*—made for a church in Siena in the 1320s. There is also Simone Martini's *Madonna and Bambino,* damaged, but one of the most famous paintings in the entire collection. Admission is 4€ ($4.60). It's open Sunday and Monday from 8:30am to 1:30pm; Tuesday to Saturday from 8:30am to 7pm.

WHERE TO DINE

On Siena's most historic square, **Al Mangia,** Piazza del Campo 43 (€ **0577/ 281121**), serves a refined Tuscan and international cuisine and offers outside tables opening onto the landmark town hall. In a building whose origins go back to the 12th century, you are served artfully prepared food, with seasonally adjusted menus. The service and the cookery are first rate, with main courses costing 18.50€ to 26€ ($21.30–$29.90). It's open daily from noon to 3:30pm and 7 to 10pm.

Equally good is **Al Marsili,** Via del Castoro 3 (€ **0577/47154**), serving a Sienese and Italian cuisine in its atmospheric setting between the cathedral and Via di Città. Some of the best *antipasti* in town is offered here, and you get such unusual but tasty dishes as smoked venison or wild boar. Their risottos—such as one made with four different cheeses—are superb, as are the tender and well-flavored meat and poultry dishes. Main courses cost 8€ to 18€ ($9.20–$20.70). It's open Tuesday to Sunday from 12:30 to 2:30pm and 7:30 to 10:30pm.

5 Venice & the Northeast

Venice is a fairy-tale city of islands and gondolas, where the canals are lined with wedding cake palaces. The "Serene Republic" of Venice had a turbulent and fascinating history. As Attila the Hun swept through 5th-century Italy toward trembling Rome, he spread proverbial death and destruction in his path. Attila was on his way to claim the emperor's stepsister, Honoria, as his "bride," and though his ultimate sack of Rome was averted, the swath of desolation he left in his wake was real enough. One particularly unfortunate town was razed to the ground, and its terrified inhabitants fled into the marshes on the shores of the Adriatic. The political climate of the times was so insecure that the population deemed it wisest to remain in the swamps and build their houses on stilts in the water, and so Venice got her start.

The Venice we know today is from a much later era though, an era rich with the accumulated spoils of Crusaders and merchantmen. The wizardlike rulers of Renaissance Venice shrewdly—sometimes unscrupulously—parlayed Venice into mistress of the Adriatic, and the many monuments and palaces erected in those days attest to the profit inherent in such a position.

The city is an excellent rail destination, though you'll naturally have to take to the water once you get to the city proper. Venice is easily reached by train from all parts of Italy (it's the northeast rail hub for Italy) and several other European countries. And rail travelers actually have the easiest time getting into the city, as the main railway station on Piazzale Roma is right in the thick of things.

Venice

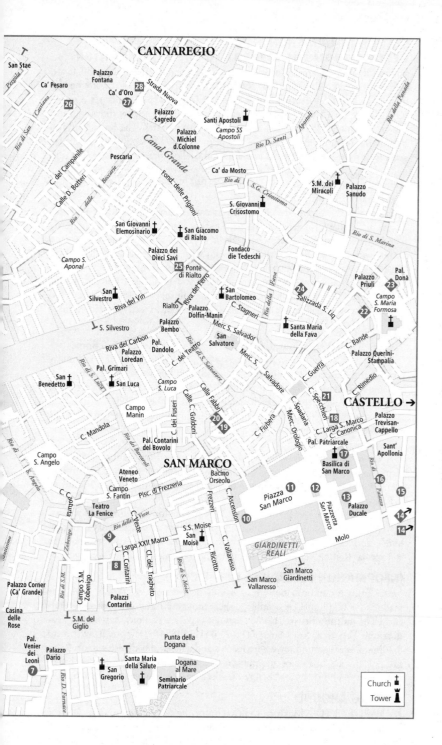

CANNAREGIO

San Stae

Palazzo
Fontana

Ca' Pesaro

26

Ca' d'Oro

28

Strada Nuova

27

Palazzo
Sagredo

Santi Apostoli

Campo SS
Apostoli

Palazzo
Michiel
d.Colonne

Rio D. Santi

Pescaria

Canal Grande

Ca' da Mosto

Rio di

S.M. dei
Miracoli

Palazzo
Sanudo

C. del Campanile

Fond. delle Prigioni

S. Giovanni
Crisostomo

Calle D. Botteri

Rio di S. Marina

San Giovanni
Elemosinario

San Giacomo
di Rialto

Campo S.
Aponal

Palazzo dei
Dieci Savi

25

Ponte
di Rialto

Fondaco
die Tedeschi

Pal.
Donà

Palazzo
Priuli

23

San
Silvestro

Riva del Vin

Rialto

San
Bartolomeo

C. Stagneri

Palazzo
Dolfin-Manin

Riva del Ferro

Salizzada S. Liq

24

Campo
S. Maria
Formosa

22

Merc S. Salvador

Santa Maria
della Fava

S. Silvestro

Palazzo
Bembo

San
Salvatore

Merc. S.

C. Bande

Palazzo Querini-
Stampalia

Riva del Carbon

Palazzo
Loredan

Pal.
Dandolo

C. del Teatro

San
Benedetto

Pal. Grimari

San Luca

Campo
S. Luca

Calle C. Goldoni

Calle Fabbri

20

19

C. Fiubera

C. Guerra

C. Rimedio

C. Specchieri

21

CASTELLO →

Campo
Manin

C. Mandola

Pal. Contarini
del Bovolo

SAN MARCO

Bacino
Orseolo

Merc. Orologio

C. Spadaria

18

C. Larga S. Marco

C. Canonica

Pal. Patriarcale

17

Basilica di
San Marco

Palazzo
Trevisan-
Cappello

Sant'
Apollonia

Campo
S. Angelo

Ateneo
Veneto

Campo
S. Fantin

Pisc. di Frezzeria

Frezzeri

C. Ascension

Piazza
San Marco

11

12

13

16

15

Teatro
La Fenice

9

Rio delle Veste

C. Larga XXII Marzo

S.S. Moise
San
Moisè

C. Ricotto

C. Vallaresso

10

Piazzetta
San Marco

Palazzo
Ducale

14

14

Molo

Palazzo Corner
(Ca' Grande)

Campo S.M.
Zobenigo

8

Cl. del Tragheto

Palazzi
Contarini

GIARDINETTI
REALI

San Marco
Vallaresso

San Marco
Giardinetti

Casina
delle
Rose

S.M. del
Giglio

Pal.
Venier
dei
Leoni

7

Palazzo
Dario

Punta della
Dogana

Santa Maria
della Salute

San
Gregorio

Dogana
al Mare

Seminario
Patriarcale

Rio D. Fornace

| Church | ✝ |
| Tower | ♜ |

605

STATION INFORMATION
GETTING FROM THE AIRPORT TO THE TRAIN STATION
You can fly nonstop from North America to Venice on Delta. You'll land at the **Aeroporto Marco Polo** (✆ 041/2606111) at Mestre, north of the city on the mainland. The **Cooperativa San Marco** (✆ 041/5222303) operates a *motoscafo* (shuttle boat) service that can deliver you from the airport directly to the center of Venice at Piazza San Marco in about 30 minutes. The boats wait just outside the main entrance, and the fare begins at 80€ ($92) for up to six passengers (if there are only two of you, find some fellow travelers to share the ride and split the fare with you). If you've got some extra euros to spend, you can arrange for a **private water taxi** by calling ✆ 041/5415084. The cost of the ride to the heart of Venice is 80€ ($92).

Buses from the airport are less expensive, though they can only take you as far as Piazzale Roma; from here you will need to take a vaporetto to reach your hotel. The **Azienda Trasporti Veneto Orientale** (✆ 041/5205530) shuttle bus links the airport with Piazzale Roma (where the main train station is located) for 2.70€ ($3.10). The trip takes about half an hour, and departures are about every 30 minutes daily 8:40am to 11:30pm. Even cheaper is a local bus company, **ACTV** (✆ 041/5287886), whose bus no. 5 makes the run for .70€ (80¢). The ACTV buses depart every half hour and take about a half hour to reach Piazzale Roma.

INSIDE THE STATION
Trains pull into the **Stazione di Santa Lucia,** at Piazzale Roma, from Rome (trip time: 5¼ hr.), Milan (3½ hr.), Florence (4 hr.), and Bologna (2 hr.). For information and timetables, contact **FS** (✆ 848/888088; www.trenitalia.it). The best and least expensive way to get from the station to the rest of town is to take a vaporetto, which departs near the main entrance to the station.

The station has all the expected amenities, including a currency exchange desk, luggage storage, restaurants, and ATMs. The vaporetto departs near the station's main entrance.

A **tourist office**(✆ 041/5298711), located just off the station's main hall, dispenses information and maps but does not make hotel reservations. Summer hours are daily from 9am to 5pm; off-season hours are daily from 9:30am to 3:30pm.

Anyone between the ages of 14 and 29 is eligible for a **Rolling Venice pass,** entitling you to discounts for museums, restaurants, stores, language courses, hotels, and bars. Valid for 1 year, it costs 2.58€ ($2.95) and can be picked up at a special Rolling Venice office set up in the train station during summer.

INFORMATION ELSEWHERE IN THE CITY
From spring to autumn hotel reservations in overcrowded Venice should be made as far in advance as possible, either through a travel agent or independently. The tourist office (see below) does not make reservations. **Azienda di Promozione Turistica,** San Marco 71F (✆ 041/5298740), is open daily 9am to 9:30pm. Posters around town with exhibit and concert schedules are more helpful. Ask for a schedule of the month's special events and an updated list of museum and church hours because these can change erratically and often.

GETTING AROUND
BY VAPORETTO Much to the chagrin of the once-ubiquitous gondoliers, Venice's **motorboats** *(vaporetti)* provide inexpensive and frequent, if not always fast, transportation in this canal city. The vaporetti are called "water buses," and

they are indeed the "buses" of Venice because traveling by water is usually faster than traveling by land. The service is operated by **ACTV (Azienda del Consorzio Trasporti Veneziano),** Calle Fisero, San Marco 1810 (✆ **041/5287886**). An *accelerato* is a vessel that makes every stop; a *diretto* makes only express stops. The average fare is 3.10€ ($3.55). Note that, in summer, the vaporetti are often fiercely crowded. Pick up a map of the system at the tourist office. They run daily up and down the Grand Canal, with frequent service 7am to midnight and then hourly midnight to 7am. To save money you can buy a 24-hour ticket for 10.50€ ($12.10) or a 3-day ticket for 22€ ($25.30).

BY MOTOR LAUNCH (WATER TAXI)   Motor launches *(taxi acquei)* cost more than public vaporetti, but you won't be hassled as much when you arrive with your luggage if you hire one of the many private ones. You might or might not have the cabin of one of these sleek vessels to yourself because the captains fill their boats with as many passengers as the law allows before taking off. Your porter's uncanny radar will guide you to one of the inconspicuous piers where a water taxi waits. The price of a transit by water taxi from the train station to Piazza San Marco begins at 60€ ($69) for up to four passengers. The captains adroitly deliver you, with luggage, to the canalside entrance of your hotel or to one of the smaller waterways within a short walking distance of your destination. You can also call for a water taxi; try the **Cooperativa San Marco** at ✆ **041/5222303.**

WHERE TO STAY

Hotel Abbazia   The benefit of staying here is that there's no need to transfer onto any vaporetto—you can walk from the rail station, about 10 minutes away. This hotel was built in 1889 as a monastery for barefooted Carmelite monks, who established a verdant garden in what's now the courtyard; it's planted with subtropical plants that thrive, sheltered as they are from the cold Adriatic winds. You'll find a highly accommodating staff and comfortable but very plain guest rooms with well-kept bathrooms. Twenty-five rooms overlook the courtyard, ensuring quiet in an otherwise noisy neighborhood.

Calle Priuli ai Cavaletti, Cannaregio 68, 30121 Venezia. ✆ **041/717333.** Fax 041/717949. www.abbazia hotel.com. 39 units. 80€–200€ ($92–$230) double. Rates include buffet breakfast. AE, DC, MC, V. Vaporetto: Ferrovia. **Amenities:** Breakfast room; lounge; laundry; nonsmoking rooms; 1 room for those with limited mobility. *In room:* Hair dryer.

Hotel ai do Mori (*Value*)   Since Venice is one of the globe's most expensive cities, many visitors put up with some inconveniences to stay at this affordable choice in the central tourist zone near Piazza San Marco. The town house dates from the mid–15th century, and you'll have to balance your need for space with your desire for a view (and your willingness to climb stairs because there's no elevator): The lower-level rooms are larger but don't have views; the third- and fourth-floor rooms are cramped but have sweeping views over the basilica's domes. Furnishings are in a simple modern style. In lieu of any food service here, numerous cafes and trattorie lie outside your door.

Calle Larga San Marco, San Marco 658, 30124 Venezia. ✆ **041/5204817.** Fax 041/5205328. www.hotel aidomori.com. 11 units. 50€–80€ ($57.50–$92) double without bathroom; 60€–135€ ($69–$155) double with bathroom. MC, V. Vaporetto: San Marco. **Amenities:** Lounge; nonsmoking rooms. *In room:* Hair dryer.

Hotel Bernardi-Semenzato   This remains a budget favorite north of the Ponte Rialto. It doesn't please everyone, and it's hardly state of the art in spite of mid-1990s renovations, but it's an affordable option in a ridiculously expensive city. The facade looks a little battered, but there is comfort to be found inside. Guests are housed in the main building, with lots of exposed hand-hewn ceiling beams, or else in an annex 3 blocks away. If you're given a room in the annex, you're not being sentenced to some Venetian Siberia; it evokes a Venetian nobleman's apartment. Bedrooms are tastefully furnished, with retiled bathrooms. Murano chandeliers and parquet floors add Venetian grace notes.

Calle de l'Oca, Cannaregio 4366, 30121 Venezia. (*) **041/5227257.** Fax 041/5222424. 26 units. 95€–105€ ($109–$121) double. AE, MC, V. Rates include breakfast. Vaporetto: Ca' D'Oro. **Amenities:** Bar; nonsmoking rooms. *In room:* Hair dryer.

Hotel do Pozzi (*)   This antique building, just a short walk from Piazza San Marco and its basilica, is more than 2 centuries old but has been modernized and brought up-to-date. The hotel is really old Venice, with lots of atmosphere, and in summer breakfast is served out on a characteristic little square surrounded by flowers. Antiques are mixed with functional modern furniture in the small to midsize bedrooms, some of which have showers in the bathrooms, others with tub and shower.

Corte do Pozzi, San Marco 2373, 30124 Venezia. (*) **041/5207855.** Fax 041/5229413. www.hoteldopozzi.it. 35 units. 130€–210€ ($150–$242) double. Rates include breakfast. AE, DC, MC, V. Vaporetto: Santa Maria del Giglio. **Amenities:** Dining room; bar; laundry; nonsmoking rooms. *In room:* Hair dryer.

Hotel Marconi   Just 50 feet from the Rialto Bridge, this old relic is still going strong. When Venice is in high season and overcrowded, it's very expensive—otherwise, it's one of the bargains in town. The building itself was constructed at the beginning of the 16th century, and the drawing room still evokes that era. The most desirable of the rooms—only four in all—open onto dramatic views of the Grand Canal. Bedrooms range from small to midsize, each with a tiled bathroom with shower. Sidewalk tables are placed outside in fair weather to take in a lovely view of the Grand Canal.

Riva del Vin, San Polo 729, 30125 Venezia. (*) **041/5222068.** Fax 041/5229700. www.hotelmarconi.it. 26 units. 70€–325€ ($80.50–$374) double; 91€–423€ ($105–$486) triple. Rates include breakfast. AE, DC, MC, V. Vaporetto: Rialto. **Amenities:** Dining room; lounge; laundry; nonsmoking rooms; rooms for those with limited mobility. *In room:* Hair dryer.

Hotel Montecarlo   Just a 2-minute walk from Piazza San Marco, this hotel is installed in a much-upgraded 17th-century town house. The owners have given it Venetian flair, lining its upper halls with the work of some of the city's most outstanding old masters and decorating the small guest rooms with Venetian-styled antique reproductions and glass chandeliers from the neighboring island of Murano. Some rooms are quite dark, the curse of many Venetian hotels. All have well-kept bathrooms.

Calle dei Specchieri, San Marco 463, 30124 Venezia. (*) **041/5207144.** Fax 041/5207789. www.venicehotel montecarlo.com. 48 units. 108€ ($124) standard double; 400€ ($460) deluxe double. Rates include buffet breakfast. AE, DC, MC, V. Vaporetto: San Marco. **Amenities:** Restaurant; bar; laundry; nonsmoking rooms. *In room:* Hair dryer.

Hotel San Cassiano Ca'Favretto (*)   San Cassiano Ca'Favretto was once the studio of 19th-century painter Giacomo Favretto. The views from the hotel's gondola pier and from the dining room's porch encompass the lacy facade of the Ca' d'Oro. The hotel was constructed in the 14th century as a palace, and many of its architectural details, including 20-foot ceilings, have been retained. There's no elevator, but the Murano chandeliers, the rooms filled with antique reproductions, the 18th-century stucco work in the breakfast room, and a wood-beamed bar with a canal view do much to compensate.

Calle della Rosa, Santa Croce 2232, 30135 Venezia. ⓒ **041/5241768**. Fax 041/721033. www.venicehotel montecarlo.com. 35 units. 70€–325€ ($80.50–$374) double. Rates include breakfast. AE, DC, MC, V. Vaporetto: San Stae. **Amenities:** Breakfast room; bar; nonsmoking rooms; rooms for those with limited mobility. *In room:* Hair dryer.

Hotel Savoia & Jolanda 𝄐   Better-heeled rail passengers seeking a taste of the Venetian luxury for which the city is renowned, will find solace here in this hotel, just a few minutes walk from Piazza San Marco right off a Venetian lagoon. It's truly a special place for lodgings and very romantic. Try for one of the midsize and well-furnished guest rooms opening onto a view of the lagoon. Well-chosen fabrics, paintings, and Venetian glass from the island of Murano add to the luster of the hotel, as do the old wooden beams and the flower-decked terraces. The suites have panoramic balconies and terraces.

Riva degli Schiavoni, Castello 4187, 30122 Venezia. ⓒ **041/5206644**. Fax 041/5207494. www.hotelsavoia jolanda.com. 51 units. 200€–300€ ($230–$345) double; from 320€ ($368) suite. Rates include buffet breakfast. AE, DC, MC, V. Vaporetto: San Zaccaria. **Amenities:** Restaurant; lounge; laundry; nonsmoking rooms. *In room:* Hair dryer.

La Residenza 𝄐𝄐   One of our all-time favorite nests in Venice occupies a *palazzo* from the 1400s overlooking an evocative square of old Venice near the swank palaces a few steps from Piazza San Marco. The legend and lore of old Venice is kept alive in this palace, and it's also kept abreast of the times, having last been renovated in 2001. Bedrooms are spacious and well furnished, with stylistic Venetian reproductions and small shower-only bathrooms. There's no elevator, so be prepared. Since the address is known by some of the world's most discerning hotel shoppers, book well in advance if arriving in season.

Campo Bandiera e Moro, Castello 3608, 30122 Venezia. ⓒ **041/5285315**. Fax 041/5238859. 15 units. 105€–155€ ($121–$178) double. Rates include breakfast. MC, V. Vaporetto: Arsenale. **Amenities:** Lounge; nonsmoking rooms.

TOP ATTRACTIONS & SPECIAL MOMENTS

You really need 2 to 3 days to properly take in the city, but if you have only 1 day, be sure to watch the sun rise over **Piazzeta San Marco** 𝄐. Adjacent to the Palace of the Doges is this landmark little square, noted for its fabulous statue of the winged lion of St. Mark. It stands atop a granite column (which was also ripped off from Constantinople), and is flanked by a similar column, on whose capital stands St. Theodore, former patron of Venice until he was supplanted by St. Mark.

In what has been called the "antechamber" of Venice, you have the best view of the southern facade of St. Mark's Basilica. Imbedded in the facade is a *Virgin and Bambino* in mosaics, honoring a poor baker—that is, Pietro Fasiol, who was unjustly accused and executed on a false charge of murder. At the left of the entrance to the Palace of the Doges stands a world-famous collection of four porphyry figures called *The Moors*. Naturally puce colored, they are huddled together in fear.

Ca' d'Oro 𝄐𝄐𝄐   The grandest setting for any art gallery is Ca' d'Oro, formerly a private palace, donated to the Italian state after the First World War by the owner, Baron Franchetti. The collection ranges from Van Dyck to Carpaccio, and the lush appointments of the palace itself compete with the works of art on the walls.

The "House of Gold" was so named because it was once gilded (imagine what that would cost today). In the ogival style, it has a lacy Gothic look, really a candy box. Opposite the entrance door you can go into a salon to see Titian's voluptuous *Venus*. The masterpiece on this floor is Andrea Mantegna's *St. Sebastian*. Another equally renowned work of art is Anthony Van Dyck's *Portrait of a Gentleman*. At some point you emerge onto a loggia where you can enjoy a panoramic view of the Grand Canal.

Cannaregio 3931–3932. © **041/5238790.** Admission 4€ ($4.60). Mon 8am–2pm; Tues–Sun 8:15am–7:15pm. Closed Jan 1, May 1, and Dec 25. Vaporetto: Ca' d'Oro.

Campanile di San Marco ★★   The bell tower of St. Mark's Basilica is a reconstruction of the original, which dramatically collapsed into the Piazza in the summer of 1902. No one was hurt, since the night before the fall, the tower had emitted a telltale groan that sent everyone within earshot racing to safety. It collapsed the next day when the populace was kept at a safe distance. The Venetians rebuilt their belfry, and it's now safe to ascend. A modern elevator takes you up for a splendid view of the city.

Piazza San Marco. © **041/5224064.** Admission 6€ ($6.90). Oct–Feb daily 9:30am–4pm; Mar–June daily 9am–7pm; July–Sept daily 9am–9pm. Closed Jan 7–31. Vaporetto: San Marco.

Ca' Rezzonico ★★   At Ca' Rezzonico, along the Grand Canal, Robert Browning lived as a widower in rooms once occupied by Clement XII. Nowadays, it's a museum of baroque furnishings and paintings. A **Throne Room** contains an allegorical ceiling by Tiepolo. Here are all the rich props that characterized Venice in the 18th century, including ebony blacks carrying torches, elaborate chandeliers, gilded furniture, and the inevitable chinoiserie. The best paintings are by Pietro Longhi, including his well-known work, *The Lady and the Hairdresser*. Majolica and Venetian costumes are exhibited on the top floor.

Fondamenta Rezzonico, Dorsoduro 3136. © **041/2410100.** Admission 6.50€ ($7.50) adults. Nov–Mar Wed–Mon 10am–5pm; April–Oct daily 10am–6pm. Vaporetto: Ca' Rezzonico.

Collezione Peggy Guggenheim ★★★   This is one of the most comprehensive and brilliant modern-art collections in the Western world, and it reveals the foresight and critical judgment of its founder. The collection is housed in an unfinished palazzo, the former home of Peggy Guggenheim. In the tradition of her family, Guggenheim was a lifelong patron of contemporary painters and sculptors. As her private collection increased, she decided to find a larger showcase and selected Venice. Displayed here are works not only by Pollock and Ernst but also by Picasso (see his cubist *The Poet* of 1911), Duchamp, Chagall, Mondrian, Brancusi, Delvaux, and Dalí, plus a garden of modern sculpture that includes works by Giacometti.

In the Palazzo Venier dei Leoni, Calle Venier dei Leoni, Dorsoduro 701. © **041/2405411.** Admission 8€ ($9.20); 4€ ($4.60) for children/students. Free for children under 10. Wed–Mon 10am–6pm. Vaporetto: Accademia.

Ducale Palace & Bridge of Sighs (Palazzo Ducale & Ponte dei Sospiri) ★★★   This Venetian landmark is around the corner from the Basilica of St. Mark. It is a 16th-century reconstruction of the original 14th-century palace, which had been gutted by a great fire. Here sat the Council of Ten, that rather arbitrary administrative body of Renaissance Venice that meted out justice at the height of the republic. Justice was unfortunately characterized largely by torture and execution, and not always for the best of reasons. The room in which the old men sat is a great gloomy chamber, decorated with somber oil paintings, and reached via an antechamber with a lion's mouth, into which letters of accusation were dropped. The famous resident of the place was the Doge himself, whose private apartments are aglow with frescoed walls and ceilings with magnificent paintings.

Dungeons are connected to the palace by the Bridge of Sighs or **Ponte dei Sospiri** 🕆🕆. The bridge was named because of the sad laments of the prisoners led across to torture and even death. Casanova was imprisoned here in 1775, but he managed to escape.

Piazzetta San Marco. 🕐 **041/2715911**. Admission 11€ ($12.65) adults. April–Oct daily 9am–7pm; Nov–Mar daily 9am–5pm. Vaporetto: San Marco.

Galleria dell'Accademia 🕆🕆🕆

The pomp and circumstance, the glory that was Venice, lives on in this remarkable collection of paintings spanning the 14th century to the 18th century. The hallmark of the Venetian school is color and more color. From Giorgione to Veronese, from Titian to Tintoretto, with a Carpaccio cycle thrown in, the Accademia has samples—often their best—of its most famous sons.

You'll first see works by such 14th-century artists as Paolo and Lorenzo Veneziano, who bridged the gap from Byzantine art to Gothic (see the latter's *Annunciation*). Next, you'll view Giovanni Bellini's *Madonna and Saint* (poor Sebastian, not another arrow), and Carpaccio's fascinating yet gruesome work of mass crucifixion. Two of the most important works with secular themes are Mantegna's armored *St. George,* with the dragon slain at his feet, and Hans Memling's 15th-century portrait of a young man. Giorgione's *Tempest* is the most famous painting at the Accademia. Lastly, seek out the cycle of narrative paintings that Vittore Carpaccio did of St. Ursula.

Campo della Carità, Dorsoduro. 🕐 **041/5222247**. Admission 6.50€ ($7.50). Mon 8:15am–2pm; Tues–Sun 8am–7:15pm. Vaporetto: Accademia.

Museo Civico Correr 🕆🕆

This museum traces the development of Venetian painting from the 14th century to the 16th century. On the second floor are the red and maroon robes once worn by the doges, plus some fabulous street lanterns. There's also an illustrated copy of *Marco Polo in Tartaria.* You can see Cosmé Tura's *La Pietà,* a miniature of renown from the genius in the Ferrara School. This is one of his more gruesome works, depicting a bony, gnarled Christ sprawled on the lap of the Madonna. Farther on, search out a Schiavone *Madonna and Child* (no. 545), our candidate for ugliest bambino ever depicted on canvas (no wonder the mother looks askance). One of the most important rooms at the Correr is filled with three masterpieces: Antonello da Messina's *Pietà,* Hugo van der Goes's *Crucifixion,* and Dieric Bouts's *Madonna and Child.* The star attraction of the Correr is the Bellini salon, which includes works by founding padre Jacopo and his son, Gentile. But the real master of the household was the other son, Giovanni, the major painter of the 15th-century Venetian school (see his *Crucifixion* and compare it with his father's treatment of the same subject).

In the Procuratie Nuove, Piazza San Marco. 🕐 **041/2405211**. Admission (including admission to the Ducal Palace above) 11€ ($12.65). Mar–Oct daily 9am–7pm; Nov–Feb daily 9am–5pm. Vaporetto: San Marco.

Scuola di San Giorgio degli Schiavoni 🕆🕆

At St. Antonino Bridge (Fondamenta dei Furlani), off the Riva degli Schiavoni, is the second important school to visit in Venice. Between 1507 and 1509, Vittore Carpaccio painted a pictorial cycle here of exceptional merit and interest. Of enduring fame are his works of **St. George and the Dragon** 🕆🕆, our favorite art in all of Venice—certainly the most delightful. In one frame, St. George charges the dragon on a

Moments **A Ride Along the Grand Canal**

The main street of town is the **Grand Canal** ✪✪✪, thronged with gondolas and *vaporetti* (those motorized boat-buses), spanned by graceful bridges and lined with palaces. Many of those palaces house fabulous museums, with collections encompassing art from the Renaissance to the present.

The best way to see the Grand Canal is to board vaporetto no. 1 (push and shove until you secure a seat at the front of the vessel). Settle yourself in, make sure that you have your long-distance viewing glasses, and prepare yourself for a view that can thrill even the most experienced world traveler.

field littered with half-eaten bodies and skulls. Gruesome? Not at all. Any moment you expect the director to call "Cut!"

Calle dei Furiani, Castello. ☎ **041/5228828.** Admission 2€ ($2.30). Nov–Mar Tues–Sun 10am–12:30pm and 3–6pm, Apr–Oct Tues–Sun 9:30am–12:30pm and 3:30–6:30pm. Last entrance 20 min. before closing. Vaporetto: San Zaccaria.

Scuola di San Rocco ✪✪✪ This dark, early-16th-century "school" was richly decorated by the great Tintoretto. *Scuole* were Venetian institutions throughout the various quarters in which the patricians met. The best-known one is San Rocco, in which Tintoretto won a commission to do 56 canvases, a task that took 18 years. Paintings cover the Upper and Lower Halls, including the well-known *Flight into Egypt.* The school owns Tintoretto's masterpiece, his huge *Crucifixion.* Other scenes also illustrate episodes from the life of Christ.

Campo San Rocco, San Polo. ☎ **041/5234864.** Admission 5.50€ ($6.35) adults, 1.50€ ($1.75) children. Mar 28–Nov 2 daily 9am–5:30pm; Nov 3–30 and Mar 1–27 daily 10am–4pm; Dec–Feb Mon–Sat 7:30am–12:30pm, Sun 7:30am–12:30pm and 2–4pm. Closed Easter and Dec 25–Jan 1. Ticket office closes 30 min. before last entrance. Vaporetto: San Tomà.

St. Mark's Basilica (Basilica di San Marco) ✪✪✪ Dominating Piazza San Marco is the **Basilica of St. Mark,** named for the patron saint of the city, whose body was carried here from Alexandria in A.D. 828. It is called the "Church of Gold" and is one of the most fabulously embellished structures in Europe. A great central dome and satellite cupolas form the silhouette, and inside is a profusion of mosaics depicting biblical scenes.

The **Presbytery** is said to contain the sarcophagus of St. Mark under a green marble "blanket." Here you'll find the *Pala d'Oro* ✪✪✪, a fabulous altar screen made of beaten gold and liberally encrusted with diamonds, rubies, emeralds, and pearls. You're also admitted to the **Treasury** ✪, filled with some of the loot the Crusaders brought back from Constantinople.

After leaving the basilica, head up the stairs in the atrium to the **Marciano Museum** and the **Loggia dei Cavalli.** The star of the museum is the world-famous *Triumphal Quadriga* ✪✪, four horses looted from Constantinople by Venetian crusaders during the sack of that city in 1204. These horses once surmounted the basilica but were removed because of pollution damage and were subsequently restored. The museum, with its mosaics and tapestries, is especially interesting, but also be sure to walk out onto the loggia for a view of Piazza San Marco.

Piazza San Marco. ℂ **041/5225205.** Basilica free; treasury 2€ ($2.30); presbytery 1.50€ ($1.75); Marciano Museum 1.50€ ($1.75). Basilica and presbytery Apr–Sept Mon–Sat 9:30am–5:30pm, Sun 2–5:30pm; Oct–Mar Mon–Sat 10am–4:30pm, Sun 2–4:30pm. Treasury Mon–Sat 9:30am–5pm; Sun 2–5pm. Marciano Museum Apr–Sept Mon–Sat 10am–5:30pm, Sun 2–4:30pm; Oct–Mar Mon–Sat 10am–4:30pm, Sun 2–4:30pm. Vaporetto: San Marco.

WHERE TO DINE

Al Covo 🕸🕸 VENETIAN/SEAFOOD   Al Covo has a special charm because of its atmospheric setting, sophisticated service, and the fine cooking of Cesare Benelli and his Texas-born wife, Diane. Look for a reinvention of a medieval version of fish soup, potato gnocchi flavored with local whitefish, seafood ravioli, linguine blended with zucchini and fresh peas, and delicious fritto misto with scampi, squid, a bewildering array of fish, and deep-fried vegetables such as zucchini flowers. Al Covo prides itself on not having any freezers, guaranteeing that all food is fresh every day.

Campiello della Pescaria, Castello 3968. ℂ **041/5223812.** Reservations recommended for dinner. All main courses 10€–35€ ($11.50–$40.25); fixed-price lunch 41€–67€ ($47.15–$77.05). No credit cards. Fri–Tues 12:45–2:15pm and 7:45–10pm. Vaporetto: Arsenale.

Al Mascaron VENETIAN   Crowd into one of the three loud, boisterous dining rooms, where you'll probably be directed to sit next to a stranger at a long trestle table. The waiters will come by and slam down copious portions of fresh-cooked local specialties: deep-fried calamari, spaghetti with lobster, monkfish in a salt crust, pastas, savory risottos, and Venetian-style calves' liver (which locals prefer rather pink), plus the best seafood of the day made into salads. There's also a convivial bar, where locals drop in to spread the gossip of the day, play cards, and order vino and snacks.

⟨ *Moments* **A Ride in a Gondola**

In *Death in Venice,* Thomas Mann wrote: "Is there anyone but must repress a secret thrill, on arriving in Venice for the first time—or returning thither after long absence—and stepping into a Venetian gondola? That singular conveyance, come down unchanged from ballad times, black as nothing else on earth except a coffin—what pictures it calls up of lawless, silent adventures in the plashing night; or even more, what visions of death itself, the bier and solemn rites and last soundless voyage!"

Mann reflected the point of view of German romanticism, but he didn't tell all the story. The voyage on a gondola isn't likely to be so soundless—at least not when time comes to pay the bill. When riding in a gondola, two major agreements have to be reached—one, the price of the ride; two, the length of the trip.

The official rate is 62€ ($71.30) per hour, but we've never known anyone to honor it. The actual fare depends on how well you stand up to the gondolier, *beginning* at 100€ ($115) for up to 50 minutes. Most gondoliers will ask at least double the official rate and reduce your trip to 30 to 40 minutes or even less. Prices go up after 8pm. Two major stations where you can hire gondolas are **Piazza San Marco** (ℂ **041/5200685**) and **Ponte di Rialto** (ℂ **041/5224904**).

Calle Lunga Santa Maria Formosa, Castello 5225. ⓒ **041/5225995**. Reservations recommended. Main courses 13€–22€ ($14.95–$25.30). No credit cards. Mon–Sat noon–3pm and 7:30–11pm. Vaporetto: Rialto or San Marco.

Le Bistrot de Venise ⋆ VENETIAN/FRENCH   Young artists and others flock to this local favorite, enjoying the change-of-pace fare, with some recipes dating back to the 14th century. Many of the dishes have been all but forgotten, such as a soup made with rice flour, pomegranates, chicken and slivered almonds, perhaps eel baked with bay leaf and a rose pepper sauce, even a prawn and Treviso red chicory tartlet in a pumpkin sauce. Of course, you can also order traditional and more familiar fare, and can virtually count on it being good.

Calle dei Fabbri, San Marco 4685. ⓒ **041/5236651**. Main courses 13€–20€ ($14.95–$23). MC, V. Daily noon–3pm and 7pm–1am. Vaporetto: Rialto.

Osteria alle Testiere ⋆ *Finds* VENETIAN/ITALIAN   A restaurant for the young at heart, this 24-seat trattoria seats you at tables covered with butcher paper and feeds you well at affordable prices. Beefed up by a wine list of some 100 selections, you can enjoy well-prepared dishes in a tavernlike setting. When you ask for a recipe here—the food is that good—you're often told it's a secret. The young couple we shared a table with claimed that they'd sampled everything on the menu, and were coming back to start all over again.

Castello 5801 (on Calle del Mondo Novo). ⓒ **041/5227220**. Reservations required. Main courses 14€–21€ ($16.10–$24.15). MC, V. Tues–Sat noon–2pm and 7–10pm. Closed: Aug and Dec 20–Jan 15. Vaporetto: San Marco or Rialto.

Ristorante Corte Sconta VENETIAN/SEAFOOD   This restaurant lies on a narrow alley, whose name is shared by at least three other streets in Venice (this particular one is near Campo Bandiere Moro and San Giovanni in Bragora). The modest restaurant's plain wooden tables are often filled with artists, writers, and filmmakers who come here for one of the biggest and most varied selection of freshly caught seafood in Venice. The fish is flawlessly fresh, including, for example, *gamberi*—tiny baby shrimp placed live on the grill.

Calle del Pestrin, Castello 3886. ⓒ **041/5227024**. Reservations required. Main courses 15€–30€ ($17.25–$34.50); fixed-price menus 55€–60€ ($63.25–$69). MC, V. Tues–Sat 12:30–2:30pm and 7:30–9:30pm. Closed Jan 7–Feb 7 and July 15–Aug 15. Vaporetto: Arsenale.

Ristorante da Raffaele ⋆ ITALIAN/VENETIAN   At Ponte delle Ostreghe, a landmark bridge, this restaurant named for the famous artist lies in a colorful setting only a 5-minute stroll from Piazza San Marco. It's been one of our favorite canal-side restaurants for so long that the maitre d' starts ordering the chef to prepare some of our favorite dishes when he sees us coming. Against an atmospheric backdrop of Old Venice, you can feast on such treats as deep-fried fish from the Adriatic or the city's best bean soup.

Calle Larga XXII Marzo (Fondamenta delle Ostreghe), San Marco 2347. ⓒ **041/5232317**. Reservations recommended Sat–Sun. Main courses 11.50€–24€ ($13.25–$27.60). AE, DC, MC, V. Fri–Wed noon–3pm and 7–10:30pm. Closed Dec 10 through Jan. Vaporetto: San Marco or Santa Maria del Giglio.

Ristorante Noemi VENETIAN   Since 1927, discerning Venetian foodies have been making their way to this typical trattoria for the friendly service, affordable mid-range prices, and market-fresh ingredients. Some of its dishes are inspired by *nuova cucina*, but many rely on old-fashioned recipes known to everybody's mamma mia. The cooks are known for their infallible skill in the kitchen and marvelous fish dishes such as "black" spaghetti with cuttlefish in its own sauce or a filet of sole Casanova (a white wine sauce, fresh mushrooms, and Adriatic shrimp).

Calle dei Fabbri, San Marco 912. *©* **041/5225238**. Reservations recommended. Main courses 17€–25€ ($19.55–$28.75). AE, DC, MC, V. Tues–Sun 11:30am–midnight. Vaporetto: San Marco.

Trattroria da Fiore ★ *(Value* VENETIAN   This affordable place is an eagerly sought out address because of its take on really typical local cookery, including some of the best regional fare served in the Accademia area. The house specialty is *pennette all Fiore*, which is served with seven fresh vegetables in season, a hearty, filling pasta dish. If you have more room, you can taste some very fresh and well-prepared fish dishes from the Adriatic, including a savory kettle of fish soup.

Calle delle Botteghe, San Marco 3461. *©* **041/5235310**. Reservations suggested. Pastas 8€–20€ ($9.20–$23); main courses 15€–35€ ($17.25–$40.25). MC, V. Wed–Mon noon–3pm and 7–10pm. Vaporetto: Accademia.

SHOPPING

There's virtually a shop—or shops—in every block, selling Venetian crafts, such as glass and lace, and oh, so much more. Most of the shopping is concentrated around **Piazza San Marco** or **Ponte Rialto.**

The best place to buy Carnevale masks is **Mondonovo,** Rio Terrà Canal, Dorsoduro 3063 (*©* **041/5287344**), where talented artisans labor to produce copies of both traditional and more modern masks, each of which is one-of-a-kind and richly nuanced with references to Venetian lore and traditions. Prices range from 25€ ($28.75) for a fairly basic model. The studio/shop **Bambole di Trilly,** Fondamenta dell'Osmarin, Castello 4974 (*©* **041/5212579**), offers dolls with meticulously painted porcelain faces (they call it a "biscuit") and hand-tailored costumes, including dressy pinafores. Prices begin at 15€ ($17.25), and reasonably priced dolls are made with the same painstaking care as their more expensive counterparts. Select outlets in Venice sell some of the greatest fabrics in the world. **Norelene,** Calle della Chiesa, Dorsoduro 727 (*©* **041/5237605**), features lustrous hand-printed silks, velvets, and cottons, plus wall hangings and clothing.

One of the oldest (founded in 1866) and largest purveyors of traditional Venetian glass is **Pauly & Co.,** Ponte Consorzi, San Marco 4392 (*©* **041/5209899**), with more than two dozen showrooms. Part of the premises is devoted to something akin to a museum, where past successes (now antiques) are displayed. Antique items are only rarely offered for sale; but they can be copied and shipped anywhere, and chandeliers can be electrified to match your standards. They begin at about 1,000€ ($1,150).

The art glass sold by **Venini,** Piazzetta Leoncini, San Marco 314 (*©* **041/5224045**), has caught the attention of collectors from all over the world. Many of its pieces, including anything-but-ordinary lamps, bottles, and vases, are works of art representing the best of Venetian craftsmanship. Its best-known glass has a distinctive swirl pattern in several colors, called a *venature*. This shop is known for the refined quality of its glass, some of which appears almost transparent. Much of it is very fragile, but the shop learned long ago how to ship it anywhere safely. To visit the furnace, call *©* **041/2737204.**

NIGHTLIFE

The tourist office distributes a free pamphlet (part in English, part in Italian), called *Un Ospite di Venezia.* A section of this useful publication lists events, including any music and opera or theatrical presentations, along with art exhibitions and local special events. *Note:* In January 1996, a dramatic fire left the fabled **Teatro de La Fenice** at Campo San Fantin, the city's main venue for performing arts, a blackened shell and a smoldering ruin. Opera lovers around the world, including Luciano Pavarotti, mourned its loss. The good news is that the restored and reconstructed theater is slated to open some time early in 2004. Check on its status at the time of your visit.

In olden days, wealthy Venetians were rowed down the Grand Canal while being serenaded by gondoliers. To date, no one has improved on that age-old but now very expensive custom. Strolling through St. Mark's Square, having a cup of espresso at one of the two famous cafes (see below) and listening to a band concert may be even better.

CAFES & BARS Venice's most famous spot is **Caffè Florian,** Piazza San Marco, San Marco 56–59 (© **041/5205641**), built in 1720 and elaborately decorated with plush red banquettes, elaborate murals under glass, and Art Nouveau lighting. The Florian has hosted everyone from Casanova to Lord Byron and Goethe. Light lunch is served noon to 3pm, and an English tea is offered 3 to 6pm, when you can select from a choice of pastries, ice creams, and cakes. It's open Thursday to Tuesday 9:30am to midnight; it's closed the first week in December and the second week in January.

Its rival, **Quadri,** Piazza San Marco, San Marco 120–124 (© **041/5222105**), stands on the opposite side of the square from Florian's and is as elegantly decorated in antique style. It should be: It was founded in 1638. Wagner used to drop in for a drink when he was working on *Tristan und Isolde.* The bar was a favorite with the Austrians during their long-ago occupation. From April to October, it's open daily 9am to 1am; off-season hours are Tuesday to Sunday from 9am to midnight.

The single most famous of all the watering holes of Ernest Hemingway is **Harry's Bar,** Calle Vallaresso, San Marco 1323 (© **041/5285777**). Harry's is known for inventing its own drinks and exporting them around the world, and it's said that *carpaccio,* the delicate raw-beef dish, was invented here. Fans say that Harry's makes the best Bellini in the world, although many old-time visitors still prefer a vodka martini. Harry's Bar is now found around the world, but this is the original (the others are unauthorized knockoffs). Celebrities frequent the place during the various film and art festivals. Harry's is open daily 10:30am to 11pm.

Among wine bars, the historic **Cantina do Spade,** Calle do Spade, San Polo 860 (© **041/5210574**), beneath an arcade near the main fish-and-fruit market, dates from 1475 and was once frequented by Casanova. The place is completely rustic and barebones, but regulars come to order *cicchetti,* the equivalent of Spanish tapas. Many diners prefer to order 1 of the 250 sandwiches. Venetians delight in the 220 types of wine; glasses begin at .80€ (90¢). Cantina do Spade is open daily from 9am to 3pm and 6 to 11pm.

CLUBS Near the Accademia, **Il Piccolo Mondo,** Calle Contarini Corfu, Dorsoduro 1056A (© **041/5200371**), is open during the day but comes alive with dance music at night. The crowd is often young. It's open daily 10pm to 4am, but the action actually doesn't begin until after midnight. Cover, including the first drink, is 7€ ($8.05) Thursday and Friday, and 10€ ($11.50) Saturday. **Martini Scala Club,** Campo San Fantin, San Marco 1980 (© **041/5224121**), is an elegant restaurant with a piano bar (and a kitchen that stays open late). The piano bar gets going after 10pm and stays open until 3am (it's closed Tues and Wed at lunch).

AN EXCURSION TO PADUA

The most popular day trip out of Venice and a spot easily reached by rail is the ancient university city of Padua, 25 miles (40km) west of Venice. Padua remains a major art center of the Venetia region. A university that grew to fame throughout Europe was founded here as early as 1222 (in time, Galileo and the Poet Tasso were to attend).

Padua itself is sometimes known as *La Città del Santo* (the city of the saint), the reference being to St. Anthony of Padua, who is buried at a basilica the city dedicated to him. *Il Santo* was an itinerant Franciscan monk (who is not to be confused with St. Anthony of Egypt, the monastic hermit who could resist all temptations of the Devil).

GETTING THERE   Padua-bound trains depart for and arrive from Venice once every 30 minutes (trip time: about 30 min.), costing 3.60€ ($4.15) for a one-way ticket. For information and schedules, call *©* 892021 toll-free in Italy. Padua's main rail terminus lies at the **Piazza Stazione,** north of the historic core and outside the 16th-century walls. Frequent buses run to the center from the station.

TOURIST INFORMATION   The **Padua Tourist Office** is at Galleria Pedrocchi (*©* 049/8767911; www.turismopadova.it), open Monday to Saturday from 9:15am to 1:30pm and 3 to 7pm. Buses 3, 8, and 12 run between the trains station and tourist office. The one-way fare is .85€ ($1). You can also go by taxi for around 10€ ($11.50).

TOP ATTRACTIONS & SPECIAL MOMENTS

Many visitors arrive just to visit **Cappella degli Scrovegni,** Piazza Eremitani 8, off Corso Garibaldi (*©* 049/2010020), to see the celebrated *Giotto frescoes* ★★★. Sometime around 1305 and 1306, Giotto did a cycle of more than 35 (remarkably well preserved) frescoes inside, which (along with those at Assisi) form the basis of his claim to fame. Like an illustrated storybook, the frescoes unfold Biblical scenes. The third bottom panel (lower level on the right) depicts Judas kissing a most skeptical Christ, perhaps the most reproduced and widely known panel in the cycle. On the entrance wall is Giotto's *Last Judgment,* with Hell winning out in sheer fascination. The chapel is open daily from 9am to 10pm, and charges an admission fee of 12€ ($13.80) for adults and 5€ ($5.75) for ages 6 to 17. The fee includes entrance to the nearby **Museo Civico di Padova** ★, Piazza Eremitani 8 (*©* 049/8204550), open Tuesday to Sunday from 9am to 7pm. Of the museums sheltered in this building, the picture gallery is the most important—filled with minor works by major Venetian artists, dating back to the 14th century.

The art world lost heavily on March 11, 1944 when Allied bombs rained down on **Chiesa degli Eremitani** ★, Piazza Eremitani 9 (*©* 049/8756410). Before that time, it housed one of the greatest art treasures in Italy, the Ovetari Chapel frescoed by Andrea Mantegna. The cycle of frescoes was the first significant work by Mantegna (1431–1506). The church was rebuilt, but you can't resurrect 15th-century frescoes, of course. Inside, in the chapel to the right of the main altar, are fragments left after the bombing, a preview of what we missed in Mantegna's work. The most interesting fresco saved is a panel depicting the dragging of St. Christopher's body through the streets. Note also the *Assumption of the Virgin.* Mantegna is recommended even to those who don't like "religious painting." In the chancel chapel are some **splendid frescoes** ★★ attributed to

Guarineto, a Venetian student of the great Giotto. Admission to the chapel is free, and it's open Monday to Saturday from 8am to 12:30pm and 4 to 7pm; Sunday from 9:30am to noon and 4 to 7pm.

At Piazza del Santo, **Basilica di Sant'Antonio** ★★ (© **049/8242811**), dates from the 13th century when it was dedicated to St. Anthony of Padua interred inside. The basilica is a hodgepodge of styles, with mainly Romanesque and Gothic features. It has as many cupolas as Salome had veils. *Campanili* and minarets combine to give it a curious Eastern appearance. Inside, the **interior** ★★ is richly frescoed and decorated—and usually swarming with pilgrims devoutly ritualistic to the point of paganism, touching "holy" marble supposed to have divine power. The greatest art treasures are the **Donatello bronzes** ★★ at the main altar, with a realistic *Crucifix* (fluid, lyrical line) towering over the rest. Seek out, too, the Donatello relief depicting the removal of Christ from the cross, a unified composition expressing in simple lines the tragedy of Christ, the sadness of the mourners—an unromantic approach.

WHERE TO DINE

At some point, head for **Caffè Pedrocchi** ★, via VIII Febbraio 15 (© **049/8781231**), off Piazza Cavour in a neoclassical landmark hailed as the most elegant coffee house in Europe when it opened its doors back in 1831. It's open Tuesday through Sunday from 8am to midnight.

For a special lunch, visit **Antico Brolo** ★★, Corso Milano 22 (© **049/664555**), across from the town's Civil Theater. Installed in a Renaissance-style dining room, with tables on its garden terrace, this restaurant serves the best food in town, a combination of the Veneto and Italian in general. Seasonal ingredients are used to shape the changing menu of classic dishes, many given a modern twist. Main courses cost 15€ to 25€ ($17.25–$28.75), and hours are Tuesday to Sunday from 12:30 to 2:30pm and 7:30 to 11pm.

AN EXCURSION TO VERONA

The fictional home of Shakespeare's "pair of star-cross'd lovers," Romeo and Juliet, Verona is 71 miles (114km) west of Venice. In the city's medieval "age of flowering" under the despotic, often cruel, Scaligeri princes, Verona reached the pinnacle of its influence and prestige, developing into a town that even today is among the great art cities of Italy. The best-known member of the ruling Della Scala family, Can Grande I, was a patron of Dante. His sway over Verona has often been compared to that of Lorenzo the Magnificent over Florence.

GETTING THERE   A total of 33 trains a day make the 2-hour run between Venice and Verona, charging 8.90€ ($10.25) for a one-way ticket. From Milan and points west, some 40 trains a day make the 2-hour journey to Verona. Tickets cost 10.59€ ($12.20) one-way. Five daily trains come up from Rome, the 5-hour journey costing 37€ ($42.55) one-way.

Trains arrive at Verona's **Stazione Porta Nuova,** Piazza XXV Aprile, south of the centrally located arena and Piazza Brà; call © **892021** toll free in Italy for schedules and information. A branch of the Verona Tourist Office (© **045/8000861**) is located at the rail station,. It's open in summer Monday to Saturday from 9am to 6pm and Sunday 9am to 3pm.

TOURIST INFORMATION   The **Verona Tourist Office** is at Via Degli Alpini 9, at Piazza Brà (© **045/8068680**). It's open Monday to Saturday from 9am to 7pm. Off-season hours are Monday to Saturday 8am to 2pm. The tourist office and its railway branch don't make hotel reservations.

TOP ATTRACTIONS & SPECIAL MOMENTS

The most famous and most beautiful square in Verona is **Piazza dei Signori** ★★, dominated by the Palazzo del Governo, where Can Grande extended the shelter of his "hearth and home" to that fleeing Ghibelline, Dante Alighieri. The marble statue in the center of the square is of the "divine poet." Facing Dante's back is the 15th-century **Loggia del Consiglio,** frescoed and surmounted by five statues. It is the most attractive building on the square. Five different arches lead into the Piazza dei Signori, the innermost chamber of the heart of Verona.

The **Arche Scaligere** are outdoor tombs surrounded by wrought-iron gates that form a kind of open-air pantheon of the Scaligeri princes. One tomb, that of Cangrande della Scala, rests directly over the door of the 12th-century **Santa Maria Antica.**

Basilica San Zeno Maggiore ★★, Piazza San Zeno (✆ **045/8006120**), is a near-perfect Romanesque church and *campanile,* graced with a stunning entrance—two pillars supported by puce-colored marble lions and surmounted with a rose window. On either side of the portal are bas-reliefs depicting scenes from the Old and New Testaments, as well as a mythological story portraying Theodoric as a huntsman lured to hell (the king of the Goths defeated Odoacer in Verona). The panels—nearly 50 in all—on the bronze doors are truly a remarkable achievement of primitive art, sculpted perhaps in the 12th century. Admission is 2€ ($2.30), and hours are Monday to Saturday from 8:30am to 6pm, and Sunday 1 to 6pm. It's closed Monday from noon to 3pm.

Arena di Verona ★★, Piazza Brà (✆ **045/8003204**), evoking the Colosseum in Rome, is an elliptically shaped amphitheatre dating from the 1st century A.D. Four arches of the "outer circle" and a complete "inner ring" still stand, which is rather remarkable because an earthquake hit this area in the 12th century. For nearly half a century, it's been the setting of a summer opera house, usually from mid-July to mid-August. More than 20,000 persons are treated to—say, Verdi, Mascagni, or a performance of *Aïda,* the latter considered by some to be "the greatest operatic spectacle in the world." Admission is 3.10€ ($3.55). It's open Tuesday to Sunday from 9am to 7:30pm (on performance days 9am–3pm), Monday 1:45 to 7:30pm.

The 14th-century **Castelvecchio (Old Castle)** ★★, Corso Castelvecchio 2 (✆ **045/594734**), is situated alongside the Adige River (and reached by heading out the Via Roma). It stands near the Ponte Scaligera, the famous bridge bombed by the Nazis in World War II and subsequently reconstructed. The former seat of the Della Scala family, the restored castle has now been turned into an **Art Museum,** with important paintings from the Veronese school. Admission is 3.10€ ($3.55), and hours are Tuesday to Sunday from 9am to 7pm.

WHERE TO DINE

While not the gourmet citadel of Italy, Verona is blessed with a series of good restaurants, notably **Ristorante 12 Apostoli** ★★, Vicolo Corticella San Marco 3 (✆ **045/596**), which is 250 years old, the city's oldest. The present owners, the Gioco brothers, keep it humming with Giorgio being the culinary whiz in the kitchen and Franco welcoming you to the table. This is Italian cookery with a flair prepared with market-fresh ingredients, with main courses costing 13€ to 22€ ($14.95–$25.30). Open Tuesday to Sunday 12:30 to 2:30pm and Tuesday to Saturday 7 to 10pm. Closed the first week in January and June 15 to July 5. Another choice, almost as good, is **Ristorante Re Teodorico** ★, Piazzale Castel

San Pietro 1 (*©* **045/834990**), serving a finely honed regional and international cuisine at a site on the edge of town, opening onto vistas of Verona and the Adige. At a table under an arbor, you can partake of some of the finest and most imaginative dishes in Verona, featuring the freshest of fish and meat dishes, with main courses costing 16€ to 25€ ($18.40–$28.75). It's open Thursday to Tuesday from noon to 3pm and 7 to 10pm. It's closed January.

Rewriting its Italian and international menu every 6 months, **Ristorante All'Aquila,** in the Due Torri Hotel Baglioni, Piazza Sant'Anastasia 4 (*©* **045/ 595044**), serves impeccably fresh ingredients fashioned into a series of palate-pleasing dishes that transcend the ordinary. Spicings and flavorings are subtle, and sometimes seemingly ill-matched ingredients are cooked into harmonious platters of delight. Main courses cost 16€ to 18.50€ ($18.40–$21.30), and hours are daily from 12:30 to 2:30pm and 7:30 to 10pm.

6 Milan & the Northwest

Busy Milan is a commercial powerhouse and, partly because of its banks and major industrial companies, Italy's most influential city. It's the center of publishing, silk production, TV and advertising, and fashion design; it's also close to Italy's densest collection of automobile-assembly plants, rubber and textile factories, and chemical plants. The industry and prosperity of the capital of the Lombardy region has imbued it with a 21st-century commercial atmosphere unlike Italy's other large cities, where the past is so tangible.

The city's commercialism, combined with World War II bombings, have spared very few of the city's oldest buildings, but those that do remain are definitely worth visiting. And Milan also boasts La Scala, one of Europe's most prestigious opera houses.

For the rail traveler, Milan is an ideal stopover during a grand tour of Europe, as several of Europe's most strategic rail lines converge here and most international trains heading into Italy stop in the city. It's also home to one of the major airports welcoming arriving traffic from North America, so many people start off their Italian rail journeys in this metropolis. From Milan, you can make connections (many of them high-speed) to all of the major cities in Italy. Though we rank this the fourth-best city in the Italian scheme of things, Milan is definitely the busiest and best of Italy's rail hubs.

STATION INFORMATION
GETTING FROM THE AIRPORT TO THE TRAIN STATION
Milan has two airports: **Aeroporto di Linate,** 4¼ miles (7km) east of the inner city and the **Aeroporto Malpensa,** 31 miles (50km) northwest. Malpensa is used for most transatlantic flights, whereas Linate is used for flights within Italy and Europe. For general airport and flight information, call *©* **02/74852200.**

Malpensa Express trains (www.malpensaexpress.it) whisk arrivals from Malpensa airport to the Central station in the heart of Milan in about 45 minutes. They run every 30 minutes daily 5:50am to 9:45pm, and every hour from 9:45pm to 1:30am. A one-way ticket costs 9€ ($10.35) for adults and 5€ ($5.75) for children 4 to 12 years old. Note that railpasses are not accepted on these trains, but Alitalia passengers ride free.

Buses run between Linate and Milan's Centrale station every 30 minutes daily from 6am to 11pm. A bus (no. 73) also runs between Piazza San Babila and Linate airport every 20 minutes daily from 5:35am to 12:30am. Buses run from Malpensa to Stazione Centrale daily every 30 to 45 minutes, and cost 5€

($5.75) one-way. For information about buses to and from the airports, call ② **800016857.** Note that both the bus and train options are much cheaper than taking a taxi, which could run you a whopping 65€ ($74.75).

INSIDE THE STATION

Milan offers the finest rail connections in Italy. The main rail station for arrivals is Mussolini's mammoth **Stazione Centrale,** Piazza Duca d'Aosta (② **892021** toll-free in Italy), where you'll find the national railways information office open daily from 7am to 9:30pm.

One train per hour arrives from both Genoa and Turin (trip time: 1½–2 hr.), costing 12.55€ ($14.45) one-way. Twenty-five trains arrive daily from Venice (trip time: 3 hr.), costing 19.16€ ($22.05) one-way, and one train per hour arrives from Florence (trip time: 2½ hr.), costing 30€ to 41.83€ ($34.50–$48.10) one-way. Trains from Rome (trip time: 4½ hr.) arrive every hour; the fare is 53.87€ ($61.95) one-way.

The station is directly northeast of the heart of town; trams, buses, and the Metro link the station to Piazza del Duomo in the very center.

At the train station, you can arrange for luggage storage daily from 4:30am to 1:30am; the cost is 2.58€ ($2.95) per 12 hours. Baggage-check facilities are labeled *Deposito Bagagli* and can be reached by taking the exit at the end of tracks #6 and #7. In the same location is a branch of the lost property office, **Ufficio Oggetti Smarriti Comune** (② **02/63712667**), open daily from 7am to 1pm and 2 to 8pm. There's also a supermarket and ATMs.

For currency exchange, head along the archway leading to tracks—called *binary* in Italian—#10 to #15 until you get to the office. Money is converted daily from 7am to 11pm.

For train information, look for a black "i" sign. The office is located at the extreme right end of the station as you enter from the tracks. The British flag indicates that an English-speaking attendant is there to help you daily from 7am to 9pm. Note, however, that this is not the office at which to make reservations for EuroCity, InterCity, Rapido Express, or Eurostar Italia trains. To reach that office, go through the main station hall and down the stairs to the foyer on the lower street level. Look for a door marked *Biglietteria Est,* meaning ticket office east, and go through that entrance, then take a number from the machine and wait your turn. The reservation office—counters #49 and #53—is called *Preno-tazioni,* and the hours are Monday to Friday from 8am to 10pm and Saturday and Sunday from 8am to 1pm. For Railpass validation, you must go to another office at the station's street level. It's marked *Biglietteria Ovest;* reservations are processed at windows #20 or #22. These windows are marked "International Tickets" (yes, in English).

A branch of the **Milan Tourist Office** at Stazione Central (② **02/72524360**), is open Monday through Saturday from 9am to 6:30pm, and Sunday from 9am to 1pm and 2 to 5pm. The staff here will give you a list of hotels but will not make reservations. Because Milan is a city of commerce that's often filled with business clients or hosting conventions, a hotel reservation should be made before you ever get to the city.

Note: The area surrounding the train station is not the best after dark; use caution when leaving or arriving here at night.

INFORMATION ELSEWHERE IN THE CITY

The main tourist office, **Azienda di Promozione Turistica del Milanese,** is at Piazza del Duomo (the very heart of Milan) at Via Marconi 1 (② **02/72524301**).

Milan

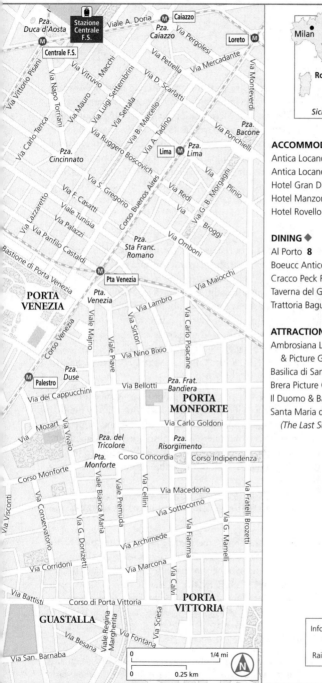

ACCOMMODATIONS ■
Antica Locanda dei Mercanti **4**
Antica Locanda Leonardo **5**
Hotel Gran Duca di York **9**
Hotel Manzoni **15**
Hotel Rovello **3**

DINING ◆
Al Porto **8**
Boeucc Antico Ristorante **13**
Cracco Peck Restaurant **11**
Taverna del Gran Sasso **1**
Trattoria Bagutta **14**

ATTRACTIONS ●
Ambrosiana Library
   & Picture Gallery **10**
Basilica di San Ambrogio **7**
Brera Picture Gallery **2**
Il Duomo & Baptistry **12**
Santa Maria delle Grazie
   (The Last Supper) **6**

Information *(i)*
Metro Ⓜ
Rail Station 🛄

It's open Monday through Friday from 8:30am to 1pm and 2 to 7pm, Saturday from 9am to 1pm and 2 to 6pm, and Sunday from 9am to 1pm and 2 to 5pm in summer (closes 1 hr. earlier in winter). The staff will provide a listing of hotels but won't make reservations.

GETTING AROUND

The **Metro subway** system is extensive and efficient, covering most of Milan; in addition, there are buses and trams, making it fairly easy to navigate. Regular tickets cost 1€ ($1.15) and are sold at Metro stations and newsstands. Some subway tickets are good for continuing trips on city buses at no extra charge, but they must be used within 75 minutes of purchase. You must stamp your ticket when you board a bus or tram, or risk incurring a fine. The tourist office and all subway ticket offices sell a **travel pass** for 3€ ($3.45) for 1 day, or 5.50€ ($6.35) for 2 days, good for unlimited use on the city's tram, bus, and subway network.

To phone a **taxi,** dial © **02/4040,** 02/8585, or 02/4000; fares start at 3.10€ ($3.55), with a nighttime surcharge of 3.10€ ($3.55).

WHERE TO STAY

Antica Locanda dei Mercanti   In the historic district, this sophisticated and reasonably priced hotel is a favorite with many movers and shakers in Milan's fashion industry. Former model Paolo Ora gutted the second floor of a building from the 1800s and turned it into this little charmer in 1996. Each midsize room comes with a marble-clad, shower-only bathroom, and the design lines are sleek and contemporary with fine use of fabrics. Some rooms have canopied beds and all feature fresh flowers, books, and magazines.

Via San Tommaso 6, 20123 Milano. © **02/8054080.** Fax 02/8054090. www.locanda.it. 14 units (showers only). 130€–250€ ($150–$288) double. AE, MC, V. Tram: 1, 14, or 24. Metro: Cairoli, Cordusio, or Duomo. **Amenities:** Laundry; nonsmoking rooms. *In room:* Hair dryer.

Antica Locanda Leonardo ⚡   If you're seeking both atmosphere and comfort, this undiscovered gem is a worthy choice. A restored 19th-century building houses the hotel, whose chief grace note is an inner courtyard and garden that features wildly blooming wisteria in summer. Many of the bedrooms open onto small balconies, and the mostly midsize rooms are individually decorated in styles ranging from Liberty to very modern. Half of the bathrooms come with shower, the rest with tub.

Corso Magenta 78, 20123 Milano. © **02/463317.** Fax 02/48014197. www.leoloc.com. 20 units. 150€–190€ ($173–$219) double. Rates include continental breakfast. AE, DC, MC, V. **Amenities:** Bar; laundry. *In room:* Hair dryer.

Hotel Gran Duca di York ⚡⚡   This Liberty-style *palazzo* dates back to the 1890s, when it was constructed by the Catholic Church to shelter the clergy from the nearby Duomo. Among them was the cardinal of Milan, who later became Pope Pius XI. Today anyone can rent one of the pleasantly furnished and well-kept rooms, ranging from small to medium in size, each with a tiled bathroom.

Via Moneta 1A (Piazza Cordusio), 20123 Milano. © **02/874863.** Fax 02/8690344. 153 units. 153€ ($176) double; 176€ ($202) triple. Rates include breakfast. AE, MC, V. Closed Aug. Metro: Cordusio or Duomo. **Amenities:** Bar; laundry. *In room:* Hair dryer.

Hotel Manzoni   The Manzoni, built around 1910 and renovated frequently since then, charges reasonable prices considering its location near the most-fashionable shopping streets. Bedrooms, although small, are color coordinated and comfortable, each tastefully furnished. The small tiled bathrooms come with showers (no tubs). A brass-trimmed winding staircase leads from the lobby into a bar and TV lounge.

Via Santo Spirito 20, 20121 Milano. ℂ 02/76005700. Fax 02/784212. 52 units. 196€ ($225) double, 252€ ($290) suite. Rates include breakfast. AE, DC, MC, V. Metro: Montenapoleone or San Babila. **Amenities:** Bar; laundry. *In room:* Hair dryer.

Hotel Rovello   This affordable hotel's location is ideal, close to the Santa Maria delle Grazie, between Castello Sforzesco and Piazza Duomo. Recent renovations added soundproofing to the windows and improved the hotel's guest rooms, which are furnished in a minimalist yet comfortable style. Hardwood floors, orthopedic mattresses, and small dressing areas in some units are part of this hotel's charm, along with immaculately kept shower-only bathrooms. The place is not luxurious but is highly commendable.

Via Rovello 18, 20121 Milano. ℂ 02/86464654. Fax 02/72023656. www.hotel-rovello.it. 120€–205€ ($138–$236) double. Children under 6 stay free in parent's room. Rates include continental breakfast. AE, DC, MC, V. Metro: Cordusio. Bus: 1, 2, 3, 4, 12, 14, 18, 19, 20, 24, or 27. **Amenities:** Bar; laundry. *In room:* Hair dryer.

TOP ATTRACTIONS & SPECIAL MOMENTS

Ambrosiana Library & Picture Gallery (Biblioteca–Pinacoteca Ambrosiana) 🎭🎭   Near the Duomo, this museum houses one of the leading art galleries in the north of Italy, stressing paintings of the 15th through the 17th centuries. Among its most famous works are *Portrait of a Musician,* by Leonardo da Vinci, and *The Fruit Basket* by Caravaggio. One of the museum's highlights is room 10, with 10 magnificent **cartoons by Raphael** 🎭🎭🎭, which he prepared for the frescoes of the School of Athens in the Vatican. Another room contains a collection of reproductions from the drawings of Leonardo da Vinci's *Codex Atlanticus.* The **Ambrosiana Library** contains many medieval manuscripts, which are shown for scholarly examination only

Piazza Pio XI 2. ℂ 02/806921. Admission 7.50€ ($8.65) adults; seniors and children under 18 are 4.50€ ($5.20). Tues–Sun 10am–5:30pm. Metro: Duomo or Cordusio.

Brera Picture Gallery (Pinacoteca di Brera) 🎭🎭🎭   A 17th-century palace houses one of the finest collections of paintings in Italy. Most of the paintings are religious works, especially by Lombard and other Northern Italian painters, but you'll also find representative paintings by El Greco, Rubens, Rembrandt, and Van Dyck. One of the gallery's prize possessions is the *Urbino Altarpiece,* by Piero della Francesca, depicting the Virgin and Child surrounded by a number of saints with the Duke of Urbino kneeling in the foreground. Also on display are Mantegna's *The Dead Christ* 🎭🎭🎭, Giovanni Bellini's *Pietà* 🎭🎭, and Bernardino's *Virgin of the Rose Bush.* Another masterpiece is Raphael's *Bethrothal of the Virgin* 🎭🎭. The Venetian School is well represented in the works of Titian, Tintoretto, and Veronese.

Via Brera 28. ℂ 02/72263229. Admission 5€ ($5.75). Tues–Sun 8:30am–7:30pm. Metro: Lanza, or Montenapoleone.

Il Duomo & Baptistery 🎭🎭🎭   Dominating the Piazza del Duomo, Milan's cathedral is the largest Gothic structure in Italy. Begun in 1386, it took nearly 500 years to complete. Work was carried on during this period by architects and master masons from France and Germany, as well as all parts of Italy, giving the Duomo a flamboyant Gothic **exterior** 🎭🎭🎭 more reminiscent of the cathedrals north of the Alps than of its sister churches in Italy. With a floor plan in the shape of a Latin cross and five naves, the cathedral is supported by 40 exterior buttresses and 50 interior columns. Its height, including the spire topped by a gilded statue of the Virgin (added in 1859), is 367 feet. More than 3,000 statues decorate the inside and outside.

To experience the Duomo at its most majestic, you must take the elevator to the **roof** or **visita ai terrazzo** ★★★, on which you can walk through a forest of pinnacles, turrets, and marble statuary.

Piazza del Duomo. ℂ **02/86463456**. Cathedral free; roof via stairs 5€ ($5.75); roof via elevator 5€ ($5.75); crypt free; baptistery 1.50€ ($1.75). Cathedral daily 6:50am–6:50pm. Roof daily 9am–4:30pm. Crypt daily 9:30am–noon and 2:30–6pm. Baptistery daily 9:30am–5pm.

Santa Maria delle Grazie & The Last Supper ★★ At the same time that Bramante was adding the purely Renaissance dome to the transitional Gothic church on the Piazza Santa Maria delle Grazie, his friend Leonardo da Vinci was working on his great fresco, *The Last Supper* ★★★, in the adjoining refectory of the Dominican convent. Bramante's vast domed crossing with its apsed transepts and choir struck an entirely original note in Milanese architecture. Visitors today often ignore the main church, however, and go directly to the simple refectory next door to gaze in awe at what is the best known and most frequently copied religious painting in the world. Although Leonardo's *Last Supper* miraculously survived such threats as a bombing attack in World War II, it is barely holding its own against the ravages of time. The painting depicts Christ at the moment when he announces that 1 of the 12 will betray him.

Piazza Santa Maria delle Grazie (off Corso Magenta). ℂ **02/4987588**. Free admission to church; 6.50€ ($7.50), plus 1€ ($1.15) for reservation to see *The Last Supper*. Church Mon–Sat 9am–noon and 3–6pm; Sun 3:30–6:30pm. *The Last Supper* viewings Tues–Sat 8:30am–6:45pm; Sun 9am–7:15pm. Reservations required for *The Last Supper;* call Mon–Sat 8am–7pm and leave your name. Metro: Cadorna or Conciliazione.

WHERE TO DINE

Al Porto ★★ SEAFOOD Since 1907, this lovely restaurant has been one of the most popular places to go for seafood. Even though Milan is an inland city, the chefs here manage to secure some of the best and freshest fish shipped daily to the local markets. Try their traditional *fritto misto,* a platter of lightly sautéed shellfish and various kinds of fish.

Piazzale Generale Cantore. ℂ **02/8321481**. Reservations required several days in advance. Main courses 9.50€–24€ ($10.95–$27.60). AE, DC, MC, V. Tues–Sat 12:30–2:30pm; Mon–Sat 7:30–10:30pm. Closed Dec 24–Jan 3 and Aug. Metro: Porta Genova or Sant'Agostino.

Boeucc Antico Ristorante INTERNATIONAL/MILANESE This longtime-favorite, opened in 1696, has a trio of rooms in an antique *palazzo,* within walking distance of the Duomo and the major shopping arteries. In summer, guests gravitate to a terrace for open-air dining. You might enjoy spaghetti in clam sauce, a salad of shrimp with arugula and artichokes, or grilled liver, veal, or beef with aromatic herbs.

Piazza Belgioioso 2. ℂ **02/76020224**. Reservations required. Main courses 15€–22.50€ ($17.25–$25.90). AE. Mon–Fri 12:40–2:30pm; Sun–Fri 7:40–10:30pm. Closed Aug, Easter, and Christmas. Metro: Duomo, Montenapoleone, or San Babila.

Cracco Peck Restaurant ★★ MILANESE/ITALIAN Peck's is owned by the famous delicatessen, viewed as the Milanese equivalent of Fauchon's in Paris. A Czech immigrant, Francesco Peck, opened the restaurant back in the 19th century and went on to build a food empire. Some of the freshest and tastiest dishes in Milan are served by an efficient staff, including a classic version of risotto Milanese.

Via Victor Hugo 4. ✆ **02/876774.** Reservations required. Main courses 30€–45€ ($34.50–$51.75). AE, DC, MC, V. Mon–Fri 12:15–2pm and 7:15–10:30pm; Sat 7:15–10:30pm. Closed 3 weeks in Jan and Aug 10–31. Metro: Duomo.

Taverna del Gran Sasso ✪ ABRUZZI   This restaurant sends out a siren call to all gourmands—no chefs serve more bountiful portions in all of Milan. Against a rustic tavern background that includes a tall open hearth, you are treated to a number of specialties from the southern province of Abruzzi. Meals are an all-you-can-eat feast. The first course offers at least 10 choices; the second, two; the third, four; the fourth, five; and there are at least 10 desserts to choose from.

Piazza Principessa Clotilde 10. ✆ **02/6597578.** Reservations not required. All-you-can-eat meal 39€ ($44.85); all-you-can-eat fish meal (reserve in advance) 44€ ($50.60). AE, DC, MC, V. Mon–Fri noon–2pm and 7–10:30pm; Sat 7:30–10:30pm. Closed Jan 1 and Aug. Metro: Repubblica.

Trattoria Bagutta ✪ INTERNATIONAL   Dating from 1927, this bustling trattoria, has long been our favorite in Milan, and we always manage to have at least one or two meals here on every visit. The cuisine is not just from Lombardy, but also borrows heavily from the kitchens of Tuscany and Bologna as well. This is generous, home-style cooking, and the interior is cozy and comfortable, amusingly decorated with caricatures of famous Italians.

Via Bagutta 14. ✆ **02/76002767.** Reservations required. Main courses 10.50€–22€ ($12.10–$25.30). AE, DC, MC, V. Mon–Sat 12:30–2:30pm and 7:30–10:30pm. Closed Dec 24–Jan 6. Metro: San Babila.

SHOPPING

London has Harrods, Paris has all the big-name boutiques you can think of, and Rome and Florence instill an acquisitional fever in the eyes of anyone who even window-gazes. Milan, however, is blessed with one of the most unusual concentrations of shopping possibilities in Europe. Most of the boutiques are infused with the style, humor, and sophistication that has made Milan the dynamo of the Italian fashion industry, a place where the sidewalks sizzle with the hard-driving entrepreneurial spirit that has been part of the northern Italian textile industry for centuries.

A walk on the fashion subculture's focal point, **via Montenapoleone,** heart of the Golden Triangle and one of Italy's great shopping streets, a mile-long (1.6 km) strip that has become a showcase for famous (and high-priced) makers of clothes and shoes, with excursions into the side streets, will quickly confirm that impression.

Early-morning risers will be welcomed only by silent streets and closed gates. Most shops are closed all day Sunday and Monday (although some open on Mon afternoon). Some stores open at 9am unless they're very chic, and then they're not likely to open until 10:30am. They remain open, for the most part, until 1pm, reopening again between 3:30 and 7:30pm.

Bargain hunters leave the Golden Triangle and head for a mile-long (1.6km) stretch of **Corso Buenos Aires,** where you can find style at more affordable prices. Start off at **Piazza Oberdan,** the square closest to the heart of Milan. Clothing abounds on Corso Buenos Aires, especially casual wear and knockoffs of designer goods. But you'll also find a vast array of merchandise, from scuba-diving equipment to soft luggage. Saturdays are unbelievably crowded here. You'll find more bargains in the **Brera,** the name given to a sprawling shopping district around the Brera Museum. This area is far more attractive than Corso Buenos Aires and has often been compared to New York's Greenwich Village because of its cafes, shops, antiques stores, and art students. Skip the main street, **Via Brera,** and concentrate on the side streets, especially **Via Solferino, Via Madonnina,** and **Via Fiori Chiari.**

NIGHTLIFE

THE PERFORMING ARTS   The most complete list of cultural events appears in the large Milan newspaper, the left-wing *La Repubblica.* Try for a Thursday edition, which usually has the most complete listings.

The world's most famous opera house, **La Scala,** Piazza della Scala (Metro: Duomo), closed December 30, 2001, for a 3-year restoration. It marks the first time since World War II that Italy's leading opera house has been closed for an extended period.

While La Scala remains closed, operas will be presented at the 2,500-seat, newly constructed auditorium, **Teatro degli Arcimboldi,** Zona Bicocca, Viale dell'Innovazione (*©* **02/72003744**), on the northern outskirts of Milan. Since the new opera house is difficult to reach by public transportation, the new theater operates shuttle buses departing from the Piazza Duomo between 6:45 and 7pm on the nights of performances. Otherwise, you have to take the Metro to the Precotto stop and from there take a bus (no. 162) to the auditorium. Tickets are extremely hard to come by and are sold out weeks in advance, costing 10€ to 155€ ($11.50–$178); tickets can be obtained only by calling the theater or by purchasing them on the Web at **www.teatroallascala.org**.

LIVE-MUSIC CLUBS   At **Le Scimmie,** Via Ascanio Sforza 49 (*©* **02/ 89402874;** bus: 59), bands play everything from funk to blues to creative jazz. Doors open nightly around 8pm, and music is presented 10pm to around 3am.

Rolling Stone, Corso XXII Marzo 32 (*©* **02/733172;** tram: 54 or 73), features head-banging rock bands. It's open every night, usually 10:30pm to 4am, but things don't get going until at least midnight. It's closed in July and August. Cover ranges from 6€ to 10€ ($6.90–$11.50).

CAFES   The decor of the **Berlin Cafe,** Via Gian Giacomo Mora 9 (*©* **02/ 8392605;** tram: 15, 19, or 24), seems straight out of turn-of-the-20th-century Berlin, with etched glass and marble-topped tables. It's a great spot for coffee or a drink, although we've had gruff service here. A variety of simple snack food is available, primarily during the day, although the cafe is open until midnight.

Boasting a chic crowd of garment-district workers and shoppers, **Café Cova,** Via Montenapoleone 8 (*©* **02/76000578;** Metro: Montenapoleone), has been around since 1817, serving pralines, chocolates, brioches, and sandwiches. The more elegant sandwiches contain smoked salmon and truffles. Sip your espresso from fragile gold-rimmed cups at one of the small tables in an elegant inner room or while standing at the prominent bar. It's closed in August and on Sunday year-round. Closing time is in the early evening.

AN EXCURSION TO LAKE COMO

Flower-bedecked promenades, lemon trees, romantic villas, parks and gardens, and crystal clear blue waters welcome you to Lake Como, lying 30 miles (48km) north of Milan and stretching 2½ miles (4km) at its widest point. "Everything noble, everything evoking love"—that's how Stendhal characterized fork-tongued Lake Como. Others have called it "the looking glass of Venus."

GETTING THERE   At the southern tip of the lake, the town of **Como,** known for its silk industry, makes a good base for exploring. Trains arrive daily at Como from Milan (trip time: 40 min.) every hour; fares cost 6.50€ ($7.50) one-way. **Stazione San Giovanni,** Piazzale San Gottardo (© **892021**), is at the end of Viale Gallio, a 15-minute walk from the center of Como.

VISITOR INFORMATION   In the exact center of town at Piazza Cavour (#17) you'll find the **tourist office** (© **031/269712;** www.lakecomo.org). It's open Monday through Saturday from 9am to 1pm and 2:30 to 6pm. The staff doesn't make hotel reservations.

TOP ATTRACTIONS & SPECIAL MOMENTS

Touring **Lake Como** ★★★ by boat is the main reason to visit the town of Como. It's easy to take a cruise around the lake; boats departing from the town's piers make calls at every significant settlement along its shores. Stroll down to the **Lungo Lario,** adjacent to Piazza Cavour, and head to the ticket windows of the **Società Navigazione Lago di Como** (© **031/304060**). Half a dozen ferries and almost as many high-speed hydrofoils embark on circumnavigations of the lake. One-way transit from Como to Colico at the northern end of the lake takes 4 hours by ferry and 90 minutes by hydrofoil, and includes stops at each of the towns or major villages en route. Transit each way costs 7.60€ to 10.80€ ($8.75–$12.40), depending on which boat you take. One-way transit between Como and Bellagio takes 2 hours by ferry and 45 minutes by hydrofoil, and costs 6€ to 8.90€ ($6.90–$10.25) per person. There's no ferry service from Como between October and Easter, but there is hydrofoil service between October and Easter.

To get an overview of the lake area, take the funicular at Lungolario Trieste (near the main beach at Villa Genio) to the top of **Brunante,** a hill overlooking Como and providing a panoramic view. Departures are every 30 minutes daily, and the trip costs 3.95€ ($4.55) round-trip.

Before rushing off on a boat for a tour of the lake, you might want to visit the **Cattedrale di Como** ★, Piazza del Duomo (© **031/265244**). Construction on the cathedral began in the 14th century in the Lombard Gothic style and continued on through the Renaissance until the 1700s. Frankly, the exterior is more interesting than the interior. Dating from 1487, the exterior is lavishly decorated with statues, including those of Pliny the Elder (A.D. 23–79) and the Younger (A.D. 62–113), who one writer once called "the beautiful people of ancient Rome." Inside, look for the 16th-century tapestries depicting scenes from the Bible. The cathedral is open Monday through Saturday from 7am to noon and 3 to 7pm.

WHERE TO DINE

Close to the cathedral, **Ristorante Imbarcadero,** in the Metropole & Suisse hotel, Piazza Cavour 19, 22100 Como (© **031/269444;** www.hotelmetropole suisse.com), serves an enticing Lombard and Italian cuisine on tables placed near the edge of the lake. All the food, including the pastas, is homemade and much of the fresh fish served here comes from the lake itself. Main courses cost 12€ to 18€ ($13.80–$20.70), with a fixed–price menu at 25€ ($28.75). It's open daily from 12:30 to 2:30pm and 7:30 to 10:30pm.

AN EXCURSION TO TURIN ★★

Also known as Torino, Turin is one of Italy's richest cities and the car capital of the country. The capital of Piedmont, Turin became the first capital of a united Italy, and much of its history is linked to the House of Savoy. Its chief treasure is the controversial Shroud of Turin, whose mysterious origins have been the subject of much controversy. Was it really the shroud that Joseph of Arimathea wrapped about the body of Christ when his body was removed from the cross?

In addition to being an economic powerhouse, Turin is also a city of grace and elegance, known for its baroque architecture, its bevy of first-rate museums, its Fiat cars, its Juventus soccer team, and its scenic location at the foothills of the Alps.

Note also that Turin has been named as the host city for the **Olympic Winter Games** in the year 2006. You can get details on the upcoming event at **www.torino2006.it**. Turin will host the opening and closing ceremonies, the Olympic Village, and the press operations, as well as some of the events.

GETTING THERE Turin is a major **rail** terminus, with arrivals at **Stazione di Porta Nuova,** Corso Vittorio Emanuele (© **011/531327;** www.trenitalia. com), or **Stazione Centrale,** Corso Vittorio Emanuele II (© **011/534435**), in the heart of the city. It takes 1¼ hours to reach Turin by train from Milan, but it takes anywhere from 9 to 11 hours to reach Turin from Rome, depending on the connection. The one-way fare from Milan is 16.20€ ($18.60); from Rome it's 76.50€ ($87.95).

TOURIST INFORMATION Go to the office of **APT,** Piazza Castello 161 (© **011/535181**), which is open Monday through Saturday from 9:30am to 7pm, and Sunday from 9:30am to 3pm. There's another office at the Porta Nuova train station (© **011/531327**), open the same hours. These offices will make "last minute" hotel reservations for free if you call 48 hours in advance— no sooner than that.

TOP ATTRACTIONS & SPECIAL MOMENTS

To begin your exploration, head first for the **Piazza San Carlo** ✦✦, the loveliest and most unified square in the city, covering about 3½ acres. Heavily bombed in the last war, it dates from the 17th century, and was built to the design of Carlo di Castellamonte. In the heart of the piazza is an equestrian statue of Emanuele Filiberto. The two churches are those of Santa Cristina and San Carlo. On the square, some of the most prestigious names in Italy have sat sipping coffee and plotting the unification of Italy. The most popular coffee house is the **Caffè Torino,** 204 Piazza San Carlo (© **011/545118**), where under the arcade you'll often see elegant Turinese who turn up for pastries, campari . . . and much talk.

The city's most interesting museums are located in the Guarini-designed, 17th-century **Science Academy Building,** 6 Via Accademia delle Scienze (© **011/4406903** or 011-5617776), whose ground floor houses an **Egyptian Museum** ✦✦✦, with a collection so vast that it's surpassed only by the ones at Cairo and the British Museum in London. Of the statuary, that of **Ramses II** is the best known, though there is one of Amenhotel II as well. In the rather crowded wings upstairs, the world of the pharaohs lives on (one of the prize exhibits is the "Royal Papyrus," with its valuable chronicling of the Egyptian monarchs from the 1st through the 17th dynasties). The funereal art is exceptionally rare and valuable, especially the chapel built for Meie and his young wife, and an entirely reassembled tomb (that of Chaie and Merie, 18th dynasty), discovered in an amazingly well-preserved condition at the turn of the 20th century.

In the same building, you can visit the **Sabauda (Savoy) Gallery** ✦✦, one of the richest in Italy, whose collection was acquired over a period of centuries by the House of Savoy. It keeps the same hours as the Egyptian Museum. The Academy has the largest exhibit of the Piedmontese masters, but is well endowed in Flemish art as well. Of the latter, the most celebrated painting is Sir Anthony Van Dyck's *Three Children of Charles I* (England). Other important works include Botticelli's *Venus,* Memling's *Passion of Christ,* Rembrandt's *Sleeping Old Man,* Titian's *Leda,* Mantegna's *Holy Conversation,* Jan van Eyck's *The Stigmata of Francis of Assisi,* Veronese's *Dinner in the House of the Pharisee,* and intriguing paintings by the Bruegels. Admission to the Egyptian Museum is 6.50€ ($7.50); to the Galleria Sabauda it's 4€ ($4.60); a combined ticket to both is 8€ ($9.20). Hours for both attractions are Tuesday through Sunday from 8:30am to 7pm. To get here, take tram 18 from the train station.

Cattedrale di San Giovanni ✶, Piazza San Giovanni (✆ **011/4360790**), is a Renaissance cathedral dedicated to John the Baptist. A tragic fire swept across the cathedral in the spring of 1997, but its major treasure, the **Holy Shroud** ✶✶✶ was not damaged. Acquired by Emanuele Filiberto (whose equestrian statue you saw in the Piazza San Carlo), the shroud is purported to be the one that Joseph of Arimathea wrapped around the body of Christ when he was removed from the cross. Detailed charts in front of the holy relic claim to show evidence of a hemorrhage produced by the crown of thorns. The shroud is rarely on view but you can see dramatically lit photographs of the amazing relic. The shroud is contained in the **Museo della Santissima Sindone,** Via San Domenico 28 (✆ **011/ 4365832**), which is open daily from 9am to noon and 3 to 7pm, and charges an admission of 5.50€ ($6.35). Entrance to the cathedral is free daily from 7am to noon and 3 to 7pm. To get here from the train station, take bus 63.

WHERE TO DINE

Turin is home to some of the best restaurants in northwest Italy, notably **Villa Sassi** ✶, in the Hotel Villa Sassi, Via Traforo del Pino 47 (✆ **011/898556**), a 17th-century villa 3¾ miles (6km) east of the town center but reached easily by tram 15 or bus 61. It's worth the extra effort to get here, as its noteworthy Piedmontese and international cuisine is served in elegant, antique-filled salons. Some of the produce for the meals comes from the villa's own farm. Main courses cost from 13€ to 24€ ($14.95–$27.60). It's open Monday to Saturday from noon to 2:30pm and 8 to 10:30pm. It's closed in August.

A fast-rising restaurant is **Vintage 1997** ✶, Piazza Solferino 16 (✆ **011/ 535948;** tram: 4 or 10; bus: 5 or 67), which specializes in regional, mainly meat-based Piedmontese fare along with a nightly offering of fresh seafood from the coast. We enjoyed some of our best meals in the region here, including some unusual but successful mixtures including scampi tails and rack rabbit in a broccoli cream sauce. Main courses cost 11€ to 22€ ($12.65–$25.30), and hours are Monday through Friday from noon to 3pm and Monday through Saturday from 8pm to midnight.

15

The Netherlands

Exploring the Netherlands by train is a snap. Few indeed are the towns and places of interest here that can't be reached directly by train, or only require a minimal amount of additional traveling to do by bus, taxi, or bike. Dutch trains are frequent, and invariably both punctual and clean, so that getting from one end of the realm to another and to points in between, is no great trial.

This means you can stay focused on getting the most out of your time spent in Amsterdam, The Hague, Haarlem, and other historic towns and cities because you won't need to spend too much time on a train. Each of these cities is no more than a short ride away from the other. Even the relatively remote Zeeland, Friesland, and Limburg provinces are within relatively easy reach, enabling you to get close to a slower-paced way of life in this country that has been wrested acre by acre from the sea.

HIGHLIGHTS OF THE NETHERLANDS

The principal highlight of the Netherlands—the city of **Amsterdam**—happens also to be one of the highlights of the entire world. That's why it's as much a fixture on any well-conceived European rail tour as London, Paris, and Rome. Just 20 minutes by train from Schiphol Airport, Amsterdam is the capital and major city of Holland, a country that's barely half the size of the state of Maine. This high-energy metropolis has a multi-ethnic population of 725,000 (and 600,000 bikes)—and it runs the cultural gamut from the heights of the Van Gogh Museum to legal prostitution and officially tolerated dope dens.

Some visitors to the Netherlands make the mistake of thinking there's no more to the country than Amsterdam. Not so. Just 15 minutes away by train is **Haarlem,** a beautiful and historic small city that's well worth a side trip. Your next stop could well be **The Hague,** cool, sophisticated, more than a little stuffy, and the seat of the Dutch government and royal family. Unless you like sharp-edged cities, there's not much call to move on to modern, hustling Rotterdam, which hosts the world's busiest seaport. Dotted between are three towns any country would be proud to own: **Delft,** Leiden, and Gouda lack for little in the way of historic interest. Each has its merited claims to distinction. Choosing between them is a tough call, but Delft, an ancient seat of Dutch royalty (and the home town of Dutch master Vermeer), ekes out in front and is our choice.

Should you feel the need to stretch your legs a bit, metaphorically speaking, head down south to handsome and occasionally raucous **Maastricht** in the province of Limburg, at the country's borders with Germany and Belgium. A different kind of Dutch spirit and some of the best eating and drinking in the land will be your rewards.

1 Essentials

GETTING THERE

Amsterdam Airport Schiphol, 8 miles (13km) southwest of the city center, is the principal airport in the Netherlands and handles virtually all of the country's international flights. Schiphol has quick, direct rail links to Amsterdam Central Station, to The Hague, Rotterdam, Utrecht, and to many more Dutch cities; to Antwerp and Brussels in Belgium; and to cities in Germany.

Carriers with flights into Amsterdam from North America include **Air Canada** (© 888/247-2262; www.aircanada.ca), **Delta Airlines** (© 800/221-1212; www.delta.com), **KLM Royal Dutch Airlines** (© 800/374-7747; www.klm.com), **Northwest Airlines** (© 800/447-4747; www.nwa.com), and **United Airlines** (© 800/538-2929; www.united.com).

THE NETHERLANDS BY RAIL

All major tourist destinations in Holland are within 2½ hours of Amsterdam, on **Nederlandse Spoorwegen (Netherlands Railways/NS; © 0900/9292;** www. ns.nl), Holland's national rail system. NS trains are a good way to travel with the Dutch, who use them even for short journeys to the next town up the line. In addition to Amsterdam, other destinations easily reached by train from Schiphol include The Hague (40 min.), Rotterdam (45 min.), and Utrecht (40 min.). The

⟮Moments⟯ Festivals & Special Events

Koninginnedag (Queen's Day), April 30, is a nationwide holiday for the House of Orange and is vigorously celebrated in Amsterdam. The city center gets so jam-packed with people it's virtually impossible to move. A street market held all over town features masses of stalls, run by everybody from kids selling old toys to professional market folk. Orange ribbons, orange-dyed hair, and orange-painted faces are everywhere, as are Dutch flags. Street music and theater combine with too much drinking, but Koninginnedag remains a good-natured if boisterous affair. For more information, contact **VVV Amsterdam** (© 0900/400-4040).

One of the world's leading gatherings of top international jazz and blues musicians, the **North Sea Jazz Festival** unfolds over 3 concert-packed days in mid-July at the giant Nederlands Congresgebouw in The Hague. Last-minute tickets are scarce, so book as far ahead as you can. Contact **North Sea Jazz Festival** (© 015/215-7756; www.northsea jazz.nl) for more information.

Lastly, the **Grachten Festival is a** 5-day festival of chamber music that plays at various intimate and atmospheric venues along Amsterdam's canals in mid-August. Part of the festival is the exuberant Prinsengracht Concert. Contact **Stichting Grachtenfestival** (© 020/421-4542) for details.

trains run so often you can usually just go to the station and wait for the next one—your wait will be short. At even the smallest stations, there is ½-hour service in both directions, and major destination points have between four and eight trains an hour in both directions. Service begins as early as 5am (slightly later on Sun and holidays) and runs until around 1am. A special Night Train runs between Utrecht and Rotterdam, via Amsterdam, Schiphol, Leiden, and The Hague.

Note: Should you wish to bike some of your travel route, Netherlands Railways has some handy arrangements for **bikers** where you can pick up a bike at one station and drop it off at another.

TICKETS & PASSES
Note that the word "return" when used in reference to trains in Holland, means round-trip.

Single & Day Return Tickets   For a return trip made within the same day, it is cheaper to buy a *dagretour* (day return) ticket than two *enkele reis* (single) tickets.

Day Card   A *dagkaart* (day card) allows unlimited travel for a day. The cards are 37€ ($42.55) in second class and 59.40€ ($68.30) in first class. Paying an additional 4.50€ ($5.20) for an *OV dagkaart* (OV are the Dutch initials for "public transportation") allows you also to use other public transportation modes, such as the tram, bus, and Metro.

Weekend Return   A *weekendretour* (weekend return), costs the same as a day return and allows you to travel between 7pm on Friday and 4am the following Monday.

Summer Tour   The *Zomertoer* (Summer Tour) pass, available between July 1 and September 9, permits unlimited 3-day travel in second class for one or two persons, over 10 consecutive days. *Zomertoer Plus* (Summer Tour Plus) allows you also to use other public transportation modes, such as the tram, bus, and Metro. The price ranges from 45€ ($51.75) for the basic pass for one, to 73€ ($83.95) for the Plus option for two.

Holland Railpass   You get two options with this multi-day pass: 3 days or 5 days of unlimited travel within 1 month. The passes are $80 for 3 days and $122 for 5 days in second class, and $120 for 3 days and $171 for 5 days in first class. Children ages 4 to 11 travel for half the adult fare, and children under 4 travel free. Discounted prices are available for those under 26.

Benelux Tourrail Pass   The pass allows 5 days of unlimited travel within 1 month in Holland, Belgium, and Luxembourg, for $163 in second class and $228 in first class. Two adults traveling together benefit from a 50% companion discount. For passengers ages 4 to 25 traveling in second class, the pass is $109. Children under 4 travel free.

The first four tickets/passes listed above can be purchased only in Holland. The Holland Railpass and the Benelux Tourrail pass are available to anyone who is not a resident of Europe and can be purchased through **Rail Europe** (© **877/ 272-RAIL** in the U.S., **800/361-RAIL** in Canada; www.raileurope.com) or your travel agent. For details on purchasing multi-country options, such as the **Eurailpass,** see chapter 2.

FOREIGN TRAIN TERMS

A *trein* is a train, and there are three kinds of trains in Holland: InterCity express trains connecting the main towns and cities; the *sneltrein* (fast train), which despite its name is slower than the InterCity trains and stops at more stations; and the *stoptrein* (stop train), which is pretty much what it says it is—a slow train that stops at every station on the route. These are in addition to high-speed Thalys trains from France, Belgium, and Germany, and high-speed ICE trains from Germany.

Klas is class; *Tweede Klas* is second class, and *Eerste Klas* is first class. A *station* is, easily enough, a station. In big cities such as Amsterdam, Rotterdam, and Den Haag (The Hague), which have more than one station, the main station is generally called Centraal Station (Central Station). The Dutch word for platform is *spoor* (it rhymes with "boar"). The bigger stations have separate, labeled counters for selling domestic tickets *(Binnenland)* and international tickets *(Buitenland,* or just plain International).

PRACTICAL TRAIN INFORMATION

Dutch trains are invariably crowded, so if you're planning to make a trip by InterCity train, it may make sense to reserve a seat; otherwise, you may need to stand. On the other hand, distances between stations are short and people are sure to get out at whatever the next one is, so you could just wait and grab a seat when it becomes vacant.

Because of the small size of the country, no Dutch trains have restaurant cars (some international trains do), but on most InterCity trains an attendant pushes around a small cart, from which coffee, tea, mineral water, sandwiches, potato chips, and other snack items are dispensed. These are more expensive than the same things bought from a supermarket, so if you are on a tight budget, buy them before boarding the train.

636   CHAPTER 15 · THE NETHERLANDS

Train Frequency & Travel Times in the Netherlands

	Amsterdam	Haarlem	The Hague	Delft	Rotterdam	Maastricht
Travel Time		15 min.	50 min.	55 min.	1 hr. 20 min.	2 hr. 36 min.
Frequency		6	6	5	6	2

* Frequency is average number of trains per hour during daytime

Similarly, a lack of long-distances means there are no sleeper cars on trains within the Netherlands.

All trains, even the smallest, have a first-class section or cars. The cars themselves are open-plan—no closed compartments. Because smoking and nonsmoking sections are usually to be found within the same car, anyone who likes to breath air free of secondhand smoke is out of luck; you can minimize the discomfort by sitting as far as possible from the dividing line.

FAST FACTS: The Netherlands

Area Codes When making local calls in Amsterdam you won't need to use the area codes shown in this book. You do need to use an area code between towns and cities. The area code for Amsterdam is **020**. Other area codes used in this book are Haarlem **023**, The Hague **070**, Delft **015**, Maastricht **043**.

Business Hours Banks are open Monday to Friday from 9am to 4pm (some stay open until 5pm). Some banks are also open on late-hour shopping nights and Saturdays. Stores generally are open Monday from 10 or 11am to 6pm, Tuesday to Friday from 8:30 or 9am to 5 or 6pm, and Saturday to 4 or 5pm. Some stores close for lunch, and nearly all have 1 full closing day or 1 morning or afternoon when they're closed. Many stores, especially in the larger towns, have late hours on Thursday and/or Friday evening, and in the cities stores along the main streets are open on Sundays.

Climate Holland has a maritime climate, with few temperature extremes in either summer or winter. Summer temperatures average 67°F (19°C); the winter average is 35°F (2°C). Winters, moderated by the North Sea and the fading glow of the Gulf Stream, most often are rainy (it's driest from Feb–May).

July and August are the best months for soaking up rays at sidewalk cafes, dining at an outdoor restaurant in the evening, and going topless on the beach. September usually has a few weeks of fine weather. There are even sunny spells in winter, when brilliant, crisp weather alternates with clouded skies.

Documents Required For stays of up to 3 months, citizens of the U.S., Canada, the U.K., Ireland, Australia, and New Zealand need only a valid passport. A visa is required for stays of longer than 3 months.

Electricity The Netherlands runs on 220 volts electricity (North America uses 110 volts). To use appliances from home without burning them out, you'll need a small voltage transformer (available at your local hardware store) that plugs into the round-holed European electrical outlet and converts the Dutch voltage for any small appliance up to 1,500 watts.

Embassies & Consulates **U.S. Embassy:** Lange Voorhout 102, Den Haag (© 070/310-9209); **U.S. Consulate** in Amsterdam: Museumplein 19 (© 020/575-5309; tram: 3, 5, 12, 16). **Canada:** Sophialaan 7, Den Haag (© 070/311-1600).

Health & Safety Call © **112** for police *(politie)*, fire department, and ambulance assistance.

Holidays January 1 (New Year's Day), Good Friday, Easter Sunday and Monday, April 30 (Queen's Day/*Koninginnedag*), Ascension Day, Pentecost Sunday and Monday, December 25 (Christmas Day), and December 26. The dates for Easter, Ascension, and Pentecost change each year.

Mail Postage for a postcard or ordinary letter to the U.S., Canada, Australia, and New Zealand is .75€ (85¢); to the U.K. and Ireland it's .45€ (50¢).

Police & Emergencies Holland's emergency number to call for the police *(politie)*, fire department, and ambulance is © **112**. For routine matters in Amsterdam, the city police headquarters are at Elandsgracht 117 (© **0900/8844**; tram: 7, 10, 17).

Telephone The international access code for the Netherlands is **011** and the country code is **31**. To call the Netherlands from the United States, dial 011, then 31, then the area code of the city you'd like to reach (20 in Amsterdam, for example), followed by the telephone number. So the whole number you'd dial would be **011-31-20-000-0000**.

To make international calls from the Netherlands, first dial 00 and then the country code (U.S. or Canada 1, U.K. 44, Ireland 353, Australia 61, New Zealand 64). Next you dial the area code and number. For example, if you wanted to call the British Embassy in Washington, D.C., you would dial **00-1-202-588-7800**.

For directory assistance: Dial © **0900/8418** for international information. Dial © **0900/8008** for multiple numbers inside Holland and © **118** for a maximum of one number per call.

For operator assistance: To make an international collect call, dial © **0800/0410**. To call collect inside Holland, dial © **0800-0101**.

Toll-free numbers: Numbers beginning with 0800 within Holland are toll-free, but calling a 1-800 number in the States from Holland is not toll-free. In fact, it is the same as an overseas call.

You can use pay phones with either a KPN or a Telfort *telekaart* (phone card)—but note that neither company's card works with the other company's phones—which are 5€ ($5.75), 12.50€ ($14.40), and 25€ ($28.75) from post offices, train ticket counters, VVV tourist information offices, and some tobacconists and newsstands. Some pay phones take credit cards. A few pay phones take coins.

To charge a call to your calling card, call **AT&T** (© **0800/022-9111**), **MCI** (© **0800/022-9122**), **Sprint** (© **0800/022-9119**), **Canada Direct** (© **0800/022-9116**), or **British Telecom** (© **0800/022-9944**).

Tipping The Dutch government requires that all taxes and service charges be included in the published prices of hotels, restaurants, cafes, discos, nightclubs, salons, and sightseeing companies. Even taxi fare includes taxes and a standard 15% service charge. To be absolutely sure in a restaurant that tax and service are included, look for the words *inclusief BTW en service* (BTW is the abbreviation for the Dutch words that mean value-added tax), or ask the waiter. The Dutch are so accustomed to having these charges included that many restaurants have stopped spelling it out.

To tip like the Dutch (no, seriously!), in a cafe or snack bar leave some small change; in a restaurant, leave 2€ to 3€ ($2.30–$3.45), and up to a generous 5€ ($5.75) if you think the service was particularly good; for expensive tabs, you may want to leave more—or maybe less! It's enough to round up taxi fares. An informal survey (I asked a taxi driver) reveals that Americans and British are the best tippers; the worst are the Dutch themselves.

2 Amsterdam ★★★

Amsterdam has never entirely shed its twofold reputation as a hippie haven and a tulips-and-windmills landmark, even with an economy that has moved far beyond these clichés. Powered more by business than by the combustion of semilegal exotic plants, prosperity has settled like a North Sea mist around the graceful cityscape of canals and 17th-century town houses.

The historic center recalls Amsterdam's golden age as the command post of a vast trading network and colonial empire, when wealthy merchants constructed gabled residences along neatly laid-out canals. A delicious irony is that the placid old structures also host brothels, smoke shops, and some extravagant nightlife. The city's inhabitants, proud of their live-and-let-live attitude, which is based on pragmatism as much as on a long history of tolerance, have decided to control what they cannot effectively outlaw. They permit licensed prostitution in the Red Light District, and the sale of hashish and marijuana in designated "coffee shops."

But don't think most Amsterdammers drift around town in a drug-induced haze. They are too busy whizzing around on bikes, jogging through Vondelpark, feasting on arrays of ethnic dishes, or simply watching the parade of street life from a sidewalk cafe. A new generation of entrepreneurs has revitalized old neighborhoods like the Jordaan, turning some of the distinctive houses into offbeat stores and bustling cafes, hotels, and restaurants.

Between dips into Amsterdam's artistic and historical treasures, be sure to take time out to absorb the freewheeling spirit of Europe's most vibrant city.

STATION INFORMATION
GETTING FROM THE AIRPORT TO THE TRAIN STATION
Netherlands Railways **trains** for Amsterdam Centraal Station depart from Schiphol Station, downstairs from Schiphol Plaza, attached to the airport. Frequency ranges from four trains an hour at peak times to one an hour at night. The fare is 3€ ($3.45) one-way, and the trip takes 20 minutes. You find **taxi** stands in front of Schiphol Plaza. All taxis from the airport are metered. Expect to pay around 38€ ($43.70) to the city center.

INSIDE THE STATION
Amsterdam Centraal Station is the mammoth hub for all rail travel and public transportation in the city. An office of **VVV Amsterdam** tourist information (© 0900/400-4040; www.visitamsterdam.nl), is inside the station on platform 2 and another office is right in front of the station on Stationsplein. Both offices have hotel reservation desks. In addition to the tourist information desks, you'll

find 24-hour currency exchange, a host of restaurants and shops, and a train information office where seat reservations can be made.

INFORMATION ELSEWHERE IN THE CITY

VVV Amsterdam also has an office at Leidseplein 1 (tram: 1, 2, 5, 6, 7, 10), on the corner of Leidsestraat, which will also reserve hotel rooms. All VVV Amsterdam offices are open daily from 9am to 5pm in the low season; evening open hours gradually increase until about 8pm and then move back to the baseline time on a somewhat unpredictable schedule as the high season proceeds.

GETTING AROUND

The city center is small enough that the best way to get around Amsterdam is on your own two feet. Be sure to wear good walking shoes, as those charming cobblestones will get under your soles and on your nerves after a while. When crossing the street, watch out for trams and bikes.

Of the city's 16 **tram (streetcar)** lines, 10 begin and end at Centraal Station. An extensive **bus** network complements the trams. Four **Metro** lines—50, 51, 53, and 54—bring people in from the suburbs. Most tram/bus shelters and all metro stations have maps that show the entire system. A detailed map is available from VVV tourist information offices and from the GVB Tickets & Info office on Stationsplein.

There are 11 public transportation fare zones in greater Amsterdam, though tourists rarely travel beyond the city-center zone 5700 (Centrum). Most tickets are valid on buses, trams, and the Metro. A **day ticket** *(dagkaart),* valid for the entire day of purchase and the following night, can be purchased from any bus or tram driver, conductor, or ticket dispenser for 5.50€ ($6.30). **Two-** to **9-day** tickets, from 8.80€ to 26.40€ ($10.10–$30.35), are available from the **GVB/ Amsterdam Municipal Transportation** Tickets & Info office on Stationsplein, in front of Centraal Station.

A **single journey ticket** *(enkeltje)* is 1.60€ ($1.85) for 1 zone and 2.40€ ($2.75) for 2 zones. For multiple journeys, buy a **strip card** *(strippenkaart).* An 8-strip card is 6.40€ ($7.35) from the driver or conductor. Discount strip cards are available from train and Metro station ticket counters, the GVB Tickets & Info office in front of Centraal Station, post offices, and many news vendors, where you pay 6.20€ ($7.15) for a card with 15 strips, and 18.30€ ($21.05) for one with 45 strips. On some trams and on Metro trains you are responsible for stamping the required number of strips for your journey, on some trams a conductor does this, and on buses the driver does it. To use the validating machines, just fold at the line and punch in; you don't need to punch in each individual strip—just count down the number of strips you need and punch in the last one.

Officially, you can't hail a **taxi** from the street, but taxis will often stop anyway if you do. Otherwise, find one of the strategically located taxi stands sprinkled around town, marked by distinctive yellow phone boxes. Alternatively, call **Taxi Centrale** (© 020/677-7777). Taxis are metered. Fares—which include a service charge—begin at 2.90€ ($3.35) when the meter starts and run up at 1.80€ ($2.10) a kilometer, or 1.12€ ($1.30) a mile (1.6km).

Two waterbus services bring you to many of the city's top museums and other attractions. A day ticket for the **Canal Bus** (© 020/623-9886) allows you to hop on and off as many times as you like on three lines until noon the next day, for 15€ ($17.25) for adults, 10.50€ ($12.10) for children ages 3 to 12, and free

Amsterdam

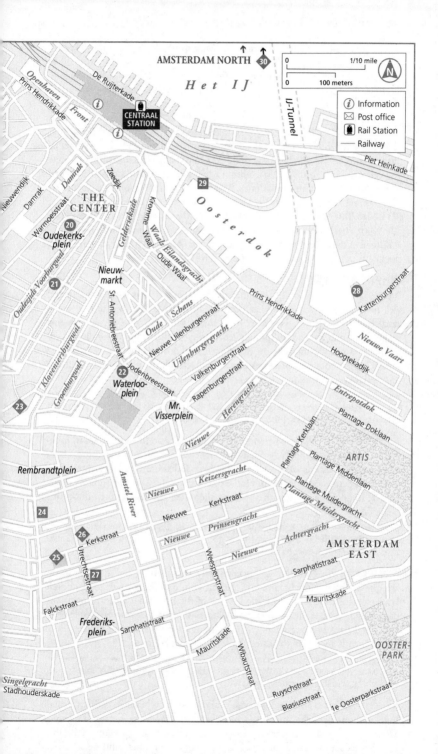

for children under 3. The **Museumboot** (**Museum Boat;** © 020/530-5412)—"*boot*" is pronounced just like "boat"—operates a scheduled service every 30 to 45 minutes from Centraal Station to Prinsengracht, Leidseplein, Museumplein, Herengracht, the Muziektheater, and the Eastern Dock. A day ticket is 14.25€ ($16.40) for adults, 9.50€ ($10.95) for children ages 4 to 12, and free for children under 4; after 1pm, tickets are, respectively, 12.50€ ($14.40) and 7.25€ ($8.35). Tickets include discounted admission to some museums and attractions.

You can also follow the Dutch example and go around by bike. Bike-rental rates are around 8€ ($9.20) a day or 32€ ($36.80) a week; a deposit is required. You can rent bikes from Centraal Station when you arrive, and from many rental stores, all of which have similar rates. **MacBike** rents a range of bikes, including tandems and six-speed touring bikes; it has branches at Mr. Visserplein 2 (© 020/620-0985), conveniently close to the Muziektheater, and Marnixstraat 220 (© 020/626-6964), a 5-minute walk from Leidseplein. **Damstraat Rent-a-Bike** is in the cellars of the Beurs van Berlage (Berlage's Stock Exchange) near the Dam, at Damstraat 22–24 (© 020/625-5029).

WHERE TO STAY

Agora ✾ Old-fashioned friendliness is the keynote at this efficiently run and well-maintained lodging, a block from the Flower Market, in a fully restored canal house from 1735. Furniture from the 1930s and 1940s mixes with fine mahogany antiques and an abundance of overstuffed furniture—nearly every room has a puffy armchair you can sink into. Those rooms that don't have a canal view look out on a pretty garden at the back. There's no elevator, and three rooms have no bathroom.

Singel 462, 1017 AW Amsterdam. © 020/627-2200. Fax 020/627-2202. www.hotelagora.nl. 16 units. 90€–127€ ($104–$146) double with bathroom; 72€ ($82.80) double without bathroom. Rates include buffet breakfast. AE, DC, MC, V. Tram: 1, 2, 5 to Koningsplein. **Amenities:** Lounge. *In room:* Hair dryer, no A/C.

Amstel Botel ✾ Where better to experience a city on the water than by lodging in a boat-hotel, moored so close to Centraal Station you could just about swim there? Its cabins are spread out over four decks connected by elevator. The bright, modern rooms are no-nonsense but comfortable, and the showers small. Be sure to ask for a room with a view on the water, and not on the uninspiring quayside.

Oosterdokskade 2–4, 1011 AE Amsterdam. © 020/626-4247. Fax 020/639-1952. www.amstelbotel.com. 175 units. 75€–86€ ($86.25–$98.90) double. AE, DC, MC, V. Tram: 1, 2, 4, 5, 9, 13, 16, 17, 24, 25 to Centraal Station. Amenities: Bar. *In room:* No A/C.

Amsterdam Wiechmann ✾ It takes only a moment to feel at home in the antique-adorned Wiechmann, a classic, comfortable, casual place beside Looiersgracht. Besides, the location is one of the best you'll find in this or any price range. Most of the rooms are standard, with good-size twin or double beds, and some have big bay windows. Furnishings are elegant. The higher-priced doubles, with a view on the canal, have antique furnishings.

Prinsengracht 328–332, 1016 HX Amsterdam. © 020/626-3321. Fax 020/626-8962. www.hotelwiechmann. nl. 38 units. 120€–140€ ($138–$161) double. Rates include continental breakfast. MC, V. Tram: 1, 2, 5 to Prinsengracht. **Amenities:** Lounge. *In room:* No A/C.

Bilderberg Hotel Jan Luyken ✾✾ This property is best described as a small hotel with many of the amenities and facilities of a big hotel. Everything here is done with perfect attention to detail. The Jan Luyken maintains a balance between its sophisticated lineup of facilities and an intimate and personalized approach that's appropriate to this 19th-century residential neighborhood. That residential feel extends to the air-conditioned guest rooms, which look much more like those in a well-designed home than a standard hotel room.

Jan Luykenstraat 58 (near the Rijksmuseum), 1071 CS Amsterdam. ✆ 800/641-0300 in the U.S. and Canada, or 020/573-0730. Fax 020/676-3841. www.janluyken.nl. 62 units. 220€–295€ double ($253–$339); add 5% city tax. AE, DC, MC, V. Tram: 2, 5 to Hobbemastraat. **Amenities:** Wine bar; laundry; nonsmoking rooms. *In room:* Hair dryer.

Canal House ✿
A contemporary approach to reestablishing the elegant canal-house atmosphere has been taken by the proprietor of this small hotel in three adjoining houses from 1630 close to Westermarkt. These were rebuilt to provide private bathrooms and filled with antiques, quilts, and Chinese rugs. A steep staircase still has its beautifully carved old balustrade. Overlooking the back garden, the magnificent breakfast room seems to have been untouched since the 17th century. On the parlor floor is a cozy Victorian-style saloon.

Keizersgracht 148, 1015 CX Amsterdam. ✆ 020/622-5182. Fax 020/624-1317. www.canalhouse.nl. 26 units. 140€–190€ ($161–$219) double. Rates include continental breakfast. DC, MC, V. Tram: 13, 14, 17 to Westermarkt. **Amenities:** Lounge. *In room:* Hair dryer, no A/C.

De Filosoof ✿✿ *(Finds)*
On a quiet street facing Vondelpark, this hotel might be the very place if you fancy yourself as something of a philosopher. Each room is dedicated to a mental maestro—Aristotle, Plato, Goethe, Wittgenstein, Nietzsche, Marx, and Einstein are among those included—or are based on motifs like Eros, the Renaissance, and astrology. Recent all-round improvements in service and amenities have been made.

Anna van den Vondelstraat 6, 1054 GZ Amsterdam. ✆ 020/683-3013. Fax 020/685-3750. www.hotel filosoof.nl. 38 units. 111€–135€ ($128–$155) double. Rates include buffet breakfast. AE, MC, V. Tram: 1, 6 to Jan Pieter Heijestraat. **Amenities:** Bar. *In room:* Hair dryer, no A/C.

Hotel Amsterdam ✿✿
Just 436 yards from Centraal Station, this hotel, housed in a 1911 building and still owned by descendants of the original proprietors, has an 18th-century facade. Its rooms are supermodern, though, featuring thick carpets, air-conditioning, and ample wardrobe space. Rooms at the front of the hotel tend to get more light, but are also subjected to more street noise; some have balconies. The award-winning De Roode Leeuw restaurant serves classic Dutch cuisine.

Damrak 93–94 (at the Dam), 1012 LP Amsterdam. ✆ 020/555-0666. Fax 020/620-4716. www.hotel amsterdam.nl. 79 units. 225€–295€ ($259–$339) double; 280€–310€ ($322–$357) suite. AE, DC, MC, V. Tram: 4, 9, 14, 16, 24, 25 to the Dam. **Amenities:** Restaurant; cafe; nonsmoking rooms. *In room:* Hair dryer.

Prinsenhof ✿
A modernized canal house close to the Amstel River, this hotel has rooms (three with bathroom) with beamed ceilings and basic yet reasonably comfortable beds. Front rooms look out onto the Prinsengracht, where houseboats are moored. The proprietors, Rik and André van Houten, take pride in their hotel and make you feel welcome (check out the hotel's website for a good dose of their humor). There's no elevator, but a pulley hauls your luggage up and down the stairs.

Prinsengracht 810, 1017 JL Amsterdam. ✆ 020/623-1772. Fax 020/638-3368. www.hotelprinsenhof.com. 10 units. 80€ double ($92) with bathroom, 60€ double ($69) without bathroom. Rates include continental breakfast. AE, MC, V. Tram: 4 to Prinsengracht. *In room:* No TV, no A/C.

Seven Bridges ✿✿
One of Amsterdam's canal-house gems, not far from Rembrandtplein, gets its name from its view of seven arched bridges. There are antique furnishings, handmade Italian drapes, hand-painted tiles and wood-tiled

floors, and Impressionist art posters on the walls. The biggest room, on the first landing, can accommodate up to four and has a huge bathroom with marble floor and double sinks. Attic rooms have sloped ceilings and exposed wood beams, and there are big, bright basement rooms done almost entirely in white.

Reguliersgracht 31, 1017 LK Amsterdam. ℂ 020/623-1329. 8 units. 110€–175€ ($127–$201) double. Rates include full breakfast. AE, MC, V. Tram: 16, 24, 25 to Keizersgracht. *In room:* Hair dryer, no A/C.

TOP ATTRACTIONS & SPECIAL MOMENTS

For sightseers in Amsterdam, the question is not simply what to see and do, but rather how much of this intriguing city's marvelous sights you can fit into the time you have.

There are miles and miles of canals to cruise, hundreds of narrow streets to wander, countless historic buildings to visit, more than 40 museums holding collections of everything from artistic wonders to obscure curiosities, not to mention all the diamond cutters and craftspeople to watch as they practice generations-old skills...the list is as long as every visitor's individual interests.

Amsterdams Historisch Museum (Amsterdam Historical Museum) ✦✦

Few cities in the world have gone to as much trouble and expense to display and explain their history, and few museums in the world have found as many ways to make such dry material as population growth and urban development so interesting. This large and fascinating museum in the restored 17th-century Burger Weeshuis, the former City Orphanage, next to the Begijnhof, gives you a better understanding of everything you see when you go out to explore the city on your own. Gallery by gallery, century by century, you learn how a small fishing village founded around 1200 became a major sea power and trading center.

The main focus is on the city's 17th century Golden Age, a period when Amsterdam was the wealthiest city in the world, and some of the most interesting exhibits are of the trades that made it rich. You can also view many of the famous paintings by the Dutch masters in the context of their time and place in history.

When you leave the museum, cut through the **Schuttersgalerij (Civic Guards Gallery),** a narrow, skylit, covered passageway that leads to the Begijnhof, and is bedecked with 15 enormous 17th-century paintings of the Amsterdam Civic Guards. The open hours are the same as for the museum, and admission is free.

Kalverstraat 92, Nieuwezijds Voorburgwal 359, and Sint-Luciënsteeg 27. ℂ 020/523-1822. www.ahm.nl. Admission 6€ ($6.90) adults, 4.50€ ($5.20) seniors, 3€ ($3.45) children 6–16, children under 6 free. Mon–Fri 10am–5pm; Sat–Sun 11am–5pm. Closed Jan 1, Apr 30, Dec 25. Tram: 1, 2, 4, 5, 9, 14, 16, 24, 25 to Spui.

Anne Frankhuis ✦✦✦

In summer you may have to wait an hour or more to get in, but no one should miss seeing and experiencing this house, beside Westermarkt, where eight people from three separate Jewish families lived together in near total silence for more than 2 years during World War II. The hiding place Otto Frank found for his family and friends kept them safe until, tragically close to the end of the war, it was raided by Nazi forces and its occupants were deported to concentration camps. It was in this house that Anne kept her famous diary as a way to deal with both the boredom and with her youthful jumble of thoughts, which had as much to do with personal relationships as with the war and the Nazi terror raging outside her hiding place. Visiting the rooms where she hid is a moving and eerily real experience.

The rooms of the building, which was an office and warehouse at that time, are still as bare as they were when Anne's father returned, the only survivor of the eight *onderduikers* (divers or hiders). Nothing has been changed, except that protective Plexiglas panels have been placed over the wall where Anne pinned up photos of her favorite actress, Deanna Durbin, and of the little English princesses Elizabeth and Margaret. As you tour the building, it's easy to imagine Anne's experience growing up in this place, awakening as a young woman, and writing down her secret thoughts in a diary.

Prinsengracht 263. © 020/556-7100. www.annefrank.nl. Admission 6.50€ ($7.50) adults, 3€ ($3.45) children 10–17, children under 10 free. Apr–Aug daily 9am–9pm; Sept–Mar daily 9am–7pm; Jan 1 and Dec 25 noon–5pm. Closed Yom Kippur. Tram: 13, 14, 17 to Westermarkt.

The Hash, Marihuana & Hemp Museum *Finds*   It wouldn't really be Amsterdam, would it, without its fascination with intoxicating weeds? This museum in the Red Light District will teach you everything you ever wanted to know, and much you maybe didn't, about hash, marijuana, and related products. The museum does not promote drug use but aims to make you better informed before deciding whether to light up and, of course, whether to inhale. One way it does this is by having a cannabis garden in the joint—sorry, on the premises. Plants at various stages of development fill the air with a heady, resinous fragrance. Some exhibits shed light on the medicinal uses of cannabis and on hemp's past and present-day uses as a natural fiber. Among several notable artworks in the museum's collection is David Teniers the Younger's painting, *Hemp-Smoking Peasants in a Smoke House* (1660).

Oudezijds Achterburgwal 130. © 020/623-5961. www.hashmuseum.com. Admission 5.70€ ($6.55). Daily 10am–5:30pm. Tram: 4, 9, 14, 16, 24, 25 to the Dam.

Koninklijk Paleis (Royal Palace) *★★*   One of the heavier features of the Dam is the solid, neoclassical facade of the Royal Palace (1648–55). Designed by Jacob van Campen—the Thomas Jefferson of the Dutch Republic—as the city's Stadhuis (Town Hall), its interior is replete with white Italian marble, sculptures, and painted ceilings. Poet Constantijn Huygens called the new Town Hall the "Eighth Wonder of the World." It was built on a foundation of a precisely tabulated 13,659 timber piles—a figure all Dutch schoolchildren are taught.

In the *Vierschaar* (Court of Justice), until the 18th century, magistrates pronounced death sentences watched over by images of Justice, Wisdom, and Mercy. Atlas holds up the globe in the high-ceilinged *Burgerzaal* (Citizen's Chamber), and maps inlaid on the marble floor show Amsterdam as the center of the world. Ferdinand Bol's painting *Moses the Lawgiver* hangs in the *Schepenzaal* (Council Chamber), where the aldermen met. On the pediment overlooking the Dam, Flemish sculptor Artus Quellien carved a baroque hymn in stone to Amsterdam's maritime pre-eminence, showing figures symbolizing the oceans paying the city homage. The weathervane on the cupola takes the form of a Dutch sailing ship.

Dam. © 020/620-4060. Admission 4€ ($4.60) adults, 3€ ($3.45) children 5–12, children under 5 free. Easter holidays and June–Aug daily 11am–5pm; Sept to mid-Dec and mid-Feb to May (except Easter holidays), generally Tues–Thurs 12:30–5pm (open days and hours vary; check before going). Guided tours usually Wed 2 and 3pm; Closed mid-Dec to mid-Feb, and during periods of royal residence and state receptions. Tram: 1, 2, 4, 5, 9, 13, 14, 16, 17, 24, 25 to the Dam.

Museum Het Rembrandthuis *★*   Bought by Rembrandt in 1639 when he was Amsterdam's most fashionable portrait painter, the house, behind Waterlooplein, has 10 rooms and is a shrine to one of the greatest artists the world has ever known. In this house, Rembrandt's son Titus was born and his wife Saskia died. The artist was bankrupt when he left in 1658. Not until 1906 was the

---

Tips **Closed for Renovations**

The Rijksmuseum (see below) isn't the only museum in Amsterdam getting a makeover. The city's premiere modern art museum, the **Stedelijk Museum** 🟊🟊, Paulus Potterstraat 13 (© 020/573-2737; www.stedelijk.nl), next to the Van Gogh Museum on the Museumplein, will be closed from January 1, 2004 through at least March 2005 for renovation work and construction. Many of the museum's works—by artists such as Willem de Kooning, Piet Mondrian, and Andy Warhol—will be displayed in other city venues while the museum is closed. To check on the progress of the renovations, see the museum's website.

---

building rescued from a succession of subsequent owners and restored as a museum. In 1998, a modern wing for temporary exhibits was added.

Restoration has returned the old house to the way it looked when Rembrandt lived and worked here, complete with a ground-floor kitchen and the maid's bedroom. Additional work has restored the artist's cabinet of art and curiosities, his combined living room and bedroom, and the studio he and his pupils used. The rooms are furnished with 17th-century objects and furniture that, as far as possible, match the descriptions in Rembrandt's 1656 petition for bankruptcy. His printing press is back in place, and you can view 250 of his etchings and drawings hanging on the walls, along with works by some of his contemporaries, like Jan Lievens. These include self-portraits and landscapes, several relating to the traditionally Jewish character of the neighborhood.

Jodenbreestraat 4. © 020/520-0400. www.rembrandthuis.nl. Admission 7€ ($8.05) adults, 5€ ($5.75) students, 1.50€ ($1.75) children 6–15, children under 6 free. Mon–Sat 10am–5pm; Sun and holidays 1–5pm. Tram: 9, 14 to Waterlooplein.

Oude Kerk (Old Church) 🟊🟊 This late-Gothic church at Oudezijds Voorburgwal—its official name is the Sint-Nikolaaskerk (St Nicholas's Church), but nobody ever calls it that—was begun in 1250 and essentially completed with the construction of the bell tower in 1566. On its southern porch, to the right of the sexton's house, is a coat of arms belonging to Maximilian of Austria, who, with his son Philip, contributed to the porch's construction. Rembrandt's wife is buried in vault 28K, which bears the simple inscription "Saskia Juni 1642." The church contains a magnificent organ from 1728 by Christian Müller that is regularly used for recitals. You can climb the church tower on an hourly guided-tour for a great view of the Old City. Nowadays, the pretty little gabled almshouses around the Oude Kerk feature red-fringed windows through which can be seen the scantily dressed ladies of the Red Light District.

Oudekerksplein. © 020/625-8284. Admission 2€ ($2.30) adults, 1.50€ ($1.75) seniors and students, children 12 and under free. Church Mon–Sat 11am–5pm; Sun 1–5pm. Tower June–Sept Wed–Sat 2–4pm. Metro: Nieuwmarkt.

Rijksmuseum 🟊🟊🟊 *Note:* Most of Holland's premier museum is closed for renovation until mid-2008. During this period, key paintings from the magnificent 17th-century Dutch Golden Age collection can be viewed in the museum's own Philips Wing. Other elements of the collection will likely be on view at other venues in the city. The three-star rating given here is justified even for the highlights of Golden Age art alone, but you need to remember that most of the museum's complete collection will be "invisible" to visitors for some time to come. During the renovation period, you can find a complete review of the Rijksmuseum at **www.frommers.com**.

Stadhouderskade 42 (at Museumplein). © **020/670-7047**. www.rijksmuseum.nl. Admission 8.50€ ($9.75) adults, children under 18 free. Daily 10am–5pm. Tram: 2, 5 to Hobbemastraat; 6, 7, 10 to Weteringschans.

Scheepvaartmuseum (Maritime Museum) ★★ A bonanza for anyone who loves ships and the sea, the museum overlooks the busy Eastern Dock and is appropriately housed in a former Amsterdam Admiralty arsenal from 1656. All the exhibits chronicle the country's abiding ties to the sea through commerce, fishing, yachting, exploration, and war. Room after room is filled with boats and ship models, seascapes and ship paintings, prints, navigational instruments, cannon and other weaponry, and old maps and charts. Among the cartographic highlights is a 15th-century Ptolemaic atlas and a sumptuously bound edition of the *Great Atlas, or Description of the World,* produced over a lifetime by Jan Blaeu, the master cartographer of Holland's Golden Age. An expansive model diorama depicts 17th-century shipping in the Rede van Texel (Texel Roads), and the father-and-son artists Willem van de Velde the Elder and Younger sketching the scene from a small boat.

A full-size replica of the United East India Company merchant ship *Amsterdam,* which foundered off Hastings, England, in 1749 on her maiden voyage to the fabled Spice Islands (Indonesia), is moored at the wharf. Re-enactors create scenes from everyday life on the ship. Sailors fire cannons, sing sea shanties, mop the deck, hoist cargo on board, and attend a solemn "burial at sea." You can watch sail-makers and rope-makers at work. In the galley, the cook prepares a real shipboard meal that you might be invited to taste.

Kattenburgerplein 1. © **020/523-2222**. www.scheepvaartmuseum.nl. Admission 7€ ($8.05) adults, 4€ ($4.60) children 6–17, children under 6 free. Tues–Sat 10am–5pm (also Mon mid-June to mid-Sept); Sun noon–5pm. Bus: 22, 32 to Kattenburgerplein.

Van Gogh Museum ★★★ More than 200 paintings by Vincent van Gogh (1853–90), along with nearly every sketch, print, etching, and piece of correspondence the artist ever produced, are housed in this museum. Van Gogh painted for only 10 years, sold only one painting in his lifetime, and was on the threshold of success when he committed suicide at age 37. You can trace this great artist's artistic development and psychological decline by viewing the

---

Moments **Special Amsterdam Experiences**

- **For outdoors types:** Rent a bike and join the flow of bikers for one of the classic Amsterdam experiences—but go carefully.
- **For shoppers:** Pick up a bunch of tulips at the floating Flower Market on the Singel, even if they're just to brighten up your hotel room.
- **For people of the night:** Stroll through the Red Light District, to examine the quaint gabled architecture along its narrow canals—oh, yes, and you might also notice certain ladies watching the world go by through their red-fringed windows.
- **For bar flies:** Spend a leisurely evening in a brown cafe, the traditional Amsterdam watering hole.

paintings displayed in chronological order according to the seven distinct periods and places of residence that defined his short career.

One particularly splendid wall, on the second floor, has a progression of 18 paintings produced during the 2-year period when Vincent lived in the south of France, generally considered to be his artistic high point. It's a symphony of colors and color contrasts that includes *Gauguin's Chair; The Yellow House; Self-Portrait with Pipe and Straw Hat; Vincent's Bedroom at Arles; Wheatfield with Reaper; Bugler of the Zouave Regiment;* and one of the most famous paintings of modern times, *Still Life Vase with Fourteen Sunflowers,* best known simply as *Sunflowers.*

Paulus Potterstraat 7 (at Museumplein). ℂ 020/570-5200. www.vangoghmuseum.nl. Admission 7€ ($8.05) adults, 2.50€ ($2.90) children 13–17, children under 13 free. Daily 10am–6pm. Tram: 2, 3, 5, 12 to Van Baerlestraat.

Westerkerk (West Church)   The Dutch Renaissance-style Westerkerk holds the remains of Rembrandt and his son, Titus, and is where in 1966 Princess (now Queen) Beatrix and Prince Claus said their marriage vows. The church was begun in 1620, at the same time as the Noorderkerk, and opened in 1631. The initial designer was Hendrick de Keyser, whose son Pieter took over after his father's death in 1621. The church's light and spacious interior has a fine organ. The 277-foot-high tower, the Westertoren, is Amsterdam's tallest, and affords a spectacular view of the city; at its top is the blue, red, and gold imperial crown of the Holy Roman Empire, a symbol bestowed by the Austrian emperor Maximilian. You can climb the tower on a guided tour.

Westermarkt. ℂ 020/624-7766. Church: Free admission. May 15–Sept 15 Mon–Sat 11am–3pm; Tower: Admission 1€ ($1.15). Jun to mid-Sept, Mon–Sat 10am–4pm. Tram: 13, 14, 17 to Westermarkt.

CANAL-BOAT TOURS

The canals are the best starting point to Amsterdam. Tours last approximately an hour and leave at regular intervals from *rondvaart* (excursion) piers in key locations around town. The majority of launches are docked along Damrak and

---

Moments Biking on the Water

A water bike is a boat you pedal with your feet. Amsterdammers look down their tolerant noses at water bikes, but tourists love the things. No prizes for guessing who has the most fun. Your water bike comes with a detailed map. It's great fun in sunny weather, and still doable when it rains and your boat is covered with a rain shield. In summer, you can even rent a water bike for evening rambles, when the canals are illuminated and your bike is kitted out with its own Chinese lantern. The canals can be busy with tour boats and other small craft, so go carefully, particularly when going under bridges.

These craft seat two or four people and can be rented daily from 10am to 10pm in summer, and to 7pm at other times, from **Canal Bike** (ℂ **020/ 626-5574**. Moorings are on Prinsengracht, beside the Anne Frankhuis (tram: 13, 14, 17); on Singelgracht, a few steps from Leidseplein (tram: 1, 2, 5, 6, 7, 10); beside the Rijksmuseum (tram: 6, 7, 10); and on Keizersgracht at Leidsestraat (tram: 1, 2, 5). You can rent a water bike at one mooring and leave it at another. Rental is 7€ ($8.05) per person hourly for one or two people; 6€ ($6.90) per person hourly for three or four people. You need to leave a deposit of 50€ ($57.50).

Prins Hendrikkade near Centraal Station, on Rokin near Muntplein, and at Leidseplein. Tours leave every 15 to 30 minutes during the summer season (9am–9:30pm), every 45 minutes in winter (10am–4pm). A basic 1-hour tour is 8€ ($9.20) for adults, 6€ ($6.90) for children 4 to 12, and free for children under 4.

WHERE TO DINE

Bolhoed ★★ VEGETARIAN   Forget the corn-sheaf 'n' brown-rice image affected by so many vegetarian restaurants. Instead, garnish your healthful habits with tangy flavors and a dash of zest. Latin style, world music, evening candlelight, and a fine view of the canal from each of the two plant-bedecked, cheerful rooms in this former hat store near Noordermarkt—*bolhoed* is Dutch for bowler hat—distinguish a restaurant for which *vegetarian* is a tad too wholesome-sounding.

Prinsengracht 60–62. ✆ **020/626-1803.** Main courses 11.50€–14.50€ ($13.25–$16.70); *dagschotel* 13€ ($14.95); 3-course menu 19€ ($21.85). No credit cards. Sun–Fri noon–11pm; Sat 11am–11pm. Tram: 13, 14, 17 to Westermarkt.

De Belhamel ★★ *Finds* CONTINENTAL   Soft classical music complements a graceful Art Nouveau setting at this split-level restaurant overlooking the photogenic junction of the Herengracht and Brouwersgracht canals. The tables fill up quickly on most evenings, so make reservations or go early. Try for a window table and take in the superb canal views. Although generally excellent, De Belhamel does have two minor flaws: The waitstaff is occasionally a bit too laidback and it can get noisy.

Brouwersgracht 60. ✆ **020/622-1095.** Main courses 18€–20€ ($20.70–$23); fixed-price menu 32€ ($36.80). AE, MC, V. Sun–Thurs 6–10pm; Fri–Sat 6–10:30pm. Tram: 1, 2, 5, 13, 17 to Martelaarsgracht.

De Jaren ★ CONTINENTAL   Large and brightly lit De Jaren, across the water from Muntplein, is fashionable without being pretentious. It occupies a solid-looking building on two stories, with unusually high ceilings and a multicolored mosaic floor. Students from the nearby university lunch here, and it's popular with the media crowd. De Jaren's unique selling point is not so much the fashionable set that hangs out here, but its two marvelous open-air patios beside the Amstel River.

Nieuwe Doelenstraat 20–22. ✆ **020/625-5771.** Main courses 7.50€–14.50€ ($8.65–$16.70); fixed-price menus 9.50€–14.50€ ($10.95–$16.70). V. Sun–Thurs 10am–1am; Fri–Sat 10am–2am. Tram: 4, 9, 14, 16, 24, 25 to Muntplein.

De Prins ★★ DUTCH/FRENCH   This companionable restaurant in a 17th-century canal house across the canal from the Anne Frank House, has a smoke-stained, brown-cafe style and food that could easily grace a much more expensive place. This is a quiet neighborhood place—nothing fancy or trendy, and the relatively few tables fill up fast. There's a bar on a slightly lower level than the restaurant. From March to September De Prins spreads a terrace out onto the canal-side.

Prinsengracht 124. ✆ **020/624-9382.** Main courses 6€–12.50€ ($6.90–$14.40); *dagschotel* 10€ ($11.50). AE, DC, MC, V. Daily 10am–1am. Tram: 13, 14, 17 to Westermarkt.

Kantjil en de Tijger ★★ INDONESIAN   Unlike the many Indonesian restaurants in Holland that wear their ethnic origins on their sleeves, literally, with waitstaff decked out in traditional costume, the "Antelope and the Tiger" is chic, modern, and cool. Moreover, this eatery near Spui attracts customers who like their Indonesian food not only chic, modern, and cool—but good as well. The 20-item *rijsttafel* for two is deservedly a bestseller.

Spuistraat 291. © **020/620-0994**. Reservations recommended on weekends. Main courses 11.50€–15.50€ ($13.25–$17.55); rijsttafels 37.50€–47.50€ ($43.15–$54.65) for 2. AE, DC, MC, V. Daily 4:30–11pm. Tram: 1, 2, 5 to Spui.

Moko ⓡ FUSION/POLYNESIAN   Named for a Maori facial tattoo, Moko mixes culinary influences from Australia, New Zealand, Asia, and Oceania, with north European and Mediterranean dishes. It occupies a converted 17th-century, timber church, the Amstelkerk, on a wide, open square set back from Prinsengracht. Be ready to go out on a limb, foodwise, in a colorful, if somewhat impersonal high-tech space with Maori-accents and images. On warm summer evenings, aim to get a table on the compact outdoor terrace.

Amstelveld 12. © **020/626-1199**. Main courses 16€–20€ ($18.40–$23). AE, DC, MC, V. May–Oct Mon–Fri 11:30am–1am, Sat–Sun 11:30am–2am; Nov–Apr Tues–Sat 11:30am–1am, Sat–Sun 11:30am–2am. Tram: 4 to Prinsengracht.

Rose's Cantina ⓡ TEX-MEX   Rose's attracts with typical American favorites such as hamburgers and meatballs, though the decor and most of the cuisine are Mexican-inspired. The tables are oak, the service is decent but slow—think the basic rate of continental drift—and the atmosphere is Latin American and buzzing with good cheer. Watch out for long waiting times for a table, during which, as likely as not, you'll sit at the bar downing one after another of Rose's deadly margaritas.

Reguliersdwarsstraat 38–40 (off Leidsestraat). © **020/625-9797**. Main courses 11€–22€ ($12.65–$25.30). AE, DC, MC, V. Daily 5–midnight. Tram: 1, 2, 5 to Koningsplein.

Spanjer & Van Twist ⓡⓡ 𝘍𝘪𝘯𝘥𝘴 CONTINENTAL   This place off Keizersgracht would almost be worth the visit for its name alone, so it's doubly gratifying to find the food good, too. The interior is typical *eetcafé*-style, with the day's specials chalked on a blackboard, a long table with newspapers at the front, and the kitchen visible in back. In fine weather, you can eat on an outdoor terrace beside the tranquil Leliegracht canal.

Leliegracht 60. © **020/639-0109**. Reservations not accepted. Main courses 11.75€–14.75€ ($13.50–$17). MC, V. Daily 10am–1am (only light snacks after 11pm). Tram: 13, 14, 17 to Westermarkt.

Tempo Doeloe ⓡⓡ INDONESIAN   For authentic Indonesian cuisine, from Java, Sumatra, and Bali—which doesn't leave out much—this place between Prinsengracht and Keizersgracht is hard to beat. You dine in a *batik* ambience that's Indonesian, but restrained. Try out one of the many little meat, fish, and vegetable dishes of the three different *rijsttafel* (rice table) options, from the 15-plate vegetarian *rijsttafel sayoeran,* and the 15-plate *rijsttafel stimoelan,* to the sumptuous 25-plate *rijsttafel istemewa.*

Utrechtsestraat 75. © **020/625-6718**. Main courses 18€–22.50€ ($20.70–$25.90); *rijsttafel* 24€–31.50€ ($27.60–$36.25); fixed-price menu 27€–43€ ($31.05–$49.45). AE, DC, MC, V. Mon–Sat 6–11:30pm. Tram: 4 to Keizersgracht.

Wilhelmina-Dok ⓡⓡ CONTINENTAL   Dining at this slightly wacky-looking waterfront eatery in Amsterdam Noord, across the IJ waterway from Centraal Station, more than justifies a short, free ferry-boat ride across the IJ followed by a 5-minute walk. Plain wood, candlelit tables, wood floors, and oak cabinets give the interior an old-fashioned maritime look, and large windows serve up views across the narrow, barge-speckled channel. Tables on the outdoor terrace are sheltered from the wind in a glass-walled enclosure.

⌒ *Moments* Spice of Life

Even if you're on a tight budget, try to have at least one **Indonesian** *rijsttafel.* This traditional "rice table" banquet of as many as 25 succulent and spicy foods served in tiny bowls, usually costs between 18€ ($20.70) and 30€ ($34.50). Pick and choose from among the bowls and add your choice to the pile of rice on your plate. It's almost impossible to eat all the food set on your table, but give it a shot—it's delicious and a true taste of multicultural Amsterdam. For an abbreviated version served on one plate, try *nasi rames.* At lunch, the standard Indonesian fare is *nasi goreng* (fried rice with meat and vegetables) or *bami goreng* (fried noodles prepared in a similar way). A great place to eat rijsttafel is Tempo Doeloe (see above).

Nordwal 1. ⓒ 020/632-3701. Main courses 15€–16.50€ ($17.25–$19). AE, DC, MC, V. Mon–Fri noon–midnight, Sat–Sun noon–1am. Ferry: IJveer from Pier 8 behind Centraal Station to the dock at IJplein, then go right along the dike-top path.

SHOPPING

Bargain-hunters won't have much luck (except at the flea markets), but shopping in Amsterdam definitely has its rewards. Best buys include diamonds and traditional Dutch products such as Delftware, pewter, crystal, and old-fashioned clocks. No matter what you're looking for, you're sure to be impressed with the range of possibilities.

By far the most ubiquitous items you'll see will be those in the familiar blue-and-white "Delft" colors that have almost become synonymous with Holland. Souvenir stores, specialty stores, and department stores feature Delftware earthenware products in the widest variety of forms imaginable. If any one object has particular appeal, by all means buy it—but be aware that unless it meets certain specifications, you are not carting home an authentic piece of the hand-painted earthenware pottery that has made the Delft name famous. A wide selection of Delftware can be found at **De Porceleyne Fles,** Prinsengracht 170 (ⓒ **020/622-7509**), opposite the Anne Frank House, and **Focke & Meltzer,** Gelderlandplein 149, Buitenveldert (ⓒ **020/644-4429**).

De Bijenkorf, Dam 1 (ⓒ **020/621-8080**), Amsterdam's premier department store, has a vast array of goods in all price ranges.

Amsterdam diamond cutters have an international reputation for high standards. When you buy from them, you'll be given a certificate listing the weight, color, cut, and identifying marks of the gem you purchase. The following stores offer diamond cutting and polishing tours, as well as sales of the finished product: **Amsterdam Diamond Center,** Rokin 1 (ⓒ **020/624-5787**); **Coster Diamonds,** Paulus Potterstraat 2–4 (ⓒ **020/676-2222**); **Gassan Diamonds,** Nieuwe Uilenburgerstraat 173–175 (ⓒ **020/622-5333**); **Stoeltie Diamonds,** Wagenstraat 13–17 (ⓒ **020/623-7601**); and **Van Moppes Diamonds,** Albert Cuypstraat 2–6 (ⓒ **020/676-1242**).

At the **Albert Cuyp Markt,** Albert Cuypstraat, you find just about anything and everything your imagination can conjure up. It's open Monday to Saturday from 9:30am to 5pm. From March to December, Thorbeckeplein hosts a **Sunday Art Market** where local artists show off their wares. **Waterlooplein Flea Market** is the classic market of Amsterdam, offering everything from cooking pots to mariner's telescopes to decent prints of Dutch cities; it's open Monday to Saturday from 10am to 5pm. And gardeners will find it well-nigh impossible to leave Amsterdam without at least one purchase from the floating **Flower Market,** on Singel at Muntplein, open daily year-round. Just be certain the bulbs you buy bear the obligatory certificate clearing them for entry into the United States.

NIGHTLIFE

Like an Indonesian *rijsttafel,* nightlife in Amsterdam is a bit of this and a bit of that. There's a strong jazz scene, good music clubs, and some enjoyable English-language shows at the little cabarets and theaters along the canals. The club and bar scene can be entertaining if not outrageous; the dance clubs may indeed seem quiet and small to anyone used to the flash of New York, L.A., or London. However, the brown cafes—the typical Amsterdam pubs—have never been better.

Amsterdam's top orchestra is the famed **Royal Concertgebouw Orchestra,** whose home is the **Concertgebouw,** Concertgebouwplein 2–6 (✆ 020/671-8345 daily from 10am–5pm, 24-hr. information line 020/675-4411). World-class orchestras and soloists are only too happy to appear at the Concertgebouw's Grote Zaal (Great Hall) because of its perfect acoustics. No matter where your seat, the listening is impeccable. Chamber and solo recitals are given in the Kleine Zaal (Little Hall). Tickets are between 12.50€ ($14.40) and 100€ ($115). The main concert season is September to mid-June, but during July and August there is the Robeco Summer Series, also world-class but with a listener-friendly price tag—all seats are just 30€ ($34.50).

The **Netherlands Opera** has established an international reputation for mounting often daring productions. The company performs at the **Muziektheater,** Waterlooplein 22 (24-hr. information ✆ 020/551-8100, box office 020/625-5455). This theater is also used by the **National Ballet,** which performs large-scale classical ballet repertoire as well as contemporary work, and by the **Netherlands Dance Theater,** which is based in The Hague and is famous for its groundbreaking contemporary repertoire. Most performances begin at 8:15pm, with opera tickets for 20€ to 60€ ($23–$69), and ballet tickets slightly less.

For several years, **Boom Chicago,** Leidspleintheater, Leidseplein 12 (✆ 020/530-7300; www.boomchicago.nl), has been bringing delightful English-language improvisational comedy to Amsterdam. *Time* magazine compared it to Chicago's famous Second City comedy troupe. Dutch audiences don't have much of a problem with the English sketches; they often seem to get the point ahead of the native English speakers in attendance. Tickets are 7.50€ to 9.50€ ($8.65–$10.95). Spectators are seated around candlelit tables for eight people and can have dinner and a drink while they enjoy the show. The restaurant is open at 7pm, and meals are 10€ to 12.50€ ($11.50–$14.40).

In Amsterdam, jazz and blues groups hold forth in bars, and the joints start jumping at around 11pm. You'll find listings in *What's On.* **BIMhuis,** Oudeschans 73–77 (✆ 020/623-1361), is for the serious contemporary jazz connoisseur; **Joseph Lam Jazz Club,** Diemenstraat 8 (✆ 020/622-8086), is Dixieland; and **Bourbon Street Jazz & Blues Club,** Leidsekruisstraat 6–8 (✆ 020/623-3440), hosts a mix of local and traveling talent. Also recommended is **Alto,** Korte Leidsedwarsstraat 115 (✆ 020/626-3249), off of Leidseplein.

Amsterdam's dance-club scene embraces every type of ambience and clientele, from the sophisticated rooms in large hotels to underground alternative spots. The scene isn't wildly volatile, but places do come and go. Leading clubs include

Mazzo, Rozengracht 114 (© **020/626-7500**), for trance and techno; **Akhna-ton,** Nieuwezijds Kolk 25 (© **020/624-3396**), for African music and salsa; **Melkweg,** Lijnbaansgracht 234A (© **020/624-1777**), for a variety of live music plus dance events; **iT,** Amstelstraat 24, near Rembrandtplein (© **020/625-0111**), which is gay on Saturday and mixed Thursday, Friday, and Sunday; **Par-adiso,** Weteringschans 6–8 (© **020/626-4521**), which has live music followed by dance parties; and **Soul Kitchen,** Amstelstraat 32, near Rembrandtplein (© **020/620-2333**), which usually has a relaxed, amicable crowd just out to swing.

BROWN CAFES

You'll find *bruine kroegen* (brown cafes) everywhere: on street corners, at the canal intersections, and down narrow little lanes. They look as if they've been there for-ever, and they have, practically. These are the favorite local haunts and are quite likely to become yours as well—they're positively addictive. Brown cafes will typi-cally sport lace half-curtains at the front window and ancient Oriental rugs on tabletops (to sop up any spills from your beer). Wooden floors, overhead beams, and plastered walls blend into a murky brown background, darkened by the cen-turies of smoke from Dutch pipes. Frequently there's a wall rack with newspapers and magazines, but they get little attention in the evening, when conversations flow as readily as *pils* (beer). *Jenever,* the potent Dutch gin, is on hand in several different flavors, some served ice cold—but never on the rocks. Excellent Dutch beers, as well as more expensive imported brews, are available.

Smoking Coffee Shops

Visitors often get confused about "smoking" coffee shops and how they differ from "no-smoking" ones. Well, to begin with, "smoking" and "no-smoking" don't refer to cigarettes—they refer to hashish and marijuana. The use of narcotic drugs is officially illegal in the Nether-lands, but Amsterdam and some other localities permit the sale in licensed premises of up to 5 grams (0.2 oz.) of hashish or marijuana for personal consumption.

Smoking coffee shops not only sell cannabis, most commonly in the form of hashish, but also provide a place where patrons can sit and smoke it all day long if they so choose. Not too long ago, before there was a small crackdown on soft drugs in Amsterdam, smoking coffee shops advertised their wares with a marijuana leaf sign. Though the practice of buying and smoking hashish in the coffee shops is still tol-erated, the marijuana leaf advertisements are now illegal. Generally, these smoking coffee shops are the only places in Amsterdam called "coffee shops"—regular cafes are called cafes or *eetcafes*—so chances are, whether or not you want to smoke, you'll be able to find what you're looking for without too much difficulty.

Some of the most popular smoking coffee shops are **The Rookies,** Korte Leidsedwarsstraat 145–147 (© **020/694-2353**); **Borderline,** Ams-telstraat 37 (© **020/622-0540**); and the several branches of the **Bulldog** chain (the **Bulldog Palace** is at Leidseplein 15; © **020/627-1908**).

Your hotel neighborhood is sure to have at least one brown cafe close at hand, and far be it for me to set any sort of rigid itinerary for a brown-cafe *kroegentocht* ("pub crawl"), but you just might want to look into the following: **Hoppe,** Spui 18–20 (© **020/623-7849**), a student and journalist hangout since 1670, which still has sawdust on the floor and is always packed and lots of fun; **Kalkhoven,** at Prinsengracht and Westermarkt (© **020/624-9649**), an atmospheric old bar that dates back to 1670; **Cafe 't Smalle,** Egelantiersgracht 12 (© **020/623-9617**), in the Jordaan district on the canal-side, a beautiful bar in a former distillery and tasting house that dates from 1786; **Café Chris,** Bloemstraat 42 (© **020/624-5942**), a tap house since 1624; **De Karpershoek,** Martelaarsgracht 2 (© **020/624-7886**), which dates from 1629 and was once a favorite hangout of sailors; and **Papeneiland,** Prinsengracht 2 (© **020/624-1989**), a 300-year-old establishment filled with character and with a secret tunnel that was used by Catholics in the 17th century.

AN EXCURSION TO HAARLEM

Traditionally the little sister city of Amsterdam, this handsome small city, has a similar 17th-century ambience but gets by fine without the hassles that go with the capital's famously tolerant and often eccentric lifestyle.

ESSENTIALS

GETTING THERE **Trains** depart at least every half hour from Amsterdam Centraal Station for Haarlem; the trip takes 15 minutes.

VISITOR INFORMATION **VVV Haarlem,** Stationsplein 1 (© **0900/616-1600;** www.vvvzk.nl), is located just outside the train station.

TOP ATTRACTIONS & SPECIAL MOMENTS

The historic center is a 5- to 10-minute walk from the graceful 1908 Art Nouveau train station (which is decorated with painted tiles and has a fine station restaurant), most of it via pedestrian-only shopping streets. First-time visitors generally head straight for the **Grote Markt** 🏵🏵🏵, the beautiful central market square. Most points of interest in Haarlem are within easy walking distance of the Grote Markt. The monumental buildings around the square date from the 15th to the 19th century and are a visual minicourse in the development of Dutch architecture. Here stands Haarlem's 14th-century **Stadhuis (Town Hall),** a former hunting lodge of the counts of Holland rebuilt in the 17th century.

Adjacent to the Grote Markt, the splendid **Sint-Bavokerk (Church of St. Bavo),** also known as the **Grote Kerk (Great Church)** 🏵🏵, Oude Groenmarkt 23 (© **023/532-4399**), soars into the sky. Finished by 1520 after a relatively short building period, it has a rare unity of structure and proportion. Mozart, Handel, and Liszt all made special visits to Haarlem to play the church's magnificent, soaring **Christian Müller Organ,** built in 1738. You can hear it at one of the free concerts given on Tuesday and Thursday from April to October. It has 5,068 pipes and is nearly 98 feet tall, and when it's going flat out, it's loud enough to blow your socks off. St. Bavo's is open Tuesday to Saturday from 10am to 4pm. Admission is 1.50€ ($1.75) for adults, and 1€ ($1.15) for children under 15.

The finest attraction in the city is the **Frans Hals Museum** 🏵🏵🏵, Groot Heiligland 62 (© **023/511-5775;** www.franshalsmuseum.nl). The galleries here are the halls and furnished chambers of a 1608 home for retired gentlemen, so the famous paintings by Frans Hals (ca. 1580–1686) and other masters of the Haarlem school hang in settings that look like the 17th-century houses they were intended to adorn. The museum is open Tuesday to Saturday from 11am to 5pm, and Sunday and holidays from noon to 5pm; closed January 1 and December 25. Admission is 5.40€ ($6.20) for adults, 4€ ($4.60) for seniors, and free for visitors under 19.

Just like in Amsterdam, an ideal way to view the town is by tour-boat on the canals. These are operated by **Woltheus Cruises** (© **023/535-7723;** www. woltheuscruises.nl), from a jetty on the Spaarne River beside the Gravenstenen-brug, a handsome lift bridge. Boats depart every hour. Cruises, from April to October at 10:30am, noon, 1:30, 3, and 4:30pm, are 6.50€ ($7.50) for adults, 4€ ($4.45) for children ages 3 to 11, and free for children under 3.

WHERE TO DINE

You can just about smell the North Sea breeze at the fine, French-inspired **De Pêcherie Haarlem aan Zee** ★★, Oude Groenmarkt 10 (© **023/531-4848**), beside Sint-Bavokerk. The nautical decor is not so original—lots of seafood eateries are bedecked with fishing nets, brass navigation lamps, and the like, but a nice touch is that you can sit on old-fashioned, high-backed wicker wind-breaker beach chairs, which enhance the seacoast ambience while creating a feel-ing of seclusion. Main courses cost 14.50€–21.50€ ($16.70–$24.75); fixed-price menus 19.50€ to 44.50€ ($22.45–$51.20).

Jacobus Pieck ★, Warmoesstraat 18 (© **023/532-6144**), a popular cafe-restaurant, has a lovely shaded terrace in the garden for fine-weather days, and inside it's bustling and stylish. Outside or in, you'll find excellent food for reason-able prices and friendly, efficient service. At lunchtime they serve generous sand-wiches and burgers, and their salads are particularly good. Main dinner courses range from pastas and Middle Eastern dishes to wholesome Dutch standards.

3 The Hague ★★

Amsterdam may be the capital of the Netherlands, but The Hague ('s-Graven-hage, or more commonly Den Haag, in Dutch) has always been the seat of gov-ernment and the official residence of the Dutch monarchs. This tradition began in 1248, when Count Willem II of Holland was crowned king of the Romans in the German city of Aachen, but he chose to live at the Binnenhof Palace in what is now The Hague. Beautiful and sophisticated, full of parks and elegant homes, the city has an 18th-century French look that suits its role as the diplo-matic center of the Dutch nation.

GETTING THERE The Hague is an easy day trip from Amsterdam, with frequent **train** service from Amsterdam Centraal Station. Note that The Hague has two main train stations, Centraal and Hollands Spoor; most of the sights are closer to Centraal Station, but some trains stop only at Hollands Spoor.

TOURIST INFORMATION VVV **Den Haag,** Koningin Julianaplein (© **0900/340-3505;** www.denhaag.nl), has an office in front of Centraal Sta-tion. The office is open September to June, Monday to Saturday from 9am to 5:30pm; July and August, Monday to Saturday from 9am to 5:30pm, and Sun-day from 11am to 5pm.

TOP ATTRACTIONS & SPECIAL MOMENTS

The most notable attraction of The Hague is the impressive **Binnenhof (Inner Court)** complex of Parliament buildings, in the city center. You can join a tour to visit the lofty, medieval **Ridderzaal (Hall of the Knights),** in which the queen delivers a speech from the throne each year. On the third Tuesday in September, be sure to be here to see her arrive and depart in her golden coach—like Cinderella—drawn by high-stepping royal horses. Depending on the volume and urgency of governmental business, you can tour one or the other of the two chambers of the **Staten-Generaal (States General)**, the Dutch Parliament. The Parliament is open Monday to Saturday from 10am to 4pm; guided tours are 2.50€ ($2.90) or 3€ ($3.45) for adults, and 2€ ($2.30) or 2.50€ ($2.90) for seniors and children ages 13 and under, depending on the exact tour being offered at the time. It's requested you book ahead by telephone (© **070/ 364-6144**) for the guided tour, and you should call ahead in any case to make sure tours are going on the day you intend to visit. Admission to the Parliament exhibit in the reception room of the Hall of Knights is free.

Adjacent to the Binnenhof is the elegant Italian Renaissance–style **Maurit-shuis,** Korte Vijverberg 8 (© **070/302-3435;** www.mauritshuis.nl), built in 1644 as the architecturally innovative home of a young court dandy and cousin of the Orange-Nassaus. Today this small palace houses the **Koninklijk Kabinet van Schilderijen (Royal Cabinet of Paintings)** ✮✮✮, and is the permanent home of an impressive art collection given to the Dutch nation by King Willem I in 1816. Highlights include 13 Rembrandts, 3 Frans Hals, and 3 Vermeers (including the famous *View of Delft*), plus hundreds of other famous works by such painters as Breugel, Rubens, Steen, and Holbein (including his portrait of Jane Seymour, 3rd wife of King Henry VIII of England). The gallery is open Tuesday to Saturday from 10am to 5pm, and Sunday from 11am to 5pm. Admission is 7€ ($8.05) for adults, 3.50€ ($4.05) for seniors, and free for visitors under 19.

Designed by Hendrik Petrus Berlage (1927–34), the **Haags Gemeentemuseum (Hague Municipal Museum)** ✮✮, Stadhouderslaan 41 (© **070/338-1111;** www.gemeentemuseum.nl), possesses a world-famous collection of works by Piet Mondrian (1872–1944), including his last work, *Victory Boogie Woogie* (1943), inspired by New York. The museum is open Tuesday to Sunday from 11am to 5pm; closed January 1 and December 25. Admission is 7€ ($8.05) for adults, 5.50€ ($6.35) for seniors, and free for children under 13.

Not far away, in the Scheveningen Woods, is enchanting **Madurodam** ✮, George Maduroplein 1 (© **070/416-2400;** www.madurodam.nl), a miniature village in 1-to-25 scale that represents the Dutch nation in actual proportions of farmland to urban areas. It presents many of the country's most historic buildings in miniature, with lights that actually work, bells that ring, and trains that run efficiently—as trains do in Holland. It's open January to mid-March and September to late December, daily from 9am to 6pm; mid-March to June, daily from 9am to 8pm; July to August, daily from 9am to 10pm. Admission is 10€ ($11.50) for adults, 9€ ($10.35) for seniors, 7€ ($8.05) for children ages 4 to 11, and free for children under 4.

SCHEVENINGEN

So close is the beach resort and fishing port of **Scheveningen** to The Hague—just 3 miles (5km) from the center—it seems part of the same city. This is probably Holland's most chic seacoast resort (though that's not saying much) and contains an array of international-name boutiques and upscale restaurants. Yet you can still catch a sight of costumed fishermen's wives near the harbor—they dress up in their traditional Dutch garb only for special events, like *Vlaggetjesdag* (Flag Day) at the end of May when the first of the new season's herring are landed.

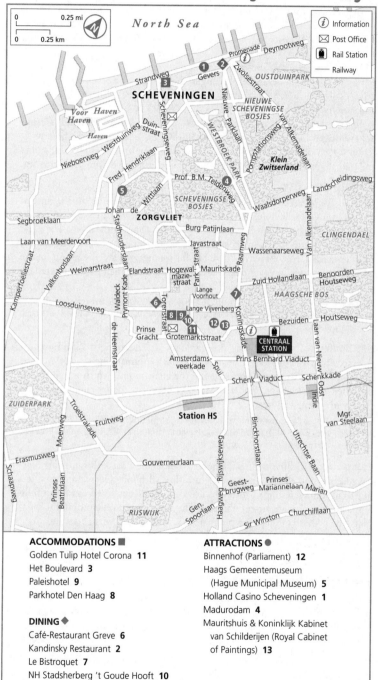

North Sea

SCHEVENINGEN

(i) Information
⊠ Post Office
🚉 Rail Station
— Railway

CENTRAAL STATION

Station HS

ACCOMMODATIONS ■
Golden Tulip Hotel Corona **11**
Het Boulevard **3**
Paleishotel **9**
Parkhotel Den Haag **8**

DINING ◆
Café-Restaurant Greve **6**
Kandinsky Restaurant **2**
Le Bistroquet **7**
NH Stadsherberg 't Goude Hooft **10**

ATTRACTIONS ●
Binnenhof (Parliament) **12**
Haags Gemeentemuseum
  (Hague Municipal Museum) **5**
Holland Casino Scheveningen **1**
Madurodam **4**
Mauritshuis & Koninklijk Kabinet
  van Schilderijen (Royal Cabinet
  of Paintings) **13**

To get there from The Hague, take tram nos. 1 or 9 from Den Haag Centraal Station to Gevers Deynootplein in Scheveningen. Tourist information is available from **VVV Scheveningen,** Gevers Deynootweg 1134 (✆ **0900/340-3505;** www.denhaag.com), at the Palace Promenade mall.

Among Scheveningen's attractions are biking, strolling on the dunes, deep-sea fishing in the North Sea, and splashing in the waves at the beach or in a heated wave pool. The beach and bathing zone is called Scheveningen Bad—but it looks pretty good to the Dutch.

Tuxedoed croupiers provide blackjack and roulette at **Holland Casino Scheveningen,** Kurhausweg 1 (✆ **070/306-7777**), across from the beautifully restored 19th-century Kurhaus Hotel. These are "complemented" by video games and pinball machines at the old Scheveningen Pier jutting out into the North Sea.

WHERE TO STAY

Golden Tulip Hotel Corona ★★ Centrally located opposite the Parliament, this charming small hotel, once a lively coffeehouse, features contemporary decor, with touches of handsome marble and mahogany in the lobby. The guest rooms are done in soft pastel colors with graceful window drapes. The elegant main restaurant, full of French Provincial furnishings, is a favorite retreat for the good and the great in government circles. In balmy weather, part of the restaurant becomes a sidewalk terrace.

Buitenhof 39–42, 2513 AH Den Haag. ✆ **070/363-7930.** Fax 070/361-5785. www.corona.nl. 36 units. 135€–190€ ($155–$219) double. Rates include buffet breakfast. AE, DC, MC, V. **Amenities:** 2 restaurants; bar; laundry. *In room:* Hair dryer, no A/C.

Het Boulevard Perched atop the sea dunes at Scheveningen within walking distance of the Palace Promenade, this hotel has a commanding sea view from its sun lounge/restaurant and from some of the guest rooms, which are all plainly furnished in a clean-cut, modern style. The hotel has special family rooms for those with young children.

Seinpostduin 1, 2586 EA Scheveningen. www.boulevard-hotel.nl. ✆ **070/354-0067.** Fax 070/355-2574. 31 units. 75€–110€ ($86.25–$127) double. Rates include continental breakfast. AE, DC, MC, V. Tram: 1 or 9 from The Hague. *In room:* no A/C.

Paleishotel Behind the royal family's Noordeinde Palace, this intimate hotel has spacious and elegant guest rooms furnished with soft chairs and settees, in a quiet city-center setting. Bathrooms are a bit small but fitted out beautifully. Some guest rooms are air-conditioned. The location is excellent both for shopping (the pedestrian shopping promenade is nearby) and for sightseeing.

Molenstraat 26, 2513 BL Den Haag. ✆ **070/362-4621.** Fax 070/361-4533. www.paleishotel.nl. 20 units. 115€–165€ ($132–$190) double. Buffet breakfast 12.50€ ($14.40) extra. AE, DC, MC, V. **Amenities:** Bar. *In room:* No A/C in standard rooms.

Parkhotel Den Haag This pleasant, centrally located, full-service hotel is on a quiet street, with doors opening from the spacious entrance lobby onto a walled-in streetside terrace in fine weather. The early-20th-century monument has original yellow brick and tile features on the staircases that demand a constant process of preservation. A grandiose breakfast room overlooks the gardens of Noordeinde Palace. The guest rooms are spacious and attractive and have full marble bathrooms.

Molenstraat 53, 2513 BJ Den Haag. ✆ **070/362-4371.** Fax 070/361-4525. www.parkhoteldenhaag.nl. 114 units. 160€–240€ ($184–$276) double. Rates include continental breakfast. AE, DC, MC, V. **Amenities:** Lounge; bar. *In room:* Hair dryer, no A/C.

WHERE TO DINE

Café-Restaurant Greve ✸ MEDITERRANEAN   What was once a car showroom is now a popular restaurant. The cafe's large windows look out on lively Torenstraat; the restaurant is more intimate with low ceiling, candlelight, and wooden tables. There's a small a la carte menu and a 3-course fixed-price option. You can choose to have a dish either as a starter or as a main course— an ideal solution for small appetites or those who want to sample the menu.

Torenstraat 138. ✆ **070/360-3919.** Main courses 12.50€–16€ ($14.40–$18.40); 3-course dinner 22.50€ ($25.90). AE, DC, MC, V. Cafe, daily 10am–1am; restaurant, Mon–Sat 6–11pm, Sun 6–10pm.

Kandinsky Restaurant ✸✸ FRENCH/MEDITERRANEAN   Save your most special Scheveningen meal for this small, exquisite restaurant. Beside the beach, the dining room overlooks the sea and its decor features signed Kandinsky lithographs. The cuisine here is classic French plus some Italian and other Mediterranean variations, and you can order vintage wines by the glass.

In the Steigenberger Kurhaus Hotel, Gevers Deynootplein 30, Scheveningen. ✆ **070/416-2636.** Main courses 22.50€–37.50€ ($25.90–$43.15); 5-course menu du chef 55€ ($63.25). AE, DC, MC, V. Mon–Fri noon–2pm; daily 6–10:30pm. No lunches served July–Aug.

Le Bistroquet ✸ CONTINENTAL   This small, popular restaurant in the city center is one of The Hague's finest, its quietly elegant dining room featuring lovely table settings. The menu, though short, is to the point, and covers lamb, fish, and poultry dishes. A fine Dutch menu choice is the three variations of Texel lamb with roasted garlic and a basil sauce.

Lange Voorhout 98. ✆ **070/360-1170.** Main courses 19€–32.50€ ($21.85–$37.40); fixed-price menus 28.50€–45€ ($32.80–$51.75). AE, DC, MC, V. Mon–Fri noon–2pm and 6–10:30pm; Mon–Sat 6–10:30pm.

NH Stadsherberg 't Goude Hooft ✸✸ DUTCH/CONTINENTAL   There's a definite old Dutch flavor to this wonderful, large restaurant overlooking the city's old market square, yet its 1600s exterior cloaks a 1939 interior installed after a disastrous fire. The wooden beams, brass chandeliers, and rustic chairs and tables blend harmoniously with the stained-glass windows, medieval banners, and wall murals. There's a large sidewalk cafe on the "Green Market" square. An extensive menu covers everything from snacks to light lunches to full dinners.

Dagelijkse Groenmarkt 13. ✆ **070/346-9713.** Main courses 13.50€–19.50€ ($15.55–$22.45); fixed-price menus 15.80€–23.80€ ($14.65–$27.40); coffee table 14.50€–15.50€ ($16.70–$17.85). AE, DC, MC, V. Mon noon–6pm; Tues–Wed and Fri–Sat 10am–7pm; Thurs 10am–9:30pm, Sun 11am–6pm.

AN EXCURSION TO DELFT ✸✸

Yes, this is the home of the famous blue-and-white porcelain, and you can visit the factory where it's produced. The small, handsome city also is the cradle of the Dutch Republic and the burial place of the royal family, and was the birthplace and inspiration of artist Jan Vermeer, the 17th-century master of light and subtle emotion.

GETTING THERE   There's frequent **train** service from Amsterdam; the trip takes about 55 minutes. The train station in Delft is only a short walk from the city center, or you can take one of the trams or taxis that stop right outside the station. **Tram** service is also available from Den Haag Centraal to Delft and costs 4 strips on a *strippenkaart*, or about 1.65€ ($1.90).

VISITOR INFORMATION   Tourist Information Delft, Hippolytusbuurt 4, 2611 HN Delft (✆ **015/215-4051;** www.delft.nl), is located in the center of town. The office is open Sunday and Monday from 10am to 4pm, Tuesday to Friday from 9am to 6pm, and Saturday from 9am to 5pm.

TOP ATTRACTIONS & SPECIAL MOMENTS

The house where Vermeer was born, lived, and painted is long gone from Delft, as are his paintings. The artist's burial place, the **Oude Kerk (Old Church)** ✸, Roland Holstlaan 753 (✆ **015/212-3015**), is noted for its 27 stained-glass windows by Joep Nicolas. You should also visit the **Nieuwe Kerk (New Church)** ✸✸, Markt (✆ **015/212-3025**), where Prince William of Orange and other members of the House of Orange-Nassau are buried. The church is open April to October, Monday to Saturday from 9am to 6pm; November to March, Monday to Saturday from 11am to 4pm. Admission is 4€ ($4.45) for adults, 2€ ($2.30) for children ages 3 to 12, and free for children under 3.

The **Prinsenhof Museum** ✸ St. Agathaplein 1 (✆ **015/260-2358**), on nearby Oude Delft, is where William I of Orange (William the Silent) lived and had his headquarters in the years when he helped found the Dutch Republic. He was assassinated here in 1584, and you can still see the bullet holes in the stairwell. Today the Prinsenhof is a museum of paintings, tapestries, silverware, and pottery, and is the site of the annual Delft Art and Antiques Fair, held in late October or early November. The museum is open Tuesday to Saturday from 10am to 5pm, and Sunday and holidays from 1 to 5pm; closed January 1 and December 25. Admission is 3.50€ ($4.05) for adults, 3€ ($3.45) for children ages 12 to 15, and free for children under 12.

In the same neighborhood you can view a fine collection of old Delft tiles displayed in the wood-paneled setting of a 19th-century mansion museum called **Lambert van Meerten,** Oude Delft 199 (✆ **015/260-2358**). The museum is open Tuesday to Saturday from 10am to 5pm, and Sunday and holidays from 1 to 5pm; closed January 1 and December 25. Admission is 2.50€ ($2.90) for adults, 2€ ($2.30) for children ages 12 to 15, and free for children under 12.

To view a demonstration of the traditional art of making and hand-painting Delftware, visit the factory and showroom of **Koninklijke Porceleyne Fles,** Rotterdamseweg 196 (✆ **015/251-2030**), founded in 1653. It's open April to October, daily from 9am to 4:30pm; November to March, Monday to Friday from 9am to 4:30pm, and Saturday and Sunday from 11am to 1pm. Admission is 2.50€ ($2.90) for adults, and free for children under 13.

WHERE TO DINE

The skillfully prepared dishes at **Le Vieux Jean** ✸, Heilige Geestkerkhof 3 (✆ **015/213-0433**), draw from the provincial French tradition, using the freshest of top-quality ingredients. The setting is a historical churchyard, and you receive a warm and friendly welcome. Main courses cost 14.50€ to 19.50€ ($16.70–$22.45); fixed-price menus 24.50€ to 49.50€ ($28.20–$56.95).

Some of the best Dutch cooking in the country is dished up at the atmospheric **Spijshuis de Dis** ✸✸, Beestenmarkt 36 (✆ **015/213-1782**), east of the market. Look out for traditional plates presented in modern variations. A good example is the *Bakke pot*—a stew made from three kinds of meat (beef, chicken, and rabbit) in a beer sauce, served in the pan. An entree will set you back 13€ to 22.50€ ($14.95–$25.90); fixed-price menu 26.50€ ($30.50).

4 Maastricht ✸

A city of cafes and churches, Maastricht (pop. 120,000) is a charming mixture of historic buildings and monuments, a lighthearted carnival famous throughout Europe, and some of the finest restaurants to be found in any Dutch city of its size. Somehow—in between eating, drinking, church-going, stepping out for

Carnival, and hanging onto their heritage—the people of Maastricht are building a modern, prosperous, and vibrant city. Discovering how they do it all can be
quite an education.

GETTING THERE   Maastricht has frequent **train** connections to Amsterdam, Rotterdam, and The Hague. Trains leave on the hour from each city to
make the 2½ hour journey to Maastricht's Centraal Station, about a 15- to 20-
minute walk from the center of the city.

VISITOR INFORMATION   The **VVV Maastricht office,** Kleine Staat 1
(© **043/325-2121;** www.visitmaastricht.nl), is right off of Grote Straat, a 15-
minute walk from the train station (head down Stationstraat, cross the St. Servaasbrug, and then bear right). It's open Monday to Friday from 9am to 6pm;
January to April and November through December, also Saturday from 9am to
5pm; and mid-May through October, also Sunday from 11am to 3pm.

TOP ATTRACTIONS & SPECIAL MOMENTS

Coming from the train station to the old center, you cross the Maas on the **Sint-
Servaasbrug (St. Servatius Bridge),** which dates from 1280 to 1289 and is one
of the oldest bridges in the Netherlands. The **Vrijthof,** the city's most glorious
square, is a vast open space bordered on three sides by restaurants and cafes with
sidewalk terraces, and on the fourth by the Romanesque Sint-Servaas Church
and the Gothic Sint-Jan's with its soaring red belfry. This is Maastricht's forum,
especially in good weather, when the terraces are filled with people soaking up
the atmosphere and watching the world go by.

The oldest parts of the majestic cruciform **Sint-Servaasbasiliek (Basilica of
St. Servatius),** Keizer Karelplein (© **043/325-2121**), adjacent to the Vrijthof,
date from the year 1000, though the church was considerably enlarged in the
14th and 15th centuries. Saint Servatius, Maastricht's first bishop, is buried in
the crypt. Over the centuries people have honored the saint with gifts, so the
Treasury has a collection of incredible richness and beauty that includes two
superb 12th-century reliquaries fashioned by Maastricht goldsmiths. The
church is open September to June, Monday to Saturday from 10am to 5pm, and
Sunday from 1 to 5pm; July and August, Monday to Saturday from 10am to
6pm, and Sunday from 1 to 5pm. Admission is 2€ ($2.30) for adults, 1.50€
($1.75) for seniors, and .50€ (60¢) for children under 13.

Next door, the sober, whitewashed interior of the city's main Dutch Reformed
(Protestant) church, **Sint-Janskerk (St. John's Church),** Henric van Veldeke-
plein (© **043/325-2121**), adjacent to the Vrijthof, dating from the 14th century and given to the Protestants in 1633, makes a study in contrasts with the
lavish Catholic decoration at St. Servatius's. But there are murals, sculpted cor-
bels of the 12 Apostles, and grave monuments of local dignitaries and wealthy
individuals. However, most people come here to climb the 218 narrow, winding
steps to the 230-foot-high belfry's windy viewing platform, 141 feet above the
streets, and the fine view of the city it provides. The church is open Easter to
mid-October, Monday to Saturday from 11am to 4pm. Admission to the church
is free; and to the tower is 1€ ($1.15).

The west wing and crypts of the Romanesque cruciform **Onze Lieve Vrouw-
basiliek (Basilica of Our Lady),** Onze Lievevrouweplein (© **043/325-2121**),
date from the 11th century, and there's evidence of an even earlier church and a
pagan place of worship on the site. But it is the side chapel sheltering the statue
of Our Lady Star of the Sea that is the focus for most pilgrims. The richly robed
statue, fronted by a blaze of candles, is credited with many miracles, even during

long years when it had to be hidden away because of religious persecution. The church Treasury contains a rich collection of tapestries, reliquaries, church silver, and other religious artifacts. The basilica is open daily from 11am to 5pm, except during services; the Treasury is open Easter to mid-October, Monday to Saturday from 11am to 5pm, and Sunday from 1 to 5pm. Admission to the basilica is free; and to the Treasury is 2€ ($2.30) for adults, and .50€ (60¢) for children.

Designed by Italian architect Aldo Rossi and opened in 1995, the otherwise restrained riverside **Bonnefanten Museum,** Av. Céramique 250 (© **043/329-0190**), is instantly recognizable from its striking, bullet-shaped dome. Works of art within from the Maasland School include sculpture, silverwork, and woodcarvings produced along the Maas Valley in Limburg and Belgium. This art dates as far back as the 13th century and had its apogee during the 15th and 16th centuries. Internationalism is illustrated in the museum's collection of Italian and Flemish masters. These include works by Filippo Lippi and Bellini, and Pieter Bruegel the Younger's *Wedding In Front Of A Farm* and *Census At Bethlehem.* The museum is open Tuesday to Sunday from 11am to 5pm. Admission is 6.50€ ($7.50) for adults, 5€ ($5.75) for seniors and children ages 13 to 18, and free for children under 13.

As over the centuries more and more marlstone was extracted from **Sint-Pietersberg (Mount St. Peter),** Fort Sint-Pieter (© **043/325-2121**), on the southwestern edge of the city, the interior became honeycombed with 20,000 passages. From Roman times to the days of medieval sieges, to the 4 years of enemy occupation during World War II, their passages have served as a place of refuge. The temperature underground is about 10°C (50°F), and it's damp, so bring a cardigan or a coat to protect against the chill. The caves are open July to September, daily at 2:45pm. Guided tours are 3€ ($3.45) for adults, and 2€ ($2.30) for children under 12.

WHERE TO STAY & DINE

There's been an inn on the site of the **Best Western Hotel du Casque** 🛠, Helmstraat 14 (© **043/321-4343;** www.bestwestern.nl/ducasque), since the 15th century. The present family-run hotel carries on the proud tradition, with modern facilities, comfortable rooms, and good old-fashioned friendliness. Renovated in 2000, it faces the lively Vrijthof square; those rooms overlooking the Vrijthof have the finest view in town. Doubles cost 110€ to 131€ ($127–$151).

At **De Poshoorn,** Stationsstraat 47 (© **043/321-7334;** www.poshoorn.nl), a small corner hotel near the train station, you register with the friendly owner in the ground-floor cafe. You needn't be afraid of being disturbed in your sleep—from the rooms you can hardly hear any of what's going on downstairs. The guest rooms aren't too large, but they're modern and have comfortable beds. Doubles cost 70€ ($80.50) double.

Sightseeing, shopping, dining, and just plain people-watching couldn't be more convenient than at the modern **Bastion Deluxe Hotel Maastricht/Centrum,** Boschstraat 27 (© **043/321-2222;** www.bastionhotels.nl), on the edge of the city center, overlooking the old inner harbor, called the *Bassin.* Guest rooms are large and have wooden furniture and comfortable box-spring beds. The hotel offers a continental breakfast buffet, and there's also a restaurant and a convivial bar overlooking a covered winter garden. A double costs 106€ ($122) per night.

You dine with pink table napkins under a timber-beamed ceiling at the refined, intimate **Au Premier** 🛠🛠, Brusselsestraat 15 (© **043/321-9761**). In summertime, you can eat outside on a pretty garden patio with a view of old

Maastricht around you. The cuisine features regional specialties utilizing local produce, in addition to provincial French dishes. Try the *Hemel en Aarde* (Heaven and Earth), a traditional Limburg stew that combines apples, potatoes, black pudding, and goose liver. Main courses cost 18€ to 22.50€ ($20.70–$25.90); fixed-price menus 32.50€–47.50€ ($37.40–$54.65).

At the breezy **Sagittarius,** Bredestraat 7 (© **043/321-1492**), off the Vrijthof, in a long, glass-lit room, the chef prepares both modern and classic variations of local and French fish dishes and grilled meats in his open kitchen as you watch. The menu changes daily. The *bouillabaisse et sa rouille,* a Provençal fish stew served with a spicy chili and garlic sauce, is excellent. In summer months, you can dine in a pleasant garden. Entrees run 16.50€ to 22.50€ ($19–$25.90); a fixed-price menu 27.50€ ($31.65).

Local favorite **'t Plenkske** ♠♠, Plankstraat 6 (© **043/321-8456**), is a fine restaurant in the Stokstraat Quarter, with a light, airy decor and an outdoor patio overlooking the site of the city's ancient Roman baths. Regional specialties from both Maastricht and Liège are prominent on the menu, along with a number of French classics thrown in for good measure. Main courses cost 13.50€ to 22.50€ ($15.55–$25.90); the fixed-price menu 19.50€ to 33.50€ ($22.45–$38.55).

16

Norway

For the rail traveler, the mountainous and elongated country of Norway is the Valhalla of Scandinavia. From its snow-capped mountains to its scenic fjords warmed by the Gulf Stream, much of the country's varied land and seascapes can be seen from your train window. The rail ride between the eastern capital city of Oslo and its western outpost of historic Bergen (gateway to the fjord district) is one of the most scenic in Europe, vying with some of the dramatic mountain rail journeys in Alpine Switzerland. See "Highlights of Norway," below, for more details on this 7-hour trip.

Norwegian rail engineers have defied nature and laid tracks once thought impossible to carry you quickly and efficiently across the dramatic but difficult terrain of their beautiful land. Routes are not comprehensive, especially as you go into the far north toward Lapland and the Midnight Sun, but rail lines are gloriously scenic, trains are efficient, and the major towns with their myriad attractions are easily accessible by train.

Scenery Norway has, but do bear in mind that it comes at a price; what Norway doesn't have is cheap living. It is, in fact, one of the world's priciest destinations, with Oslo enjoying the dubious distinction of being named the most expensive city on the planet in 2003. High prices, however, shouldn't deter the value-minded rail traveler. In this chapter, we provide some budget-saving tips along with recommendations of moderately priced hotels and restaurants.

Note: A map detailing Norway's rail routes as well as the rail lines of the three major Scandinavian countries can be found on p. 189.

HIGHLIGHTS OF NORWAY

The weather will be the key determining factor in timing your rail visit to Norway. The summer season is very short, beginning in June (May is still quite cold) and ending by late August, when it's often possible to see snow flurries whirling about your head. Expect long days of sunlight, even at night. North of the Arctic Circle, the Midnight Sun is clearly visible.

The average rail passengers will not have much time for exploring the northern reaches of this ancient land of the Vikings and can confine themselves to the two greatest cities in Norway—Oslo, the capital, and the "second city" of Bergen. These cities spring to their business, cultural, and commercial life when September arrives, but the days quickly grow cold. Open-air museums close down, and attractions, including tourist offices, go on reduced hours, and—most important for the rail traveler—trains begin running on less frequent schedules. Winter sports under dark, foreboding skies provide dog-sledding, ice-fishing, and cross-country and Alpine skiing, but these attract only the most adventurous and esoteric of travelers.

Oslo, one of the world's most beautifully sited capitals, deserves at least 2 or 3 days of your time, as does Bergen, particularly if you want to use it as a launch pad for sampling some of the scenic highlights of the western fjord district.

⌢ *Moments* Festivals & Special Events

Norway's cities and towns stage numerous festivals and special events throughout the year (check with the local tourist office to see what's going on during your visit), but the following three are definitely worth a look if you're in town for them:

The **Holmenkollen Ski Festival** held on the outskirts of Oslo in early March is one of Europe's largest ski festivals, with World Cup Nordic skiing and biathlons, international ski-jumping competitions, and Norway's largest cross-country race for amateurs. For more information, contact Skiforeningen, Kongeveien 5, Holmenkollen, N-0390 Oslo 3 (© **22-92-32-00;** www.skiforeningen.no).

From mid-May to early June, the world-class **Bergen International Festival (Bergen Festspill)** features musical artists from Norway and around the world. It's is one of the largest annual musical events in Scandinavia. For information, contact the Bergen International Festival, Slottsgaten 1, 4055, Dregen N-5835 Bergen (© **55-21-06-30**).

The major event on the Oslo calendar, the **Nobel Peace Prize Ceremony** is held annually at Oslo City Hall on December 10. Attendance is by invitation only. For information, contact the Nobel Institute, Drammensveien 19, N-0255 Oslo 2 (© **22-44-36-80;** www.nobel.se).

Most flights to the country land in Oslo, one of the world's most beautifully sited capitals, making it the obvious starting point for a rail trip in Norway. A number of world-class attractions await you: **Akershus Castle,** one of the oldest historical monuments in Oslo; the 17th-century Oslo Cathedral; **Vigelandsparken** (a field of sculpture by Norway's greatest, Gustav Vigeland); the **Kon-Tiki Museum** housing the world-famous balsa log raft from 1947; the open-air **Norwegian Folk Museum; the Viking Ship Museum** (with a trio of Viking burial vessels); and, outside of town, the **Henie Onstad Kunstsenter,** a treasure trove of art acquired by former movie star and skating champion, Sonja Henie. The city deserves at least 2 days, if not more of your time.

One of the great adventures of Norway is to make the 7-hour, 305-mile (490km) rail journey from Oslo to Bergen, one of the most startlingly beautiful in all of Europe. The train after leaving Oslo climbs to the little town of **Gol** at 679 feet before beginning a much steeper ascent. It reaches the winter resort of **Geilo** at 2,605 feet and continues to climb until it approaches the village of **Ustaoset** at 3,248 feet. After that the train crosses a foreboding landscape of icy mountain lakes and rock-strewn ridges wearing "snow bonnets."

At the tiny mountain village of **Finse,** in the vicinity of the **Hardangerjøkulen Glacier,** you are virtually in polar conditions. At 4,009 feet, Finse is the highest station in Norway.

Leaving Finse, the Oslo-Bergen line goes through a 6.2-mile (10km) tunnel emerging near **Hallingskeid** before going on to its next stop at **Myrdal.** The descent then is to the lake town of **Voss,** only 184 feet above sea level and both a winter and summer sports resort. The scenery grows tamer as the train begins its descent onto Bergen, the last lap of this journey taking about an hour.

The final destination of **Bergen** is one of the great historic centers of Scandinavia, an old Hanseatic port and Norway's second city, the gateway to the fjords. Situated on a peninsula, this UNESCO World Heritage Site is surrounded by towering mountains and filled with old cobblestone streets flanked by weather-beaten clapboard houses in various hues. Be sure to see the aquarium here (one of the largest and best in Scandinavia), and to tour old Bryggen, a district of Hanseatic timbered houses along the waterfront. Allot at least 2 to 3 days to this city, particularly if you want to use it as a launch pad for sampling some of the scenic highlights of the western fjord district.

1 Essentials

GETTING THERE

All transatlantic flights from North America land at Oslo's Fornebu Airport. **SAS** (© **800/221-2350** in the U.S.; www.scandinavian.net) flies nonstop daily from Newark, NJ, to Oslo. Most other SAS flights from North America go through Copenhagen. Note that transatlantic passengers on SAS are occasionally allowed to transfer to a Norwegian domestic flight from Oslo to Bergen for no additional charge.

Other airlines that fly to Norway through a gateway city in Europe, include **British Airways** (© **800/AIRWAYS** in the U.S.), **Icelandair** (© **800/223-5500** in the U.S.; www.icelandair.com) and **KLM** (© **800/347-7747** in the U.S.; www.nwa.com).

NORWAY BY RAIL
PASSES

For information on the **Eurailpass, Eurailpass Flexi, Scanrail Pass,** and other multi-country options, see chapter 2.

In addition to the multi-country passes, there is the national **Norway Rail Pass.** The pass offers 3 days of unlimited second-class train travel in a 1-month period for $209 for adults. There's no need to splurge on a first-class pass, as the comfort level of second-class on Norwegian trains is equal to first-class in many other European countries. Similar passes for travelers under 26 and for seniors (over 60) cost $151.

FOREIGN TRAIN TERMS

Don't bother learning a lot of train terms in difficult-to-pronounce Norwegian. Norwegians start learning English while in grade school, and you can usually learn what you need to know by asking train personnel for help in English. That said, here are a few common terms you may find: *Avgaende tog* means departure and *Ankommende tog* means arrival. *Billetter* are tickets.

PRACTICAL TRAIN INFORMATION

The **Norwegian State Railways (NSB)** operates the major rail lines of Norway. Call © **81-50-08-88** for timetable information and for bookings. For information on the Web, log on to **www.nsb.no**.

Norway's 2,500-mile (4,044km) network of electric and diesel-electric trains runs as far as Bodø, 62 miles (100km) north of the Arctic Circle. (Beyond that, visitors must take a coastal steamer, plane, or bus to Tromsø and the North Cape.) Recently upgraded express trains, called **Signatur-tog** (the fastest in the country—they "tilt" as they take corners), crisscross the mountainous terrain between Oslo, Stavanger, Bergen, and Trondheim. Note that these Signatur-tog are faster than the quick trains labeled **Expresstog** and that railpasses will only get you free access to second-class seats on these speedy trains. Holders of first-class railpasses get a 50% reduction on first-class seating supplements, but we say don't bother as second-class is just fine on these trains.

The most popular and most scenic run in the country covers the 305 miles (490km) between Oslo and Bergen. Visitors with limited time often choose this route for its fabled mountains, gorges, white-water rivers, and fjords. The trains often stop for passengers to enjoy breathtaking views. The one-way second-class fare from Oslo to Bergen is 633NOK ($85), plus a mandatory seat reservation of 40NOK ($5.40). Another popular run, from Oslo to Trondheim, costs 707NOK ($95) one-way in second class.

One of the country's obviously scenic trips, from Bergen to Bodø, is not possible by train because of the terrain. Trains to Bodø leave from Oslo (see "The Essence of Norway," below).

If you're traveling direct between cities separated by a long distance and don't have a rail pass, a **Minipris Ticket** might be a good option. With this ticket, you can travel in second class for 360NOK ($49) one-way, but only on routes that

---

Moments **The Essence of Norway**

The must-do rail experience in this country is the trip from Oslo to Bergen, but those with more time—a total of 24 hours—will find another wonderful option that cuts through the heart of Norway on a northward trek: **A train trip from Oslo to Bodø** that captures what local tourist promoters accurately bill as "the essence" of Norway.

As the train heads north from Oslo, the scenery is bucolic with rolling hills, farmlands, and small villages. The farther north you go, the more dramatic the scenery becomes, especially as you continue north from the resort of Lillehammer, famed for hosting the 1992 Winter Olympics. When you reach Dombås—instead of going to Trondheim—you can detour to the northwest and the town of Åndalsnes. This leg is one of the grandest of all rail journeys in Scandinavia: Your train will plunge through tunnels carved through foreboding mountains, and whiz over bridges and past waterfalls and the highest vertical canyon in Norway.

After arriving in Åndalsnes, you can return to Dombås for a final journey to the north. If possible, plan an overnight stopover in the medieval city of Trondheim, one of the most historic and beautiful in Scandinavia and the ancient capital of Norway.

From Trondheim you can travel to the northern terminus of the rail line at Bodø, a city that lies north of the Arctic Circle. Many rail passengers in summer take this journey to Bodø just to bask in the Midnight Sun.

At Bodø, you can return on the same train to Oslo, or, as an alternative, you can take a bus northeast from Bodø to the city of Narvik. The bus is half price for all railpass holders (free for Eurail passholders). After a stopover in Narvik, you can once again board a train, the Ofoten Line, for a plunge eastward into Sweden, where most passengers head southeast to the capital city of Stockholm.

take you more than 93 miles (150km) from your point of origin. No stopovers are allowed except for a change of trains. Tickets are valid only on select trains, for boarding that begins during designated off-peak hours. You can buy Minipris Tickets at any railway station in Norway.

Travelers over age 67 are entitled to a 50% discount, called an **Honnorrabatt,** on Norwegian train trips of more than 31 miles (49km). Regardless of age, the spouse of someone over 67 can also receive the 50% discount.

RESERVATIONS   Reservations are compulsory on most InterCity and Signatur-tog trains and on all overnight and international services. A reservation costs 40NOK ($5.40) above the price of your regular ticket or railpass if made in Norway. Sleepers on overnight trains should also be reserved (see below). It's not always necessary to make a reservation on secondary trains, but it's always advised in the summer season, as trains are likely to be filled to capacity.

Timetables are distributed free at all rail stations under the name of *NSB Togruter.* On the more scenic routes, you can often get data in English describing the highlights of the trip.

SERVICES & AMENITIES   Second-class travel on Norwegian trains is recommended. In fact, second class in Norway is as good as or better than first-class travel anywhere else in Europe, with reclining seats and lots of unexpected comforts. First-class coaches cost 50% more than second-class and are considered "not worth the investment" by the majority of rail riders in Norway.

The affordably priced sleepers on night trains (called InterNordNight) are a good investment because you'll be saving on a regular hotel accommodation. Sleepers are priced according to the number of berths in each compartment. A bed in a 3-berth cabin costs from 150NOK ($20); in a 2-berth cabin, from 290NOK ($39); and in a 1-berth cabin, from 600NOK ($81). *Couchettes* can be booked through Rail Europe in North America; a reservation costs $28 for one in either first or second class. Children 4 to 15 years of age and senior citizens pay 50% of the regular adult fare. Group and mid-week tickets are also available.

There are special compartments for persons with disabilities on most medium- and long-distance trains. People in wheelchairs and others with physical handicaps, and their companions, may use the compartments. Some long-distance trains offer special playrooms ("Kiddie-Wagons") for children, complete with toys and educational items.

The express trains running between Oslo and Bergen (or vice versa) have excellent dining cars, some of the best in Northern Europe, but meals are terribly expensive. The secondary express trains have buffets, serving both hot meals and snacks. On the *Regionaltogs* or smaller regional trains, expect food wheeled through the cabin in a trolley.

Trains & Travel Times in Norway

From	To	Type of Train	# of Trains	Frequency	Travel Time
Oslo	Bergen	Signatur-tog	2	Daily	6 hr. 24 min.– 6 hr. 41 min.
Oslo	Bergen	InterNordNight	1	Daily	7 hr. 46 min.
Oslo	Bergen	Expresstog	2	Daily	7 hr. 9 min.– 7 hr. 23 min.

FAST FACTS: Norway

Area Code The international country code for Norway is **47**. If you're call-ing from outside the country, the city code is **2** for Oslo and **5** for Bergen. Inside Norway, no area or city codes are needed. Phone numbers have eight digits.

Business Hours Most **banks** are open Monday to Friday from 8:15am to 3:30pm (Thurs to 5pm), and are closed Saturday and Sunday. Most **busi-nesses** are open Monday to Friday from 9am to 4pm. **Stores** are generally open Monday to Friday from 9am to 5pm (many stay open Thurs until 6 or 7pm) and Saturday 9am to 1 or 2pm. Sunday closings are observed.

Climate In the summer, the average temperature in Norway ranges from 57°F to 65°F (14°C–18°C). In January, it hovers around 27°F (3°C), ideal for winter sports. The Gulf Stream warms the west coast, where winters tend to be temperate. Rainfall, however, is heavy.

Above the Arctic Circle, the sun shines night and day from mid-May until late July. For about 2 months every winter, the North Cape is plunged into darkness.

Documents Required Citizens of the United States, Canada, Ireland, Aus-tralia, and New Zealand, and British subjects, need a valid **passport** to enter Norway. You need to apply for a visa only if you want to stay more than 3 months. A British Visitor's Passport is also valid for holidays and some business trips of less than 3 months. The passport can include your spouse, and it's valid for 1 year. Apply in person at a main post office in the British Isles, and the passport will be issued that day.

Electricity Norway uses 220 volts, 30 to 50 cycles, A.C., and standard con-tinental two-pin plugs. Transformers and adapters are needed to use Canadian and American equipment. Always inquire at your hotel before plugging in any electrical equipment.

Embassies & Consulates In case you lose your passport or have some other emergency, contact your embassy in Oslo. The Embassy of the **United States** is at Drammensveien 18, N-0244 Oslo (© **22-44-85-50**); and **Canada**'s is at Wergelandsveien 7, N-0244 Oslo (© **22-99-53-00**).

Health & Safety Norway offers some of the best medical facilities in Europe, with well-trained, English-speaking doctors. Norway's national health plan does not cover American or Canadian visitors; medical expenses must be paid in cash and costs are generally more reasonable than elsewhere in western Europe.

You're probably safer in Norway than in your home country; however, you should take the usual precautions you would when traveling any-where. Guard your possessions and don't become blasé about security. One of the least safe places at night is east Oslo, which has a growing drug problem; but even there it's reasonably safe to walk around at night, though you may encounter some hassle from drug addicts, alcoholics, or beggars (many of them recently arrived foreigners).

Holidays Norway celebrates the following public holidays: New year's Day (Jan 1), Maundy Thursday, Good Friday, Easter, Labor Day (May 1), Ascen-sion Day (mid-May), Independence Day (May 17), Whitmonday (late May), Christmas (Dec 25), and Boxing Day (Dec 26).

Legal Aid If arrested or charged with a crime in Norway, you can obtain a list of private lawyers from the U.S. Embassy to represent you.

Mail Airmail letters or postcards to the United States and Canada cost 7NOK (95¢) for up to 20 grams (⁷/₁₀ oz.). Airmail letters take 7 to 10 days to reach North America. The principal post office in Norway is **Oslo Central Post Office,** Dronningensgate 15, N-0101 Oslo. Mailboxes are vibrant red, embossed with the trumpet symbol of the postal service. They're found on walls, at chest level, throughout cities and towns. Stamps can be bought at the post office, at magazine kiosks, or at some stores. Only the post office can weigh, evaluate, and inform you of the options for delivery time and regulations for sending parcels. Shipments to places outside Norway require a declaration on a printed form stating the contents and value of the package.

Police & Emergencies Call ⓒ **112** for the **police,** ⓒ **110** to report a **fire,** or ⓒ **113** to request an **ambulance** throughout Norway.

Telephone & Telegrams Direct-dial long-distance calls can be made to the United States and Canada from most phones in Norway by dialing ⓒ **00** (double zero), then the country code (**1** for the U.S. and Canada), followed by the area code and phone number. Check at your hotel's front desk before you place a call. Norwegian coins of 1NOK (15¢), 5NOK (70¢), and 10NOK ($1.35) are used in pay phones.

Tipping Hotels add a 10% to 15% service charge to your bill, which is sufficient unless someone has performed a special service. Most bellhops get at least 10NOK ($1.35) per suitcase. Nearly all restaurants add a service charge of up to 15% to your bill. Barbers and hairdressers usually aren't tipped, but toilet attendants and hatcheck people expect at least 4NOK (55¢). Don't tip theater ushers. Taxi drivers don't expect tips unless they handle heavy luggage.

2 Oslo

The oldest Scandinavian capital, founded by Harald Hardrade in 1048, Oslo is renowned for its spectacular natural beauty, with subways in a few minutes connecting you to mountain lakes, evergreen forests, and hiking trails—all within the city limits. Oil rich, it is no longer a provincial capital but has risen to become a metropolis and is one of the most cosmopolitan cities of Europe with a vibrant nightlife.

At the top of the 60-mile (97km) Oslofjord, Norway encompasses 175 square miles (453 sq. km), although its urban growth covers only about a tenth of that. The rest is a vast outdoor playground.

More and more of Oslo's old wooden structures have given way to tall modern buildings and glass-roofed atriums. It's a great city for wandering as it has incorporated art to decorate both its public and private buildings, with sculpture integral to its public squares and parks, especially the Vigeland Sculpture Park.

STATION INFORMATION
GETTING FROM THE AIRPORT TO THE TRAIN STATION
International air traffic lands at **Oslo International Airport** in Gardermoen (ⓒ **81-55-02-50**), about 31 miles (50km) east of downtown Oslo. All domestic

and international flights coming into Oslo arrive through this much-upgraded airport, including aircraft belonging to SAS, British Airways, and Icelandair.

High-speed trains *(Flytoget)* run between the airport's train station (right at the air terminal) and Oslo's Central Station. The trip takes only 20 minutes and costs 180NOK ($24) per person each way. *Note:* A Eurailpass does not cover this train.

There's also frequent bus service, departing at intervals of between 15 and 30 minutes throughout the day, for downtown Oslo (trip time is about an hour). It's maintained by both SAS (whose buses deliver passengers to the Central Station and to most of the SAS hotels within Oslo) and the **Norwegian Bus Express** (*©* **81-54-44-44**), whose buses head for Central Station. Both companies charge 110NOK ($15) per person, each way.

If you want to take a taxi (and we don't recommend it unless you're traveling in a very large group), be prepared for a lethally high charge of around 575NOK ($78) for up to four passengers plus their luggage. If you need a "maxi-taxi," a minivan that's suitable for between 5 and 15 passengers, plus your luggage, you'll be assessed 800NOK ($108).

INSIDE THE STATION

Trains from the Continent, Sweden, and Denmark arrive at **Oslo Sentralstasjon,** Jernbanetorget 1 (*©* **81-50-08-88** for train information). At the beginning of Karl Johans Gate (the main street of Oslo), the terminal is in the center of the city and is open daily from 6am to 10pm. From the Central Station, trains leave for Stockholm, Copenhagen, Bergen, Stavanger, Trondheim, and Bodø (the last stop on Norway's northern rail line). You can also catch trams here to all major sections of Oslo (see "Getting Around," below).

The **Tourist Information Office** here is open daily from 8am to 10pm and is located next to the money exchange office. In addition to offering tourist information, it makes hotel reservations at a cost of 45NOK ($6.10). To request information or accommodations in advance, write to Tourist Information, Oslo Sentralstasjon, Jernbanetorget 1, N-0154 Oslo.

A money exchange kiosk lies on the mezzanine directly across from the ticket windows. It is open June to September from 7am to 6pm on Monday to Friday, and 9am to 3pm Saturday. Train information can be found on the main concourse, where staff members are available for assistance Monday to Saturday from 7am to 10pm and Sunday daily. Arrival and departure times for trains are displayed on digital bulletin boards inside the station.

For train reservations—or to validate a rail pass—go to window #4 in the main lobby's ticket office. If #4 is closed, go to any window marked *Billetter.* These kiosks make sleeping car reservations, too, and sell both domestic and international tickets.

Baggage storage lockers are located on a balcony to the right of the station's main exit. The cost is 20NOK ($2.70) for 24 hours, with a 7-day maximum. The office is open Monday to Friday 9am to 3pm. One other amenity of note inside the station: terminals offering free Internet access.

INFORMATION ELSEWHERE IN THE CITY

The **Oslo Tourist Information Office,** Fridtjof Nansens Plass 5, entered on Roald Amundsen Street (*©* **24-14-77-00**), is open April and May, Monday to Saturday 9am to 5pm; June to August, daily 9am to 7pm; September, Monday to Saturday 9am to 5pm; and October to March, Monday to Friday 9am to 4pm. The staff will give you free maps, brochures, and make hotel reservations

Oslo

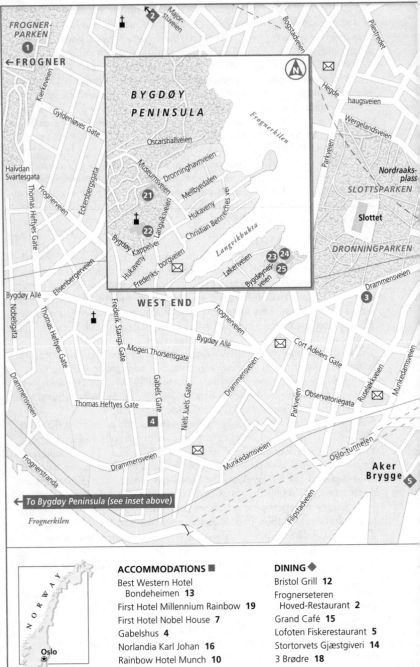

ACCOMMODATIONS ■

Best Western Hotel
  Bondeheimen **13**

First Hotel Millennium Rainbow **19**

First Hotel Nobel House **7**

Gabelshus **4**

Norlandia Karl Johan **16**

Rainbow Hotel Munch **10**

DINING ◆

Bristol Grill **12**

Frognerseteren
  Hoved-Restaurant **2**

Grand Café **15**

Lofoten Fiskerestaurant **5**

Stortorvets Gjæstgiveri **14**

3 Brødre **18**

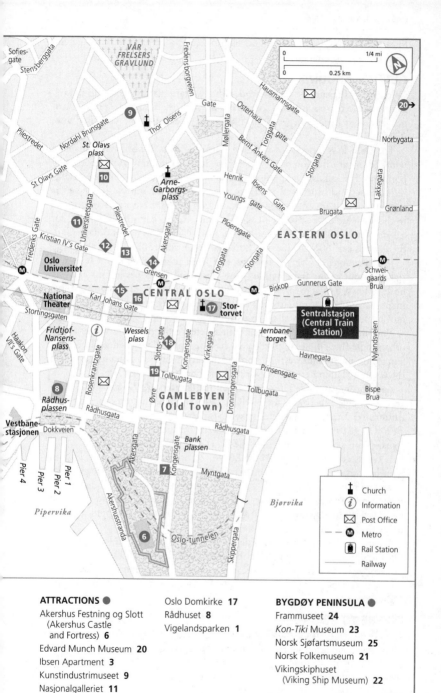

for a fee of 45NOK ($6.10). Sightseeing tickets can be purchased and guided tours can also be arranged.

GETTING AROUND

Oslo has an efficient citywide network of buses, trams (streetcars), and subways. Buses and electric trains take passengers to the suburbs; from mid-April to October, ferries to Bygdøy depart from the harbor in front of the Oslo Rådhuset (City Hall).

The **Oslo Pass** (also called the Oslo Card) can help you become acquainted with the city at a fraction of the usual price. It allows free travel on public transportation, free admission to museums and other top sights, discounts on sightseeing buses and boats, and special treats in restaurants. You can purchase the card at hotels, many shops, tourist information offices, from travel agents, and in the branches of Sparebanken Oslo Akershus. Adults pay 190NOK ($26) for a 1-day card, 280NOK ($38) for 2 days, and 370NOK ($50) for 3 days. Children's cards cost 60NOK ($8.10), 80NOK ($11), and 110NOK ($15).

Jernbanetorget is Oslo's major **bus and tram** terminal stop, and is located right in front of the train station. Most buses and trams passing through the heart of town stop at Wessels Plass, next to the Parliament, or at Stortorget, the main marketplace. Many also stop at the National Theater or University Square on Karl Johans Gate, as well as Oslo's suburbs.

The **subway (T-banen)** has four branch lines to the east. The Western Suburban route (including Holmenkollen) has four lines to the residential sections and recreation grounds west and north of the city. Subways and trains leave from the Central Station near the National Theater on Karl Johans Gate.

For schedule and fare information, call **trafikanten** (© 22-05-70-37). Drivers sell single-trip tickets for 30NOK ($4.05); children travel for half fare. Automated machines validate tickets. An eight-coupon **Maxi card** costs 140NOK ($19), half price for children. Maxi cards can be used for unlimited transfers for 1 hour from the time the ticket was stamped.

If you need a taxi, call © **22-38-80-90,** 24 hours a day. Reserve at least an hour in advance. All taxis have meters, and Norwegian cab drivers are generally honest. When a cab is available, a roof light goes on. Taxis can be hailed on the street, provided they're more than 300 feet from a taxi rank. The worst time to hail a taxi is Monday through Friday from 8:30 to 10am and 3 to 5pm, and Saturday from 8:30 to 10am.

Beginning in mid-April, ferries depart for Bygdøy from Pier 3 in front of the Oslo Rådhuset. For schedules, call **Båtservice** (© 23-35-68-90). The ferry or bus to Bygdøy is a good choice because parking there is limited. Other ferries leave for various parts of the Oslofjord. Inquire at the **Tourist Information Office** (see above).

WHERE TO STAY

Best Western Hotel Bondeheimen   This restored 1913 building is today an affordable hotel just a short walk from the Students' Grove at Karl Johans Gate and less than a mile from the train station. In spite of modernization, a certain old-fashioned charm and comfort still prevail. The rooms are a bit small but space is well used and they are furnished in pine-wood pieces. Most bathrooms have showers only (some with tubs).

Rosenkrantzgate 8 (entrance on Kristian IV's Gate), N-0159 Oslo. © **800/528-1234** in the U.S. or 23-21-41-00. Fax 22-41-94-37. 127 units. www.bondeheimen.com. Mon–Thurs 2,105NOK ($284) double;

Fri–Sun 990NOK ($134) double. Rates include breakfast. Tram: 7 or 11. **Amenities:** Restaurant; bar; laundry; nonsmoking rooms; rooms for those with limited mobility. *In room:* Hair dryer.

First Hotel Millennium ✮ *Finds*   Created in 1998 out of a 1930s Art Deco office building, this hotel is both minimalist and stylish and is hailed for its atmosphere and character. At ¼ mile (.4km) from Central Station, it's close to most of Central Oslo's major attractions. Bedrooms are generally spacious with good-size bathrooms, and combine Art Deco touches with Nordic modern decor.

Tollbugate 25, N-0157 Oslo. © **21-02-28-30.** Fax 21-02-28-30. www.firsthotels.no. 112 units. Mon–Thurs 1,103NOK–1,510NOK ($149–$204) double; Fri–Sun 703NOK–853NOK ($95–$115) double. AE, DC, MC, V. Tram: 30, 42. **Amenities:** Restaurant; bar; laundry; nonsmoking rooms; rooms for those with limited mobility. *In room:* Hair dryer.

First Hotel Nobel House ✮ *Finds*   This rather elegant boutique hotel near the Old Town was recycled from a commercial structure, and turned into an inviting oasis of charm and grace, with a glassed-in atrium, Oriental carpets, and Ionic-style columns. Suites are themed on mementos of the life of a famous Scandinavian, but the regular rooms are just as good, each equipped with a tiled bathroom. You'll get a personalized welcome from the friendly, helpful staff.

Kongensgaten 5, N-0153 Oslo. © **23-10-72-01.** Fax 23-10-72-10. 69 units. 1,249NOK ($169) double; 1,602NOK ($216) suite. Rates include breakfast. AE, DC, MC, V. T-banen: Stortinget. **Amenities:** Restaurant; bar; laundry; nonsmoking rooms. *In room:* Hair dryer.

Gabelshus ✮ *Finds*   Built in 1912, but renovated in 2000, this old-time favorite attracts only discerning travelers who know of its relatively secluded location. It's a schlep from the train station, but a worthwhile one. The aura of an English manor house is evoked by public lounges filled with art and antiques along with burnished copper and working fireplaces. Both antique reproductions and Nordic design dominate the midsize to spacious bedrooms, some of which have terraces.

Bogstadveien 20, N-0355 Oslo. © **23-27-65-00.** Fax 23-27-65-60. www.gabelshus.no. July and Fri–Sun year-round 950NOK ($128) double; rest of year 1,495NOK ($202) double. Year-round 1,790NOK ($242) suite. Rates include breakfast. AE, DC, MC, V. Tram: 10. **Amenities:** Breakfast room; laundry; nonsmoking rooms. *In room:* Hair dryer.

Norlandia Karl Johan ✮   A recent renovation has made this hotel—a 10-minute walk from Central Station—better, brighter, and more welcoming than ever. Decorators use Norwegian folk art to give it an atmospheric feel, along with some Oriental carpets, antiques, or reproductions. The medium-size bedrooms have double-glazed windows and comfortable furnishings, along with marble bathrooms.

Karl Johans Gate 33, N-0162 Oslo. © **23-16-17-00.** Fax 22-42-05-19. www.norlandia.no. Mon–Thurs 1,570NOK ($212) double, 2,300NOK ($311) suite; Fri–Sun 990NOK ($134) double, 1,890NOK ($255) suite. Rates include breakfast. AE, DC, MC, V. T-banen: Stortinget. **Amenities:** Restaurant; bar; laundry; nonsmoking rooms. *In room:* Hair dryer.

Rainbow Hotel Munch   This nine-floor hotel, built in 1983, is just a 5-minute walk north of Karl Johans Gate. The comfortable bedrooms run from small to midsize, and come with small bathrooms. Rooms are decorated with reproductions of the paintings of Edvard Munch, Norway's greatest artist, for whom the hotel is named.

Munchsgaten 5, N-0130 Oslo. © **23-21-96-00.** Fax 23-21-96-01. www.rainbow-hotels.no. 180 units. Mon–Thurs 1,145NOK ($155) double; Fri–Sun 720NOK ($97) double. Rates include breakfast. AE, DC, MC, V. T-banen: Stortinget. Tram: 7 or 11. Bus: 37. **Amenities:** Lounge; laundry; nonsmoking rooms; rooms for those with limited mobility. *In room:* Hair dryer.

TOP ATTRACTIONS & SPECIAL MOMENTS

There are those who say that a visit to Oslo would be worthwhile even if you came only to view its harbor and to take a boat ride along the Oslofjord. Because this is the most scenically located capital of Europe, panoramic views are important, especially the one from **Tryvannstårnet,** a 390-foot observation tower atop 1,900-foot Tryvann Hill.

On even the most cursory visit, you should see the Viking ships on Bygdøy peninsula; explore such famous vessels as the polar ship, *Fram,* or the balsa raft, *Kon-Tiki;* and take in the Norwegian Maritime Museum and the Folk Museum. If you're an art lover, visit the Munch Museum and go to the outskirts of town to see the famous Henie Onstad Art Center.

Akershus Festning og Slott (Akershus Castle and Fortress)   Built by King Haakon V about 1300, Akershus Castle and Fortress is one of the most important relics of Norway in the Middle Ages, though what you'll see when you visit is mostly a Renaissance palace. A fire in 1527 devastated the northern wing, and the castle was rebuilt and transformed under the Danish-Norwegian

Moments Scandinavia's Greatest Painter

Oslo is the city of the great artist, Edvard Munch (1863–1944), and many aficionados make a special pilgrimage here to see his finest works. Although he would grow up to become hailed as "the handsomest man in Norway," he suffered through many childhood illnesses and tragic deaths (such as the early death of his mother). Much of that grief later found expression in his works such as the world-famous *The Scream.* Heavily influenced by French Realism, he studied in Paris in 1885. In time he would reject that movement, succumbing to Impressionism and later Symbolism. His first exhibition in Berlin in 1892 touched off a nationwide scandal. Critics screamed "anarchistic provocation," and the show was forced to close. But Munch was not deterred. He was on a roll in the 1890s, creating some of his most memorable works, including the cycle, *The Frieze of Life,* dedicated to love, death, anxiety, and darkness.

Returning to Norway in 1908, he fell in love with the Oslofjord and painted many memorable seascapes. After a love affair went sour, he suffered a nervous breakdown. Although he helped decorate the auditorium of Oslo University, by 1916 he'd turned inward and led the life of a hermit in a home outside Oslo. He continued to paint, however, often landscapes hailed by critics as "sensuous," and always in bold colors.

The best showcase of Munch's paintings are found at **Edvard Munch Museum** ✪✪, Tøyengate 53 (✆ **23-24-14-00).** The museum traces Munch's works from early Realism to latter-day Expressionism. The rotating collection features 1,100 paintings, some 4,500 drawings, and around 18,000 prints, numerous graphic plates, and six sculptures.

Admission to the museum costs 60NOK ($8.10) for adults and 30NOK ($4.05) for children. It is open June to mid-September daily 10am to 6pm; mid-September to May Tuesday to Friday 10am to 4pm, Saturday and Sunday 10am to 6pm (T-banen: Tøyen).

king Christian IV in the 1600s. The castle is infamous for having served as a prison during the Nazi regime. Commemorating those dreadful years is the on-site Norwegian Resistance Museum, showing underground printing presses and radio transmitters among other illegal artifacts that trace the German attack on Norway in 1940 until that country's liberation in 1945.

Festnings-Plassen. ℂ **22-41-25-21.** Admission 30NOK ($4.05) adults, 10NOK ($1.35) children. Family ticket 70NOK ($9.45). May–Sept 15 Mon–Sat 10am–4pm; Sun 12:30–4pm. Closed Sept 16–Apr 14. Tram: 10 or 12. Bus: 60.

Henie Onstad Kunstsenter ⚐⚐   On a site beside the Oslofjord 7 miles (11km) west of Oslo, ex-movie star and skating champion Sonja Henie and her husband, Niels Onstad, a shipping tycoon, opened this museum in 1968 to display their art collection. The center's especially good 20th-century collection includes some 1,800 works by Munch, Picasso, Matisse, Léger, Bonnard, and Miró. Henie's Trophy Room is impressive, with 600 trophies and medals, including 3 Olympic gold medals and 10 world skating championships. In addition to its permanent exhibition, the foundation presents cultural activities—music, theater, film, dance, and even poetry readings.

Sonja Henies Vei 31. ℂ **67-80-48-80.** Admission 75NOK ($10). Free for children under 16. Tues–Thurs 11am–7pm; Fri–Sun 11am–6pm. Bus: 151, 161, 251, or 261.

Nasjonalgalleriet ⚐⚐⚐   Situated behind Oslo University, this is Norway's greatest art gallery and one of the finest in Northern Europe. It specializes in Norwegian artists, though there is a noteworthy collection of old European masters, including works by van Gogh, Gauguin, Cézanne, and Degas. Norwegian artists whose work is on display include Johan Christian Dahl, Harriet Backer, and Christian Krohg, the latter earning his fame by painting everyone from mariners to prostitutes. The two most notable homegrown artists featured in the collection are Gustav Viegeland, Norway's greatest sculptor, and Edvard Munch, Scandinavia's greatest painter. Munch's *The Scream* is one of the world's most reproduced paintings.

Universitetsgata 13. ℂ **22-20-04-04.** Free admission. Mon, Wed, Fri 10am–6pm; Thurs 10am–8pm; Sat 10am–4pm; Sun 11am–4pm. Closed Tues. Tram: 7 or 11.

Vigelandsparken ⚐⚐⚐   The work of Norway's greatest sculptor, Gustav Vigeland (1869–1943) is spread across the 75-acre Frogner Park, whose main entrance is on Kirkeveien. Vigeland died a year before the park was completed but left behind a total of 227 monumental sculptures, of which the most celebrated work is the 52-foot monolith composed of 121 colossal figures, all carved into one piece of stone. However, the most photographed sculpture is *The Angry Boy.*

Also at the park is the **Vigeland-museet,** to the south in Nobelsgate. Vigeland's former studio, where he lived and worked from 1924 until his death, features his drawings, plaster casts, and woodcuts among other memorabilia.

Frogner Park, Nobelsgate 32. ℂ **22-54-25-30.** Free admission to the park. Museum 40NOK ($5.40) adults, 20NOK ($2.70) children. Park daily 24 hours. Museum, May–Sept Tues–Sat 10am–6pm, Sun noon–7pm; Oct–Apr Tues–Sat noon–4pm, Sun noon–4pm. Tram: 12 or 15. Bus: 20, 45, or 81.

MUSEUMS ON THE BYGDØY PENINSULA

Located south of the city, the peninsula is reached by commuter ferry (summer only) leaving from Pier 3, facing the Rådhuset (Town Hall). Departures during the day are every 40 minutes, and a one-way fare costs 22NOK ($2.95). The no. 30 bus from the National Theater also runs to Bygdøy; the museums are only a short walk from the bus stops on Bygdøy.

⌒ *Moments* Ringing the Doorbell at Ibsen's Apartment

Although he sometimes had a troubled relationship with his native country of Norway, Henrik Ibsen (1828–1906) is today hailed as that country's foremost dramatist and is duly honored. Since 1993, it's been possible to visit his **apartment,** which lies just a short walk from the National Theater in Stortingsgate where so many of his greatest plays, including the 1879 *A Doll's House* and the 1881 *Ghosts,* are still performed with a certain devotion.

A blue plaque on the building at the corner of Arbinsgate and Drammensveien marks the apartment where Ibsen lived from 1895 until his death. He often sat in the window, with a light casting a glow over his white hair. People lined up in the street below to look up at him, and he seemed to take delight in the adulation, so long overdue, as far as he was concerned. Italy's greatest actress, Eleanora Duse, came here to bid him a final adieu, but he was too ill to receive her. She stood outside in the snow, blowing him kisses.

The only time Ibsen broke with Norway was when his country did not come to the aid of Denmark in its war with Prussia. Outraged, Ibsen went into a self-imposed exile in 1864 and stayed away in protest for 27 years, returning to settle in Christiania (the old name for Oslo) when memories of his resentment had faded. All is forgiven now, and his memorable *Peer Gynt* is hailed around the world as a forerunner of contemporary drama.

It's an amazing moment to wander through the apartment, which still has its original furniture. It's as if Ibsen still resides in this truly "living museum." The entrance is at Arbingsgate 1 (⌀ **22-55-20-09**), and admission is 50NOK ($6.75) for adults, 20NOK ($2.70) for children. The apartment is open Tuesday to Sunday noon to 3pm, with guided tours in English at noon, 1pm, and 2pm. T-banen: Nationaltheatret.

Frammuseet ⌀   There's only one exhibit here, but it's world famous: the polar ship *Fram.* The sturdy exploration ship was the vessel Fridtjof Nansen used to sail across the Arctic Ocean (1893–96) at the age of 27. The vessel was later used in the Antarctic by Norwegian explorer Roald Amundsen, when he became the first man to reach the South Pole in 1911.

Bygdøynesveien. ⌀ **23-28-29-50.** Admission 30NOK ($4.05) adults, 15NOK ($2.05) children. Nov–Feb Mon–Fri 11am–2:45pm; Sat–Sun 11am–3:45pm.

Kon-Tiki Museum ⌀⌀   *Kon-Tiki* is the world-famed balsa-log raft that the young Norwegian scientist Thor Heyerdahl and his five comrades sailed on for 4,300 miles (7,000km) in 1947—all the way from Callao, Peru, to Raroia, Polynesia. The museum also houses the papyrus *Ra II,* which Heyerdahl and his comrades used in 1970 to cross the Atlantic from Safi in Morocco to Barbados in the southern Caribbean.

Bygdøynesveien 36. ⌀ **23-08-67-67.** Admission 35NOK ($4.75) adults, 20NOK ($2.70) children. Family ticket 90NOK ($12). Apr–May and Sept daily 10:30am–5pm; June–Aug daily 9:30am–5:45pm; Oct–Mar daily 10:30am–4pm.

Norsk Folkemuseum ★★★   In a beautiful 35-acre park, this 110-year-old museum traces Norwegian cultural history with both indoor and outdoor exhibitions. Preservation-minded Norwegians scoured the countryside, finding more than 140 old buildings, mostly from the 1600s and 1700s, and moved them to Oslo where they are arranged almost like a time capsule dedicated to a memory of "the way it was." Of special note is the museum's **Gamlebyen** (old town), the reproduction of an early-20th-century small village, and a medieval wooden stave church built in 1200.

Museumsveien 10. ℂ **22-12-37-00**. Admission 55NOK ($7.45) adults, 20NOK ($2.70) children under 17. Jan–May 14 and Sept 15–Dec 31 Fri–Sat 11am–3pm, Sun 11am–4pm; May 15–June 14 and Sept 1–14 daily 10am–5pm; June 15–Aug 31 daily 10am–6pm.

Norsk Sjøfartsmuseum ★★   This museum, which contains a complete ship's deck with helm and chart house, and a three-deck-high section of the passenger steamer *Sandnaes,* chronicles the maritime history and culture of Norway. The Boat Hall features a fine collection of original small craft. Especially intriguing are the sailing ships used in 18th- and 19th-century polar expeditions, including the vessel *Gjøa,* which Roald Amundsen used to sail through the Northwest Passage from 1903 to 1906.

Bygdøynesveien 37. ℂ **24-11-41-50**. Admission to museum and boat hall 40NOK ($5.40); free for kids under 16. May 15–Aug daily 10am–6pm; Sept–May 14 Mon–Wed, Fri–Sun 10:30am–4pm, Thurs 10:30am–6pm.

Vikingskiphuset (Viking Ship Museum) ★★★   This museum is devoted to one of the rarest finds in the world: three Viking burial vessels that were excavated on the shores of the Oslofjord and preserved in clay. The most spectacular find is the 9th-century *Oseberg* ★, discovered near Norway's oldest town. This 64-foot dragon ship features a wealth of ornaments and is the burial chamber of a Viking queen and her slave. The *Gokstad* find is an outstanding example of Viking vessels because it's so well preserved. The smaller *Tune* ship was never restored.

Huk Aveny 35, Bygdøy. ℂ **22-13-52-80**. Admission 40NOK ($5.40) adults, 20NOK ($2.70) children. May–Sept daily 9am–6pm; Oct–Apr daily 11am–4pm

WHERE TO DINE

Bristol Grill ★★ CONTINENTAL   Located in the prestigious Hotel Britsol and open since 1924, this grill has attracted its fair share of celebrities, including Frank Sinatra and Sophia Loren. It's one of the last bastions in Oslo of

---

Moments Down by the Old Waterfront

On the waterfront near Rådhusplassen, the town hall, Oslo's Fishermen's Wharf—called **Aker Brygge**—is a favorite rendezvous point for visitors and Oslovians alike. One of our favorite pastimes is to head down here and approach one of the shrimp boats where you can purchase a bag of freshly caught and cooked shellfish from a fisherman. Buy a beer at the harbor-fronting **Aker Brygge Café** and find a scenic spot where you can shell your feast and eat while taking in a view of the harbor.

After your snack, wander among the little shops, the ethnic food joints, the fast-food stands, or see what's playing in the on-site theater and a multi-cinema complex. In summer, jazz concerts are often staged in the outdoors.

courtly formal service, everything taking place against a backdrop that evokes a 1920s hunting lodge. The best Nordic version of bouillabaisse is served here, along with time-tested favorites such as medallions of venison.

In the Hotel Bristol, Kristian IV's Gate 7. ℭ **22-82-60-00.** Reservations recommended. Main courses 210NOK–285NOK ($28–$38). AE, DC, MC, V. Daily 5–11pm. Closed July. Tram: 10, 11, 17, or 18.

Grand Café ⊛⊛ NORWEGIAN   This is the most famous cafe in Oslo, once patronized by Edvard Munch and Henrik Ibsen, the latter a devotee of whale steak. Installed on the ground floor of Oslo's grandest hotel, the restaurant serves tasty traditional Norwegian country cuisine (where can you get a good elk stew today if not here?) in an elegant setting. This is unpretentious cooking that will win you over if you like solid, honest, and earthy flavors

In the Grand Hotel, Karl Johans Gate 31. ℭ **23-21-20-00.** Reservations recommended. Main courses 160NOK–280NOK ($22–$38). AE, DC, MC, V. Mon–Sat 11am–11pm; Sun noon–11pm. T-banen: Stortinget.

Frognerseteren Hoved-Restaurant NORWEGIAN   This longtime favorite is set on the mountain plateau of Holmenkollen, and offers a sweeping panorama of the city and the Oslofjord. In a landmark Viking-Revival lodge constructed in 1896, guests can choose between an affordable cafe and a more formal restaurant, or else opt for beer and snacks on the breezy terrace outside. Specialties, served 1,600 feet above sea level and 1,000 feet downhill from the Holmenkollen railway stop, include such country favorites such as filet of elk and smoked Norwegian salmon.

Holmenkollveien 200. ℭ **22-92-40-40.** Reservations recommended. Cafe platters 80NOK–110NOK ($11–$15). Restaurant main courses 265NOK–300NOK ($36–$41). Set-price menus 455NOK–625NOK ($61–$84). DC, MC, V. Restaurant Tues–Fri noon–3pm, Mon–Sat 5–10pm, Sun 1–8pm; Cafe daily 11am–10pm. T-banen: 15 to Frognerseteren.

Lipp INTERNATIONAL   A touch of Paris in the Roaring Twenties is recaptured in this restored brasserie, where black-vested waiters serve a savory cuisine that roams Europe for inspiration. The chefs wisely change the menu every season to take advantage of what's best and freshest from both field and stream—roasted grouse in the fall or the freshest of summer produce in July. Expect succulent pastas or freshly caught fish grilled to perfection.

In the Hotel Continental, Stortingsgaten 24. ℭ **22-82-40-60.** Reservations recommended. Main courses 218NOK–298NOK ($29–$40). AE, DC, MC, V. Daily 4–11:30pm. T-banen: Nationaltheatret.

Lofoten Fiske Fiskerestaurant ⊛ SEAFOOD   Located in the Aker Brygge complex, this restaurant is one of the best choices for dining along the waterfront of Oslo, combining a top-notch seafood dinner with one of the most panoramic views of the city's seascape. Nautical accessories decorate the interior, and when the weather's fair guests prefer a table on the outdoor terrace. Scrupulously seasonal and rigorously precise, the cuisine is based on the favorite fish of the Norwegian palate: lobster, oysters, salmon, halibut, and trout.

Stranden 75, Aker Brygge. ℭ **22-83-08-08.** Reservations recommended. Main courses 243NOK–280NOK ($33–$38) at lunch or dinner. AE, DC, MC, V. Mon–Sat 11am–1am; Sun noon–midnight. Bus: 27.

Stortorvets Gjaestgiveri ⊛ NORWEGIAN   The oldest restaurant in Oslo, this is one of the city's most atmospheric dining spots. Many of its dining rooms haven't changed much since the early 18th century, when this was an inn for wayfarers, offering both food and lodging. The venue remains a top choice for the traditional Norwegian cuisine served in both the cafe up front and a more formal restaurant in the rear. To illustrate just how authentic the food is, *Lutefisk*—aged, air-dried cod—a dish abandoned by most chefs as too time-consuming, is still prepared here.

Grensen 1. (✆ **23-35-63-60.** Small platters and snacks in cafe 92NOK–160NOK ($12–$22). Main courses 170NOK–260NOK ($23–$35). AE, DC, MC, V. Mon–Sat 11am–10:30pm.

3 Brødre ⭐ *Finds* NORWEGIAN   Taking its name from three brothers who used to manufacture gloves here, this restaurant attracts both locals and visitors seeking an authentic "taste of Norway." Affordable prices, fresh ingredients, and well-prepared and hearty portions are the hallmarks of this long-time favorite, with a lively bar on the ground floor and more dining upstairs and on a summer terrace.

Øvre Slottsgate 14. (✆ **23-10-06-70.** Reservations recommended. Main courses 150NOK–250NOK ($20–$34). AE, DC, MC, V. Restaurant Mon–Sat 4pm–1am; bar Mon–Sat 11pm–2:30am. Bus: 27, 29, or 30.

SHOPPING

Many of the leading stores are found along **Karl Johans Gate,** the main street of Oslo, and its many side streets. In the core of the city, there are many other shops ringing **Stortovet,** the main square of town. These shops tend to special-ize in local goods such as enameled silver jewelry and handcrafts. If you're inter-ested in Norwegian crafts, check out **Baerum Verk,** Verksgata 15, Baerum Verk (✆ **67-13-00-18**), where you'll find some 65 different shops hawking hand-crafts on-site, especially jewelry and woolens. Some of the best crafts are on dis-play at **Den Norske Husfliden,** Møllergata 4 (✆ **22-42-10-75**), near the marketplace and the cathedral. This is the retail outlet of the Norwegian Asso-ciation of Home Arts and Crafts, an organization founded in 1891 and devoted to quality work. Here you'll find the finest in Norwegian designs, including fur-nishings, woodworking, gifts, textiles, glassware, ceramics, embroidery, and wrought iron. Another fine showcase of crafts is **Norway Designs,** Stortings-gaten 28 (✆ **23-11-45-10**), with its mostly upmarket merchandise with good buys in pewter, jewelry, crystal, and knitwear.

Folk costumes often interest those with Norwegian ancestors, and the best purveyor is **Heimen Husflid,** Rosenkrantzgate 8 (✆ **22-41-40-50**), which offers folkloric clothing from all the different regions of the nation, both north and south. The hand-knit sweaters in traditional Norwegian patterns are an especially good buy.

Hadeland Glassverk, Jevnaker (✆ **61-31-64-00**), is the most famous name in Norwegian glass and has been since 1762. Craftspeople on-site will show you how glass is blown and shaped, and you can also visit an on-site glass museum. All the items here are of the highest quality and are guaranteed.

A lot of hawked souvenirs are pure junk, but not at **William Schmidt,** Fr. Nansens Plads 9 (✆ **22-42-02-88**), the leading vendor of quality Norwegian souvenirs since 1853. Its pewter items range from Viking ships to beer goblets, and many sealskin items, such as moccasins and handbags, are also sold. Prepare for winter with one of the first-class hand-knit cardigans, pullovers, or gloves. All the sweaters are made from 100% Norwegian wool.

NIGHTLIFE

With more than 100 night cafes, restaurants, and clubs, Oslo rocks around the clock. From the tourist office or your hotel reception desk, pick up a copy of *What's On in Oslo* to see what's happening at the time of your visit. Tickets to many events, including ballets, opera, and the theater are sold at **Billettsentralen,** Karl Johans Gate 35 (✆ **81-53-31-33**). Note that from June 20 to the middle of

August, Oslo goes into a cultural slumber—Oslovians are too busy enjoying their natural surroundings while the summer sun shines to go to the theater.

Their city's **Nationaltheatret,** Johanne Dybwads Plass 1 (*✆* **81-50-08-11**), is world famous, but it's only for theater buffs who want to see Ibsen or Bjørnson performed in the original Norwegian language. There are no performances in July and August; otherwise, tickets range from 180NOK to 300NOK ($24–$41) for adults or 85NOK to 170NOK ($11–$23) for students and seniors.

Even if you don't speak Norwegian, you might want to attend a performance of **Den Norske Opera,** the Norwegian National Opera Company at Storgaten 23 (*✆* **23-31-50-00**), the leading venue for ballet and opera, although there are no performances from mid-June to August. Tickets cost 170NOK to 320NOK ($23–$43) except for galas.

Visitors should catch a performance of **Det Norske Folkloreshowet (Norwegian Folklore Show)** performed from July to early September at the **Oslo Konserthus,** Munkedamnsveien 15 (*✆* **23-11-31-11**). One-hour performances are at 8:30pm on Monday and Thursday, with tickets costing 160NOK ($22) for adults, 90NOK to 110NOK ($12–$15) for children. The ensemble at the **Norwegian Folk Museum** (p. 679) often presents folkloric performances at its open-air theater in summer. Check *What's On in Oslo* for details.

Although not the equal of Stockholm or Copenhagen, Oslo has its fair share of dance clubs, including the hottest ticket, **Smuget,** Rosenkrantzgate 22 (*✆* **22-42-52-62**), behind the Grand Hotel in the center of town. It offers the liveliest dance floor in town and a stage where live bands perform. Live music plays from 11pm to 3am, and there's recorded music from 10pm till very late. Cover ranges from 60NOK to 100NOK ($8.10–$14).

A conventional pub most evenings, **Herr Nilsen,** C. J. Hambros Plass 5 (*✆* **22-33-54-05**), is also a venue for the best recorded jazz in the city—everything from prospective to Dixieland. The cover ranges from 75NOK to 100NOK ($10–$14). Open Monday to Saturday noon to 3am, Sunday 3pm to 3am. One of the largest venues for jazz and rock is the **Rockefeller Music Hall,** Torggata 16 (*✆* **22-20-32-32**), where tickets for live concerts range from 100NOK ($14) to as much as 700NOK ($95), the latter price charged only for big groups. The convert hall and club is open Sunday to Thursday 8pm to 2:30am, Friday and Saturday 9pm to 3:30am.

Buddha Bar, Klingenberggata 4 (*✆* **22-82-86-50**), evokes memories of New York's Studio 54 in its heyday in the 70s. Long lines of hipsters form on weekends, a combination of gay and straight, and various hues in between. Recorded music blasts away, and the on-site restaurant late at night is the liveliest in Oslo. Sometimes a cover of 70NOK ($9.45) is charged, and hours are Tuesday to Sunday 7pm to 3am.

Our favorite Oslovian night cafe is **Lorry,** Parkveien 12 (*✆* **22-69-69-04**), a suds-drenched cafe/restaurant established 120 years ago and still going strong at its location across the street from a park flanking the Royal Palace. An outdoor terrace is a magnet in summer, or else you can retreat inside to enjoy 130 different kinds of beer and a young convivial crowd of both locals and visitors. Open Monday to Saturday 11am to 3am, Sunday noon to 1am.

3 Bergen

Many rail passengers head straight for Bergen, bypassing Oslo altogether for Norway's second city because it's the gateway to the western fjord district. In spite of the fact it's swarming with thousands of visitors and cruise-ship passengers during

Bergen

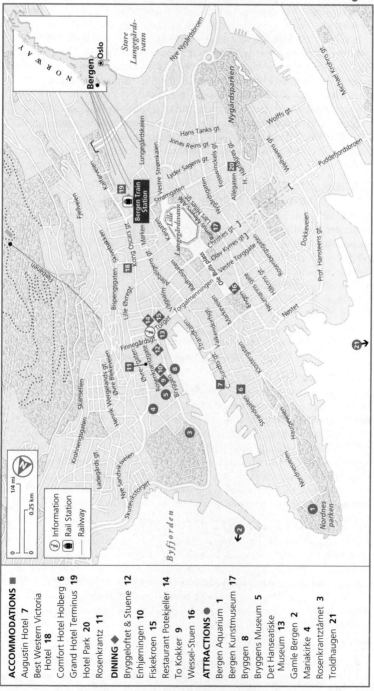

NORWAY

Store
Lungegårds-
vann

●Oslo

Bergen
●

Nye Nygårdsbroen

Lungegårdskaien

Nygårdsparken

Hans Tanks gt.

Jonas Reins gt.

Wolffs gt.

Vestre Strømkaien

Lyder Sagens gt.

Puddefjordsbroen

Strømgaten

Bergen Train
Station **19**

Marken

18 Kong Oscars gt.

Skivebakken

Lille Øvregt.

Bispengsgaten

Kalfarveien

Fjellveien

Fløibanen

17

Christies gt.

Olav Kyrres gt.

16

Rådhusgaten

Torgalmenningen

Ole Vestre Torggate

Vågsbunn

14

15

Torget

13

i

12

11

Øvre-
gaten

Rosenkrantzgate

9 **10**

8

Bryggen

5

4

7

6

3

Strandgaten

Kloostergaten

Nøstet

Skuteviksveien

Henrik Wergelands gt.
Øvre Blekeveien

Skanselien

Krohengaten

Ladegårds gt.

Nye Sandviksveien

Skuteviksstorget

1

*Nordnes
parken*

2

Byfjorden

21 →

Neumanns gate

Prof. Hansteens gt.

N

1/4 mi

0.25 km

0

i Information

🚉 Rail Station

— Railway

ACCOMMODATIONS ■
Augustin Hotel **7**
Best Western Victoria
    Hotel **18**
Comfort Hotel Holberg **6**
Grand Hotel Terminus **19**
Hotel Park **20**
Rosenkrantz **11**

DINING ◆
Bryggeloftet & Stuene **12**
Enhjørningen **10**
Fiskekroen **15**
Restaurant Potekjeller **14**
To Kokker **9**
Wessel-Stuen **16**

ATTRACTIONS ●
Bergen Aquarium **1**
Bergen Kunstmuseum **17**
Bryggen **8**
Bryggens Museum **5**
Det Hanseatiske
    Museum **13**
Gamle Bergen **2**
Mariakirke **4**
Rosenkrantztårnet **3**
Troldhaugen **21**

its short summer, the city at its core manages to retain the feeling of a large country town.

In history, it was the former capital of Norway, having been founded in 1170, and Bergen enjoyed its heyday as the most important trading center for the powerful Hanseatic League of the Middle Ages. Like Oslo, Bergen is scenically located in a sheltered position between a string of islands to its west and the famous silhouette of seven mountains to its east.

Still a maritime city, it is known even today for its fishing industries and shipbuilding. Its unique harborfront, with its old Hanseatic buildings, is today one of UNESCO's World Heritage Sites. Increasingly cosmopolitan in spite of its villagelike center, Bergen is more and more becoming a city of culture—in fact, it launched the new millennium as the "European City of Culture" in 2000.

STATION INFORMATION
GETTING FROM THE AIRPORT TO THE TRAIN STATION
Should you opt to fly into Bergen, say, from London or Copenhagen, you'll land at the **Bergen Airport** in Flesland, 12 miles (19km) south of the city. Planes operated by airlines such as **SAS** (© **67-59-60-50**) and **Braathens SAFE** (© **55-99-82-50**) service Bergen.

Frequent buses connect the airport to the center of town, departing every 20 minutes Monday to Friday or every 30 minutes Saturday and Sunday; a one-way ticket costs 60NOK ($8.10). A taxi from the airport to the city center, including the rail station, costs from 265NOK ($36). However, chances are that you will not be flying into Bergen and quickly boarding a train for some other destination in Norway, since most visitors head to Bergen and the fjord country as a destination unto itself and not necessarily a stopover en route to somewhere else.

INSIDE THE STATION
The stone-constructed **Bergen Train Station** (© **81-50-08-88**), is a 7- to 10-minute walk south of the harbor, along the street from the entrance to the Bergen Storsenter Shopping Mall, which also houses the city's bus station. Trains from Oslo pull in here. On-site is a luggage storage facility, open daily 7am to 10:50pm, that charges 20NOK to 40NOK ($2.70–$5.40) per day. Because the station is so close to the city center, services such as ATMs, restaurants, currency exchange, pharmacies, and more, are in the immediate vicinity of the station.

There is no tourist office within the station itself, but the city's visitor information center is just a 10-minute walk away (see below).

INFORMATION ELSEWHERE IN THE CITY
The **Bergen Tourist Office,** Bryggen 7 (© **55-32-14-80**), in the center of town, provides information, maps, and brochures about Bergen and the fjord district. It also makes hotel reservations for 50NOK ($6.75). You can exchange foreign currency and cash traveler's checks here when the banks are closed. You can also purchase city sightseeing tickets here or book tours of the fjords. Open June to August daily 8:30am to 10pm; May and September daily 9am to 8pm; October to April Monday to Saturday 9am to 4pm.

GETTING AROUND
The **Bergen Card** entitles you to free bus transportation and (usually) free museum admission throughout Bergen, plus discounts on car rentals, parking, and some cultural and leisure activities. It's a good value. Ask for it at the Bergen Tourist Office (see above). A 24-hour card costs 165NOK ($22) for adults,

70NOK ($9.45) for children 3 to 15. A 48-hour card is 245NOK ($33) or 105NOK ($14). Children under 3 generally travel or enter free.

The **Central Bus Station** (Bystasjonen), Strømgaten 8 (✆ 55-55-90-70), is the terminal for all buses serving the Bergen and Hardanger areas, as well as the airport bus. The station has luggage storage, shops, and a restaurant. City buses are marked with their destination and route number. For **bus information** in the Bergen area, call ✆ **177.** A network of yellow-sided city buses serves the city center only. For information, call ✆ **55-59-32-00.**

You can call a **taxi** by dialing **07000.** Sightseeing by taxi, a bit of a luxury, costs 390NOK ($53) for the first hour and 300NOK ($41) for each additional hour.

You can take a ferry across the harbor Monday to Friday from 7am to 4:15pm; they don't run on Saturday or Sunday. One-way fares are 12NOK ($1.60) for adults, 6NOK (80¢) for children. Ferries arrive and depart from either side of the harbor at Dreggekaien and Munkebryggen. For information, call ✆ **55-32-14-80.**

WHERE TO STAY

Augustin Hotel ⭐ *Finds*   Right on the harborfront, this well-run hotel enjoys some of the best scenic views in the city. Managed by the same family for four generations, it was built in 1909 in the Art Nouveau style but added a new wing in 1999. For tradition and old-fashioned comfort, book one of the rooms in the old section; for the latest in amenities, opt for the new wing.

Carl Sundts Gate 24, N-5004 Bergen. ✆ **55-30-40-40.** Fax 55-30-40-10. www.augustin.no. 109 units. 1,550NOK ($209) double, 1,890NOK ($255) suite. AE, DC, MC, V. Bus: 2 or 4. **Amenities:** Restaurant; bar; laundry; nonsmoking rooms; rooms for those with limited mobility. *In room:* Hair dryer.

Best Western Victoria Hotel ⭐ *Value*   A family-run hotel in the center of town, this Best Western affiliate is close to the train station, the fish market, and the historic Hanseatic buildings at Bryggen. You can walk to virtually any point of interest in town. Small and offering personalized service, the hotel features recently redecorated and comfortable bedrooms, containing pieces of birch veneer furnishings, modern artwork, and midsize bathrooms with showers.

Kong Oscarsgt. 29, N-5017 Bergen. ✆ **800/528-1234** in the U.S., or 55-21-23-00. Fax 55-21-23-60. www. victoriahotel.no. 43 units. Mid–May to mid–Sept 1,490NOK ($201) double; mid–Sept to mid–May Mon–Thurs 1,030NOK ($139) double, Fri–Sun 1,490NOK ($201) double. Rates include breakfast. Bus: 2 or 4. **Amenities:** Greek restaurant under separate ownership; bar; laundry; nonsmoking rooms. *In room:* Hair dryer.

Comfort Hotel Holberg ⭐   This hotel, a 15-minute walk from Bergen's Fish Market, is named for Holberg, the famous 18th-century Norwegian writer and dramatist and the lobby is a virtual shrine to the author. The midsize bedrooms are decorated in a modernized Norwegian farmhouse style, with wooden floors, half-paneling stained in forest green, and large windows. Half the tiled bathrooms have tubs and showers; the rest have showers only.

Strandgaten 190, Nordnes, N-5817 Bergen. ✆ **55-30-42-00.** Fax 55-23-18-20. www.choicehotels.no. 140 units. Mon–Thurs 790NOK–1,560NOK ($107–$211) double; Fri–Sat 890NOK ($120) double. Rates include breakfast. AE, DC, MC, V. **Amenities:** Restaurant; bar; laundry; nonsmoking rooms; rooms for those with limited mobility.

Grand Hotel Terminus   Opposite the rail station, this enduring favorite and Bergen landmark opened in 1928 as the city's first luxury hotel. The great explorer of the Arctic wastelands, Roald Amundsen, used to be a guest. The classically elegant atmosphere of the old days remains despite an upgrade in the mid-1990s. The small to midsize bedrooms are comfortably and traditionally furnished and have a host of modern amenities.

Zander Kaaesgate 6, N-5001 Bergen. ✆ **55-31-16-55**. Fax 55-21-25-01. www.grand-hotel-terminus.no. 131 units. 1,460NOK ($197) double; 1,660NOK ($224) suite. Rates include breakfast. AE, DC, MC, V. Bus: 2 or 4. **Amenities:** Restaurant; bar; laundry; nonsmoking rooms; rooms for those with limited mobility. *In room:* Hair dryer.

Hotel Park ✯   A 10-minute walk from the rail station, this family-run hotel is set in a converted 1890 town house. The spacious to midsize rooms are traditionally furnished, and with antiques. Bathrooms are tiny. The bountiful Norwegian breakfast is one of the reasons to stay here. *Note:* In summer, the Park uses a nearby building (furnished in the same style) to accommodate its overflow.

Harald Hårfagresgaten 35 and Allegaten 20, N-5007 Bergen. ✆ **55-54-44-00**. Fax 55-54-44-44. www.park hotel.no. 33 units. 980NOK ($132) double. Rates include breakfast. **Amenities:** Breakfast room; lounge; nonsmoking rooms. *In room:* Hair dryer.

Rosenkrantz ✯   Near Bryggen, the historic Hanseatic port, this restored 1921 hotel enjoys a bull's-eye central location. For such a small place, it offers a surprising array of entertainment possibilities ranging from a piano bar to a nightclub with live music, and its notable on-site restaurant, Harmoni, is patronized by locals and visitors alike. The midsize bedrooms are pleasantly and comfortably furnished, each with a good-size bathroom.

Rosenkrantzgate 7, N-5003 Bergen. ✆ **55-31-50-00**. rosenkrantzrainbow-hotels.no. 129 units. 1,540NOK ($208) double. Rates include breakfast. AE, DC, MC, V. Bus: 1, 5, or 9. **Amenities:** Restaurant; bar; laundry; nonsmoking rooms; rooms for those with limited mobility. *In room:* Hair dryer.

TOP ATTRACTIONS & SPECIAL MOMENTS

On your first day, explore the top attractions of Bergen, including the old Hanseatic Bryggen and its museums, and discover the shops and artisans' workshops along the harborfront. End your day by taking a funicular to Fløien for a panoramic view of Bergen and its waterfront and have a fish dinner in an old tavern. On day 2, head out to Troldhaugen, the summer villa of the fabled composer, Edvard Grieg, and return to Bergen in time to walk through Gamble Bergen, a re-created old town from the 18th and 19th centuries.

For orientation purposes and to gain a convenient overview of the attractions of Bergen, you can take a 3-hour city tour offered daily at 10am May to September, costing 300NOK ($41) for adults or 160NOK ($22) for children. The tour covers all the major attractions, including Troldhaugen and Bryggen. For information and tickets, contact **Tourist Information** at Bryggen 7 (✆ **55-32-14-80**).

Akavriet (Bergen Aquarium) ✯✯   One of the biggest and most impressive aquariums in Scandinavia is only a 15-minute walk from the historic center. If it swims off the coast of Bergen, it's swimming here. The aquarium's mammoth outdoor tank holds seals and penguins, and some 70 indoor tanks are home to a host of colorful sea life. It's almost mesmerizing to watch the schools of herring or anglerfish glide by in complete synchronization. Most popular are the penguin feedings scheduled May to September at 11am, 3pm, and 6pm, or October to April at noon and 3pm.

Nordnesbakken 4. ✆ **55-55-71-71**. Admission 100NOK ($14) adults, 50NOK ($6.75) children; 200NOK ($27) family ticket. May–Aug daily 9am–7pm; Sept–Apr daily 10am–6pm. Bus: 11 from the Fish Market.

Bergen Kunstmuseum (Bergen Art Museum)   The museum is composed of three galleries situated in three separate buildings overlooking the lake, Lille Lungegardsvann. This is really three museums in one—Bergen Billedgalleri,

Moments Strolling Medieval Bergen

Bryggen ⭐⭐⭐, a row of Hanseatic timbered houses rebuilt along the waterfront after the disastrous fire of 1702, is all that remains of medieval Bergen. Fires have damaged this area repeatedly over the centuries (last in 1955) because of the wooden structures, but much has been restored, enough so that the site has been added to UNESCO's World Heritage List. It's now a center for arts and crafts, where painters, weavers, and craftspeople have their workshops. You'll need at least 2 hours to walk and explore the old wharf.

To see what Bergen was like in the Middle Ages, enter **Det Hanseatiske Museum** ⭐, Finnegårdsgaten 1A, Bryggen (✆ **55-31-41-89**), which is the best preserved of the wooden buildings of old Bryggen. Today the building is furnished with authentic artifacts from the early 18th century. Living conditions, as you can clearly see, were sparse. No heating or lighting was allowed in these old buildings because of the danger of fire. Hours June to August are daily 9am to 5pm; September to May daily 11am to 2pm. Admission is 25NOK ($3.40) for adults, free for children. Bus: 1, 5, or 9.

Also at Bryggen, you can visit the **Bryggens Museum** (✆ **55-58-80-10**), displaying artifacts uncovered in excavations from 1955 to 1972. This museum illustrates the daily life of Bergensers in the medieval times. Foundations more than 8 centuries old have been incorporated into today's exhibits. Admission is 30NOK ($4.05) for adults, free for children. Open May to August Tuesday to Sunday 10am to 5pm; September to April Tuesday to Saturday 11am to 2pm, Sunday 11am to 3pm. Bus: 1, 5, or 9.

Stenersen Collection, and the Rasmus Meyers Collection. The collection of 18th and 19th-century international art is superb and wide ranging with some of the finest artists in Europe on display here, including Joan Miró, Picasso, Braque, and Kandinsky. The Stenersen Collection, for example, has one of Europe's finest assemblages of the **works of Paul Klee** ⭐⭐. In the Rasmus Meyers collection is a parade of **Edvard Munch masterpieces** ⭐⭐. Turn to the Billed-galleri to see the works of Norway's old masters, including Edvard Munch (the leader of the pack), I.C. Dahl, Lars Hertevig, Harreit Backer, and Christian Krohg.

Rasmus Meyers Allé, 3-7 and Lars Hillesgate 10. ✆ **55-56-80-00**. Admission 35NOK–50NOK ($4.75–$6.75) adults, free for children. May 15–Sept 15 daily 11am–5pm; Sept 16–May 14 Tues–Sun 11am–5pm. Bus: 1, 5, or 9.

Gamle Bergen ⭐   North of the city center, this open-air museum is one of the finest along the western coast of Norway, re-creating life as lived in the 18th and 19th centuries in a parklike setting. More than 40 wooden buildings were moved here from western Norway and reassembled. This Old Town comes with old-fashioned streets as well as narrow cobblestone alleyways, converging on an open square. The houses are furnished with pieces authentic to the era. You can visit such sites as a photographer's studio from the turn of the 20th century, a merchant's living room in the style of the 1870s, a baker's house and shop, even the abode of a poor seamstress circa 1860.

Elsesro and Sandviken. ℂ **55-39-43-00**. Admission 50NOK ($6.75) adults, 25NOK ($3.40) children and students. Houses mid–May to Aug only, guided tours daily on the hour 10am–5pm. Park and on-site restaurant daily noon–6pm. Bus: 1 or 9 from the city center every 10 minutes.

Mariakirke ★★ The oldest building in Bergen (its exact date is unknown, but it was built sometime in the 12th c.) is this Romanesque church, one of the most beautiful in Norway. It's been in continuous use since the day it opened, having been spared destruction from the numerous fires that swept over this "city of wood." The oldest artifact is an impressive 15th-century triptych behind the altar, and there's a baroque pulpit, donated by Hanseatic merchants, with carved figures depicting everything from Chastity to Naked Truth.

Dreggen. ℂ **55-31-59-60**. Admission 10NOK ($1.35) for adults, free for children. May 18–Sept 9 Mon–Fri 11am–4am; Sept 10–May 17 Tues–Fri noon–1:30pm. Bus: 5, 9, 20, 21, or 22.

Rosenkrantztårneet ★ Scottish masons, who incorporated a mammoth keep from 1270, designed this tower in the 1560s as both a defensive tower and a residence. The tower was named for Erik Rosenkrantz, the governor of Bergen Castle. In 1560, the tower and residence were reconstructed and enlarged. A small octagonal tower, crowned by a cupola, surmounts the Renaissance facade

---

⌐ Moments Norway's Most Dramatic Train Ride

The train ride from Bergen to the little resort of Flåm has been called "Norway in a Nutshell." This **12-hour tour** ★★★ is the most scenically captivating in the entire country, the breadth and diversity of its landscapes encapsulating the majesty of the country's fjords and mountains. Year-round, the train to Flåm departs daily at 8:11am from the Bergen Rail Station. After a 2-hour ride, you disembark in the mountaintop hamlet of Myrdral where you can sightsee for 20 minutes. In Myrdal, you board a cog railway for one of the world's most dramatic inclined train rides. On the 1-hour trip down to the village of Flåm, you'll drop a steep 2,900 feet while passing roaring streams and seemingly endless waterfalls.

After a 1-hour stopover in Flåm, where you can have lunch or take a brief hike, you can board a fjord steamer for a ride along **Sognefjord** ★★★, Norway's longest and deepest fjord, a geologic and panoramic marvel. You reach the fjord-side town of Gudvangen after a 2-hour ride. After a 30-minute break in Gudvangen, you board a bus for the 75-minute ride to the summer and winter resort of Voss, where you can spend half an hour or so before boarding a train for the 75-minute ride back to Bergen, where you'll arrive at 8:18pm.

On the downside, you can expect only a rushed overview at each stopover. And know also that there is more scenery here than you can really digest in just a 12-hour day. The round-trip fare, excluding meals, is 705NOK ($95) for adults or 355NOK ($48) for children under 12. Eurail and Scanrail passholders get a 30% discount. For more information, call the **Bergen Tourist Office** at ℂ **55-32-14-80** or contact Rail Europe.

Moments Something Fishy

There is no livelier place in Bergen than the open-air **Fisketorget (Fish Market)** held every Monday to Saturday 7am to 3pm at the **Torget** along the harborfront. You can wander at will through the crowds drawn to the colorful stands where a wide variety of fresh fish is hawked, especially kippers, smoked salmon, and shellfish. We prefer to feast here at lunch on freshly made smoked salmon sandwiches. In addition to fish, there is fruit as well as hawkers peddling flowers, vegetables, and even handcrafts and souvenirs. You can also pick up the makings of a picnic lunch here. And bring your camera—the sight of the vendors in their bright orange rubber overalls makes a great photo op.

of this five-floor building. Although heavily damaged in an explosion in the harbor during the Nazi era, the tower was reconstructed. From the battlements, a panoramic view of Bergen can be enjoyed.

Bergenhus Bradbenken. © **55-31-43-80.** Admission 20NOK ($2.70) adults, 10NOK ($1.35) children. May 15–Aug 31 daily 10am–4pm; Sept 1–May 14 Sun noon–3pm. Bus: 1, 5, or 9.

Troldhaugen   This Victorian house, high on a hill overlooking Lake Nordås just outside of Bergen, was the summer villa of composer Edvard Grieg. The house contains Grieg's own furniture, paintings, and other mementos. His Steinway grand piano is frequently used at concerts given in the house during the annual Bergen festival, as well as at Troldhaugen's own summer concerts. Grieg and his wife, Nina, are buried in a cliff grotto on the estate—follow the marked pathway across the wooded grounds.

Troldhaugveien 65, Hop. © **55-91-17-91.** Admission 50NOK ($6.75) adults, free for children. May–Sept daily 9am–6pm; Oct–Apr Mon–Fri 10am–2pm, Sat–Sun noon–4pm (anticipate some off-season closings and check before going here). Take the bus to Hop at the Central Bus Station (platforms 18–20). Hop is 3 miles (4.8km) from Bergen.

WHERE TO DINE

Bryggeloftet & Stuene *Value* NORWEGIAN   One of the town's better bargains, this harborfront restaurant is an atmospheric choice, with a street-level bar and eating area, evoking 19th-century Bergen, and a more formal restaurant upstairs resting under high ceilings and paneled in wood. Meals here are quintessentially Norwegian—try the grilled filet of reindeer with a creamy wild game sauce.

Bryggen 11. © **55-31-06-30.** Reservations recommended. Main courses 159NOK–275NOK ($21–$37); lunch smørrebrød 85NOK–149NOK ($11–$20). AE, DC, MC, V. Mon–Sat 11am–11:30pm; Sun 1–1:30pm. Bus: 1, 5, or 9.

Enhjørningen (The Unicorn)   SEAFOOD/CONTINENTAL   This is one of the best restaurants in town and one of the most atmospheric. You'll dine in one of several old-fashioned rooms set end-to-end railroad-car style in an old Hanseatic clapboard structure on the Bryggen harborfront. The lunchtime buffet is one of the best dining bargains of town, loaded with meat and fish dishes. The seafood and continental menu in the evening is more refined with such delights as a cognac-marinated Norwegian salmon.

Bryggen. © **55-32-79-19.** Reservations required. Main courses 240NOK–350NOK ($32–$47); set-price buffet lunch 175NOK ($24); set-price menus 395NOK–520NOK ($53–$70). AE, DC, MC, V. June–Sept daily noon–4pm; year-round daily 4–11pm. Closed 2 weeks at Christmas. Bus: 5 or 21.

Fiskekroen ★★★ SEAFOOD/GAME/NORWEGIAN   This 36-seat restaurant—the most exclusive in Bergen—occupies elegant premises at the harborfront complex, with panoramic views of the ships at anchor. The attention to detail and the choice of luxury ingredients ensure our return to this citadel of refined dining and formal service. The menu changes seasonally but may feature game, such as venison, in several different preparations, along with some of the best and freshest fish caught in Norwegian waters.

Zacchariasbrygge 50. ℭ **55-55-96-46.** Reservations required. Main courses 285NOK–345NOK ($38–$47). AE, DC, MC, V. May–Aug Mon–Sat 11am–11pm, Sun 11am–10pm; Sept–Apr Mon–Sat 4–11pm. Bus: 1, 5, or 9.

Restaurant Potekjeller ★ *Finds* NORWEGIAN/ITALIAN   For deluxe dining, Bergen style, this citadel of fine food and formal service is worth every krone. Set inside an antique wood building just steps from the Fish Market, this is one of the city's oldest restaurants, its foundations going back to the mid–15th century. Guests, dining either in the ancient cellar or the more formal dining room upstairs, can partake of an unusual, yet excellent, cuisine that combines some of the best dishes from both the Norwegian and Italian kitchens. Light, inventive cookery is the rule of the day.

Kong Oscargate 1A. ℭ **55-32-00-70.** Reservations required. Set menus 395NOK–585NOK ($53–$79). AE, DC, MC, V. Mon–Sat 4–10pm; bar Mon–Sat till 1am. Bus: 1, 5, or 9.

To Kokker (Two Cooks) ★ FRENCH/NORWEGIAN   Visiting celebrities and savvy local foodies frequent this bastion of good eating, set in a 1703 building adjacent to the old piers and wharves along the harborfront. Start, perhaps, with the velvety smooth lobster soup before going on to—say, reindeer with lingonberry sauce. The chefs here know their craft well and the solid staff offers delightful service in a lovely antique setting.

Enhjørninggarden. ℭ **55-32-28-16.** Reservations required. Main courses 350NOK–695NOK ($47–$94). AE, DC, MC, V. Mon–Sat 5–10pm. Bus: 1, 5, or 9.

Wessel-Stuen NORWEGIAN   Named for the 18th-century humorist, Johan Herman Wessel, this local favorite evokes a wine cellar from the 1700s and is decorated in an old tavern style, with beamed ceilings and an adjoining pub. We are impressed with the recent menu changes, noting that the chefs are becoming more inventive and more attuned to modern taste. You'll still find the classic sirloin steak with Béarnaise sauce, but also a pesto-gratinéed filet of lamb with ratatouille.

Engen 14. ℭ **55-55-49-49.** Reservations recommended. Main courses 139NOK–290NOK ($19–$39); fixed-price menu 85NOK–120NOK ($11–$16). AE, DC, MC, V. Mon–Sat 3–11pm; Sun 11:30am–10pm. Bus: 2, 3, or 4.

SHOPPING

One of the best displays of handcrafts from the western fjord district is the **Torget** or marketplace (p. 689) along the waterfront, the site of a lively fishing market Monday to Saturday. Good buys here include rugs, handmade tablecloths, and woodcarvings.

For one-stop shopping, the leading department store is **Sundt & Co.,** Torgalmenningen (ℭ **55-32-31-00**), although it now has competition from **Galleriet,** Torgalmenningen 8 (ℭ **55-30-05-00**), the largest shopping complex in western Norway, with some 70 different shops.

For good buys in local clothing, head for **Berle Bryggen,** Bryggen (ℭ **55-31-73-00**), along the harbor at the historic core of the old waterfront. The well-stocked emporium offers great buys in sweaters for both men and women as well as souvenirs such as troll dolls, pewter, and other gift items.

Close to the fish market and harbor, the four-floor **Kloverhuset,** Strandgaten 13–15 (✆ **55-31-37-90**), offers the biggest inventory of fashion, including gloves, wool sweaters, and Sami jackets from the north of Norway. Opposite the Flower Market, **Viking Designs,** Strandkaien 2A (✆ **55-31-05-20**), has a prize-winning selection of upmarket knitwear.

The best outlet for handcrafts is in and around **Bryggen Brukskunst,** the Old Town near the wharf. Here local craftspeople have taken over the old buildings and ply their trades in this colorful atmosphere. Some of the items being crafted are based on designs that might go back 3 centuries, even as much as 1,500 years, the latter exemplified by a Romanesque-style cruciform pilgrim's badge.

The leading purveyor of glassware and ceramics is **Prydkunst–Hjertholm,** Olav Kyrres Gate 7 (✆ **55-31-70-27**), much of the merchandise coming directly from artisans' studios, including textiles, pewter, and wood items, along with gifts and souvenirs.

NIGHTLIFE

From June to August, **Bergen Folklore** performs at the Bryggens Museum at Bryggen (✆ **97-52-86-30**), with tickets costing 95NOK ($13) for adults, free for children. The 1-hour program consists of traditional folk dances and music from rural Norway, with tickets on sale at the tourist office (see above). The major cultural venue is **Grieghallen,** Lars Hillesgate 3A (✆ **55-21-61-50**), the 1978 performance hall that is the most prestigious venue in western Norway for music, drama, and other cultural events. The Bergen Symphony Orchestra, founded in 1765, performs here from August to May on Thursday at 7:30pm and Saturday at 12:30pm. It's also the setting for visiting opera productions, with international conductors and soloists performing as well. Tickets cost 100NOK to 350NOK ($14–$47).

The best dance club is **Engelen,** in the Radisson SAS Royal Hotel, Bryggen (✆ **55-54-30-00**; Bus: 1, 5, or 9), open Wednesday to Saturday 9am to 3am, with hot DJs handling the music. Covers range from 60NOK to 80NOK ($8.10–$11). **Rick's Café,** Veiten 3 (✆ **55-55-31-31**; Bus 1, 5, or 9), is also popular locally, with its rooms devoted to cabaret, comedy, or just drinking. Open daily 10pm to 3am; no one under 24 permitted.

The biggest sports pub in Bergen is **Fotballpuben (Football Pub),** Vestre Torggate 9 (✆ **55-35-66-61**; Bus: 1 or 9), a sudsy joint where soccer and rugby ignite passions. Its inner rooms are crowded with a heavy-drinking, sports-loving crowd who watches games on the TV screens up above. Known for its inexpensive beer, the club is open Monday to Thursday 9am to 1am, Friday and Saturday 9am to 2am, and Sunday noon to 1am. The town's most frequented pub is **Kontorget Pub,** in the Hotel Norge, Ole Bulls Plass 8–10 (✆ **55-36-31-33**; Bus: 2, 3, or 4), next to the Dickens Restaurant and Pub. You can order the same food at the Kontoret as in the Dickens, though most people come here to drink. It's open Sunday to Thursday 4pm to 1am, and Friday noon to 2am.

17

Portugal

Occupying the Iberian Peninsula with the much larger country of Spain, Portugal is a world unto itself, lying in one of the remotest and the least-explored corners of western Europe. In no way are you visiting a "suburb of Spain," as Portugal's harshest critics charge. In history, in language, in culture, and in cuisine, Portugal, in spite of its diminutive size, is very much a nation with a distinctive and remarkable heritage and identity.

For such a small country, the regional diversity is immensely varied and of compelling interest from the beach resorts of the Algarve to the historic capital of Lisbon and onward into the north, embracing not only the city of Porto but the rural Minho where old traditions still prevail and even the most remote province, Trás–os–Montes, where country life goes on much as it did for decades.

Of all the western European countries reviewed in this book, Portugal has the least developed rail system, but what there is will easily, quickly, conveniently—and cheaply—get the train traveler to the country's scenic highlights stretching from Porto, a city famed for its port wine, in the north, to the beach resorts of the Algarve in the south, opening onto the Mediterranean. Portugal's rail system, **Caminhos de Ferro Portugueses (CP),** runs InterCidade trains that link a total of 60 Portuguese cities to Lisbon. To rush you to the north, the high-speed Alfa train connects Lisbon, Porto, and the far northern city of Braga and offers both first- and second-class seating. If there is a real downside to the country for the international rail traveler, it's that Portugal's only international trains links are between Lisbon and Badajoz, Spain, and Porto and the northwestern Galician city of Vigo, Spain. So though we totally recommend a journey to this lovely country, it's best to make it either your first or last stop on a train tour of Europe.

HIGHLIGHTS OF PORTUGAL

The areas of Portugal most easily reached by rail, and most likely to leave lasting and evocative memories, are the capital city of **Lisbon** (of course), situated on the western coast of the country; the sun belt southern coast of the **Algarve;** the enchanting medieval walled town of **Óbidos;** the university city of **Coimbra,** seat of one of the oldest universities in the world and the center of the Portuguese Renaissance; and **Porto,** at the mouth of the River Douro, whose vineyards in the hinterlands beyond produce port wine.

In Portugal, your choice of rail itineraries is more limited: From Lisbon you can go south to the Algarve or north to Óbidos, Coimbra, Porto, and beyond, unless you plan to visit the remote provinces in the eastern plains. No matter which route you choose to take, you won't feel deprived.

The northern route is the most scenic, taking you up the Atlantic coast to the walled town of Óbidos and on to Coimbra, one of the most enchanting university cities in Europe, and even farther north to Porto, center of the country's thriving port wine trade.

Portugal

The journey south from Lisbon to the Algarve doesn't go through the lush green countryside of Portugal the way the trip north does. It takes you across the drier but dramatic plains of Portugal in a land that its former Moorish rulers called *Al-Gharb.* Much of the terrain you'll see outside your train window evokes the northern tier of the African coastline. You'll pass a countryside fabled for its rice paddies, wheat fields, Arabian horses, and black bulls, and can often gaze upon *campinos,* the region's sturdy horsemen dressed in regional garb.

The capital city of Lisbon, even though not central to Portugal the way Madrid is to Spain, is nonetheless the hub of its vast rail networks. Regardless of where you're going in Portugal by rail, you can reach the destination from Lisbon by riding the rails. When the rail lines run out, buses take over to carry you the rest of the way, but that holds true only for the remotest towns and villages.

To make the most of your trip, here's the best way to go about your journey. Spend 3 days in Lisbon. Most of the first day will be used up merely getting to Lisbon. If you arrive in time, you can walk around the **Alfama** (the oldest and most historic district) and end your tour seeing the fantastic panorama afforded by a sunset visit to Castel de São Jorge (St. George's Castle). Start off your next day with a tour of Belém, a suburb of Lisbon, and view the famous Mosteiro dos Jerónimos (Jerónimos Monastery). Toss in some artistic highlights in the afternoon, including the must-see **Museu da Fundacão Calouste Gulbenkian,** one of Europe's artistic treasure troves. Your third day can be spent exploring the satellite town of **Sintra,** Lord Byron's "glorious Eden," and visiting its two national palaces.

⌢Moments Festivals & Special Events

The **Festas dos Santos Populares** is celebrated throughout Lisbon. Celebrations begin on June 13 and 14 in the Alfama, with feasts honoring Saint Anthony. Parades commemorating the city's patron saint feature marchas (parading groups of singers and musicians) along Avenida da Liberdade, singing, dancing, drinking wine, and eating grilled sardines. On June 23 and 24, for the Feast of St. John the Baptist, bonfires brighten the night and participants jump over them. The night of the final celebration is the Feast of St. Peter on June 29. The Lisbon Tourist Office (© **21/346-6307**) supplies details about where some of the events are staged, although much of the action is spontaneous. Mid-June to June 30.

On the first weekend in July, the **Colete Encarnado ("Red Waistcoat")** takes place at Vila Franca de Xira, north of Lisbon on the River Tagus. Like the more famous feria in Pamplona, Spain, this festival involves bulls running through narrow streets, followed by sensational bullfights in what aficionados consider the best bullring in Portugal. Fandango dancing and rodeo-style competition among the Ribatejo campinos (cowboys) mark the event. For more information, call © **26/ 327-6053**.

The **Estoril Festival,** at the seaside resort outside of Lisbon, is a festival of classical music usually run from mid-July to the first week in August (dates vary), which occupies two concert halls that were built for the 500th anniversary of Columbus's first voyage to the New World. For information, write **Associação International de Música da Costa do Estoril,** Casa–Museu Verdades de Faria, Av. Do Faboia 1146, Monte Estoril, call © **21/466-3813**.

For many rail travelers, that will be all the time allotted for Portugal. Those with another 3 days will usually explore the history-rich **Algarve** coast, which stretches for some 100 miles (160km) from Henry the Navigator's Cape St. Vincent to the border town of Vila Real de Santo Antonio adjacent to Spain. This is the region we focus on most in this chapter. To reach the Algarve, take a train from Lisbon to either **Lagos** or **Faro.** Both of these cities make logical bases because of their convenient rail links to Lisbon. By going both east and west from either town you can also explore the more remote villages of interest along the coast. A distinct Arabic flavor still prevails in the region, with its fret-cut chimneys, mosque-like cupolas, and cubist houses.

If you seek culture more than R & R time at a beach, you can spend your remaining 3 days taking in 3 of the major sightseeing targets north of Lisbon, including Óbidos, Coimbra, and Porto. If you only have 1 day, we'd cast our vote for Coimbra. If you have 2 days, then go to Coimbra followed by Porto, and if you have 3 days, then see all three. The rail connections from Coimbra and Porto are easy, less so for Óbidos, although the latter is worth the effort to reach it. See "Northward Ho!" on p. 718 for more information on Portugal's northern highlights.

1 Essentials

GETTING THERE

The major gateway city for flights into Portugal from all over the world is the capital city of Lisbon. International flights land at **Aeroporto de Lisboa** (© 21/ **841-3500**) on the northern edge of Lisbon. The location is 4 miles (6.4km) from the heart of the city. (Instead of flying, however, many rail passengers prefer to get to Lisbon by taking the train west from Madrid after their visit to Spain.)

Flying time from New to York to Lisbon is about 6½ hours.

When it was established in 1946, **TAP** (© 800/221-7370; www.tap-air portugal.us), the national airline of Portugal, flew only between Lisbon and Angola and Mozambique (then Portuguese colonies). Today, TAP flies to four continents and has one of the youngest fleets in the airline industry—its aircraft have an average age of only 4 years. Its U.S. gateway is Newark, New Jersey. In Portugal, it flies to 3 destinations, the most popular of which are Lisbon, Porto, and Faro. Porto is the headquarters of the port wine industry, and Faro is the capital of the Algarve along Portugal's southern coast.

Continental Airlines (© 800/525-0280; www.continental.com) began flying to Lisbon out of Newark International Airport in 1997. The increased capacity comes as a welcome addition to existing air service, particularly during heavy travel periods in summer.

Air Canada (© 800/247-2262; www.aircanada.ca) no longer offers direct flights to Lisbon, but it does offer daily flights from Toronto and Montréal to Paris, where you can transfer to another carrier to reach Lisbon.

For flights from the U.K., contact **British Airways** (© 0845/773-3377, or © 0345/222-111 outside London; www.british-airways.com) or **TAP**, Gillingham House, 3844 Gillingham St., London SW1V 1JW (© 0845/601-0932).

TAP also has frequent flights on popular routes from major cities in western Europe. Its flights to Lisbon from London are an especially good deal; sometimes they're priced so attractively that one might combine a trip to England with an inexpensive rail excursion in Portugal.

PORTUGAL BY RAIL

PASSES

Both the **Eurailpass** and **Eurailpass Flexi** are good for use on Portuguese trains; the **Iberic Railpass** is good on both Spanish and Portuguese trains. See chapter 2 for more details on these passes.

Portugal also has its own railpass: the **Portuguese Railpass** allowing any 4 days of unlimited first-class train travel in a 15-day period, costing $105 per person. Children, ages 4 to 11, are charged half the adult fare. Kids under 4 ride for free. Portuguese trains are run by **Caminhos de Ferro Portugueses** (© 800/ **200-904**; www.cp.pt), the national railway.

Note: All of the passes we mention above must be purchased in North America prior to your departure. Passes can be ordered in North America through **Rail Europe** (© 877/272-RAIL in the U.S., 800/361-RAIL in Canada; www.raileurope.com) or your travel agent.

FOREIGN TRAIN TERMS

Posted schedules—called *horarios* in Portuguese—aren't always accurate, so you should go to the station ticket windows, called *bilheteiras,* instead.

Suburbano trains, as you might have guessed, run to the environs of any city, such as Lisbon. On timetables, the rail line's long-distance international links are marked *IN.*

If you prefer to purchase your rail tickets abroad, when you see the words *Bilhetes turisticos,* that means a tourist ticket and invariably it offers a discount. Families should ask about a *cartão de família,* which offers good discounts to families traveling together.

The complete rail timetable in Portugal, available at train stations, is called *Guia Horario a Oficial.* In larger stations, you'll see ticket windows divided between *Camboios de amanhã e doas segiomtes,* meaning ticket offices for purchasing advance tickets, and *Só para comboios de hoje,* meaning offices in which you buy tickets on the day of travel. Travelers 65 or over might inquire about a *cartão dourado* or senior citizens card. At rail stations, know that *partida* indicates a departure gate and that *chegada* means arrival.

PRACTICAL TRAIN INFORMATION

Originally built by the British, the country's network of rail lines consists mostly of wide-gauge lines for more comfort, and much of the 2,236-mile (3,600km) network is electrified. In some of the more remote parts of Portugal, however, the rail lines are narrow-gauge, resulting in slow travel times.

Whenever possible, board an **Alfa** train. These high-speed carriers run between the most important cities in the north and make only major stops. The best of these trains are the new **Alfa Pendular** express trains racing between Lisbon and Porto, and these trains are as good as any competitor in Europe, with air-conditioning, fine food service, and airline-type seating. Far less luxurious and much slower are the **InterCidade** or **InterCity (IC)** trains linking most major towns and cities of Portugal. These IC trains offer dining and drinking facilities, but passengers for years have complained about the poor quality of the cuisine. The fastest trains that carry no supplements are the **Inter-Regionals (IR).** On less popular routes, you'll likely find yourself aboard one of the slow-moving **Regionals** or **Suburbanos** trains, which stop at every hamlet. Not only that, but travel aboard these lines is spartan at best.

RESERVATIONS These are mandatory on Portuguese trains, and should be made as far in advance as possible. Likewise, railpass validation should be made at designated windows at rail stations. Tickets for IC or Alfa trains can often be booked up to 20 days ahead; in some cases, only 10-day advance bookings are allowed. You can make reservations through travel agents or else go to the station yourself where you'll often have to wait in long lines. You can also make reservations for most Portuguese trains in the U.S. through **Rail Europe (© 877/272-RAIL** in the U.S., 800/361-RAIL in Canada; www.raileurope.com). If you don't have a ticket before boarding, the conductor may fine you. Riding without a ticket *(sem bilhete)* can lead in some cases to exorbitant fines. Reservations are essential on international and express trains, but on many trains they are optional; nevertheless, because all Portuguese trains are likely to be crowded, reservations are advised. They are free if made on the day before departure, though you'll pay $11 if you make them in the U.S. Also note that even if you hold a Eurailpass, you'll need to pay a supplement when traveling the express routes.

SERVICES & AMENITIES *Couchettes*—actually foldout bunk beds—are available in Portugal, and advance reservations are absolutely essential for one of these compartments. Couchettes are rented on the Sud Expresso from Paris to Lisbon and on the Lusitania Express from Madrid to Lisbon. On most trains,

Trains & Travel Times in Portugal

From	To	Type of Train	# of Trains	Frequency	Travel Time
Madrid	Lisbon	Talgo	2	Daily	9 hr. 30 min.
Lisbon	Lagos	IC	5	Daily	5 hr. 30 min.
Lisbon	Faro	IC	4	Daily	4 hr. 15 min.–5 hr. 15 min.
Lisbon	Óbidos	Suburbanos	13	Mon–Fri	1 hr. 46 min.–2 hr. 52 min.
Lisbon	Óbidos	Suburbanos	10	Sat–Sun	1 hr. 55 min.–2 hr. 56 min.
Lisbon	Coimbra	ALFA	7	Daily	1 hr. 51 min.–1 hr. 59 min.
Lisbon	Coimbra	IC	7	Daily	2 hr. 3 min.–2 hr. 6 min.
Lisbon	Porto	ALFA	7	Daily	3 hr. 1 min.–3 hr. 11 min.
Lisbon	Porto	IC	6	Daily	3 hr. 31 min–5 hr. 14 min.
Coimbra	Porto	ALFA	7	Daily	1 hr. 8 min.–1 hr. 11 min.
Coimbra	Porto	Regionals	19	Daily	1 hr. 50 min.–2 hr. 4 min.
Coimbra	Porto	IC	3	Daily	1 hr.–2 hr.

couchettes cost $28 per person. On major runs, you'll also encounter *wagons-lit* or sleepers—bedroom compartments with one to three beds. Most night trains offer full restaurant service, and stewards provide drinks and snacks around the clock. If you need food and drink, always inquire before boarding a train because there's no guarantee they will be available on Portuguese trains. If services aren't available, carry the food and drink you'll need for the journey. Most trains in Portugal are air-conditioned and have adequate restroom facilities.

FAST FACTS: Portugal

Area Codes The most used area code in Portugal is **21** in Lisbon. Other area codes include **28** for both Lagos and Faro (the capital of the Algarve).

Business Hours Hours vary throughout the country, but there is a set pattern. Banks generally are open Monday to Friday from 8:30am to 3pm. Currency exchange offices at airports and rail terminals are open longer hours, and the office at Portela Airport outside Lisbon is open 24 hours a day. Most museums open at 10am, close at 5pm, and often close for lunch between 12:30 and 2pm. Larger museums with bigger staffs can remain open at midday. Shops are open, in general, Monday to Friday from 9am to 1pm and from 3 to 7pm, and Saturday from 9am to 1pm. Most restaurants serve lunch from noon until 3pm and dinner from 7:30 to 11pm; many close on Sunday. Many nightclubs open at 10pm, but the action doesn't really begin until after midnight, and often lasts until the wee hours of the morning.

Climate Summer may be the most popular time to visit Portugal, but for the traveler who can chart his or her own course, spring and autumn are the most delectable seasons. To use a North American analogy, the climate of Portugal most closely parallels that of California. There are only slight fluctuations in temperature between summer and winter; the overall mean ranges from 77°F (25°C) in summer to about 58°F (14°C) in winter. The rainy season begins in November and usually lasts through January. Because of the Gulf Stream, Portugal's northernmost area, Minho, enjoys mild (albeit very rainy) winters, even though it's at approximately the same latitude as New York City.

Snow brings many skiing enthusiasts to the Serra de Estrêla in north central Portugal. For the most part, however, winter means only some rain and lower temperatures in other regions. The Algarve enjoys temperate winters and is somewhat of a winter Riviera that attracts sun worshippers from North America and Europe. Summers in both tend to be long, hot, clear, and dry.

Lisbon and its satellite resort of Estoril enjoy 46°F to 65°F (8°C–18°C) temperatures in winter and temperatures between 60°F and 82°F (16°C–28°C) in summer.

Documents Required If you have a valid passport from the U.S. or Canada and plan to stay no more than 90 days, you do not need a visa to enter Portugal. If you'd like to stay more than 90 days, you can apply for an additional stay at the nearest Portuguese embassy. As a rule, the extension is granted immediately.

Electricity Voltage is 200 volts AC (50 cycles), so you'll need a transformer and an adapter plug—available at most hardware stores in North America—to use your electrical appliances from home in Portugal. The concierge desks of most large hotels can often lend you a transformer and plug adapters, or tell you where you can buy them nearby. If you have any doubt about whether you have the appropriate transformer, ask at your hotel desk before you try to plug in anything.

Embassies & Consulates If you lose your passport or have some other pressing problem, you'll need to get in touch with your embassy. The Embassy of the **United States,** on Avenida das Forças Armadas (Sete Rios), 1600 Lisboa (© 21/727-3300), is open Monday to Friday from 8am to 12:30pm and from 1:30 to 5pm. The Embassy of **Canada** is at Avenida da Liberdade 200,1269 Lisboa (© 21/316-4600). It's open Monday to Friday from 9am to noon and from 2 to 4pm (in July and Aug, the embassy closes at 1pm on Fri).

Health & Safety You should encounter few health problems traveling in Portugal. The tap water is generally safe to drink, the milk is pasteurized, and health services are good. Occasionally, the change in diet may cause some minor diarrhea, so you may want to take some anti-diarrhea medicine along.

Limit your exposure to the sun, especially during the first few days of your trip and, thereafter, from 11am to 2pm. Use a sunscreen with a high protection factor and apply it liberally. Remember that children need more protection than adults do and should wear a hat.

Though Portugal has a relatively low rate of violent crime, petty crime against tourists is on the rise in continental Portugal. Travelers may become targets of pickpockets and purse-snatchers, particularly at popular tourist sites, restaurants, and on public transportation such as trains. Travelers should also avoid using ATMs in isolated or poorly lit areas. In general, visitors to Portugal should carry limited cash and credit cards, and leave extra cash, credit cards, and personal documents at home or in a hotel safe.

Pickpocketing and purse-snatching in the Lisbon area occur in buses, restaurants, the airport, trains, train stations, and trams, *especially tram number 28 to the Castle of São Jorge*. Gangs of youths have robbed passengers on the Lisbon-Cascais train. At restaurants, thieves snatch items hung over the backs of chairs or placed on the floor, so keep a careful eye on your belongings. There have been reports of theft of unattended luggage from the Lisbon Airport. Special care should also be taken at the Santa Apolónia and Rossio train stations, the Alfama and Bairro Alto districts, the Castle of São Jorge, and Belém.

Holidays Watch for these public holidays, and adjust your banking needs accordingly: January 1 (New Year's Day and Universal Brotherhood Day); Carnaval, early March (dates vary); Good Friday, March or April (dates vary); April 25 (Liberty Day, anniversary of the revolution); May 1 (Labor Day); Corpus Christi, June (dates vary); June 10 (Portugal Day); August 15 (Feast of the Assumption); October 5 (Proclamation of the Republic); November 1 (All Saints' Day); December 1 (Restoration of Independence); December 8 (Feast of the Immaculate Conception); and December 25 (Christmas Day). June 13 (Feast Day of St. Anthony) is a public holiday in Lisbon, and June 24 (Feast Day of St. John the Baptist) is a public holiday in Porto.

Legal Aid Contact your local consulate for a list of English-speaking lawyers if you run into trouble with the law. After that, you're at the mercy of the local courts.

Mail While in Portugal, you may have your mail directed to your hotel (or hotels), to the American Express representative, or to General Delivery *(Poste Restante)* in Lisbon. You must present your passport to pick up mail. The general post office in Lisbon is on Praça do Comércio, 1100 Lisbon (© 21/346-3231); it's open daily from 8am to 10pm.

Police & Emergencies For the police (or an ambulance) in Lisbon, call **115.** In case of fire, call © 32-22-22 or 60-60-60. For the Portuguese Red Cross, call © 61-77-77. The national emergency number in Portugal is **115.**

Telephone Portugal Telecom phones accept coins or a prepaid phone card. Calling from a booth with the right change or card allows you to avoid high hotel surcharges. Put coins in a slot at the top of the box while you hold the receiver, then dial your number after hearing the dial tone. Once a connection is made, the necessary coins will automatically drop. If enough coins are not available, your connection will be broken. A warning tone will sound and a light over the dial will go on if more coins are needed. For long-distance (trunk) calls within the country, dial the city code, followed by the local number. *Note:* If you see a city code that begins with a zero, drop this initial zero and substitute a "2."

At "CrediFone" locations and at post offices, special phones take pre-paid cards sold at post offices.

Telephone calls can also be made at all post offices, which also send telegrams. International calls are made by dialing **00** (double zero), followed by the country code, the area code (not prefaced by 0), then the local phone number. The country code for the United States and Canada is **1**. The country code for Portugal is **351**.

Tipping   Most service personnel in Portugal expect a good tip rather than a small one, as in the past. Hotels add a service charge (known as *serviço*), which is divided among the entire staff, but individual tipping is also the rule. Tip .75€ (85¢) to the bellhop for running an errand, .50€ (60¢) to the doorman who hails you a cab, .75€ to 1€ (85¢–$1.15) to the porter for each piece of luggage carried, 2.50€ ($2.90) to the wine steward if you've dined often at your hotel, and 1.50€ ($1.75) to the chambermaid. In first-class or deluxe hotels, the concierge will present you with a separate bill for extras, such as charges for bullfight tickets. A gratuity is expected in addition to the charge. The amount will depend on the number of requests you've made.

Figure on tipping about 20% of your taxi fare for short runs. For longer treks—for example, from the airport to Cascais—15% is adequate. Restaurants and nightclubs include a service charge and government taxes of 17.5%. As in hotels, this money is distributed among the entire staff—not to mention the waiter's mistress and the owner's grandfather—so extra tipping is customary. Add about 5% to the bill in a moderately priced restaurant, up to 10% in a deluxe or first-class establishment. For hat-check in fado houses, restaurants, and nightclubs, tip at least .50€ (60¢). Washroom attendants also get .50€ (60¢).

2 Lisbon

This capital city's greatest glory came in the 15th and 16th centuries during Portugal's Age of Discovery when mariners such as Vasco da Gama sailed from here to explore the uncharted seas of the world. Those discoveries, such as the first sea route from western Europe around Africa to the Indies, launched the spice trade and brought great wealth to the city, ushering in the golden age of Lisbon when it became known as the "Queen of the Tagus River."

Trouble was on the way in the centuries ahead, including a devastating earth-quake in 1755, but Lisbon has bounced back from its many disasters and is waiting to greet you today. In spite of extensive rebuilding and modernization, the old charm of Lisbon still remains, especially in its most traditional quarter, the Alfama.

Lisbon is still benefiting from the 1998 face-lift it gave itself when it hosted the World Expo. Many construction projects were completed for that spectacle, and most of these have been recycled to benefit today's visitor.

Lisbon

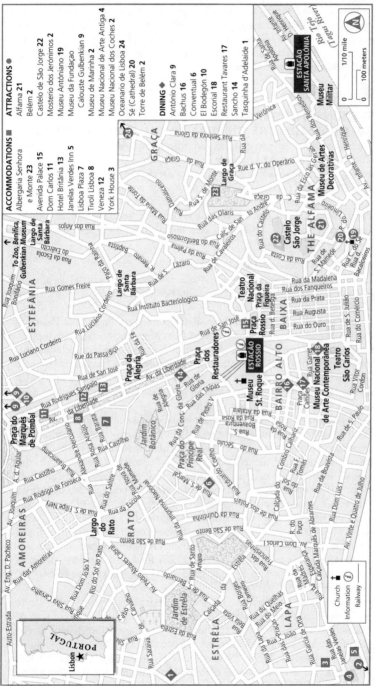

ACCOMMODATIONS ■
Albergaria Senhora
e Monte 23
Avenida Palace 15
Dom Carlos 11
Hotel Britânia 13
Janelas Verdes Inn 5
Lisboa Plaza 7
Tivoli Lisboa 8
Veneza 12
York House 3

ATTRACTIONS ●
Alfama 21
Belém 2
Castelo de São Jorge 22
Mosteiro dos Jerónimos 2
Museu Antóniano 19
Museu da Fundação
  Calouste Gulbenkian 9
Museu de Marinha 2
Museu Nacional de Arte Antiga 4
Museu Nacional dos Coches 2
Oceanario de Lisboa 24
Sé (Cathedral) 20
Torre de Belém 2

DINING ◆
António Clara 9
Bachus 16
Conventual 6
El Bodegón 10
Escorial 18
Restaurant Tavares 17
Sancho 14
Tasquinha d'Adelaide 1

Allow at least 3 days to skim the highlights of Portugal's capital, sitting on the north bank of the Tagus estuary, some 10 miles (16km) from the Atlantic. With a population of some 700,000, it is a busy, bustling metropolis and port, noted for its cuisine (especially seafood), monuments, great art, fado music cafes, fashionable bars and clubs, and great shops. It is also the best center for touring anywhere in Portugal by rail, including spectacular Sintra, located in the immediate environs of Lisbon.

STATION INFORMATION
GETTING FROM THE AIRPORT TO THE TRAIN STATIONS
There is no direct rail service from Portugal's airport. After a long flight many passengers arriving at the Aeroporto de Lisboa prefer to take a taxi to meet a connecting train. The average taxi fare to one of the city's main train stations ranges from 10€ to 15€ ($11.50–$17.25), depending on how heavy traffic is; an additional charge of 1.50€ ($1.75) is leveled for each piece of luggage. Less expensive is the AERO-BUS that takes passengers between the airport and the Cais do Sodré train station, departing every 20 minutes from 7am to 9pm. The cost is 2.45€ ($2.80) one-way.

INSIDE THE STATIONS
Lisbon has a confusing number of rail stations—some with a full range of services such as Estação Rossio or Estação Santa Apolónia, others with more meager offerings.

Estação Rossio lies between Praça Restauradores and Praça Dom Pedro IV (Metro: Rossio or Restauradores). Trains from here mostly service day-trippers and commuters from the bedroom communities around Lisbon, including the former royal palaces at Quéluz and Sintra. Rossio is the smallest, oldest, and most lavishly decorated of the stations of Lisbon, and the site of that grand dowager hotel, Avenida Palace. It's set in the heart of the city so you don't need to worry about public transport links to it.

Rossio remains a vintage, somewhat outmoded piece of architecture, evoking the Manueline architecture of the great Portuguese kings, and is a sightseeing attraction in its own right. There is no tourist office here but one lies nearby (see below). You will find money exchange kiosks, restaurants, and bars. On the ground floor is a little information office, dispensing routine advice daily from 10am to 1pm and 2 to 7pm. For domestic travel, a window is open daily from 7am to 3:30pm, with an international window open daily from 9:15am to noon and 1 to 5:30pm. Both of these offices are staffed by English-speaking attendants. Most visitors to Lisbon pass through here to catch a train to Sintra. Trains depart on tracks 4 and 5 every 15 to 30 minutes from 6am to 2am daily, the trip taking 45 minutes and costing 1.10€ ($1.25) for a one-way ticket. Luggage storage is available here daily from 8:30am to 11:30pm, a locker costing 3€ ($3.45) for 48 hours.

Estação Santa Apolonia, Av. Infante Dom Henrique, lies east of the Alfama on the banks of the Tagus River, 2 miles (2½km) east of the center of Lisbon. Depending on traffic, it takes a taxi from 5 to 10 minutes to reach the center of town from this station, with an average fare costing 5€ ($5.75). It's also possible to go by buses 9, 28, 46, 59, and 90, a one-way fare going for 1€ ($1.15). Major national and international trains pull in here, including those from Paris and Madrid. Major cities of Lisbon are also served, including Coimbra (the university city) and Porto (home of port wine). Facilities here include ATMs, restaurants, bars, and money exchange kiosks. Luggage storage is also available daily from 8:30am to 11:30pm, and costs 3€ ($3.45) for a locker for 48 hours. You can get both rail information and tourist information at offices to the right as you exit from the trains and walk past Ticket Window #1. These offices are open daily from 9am to 10pm. Hotel reservations can be made at the tourist office here, and there is no commission charged.

Estação Oriente (Metro: Oriente) is Lisbon's newest and most modern railway station. Designed by a Spanish architect in 1998 as part of the city's Expo 98 improvements, it links together railway spurs and railway lines that previously were never connected. Set in the Olivais neighborhood, near Lisbon's southern edge within the showplace park, Parque das Naçaos, it's an industrial-looking structure made of white-painted steel that looks both stylish and postmodern. Prior to its construction, passengers arriving in Rossio had to take a bus, tram, or taxi, with their luggage, if they wanted to continue their rail journey from the north to the south of the country. Today some long-distance and suburban trains stop here. For example, all trains heading for Santa Apolónia make a brief stop here. Trains leave from here to such northern destinations as Porto, the Beiras (Central Portugal), the Minho (in the north), and the Douro of port wine fame. This is also a departure point for Sintra. This railway station's opening coincided with the construction of 10 additional subway stations, and Oriente Station is interconnected with the entire subway system.

Estação Cais do Sodré (Metro: Cais do Sodré) lies just beyond the end of Rua Alecrim, to the west of Praça Comércio. The station, a 5-minute walk from the Baixa district, is so small in scale that it's easy to mistake it for a tram station. To reach the center, such as the landmark Praça dos Restauradores, take the Metro or else buses 1, 44, or 45. If you're connecting with trains at the Estação Santa Apolónia, take bus 28. Most passengers exploring Lisbon stop off here to reach the many attractions of Belém, including Mosteiro dos Jerónimos. Trains depart for Belém every 15 minutes during the day, costing .70€ (80¢) for the one-way, 10-minute trip. It's also possible to get trains here for the country's two most famous resorts along the Costa do Sol, Estoril and Cascais, both lying to the immediate north of Lisbon.

Estação Entre Campos (Metro: Entre Campos) is an intermediate railway station, a sort of "way station" that's set strategically on a spur line emanating outward from the city's newest, blockbuster railway station, Estação Oriente (see above). Passengers departing from Lisbon for points south of the Tagus, including Faro and Lagos, can board their trains here. They are routed on the lower level of the older of the two bridges traversing the Tagus, Ponte XXV Abrile (locals also refer to this bridge as the "Ponte Sobre Tejo"; its upper level is reserved for cars). A few of the trains stopping at this station continue to their final destination on the south bank of the Tagus. But for passengers headed to the Algarve (and Faro), they require a transfer of trains in the railway station at Barreiro, on the Tagus' south bank. At Barreiro, passengers cross a platform to board trains headed to points in Portugal's "Deep South." Barreiro on the opposite bank of the Tagus is also linked by a ferry to Lisbon. Ferries depart from Terminal Fluvial (also known as Sul e Sueste), adjacent to Praça do Comércio. The ferry ride is included in rail tickets to the Algarve, and departures are every half hour (trip time: 30 min.).

For rail information at any of these terminals, call ⓒ **80/820-8208.**

INFORMATION ELSEWHERE IN THE CITY

Hotel reservations, for which no commission is levied, can be made at all local tourist offices. The main office is at Palacio da Foz, Praça dos Restauradores

(℃ 21/346-6307), at the Baixa end of Avenida da Liberdade. The office dispenses information about Lisbon but also about Portugal in general, and is open daily from 9am to 8pm (Metro: Restauradores). Go here also to purchase the **Lisbon Card,** which provides free city transportation and entrance fees to many museums and attractions, plus discounts to certain events. For adults, a 1-day pass costs 12€ ($13.80); 2 days, 21.50€ ($24.75); 3 days, 26.55€ ($30.55). Children 5 to 11 pay 5.70€ ($6.55), 8.55€ ($9.85), and 11.40€ ($13.10), respectively.

GETTING AROUND

Lisbon is a vast urban sprawl, with many of its most visited attractions, including Belém and Sintra, lying in the environs. You'll need to rely on public transportation, which more or less runs pretty well. In the heart of town, the best way to cover Lisbon, especially the ancient districts of the Alfama and Baixa, is on foot. Wear sturdy walking shoes along these often cobbled and narrow streets, left over from the days when donkeys walked them.

The public transportation system is operated by **CARRIS** (℃ 21/361-3000), supervising the network of funiculars, trains, subways (the Metro), and buses. Consider buying a *bilhete de assinature turistico* good for 4 days of unlimited travel on the whole network; it costs 9.95€ ($11.45). A 1-day pass sells for 2.75€ ($3.15); a 7-day pass goes for 14.10€ ($16.20). Passes can be purchased at CARRIS booths in terminals and transportation hubs, which are open daily from 9am to 5pm, and at most Metro stations.

The Metro subway system's stations are designated by large M signs. A single ticket costs .65€ (.75¢); a packet of 10 tickets goes for 5.10€ ($5.85). Service is daily from 6:30am to 1am. For more information call ℃ **21/355-8457.**

Lisbon still operates an old-fashioned tram system, with trolley cars called *eléctricos,* making the steep run from the heart of town up to the Bairro Alto section. Buses or tram tickets cost from 1€ ($1.15) each, and you can purchase tickets from the driver. Actually, the fare depends on how far you're traveling, as Lisbon is divided into five different zones. Buses and *eléctricos* run daily from 6am to 1am.

The city is linked to its Riviera by a smooth-running, electric train system that will take you from Lisbon to such resorts as Estoril and Cascais. There's only one class of service, with a one-way fare ranging from 1.25€ to 2.50€ ($1.45–$2.90). There is also a trio of funiculars, including the Glória, which goes from Praça dos Restauradores to Rua São Pedro de Alcântara; the Bica, from Calçada do Combro to Rua do Boavista; and the Lavra, from the eastern side of Avenida da Liberdade to Campo Martires de Pátria. A one-way ticket on any of these funiculars costs 1€ ($1.15).

Finally, taxis are often the preferred means of transport, as fares are reasonable, beginning with a basic charge of 1.80€ ($2.10) with increments thereafter. Between 10pm to 6am daily, fares go up by 20%. For a **Radio Taxi** call ℃ **21/ 811-9000.**

WHERE TO STAY

Albergaria Senhora de Monte ★ *Finds*   Near St. George's Castle, in the oldest part of Lisbon, this inn is inviting and unpretentious, standing on a belvedere, opening onto panoramic views in all directions. Opt if you wish for one of the junior suites, as these have terraces, although all the bedrooms are inviting. The recently restored accommodations are imbued with decorator's touches such as gilt-edged door panels.

Calçada do Monte 39, 1170-250 Lisboa. ℂ **21/886-6002.** Fax 21/887-7783. 28 units. 105€–120€ ($121–$138) double; 150€–175€ ($173–$201) suite. Rates include continental breakfast. AE, DC, MC, V. Metro: Socorro. **Amenities:** Breakfast room; bar; laundry. *In room:* Hair dryer.

Avenida Palace ⭐   Right at the Rossio train station, this is the grand dame of luxury hotels in Lisbon, dating from 1892 and still imbued with the aura of its original Belle Epoque decorators, though it's been renovated and brought up-to-date. Nowhere in Lisbon is regal and elegant architecture combined with such modern comforts and personalized service. It's in a noisy, traffic-congested part of Lisbon, but rooms are soundproof and furnished in the styles of Louis XV or his ill-fated son, Louis XVI, even in Empire, and many of the accommodations are as spacious as they were at the turn of the 20th century.

Rua 1er Dezembro 123, 1200-359 Lisboa. ℂ **21/321-8100.** Fax 21/342-2884. www.hotel-avenida-palace. pt/rooms.htm. 82 units. 165€–200€ ($190–$230) double; from 240€ ($276) junior suite. Rates include breakfast. AE, DC, MC, V. Metro: Restauradores. **Amenities:** Breakfast room; bar; laundry. *In room:* Hair dryer.

Dom Carlos *(Value)*   Just off the landmark Praça do Marquês de Pombal, this hotel is known for its central location and affordable prices. Bedrooms are mid-size and paneled in Portuguese redwood, each more functional than stylish. Facing a little park, the hotel is well run with a friendly, accommodating staff who will direct you to all the points of interest and tell you the best way to get to where you're going.

Av. Duque de Loulé 121, 1050-089 Lisboa. ℂ **21/351-2590.** Fax 21/352-0728. hdcarlos@mail.telepac.pt. 76 units. 118€ ($136) double, 135€ ($155) triple, 150€ ($173) suite. Rates include buffet breakfast. AE, DC, MC, V. Metro: Marquês de Pombal. **Amenities:** Restaurant; bar; laundry. *In room:* Hair dryer.

Hotel Britânia ⭐ *(Value)*   Only 1,640 feet from the Rossio, a block from Avenida da Liberdade (the main boulevard), this long-time favorite was carved out of a 1942 Art Deco office building. In the mid-1990s all the spacious bedrooms were massively upgraded and renovated, although many of its vintage architectural features were retained. Rooms have high ceilings, tasteful carpeting, comfortable furnishings, and carved headboards on twin- or king-size beds. The hotel's service is like that provided by a small, well-run inn.

Rua Rodrigues Sampaio 17, 1150-278 Lisboa. ℂ **21/315-5021.** www.heritage.pt. 30 units. 148€–225€ ($170–$259) double. AE, DC, MC, V. Metro: Avenida. **Amenities:** Bar; laundry, nonsmoking rooms. *In room:* Hair dryer.

Janelas Verdes Inn ⭐⭐ *(Finds)*   Set 1¼ miles (2km) from Rossio, between the harbor and Bairro Alto, this is one of Lisbon's most atmospheric and charming hotels, installed in the 18th-century town house that was once home to Eca de Queiroz, the Portuguese novelist. Rooms are spacious and elegantly furnished, with a combination of antiques and reproductions. The best rooms are in the rear and on the upper levels, as they open onto sweeping views of the Tagus River.

Rua das Janelas Verdes 47, 1200-690 Lisboa. ℂ **21/396-8143.** Fax 21/396-8144. www.heritage.pt. 165€–245€ ($190–$282) double. AE, DC, MC, V. Bus: 27, 40, 49, or 60. **Amenities:** Bar; laundry, nonsmoking rooms, rooms for those with limited mobility. *In room:* Hair dryer.

Lisboa Plaza ⭐⭐   In the heart of the city, this family-owned, government-rated, 4-star hotel rises seven floors on a quiet side street ½ mile (1km) north of Rossio. A tradition since 1953, the hotel was extensively restored by top designers in the 90s, and much of its charm, evoking Edwardian elegance, was retained and touched up. With double-glazed windows and marble bathrooms, the mid-size bedrooms are refined with traditional styling, ranging from standard, to the much larger superior units, to roomy and tastefully furnished suites (try for one at the rear overlooking botanical gardens).

Travessa do Salitre 7, Avenida da Liberdade, 1269-066 Lisboa. ℭ **21/321-8218.** Fax 21/347-1630. www. heritage.pt. 112 units. 148€–225€ ($170–$259) double; from 250€ ($288) suite. Children under 13 free in parent's room. AE, DC, MC, V. Metro: Avenida. **Amenities:** Restaurant; bar; laundry, nonsmoking rooms. In room: Hair dryer.

Tivoli Lisboa ★★ In a prime spot about ⅔ mile (1.1km) north of Rossio, this hotel, opened in 1933, is a conservative, cosmopolitan, and enduring favorite of both vacationers and business travelers, offering such enticing features as the only hotel pool in central Lisbon. A large, dramatically decorated two-floor lobby sets the style tone, and a top-floor restaurant opens onto a terrace for panoramic dining. Tasteful carpeting, stylish chintz, and comfortable furnishings decorate the spacious, bright, and inviting bedrooms with many amenities including chic marble bathrooms.

Avenida da Liberdade 185, 1269-050 Lisboa. ℭ **21/319-8900.** Fax 21/319-8950. www.tivolihotels.com. 329 units. 195€–255€ ($224–$293) double; from 402€ ($462) suite. Rates include continental breakfast. AE, DC, MC, V. Metro: Avenida. **Amenities:** 2 restaurants; 2 bars; laundry; nonsmoking rooms, rooms for those with limited mobility. In room: Hair dryer

Veneza ★ *Finds* Opened as a hotel in 1990 in a grand old building from 1886, this splendid structure is a real discovery, as it's housed in one of the few remaining old palaces that once lined Avenida da Liberdade, Lisbon's main boulevard. A grand staircase leads to a trio of upper floors where you'll find handsomely furnished and up-to-date guest bedrooms. The service and friendly welcome are top rate.

Avenida Da Liberdade 189, 1250-141 Lisboa. ℭ **21/352-2618.** Fax 21/352-6678. www.3khoteis.com. 37 units. 130€–150€ ($150–$173) double. Rates include continental breakfast. AE, DC, MC, V. Metro: Avenida. **Amenities:** Bar; laundry. In room: Hair dryer.

York House ★★ An even more atmospheric choice than Janelas Verdes (see above), the York House was carved out of a 17th-century convent and is filled with more charm and character than any other hotel in Lisbon. Long a celebrity favorite, it lies on a cobbled street between Bairro Alto and the waterfront 1¼ miles (2km) west of the Rossio. Mazelike public rooms, filled with antiques, lead to bedrooms that vary in size, although each is beautifully furnished, often with a four-poster bed and antiques.

Rua das Janelas Verdes 32, 1200-691 Lisboa. ℭ **21/396-2435.** Fax 21/397-2793. 34 units. 140€–200€ ($161–$230) double. AE, DC, MC, V. Bus: 27, 40, 49, 54, or 60. **Amenities:** Restaurant; bar; laundry. In room: Hair dryer.

TOP ATTRACTIONS & SPECIAL MOMENTS

If you're in Lisbon just for the day, and that's all the time you have, take a stroll through the Alfama, the most interesting district of Lisbon. Visit the 12th-century **Sé (cathedral),** and take in a view of the city and the River Tagus from the **Santa Luzia Belvedere.** Climb up to the **Castelo de São Jorge (St. George's Castle).** Take a taxi or bus to Belém to see the **Mosteiro dos Jerónimos (Jerónimos Monastery)** and the **Torre de Belém.** While at Belém, explore one of the major sights of Lisbon, the **Museu Nacional dos Coches (National Coach Museum).**

IN THE ALFAMA

Castelo de São Jorge ★★ This hilltop fortress, a former citadel of Portuguese kings, towers over the Alfama and Lisbon in general. Since Afonso Henriques chased out the Moors in 1147, it was a royal abode until Manuel I in

Moments **Strolling the Alfama**

It's old and decaying but the **Alfama** 🟊🟊 is one of the most history-rich and evocative old quarters of any European capital. Give it at least a morning or an afternoon. Now mired in large part in poverty, the Alfama used to be the toniest neighborhood in Lisbon, inhabited in part by the aristocracy, its closely-knit alleyways built around a fortified castle on the hilltop.

The rich fled after Lisbon's 1755 earthquake leaving the district to the families of fishermen and paupers. The Alfama was allowed to decay gracefully, and it is because of this poverty that its Casbah-like layout remains intact today.

Balconies are strung with laundry; music emanates from *tavernas* filled with immigrants from such former colonies as Mozambique or Cape Verde; crumbling churches have terraces with panoramic views; hidden restaurants spill out onto open-air courtyards; and black-shawled widows grill sardines on open braziers, tossing a fish head to a passing cat.

One of the best views is from **Largo das Portas do Sol** 🟊, one of the gates to the old city. A lively fish market takes place every morning at Rua de São Pedro.

Another great panoramic sweep is possible from **Miradouro de Santa Luzia** 🟊🟊, whose bougainvillea-clad terrace spans the tiled roofs of the Alfama toward the Tagus River.

1511 constructed a more lavish palace closer to the harbor. The 1755 earthquake struck it badly, but in 1938 the dictator, Salazar, ordered the old walls rebuilt and gardens added.

Today's visitors can climb the towers and walk along the **battlements** 🟊, the reconstructed ramparts, later taking in the **view from the Observation Platform** 🟊🟊, a large shaded square opening onto Lisbon and the river beyond. You can stroll the grounds, enjoying the landscaping of olive, pine, and cork trees, all graced by elegant peacocks showing off their feathers or white-bodied swans gliding by.

Rua da Costa do Castelo. ✆ 21/887-7244. Free admission. Apr–Sept daily 9am–9pm; Oct–Mar daily 9am–6pm. Bus: 37. Tram: 12 or 28.

Museu Antóniano   This Alfama church, so it is said, stands on the spot where St. Anthony of Padua, an itinerant Franciscan monk who became the patron saint of Portugal, was born in 1195. Only the crypt remains from the original church. The present structure dates from 1757 and was based on the design of the architect Mateus Vicente. The church is a medley of styles including Baroque overtones and neoclassical Ionic columns standing on each side of the principal portal. Married couples visit the church on their wedding day, leaving flowers for St. Anthony. He was born and reared in Lisbon but spent the last months of his life in Padua. Next to the church, the museum displays ancient manuscripts, ex-votos, and images, all related to St. Anthony.

Largo de Santo António de Sé. ✆ 21/886-9145. Free admission. Daily 7:30am–7:30pm. Metro: Rossio. Bus: 37.

Sé (Cathedral) ✦   It's not one of the grand cathedrals of Europe, but this blend of Romanesque and Gothic architecture, characterized by twin towers flanking its entrance, merits 30 or so minutes of your time if you're exploring the Alfama. The cathedral was begun in 1150 when Afonso Henriques ordered it built for the first bishop of Lisbon after he'd kicked out the Moors. Over the years the cathedral has had a rough time of it, as it was devastated by a series of earth tremors in the 14th century, and it shook at its foundations during the earth-quake of 1755. The austere interior is a bit gloomy, but there are treasures here, including the font where St. Anthony of Padua is said to have been christened in 1195. Other notable features include the Gothic chapel of Bartholomeu Joanes plus a crib by Machado de Castro. If time remains, visit the cloister, built on the orders of King Dinis in the 14th century. It's of ogival construction with garlands and a Romanesque **wrought-iron grille** ✦. The sacristy contains valuable images, relics, and other treasures from the 15th and 16th centuries.

Largo de Sé. ✆ 21/886-6752. Cathedral, free; cloister .50€. (60¢) Mon–Sat 10am–6pm. Tram: 28. Bus: 37.

IN BELEM

At the mouth of the Tagus River, Portuguese caravels set sail on their voyages of discovery, changing the maps of the world and even the world itself. These voyages led to trade with India and the East, the capture of Goa, the colonization of Brazil, and the granting of Macao as a trading post with China, among other adventures. Portugal was indeed launched upon its golden age.

You can journey to the suburb of Belém in the southwestern district to see where Portuguese mariners such as Ferdinand Magellan, Vasco de Gama, and Barolomeu Dias set out on their voyages across the Sea of Darkness.

Belém is easily reached by public transportation. Take tram 15 for the 20-minute ride from Praça do Comércio in the center of Lisbon, or else buses 29 and 43 also leaving from Praça do Comércio. The slow trains from Cais do Sodré marked Cascais also stop at Belém.

You can spend an entire day at Belém enjoying its monuments, parks, and gardens, as well as strolling its setting along the Tagus. If time is very limited, try to see at least Mosteiro dos Jerónimos, Museu da Marinha, and Museu Nacional dos Coches—all previewed immediately below along with some more minor attractions.

Mosteiro dos Jerónimos ✦✦   This is the jewel of the age of Manueline art. Manuel I, called "The Fortunate," launched this monastery to commemorate the success of Vasco da Gama's voyage to India. Bearing the king's name, Manu-eline architecture blends the most flamboyant Gothic aspects with Moorish influences. "Pepper money," meaning profits from the spice trade with India, helped finance this magnificent monument.

A former small chapel built by Henry the Navigator is today **Ingreja de Santa Maria** ✦✦, with one of the most beautiful interiors of any of Lisbon's churches, particularly evocative for its **network vaulting** ✦ over the aisles and naves. The pinnacle of Manueline expression is achieved in the **Cloisters** ✦✦✦, reached through the west door. Completed in 1544, these cloisters are filled with deli-cate tracery and lushly carved images adorning their arches and balustrades. The church boasts three naves noted for their delicate columns, and many of the ceil-ings are graced with ribbed barrel vaulting. Many of Portugal's greatest national heroes are entombed here, including Vasco da Gama and the land's national poet, Luís Vas de Camões, author of the epic, *Os Lusíadas* (The Lusiads), in which he glorified the triumphs of his compatriots.

Praça do Império. ℂ **21/362-0034.** Free admission to church; admission to cloisters 3€ ($3.45), free for children under 12. May–Sept Tues–Sun 10am–6pm; Oct–Apr Tues–Sun 10am–5pm.

Museu de Marinha ★★ One of Europe's greatest maritime museums depicts Portugal's seafaring past and is installed in the west wing of Mosteiro dos Jerónimos. It was in the chapel here that mariners took mass before embarking on their fabled voyages, including Vasco da Gama's sail around the Cape of Good Hope to open the sea route to India. Navigational instruments, replicas of maps from the 1500s, and astrolabes evoke the mariner's past and what was known at the time of their discoveries. Royal galleys re-create an age of opulence, with depictions of everything from the heads of dragons to sea monsters. The most elaborate of these galleys was the one ordered built by Queen Maria I in honor of her son's marriage in 1785 to a Spanish princess—the crew consisted of 80 oarsmen. On display are many models of sailing ships ranging from the 15th to the 19th centuries, including pleasure boats and river craft. Of special interest is a model of the queen's stateroom on the royal yacht of Carlos I, the Brangança king assassinated at Praça do Comércio in 1908. On this craft the queen mother, Amélia, and her son, Manuel II, escaped to Gibraltar.

Praça do Império. ℂ **21/362-0019.** Admission 3€ ($3.45) adults, 1.50€ ($1.75) students. Free for children under 5. Peak season Tues–Sun 10am–6pm; winter Tues–Sun 10am–5pm.

Museu Nacional dos Coches ★★ This is the world's greatest coach museum, and is one of the most visited attractions in Portugal. Founded by Amélia, wife of Carlos I, it's installed in a riding academy built in the 1700s. Gilded coaches, four-wheelers, litters, they are all here. The most ancient is the splendidly painted **four-wheeler** ★ that Philip of Spain brought to Portugal in the late 16th century. The coaches range from the very simple to the most ostentatious, the latter being the three outrageously adorned coaches built in 1716 for the Marquês de Abrantes, Portugal's ambassador to Pope Clement XI. Interiors are lined with gold and red velvet, and the coaches are carved and decorated with royal coats-of-arms along with allegories.

Praça de Afonso de Albuquerque. ℂ **21/361-0850.** Admission 3€ ($3.45) adults, I.50€ ($1.75) students 14–25, free for children under 14. Tues–Sun 10am–5:30pm.

Torre de Belém ★★ This quadrangular tower is one of Portugal's greatest monuments to its Age of Discovery. Built by Manuel I, the tower was a fortress in the early 16th century and the starting point for the famous Portuguese mariners. The **decoration** ★★ of the tower's exterior is magnificent, adorned with rope carved of stone and balconies. Moorish-styled watchtowers guard it and the battlements appear in the shape of shields. A monument to Portugal's great naval past, the tower is often used to symbolize Portugal itself. Along the balustrade of the loggias, stone crosses represent the Portuguese crusaders. From the ramparts you're rewarded with a **panorama** ★★ of the Tagus and its vessels. In the center of the square on which the tower sits is the **Fonte Luminosa** ★ or Luminous Fountain with its patterns of water jets that strike up some 70 original designs, making for a show every evening that lasts for about an hour.

Praça do Império, Av. de Brasília. ℂ **21/362-0034.** Admission 4€ ($4.60) adults, 1.50€ ($1.75) children. On Sun free until 2pm. May–Sept Tues–Sun 10am–6pm; Oct–Apr Tues–Sun 10am–5pm.

OTHER GREAT MUSEUMS
Museu da Fundaçao Calouste Gulbenkian ★★★ Hailed by art critics as
one of the world's finest private art collections, this magnificent treasure trove

was formed from a nucleus of art acquired by Calouste Gulbenkian, an oil magnate with an eye for art, who died in 1955 and willed his collection to the state. The modern museum was constructed on a former private estate that once belonged to the Count of Vilalva and opened in 1969. Allow at least 3 hours for a romp through this varied collection, which covers Egyptian, Greek, and Roman antiquities among other treasures, even a rare (for Europe) assemblage of Islamic art, including Syrian glass and ceramics and textiles from Turkey and old Persia. The **medieval illuminated manuscripts and ivories** form a stunning display, as do the French Impressionist paintings, 18th-century decorative works, antiques, silverware, and jewelry.

In a move requiring great skill in negotiation, Gulbenkian managed to buy art from the Hermitage in St. Petersburg. Among his most notable acquisitions are two Rembrandts: *Portrait of an Old Man* and *Alexander the Great*. Two other well-known paintings are *Portrait of Hélène Fourment* by Peter Paul Rubens and *Portrait of Madame Claude Monet* by Pierre-August Renoir. In addition, we suggest that you seek out Mary Cassatt's *The Stocking*. The French sculptor Jean-Antoine Houdon is represented by a statue of Diana. Silver made by François-Thomas Germain, once used by Catherine the Great, is here, as well as one piece by Thomas Germain, the father.

As a cultural center, the Gulbenkian Foundation sponsors plays, films, ballets, and concerts, as well as a rotating exhibition of works by leading modern Portuguese and foreign artists.

Av. de Berna 45. ℂ **21/782-3000.** Admission 3€ ($3.45), free for seniors (65 and over) and students and teachers. Free to all Sun. Wed–Sun 10am–6pm. Metro: Sebastião.

Museu Nacional de Arte Antiga In the 17th century palace of the Counts of Alvor, this great museum, one of the finest in Iberia, was founded in part from rare collections taken from monasteries that were suppressed in 1833. The greatest paintings to be found in Portugal are displayed here in a carefully laid out collection, with the major European paintings from the 14th to the 19th centuries on the ground floor. On the top floor is one of the country's

---

Finds **If It Swims, It's Here**

A legacy left by Expo 98, the second biggest aquarium in the world (the largest is in Osaka, Japan), **Oceanario de Lisboa** (ℂ **21/891-7002**), truly makes you realize what a seafaring nation Portugal was and still is. The centerpiece of this amazing glass-and-stone building is a 1.3-million-gallon holding tank. That's about the equivalent of four Olympic swimming pools strung together. From shoals of sardines to menacing sharks, the displays consist of four distinct ecosystems that replicate the Atlantic, Pacific, Indian, and Antarctic oceans. Each is supplemented with above-ground portions on which birds, amphibians, and reptiles flourish. Look for otters in the Pacific waters, penguins in the Antarctic section, trees and flowers that might remind you of Polynesia in the Indian Ocean section, and puffins, terns, and seagulls in the Atlantic division.

Don't underestimate the national pride associated with this huge facility. Most Portuguese view it as a latter-day reminder of their former mastery of the seas. Admission is 9€ ($10.35) adults, 4.60€ ($5.30) students and children under 13. Open daily 10am to 7pm. Metro: Estaçao do Oriente.

finest displays of Portuguese art and sculpture. The gallery has some celebrated works, including a **polyptych** ★★★ from St. Vincent's monastery, a work attributed to Nuno Gonçalves between 1460 and 1470. A triptych, *The Temptation of St. Anthony* ★★★, is the gallery's other celebrated treasure. Other notable works include the portrait of St. Jerome in his old age by Albrecht Dürer, a great work of Renaissance humanism from 1521. Hans Holbein the Elder weighs in with his masterly *The Virgin and Child and Saint* from 1519. A series of 16th-century **Namban screens** ★ form one of the museum's other treasures, as does a ceramics collection, many decorative items made for the royal family, including a strikingly unusual Faïence violin.

Rua das Janelas Verdes. ℂ **21/391-2800**. Admission 3€ ($3.45) adults, 1.50€ ($1.75) students. Free for children under 14. Tues 2–6pm, Wed–Sun 10am–6pm. Tram: 15 or 18.

WHERE TO DINE

Antonio Clara ★★ PORTUGUESE/INTERNATIONAL   One of the most celebrated restaurants in Lisbon, lying off the Praça do Marquês de Pompal, this upmarket restaurant occupies a late-19th-century villa that was the home of the Miguel Ventura Terra (1866–1918), a famous architect of his day. In one of the most beautiful dining rooms of the city, you can enjoy top-notch cooking that is a modern and inspired rendition of classic recipes. In a refined atmosphere, market-fresh ingredients are fashioned into sublime fare by chefs whose techniques are exemplary. The seafood is especially good here.

Av. da República 38. ℂ **21/799-4280**. Reservations required. Main courses 12.50€–17.50€ ($14.40–$20.10). AE, DC, MC, V. Mon–Sat noon–3pm and 7–10:30pm. Metro: Saldainha.

Bachus ★★ INTERNATIONAL   In Bairro Alto, a short distance south of Rossio station, this amusing and sophisticated restaurant has an ambience evocative of a turn-of-the-20th-century British club. Classic favorites are dished up by classy waiters who service the tables well. The menu is adjusted to take advantage of seasonal produce, and old and new influences are combined to produce appetizing fare that might range from shrimp Bachus to mountain goat.

Largo da Trindade 9. ℂ **21/342-28-28**. Reservations recommended. Main courses 15€–20€ ($17.25–$23). AE, DC, MC, V. Tues–Fri noon–3pm and Tues–Sun 7pm–midnight. Metro: Chiado.

Conventual ★★ *Finds* PORTUGUESE   One of Lisbon's finest yet undiscovered restaurants lies to the west of Rossio, off Praça de Principe Real. This exemplary restaurant is comfortably spaced with white-clothed tables evoking a 1930s style and is overseen by a graceful, welcoming staff. The menu is beautifully balanced between rich game favorites such as stewed partridge in port and fish dishes, such as the grilled monkfish in an herb-flavored cream sauce.

Praça das Flores 45. ℂ **21/390-9196**. Reservations required. Main courses 15€–22€ ($17.25–$25.30). AE, DC, MC, V. Mon–Fri 12:30–3:30pm; Mon–Sat 7:30–11:30pm. Closed Aug. Metro: Avenida.

El Bodegón PORTUGUESE/SPANISH/INTERNATIONAL   At the top of the Avenida da Liberdade, this hotel dining room serves some of the finest Spanish dishes in town, plus an array of regional and international—mainly continental—selections. Many of the offerings come from the rich bounty of the Portuguese countryside, especially in the north, including such items as fresh salmon, quail, and partridge. From the plains of Ribatejo comes acorn-sweetened pork, along with other reliable dishes. If they're on the menu, try the succulently fresh strawberries from Sintra.

In the Hotel Fénix, Praça do Marquês de Pombal 8. ℂ **21/386/3155**. Reservations required. Main courses 12€–20€ ($13.80–$23). AE, DC, MC, V. Daily 12:30–3pm and 7:30–10:30pm. Metro: Rotunda.

Escorial ⚔ INTERNATIONAL   Near Rossio station in the heart of Lisbon's restaurant district, this Spanish-owned dining room serves some of the best Iberian cuisine known to Lisboans. It's been a rousing success ever since it opened years ago because of its opulent repertoire of the classic and perfectly prepared dishes that range from barbecued baby goat to a mixed shellfish grill. This inviting and stylish restaurant *par excellence* is an enduring favorite despite its increasingly sleazy neighborhood because of its time-tested professionalism.

Rua das Portas de Santo Antão 47. ℂ **21/346-4429.** Reservations recommended. Main courses 10€–30€ ($11.50–$34.50). AE, DC, MC, V. Daily noon–4pm and 7pm–midnight. Metro: Rossio or Restauradores.

Restaurant Tavares ⚔⚔⚔ PORTUGUESE/CONTINENTAL   Established as a cafe in the 18th century, Lisbon's oldest restaurant is still going strong and still serving some of the city's most refined meals even though it has many challengers today whereas in the past it used to reign supreme. Against an elegant backdrop with splendid furnishings, the restaurant serves the finest interpretation of regional cuisine mixed harmoniously with classic French-inspired dishes from the Continent. The cooking and market shopping is firmly rooted to the seasons, and the top-notch welcome and service continue to attract the diplomats and literati who patronize this swank rendezvous.

Rua das Misericórdia 37. ℂ **21/342-1112.** Reservations required. Main courses 20€–30€ ($23–$34.50). AE, DC, MC, V. Mon–Fri 12:30–3pm; Sun–Fri 7:30–11pm. Bus: 15.

Sancho PORTUGUESE/INTERNATIONAL   This cozy and rustic dining room in the heart of Lisbon, close to Rossio, is one of the city's most atmospheric. With blessed air-conditioning in summer and a roaring fireplace in winter, the restaurant serves long-time favorite dishes such as pan-broiled Portuguese steak. Their shellfish is some of the best and freshest in town, and for something really local, opt for *churrasco de cabrito ao piri-piri* (goat with a fiery pepper sauce).

Travessa da Glória 14. ℂ **21/346-9780.** Reservations recommended. Main courses 10€–12€ ($11.50–$13.80). AE, DC, MC, V. Mon–Sat noon–3pm and 7–10:30pm. Metro: Avenida or Restauradores.

Tasquinha d'Adelaide ⚔ *Finds* PORTUGUESE   This unusual restaurant is known for serving the culinary specialties of Trás-os-Montes, the most rugged and remote province of Portugal, lying in the northeast. The restaurant itself is on the western edge of the Bairro Alto, and a table here is a coveted commodity among Lisboan foodies, who appreciate its home-like atmosphere and unpretentious but good-tasting cuisine. This food is not for the faint of heart but attracts those who deliberately seek out its hearty regional fare, including such daunting courses as tripe with collard greens and rice, though there are options for less adventurous palates as well.

Rua do Patrocinio 70–74. ℂ **21/396-2239.** Reservations recommended. Main courses 14€–21€ ($16.10–$24.15). AE, DC, MC, V. Mon–Sat noon–2am. Metro: Rato.

SHOPPING

Portugal is known for its handcrafts, including exquisite embroideries, decorative glazed tiles, china, fishermen's sweaters, fado recordings, lightweight baskets—and the best buys of all, regional pottery in all types, shapes, and forms. The single best buy in the country is gold, as jewelers are required by law to put in a minimum of 19.2 karats into each piece of jewelry. Many of the ornamental designs of fine gold or silver pieces date from ancient times.

The two leading centers for silver, gold, and filigree include **W.A. Sarmento,** Rua Aurea 251 (ℂ **21/347-0783**), at the foot of the Santa Justa elevator. Run by the same family for more than a century, these are the most distinguished silver- and goldsmiths in Portugal. Their specialty is lacy filigree jewelry. Also worthy is the competitor, **Joalharia do Carmo,** Rua do Carmo 87B (℃ **21/342-4200**), selling handmade silver pieces and even platinum jewelry in stunning designs.

Just for fun, even if you don't buy anything, head for the open-air street market, **Feira da Ladra** ⚜⚜, the sprawling flea market where Portuguese vendors peddle their wares on Tuesday and Saturday. It's best to go in the morning. One of the best selections of Portuguese baskets and one of the widest displays of regional handcrafts are sold here. The market activity begins about a 5-minute stroll from the Lisbon waterfront as you head into the Alfama sector, beginning your search at Campo de Santa Clara and just following your instinctive shopping nose from here up and down the hilly streets.

Carpet aficionados around the world value the beautifully woven Arraiolos carpets sold at **Casa Quintão,** Rua Serpa Pinto 12A (℃ **21/346-5837**), where rugs are priced by the square foot. Many of the finest carpets are based on designs popular in the Middle Ages.

In the same building as the Hotel Avenida Palace near Rossio train station, **Casa Bordados da Madeira,** Dezembro 137 (℃ **21/342-1447**), features the city's best selection of the exquisite and valuable embroideries from the island of Madeira. The same exquisite work is also sold at **Madeira House,** Av. Da Liberdade 159 (℃ **21/315-1558**). In contrast, **Casa Regional da Ilha Verde,** Rua Paiva de Andrade 4 (℃ **21/342-5974**), specializes in hand embroideries from the Azores, each piece sold here carrying a made-by-hand guarantee.

The recordings of Portugal's most popular fadistas are sold at **Valentim de Carvalho,** Rua Ventu du Jesus Caracas 17 (℃ **21/392-9750**). Fado, of course, is the most quintessential music of Portugal.

Moments **To Market, to Market . . .**

The big market of **Ribeira Nova** ⚜⚜ is as close as you can get to the heart of Lisbon. Behind the Cais do Sodré train station, an enormous roof shelters a collection of stalls offering the produce used in Lisbon's finest restaurants. Foodstuffs arrive each morning in wicker baskets bulging with oversize carrots, cabbages big enough to be shrubbery, and stalks of bananas. Some of the freshly plucked produce arrives by donkey, some by truck, some balanced on the heads of Lisboan women in the Mediterranean fashion. The country's rich soil produces the juiciest peaches and the most aromatic tomatoes.

At the market, women festively clad in voluminous skirts and calico aprons preside over the mounds of vegetables, fruit, and fish. On cue, the vendors begin howling about the value of their wares, stopping only to pose for an occasional snapshot. Fishing boats dock at dawn with their catch. The fishermen deposit the cod, squid, bass, hake, and swordfish on long marble counters. The *varinas* (fishwives) balance wicker baskets of the fresh catch on their heads. They climb the cobblestone streets of the Alfama or the Bairro Alto to sell fish from door to door.

Moments   The Songs of Sorrow

Unless you have experienced the nostalgic sounds of **fado,** the songs of sorrow, you do not know Portugal—certainly not its soul. Fado is Portugal's most vivid art form; no visit to the country should be planned without at least 1 night spent in a local tavern where this traditional folk music is heard.

A rough translation of *fado* is "fate" from the Latin *fatum,* meaning "prophecy." Fado usually tells of unrequited love, jealousy, a longing for days gone by. As one expert put it, it speaks of "life commanded by the Oracle, which nothing can change." It's usually sung by females but is also performed by male singers, both known as *fadistas.*

Fado found its earliest fame in the 19th century when Maria Severa, the beautiful daughter of a gypsy, took Lisbon by storm, singing her way into the hearts of the people—and especially the heart of the count of Vimioso, an outstanding bullfighter of his day. Legend has it that she is honored by present-day fadistas who wear a black-fringed shawl in her memory.

In this century the most famous exponent of fado has been Amália Rodrigues, who was introduced to American audiences in the 1950s at the New York club La Vie en Rose. She was discovered while walking barefoot and selling flowers on the Lisbon docks, near the Alfama.

Clutching black shawls around themselves, the female fadistas pour out their emotions, from the tenderest whisper of hope to a wailing lament of life's tragedies. As they sing, accompanied by a guitar and a viola, standing against a black gas street lamp, without benefit of backdrops or makeup, they seem to lose all contact with the surrounding world—they just stand there, seemingly outdoing the Rhine's Lorelei in drawing you into their world of tenderness and fire. Though much enjoyment can be derived from understanding the

NIGHTLIFE

What's on in Lisbon, available at most newsstands, is your best companion for an up-to-the-minute preview of what's going on in the Portuguese capital.

Cultural Lisbon is best showcased at **Teatro Nacional São Carlos,** Rua Serpa Pinto 9 (© **21/325-3000**), attracting opera and ballet lovers from across the country, its season lasting from mid-September to July. Some of the best concerts and recitals are presented at **Museo da Fundacão Calouste Gulbenkian,** Av. De Berna 45 (© **21/782-3000**), which stages occasional ballets or jazz concerts as well.

To get your evening in Lisbon going, you can head for one of two evocative institutions. **A Brasileira,** Rua Garrett 120 (© **21/346-9541**), in the Chiado district, is the oldest surviving coffeehouse in Lisbon, a tradition since 1905 when it was the gathering place for the city's literati. Sitting here having a demitasse of strong coffee is like wandering back in a time capsule to Lisbon's yesterday. Other than coffee, the most typical drink of Lisbon is port wine, and **Solar do Vinho do Porto,** Rua de São Pedro de Alcântara 45 (© **21/347-5707**), is poetic imagery, a knowledge of Portuguese is not essential. The power of the lyrics, the warmth of the voices, and the personalities of the singers communicate a great deal.

Fado is sung all over Lisbon and its environs, but the best clubs for this art form include **Adega Machado,** Rua do Norte 91 (ⓒ **21/347-0550**), the city's most beloved fado club where some of the greatest of today's fadistas appear. A dinner show starts at 8pm with music beginning at 9:15pm. Open Tuesday to Sunday, the club charges 15.50€ ($17.85), including two drinks.

Another cherished favorite is **A Severa,** Rua das Gaveas 51 (ⓒ **21/346-4006**), featuring top-notch male and female fadistas, alternating with folk dancers. You can also dine here on fine regional dishes. The cost of a meal with wine is 35€ ($40.25), or else for 17.50€ ($20.15) cover, including two drinks, you can come only for the show daily from 8pm to 3:30am.

One of the most famous and enduring clubs in Bairro Alto is **Luso,** Travessa de Queimada 10 (ⓒ **21/342-2281**), converted from a vaulted network of 17th-century stables. Great fado shows and good regional food is served, with dinners costing 35€ ($40.25). For a cover of 20€ ($23), including two drinks, you can come just for the shows, which are Monday to Saturday at 9pm and 2am (a real late show).

Close to the waterfront and the Alfama, **Parreirinha da Alfama,** Beco do Espirito Santo 1 (ⓒ **21/886-8209**), is an old-time cafe that offers one of the purest forms of fado (no folkloric shows here). A favorite since the 1950s, it presents classic fado and serves a good regional dinner for 25€ ($28.75). If you don't want to dine, you pay a modest cover of 10€ ($11.50), which is credited toward your drink bill. Open daily from 8:30pm to 1am, with music beginning at 9:30pm.

devoted just to this enticing drink. In a setting from 3 centuries ago, you can peruse the menu of 200 types of port wine—sweet or dry, red or white.

Lisbon abounds with bars and dance clubs, many offering live music. In a former factory and warehouse beside the river, **Bar of the Café Alcántara,** Rua Maria Luisa Holstein 15 (ⓒ **21/363-7176**), evokes a railway car in turn-of-the-20th-century Paris. The club is a lot of fun, and caters to gay, straight, and everything in between. Another cafe, **Blues Café,** Rua Cintura do Puerto do Lisboa 3-4 (ⓒ **21/395-7085**), is also by the river with an eagle's nest balcony encircling one floor. The latest hip-hop and garage music is played here every night except Sunday.

A two-story warehouse near the Apolónia has been converted into **Lux,** Avenida Infante Don Henrique (ⓒ **21/882-0890**), on the banks of the Tagus. This counterculture joint is filled with hip patrons and cutting-edge music, including both a disco and a bar, with the dance club charging 12€ ($13.80) cover after midnight.

If you like a drink with a view, there is no better spot than the aptly named **Panorama Bar,** in the Lisboa Sheraton Hotel, Rua Latino Coelho 1 (© **21/357-5757**), on the top floor of Portugal's tallest building (30 stories high). Against the backdrop of a cosmopolitan décor, you can enjoy views over the city and the Tagus. The bar stays open nightly until 2am. One of the most popular watering holes in the Barrio Alto is **Portas Largas,** Rua da Atalaia 105 (© **21/346-6379**), a hip hangout attracting a mixture of straight and gay that's open until 3:30am daily. The most charming bar of Lisbon is **Procópio,** Alto de São Francisco 21 (© **21/385-2851**), which attracts actors, journalists, and politicos.

AN EXCURSION TO SINTRA

To Lord Byron, it was a "glorious Eden." To today's visitor, it is the single most rewarding day trip from any city within Portugal. Once a favorite retreat in summer for Portuguese kings, Sintra is set among fresh water springs, wooded ravines, and lush vegetation of exotic trees and shrubs. In the blistering summer months, Sintra is a cool mountain retreat, especially in the evening.

The natural beauty of this land, located 18 miles (29km) northwest of Lisbon, is enhanced by country manor houses, cobbled streets, horse-drawn carriages, and national palaces. In 1995, UNESCO recognized its charm by naming it a World Heritage Site.

GETTING THERE   Trains depart from Estaçao Rossio (p. 702) from tracks 4 and 5, leaving every 15 to 30 minutes daily from 6am to 2am. The trip time is 45 minutes, and a one-way ticket costs 1.10€ ($1.25). Trains arrive in Sintra at **Estação de Caminhos de Ferro,** Av. Dr. Miguel Bombarda (© **21/923-2605**). The station is ⅔ mile (1.1km) downhill from the center of town. Buses run frequently back and forth; the fare is .50€ (60¢). A taxi into town costs 4€ ($4.50) for up to 4 passengers. For more information, call © **808/820-8208.**

TOURIST INFORMATION   The **Sintra Tourist Office** is at Praça da República 23 (© **21/923-1157**), in the center of town. From June to September it is open daily 9am to 8pm; October to May, daily 9am to 7pm.

TOP ATTRACTIONS & SPECIAL MOMENTS

Even those on the most rushed of schedules try to budget time to see two of Portugal's greatest palaces, especially **Palacio Nacional de Sintra** ☆☆☆, Largo da Rainha Dona Amélia (© **21/910-6840**), a royal palace until 1910, when the Portuguese monarchy fled town in face of revolution. In the heart of *Sintra Vila,* the old town, the landmark structure is dominated by a pair of conical chimneys rising above it. Much of it was constructed by João I in the late 1300s and built upon the site of a palace constructed by Moorish sultans that had been torn down. A favorite summer retreat of Portuguese royalty, it has seen much rebuilding and enlarging over the years, and the building is now an interesting conglomeration of architectural styles. Inside, the domed ceiling of **Sala does Brasões (Stag Room)** ☆ makes for a splendid salon. Stags hold the coats-of-arms of nearly 75 Portuguese noble families, and the lower walls are lined with Delft-like tiled panels from the 1700s. The other splendid chamber is the **Sala dos Cisnes (Swan Room)** ☆ of the former banquet hall, painted in the 17th-century. This room was a favorite of King João I, the father of Prince Henry the Navigator. The ceiling was covered with magpies, a reference to the gossipy ladies of the courts. The **Room of the Sirens or Mermaids** is one of the most elegant in the palace. It's decorated with intricate Arabesque designs. Admission is 3€ ($3.45) for adults, 1.50€ ($1.75) for children 14-25. Free for kids under 13. Open Thursday through Tuesday 10am to 1pm and 2 to 5pm.

> *Moments* **Back to Glorious Eden**
>
> If you'd like to see Sintra the way Lord Byron did when working on his autobiographical *Childe Harold's Pilgrimage*, you can rent a horse-drawn carriage in front of the National Palace of Sintra at Largo da Rainha Dona Amélia. Carrying up to five passengers, these romantic tours last less than an hour but are worth the price for a most agreeable ride under shade trees. You'll be following trails blazed by Moorish sultans centuries ago along bougainvillea-lined streets. You can look up at little balconies aflame with red geraniums. Once you've gotten the view the horse has shown you, you can wander about on your own making your own discoveries. Prices must be negotiated with the driver as there are no fixed rates, but an average ride through town usually costs about 10€ to 20€ ($11.50–$23).

The other great palace in Sintra is **Palacio Nacional de Pena** ★★, Estrada de Pena (© **21/910-5340**), standing on a plateau of 1,500 feet on one of the loftiest peaks in the Serra de Sintra mountain chain. Built in the 19th century, the palace is a blend of various architectural styles and was the royal abode of the young queen, Maria II, and her husband, Ferdinand Saxe-Coburg-Gotha. Ferdinand took charge of the building, appointing Baron Von Eschwege, a German architect to construct this cool summer place for the royal family.

It's set on parklike grounds and is a monument to a faded royal life. Allow 2 hours to tour the whole place, including Manuel II's oval-shaped bedroom adorned with bright red walls. He was the last king of Portugal. Decorated with German stained-glass windows, the elegant **Ballroom** ★ is a major highlight, with its Asian porcelain and life-size torchbearers supporting mammoth candelabra. The **Arab Room** ★ is a stunner with its magnificent *trompe l'oeil* frescoes.

The notable **Chapel Altarpiece** ★ is from the 16th century and is built from alabaster and marble, each niche depicting a scene from the life of Christ. If time remains, explore the gardens.

Admission is 5€ ($5.75) for adults, 3.50€ ($4.05) children 6 to 17 years old, and free for children 5 and under. The palace is open June to September Tuesday to Sunday, from 10am to 6:30pm; October to May Tuesday to Sunday, 10am to 5pm.

WHERE TO DINE

In the hillside village right below Sintra, **Cantinho de São Pedro,** Praça Dom Fernando II 18 (© **21/923-0267**), is known for its savory French and Portuguese-inspired cuisine, and is found right off the main square of this little satellite to Sintra. Daily specials *(pratos do dia)* are some of the finest fare in the area, and the menu always offers something enticing, perhaps salmon and shrimp au gratin or pork with an unusual mixture of clams. Main courses cost 14€ to 27.50€ ($16.10–$31.65), with a fixed-price menu going for 18€ ($20.70). Open daily noon to 3pm and 7:30 to 10pm.

Uphill from the Praça de República in Sintra, **Tacho Real** ★★ Rua da Ferraria 4 (© **21/923-5277**), serves well-prepared Portuguese and French meals in a stylish setting reached after climbing some steep steps. Both meat and fish dishes are handled equally well by a well-trained staff. The fish stew is the best in the area, and the fixed-price menu is one of Sintra's dining bargains. Main courses cost 8€ to 19€ ($9.20–$21.85), with a fixed-price menu cost of 12€ ($13.80). Open Thursday to Tuesday noon to 3pm and 7:30 to 10:30pm.

Moments   Northward Ho!

Although we focus more on Portugal's southern region in this chapter because its northern region really is more suited to a driving tour than a rail trip, if you have 3 days to play with on your itinerary, you can ride the rails north from Lisbon to experience three widely different jewels in the Portuguese crown: the walled medieval city of **Óbidos**, followed by the ancient university city of **Coimbra**, and topped by several glasses of port wine drunk on home turf in the old city of **Porto** (2nd largest in Portugal). Unlike the arid but historical plains to the south, these towns and cities lie in lush "Atlantic green" Portugal.

Óbidos

Dominated by the keep and towers of its ancient castle, the walled city of **Óbidos** ★★ is only 58 miles (93km) north of Lisbon, but it's a comparatively long train ride away. From the Estaçao do Rossio in Lisbon, frequent daily commuter trains run to the rail junction at Cacém where you can change trains for the final lap into Óbidos. The entire trip takes 2 to 3 hours and costs 5.10€ ($5.85) for a one-way ticket.

Óbidos so captivated Queen Isabella in 1228 that her husband, King Denis, presented it to her as a gift, a token of his devotion. You can spend 3 or 4 hours wandering behind its 14th-century castellated walls, viewing the whitewashed houses and old churches, and finding good food and overnight lodgings at its converted stone castle, now the **Pousada do Castelo,** Paço Real (© **26/295-5080;** www.pousadas. pt), offering 12 air-conditioned rooms and suites. Rates range from 149€ to 237€ ($171–$273).

Coimbra

Most rail passengers, however, skip Óbidos and head straight from Lisbon to the romantic city of **Coimbra** ★★★, 123 miles (198km) to the north. Some 14 high-speed trains per day make the 2-hour trek north from Lisbon to Coimbra at a cost of 9.40€ ($10.80) for a one-way ticket.

The birthplace of six kings and the seat of Portugal's oldest university, Coimbra, on the right bank of the Mondego River, is a city rich in attractions—not only its university, but one of the country's greatest Romanesque cathedrals, **Sé Velha;** and a 12th-century Gothic monastery. The renowned 18th-century **Quinta das Lagrimas** (Estate of Tears), or "Garden of Tears," was the former abode of the ill-fated Inês de Castro, mistress of Pedro the Cruel, who was murdered here on order of Pedro's father, King Alfonso IV. The gardens are a favorite pilgrimage spot for romantics and the house is now the best hotel in the region (see below).

Stop in at the **Coimbra Tourist Office,** Largo da Portagem (© **23/ 948-8120**), a 5-minute walk from the train station, and you'll be given

3 The Algarve

This strip of beachfront property is a great amphitheater facing the sea and stretching for 100 miles (160km) from Cape St. Vincent of Prince Henry the a map of the town, a list of the monuments with hours and times of opening, and the names of the leading hotels and restaurants. Our favorite place to stay in town is the luxurious and romantic 35-room manor **Quinta das Lagrimas,** Rue Antonio Agusto Gonçalves (② 23/980-2380; www.quintadaslagrimas.com) The romantic rooms are decorated in traditional Portuguese style but offer every modern comfort. Rates are 133€ to 170€ ($153–$196) double; 300€ to 375€ ($345–$431) suite.

Porto

The final stop on your rail journey north is **Porto** ★★, 195 miles (314km) north of Lisbon. A settlement known as Portucale since the 8th century B.C., the town eventually lent its name to the whole country. Once the base of the Portuguese shipping fleet, Porto (literally, "the port") helped Portugal evolve into a great maritime power. Today, however, the city on the Douro River is known mainly for housing the lodges or wine storehouses of the world-famous port wine made across Ponte Dom Luis in the satellite suburb of Vila Nova de Gaia.

The rail traveler can explore some of Porto's notable tourist highlights, including its Romanesque **Sé (Cathedral);** its 15th-century church, **Ingreja de Santa Clara;** its even more impressive 14th-century Gothic **Ingreja de São Francisco;** and its **Fundaçao de Serralves** museum devoted to modern art. Later in the day, you can take a boat trip up the Douro to sail by the vineyards where the grapes used to make the port are grown.

From Lisbon, seven daily Alfa trains make the trip to Porto. The journey takes about 2 hours, and costs 21€ ($24.15) for a one-way ticket. If you spend the night in Coimbra (see above), you can take one of several high-speed trains to Porto (trip time: 1–2 hr.); a one-way ticket costs 11€ ($12.65). Be sure to take a train to the **Estação de Sãu Bento** station, which is in the center of town, and not Porto's other rail station, which is south of the city.

For a list of hotels, restaurants, and the addresses and times to visit all the attractions, stop in at the **Porto Tourist Board,** Rua do Clube Fenianos 25 (② 22/205-2740), just a few minutes walk from the train station. One good hotel within 5 or 10 minutes' walk of the station is the 149-room **Mercure Batalha Hotel,** Porto Praca de Batalha (② 22/200-0571). It offers traditional and tastefully decorated rooms. Rates run 75€ to 85€ ($86.25–$97.75) double, but the hotel often discounts it prices.

Navigator fame to the border town of Vila Real de Santo António overlooking the Spanish frontier. Called *Al-Gharb* by the Moorish conquerors, the Algarve is celebrated for the pink blossoms of its almond trees in bloom from the middle of January until the end of February.

Fishing is still a buoyant source of income for this region, although nearly all the coast has been given over to tourism. Those lonely beaches backed up by tiny, whitewashed fishing hamlets are getting harder and harder to find as developers take over. The Algarve consists of two sections. The *barlavento* lying to the west of Portimão is a coastal strip—mainly a rock-strewn coast—that is humid and has cliffs rising 246 feet, with sandy shores and hidden coves often separated by strange grottoes. East of Faro (the capital), the *sotavento* is riddled with salty lagoons, sandy dunes, and broken spits of beaches filled mainly with European sunbathers from June to October.

Lagos and Faro are the best base cities in the Algarve for train travelers because both offer easy rail access to Lisbon.

GETTING THERE

Faro, 192 miles (309km) southeast of Lisbon, is the rail hub of the Algarve with four IC trains arriving daily from Lisbon. The trip takes 4 to 5 hours and a one-way ticket costs about 12.50€ ($14.40). If you're connecting with Lagos in the west, nine trains make the 2-hour journey out of Faro each day. Fares cost 4.20€ ($4.85) one-way.

Estación Faro, Largo Estaçao (☎ **28/980-1726**), lies near the town center, adjacent to the bus station and close to the intersection of Av. de República and Praça de Estação. Built as an architectural showcase in the 1890s, but dimmed by age, it is the most important and strategic rail junction in the south of Portugal thanks to its position astride lines that interconnect it to the north–south lines from Lisbon and the east–west lines from Vila Real in the east and Lagos in the west. Faro is the second most used railway transfer point after Lisbon.

There are no tourist offices within the station, but the **Faro Tourist Office,** Rua da Misericórdia 8 (☎ **28/980-3604**), is just a few minutes walk away. It's open June to August daily 9:30am to 7pm, September to May daily 9:30am to 5:30pm. The staff does not make hotel reservations but will provide data about what lodging is available: what's cheap, what's luxurious, and so forth. Although there is no ATM at the station, there are banks along Av. de Rua de Santo António and Av. de República, all a short walk from the station. For luggage storage, you'll have to go next door to the bus station, which doesn't store bags for more than 24 hours. Depending on size, the cost is from 2€ to 4€ ($2.30–$4.60) per bag. Note that the kiosk here isn't staffed on Saturday and Sunday. Taxis line up outside the rail station, with fares to most points within the environs of Faro ranging from 5.50€ to 19€ ($6.35–$21.85).

Caminho Ferro Portugués, Largo da Estação (☎ **28/276-2987**), is the second major rail hub for the Algarve. It's in Lagos and lies across the river from the main part of town, which is reached by a pedestrian suspension bridge. Lagos is 43 miles (69km) west of Faro and 164 miles (264km) south of Lisbon. The station lies in the eastern part of Lagos about 700 yards from the town's main square, at Praça Gil Eanes. Five IC trains arrive daily from Lisbon. The trip takes 4½ hours and a one-way ticket costs 12.60€ ($14.50). Lagos also enjoys easy rail links to Faro in the east (see above), and is the westernmost terminus of rail lines that stretch east to west across the Algarve. Points farther west, including Sagres, require access by bus from either Lagos or Faro.

There are no ATMs within the station, but there are a number of them along Avenida dos Descobrimentos, one of the city's busiest and most visible avenues, just a short walk away. The bus station lies directly across the street; neither station offers luggage storage. Taxis are available at the entrance to the station; it will cost about 5€ to 13€ ($5.75–$14.95) to go virtually anywhere within Lagos.

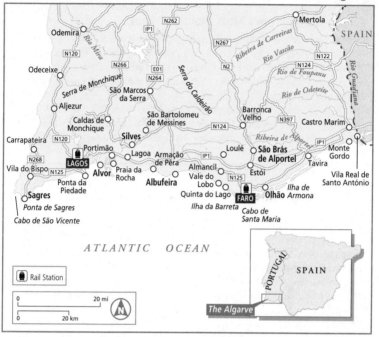

There is no tourist office within the station. The **Lagos Tourist Office** lies along Rua Vasco da Gama, Sitio de São João (© **28/276-3031**), open daily from 9:30am to 1pm and 2 to 5:30pm. The staff will make reservations but only if the client shows up in person or only if the client requests this service by phone at least 2½ weeks in advance. Reservations cost 2€ ($2.30) per person.

TOP ATTRACTIONS & SPECIAL MOMENTS

Other than the beaches, the chief man-made attractions in the Algarve lie within the towns of Faro and Lagos. The exception to this is **Sagres** ★, or "The End of the World," lying 21 miles (34km) west of Lagos and 71 miles (114km) west of Faro. At the extreme southwestern corner of Europe, it is a rocky escarpment jutting into the Atlantic Ocean. It was from this remote point that Prince Henry the Navigator launched Portugal onto the seas of exploration, establishing a school where mariners such as Vasco da Gama, Magellan, Diaz, and Cabral apprenticed. We find the sunsets here among the most dramatic in Europe. Ancient mariners thought that when the sun sank from here beyond the cape, it plunged over the edge of the world.

Henry's windswept fortress, **Fortaleza de Sagres,** has been reconstructed and turned into a small museum documenting the area's naval history. It's open May to September daily from 10am to 8:30pm; October to April daily from 10am to 6:30pm. Admission is 3€ ($3.45) for adults or 1.50€ ($1.75) for ages 24 and under. Far more dramatic than this man-made attraction is the surrounding pathways that open onto vertigo-inducing panoramas of the turbulent sea and towering cliffs.

Lying 3 miles (4.8km) to the west is the lonely **Cabo de São Vicente,** with the second most powerful lighthouse in Europe. This lighthouse beams illumination

---

Finds **The Algarve's Most Beautiful Spot**

Directly south of the port of Lagos stands **Ponta da Piedade** ⭐⭐⭐, an area of such stunning beauty that it's unmatched anywhere along the coast. This gem is filled with towering cliffs and hidden grottoes carved eons ago by turbulent waves, which make them look like flamboyant examples of Manueline architecture.

At the lighthouse here, the **view** ⭐⭐ stretches from Cabo de São Vincente on the west to Cabo Carvoeiro in the east. Ponta de Piedade is 2 miles (3km) south of the Lagos harbor. To get here, take a taxi down from Lagos.

---

60 miles (97km) across the ocean. Tours are not generally available of the actual lighthouse itself.

Lagos ⭐, your rail hub for the western Algarve, is also the principle resort of the western Algarve, opening onto Baia de Lagos, one of the widest bays of the Portuguese coast. You can spend a morning or an afternoon exploring its attractions, including **Antigo Mercado de Escravos,** Praça do Infante Dom Henríques, an arcaded slave market, the only one of its kind in Europe. Captives were once sold here to the highest bidder. Charging no admission, it can be viewed at any time.

Sitting just off the waterfront stands the 18-century church, **Igreja de Santo António** ⭐, Rua General Alberto Carlos Silveira (© **28/276-2301**). This church is a real Algarvian gem, its lower part covered with the blue-and-white tiles or *azulejos* of Portugal. The rest is in carved, painted, or gilded wood. A series of eight paneled paintings depict so-called miracles performed by Saint Anthony. At the altar are impressive **gilt carvings** ⭐, created with gold imported from Brazil. Admission is free and hours are Tuesday to Sunday 9:30am to 12:30pm and 2 to 5pm.

Next door to the church of Saint Anthony stands the **Museu Municipal Dr. José Formoshinho,** Rua General Carlos Silveira (© **28/276-2301**), the regional museum of the western Algarve. Of particular interest here are the replicas of the fret-cut chimneys of the Algarve, with exhibitions of various regional handcrafts and artifacts ranging from ecclesiastical sculpture to a numismatic collection. Pickled freak animals are among its more exotic attractions, and there's even a funky pair of 19th-century sunglasses. Admission is 2€ ($2.30) for adults, 1€ ($1.15) for kids 11 to 14, free for children under 11. Hours are Tuesday to Sunday 9:30am to 12:30pm and 2 to 5pm.

The capital city of **Faro** is a bit lean on man-made attractions. If you're caught between trains, you can occupy 2 to 3 hours of time by visiting such sights as **Igreja de Nossa Senhora do Monte do Carmo do Faro,** Largo do Carmo, erected in the 19th century. The church could be easily skipped were it not for its bizarre **Capela d'Ossos** or "Chapel of Bones." The chapel is lined with an estimated 1,245 human skulls and bones. These bones were dug up from graves around the church in 1816. Entrance to the chapel costs .75€ (85¢). Open May to September 10am to 1pm and 3 to 5pm, Saturday 10am to 1pm; October to April Monday to Friday 10am to 1pm and 3 to 5pm, Saturday 10am to 1pm.

The **Sé (Cathedral),** Largo da Sé (© **28/980-6632**), should be more impressive than it is as it's the major cathedral for the Algarve. Nonetheless, it merits 30 minutes or so of your time. This Renaissance cathedral took the tower of its

Gothic predecessor, and its wide nave is flanked by tiles *(azulejos)* from the 18th-century. Its chief attraction is its Capela do Rosário, which is loaded with *azulejos* from the 17th-century. Admission is free and the building is open Monday to Friday 10am to noon, Saturday at 5pm for services, and Sunday 8am to 1pm for services.

The **Museo Municipal,** Praça Afonso III 14 (© **28/989-7400**), is housed in the 16th-century edifice of the former Convento de Nossa Senhora da Assuncão. Artifacts recovered from the Algarve are on display in the cloister galleries with some intriguing sights—including a tomb—excavated at nearby Milreu, where the Romans built a temple dedicated to Ossonoba in the 1st century A.D. Other displays include Mudéjar *azulejos* or tiles from the Muslim era, ancient weapons and coins, and a 16th-century bishop's throne. Admission is 2€ ($2.30) adults or 1€ ($1.15) for children ages 13 to 18. Free 12 and under. Open Tuesday to Friday 10am to 6pm.

WHERE TO STAY & DINE

A good choice for Lagos-bound travelers is the 334-room **Tivoli Lagos** ★, Rua António Crisógano dos Santos, Lagos 8600-678 (© **28/279-0079**), the town's leading hostelry, housed in a 20th-century castle of Moorish and Portuguese design lying within its own ramparts and moats. Removed from the beach, the hotel lies at the eastern side of town, but with its own pool, on 3 acres of prime hilltop real estate. Both standard and deluxe rooms are rented and each is well maintained and attractively furnished. Doubles average 165€ ($190), with suites going for 218€ ($251).

Down the scale a bit, but still very inviting, is **Albergaria Marina Rio,** Av. dos Descobrimentos, Lagos 8600 (© **28/276-9859**), in the very heart of Lagos opposite the marina. Its most dramatic feature is a panoramic top-floor swimming pool with a broad sun terrace. A courtesy bus takes guests to the beaches. Bedrooms are neatly kept and range in size from small to medium, with doubles averaging 90€ ($104), rates including a buffet breakfast.

For the finest lodgings in the Lagos area, head over to **Romantik Hotel Vivenda Miranda** ★★★, Porto de Mos, Lagos 8600-282 (© **28/276-3222**), a Moorish-inspired hotel standing on a cliff that opens onto the rugged coastline, 1¾ miles (2.8km) south of Lagos, close to a good sandy beach at Praia do Porto de Mos. The hotel offers well-furnished and somewhat stylish bedrooms ranging from midsize to spacious, and its outdoor pool opens onto lush gardens and sun terraces. Doubles rent for 134€ to 184€ ($154–$212), with a suite costing 175€ to 245€ ($201–$282).

Even though a bit uninspired, **Eva** ★, Av. da República, Faro 8000-078 (© **28/900-1000**), is the best of the lodgings lot in the capital city of Faro. This modern, eight-floor, 148-room hotel stands at the harborfront, not at the beach, but offers a rooftop swimming pool. Bedrooms are furnished in a restrained style, the finer accommodations containing balconies opening onto the water. Doubles average 133€ ($153), with suites costing 213€ ($245), rates including breakfast. The best overnight value in town is found at **Residential Algarve** ★, Rua Infante Dom Henrique 62, Faro 8000-363 (© **28/989-5700**), which opened in 1999, having been created from an 1880s private home that was once owned by a local mariner. Before it became a hotel, it had to be practically demolished but was reconstructed in the original style. The hotel, only a short walk from the center of town, offers midsize to spacious bedrooms, each well-furnished. Rates average 70€ ($80.50) double and 83€ ($95.45) triple.

In the very heart of Lagos, the undiscovered **A Lagosteira,** Rua do 1 de Maio 20 (℗ **28/276-2486**), is one of the best restaurants in town, serving a regional Portuguese cuisine with an Algarvian slant. We always gravitate to this place for our first meal in town, devouring the fish soup and the savory clams—lobster is also a specialty. Main courses cost from 7€ to 14€ ($8.05–$16.10). Another local favorite is **Don Sebastiã,** ⭐ Rua do 25 de Abril 20 (℗ **28/276-2795**), which serves a savory Portuguese and Algarvian cuisine that's an equal match for the food dished out at A Lagosteira. It, too, is in the heart of town, lying to the west of the main waterfront, bordering Avenida dos Descobrimentos on the opposite bank from the rail station. The menu is varied and tasty, with a good selection of local wines. In summer, there's outdoor dining. Main courses cost from 7€ to 25€ ($8.05–$28.75).

The greatest restaurants in the Algarve are not found in Faro, but you are likely to find yourself here because it's a rail hub. Don't despair, as you can order hearty, typical Algarvian cuisine at **Adega Nortenha,** Praça Ferreira de Almeida 25 (℗ **28/982-2709**), in the heart of the city and convenient to bus and rail connections. The restaurant's regional dishes, such as bits of seafood cooked with chunks of pork in a casserole, also make it one of the most affordable bargains in town, with main courses costing 5.50€ to 10.50€ ($6.35–$12.10). A tradition since 1925, **Dois Irmãos,** Largo do Terreiro do Bispo 13-15 (℗ **28/982-3337**), is modesty itself but a good choice for its Algarvian cuisine of freshly grilled fish and shellfish dishes—most likely the catch was harvested that morning. Service is slow but it's worth the wait, with main courses costing 10€ to 20€ ($11.50–$23).

To avoid a constant diet of regional fare, you can retreat to **Casa Velha** ⭐⭐⭐ (℗ **28/939-4983**), outside Faro, 12 miles (20km) to the east, in the direction of Almancil. This is one of the grand restaurants along the coast, serving a refined French cuisine based on market-fresh ingredients deftly handled by an experienced kitchen staff. Dishes are beautifully balanced, featuring everything from foie gras or lobster to sea bass or a delectable breast of duck seasoned with a dozen spices. Main courses cost 15€ to 28€ ($17.25–$32.20).

Spain

Riding the rails in Spain is a grand adventure that offers travelers an ideal way to see one of the most diverse landscapes in Europe—from the snow-capped peaks surrounding Granada to the rivers enveloping Toledo and the Moorish-flavored Andalusia to the modern artistry of Catalonia. Traveling through Spain by rail is both the cheapest way to see the country—especially if you opt for a railpass—and a relatively inexpensive venture when compared to train travel in other western European countries. Value-conscious travelers looking for a diverse destination without sacrificing comfort will be hard-pressed to find a better choice on the Continent.

Since the mid-1990s, there has been an almost Herculean improvement in the Spanish state railway system, aka **RENFE** *(Red Nacional de Ferrocarriles Espanoles)*. Spain now offers more options for the rail traveler than ever before. Its high-speed TALGO trains, and the speedy and luxurious AVE trains running between Madrid and Seville, have almost buried the country's reputation for sluggish rail service, though the notoriously slow *regionales y cercanías* (regional and local trains) still remain.

RENFE's network of trains is now so vast that all the major sections of Spain are linked to Madrid with efficient high-speed trains. To reach some of the more remote provinces or areas, you still must rely on slow-moving trains, but if you stick to the main cities, you can be anywhere in Spain within a matter of hours, including Andalusia in the south (Seville and Granada) or Barcelona (the country's 2nd major rail hub) in the east.

HIGHLIGHTS OF SPAIN

Every major region of Spain from the Basque country in the northeast to the southern cities of Andalusia, such as Granada and Seville, are within hours of **Madrid** by rail. The capital of Spain is at the geographical center of the country and is the hub of all its major rail networks. Madrid makes the best base for a rail tour of Spain because you can branch out to virtually anywhere in the country.

The country's second major rail transportation hub, **Barcelona,** is in the remote northeast of the country and is a long way from some of Spain's frequently visited cities, such as Toledo. Barcelona is a good launch pad for rail travelers only if they are coming from the east, through the south of France, or are flying first into Barcelona to begin their rail journey.

Madrid's attractions are year-round, including three internationally famous art galleries—**the Prado, Centro de Arte Reina Sofia, and Museo Thyssen–Bornemisza**—along with a royal palace, grand public squares, and museum after museum stuffed with treasures. Its 17th-century square, **Plaza Mayor,** lies at the focal point of Madrid's historic core. While in Madrid, be sure to budget a 1-day trip by rail to **Toledo,** the capital of old Castile and one of the five most fascinating cities of Spain.

After seeing Madrid, most rail passengers head south to Andalusia, specifically Seville. Those with an extra 2 or 3 days to spare, however, can continue to take train rides from Madrid to several art cities that lie on its doorstep. In just 2 hours you can travel 54 miles (87km) northwest of Madrid to **Segovia.** If you leave early enough from Madrid, you can visit Segovia's Cabildo Catédral de Segovia, the last Gothic cathedral built in Spain (1515) and its fabled Alcázar dating from the 12th century. Although it would be a long day, you can return to Madrid by nightfall. Another longer day trip from Madrid is the walled city of **Avila,** 68 miles (109km) northwest of Madrid. Some two dozen trains leave daily from Madrid for Avila, taking 1½ to 2 hours each way. The main attractions in this city forever linked to St. Teresa, born here in 1515, are the medieval walls of Avila averaging 33 feet in height.

An even longer day trip out of Madrid is an excursion to the ancient university city of **Salamanca,** 127 miles (204km) northwest of Madrid. Labeled a World Heritage City by UNESCO, Salamanca's major attractions, including its Plaza Mayor (the most beautiful in Spain) and both its old and new cathedrals can be visited in 3 hours.

Although the city of **Bilbao,** capital of the Basque country, is a popular tourist destination now that its Guggenheim Museum has opened, a train ride here from Madrid can take 6½ to 8½ hours, making it very inconvenient for rail travelers exploring Spain for the first time and with limited time on their hands. The

---

⌒ *Moments*   Festivals & Special Events

One of the biggest draws on Spain's cultural calendar, **ARCO** (Madrid's International Contemporary Art Fair) showcases the best in contemporary art from Europe and America. At the Nuevo Recinto Ferial Juan Carlos I, the exhibition draws galleries from throughout Europe, the Americas, Australia, and Asia, who bring with them the works of regional and internationally known artists. To buy tickets contact Parque Ferial Juan Carlos I at ℭ **91-722-5000.** The cost is between 19€ and 23€ ($22–$26.50). You can get schedules from the tourist office closer to the event. Dates vary, but it's usually held mid-February. For more information, call ℭ **90-240-0222.**

The **Feria de Sevilla (Seville Fair)** is the most celebrated week of revelry in all of Spain, with all-night flamenco dancing, entertainment booths, bullfights, horseback riding, flower-decked coaches, and dancing in the streets. The action takes place the second week after Easter and you'll need to reserve a hotel well in advance. For general information and exact festival dates, contact the Office of Tourism in Seville (ℭ **95-422-14-04).**

Madrileños run wild during the 10-day **Fiesta de San Isidro** celebration honoring their city's patron saint. Food fairs, Castilian folkloric events, street parades, parties, music, dances, bullfights, and other festivities mark the occasion, which starts the second week of May. Make hotel reservations early. Expect crowds and traffic (and beware of pickpockets). For information, write to **Oficina Municipal de Información y Turismo,** Plaza Mayor 3, 28014 Madrid, or call ℭ **91-588-1636.**

same goes for the sea resort of San Sebastian and for the medieval city of Pamplona, made famous by its running of the bulls.

It's far easier for rail travelers to head south, and we concentrate on options in that area of the country. From Madrid, high-speed trains rush you south to the vast sprawling lands of Andalusia, which takes up all of the southern tier of Spain, opening onto the Mediterranean. This once-great stronghold of Muslim Spain is rich in history and tradition, containing some of the country's most celebrated treasures: the world-famous Mezquita (mosque) in Córdoba, the Alhambra in Granada, and the great Gothic cathedral in Seville. It also has many smaller towns just waiting to be discovered—Ubeda, Jaén, gorge-split Ronda, Jerez de la Frontera, and the gleaming white port city of Cádiz. Give Andalusia at least a week and you'll still have only skimmed the surface.

This dry mountainous region also embraces the overbuilt and often tacky Costa del Sol (Málaga, Marbella, and Torremolinos), or Sun Coast, a strip of beach resorts that's popular with Europeans, but one that we suggest skipping.

Seville, the capital of Andalusia, is a major goal of the rail passenger, as this city ranks along with Madrid, Barcelona, and Toledo as one of the five most visited—and justifiably so—cities of Spain.

On the banks of Río Guadalquivir, Seville flourished under Muslim rule and again in the 16th century. Many architectural treasures remain from those epochs, including a celebrated cathedral and **La Giralda,** the minaret of a mosque constructed from 1184 to 1198. This is Spain's most perfect Islamic building. The cathedral contains the tomb of Columbus. Seville's **Barrio de Santa Cruz,** or medieval Jewish quarter, is alone worth the train ride from Madrid, with its tangle of quaint and winding streets. Because of the sultry climate, July and August are the worst months to visit here.

Eighteen AVE trains make the 45-minute trip from Seville to the historic city of **Córdoba,** each day. A visit to the city's famous mosque is one no rail traveler will likely forget.

After a visit to Seville, passengers wanting to see the world famous **Alhambra,** a palace left over from the days of Moorish occupation, can take one of four trains heading east from Seville along one of Andalusia's most scenic train rides into the snow-capped Sierra Nevada mountains before reaching the palace's home, the city of **Granada.** After Granada, a traditional rail tour of Spain heads northeast to **Barcelona,** although this is a long journey that will take 11 to 15 hours depending on the train.

Barcelona, the capital of Catalonia, is one of the busiest ports in the Mediterranean. In culture, business, and sports, it rivals Madrid and is on par with some of the grandest capitals of Europe. Barcelona is known for its **Las Ramblas,** the most famous street in Spain, alive at all hours, and for the architecture of Gaudí, best represented by his unfinished masterpiece, **Sagrada Familia,** a cathedral. In the heart of town, the evocative **Barri Gotic** or Gothic quarter is reason enough to visit the city, crowned by the 14th-century **Barcelona Cathedral.** Historical monuments and museums, including one dedicated to Picasso, abound here, but the city is celebrated for the scores of structures in its Eixample District, left over from the artistic explosion of *Modernisme.*

Once Barcelona is visited, rail passengers can either fly out of the city or can continue by train up the rugged coastline, **Costa Brava,** and into France.

1 Essentials

GETTING THERE

The major gateway cities for flights into Spain from all over the world are Barcelona and Madrid. Madrid's international airport, **Barajas** (© **91-305-8343**), lies 9 miles (15km) east of the center with two terminals, one for international flights, the other for domestic traffic. The airport for Barcelona is El Prat de Llobregat, Prat de Llobregat (© **93-298-3838**), about 7½ miles (12km) southwest of the city.

Iberia Airlines (© **800/772-4642;** www.iberia.com) offers more routes into and within Spain than any other airline. It features daily nonstop service to Madrid from such North American cities as New York, Chicago, and Miami. **Air Europa** (© **888/238-7672;** www.air-europa.com), is Iberia's chief Spanish-based competitor, serving Madrid from New Jersey's Newark Airport, with continuing service to major cities in Spain.

Note: Barcelona-bound passengers often land in Madrid, which is linked by Iberia flights leaving at 15-minute intervals during peak hours on weekdays. Iberia flights also leave Madrid frequently for Seville, which is the gateway air city to Andalusia.

Other North American carriers with direct service to Spain include **American Airlines** (© **800/433-7300;** www.aa.com), **Delta** (© **800/241-4141;** www.delta.com), **Continental Airlines** (© **800/231-0856;** www.continental.com), and **US Airways** (© **800/428-4322;** www.usairways.com).

Moments **The Orient Express . . . Spanish Style**

The most luxurious way to see Spain by rail is aboard the "Belle Epoque hotel on wheels," more commonly known as the **Al Andalus Expreso** (**www.lugaresdivinos.com**), an Orient Express–style train which departs either from Madrid or Seville and passes through several cities in Andalusia, including Cordoba and Granada. The train features 14 carefully restored antique carriages that were built in 1929 but now feature all the modern comforts. From its brass fittings to its antique veneers, this is rail travel in grand style, complete with gourmet dining, flamenco shows, and elegant sleeping carriages. The cost of a basic package of 6 days and 5 nights begins at 2,547€ ($2,929) per person based on double occupancy.

United Airlines (℃ **800/241-6522;** www.ual.com) does not fly into Spain directly but offer airfares from the United States to Spain in conjunction with a host of European airlines.

SPAIN BY RAIL
PASSES

Both the **Eurailpass** and **Eurailpass Flexi** are good for use on Spanish trains. For information on the Spain Flexipass, Iberic Railpass, Spain Rail 'n Drive Pass, and the France 'n Spain Pass, see chapter 2. All rail passes should be purchased in North America before you depart for Europe. Passes can be ordered in North America through **Rail Europe** (℃ **877/272-RAIL** in the U.S., **800/361-RAIL** in Canada; www.raileurope.com) or your travel agent.

Spain also has its own national rail passes, all issued by RENFE. For information on train fares, schedules, and destinations, call RENFE at ℃ **902-24-0202** or see its website at **www.renfe.es**. Children 4 to 11 pay half the adult fare, and tots under 4 ride free. For train tickets, go to the principal office of RENFE in Madrid at Alcalá 44 (℃ **91-506-6329;** Metro: Banco de España), open Monday to Friday 9:30am to 8pm.

Warning: If you purchase a round-trip ticket in Spain, you must hang onto both parts of the ticket until you've completed your entire journey or you might be fined severely when the conductor comes around to check tickets on your return leg.

FOREIGN TRAIN TERMS

All stations in Spain post train timetables, *llegadas* indicating arrivals and *salidas* meaning departures. For other information, ask at a ticket window or *taquilla*. Nearly all long-distance trains *(largo recorrido)* offer first- and second-class tickets, the slowest (also the least expensive) of these being the *regionales*.

Regular long-distance inter-regional trains are known as *diurnos*. When these trains travel at night, they become *estrellas*. *Talgo* (Tren Articulado Ligero Giocoechea Oriol) are the fastest, most expensive, and also the most comfortable trains in Spain. Talgos stop only at major cities, not outposts. The classic and best version is a **Talgo 200,** featuring both a *turista* class and a luxurious *preferente* class. The high-speed train between Madrid and Seville is called AVE. Bigger cities such as Madrid have trains making short runs, and these local networks are called *cercanias*.

PRACTICAL TRAIN INFORMATION

TALGO and **AVE** trains are the fastest and most efficient in Spain, but there are a number of other special trains that run in Spain as well. Altaria trains are high-speed lines that will get you from Madrid to Córdoba in a little more than 2 hours, or Madrid to Seville in slightly more than 3 hours.

For speed, stick to the fast TALGO trains linking Barcelona with Madrid. Sometimes a train carries a special name such as *Extremadura*, which gets you to Madrid at about the same time as a TALGO. Try to avoid the two slow-moving trains, *Costa Brava* and *Trenhotel* (unless it's the overnight train), which take about 9 hours to get between the two cities. You should also try to avoid the slow InterCity trains and even slower *Estrecho* trains that run between Madrid and Córdoba, and the slow Trian trains that run between Madrid and Seville. The two most important cities of Andalusia, Seville and Granada, are linked by TRD trains (Regional Diesel Trains), incorporating the latest technology in the field of diesel engines.

If you're on a strict budget, opt for second-class seats on trains; they are reasonably comfortable and usually well maintained.

RESERVATIONS   Reservations are required on Spanish trains. If you're traveling on the same day you purchase your ticket, go to the window marked *venta immediata*. For future travel, head for the window called *venta anticipada*. Expect long lines at either window. Sometimes you'll have to take a number from a vending machine and watch for that number to appear on a digital display board.

Reservations should be made as far in advance as possible, and railpass validation can also be made at any of these designated windows. Before leaving the window, be certain that the *fecha* (date) and the *hora salida* (departure time) are correct on your reservation.

SERVICES & AMENITIES   *Couchettes*—actually foldout bunk beds—are called *literas* in Spain. We have found that many of these couchettes, which sleep six, are old and dirty. They're inexpensive but you might not feel comfortable sleeping in them. If you're taking a long-distance night train—called an *estrella*—you can see if a *Trenhotel* (train hotel) option is available for you. These are clean sleeping compartments with their own shower and toilet. Advance reservations are absolutely essential for one of these compartments.

For both regular ticket holders and passholders, standard seat reservations start at 9.55€ ($11) per passenger for both adults and children and are non-refundable. Reservation prices for more luxurious trains can be higher, beginning at 13.90€ ($16) per passenger. Based on distance, sleeper fares—in addition to the regular ticket—range from 21.75€ to 175€ ($25–$201) per passenger, with couchette reservations costing a flat 24.35€ ($28) per person. Reservations can be confirmed up to 2 months prior to the date of travel, but are non-refundable and non-exchangeable.

Most night trains have full restaurant service, and stewards also provide drinks and snacks at all hours. Inquire in advance about dining facilities or services. If they don't exist, bring your own food and drink to be on the safe side.

Most Spanish trains are air-conditioned with adequate toilet facilities. Tickets for *gran clase* (*preferente* on the Talgo) feature sleeping cars with private showers and toilets. In *turista* class cars, you'll find berths that sleep four. In economy class, expect a "sleeperette" seat.

Trains & Travel Times in Spain

From	To	Type of Train	# of Trains	Frequency	Travel Time
Madrid	Barcelona	Talgo	6	Daily	6 hr. 45 min.– 7 hr. 5 min.
Madrid	Barcelona	Extremadura	1	Daily	7 hr. 3 min.
Madrid	Barcelona	Costa Brava	1	Daily	9 hr.
Madrid	Barcelona	Trenhotel	1	Sun–Fri	8 hr. 58 min.
Madrid	Cordoba	AVE	18	Daily	1 hr. 42 min.
Madrid	Cordoba	Talgo 200	5	Daily	2 hr. 10 min.
Madrid	Cordoba	Talgo 200	1	Mon–Sat	1 hr. 57 min.
Madrid	Cordoba	Altaria	2	Daily	2 hr. 5 min.– 2 hr. 9 min.
Madrid	Cordoba	Intercity	1	Daily	4 hr. 38 min.
Madrid	Cordoba	Triana	1	Daily	2 hr. 10 min.
Madrid	Cordoba	Estrecho	1	Daily	5 hr. 32 min.
Madrid	Seville	AVE	19	Daily	2 hr. 20 min.– 2 hr. 30 min.
Madrid	Seville	Altaria	1	Daily	3 hr. 12 min.
Madrid	Seville	Triana	1	Daily	3 hr. 25 min.
Madrid	Algeciras	Altaria	1	Daily	5 hr. 50 min.
Madrid	Algeciras	Estrecho	1	Daily	10 hr. 20 min.
Madrid	Malaga	Talgo 200	6	Daily	4 hr. 2 min.– 4 hr. 20 min.
Madrid	Malaga	Talgo 200	1	Mon–Sat	4 hr. 15 min.
Madrid	Malaga	Intercity	1	Daily	6 hr. 2 min.
Madrid	Granada	Talgo	2	Daily	5 hr. 55 min.– 6 hr. 2 min.
Seville	Granada	T.R.D.	4	Daily	3 hr. 12 min.– 3 hr. 22 min.
Seville	Cordoba	AVE	18	Daily	45 min.
Granada	Barcelona	Trenhotel	1	Daily	11 hr. 40 min.

FAST FACTS: Spain

Area Codes In Spain the entire number must be dialed, including the area code, even in the city in which you are located. Area codes are as follows: **91** for Madrid; **93** for Barcelona; **95** for Seville, Córdoba, Marbella, and Málaga.

Business Hours Banks are open Monday through Friday from 9:30am to 2pm and Saturday from 9:30am to 1pm. Most offices are open Monday through Friday from 9am to 5 or 5:30pm; the long-time practice of early closings in summer seems to be dying out. In restaurants, lunch is usually from 1 to 4pm and dinner from 9 to 11:30pm or midnight. There are no set rules for the opening of bars and taverns, many opening at 8am, others at noon; most stay open until 1:30am or later. Major stores are open Monday to Saturday 9:30am to 8pm; smaller establishments, however, often take a siesta, doing business from 9:30am to 1:30pm and 4:30 to 8pm. Hours can vary from store to store.

Climate Spring and fall are ideal times to visit nearly all of Spain, with the possible exception of the Atlantic coast, which experiences heavy rains in

October and November. May and October are the best months, in terms of both weather and crowds. In summer it's hot, hot, and hotter still, with the cities in Castile (Madrid) and Andalusia (Seville and Córdoba) heating up the most. Madrid has dry heat; the average temperature can hover around 84°F (29°C) in July and 75°F (24°C) in September. Seville has the dubious reputation of being about the hottest part of Spain in July and August, often baking under average temperatures of 93°F (34°C). Barcelona, cooler in temperature, is very humid in July and August.

Documents Required Visas are not needed by U.S. and Canadian citizens for visits of less than 3 months.

Electricity Most hotels have 220 volts AC (50 cycles). Some older places have 110 or 125 volts AC. Carry an adapter with you, and always check at your hotel desk before plugging in any electrical appliance. It's best to travel with battery-operated equipment; check to see if your hotel has an adaptor, or just buy a new hair dryer in Spain.

Embassies & Consulates If you lose your passport, fall seriously ill, get into legal trouble, or have some other serious problem, your embassy or consulate can help. These are the Madrid addresses and hours: The **United States Embassy,** Calle Serrano 75 (© **91-587-2200**; Metro: Núñez de Balboa), is open Monday through Friday from 9am to 6pm. The **Canadian Embassy,** Núñez de Balboa 35 (© **91-423-3250**; Metro: Velázquez), is open Monday through Friday from 8:30am to 5:30pm.

Health & Safety Spain should not pose any major health hazards. The rich cuisine—garlic, olive oil, and wine—may give some travelers mild diarrhea, so take along some anti-diarrhea medicine; moderate your eating habits; and even though the water is generally safe, drink mineral water only. The water is safe to drink through Spain; however, do not drink the water in mountain streams, regardless of how clear and pure it looks. Fish and shellfish from the horrendously polluted Mediterranean should only be eaten if cooked.

If you are traveling around Spain (particularly southern Spain) over the summer, limit your exposure to the sun, especially during the first few days of your trip and, thereafter, from 11am to 2pm. Wearing a hat is probably a good idea, and you should use a sunscreen with an SPF rating of at least 25 and apply it liberally and often. Remember, if you're traveling with kids, that they need more protection than adults do.

While most of Spain has a moderate rate of crime, and most of the estimated one million American tourists who visit it each year have trouble-free visits, the principal tourist areas have been experiencing an increase in violent crime. Madrid and Barcelona, in particular, have reported growing incidents of muggings and violent attacks, and older tourists and Asian Americans seem to be particularly at risk. Criminals frequent tourist areas and major attractions such as museums, monuments, restaurants, hotels, beach resorts, trains, train stations, airports, subways, and ATMs. In Barcelona, violent attacks have occurred near the Picasso Museum and in the Gothic Quarter, Parc Guell, Plaza Real, and Mont Juic. In Madrid, reported incidents occurred in key tourist areas, including the area near the Prado Museum and Atocha train station, and areas of old Madrid such as Sol, the El Rastro flea market, and Plaza Mayor. Travelers should exercise caution both day and night, carry limited cash and credit cards, and leave extra cash, credit cards, passports, and personal documents in a safe location.

Holidays These include January 1 (New Year's Day), January 6 (Feast of the Epiphany), March 19 (Feast of St. Joseph), Good Friday, Easter Monday, May 1 (May Day), June 10 (Corpus Christi), June 29 (Feast of St. Peter and St. Paul), July 25 (Feast of St. James), August 15 (Feast of the Assumption), October 12 (Spain's National Day), November 1 (All Saints' Day), December 8 (Immaculate Conception), and December 25 (Christmas).

Legal Aid If you're in trouble with the law, contact your nearest embassy or consulate, who will provide a list of English-speaking lawyers in your area.

Mail Airmail letters to the United States and Canada cost .75€ (85¢) up to 15 grams, and letters to Britain or other EU countries .50€ (60¢) up to 20 grams; letters within Spain .25€ (30¢). Postcards have the same rates as letters. Allow about 8 days for delivery to North America, generally less to the United Kingdom; in some cases, letters take 2 weeks to reach North America. Rates change frequently, so check at your local hotel before mailing anything. As for surface mail to North America, forget it. Chances are you'll be home long before your letter arrives.

Police & Emergencies The national emergency number is **006** throughout Spain, except in the Basque country where it is **088**.

Telephones If you don't speak Spanish, you'll find it easier to telephone from your hotel, but remember that this is often very expensive because hotels impose a surcharge on every operator-assisted call. In some cases it can be as high as 40% or more. On the street, phone booths (known as *cabinas*) have dialing instructions in English; you can make local calls by inserting a .25€ (30¢) coin for 3 minutes.

For directory assistance: Dial **1003** in Spain.

For operator assistance: If you need operator assistance in making an international call, dial **025**.

Toll-free numbers: Numbers beginning with **900** in Spain are toll-free, but calling an 800-number in the States from Spain is not toll-free. In fact, it costs the same as an overseas call.

Each number is preceded by its provincial code for local, national, and international calls. For example, when calling to Madrid from Madrid or another province within Spain, telephone customers must dial **91-123-45-67**. Similarly, when calling Valladolid from within or outside the province, dial **979-123-45-67**.

When in Spain, the access number for an **AT&T** calling card is ℂ **800/CALL-ATT**. The access number for **Sprint** is ℂ **800/888-0013**.

More information is also available on the Telefónica website at **www.telefonica.es**.

To call Spain: If you're calling Spain from the United States, dial the international access code (**011**), then the country code for Spain (**34**), followed by the city code and the telephone number. So the whole number you'd dial would be **011-34-93-000-0000**.

To make international calls: To make international calls from Spain, first dial **00** and then the country code (U.S. or Canada **1**), followed by the city area code and number.

Tipping The government requires restaurants and hotels to include their service charges—usually 15% of the bill. However, that doesn't mean you should skip out of a place without dispensing an extra euro or two. The following are some guidelines:

Your hotel porter should get 1€ ($1.15) per bag. Maids should be given 1.50€ ($1.75) per day, more if you're generous. Tip doormen 1€ ($1.15) for assisting with baggage and .50€ (60¢) for calling a cab. In top-ranking hotels the concierge will often submit a separate bill, showing charges for newspapers and other services; if he or she has been particularly helpful, tip extra. For cab drivers, add about 10% to the fare as shown on the meter. At airports, such as Barajas in Madrid and major terminals, the porter who handles your luggage will present you with a fixed-charge bill.

In both restaurants and nightclubs, a 15% service charge is added to the bill. To that, add another 3% to 5% tip, depending on the quality of the service. Waiters in deluxe restaurants and nightclubs are accustomed to the extra 5%, which means you'll end up tipping 20%. If that seems excessive, you must remember that the initial service charge reflected in the fixed price is distributed among all the help.

Barbers and hairdressers expect a 10% to 15% tip. Tour guides expect 2€ ($2.30), although a tip is not mandatory. Theater and bullfight ushers get .50€ (60¢).

2 Madrid

At an altitude of 2,165 feet, lofty Madrid is the geographical center of Spain and the hub of both its rail and highway networks. Since 1561, the city has presided over one of the most volatile and fast-changing countries in the world, going from kingdom to dictatorship to democracy.

Madrid is not the most beautiful or charming of European capitals, but it is home to some of the greatest art museums in the world, and it is also a good base for exploring some of the finest art cities of antiquity, especially Toledo to its immediate south.

Even more than museums, it is the spirit and lifestyle of the Castilians that provoke interest, even passion, in those who view the city as a grand place to visit. Once night falls, *la movida* (roughly, "the movement") flows until dawn in more bars, cafes, *tascas,* and clubs than there would seem to be stars in heaven.

For the train traveler, Madrid is Valhalla, the "center of the universe" for riding the rails. Trains fan out from Madrid to all the major cities, regions, and provinces of Spain. There are good connections to the "cities of the heartland," such as Segovia and Toledo, and express links to such major cities and attractions as Seville or Barcelona.

STATION INFORMATION
GETTING FROM THE AIRPORT TO THE TRAIN STATIONS

In lieu of adequate bus connections, many passengers arriving in Madrid at its Barajas airport rely on a taxi to take them to the two major rail terminals. To the station at Chamartín, the cost of a ride ranges from 20€ to 25€ ($23–29). Trip time is 15 to 20 minutes, depending on traffic. From Barajas to the Atocha station, the cost ranges from 25€ to 30€ ($29–$34.50), with trip time varying from 20 to 40 minutes, based entirely on traffic conditions.

If you are traveling light and want to save money, you can take a subway from Barajas into central Madrid. Take line 8 to Mar de Cristal and switch to line 4, a one-way trip costing 1.10€ ($1.25). Air-conditioned buses also take you from the arrivals terminal to the bus depot under Plaza de Colón, a central point. The fare is 2.50€ ($3), and buses leave every 10 to 15 minutes daily from 6am to 10pm. Unless you can make adequate Metro connections, you'll still need a taxi to take you to Atocha or Chamartín once you arrive in central Madrid.

INSIDE THE STATIONS

Madrid has two major rail stations, Atocha and Chamartín.

At **Estación Atocha,** Glorieta Carlos V (© **90-224-0202;** Metro: Atocha), high-speed Talgo 200 and AVE trains link Madrid with major points in Andalusia (Córdoba, Seville, and the Costa del Sol, for example). Atocha is linked to the city's second major station, Chamartín (see below) by Madrid's Metro system.

The local **RENFE ticket office** (© **90-224-0202**) in the station is open daily from 7:15am to 10:15pm. Go here for train information, seat reservations, and railpass validation. For money exchange, use the on-site offices of **Caya Madrid** (© **91-506-2800**), open Monday to Friday 8:15am to 7pm.

A branch of the Madrid Tourist Office (© **91-528-4630**), is also found here, and is open daily from 9am to 9pm. This office doesn't make hotel reservations. For that, go to the on-site travel agency, **Viajes El Corte Inglés** (© **91-528-4408**), open daily from 7am to 10pm. You pay your hotel bill on the spot and are issued a voucher. There is no charge for hotels booked within Madrid; outside of the city, the cost is 13€ ($15) per booking. **Luggage lockers** *(consignas automáticas),* operated by RENFE, are also at the station. Luggage can be stored daily from 8am to 10:30pm.

Atocha is a virtual tourist attraction in itself, a 19th-century palace built of iron and glass, with a restaurant, a botanical garden, along with numerous cafes and bars. Signs are clearly marked throughout the station, and there are excellent links to public transport such as the Metro. Atocha is far more central than Charmartín, lying directly south of the famous Parque del Buen Retiro and within walking distance of such attractions as Museo del Prado.

Estación Charmartín, San Agustin de Foxa (© **902-24-0202;** Metro: Charmartín), is the international rail station for Madrid, linking it with most European capitals to the east, with connections to Barcelona and beyond. Major destinations from here include Lisbon as well as Paris. Chamartín is the depot for domestic destinations in the northeast and parts of southern Spain. For **train information,** seat reservations, and railpass validation, go to the local RENFE office (© **902-24-0202**), in the center of the station between tracks 11 and 12. Hours are daily from 6:30am to 10:55pm.

Opposite track 19 is the **tourist information office** (© **91-315-9976**), open Monday to Saturday 8am to 8pm. Next to the tourist office is **Viajes Brujula** (© **91-315-7894**), a travel agent that will make reservations in Madrid hotels for 2.50€ ($3) per person. Daily 7am to 9:30pm. For **money exchange,** go to Caja Madrid (© **91-732-0155**), open Monday to Friday 8am to 8pm and Saturday 10am to 2pm.

RENFE runs the local luggage storage *(consignas automáticas),* charging 2.40€ to 4.50€ ($2.75–$5.25) per bag.

Chamartín lies in the north of Madrid, a 15- to 20-minute ride from the center (longer if traffic is bad).

Madrid

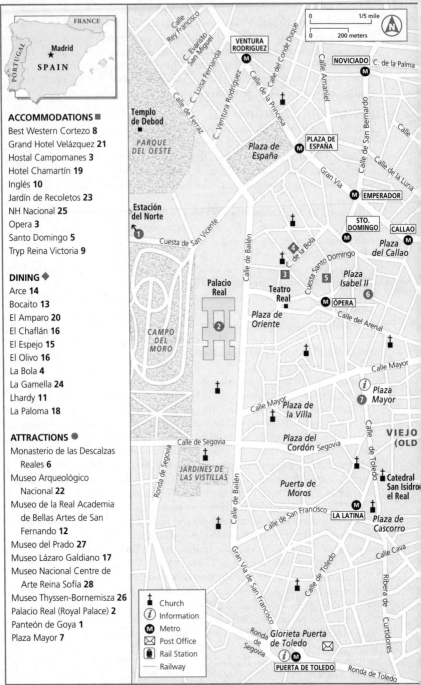

ACCOMMODATIONS ■
Best Western Cortezo **8**
Grand Hotel Velázquez **21**
Hostal Campomanes **3**
Hotel Chamartín **19**
Inglés **10**
Jardín de Recoletos **23**
NH Nacional **25**
Opera **3**
Santo Domingo **5**
Tryp Reina Victoria **9**

DINING ◆
Arce **14**
Bocaito **13**
El Amparo **20**
El Chaflán **16**
El Espejo **15**
El Olivo **16**
La Bola **4**
La Gamella **24**
Lhardy **11**
La Paloma **18**

ATTRACTIONS ●
Monasterio de las Descalzas
  Reales **6**
Museo Arqueológico
  Nacional **22**
Museo de la Real Academia
  de Bellas Artes de San
  Fernando **12**
Museo del Prado **27**
Museo Lázaro Galdiano **17**
Museo Nacional Centre de
  Arte Reina Sofía **28**
Museo Thyssen-Bornemisza **26**
Palacio Real (Royal Palace) **2**
Panteón de Goya **1**
Plaza Mayor **7**

† Church
ⓘ Information
Ⓜ Metro
✉ Post Office
🚉 Rail Station
---- Railway

Estación
Chamartín

Calle de la Palma

Calle de Fuencarral

C. de El Escorial

del Pez

Corredera Baja de San Pablo

Calle de Valverde

Calle de Fuencarral

Calle Fernando VI

Calle
de Augusto

Hortaleza

Calle de Genova

Plaza de
la Villa

Calle Bárbara
de Braganza

Gravina

Ⓜ CHUECA

San Marcos

Figueroa **14**

13

Infantas

Ⓜ **GRAN VÍA**
Red. de
San Luis

Gran Vía

Calle Montera

C. del Carmen

C. de Preciados

Calle de la Cruz

Puerta
del Sol
Ⓜ SOL

Calle de Alcalá

12

Carrera de San

Jerónimo **11**

10

9 Calle del Prado

Plaza Jacinto
Benavente
MADRID
MADRID)8

Ⓜ TIRSO DE MOLINA
Calle de la Magdalena
✉ Calle de la Cabeza

Calle Jesús y María Levapiés

Calle del Amparo

Baja

Calle Mesón de Paredes

Calle de Embajadores

C. Miguel Servet

Calle de Santa Isabel

Plaza
Lavapiés
Ⓜ LAVAPIES

Calle de las Huertas

Calle Atocha

ANTÓN
MARTÍN Ⓜ

Calle de la Cabeza

Calle de Cervantes

Plaza
de las
Cortes
ⓘ

Calle de Prim

Paseo de Recoletos

Plaza de
la Cibeles

Calle de Alcalá

BANCO
DE ESPAÑA Ⓜ

Ⓜ SEVILLA

Palacio de
Villahermosa

25

Paseo del Prado

26

Plaza C.
del Castillo

Calle de Gobernador

Calle Atocha

Paseo del Prado

Plaza de la
Castellana

16 **17**

■ Wax Museum

Plaza
de Colón

Calle de Goya

COLÓN
Ⓜ **15**

SERRANO

18→
Ⓜ
19

JARDINES
DEL
DESCUBRIMIENTO

20→

Calle de Serrano

Coello

Claudio

23
22

BARRIO
DE SALAMANCA

21→

Plaza de la
Independencia

Calle de Montalban

24

■ Naval
Museum

Plaza de
la Lealtad

Calle A. Maura

Calle de Alfonso XII

■ Army
Museum

27

Museo del
Prado

Calle de Espalter

PARQUE
DEL
BUEN
RETIRO

REAL
JARDIN
BOTANICO

Calle de Alfonso XII

28 Reina
Sofía

✉

Ⓜ ATOCHA

Sta. María
de la Cabeza

Paseo de la
Infanta Isabel

Estación
de Atocha

✉

Ronda de Atocha

Madrid Metro

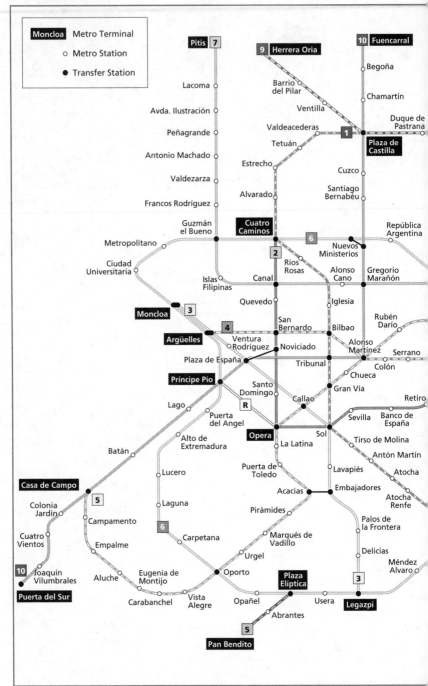

Moncloa Metro Terminal
○ Metro Station
● Transfer Station

Pitis 7
Herrera Oria 9
Fuencarral 10
Lacoma
Barrio del Pilar
Begoña
Avda. Ilustración
Ventilla
Chamartín
Peñagrande
Valdeacederas
Duque de Pastrana
Antonio Machado
Tetuán
1
Valdezarza
Estrecho
Plaza de Castilla
Francos Rodríguez
Alvarado
Cuzco
Guzmán el Bueno
Cuatro Caminos
Santiago Bernabéu
Metropolitano
6
República Argentina
Ciudad Universitaria
2
Ríos Rosas
Nuevos Ministerios
Islas Filipinas
Canal
Alonso Cano
Gregorio Marañón
Quevedo
Iglesia
Moncloa 3
San Bernardo
Rubén Darío
Argüelles 4
Ventura Rodríguez
Noviciado
Bilbao
Alonso Martínez
Plaza de España
Tribunal
Serrano
Príncipe Pío
Santo Domingo
Callao
Chueca
Colón
Lago
Gran Vía
Retiro
Puerta del Angel
R
Sevilla
Banco de España
Alto de Extremadura
Opera
La Latina
Sol
Tirso de Molina
Batán
Lucero
Puerta de Toledo
Lavapiés
Antón Martín
Atocha
Casa de Campo
Acacias
Embajadores
Atocha Renfe
Colonia Jardín
5
Laguna
Pirámides
Palos de la Frontera
Cuatro Vientos
Campamento
6
Carpetana
Marqués de Vadillo
Delicias
Empalme
Urgel
Méndez Alvaro
10 Joaquín Vilumbrales
Aluche
Eugenia de Montijo
Oporto
3
Puerta del Sur
Carabanchel
Vista Alegre
Opañel
Plaza Elíptica
Usera
Legazpi
Abrantes
5
Pan Bendito

738

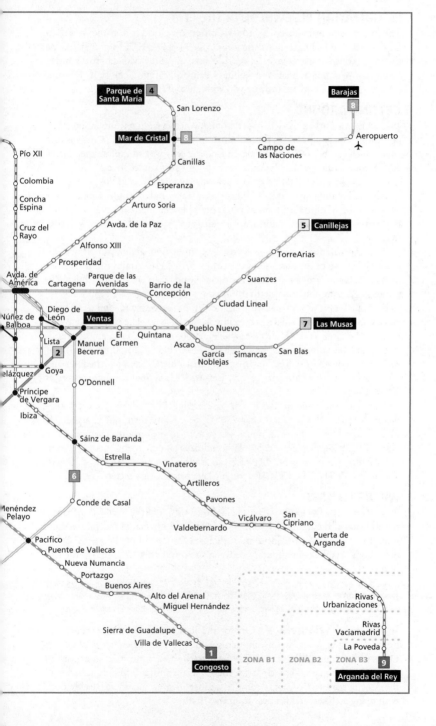

INFORMATION ELSEWHERE IN THE CITY

The major and most convenient **tourist office** in Madrid is near the American Express office on Duque de Medinaceli 2 (© **91-429-3177**; Metro: Banco de España). Ask for a street map of Madrid here any time Monday to Saturday from 9am to 7pm; Sunday and holidays 9am to 2:30pm. The staff does not make reservations but will provide you with a list of hotels and *hostales.*

GETTING AROUND

Madrid is a vast urban sprawl. To get around, you'll need to rely on public transportation. The good news is that so much of tourist interest lies in the historic core, which can be covered on foot. In fact, the only way to explore the narrow cobblestone streets of old Madrid is by walking (wear sturdy shoes).

For most attractions, the Metro (or subway) system is the way to go. It's safe, speedy, well maintained, and also inexpensive. Fares and schedules are posted at every one of Madrid's 158 subway stations. Eleven lines, totaling 106 miles (171km) service Greater Madrid, with individual Metro tickets costing 1.10€ ($1.25).

It's cheaper to purchase a *bonotransporte* at any station, giving you 10 rides on either the Metro or the bus system at a cost of 5.20€ ($6). Trains run daily from 6am to 1:30am. Violent crime is almost unheard of in the subway, but pickpocketing is common. For Metro information, call © **90-244-4403**.

Buses pick up the slack caused by gaps in the Metro system, and these vehicles are usually fast and efficient, traveling in special lanes. The cost of a one-way ticket is the same as the Metro (see above). A bus guide, *Madrid en Autobús,* is distributed free at bus kiosks. Buses run daily from 6am to 11:30pm. Late-night revelers rely on the *Búho* or "owl," a late-night bus service. For schedules and information about Madrid buses, call **Empresa Municipal de Transportes** at © **91-406-8810**.

Taxis operate around the clock. The base fare is 1.45€ ($1.75); for every kilometer thereafter, the fare increases by .85€ ($1). Supplements are charged: 2€ ($2.30) to a bus or train station or 4€ ($4.50) to the airport. There is also a .95€ ($1.10) supplement on Sundays, holidays, and at night. Taxis are most often hailed in the street; otherwise, call **Radio Taxi** at © **91-447-5180**; or **Teletaxi** at © **91-371-3711**. *Warning:* Make sure the taxi meter is turned on.

WHERE TO STAY

Best Western Cortezo   This chain hotel, just off the Calle de Atocha, remains one of the most affordable choices near the Atocha train depot. A short walk from the center of Madrid, near the Plaza Mayor and the Puerta del Sol, it offers comfortable, contemporary bedrooms that were last renovated at the end of the 90s.

Doctor Cortezo 3, 28012 Madrid. © **91-369-0101**. Fax 91-369-3774. www.bestwestern.com. 85 units. 120€–125€ ($238–$144) double; 150€–180€ ($173–$207) suite. Metro: Tirso de Molina. **Amenities:** Restaurant; bar; laundry; nonsmoking rooms; rooms for those with limited mobility. *In room:* Hair dryer.

Grand Hotel Velázquez ★   One of the most attractive of the moderately priced hotels of Madrid, this appealing choice is found behind a 1930s Art Deco–style facade. It lies in the chic Salamanca shopping district, northeast of the landmark square, Plaza de la Independencia within a 5-minute taxi ride of the Atocha station. Bedrooms come in a range of sizes, but all are sleekly done with many architectural features from the 1940s.

Calle de Velázquez 62, 28001 Madrid. © **91-575-2800.** Fax 91-575-2809. www.chh.es. 149 units. 125€–175€ ($144–$201) double; 175€–200€ ($201–$230) junior suite; 200€–240€ ($230–$276) executive suite. AE, DC, MC, V. Metro: Velázquez. **Amenities:** 2 restaurants; laundry. *In room:* Hair dryer.

Hostal Campomanes *(Value)*   A great location near the opera house and Palacio Real (Royal Palace) and affordable prices combine to make this one a winner. It's a clean, decent choice with Philippe Stark minimalist furnishings. The folks at the desk are especially helpful in decoding rail timetables.

Calle Campomanes 4, 28013 Madrid. © **91-548-8548.** Fax 91-559-1288. www.hhcampomanes.com. 30 units. 90€–115€ ($104–$132) double; 115€–154€ ($132–$177) suite. Rates include continental breakfast. AE, DC, MC, V. Metro: Opera. **Amenities:** Laundry; rooms for persons with limited mobility. *In room:* Hair dryer.

Hotel Chamartín   If you're staying overnight near the Chamartín station, this is your best bet. The hotel is part of a massive shopping center linked to the actual station—in fact, its owner is RENFE, the Spanish government rail system. A 15-minute taxi ride from the airport, the hotel offers good-size and well-appointed bedrooms.

Augustin de Foxá, 28036 Madrid. © **91-334-4900.** Fax 91-733-0214. www.hotelchamartin.com. 378 units. 84€–165€ ($97–$190) double; 172€–264€ ($198–$304) suite. AE, DC, MC, V. Métro: Chamartín. **Amenities:** Restaurant; cafeteria, bar/lounge; laundry; rooms for those with limited mobility. *In room:* Hair dryer.

Inglés   Near the Puerta del Sol, the heart of Madrid, this hotel lies on a small street of inexpensive restaurants and bars. Rooms come in various shapes and sizes—many are small—and Inglés is a long-time friend of the budget traveler. Even Virginia Woolf once checked in.

Calle Echegaray 8, 28014 Madrid. © **91-429-6551.** Fax 91-420-2423. www.hotelingles.com. 58 units. 90€ ($104) double; 112€ ($129) suite. AE, DC, MC, V. Metro: Puerta del Sol or Sevilla. **Amenities:** Cafeteria; laundry. *In room:* Hair dryer, no A/C.

Jardín de Recoletos ★ *(Value)*   This 1999 hotel, known for its affordable prices, stands in the elegant Salamanca district, lying close to the Plaza Colón, one of Madrid's major traffic arteries. Rooms are rather spacious and attractively and comfortable decorated. The added advantage of having a well-equipped kitchenette makes this hotel popular with families.

Gil de Santiváñes 6, Madrid 28001. © **91-781-1640.** Fax 91-781-1641. 36 units. 170€ ($196) double; 231€ ($266) suite. Rates include buffet breakfast. AE, DC, MC, V. Metro: Colón. **Amenities:** Restaurant; cafe; laundry. *In room:* Hair dryer.

NH Nacional   At the turn of the 20th century, this hotel was built to service overnight passengers arriving at the nearby Atocha rail station. In its restored format, the hotel continues to do so a century or so later. Although not the grand monument it used to be, it still offers comfortable, modernized bedrooms and a welcoming ambience.

Paseo del Prado 48, 28014 Madrid. © **91-429-6629.** Fax 91-369-1564. www.nh-hotels.com. 214 units. 97€–164€ ($112–$189) double; 217€–440€ ($250–$506) junior suite. AE, DC, MC, V. Metro: Atocha. **Amenities:** Restaurant; bar-cafeteria; laundry; rooms for those with limited mobility. *In room:* Hair dryer.

Opera ★★ *(Finds)*   Set close to the royal palace and the opera house, this hotel offers first-rate comfort and a warm welcome from its English-speaking staff. Guest rooms range from medium to surprisingly spacious, each with first-rate furnishings. The Opera remains one of Madrid's relatively undiscovered boutique hotels.

Cuesta de Santo Domingo 2, 28013 Madrid. © **91-541-2800.** Fax 91-541-6923. www.hotelopera.com. 79 units. 120€–132€ ($138-$152) double. AE, DC, MC, V. Metro: Opera. **Amenities:** Restaurant; bar; laundry; rooms for persons with limited mobility. *In room:* Hair dryer.

Santo Domingo ★★   A 2-minute walk from the Plaza de España, in the center of Madrid, this 1994 hotel rises five floors. The guest rooms are the strong point here, impressively decorated with tapestry wall coverings, marble bathrooms, fine bedding, and brocade draperies. Floors 2 and 3 open onto private balconies, and for the price, the lodgings are lush.

Plaza Santo Domingo 13, 28013 Madrid. © **91-547-9800.** Fax 91-547-5995. www.hotelsantodomingo.com. 120 units. 153€–209€ ($178–$240) double. Breakfast free Sat–Mon mornings; otherwise, 11€ ($12.75) extra. AE, DC, MC, V. Metro: Santo Domingo. **Amenities:** Restaurant; bar; laundry; nonsmoking rooms. *In room:* Hair dryer.

Tryp Reina Victoria ★   Built in 1923 in the bull's-eye center of the city, this first-class hotel has stayed abreast of the times though the flavor of old Madrid lives on here. Housed in the former palace of the Counts of Teba, it remains a favorite of bullfighters (there's a bar named for the great Matador, Manolete, a former patron). Guest rooms are simply but comfortably furnished.

Plaza Santa Ana 14, 28012 Madrid. © **91-531-4500.** Fax 91-522-0307. www.solmelia.com. 201 units. 218€ ($251) double; from 287€ ($331) suite. AE, DC, MC, V. Metro: Tirso de Molina or Puerta del Sol or Sevilla. **Amenities:** Restaurant; bar; laundry; nonsmoking rooms; rooms for persons with limited mobility. *In room:* Hair dryer.

TOP ATTRACTIONS & SPECIAL MOMENTS

Monasterio de las Descalzas Reales ★★   This magnificent building was once a royal palace. In 1559, Juana of Austria, sister of Felipe II, converted the building into a convent where aristocratic women could retreat to become "the bride of Christ." When the Pope learned that the sisters in the convent were starving, he allowed them to open the monastery to visitors wanting to see its rich treasure trove of art. Each noblewoman who entered the convent brought a dowry, and those precious relics form the nucleus of the collection today. The most valuable painting is Titian's *Caesar's Money,* along with art works from old masters such as Breugel the Elder sheltered in The Flemish Hall. Tapestries on display are from Ruben's cartoons with his chubby matrons. A small cloister on the second floor is ringed with chapels containing art works and precious objects, including bits of wood said to be from the cross on which Christ was crucified.

Plaza de las Descalzas Reales s/n. © **91-542-0059.** Admission 4.80€ ($5.50) adults, 2.40€ ($2.75) children. Mon–sat 9am–6pm; Sun 9am–3pm. Bus: 1, 2, 5, 20, 46, 52, 53, 74, M1, M2, M3, or M5. From Plaza del Callao, off Gran Via, walk down Postigo de San Martín to Plaza de las Descalzas Reales; the convent is on the left.

Museo Arqueológico Nacional ★★   This stately mansion houses one of the great archaeological museums of Iberia. Founded by Queen Isabella II in 1867, the museum features exhibits spanning history from unrecorded times to the 19th century. The Iberian artifacts are supplemented by finds at digs from Ancient Greece, Italy at the time of the Etruscans, and Egypt.

The most notable and impressive sculpture is *La Dama de Elche,* a primitive carving from the 4th century B.C. discovered along the southeastern coast of Spain. The austere beauty of the statue reveals traces of Greek influence. Another notable sculpture is *La Dama de Baza.* The museum is especially rich in artifacts in the epoch between Roman and Mudéjar Spain.

The mosaics from the Roman period are notable, especially *Monks and Seasons* from the Albacete period, with outstanding pieces from the Visigothic era also on display. Outside the museum is an exact reproduction of the Altamira cave paintings discovered near Santander in northern Spain in 1868.

Calle Serrano 13. © **91-577-7912.** Admission 3€ ($3.50), free for children and adults over 65, free on Sat–Sun. Tues–Sat 9:30am–8:30pm; Sun 9:30am–2:30pm. Metro: Serrano or Colón. Bus: 1, 9, 19, 51, or 74.

Museo de la Real Academia de Bellas Artes de San Fernando ✫ A
short stroll from the Puerta del Sol (the exact center of Madrid), this is one of
Iberia's leading fine arts museum, lying in a 17th-century baroque palace. When
the building was an art academy, its alumni numbered the likes of Salvador Dalí
and Picasso. This is hardly the grandest art museum in Madrid, but there are
superb works, including a collection of Old Masters paintings ranging from
Rubens to Van Dyck, plus excellent drawings by Titian and Raphael. The best
selection is the array of Spanish paintings from the 1500s to the 1800s, including works by Velázquez, El Greco, Ribera, and Murillo. One of the best monk
paintings Zurbarán ever did, *Fray Pedro Machado,* is here. A former director of

---

(*Moments* **Death in the Afternoon**
_____

Blood sports may not be your thing, and that's very understandable.
Yet the art of bullfighting is as old as pagan Spain, and has much to
reveal about the character of the Spaniard. Bullfighting's most avid
aficionados claim it is a "microcosm of death, catharsis, and rebirth."
It remains one of the most evocative and memorable events in Spain,
although the action at the *corrida* may horrify the faint-of-heart.

Madrid draws the finest matadors in Spain. If a matador hasn't
proved his worth in the **Plaza Monumental de Toros de las Ventas,**
Alcalá 237 (② **91-356-2200;** Metro: Ventas), he just hasn't been recognized as a top-flight artist. The major season begins during the Fiestas
de San Isidro, patron saint of Madrid, on May 15. This is the occasion
for a series of fights with talent scouts in the audience. Matadors who
distinguish themselves in the ring are signed up for Majorca, Málaga,
and other places.

The best way to get tickets to the bullfights is at the stadium's box
office (open Fri–Sun 10am–2pm and 5-8pm). Alternatively, you can
contact one of Madrid's most competent ticket agents, **Localidades
Galicia,** Plaza del Carmen 1 (② **91-531-2732;** Metro: Puerta del Sol). It's
open Tuesday through Saturday from 9:30am to 1:30pm and 4:30 to
7pm, Sunday from 9:30am to 3pm. Regardless of where you buy them,
tickets to bullfights range from 20€ to 140€ ($23–$161), depending on
the event and the position of your seat within the stadium. Concierges
for virtually every upper-bracket hotel in Madrid can acquire tickets,
through inner channels of their own, to bullfights and other sought-
after entertainment. Front-row seats at the bullfights are known as
barreras. Delanteras (3rd-row seats) are available in both the *alta*
(high) and the *baja* (low) sections. The cheapest seats sold, *filas,* afford
the worst view and are in the sun *(sol)* during the entire performance.
The best seats are in the shade *(sombra).*

Bullfights are held on Sunday and holidays throughout most of the
year, and every day during certain festivals, which tend to last around
3 weeks, usually in the late spring. Starting times are adjusted according to the anticipated hour of sundown on the day of a performance.
Late-night fights by neophyte matadors are sometimes staged under
spotlights on Saturday around 11pm.

the academy, Goya has a room devoted entirely to his art. Our favorite is his *Burial of a Sardine.*

Alcalá 13. (📞 **91-524-0864**. Admission 2.40€ ($2.75) adults, 1.20€ ($1.40) students, free Wed and for children 17 and under. Tues–Fri 9am–7pm; Mon 10am–2pm. Metro: Puerta del Sol or Sevilla. Bus: 3, 15, 20, 51, 52, 53, or 150.

Museo del Prado ⭐⭐⭐ This museum, one of the world's greatest repositories of art, began as a royal collection and was later beefed up by the Hapsburgs. The range of art is mainly from the 12th to the 19th centuries, and the collection quite naturally features the greatest assembly of Spanish paintings in the world, notably impressive works by the great Velázquez and Goya. The annex of the Prado, Cason del Buen Retiro, contains late-19th-century and 20th-century sculpture and painting.

Those who can't see everything might want to enter through the Puerta de Goya, opening onto Calle Felipe IV. This leads to the second floor (called 1st floor in Spain). The artworks are arranged by schools, with the oldest works displayed on the lower floors. Especially notable is the Goya Collection featuring both his *Clothed Maja* and *Naked Maja* (both ca. 1800). The artist who depicted "blatant" nudity was charged with obscenity.

You'll find a splendid array of works by the incomparable Diego Velázquez (1599–1660). The museum's most famous painting, in fact, is his *Las Meninas,* a triumph for its use of light effects and perspective. The faces of the queen and king are reflected in the mirror in the painting itself. The artist in the foreground is Velázquez, of course.

The Prado is a trove of the work of El Greco (ca. 1541–1614), the Crete-born artist who lived much of his life in Toledo. You can see a parade of "The Greek's" saints, Madonnas, and Holy Families—even a ghostly *John the Baptist.*

The Flemish painter Peter Paul Rubens (1577–1640), who met Velázquez while in Spain, is represented by the peacock-blue *Garden of Love* and by the *Three Graces.* Also worthy is the work of José Ribera (1591–1652), a Valencia-born artist and contemporary of Velázquez, whose best painting is the *Martyrdom of St. Philip.* Seville-born Bartolomé Murillo (1617–82)—often referred to as the "painter of Madonnas"—is represented by three versions of the Immaculate Conception.

The Prado has an outstanding collection of the work of Hieronymus Bosch (1450?–1516), the Flemish genius. *The Garden of Earthly Delights,* the best-known work of "El Bosco," is here. You'll also see his *Seven Deadly Sins* and his triptych *The Hay Wagon. The Triumph of Death* is by another Flemish painter, Pieter Breugel the Elder (1525?–69), who carried on Bosch's ghoulish vision.

Major Italian works are exhibited on the ground floor. You'll see art by Italian masters—Raphael, Botticelli, Mantegna, Andrea del Sarto, Fra Angelico, and Correggio. The most celebrated Italian painting here is Titian's voluptuous Venus being watched by a musician who can't keep his eyes on his work.

Paseo del Prado. (📞 **91-330-2800**. http://museoprado.mcu.es. Admission 3€ ($3.50) adults, 1.50€ ($1.75) students and seniors, free for kids 17 and under and free for everybody on Sun. Tues–Sun 9am–7pm. Closed Jan 1, Good Friday, May 1, and Dec 25. Metro: Atocha or Cibeles. Bus: 10, 14, 27, 34, 37, or 45.

Museo Lázaro Galdiano ⭐⭐ *Finds* Bequeathed to the nation in 1947, this is one of the grandest collections of art in Castile, housed in the former manse of the author, José Lázaro Galdiano. The original museum, added to over the years, began from the writer's own impressive collection of fine and applied art. Imagine 37 rooms bulging with art, including many of the most famous and reproduced masters of Europe.

We like to take the elevator to the top floor and work our way down, taking in at our leisure everything from Goya portraits to a cross-shaped pocket watch worn by Charles V. The *Saviour* is a portrait attributed to Leonardo da Vinci. Surprisingly, the collection is rich in English landscapes, notably by Turner, Gainsborough, and Constable, and also contains paintings from Spain's greatest masters, notably El Greco, Murillo, Velázquez, and Zubarán. Of macabre interest is Salon 30 devoted to Goya, including some notorious paintings from his "black period."

Serrano 122. ℭ **91-561-60-84.** Admission 3€ ($3.50). Tues–Sun 10am–2pm. Closed holidays and August. Metro: Ruben Dario or Nunez de Balboa. Bus: 9, 16, 19, 27, 45, 51, 61, 89, or 114.

Museo Nacional Centro de Arte Reina Sofia ★★

A former 18th-century general hospital, once called "the ugliest building in Spain," is today the repository of modern art in Spain. It's worth the trip alone just to see Picasso's ***Guernica*** ★★★, the single most famous work of the 20th century. Taking his inspiration from the German attack on the Basque town of Guernica in 1937, this masterpiece represents Picasso's glaring indictment of the destruction of war.

Picasso is represented by other works, too, including one of our all-time favorites, *Woman in Blue,* painted in 1901. When it failed to win in a national competition, Picasso disowned the work. The permanent collection of works is found on the second and fourth floors, featuring such famous Spanish artists as Dalí and Miró. Sometimes the temporary exhibits shown here are even more stunning than the permanent collection.

Santa Isabel 52. ℭ **91-467-5062.** Admission 3€ ($3.50) adults, 1.50€ ($1.75) students, free after 2:30pm on Sat, all day Sun, and for ages 17 and under. Wed–Sat and Mon 10am–9pm; Sun 10am–2:30pm. Free guided tours Mon and Wed at 5pm; Sat at 11am. Metro: Atocha.

Museo Thyssen-Bornemisza ★★★

Installed in Madrid's 18th-century Villahermosa Palace in 1992, this collection grew from one of the greatest private art collections in the world, the assemblage of the late Baron Heinrich Thyssen-Bornemisza and his son, Hans Heinrich. Beginning in the 1920s, the collection was intended to illustrate the history of Western art, and it succeeds brilliantly with some 800 representative works of art, including masterpieces by the likes of Picasso, Goya, van Gogh, and Titian, towering among others.

As a privately owned collection, the Thyssen museum's treasure trove was rivaled only by that of Queen Elizabeth II. Spain acquired the collection for $350 million, outbidding Walt Disney World and others. Rooms are arranged so that the logical sequence of European paintings can be traced from the 13th to the 20th centuries, a parade of greatness from El Greco to Velázquez, from Rembrandt to Caravaggio. The walls are rich with the work of notable French Impressionists, including major American works by the likes of Jackson Pollock and Edward Hopper.

The galleries are arranged around a covered central courtyard, the top floor starting with early Italian and going on to the 1600s. By the time you reach the ground floor you'll be surrounded by works from the 20th century.

Palacio de Villahermosa, Paseo del Prado 8. ℭ **91-369-0151.** www.museothyssen.org. Admission 4.80€ ($5.50) adults, 3€ ($3.50) students and seniors, free for children 12 and under. Tues–Sun 10am–7pm. Metro: Banco de España. Bus: 1, 2, 5, 9, 10, 14, 15, 20, 27, 34, 45, 51, 52, 53, 74, 146, or 150.

Palacio Real (Royal Palace) ★★

During the reign of the dictator, Franco, this palace was just a monument, but now has taken on more meaning after the restoration of the monarchy. The lavishly decorated complex is vast, constructed high on a bluff opening onto Río Manzanares. For centuries the site was a royal fortress, but following a fire in 1734, the present palace was built on orders of Felipe V.

Today's royal family resides elsewhere, but this palace was occupied until 1931 when Alfonso XIII abdicated. King Juan Carlos comes here only for state occasions.

Most impressive is the **Throne Room** 🟊, with its gold and scarlet thrones, exact reproductions of those once used by Charles V. The **Porcelain Room** 🟊 is a stunner, both its walls and ceiling entirely covered by porcelain from the royal factory. It's a romp of cherubs and wreaths.

Decorated in 1879, the **Dining Gallery** 🟊, with its ceiling paintings and handsome tapestries, evoke the heyday of the Bourbon dynasty. Today, there are some 2,000 rooms in the palace, not all of them open to the public. You can visit such highlights as the Reception Room, the State Apartments, the Armory, and the Royal Pharmacy. A special discovery, often overlooked, is the **Gasparini Room** 🟊, named after the Neapolitan designer and decorated with rococo and chinoiserie. In the antechamber is a portrait of Charles IV by Goya. After touring the palace, you can stroll through its garden, Campo del Moro.

Plaza de Oriente, Calle de Bailén. ℂ **91-454-8700.** Admission 8€ ($9.25) adults, 3.30€ ($3.75) students and children. Mon–Sat 9am–6pm; Sun 9am–3pm. Metro: Opera or Plaza de España.

Panteón de Goya   Outside the city center, Goya's Tomb still attracts his fans, as it contains one of his masterpieces, an elaborate **fresco** 🟊🟊🟊 depicting the miracles of St. Anthony on the dome and cupola of this little hermitage of San Antonio de la Florida. Critics have hailed the work as "Goya's Sistine Chapel." Built in the reign of Carlos IV in the neoclassical style, the hermitage is dedicated to St. Anthony. In 1798, Goya spent 4 months painting the cupola with this mammoth fresco. In the background the artists peopled his work with ordinary street characters from the 1700s. In the chapel rests the tomb of the artist, his remains shipped here from Bordeaux where he died as an expatriate in 1828. In 1799, Goya became court painter to Carlos IV but pictured the royal family with grotesque accuracy.

Glorieta de San Antonio de la Florida 5. ℂ **91-542-0722.** Free admission. Tues–Fri 10am–2pm and 4–8pm; Sat–Sun 10am–2pm. Metro: Principe Pio. Bus: 41, 45, 46, or 75.

Plaza Mayor 🟊🟊🟊   This is the most famous and most historic square in Spain. The plaza is enveloped by 17th-century, three-story buildings with arcades at their base. These arcades are filled with cafes and craft shops. Some of the building facades are graced with allegorical paintings, as well as balconies, pinnacles, and dormer windows. The square was the center of life in old Madrid, staging everything from bullfights to executions, from pageants to trials by the Inquisition. In 1621, the square was the venue for the beautification of St. Isidore, Madrid's patron saint. In the center of the plaza stands a statue of Felipe III who is responsible for the construction of the square. A coin and stamp market is held every Sunday morning, along with stalls hawking used books, old badges, and other collectibles.

In the southwest corner of the square you can take a flight of steps leading down to the Calle de Cuchilleros, site of a bevy of *mesones* (traditional restaurants). The most famous of these is **Sobrino de Botín,** Calle de Cuchilleros 17 (ℂ **91-366-4217**), which Hemingway made famous in the pages of *The Sun Also Rises.* Dating from 1725, the kitchen specializes in roast suckling pig.

Plaza Mayor. Open 24 hours. Metro: La Latina or Opera.

WHERE TO DINE

Arce SPANISH   Close to the Gran Vía (Madrid's main street) the owner and chef, Iñaki Camba and his wife, Theresa, prepare a traditional cuisine, taking culinary inspiration from all of Spain, especially the Basque country. In a graceful setting, this renovated restaurant continues to please discerning diners year after year with dishes that bring out natural flavors. This is virile, self-assured cookery, and each dish has a distinct personality and is given a "signature" purely its own.

Augusto Figueroa 32. © 91-522-5913. Reservations recommended. Main courses 12€–25€ ($14–$28.75). AE, DC, MC, V. Mon–Fri 1:30–4pm; Mon–Sat 9pm–midnight. Closed Easter week and Aug 15–31. Metro: Chueca.

Bocaito SPANISH/TAPAS   We are so in love with the perfectly prepared and tasty tapas served here that it's hard to get around to ordering a main course. In a typical Madrid tavern with bullfighting posters, the chefs prepare tapas "to die for," including the likes of such delicacies as salt cod pâté with caviar. Don Luis Benavente, the chef and owner, has a devoted following who like his imaginative take on typical Andalusian and Castilian dishes.

Calle Libertad 4–6. © 91-532-1219. Reservations recommended. Tapas 5.40€–7.20€ ($6.25–$8.25), main courses 15€–20€ ($17.25–$23). MC, V. Mon–Fri 1–4pm; Mon–Sat 8:30pm–midnight. Closed last 2 weeks in Aug. Metro: Banco de España.

El Amparo 🏵🏵 BASQUE   A former carriage house was converted to establish this elegant enclave of a refined Basque cuisine, which some food critics hail as the finest provincial food in Spain. The cuisine has a real modern accent, made with top-notch ingredients that are fashioned into imaginative and flavorful platters. Under rough-hewn wooden beams, you can partake of such specialties as ravioli with crayfish or roulades of lobster flavored with soy sauce.

Callejón de Puigcerdà 8. © 91-431-6456. Reservations required. Main courses 24€–30€ ($27.50–$34.50). AE, MC, V. Mon–Sat 2–3:30pm and 9–11:30pm. Closed Easter week. Metro: Serrano. Bus: 19 or 45.

El Chaflán 🏵 SPANISH   This restaurant is the showcase for the culinary talents of one of Madrid's hottest chefs, Jean Pablo Felipe Tablado, who draws enthusiastic diners and rave reviews. He puts his own spin on every dish that comes out of his kitchen, emphasizing flavor and texture. The best fish, local meats, and produce attract native foodies and discerning visitors alike—try the roast suckling pig.

Av. Pio XII 34. © 91-350-6193. Reservations required. Main courses 26€–40€ ($30–$46). Fixed-price menu 77€ ($88.50). AE, DC, MC, V. Mon–Fri 1:30–4pm; Mon–Sat 9–11:30pm. Metro: Pio XII.

El Espejo 🏵 *Value* INTERNATIONAL   In a location near Plaza de las Cortés, this restaurant features one of the best menu values in town, the list of international specialties changing daily. The chefs enhance the pristine flavors of food with skill and restraint, and dish after dish, such as guinea fowl flavored with Armagnac, have won our enthusiasm. The setting is a beautiful Art Nouveau dining room, with outside tables for most months of the year.

Paseo de Recoletos 31. © 91-308-2347. Reservations required. Fixed-price menu 22€. ($25.25) AE, MC, V. Daily 1–4pm and 9pm–midnight. Metro: Colón. Bus: 14, 27, 45, 145, and 150.

El Olivo 🏵🏵 MEDITERRANEAN   This chic restaurant is for devotees of olive oil and Spanish sherry. It took a Frenchman, Jean-Pierre Vandelle, to exploit two of Spain's culinary highlights in this showcase of fine cuisine, where

Moments Tasca Hopping

Madrid's equivalent of London's pub-crawl is *tasca* hopping. Tascas are local taverns serving tapas along with beer and wine (the hard stuff, too). Many tascas specialize in one dish, perhaps mushrooms or else shrimp, although most of them serve a wide array of tasty appetizers. Since the dining hour is late in Madrid, often around ten o'clock at night, Madrileños patronize these tascas and satisfy their pre-dinner appetites with one "small plate" after another. It's amazing they are still hungry when it's time for dinner.

Our favorite tascas include **Casa Mingo,** Paseo de la Florida 34 (✆ **91-547-7918**), which Madrileños patronize for the best cider in town, often consuming it with a piece of *cabrales* or goat cheese from the northwestern province of Asturias. Roast chicken, served at communal tables, is the other specialty of the kitchen. A tankard of cider goes for 3.90€ ($4.50), a serving of *cabrales* for 5€ ($5.75), and a whole roasted chicken for 7€ ($8). Service is daily 11am to midnight. No credit cards. Metro: Principe Pio, then a 5-minute walk.

One of the most patronized tascas in old Madrid is **Taberna Toscana,** Manuel Fernández y Gonzales 10 (✆ **91-429-6031**), where you sit on country stools and order some of the best tapas in town. These include *chorizo* (the spicy Spanish sausage), *lacón y cecina* (boiled ham), and tasty *habas* or broad beans. The kidneys in sherry sauce and the snails in hot sauce are also delectable. A glass of wine costs from .90€ ($1.10), and tapas range from 3€ to 11€ ($3.50–$12.75). MasterCard and Visa are accepted, and hours are Tuesday to Saturday noon to 4pm and 8pm to midnight. Metro: Puerta del Sol or Sevilla.

Cervecería Santa Barbara, Plaza de Santa Barbara 8 (✆ **91-319-0449**), is the outlet for a beer factory, lying on one of old Madrid's most colorful squares. The two most popular brews are *cerveza negra* (black beer) and *cerveza dorada* (golden beer). This cerveza is consumed with homemade potato chips and such seafood delights as barnacles, fresh lobster or shrimp, or crabmeat. Tapas cost 6€ to 10€ ($7–$11.50), with a beer going for 1.55€ ($1.80). MasterCard and Visa are accepted. Open daily 11:30am to midnight. Metro: Alonzo Martínez. Bus: 3, 7, or 21.

Another well-patronized tapas outlet, **Cervecería Alemania,** Plaza de Santa Ana 6 (✆ **91-429-7033**), opens onto an even more colorful square. Evocative of the turn of the 20th century, it offers little tables that are jam-packed nightly with locals sampling the fried sardines or a Spanish omelet. A beer costs 1.75€ to 2.25€ ($2–$2.75), with tapas going from 4€ to 13€ ($4.75–$15). No credit cards. Open Sunday and Thursday 11am to 12:30am, Friday and Saturday 11am to 2am. Metro: Tirso de Molina or Puerta del Sol.

a cart stocked with 40 regional olive oils is wheeled from table to table. Cookery shows imagination and solid technique, and the sherry bar features 100 different brands.

General Gellgos 1. ℂ **91-359-1535.** Reservations recommended. Main courses 19€–27€ ($21.75–$31). Fixed-price menus 45€ ($51.75). AE, DC, MC, V. Tues–Sat 1–4pm and 9pm–midnight. Closed Aug 15–31 and 4 days around Easter. Metro: Plaza de Castilla.

La Bola *(Finds)* MADRILEÑA   Ava Gardner in *The Barefoot Contessa* (an old movie she made with Bogie), no longer shows up barefoot and surrounded by matadors, but this remains one of the most evocative of the 19th-century red-doored restaurants of Madrid. Against a backdrop of Venetian crystal, ever-loyal fans show up to dine on *cocido madrilène,* the traditional Castilian Sunday boiled dinner. The tried-and-true recipes of Old Castile are still served here.

Calle de la Bola 5. ℂ **91-547-6930.** Reservations required. Main courses 10€–20€ ($11.50–$23). No credit cards. Daily 1–4pm; Mon–Sat 8:30–11pm. Metro: Opera or Santo Domingo. Bus: 25 or 39.

La Gamella *(Finds)* CASTILIAN   An unusual mix and successful offering of Californian and Castilian cuisine is delectably served at this expat outpost under the guidance of Ohio-born Dick Stephens. In the 19th-century building where Ortega y Gasset, the Spanish philosopher, was born, Stephens has cooked for such notable palates as the king and queen of Spain. The chefs here know just how to coax the most flavor out of the premium ingredients used—and you can invariably count on a delightful evening.

Alfonso XII 4. ℂ **91-532-4509.** www.lagamella.com. Reservations required. Main courses 12€–19€ ($13.75–$21.75). AE, DC, MC, V. Mon–Fri 1:30–4pm; Mon–Sat 9pm–midnight. Metro: Retiro or Banco de España. Bus: 19.

Lhardy *(*★★*)* SPANISH/INTERNATIONAL   A Madrid legend since its opening back in 1839, this was once the preferred dining choice of the capital's cognoscenti, especially it's literary and political leaders. In an antique setting of marble and hardwood, there is a ground floor deli still dispensing cups of steaming consommé dispensed from silver samovars into little porcelain cups. On the second floor, in an ornate Belle Epoque–styled restaurant, specialties that might have been known to Queen Isabella II are still dispensed—and done so exceedingly well.

Carrera de San Jerónimo 8. ℂ **91-521-3385.** Reservations recommended for the upstairs dining room. Main courses 20€–30€ ($23–$34.50). AE, DC, MC, V. Daily 1–3:30pm; Mon–Sat 8:30–11pm. Closed Aug. Metro: Puerta del Sol.

La Paloma *(*★*)* BASQUE/FRENCH   Two of Europe's greatest cuisines from France and the Basque provinces are wed harmoniously at this exclusive retreat in the elegant Salamanca district. The chef and owner, Segundo Alonso, is known for his perfectly prepared and "robust" dishes, specializing in various meats, such as pigs' trotters, which he fashions into divine concoctions. The welcome and the service are flawless.

Jorge Juan 39. ℂ **91-576-8692.** Reservations required. Main courses 12€–25€ ($13.75–$28.75). Menú de degustación 51€ ($58.75). AE, DC, MC, V. Mon–Sat 1:30–3:45pm and 9–11:45pm. Metro: Vergara and Velázquez.

SHOPPING

Some call it Madrid's **El Rastro** ★ or flea market. Other more discerning critics refer to it as the thieves market. It's said that virtually everything stolen in Madrid turns up here at some point. Lying in a triangle of streets a few minutes' walk south of Plaza Mayor, this flea market dates from the Middle Ages and is centered around Plaza de Cascorro. The main action takes place along Calle Ribera de Curtidores or "tanner's riverbank," once the headquarters of the tanning industry and the slaughterhouse district. The other major street of vendors hawking their wares is along Calle de Embajadores. The time to go is after 8am on a Sunday morning. What's for sale? Everything from an "original" El Greco for 21.75€ ($25) to antiques, bric-a-brac, and a vast array of fascinating junk. Plaza de Cascorro and Ribera de Curtidores. Metro: La Latina. Bus: 3 or 17.

The leading department store of Madrid—in fact, the flagship of the largest department store chain—is **El Corte Inglés,** Preciados 3 (© **91-379-8000**). A lot of the merchandise here is of interest mainly to locals, but you'll also find a large selection of Spanish handcrafts, including damascene steelwork from Toledo, embroidered shawls, and flamenco dolls. You can also preview a wide selection of Spanish fashions for both women and men. Monday to Saturday 10am to 10pm; Metro: Puerta del Sol.

A truly excellent center for crafts is **El Arco de los Cuchilleros Artesania de Hoy,** Plaza Mayor 9 (© **91-365-2680**), set within one of the 17th-century vaulted cellars off the historic Plaza Mayor. An unusual and varied collection of one-of-a-kind merchandise from all over Spain has been assembled here, including everything from textiles to pottery and leather items. Daily 11am to 9pm. Metro: Puerta del Sol or Opera. The devotees of antiques, Iberian style, gravitate to **Centro de Anticuarios Lagasca,** Lagasca 36 (© **91-577-3752**), where they discover about a dozen different outlets under one arcade. The attics of Spain were raided for this assemblage of furnishings, porcelain, and bric-a-brac. Open Monday to Saturday 10am to 2pm and 5 to 8pm. Metro: Serrano or Velázquez.

The quality leather products of **Loewe,** Serrano 26 (© **91-577-6056**), have made this exclusive outlet a Madrid legend since 1846. Its designers have won many gold medals for their tasteful, chic designs in leather. The store carries a deluxe assortment of luggage and handbags along with both leather and suede jackets for men and women. Open Monday to Saturday 9:30am to 8:30pm. Metro: Banco de España or Gran Vía.

One of the leading art galleries of Madrid is **Galeria Kreisler,** Hermosilla 8 (© **91-431-4264**), operated by the Ohio-born Kreisler family who specialize in both figurative and modern paintings as well as sculpture and graphics. Open Monday to Friday 10:30am to 2pm and 5 to 9pm. Metro: Serrano. Bus: 19 or 51.

NIGHTLIFE

Following a $157 million renovation in the late 1990s, **Teatro Real,** Plaza Isabel II (© **91-516-0660**), is the showcase for cultural Madrid. It first opened in 1850 under the reign of Queen Isabel II, and its acoustics are the best in Iberia. The building is the home for Compañía del Teatro Real, which specializes in opera but is also a major venue for classical music, with tickets beginning as low as 14€ ($16), although they might also range upward to 226€ ($260). Metro: Opera.

Palacio Gaviria, Calle Arenal 9 (© **91-526-6069**), was built in 1847 by Marqués de Gaviria, one of the paramours of Queen Isabella II. It remains today as of one the greatest *Isabelino* (a jumble of neoclassical and baroque) palaces in Madrid. Today it is both a venue for classical music and a late-night cocktail bar. Guests wander from one elegant salon to elegant salon. Wednesday is cabaret night. The cover ranges from 9€ to 15€ ($10.25–$17.25), including a first drink. Open Monday to Wednesday 9:30pm to 3am, Thursday to Saturday 9:30pm to 5am, and Sunday 11pm to 2am. Metro: Puerta del Sol or Opera.

The mammoth **Kapital,** Atocha 125 (© **91-420-2906**), is one of the top dance clubs of Madrid, drawing an under-35 crowd of dancing fools. From hip-hop to house, from terrazas to cinemas, there is action going on at all times on seven floors of this "mad, mad world" *discoteca.* The action doesn't really get going until 2am. Open Thursday to Sunday midnight to 7am, with afternoon sessions Saturday and Sunday from 5:30 to 11pm. Admission ranges from 12€ to 15€ ($13.75–$17.25), including the first drink. Metro: Atocha.

Another hot, hot dance club set near the Puerta del Sol is **Joy Eslava,** Arenal 11 (© **91-366-3733**), which goes on in spite of passing fads and fancies. Attracting a wide range of clients, mostly in their 30s and 40s, it pulsates to a lively disco beat nightly from 11:30pm to 6:30am. Admission is 15€ ($17.25), including your first drink. Metro: Puerta del Sol.

Jazz aficionados flock to **Café Central,** Plaza del Angel 10, off Plaza de Santa Ana (© **91-369-4143**), which has a turn-of-the-20th-century Art Deco decor. Some of the country's leading jazz performers entertain you at their nightly sessions. Open Sunday to Thursday 1:30pm to 2:30am, Friday and Saturday 1:30pm to 3am. Live jazz is featured daily from 10pm to midnight, with a cover ranging from 8€ to 12€ ($9.25–$13.75), depending on the show. Metro: Antón Martín. Those seeking jazz also descend on **Clamores,** Albuquerque 14 (© **91-445-7938**), with its dark and smoky interior. Dating from the 1980s, this is one of the biggest and most frequented jazz clubs in Iberia. Spanish jazz bands appear regularly but so do some excellent artists from the United States as well. Jazz is presented only Tuesday to Saturday; call for times. Jam sessions are staged on Sunday night. A cover of 6€ to 20€ ($7–$23) is imposed Tuesday to Saturday. Metro: Bilbao.

Casino action is found at **Casino Gran Madrid,** Km29 Carretera La Coruña, Apartado 62 (© **91-856-1100**), the A-6 highway running between Madrid and La Coruña. The largest casino in Spain, it also attracts non-gamblers to its restaurant and entertainment facilities, featuring everything from 3 bars to a disco. Games of chance include both French and American roulette, blackjack, punto y banco, baccarat, and chemin-de-fer. Entrance costs 3€ ($3.50), and you must present a passport. Open daily 4pm to 5am.

AN EXCURSION TO TOLEDO

Reached by train in only 1½ hours from Madrid, this is Iberia's greatest imperial city, lying 42 miles (68km) to the south. Toledo stands atop a hill enveloped on three sides by a bend in the River Tagus, a scene immortalized by the city's most famed painter, El Greco, in his *View of Toledo,* hanging in the Metropolitan Museum of Art in New York.

Toledo's history is ancient. The Visigoths made it their capital in the 6th century A.D., leaving behind churches still present today. In medieval times, Toledo was a melting pot of Muslim, Jewish, and, of course, Christian cultures. The Toledo cathedral, one of the greatest in Europe, dates from those times. Even on the most rushed of schedules, try to visit this cathedral along with the Iglesia de Santo Tomé (with El Greco's masterpiece), and most definitely Charles V's fortified palace, the Alcázar. With time remaining, you can see El Greco's house in the old Jewish quarter.

GETTING THERE

From either the Atocha or Chamartín stations in Madrid, 9 to 10 trains per day run to Toledo. The earliest departures Monday to Friday are 6:30am, but not until 8:25am on Saturday and Sunday, a one-way fare costing 4.90€ ($5.75). For schedules and more information, call RENFE at © **90-224-0202.**

Arrivals are at **Estación Toledo,** Paseo de la Rosa 2 (© **90-224-0202**), a beautiful neo-Mudéjar station lying just over the bridge, Puente de Azarquiel, from the center of town. From the station, buses 5 or 6 run into the center.

Moments   The Exotic Sound of Flamenco

No art form, other than bullfighting, is more evocative of Spain than flamenco dancing. Although it may have been created by "lowlife roots," including taverns catering to hoodlums, brothels, gypsies, and what one critic called "whoopee hedonism," flamenco has long since grown respectable and is heard in the most elegant of clubs today.

The finest flamenco singers and dancers appear in Madrid, accompanied by the guitar music, castanets, and the ritualized clapping of the audience. The earliest performers might have been dancer-prostitutes, but today some of the finest talent in all the land, both female and male, pursue the art of flamenco. If you have only 1 night in Madrid, try to take in a flamenco show, notably at the sizzling **Corral de la Morería,** Morería 17 (© **91-365-8464**), charging a 30€ ($34.50) cover, including one drink. Although it's touristy, some of the best flamenco performers in Spain appear here nightly in colorful costumes. Open daily 8:30pm to 2am. Metro: Puerta del Sol or La Latina.

If you prefer a less touristy atmosphere, check out the scene at **Casa Patas,** Cañizares 10 (© **91-369-0496**), which is also a bar and restaurant. Perhaps the best flamenco shows in Madrid are presented here daily. The cover ranges from 23€ to 28€ ($26.50–$32.25), and two shows are presented Friday and Saturday at 9pm and midnight, with one show Monday to Thursday at 10:30pm. Metro: Tirso de Molina.

Should you become crazed for flamenco during your stay in Madrid, you might also head for **Café de Chinitas,** Torija 7 (© **91-559-5135**), a club of long-enduring popularity. One of Madrid's best flamenco clubs, the cafe lies in an old structure set at midpoint between the Gran Vía (the main drag) and the Opera. Some of the best of gypsy flamenco dancers from Andalusia appear here. A dinner and show costs 70€ ($80.50), although the cover for the show without dinner, but with one drink included, is 32€ ($36.75). Shows are presented Monday to Saturday from 10:30pm to 2am. Metro: Santo Domingo. Bus: 1 or 2.

Buses depart every 15 minutes from the station during the day, taking you to the main square of town, Plaza de Zocodover, the ancient marketplace. A one-way fare costs .78€ (90¢), the ride into the center taking only 5 minutes. The train station has drinking and dining facilities but no tourist information office. There is a luggage storage kiosk, however, charging 3€ ($3.50) per bag. Open daily 7am to 9:30pm.

TOURIST INFORMATION

The **Toledo Tourist Office** is at Puerta de Bisagra (© **92-522-0843**), and is open Monday to Friday 9am to 6pm, Saturday 9am to 7pm, and Sunday 9am to 3pm.

TOP ATTRACTIONS & SPECIAL MOMENTS

One of the great Gothic structures of the world, the **Catedral de Toledo** ★★★, Cardenal Cisneros 1 (© **92-522-2241**), dates from 1226 when King Ferdinand III laid the first stone. Today, the cathedral is renowned for its art and architecture, along with its five naves and stunning stained glass. It makes no apologies for its ostentation. The cathedral is the seat of the primate of Spain and the spiritual heart of the Spanish Catholic church. Its chief treasures are its **choir stalls** ✹✹✹, the carvings on its wooden lower stalls depicting the fall of Granada, and a **series of paintings by El Greco** ✹ in the Sacristy. The masterpiece here is El Greco's *Denuding of Christ* above the marble altar. A splendid 16th-century **silver gilt monstrance** ✹✹ by Enrique de Arfe is found beneath a Mudéjar ceiling in the Treasury. At the High Altar, a **polychrome reredos** ✹ is one of the most magnificent in Spain, depicting scenes from the life of Christ. Admission to the cathedral is free but if you visit its treasury the cost is 4.95€ ($5.75). Open Monday to Saturday 10:30am to 6:30pm and Sunday 2 to 6:30pm.

The second great edifice of Toledo is the **Alcázar,** Cuesta de Carlos V, 2, near Plaza de Zocodover (✆ **92-522-1673**), close to the eastern edge of the old city, its architectural line dominating the skyline. Charles V ordered this fortified palace built on the site of Roman, Visigoth, and even Muslim fortifications. The Alcázar became world famous in 1936 when it was practically destroyed by Republicans. Holding down the fortress, the Nationalists survived a 70-day siege. Today the Alcázar houses an army museum. Check the status of the Alcázar with the tourist office before heading here. It is currently closed for renovations but should reopen again during the lifetime of this edition.

In a 16th-century hospital founded by Cardinal Mendoza, **Museo de Santa Cruz** ✹✹, Calle Miguel de Cervantes 3 (✆ **92-522-1036**), is a museum of art and sculpture, one of the finest in Seville. The museum is celebrated for its **collection of 16th and 17th century paintings** ✹, 18 of which are by El Greco himself. *The Assumption of the Virgin* ✹ is El Greco's last known work. Paintings by Ribera, Goya, and other great Spanish artists are also on display, along with medieval and Renaissance tapestries and masterful sculptures. Admission is free, and the museum is open Monday to Saturday 10am to 6pm, Sunday 10am to 2pm.

At **Iglesia de Santo Tomé,** Plaza del Conde 4 (✆ **92-525-6098**), you can gaze upon El Greco's masterpiece, *The Burial of the Count of Orgaz* ✹✹✹, painted in 1586. The chapel itself is modest, dating from the 14th century and standing in the old Jewish quarter. Admission is 1.50€ ($1.75), and hours are daily 10am to 6:45pm (closes at 5:45pm in winter).

Founded by Queen Isabella and King Ferdinand in 1477, **Monasterio de San Juan de los Reyes** ✹, Calle Reyes Católicos 17 (✆ **92-522-3802**), is in the Isabelline style, with flamboyant Gothic, traces of Mudéjar, and even Renaissance influences. The church is noted for its **sculptured decoration** ✹ by Juan Guas, the Flemish architect who designed the church. Its Gothic cloister from 1510 is stunningly beautiful with a multi-colored Mudéjar ceiling. Admission is 1.50€ ($1.75) and hours are daily 10am to 6:45pm. From November to March hours are daily 10am to 5:45pm.

Moments   **Toledo Through El Greco's Eyes**

Fleeing for the moment the narrow medieval streets of Toledo, hail a taxi and ask to be taken along the **Carretera de Circunvalación,** the highway that runs for 2 miles (3km) on the far bank of the Tagus. The road makes a circular loop of the river from Alcántara to San Martín Bridge. This same view was painted and immortalized by El Greco in his *A View of Toledo.*

It's not known for sure if El Greco actually lived at this address, but even so **Casa y Museo de El Greco,** Calle Samuel Leví 3 (© **92-522-4046**), remains one of the most enduring attractions of Toledo. In the old Jewish quarter, the house is a museum sheltering a collection of the Crete-born artist's works, including his magnificent series, *Christ and the Apostles* ✦. The museum also displays a copy of his famous *A View of Toledo,* plus three portraits and many other works of art. Admission is 2.40€ ($2.75), and hours are Tuesday to Saturday 10am to 2pm and 4 to 6pm, Sunday 10am to 2pm.

The oldest and largest of Toledo's eight original synagogues, **Sinagoga de Santa Maria la Blanca,** Calle Reyes Católicos 2 (© **92-522-7257**), dates from the 12th century. By 1405 it was taken over by the Catholic Church, but in modern times it has been restored, as much as it's possible, to its pristine beauty, with carved stone capitals and white horseshoe arches, along with ornamental, horizontal moldings. Its five naves and much of its elaborate Mudéjar decorations remain. Admission is 1.50€ ($1.75). Hours April to September are daily 10am to 1:45pm and 3:30 to 6:45pm (otherwise daily 10am–2pm and 3:30–5:45pm).

WHERE TO DINE

In the heart of the city, a minute's walk north of the cathedral, stands **Asador Adolfo** ✦, Calle Hombre de Palo 7 (© **92-522-7321**), serving the best of a typical Toledan cuisine. In a building dating in part from the Middle Ages, chefs turn out a savory cuisine, including some of the province's best game dishes, such as partridge or venison. Reservations are recommended, and main courses range from 18€ to 26€ ($20.75–$30). Open Tuesday to Saturday 1 to 4pm and 8pm to midnight, Sunday 1 to 4pm.

As you're in the heart of old Castile, you might want to sample some of that province's fabled fare. It doesn't get any better than that served at **Casón de los López** ✦✦, Silleria 3 (© **92-527-4774**). A short walk from the exact center of town, Plaza de Zocodover, this restaurant serves the lightest and most sophisticated cuisine in Toledo. The building itself is a virtual antique museum, but it's the fresh food from the bounty of the agricultural countryside that keeps packing them in here. Reservations are required. Main courses cost 15€ to 22€ ($17.25–$25.25), with set-price menus ranging from 33€ to 45€ ($38–$51.75). Open daily 1:30 to 4pm and Monday and Saturday 9 to 11:30pm.

SHOPPING

Toledo is known for its *damasquinado* or damascene work—that is, the Moorish art of inlaying gold, and even copper or silver threads, against a matte black steel backdrop. Stores all over town hawk these objects, none better than **Casa Bermejo,** Calle Airosas 5 (© **92-528-5367**), established in 1910 and still going strong. Some 50 artisans here turn out beautiful objects in Mudéjar designs, including platters, pitchers, swords, and other gift items. Open Monday to Friday 9am to 1pm and 3 to 6pm, Saturday 10am to 6pm. A worthy rival is **Felipe Suarez,** Circo Romano 8 (© **92-522-5615**), in business since 1920s. It also turns out quality damascene work, some objects of rare beauty. Open daily 10am to 7pm. Toledo is also famous for its marzipan, a treat made of sweet almond paste. The best marzipan is sold at **Casa Telesforo,** Plaza de Zocodover 13 (© **92-522-3379**). The confection is often shaped into such whimsical forms as hearts, diamonds, flowers, and fish. From June to September hours are daily 9am to midnight (closes at 9pm off season).

3 Seville

The capital of Andalusia, Seville launched itself into greatness after the Christian conquest of the south in the 13th century. The most exciting times to visit is during *Semana Santa* (Holy Week which leads up to Easter) and for the *Feria de Abril* (April Fair). The religious processions at Holy Week when sacred images are paraded through the streets are world famous.

Visitors flock to Seville to see its *Catedral* (3rd largest in the world) and its Alcázar complex, the Moorish fortress enlarged by the Christians in the 14th century to resemble the Alhambra in Granada. The maze of streets east of the cathedral and the Alcázar is called the Barrio de Santa Cruz, the old Jewish quarter. It's Seville at its most romantic, filled with strolling guitarists, secret plazas, flower-bedecked patios, and tapas bars. This old ghetto is reason enough to visit here.

GETTING THERE   Located to the north of the city, **Estación Santa Justa,** Av. Kansas City (© **95-454-0202**), is the major transportation hub of Andalusia with arriving trains, including AVE and Talgo runs, coming in from all over Spain, with especially good connections to Córdoba, Madrid, Barcelona, and Málaga, even Valencia and Granada. For a preview of trains serving the area, refer to the "Trains & Travel Times in Spain" chart on p. 731.

The tourist information office at the train station (© **95-454-1952**) is open daily from 8am to 10pm. The staff provides information about hotels available in the area but do not make reservations themselves. The station is easy to navigate, with 3 ATMs available as well as a money exchange kiosk. There are 3 bars and a cafe, plus a restaurant. Bus 32 runs to the center, costing .90€ ($1.10). You can also take TeleTaxi (© **95-462-2222**) or Radio Taxi (© **95-458-0000**), whose base rate is 2.15€ ($2.50). There is a luggage storage facility at the station that charges 3€ ($3.50) per bag per day.

VISITOR INFORMATION   The main office for tourist information is at Av. De la Constitución 21 (© **95-422-1404**), open Monday to Friday 9am to 7pm, Saturday 10am to 2pm and 3 to 7pm, Sunday and holidays 10am to 2pm. The staff here doesn't make hotel reservations.

TOP ATTRACTIONS & SPECIAL MOMENTS

Catedral de Sevilla ✻✻✻, Plaza del Triunfo, Av. De la Constitución (© **95-421-4971**), was constructed in the 12th century on the site of the great mosque of the Almohads. The celebrated cathedral is the largest Gothic building in the world and the third largest church in Europe. Lasting for 1 century, construction began in 1401. The stated goal of its architects was simply this: "Those who come after us will take us for madmen." The towering edifice claims to shelter the Tomb of Columbus, his coffin held up by bearers evoking the kings of Navarra, Aragón, Castile, and León. The towering monument to Christian beliefs is filled with *objets d'arts* and architectural monuments, including the **Capilla Mayor** ✻, with its huge iron grilles forged in the 16th century. At the Retablo Mayor, a statue of Santa Maria de la Sede, the patron saint of the cathedral, sits at the main altar before a "waterfall" of gold brought back from the New World. Other treasures include **15th-century stained-glass windows** ✻, elaborate choir stalls from the same century, and paintings by Murillo, Goya, and Zurbarán among other Spanish artists. After touring the dark cathedral, you can take delight in the **Patio de los Naranjos** ✻, with its fresh citrus scent of orange blossoms and sound of chirping birds.

The major landmark on the Seville skyline is **La Giralda** ⚜⚜⚜, the bell tower that adjoins the cathedral. Visitors climb this tower for one of the most panoramic city views in Andalusia. The Arabs built the tower as a minaret in 1198, crowning it with bronze spheres. Instead of tearing the tower down as a pagan monument, the Catholic conquerors removed these spheres and crowned La Giralda with Christian symbols such as a bronze weathervane (called *giraldillo*) portraying Faith. The tower has seen other additions over the centuries, including the addition of bells in the 1500s. To ascend it, you walk a seemingly endless ramp.

Admission to the tower and cathedral is 6€ ($6.90) for adults, 1.50€ ($1.75) for children and students. There is free admission to all on Sunday. Hours in July and August are daily 9:30am to 4:30pm; September to June daily 11am to 5pm.

Hospital de Santa Caridad, Calle Temprado 3 (✆ **95-422-3232**), was once the haunt of Miguel de Manara, whose notorious life was said to have been the inspiration for the story of Don Juan. A charity hospital founded in 1674, it still cares for the elderly and the infirm. It can be visited by the general public, who come here to delight in the glory of the building's baroque Sevillana style. Nuns will show you through two beautiful courtyards filled with plants. On the tour you can see some Dutch tiles from the 18th century and impressive fountains. In the church itself are many Old Masters–type paintings by some of the leading artists of the 17th century. Especially ghoulish is the *End of the World's Glory* by Valdés Leal, picturing an archbishop being devoured by maggots. Admission is 3€ ($3.50); free for children under 13. Open Monday to Saturday 9:30am to 1:30pm and 3:30 to 7:30pm, Sunday 9am to 1pm.

Museo Provincial de Bellas Artes de Sevilla ⚜⚜, Plaza del Museo 9 (✆ **95-422-0790**), lies off a main artery, Calle de Alfonso XII, and is a former convent. Today it shelters a gallery devoted to some of the most important works of art in Seville. One gallery showcases two of El Greco's best-known works, and many other leading Spanish painters are on parade, including Zurbarán. Note especially Zurbarán's *San Hugo en el Refectorio* (1655), painted for the monastery at La Cartuja. The most fascinating of these artists is Valdés-Leal, a 17th-century painter with a macabre style as exemplified by his painting of John the Baptist's head. More contemporary paintings are displayed on the top floor. Admission is 1.50€ ($1.75); free for students and children under 12. Open Tuesday 3 to 8pm, Wednesday to Saturday 9am to 8pm, Sunday 9am to 2pm.

Reales Alcázares ⚜⚜⚜, Patio de Bandera (✆ **95-450-2323**), is a complex of magnificent buildings that has been the home of Spanish royalty for almost 7 centuries. The palace was the sometimes residence of Queen Isabella I, who sent navigators from Seville to the New World in search of gold and other treasures. Mudéjar courtyards and elegantly decorated corridors remain from the Alcázar's imperial heyday. Over the years subsequent monarchs have added their own architectural touches, including the lavishly decorated **state apartments** ⚜ ordered built by Charles V. Beautiful 16th-century tiles and elaborate tapestries decorate the halls where Charles once trod. The palace contains many notable features such as the **Patio de las Doncellas** ⚜ or maidens, with its elaborate plasterwork by the top artisans brought in from Granada, and the **Salon de Embajadores** ⚜, dating from 1427. This salon is celebrated for its splendid dome of carved and gilded, interlaced wood. Wind down in the sumptuous **gardens** ⚜ with their Moorish fountains, pavilions, and terraces. Admission is 5€ ($5.75); free for students and children under 14. Open April to September Tuesday to Saturday 9:30am to 7pm, Sunday 9:30am to 5pm. October to March Tuesday to Saturday 9:30am to 5pm, Sunday 9:30am to 1:30pm.

Seville

ACCOMMODATIONS ■
Doña María **6**
La Casa de la Judería **8**

DINING ◆
La Albahaca **7**
Rincón de la Casana **9**
Taverna del Alabardero **2**

ATTRACTIONS ●
Catedral de Sevilla **4**
Hospital de la Santa
  Caridad **3**
Museo Provincial de Bellas
  Artes de Sevilla **1**
Reales Alcázares **5**

WHERE TO STAY & DINE

At the 64-unit **Doña Maria** ⭐, Don Remondo 19, 41004 Sevilla (© **95-422-4990;** www.hdmaria.com), the cathedral is dramatically on view from the rooftop terrace of this well-run hotel, graced by an elaborate neoclassical entryway. A pool plus Iberian antiques in the stone-faced public lobby and upper hallways add a grace note, and iron balconies and other architectural features remain from the building's heyday as a private town house in the 1840s. Bedrooms are midsize and comfortably furnished, each individually decorated, a few containing four-poster beds. Rates are 99€ to 165€ ($114–$190) in a double; rooms are equipped with a hair dryer, and on-site facilities include a bar.

La Casa de la Judería ⭐⭐, Plaza Santa Maria la Blanca, Callejón de dos Hermanos 7 (© **95-441-5150;** www.casasypalacios.com), a 17th-century palace and the former abode of the dukes of Beja, lies in the Santa Cruz *barrio* and is within an easy walk of the cathedral and Seville's other major attractions. The 116 bedrooms are individually decorated, most often with antiques or reproductions, and some have four-poster beds. All the units have balconies, and some of the better units also contain whirlpool tubs and living rooms. Doubles cost 129€ to 235€ ($148–$270), with suites going for 210€ to 346€ ($242–$298). Amenities include a restaurant and bar, and all rooms have hair dryers.

La Albahaca ⭐⭐, Plaza Santa Cruz 12 (© **95-422-0714**), serving grand Andalusian and Basque cuisine, is housed in one of the best-preserved structures in the Santa Cruz *barrio.* The house was designed by famed architect Juan Talavera, and the setting is elegant—it's long been a favorite of visiting royalty, including the king and queen of Spain. The menu is skillfully tailored from an array of bounty found in the Andalusian countryside, and no chef in town does better desserts—wait until you try the fig soufflé or the bitter orange mousse. Main courses cost 16€ to 20€ ($18.50–$23), and hours are Monday to Saturday 1 to 4pm and 8pm to midnight. Closed Monday lunch in July and August.

An unusual blend of Argentine and Andalusian cuisine is served at the relatively unknown **Rincón de la Casana** ⭐, Santo Domingo de la Calzeda 13 (© **95-453-1710**). It's located near the old town, with a setting of antique tiles and regional artifacts forming an appropriate backdrop for the skilled cooking of some talented chefs who turn out savory dishes night after night. Inside the two-story interior you can stop at the entrance and pay your respects to the mounted head of the last bull killed in the ring by José Luís Vasquez, the celebrated bullfighter. The meat dishes, such as ox steak, are especially succulent. Main courses cost 12€ to 16€ ($13.75–$18.50), and hours are Monday to Saturday 1 to 4:30pm and 8:30pm to 12:30am

Three blocks from the cathedral, **Taverna del Alabardero** ⭐⭐, Calle Zaragoza 20 (© **95-450-2721**), is one of the city's leading restaurants. Housed in a 19th-century town mansion, the restaurant serves a refined Andalusian cuisine based on quality ingredients to politicians, diplomats, and royalty. Against a backdrop of art and antiques, formalized service takes place in two main salons, with additional seating in the rear garden. Devotees of fine food in Seville swear by this place. Main courses cost 13€ to 23€ ($15–$26.50). Hours in June and July are daily 1:30 to 4:30pm and 8:30pm to 12:30am; September to May 1pm to 3:30pm and 8pm to midnight. Closed in August.

SHOPPING

One of the best selections of Andalusian ceramics is found at **El Postigo,** Calle Arfe (© **95-456-0013**), in the vicinity of the cathedral. The display of hand-painted tiles is exceptional. Open Monday to Saturday 10am to 2pm and

Monday to Friday 5:30 to 8:30pm. Another good selection of ceramics from southern Spain is found at **Martian,** Calle Sierpes 74 (© 95-421-3413), close to the town hall. Many of the designs were taken from ancient geometric patterns of Andalusia, and all the ceramics are made in the Greater Seville area. Open Monday to Saturday 10am to 2pm and 5 to 8:30pm. If you'd like a fan like Carmen might have fluttered about, the best selection is at **Casa Rubio,** Sierpes 56 (© 95-422-6872), open Monday to Saturday 9:30am to 1:30pm and Monday to Friday 4:30 to 8:30pm.

For general merchandise, head for **El Corte Inglés,** Plaza Duque 8 (© 95-459-7000), in the commercial center of town. In addition to its regular line of items for the home, it also hawks a vast array of handcrafts as well. Open Monday to Saturday 10am to 10pm.

Works by some of the best of the southern Spanish artists are on display at **Rafael Ortiz,** Marmolles 12 (© 95-421-4874), where exhibitions are frequently changed. Open Monday to Saturday 11am to 1:30pm and Monday to Friday 6 to 9pm.

The fashions of southern Spain are showcased at **Iconos,** Av. de la Constitución 21A (© 95-422-1408), a boutique appealing to a wide age group of women, with its array of every item from costume jewelry to silk scarves. Open Monday to Saturday 10am to 9pm. More upscale and chic fashion is sold at **Victorio & Lucchino,** Sierpes 87 (© 95-422-7951). Open Monday to Friday 10am to 1:30pm and 5:30 to 8:30pm and Saturday 10:30am to 1:30pm and 5:30 to 8:30pm.

NIGHTLIFE

The people of Seville begin their evening early by touring all the tapas bars. The most typical of the old-fashioned tapas joints is **Casa Ramón,** Plaza de los Venerables 1 (© 95-422-8483), in Barrio de Santa Cruz. Since 1934, this has been a landmark bar serving delectable tapas along with local wine, and doing so exceedingly well. Try *pata negra,* a ham from the fabled black-hoofed Iberian breed of pig, celebrated for its sweet flavor caused by a diet of acorns. If you become addicted to this, you'll find more *pata negra* offerings at **Casa Ruitz,** Calle Francos 59 (© 95-422-8624). On the northern edge of Barrio de Santa Cruz stands **El Rinconcillo,** Gerona 40 (© 95-422-3182), a tasca with a history going back to 1670, making it the oldest bar in town. The selection of cheese here is especially tempting. For the best seafood tapas, head over to **La Alicantina,** Plaza del Salvador 2 (© 95-422-6122), lying 5 blocks north of the cathedral. We can personally vouch for the fried calamari, the clams marinara, and the garlic-flavored grilled shrimp.

If you like bars instead of tascas, head for **Abades,** Calle Abades 13 (© 95-422-5622), set in a mansion in the Santa Cruz *barrio* that dates from the 1800s. It is an architectural jewel box from the Spanish *Romantico* era, with classical music playing in the background. Later you can enjoy authentic Andalusian flamenco at **Club Los Gallos,** Plaza de Santa Cruz 11 (© 95-421-6981), which is one of the most reputable of the joints, attracting top talent for its impassioned performances. The cover charge of 27€ ($31) includes the first drink.

Its major competition, with shows almost equally as good, is **El Arenal,** Calle Rodó 7 (© 95-421-6492). It charges the same cover as Los Gallos. Show times at both clubs are usually nightly at 9 and 11, but call to confirm that. For a fiesta every night, head for **El Patio Sevillano,** Paseo de Cristobal Colón 11 (© 95-421-4120), where exotically costumed Andalusian dancers entertain you with flamenco songs and dance, Spanish folk songs and dance, and occasional classical pieces such as by such composers as Chueca. Two shows nightly begin at 7:30 and 10pm, and the cover of 29€ ($33.50) includes the first drink.

There's something really special about attending operas inspired by Seville, especially Mozart's *Marriage of Figaro* or Verdi's *La Forza del Destino* in Seville itself. Since the 1990s, the city has boasted its **Teatro de la Maestranza,** Paseo de Colón 22 (© **95-422-6573**), which is also the setting for other musical presentations ranging from jazz to classical. Spanish *zarzuelas* (operettas) are also performed here. Tickets depend on the event and can be purchased at the box office, open daily from 10am to 2pm and 6 to 9pm.

AN EXCURSION TO CORDOBA

Julius Caesar, Pompey, and Agrippa used to stop off in Córdoba when it was the capital of a Roman province called Baetica established in 151 B.C. But it was under the Moors in the 8th century that the city reached the apex of its power of glory, second in glitter only to glittering Constantinople. A pilgrimage to its Mezquita or Great mosque—still standing today—was said to have been comparable to a pilgrimage to Mecca.

GETTING THERE   Eighteen daily AVE trains depart from Seville for Córdoba—a trip of only 45 minutes. For more information and schedules, contact RENFE (© **90-224-0202;** www.renfe.es).

Trains arrive at Estación Córdoba, Glorieta de las Tres Culturas, which has a 24-hour luggage storage area with coin-operated lockers. The cost ranges from 2.40€ to 4.50€ ($2.75–$5.25) depending on your type of luggage. Also inside the station is a restaurant and cafeteria but no tourist information office.

The train station is a 10-minute walk from the city center. If you don't want to walk, you can head into town by taxi for about 6€ to 7€ ($7–$8). Taxis usually meet arriving trains or else you can call **Radio Taxi** at © **95-776-4444.**

Bus 3 makes the run from the train station through Plaza Tendillas and along the river up Calle Doctor Fleming. A one-way ticket costs .80€ (90¢).

TOURIST INFORMATION   The **Córdoba Tourist Office** is at Calle Torrijos 10 (© **95-747-1235**), open Monday to Saturday from 9:30am to 6:30pm, Sunday 10am to 2pm. The staff does not make hotel reservations.

TOP ATTRACTIONS & SPECIAL MOMENTS

It's worth the train trip to Andalusia to visit the **Mezquita-Catedral de Córdoba** ✸✸✸, Torrijos and Calle Cardenal Herrero (© **95-747-0512**). This magnificent edifice was the Arabs' crowning architectural achievement in the West during their 8th-century heyday. The original mosque, built between 785 and 787, changed and evolved over the centuries using many different styles. The field of more than **850 columns** ✸✸✸ was crafted mainly from jasper, granite, and marble, building material often taken from Roman and Visigothic structures. The richly ornamented prayer niche, the **mihrab** ✸✸✸, is a stunning work. This domed shrine of Byzantine mosaics once housed the Koran.

In the 16th century, a cathedral was placed awkwardly in the middle of this mosque. Highlights of the cathedral include **two pulpits** ✸✸ of mahogany, jasper, and marble, and the **baroque choir stalls** ✸✸ of Pedro Duque Cornejo from the mid–18th century. Not quite as impressive is the **Capilla de Villaviciosa** ✸, the first Christian chapel constructed in the mosque in 1371 with magnificent multi-lobed arches. The Patio de los Naranjos, a courtyard of orange trees where the faithful once washed before prayer, is quite charming. Admission is 6.50€ ($7.50) adults, 3.25€ ($3.75) children (ages 10–14). Kids

9 and under free. Open June to September daily 10am to 7pm, October to April daily 10am to 6pm.

The second great edifice of Córdoba is the **Alcázar de los Reyes Cristianos** (⭐), Plaza Santo de los Mártires (𝒞 **95-742-0151**), lying 2 blocks southwest of the Mezquita. This fortress was commissioned in 1328 by Alfonso XI and remains one of the finest examples of military architecture in all of Iberia. It became the palace-fortress of the Catholic monarchs, its severity softened by its beautiful gardens, fountains, and water terraces. Wander at leisure across the Moorish patios, taking in salons with **Roman mosaics** (⭐) and an impressive **sarcophagus** (⭐) from the 3rd century A.D. Admission to the Alcázar is 2€ ($2.30) adults; free for children under 18. Hours in June are Tuesday to Saturday 10am to 2pm and 5:30 to 7:30pm, Sunday 9:30am to 2:30pm; July and August Tuesday to Sunday 8:30am to 2:30pm and 8pm to midnight; September to May Tuesday to Saturday 9:30am to 3pm and 4:30 to 6:30pm, Sunday 9:30am to 3pm. Gardens are illuminated May to September daily 10am to 1am.

After seeing the city's two major edifices, you will have viewed the best of Córdoba. If you still have some time remaining before you have to head back to Seville, check out the narrow streets of the old **Judería** (⭐⭐), the former Jewish quarter. This ancient *barrio* lies directly north of the Mezquita, and is filled with 18th-century whitewashed houses with delicate window grilles.

Of the private palaces of Córdoba, one is open to the public, **Palacio Museo de Viana** (⭐⭐), Plaza de Don Gome 2 (𝒞 **95-749-6741**), an impressive example of the civil architecture of Córdoba in the 15th century. With its beautiful garden and a dozen courtyards, it's a stunner outside and in, as it's filled with opulently rich furnishings and objets d'art. Note especially the stunning **Mudéjar** *artesonado* **ceiling** (⭐) constructed of cedar. The tapestry collection is rich and evocative—many of the hangings made in royal workshops after cartoons by Goya. Admission is 6€ ($7). It's open June to September Monday to Saturday 9am to 2pm; October to May Monday to Friday 10am to 1pm and 4 to 6pm, Saturday 10am to 1pm. Closed June 7 to 22.

Other minor museums include the **Museo Arqueológico Provincial** (⭐), Plaza Jerónimo Páez 7 (𝒞 **95-747-4011**), 2 blocks northeast of the Mezquita. This is one of Andalusia's most important treasure troves of archaeological digs in the area. In a palace from 1505, it displays artifacts, many from Paleolithic and Neolithic times, along with Roman sculptures, bronzes, mosaics, and ceramics, even some Visigothic finds. Admission is 1.50€ ($1.75). Children 17 and under free. Open Tuesday 3 to 8pm, Wednesday to Saturday 9am to 8pm, and Sunday 9am to 3pm.

Another distinguished museum is **Museo de Bellas Artes de Córdoba,** Plaza del Potro 1 (𝒞 **95-747-1314**), housed in an old hospital. This is an impressive regional fine arts museum, housing some outstanding examples of Spanish baroque art, along with sculpture, and other art objects. The museum lies to the immediate east of the Mezquita. Admission is 1.50€ ($1.75). Free for children under 18. Open Tuesday 3 to 8pm, Wednesday to Saturday 9am to 8pm, and Sunday 9am to 3pm.

WHERE TO DINE

Just a 10-minute walk from the Mezquita, **Campos de Córdoba** (⭐), Calle de los Lineros 32 (𝒞 **95-749-7500**), is a wine cellar *(bodega)* and top-notch restaurant that's been around since 1908, so it must be doing something right. In the front is a tapas bar filled with wine drinkers, or else you can retreat to the rear following in the footsteps of numerous celebrities who have come to dine on the well-prepared, fresh Spanish and Andalusian cuisine. Main courses cost 12€ to 18€ ($13.75–$20.75), and reservations are recommended. Open daily 1:30 to 4:30pm and Monday to Saturday 8:30pm to midnight.

Serving even better but more expensive food is **La Almudaina** ★★★, Plaza de los Santos Mártires 1 (✆ **95-747-4342**), lying near the Alcázar in a 15th-century palace. Fronting the river in the former Jewish *barrio*, this is one of the finest restaurants of Andalusia but moderate in price considering its quality. Highly personal cuisine served in generous portions is the hallmark of the place. Reservations are required, with main courses costing 16€ to 40€ ($18.50–$46), a fixed-price menu going for 21€ ($24.15). Hours are daily from noon to 4pm and Monday to Saturday 8:30pm to midnight. In July and August the restaurant closes on Sunday and for the rest of the year only on Sunday night.

Around the corner from the Mezquita, **Casa Pepe de la Judería,** Calle Romero 1 (✆ **95-720-0744**), is a typical looking restaurant that serves Córdoban recipes of exceptional merit. Spread across three floors, its special feature is rooftop dining from May to October. The fare is hearty and regional, with first-rate ingredients used. Try the Andalusian gazpacho for starters. Reservations are recommended, and main courses cost 13€ to 18€ ($15–$20.75). Open daily Sunday to Thursday 1 to 4pm and 8:30 to 11:30pm; Friday and Saturday 1 to 4:30pm and 8:30pm to midnight.

4 Granada ★★★

In the foothills of the snowcapped Sierra Nevada, Granada, at 2,200 feet, sprawls over two main hills, the Alhambra and the Albaicín, and is crossed by two rivers, the Genil and the Darro. The location is 258 miles (415km) south of Madrid, 164 miles (261km) east of Córdoba, and 155 miles (250km) southeast of Seville. This former stronghold of Moorish Spain is full of romance and folklore. Washington Irving *(Tales of the Alhambra)* used the symbol of this city, the pomegranate *(granada),* to conjure up a spirit of romance.

Most visitors head to this city with one goal in mind—to see the famous Alhambra Palace. Though the palace is the city's must-see attraction, visitors should definitely take the time to soak up the city's Moorish atmosphere in the old Arab Quarter and take in its other top sites. *Tip:* A good way to tour the city for the rail traveler heading here from Seville (the most popular departure point for Granada) is to schedule one's arrival in the city for late afternoon, overnight in Granada, and then spend the next day touring the wonders of the city before departing on the overnight *Trenhotel* to Barcelona. Just be sure to reserve a spot on the overnight train well in advance.

GETTING THERE Most rail passengers head east to Granada after a visit to Seville (see above). Four T.R.D. trains run from Seville to Granada daily taking slightly more than 3 hours, sometimes just under 3½ hours. Instead of launching your Andalusian rail adventure in Seville, you can also take one of two daily TALGO trains leaving from Madrid's Atocha Rail Station and heading south to Granada daily, the trip taking around 6 hours.

The train station in Granada is at Avenida de Los Analuces (✆ **90-224-0202**) in the southwesterly part of the city, away from the city center. A taxi from the train station to the center of Granada costs 3€ to 5€ ($3.45–$5.75), but a one-way bus fare is only .85€ ($1). A stop for bus lines 1, 3, 4, 5, 6, 7, 9, 11, or 33 is about 330 feet from the entrance to the train station.

Granada & the Alhambra

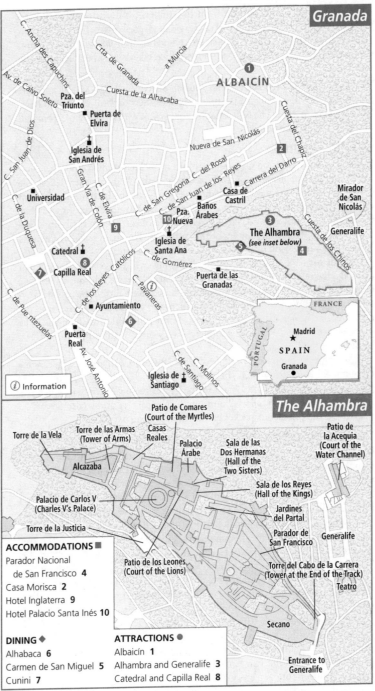

Granada

- Pza. del Triunto
- Puerta de Elvira
- Iglesia de San Andrés
- Universidad
- **ALBAICÍN** 1
- Nueva de San Nicolás
- 2
- Casa de Castril
- Baños Árabes
- Pza. Nueva 10
- Iglesia de Santa Ana
- Mirador de San Nicolás
- **The Alhambra** *(see inset below)* 3 5 4
- Generalife
- Catedral 8
- Capilla Real
- 7
- 9
- Puerta de las Granadas
- Ayuntamiento
- 6
- Puerta Real
- Iglesia de Santiago
- i Information

Spain inset
- FRANCE
- PORTUGAL
- Madrid ★
- SPAIN
- Granada ●

The Alhambra

- Torre de la Vela
- Torre de las Armas (Tower of Arms)
- Casas Reales
- Patio de Comares (Court of the Myrtles)
- Palacio Árabe
- Sala de las Dos Hermanas (Hall of the Two Sisters)
- Patio de la Acequia (Court of the Water Channel)
- Alcazaba
- Sala de los Reyes (Hall of the Kings)
- Palacio de Carlos V (Charles V's Palace)
- Jardines del Partal
- Torre de la Justicia
- Patio de los Leones (Court of the Lions)
- Parador de San Francisco
- Generalife
- Torre del Cabo de la Carrera (Tower at the End of the Track)
- Teatro
- Secano
- Entrance to Generalife

ACCOMMODATIONS ■
Parador Nacional
   de San Francisco **4**
Casa Morisca **2**
Hotel Inglaterra **9**
Hotel Palacio Santa Inés **10**

DINING ◆
Alhabaca **6**
Carmen de San Miguel **5**
Cunini **7**

ATTRACTIONS ●
Albaicín **1**
Alhambra and Generalife **3**
Catedral and Capilla Real **8**

The station is open daily from 7am to 11:30pm. Immediate tickets can be purchased daily from 7:15am to 11:25pm, and advance tickets from 8:30am to 11:30pm. There is a luggage storage office open daily from 7am to 11:15pm, which costs 2.40€ ($2.75), but no tourist office. ATMs are available inside the station.

VISITOR INFORMATION   The **tourist office,** Calle de Mariana Pineda (© **95-822-5990;** www.granada.org), is open Monday to Saturday 9am to 7pm, Sunday 10am to 2pm. The staff here will supply you with a list of hotels but will not make hotel reservations.

GETTING AROUND

Walking is a viable option once you arrive in the center of town, and is the preferred method for exploring Old Granada and the Arab Quarter. Cuesta de Gomérez is one of the most important streets in Granada. It climbs uphill from the Plaza Nueva, the center of the modern city, to the Alhambra. At the Plaza Nueva the east–west artery, Calle de los Reyes Católicos, goes to the heart of the 19th-century city and the towers of the cathedral. The main street of Granada is the Gran Vía de Colón, the principal north–south artery.

Calle de los Reyes Católicos and the Gran Vía de Colón meet at the circular Plaza de Isabel la Católica, graced by a bronze statue of the queen offering Columbus the Santa Fe agreement, which granted the rights to the epochal voyage to the New World. Going west, Calle de los Reyes Católicos passes near the cathedral and other major sights in the downtown section of Granada. The street runs to Puerta Real, the commercial hub of Granada with many stores, hotels, cafes, and restaurants.

Taxis can be summoned by calling © **95-828-06-54.** Otherwise, you can rely on public buses (© **95-881-37-11** or 900-710-900). The most useful bus is Bus Alhambra going from Plaza Nueva in the center to the Alhambra (which is a steep climb of almost ¾ mile/1.2km from the city center). Rides cost .85€ ($1), or else you can purchase a packet of 10 tickets costing 5€ ($5.75).

TOP ATTRACTIONS & SPECIAL MOMENTS

Later enriched by Moorish occupants into a lavish palace, the **Alhambra and Generalife** ✹✹✹, Palacio de Carlos V (© **95-822-0912;** www.Alhambra.org), was originally constructed for defensive purposes on a rocky hilltop outcropping above the Darro River. The modern city of Granada was built across the river from the Alhambra, about half a mile (.8km) from its western foundations.

When you first see the Alhambra, you may be surprised by its somewhat somber exterior. You have to walk across the threshold to discover the true delights of this Moorish palace. Tickets are sold in the office at the Entrada del Generalife y de la Alhambra. Enter through the incongruous 14th-century **Gateway of Justice** ✹. Most visitors don't need an expensive guide but will be content to stroll through the richly ornamented open-air rooms, with their lacelike walls and courtyards with fountains.

The most-photographed part of the palace is the **Court of Lions** ✹✹✹, named after its highly stylized fountain. This was the heart of the palace, the most private section where the sultan enjoyed his harem. Opening onto the court are the Hall of the Two Sisters, where the favorite of the moment was kept, and the Gossip Room, a factory of intrigue. In the dancing room in the Hall of Kings, entertainment was provided nightly to amuse the sultan's party.

Charles V built a Renaissance palace at the Alhambra—which, although quite beautiful, is terribly out of place in such a medieval Moorish setting. Today it

> **Tips** **Reserving for the Alhambra**
>
> Because of the overwhelming crowds, the government limits the number of people who can enter the Alhambra. Go as early as possible, but even if you get here at 10am, you may not be admitted until 1:30pm. If you arrive after 4pm, it's unlikely you'll get in at all. Your best bet is to make arrangements for tickets before you arrive by calling the Banco Bilbao Vizcaya at ℭ **90-222-4460** within Spain. Tickets can also be reserved online at **www.alhambratickets.com**. You can charge tickets to your MasterCard or Visa. Tickets cost the regular 8€ ($9.20) but with an additional service fee of .88€ ($1). Once reserved, these tickets can be picked up at the main entrance to the Alhambra.

houses the **Museo Bellas Artes en la Alhambra** (ℭ **95-822-4843**), open Tuesday to Saturday 9am to 8pm, Sunday 9am to noon. Of minor interest, it displays mostly religious paintings and sculpture from the 1500s to the present. It also shelters the Museo de la Alhambra (ℭ **95-822-7527**), devoted to Hispanic-Muslim art and open Tuesday to Saturday from 9am to 2pm, and Sunday 9am to 2pm.

Exit from the Alhambra via the Puerta de la Justicia, then circumnavigate the Alhambra's southern foundations until you reach the gardens of the summer palace, where Paseo de los Cipreses quickly leads you to the main building of the **Generalife** ✸✸, built in the 13th century to overlook the Alhambra. The sultans used to spend their summers in this palace (pronounced Heh-neh-rah-*lee-feh*), safely locked away with their harems. The Generalife's glory is its gardens and courtyards. Don't expect an Alhambra in miniature: The Generalife was always meant to be a retreat, even from the splendors of the Alhambra. A comprehensive ticket, including Alhambra and Generalife (above), is 8€ ($9.20); Museo Bellas Artes 1.50€ ($1.75); Museo de la Alhambra free; illuminated visits 8€ ($9.20). March to October, daily 8:30am to 8pm, floodlit visits daily 10pm to midnight; November to February, daily 8:30am to 6pm, floodlit visits daily 8 to 10pm. Bus: 30.

Once you've finished touring the Alhambra, head for the **Albaicín** ✸. The city's old Arab quarter is on one of the two main hills of Granada and stands in marked contrast to the city center's 19th-century buildings and wide boulevards. It and the surrounding gypsy caves of Sacromonte are holdovers from an older past. The Albaicín once flourished as the residential section of the Moors, even after the city's reconquest, but it fell into decline when the Christians drove them out. This narrow labyrinth of crooked streets escaped the fate of much of Granada, which was torn down in the name of progress. Fortunately it has been preserved, as have its cisterns, fountains, plazas, whitewashed houses, villas, and the decaying remnants of the old city gate. To begin your tour of the Albaicín, take bus 31.

In the center of town, **Catedral and Capilla Real** ✸✸, Plaza de la Lonja, Gran Vía de Colón 5 (ℭ **95-822-2959**), is a richly ornate Renaissance cathedral begun in 1521 and completed in 1714. Its **spectacular altar** ✸✸ is one of the country's architectural highlights, acclaimed for its beautiful facade and gold-and-white interior. Behind the cathedral (entered separately) is the flamboyant Gothic **Royal Chapel** ✸✸, where the remains of Queen Isabella and her husband Ferdinand lie. It was their wish to be buried in recaptured Granada, not

Castile or Aragón. Accenting the tombs is a wrought-iron grille, itself a master-piece. In the sacristy you can view Isabella's personal **art collection** 🏵🏵🏵, including works by Rogier Van der Weyden and various Spanish and Italian masters such as Botticelli. Admission to cathedral is 2.50€ ($2.90); chapel 2.50€ ($2.90). Cathedral and chapel are open Monday to Saturday 10:30am to 1:30pm and 4 to 8pm (4–7pm in winter).

WHERE TO STAY & DINE

Because the rail station is inconveniently located with respect to the center of the city, all of the following hotels and restaurants are about a 10- to 12-minute taxi or bus ride from the train depot.

Parador Nacional de San Francisco 🏵🏵🏵, Alhambra, 18009 Granada (© **95-822-1440**), is the most famous *parador* (special state-owned inns) in Spain—and the hardest to get into—set on the grounds of the Alhambra. The decor is tasteful and the place evokes a lot of history with its rich Andalusian ambience. The 36-room parador is housed within a former convent founded by the Catholic monarchs after they conquered the city in 1492. The guest rooms are generally roomy and comfortable; rooms in the older section are furnished with antiques. Units in the more modern wing are less inspired. Rates are 208€ ($239) double.

A real find, the 14-room **Casa Morisca** 🏵🏵, Cuesta de la Victoria 9, 18010 Granada (© **95-822-1100;** www.hotelcasamorisca.com), is in the historic lower district of Albaicín, at the foot of the Alhambra. The house dates from the end of the 15th century and the interior was kept and restored, although the facade was given a 17th-century overlay. Local craftsmen worked only with the original materials of the building, including clay tiles and lime mortar. Bedrooms are individually decorated in an old style but with all modern comforts. Rates are 140€ ($161) double; 190€ ($219) suite.

The NH chain runs the 36-room **Hotel Inglaterra,** Cettie Meriem 4, 18010 Granada (© **95-822-1559;** www.nh-hoteles.es), 2 blocks northeast of the cathedral and 5 minutes from the Alhambra. In 1992, they completely refurbished the run-down place. Its five-floor property is set well back from the thundering traffic of the main drag, Gran Vía de Colón. The air-conditioned rooms are moderately spacious and comfortably furnished with good beds and bright decorations. Rates are 120€ ($138) for a double.

Hotel Palacio Santa Inés 🏵🏵, Cuesta de Santa Inés 9, 18010 Granada (© **95-822-2362;** www.lugaresdivinos.com), in the colorful Albaicín district, is one of the most enchanting places to stay in Granada and about a 5-minute walk from the Alhambra. The painstakingly restored little palace was in complete ruins until the mid-1990s. Now it's a lovely, graceful inn that's even a bit *luxe.* The 35 medium-size rooms have air-conditioning and lots of antique furniture; some are duplexes and have small sitting rooms, and several open onto views of Granada. The suites have full kitchens. Rates are 100€–120€ ($115–$138) for a double; 155€–225€ ($178–$259)for a suite.

Alhabaca 🏵, Calle Varela 17 (© **95-822-4923**), is a little bistro in a century-old building owned by Javier Jiménez, who seats 30 diners at 10 tables in this old-fashioned restaurant decorated in a rustic style with bare white walls. The traditional dishes he serves are unpretentious and tasty, especially the *salmorejo* (creamy tomato gazpacho). It's a real find! Main courses run 7€–13€ ($8.05–$14.95).

On the sloping incline leading up to the Alhambra, **Carmen de San Miguel,** Plaza de Torres Bermejas 3 (© **95-822-6723**), offers spectacular views of the city center. The restaurant is proud of its glassed-in dining room and patio-style terrace. The food, although good, doesn't quite match the view. Main courses are 15€ to 20€ ($17.25–$23); tasting menu 37€ ($42.55).

The array of seafood served at **Cunini,** Plaza de la Pescadería 14 (© **95-825-0777**), perhaps 100 selections, extends even to the tapas offered at the long stand-up bar. Even though Granada is inland, it's not that far from the Mediterranean, and some of the freshest and best fish in town is served here. Specialties include both a *zarauela* (seafood stew) and rice studded with tasty morsels of fish as well. Main courses cost 16€ to 25€ ($18.40–$28.75).

NIGHTLIFE

A good place to begin your night is along the **Campo del Príncipe,** where at least seven old-fashioned tapas bars do a rollicking business during the cool of the evening. Our favorite is **La Esquinita,** Campo del Príncipe (© **95-822-7106**). Small, atmospheric, and sometimes claustrophobic, it serves a crowd that mostly eats standing up, sometimes spilling into the street. A perennial favorite directly in front of the cathedral is **Antigua Bodega Cartañeda,** Elvira 5 (© **95-822-9706**). Inside, rows of antique wine barrels and exposed masonry attract the city's wine connoisseurs. Another contender for your bar business is **Casa Henrique,** Calle Acero de Darro 8 (© **95-812-3508**), an old-fashioned masonry-sided hole-in-the-wall lined with antique barrels of wine and sherries. Its specialty tapas consist of thin-sliced Serrano ham and heaping platters of steamed mussels with herbs and white wine.

The best flamenco show in Granada is staged at **Sala de Fiesta Alhambra,** Carretera de Jaén, Polígono Industrial Olinda (© **95-841-2269**), nightly at 10:15pm. In addition to flamenco, performers attired in regional garb do folk dances and present guitar concerts. The show takes place in a garden setting. There's a high cover charge of 25€ ($28.75), which includes a drink you can nurse all evening. *Note:* It's best to take a taxi here.

5 Barcelona

One of the Mediterranean's busiest and most bustling ports, Barcelona is the capital of Catalonia, a province with its own rich language and culture that lies in the northeast of Spain and leans more to continental Europe in spirit than it does to the peninsula of Iberia.

If your schedule is so rushed that you might make it Barcelona or Madrid, that's a tough call. It's like saying should someone visit London or Paris. In sights, food, monuments, and shopping, the rival cities are in a neck-and-neck race. If you want to see the traditional land of bullfights and flamenco, make it Madrid. For wild nightlife, bronzed nude beaches, whimsical and daring *Modernisme* architecture, Surrealistic painters such as Dalí or Joan Miró, then make it Barcelona, home of the 1992 Olympics when the world became aware of a post-Franco and "new" Barcelona.

Barcelona is also the gateway to Catalonia, eastern coast Spanish ports along the Mediterranean, such as Valencia, and the Pyrenees, which are not that distant.

However, it is not a good center for touring much of Spain. Madrid is in the very exact center and is a better rail hub to the old imperial city of Toledo, the leading art cities of Andalusia such as Seville and Córdoba, and the fleshpot resorts of the Costa del Sol.

Barcelona

Plaça de
Francesc Macia

Carrer de Buenos Aires

Carrer de Londres

Carrer de Paris

Travessara de Gràcia

Gran de Gràcia

Avinguda Diagonal

29

Information
Rail Station

Travessara de Gràcia

Av. de Sant Antoni Maria Claret

Carrer de la Industria

Carrer de Còrsega

EIXAMPLE (i)

28

Carrer de Rosselló

Carrer de Roger de Flor

Plaça de la
Sagrada
Família
24

Carrer de Provença

Carrer Enric Granados

Carrer de Balmes

Rambla de Catalunya

27

Passeig de Gràcia

25

Carrer de Pau Claris

Avinguda Diagonal

Carrer de Mallorca

Carrer de València

Carrer d'Aragó

26

Carrer del Consell de Cent

Carrer de la Diputació

Gran Via de les Corts Catalanes

Carrer de Comte Borrell

Carrer del Comte d'Urgell

Carrer de Villarroel

Carrer de Casanova

Carrer de Muntaner

Carrer d'Aribau

Carrer de R. Llúria

Carrer del Bruc

Carrer de Girona

23

Carrer de Bailèn

Passeig de Sant Joan

Carrer de Nàpols

Carrer de Sicília

Plaça de la
Universitat

Ronda Universitat

Carrer de Pelai

22

Plaça
Catalunya

Plaça de
Tetuan

Carrer   de Casp

Carrer   d'Ausias Marc

Carrer   d'Alí Bei

Carrer de Ribes

Carrer de Sardenya

Ronda de Sant Antoni

RAVAL

21

20

(i)

Plaça
Urquinaona

Ronda de Sant Pere

Ronda Sant Pau

Carrer de Hospital

La Rambla

19

Av. Portal de l'Àngel

17   16

18

Via Laietana

Palau de la
Música Catalana

Passeig de Lluís Companys

Carrer de la Marina

14

La Rambla

BARRI GÒTIC

13 12

15

11

Passeig de Pujades

Carrer de Sant Pau

Gran Teatre
del Liceu

C. de   Ferran   C. de la Princesa

8

Passeig de Picasso

Passeig de Pujades

PARC DE LA
CIUTADELLA

Carrer Nou de la Rambla

9

7   6

Carrer del Comerç

Avda. de les Drassanes

La Rambla

10

LA RIBERA

4

5

Carrer de Wellington

Carrer Ample

3

Passeig de Colom

Pg. Isabel II

Estacio de
Francia

Plaça Portal
de la Pau

Moll de la Fusta

Moll d'Espanya

Port
Vell

Avinguda d'Icaria

PARC
ZOOLOGIC

Villa →
Olímpica

BARCELONETA

Passeig   Marítim

STATION INFORMATION
GETTING FROM THE AIRPORT TO THE TRAIN STATIONS
You can reach Estaçio Barcelona-Sants by a local train that runs at half-hour intervals between the airport and the train station daily from 6am to 10:15pm, the 21-minute trip costing 2.15€ ($2.50). For 3€ ($3.50), you can also take one of the **Aeróbuses** running daily from the airport to the Estaçio Sants every 15 minutes Monday to Friday 5:30am to 11pm, Saturday and Sunday 6pm to 10:15pm. To get to the station by taxi, expect a fare ranging from 15€ to 18€ ($17.25–$20.75).

There is no Metro that runs into the Estaçio de França station, however, and no Aérobus. Taxis meet all arriving flights at the Barcelona airport and a trip to Estaçio de França by taxi costs 20€ to 22€ ($23–$25.25). You can, of course, reach Plaça de Catalunya by bus or Metro. From this transportation hub, bus 17 runs out to the Estaçio França. Of course, if you're carrying heavy luggage, this will be a difficult jaunt.

INSIDE THE STATIONS
Like Madrid, Barcelona has two major rail stations: Estaçio Barcelona-Sants and Estaçio França.

Estaçio Barcelona-Sants, in Plaça Paisos Catalans (Metro: Sants-Estaçio; ✆ 93-491-3183), is Barcelona's public transportation hub, with most bus lines, all Metro (subway to Americans) lines, and both long distance and regional trains converging here. Direct trains link you to Montpellier, France, with ongoing connections to Paris and Geneva on TGVs or high-speed trains.

You can also catch trains here for Valencia and the Levante, Zaragoza, Madrid, Seville, and faraway Milan in Italy. For general rail information call ✆ 90-224-0202 or see **www.renfre.es** on the Web.

The two-level station offers many services and facilities, including banks for exchanging money, ATMs, a pharmacy, travel agents for making hotel reservations, restaurants, a phone center, and tourist shopping. The tourist office (no phone) is open daily Monday to Friday from 8am to 8pm, Saturday and Sunday 8am to 2pm. Luggage storage is available: Large lockers rent for 4.50€ ($5.25), small lockers for 3€ ($3.50). The luggage storage facility is open daily from 7am to 11pm.

The station's 12 tracks lying beneath the main floor of the station are accessible by both elevators and escalators. Video screens posted over the tracks list information.

Estacio de França, Av. Marqués de l'Argentera (✆ 90-224-0202), lies southeast of the center of Barcelona, close to Ciutadella Park, the zoo, the port, and Vila Olímpica. It is linked by frequent buses to the Plaça de Catalunya. Take bus 17, costing 1.05€ ($1.20) for a one-way fare. There is neither a tourist office here nor travel agents for making hotel reservations, and no currency exchange is available either. There are, however, ATMs, a restaurant, a bar, and a cafe at this two-level station. RENFE trains serving such regional cities as Girona or Tarragona in Catalonia or else Zaragoza in Aragón are the ones that frequent França. Express night trains from Paris, Zurich, Milan, and Geneva also pull in here.

INFORMATION ELSEWHERE IN THE CITY
The main tourist office for Barcelona is at **Palau de Rubert,** Passeig de Gràcia 107 (✆ 93-238-4000), open daily 10am to 7pm. The staff does not make hote reservations but will provide a list of dozens of local travel agents who do. They will also give you a list of Barcelona hotels in all price ranges. Another

Barcelona Metro

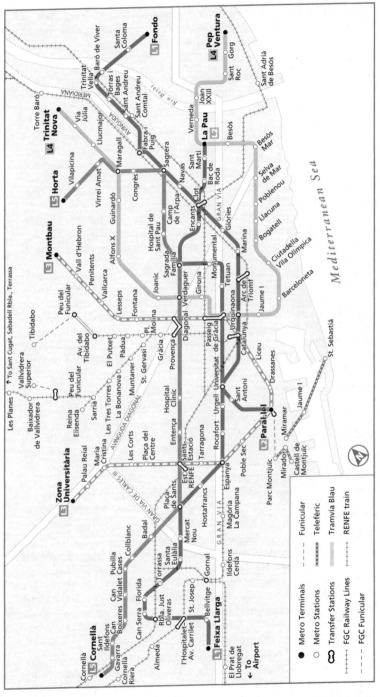

organization, **Oficina de Informaçio de Turisme de Barcelona,** Plaça de Catalunya 17-S (© **93-304-3134**), also provides detailed information—but no hotel reservations—daily from 9am to 9pm.

GETTING AROUND

To save money on public transportation, a *carte* good for 10 trips, the *Tarjeta T-10,* sells for 5.90€ ($6.75). This pass is available at Transports Metropolita de Barcelona, Plaça de la Universitat, open Monday to Friday 8am to 5pm, Saturday 8am to 1pm.

Another money-saver is a ride on *Bus Turistic,* which travels by 24 of the city's most visited attractions. You can get on and off the bus as you please, and your single ticket also covers the Montjuïch and Tibidabo cable car and funicular. The *Bus Turistic* can be purchased on the bus or at the tourist office at Plaça de Catalunya, and costs 15€ ($17.25) for 1 day or 19€ ($21.75) for 2 days. Children pay 9€ ($10.25) for 1 day or 12€ ($13.75) for 2 days.

Five Metro (subway) lines service Greater Barcelona on Monday to Thursday from 5am to midnight, Saturday 5am to 2am, and Sunday 6am to 2am. A one-way fare is 1.10€ ($1.25), and all major Metro lines converge at Plaça de Catalunya.

Barcelona also has daily bus service from 6:30am to 10pm, with some night buses running between 11pm and 4am. The one-way fare is 1.05€ ($1.20).

Look for the letters SP (meaning *servicio público*), the designation for taxis, which charge a basic rate of 1.15€ ($1.30), with each additional kilometer costing .69€ (80¢). Supplements are assessed for certain items, including rides to the airport and charges for extra large pieces of luggage. Most taxis can be hailed on the street or you can call **Autotaxi Mercedes** at © **93-303-3266** or **Miramar** (© **93-433-1020**).

WHERE TO STAY

Duques de Bergara ⊕   This town house, built for the Duke of Bergara in 1899, has been successfully transformed into an inviting five-story hotel with a modern, seven-story tower. Bedrooms are generally large and sport elegant fabrics and traditional comforts, including some especially inviting marble bathrooms. The public rooms are dramatically furnished in a decorative *Modernismo* style, and this is that rare Barcelona hotel that has a pool.

Bergata 11, 08002 Barcelona. © **93-301-5151.** Fax 93-317-3442. 149 units. 171€–235€ ($197–$270) double; 201€–259€ ($231–$298) triple. AE, DC, MC, V. Metro: Plaça de Catalunya. **Amenities:** Restaurant; bar; laundry; rooms for those with limited mobility. *In room:* Hair dryer.

Hotel Balmes   In the Eixample district, north of Plaça de Catalunya, this seven-story, hotel from the 1980s is chain-operated but highly efficient and welcoming. Bedrooms are the strong attraction here, as they are exceedingly comfortable, tastefully furnished, and contain marble-trimmed bathrooms. The more tranquil units open onto a small garden in the rear, and there is also a pool.

Carrer Mallorca 216, 08008 Barcelona. © **93-451-1914.** Fax 93-451-0049. www.derbyhotels.es. 100 units. 136€–186€ ($156–$214) double. AE, DC, MC, V. Metro: Diagonal. **Amenities:** Restaurant; bar; laundry. *In room:* Hair dryer.

Hotel Colón ⊕⊕   If you want to stay in the heart of Gothic Barcelona, there is no better location than this hotel opposite the main entrance to the cathedral. You parade through old-fashioned public rooms to modernized and good-size bedrooms that are comfortably and traditionally furnished. The sixth-floor rooms with balconies overlooking the square are the most sought after.

Avinguda de la Catédral 7, 08002 Barcelona. ✆ **800/845-0636** in the U.S. or 93-301-1404. Fax 93-317-2915. www.hotelcolon.es. 147 units. 220€–245€ ($253–$282) double; from 350€ ($403) suite. AE, DC, MC, V. Bus: Plaça de Catalunya or Urquinaona. **Amenities:** Restaurant; bar; laundry. *In room:* Hair dryer.

Hotel España   Stay here for the low rates, although you will get plenty of comfort and some architectural style. The hotel dates from 1902 and is the work of the famed architect, Doménech I Montaner; guests have included Salvador Dalí and other luminaries. Bedrooms are mostly medium in size and are comfortably but rather functionally furnished.

Carrer Sant Pau 11, 08001 Barcelona. ✆ **93-318-1758.** Fax 93-317-1134. 60 units. 86€ ($99) double. AE, DC, MC, V. Metro: Liceu or Drassanes. **Amenities:** 2 restaurants; bar; nonsmoking rooms; rooms for those with limited mobility. *In room:* Hair dryer.

Hotel Majestic ⭐   A landmark since 1920, this hotel stands in the center of Barcelona, only a 10-minute walk from the transportation hub at Plaça de Catalunya. A government-rated four-star hotel, it has been considerably modernized and upgraded. Bedrooms are better than many nearby competitors, with tasteful color schemes, chic upholsteries and carpets, and even artwork. Special amenities include a pool, fitness center, and sauna.

Passeig de Gràcia 68, 08007 Barcelona. ✆ **93-488-1717.** Fax 93-488-1880. www.hotelmajestic.es. 322 units. 175€–320€ ($201–$368) double; 360€–435€ ($414–$500) suite. AE, DC, MC, V. Metro: Passeig de Gràcia. **Amenities:** 2 restaurants; bar; laundry. *In room:* Hair dryer.

Hotel Regencia Colón ⟨Value⟩   In back of the Hotel Colón (see above) this property is a less expensive sibling, though it still enjoys a great location in the Gothic old town near the cathedral. It's a bit stodgy but a long enduring favorite and is most comfortable. Rooms are insulated against sound and are well maintained and inviting, as is the welcome from the staff here.

Sagristans 13-17, 08002 Barcelona. ✆ **93-318-9858.** Fax 93-317-2822. 55 units. www.hotelregenciacolon. com. 148€ ($170) double; 170€ ($196) triple. AE, DC, MC, V. Metro: Plaça de Catalunya or Urquinaona. **Amenities:** Bar; laundry. *In room:* Hair dryer.

HUSA Oriente   If you want to find lodgings on Barcelona's colorful and most famous boulevard, the Rambles, consider this hotel. In its heyday it was one of the grand hotels of the city, and dates from 1842. Considerably modernized and changed over the decades, it offers modestly furnished but tasteful and comfortable bedrooms. Much of its original architectural grandeur remains.

Les Rambles 45, 08002 Barcelona. ✆ **93-302-2558.** Fax 93-412-3819. www.husa.es. 142 units. 144€ ($166) double; 180€ ($207) triple. Rates include breakfast. AE, DC, MC, V. Metro: Liceu. **Amenities:** Restaurant; bar. *In room:* No hair dryer.

Jardí ⟨Value⟩   In the heart of the Gothic quarter, this hotel is located near many of the city's most visited monuments. The five-story hotel itself rests on ancient Roman foundations and has been considerably modernized and improved. Rooms, although simple, are furnished comfortably; the quieter accommodations are on the upper floors.

Plaça Sant Josep Oriols 1, 08002 Barcelona. ✆ **93-301-5900.** Fax 93-342-5733. 42 units. 75€–80€ ($86.25–$92) double; 90€ ($104) triple. AE, DC, MC, V. Metro: Liceu. **Amenities:** Lounge. *In room:* No hair dryer.

Mesón Castilla ⭐ ⟨Value⟩   Operated by the Spanish hotel chain, HUSA, this hotel, a real bargain, was carved out of a former apartment building near the center of Les Rambles, the main boulevard of Barcelona. Bedrooms are medium in size and quite comfortable, furnished with tasteful pieces such as Catalán-style headboards. The best accommodation open onto private terraces.

Valldoncella 5, 08001 Barcelona. © **93-318-2182**. Fax 93-412-4020. 57 units. 117€ ($135) double; 156€ ($179) triple. AE, DC, V. Metro: Plaça de Catalunya. **Amenities:** Breakfast room; lounge; laundry. *In room:* Hair dryer.

Rivoli Ramblas 👁   On the upper part of the Rambles, this hotel is housed in an Art Deco town mansion lying a block south of Plaça de Catalunya in the heart of Barcelona. The property has been recently renovated and its stylish interior is a good example of Catalán design. Bedrooms are neatly kept, a bit small for the most part, but carpeted and soundproof.

Les Rambles, 08002 Barcelona. © **93-302-6643**. Fax 93-317-5053. www.rivolihotels.com. 129 units. 246€ ($283) double; from 300€ ($345) suite. Rates include breakfast. AE, DC, MC, V. Metro: Plaça de Catalunya or Liceu. **Amenities:** Restaurant; bar; laundry; rooms for nonsmokers; rooms for those with limited mobility. *In room:* Hair dryer.

TOP ATTRACTIONS & SPECIAL MOMENTS

Before wandering the narrow, labyrinthine streets of old Barcelona, consider a panoramic view of it first just to get your bearings. That's possible from **Tibidabo Mountain** 👁, just north of the port, and reached by a funicular taking you up to 1,600 feet. **Mirador Torre de Collserola** (© **93-406-9354**) was built at the time of the 1992 Barcelona Olympics, and from it the most stunning vistas unfold. It costs 3€ ($3.50) to climb the tower. From Plaça de Catalunya, take bus 58 to Avinguda del Tibidabo, where you can board a special bus to take you to the funicular. The funicular runs daily and costs 4.40€ ($5) one-way. The tower is open July to September Monday to Friday 11am to 2:30pm and 3:30 to 8pm, Saturday and Sunday 11am to 8pm. During other months, hours are more limited, with most closings at 6pm.

Catedral de Barcelona 👁👁👁   The most acclaimed example of Catalán architecture, this is one of the great Gothic cathedrals of Europe and was begun in 1298 under the reign of Jaime II, although not completed until 1889. Called "the loveliest oasis in Barcelona" by historian Cirici, it is distinguished by a Gothic interior with a single, wide nave, with 28 side chapels branching off of it. Among the most distinguished of these is Capella de Sant Benet, dedicated to the patron saint of Europe and housing a splendid altarpiece depicting the *Transfiguration* by Bernat Martorell in 1452. The **choir stalls** 👁 are especially notable, the top tier of this 15th-century art displaying the coats-of-arms of the 12 knights of the Order of Toisón del Oro. The **cloisters** 👁 are another notable feature; they're in the Gothic style and decorated with a statue of St. George slaying the dragon. The cloister contains a museum of medieval art. Beneath the main altar is the impressive **crypt** 👁, with its alabaster sarcophagus (1339) of the martyred St. Eulalia. The twin octagonal bell towers date from 1386, although the bells were installed in 1545. You can take an elevator to the roof for one of the grand panoramic views of Barcelona's Gothic *barrio*. At noon on Sunday, the most typical folkloric dance of Catalonia, the *sardana,* is performed in front of this edifice.

Plaça de la Seu. © **93-315-1554**. Free admission to the cathedral; admission to museum 1€ ($1.15). Global ticket to museum, rooftop terraces, and towers 4€ ($4.50). Cathedral daily 9am–1pm and 5–7pm. Cloister museum daily 10am–1pm and 4–7pm. Metro: Jaume I.

Fundació Antoni Tàpies 👁   This museum is devoted to the work of a single artist, Antoni Tàpies. Born in 1923, Tàpies has become one of the best-known artists in Catalonia. He was a devotee of Surrealism and used any number of unconventional materials in the creation of his work, including concrete and metal. A landmark building, the museum lies near Passeig de Gràcia in the

Eixample district, and was designed by Lluis Domenech I Montaner, the leading exponent of Catalán Art Nouveau. A full range of Tàpies's work is on show, including drawings, sculptures, and ceramics, as well as paintings. His most controversial and rather gigantic sculpture, *Cloud and Chair*, is on top of the building. It was made from 9,000 feet of metal wiring and tubing.

Aragó 255. (✆ **93-487-0315**. Admission 4.20€ ($4.75) adults, 2.10€ ($2.50) students, free for children under 16. Tues–Sun 10am–8pm. Metro: Passeig de Gràcia.

Fundació Joan Miró ✿ One of Spain's greatest artists, Joan Miró (1893–1983) was from Catalonia. A stark white building was designed by Josep Lluís Sert to house a permanent collection of the paintings, sculptures, graphics, and tapestries of this world-class artist, including his amusing *Flame in Space* and *Named Woman*, painted in 1932. Trained in Paris and an admirer of Gaudí's Modernisme, Miró donated many of these works. Using multi-media, one wing charts the evolution of Miró's art from the age of 8 until his final works in the 1970s.

Plaça de Neptú, Parc de Montjuïc. (✆ **93-443-9470**. Admission 7.20€ ($8.25) adults, 3.60€ ($4) students, free for children under 15. July–Sept Tues–Wed and Fri–Sat 10am–8pm, Thurs 10am–9:30pm, Sun 10am–2:30pm; Oct–June Tues–Wed and Fri–Sat 10am–7pm, Thurs 10am–9:30pm. Sun 10am–2:30pm. Bus: 50 at Plaça d'Espanya.

La Sagrada Família ✿✿ This, the symbol of Barcelona, is Antoni Gaudí's unfinished masterpiece and the most unconventional church in Europe. The architect lived like a recluse at the site for 16 years and is buried in the **crypt** ✿, which was actually constructed by the cathedral's original architect, Francesc de Paula Villar I Lozano. Those who have seen Gaudí's finished plan for Sagrada Família can only lament that the architect died before carrying out his final dream. At the time of his death only one tower on the Nativity Facade had been completed. Financed by public contributions, work continues to this day. The apse remains the first part of the church completed by Gaudí. The controversial **Passion Façade** ✿ was finished in the late 1980s by Josep María Subirach. It is often criticized because of its "sinister" figures. Finished in 1904, the **Nativity Façade** ✿ is the most complete part of the church, its doorways representing faith, hope, and charity. A steep climb, 400 steps lead to the towers and upper galleries, opening onto **panoramic views of Barcelona** ✿✿. Or else you can take an elevator.

Majorca 401. (✆ **93-207-3031**. Admission 8€ ($9.25). Elevator 1.50€ ($1.75). Apr–Oct daily 9am–8pm. Nov–Mar daily 9am–6pm. Metro: Sagrada Família.

Museo Barbier-Mueller Art Precolombí ✿✿ In the medieval Palacio Nadal, this 1997 museum showcases one of the most important collections of pre-Columbian art. On display are some 6,000 exhibitions of tribal art, the first pieces acquired by the museum's namesake, Josef Mueller (1887–1977) in 1908. Of much interest are the artifacts left over from the Mayan culture, dating from 1000 B.C. A vast array is on display, including stone sculpture, ceramic and ornamental objects of great style, and funerary artifacts. Seek out, in particular, the artifacts of the Olmecs, a tribe who settled on the Gulf of Mexico at the first millennium B.C. and were known for their impressive stone sculpture and figures carved out of jade.

Carrer de Montcada 12–14. (✆ **93-310-4516**. Admission 3€ ($3.50) adults, 1.50€ ($1.75) students and seniors; free for children under 16. Free to all first Sun of every month. Tues–Sat 10am–6pm; Sun and holidays 10am–3pm. Metro: Jaume I.

> ## *Moments*   A Journey Back in Time
>
> Barcelona's **Barri Gòtic** ★★★ or Gothic quarter is filled with narrow, winding streets that take you back to the Middle Ages. Every street you turn down offers something of interest, a historic sight and most definitely dozens of shops, restaurants, and cafes, some of which may have been patronized by Picasso. The chief attraction is the Cathedral of Barcelona (p. 774), but there are dozens of other historic buildings as well, along with countless squares to discover on your own. None is more notable than Plaça de Sant Jaume, which has been the city's political center since Roman times. Today this square is dominated by the **Palau de la Generalitat**, headquarters of the autonomous government of Catalonia, and the **Ajuntament**, the Barcelona city hall. If you need guidance in approaching this warren of fascinating old streets, the tourist office leads walking tours of the *barrio*. You can purchase tickets at the Ajuntament in Plaça St. Jaume. Tours, costing 7€ ($8) for adults and 3€ ($3.50) for children under 12, are conducted Saturday and Sunday at 10am in English. For more information call ✆ **90-630-1282.**

Museu d'Art Contemporani de Barcelona ★   One of the leading showcases of modern art in eastern Spain, this museum houses masterpieces from a wide range of artists, including Tàpies and Paul Klee. It is especially rich in the works of Catalan painter Joan Miró, who was known for his Surrealistic style, his vivid colors, and fantastical forms. The museum itself is an architectural statement of Richard Meier, an American architect. Some critics say, and we agree, that the building itself is a work of art, particularly in its manipulation of natural light.

Plaça dels Angels 1. ✆ **93-412-0810.** Admission 7€ ($8) adults, 5.50€ ($6.25) students, free for children under 14. Wed–Fri 11am–7:30pm; Sat 10am–8pm; Sun 10am–3pm. Metro: Plaça de Catalunya.

Museo Nacional d'Art de Catalunya ★★★   Built for the 1929 World's Fair, in Montjuïc Park, this museum is not only Spain's major repository of Catalán art, but also displays the most significant collection of Romanesque art in the world. Some 100 Romanesque pieces range from icons to sculptures, and also include some splendid frescoes from the 12th century. To round out the collection, churches, monasteries, and other centers were "raided" throughout Catalonia for their treasures. One of the most remarkable exhibitions here are wall paintings from Sant Climent de Taüll and Santa Maria de Taüll. The museum is also rich in Gothic art, especially from Catalonia. Paintings by many great Spanish masters, from Velázquez to Zurbarán, are featured.

Palau Nacional, Parc de Montjuïc. ✆ **93-622-0360.** Admission 4.80€ ($5.50) adults, 3.30€ ($3.75) youths 7–20, free for children 6 and under. Tues–Sat 10am–7pm; Sun 10am–2:30pm. Metro: Espanya.

Museu Picasso ★★   Pablo Picasso (1881–1973) was born in Málaga but arrived in Barcelona at the age of 14. He fell in love with the city and in time would donate some 2,500 of his paintings, drawings, and engravings. They are now housed in this museum carved out of several old mansions on this street from the Middle Ages. The greatest attraction here is in the early drawings of the teenage Picasso, including *The First Communion* painted in 1896. A few paintings from his Blue and Rose periods are displayed, but his most celebrated work is the series, *Meninas,* based on the Velázquez masterpiece hanging in Madrid's

Prado (p. 744). Scenes from Picasso's old notebooks depict street life in Barcelona. It is said that Picasso found inspiration among Barcelona's prostitutes for his *Les Demoiselles d'Avignon,* which some art historians view as the well-spring of modern art.

Montcada 15–23. (✆ **93-319-6310**. Admission 5€ ($5.75) adults, 2.50€ ($3) students and people under 25, free for children under 16. Tues–Sat 10am–7:30pm; Sun 10am–2:30pm. Metro: Jaume I.

Parc Güell 🎢🎢 Like Sagrada Família, Gaudí's eccentric park was never completed. Even so, UNESCO has designated it as a World Heritage Site. The park was commissioned in the 1890s by Count Eusebi Güell and set on 50 acres as a "garden city." Even though the park opened in 1922, little of Gaudí's grand design had been realized. On-site today is **Casa-Museu Gaudí,** Carrer del Carmel 28 (✆ **93-219-3811**), designed by the architect, Ramon Berenguer. The museum contains drawings and furnishings by Gaudí. Admission to the museum is 4€ ($4.50), and it is open May to September daily 10am to 9pm, October to April daily 10am to 6pm. Gaudí did complete several of the public areas in the park, which evoke a Surrealist Disney World, complete with a mosaic pagoda and a lizard fountain spitting water. A mosaic-encrusted chimney by Gaudí can be seen at the entrance to the park, and the Room of a Hundred Columns with 84 crooked pillars, is the most atmospheric attraction.

Carrer d'Olot. (✆ **93-424-3809**. Free admission. May–Sept daily 10am–9pm; Oct–Apr daily 10am–6pm. Bus: 24, 25, 31, or 74.

Poble Espanyol 🎢 This re-created Spanish village was originally constructed for the 1929 World's Fair. A total of 116 houses illustrate architectural styles from all the Spanish provinces, ranging from Galicia in the northwest to Valencia along the southeastern coast, known as the Levante. Some of these life-size reproductions of typical buildings go back in style to the 10th century. The living museum is an entertainment complex with more than a dozen restaurants, "musical" bars, and even a dance club, along with numerous shops selling typical Spanish handcrafts. In some of these artisan havens, you can see craftspeople at work, perhaps blowing glass or printing colorful fabrics. Toledo damascene

---

Moments **Rambling Les Rambles**

Commonly called **La Rambla** 🎢🎢🎢, this winding street is the most famous promenade in Spain. It actually consists of five different sections—each a rambla—Rambla de Canaletes, Rambla dels Estudis, Rambla de Sant Josep, Rambla dels Caputxins, and Rambla de Santa Mónica. It begins in the north at the transportation hub, Plaça de Catalunya, and runs all the way to the port and the monument to Columbus. Day and night, this is the most active street in Barcelona. It can be walked at any time because you'll always see something new, as the street is forever changing. Caged birds and flower stalls greet you, as do street musicians and mime *artistes,* even tarot card readers. Hotels, town mansions, endless shops, and many cafes and restaurants also flank this fabled boulevard. The most famous building you'll pass along the 1-mile (1.6km) boulevard is Gran Teatre del Liceu on Rambla dels Caputxins.

work along with sculpture, and even Catalán canvas sandals are made here. There's also a children's theater.

Marqués de Comillas, Parc de Montjuïc. ⓒ 93-325-7866. Admission 7€ ($8) adults, 3.70€ ($4.25) children 7–12; free for children 6 and under. Mon 9am–8pm; Tues–Thurs 9am–2am; Fri–Sat 9am–4am, Sun 9am–midnight. Metro: Espanya.

WHERE TO DINE

Agut 🟆 (Finds) CATALAN   Only 3 blocks from the waterfront, this moderately priced long-time favorite lies in the colorful Barri Xinés district. A family-run business for most of the 20th century, the place is decorated with paintings by Catalán artists. It serves good food at very reasonable prices, the cuisine based on time-tested recipes and fresh ingredients.

Gignas 16. ⓒ 93-315-1709. Reservations required. Main courses 6€–18€ ($7–$20.75). Fixed-price lunch 9€ ($10.25). MC, V. Tues–Sun 1:30–4pm; Tues–Sat 9pm–midnight. Closed Aug. Metro: Jaume I.

Agut d'Avignon 🟆 CATALAN   Near Plaça Reial in the old town, this is one of the oldest and most enduring restaurants of Barcelona, still turning out a savory Catalán cuisine while keeping its devotees but gaining new converts every year. Long a choice of writers, newspaper people, artists, and politicians, it offers time-tested meals served in generous portions and made with quality ingredients. Start with the fishermen's soup and proceed through the menu—whatever you order, you can expect something special here.

Trinitat 3. ⓒ 93-302-6034. Reservations required. Main courses 11€–22.50€ ($12.75–$26). AE, DC, MC, V. Daily 1–3pm and 9–11:30pm. Metro: Jaume I or Liceu.

Café de L'Academia 🟆 (Value) MEDITERRANEAN   A short walk from Plaça Sant Jaume, one of the most famous squares in the Gothic quarter, this affordable restaurant housed in a 15th-century building presents succulent Catalán and Mediterranean dishes. The chef terms his cuisine "kitchen of the market," an accurate appraisal of his use of the freshest of ingredients gathered early in the morning on shopping rounds. Recipes are imaginative and nearly always palate pleasing, as exemplified by the partridge stuffed with onions and duck liver.

Carrer Lledó 1. ⓒ 93-315-0026. Reservations required. Main courses 8.25€–12.50€ ($9.50–$14.25). AE, MC, V. Mon–Fri 9am–noon, 1:30–4pm, and 8:45–11:30pm. Closed last 2 weeks Aug. Metro: Jaume I.

Comerç 24 🟆 (Finds) INTERNATIONAL   Chef Carles Abellan earns culinary laurels with his imaginative and original renderings of old-time Catalonia favorites, most often creating lighter fare. Against a backdrop of minimalist design, the restaurant is found along the Barceloneta waterfront. Dishes are cooked to order as the chef believes in "split-second" timing. Try the fresh salmon perfumed with vanilla and served with yogurt.

Carrer Comerç 24, La Ribera. ⓒ 93-319-2102. Reservations required. Main courses 5€–16€ ($5.75–$18.50). Tasting menu 42€ ($48.25). MC, V. Tues–Sat 1:30–3:30pm and 8:30pm–12:30am. Closed 10 days in Dec, 10 days in Aug. Metro: Arco de Triompho.

Coses de Menjar 🟆 (Finds) MEDITERRANEAN   This hip restaurant is one of the favorite, fun eating spots of Barcelona, known for its young clientele and its savory blend of fusion and Mediterranean cuisine. Everything is a bit wacky here, including the napkin rings made from bent forks, but it's not so gimmicky that it loses sight of why people come here—and that's for the good food. Dishes are wildly imaginative and good tasting as exemplified by the red mullet in almond sauce with a side dish of fresh figs.

Pla de Palau 7. ☎ **93-310-6001**. Reservations required. Fixed-price lunch (Mon–Fri only) 11€–14€ ($12.75–$16). Main courses 30€–33€ ($34.50–$38). MC, V. Mon–Thurs 1:30–4pm and 9–11:30pm; Fri–Sat 1:30–4pm and 9pm–midnight; Sun 1:30–4pm and 9–11:30pm. Metro: Jaume I.

Els Quatre Gats *Value* CATALAN   Since 1897, this gathering place of the former literati and artistic elite, including Picasso, has been a favorite for drinking and dining in the Gothic *barrio* close to the cathedral. Today the restored fin-de-siècle cafe is visited for its atmosphere, good food, and reasonable prices. The cookery is unpretentious but prepared from fresh ingredients, and the menu is seasonally adjusted.

Montsió 3. ☎ **93-302-4140**. Reservations required Sat–Sun. Main courses 12€–22€ ($13.75–$25.25). Fixed-price menu Mon–Fri 10€ ($11.50); Sat 16€ ($18.50). AE, DC, MC. Daily 8am–2pm. Metro: Plaça de Catalunya.

Garduña *Value* CATALAN   In the rear of Catalonia's most famous food market, La Bouquería, this somewhat ramshackle eatery is known for its crowd-pleasing food, large portions, and reasonable prices. Food here is super-fresh—you'll likely pass some of the produce stalls that provided the ingredients for your meal as you walk through the market. The restaurant offers you a choice of dining downstairs at a bustling bar or more formally in the room upstairs.

Jerusalem 18. ☎ **93-302-4323**. Reservations recommended. Main courses 6€–24.50€ ($7–$28.25). Fixed-price lunch 9€ ($10.25). Fixed-price dinner 12€ ($13.75). AE, DC, MC, V. Mon–Sat 1–4pm and 8pm–midnight. Metro: Liceu.

Jean Luc Figueras ★★★ CATALAN   Jean Luc Figueras is one of our favorite chefs in Catalonia—and of most local food critics, too. The former studio of Balenciaga in the Gràcia district has been elegantly converted into a backdrop for the refined cuisine of this talented chef who respects tradition but is also innovative. The emphasis is on seafood and market-fresh ingredients are cleverly fashioned into velvety smooth dishes. Be sure to try the homemade desserts, and definitely sample one of the seven varieties of freshly made bread.

Santa Teresa 10. ☎ **93-415-2877**. Reservations required. Main courses 19€–32€ ($21.75–$36.75). AE, DC, MC, V. Mon–Sat 1:30–4:30pm and 8:30pm–midnight. Metro: Diagonal.

La Rosca *Value* SPANISH/CATALAN   In the Gothic *barrio,* close to the transportation hub of Plaça de Catalunya, this is an old-fashioned restaurant where the owner, Don Alberto Vellve, respects Catalan traditions of good food and service. Against a nostalgic backdrop of bullfighter posters and pictures of old Barcelona, a hearty, regional fare is served at most affordable prices. Most of the dishes served here would have been familiar in the kitchen of Grandmother Catalonia—and that's a very good thing.

Julía Portet 6. ☎ **93-302-5173**. Reservations recommended. Main courses 6€–12€ ($7–$13.75). Fixed-price menu 7.50€–10€ ($8.50–$11.50). No credit cards. Sun–Fri 9am–4pm and 8–9:30pm. Closed Aug 20–30. Metro: Plaça de Catalunya.

Pla de la Garsa ★ *Value* CATALAN   Close to the cathedral in the Gothic quarter, Ignacio Sulle, an antiques seller, has assembled an intriguing collection of furnishings and objets d'art that serve as a mere backdrop for his succulent menu of old-time Mediterranean and Catalan favorites. Backed up by one of the best wine lists in Barcelona, he searches far and wide for choice ingredients, which his chefs concoct into a series of imaginative dishes, beginning with marvelous terrines and the fish and meat pâtés.

Assaonadors 13. ☎ **93-315-2413**. Reservations recommended Sat–Sun. Main courses 5€–10€ ($5.75–$11.50). AE, MC, V. Daily 8pm–1am. Metro: Jaume I.

Moments A Taste of Catalán Bubbly

Catalonia is famous for its *cava*, the local name for champagne. Throughout Barcelona champagne bars are called *xampanyerías*. For a fun night on the town, go on a champagne bar crawl sampling the local bubbly. Our favorites include **El Xampanyet,** Carrer Montcada 22 (© **93-319-7003;** Metro: Jaume I), close to the Picasso Museum in the old town on an ancient street. Revelers go here to drink the champagne at marble tables and to feast on tapas. Open Tuesday to Saturday noon to 4pm and 7 to 11:30pm, Sunday noon to 4pm. Closed in August. Another favorite, **Xampanyería Casablanca,** Bonavista 6 (© **93-237-6399;** Metro: Passeig de Gràcia or Diagonal), honors the World War II classic film starring Bogart and Ingrid Bergman. It offers four types of the house *cava* that can be purchased by the glass. Open Monday to Saturday 8am to 3pm. At the corner of Plaça de Tetuan is a final choice, **Xampú Xampany,** Gran Vía de les Corts Catalanes 702 (© **93-265-0483;** Metro: Girona). Against a backdrop of abstract paintings, you can enjoy glass after glass of the bubbly Monday to Saturday 8pm to 1:30am.

SHOPPING

The best one-stop shopping is at **El Corte Inglés,** at Avinguda Diagonal 617–619 (© **93-366-7100;** Metro: Cristina), one of the finest department stores along the eastern Spanish seaboard, selling everything from high fashion to regional handcrafts. Enjoy food and drink in a rooftop cafe. Open Monday to Saturday 10am to 10pm. There's a branch at Avinguda Diagonal 471 (© **93-493-4800;** Metro: Hospital Clinic), which keeps the same hours.

As a city of art, Barcelona is known for its galleries. Especially interesting for visitors is **Art Picasso,** Tapinería 10 (© **93-310-4957;** Metro: Jaume I), which has excellent lithographic reproductions of works by Joan Miró, Dalí, and Picasso, all the homegrown artists. Open daily 10am to 7:30pm. The best artwork by Catalonia's living artists and sculptors is sold at **Sala Parés,** Petritxol 5 (© **93-318-7020;** Metro: Liceu), established in 1840. Artwork is shown in a two-floor amphitheater, and exhibitions of contemporary works change every 3 weeks. Open Monday to Saturday 10:30am to 2pm and 4:30 to 8:30pm. Antique collectors head for **Sala d'Art Artur Ramón,** Palla 23 (© **93-302-5970;** Metro: Jaume I), a three-story emporium filled with rare pieces from the attics of Catalonia, and also 19th- and 20th-century artwork and sculpture, including many decorative objects and rare ceramics. Open Monday to Friday 10am to 1:30pm and 5 to 8pm.

Barcelona is not Milan or Paris but is increasingly known for its fashion, best represented by **Adolfo Domínguez,** Passeig de Gràcia 32 (© **93-487-4170;** Metro: Passeig de Gràcia), an outlet celebrated as the Spanish Armani. Their style as summed up by one local fashion critic—"Austere but not strict, forgivingly cut in urbane earth tones." Open Monday to Saturday 10am to 8:30pm.

Catalonia has long been celebrated for its handmade pottery, which is showcased best at **Itaca,** Carrer Ferran 26 (© **93-301-3044;** Metro: Liceu), which has a wide array of ceramics and other works. Open Monday to Saturday 10am to 8:30pm. **Textil I d'Indumentaria,** Carrer Montcada 12 (© **93-310-7403;** Metro: Jaume I), is a showcase of regional design under the auspices of the Museum of Textile and Fashion. Across from the Picasso Museum, it sells well-designed clothing, shoes for men and women, jewelry, and an array of other merchandise. Open Tuesday to Saturday 10am to 8:30pm and Sunday 10am to 3pm. The best center for designer housewares is **Vincón,** Passeig de Gràcia 96 (© **93-215-6050;** Metro: Diagonal), selling some 10,000 different wares, including beautifully designed household items along with sleekly designed modern furnishings. Open Monday to Saturday 10am to 8:30pm.

The hurried rail passenger on a tight schedule may have time to visit only the pick of the city's malls, which display a wide variety of Catalonian merchandise under one roof. The best of these include **Maremagnum,** Moll d'Espanya (© **93-225-8100;** Metro: Drassanes), near the Columbus Monument. In addition to its many shops, there are also a dozen theaters, an IMAX theater, and many restaurants, pubs, and dance clubs. Open daily 11am to 10pm. The largest shopping center in Barcelona is **Centre Comercial Barcelona Glòries,** Avinguda Diagonal 208 (© **93-486-0404;** Metro: Glòries), a three-story emporium with some 100 shops, many of them posh. This mall is filled with some treasures, but also lots of lesser merchandise. Open Monday to Saturday 10am to 10pm.

NIGHTLIFE

Begin your tasca crawl of the Gothic *barrio* by sitting on the terrace of **La Vinya del Senyor,** Plaça Santa María 5 (© **93-310-3379**), enjoying the magnificent facade of Santa María del Mar. There are some 300 selections of wine here (many sold by the glass), along with select *cavas* (Catalán champagne), *moscatells,* and sherries. Open Tuesday to Saturday noon to 1:30am and Sunday noon to midnight. Metro: Jaume I or Barceloneta.

Before attending the theater, head for **Café de la Opera,** La Rambla 74 (© **93-317-7585;** Metro: Liceu), virtually the city's most fabled cafe having been in business during all of the 20th century. Operagoers flock here, as do one of the widest cross sections of people. It's open daily from 8:30am until the early morning hours. After a drink, head for the **Gran Teatre del Liceu,** Rambla dels Caputxins (© **93-485-9913;** Metro: Liceu), a Belle Epoque–style, 2,700-seat opera house, one of the greatest theaters in the world. It was rebuilt following a devastating fire in 1994. Today, it's the venue for the major cultural events of Catalonia.

At the top of the Ramblas, you can patronize **Café Zurich,** Plaça de Catalunya (© **93-317-9153;** Metro: Plaça de Catalunya), another traditional meeting point and one of the best places in the old city for people-watching. Going strong since the early 1920s, it's known for its *bocadillos* or little sandwiches.

The evening begins early in Barcelona in the bars, with **Molly's Fair City,** Carrer Ferran 7 (© **93-342-4026;** Metro: Liceu), being the favorite hangout of ex-pats. Evoking a Dublin beer hall, it is open daily from 8pm till 2:30am Monday to Friday or 3am Saturday and Sunday. For a typical old town bar, head for **El Born,** Passeig del Born 26 (© **93-319-5333;** Metro: Jaume I) a converted former fish shop. You can also enjoy an inexpensive dinner here beginning at 16€ ($18.50). Open Monday to Saturday 6pm to 3am. Near Plaça Reial, **Schilling,** Carrer Ferran 23 (© **93-317-6787;** Metro: Liceu), is an old cafe and bar that's like something from Gaudí's era, with its iron columns and marble tables. Both gays and straights mix harmoniously here. Open Monday to Saturday 10am to 2:30am and Sunday noon to 2am.

As the evening grows later, the cabarets and jazz clubs start to fill up. One of the oldest and best jazz clubs is **Harlem Jazz Club,** Comtessa de Sobradiel 8 (© **93-310-0755;** Metro: Jaume I). Small and intimate, the club often attracts top jazz artists from Europe and America. Open Tuesday to Thursday 8pm to 4am, until 5am Friday to Sunday. There's a one-drink minimum but no cover. Closed 2 weeks in August. Another premier venue for good blues and jazz is **Jamboree,** Plaça Reial 17 (© **93-301-7564;** Metro: Liceu), in the heart of the Gothic old city. Jazz is not always scheduled here; sometimes a Latin dance band will perform. Cover is 6€ to 12€ ($7–$13.75), and it's open daily 10:30pm to 5am, with shows beginning at 11pm.

In the showplace rooms of the Palau Dalmases, **Espai Barroc,** Carrer Montcada 20 (© **93-310-0673;** Metro: Jaume I), holds forth in the Barri Gòtic. It's one of the most elegant venues on the after-dark circuit. The best night is Thursday at 11pm when nearly a dozen singers perform from assorted operas. For the opera aficionado, this is a grand evening out. Cover is charged only on Thursday, costing 18€ ($20.75) and including a drink. Open Tuesday to Sunday 8pm to 2am.

Luz de Gas, Carrer de Muntaner 246 (© **93-209-7711**), is a theater and cabaret with some of the best jazz in Barcelona on weekends. Days of the week at this Art Nouveau club are given over to cabaret. A wide range of music is presented here weekly, including pop, soul, jazz, rhythm, and blues, along with salsa. The cover of 15€ ($17.25) includes the first drink. Open Friday to Wednesday 11pm to 4am, Thursday 11pm to 5am. **Barcelona Pipa Club,** Plaça Reial 3 (© **93-302-4732;** Metro: Liceu), is a final venue for jazz devotees. You ring the buzzer as if being admitted to an old speakeasy, and inside the music ranges from Brazilian rhythms to New Orleans jazz. There's no cover, and hours are daily 10pm to 4am.

Barcelona is not associated with flamenco the way Madrid or Andalusia is, but there are some excellent clubs, including a highly rated flamenco cabaret at **El Tablao de Carmen,** Poble Espanyol de Montjuïc (© **93-325-6894;** Metro: Espanya). You can go early and explore this re-created Spanish village. The first show is presented at 9:30pm, the second show at 11:30pm on Tuesday, Wednesday, Thursday, and Sunday, or else midnight on Friday and Saturday. A drink and show costs 28€ ($32.25). The oldest flamenco club in Barcelona is **Los Tarantos,** Plaça Reial 17 (© **93-318-3067**), which presents the best of Andalusian flamenco. Each show lasts around 1¼ hours, beginning at 10pm and midnight Monday to Saturday. The 24€ ($27.50) cover includes your first drink.

Late at night, especially into the early hours, dance clubs prevail, including **La Paloma,** Tigre 27 (© **93-301-6897;** Metro: Universitat), the most famous dance hall in Barcelona. It's for an older crowd who remember the mambo or the fox trot. The hall is open Thursday to Sunday with matinees lasting from 6 to 9:30pm, and night dances taking place from 11:30pm to 5am. A much younger crowd is drawn to **Up and Down,** Numancia 179 (© **93-205-5194;** Metro: Maria Cristina). This is a two-level dance club, with the members of the flaming youth hanging out downstairs. A cosmopolitan place, the dance club is open Tuesday to Saturday midnight to 6am, charging a cover ranging from 12€ to 17€ ($13.75–$19.50), including your first drink.

AN EXCURSION TO MONTSERRAT

At a point 35 miles (56km) northwest of Barcelona, the monastery of Montserrat is the most visited attraction outside Barcelona. One of the major pilgrimage centers in Spain, it sits atop a 4,000-foot-high mountain that's 7 miles (11km) long and 3¼ miles (5.5km) wide. A popular venue for weddings, the site possesses the medieval statue of "The Black Virgin" *(La Moreneta)*, the patron saint of Catalonia. Thousands upon thousands of the faithful flock here annually to touch the statue.

GETTING THERE   From Barcelona, Montserrat is reached via the Manresa line of Ferrocarrils de la Generealitat de Catalunya, with 10 trains leaving daily from Plaça d'Espanya in Barcelona. The central office at Plaça de Catalunya (© **93-205-1515**) sells tickets for 12€ ($13.75) round-trip. The train connects with the aerial cable car, Aeri de Montserrat, whose fare is included in the round-trip. *Note:* Rail passes are not accepted for this journey, so passholders will have to purchase a ticket.

VISITOR INFORMATION   The visitor information center is at Plaça de la Creu (© **93-490-4000**). It's open daily 9am to 7pm.

TOP ATTRACTIONS & SPECIAL MOMENTS

Consecrated in 1592, the Montserrat Monastery is entered at Plaça Santa María. Although the French destroyed the monastery in 1811 during their attack on Catalonia, it was reconstructed and repopulated in 1844. During the Franco regime, when the dictator tried to obliterate Catalán culture, the monastery remained a beacon of enlightenment.

One of its noted attractions is the 50-member **Escolania** ★★, one of the oldest and most renowned boys' choirs in Europe, having been founded in the 13th century. Crowds flock here at 1pm daily to hear the choir sing *"Salve Regina"* and *"Virolai"* in the basilica. Hours are daily 8 to 10:30am and noon to 6:30pm, charging no admission. For a view of the **Black Madonna,** enter the church through a side door to the right and follow the crowds.

Museu de Montserrat stands at Plaça de Santa María (© **93-877-7777**). It contains important works of art, including paintings by old masters such as El Greco or Caravaggio. Even more modern painters such as Picasso are also shown here, as well as works by such French Impressionists as Monet and Degas. Many ancient artifacts are also shown, and hours are daily Monday to Friday 10am to 7:30pm and Saturday and Sunday 9:30am to 7:30pm. Admission is 4.50€ ($5.25) for adults or 3€ ($3.50) for students and children.

A funicular in just 9 minutes takes you to the peak, **Sant Jeroni,** at 4,119 feet; it operates every 20 minutes daily from 10am to 6pm, costing 6.10€ ($7) round-trip. One of the **greatest panoramas in all of Spain** ★★★ can be seen from here—from the distant Pyrenees to the Balearic Islands.

19

Sweden

Twice the size of Britain, Sweden sits along the northern edge of Europe. It's a bit of an effort for the rail traveler to get to this land of natural beauty, but once you arrive, you'll find that your efforts were well worth the trouble. From the mountainous Arctic reaches of northern Lapland to the sandy white beaches of Skåne in the south, this is one varied landscape.

The good news for rail travelers in Sweden is that Sweden's trains are among the most efficient and high tech in Europe, with easy rail access to all the top sites, along mostly scenic routes in a country that is relatively underpopulated as Europe goes. English speakers will have no trouble finding someone to help them out—nearly the whole country speaks English—making this a trouble-free destination in the language department.

The bad news: Its trains run on time with utter efficiency, and the natural sights are great, but the prices in Scandinavia are a killer. To travel deluxe or first class in Sweden is a costly undertaking (though cheaper than in other Scandinavian countries). We do, of course, recommend a number of moderate choices in this chapter, but one should keep in mind that Sweden's not the best place for a rail trip on a strict budget.

If you have a choice, come here in summer when the Midnight Sun extends the days in June and July. The climate is generally cool, though. As a shock to some, the south coast resorts can heat up like the Mediterranean during this brief summer, thanks to the temperate effects of the Gulf Stream. Winter, on the other hand, when the days are gray and too short, can be a horrible experience, and even Stockholm can feel like the deep freeze. On the positive side, the air is clean, crisp, and fresh.

Note: For a detailed look at Sweden's rail routes, as well as the rail lines in all of the major Scandinavian countries, see the map on p. 189.

HIGHLIGHTS OF SWEDEN

The average rail traveler usually allots 3 to 5 days for Sweden. If all you have is 3 days and Sweden's the first stop on your rail itinerary, we recommend that you fly immediately to Stockholm, which is the air transportation hub of the country. You can also travel in by rail from Copenhagen to Stockholm but note that you'll lose an extra day in transit. If you have 5 days, we suggest you spend your extra time on the country's west coast in Gothenburg. The rail journey from Gothenburg to Stockholm takes slightly more than 3 hours and you'll cut across the heartland of the country, passing some of its most evocative landscapes, including rich forestland and glistening blue lakes.

Even those doing the most cursory tour of Europe are advised to include **Stockholm,** the capital of Sweden, in their rail itineraries. The city is the rail hub of Sweden, with high-speed trains branching out to the south, north, and west.

Though a city of one-and-a-half million—Ingmar Bergman calls it "simply a rather large village"—Stockholm is filled with wide open spaces and expanses of

Moments   Festivals & Special Events

Some 30 operas and ballets, from the baroque to early romantic era, are presented in Stockholm's unique 1766 **Drottningholm Court Theater,** with original decorative paintings and stage mechanisms. Call ℂ **08/660-82-25** for tickets. The season runs from late May to late September. Take the T-bana to Brommaplan, then bus no. 301 or 323. A steamboat runs here from Stockholm in the summer; call ℂ **08/411-70-23** for information.

Swedes celebrate **Midsummer Eve** all over the country with maypole dances to the sound of a fiddle and accordion, among other events. It's celebrated on the Saturday that falls between June 20 and June 26.

A tradition since 1989, the weeklong **Stockholm Waterfestival** on the city's shores serves up fireworks and concerts, as well as information about the care and preservation of water. Call the Stockholm tourist office for information. The fun takes place during the second week in August.

water in which Stockholmers fish. The city spreads across 14 islands in Lake Mälaren, marking the beginning of a mammoth archipelago that takes in 24,000 islands, skerries, and islets stretching all the way to the Baltic Sea. Founded more than 7 centuries ago, it didn't become the official capital until the mid-1600s.

As cities go, Stockholm is one of the most beautiful in Europe, and you can easily budget 3 days to take in the highlights, especially if you include a side trip to Uppsala. Walk the streets of its old town, **Gamla Stan,** visit one of the city's many fine museums, and tour the must-see Royal Warship *Wasa,* a 17th-century man-of-war pulled from the sea and the top attraction of Scandinavia. The open-air park, **Skansen,** filled with some 150 old dwellings, is another attraction that is well worth your time.

And when you need a change of scenery, take a train from Stockholm on a day trip to the ancient city of **Uppsala,** Sweden's major university town, which is easily reached by train. It not only has a great university but a celebrated 15th-century cathedral that is still the seat of the archbishop. If you have time, visit nearby **Gamla Uppsala,** which was the capital of the Svea kingdom about 15 centuries ago.

If you have the time and you've finished touring the east coast of Sweden, hop on a train and head west to the city of **Gothenburg** (Göteborg in Sweden), the best center for exploring the western coast of Sweden, and the country's major port. Stockholm, of course, is the far greater attraction, but Gothenburg is not without its charm. Like Stockholm, it is a lively, bustling place riddled with canals, parks, and flower gardens, a wealth of museums, and the largest amusement park in Northern Europe. And from here, you can easily catch an international train that will whisk you off to your next international destination.

1 Essentials

GETTING THERE

Travelers from the U.S. East Coast usually choose **SAS** (ℂ **800/221-2350** in the U.S.; www.scandinavian.net). Another major competitor is **American Airlines**

(© **800/443-73** in the U.S.; www.aa.com), which offers daily flights to Stockholm from Chicago, and excellent connections through Chicago from American's vast North American network.

Other airlines fly to gateway European cities and then connect to other flights into Stockholm. **British Airways** (© **800/247-9297** in the U.S.; www.british airways.com) and **Northwest** (© **800/225-2525** in the U.S.; www.nwa.com) both fly to London and offer connecting flights to Sweden. **Icelandair** (© **800/ 223-5500** in the U.S.; www.icelandair.com) is an excellent choice for travel to Stockholm, thanks to connections in Reykjavik, and usually offers good deals.

To reach Stockholm or Gothenburg by rail, you'll likely pass through Copenhagen, which is the main rail hub connecting Scandinavia to the rest of Europe. There are seven daily trains from Copenhagen to Stockholm and six from Copenhagen to Gothenburg. All connect with the Danish ferries that travel to Sweden via Helsingør or Frederikshavn (p. 214).

If you're traveling out of Norway, there are at least three trains a day that go from Oslo to Stockholm. Travel time is about 6½ hours. There are also three trains a day from Oslo to Gothenburg. Travel time is about 4 hours.

SWEDEN BY RAIL
PASSES
For information on the **Eurailpass,** the **Eurailpass Flexi,** the **Scanrail Pass,** and other multicountry options, see chapter 2. Sweden has no country-specific railpasses.

FOREIGN TRAIN TERMS
The Swedish word for train is *tåg,* Beyond that one word, don't bother learning a lot of train terms in difficult-to-pronounce Swedish. Swedes start learning English in grade school, and you can usually find out what you need to know by asking train personnel for help.

PRACTICAL TRAIN INFORMATION
Swedish trains follow tight schedules and travel often—usually every hour, or every other hour—between most of the big Swedish towns. Trains leave Malmö,

---

Moments Sweden's Most Famous Rail Journey

The most famous rail route in Sweden during summer is the 621-mile (1,000km) run from Mora to Gallivare—called *Inlandsbanan* (© **63/ 19-44-09**) or "Inland Railway." It crawls around at a speed of 30 mph (48kmph) through unspoiled Swedish landscapes of blue lakes and deep green forests. From your window you can often see bear, reindeer, and elk. The train makes several stops along the way for photo ops. Passengers get off and pick wild berries or can take a quick dip in a mountain lake (take care to avoid hungry bears!). You can reach Mora from Stockholm by train in 3 to 4 hours. If you figure in a return-trip to Stockholm, the whole journey will take about a week, and cost around 7,871SEK ($990) per person double with a 3,379SEK ($425) single supplement, including hotels, breakfasts, and rail fare. The final return to Stockholm is on an overnight train in a two-bed sleeping compartment.

Helsingborg, and Gothenburg for Stockholm every hour throughout the day, Monday through Friday.

Swedish trains are among the most modern and efficient in Europe, spanning the entire country. The Swedish high-speed train is called the **X2000,** and travels at speeds of 125 mph (200kmph) on all major routes. Modern and comfortable overnight trains, including *Nordpilen* (Northern Arrow), operate only on the longer routes that go from north to south, or to international destinations such as London, Paris, Oslo, and Helsinki.

Children under 12 travel free when accompanied by an adult, and those up to age 18 are eligible for discounts.

Trains are operated by **Swedish State Railways (Statens Järnvagär).** For train information, call ℂ **0771/75-75-75;** or surf the Web to **www.sj.se.**

RESERVATIONS At train stations in Sweden, ask for a free copy of *SJ Tagtider,* the rail timetable. Unlike many of its fellow European countries, Swedish trains are generally devoid of surcharges even though reservations are mandatory. For example, if you purchase a regular rail ticket, a seat reservation is included. If you've purchased a reservation on a night train, a seat—or else a sleeper—is also included in the price.

Many high-speed SJ trains do require a supplement, however, including X2000, InterCity (IC), and InterRegio trains. Typical reservations costs—for example, for an InterCity train—are $28 in both first and second class for a *couchette* or else $11 for a seat in either first or second class. For some SJ trains, supplements are waived if the rail trip is less than 93 miles (150km). Railpass holders don't have to pay a supplement on regional trains and often aren't charged on IC trains either.

Policies may different slightly on non-SJ trains in Sweden. More than two dozen regional train services are called *Länstrafik* and are run by the various provinces of Sweden, though these are often run in close cooperation with SJ. Your international railpass should be valid on most regional trains.

SERVICES & AMENITIES In first-class compartments, passengers are served hot meals in their seats. In second-class cars, meals are served in a bistro coach. All InterCity trains offer meals and refreshments such as snacks and drinks, and many have family cars with play facilities for kids. Some long routes even have a movie-theater coach, and the X2000 trains offer audio channels and computer outlets.

Overnight accommodation, where available ranges from clean and comfortable couchettes to exclusive 2-bed compartments with a shower and toilet. Generally speaking, sleepers in Scandinavia aren't a particularly expensive venture and cost less than in other European countries.

Note: Second class on Swedish trains is the same as first class in many countries to the south so you may want to save the extra kronor.

Trains & Travel Times in Sweden

From	To	Type of Train	# of Trains	Frequency	Travel Time
Stockholm	Uppsala	SJ	18	Daily	40 min.
Stockholm	Gothenburg	X2000	1	Mon–Fri	3 hr. 15 min.
Stockholm	Gothenburg	X2000	2	Sun–Fri	3 hr. 15 min.
Stockholm	Gothenburg	X2000	1	Sat–Sun	3 hr. 15 min.
Stockholm	Gothenburg	InterCity	6	Daily	5 hr. 15 min.

FAST FACTS: Sweden

Area Code The international country code for Sweden is **46**. The local city code for Stockholm is **08**; for Uppsala, it's **18**; and for Gothenburg, it's **31**.

Business Hours Generally, **banks** are open Monday through Friday from 9:30am to 3pm. In some larger cities banks extend their hours, usually on Thursday or Friday, until 5:30 or 6pm. Most **offices** are open Monday through Friday from 8:30 or 9am to 5pm (sometimes to 3 or 4pm in the summer); on Saturday, offices and factories are closed, or open for only a half day. Most **stores and shops** are open Monday through Friday between 9:30am and 6pm, and on Saturday from 9:30am to somewhere between 1 and 4pm. Once a week, usually on Monday or Friday, some of the larger stores are open from 9:30am to 7pm (during July and Aug to 6pm).

Climate It's hard to generalize about Sweden's climate. The country as a whole has many sunny summer days, but it's not super-hot. July is the warmest month, with temperatures in Stockholm and Gothenburg averaging around 64°F (17°C). February is the coldest month, when the temperature in Stockholm averages around 26°F (–3°C), and Gothenburg is a few degrees warmer. It's not always true that the farther north you go, the cooler it becomes. During the summer, the northern parts of the country (Halsingland to northern Lapland) may suddenly have the warmest weather and bluest skies.

Documents Required U.S. and Canadian citizens with a **valid passport** don't need a visa to enter Sweden if they don't expect to stay more than 90 days and don't expect to work there.

Electricity In Sweden, the electricity is 220 volts AC (50 cycles). To operate North American hair dryers and other electrical appliances, you'll need an electrical transformer (sometimes erroneously called a converter) and plugs that fit the two-pin round continental electrical outlets that are standard in Sweden. Transformers can be bought at hardware stores.

Embassies & Consulates All embassies are in Stockholm. The Embassy of the **United States** is at Strandvägen 101, S-115 89 Stockholm (✆ **08/783-53-00**); the **Canadian Embassy** is at Tegelbacken 4, S-101 23 Stockholm (✆ **08/453-30-00**).

Health & Safety Sweden is viewed as a "safe" destination, although problems, of course, can and do occur anywhere. You don't need to get shots; most foodstuff is safe, and the water in cities and towns potable. If you're concerned, order bottled water. It is easy to get a prescription filled in towns and cities, and nearly all cities and towns throughout Sweden have hospitals with English-speaking doctors and well-trained medical staffs.

Holidays Sweden celebrates the following public holidays: New Year's Day (Jan 1); Epiphany (Jan 6); Good Friday; Easter Sunday; Easter Monday; Labor Day (May 1); Ascension Day (mid-May); Whitsunday (late May); Whitmonday; Midsummer Day (June 21); All Saints' Day (Nov 1); and Christmas Eve, Christmas Day, and Boxing Day (Dec 24, 25, and 26). Inquire at a tourist bureau for the dates of the holidays that vary.

Legal Aid While traveling in Sweden, you are, of course, subject to that country's laws. If arrested or charged, you can obtain a list of private lawyers from the U.S. Embassy to represent you.

Mail Post offices in Sweden are usually open Monday through Friday from 9am to 6pm and on Saturday from 9am to noon. To send a postcard to North America costs 6.50SEK (80¢) by surface mail, 8SEK ($1) by airmail. Letters weighing not more than 20 grams (⁷⁄₁₀ oz.) cost the same. Mailboxes can easily be recognized—they carry a yellow post horn on a blue background. You can buy stamps in most tobacco shops and stationers.

Police & Emergencies In an emergency, dial ✆ **90-000** anywhere in the country.

Telephone Instructions in English are posted in public phone boxes, which can be found on street corners. Very few phones in Sweden are coin operated; most require a phone card, which can be purchased at most newspaper stands and tobacco shops. The price of a phone card depends on the number of minutes purchased; 35SEK ($4.40) will get you 30 minutes. Post offices throughout Stockholm now offer phone, fax, and telegram services.

Tipping Hotels include a 15% service charge in your bill. Restaurants, depending on their class, add 13% to 15% to your tab. Taxi drivers are entitled to 8% of the fare, and cloakroom attendants usually get 6SEK (75¢).

2 Stockholm

Although a long rail journey from the heartland of Europe, Stockholm has the biggest airport in the country; many rail passengers, with precious little time to spare, fly into Stockholm and then use the time saved to explore not only Sweden's capital, but other major rail destinations in the country, including Gothenburg. And, as the country's rail hub, Stockholm also has the best rail connections in Sweden; all of the major tourist destinations are within easy reach, many no more than 3 hours or so away. And because of the natural beauty of the country, every major train journey out of the capital is scenic.

It may be old, at least 7 centuries, but the capital of Sweden is one of the most beautiful on earth, from the cobblestone streets of its medieval old town to its granite, marble, and glass new town. Built at a point where the waters of Lake Mälaren join the Baltic Sea, it is the Baltic's largest port, right on the doorstep of an archipelago of 24,000 islands, skerries, and islets. Though it pays homage to its past, romantic Stockholm is also a world showcase of democratic socialism. It is a city that is both clean and well planned, a savvy, sophisticated metropolis that has moved along with Paris and Berlin to the cutting edge of excitement.

Give it at least 3 days and know that you will have scratched only the surface of its allure. Note, however, that rail passengers should avoid a winter visit when many of Stockholm's major attractions, including all the outdoor ones, close down. The cold weather sets in by October, and you'll need to keep bundled up heavily until long past April.

STATION INFORMATION
GETTING FROM THE AIRPORT TO THE TRAIN STATION
You'll wing your way into Stockholm's **Arlanda Airport** (✆ **08/797-61-00**), 28 miles (45km) north of the city center on E4 highway. A long covered walkway

Stockholm

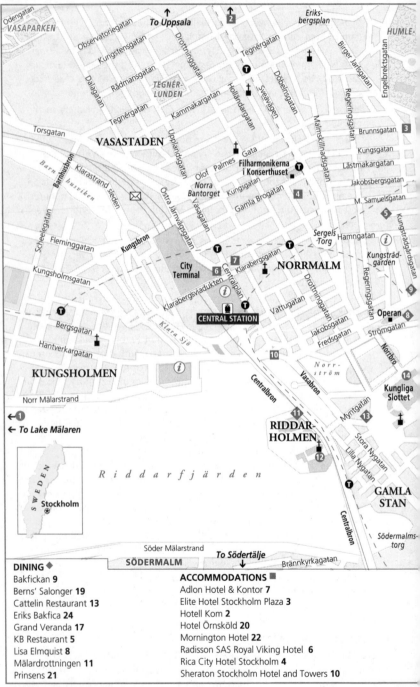

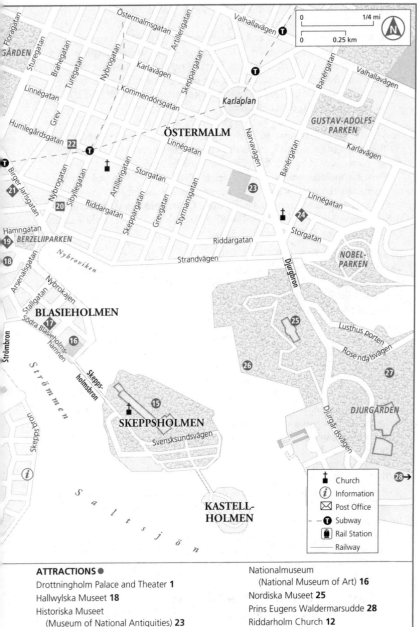

ATTRACTIONS ●

Drottningholm Palace and Theater **1**

Hallwylska Museet **18**

Historiska Museet
(Museum of National Antiquities) **23**

Kungliga Slottet (Royal Palace)
& Museums **14**

Moderna Museet
(Museum of Modern Art) **15**

Nationalmuseum
(National Museum of Art) **16**

Nordiska Museet **25**

Prins Eugens Waldermarsudde **28**

Riddarholm Church **12**

Skansen **27**

Vasamuseet **26**

connects the international and domestic terminals should you be flying in from Gothenburg or some other Swedish city.

For rail travelers, the fastest and cheapest way to go from the airport to the Central Station within Stockholm is on the high-speed **Arlanda Express** train (trip time: 20 min.), which is covered by the Eurailpass. Trains run every 15 minutes daily from 5am to midnight. If you don't have a railpass, the cost of a one-way ticket is 140SEK ($18). For more information, call **020/22-22/24** or go online to **www.arlandaexpress.com**.

Another option is to take the **Flygbussarna Bus** (www.flygbussarna.com) outside the airport entrance to Central Station. The one-way fare is 80SEK ($10), and the trip takes 40 minutes or so depending on traffic. A taxi from the airport costs 400SEK to 500SEK ($50–$63), maybe more.

At the **Centralstationen** (Central Station; ☎ **07/175-75-75**), you can connect with Stockholm's efficient subway system, called the T-bana. The Central Station is directly across from the bus station, **Cityterminalen (City Terminal)** at Klarabergsviadukten 72 (☎ **08/440-85-70**). Both the bus and train stations are serviced by the T-bana Centralen stop.

INSIDE THE STATION

The ground level of the tri-level Central Station is home to a branch of the tourist office and the **Hotell Centralen** (☎ **08/789-24-25**), which can reserve you a hotel room, for a booking fee of 50SEK ($6.25) daily June to August 8am to 8pm and September to May daily 9am to 6pm. This agency sometimes offers discounted room rates for same-day occupancy during slow periods. Of course, not all hotels discount rooms, but those that do usually lower their rates as the day wears on. You can also have the main tourist office (see below) reserve you a room for no fee.

The Central Station is convenient to any number of affordable hotels in the area, and is one of the better equipped stations in the north of Europe, featuring a number of shops on its lower level, and kiosks selling everything from food and beverage to tobacco and newspapers. On-site is a **Konsum,** evocative of an American supermarket. The food service ranges from a cafeteria to a first-class restaurant. The all-you-can-eat breakfast buffet in the restaurant, **Centralens Resaurang,** is an especially good deal.

Train information is prominently displayed on bulletin boards in several key places just inside the main entrance to the Central Station. In the main hall is a large ticket office where train reservations can be made, including reservations for sleeper-car accommodations. Hours are Monday to Friday 5:45am to 9pm, Saturday 5:45am to 7pm, and Sunday 8am to 9pm.

Also at the station is a currency exchange kiosk, **Forex** (☎ **08/24-88-00**), open daily 7am to 9pm. Lockers at the station cost 20SEK to 60SEK ($2.50–$7.50) per 24 hours.

INFORMATION ELSEWHERE IN THE CITY

The main **Tourist Center** is at Kungsgatan 37 (☎ **08/789-24-00**), a 10-minute walk east of Central Station. It's open June to August Monday to Saturday 9am to 7pm; Saturday and Sunday 9am to 5pm; September to May Monday to Friday 9am to 6pm; Saturday and Sunday 10am to 3pm. Maps and other free materials are available, and the English-speaking staff here will reserve you a hotel room at no charge.

GETTING AROUND

You can travel throughout Stockholm by bus, local train, subway (T-bana), and tram, going from Singö in the north to Nynäshamn in the south. Routes are divided into zones, and one ticket is valid for all types of public transportation in the same zone within an hour of being stamped. Subway entrances are marked with a blue T on a white background.

The basic fare for public transportation (subway, tram, streetcar, or bus) is 20SEK ($2.50). Purchase a ticket for a tram or streetcar at the tollbooth found at every stop. On buses, you pay the driver. To travel in most of Stockholm, all the way to the borders of the inner city, requires two tickets. The maximum ride, to the outermost suburbs, requires five tickets. You can transfer free (or double back and return to your starting point) within 1 hour of your departure.

For information on all services, including buses, subways *(Tunnelbana),* and suburban trains *(pendeltåg),* call ✆ **08/600-10-00.** The SL Center, on the lower level of Sergels Torg (5 min. east of Central Station), provides transportation information. It also sells a map of the city's system, including suburban trains, and day and discount passes for public transportation. It's open in summer, Monday to Thursday from 9am to 6pm, Friday 9am to 5:30pm, Saturday 9am to 4pm, Sunday 10am to 3pm; the rest of the year, Monday to Friday 9am to 5pm. Your best transportation bet is to get a **tourist season ticket.** A 1-day card costs 80SEK ($10) and is valid for 24 hours of unlimited travel by T-bana, bus, and commuter trains within Stockholm. It also includes passage on the ferry to Djurgården. Most visitors will probably prefer the 3-day card for 150SEK ($19), valid for 72 hours in Stockholm and the adjacent county. The 3-day card is also valid for admission to the Skansen Museum, the Kaknäs Tower, and Gröna Lunds Tivoli. A card for a child 8 to 17 costs 50SEK to 90SEK ($6.25–$11), and kids under 8 travel free with an adult. Tickets are available at tourist information offices, in subway stations, and from most news vendors.

Stockholmskortet (Stockholm Card) is a discount card that allows unlimited travel by bus (except airport buses), subway, and local trains throughout the city and surrounding county. Admission to 70 attractions is included in the package. You can also take a sightseeing tour with City Sightseeing, getting on and off as often as you please. Tours are available daily from mid-June to mid-August. The card is good for a 50% discount on a boat trip to the Royal Palace of Drottningholm. The card is an excellent buy, especially if you plan to do a lot of traveling by public transport around Stockholm to visit a lot of attractions.

You can buy the card at several places in the city, including the Tourist Center in Sweden House, HotellCentralen, the Central Station, the tourist information desk in City Hall (summer only), the Kaknäs TV Tower, SL-Center Sergels Torg (subway entrance level), and Pressbyrån newsstands. The cards are stamped with the date and time of the first use. For a 24-hour card adults pay 220SEK ($28), for 48 hours 380SEK ($48), and for 72 hours 540SEK ($68), with children paying 60SEK ($7.50), 120SEK ($15), and 180SEK ($23), respectively.

Taxis in Stockholm are the most expensive in the world. The meter starts at 36SEK ($4.50), and a short ride can easily cost 80SEK ($10) or far more. You can hail cabs that display the sign LEDIG, or you can order one by phone. **Taxi Stockholm** (✆ **08/15-00-00** or 08/15-04-00) is a large, reputable company.

WHERE TO STAY

Adlon Hotell & Kontor   Last renovated in 2002, this 1890s structure has known many improvements and changes over the years. The hotel is just a few blocks away from Central Station and is convenient to public transportation. Much of the old architecture has been retained, although all the small to mid-size bedrooms sport small bathrooms and have been modernized with functional Nordic furnishings. It's a little short on style but big on comfort.

Vasagatan 42, S-111 20 Stockholm. (℃) **08/402-65-00.** Fax 08/20-86-10. www.adlon.se. 78 units. 1,350SEK–1,995SEK ($169–$249) double. Rates include breakfast. T-bana: Centralen. **Amenities:** Bar; lounge; laundry; nonsmoking rooms. *In room:* Hair dryer.

Elite Hotel Stockholm Plaza ★

This top-rated and well-run hotel is set on a triangular piece of land about a half mile (.8km) northeast of Central Station. The building is more than a century old but has kept abreast of the times with frequent modernizations. Since 1984, it's been one of the most respectable mid-bracket hotels of central Stockholm. The renovated bedrooms are small to mid-size, and furnished functionally but comfortably, each with a tiled bathroom.

Birger Jarlsgatan 29, S-103 95 Stockholm. (℃) **08/566-22-000.** Fax 08/566-22-020. www.elite.se. 151 units. 1,290SEK–2,395SEK ($161–$299) double, from 2,795SEK ($349) suite. Rates include breakfast. AE, DC, MC, V. T-bana: Hötorget or Östermalmstorg. **Amenities:** Restaurant; bar; laundry. *In room:* Hair dryer.

Hotel Kom *Value*

In the city center, about a 20-minute walk to Central Station, this hotel was carved out of a modernized hostel built in 1972 and it's still owned by the YMCA and YWCA. In May 2003, the hotel also added 29 new rooms in a nearby building equipped with its own breakfast room. Reflecting their hostel background, many rooms are still quite small but are nicely furnished with a host of modern amenities and immaculate shower-only bathrooms.

17 Döbelnsgatan, S-111 40 Stockholm. (℃) **08/412-23-00.** Fax 08/412-23-10. www.komhotel.se. 128 units. Mon–Thurs 1,670SEK–1,890SEK ($209–$236) double; Fri–Sun 1,150SEK ($144) double. Rates include breakfast. **Amenities:** Breakfast room; bar; laundry; nonsmoking rooms; rooms for those with limited mobility. *In room:* Hair dryer.

Hotel Örnsköld *Value*

Near the Royal Dramatic Theatre, this hotel is east of Central Station but is convenient to the attractions in the heart of town. Built in 1910, it has been frequently renovated but still has a slightly old-fashioned appeal. Its high-ceilinged rooms, on the floor above street level, have modern furnishings, some a little worn, but all immaculately kept. Some of the larger rooms are spacious enough to hold extra beds, and each room comes with a neat little shower-only bathroom. Its affordable prices are its chief asset in super-expensive Stockholm.

Nybrogatan 6, S-111 34 Stockholm. (℃) **08/667-02-85.** Fax 08/667-69-91. 27 units. 1,275SEK–1,975SEK ($159–$247) double. Rates include breakfast. AE, MC, V. T-bana: Östermalmstorg. **Amenities:** Breakfast room; lounge; nonsmoking rooms. *In room:* Hair dryer.

Mornington Hotel ★

Renovated frequently throughout its long career, this well-run, Best Western affiliate is warm and welcoming. We find its Library Bar its chief asset. You can enjoy drinks or else a good book in a room that evokes a gentleman's club in London. Although the decor is a bit standard, the small to midsize bedrooms are comfortable, each with an immaculately kept bathroom. The hotel is conveniently located right near a T-bana stop.

Nybrogatan 53, S-102 44 Stockholm. (℃) **800/528-1234** in the U.S., or 08/663-12-40. Fax 08/507-33-000. www.morningtonhotel.com. 141 units. June 26–Aug 9, 1,295SEK ($162) double; Aug 10–June 25, 2,020SEK ($253) double. Rates include buffet breakfast. AE, DC, MC, V. T-bana: Östermalmstorg. Bus: 49, 54, or 62. **Amenities:** Restaurant; bar; laundry; nonsmoking rooms; rooms for those with limited mobility. *In room:* Hair dryer.

Rica City Hotel Stockholm

This first-class hotel is just 430 yards and an easy walk from Central Station. Built in the early 1980s, and still very evocative of that era, it offers rooms large on international style and comfort but short on local charm. The midsize bedrooms are tastefully though functionally furnished. The large bountiful breakfast buffet is served in a lovely winter garden.

Slöjdgatan 7, S-111 40 Stockholm. 🕐 08/723-72-00. Fax 08/723-72-09. www.rica.se. 292 units. 1,220SEK–1,900SEK ($153–$238) double. Rates include breakfast. AE, DC, MC, V. **Amenities:** Lunch restaurant; lounge; laundry; nonsmoking rooms; rooms for those with limited mobility. *In room:* Hair dryer.

Sheraton Stockholm Hotel and Towers   Just a 2-minute walk from the Central Station, this 8-story hotel opens onto views of the old town, Lake Mälaren, and the City Hall. What it lacks in old-fashioned Swedish charm, it makes up for with its strikingly modern rooms and facilities. Bedrooms are spacious and rather luxuriously furnished; from bedside room controls to large closets with mirrored doors, all the important amenities—and them some—are here.

Tegelbacken 6, S-101 23 Stockholm. 🕐 800/325-3535 in the U.S., or 08/412-34-00. Fax 08/12-34-09. www.sheraton.com. 461 units. 3,380SEK ($423) double; from 4,300SEK ($538) suite. Rates include breakfast. AE, DC, MC, V. T-bana: Centralen. **Amenities:** 2 restaurants; bar; laundry; nonsmoking rooms; rooms for those with limited mobility. *In room:* Hair dryer.

TOP ATTRACTIONS & SPECIAL MOMENTS

Even on the most cursory visit to the city, take the ferry to **Djurgården** to visit the **Vasa Ship Museum,** the city's most celebrated attraction, and the open-air **Skansen Folk Museum.** In the afternoon take a walking tour of **Gamla Stan (Old Town)** and perhaps have dinner here. On the second day get up early and go for a boat cruise of the archipelago and catch such cultural highlights as **Kungliga Slottet (Royal Palace),** or the **National Museum of Art.** If you have a third day, prepare to descend on the **Drottningholm Palace and Theater** or take a day tour to the ancient university city of **Uppsala.**

Drottningholm Palace and Theater 🌟🌟🌟   On an island in Lake Mälaren, Drottningholm (Queen's Island)—dubbed the Versailles of Sweden though it actually takes after the French baroque trends of the 18th century—is about 7 miles (11km) from Stockholm and is easily reached by boat, bus, or subway. The palace—loaded with courtly art and furnishings—is surrounded by fountains and parks, and still functions as one of the official residences of the country's royal family.

Nearby is the **Drottningholm Court Theater,** which grew to fame under Gustavus III, himself an accomplished playwright and actor. The best-preserved 18th-century theater in the world, it still uses its original stage machinery. Each summer, between May and September, operas and ballets are staged in full 18th-century regalia, complete with period costumes and wigs. In addition to touring the stage, the auditorium, and the dressing rooms, visitors can also pop into a museum charting the growth of the stage between the 1500s and 1700s.

One other item of interest: The **Chinese Pavilion** located on the palace grounds. It was built during the rococo conquest of Europe, when everything Oriental came into fashion.

Ekerö, Drottningholm. 🕐 08/402-62-80. Palace, 60SEK ($7.50) adults, 50SEK ($6.25) students and persons under 26; theater, guided tour 60SEK ($7.50) adults, 30SEK ($3.75) students and persons under 26; Chinese Pavilion, 50SEK ($6.25) adults, 25SEK ($3.15) students. All free for children under 7. Palace, Oct–Apr, Sat–Sun noon–3:30pm; May–Aug, daily 10am–4:30pm; Sept, daily noon–3:30pm. Theater, guided tours in English, May, daily 12:30pm, 1:30pm, 2:30pm, 3:30pm, and 4:15pm; June–Aug, daily 11:30am, 12:30pm, 1:30pm, 2:30pm, 3:30pm, and 4:15pm; Sept, daily 1:30pm, 2:30pm, 3:30pm. Chinese Pavilion, May–Aug, daily 11am–4:30pm; Sept, daily noon–3:30pm. T-bana: Brommaplan, then bus no. 301 or 323 to Drottningholm. Ferry from the dock near City Hall.

> **Moments** The Changing of the Royal Guard
>
> In summer, you can watch the **parade of the military guard** daily. In winter it takes place on Wednesday and Sunday; on other days there's no parade, but you can still see the **changing of the guard** at Kungliga Slottet. For information on the time of the march and the parade route, ask at the Tourist Office. The changing of the guard takes place at noon Monday through Saturday and at 1pm on Sunday in front of the Royal Palace.

Hallwylska Museet (Hallwyl Museum) ⊛ *Finds* To visit the former home of Countess Wilhelmina von Hallwyl is to wander back into a time capsule from yesteryear. The countess was a world-class collector of art and *objets d'art,* and she spent the better part of 7 decades acquiring an astonishing collection of priceless paintings, silver, armor, weapons, rare tapestries, glass, or whatever— she collected virtually anything, even buttons and umbrellas. Wilhelmina installed a private bathroom in the house—complete with running water—even before the royal palace got plumbing. This is surely the most eccentric of Stockholm museums, but one of real splendor.

Hamngatan 4. ⓒ **08/519-55-599.** Guided tours 65SEK ($8.15) adults, 30SEK ($3.75) students, free for children under 7. Guided tours in English July–Aug, daily on the hour starting at 1pm; Sept–June, Sun starting at 1pm. Tues–Sun 1pm. T-bana: Östermalmstorg.

Historiska Museet (Museum of National Antiquities) ⊛⊛ Among other allures, this museum boasts one of the most precious collections of gold in the world. The *Guldrummet* or **Gold Room** ⊛⊛⊛ is an underground vault accessed to the right of the main entrance. In all, there are 3,000 gold and silver objects displayed in this room, dating from about 2,000 B.C. to A.D. 1520. The room also displays Viking silver and gold jewelry, and other precious items, many unearthed from ancient burial sites. Collections include Viking stone inscriptions and coins minted in the 10th century.

Narvavägen 13–17. ⓒ **08/519-556-00.** Admission 60SEK ($7.50) adults, 50SEK ($6.25) seniors and students, 35SEK ($4.40) children 7–15, free for children under 7, 140SEK ($18) family. Apr–Sept, daily 11am–5pm; Oct–Mar, Tues–Sun 11am–5pm, Thurs 11am–8pm. T-bana: Karlaplan or Östermalmstorg. Bus: 44, 47, or 56.

Kungliga Slottet (Royal Palace) & Museums ⊛⊛ The pride of Gamla Stan (Old Town), this 608-room showcase is one of the few palaces in Europe still in use as the official home for a monarch (though the king and queen actually prefer Drottningholm) that may be visited by the general public. Built principally in the Italian baroque style, between 1691 and 1754, it can easily take up 2 to 3 hours of your time.

The highlight here is the **Royal Apartments** ⊛⊛, with their magnificent baroque ceilings and fine tapestries. The State Apartments have the oldest palace interiors, having been decorated in 1690 by French artists; look for at least three magnificent baroque ceiling frescoes and fine tapestries.

Nearly all visitors head for the **Royal Armoury** *(Livrustkammaren)* ⊛⊛ in the cellars of the palace. You can view weapons and armor, check out the gilded coaches ridden in by kings, and look at coronation outfits, some dating from the 16th century. *Skattkammaren,* the **Royal Treasury** ⊛⊛, contains one of the best-known collections of crown jewels in Europe, including a dozen crowns, scepters, and orbs along with stunningly beautiful pieces of antique jewelry. The most outstanding exhibit here is King Erik XIV's coronation royal regalia from 1561. Gustav III's collection of sculpture from the days of the Roman Empire can be viewed in the **Antikmuseum (Museum of Antiquities).**

Kungliga Husgerådskammaren. (C) **08/402-61-30** for Royal Apartments & Treasury, 08/402-61-34 for the Skattkammaren, 08/10-24-88 for Royal Armory, or 08/402-61-30 for Museum of Antiquities. Royal Apartments, 70SEK ($8.75) adults, 50SEK ($6.25) students, free for children under 7; Royal Armory, 65SEK ($8.15) adults, 50SEK ($6.25) seniors and students, 20SEK ($2.50) children, free for children under 7; Museum of Antiquities, 70SEK ($8.75) adults, 35SEK ($4.40) seniors and students, free for children under 7; Treasury, 70SEK ($8.75) adults, 60SEK ($7.50) seniors and students, free for children under 7. Combination ticket to all parts of palace 110SEK ($14) adults, 65SEK ($8.15) students and children. Apartments and Treasury, Feb 1–May 14 Tues–Sun noon–3pm, May 15–Aug 31 daily 10am–4pm, Sept 1–Dec 31 Tues–Sun noon–3pm, closed Jan 7–Jan 31 and during government receptions. Museum of Antiquities, May 15–Aug 31 daily 10am–4pm. Royal Armory, Sept–Apr, Tues–Sun 11am–4pm; May–Aug, daily 11am–4pm. T-bana: Gamla Stan. Bus: 43, 46, 59, or 76.

Moderna Museet (Museum of Modern Art) ✶✶   On the tiny island of Skeppsholmen, this museum focuses on contemporary works by Swedish and international artists, including kinetic sculptures. It's the most controversial in town. In addition to changing exhibitions, there is a small but good collection of Cubist art by Picasso, Braque, and Léger; Matisse's *Apollo* decoupage; the famous *Enigma of William Tell* by Salvador Dalí; and works by Brancusi, Max Ernst, Giacometti, and Arp, among others. Other works include the 12-foot-high *Geometric Mouse* by Claes Oldenburg; *Fox Trot,* an early Warhol; and *Total Totality All,* a large sculpture by Louise Nevelson.

Moments **A Walk Back into Time**

Gamla Stan ✶✶✶, or the Old Town of Stockholm, contains two of our top sights: the Royal Palace and Riddarholm Church. But with its narrow lanes and medieval buildings, Gamla Stan is a major attraction in its own right. The old shops are well worth the trip, and they are backed up by a number of attractive, mainly expensive restaurants.

Stortorget, the old marketplace, is the center of Gamla Stan. Dominated by a rococo palace, the square bears a resemblance to the Grand Place in Brussels—minus the pure gold leaf. Most of its buildings date from the 16th and 18th centuries (the red building was constructed during the reign of the oft-mentioned Christina). The **Stock Exchange** (open weekdays; free) is housed in an 18th-century building.

The **Storkyrkan Church** ✶✶, or **Great Church,** the oldest church in Stockholm (near the Royal Palace), was founded in the 13th century, but it has been rebuilt many times since. It is the scene of royal coronations, christening, and weddings. The most celebrated sculpture is the immense *St. George and the Dragon* ✶✶✶, dating from 1489. The royal pews have been in service for 3 centuries, and the altar, mainly in ebony and silver, is stunning, dating from 1652. You can also see the *Last Judgment,* a large painting (said to be one of the largest on earth) and the oldest preserved one in Stockholm. This is still an operating church, so confine your sightseeing to times when no services are being conducted. It's open from 9am to 7pm Monday through Saturday, 9am to 5:30pm on Sunday; admission is free.

Klaravergsviadukten 61. ℭ 08/519-55-200. Free admission. Tues–Wed 10am–8pm; Thurs–Sun 10am–6pm. T-bana: T-Centralen. Bus: 65.

Nationalmuseum (National Museum of Art) ★★

Had Queen Christina retained her crown and continued building her collection, Stockholm would surely have had a Prado or a Louvre. This museum isn't the Prado—nor is it the Uffizi, but it does contain a vast Swedish collection of masterpieces and is one of the most outstanding art museums in northern Europe, filled with the works of Old Masters such as Rembrandt or Rubens.

Located at the tip of a peninsula on Södra Blasieholmshamnen, a short walk from the Royal Opera House, the Renaissance-style building houses world-class masterpieces from the early Renaissance to the beginning of the 20th century.

The first floor is devoted to applied arts (silverware, handcrafts, porcelain, Empire furnishings, and the like), but first-time visitors may want to head directly to the second-floor collection of masterpieces, which includes a notable collection of rare 16th-century Russian icons and Lucas Cranach's most amusing painting, *Venus and Cupid.*

The most important room in the entire gallery has one whole wall devoted to the works of Rembrandt (*Portrait of an Old Man* and *Portrait of an Old Woman*), along with his impressions of a maid (one of the more famous works in Stockholm). Other rooms offer exceptional paintings by Flemish, English, and Venetian masters. Exhibited also are important modern works—Manet's *Parisienne;* Degas's dancers; Rodin's nude male *(Copper Age);* van Gogh's *Light Movements in Green;* and paintings by Renoir, notably *La Grenouillère.*

Södra Blasieholmshamnen. ℭ 08/519-54-300. Admission 75SEK ($9.40) adults, 60SEK ($7.50) seniors and students, free for children under 16. Tues and Thurs 11am–8pm, Wed and Fri–Sun 11am–5pm. T-bana: Kungsträdgården. Bus: 46, 62, 65, or 76.

Nordiska Museet ★★

On the island of Djurgården, the outstanding Nordic museum houses an impressive collection of more than a million implements, costumes, and furnishings depicting life in Sweden from the 1500s to the present day. Highlights of the rich and varied collection include dining tables laid with food and all the implements, one from each century; period costumes ranging from matching garters and ties for men to the purple flowerpot hats of the strolling ladies of the 1890s. Anglers head for the basement, where there's an extensive exhibit of the tools of the Swedish fishing trade, plus relics once used by nomadic Lapps.

Djurgårdsvägen 6–16, Djurgården. ℭ 08/519-56-000. Admission 70SEK ($8.75) adults, 50SEK ($6.25) seniors, 30SEK ($3.75) students, free for children up to age 18. Daily 10am–5pm. Bus: 44, 47, or 69.

Prins Eugens Waldermarsudde ★★

The once-royal residence of the "painting prince," Prince Eugen (1865–1947), is today an art gallery, surrounded by a sculpture garden and overlooking the water. Donated by the prince to the city, Waldemarsudde is on Djurgården. The prince was one of Sweden's major landscape painters, and his most visible works are the murals on the inner walls of City Hall. At one time Prince Eugen possessed the largest art collection in Sweden, and some of it—works by Edvard Munch, for one—is on display.

Prins Eugens Väg 6. ℭ 08/545-837-00. Admission 75SEK ($9.40) adults, 55SEK ($6.90) seniors and students, free for children under 17. June–Aug Tues and Thurs 11am–8pm, Wed and Fri–Sun 11am–5pm; Sept–May Tues–Sun 11am–4pm. Bus: 47 to the end of the line.

Riddarholm Church ★

The second-oldest church in Stockholm is on the tiny island of Riddarholmen, next to Gamla Stan. It was founded in the 13th century as a Franciscan monastery. Almost all the royal heads of state are entombed here, except for the elusive Christina, who is buried in Rome. Her father, Gustavus Adolphus II, who saw Swedish power reach its peak, is buried in a Dutch Renaissance chapel. There are three principal royal chapels, including one, the Bernadotte wing, that belongs to the present ruling family.

Riddarholmen. ℂ **08/402-61-30.** Admission 20SEK ($2.50) adults, 10SEK ($1.25) students and children. May–Aug daily 10am–4pm; Sept Sat–Sun noon–3pm. Closed Oct–Apr. T-bana: Gamla Stan.

Skansen 🏵🏵🏵   Stockholmers call this 75-acre open-air museum, with more than 150 antique buildings from the 17th and 18th centuries, "Old Sweden in a Nutshell" because it represents all of Sweden's provinces, from Lapland in the north to Skåne in the south. Founded in 1891, Skansen is the world's oldest open-air museum and comes complete with a zoo featuring Scandinavian fauna. Exhibits range from a windmill to a manor house to a complete town quarter. Browsers can explore the old workshops where craftspeople such as silversmiths or glassblowers plied their trade. Handcrafts (glassblowing, for example) are demonstrated here, along with peasant crafts such as weaving and churning. In summer, international stars perform at the auditorium here, and many special events such as folk dancing and concerts are staged.

Djurgården 49–51. ℂ **08/442-80-00.** Admission 70SEK ($8.75) adults; 30SEK ($3.75) children 6–15; free for children 5 and under. Historic buildings, Jan–Apr and Oct–Dec daily 10am–4pm; May daily 10am–8pm; June–Aug daily 10am–10pm; Sept daily 10am–5pm. Closed Dec 24. Bus: 47 from central Stockholm. Ferry from Slussen.

Vasamuseet (Royal Warship Wasa) 🏵🏵🏵   On a bright sunny Sunday, August 10, 1628, the Royal Flagship *Wasa*—ordered built by Gustavus Adolphus II—set sail on her maiden voyage and, much to the horror of onlookers, she promptly keeled over sank into the murky Stockholm harbor.

The *Wasa* was finally salvaged by Anders Franzén, an amateur marine archaeologist, in 1961. To everyone's amazement, she was fantastically well preserved. More than 4,000 coins, carpenter's tools, "Lübeck gray" sailor pants, fish bones, and what have you were found aboard. All of the *Wasa* sculptures—97% of the 700 were found—are back on the ship, which looks stunning now that it is once again carrying grotesque faces, lion masks, fish-fashioned bodies, and other carvings, some still with the original paint and gilt left.

The great cabin of the ship has been rebuilt with the original oak panels decorated with elegant woodcarvings and ingenious foldout beds. Visitors can walk right through the cabin. Also, a 16-foot-long interior cut-through model has been built; 90 dolls representing soldiers and crew show life aboard.

Galärvarvsvägen, Djurgården. ℂ **08/519-54-800.** Admission 70SEK ($8.75) adults, 40SEK ($5) seniors and students, 10SEK ($1.25) children 7–15, free for children under 7. Jan 2–June 9 and Aug 21–Dec 30 Mon, Tues, Thurs–Sun 10am–5pm, Wed 10am–8pm; June 10–Aug 20, daily 9:30am–7pm. Closed Jan 1, May 1, Dec 23–25. Bus: 44, 47, or 69. Ferry from Slussen year-round, from Nybroplan in summer only.

WHERE TO DINE

Bakfickan 🏵 *Finds* SWEDISH   In-the-know local foodies gravitate to Bakfickan, which is far more affordable than it's more glamorous neighbor, Operakällaren, even though both restaurants use the same kitchen. Some of the best and most authentic Swedish specialties are served with a certain flair, and in season you can feast on such delights as reindeer, elk, and even delectable saffrongold Arctic cloudberries.

Jakobs Torg 12. ℂ **08/676-58-09.** Reservations not accepted. Main courses 105SEK–199SEK ($13–$25). AE, DC, MC, V. Aug–June Mon–Sat noon–11:30pm. T-bana: Kungsträdgården.

Berns' Salonger ⭐ SWEDISH   This restaurant enjoys one of the city's most elegant settings, with a trio of mammoth chandeliers lighting its main salon. In its day, it was frequented by August Strindberg who described it in his novel, *Röda Rummet* (Red Room). The chefs are known for their use of market-fresh ingredients in preparing Swedish specialties and a few more exotic temptations, such as filet of ostrich with mushroom cannelloni and Marsala sauce.

Näckströmsgatan 8. ✆ 08/566-32-200. Reservations recommended. Main courses 165SEK–350SEK ($21–$44). AE, DC, MC. Mon–Sat 11:30am–3pm and 5pm–1am. T-bana: Östermalmstorg.

Cattelin Restaurant *(Value)*   Since 1897, this old favorite has been feeding frugal Stockholmers—and feeding them well—from its location on a historic street about a half mile (.8km) south of Central Station. Cattelin has survived not only wars but also changing tastes and still sticks to the tried and true, using market-fresh ingredients laced into grandmother's favorite salmon, veal, chicken, and beef dishes. The lunch crowd often opts for the daily specials prepared that morning and dished out in a convivial but noisy setting.

Storkyrkobrinken 9. Reservations recommended. Main courses 110SEK–185SEK ($14–$23). *Dagens* (daily) menu 72SEK ($9). AE, DC, MC, V. Mon–Fri 11am–10pm, Sat–Sun noon–11pm. T-bana: Gamla Stan.

Eriks Bakfica *(Value)* SWEDISH   A favorite launched in 1979, Eriks "Back Pocket" is beloved by locals who come here for what the Swedes call *husmanskost* or wholesome home cooking, the type your Swedish mother (if you had one) might serve. In a warm, cozy, and inviting setting, fresh ingredients are cleverly prepared to bring out their natural flavor instead of being buried under sauces. Our recent order of roast prime veal with fresh morels and a ragout of fresh green asparagus and broad beans was a masterful accomplishment.

Fredrikshovsgatan 4. ✆ 08/660-15-99. Reservations recommended. Main courses 145SEK–298SEK ($18–$37). AE, DC, MC, V. Mon–Fri 11:30am–midnight, Sat–Sun 5–11pm. Bus: 47.

Grand Veranda ⭐   Opposite the Royal Palace, the 1874 Grand Hotel, the finest in Sweden, is the setting for this first-class, veranda-like restaurant opening onto panoramic views of the harbor. The chefs here are celebrated for their buffets, which more or less parallel the fabled Swedish smörgåsbord. Waiting to dazzle you is a parade of first-rate dishes that range from filet of reindeer marinated in red wine to braised wild duck in an apple cider sauce.

In the Grand Hotel, Södra Blasieholmshamnen 8. ✆ 08/679-35-86. Reservations required. Main courses 125SEK–295SEK ($16–$37). Swedish buffet 325SEK ($41). AE, DC, MC, V. Daily 11am–11pm. T-bana: Kungsträdgården. Bus: 46, 55, 62, or 76.

KB Restaurant SWEDISH/CONTINENTAL   About a half mile (.8km) from Central Station, this restaurant has long been a favorite of artists and those who like good food at affordable prices. The cuisine is skillful in that it blends the best and most authentic of Swedish dishes with the refined cuisine of the Continent, mostly from France. The fish dishes are the best on the menu, especially those caught in local waters such as salmon, trout, or turbot. What could be better for dessert than their lime soufflé with orange blossom honey?

Smålandsgatan 7. ✆ 08/679-60-32. Reservations recommended. Main courses 220SEK–310SEK ($28–$39); fixed-price lunch 280SEK–345SEK ($35–$43); fixed-price dinner 385SEK–480SEK ($48–$60). AE, DC, MC, V. Mon–Fri 11:30am–11:30pm, Sat 5–11:30pm. Closed June 23–Aug 7. T-bana: Östermalmstorg.

Lisa Elmquist ⭐ SEAFOOD/SWEDISH   Stockholm's bustling food produce market, Östermalms Saluhall, is filled with hawkers of fresh food and a number of restaurants and cafes, our long-time favorite being Lisa Elmquist. The eatery, right in the midst of the market, is owned by one of Stockholm's leading fish-mongers, and naturally seafood is the item to order from its carefully chosen menu. There is real "taste of Sweden." You'll find the best fish soup at the market, along with fresh-from-the-boats shrimp and such choice platters as filet of lemon sole and thick salmon cutlets.

Östermalms Saluhall, Nybrogatan 31. © **08/553-404-10.** Reservations recommended. Main courses 150SEK–400SEK ($19–$50). AE, DC, MC, V. Mon–Thurs 10am–6pm. Fri 10am–6:30pm, Sat 10am–2pm. T-bana: Östermalmstorg.

Mälardrottningen ★ *(Finds* INTERNATIONAL   This is a rare chance to dine aboard the famous motor yacht once owned by Woolworth heiress Barbara Hutton, who entertained her husbands, including Cary Grant, aboard this vessel. Converted into a hotel and restaurant, it is now an atmospheric dining choice with an international menu that changes seasonally but always uses very fresh produce. Service is formal and you can feast upon an array of top-notch dishes.

Riddarholmen. © **08/545-187-80.** Reservations recommended. Main courses 160SEK–265SEK ($20–$33). AE, DC, MC, V. Mon–Fri 11am–2pm and 3–11pm; Sat 5–11pm. Closed July 5–Aug 4. T-bana: Gamla Stan.

Prinsens ★ SWEDISH   This enduring (it opened in 1897) and atmospheric restaurant has long been popular with artists and what used to be called "the bohemian fringe," and forcefully emphasizes good Swedish home cooking. Delights such as homemade lingonberry preserves go great with the game dishes of autumn. Seating is on two levels, but spills out onto the pavement with sidewalk tables when the summer sun shines.

Mäster Samuelsgatan 4. © **08/611-13-31.** Reservations recommended. Main courses 124SEK–285SEK ($16–$36). AE, DC, MC, V. Mon–Fri 11:30am–11:30pm; Sat 1–11:30pm; Sun 5–10pm. T-bana: Östermalmstorg.

SHOPPING

The quality of Swedish glass is known around the world, and functional Swedish design in furniture, often made of blond pine or birch, enjoys equal renown. Many visitors shop for handcrafts, especially woolen items. The favorite place for shopping is the network of cobblestone streets in **Gamla Stan** or old town near the Royal Palace, especially along **Västerlånggatan.** In central Stockholm, one of the main shopping drags is **Hamngatan.**

In ceramics, **Blås & Knåda,** Hornsgatan 26 (© **08-642-77-67**), is a cooperative of more than 50 Swedish ceramic artists and glassmakers, selling high-quality products.

For one-stop shopping, visit one of Stockholm's major department stores, including its largest, **Åhléns City,** Klarabergsgatan 50 (© **08/676-60-00**), with its celebrated food department and first-class gift shop, along with a department selling Orrefors and Kosta Boda crystal ware. Its major competitor, in business since 1902, is **Nordiska Kompanient (NK),** Hamngatan 18–20 (© **08/762-80-00**), which also has a major department devoted to the sale of Swedish glass, especially Orrefors and Kosta Boda. In the basement you'll find thousands of handcrafts. A final department store that might interest you is **PUB,** Hötorget 13 (© **08/789-19-39**), filled with boutiques and specialty departments, selling a lot of middle-priced clothing and high-quality housewares.

Just for fun, you can visit the Stockholm Flea market, **Loppmarknaden i Skärholmen,** Skärholmen (© **08/710-00-60**), the largest flea market in northern Europe, where everything is likely to turn up. One of the great showcases of Swedish handcrafts is **DesignTorget,** in the Kulturhuset, Sergels Torg 3

(© **08/508-31-520**), a shop displaying the work of nearly 200 Swedish crafts-people. This center is especially rich in pottery, furniture, textiles, clothing, pewter, and crystal.

Yet another outlet is **Svensk Hemslojd,** Sveavägen 44 (© **08/23-21-15**), headquarters for the Society for Swedish Handcrafts, with a wide selection of elegant glassware, pottery, gifts, and wooden and metal handcrafts by some of Sweden's best-known artisans.

For home furnishings, Swedish style, the best outlet is **Nordiska Galleriet,** Nybrogatan 11 (© **08/442-83-60**), with two floors of beautifully styled yet functional furniture. One of Sweden's most prominent stores for home furnish-ings, **Svenskt Tenn,** Standvägen 5 (© **08/670-16-00**), has been a tradition since 1924. Look for one of Stockholm's best selections of furniture, printed textiles, lamps, glassware, china, and gifts.

Finally, and just for fun, head for **Östermalms Saluhall,** Nybrogatan 31, Sweden's most colorful indoor market, filled with vendors hawking cheese, meat, fresh vegetables, and fish just caught, along with everything else. Plan to have lunch at one of the food stalls.

NIGHTLIFE

The greatest after dark event is to attend a performance at **Drottningholm Court Theater,** Drottningholm (© **08/660-82-25**), founded by Gustavus III in 1766 (p. 795). On Lake Mälaren, outside Stockholm, but easily reached by pub-lic transportation, it stages operas and ballets with performances in regalia, wigs, and period costumes from the 1700s. The theater's original machinery and nearly three dozen sets are still in use. Seating 450 patrons, the theater charges 165SEK to 600SEK ($21–$75) for its hard-to-get tickets. The season runs from May to September, with performances beginning at 7pm. Another major cul-tural venue, **Operahuset (Royal Opera House),** Gustav Adolfs Torg (© **08/24-82-40**), was also founded by Gustavus III, who was later assassinated here at a masked ball. This is the home of the Royal Swedish Opera and Royal Swedish Ballet. Tickets cost 100SEK to 400SEK ($13–$50) for most performances.

In summer, head for **Skansen,** Djurgården 49–51 (© **08/442-80-00**), which stages folk dancing from June to August Monday to Saturday at 7pm and Sun-day at 2:30pm and 4pm. During the same period, outdoor dancing is presented with live music Monday to Friday 8:30 to 11:30pm. In summer there are also concerts, singalongs, and guest performances by leading artists. Admission ranges from 30SEK to 70SEK ($3.75–$8.75) for adults or 20SEK to 30SEK ($2.50–$3.75) for children 6 to 15. Take bus 47 or the ferry from Slussen.

Another summer delight is the amusement park, **Gröna Lunds Tivoli,** Djurgården (© **08/587-501-00**), for those who like Coney Island–type amuse-ments. Its major adventure is a ride on a revolving tower for a nighttime panorama of Stockholm. The park is open daily from the end of April to August, most often from noon to 11pm, charging 60SEK ($7.50), free for children under 17; bus 47 from Slussen.

MUSIC CLUBS   One of the most frequented nightclubs in Stockholm is **Café Opéra,** Operahuset, Kungsträdgården (© **08/676-58-07**), an elegant dance floor open nightly from 5pm to 3am, charging a cover of 100SEK ($13) after 11pm. Another major entertainment emporium is **The Daily News,** in Sweden House, Kungsträdgården (© **08/21-56-55**), both a dance club upstairs with a much-frequented pub in the cellar. It's open Wednesday to Monday 9am to between 4 or 5am; cover is 60SEK to 160SEK ($7.50–$20).

The leading jazz club in town is **Stampen,** Stora Nygatan 5 (℃ **08/20-57-93**), attracting lovers of Dixieland along with swing music from the 1920s to the 1940s. On Tuesday it's rock and roll from the Elvis's heyday. In summer, an outdoor terrace is in use, and there's always dancing downstairs. It's open Monday to Saturday 8pm to 1am, with a cover of 100SEK ($13). Yes, Virginia, Stockholm has a **Hard Rock Cafe** at Sveavägen 75 (℃ **08/545-494-00**); it charges no cover and serves the best burgers in town from Sunday to Thursday 11am to midnight and Friday and Saturday 11am to 1am. Both the **Pub Engelen** and the **Nightclub Kolingen** share the same address: Kornamnstorg 59B (℃ **08/20-10-92**), with the nightclub charging a cover of 40SEK to 60SEK ($5–$7.50) after 8pm. Live performances—soul, funk, rock, whatever—fill the night. The pub is open Tuesday to Thursday 4pm to 1am, Friday and Saturday 4pm to 3am, Sunday 5pm to 3am; the nightclub daily from 10pm to 3am.

BARS   As you're barhopping, call at **Café Victoria,** Kungsträdgården (℃ **08/10-10-85**), which has one of the liveliest bars in town and also serves food. It's open Monday to Saturday noon to 3am, Sunday noon to 1am.

Stockholm's most unusual bar is **Icebar,** Nordic Sea Hotel 4–7 Vasaplan (℃ **08/217-177**), the world's first permanent ice bar, with temperatures kept at 27°F (–5°C) year-round. Even the cocktail glasses here are made of pure, clear ice shipped down from the Torne River in Sweden's Arctic north. The bartender will make you a Bahama Mama to warm you up. Perhaps Stockholm's favorite bar—certainly its most central—is **Sturehof,** Stureplan 2 (℃ **08/440-57-30**), a tradition since 1897. Housed in a covered arcade, it is open Monday to Friday 11am to 1am, Saturday noon to 1am, and Sunday 1pm to 1am. Supermodels and a bevy of TV actors flock to **Blue Moon Bar,** 18 Kungsgatan (℃ **08/244-700**), with its black leather upholstery and chic atmosphere. Recorded dance music is often played and there's a cover of 120SEK ($15). It's open Thursday to Sunday 10pm to 5am.

AN EXCURSION TO UPPSALA

On the Fyrisån River, the ancient university city of Uppsala—easily reached by train—is 42 miles (68km) north of Stockholm and is the most popular day trip outside the capital. An important Viking settlement, Uppsala is also visited for its celebrated 15th-century cathedral and its 16th-century castle.

With its 20,000 students, Uppsala enjoys a lovely setting in an urban environment of grand old churches, footbridges, and the gardens and former home of Swedish botanist Carl von Linné. Uppsala still reigns as the ecclesiastical capital of Sweden and one of the greatest centers of learning in Europe. Film buffs already know it as the birthplace of Ingmar Bergman and the setting for his film classic, *Fanny and Alexander.*

GETTING THERE   During the day, trains leave every half hour going from Stockholm's Central Station to Uppsala, making the trip in just 45 minutes. It's possible to go to Uppsala early in the morning, see the major attractions, and be back in Stockholm for dinner. Eurail Passholders ride for free; otherwise, a one-way ticket costs 70SEK ($8.75).

Trains arrive in the heart of the city at the Uppsala Central Station, which is within easy walking distance of all the city's major attractions except for Gamla Uppsala (see below). The latter can be reached by bus 2 or 24 departing from the train terminal. The bus costs 20SEK ($2.50) per ride. Buy your ticket directly aboard the bus, but note that the driver won't change any bill larger than 100SEK ($13).

VISITOR INFORMATION   The **Uppsala Tourist Information Office** is at Fyris torg 8 (© **018/727-48-00**), a 5-minute walk from the train station. It's open Monday to Friday 10am to 6pm, Saturday 10am to 3pm.

TOP ATTRACTIONS & SPECIAL MOMENTS

The crowning glory of Uppsala is **Domkyrkan** ✦✦, Domkyrkoplan 2 (© **018/ 18-72-01**), a Gothic cathedral—the largest in Scandinavia—whose twin spires dominate the skyline at 400 feet. Once severely damaged in a fire in 1702, it has been restored in the old style. Finished in 1270, the cathedral for 3 centuries was the coronation church for Sweden's monarchy and 11 Swedish kings and 1 queen were crowned under the Coronation Vault between 1441 and 1719. Much of the original Gothic work can still be seen in the doorways.

The cathedral's greatest treasure is the 1710 **Baroque pulpit** ✦✦✦, which was carved by Burchardt Precht based on designs of Nicodemus Tessin the Younger. King Gustav Vasa is buried in the medieval Lady Chapel, and the Finsta Chapel is the setting for the display of the gilt and silver **Reliquary of St. Erik** ✦✦✦ from 1579, dedicated to the patron saint of Sweden. A **Museum** ✦✦ in the north tower shelters a splendid collection of rare textiles, which go back to the 12th century, as well as royal burial regalia from the Vasa tombs. Rare artifacts include a gold embroidered brocaded robe from the early 15th century that once belonged to Queen Margrethe.

Admission to the cathedral is free; admission to the museum costs 30SEK ($3.75) adults, 15SEK ($1.90) seniors and students. Children up to 16 enter free. The cathedral is open daily 8am to 6pm. The museum is open May to September Monday to Saturday 10am to 5pm, Sunday 12:30 to 5pm. From October to April hours are Tuesday to Saturday 11am to 3pm, Sunday 12:30 to 3pm.

The Swedish botanist, Carl von Linné—also known worldwide as Carolus Linnaeus—lived and worked at the **Linnaeus Garden & Museum,** Svartbacksgatan 27 (© **018/13-65-40**), where he developed a classification system for the world's plants and flowers still used today. His house is now a museum adjacent to a botanical garden with some 1,600 different plants. When von Linné died, curators found detailed sketches and descriptions of his garden, which has been authentically restored. The museum of mementos costs 25SEK ($3.15) for adults, free for children. To enter the gardens costs 20SEK ($2.50), free for children 14 and under. The museum is open June to mid-September Tuesday to Sunday noon to 4pm. The gardens are open May to August daily 9am to 9pm; September daily 9am to 7pm (closed in other months).

At the end of Drottinggatan is the **Carolina Rediviva (University Library),** Drottninggatan (© **018/471-39-00**), which houses more than 2 million volumes and more than 40,000 manuscripts, many from the medieval era and among the rarest in Europe. This is the largest library in Sweden, and the home of the celebrated **Silver Bible Codex Argenteus** ✦✦, written in silver and gold letters on 187 leaves of purple parchment sometime around A.D. 520. It is the only book in the world that's extant in the old Gothic script. Among other rare treasures is the **Carta Marina,** a fairly accurate map of Scandinavia from 1539. Another rare treasure is **Codex Uppsaliensis,** the oldest manuscript (around 1300) of Snorre Sturtasson's *Edda*. Admission is 20SEK ($2.50) adults; free for children under 12. It's open June 16 to August 17 Monday to Friday 9am to 5pm, Saturday 10am to 5pm, and Sunday 11am to 4pm. It is also open June 2 to 15 and August 18 to September 15 but only on Sunday 1 to 3:30pm.

If you have time, make your way to **Gamla Uppsala** ✦, 3 miles (4.8km) north of the center of Uppsala. Little remains of the city, which some 15 centuries ago was the capital of the Svea kingdom, with a grove set aside for both human and animal sacrifices. An archaeological site includes a trio of **Royal Mounts** ⭐⭐⭐ dating from the 6th century and believed to contain the pyres of three Swedish kings. On the site of an early pagan temple stands a badly damaged 12th-century parish church that was never properly restored—"a stave church turned to stone," some have called it. Swedish kings were crowned here before that role fell to Uppsala Cathedral. Across from the church stands **Stifelsen Upplandsmuseet,** Sankt Eriksgrand 6 (℗ **018/16-91-00**), an open-air museum with reconstructed buildings moved to this site from various parts in Uppland. Admission is 30SEK ($3.75) for adults, 15SEK ($1.90) for seniors, and free for those ages 17 and under.

WHERE TO DINE

If you're in Uppsala for lunch, head for the **Domtrappkällaren** ⭐⭐, Sankt Eriksgrand 15 (℗ **018/13-09-55**), in the center city, an atmospheric choice constructed on the remains of an ecclesiastical compound from the 12th century. You dine in a series of rooms, including some with vaulted ceilings, or else in a narrow room where unruly students were imprisoned in medieval times. The chefs don't depend on a mellow old atmosphere alone but turn out finely tuned Swedish cuisine made with market-fresh ingredients, including freshly caught salmon or else reindeer from the north, with game being a specialty in autumn. Main courses cost 195SEK to 290SEK ($24–$36), and hours are Monday to Friday 11:30am to 11pm, Saturday 5 to 11pm.

An alternative choice is **Restaurant Odinsborg** ⭐, near the burial grounds in Gamla Uppsala (℗ **018/323-525**), housed in a farmhouse built in the late 1890s. As befits its setting near a Viking royal graveyard, the restaurant uses the same early medieval theme for its decor. Order traditionally prepared Swedish favorites, including smoked eel, fried herring, or marinated salmon. The Sunday smörgåsbord is the best value in town. Main courses cost 150SEK to 400SEK ($19–$50), with the Sunday smorgasbord going for 150SEK ($19). It's open daily from 10am to 6pm.

3 Gothenburg

Göteborg (in Swedish) is the gateway to northern Europe and Sweden's major port and largest city. At the mouth of the Göta River, it is especially convenient for the rail traveler as it lies equidistant from three Scandinavian capitals. Stockholm can be reached in 3 hours and 15 minutes, and Oslo in 4 hours. To get here from Copenhagen, you can take a train to the Swedish city of Malmö every 20 minutes (trip time: 35 min.), and then travel north by train to Gothenburg (trip time: 3½ hr.).

Although filled with heavy industry, there is much in Gothenburg of interest to the visitor, including numerous museums and a summer amusement park that is the largest in northern Europe. Gothenburg also makes the best center for excursions to the fishing villages and holiday resorts strung along the western coast of Sweden.

STATION INFORMATION
GETTING FROM THE AIRPORT TO THE TRAIN STATION

Many residents of Sweden's west coast consider Copenhagen's airport more convenient than Stockholm's when heading for Gothenburg. For information on getting to Copenhagen, see "Getting There" in chapter 6.

Gothenburg

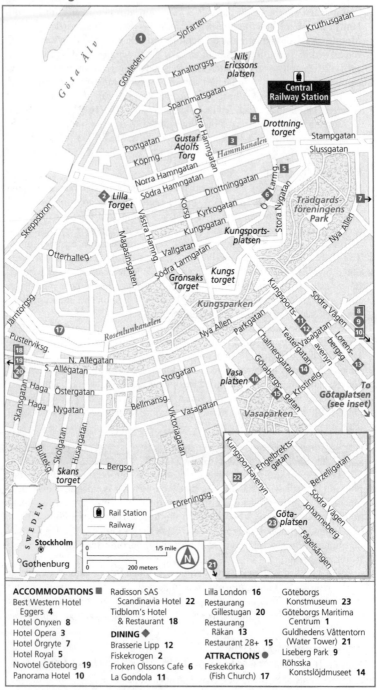

Planes arrive from other areas of Europe at **Landvetter Airport** (✆ **031/94-10-00**), 16 miles (26km) east of Gothenburg. An airport bus *(Flygbuss)* departs every 30 minutes for the half-hour ride to the city's central bus terminal, just behind Gothenburg's main railway station. Buses run daily between 5am and 11:30pm. A one-way trip costs 50SEK ($6.25). For more information, see **www.flygbussarna.com**.

INSIDE THE STATION

Trains arrive from all over Scandinavia at **Central Station** (✆ **031/10-44-45**), on one side of Drottningtorget. The station has an office of the Swedish National Railroad Authority (SJ), which sells rail and bus tickets for connections to nearby areas. Office hours are 7am to 10pm daily. You will also find a Forex currency-exchange bureau, a small supermarket, a post office, and a luggage storage kiosk. The station also has newsstands and reasonably priced restaurants.

INFORMATION ELSEWHERE IN THE CITY

The **Gothenburg Tourist Office** is at Kungsportsplatsen 2 (✆ **031/61-25-00; www.goteborg.com**). Open June to August daily 9am to 8pm; September to may Monday to Friday 9am to 5pm, Saturday 10am to 2pm. The English-speaking staff here will make you a hotel reservation in either a hotel or else a room in a private home for 60SEK ($7.50) per person.

Warning: The area around the station attracts a lot of unsavory characters at night, many intent on baiting visitors into hookups with prostitutes or else mugging them. Take precautions or a cab if you need to get to the station at night.

GETTING AROUND

Visitors usually find that the cheapest way to explore Gothenburg (except on foot) is to buy a **Göteborgskortet (Gothenburg Pass).** Available at hotels, newspaper kiosks, and the city's tourist office (see above), it entitles you to unlimited travel on local trams, buses, and ferries. The card also covers certain sightseeing attractions; discounts at some shops; and several other extras, which usually make the card worthwhile. A ticket valid for 24 hours costs 175SEK ($22) for adults, 95SEK ($12) for children; a 48-hour ticket is 295SEK ($37) for adults and 190SEK ($24) for children.

A single tram ticket costs 20SEK ($2.50); a 24-hour travel pass is 50SEK ($6.25). If you don't have an advance ticket, board the first car of the tram—the driver will sell you a ticket, and stamp one-way tickets. Previously purchased tickets must be stamped in the automatic machine as soon as you board the tram.

Taxis are not as plentiful as you might like. However, you can always find one by going to the Central Station. To call a taxi, dial ✆ **031/27-27-27.** A taxi ride within the city limits costs 155SEK to 275SEK ($19–$34). With the Gothenburg Pass, you get a 10% reduction.

WHERE TO STAY

Best Western Hotel Eggers ⭐ *(Finds)*   Built in 1859, this is the second oldest hotel in Gothenburg, and it's still a favorite and going strong. Even better for rail travelers—it's right near Central Station. The hotel retains some of its old architectural allure—wood paneling, elaborate staircases, and stained-glass windows—though everything has been modernized. The individually decorated bedrooms vary in size but are attractive and comfortable, and sport large bathrooms.

Drottningtorget, S-401 25 Göteborg. ✆ **800/528-1234** in the U.S. and Canada, or 031/80-60-70. Fax 031/15-42-43. 67 units. June 29–Aug 6 and Fri–Sat year-round, 980SEK–1,350SEK ($123–$169) double; rest of year, 1,790SEK–1,990SEK ($224–$249) double. Rates include breakfast. AE, DC, MC, V. Tram: 1, 2, 3, 4, 5, 6, 7, 8, or 9. Bus: 40. **Amenities:** Restaurant; bar; laundry; nonsmoking rooms. *In room:* Hair dryer.

Hotel Onyxen *Value* This family-owned and -run hotel is set inside a late-19th-century building that has been reconfigured into a more modern format. It's good value choice that's a short tram ride from Central Station, though the decor is more efficient than stylish. The midsize bedrooms rest under white, high ceilings and have shower-only bathrooms that are small but clean.

Sten Sturegatan 23, S-412 52 Göteborg. (C) **031/81-08-45.** Fax 031/16-56-72. www.hotelonyxen.com. 34 units. July–Aug and Fri–Sat year-round 990SEK ($124) double; rest of year 1,390SEK ($174) double. Extra bed 200SEK ($25). Rates include breakfast. AE, DC, MC, V. Tram: 4, 5, 6, 8. **Amenities:** Bar; laundry; nonsmoking rooms. *In room:* Hair dryer.

Hotel Opera Created from two hotels that were joined together in 1994, this well-run hotel is housed in two much-renovated and modernized 19th-century buildings and appeals equally to business and leisure travelers. It's ideal for rail travelers, as it's only a couple of minutes' walk from Central Station. The mid-size bedrooms are individually decorated and comfortably furnished; each has a small bathroom.

Norra Hamngatan 38, S-411 06 Göteborg. (C) **031/80-50-80.** Fax 031/80-58-17. www.hotelopera.se. 145 units. June 26–Aug 17 and Fri–Sat year-round 695SEK–895SEK ($87–$112) double; rest of year 1,295SEK–1,450SEK ($162–$181) double. Rates include breakfast. AE, DC, MC, V. Tram: 1, 4, 5, 6, 7, 8, or 9. **Amenities:** Restaurant, bar; laundry, nonsmoking rooms. *In room:* Hair dryer.

Hotel Örgryte This family-owned and -run hotel is a local favorite that dates back to the 1960s but was massively upgraded in the 1990s. It's in the residential district of Örgryte, 1 mile (1.6km) east of the historic district but is easily reached by a quick bus ride. The hotel has streamlined, rather functional midsize bedrooms, although some are large enough to have sitting areas. The bathrooms are a bit small. The place is decent, well maintained, and affordable.

Danska Vägen 68–70, S-416 59 Göteborg. (C) **031/707-89-00.** Fax 031/707-89-99. www.hotelorgryte.se. 70 units. Sun–Thurs 1,375SEK ($172) double; Fri–Sat 850SEK ($106) double. Daily 1,550SEK–1,930SEK ($194–$241) suite. Rates include breakfast. AE, DC, MC, V. Bus: 60 or 62. **Amenities:** Restaurant; bar, laundry; nonsmoking rooms. *In room:* Hair dryer.

Hotel Royal Just a quarter-mile (.4km) from the train station, this is the oldest hotel in Gothenburg, dating back to 1852. The owners, the Oddestad family, have completely renovated it and added all the modern comforts though the entrance hall is still imbued with a rich aura of the 1800s, with a painted glass ceiling and a staircase with wrought-iron banisters. The guest rooms come in various shapes and sizes, each with a good-size shower-only bathroom.

Drottninggatan 67, S-411 07 Göteborg. (C) **031/700-11-70.** Fax 031/700-11-79. www.hotel-royal.com. 82 units. June 22–Aug 14 and Fri–Sat year-round 890SEK–990SEK ($111–$124) double; rest of year; 1,295SEK–1,395SEK ($162–$174) double. Rates include buffet breakfast. AE, DC, MC, V. Tram: 1, 2, 3, 4, 5, or 6. Bus: 60. **Amenities:** Nonsmoking rooms. *In room:* Hair dryer.

Novotel Göteborg ⭐ A converted brewery—now one of the best hotels in Gothenburg—was successfully converted to receive guests. Even though it lies 2½ miles (4km) from the center, it is easily reached by a series of trams and buses. It's worth the trek outside the inner core of the city to stay here in style and comfort. The 148 bedrooms contain many built-in pieces, all tasteful and inviting, each with a small bathroom with tub and shower. The sauna is a popular facility here.

Klippan 1, S-414 51 Göteborg. ℂ 800/221-4542 in the U.S., or 031/14-90-00. Fax 031/42-22-32. www. novotel.se. June 26–Aug 10 and Fri–Sat year-round 860SEK ($108) double, 1,530SEK ($191) suite; rest of year 1,370SEK ($171) double, 1,840SEK ($230) suite. Rates include breakfast. AE, DC, MC, V. Tram: 3 or 9. Bus: 91 or 92. **Amenities:** Restaurant; bar; laundry; nonsmoking rooms; rooms for those with limited mobility. *In room:* Hair dryer.

Panorama Hotel ⭐ *Finds* Only a 10-minute walk from the center, this 13-story, 338-unit hotel is one of the tallest buildings in Gothenburg. The best and most accessorized rooms are on floors 7 to 13. The plant-filled lobby, lit by a skylight, is home to a mezzanine restaurant and a piano bar. Bedrooms are well furnished and lit, each with wooden floors and double-glazed windows. Bathrooms, though small, are neatly kept with adequate shelf space.

Eklandagatan 5153, S-400 22 Göteborg. ℂ 031/767-70-00. Fax 031/767-70-73. www.panorama.se. June 20–Aug 10 and Fri–Sat year-round 990SEK ($124) double, 1,330SEK ($166) suite; rest of year 1,650SEK ($206) double, 2,100SEK ($263) suite. Rates include breakfast. AE, DC, MC, V. Closed Dec 21–Jan 7. Tram: 4 or 5. Bus: 40 or 51. **Amenities:** Restaurant; bar; laundry; nonsmoking rooms.

Radisson SAS Scandinavia Hotel ⭐⭐⭐ If your budget can afford it, this is one of your best options for living well in Gothenburg, and it's ideally located opposite the rail station. Surrounding a large atrium, it is one of the best-run and -equipped hotels in town; it opened in 1986, but has kept abreast of the times ever since. The bedrooms are spacious and rather luxuriously appointed, with well-maintained bathrooms. The hotel's health club has an indoor pool.

Södra Hamngatan 59–65, S-401 24 Göteborg. ℂ 800/333-3333 in the U.S., or 031/758-50-50. Fax 031/758-50-01. www.radissonsas.com. 349 units. 1,450SEK–2,150SEK ($181–$269) double; from 2,300SEK ($288) suite. Rates include breakfast. AE, DC, MC, V. Tram: 1, 2, 3, 4, 5, or 7. Bus: 40. **Amenities:** Restaurant; bar; laundry; nonsmoking rooms; rooms for those with limited mobility. *In room:* Hair dryer.

Tidblom's Hotel & Restaurant ⭐ *Finds* There aren't enough affordable hotels in the city center, so if you're here in summer, you may want to take a tram to this hotel, located in a residential neighborhood 2 miles (3.2km) east of the rail station. The hotel dates from 1897 but has been completely modernized and enjoys the benefits of a tranquil and safe neighborhood. A conical tower, elaborate brickwork, and other 19th-century adornments are still in place. The midsize bedrooms sport wood floors and are comfortably furnished, each equipped with a good-size bathroom. Guests like to meet each other in the little British-style library. The on-site restaurant, inspired by Scottish design and set in a cozy and inviting vault, is a local favorite.

Olskrosgatan 23, S-416 66 Göteborg. ℂ 031/707-50-00. Fax 031/707-50-99. www.tidbloms.com. 42 units. Sun–Thurs 1,200SEK–1,500SEK ($150–$188) double; Fri–Sat 940SEK ($118) double. Rates include breakfast. AE, DC, MC, V. Tram: 1, 3, or 6. **Amenities:** Restaurant; bar; laundry; nonsmoking rooms; rooms for those with limited mobility. *In room:* Hair dryer.

TOP ATTRACTIONS & SPECIAL MOMENTS

If you're here in summer, be sure to enjoy a cup of coffee at one of the cafes along **Kungsportsavenyn** ⭐, the pulsating artery of Gothenburg, which stretches from Götaplatsen north for ⅔ mile (1km) to the canal and Kungsportsplatsen. To walk this tree-lined boulevard (known locally as "The Avenyn") is to experience the "living room" of Gothenburg. Winter visitors can explore some of Gothenburg's numerous museums, including Göteborgs Konstmuseum, the Göteborg Maritime Center, and the East India House.

Göteborgs Konstmuseum ⭐⭐⭐ This is the leading art museum of Western Sweden. If your time is limited, take the elevator to the **Fürstenberg Gallery** ⭐⭐⭐, established by arts patron Pontus Fürstenberg (1827–1902) to display works by Scandinavian artists living as expats in Paris in the 1880s. All the big names in Swedish art, including Prince Eugen and Carl Larsson, are on parade here, and the collection is also rich in the National Romantic movement of the 1890s. The other highlight of the museum is the octagonal **Arosenium Room** ⭐⭐⭐, which is a delightful romp showcasing the whimsical paintings of artist Ivar Arosenius (1878–1909).

Colorful lyricism explodes in the rooms beyond, as they are devoted to the "Göteborg Colorists," including Karl Isakson (1878–1922) and Carl Kylberg (1878–1952). Old masters, including Rembrandt and Rubens, are also on exhibit, as are such contemporary achievers as Henry Moore and Francis Bacon. The gallery also has an impressive collection of international art, notably French Impressionists, along with Bonnard, Cézanne, van Gogh, and Picasso, as well as sculptures by Carl Milles and Rodin.

Götaplatsen. ℂ 031/61-29-80. ww.konstmuseum.goteborg.se. Admission 60SEK ($7.50) adults, children up to age 19 are free. May–Aug Mon–Fri 11am–4pm, Sat–Sun 11am–5pm; Sept–Apr Tues and Thurs–Fri 11am–6pm, Wed 11am–9pm, Sat–Sun 11am–5pm. Tram: 4 or 5. Bus: 40.

Göteborgs Maritima Centrum   This maritime museum is rather appropriately located on the harbor. This is a true floating museum of nearly a dozen ships, of which the destroyer, *Småland,* is the most formidable. Other highlights of the fleet include the submarine *Nordkaparen,* along with tugboats, a lightship, steamships, and other watercraft. When not sailing to Stockholm, the famous Göta Canal boats are berthed here, including the 1874 *Juno,* the 1912 *Wilhelm Tell,* and the 1931 *Diana.*

Packhujkajem 8. ℂ 031/10-59-50. www.goteborgsmaritimacentrum.com. Admission 70SEK ($8.75) adults, 30SEK ($3.75) children 7–15. Free for children under 7. July daily 10am–9pm; May–June and Aug daily 10am–6pm. Mar–Apr and Sept–Nov daily 10am–4pm. Closed Dec–Feb. Tram: 5 to Lilla Bommen.

Liseberg Park ⭐⭐   Believe it or not, this amusement park, the largest in Scandinavia, is Sweden's number-one tourist attraction, drawing more than three million visitors annually. Launched in 1923, it has been amusing, wining,

---

Moments   **Scenes from Gothenburg Life**

Early risers can visit the daily **Fish Auction** ⭐ at the harbor, the largest fishing port in Scandinavia. The entertaining sale begins at 7am sharp. You can also visit the **Feskekörka (Fish Church),** on Rosenlundsgatan, which is in the fish market. It's open Tuesday through Friday from 9am to 5pm, Saturday from 9am to 1pm.

The traditional starting point for seeing Gothenburg is the cultural center, **Götaplatsen.** Its Poseidon Fountain is the work of Carl Milles, one of Sweden's most important sculptors. The big trio of buildings here are the Concert Hall, the municipally owned theater, and the Göteborgs Konstmuseum (see above).

For a quick orientation to Gothenburg, visit the 400-foot-tall **Guldhedens Våttentorn (water tower),** Syster Estrids Gata (ℂ 031/82-00-09); take tram no. 6 or 7 from the center of the city, about a 10-minute ride. The elevator ride up the tower is free, and there's a cafeteria/snack bar at the top. The tower is open May to September daily noon to 10pm.

and dining Gothenburgers ever since, with its "gardens of delight," including splashing fountains, pleasure pavilions, festive lighting, and beds of flowers. Open-air vaudeville shows and musical performances are presented on various stages, and there are dozens of rides, including a brand-new wooden roller coaster—Scandinavia's largest. The park is dominated by the 492-foot-high **Liseberg Tower** ✈; the ride to the top is accompanied by sound and light and it climaxes with a vast panoramic view of Gothenburg.

Korsvägen. ℂ **031/40-01-00**, or 031/40-02-20 for daily programs and times. www.liseberg.se. Admission 50SEK ($6.25), free for children under 7. June–Aug Mon–Fri 11am–11pm, Sat 11am–midnight, Sun 11am–10pm; Sept–Nov Thurs-Sun 4-10pm. Tram: 4 or 5 from the city.

Röhsska Konstslöjdmuseet ✈✈ Two Gothenburgers, the Röhss brothers, launched this leading arts and crafts museum in 1916 with a bequest to the city. Pass through the entrance to this National Romantic–style building—flanked by a pair of marine lions from the Ming dynasty—and you'll find temporary exhibitions of modern arts and crafts on the main floor. The highlights of the permanent collection of contemporary arts and crafts are on the second landing, where the exhibits are particularly rich in the era from the 17th to the 19th centuries. Upstairs are exhibits devoted to silver, glassware, exquisite porcelain, furnishings, and antique textiles. On the top floor is an array of East Asian art.

Vasagatan 37–39. ℂ 031/61-38-50. www.designmuseum.se. Admission 40SEK ($5) adults, free for children up to age 19. Wed–Sun noon–5pm, Tues noon–3pm. Tram: 1, 4, 5, 6, or 8. Bus: 40.

WHERE TO DINE

A Hereford Beefstouw ✈ *Value* STEAK Gothenburg's best steakhouse most often serves Australian beef, specializing in a 17-ounce T-bone—finish it at your own risk. Backed up by a copious salad bar—the best in town—the menu offers a series of sauces to go with your beef, including the classic Béarnaise but also a garlic butter or parsley sauce. A wide array of other cuts, including filet steaks, tenderloins, and veal sirloins are also featured.

Linnégatan. ℂ **031/775-04-41**. Reservations recommended. Main courses 120SEK–315SEK ($15–$39); salad bar as a main course 85SEK ($11). AE, DC, MC, V. Mon–Thurs 11:30am–2pm and 5–10pm; Fri-Sat 5–11pm; Sun 3–9pm. Tram: 1, 3, 4, 9.

Brasserie Lipp SWEDISH/FRENCH On Gothenburg's main promenade, this bustling eatery, established in 1987, is as close as the city gets to having a bistro evocative of the Left Bank in Paris. Although much of the menu is French inspired, including escargots in garlic butter and entrecôte of beef with a Dijon mustard sauce, other dishes are strictly homegrown, including fresh fish caught off the coastal waters of Gothenburg. The best *choucroute garnie* (sauerkraut with sausage and pork) in the city is served here.

Kungsportsavenyn 8. ℂ 031/711-50-58. Reservations required. Main courses 159SEK–229SEK ($20–$29); daily platters 75SEK ($9.40). AE, DC, MC, V. Daily 11:30am–2am. Tram: 1, 4, 5, or 6. Bus: 40.

Fiskekrogen ✈✈ SEAFOOD Across the canal from the Stadtsmuseum, this restaurant is your best choice for seafood in the central city. Against a nautical backdrop, the restaurant offers a well-stocked fresh seafood bar, with plenty of lobster, clams, crayfish, mussels, and oysters. The chefs take a bold approach to harmonizing flavors, have admirably accurate cooking times, and offer fragrant, light sauces as part of their finely tuned repertoire.

Lilla Torget 1. ℂ 031/10-10-05. Reservations recommended. Main courses 255SEK–335SEK ($32–$42); vegetarian menu 315SEK ($39); small menu 595SEK ($74); big menu 795SEK ($99). AE, DC, MC, V. Mon–Fri 11:30am–2pm and 5:30–11pm; Sat 1–11pm. Tram: 2 or 5.

Moments   A Picnic in the Park

Right across the canal from the Central Station is an ideal spot for a picnic: **Trädgårdsföreningen** ⭐⭐, with entrances on Slussgatan. This park boasts a large *rosarium* with some 10,000 rose bushes of 4,000 different species, the centerpiece being a Palm House, a large greenhouse where subtropical plants grow even in winter. The other attraction is a Butterfly House where these stunning creatures live in a simulation of a natural habitat. The park costs 15SEK ($1.90) to enter, free for children under 17. The Butterfly House charges 35SEK ($4.40) for adults, 10SEK ($1.25) for children, and the Palm House costs 20SEK ($2.50) for both adults and children. The park is open daily from 10am to 5pm.

For the makings of an elegant picnic, go to **Sulhallen,** Kungstorget, which was built in 1888. This is the city's colorful indoor market. Shops sell meat, fruit, vegetables, and delicatessen products. You can buy, for example, quail and all sorts of game, including moose and reindeer, and even lamb from Iceland. The produce (including exotic fruit) comes from all over the world. There are, in addition, four restaurants and one coffee bar in the building. Much of the food is already cooked and can be packaged for you to take out. The hall is open Monday to Thursday 9am to 6pm, Friday 8am to 6pm, and Saturday 8am to 1pm. Take tram no. 1, 4, 5, or 6 to Kungsportsplatsen.

Froken Olssons Café SWEDISH   This local favorite is conveniently located 2 blocks from Kungsportsavenyn, the major city artery. In summer, tables overflow onto a wide terrace, although there is ample space inside as well. Come here to feast on light cafe cuisine: well-stuffed baguettes, hot pies, and an array of homemade soups and freshly made salads. It can get a bit noisy and crowded at lunchtime.

Östra Larmgatan 14. ⓒ **031/13-81-93.** Coffee 22SEK ($2.75); *dagens* (daily) menu 60SEK–69SEK ($7.50–$8.65); hot pies with salad 55SEK ($6.90); sandwiches 25SEK–65SEK ($3.15–$8.15). MC, V. Mon–Fri 9am–10pm. Tram: 1, 4, 5, or 6. Bus: 40.

La Gondola ITALIAN   Some of the best pizzas and classic Italian dishes in Gothenburg are dished up here. The cuisine may lack a certain authenticity given the Scandinavian location, but it remains as vivid and modern as ever. All the old favorites turn up, including the house specialty, *saltimbocca* (veal and ham), along with such grilled specialties as tender and juicy steaks. Try the freshly made minestrone and save room for one of the succulent desserts.

Kungsportsavenyn 4. ⓒ **031/711-68-28.** Reservations recommended. Main courses 85SEK–400SEK ($11–$50); *dagens* (daily) lunch 65SEK–150SEK ($8.15–$19). AE, DC, MC, V. Daily 11:30am–11pm. Tram: 1, 4, 5, or 6. Bus: 38 or 75.

Lilla London SWEDISH/FRENCH   This local tavern, down a flight of steps, is attractively designed with a nautical decor that includes paintings of clipper ships. Don't let the decor scheme fool you into thinking this is a typical seafood restaurant; where it excels is in the meat and poultry categories. Try the beef or lamb filet in a mustard cream sauce or the grilled chicken delectably prepared with fresh morels. This is good though not sublime standard fare that is both filling and affordable.

Avenyn/Vasagatan 41. ℭ **031/18-40-62**. Reservations recommended. Main courses 79SEK–210SEK ($9.90–$26). AE, DC, MC, V. Mon-Fri 11:30am–2pm and 6pm–midnight; Sat 5–10pm; Sun 2–8pm. Tram: 1, 4, 5, or 6. Bus: 40.

Restaurang Gillestugan SWEDISH/INTERNATIONAL   This longtime favorite began life in 1918 and was transformed into a golden oldie in the 1990s, featuring a cabaret, a supper club, and the Tullen Pub, one of the most frequented bars in town. You can visit throughout the day for good tasting but rather standard fare served by a hard-working staff in generous portions. In the evening, from 9 to 11pm, a revolving series of musical or theatrical events take place here on a small stage (sometimes in English). There's no cover charge for the entertainment.

Järntorget 6. ℭ **031/24-00-50**. Reservations recommended. Main courses 100SEK–200SEK ($13–$25); fixed-price menus 250SEK–275SEK ($31–$34). AE, DC, MC, V. Daily 11:30am–2pm and 5–11:30pm; bar, Sun–Thurs 11am–1am, Fri–Sat 11am–3am. Entertainment 9pm–midnight. Tram: 1, 3, 4, and 9.

Restaurang Räkan ⚓ SEAFOOD   Also called the "Yellow Submarine," this is one of the city's finest seafood joints, with a nautical decor with wooden plank tables, buoy lamps, and the re-creation of a Swedish "lake." Your seafood platter arrives on a battery-powered boat with you directing the controls. If all this sounds too gimmicky, know that the fish is fresh, perfectly cooked, and lightly seasoned, especially the prawns, mussels, and Swedish lobster.

Lorensbergsgatan 16. ℭ **031/16-98-39**. Reservations recommended. Main courses 135SEK–265SEK ($17–$33). AE, DC, MC, V. Mon–Sat 5–11pm; Sun 3–11pm. Tram: 1, 4, 5, or 6. Bus: 40.

Restaurant 28+ ⚓⚓⚓ INTERNATIONAL   Chic and stylish, this restaurant's three dining salons are romantically lit by candles and have soaring ceiling vaults. It's hip, it's fashionable, the service is exceptional, and the food is good if a little pricey. That said, you get some of the most imaginative and fabulously fresh cuisine in town, so it's worth spending the extra money if you have a demanding palate that needs satisfying.

Götabergsgatan 28. ℭ **031/20-21-61**. Reservations recommended. Fixed-price menus 725SEK–845SEK ($91–$106); main courses 285SEK–405SEK ($36–$51). AE, DC, MC, V. Mon–Sat 6–11pm. Tram: 1, 4, 5, or 6. Bus: 40.

SHOPPING

For one-stop shopping, visit **Nordstan,** the largest shopping mall in Scandinavia with more than 150 shops, stores, restaurants, coffee shops, banks, a post office, and travel agencies. **Kungsgatan** and **Fredsgatan** comprise the longest pedestrian mall in Sweden, stretching for 2 miles (3.2km). Another major shopping artery is **Kungsportsavenyn,** called the "Avenyn" by Gothenburgers. From early spring to autumn, this is the most bustling avenue in Gothenburg, and it's flanked with shops, restaurants, and cafes.

The biggest department store is **Bohusslöjds,** Kungsportsavenyn 25 (ℭ **031/16-00-72**), with one of the city's most carefully chosen selection of Swedish handcrafts including hand-woven rugs and pine or birch bowls. Since 1866, **C.J. Josephssons Glas & Porslin,** Korsgatan 12 (ℭ **031/17-56-15**), has been a leading name in Swedish glassmaking. Many of its best pieces are the work of some of the country's best-known designers.

Seemingly every Gothenburger's favorite store is **Nordiska Kompaniet (NK),** Östra Hamngatan 42 (ℭ **031/710-10-00**), carrying more than 200,000 items for sale. It's especially well stocked in Kosta Boda and Orrefors crystal, along with pewter items, and many, many crafts.

An exhibit for some 30 potters and glassmakers, **Lerverk,** Västra Hamngatan 24–26 (✆ **031/13-13-49**), offers carefully crafted items of the highest quality.

NIGHTLIFE

Liseberg Park (see "Top Attractions & Special Moments," above) is the leading nighttime venue in summer, with all sorts of family-style entertainment. The cultural highlight is **Göteborgsoperan** (the Gothenburg Opera House), Pack-huskajen (✆ **031/10-80-00**), a relatively new opera house opened by the king in 1994 that features opera, operettas, musicals, and ballet. A short walk from Central Station, it opens onto views of the water, and has five bars and a cafe in its lobby. Prices depend on the event being staged.

The largest and most comprehensive nightclub in Gothenburg is **Trädgoärn,** Allegatan 8 (✆ **031/10-20-80**), where no one under 25 is admitted. Its two-story interior is filled with a dance club, a cabaret, and a restaurant. The cover charge for the dance club is 100SEK ($13), with a dinner and access to the cabaret going for 530SEK ($66). The dance club is open Friday and Saturday 11pm to 5am, the restaurant Monday to Friday 11:30am to 3:30pm, and Wednesday to Saturday 6 to 10:30pm, with the cabaret beginning at 8pm.

Unlike Trädgoärn, **Bubbles,** Kungsportsavenyn 8 (✆ **031/10-58-20**), charges no cover and is a small, intimate nightclub and cocktail lounge. For the over-30 age group, it's one of the most popular gathering points at night, with a small dance floor and recorded music. It's open daily 8pm to 5am. In a former fire station, **Oakley's Country Club,** Tredje Långgatan 16 (✆ **031/42-60-80**), evokes the American West with female students from a nearby ballet academy dressed as Gold Rush–era can-can girls. From 9pm on, there's live entertainment of the *Annie Get Your Gun* variety. A swankier joint is the **Park Lane Nightclub,** in the Radisson SAS Hotel Park Avenue Hotel, Kungsportsavenyn 36–38 (✆ **031/20-60-58**), the leading nightclub on the west coast of Sweden. Some of the best known of international performers, including Prince, have appeared here. It's open Wednesday to Sunday 11pm to 3am, and charges a cover of 80SEK ($10). No cover for hotel guests.

Finally, **Valand,** Vasagatan 41 (✆ **031/18-30-93**), is a dance club and restaurant, one of the largest and best known in Gothenburg, but you must be 23 or older to enter. There is also a small-stakes casino on-site. The cover is 83SEK to 103SEK ($10–$13).

Switzerland

Switzerland occupies a position on the rooftop of the continent of Europe, with the drainage of its mammoth Alpine glaciers becoming the source of such powerful rivers as the Rhine and the Rhône. The appellation "the crossroads of Europe" is fitting, as all rail lines, road passes, and tunnels through the mountains lead here. From the time the Romans crossed the Alps, going through Helvetia (the old name for today's Switzerland) on their way north, the major route connecting northern and southern Europe has been through Switzerland. The old roads and paths have developed into modern highways and railroads.

The tourist industry as we know it started in Switzerland, and the tradition of welcoming visitors is firmly entrenched in Swiss life. The first modern tourists, the British, began to come here "on holiday" in the 19th century, and other Europeans and some North Americans followed suit, so that soon the small federal state became known as "a nation of hotelkeepers." Swiss catering, based on years of experience, has gained a worldwide reputation, and the entire country is known for its cleanliness and efficiency.

Switzerland has many great museums and a rich cultural life, but that's not why most people visit. They come mainly for the scenery, which is virtually unrivaled in the world, from Alpine peaks to mountain lakes, from the palm trees of Ticino to the "Ice Palace" of Jungfrau. And, especially important to the rail traveler, Switzerland is renowned for the breadth and number of its scenic train routes (see "Switzerland's Famous Scenic Rail Lines," at the end of this chapter, for the lowdown on eight of our favorites).

HIGHLIGHTS OF SWITZERLAND

Most European capitals completely dominate the attractions list of their countries as in the case of London or Paris. Not so in Switzerland, which has four cities of equal tourist allure—Zurich, Geneva, Bern, and Lausanne—all of which we'll explore by rail in this section. Each city deserves at least 2 days of your time and because Switzerland is so small, you can travel quickly by rail from one city to another in just a matter of a few hours.

Most airplanes from North America arrive in **Zurich,** which is the major rail transportation hub of Switzerland and an ideal place to embark upon your train tour of the Alps. At the foot of the large **Lake Zurich,** the city of Zurich is one of the most beautiful in Europe, spreading out along both banks of the Limmat River. Zurich can be visited for its remarkably preserved **Altstadt** or old town alone. You can spend a morning walking the Limmat's right bank and exploring its guild houses from the 16th and 17th centuries.

Switzerland's largest city, former home of Thomas Mann, James Joyce, and Lenin, is filled with attractions, none more notable than its quays along the river. Its two chief churches are **Fraumünster** and **Grossmünster,** and its greatest museums are the **Landesmuseum (Swiss National Museum)** and **Kunsthaus**

Switzerland

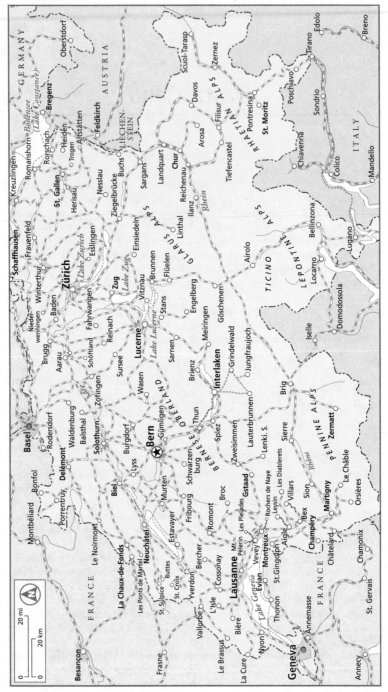

> (*Moments* **Festivals & Special Events**
>
> On the third Monday in April, members of all the guilds dress in costumes and celebrate the arrival of spring at **Sechseläuten** ("Six O'Clock Chimes") in Zurich. The festival climaxes with the burning of Böögg, a straw figure symbolizing winter. There are also children's parades. The **Zurich Tourist Office** (② **01/215-40-00**) shows the parade route on a map. (Böögg is burned at 6pm on Sechseläutenplatz, near Belevueplatz.)
>
> At the **Fêtes de Genève**, in Geneva, highlights include flower parades, fireworks, and live music all over the city. Call ② **022/909-70-00** for more information. The festival takes place in early August.
>
> Lastly, the famous "onion market" fair, **Zibelemärit**, takes place in Bern in mid-November. Call ② **031/311-66-11** for more information.

Zurich, a fine arts museum that is one of the most important in Europe. Even on the shortest of visits, save time to walk the beautiful—and super expensive— **Bahnhofstrasse,** the world's greatest shopping street, which runs from the main train station to the lake.

It's an hour's ride from Zurich to the capital city of **Bern,** which is even lovelier than Zurich because it embraces one of the greatest medieval districts in Europe. In Bern you get scenery, culture, and history, and the most idyllic gateway for exploring the **Bernese Oberland,** a summer and winter playground with its Alpine skiing, clear blue lakes, and **Jungfraujoch** at 11,333 feet, where a train from **Interlaken** will take you to the highest railway station in Europe.

Walking the arcaded streets of the **Altstadt** is Bern's major drawing card. The special places include **Bärengraben (Bear Pits),** the **Cathedral of St. Vincent** dating from 1421, and the **Kunstmuseum** or Fine Arts Museum, with one of the largest collections of the works of Paul Klee. For a final goodbye to the city, head for the belvedere atop **Mount Gurten** at 2,815 feet.

On your fifth day in Switzerland head by rail to the lakeside town of **Lausanne,** usually a 90-minute ride. This is your best base for exploring **Lake Geneva,** one of the world's most beautiful bodies of water. You can spend 1 day discovering Lausanne itself, including Switzerland's most impressive Gothic building **(Lausanne Cathedral),** and the next day touring the lake by boat.

Your final 2 days in Switzerland can be devoted to the serene city of **Geneva,** which is located near the French border and can be reached from Lausanne in about 30 minutes. Called the most international city in the world, Geneva is the center of the European United Nations, the birthplace of the International Red Cross, and the capital of French-speaking Switzerland.

Although devoid of world-class attractions, the city and its beautiful lakeside setting is an attraction in and of itself. You come here to buy a watch, walk the lakeside quays, and spend a night in *Vieille Ville* (Old Town) clustered in narrow streets around **Cathédrale St-Pierre.** Geneva is also a good base for exploring the Alps and Lake Geneva.

1 Essentials

GETTING THERE

Switzerland is situated at the center of Europe and is therefore a focal point for international air traffic. The busy intercontinental airports of Zurich and Geneva can be reached in 7 to 8 hours from the east coast of North America and in less than 2 hours from London or Paris.

Swiss International Air Lines Ltd. (simply called **Swiss**) has taken over as the major carrier for Switzerland in the wake of the famous Swissair bankruptcy. For information, contact Swiss at $\textcircled{C}$ **800/221-4750** in the U.S.; 0848/85-20-00 in Switzerland, or 0845/601-90-56 in London. For online information, check out **www.swiss.com**. Most flights from North America land in Geneva or Zurich.

Other airlines that offer service to Switzerland out of North America include **American Airlines** ($\textcircled{C}$ **800/433-7300;** www.aa.com), **Delta Airlines** ($\textcircled{C}$ **800/ 221-1212;** www.delta-air.com), and **Air Canada** ($\textcircled{C}$ **888/247-2262;** www. aircanada.com).

If none of the major carriers above services your airport, you can also fly into London or Manchester, and from there connect to either Zurich or Geneva on **British Airways** ($\textcircled{C}$ **0845/773-3377;** www.britishairways.com), **easyJet** ($\textcircled{C}$ **0870/600-000;** www.easyjet.com), or **Aer Lingus** ($\textcircled{C}$ **020/8899-4747;** www.aerlingus).

SWITZERLAND BY RAIL

PASSES

For information on the **Eurailpass, Eurailpass Flexi,** and other multi-country options, including the new France 'n Switzerland and Switzerland 'n Austria passes, see chapter 2.

SWISS PASS/SWISS FLEXIPASS The most practical and convenient ticket for your trip to Switzerland is the **Swiss Pass,** which entitles you to unlimited travel on the entire network of the Swiss Federal Railways, as well as on lake steamers and most postal motor coaches linking Swiss cities and resorts. For prices and more information on the Swiss Pass, **Swiss Flexipass,** and the free **Swiss Family Card** that allows children under 16 to travel free with a paying parent (and only a parent), see chapter 2. All of these passes must be purchased in North America before you leave on your trip, and can be obtained through **Rail Europe** ($\textcircled{C}$ **877/257-2887** in the U.S., **800/361-RAIL** in Canada; www.raileurope.com) or your travel agent.

SWISS REGIONAL RAILPASSES One of the country's most unusual transportation bargains is offered in the form of regional passes that divide Switzerland into about half a dozen districts. Passes, most of which are good for 5 days of unrestricted rail travel, are offered for the Lake Geneva region, the Graubunden (Grisons), the Ticino, central Switzerland, and the Bernese Oberland. If you plan to devote a block of days to exploring one of these specific regions, you might find one of these passes a great savings. They can be purchased at most major Swiss railstations.

One of the most popular of these passes is the **Bernese Oberland Regional Pass** (Regional Pass für das Berner Oberland) which allows for 3 travel days out of 7, and 5 travel days out of 15. They're available from any railway station in the Bernese Oberland. The 3-day option sells for 195F ($127) in second class and 233F ($151) in first class. The 5-day option costs 240F ($156) in second class and 287F ($187) in first class. The pass provides free transport during the appropriate time frames on all but a handful of the cog railways, buses, cable cars, ferryboats, and SBB trains within the region.

SWISS CARD   This pass, valid for 1 month, entitles the holder to a free transfer from any Swiss airport or border point to any destination within Switzerland and a second free transfer from any destination in Switzerland to any Swiss airport or border point. Each transfer must be completed within 1 day. Additionally, the Swiss Card gives the holder unlimited half-fare trips on the entire Swiss travel system, including trains, postal coaches, lake steamers, and most (but not all) excursions to mountaintops. The pass costs $166 for first class or $124 for second class and is available from Rail Europe. Children under 16 ride free with a *parent* if you request the free **Swiss Family Card** (see above) when you purchase your Swiss Card.

FOREIGN TRAIN TERMS

Though the two most popular languages in Switzerland are German and French, English is widely spoken and understood by Swiss nationals, who learn to speak it in grade school, so there's no need to trouble yourself learning any foreign train terms. Most Swiss timetables in railway stations usually have a section written in English.

PRACTICAL TRAIN INFORMATION

The **Swiss Federal Railway** sports one of the most extensive rail systems on the Continent and its trains are noted for their comfort and cleanliness. Most of the electrically operated trains have first-class and second-class compartments. International trains link Swiss cities with other European centers. InterCity trains arriving from Holland, Scandinavia, and Germany usually require a change at Basel's station, where a connection is usually available on the same platform. Most InterCity trains offer the fastest connections, and because trains leave the Basel station hourly, there's never too long a wait.

One of the busiest rail links in Europe stretches from Paris to Geneva and Lausanne. Almost as busy are the rail routes between Paris and Zurich. Most of the trains assigned to these routes are part of Europe's network of high-speed trains. (The French refer to them as *trains à grande vitesse,* or TGV.) From Paris's Gare de Lyon, about four trains a day depart, respectively, for both Geneva and Lausanne. Travel time to Geneva is about 4 hours; travel time to Lausanne is about 4½ hours. Trains from Paris to Basel, with connections to Zurich, depart three times a day from Paris's Gare de l'Est.

Ironically, kilometers traveled by train within Switzerland are proportionately more expensive than equivalent distances within France, so ongoing fares from Zurich or Geneva to other points within Switzerland might come as an unpleasant surprise. Consequently, many travelers who anticipate lots of rail travel are well-advised to consider the purchase of any of Rail Europe's passes, or one of the Swiss Passes. Note, however, that a number of Switzerland's best-known trains are privately owned and do not accept Eurailpasses, though passholders will get a discount on fares.

RESERVATIONS   These are absolutely necessary on Switzerland's special scenic trains (see the last section in this chapter for details). On most Swiss trains, however, reservations aren't usually necessary, although you can make one for about $11 through Rail Europe if you want to ensure yourself a seat, especially during the busy holiday season. Having a railpass doesn't guarantee you a seat,

Trains & Travel Times in Switzerland

From	To	Type of Train	# of Trains	Frequency	Travel Time
Zurich	Bern	InterCity	17	Daily	1 hr. 11 min.
Zurich	Geneva	InterCity	8	Daily	2 hr. 56 min.
Zurich	Lausanne	InterCity	7	Daily	1 hr. 37 min.
Zurich	Lausanne	InterRegional	9	Daily	2 hr. 20 min.

of course. Fares for EuroCity and InterCity trains within Switzerland are included in a railpass, but on most international trains you'll be assessed another $11 supplement.

Since rail journeys are short in Switzerland, it will rarely be necessary to book a *couchette* or sleeper, for which reservation fees begin at $28 and climb higher. Wagon-Lits does operate sleepers on all international routes running through Switzerland, and accommodations on these trains can be reserved at least 3 months in advance through Rail Europe. These sleeper services aren't available on inland runs within Switzerland itself.

SERVICES & AMENITIES   All major train stations in Switzerland have food and drink for sale. We'd recommend that you avail yourself of their offerings, taking along bottled water or a picnic lunch to enjoy as you watch the Alpine scenery fly by. Of course, most trains have minibars but they are expensive and not for the frugal rail traveler.

Many trains making longer runs also have self-service buffets, which are far more affordable than eating in one of the dining cars where prices are lethal. If your train has it, a self-service buffet is the way to go if you didn't bring a picnic lunch.

FAST FACTS: Switzerland

Area Code The country code for Switzerland is **41**. City area codes are as follows: **01** for Zurich, **031** for Bern, **021** for Lausanne, and **022** for Geneva.

Business Hours **Banks** are usually open Monday through Friday from 8:30am to 4:30pm (closed on legal holidays). Foreign currency may be exchanged at major railroad stations and airports daily from 8am to 10pm. Most **business offices** are open Monday through Friday from 8am to noon and 2 to 6pm. **Shops** are usually open Monday through Friday from 8am to 12:15pm and 1:30 to 6:30pm, and on Saturday from 1:30 to 4pm. In large cities, most shops don't close during the lunch hour, although many do so on Monday morning.

Climate The temperature range is about the same as in the northern United States, but without the extremes of hot and cold. Summer temperatures seldom rise above 80°F (27°C) in the cities, and humidity is low. Because of clear air and lack of wind in the high Alpine regions, sunbathing is sometimes possible even in winter. In southern Switzerland, the temperature remains mild year-round, allowing subtropical vegetation to grow. June is the ideal month for a tour of Switzerland, followed by either September or October, when the mountain passes are still open. During summer, the country is usually overrun with tourist traffic.

Documents Required Every traveler entering Switzerland must have a valid passport, although it's not necessary for North Americans to have a visa if they don't stay longer than 3 continuous months. For information on permanent residence in Switzerland and work permits, contact the nearest Swiss consulate.

Electricity Switzerland's electricity is 220 volts, 50 cycles, AC. Some international hotels are specially wired to allow North Americans to plug in their appliances, but you'll usually need a transformer for your electric razor, hair dryer, or soft-contact-lens sterilizer. You'll also need an adapter plug to channel the electricity from the Swiss system to the flat-pronged American system. Don't plug anything into the house current in Switzerland without being certain the systems are compatible.

Embassies & Consulates Most embassies are located in the national capital, Bern; some nations maintain consulates in other cities such as Geneva. The **Canadian embassy** is at 5 Avenue Del 'Ariana, Bern (© **031/ 357-32-00**). The embassy of the **United States** is located at Jubilaumstrasse 93, Bern (© **031/357-70-11**), with consulates in Zurich at Dufourstrasse 101 (© **01/422-25-66**), and in Geneva at World Trade Center Building no. 2 (© **022/840-51-61**).

Health & Safety Medical care and health facilities in Switzerland are among the best in the world. Swiss authorities, however, require immunization against contagious diseases if you have been in an infected area during the 14-day period immediately preceding your arrival in Switzerland.

Crimes of violence, such as muggings, are rare in Switzerland. It is generally safe to walk the streets of cities day and night. The most common crime reported by visitors is a picked pocket.

Holidays The legal holidays in Switzerland are New Year's (Jan 1–2), Good Friday, Easter Monday, Ascension Day, Whit Monday, Bundesfeier (the Swiss "Fourth of July"; Aug 1), and Christmas (Dec 25–26).

Legal Aid This may be hard to come by in Switzerland. The government advises foreigners to consult their embassy or consulate (see "Embassies & Consulates," above) in case of a dire emergency, such as an arrest. Even if your embassy or consulate declines to offer financial or legal help, it will generally offer advice on how to obtain help locally.

Mail Post offices in large cities are open Monday through Friday from 7:30am to noon and 2 to 6:30pm, and on Saturday from 7:30 to 11am. If you have letters forwarded to a post office to be collected after you arrive, you'll need a passport for identification. The words *"Poste Restante"* must be clearly written on the envelope. Letters not collected within 30 days are returned to the sender. Letters are either first class, meaning airmail, or surface mail, rated second class. To send letters and postcards to America, weighing up to 20 grams, the cost is 1.80F ($1.15) in first class or 1.40F (90¢) for surface. To Great Britain, the charge is 1.30F (85¢) in first class or 1.20F (80¢) for surface.

Police & Emergencies Dial © **117** for the police (emergencies only) and © **118** to report a fire.

Telephone The telephone system is entirely automatic and connects the entire country. **Helpful numbers** to know are: **111** for directory assistance, **120** for tourist information and snow reports, **140** for help on the road, **162** for weather forecasts, and **163** for up-to-the-minute information on road conditions. Hotels add substantial service charges for calls made from your room; it's considerably less expensive to make calls from a public phone booth.

To use a **coin-operated telephone,** lift the receiver and insert 40 centimes to get a dial tone. Be sure to have enough coins on hand, as you must insert more for each message unit over your initial deposit. If you insert more coins than necessary, the excess amounts will be returned. A pay phone will accept up to 5F ($3.25).

To make a local call, dial directly after you hear the dial tone (no area code needed); for other places in Switzerland, dial the area code and then the number. To call a foreign country, dial the code of the country first, then the area code, and then the number.

Tipping A 15% service charge is automatically included in all hotel and restaurant bills, although some people leave an additional tip for exceptional service. For taxis, a tip is usually included in the charges (a notice will be posted in the cab).

2 Zurich ★★★

Zurich is not only the largest city in Switzerland and one of the most beautiful on the Continent, but it is also Switzerland's major rail hub and one of the country's two major airport terminals for air traffic from North America. Most rail passengers fly into Zurich to begin their rail tour of Switzerland.

Zurich is well-connected to many of Europe's major cities, with 4 trains per day arriving from Munich (trip time: 4 hr.); trains arriving every hour from Milan (trip time 4½ hr.); 2 trains per day from Paris (trip time: 6–8 hr.); 5 trains from Salzburg (trip time: 6 hr.); and 4 trains from Vienna (trip time: 9 hr.). From Zurich, high-speed trains also race you anywhere you're going within Switzerland.

Called the city by the lake, Zurich lies on both banks of the Limmat River and its tributary, the Sihl. Quays line the riverbanks and the lake making for some of the grandest scenic promenades in Europe. Though the capital of a canton (district), Zurich has not been the capital of Switzerland since 1848 (that's Bern). It was, however, a great center of liberal thought, having attracted Linen, Carl Jung, James Joyce, and Thomas Mann. The Dadaist school was founded here in 1916.

Even though it's a German-speaking city, nearly all Zurichers speak English. Although there is much here of interest to the visitor, Zurich is essentially a city of commerce and industry, with briefcase-carrying, Armani-attired executives heading for the world's fourth largest stock exchange or the world's largest gold exchange. Because of all this money changing hands, Zurich also offers some of the most upper-crust shops in Europe along with a bevy of top quality, posh restaurants. On the downside, the city caters to the wealthy and prices are appropriately up there. No need to worry though—we recommend dining and hotel options for all budgets in this section.

STATION INFORMATION
GETTING FROM THE AIRPORT TO THE TRAIN STATION

Kloten Airport (© 01/816-22-11), the international airport of Zurich, is the biggest airport in Switzerland and the most popular gateway to the country; in fact, it's among the 10 busiest airports in Europe. It's located approximately 7 miles (11km) north of the city center.

The best and cheapest way to get to the center of the city is to hop a train at the airport; for 7.50F ($4.90), you'll arrive in less than 10 minutes at the Zurich Hauptbahnhof, the main railway station. The train runs every 15 to 20 minutes between 5:36am and 12:20am.

A trip to the central rail station by taxi will cost you between 55F and 60F ($36 and $39).

INSIDE THE STATION

Zurich Hauptbahnhof (© 0900/300-300) is a major European rail hub and one of the cleanest and safest stations on the Continent. Trains arrive and depart to a number of major European cities, including Munich, Milan, and Paris, from this station.

On the same level as the train tracks is the **Rail Travel Centre,** situated in the main hall on the left side. You can get your railpass validated here, and the staff provides information for rail travel throughout Switzerland, sells tickets, and makes reservations. It's open daily from 6:30am to 9:30pm. Take a number from the machine as you enter, and wait your turn. A list of departing trains is displayed on digital boards within the station.

On the right side of the Rail Travel Centre is a **Money Exchange** kiosk open daily from 6:30am to 10:45pm. The staff will convert your currency into Swiss francs. The Swiss prefer to use their own francs in transactions, shunning the euro and the dollar. You can store your luggage in lockers one level below (take the escalator). The cost is 8F ($5.25) per day, and the counter is open daily from 6am to 10:50pm. There are also public showers at the train station, costing 12F ($7.75) and open 6am to midnight.

The **Zurich Tourist Office,** Bahnhofplatz 15 (© 01/215-40-00; www. zuerich.com), is based inside the main railway station and offers tourist information, maps, and brochures. It's open November through March, Monday through Friday from 8am to 8:30pm and on Saturday and Sunday from 8:30am to 6:30pm; April through October, Monday through Saturday from 8am to 8:30pm and on Sunday from 8:30am to 6:30pm.

Hotel reservations can be made here, or you can e-mail the staff in advance at **information@zurichtourism.ch.**

On the bottom level of the station are a number of shops and fast-food outlets.

The Bahnhof is also the hub for Zurich's public transportation system. You can catch trams or buses here to wherever you are going in the city.

GETTING AROUND

The public transport system of Zurich is operated by VBZ Züri–Linie, or **Zurich Public Transport** (© 01/212-37-37 for information) and is the best and cheapest way to get around town. The modern and extensive network of trams and buses (there is no subway) runs daily from 5:30am to midnight. You shouldn't have to wait longer than 6 minutes during rush hours. Most trams and buses connect at the Zurich Hauptbahnhof, in the heart of the city.

Zurich

Basel   ● **Zurich**

Bern ★   SWITZERLAND

○ Geneva

ACCOMMODATIONS ■
Hotel Bristol **2**
Hotel Kindli **7**
Hotel Rössli **13**
Hotel Walhalla **1**
Lady's First **17**

DINING ◆
Bierhalle Kropf **11**
Brasserie Lipp **5**
Fischstube Zürichhorn **18**
Kaufleuten **8**
Mére Catherine **12**
Restaurant Reithalle **4**

ATTRACTIONS ●
Fraumünster **9**
Grossmünster **14**
Kunsthaus Zurich
   (Fine Arts Museum) **16**
Landesmuseum
   (Swiss National Museum) **3**
Lindenhof **6**
Münsterhof **10**
Rathaus **15**

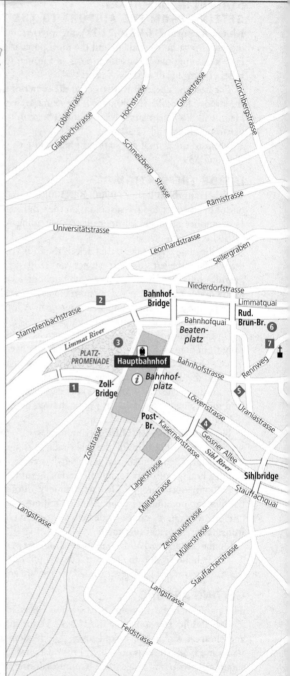

✝   Church
ⓘ   Information
🛄   Rail Station
—   Railway

RIGHT BANK

Plattenstrasse
Freiestrasse
Klosbachstrasse
Asylstrasse
Zollikerstrasse
Minervastrasse
Kreuzplatz
Feldeggstrasse
Seefeldstrasse
Dufourstrasse
Hottingerstrasse
Zeltweg
Mühlebachstrasse
Bellerivestrasse
Stadelhofer-platz
17
Rämistrasse
Falken strasse
Kreuzstrasse
18
16
Hirschengraben
Theaterstr.
Goethestr.
Utoquai
Grossmünster-platz
Oberdorfstr.
14
Bellevueplatz
Münsterg.
13
15
Limmatquai
12
Quaibr.
Limmat River
Lake Zurich
11
Stadthausquai
Bürkli-platz
10
Münster-Bridge
9
Bahnhof-strasse
Börsenstrasse
Tal strasse
Paradeplatz
Bleicherweg
Claridenstrasse
Gen. Guisan-Quai
ARBORETUM
Beethovenstrasse
Dreikönigstrasse
Mythenquai
Bastei-platz
8
Alikanstrasse
Stocker strasse
Gotthard strasse
Alfred-Escher-Strasse
BELVOIR PARK
Tödistrasse
Lavaterstrasse
Seestrasse
Brandschenk estrasse
Freigutstrasse
Tessinerplatz
Seestrasse
Schulhausstrasse
Gablerstrasse
RIETER PARK
Stauffbridge
Tunnelstrasse
Bürglistrasse
Scheideggstrasse
Enge
HugelstrasseKurf
Bederstrasse
Waffenplatzstrasse
Sihl River
Lessingstrasse
LEFT BANK
Nationalstrasse 3

You can buy tickets from automatic-vending machines located at every stop. You must have a ticket before you get on a vehicle; if you're caught without one, you'll pay a fine of 60F ($39) on the spot.

For a trip of up to four stops, the fare is 3.30F ($2.15), and 4.10F ($2.65) for longer journeys. Visitors will get the most for their money by buying a *Tageskarte* (1-day ticket), which costs 7.50F ($4.90) and allows you to travel on all city buses and trams for 24 hours.

Taxis are very expensive in Zurich. The budget-conscious will want to use them only as a last resort. Your hotel will usually be glad to call a taxi for you, but if you're making the call yourself, call **Taxi–Zentrale Zurich** (✆ **01/272-44-44**). The basic charge before you even get into the vehicle is 6F ($3.90), plus 3.50F ($2.30)for each kilometer you travel.

Biking is a good way to get around Zurich, especially in the outlying areas. Bicycles can be rented at the baggage counter of the railway station, the **Hauptbahnhof** (✆ **051/222-29-04**), for 27F ($18) per day for a city bike or 21F ($14) for a half day. The rental office is open daily from 7am to 7:30pm.

WHERE TO STAY

Hotel Bristol ★ *Value*   Close to the Bahnhof, this affordable (a rarity in super-expensive Zurich!) hotel is a bit lean on facilities, but the helpful staff will quickly ease you into life in Zurich. The midsize bedrooms are well maintained, and are subject to frequent renovation. This is also one of the few lower-priced hotels that is accessible to those with limited mobility.

Stampfensbachstrasse 34, CH-8035 Zurich. ✆ **01/258-44-44**. Fax 01/258-44-00. www.hotelbristol.ch. 53 units. 150F–185F ($98–$120) double; 200F–240F ($130–$156) triple. Rates include cold buffet breakfast. AE, DC, MC, V. Tram: 11 or 14. **Amenities:** Laundry; rooms for those with limited mobility. *In room:* Hair dryer.

Hotel Kindli ★   In the Altstadt's (Old Town) pedestrian zone, this hotel is set inside a restored 16th-century building. The structure might be antique but the hotel was drastically overhauled in the '90s and turned into one of the better choices for those seeking good comfort and a bit of atmosphere, enhanced by the use of Laura Ashley fabrics throughout. Bedrooms are midsize, each with a different color scheme and completely modern plumbing.

Pfalzgasse 1, CH-8001 Zurich. ✆ **01/211-59-17**. Fax 01/211-65-28. 20 units. 330F–360F ($215–$234) double. Rates include continental breakfast. AE, DC, MC, V. Tram: 7, 11, or 13. **Amenities:** Restaurant. *In room:* Hair dryer.

Hotel Rössli ★   This antique building in the Oberdorf section of Zurich, about a mile (1.6km) from the train station, was massively overhauled in the past decade and turned into a hotel that attracts a hip, young crowd. The midsize bedrooms are tastefully and comfortably furnished. A special feature here is a suite with a separate living room, three bedrooms, and a roof terrace offering lovely views. The bar is a popular gathering point for Zurich's artists and musicians.

Rössligasse 7, CH-8001 Zurich. ✆ **01/256-70-50**. Fax 01/256-70-51. www.hotelroessli.ch. 18 units. 280F ($182) double; 360F ($234) suite. Rates include breakfast. AE, DC, MC, V. Tram: 4 or 15. **Amenities:** Bar. *In room:* Hair dryer.

Hotel Walhalla *Value*   Only a short walk from the Bahnhof, this hotel is a bargain by Zurich standards. It is spread across two five-floor buildings. One of these structures was renovated in 1997; the other is still a bit more antiquated, although some prefer its higher ceilings and architectural details. The midsize bedrooms are comfortably furnished and well maintained, though beyond a bathroom, expect almost no in-room amenities but a TV.

Limmatstrasse 5, 8005 Zurich. © **01/446-54-00.** Fax 01/446-54-54. www.walhalla-hotel.ch. 48 units. 200F ($130) double. AE, DC, MC, V. Tram: 3 or 14. **Amenities:** Restaurant; nonsmoking rooms; rooms for those with limited mobility.

Lady's First ★ *Finds*   Pia Schmid, a well-known local architect, took an 1880s town house and successfully converted it into this charming boutique hotel, equipped with a first-class spa and a rooftop terrace with panoramic views of the cityscape. The midsize to spacious bedrooms are handsomely furnished with high ceilings and parquet floors. The summer rose garden is an allure, as is the blazing fireplace in the winter lounge. One other special feature: The hotel reserves its top two floors just for women.

Mainaustrasse 24, Kreis 8, CH-8008 Zurich. © **01/380-80-10.** Fax 01/380-80-20. www.ladysfirst.ch. 28 units. 280F ($182) single; 365F ($237) suite. Rates include breakfast. AE, DC, MC, V. Tram: 2 or 4. **Amenities:** Breakfast room. *In room:* Hair dryer.

TOP ATTRACTIONS & SPECIAL MOMENTS

In the center of Zurich, the world-famous **Bahnhofstrasse** ★★★ is the world's most beautiful shopping street. Planted with linden trees, the street was built on the site of what used to be a "frogs' moat." The exclusive street is relatively free of traffic, except for trams, which Zurichers have labeled "holy cows."

Beginning at the Bahnhofplatz, the street extends for nearly 4,000 feet until it reaches the lake. The drab **Bahnhofplatz,** the hub of Zurich's transportation network, is the railway station square and is home to the Hauptbahnhof (the German word for central railway station), which was built here in 1871.

With your back to this railway terminus, head up Bahnhofstrasse, which is filled with shops selling luxury merchandise, such as Swiss watches, and banks. Select a favorite cafe and people-watch when you get tired of shopping. Incidentally, if you do shop, take along plenty of cash or else a gold-plated credit card. The merchandise here is exquisite, but it's also some of the most expensive in the world.

Moments   **A Summer Walk Along the Quays of Zurich**

To walk the **Quays of Zurich** ★★★ is an attraction rivaled in the city only by the Swiss National Museum. These promenades have been built along the Zurichsee (Lake Zurich) and the Limmat River. The most famous is **Limmat Quai,** in the virtual heart of Zurich, beginning at the Bahnhof Bridge and extending east to the Rathaus (town hall) and beyond. These quays have lovely gardens planted with beautiful trees such as the linden. The Swiss are known for their love of flowers, which is much in evidence as you join Zurichers for a stroll on the promenade, an especially invigorating experience when spring comes to the city.

Uto Quai is the major lakeside promenade, running from Badeanstalt Uto Quai, a swimming pool, to Bellevue Square and Quai Brucke. The graceful swans you see in the lake aren't just a scenic attraction. Zurichers have found that they're an efficient garbage disposal system, keeping the lake from being polluted as it laps up on their shores. If you stroll as far as **Mythen Quai,** you'll be following the lake along its western shore and out into the countryside where vistas open onto the Alps and, on the far horizon, the Oberland massifs.

Moments   Sailing Lake Zurich

At some point during your stay in Switzerland's largest city, you'll want to take a lake steamer for a tour around Lake Zurich. Walk to Bahnhofstrasse's lower end and buy a ticket at the pier for any of the dozen-or-so boats that ply the lake waters from late May to late September. The boats are more or less the same so it doesn't matter which one you take. Most of the steamers contain simple restaurant facilities, and all have two or three levels of decks and lots of windows for wide-angle views of the Swiss mountains and shoreline. During peak season, boats depart at approximately 30-minute intervals. The most distant itinerary from Zurich is to **Rapperswil,** a historic town near the lake's southeastern end. A full-length, round-trip tour of the lake from Zurich to Rapperswil takes 2 hours each way, plus whatever time you opt to spend exploring towns en route. Many visitors opt for shorter boat rides encompassing only the northern third of the lake, where the total trip takes about 90 minutes.

A full-length tour of the lake costs 20F ($13) in second class and 33F ($21) in first class. The shorter boat ride on the northern third of the lake costs only 5.40F ($3.50).

Fraumünster   Rising on the left bank, this church, with its slender blue spire, overlooks the Münsterhof, the former pig market of Zurich. It was founded as an abbey by the Emperor Ludwig (Louis the German, grandson of Charlemagne) in 853, but dates mainly from the 13th and 14th centuries in its present incarnation. In the undercroft are the remains of the crypt of the old abbey church. The chief attractions here are five **stained-glass windows** ⊛—each with its own color theme—by Marc Chagall dating from 1970. Obviously they are best seen in bright morning light. The Münster is also celebrated for its elaborate organ. The Gothic nave is from the 13th to the 15th centuries, and the basilica has three aisles. In the Romanesque and Gothic cloisters are 1920s paintings depicting old Zurich legends about the founding of the abbey.

Fraumünsterstrasse. Free admission. May–Sept Mon–Sat 9am–noon and 2–6pm; Sun 2–6pm; Oct, Mar–Apr Mon–Sat 10am–noon and 2–5pm, Sun 2–5pm; Nov–Feb Mon–Sat 10am–noon and 2–4pm, Sun 2–4pm. Tram: 4 to City Hall.

Grossmünster ⊛   The Romanesque and Gothic cathedral of Zurich, Grossmünster, was, according to legend, founded by Charlemagne, whose horse bowed down on the spot marking the graves of three early Christian martyrs. Rising on a terrace above the Limmatquai, the cathedral has twin three-story towers, a city landmark. On the right bank of the Limmat, the present structure dates principally from 1090-1180 and from 1225 to the dawn of the 14th century. The cathedral is dedicated to those Christian missionaries and the patron saints of Zurich: Felix, Regula, and Exuperantius.

The cathedral was once the parish church of Zwingli, one of the great leaders of the Reformation. He urged priests to take wives (he'd married one himself) and attacked the "worship of images" and the Roman doctrine of Mass. This led to his death at Kappel in a religious war in 1531. The public hangman quartered his body, and soldiers burnt the pieces with dung. That spot at Kappel is today

Moments   Discoveries Along Medieval Streets

Even if you have to skip a museum or two, head for the **Alstadt (Old Town)** ✦✦✦, known for its romantic squares, narrow cobblestone streets, winding alleyways that aren't as sinister as they look, fountain-decorated corners, medieval houses, art galleries, boutiques, colorfully quaint restaurants, shops, a scattering of hotels, and antiques stores. The old town lies on both sides of the Limmat River, and you might begin your exploration at the **Münsterhof** or former swine market. Excavations have turned up houses here that date back to the 1100s. Once it was the tarrying place of Charlemagne, and to walk its old streets is to follow in the footsteps of everybody from Mozart and Lenin to Einstein and Carl Jung.

Shaded by trees, the belvedere square of **Lindenhof** is one of the most scenic spots in Zurich, especially favored at twilight time by those who believe in "young love." It can be reached by climbing medieval alleyways from the Fraumünster. Once the site of a Celtic and Roman fort, Lindenhof is a good point to view the Limmat River. The lookout point is graced with a fountain, of course. There's also a good view of the medieval Old Quarter, which rises in layers on the right bank. Many excellent restaurants are located in this vicinity.

Weinplatz is another landmark square you'll invariably reach in your exploration of Zurich. It lies right off the 1878 Rathausbrücke (town hall bridge) spanning the Limmat. Once, this was the only river crossing in Zurich (not the present structure, however). The Weinplatz is named for its 1909 Weinbauer fountain depicting a "little ole Swiss wine-grower," basket of grapes in hand. Many visitors like to stop here to take a picture of the old burghers' houses with Flemish-style roofs on the opposite bank.

Directly south of Münsterbrücke is a Gothic church, rather austere, called the **Wesserkirche** or "water church." When it was built in 1479, it was surrounded by water.

marked with an inscription: "They may kill the body but not the soul." If you visit the choir, you'll come upon stained-glass windows Giacometti completed in 1933. In the crypt is the original (but weather-beaten) statue of a 15th-century figure of Charlemagne. A copy of that same statue crowns the south tower.

Grossmünsterplatz. ☎ 01/252-59-49. Cathedral, free; towers, 2F ($1.30). Cathedral, Mar 15–Oct daily 9am–6pm; Nov–Mar 14 daily 10am–4pm. Towers, Mar–Oct daily (when weather permits); off season Sat–Sun when weather permits. Same hours as cathedral. Tram: 4.

Landesmuseum (Swiss National Museum) ✦✦✦   This museum, located in a big, sprawling gray stone Victorian building in back of the Zurich Hauptbahnhof, offers an epic survey of Swiss culture, art, and history. The collection of artifacts starts off in dim unrecorded time and carries you up to the present day. It's like a storybook history of all the cantons that you turn page by page as you go from gallery to gallery.

Religious art sounds a dominant theme, and especially noteworthy are the 16th-century stained glass that was removed from Tänikon Convent, and the frescoes from the church of Müstair. Some of the museum's Carolingian art dates back to the 9th century. Altarpieces—carved, painted, and gilded—bring back the glory of the Swiss medieval artisan. Several rooms from Fraumünster Abbey are also on view.

The museum's prehistoric section is exceptional, dipping back to the 4th millennium. Switzerland's history as a Roman outpost is explored in several exhibits. And the displays of utensils and furnishings of Swiss life over the centuries are staggering: medieval silverware, 14th-century drinking bowls, tiled 18th-century stoves, 17th-century china, Roman clothing, painted furniture, costumes, even dollhouses. Naturally, arms and armor revive Switzerland's military legacy, from 800 to 1800, although some weapons date from the late Iron Age.

Museumstrasse 2. ✆ 01/218-65-11. Admission 5F ($3.25), 3F ($1.95) students and seniors; special exhibitions 8F–12F ($5.20–$7.80). Tues–Sun 10:30am–5pm. Tram: 3, 4, 5, 11, 13, or 14.

Zurich Kunsthaus (Fine Arts Museum) ✿ This museum is devoted to works mainly from the 19th and 20th centuries, although many of its paintings and sculpture dip back to antiquity. Dating back to Victorian times, the collection has grown and grown and is today one of the most important in Europe.

As you enter, note Rodin's *Gate of Hell*. Later on you can explore one of our favorite sections, the **Giacometti wing** ✿, showcasing the artistic development of the amazing Swiss-born artist (1901–66), whose works are characterized by surrealistically elongated forms and hallucinatory moods.

All the legendary names of modern art can be found in the galleries, including a collection of the works of Norwegian artist **Edvard Munch** ✿✿, the largest outside of Oslo. Old masters such as Rubens and Rembrandt are suitably honored, and one salon contains 17 Rouaults.

Heimplatz 1. ✆ 01/253-84-97. Admission 6F ($3.90) adults, 4F ($2.60) children, free for children 5 and under; special exhibitions 14F ($9.10) adults, 7F ($4.55) children. Tues–Thurs 10am–9pm; Fri–Sun 10am–5pm. Tram: 3 (marked "Klusplatz").

WHERE TO DINE

Bierhalle Kropf ✿ SWISS/BAVARIAN *Der Kropf* is the everyone's favorite beer hall, installed in one of the oldest burgher houses in Zurich, only a short walk from Paradeplatz. Locals flock here for the large portions and affordable prices. Against an old-fashioned Swiss backdrop of stag horns and stained glass, robust and well-prepared platters of mountain favorites, such as mammoth pork shanks, stewed meats, chopped veal, and the famous rösti or Swiss-style hash browns are served.

In Gassen 16. ✆ 01/221-18-05. Reservations recommended. Main courses 20F–43F ($13–$28). AE, MC, V. Mon–Sat 11:30am–11:30pm. Closed Easter, Dec 25, and Aug 1. Tram: 2, 8, 9, or 11.

Brasserie Lipp SWISS/FRENCH This bustling bistro was inspired by the world-famous Art Nouveau Brasserie Lipp in Paris. The atmosphere of Paris is re-created here, as is the cuisine; you'll find such old-time classics as peppery steaks and sole meunière on the menu. It's a bustling place, with waiters scurrying about, often bringing in heaping platters of sauerkraut with pork products just as they do in the real thing on the Left Bank of Paris.

Uraniastrasse 9. ✆ 01/211-11-55. Reservations recommended, especially Fri–Sat. Main courses 30F–50F ($20–$33). AE, DC, MC, V. Mon–Sat 11:30am–11pm (to 1am Fri–Sat). Tram: 6, 7, 11, or 13.

Fischstube Zurichhorn SWISS/SEAFOOD Tables at this restaurant are placed outside on a terrace held up by pilings anchored into the lake, making it an idyllic choice for a fresh fish dinner in Zurich. It's perfect on a summer evening when you can devour the lake fish fried in butter, accompanied by fresh vegetables grown in the province and rushed to market that day. The chefs believe in simplicity and accurate seasoning of their dishes, some of which will appeal to meat fanciers.

Bellerivestrasse 160. ℂ 01/422-25-20. Reservations required. Main courses 26F–42F ($17–$27); fixed-price lunch 39F ($25). AE, MC, V. Daily 9:30am–11pm. Closed Sept 26–Easter. Tram: 2 or 4.

Kaufleuten *Finds* INTERNATIONAL   Only a few steps from the Bahnhofstrasse, this enduring favorite roams the globe for its culinary inspiration, serving everything from a platter-size Wiener schnitzel fried a golden brown to a fiery coconut and chicken curry from Thailand. It is strong in its freshwater fish dishes, especially salmon, sole, and sea bass, which are prepared almost close to perfection and never allowed to dry out. The restaurant is also a nightlife venue.

Pelikanstrasse 18. ℂ 01/225-33-33. Reservations recommended. Main courses 22F–47F ($14–$31). AE, DC, MC, V. Mon–Fri 11:30am–2pm; daily 7pm–2am (to 3am Fri–Sat). Tram: 6, 7, 11, or 13.

Mère Catherine PROVENÇAL/FRENCH   One of Alstadt's favorite bistros is nestled in a quiet courtyard, its tranquil cafe tables evoking the left Bank of Paris. The unpretentious French cooking features fresh fish along with an ever-changing roster of daily specials. Try to arrive early for an aperitif at the Bar Philosophe next door before going to your table to partake of delights that will make you salivate with pleasure.

Nägelihof 3. ℂ 01/250-59-40. Reservations required. Main courses 24F–38F ($16–$25); surprise lunch Mon–Fri 16.50F–24F ($11–$16). AE, DC, MC, V. Daily 11:30am–2:30pm and 6–11:30pm. Tram: 4 or 15.

Restaurant Reithalle *Value* INTERNATIONAL   In a former stable on a small island in the heart of Zurich, this local favorite is a friend of the frugal rail passenger. In fair weather, its cobblestone courtyard is mobbed with fun-loving drinkers and diners. Expect a robust and hearty cuisine prepared with fresh ingredients, based on recipes from around the world—even from as far away as Iran. The interior becomes a dance club every Saturday from 11pm to 3am, and restaurant patrons enter free (otherwise there's a cover of 12F/$7.80).

In the Theaterhaus Gessnerallee, Gessnerallee 8. ℂ 01/212-0766. Reservations not necessary. Lunch main courses 14.50F–32F ($9.45–$21); dinner main courses 20F–32F ($13–$21). AE, DC, MC, V. Mon–Fri 11am–midnight, Sat–Sun 6pm–midnight. Tram: 3.

SHOPPING

Zurich has been called a shopper's Valhalla, if that's not too pagan a term for such a Protestant city. Within the heart of Zurich are 25 acres of shopping, including the exclusive stores along the **Bahnhofstrasse,** previewed on p. 827. Along this gold-plated street you can walk with oil-rich sheiks and their families in your search for furs, watches, jewelry, leather goods, silks, and embroidery. If your own oil well didn't come in, you can still shop for souvenirs.

Your shopping adventure might begin more modestly at the top of the street, the **Bahnhofplatz.** Underneath this vast transportation hub is a complex of shops known as **"Shop Ville."**

Bally Capital, Bahnhofstrasse 66 (ℂ 01/224-39-39), is the largest official outlet of the famous Swiss chain, occupying a prominent place in a big-windowed store on this shopping artery. For lovers of Bally shoes, this is the place to buy them, although the merchandise is not necessarily cheaper than at other Bally outlets. Here, you'll find the most complete line of Bally shoes in the world, along with accessories and clothing (most, but not all, of which are made in Switzerland).

If your heart is set on buying a timepiece in Zurich, try **Beyer,** Bahnhofstrasse 31 (© **01/221-10-80**), located midway between the train station and the lake. Besides carrying just about every famous brand of watch made in Switzerland, such as Rolex and Patek Philippe, they also have a surprising museum in the basement, containing timepieces from as early as 1400 B.C. Another sure bet in Zurich would be **Bucherer,** Bahnhofstrasse 50 (© **01/211-26-35**). A longtime name in the Swiss watch industry, this store carries an impressive collection of jewelry as well.

Jelmoli Department Store, Bahnhofstrasse 69 (© **01/220-44-11**), is a Zurich institution, having everything a large department store should, from cookware to clothing. Founded 150 years ago by the Ticino-born entrepreneur Johann Peter Jelmoli, the store and the success of its many branches is a legend among the Zurich business community.

Musik Hug, Limmatquai 28–30 (© **01/251-68-50**), is the kind of shop that musicians will love, particularly if they need sheet music for anything from flugelhorn concertos to yodeling duets. It might be the largest repository of Alpine musical tradition anywhere, as well as a commercial music shop stocking woodwind recorders of all sizes and pitches along with flugelhorns and French horns.

Schweizer Heimatwerk, Bahnhofstrasse 2 (© **01/221-08-37**), is only one of a chain of similar stores throughout Zurich. Most of them have the same basic collection of, for example, hand-painted boxes in charmingly naïve patterns with or without music mechanisms, bookends, china, decorative stoneware plates, a wide range of textiles, and the obligatory cowbells in all sizes. This particular store has a large selection of glass, embroidery, and woodcarvings, among other items. The English-speaking staff is particularly helpful in suggesting "little gifts."

NIGHTLIFE

The Zurich Opera, the most outstanding local company, performs at the **Opernhaus,** Falkenstrasse 1 (© **01/268-66-66**), near Bellevueplatz in the center of the city. The opera house is also a repertory theater, hosting ballets, concerts, and recitals, although it shuts down in July and August. Tickets cost 35F to 210F ($23–$137), and the box office is open daily 10am to 6:30pm. The **Zurich Tonhalle Orchestra** performs at the Tonhalle Gesellschaft, Claridenstrasse 5 (© **01/206-34-34**), a 1,500-seat theater, which is also the venue for many internationally known soloists. Tickets range from 17F to 160F ($11–$104), and the box office is open daily 10am to 6pm.

More boisterous nightlife is found at the 160-seat **Bierhale Wolf,** Limmatquai 132 (© **01/251-01-30**), the best-known beer hall in the city, known for its "evergreen music" (folk) played by an oompah band. You can also dine here on the kitchen's robust fare. Cover ranges from 4F to 6F ($2.60–$3.90), and hours are daily 11am to 2am. The largest nightclub in Zurich, and one of the best, is **Palais X-tra,** in the Limmathaus, Limmatstrasse 118 (© **01/448-15-00**). With a long bar and an outdoor terrace, it features some of the best rock groups in Europe. The cover ranges from 30F to 45F ($20–$29), depending on the performers.

For the best New Orleans style jazz, head for **Casa Bar,** Münstergasse 30 (© **01/261-20-02**), where Dixieland is heard nightly from 5pm to 2am. Some 60 patrons a night, of various ages, crowd into this bar. House and garage music

---

Value **An Open Sesame & Bargain Pass**

In 2003, the **ZurichCARD** (www.zuerich.com/e/zuerichcard.htm) was launched to great success. The card costs 15F ($9.75) for 24 hours or 30F ($20) for 72 hours. It's a great deal offering 50% reduction on public transportation, free visits to 43 museums, reduced prices at the local zoo, and a welcome drink at more than two dozen restaurants. The pass is widely available, and is sold at the Zurich Hauptbahnhof, the airport, and at certain hotels.

---

are featured at **Kaufleuten,** Pelikanstrasse 18 (✆ **01/225-33-33**), which has four different bar areas and an on-site restaurant. British or Irish pubs are all the rage in Zurich, including **James Joyce Pub,** Pelikanstrasse 8 (✆ **01/221-18-28**), boasting the furnishings and paneling of an 18th-century pub in Dublin, and **Oliver Trist,** Rindermarkt 6 (✆ **01/252-47-10**), attracting a fun-loving young crowd that overflows into a summer courtyard.

3 Bern ★★★

Bern lies in the heart of Switzerland and has been the country's capital since 1848. A city of diplomats, it is one of the loveliest places to visit in the country, surrounded on three sides by the River Aare, a body of water to which it is linked symbolically as much as Paris is to the Seine.

Built between the 12th and 18th centuries, Bern is one of the few great medieval cities left in Europe that hasn't been destroyed, torn down, or bombed in wars. In 1983, the United Nations declared it a "World Landmark." It's a city of arcades, nearly 4 miles (6.4km) of them running along the streets of the old sector, and they're weatherproof and traffic free. Underneath these arcades are shop windows, everything from exclusive boutiques to department stores, from antiques dealers to jewelers. It's a city of fountains and oriel windows, and its old sandstone steps have been trodden for centuries.

The city is a stop on many international rail routes. Trains from France, Italy, Germany, the Benelux countries, and even Scandinavia and Spain all pass through Bern, making it a great stopover point on a cross-continental train trip. The TGV high-speed train, for example, connects Paris with Bern in just 4½ hours. Bern is also situated on most major rail lines in Switzerland, particularly those connecting Geneva (90 min.) and Zurich (1 hr. 11 min.). We rank it third on a rail trip through Switzerland because most people fly into Zurich or Geneva first though Bern has its own airport at Belpmoos.

Bern can also be your gateway to the Alpine region of Central Switzerland, the Bernese Oberland. Trains leave every hour for Interlaken, the capital of the Bernese Oberland, where you can make all sorts of rail connections into the mountains, especially if you want to take the train trip to Jungfraujoch, which for many rail passengers is the most dramatic and scenic trip in all of Switzerland.

STATION INFORMATION
GETTING FROM THE AIRPORT TO THE TRAIN STATION
The **Bern-Belp Airport** (✆ **031/960-21-11**) is 6 miles (9.6km) south of the city in the town of Belpmoos. International flights arrive from London, Paris,

and Nice, but transatlantic jets are not able to land here. Fortunately, it's a short hop to Bern from the international airports in Zurich and Geneva.

A taxi from the airport to the city center costs about 45F to 50F ($29–$33), so it's better to take the shuttle bus that runs between the airport and the Bahnhof (train station) in the city center. The shuttle trip costs 15F ($9.75) one-way.

INSIDE THE STATION

The **Bahnhof** rail station, on Bahnhofplatz, is right in the center of town near all the major hotels.

The **Rail Information Center** inside the station is open Monday to Friday 8am to 7pm and Saturday 9am to 5pm. Here you can also make reservations and validate your railpasses. The location of the office is across the passageway from the tourist center. Many visitors who arrive in Bern choose to visit the Jungfrau, the famous mountain outside Interlaken, whose train station, at 11,133 feet is the highest in Europe. Your Eurailpass will take you from Bern to Interlaken, but at the Interlaken station you must purchase a separate ticket on a private railroad for the final trip to Jungfrau. The base fee for a ticket is 6.80F ($4.40) plus 3.10F ($2) per .6 miles (1km) traveled.

For more rail information and schedules, call ✆ **0900/300-300.**

On the ground level of the station there are money exchange offices including an ATM. The Swiss Railroad operates one of these offices, labeled *Change SBB,* which is open daily from 6:30am to 9pm. The station also offers a 24-hour baggage storage facility downstairs, charging 4F to 8F ($2.60–$5.20) for lockers.

The **Bern Tourist Office,** is located inside the Bahnhof, on Bahnhofplatz (✆ **031/328-12-12;** www.bernetourism.ch). It's open June through September daily from 9am to 8:30pm; October through May Monday through Saturday from 9am to 6:30pm and on Sunday from 10am to 5pm. If you need help finding a hotel room, the tourist office can make a reservation for you in the price range you select. The office also sells hotel packages for 2, 3, or 4 nights in hotels rated anywhere from 2 to 5 stars, the latter almost paralyzingly priced.

If your luggage is light, you can walk to your hotel; otherwise, take one of the taxis waiting outside the station.

GETTING AROUND

The public transportation system, **Stadtische Verkehrsbetriebe (SVB),** is a reliable, 48-mile (77km) network of buses and trams. Before you board, purchase a ticket from one of the automatic machines (you'll find one at each stop) because conductors don't sell tickets. If you're caught traveling without one, you'll be fined 60F ($39) on the spot in addition to the fare for the ride. A short-range ride (within six stations) costs 1.70F ($1.10); a normal ticket, valid for 45 minutes one-way, goes for 2.60F ($1.70).

To save time and money purchase a tourist ticket for 9F ($5.85), which entitles you to unlimited travel on the SVB network. Just get the ticket stamped at the automatic machine before beginning your first trip. One-day tickets are available at the **ticket offices** at Bubenbergplatz 5 (✆ **031/321-88-88**).

You can catch a taxi at the public cab ranks, or call a dispatcher; two cab companies you can try are **Nova Taxi** (✆ **031/301-11-11**) and **Bären Taxi** (✆ **031/371-11-11**). The first kilometer (.6 miles) of any taxi ride in Bern costs from 9F to 10F ($6.75–$7.50), and every kilometer after that costs an additional 3F to 4F ($2.25–$3), depending on how fast the traffic is moving and the time of day. The "average" taxi ride within Bern will probably cost about 15F to 20F ($11–$15).

Bern

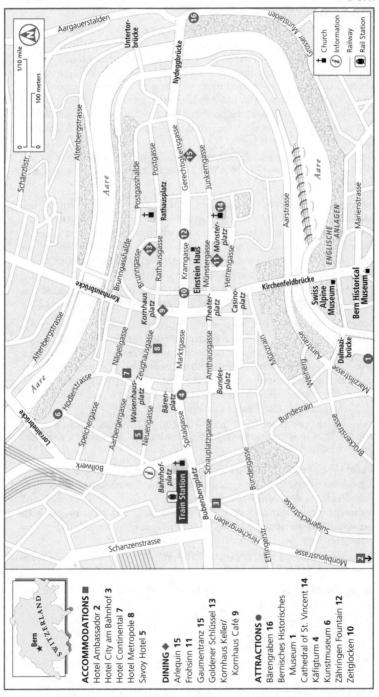

0   1/10 mile
0   100 meters

Church ✝
Information ⓘ
Railway |
Rail Station 🚉

ACCOMMODATIONS ■
Hotel Ambassador **2**
Hotel City am Bahnhof **3**
Hotel Continental **7**
Hotel Metropole **8**
Savoy Hotel **5**

DINING ◆
Arlequin **15**
Frohsinn **11**
Gaumentranz **15**
Goldener Schlüssel **13**
Kornhaus Keller/
   Kornhaus Café **9**

ATTRACTIONS ●
Bärengraben **16**
Bernisches Historisches
   Museum **1**
Cathedral of St. Vincent **14**
Käfigturm **4**
Kunstmuseum **6**
Zähringen Fountain **12**
Zeitglocken **10**

WHERE TO STAY

Hotel Ambassador ★   This 9-floor hotel close to the Bundeshaus, the seat of the Swiss government is one of the best and most affordable of the moderately priced hotels in Bern. True, its rooms are a bit small and the furnishings are only functional, but they are reasonably comfortable and very well maintained. Rooms like this you expect in Switzerland, but what comes as a surprise is the on-site teppan restaurant with Japanese specialties, including a garden evocative of Tokyo. Unusual for Bern, the hotel also has a private pool with sauna. It's a 5-minute tram ride from the train station (the tram stops right in front of the hotel).

Seftigenstrasse 99, CH-3007 Bern. ℂ 031/370-99-99. Fax 031/371-41-17. www.fhotels.ch. 97 units. 21F5–225F ($140–$146) double. AE, DC, MC, V. Tram: 9. **Amenities:** 2 restaurants; laundry service. *In room:* Hair dryer.

Hotel City am Bahnhof   This hotel takes its name from the train station, which is only 2 blocks away. If your luggage is light, you can walk straight here from the depot. The hotel is equally popular with business clients and visitors to Bern. The midsize bedrooms with acceptable—hardly exciting—furnishings are far from luxurious, but the maintenance level is high. Rooms come with a minibar and TV but little else. Breakfast is the only meal served.

Bahnhofplatz 7, CH-3011, Bern. ℂ 031/311-53-77. Fax 031/311-06-36. www.fhotels.ch. 58 units. 170F–205F ($111–$133) double. AE, DC, MC, V. Free parking. **Amenities:** Breakfast lounge; laundry.

Hotel Continental   This is one of the better, though still fairly impersonal, government-rated three-star hotels clustered around the Bern Bahnhof. Last renovated in 1997, it charges very fair prices—at least by the standards of high-priced Bern—for its comfortably furnished bedrooms. The rooms, although small, are well maintained and outfitted in both contemporary and traditional pieces; flower boxes outside the bedroom windows are a nice touch. In fair weather, breakfast is taken under a canopied terrace.

Zeughausgasse 27, CH-3011 Bern. ℂ 031/329-21-21. Fax 031/329-21-99. www.hotel-continental.ch. 43 units. 150F–180F ($98–$117) double. Rates include buffet breakfast. AE, DC, MC, V. Tram: 3 or 9. **Amenities:** Breakfast lounge.

Hotel Metropole   This hotel is situated between the Bern Bahnhof and the Altstadt, so it's convenient to most attractions and all transportation. The hotel was given a much-needed renovation in 1998, and today it offers rather small bedrooms comfortably furnished in both traditional and contemporary style with equally small bathrooms. Don't expect too many amenities—minimalism is the word here.

Zeughausgasse 26, CH-3011 Bern. ℂ 031/311-50-21. Fax 031/312-11-53. www.hotelmetropole.ch. 58 units. 170F–195F ($111–$127) double. Rates include buffet breakfast. AE, DC, MC, V. Tram: 9.

Savoy Hotel ★ *Value*   Close to the Bern Bahnhof, this traditional and welcoming hotel earns a 4-star rating from the government instead of the usual 2 or 3. Its most devoted fans call it a "budget version" of the Hotel Schweizerhof, one of the more elegant and expensive hotels in Bern. The five-story property offers midsize renovated bedrooms that are comfortably and tastefully furnished, with soundproof windows. The shopping arcade streets of Bern begin just outside the door.

Neuengasse 26, CH-3011 Bern. ℂ 031/311-4405. Fax 031/312-1978. www.zghotels.ch. 56 units. 230F–250F ($150–$163) double; 270F ($176) junior suite. AE, DC, MC, V. **Amenities:** Bar; laundry. *In room:* Hair dryer.

TOP ATTRACTIONS & SPECIAL MOMENTS

Marktgasse is the principal artery of the old town, and it's lined with luxurious shops and boutiques—the number of florists reveals the Bernese love of flowers. In this traffic-free sector you can stroll at your leisure, shopping and admiring the 17th- and 18th-century houses. Eventually you'll come to **Junkerngasse,** the most prestigious street in Bern, lined with patrician houses.

Marktgasse rolls on until it becomes **Kramgasse,** the first street to the right of the city's clock tower. It has many antiques shops and art galleries. You'll also view many turrets and oriel windows, and you'll come upon the 1535 **Zähringen fountain,** showing a bear, the city's mascot, in armor.

The **Käfigturm** (prison tower) on Marktgasse in the 13th century marked the boundary line of Bern. Restored in the 18th century, it stands at the top of the Marktgasse.

To the east stands the **Zeitglocken** or clock tower, which was built in the 12th century and restored in the 16th century. Until 1250 it was the west gate of Bern. Four minutes before every hour, crowds gather for what has been called "the world's oldest and biggest horological puppet show." Mechanical bears (the little bear cubs are everybody's favorite), jesters, and emperors put on an animated show, and it's one of the longest running acts in show business, staged since 1530.

Bärengraben ⚑ The famous bear pits are a deep, moon-shaped den where the bears, those mascots of Bern, have been kept since 1480. Beloved by the Bernese, the bears are pampered and fed. Everybody seemingly drops by here, throwing these hungry beasts a carrot. The pits are reached by going across Nydegg Bridge, which has a great view of the city. It was built over a gorge of the river and its major stone arch has a span of 180 feet. The bears have long been adopted as the heraldic symbol of Bern.

East end of Nydeggbrücke. Free admission. 3F ($1.95) to feed the bears. June–Sept daily 9am–5:30pm; Oct–May daily 10am–4pm.

⌢Moments On the Hoof Through Bern

Bern is a walking city and your own two feet are the only practical means of exploring Altstadt and its many attractions. You can see what there is to see here in about 2½ hours.

Don't overlook the possibility of walks in Greater Bern, including Bern's own mountain, **Gurten,** a popular day trip destination reached in 25 minutes by tram no. 9 and a rack railway. Eurailpass and Swiss Passholders get a 50% discount on the railway. Once here, you'll find many walking paths and can enjoy a panorama over the Alps. There's also a children's playground.

In and around Bern you'll find 155 miles (250km) of **marked rambling paths.** One of the most scenic runs along the banks of the Aare through the English gardens, the Dählhölzli Zoological Gardens, Elfenau Park, and the Bremgarten woods.

For **jogging and running,** the best spots are the Aare River Run (Dalmaziquai), stretching 2¼ miles (4km), or the Aare River Run–Bear Pits, which is 3 miles (5km) long.

Bernisches Historisches Museum (Bern Historical Museum) ★★ This neo-Gothic castle, built in the Swiss fortress style of the 16th century, contains historical relics, along with archaeological, ethnographic, and numismatic collections. The main attraction is a series of seven 15th-century tapestries. A tapestry called *The Thousand Flowers,* plus four others telling the story of Julius Caesar, once belonged to the dukes of Burgundy. A number of rural and urban rooms, filled with period furnishings and artifacts, are also open to the public.

Helvetiaplatz 5. ✆ 031/350-77-11. Admission 13F ($8.45) adults, 8F ($5.20) students and seniors, free for children 16 years and under. Tues–Sun 10am–5pm. Tram: 3 or 5.

Cathedral of St. Vincent ★ The Münster was begun in 1421, although its tower wasn't completed until 1893. Its **belfry** ★★, dominating Bern, is 300 feet high, and at the top a panoramic sweep of the Bernese Alps unfolds. You can climb a staircase, some 270 steps, to the platform tower. You'll also have a great vista over the old town and its bridges and a view of the **Aare.**

The Münster is one of the newer of the Gothic churches of Switzerland. Its most exceptional feature is the **tympanum** ★★ over the main portal, with more than 200 figures. Some of them are painted, and the vanquished ones in this Last Judgment setting are singled out for particularly harsh treatment. The mammoth stained-glass windows in the chancel were created in the 15th century. The choir stalls from 1523 brought the Renaissance to Bern, and in the Matter Chapel is a curious stained-glass window, the *Dance of Death,* constructed in the closing year of World War I but based on a much older design.

Münsterplatz. ✆ 031/312-04-62. Cathedral, free; viewing platform, 3F ($1.95) adults, 1F (65¢) children. Cathedral Easter Sun–Oct Tues–Sat 10am–5pm, Sun 11:30am–5pm; off season Tues–Fri 10am–noon and 2–4pm, Sat 10am–noon and 2–5pm, Sun 11:30am–2pm. Viewing platform closes half an hour before cathedral. Bus: 12.

Kunstmuseum ★★★ This 1879 Fine Arts Museum is known for its **collection of the works of Paul Klee** ★★★, the largest such treasure trove in the world. A German painter, born in Switzerland in 1879, Klee had a style characterized by fantasy forms in line and light colors. He combined abstract elements with recognizable images. The museum has both Swiss and foreign works, placing its emphasis on the 19th and 20th centuries. However, some of its painting goes back to the 14th century. There is a collection of Italian "primitives," such as Fra Angelico's *Virgin and Child.* Swiss primitives include one from the Master of the Carnation (Paul Löwensprung, who died in 1499), who signed his work with either a red or white carnation.

The romantic painter, Hodler, is represented by allegorical frescoes, depicting *Day* and, conversely, *Night.* Several Impressionists are represented, including Monet, Manet, Sisley, and Cézanne, and you'll find such other artists as Delacroix and Bonnard.

Hodlerstrasse 12. ✆ 031/328-09-44. Permanent collection, 7F ($4.55) adults, 5F ($3.25) seniors; special exhibitions, 14F–16F ($9.10–$10) extra. Tues 10am–9pm; Wed–Sun 10am–5pm. Bus: 20.

WHERE TO DINE

Arlequin SWISS/ITALIAN Artists, writers, and frugal diners frequent this informal restaurant, which sets out tables on a pergola-shaded, open-air terrace in summer. From Wednesday to Friday, the chef sautés a platter-wide Wiener schnitzel—the best in town—a golden brown. At other times of the week you can dig into a lot of old-time Swiss favorites, such as goulash soup, and even some specialties from south of the border in Italy.

Gerechtigkeitsgasse 51. ⒸÂ **031/311-39-46.** Reservations recommended. Main courses 15F–30F ($9.75–$20); fixed–price meal 20F ($13). MC, V. Daily 11am–1pm and 5–10pm. Tram: 9.

Frohsinn ✸ *Finds* SWISS/CONTINENTAL   Small and intimate, this bistro is close to the Bern Clock Tower. Its intimate atmosphere and good, moderately priced food has attracted a loyal following of journalists and national politicians. Sometimes the chefs dip across the borders into neighboring countries, especially France and Italy, for their recipes, which are prepared with first-rate ingredients purchased at the market that day.

Münstergasse 54. ⒸÂ **031/311-37-68.** Reservations required. Main courses 20F–43F ($13–$28). AE, DC, MC, V. Tues–Sat 8am–2pm and 6–11:30pm. Closed July 15–Aug 15. Tram: 54.

Gaumentranz SWISS/PACIFIC RIM   Intimate and artsy, this modern, hip restaurant has gained a foothold among serious Bern foodies, attracted to the refined cuisine of chef Max Zwahlen. He not only prepares good-tasting Swiss specialties in the restaurant's open-kitchen, but also draws inspiration from around the globe, including Asia (especially Thailand). The menu changes about every 6 weeks, but regardless of what's offered, count on something special.

Gerechtigkeitsgasse 56. ⒸÂ **031/311-64-84.** Main courses 24F–30F ($16–$20); set–price lunch 15F–17F ($9.75–$11). AE, MC, V. Tues–Sat 11am–2pm and 6–10pm.

Goldener Schlüssel ✸ SWISS   On the street level of an inexpensive hotel of the same name, this longtime favorite caters to local workers, who gravitate here for the well-prepared yet unpretentious food served in generous portions. In a building whose origins go back to the 1200s, the interior features antique planking and stonework, a rustic backdrop for time-tested recipes, many of which have emerged relatively intact from Grandmother Alpine's kitchen, including butter-fried Swiss sausage with onion sauce accompanied by *Rösti* (hash browns).

Rathausgasse 72. ⒸÂ **031/311-02-16.** Reservations recommended. Main courses 23F–32F ($15–$21); fixed–price lunch 20F–24F ($13–$16). AE, MC, V. Sun–Thurs 7am–11:30pm; Fri–Sat 7am–12:30am. Tram: 9. Bus: 12.

Kornhaus Keller/Kornhaus Café SWISS/MEDITERRANEAN   With a pedigree dating back to the 1700s, this is the most famous restaurant and beer cellar in Bern. Installed in a converted grain warehouse, this veteran favorite hardly serves the best food in Bern, although the acceptable, rib-sticking fare is dished out in heaping portions. The 450-seat-plus dining room is filled every night, and the restaurant keeps patrons in a convivial mood by presenting folk music from the Alps. Most diners come here for the good times under the soaring vaulted ceilings—you won't find a more jovial atmosphere elsewhere in Bern.

Kornhausplatz 18. ⒸÂ **031/327-72-70.** Reservations recommended in cellar-level restaurant, not necessary in cafe. Main courses in cellar 35.50F–43.50F ($23–$28); platters and snack items in cafe 10F–26F ($6.50–$17); glasses of wine and tea in cafe 5F–7F ($3.25–$4.55) each. AE, DC, MC, V. Cafe daily 8:30am–12:30am. Cellar Mon–Sat noon–2pm; daily 6–11pm (last order). Cellar–level bar 6pm–12:30am or 2am, depending on business.

SHOPPING

With 4 miles (6km) of arcades, you'll find stores of all types in Bern. The main shopping streets are **Spitalgasse, Kramgasse, Postgasse, Marktgasse,** and **Gerechtigkeitsgasse.**

With a few exceptions, stores in the city center are open on Monday from 2 to 6:30pm; on Tuesday, Wednesday, and Friday from 8:15am to 6:30pm; on Thursday from 8:15am to 9pm; and on Saturday from 8:15am to 4pm. They're closed on Sundays.

You might begin your shopping excursion at **Globus,** Spitalgasse 17 (© **031/ 313-40-40**), a major department store that has been compared to Bloomingdale's, with departments for everything. Many people from the Bernese Oberland come into Bern just to shop at Globus.

The best handcrafts, souvenirs, and gifts are found at **Oberlander Heimat,** Kramgasse 61 (© **031/311-30-00**), located on a historic street near the Clock Tower. This outlet sells handcrafts from all over Switzerland, including textiles, woodcarvings, music boxes, and jewelry.

NIGHTLIFE

This Week in Bern, distributed free by the tourist office, keeps a current list of cultural events.

The **Bern Symphony Orchestra,** one of the finest orchestras in Switzerland, is conducted by the acclaimed Russian-born Dmitrij Kitajenko, whose services are supplemented by frequent guest conductors from around the world. Concerts by the orchestra are usually performed at the concert facilities in the **Bern Casino,** Herrengasse 25 (© **031/311-42-42**). Except for a summer vacation usually lasting from July until mid-August, the box office is open Monday through Friday from 12:30 to 3pm. Tickets range from 18F to 55F ($12–$36).

Concerts with fewer musicians, especially chamber music, are often performed in any of four or five churches; in the auditorium at the **Konservatorium für Musik,** Kramgasse 36 (© **031/311-62-21**); or in the concert and recording facilities of **Radio Studio Bern,** Schwarztorstrasse 21 (© **031/ 388-91-11**).

Major opera and ballet performances are usually staged in what is Bern's most beautiful theater, the century-old **Stadttheater,** Kornhausplatz 20 (© **031/329-51-11**). Performances are usually in German, and to a lesser degree in French, but the language barrier usually won't get in the way of enjoying a performance.

Klötzlikeller, Gerechtigkeitsgasse 62 (© **031/311-74-56**), the oldest wine tavern in Bern, is near the Gerechtigkeitsbrunnen (Fountain of Justice), the first fountain you see on your walk from the Bärengraben (Bear Pits) to the Zytgloggeturm (Clock Tower). Watch for the lantern outside an angled cellar door. The well-known tavern dates from 1635 and is leased by the city to an independent operator. Some 20 different wines are sold by the glass, with prices starting at 8.50F ($5.55). The menu is changed every 6 weeks. Open Tuesday to Saturday 4pm to 12:30am.

Marians' Jazzroom, Engerstrasse 54 (© **031/309-61-11**), has its own separate entrance from the Innere Enge Hotel. Unique in Bern, it serves up not only food and drink, but the finest traditional jazz performed live by top artists from around the world. From Tuesday through Thursday, hours are 7:30pm to 1am, Friday and Saturday 7:30pm to 2am. On Saturday, there is a Concert Apéro from 4 to 6:30pm, and on some Sundays there is a Jazz Brunch from 10am to 1:30pm. Cover ranges from 15F to 47F ($9.75–$31), depending on the act. Closed June 6 to September 7.

Temple, Aarbergergasse 61 (© **031/311-50-41**), is one of the biggest and best-known discos in Bern. It's sweet and sexy, drawing a young crowd (especially on Fri and Sat nights when there's usually a live band). Wednesday is golden-oldie night; on other days there's a DJ spinning. Cover (including the 1st drink) is 12F ($7.80) Monday to Thursday, 17F ($11) Friday to Saturday. It's open Monday to Thursday 9pm to 3am, and Friday to Saturday 9pm to 3:30am. Closed July to August.

4 Lausanne ★★★

Lausanne, the second largest city on Lake Geneva and the fifth largest city in Switzerland, rises in tiers from the lake. A haunt of international celebrities, Lausanne is 134 miles (214km) southwest of Zurich and is easily reached by rail. Either Lausanne or Geneva (see below) can be your base for exploring Lake Geneva, which the Swiss call Lac Léman.

Many rail passengers even use Lausanne as a base for a day trip to Geneva, as trains connect these two lakeside cities every 20 minutes (trip time: 50 min.). If you're in France and want to visit Switzerland next door, you can also take one of four trains per day (trip time between Paris and Lausanne is 4 hr.).

This university city has been inhabited since the Stone Age, and was the ancient Roman town of *Lousanna*. In 1803, it became the 19th canton to join the Confederation, and is today the capital of the canton of Vaud.

Ouchy, once a sleepy fishing hamlet, is now the port and hotel resort area of Lausanne. The lakefront of Lausanne consists of shady quays and tropical plants spread across a lakefront district of about half a mile (.8km). The **Château d'Ouchy** stands on place de la Navigation; from here, place du Port adjoins immediately on the east. **Quai de Belgique** and **quai d'Ouchy** are lakefront promenades bursting with greenery and offering the best views of the lake.

Haute Ville or the Upper Town is the most ancient part of Lausanne and is best explored on foot (see box, below). The upper and lower towns are connected by a small metro or subway.

STATION INFORMATION
GETTING FROM THE AIRPORT TO THE TRAIN STATION
Lausanne doesn't have an airport, so most visitors fly to Geneva–Cointrin Airport in Geneva (see later in this chapter) and then travel on to Lausanne. The train from Geneva leaves for Lausanne every 20 minutes and the trip takes 45 minutes. Call ✆ **0900/300-300** for **train** schedules.

In addition, between late May and late September a lake steamer cruises several times a day in both directions between Geneva and Saint-Gingolph, Lausanne, Vevey, Montreux, and Nyon. Sailing time from Geneva is about 3½ hours. Round-trip transit from Geneva costs 72F ($39.60) in first class, 52F ($28.60) in second class, with 50% discounts for children 16 and under. For information, contact the **Compagnie Générale de Navigation (CGN),** 17 av. de Rhodanie (✆ **0848-811-848**).

Lausanne's railway station is a steep, 20-minute uphill climb from the ferryboat terminal and recommended only for the enthusiastic and the very fit. More appealing is a 7-minute metro ride, priced at 2.40F ($1.55) per person, between the stations of **Embarcadère** (immediately adjacent to the ferryboat terminal) and **Gare SFF.**

INSIDE THE STATION
Trains arrive at the **Lausanne Train Station,** place de la Gare (✆ **021/157-22-22**), with arrivals from Basel every hour (trip time: 2½ hr.) or from Zurich via Biel at the rate of 3 trains per hour (trip time: 2½ hr.).

The **Lausanne Tourist Office** (✆ **21/614-73-73**; www.lausanne-tourisme. ch) is located in the main hall of the train station and is open daily 9am to 7pm. Off season, Monday to Friday 8am to 5pm and Saturday 8am to noon and 1 to 5pm. The multilingual staff here will make hotel reservations for a 3% commission. They'll also sell you one of two distinctly different passes. The **Lausanne**

Pass (also known as a *carte journalière,* a **Lausanne Daily Ticket,** or a **24-Hour Pass**), priced at 7.20F ($4.20), is good for 24 consecutive hours of free travel on any bus or metro line within the town center. In distinct contrast, the **Lausanne Card,** priced at 15F ($9.75) gives its owner free transportation over any consecutive 2-day period on any bus or metro line within the town center, discounts of between 25% and 30% on museum entrances throughout the city, discounts on some city tours, and occasional discounts at a limited number of specially designated restaurants.

There is also a **currency exchange kiosk** at the station (✆ 021/312-38-24), which charges only a 2F ($1.30) commission or else no commission on traveler's checks. If your credit card allows it, the office also makes cash advances during its daily business hours of 6:30am to 7:30pm. The luggage storage (✆ 021/24-21-62) office is open daily from 6:40am to 7:40pm, and charges 5F to 7F ($3.25–$4.55) for lockers.

GETTING AROUND

To avoid the crawling pace of the city's trams, take the metro, the city's subway system. The trip between the heart of the Haute Ville and Ouchy takes 6 minutes. Departures are every 7½ minutes Monday to Friday from 6:15am to 11:45pm. During off–hours and on weekends and holidays, trains run every 15 minutes. A one-way ride from the town center to Ouchy costs 2.40F ($1.55); a 24-hour ticket sells for 7.20F ($4.70).

The **TL (Lausanne Public Transport Company)** has a well-designed network of trams and buses whose routes complement the city's subway line. The tram or bus fare is 2.40F ($1.55), regardless of the distance, for a single trip completed within 60 minutes on lines 1 to 50 of the TL urban network on the Lausanne-Ouchy metro.

You can purchase or stamp your tickets at the automatic machines installed at most stops, or just ask the driver. (A surcharge is collected if you get your ticket from the driver at a stop that has a machine.) A 1-day ticket for unlimited rides costs 7F ($4.55) for adults, 3.75F ($2.45) for children.

Lausanne has dozens of taxi stands, where you'll usually find a long line of people waiting for a cab. Alternatively, you can telephone **Taxibus** (✆ 0800/800-312) or **Taxiphone** (✆ 0800/80-18-02) for a cab. The meter starts at 7.50F ($4.90); each kilometer (.6 miles) traveled adds 3F ($1.95) during daylight hours in town, or 3.50F ($2.30) in town on weekends or at night between 8pm and 6am. For trips outside the town limits, each kilometer traveled costs 4F ($2.60), regardless of the time of day. The first 22 pounds of luggage is free, with 1F (65¢) charged for every suitcase thereafter.

You can rent bikes at the baggage-forwarding counter of the **railroad station** (✆ 0900-300-300). It's open daily from 6:50am to 7:50pm. The cost is 17F ($11) per day. You can easily bike around the lower town—the part that borders the lake is relatively flat—but it isn't recommended in the upper town where the streets are very steep.

WHERE TO STAY

Hotel Agora ✦   For rail travelers, this government-rated four-star hotel is the most convenient base in town as it's only 300 yards from the Lausanne train depot. Opened in 1987, the six-story structure brings a startlingly modern look to old Lausanne; its architecture of sculpted marble has been compared by locals to the facade of a spaceship. The small to midsize bedrooms are set behind soundproof windows and offer comfortable furnishings and modern plumbing.

9 av. du Rond-Point, CH-1006 Lausanne. © **021/617-12-11**. Fax 021/616-26-05. www.fhotels.ch. 82 units. 207F–257F ($135–$167) double; 262F ($170) junior suite. AE, DC, MC, V. Bus: 1, 3, or 5. **Amenities:** Restaurant; laundry; nonsmoking rooms. *In room:* Hair dryer.

Hotel Aulac *(Value*   This hotel lies along the Ouchy lakefront in a mellow old baroque styled mansion with a three-story Renaissance-influenced porch. It dates from the turn of the 20th century as evoked by its mansard roof with tiles and its towering Victorian clock tower. Last renovated in the 1990s, the bedrooms are among the least expensive along the waterfront, although hardly the best. They never rise to more than those found in a low-rent motel, but maintenance is high and the furnishings comfortable.

4 place de la Navigation, CH-1000 Lausanne-Ouchy. © **021/613-15-00**. Fax 021/613-15-15. www.aulac.ch. 84 units. 200F–260F ($130–$169) double. Rates include continental breakfast. AE, DC, MC, V. Metro: Ouchy. **Amenities:** Restaurant; laundry.

Hotel Continental   Across from the Lausanne train station, the Continental competes with the Agora (see above) for the most convenient hotel for passengers arriving by train. Because it's cheaper, the Agora is often fully booked, so the larger Continental is a viable alternative, as it, too, is a contemporary first-class hotel. The accommodations here range from midsize to large, and are well maintained and comfortably furnished with modern pieces, soundproof windows, and a tiled bathroom.

2 place de la Gare, CH-1001 Lausanne. © **021/321-88-00**. Fax 021/321-88-01. www.hotelcontinental.ch. 1,230 units. 289F ($188) double; 306F ($199) junior suite. AE, DC, MC. Rates include buffet breakfast. **Amenities:** 2 restaurants; bar; laundry; nonsmoking rooms. *In room:* Hair dryer.

Hotel Elite *Q*   Though located in the center of Lausanne and a short uphill walk from the train station, this white-painted, five-story hotel has a tranquil atmosphere and a small garden with fruit trees. Originally built as a villa in the late 1890s, it was turned into a hotel in 1938 and has been successfully run by the same family ever since. The midsize bedrooms, some with air-conditioning and one with a kitchenette, are clean and neatly furnished. Bathrooms have either a shower, a bath, or both. All bedrooms are nonsmoking. The best rooms are those on the fourth floor, as they open onto views of the lake.

1 av. Sainte-Luce, CH-1003 Lausanne. © **021/320-23-61**. Fax 021/320-39-63. www.elite-lausanne.ch. 33 units. 170F–255F ($111–$166) double. Rates include buffet breakfast. AE, DC, MC, V. Bus: 1, 3, or 5. **Amenities:** Breakfast lounge; laundry; nonsmoking rooms. *In room:* Hair dryer.

Minotel AlaGare   Taking its name from the nearby train station *(gare)*, this government-rated three-star hotel offers affordable and convenient, if basic, accommodations for rail travelers. It's especially inviting in summer when its window boxes burst into bloom with geraniums. The paneled public rooms lead to a series of small but clean and comfortable bedrooms, each with modern plumbing.

14 rue du Simplon, CH-1006 Lausanne. © **021/617-92-52**. Fax 021/617-92-55. www.alagare.com. 45 units. 160F–250F ($104–$163) double. Rates include buffet breakfast. AE, DC, MC, V. Closed Dec 29–Jan 5. Bus: 1, 3, or 5. **Amenities:** Restaurant.

TOP ATTRACTIONS & SPECIAL MOMENTS

Château de Beaulieu et Musée de l'Art Brut *Q*   If you find the bizarre art in this gallery "disturbing," know that it was painted by disturbed individuals. Located on the northwestern side of town, this chateau dates from 1756 and was once occupied by Madame de Staël. The museum displays what the artist Jean Dubuffet called *art brut* in the 1940s. This curious mélange of artwork was

Moments **A Walk Through the Middle Ages**

Lausanne's Upper Town or **Haute Ville** ★★ still evokes the Middle Ages—a night watchman even calls out the hours from 10pm to 2am from atop the cathedral's belfry. Walking through the old town of Lausanne is one of its major attractions and the best way to absorb the Medieval atmosphere. It's easy to get lost—and that's part of the fun. If you don't want to be so carefree, you can also take an organized walking tour (see below). This area is north of the railroad station; you can reach it by strolling along rue du Petit-Chêne.

The focal point of the Upper Town, and the shopping and business heart of Lausanne, is **place Saint-François.** The Church of St. François, from the 13th century, is all that remains of an old Franciscan friary. Today the square is regrettably filled with office blocks and the main post office. While vehicles are permitted south of the church, the area to the north is a pedestrian-only zone; it has more than 1¼ miles (2km) of streets, including **rue de Bourg,** northeast of the church, the best street for shopping. Rue de Bourg leads to the large, bustling rue Caroline, which winds north to **Pont des Bessières,** one of the three bridges erected at the turn of the century to connect the three hills on which Lausanne was built. From the bridge, you'll see the Haute Ville on your right, with the 13th-century **Cathedral of Lausanne,** opening onto place de la Cathédrale. From the square, rue du Cité-de-Vant goes north to the 14th-century **Château Saint-Marie,** on place du Château—once the home of bishops and now housing the offices of the canton administration.

From here, avenue de l'Université leads to **place de la Riponne,** with the **Palais de Rumine** on its east side. From place de la Riponne, rue Pierre-Viret leads to the **Escaliers du Marché,** a covered stairway dating back to the Middle Ages. You can also take rue Madeleine from the place de la Riponne, continuing south to place de la Palud. On the side of place de la Palud stands the 17th-century **Hôtel de Ville** (town hall).

South of place de la Palud is rue du Pont, which turns into rue Saint-François (after crossing rue Centrale). Nearby, at **place du Flon,** you can catch the subway to Ouchy. In recent years place du Flon, with its cafes and bars, has become a favorite evening hangout.

Lausanne's civic authorities conduct a **guided walking tour** of their city, lasting 1 to 2 hours, Monday through Saturday. Departure is from place de la Palud, adjacent to the city hall, at 10am and 3pm. The cost is 10F ($6.50) for adults, 5F ($3.25) for seniors and students. Children are free. For data, call the city's tourist office (see above).

collected by the painter from prisoners, the mentally ill, and the criminally insane. It's a bizarre *Twilight Zone* of art, often dubbed "psychopathological," especially the art by schizophrenics. Dubuffet despised the pretentiousness of the avant-garde art scene around him, and as a form of protest decided to begin this collection of the works of "non-artists," many of whom he found superior to the more established artists of his day.

11 av. des Bergières. ✆ **021/647-54-35**. www.artbrut.ch Admission 6F ($3.90) adults, 4F ($2.60) seniors, students, and children. Tues–Fri 11am–noon and 2–6pm; Sat–Sun 11am–6pm. Bus: 2 to Beaulieu.

Lausanne Cathédrale ★★★   The focal point of the Upper Town is one of the finest medieval churches in Switzerland—in fact, one of the most beautiful Gothic structures in Europe, standing 500 feet above Lake Geneva. Construction began in 1175; in 1275, the church was consecrated by Pope Gregory X. The doors and facade of the cathedral are luxuriously ornamented with sculptures and bas-reliefs. The architect, Eugène Viollet-le-Duc, began a restoration of the cathedral in the 19th century—and it's still going on. The interior is relatively austere except for some 13th-century choir stalls; the rose window also dates from the 13th century. The cathedral has two towers; you can climb the 225 steps to the observation deck of one of the towers.

Place de la Cathédrale. ✆ **021/316-71-61**. Admission cathedral, free; tower, 2F ($1.30). Apr–Sept Mon–Fri 8am–6:30pm, Sat 8:30am–6pm, Sun 2–7pm; Oct–Mar Mon–Fri 7:30am–6pm, Sat 8:30am–5pm, Sun 2–5:30pm. Visits not permitted Sun morning during services. Bus: 7 or 16.

WHERE TO DINE

Buffet de la Gare CFF SWISS/FRENCH   Surprising as it may seem, one of the town's best inexpensive restaurants is inside the Lausanne railway station itself, and frugal city dwellers often come here for a good brasserie dinner. This is not a rail station fast-food joint, but an informal restaurant offering well-prepared dishes cooked to order and made from market-fresh ingredients. There is both a brasserie section for more casual dining (it's more fun), as well as a more formal restaurant area (more sedate), although the prices and the kitchens are the same.

In the train station, 11 place de la Gare. ✆ **021/311-49-00**. Reservations recommended in the restaurant only. Main courses 25F–59F ($16–$38); fixed–price menu 28F ($18). MC, V. Restaurant, daily 7am–midnight. Brasserie, daily 11am–midnight. Bus: 1, 3, or 5.

Café Beau-Rivage ★ SWISS   Reached through the exquisitely maintained gardens of the plush hotel, the Beau-Rivage Palace, this inviting restaurant is sheltered in a lakeside pavilion, its dining room evoking a Parisian cafe with a flower-filled summer terrace. In addition to its elegant dinner service, the cafe serves coffee, tea, pastries, and a light menu from Monday to Friday 11am to 1am and on Saturday and Sunday 9am to 1am. After 7:30pm, it also becomes a piano bar. If you come here for food, expect a light and tasty cuisine prepared with the freshest of ingredients, followed by luscious desserts wheeled around on a trolley.

In the Beau-Rivage Palace, 18 place du Général-Guisan, Ouchy. ✆ **021/613-33-33**. Reservations recommended. Main courses 35F–50F ($23–$33); fixed–price dinner 70F ($46). AE, DC, MC, V. Daily 11:30am–1am. Metro: Ouchy.

Le Jardin d'Asie ★ PAN-ASIAN   This is the best pan-Asian restaurant in the city, drawing heavily from the culinary influences of both Japan and China, but also including some zesty Malaysian specialties for greater variety. The atmosphere appropriately evokes a garden setting and the widely spaced tables allow for private conversations. Servers stylishly present sushi, sashimi, and many specialties such as chicken in peanut sauce to a satisfied clientele. There are also uniformed *teppanyaki* chefs standing by, knives at the ready, to prepare your dinner in front of you.

7 av. du Théâtre. ✆ **021/323-74-84**. Reservations recommended. Main courses 22F–30F ($14–$20); fixed-price Chinese menu 45F ($29); fixed-price Japanese menu 45F ($29). AE, DC, MC, V. Mon–Sat 11:45am–2pm and 7–10pm. Bus: 7 or 16.

Pinte Besson ★ *Finds* VAUD/SWISS   This intimate restaurant, whose interior masonry dates back to 1780, is a closely guarded secret among locals, who don't want it to become too known or too overrun with visitors. Its chefs concentrate on seasonal dishes, and offer some of the best local specialties in town, including cheese fondues and dried Alpine beef. For your big steak dinner, you can request that the meat come from either a horse or a cow.

4 rue de l'Ale. ⓒ 021/312-72-27. Main courses 20F–37F ($13–$24). MC, V. Mon–Fri noon–2pm and 6pm–midnight; Sat–Sun noon–2pm. Closed Aug. Bus: 1 or 9.

SHOPPING

Shoppers in Lausanne tend to be much more concerned with the commercialized glamour of Paris than with kitschy mountain souvenirs. That being the case, you'll find lots of emphasis on high-profile outfits such as luggage and leather maker **Louis Vuitton,** 30 rue de Bourg (ⓒ **021/312-76-60**), or haute jeweler **Cartier,** 6 rue de Bourg (ⓒ **021/320-55-44**).

But if handmade souvenirs from the region appeal to you, head for **Heidi's Shop,** 22 rue du Petit-Chêne (ⓒ **021/311-16-89**). For artifacts with deeper patinas that sell for a lot more money, check out the art and antiques at two intriguing, relentlessly upscale antiques shops: **Antiquités R.S.,** 17 av. de la Gare (ⓒ **079/210-45-61**), and the **Galerie du Château,** 2 place du Tunnel (ⓒ **021/ 647-2142**), both of which specialize in 18th- and 19th-century furniture. A worthy competitor, with a greater emphasis on paintings and sculpture, is the **Galerie de la Belle Fontaine,** 9–13 rue Cheneau-de-Bourg (ⓒ **021/323-47-87**).

The biggest jeweler in Lausanne, with a well-established international recommendation, is **Bucherer,** 5 place St-François (ⓒ **021/320-63-54**). Competitors, especially for Swiss watches, include **Roman Mayer,** 12 place St-François (ⓒ **021/312-23-16**), which has especially good buys in Omega watches, and **Junod,** 8 place St-François (ⓒ **021/312-27-45**), carrying Blancpain watches among others.

NIGHTLIFE

A good way to spend an evening in Lausanne is by hanging out in any of the cafes and bars ringing the **Espace Flon,** a cluster of restaurants and shops at place Flon. Lots of hideaways, frequented by strollers of all ages, will be here to tempt you, but one of the most appealing is **Le Grand Café,** esplanade de Mont-Benon (ⓒ **021/320-40-30**). Here, in an American-inspired space that contains some of the glitz and razzle-dazzle of a celebrity haunt, you can meet a cross section of virtually every night owl in town.

Attractive and popular discos include **Le Mad,** route de Genève (ⓒ **021/340-69-69**), where the fads and preoccupations of nocturnal Paris filter quickly in from the west via an under-30 crowd. **Ouchy White Horse Pub,** 66 av. d'Ouchy (ⓒ **021/616-75-75**), draws the crowds at night who in summer enjoy the terrace with views of the water. There's beer on tap, and a range of tapas and burgers are sold. It's the most authentic pub atmosphere in town.

Lausanne is also a city of culture. With Geneva it shares the Orchestre de la Suisse Romande and also occasionally hosts the legendary ballet company of Maurice Béjart. For information on what's happening during the time your visit, contact the local tourist office (see above). Most performances of major cultural impact take place at the **Théâtre-Municipal Lausanne,** avenue du Theatre (ⓒ **021/310-16-00**). **Beaulieu,** at 10 av. des Bergières (ⓒ **021/643-21-11; www.beaulieu.org**), is also a venue for dance concerts, operas, and orchestral music presentations. Tickets can be purchased at **Billetel** (ⓒ **021/625-35-85**), which has various locations over Lausanne. For more information contact the Théâtre-Municipal Lausanne.

5 Geneva ★★★

Switzerland's second largest city, French-speaking Geneva is situated at the lower end of Lake Geneva aka Lac Léman. Located on the Rhône at the extreme western tip of Switzerland, but right in the heart of Europe, Geneva lies at the crossroads of the continent. Often deemed the "most international of cities" because of all the international organizations (such as the Red Cross) that have their headquarters in the city, Geneva is linked to the outside world by a vast network of airlines and railways, and is an ultra-convenient stop on any rail passenger's itinerary.

In addition to enjoying good rail connections to all of Switzerland, Geneva receives four trains per day from Vienna (trip time: 10–12 hr.), and eight trains per day from Milan (trip time: 4 hr.). The city is also the terminal point for the Paris–Geneva train, 10 of which arrive daily in the city after a journey of only 3¾ hours. Geneva also rivals Lausanne (see above) as the best base for exploring Lake Geneva.

A lively, cosmopolitan atmosphere prevails in Geneva, a city of parks and promenades. In summer it becomes a virtual garden. It's also one of the healthiest cities in the world—the north wind blows away any pollution. The situation, in a word, is magnificent, not only lying on one of the biggest Alpine lakes, but within view of the pinnacle of Mont Blanc.

Geneva is virtually surrounded by French territory. It's connected to Switzerland only by the lake and a narrow corridor. For that and other reasons—the city was actually unwillingly annexed by France in 1798 before being set free during Napoleon's collapse in 1814—Geneva is definitely a Swiss city, but with a decided French accent.

STATION INFORMATION
GETTING FROM THE AIRPORT TO THE TRAIN STATION

The **Geneva-Cointrin Airport** (✆ 022/717-71-11), although busy, is quite compact and easily negotiated. The national airline, **Swiss** (✆ 877/359-7947) serves Geneva more frequently than any other airline. Other international airlines that partner with North American–based airlines and fly into Geneva include **Air France** (✆ 022/827-87-87), with seven flights daily from Paris, and **British Airways** (✆ 022/710-61-00), with seven daily flights from London. **Crossair** (✆ 0848/852-000) offers connection to several European capitals.

You can easily get to the center of Geneva from the airport by rail. Trains leave from the airport terminal about every 8 to 20 minutes from 5:39am to 11:36pm for the 15-minute trip to **Gare Cornavin,** the main train station. The one-way fare is 8.60F ($5.60) in first class and 5.20F ($3.40) in second class. Railpasses cover this line, though you may not want to waste a day on a Flexipass for such a short and inexpensive trip.

A taxi into town will cost 42F ($27) and up, or you can take bus no. 10 for 12F ($7.80).

Note: From late May to late September there are frequent daily arrivals in Geneva by Swiss lake steamer from Montreux, Vevey, and Lausanne (you can use your Eurailpass for the trip). If you're staying in the Left Bank (Old Town), get off at the Jardin Anglais stop in Geneva; Mont Blanc and Pâquis are the two Right Bank stops. For more information, call ✆ 022/312-52-23. To get to the Jardin Anglais stop from the railway station, take bus no. 8, getting off (both stops are appropriate) at either the quai du Mont-Blanc stop or the Metropole stop. If you prefer to go on foot, the walk from the railway station to the quays will take only 5 to 10 minutes.

Geneva

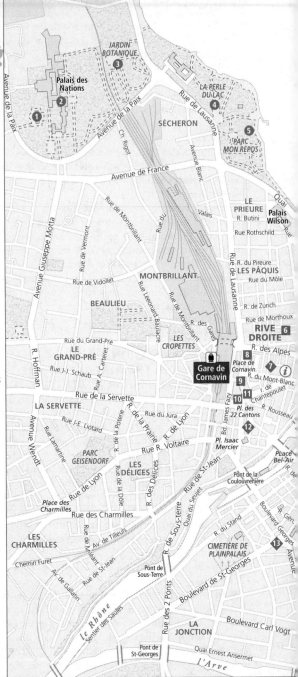

ⓘ Information

🚉 Rail Station

—— Railway

Lac Léman

FRONTENEX

Quai Cologny

Rampe de Cologny

Route de Vandoeuvres

PARC DES
EAUX-VIVES

Plateau de Frontenex

PARC
LA GRANGE

Avenue W. Favre

Chemin Frank Thomas

Av. Rosemont

MONTCHOISY

Rade de
Genève

27
Jet d'Eau

Rue des Vollandes

Rue des Eaux-Vives

rue du 31 Décembre

R. de la Mairie

Route de Frontenex

Gare des
Eaux-Vives

Route de Chêne

Ch. de la Petite Boissière

26

Rue Plantamour

Quai du Mont-Blanc

Woodrow Wilson

Jacquet

25

Pont du-
Mont-Blanc

JARDIN
ANGLAIS

22 **23**

Pont des
Bergues

24

ILE
ROUSSEAU

Quai Général Guisan

RIVE
GAUCHE

rd.-pt
de Rive

Av. Pictet De Rochemont

Rue Agasse

Promenade Martin

Av. de l'Amandolier

Rue du Rhône

21

R. De Rive

Rue de la Terassière

R Lachenal

Route de Malagnou

Chemin Rieu

RUES BASSES

les Rues Basses **19**

20

VIELLE VILLE
(OLD TOWN)

18 **15**

Grand Rue

17 **16**

R. de l'Hôtel de Ville

Hôtel de
Ville

R. de la Croix Rouge

R. la Fontaine

Rue Hodler

Pl. Em.
Guyenot

Ch. Galland

Bd. des Tranchées

FLORISSANT

la Corraterie

Place
Neuve

Dufour

Promenade
des Bastions

Université

R. de Candolle

Rue St. Léger

Bd. Jacques Dalcroze

Boulevard Helvétique

Rue de l'Athénée

Cours ses Bastions

Place Ed.
Claparède

14

Route de Florissant

PARC
A. BERTRAND

Avenue Bertrand

Favon

PLAINE DE
PLAINPALAIS

Rd-pt. de
Plainpalais

Philosophes

Rue A. Lombard

Avenue de l'Athénée

Avenue Peschier

CHAMPEL

Avenue de Miremont

Avenue Louis Aubert

Mail

Henri Dunant

Boulevard du Pont d'Arve

R. Prévost-Martin

R. de Carouge

Bd. de la Cluse

LA CLUSE

Avenue de Champel

Av. Calas

0   1/5 mile
0   200 meters

INSIDE THE STATION

Geneva's **CFF (Chemins de Fer Fédéraux)** train station in the town center is **Gare Cornavin,** place Cornavin (© **0900/300-300** for ticket information), which is a major international and local hub.

The city's tourist office maintains a free direct phone line to most Geneva hotels at the station, with a digital board listing accommodations available. For comprehensive service and general information, however, you'll need to head for the main tourist office (see below).

In the center of the station is a **Reservations and Information Counter** (© **022/157-22-22**), open Monday to Friday 8:30am to 6:30pm, Saturday 8:30am to 6:30pm. You can buy tickets, make seat reservations, and have rail-passes validated here.

Also on-site is a luggage storage kiosk open Monday to Friday 7am to 7:40pm, Saturday and Sunday 8am to 12:30pm and 1:30 to 6:45pm, which charges 6F ($3.90) per day. The locker area charges from 4F to 7F ($2.60–$4.55) and is open daily 4:30am to 12:45am. There are also several ATMs at the station.

Public transportation is readily available right outside the train station.

INFORMATION ELSEWHERE IN THE CITY

A 5-minute walk from the rail station, Geneva's tourist office, the **Office du Tourisme de Genève,** is located at 3 rue du Mont-Blanc (© **022/909-70-00;** www.genevetourisme.ch). The staff provides information about the city, and can also arrange hotel reservations for a 5F ($3.25) fee, both in Geneva and through-out Switzerland, and refer you to other establishments specializing in tour bookings. They can also give you details about audio-guided visits to the city's Old Town. The tourist office is open from June 15 to September 15, Monday to Friday from 9am to 6pm and Saturday and Sunday from 8am to 5pm; the rest of the year, Monday to Saturday from 10am to 6pm.

GETTING AROUND

Walking is the cheapest and most practical form of transportation within Geneva, and it's also the most advantageous method for the rail traveler to view this beautiful city. That said, there will be times you'll need to get someplace a little more quickly than a leisurely stroll will allow, and the city has a couple of transportation methods to choose from.

BY PUBLIC TRANSPORTATION   Most of Geneva's public tram and bus lines begin at the central place Cornavin in front of the main railroad station. From here, you can take bus F or 8 to the Palais des Nations. Local buses and trams operate daily from 5am to midnight, and you can purchase a ticket from a vending machine before you board; instructions are given in English. **Transport Publics Genevois** (© **022/308-34-34**), next to the tourist office in Gare Cornavin, offers free maps of local bus routings. Trips that stay within zone 10, enveloping most of Geneva, cost 2.20F ($1.45), with unlimited use of all zones costing 12F ($7.80) for 1 day. The latter is particularly useful as most of the city's noteworthy attractions are in the suburbs.

BY TAXI   The meter on whatever cab you take in Geneva will automatically begin calculating your fare at 6.30F ($4.10), and then add between 2.70F ($1.75) and 3.30F ($2.15) for every kilometer (.6 miles) you travel, depending on the time of day or night. No tipping is required. To call for a **taxi,** call © **022/331-41-33** or 022/320-20-20.

WHERE TO STAY

Best Western Strasbourg & Univers ⚘   A 2-minute walk from Gare Cornavin, this is one of Geneva's best moderately priced hotels. The building itself dates from 1900 but has been renovated and modernized over the years (last in 2000). Bedrooms range from large (on the lower floors) to a bit cramped. Rooms are comfortably furnished with a lot of wood pieces, and have decent tiled bathrooms. The hotel is run by a local family and doesn't have the feel of a chain hotel despite its affiliation with Best Western.

10 rue J–J–Pradier, CH-1201 Genève. ℂ **800/528-1234** in the U.S. or 022/906-58-00. Fax 022/738-42-08. www.strasbourg-geneva.ch. 51 units. 250F ($163) double; 400F–500F ($260–$325) suite. Rates include continental breakfast. AE, DC, MC, V. Bus: 1, 2, 3, 4, 8, 12, 13, or 44. **Amenities:** Breakfast lounge. *In room:* Hair dryer.

Hotel Bernina   Rail passengers often check in here because of the convenience of its location across from Gare Cornavin and its reasonable prices (considered inexpensive in this costly town). Although guests get clean, comfortably furnished bedrooms under high ceilings, they don't enjoy a lot of style as the place is rather sterile, especially its lobby, which evokes a dull airport waiting room. The soundproof windows, however, are welcome in this heavily congested part of Geneva.

22 place de Cornavin, CH-1211 Genève. ℂ **022/908-49-50.** Fax 022/908-49-50. www.bernina-geneve.ch. 80 units. 150F–180F ($98–$117) double. Rates include breakfast. AE, DC, MC, V. Bus: 10.

Hotel Edelweiss   This hotel enjoys a scenic location near quai du President Wilson, one of the most scenic quays of Geneva, and is about a half mile (.8km) from Gare Cornavin. Built in the 1960s, it was upgraded and renovated in the '90s and is a winning choice for its blend of rustic Alpine decor, modern exterior, and completely up-to-date amenities. Most of the bedrooms are small and rather functionally furnished, but they are well kept and comfortable. The friendly staff greets guests in traditional costumes.

2 place de la Navigation, CH-1201 Genève. ℂ **022/544-51-51.** Fax 022/544-51-99. www.manotel.com. 42 units. 315F ($205) double. Rates include buffet breakfast. AE, DC, MC, V. Bus: 1. **Amenities:** Restaurant; bar; laundry. *In room:* Hair dryer.

Hotel International & Terminus   This hotel, originally built in 1900, is a winning choice for rail travelers as it's just across the street from the main entrance to Gare Cornavin. The property completed a much needed and massive overhaul in 2001, doing away with some of its really small units and turning them into more spacious accommodations, while adding double-glazing to the windows. Maintenance is high, and the furnishings are comfortable and modern, although the bathrooms are rather cramped. The hotel's La Veranda restaurant is frequently patronized by rail travelers tired of the train depot's fast-food outlets.

20 rue des Alpes, CH-1201 Genève. ℂ **022/732-80-95.** Fax 022/906-97-78. www.international-terminus.ch. 60 units. 190F–280F ($124–$182) double. Rates include continental breakfast. AE, DC, MC, V. Bus: 6, 10, or 33. **Amenities:** Restaurant.

Hotel Lido   Only 2 blocks from Gare Cornavin, this hotel dates from 1963 and has never overcome the architectural dullness of that era, despite a slew of renovations in the 1990s. Nonetheless, the hotel is convenient for train travelers and charges reasonable rates for its government-rated two-star bedrooms. Furnishings are functional—not stylish—but there is comfort and cleanliness here, along with full bathrooms. Expect very few amenities, however, especially in the rooms.

8 rue Chantepoulet, CH-1201, Genève. ⓒ **022/731-55-30.** Fax 022/731-65-01. www.hotel-lido.ch. 31 units. 180F ($117) double. Rates include continental breakfast. AE, DC, MC, V. Bus: 10. **Amenities:** Breakfast room; laundry.

Hotel Moderne   One of many acceptable choices near Gare Cornavin, this seven-story hotel is within easy walk of the quays. Last renovated in 1999, the hotel's public areas are Nordic-style and modern. Behind soundproof windows, the midsize bedrooms are sunny and furnished in a standard but comfortable manner, and the small bathrooms are spotless and have either shower or bath. Breakfast is served in a glassed-in extension.

1 rue de Berne, CH-1211 Genève. ⓒ **022/732-81-00.** Fax 022/738-26-58. www.hotelmoderne.ch. 55 units. 160F–200F ($104–$130) double. Rates include buffet breakfast. AE, DC, MC, V. Bus: 10. **Amenities:** Laundry; nonsmoking rooms.

TOP ATTRACTIONS & SPECIAL MOMENTS

If you arrive in Geneva in summer, begin your tour of the city by heading east from the rail station along rue du Mont-Blanc until you arrive at quai du Mont Blanc and begin a long promenade along the **Quays of Geneva** ★★★. The one sight you can't miss—even if you tried—is the **Jet d'Eau** ★★, the famous fountain that is the trademark of the city and is located on a concrete platform in the middle of the lake. Visible for miles around from April to September, it throws water 460 feet into the air above the lake. The *bise* (wind) blows the spume into a feathery, fluttery fan, often wetting those below who stand too close. The Genevese call the fountain the *jeddo.* It dates from 1891, but was much improved in 1951. Many cities have sent engineers to Geneva to discover the workings of the fountain, but it remains a carefully guarded state secret. It pumps 109 gallons of lake water at 125 mph (200kmph).

The quays, with their luxuriantly planted flower gardens, are dotted with ancient buildings. The aquatic population consists of seagulls, ducks, and swans. A fleet of small boats, called *Mouettes genevoises,* shuttles visitors from one quay to another from mid-March to mid-October. For rides that last 30 minutes or less, the cost is 1.80F ($1.15) adults, and 1.50F ($1) children; rides lasting 30 to 60 minutes cost 2.20F ($1.45) adults and 1.80F ($1.15) children.

Like the water jet, the **Flower Clock** in the **Jardin Anglais (English Garden)** is another Geneva trademark. Its face is made of flowers, and it keeps perfect time (but what else in this world-famed center of watchmaking?). The Jardin Anglais is at the foot of the Mont Blanc Bridge, which spans the river at the point where the Rhône leaves Lake Geneva. It was rebuilt in 1969. To get here from the Jet d'Eau stroll south on quai Gustave-Ador and then bear right.

After leaving the garden, cross the Mont Blanc bridge and turn left onto the quai des Bergues and stroll as far as the bridge, Pont des Bergues. If you cross this bridge, you'll come to **Ile Rousseau,** with a statue of Geneva's most famous son done by Pradier in 1834. This island, the former stamping ground of the philosopher, is home to any number of ducks, swans, and other aquatic fowl such as grebes. In the middle of the Rhône, it was once a bulwark of Geneva's river defenses.

You can continue crossing the bridge and can then turn right on the Bezanson Hugues quay until you reach rue de Moulins and the **Tour-de-l'Ile,** farther downstream. Built in 1219, a château that once stood here was used as a prison by the Counts of Savoy. A wall plaque commemorates the visit of Caesar in 58 B.C. The tower is all that remains of the 13th-century castle. It was here that freedom fighter Philibert Berthelier was decapitated in 1519. Nowadays, the Geneva

Tourist Office is located on the island. You can also explore the old markets, where there are often exhibitions of the works of contemporary Genevese artists.

If you walk east along the quai des Bergues, you'll return to the Pont du Mont-Blanc. To your left, when facing the lake, is the **Brunswick Monument,** the tomb of Charles II of Brunswick who died in Geneva in 1873. The duke left his fortune to the city provided it built a monument to him. Geneva accepted the fortune and modeled the tomb after the Scalieri tombs in Verona, Italy.

VIEILLE VILLE ✮✮✮

"Old Town" in Geneva is one of the most remarkable in Switzerland and has been called "Europe's best kept secret." It's situated on the city's Left Bank, where the cultural life of Geneva flourishes. Its ancient streets are home to art galleries, antiques shops, booksellers, and tiny bistros. Follow the Grand Rue, about ¾-mile from Gare Cornavin, where Jean-Jacques Rousseau was born, and wander back into time.

The old quarter is dominated by the **Cathedral of St. Pierre** ✮, Cour St–Pierre (© **022/311-75-75**), originally built between the 10th and 13th centuries and partially reconstructed in the 15th century. The church looks out over Geneva from its hilltop perch. It became protestant in 1536. The interior is austere, just the way Calvin preferred it (his seat is on the north side). The church has seen much recent renovation, and it has a modern organ with 6,000 pipes. If you don't mind 145 steps, you can climb to the north tower for a splendid vista of the city, its lake, the Alps, and the Jura mountains.

Recent excavations have disclosed that a Christian sanctuary was here as early as A.D. 400. To enter the St. Pierre archaeological site, called **Site Archéologique de St-Pierre,** go through the entrance in Cour St-Pierre, at the right-hand corner of the cathedral steps. The underground passageway extends under the present cathedral and the High Gothic (early-15th-c.) **Chapelle des Macchabées,** which adjoins the southwestern corner of the church. The chapel was restored during World War II, after having been used as a storage room following the Reformation. Excavations of the chapel have revealed baptisteries, a crypt, the foundations of several cathedrals, the bishop's palace, 4th-century mosaics, sculptures, and geological strata.

The cathedral and the chapel are open June to September daily from 9am to 7pm; March to May and in October daily from 9am to noon and 2 to 6pm; in January, February, November, and December daily from 9am to noon and 2 to 3pm. There is no admission charge to visit the cathedral, although donations are welcome; tower admission is 3F ($1.95). Sunday service is held in the cathedral

---

Moments A Lakeside City of Parks & Gardens

If you walk heading north along rue de Lausanne from Gare Cornavin, you'll arrive at some of the lushest parks in Geneva. **Parc Mon-Repos** ✮✮ is off avenue de France and **La Perle du Lac** is off rue de Lausanne. Directly to the right is the **Jardin Botanique (Botanical Garden),** which was established in 1902. It has an Alpine garden, a little zoo, greenhouses, and exhibitions, and can be visited free from May to September, daily from 8am to 7:30pm; and October to April, daily from 9:30am to 5pm.

If you leave the **Jardin Botanique** on the Left Bank, you can head west, along avenue de la Paix, to the Palais des Nations in the **Parc de l'Ariana.** It's located about a mile (about 1.6km) north of Gare Cornavin.

at 10am, and an hour of organ music is presented on Saturdays at 6pm from June to September. The archaeological site is open Tuesday to Saturday from 11am to 1pm and 2 to 5pm; the admission charge is 5F ($3.25) adults, 3F ($1.95) students and seniors. Take bus no. 3, 5, or 17, or tram no. 12.

Next door to the cathedral is a Gothic church where Calvin preached, known as the **Temple de l'Auditoire,** or Calvin Auditorium. It was restored in 1959 in time for Calvin's 450th anniversary.

After leaving the cathedral, strike out across the Cour St-Pierre, turning left onto the rue St-Pierre, where at no. 4 you'll encounter **Maison Tavel,** 6 rue du Puits-St-Pierre (℃ 022/418-37-00), the oldest house in Geneva. First built in 1303, according to dim records, it was apparently rebuilt in 1334. It's decorated with amusing carved heads and a fine turret, and has a 12th-century cellar, which predates the original building. It's open Tuesday to Sunday 10am to 5pm; admission is free.

Hôtel de Ville (city hall), a short walk from the cathedral, dates from the 16th and 17th centuries. It has a cobbled ramp instead of a staircase. The **Salle d'Alabama** is the salon where arbitration between America and England in 1872 was peacefully resolved. Its Baudet Tower was constructed in 1455. Incidentally, the Red Cross originated here in 1864.

Across from the city hall is the **Arsenal,** an arcaded structure dating from 1634. In the courtyard of the building is a cannon cast in 1683.

OTHER ATTRACTIONS

Musée d'Art et Histoire (Museum of Art & History) ★★   This is the city's
most important museum—if you can only visit one museum while in Geneva, make it this one. The collections offer a little bit of everything, and include prehistoric relics, Egyptian relics, Greek vases, medieval stained glass, 12th-century armory, and many paintings of the Flemish and Italian schools. The Etruscan pottery is impressive, as is the medieval furniture. See the altarpiece by Konrad Witz from 1444, showing the "miraculous" draught of fishes. Swiss timepieces are duly honored, and many galleries contain works by such world-famed artists as Rodin, Renoir, Hodler, Vallotton, Le Corbusier, and Picasso.

2 rue Charles-Galland (between bd. Jacques-Dalcroze and bd. Helvétique). ℃ 022/418-26-00. Free admission; 4.50F ($2.50) temporary exhibitions. Tues–Sun 10am–5pm. Bus: 1, 3, 5, 8, or 17.

Musée de l'Ariana ★★   This is one of the top three museums devoted to
porcelain and pottery in Europe and the headquarters for the international academy of ceramics. Located west of the Palais des Nations, the museum building is in the Italian Renaissance style, and was built in 1877 for P. F. Revilliod, the 19th-century Genevese writer who began the collection. Here you'll see Sèvres at its best, along with the celebrated Delft faïence, Meissen porcelain, and many superb pieces from Japan and China.

10 av. de la Paix. ℃ 022/418-54-50. http://mah.ville-ge.ch. Free admission to permanent collection; temporary exhibitions 5F ($3.25) adults, free for children under 18. Wed–Mon 10am–5pm. Bus: 8 or F.

Palais des Nations ★★   The former home of the defunct League of Nations,
about a mile (1.6km) north of Mont Blanc Bridge, is the present headquarters of the United Nations in Europe. The monumental compound was constructed between 1929 and 1936, and the complex of buildings is the second largest in Europe after Versailles. Tours, conducted in English, last about an hour and depart from the visitors' entrance at 14 av. de la Paix, opposite the Red Cross building. To join the tour you'll need to show your passport. The highlight of the tour is the Assembly Hall, with a balcony made entirely of marble and lofty

> ## ⟨Moments⟩ Sailing the Waters of Lac Léman
>
> More interesting than the monuments of Geneva itself is a sail across
> Lake Geneva (Lac Léman). You'll enjoy sweeping waterside views of
> the surrounding hills, and some of the most famous vineyards in
> Switzerland, many of which seem to roll down to the historic waters.
> Because of bad weather and low visibility in winter, cruises only run
> between April and late October, and, in some cases, only between May
> and September.
>
> **Mouettes Genevoises Navigation,** 8 quai du Mont-Blanc (✆ **022/
> 732-29-44;** www.swissboat.com), specializes in small-scale boats carry-
> ing only 100 passengers at a time. An easy excursion that features the
> landscapes and bird life along the uppermost regions of the river
> Rhône draining into the lake is the company's **Tour du Rhône (Rhône
> River Tour).** The trip originates at a point adjacent to Geneva's Pont de
> l'Ile, and travels downstream for about 9 miles (15km; 2 hr. 45 min.) to
> the Barrage de Verbois (Verbois Dam) and back.
>
> Between April and October, departures are daily at 2:15pm, and also
> on Wednesday, Thursday, Saturday, and Sunday at 10am. The tour
> costs 15F ($9.75) for adults and 10F ($6.50) for children 4 to 12; it's free
> for children under 4. The same company also offers 1¼-hour tours
> (four times a day) and 2-hour tours (twice a day) out onto the lake. The
> longer tour includes a prerecorded commentary on the celebrity resi-
> dences and ecology of the lake en route. These tours cost 12F ($7.80)
> for the shorter tour and 22F ($14) for the longer tour. No stops are
> made en route.

bays looking out over the Court of Honor. A Philatelic Museum displays collections of stamps relating to the League of Nations or the United Nations, and
a League of Nations Museum documents the history of the precursor to the
United Nations.

Parc de l'Ariana, 14 av. de la Paix. ✆ 022/907-48-96. www.unog.ch. Admission 8.50F ($5.55) adults, 6.50F
($4.25) students, 4F ($2.60) for children 5 and under. July–Aug daily 9am–6pm; Sept–June daily 10am–noon
and 2–4pm. Bus: 5, 8, 18, F, V, or Z.

WHERE TO DINE

Brasserie International INTERNATIONAL   Though slightly battered,
this century-old and cozy brasserie in the Old Town is still inviting, with varnished paneling, gilt mirrors, and other remnants of its Belle Epoque days. The
cooking is what the French call honest and straightforward, made with fresh
ingredients from time-tested recipes. Our favorite dish here is the chef's *pot-au-
feu,* a stew of beef and vegetables pressed into a cold terrine and sliced. It's a
short tram ride or a 15-minute walk from the train station.

Rue Bovy–Lysberg 2, place du Cirque. ✆ 022/807-11-99. Reservations recommended. Main courses
22.50F–38F ($15–$25). Set-price menus 38F ($25) AE, DC, MC, V. Mon–Fri noon–2:30pm and 7–10pm;
Sat–Sun 11:30am–10pm. Closed 1st 2 weeks of Aug. Tram: 13.

Brasserie Lipp FRENCH/SWISS   Named after the most famous brasserie on
the Left Bank of Paris, this restaurant serves a similar type of cuisine, specializing in fresh oysters—the best in the city—and large platters of sauerkraut, as

does the original. When you see the waiters in long white aprons and black jackets, you'll think you've been miraculously transported over the border. That impression is reinforced when the actual food is served, including all our favorite classics such as a Toulousian cassoulet and three kinds of pot-au-feu.

In Confédération-Centre, 8 rue de la Confédération. ℭ **022/311-10-11.** Reservations recommended. Main courses 25F–50F ($16–$33); plats du jour 25F ($16) lunch only; fixed-price menus 60F–80F ($39–$52). AE, DC, MC, V. Daily 11:45am–12:15am. Bus: 12.

Café du Centre CONTINENTAL/SWISS Established in 1871, this is still the busiest cafe in Geneva, with an outdoor terrace that's always packed in fair weather. The atmosphere inside evokes a time-blackened brasserie in Old Lyon. The menu (it comes in English) is the largest in town, with nearly 140 different items offered every day. Carnivores will be especially happy with the tender and well-flavored meat platters (the best and most tender cut is called *onglet*).

5 place du Molard. ℭ **022/311-85-86.** Reservations recommended. Main courses 40F–55F ($26–$36); fixed-price assiette du jour 22.50F ($15) at lunch Mon–Fri only. AE, DC, MC, V. Daily 7am–midnight. Tram: 12.

Chez Jacky ⭐⭐ *Finds* VALAIS/SWISS Jacky Gruber is a marvelous chef from the Valais region of Switzerland who should be better known, and he brings his expertise on Swiss cooking to this local favorite, where every dish is prepared to order (so a wait for one's food isn't unheard of). In a bistro setting, you can enjoy some of the imaginative and innovative regional dishes in Monsieur Gruber's repertoire. The chef tirelessly seeks to find the most select produce, and his efforts continue to dazzle old and new clients alike.

9–11 rue Necker. ℭ **022/732-86-80.** Reservations recommended. Main courses 42F–44F ($27–$29); fixed-price meal 48F ($31) at lunch; 60F–90F ($39–$59) at dinner. AE, DC, MC, V. Mon–Fri 11am–2pm and 6:30–11pm. Closed the 1st week of Jan and 3 weeks in Aug. Bus: 5, 10, or 44.

Jeck's Place ⭐ PAN ASIAN Sitting at a table at this restaurant near Gare Cornavin is like taking a culinary tour of southeast Asia, with stopovers in India, Thailand, and Malaysia. Jeck Tan of Singapore has brought some of his choicest Pan-Asian recipes with him to Geneva. He delights palates nightly with his delicate seasonings and his innovative use of food combinations, such as whiting spread with a spicy lemongrass sauce and grilled on a banana leaf. You can often make a meal out of the excellent appetizers alone.

14 rue de Neuchâtel. ℭ **022/731-3303.** Reservations recommended. Main courses 21F–33F ($14–$21). Special lunch platter 15F ($9.75). Mon–Fri 11:30am–2pm and 6:30–10pm; Sat–Sun 6:30–10pm. AE, DC, MC, V. Bus: 4, 5, or 9.

La Favola ⭐ TUSCAN/ITALIAN Habitués of the finest Italian restaurant in the city, just a few steps from the Cathedral of St. Pierre, complain only that it doesn't serve on weekends. The family-run restaurant is warm and inviting, its tables placed in two cramped—and always packed—rooms, through which waiters scurry back and forth while carrying heaping platters of food. The seasonal menu is small and deliberately limited to ensure fresh ingredients. Don't even think of coming here without making reservations well in advance.

15 rue Jean-Calvin. ℭ **022/311-74-37.** Reservations are a must. Main courses 45F–60F ($29–$39). AE, MC, V. Mon–Fri noon–2pm and 7:15–10pm. Closed 2 weeks in July–Aug and 1 week at Christmas. Tram: 12.

SHOPPING

Geneva practically invented the wristwatch. In fact, watchmaking in the city dates from the 16th century. Be sure to avoid purchasing a Swiss watch in one of the souvenir stores; legitimate jewelers will display a symbol of the Geneva

Association of Watchmakers and Jewelers. Here, more than in any other Swiss city perhaps, you should be able to find all the best brands, including Vacheron & Constantin, Longines, Omega, and Blancpain, to name just a few. Most salespeople you'll encounter speak English and are very helpful.

A shopping spree might begin at **place du Molard,** once the harbor of Geneva before the water receded. Merchants from all over Europe used to bring their wares to trade fairs here in the days before merchants immigrated to richer markets in Lyon.

If you walk along rue du Rhône and are put off by the prices, go 1 block south to rue du Marché, which in various sections becomes rue de la Croix-d'Or and rue de Rive, and is sometimes referred to by locals as "la rue du Tram" because of the many trolleys which run along its length. Comparison-shopping is the way to go in Geneva—many stores jack up prices for visitors.

Store hours vary. Most are open Monday to Friday from 8am to 6:30pm and Saturday from 8am to 5pm. For one-stop shopping, head for one of the big department stores such as **Bon Genie,** 34 rue du Marché (✆ **022/818-11-11**), located on place du Molard. This department store sells mostly high-fashion women's clothing. Its storefront windows display art objects from local museums alongside designer clothes. There's also a limited selection of men's clothing, as well as furniture, cosmetics, and perfumes. **Magazine zum Globus,** 48 rue du Rhône (✆ **022/319-50-50**), is one of the largest department stores in Geneva, with many boutique-style departments and a self-image that's firmly patterned after the Galeries Lafayette in Paris. Expect glamour, and lots of upbeat cheerfulness.

Come Prima, 17 rue de la Cité (place Bémont; ✆ **022/310-77-79**), is our favorite Geneva shop with a spectacular array of gift and leather items. This boutique is loaded with top-quality leather bags and carry-ons.

Edgar Affolter's Swiss Tradition, 17 rue du Mont-Blanc (✆ **022/731-65-44**), identifies itself as a souvenir shop, but its collection of watches is extensive, often at prices less expensive than you might find within more glamorous and sophisticated-looking shops. Expect lots of cuckoo clocks, woodcarvings, tablecloths, and T-shirts, as well as items from the Swiss military line of watches.

Bucherer, 45 rue du Rhône (✆ **022/319-62-66**), located opposite the Mont Blanc Bridge, is a chrome-and-crystal store selling deluxe watches and diamonds. The store offers such name brands as Rolex, Piaget, Ebel, Baume & Mercier, Omega, Tissot, Rado, and Swatch. The carpeted third floor is filled with relatively inexpensive watches. You'll also find a large selection of cuckoo clocks, music boxes, embroideries, and souvenirs, as well as porcelain pillboxes and other gift items.

Gübelin Jewelers, 1 place du Molard (✆ **022/310-86-55**), dates from 1854. This family-run establishment is known mainly for its brand-name watches, although it also sells beautiful precious stones and jewelry. You can also buy reasonably priced gifts, such as pen and pencil sets.

NIGHTLIFE

Geneva has more nightlife than any other city in French-speaking Switzerland. Most activity centers around **place du Bourg-de-Four,** which used to be a stagecoach stop during the 19th century and is located in the Old Town. Here, you'll find a host of outdoor cafes in the summer.

Geneva has always attracted the culturally sophisticated, including Byron, Jean-Baptiste, Corot, Victor Hugo, Balzac, George Sand, and Franz Liszt. Ernst

Ansermet founded Geneva's great **Orchestre de la Suisse Romande,** whose frequent concerts entertain music lovers at **Victoria Hall,** 14 rue du Générale-Dufour (© **022/418-35-00;** www.osr.ch). For opera there's the 1,500-seat **Grand Théâtre,** place Neuve (© **022/418-31-30;** www.geneveopera.ch), which welcomes Béjart, the Bolshoi, and other ballet companies, in addition to having a company of its own. For a preview of events at the time of your visit, pick up a copy of the monthly *List of Events* issued by the tourist office.

On the club and music scene, the largest after-dark venue is **Arthur's Club,** Centre I.C.C., 20 route des Près-Bois (© **022/318-60-90**), near the Geneva airport (take bus 10 from the center). Attracting an age group ranging from 18 to 45, it can hold up to 2,500 dancers gyrating to the recorded music and patronizing 1 of 10 different bars. The cover charge of 27F ($18) includes the first drink, and Arthur's is open only Friday to Sunday 11pm to 5am. Back in town, **Le Dancing de la Coupole,** 116 rue du Rhône (© **022/787-50-12**), is a well–frequented brasserie that is also a dance club, focusing mainly on the music of the '60s, and doing so Tuesday to Saturday 5pm to 2am, charging no cover.

If you're barhopping, drop in at **Mr. Pickwick Pub,** 80 rue de Lausanne (© **022/731-67-97**), which also serves British food. Mostly patrons come here to drink and converse, listen to American or British music, or enjoy an Irish coffee. The best piano bar at night is **Le Francis,** 8 bd. Helvetique (© **022/346-32-52**), which is an elegant place for a rendezvous with live music beginning at 10pm.

6 Switzerland's Famous Scenic Rail Lines ✦✦✦

Switzerland not only offers Europe's most dramatic Alpine scenery, but eight of the greatest train rides in the world. If you take one or all of these train trips, be assured that they will be among the most memorable of your life. All of the trains below can be booked through **Rail Europe** (© **877/272-RAIL** in the U.S., **800/361-RAIL** in Canada; www.raileurope.com) or your travel agent.

GLACIER EXPRESS   One of the most evocative trains in the country, the **Glacier Express** connects two fabled ski resorts—St. Moritz in the east and Zermatt in the west—while passing through the resorts of Chur, Andermatt, and Brig. On the 7½-hour trip, your train will pass through 91 tunnels and cross 291 bridges, peaking at 6,669 feet at the towering Oberalp Pass. There is no more memorable way to travel across the Alpine heartland of the country, past mountain lakes, vast forests, and cow-filled pastures.

The train ride is covered by Swiss Passes; Eurailpasses are valid only from St. Moritz to Disentis. Seat reservations are required and cost an additional $18. If you begin your trip in Zermatt, you can reach the resort by rail from Geneva in just 2 hours; otherwise, tack on an additional 7½ hours for the trip from Zurich to St. Moritz.

BERNINA EXPRESS   Another dramatic ride is the **Bernina Express,** a 2½-hour trip from St. Moritz through a lunar landscape of ice-age glaciers and stone-studded fields and pastureland to the palms and foliage of Tirano in Italy. All cars on this train (run by the Rhäetische Bahn Authority) have panoramic windows so you won't miss the views. The ride may be short, but you won't soon forget the breathtaking scenery passing by your window as you go through wild gorges, across towering bridges, and into foreboding loop tunnels, moving past dozens upon dozens of snow-capped glaciers. At the rail junction in Tirano, a bus will take you on the 3-hour journey to Lugano, one of the finest lake resorts of Switzerland's Italian-speaking Ticino district. *Note:* Although we recommend you pick up the Bernina Express in St. Moritz, it actually starts off in Chur.

A one-way fare from St. Moritz to Lugano, including the bus fare is 69F ($52) in first class or 52F ($39) in second class; the trip is covered by the Eurailpass and the Swiss Pass. Seat reservations are required and cost an additional $12. St. Moritz is a 3½-hour train ride from Zurich. For more information on the Bernina Express, head online to **www.rhb.ch**.

CENTOVALLI RAILWAY   The **Centovalli Railway** offers one of the most dramatic train rides in Ticino, the Italian-speaking part of Switzerland in the south of the country bordering Italy. Running through the region's scenic "Hundred Valleys," the railway links Locarno (one of the country's most popular resorts) with the town of Domodossola in northern Italy, on the southern side of the Alps at the foot of the Simplon Pass.

The 2-hour trip features the lush, wonderful countryside of southern Switzerland, filled with mountain landscapes, flowering meadows, and magnificent forests.

No reservations are required. The trip is covered by the Eurailpass and the Swiss Pass; otherwise, it costs $128 in first class or $75 in second class. Locarno, the starting point of the trip, is about a 3-hour train ride from Zurich.

GOLDEN PASS LINE   The **Golden Pass Line** is the natural and panoramic route linking Central Switzerland with Lake Geneva, and because it features some of the country's greatest lakes and evocative mountain scenery, the line is often called "Switzerland in a Nutshell." The train ride covers 149 miles (239km), from the shores of Lake Lucerne and over the Brünig Pass to the chic resort of Montreux on Lake Geneva. Three trains run along various legs of the route and to cover the entire route, you'll need to change trains twice (track variances prevent a single train from running the entire length of the route). The **Brünig Panoramic Express** runs from Lucerne to Interlaken, the **Salon Bleu** from Interlaken to Zweisimmen, and the **GoldenPass Panoramic–MOB** from Zweisimmen to Montreux.

Reservations are required for each leg of the trip (they cost 5F/$3.75 per leg), though if you plan on traveling the whole route, you can get them all for 11F ($8.25). If you buy in advance from Rail Europe, it will cost you $18 per leg. The trip is covered by the Eurailpass and the Swiss Pass; otherwise, the cost for all three legs is 129F ($97) in first class or 78F ($59) in second class. To start your run in Lucerne, take a 50-minute train to the city out of Zurich. For more schedules and more information on this railway line, see **www.golden pass.ch** and **www.mob.ch**.

CHOCOLATE TRAIN   A real novelty is the so-called **"Chocolate Train,"** which offers luxurious first-class travel in vintage Belle Epoque 1915 Pullman cars or modern panoramic cars from June through October only. You depart from Montreux on Lake Geneva for the medieval city of Gruyères, where you are given time to tour the city's castle and famous cheese factory. Then it's back on the train and off to the Cailler-Nestlé chocolate factory in Broc, where you're given a tour and a tasting of some of the factory's delicious chocolate before reboarding your train and returning to Montreux. Along the way your train will pass stunning views of the Lake Geneva vineyards and other beautiful landscapes. Complimentary croissants and coffee are served on the train.

You can take the trip only if you hold a first-class Swiss Pass or Eurailpass, which covers the train ride and all entrance fees. Seat reservations ($22) are mandatory. The round-trip train ride, including stopovers, takes more than 8 hours to complete, and there's only one train per day. Montreux, the starting point of the trip, is a 1-hour train ride from Geneva. For more information on the train, see **www.mob.ch**.

WILLIAM TELL EXPRESS   The **William Tell Express** links the German-speaking part of the Switzerland with the Italian-speaking Ticino region from May to October. Your trip begins in Lucerne when you board a historic paddle-steamer for a 3-hour cruise of Lake Lucerne and a first-rate meal. At the little town of Fluelen, you'll abandon ship and board a panoramic train that runs through towering cliffs and steep ravines of the Reuss Valley, including passage through the Gotthard Tunnel—an historic railway tunnel that is Europe's most important north/south gateway. After passing a number of old-fashioned Swiss villages, the train plunges south into the valleys that open onto the lakeside resorts of Lugano and Locarno.

The journey takes a total of 6 hours and 10 minutes. The trip is free for holders of the Swiss Pass or Eurailpass, though reservations are required, and cost $42 (which includes your meal on the boat, and a souvenir). The trip costs $78 for adults in first class or $52 in second class. To get to the starting point in Lucerne, take a 50-minute train out of Zurich.

MOUNT PILATUS COG RAILWAY   One of the most stunning mountain rail journeys in Switzerland is the **Mt. Pilatus Cog Railway,** located about 9 miles (15km) south of Lucerne, a city only a 50-minute train ride from Zurich. The regular round-trip fare on the cog railways is 58F ($44), which includes a mandatory reservation. With a Swiss Pass, the round-trip fare is 40.60€ ($46.70), including the reservation.

Between May and November, weather permitting, the cog railway operates between Alpnachstad, at the edge of the lake, and the very top of Mount Pilatus. From the quays of Lucerne, take a lake steamer for a scenic 90-minute boat ride to Alpnachstad. If you have a railpass, it will cover this steamer.

At Alpnachstad, transfer to the electric cog railway, which runs at a 48% gradient—the steepest cogwheel railway in the world. Departures are every 45 minutes daily from 8:50am to 4:30pm May to September only, the trip taking 1 hour and 20 minutes. At Pilatus-Kulm you can get out and enjoy the view. There are two mountain hotels and a belvedere offering views of Lake Lucerne and many of the mountains around it. For the descent from Mount Pilatus, some visitors prefer to take a pair of cable cars that terminate at Kriens, a suburb of Lucerne. Here you can take bus no. 1 (covered by the Swiss Pass), which will carry you into the heart of Lucerne. If you opt to go down by the cable cars, the round-trip fare on the cog railway and cable cars is 78.40F ($51). Eurail passholders get a 30% reduction on the cable cars.

A similar excursion to Pilatus is possible in the winter, but because the cog railway is buried in snow, you must alter your plans. You'll have to ascend and descend by cable car, which many visitors find exhilarating. From the train station at Lucerne, take bus no. 1 to the outlying suburb of Kriens. At Kriens, transfer to a cable car that glides over meadows and forests to the village of Fräkmüntegg, 4,600 feet above sea level. The trip takes half an hour. At Fräkmüntegg, switch to another cable car, this one much more steeply inclined than the first. A stunning feat of advanced engineering, it swings above gorges and cliffs to the very peak of Mount Pilatus (Pilatus-Kulm). Unlike the cog railways, these cable cars operate year-round. The round-trip ride by cable car from Kriens to Fräkmüntegg costs 36F ($23).

JUNGFRAUJOCH   A train trip from Interlaken to **Jungfraujoch,** at an elevation of 11,333 feet, is the most dramatic rail journey in Switzerland. For more than a century it's been the highest railway station in Europe. It's also one of the most expensive: A ticket costs $154 in first class or $143 in second class. Holders of Eurail or Swiss railpasses are granted a 25% discount; Swiss Card holders get a 50% discount. Note that families can fill out a Family Card form, available at the railway station, which allows children 16 and under to ride free.

Take a train from either **Zurich** (3 hr.) or **Geneva** (4½ hr.) to get to Interlaken and then allow 2 hours and 20 minutes for the journey from Interlaken to the Jungfraujoch. Departures are usually daily at 8am from the east station in Interlaken; expect to return around 4pm. To check times, contact the sales office of **Jungfrau Railways,** Höheweg 37 (© **033/828-71-11** or 033/828-72-33; www.jungfraubahn.ch).

The trip is comfortable, safe, and packed with adventure. First you'll take the **Wengernalp railway (WAB),** a rack railway that opened in 1893. It will take you to Lauterbrunnen, at 2,612 feet, where you'll change to a train heading for the Kleine Scheidegg station, at 6,762 feet—welcome to avalanche country. The view includes the Mönch, the Eiger Wall, and the Jungfrau, which was named for the white-clad Augustinian nuns of medieval Interlaken (Jungfrau means "virgin").

At Kleine Scheidegg, you'll change to the highest rack railway in Europe, the **Jungfraubahn.** You have 6 miles (9.6km) to go; 4 (6.4km) of them will be spent in a tunnel carved into the mountain. You'll stop briefly twice, at **Eigerwand** and **Eismeer,** where you can view the sea of ice from windows in the rock (the Eigerwand is at 9,400 ft. and Eismeer is at 10,368 ft.). When the train emerges from the tunnel, the daylight is momentarily blinding, so bring a pair of sunglasses to help your eyes adjust. Notorious among mountain climbers, the Eigernordwand (or "north wall") is incredibly steep.

Once at the Jungfraujoch terminus, you may feel a little giddy until you get used to the air. There's much to do in this eerie world up in the sky, but take it slow—your body's metabolism will be affected and you may tire quickly.

Behind the post office is an elevator that will take you to a corridor leading to the famed **Eispalast (Ice Palace).** Here you'll be walking inside "eternal ice" in caverns hewn out of the slowest-moving section of the glacier. Cut 65 feet below the glacier's surface, these caverns were begun in 1934 by a Swiss guide and subsequently enlarged and embellished with additional sculptures by others. Everything in here is made of ice, including full-size replicas of vintage automobiles and local chaplains.

After returning to the train station, you can take the Sphinx Tunnel to another elevator. This one takes you up 356 feet to an observation deck called the **Sphinx Terraces,** overlooking the saddle between the Mönch and Jungfrau peaks. You can also see the **Aletsch Glacier,** a 14-mile (23km) river of ice—the longest in Europe. The snow melts into Lake Geneva and eventually flows into the Mediterranean.

Have a meal in one of the five **restaurants** at the top of the peak. As a final adventure, you can take a **sleigh ride,** pulled by stout huskies.

On your way back down the mountain, you'll return to Kleine Scheidegg station, but you can vary your route by going through **Grindelwald,** which offers panoramic views of the treacherous north wall.

Index

—— RAIL EUROPE ——
BECAUSE GETTING AROUND EUROPE IS AS IMPORTANT AS GETTING TO EUROPE...

Europe Your Way

For over 50 years, we've been putting people like you on the right track, responding to every possible travel need. From railpasses covering multiple countries to simple point-to-point tickets, experience the real Europe with Rail Europe.

Discover how easy getting around Europe can be

Relaxing, convenient, and an outstanding value, no other form of transportation offers you so much of Europe for so little. The European rail network stretches over 160,000 miles, so there's always a train going your way. It's how Europeans travel!

Get on track before you go

Designed exclusively for North American travelers, our passes and tickets must be purchased before you leave home (they're not available in Europe). Be sure to stop by www.raileurope.com—one of the top-rated travel sites on the web—to start planning your rail journey today and discover how easy getting around Europe can be.

RE RailEurope

It's better on the train!

1-800-438-RAIL
www.raileurope.com

NOBODY KNOWS EUROPE LIKE EUROVACATIONS!

We offer:

- More than 1,000 hand-picked boutique hotels in railway cities
- Multi-city vacations including premier, high-speed train rides
- Rental cars right at the railway stations
- Value-priced packages to major European cities with hotel and air
- Unique city and sightseeing tours and day trips
- Terrific savings when you book more than one item with us
- Expertise and advice from our seasoned team of travel professionals

Visit EuroVacations.com and book a hotel, rent a car, buy a tour, or select from one of many exciting vacations with romantic train rides:

Speed underneath the English Channel between London & Paris on the famous Eurostar

Race from Paris to the sunny, glamorous Riviera on the amazing TGV Méd

Dash from Amsterdam to Brussels and back on Thalys, Europe's "Red Train"

Your first stop: **www.EuroVacations.com**

EURO**V**acations.com

Travel's not just our business, it's our passion

A member of the Rail Europe Group.

Booked aisle seat.

Reserved room with a view.

With a queen – no, make that a king-size bed.

With Travelocity, you can book your flights and hotels together, so
you can get even better deals than if you booked them separately.
You'll save time and money without compromising the quality of your
trip. Choose your airline seat, search for alternate airports, pick your
hotel room type, even choose the neighborhood you'd like to stay in

Travelocity

Visit www.travelocity.com
or call 1-888-TRAVELOCITY

Fly.
Sleep.
Save.

Now you can book your flights and
hotels together, so you can get even better deals
than if you booked them separately.

Travelocity
Visit www.travelocity.com
or call 1-888-TRAVELOCITY

Travelocity.® Travelocity.com® and the Travelocity skyline logo are trademarks and/or service
marks of Travelocity.com LP. © 2003 Travelocity.com LP. All rights reserved.